THE OXFORD HANDBOOK OF

SHAKESPEAREAN TRAGEDY

THE OXFORD HANDBOOK OF

SHAKESPEAREAN TRAGEDY

Edited by

MICHAEL NEILL

and

DAVID SCHALKWYK

OXFORD

UNIVERSITY PRESS

OXFORD
UNIVERSITY PRESS

Great Clarendon Street, Oxford, OX2 6DP,
United Kingdom

Oxford University Press is a department of the University of Oxford.
It furthers the University's objective of excellence in research, scholarship,
and education by publishing worldwide. Oxford is a registered trade mark of
Oxford University Press in the UK and in certain other countries

Published in the United States of America by Oxford University Press
198 Madison Avenue, New York, NY 10016, United States of America

British Library Cataloguing in Publication Data

Data available

Library of Congress Control Number: 2016933510

ISBN 978–0–19–872419–3

Printed and bound by CPI Group (UK) Ltd, Croydon, CR0 4YY

CONTENTS

PART II   TEXTUAL ISSUES

PART III   READING THE TRAGEDIES

PART IV STAGE AND SCREEN

PART V THE TRAGEDIES WORLDWIDE: (I) EUROPEAN RESPONSES

PART VI THE TRAGEDIES WORLDWIDE: (II) THE WIDER WORLD

LIST OF FIGURES

LIST OF CONTRIBUTORS

Khalid Amine is Professor of Performance Studies, Faculty of Letters and Humanities at Abdelmalek Essaadi University, Tetouan, Morocco, Research Fellow at the Institute of Interweaving Performance Cultures, Free University, Berlin, Germany (2008-10). Amine is co-author with Marvin Carlson of *The Theatres of Morocco, Algeria and Tunisia: Performance Traditions of the Maghreb*, Studies in International Performance (2012).

Philip Armstrong is an Associate Professor of English at the University of Canterbury in Christchurch, New Zealand. He is the author of *Shakespeare's Visual Regime* (2000), *Shakespeare in Psychoanalysis* (2001), *What Animals Mean* (2008), and *A New Zealand Book of Beasts* (with Annie Potts and Deidre Brown, 2013).

Emily C. Bartels is Professor of English at Rutgers University and Director of the Middlebury Bread Loaf School of English. Her publications include *Spectacles of Strangeness, Imperialism, Alienation, and Marlowe* (1993), which won the 1993-4 Roma Gill Prize for Best Work on Christopher Marlowe, and *Speaking of the Moor: From* Alcazar *to* Othello (2008). She has edited *Critical Essays on Christopher Marlowe* and co-edited with Emma Smith *Christopher Marlowe in Context* (2013). Her newest project centres on Shakespearean intertextuality.

Crystal Bartolovich is an Associate Professor of English at Syracuse University where she teaches courses in early modern literature and Marxist theory. She is the author of *Marx and Freud: Great Shakespeareans* (2012) with Jean Howard and David Hillman. With Neil Lazarus, she edited *Marx, Modernity and Postcolonial Studies* (2003). Her essays have appeared in journals such as *PMLA, Shakespeare Studies, Cultural Critique*, and *New Formations* as well as numerous edited collections. From 2000 to 2014 she was the editor of *Early Modern Culture*.

Shaul Bassi is Associate Professor of English at Ca' Foscari University of Venice. His publications include *Visions of Venice in Shakespeare* (with Laura Tosi, 2011), *Experiences of Freedom in Postcolonial Literatures and Cultures* (with Annalisa Oboe, 2011), and *Shakespeare's Italy and Italy's Shakespeare. Place, 'Race', and Politics* (2016).

Catherine Belsey is Professor Emeritus in English at Swansea University and Visiting Professor at the University of Derby. Her books include *The Subject of Tragedy* (1985), *Shakespeare and the Loss of Eden* (1999), *Why Shakespeare?* (2007), *Shakespeare in Theory and Practice* (2008), and *Romeo and Juliet: Language and Writing* (2014).

Tom Bishop is Professor of English at the University of Auckland, New Zealand. He is the author of *Shakespeare and the Theatre of Wonder* (1996), the translator of Ovid's *Amores* (2003), and a general editor of *The Shakespearean International Yearbook*. He has published articles on Elizabethan music, Shakespeare, Jonson, medieval drama, Australian literature, and other topics. He is currently editor of *Pericles, Prince of Tyre* for the Internet Shakespeare Editions, and is writing a book on Shakespeare's Theatre Games.

Peter Byrne is Associate Professor of English at Kent State University at Trumbull. He received his doctorate at the University of California, Irvine, in 2004. His research focuses on the role of genre in theatrical composition and performance. His most recent published articles include ' "Titles are jests": The Challenge to Generic Dialectic in *A King and No King*' in *Medieval and Renaissance Drama in England* 28 (2015) and ' "The cunning of their ground": The Relevance of *Sejanus* to Renaissance Tragedy' in *Early Theatre* (2014).

Pavel Drábek is Professor of Drama and Performance at the University of Hull. His interests range from Shakespeare and early modern theatre in Europe, through drama translation, music theatre to theatre theory. He has published a monograph on cultural history and translations of Shakespeare (*České pokusy o Shakespeara* (Czech Attempts at Shakespeare), 2012), on John Fletcher (*Fletcherian Dramatic Achievement: The Mature Plays of John Fletcher*, 2010), on seventeenth-century English comedy in Germany, on puppet theatre, and on theatre structuralism. He is an opera librettist (mostly for composer Ondřej Kyas), playwright and translator.

Pascale Drouet is Professor of English Literature at the University of Poitiers. Her publications include *Le vagabond dans l'Angleterre de Shakespeare* (2003), *Mise au ban et abus de pouvoir. Essai sur trois pièces tragiques de Shakespeare* (2012), *De la filouterie dans l'Angleterre de la Renaissance. Études sur Shakespeare et ses contemporains* (2013), *Shakespeare's Love's Labour's Lost* (2014). She is the general editor of the online journal *Shakespeare en devenir* and the textual editor of *Henry VIII* for *The Norton Shakespeare* (Third Series, 2015). She also translates twentieth and twenty-first-century drama for the French stage.

Lee Edelman, Fletcher Professor of English Literature at Tufts University, is the author of *No Future: Queer Theory and the Death Drive* (2004) and, most recently, with Lauren Berlant, of *Sex, or the Unbearable* (2014).

Bridget Escolme is Reader in Drama at Queen Mary University of London where she she teaches and researches early modern drama in historical and recent performance; costume theory and practice; the history of emotions in performance. Her publications include *Emotional Excess on the Shakespearean Stage: Passion's Slaves* (2013) and *Talking to the Audience: Shakespeare, Performance, Self* (2005). She is co-editor of the series Shakespeare in Practice (Palgrave) and Shakespeare in the Theatre (Arden).

William Germano is Professor of English Literature and Dean of the Faculty of Humanities and Social Sciences at Cooper Union. He has written *The Tales of Hoffmann* (BFI Film Classics) and two books on writing and publishing: *Getting It Published* and *From Dissertation to Book* (University of Chicago Press). He is completing a book entitled *Shakespeare at the Opera: A History of Impossible Projects* and a book-length essay on the history of the eye chart.

John Givens is Associate Professor of Russian at the University of Rochester. He is the author of a study of the Soviet writer and film maker Vasily Shukshin (*Prodigal Son: Vasily Shukshin in Soviet Russian Culture*), the co-translator of a volume of Shukshin's prose

(*Stories from a Siberian Village*) and, from 1999 to 2015, the editor of *Russian Studies in Literature*, a quarterly journal of translations of Russian literary scholarship. He has recently completed his second book, *The Image of Christ in Russian Literature: Dostoevsky, Tolstoy, Bulgakov, Pasternak*.

Michael Gleicher is a professor in the Department of Computer Sciences at the University of Wisconsin-Madison. He is founder of the department's Computer Graphics Group. His research interests span the range of visual computing, including data visualization, image and video processing tools, virtual reality, and character animation techniques for films, games, and robotics. Prior to joining the university, he was a researcher at The Autodesk Vision Technology Center and in Apple Computer's Advanced Technology Group. He earned his PhD in computer science from Carnegie Mellon University and holds a BSE in electrical engineering from Duke University. For the 2013-14 academic year, he was visiting researcher at INRIA Rhone-Alpes. He is an ACM Distinguished Scientist.

Colette Gordon is a Lecturer in the Department of English at the University of the Witwatersrand. The focus of her research is the interaction between early modern credit culture and stage performance, but she has interrogated various aspects of Shakespearean performance in articles in *Shakespeare, Cahiers Élisabéthains, African Theatre, Shakespeare in Southern Africa, Borrowers and Lenders*, and, most recently, in *Shakespeare and the Global Stage* (Bloomsbury).

Andrew Hadfield is Professor of English at the University of Sussex and author of a number of works on early modern literature and culture including *Edmund Spenser: A Life* (2012, paperback 2014) and *Shakespeare and Republicanism* (2005, paperback 2008). He is working on a study of lying in early modern England and is editing the Works of Thomas Nashe for Oxford University Press with Jennifer Richards, Joe Black, and Cathy Shrank. He is vice-chair of the Society for Renaissance Studies.

Richard Halpern is Erich Maria Remarque Professor of Literature at New York University. He is the author of four books, including *The Poetics of Primitive Accumulation* (1990), *Shakespeare among the Moderns* (1997) and *Shakespeare's Perfume* (2002).

Sarah Hatchuel is Professor of English Literature and Film at the University of Le Havre (France), President of the Société Française Shakespeare and head of the 'Groupe de recherche Identités et Cultures'. She has written extensively on adaptations of Shakespeare's plays. She is the author of *Shakespeare and the Cleopatra/Caesar Intertext: Sequel, Conflation, Remake* (2011), *Shakespeare, from Stage to Screen* (2004) and *A Companion to the Shakespearean Films of Kenneth Branagh* (2000). She also edited *Julius Caesar* and *Antony and Cleopatra* in *The New Kittredge Shakespeare* collection (2008) and from 2003 co-edited, with Nathalie Vienne-Guerrin, the Shakespeare on Screen series.

David Hillman is a Senior Lecturer in the Faculty of English at the University of Cambridge, and Fellow and Director of Studies at King's College, Cambridge. He is the author of *Shakespeare's Entrails: Belief, Scepticism and the Interior of the Body* (2007) and of *Shakespeare and Freud* in The Great Shakespeareans series (2012); he is the co-editor of *The Cambridge Companion to the Body in Literature* (2015) and of *The Body in Parts: Fantasies of Corporeality in Early Modern Europe* (1997). He is currently working on a monograph, *Greetings and Partings in Shakespeare and Early Modern England*.

Andreas Höfele is Professor of English at Munich University. He is author of *Stage, Stake, and Scaffold: Humans and Animals in Shakespeare's Theatre* (2011), which won the 2012 Roland H. Bainton Prize for Literature. His publications in German include books on Shakespeare's stagecraft, late nineteenth-century parody, and on Malcolm Lowry, as well as six novels. He served as President of the German Shakespeare Society 2002–11.

Peter Holland is McMeel Family Professor in Shakespeare Studies in the Department of Film, Television and Theatre, and Associate Dean for the Arts at the University of Notre Dame. He was Director of the Shakespeare Institute in Stratford-upon-Avon from 1997 to 2002. He is editor of *Shakespeare Survey*, co-General Editor of *Oxford Shakespeare Topics*, *Great Shakespeareans* and the Arden Shakespeare 4th series. His edition of *Coriolanus* for the Arden 3rd series appeared in 2013.

Jonathan Hope is Professor of Literary Linguistics at Strathclyde University in Glasgow. He has published widely on Shakespeare's language and the history of the English language. His most recent book, *Shakespeare and Language: Reason, Eloquence and Artifice in the Renaissance* (2010), seeks to reconstruct the linguistic world of Shakespeare's England and measure its distance from our own. With Michael Witmore (Folger Shakespeare Library), he is part of a major digital humanities project, funded by the Mellon Foundation, to develop tools and procedures for the linguistic analysis of texts across the period 1450-1800. Early work from this project is blogged at: winedarksea.org.

Mark Houlahan is Senior Lecturer in English at the University of Waikato, Hamilton, New Zealand. Currently he is President of the Australia and New Zealand Shakespeare Association (*ANZSA*). Recently he has edited *Shakespeare and Emotions: Histories, Re-Enactments, Legacies* (2015), with R. S.White and Katrina O'Loughlin, and *Twelfth Night* (2014), with David Carnegie, in the Broadview/Internet Shakespeare series.

Alexa Huang teaches in the English department at George Washington University; she co-founded the GW Digital Humanities Institute and directs the Dean's Scholars in Shakespeare. Her latest book is *Shakespeare and the Ethics of Appropriation* (co-edited with Elizabeth Rivlin, 2014). She is co-general editor of *The Shakespearean International Yearbook*.

Sujata Iyengar, Professor of English at the University of Georgia, is the author of *Shades of Difference: Mythologies of Skin Color in Early Modern England* (2005), *Shakespeare's Medical Language* (2011), and editor of *Disability, Health, and Happiness in the Shakespearean Body* (2015). She is currently at work on two book projects, a monograph called 'Shakespeare and the Art of the Book' and an edited essay collection on Shakespearean transformations, and a suite of essays about Shakespeare, intermediality, and bodily differences. With Christy Desmet, she co-founded and co-edits the award-winning multimedia scholarly periodical *Borrowers and Lenders: The Journal of Shakespeare and Appropriation*.

MacDonald P. Jackson is an Emeritus Professor of English at the University of Auckland and a Fellow of the Royal Society of New Zealand. He was an associate general editor of the Oxford Middleton and is a co-editor of the Cambridge Webster. His most recent book is *Determining the Shakespeare Canon: 'Arden of Faversham' and 'A Lover's Complaint'*.

Russell Jackson is Allardyce Nicoll Professor of Drama in the University of Birmingham. His recent publications include *Shakespeare Films in the Making: Vision, Production* *and Reception* (2007), *Theatres on Film: how the Cinema Imagines the Stages* (2013) and *Shakespeare and the English-speaking Cinema* (2014).

Bernhard Klein is Professor of English at the University of Kent, United Kingdom. He has published monographs and articles, and edited and co-edited essay collections on various early modern topics, including cartography, the sea, and travel writing. He is currently co-editing one volume in the forthcoming critical edition of Richard Hakluyt's *Principal Navigations*.

Paul A. Kottman is Associate Professor of Comparative Literature at the New School for Social Research. He is the author of *Tragic Conditions in Shakespeare* (2009), *A Politics of the Scene* (2008) and the editor of *Philosophers on Shakespeare* (2009). He is also the editor of a new book series at Stanford University Press, called Square One: First-Order Questions in the Humanities.

Peter Lake is University distinguished professor of early modern English history at Vanderbilt University. His most recent book (written with Isaac Stephens) is *A Northamptonshire Maid's Tragedy*. A revised version of his 2011 Ford Lectures (*Bad queen Bess?*) will be published by Oxford University Press in 2016. He is currently completing s study of Shakespeare's history plays and the politics of the 1590s.

Douglas Lanier is Professor of English and Director of the London Program at the University of New Hampshire. He is the author of *Shakespeare and Modern Popular Culture* (2002) and many articles and chapters on modern appropriation of Shakespeare. He is currently working on a book-length study of *Othello* on screen and a book on *The Merchant of Venice* for the Arden Language & Writing series.

Hester Lees-Jeffries is a University Lecturer in English at Cambridge University and a Fellow of St Catharine's College. She is the author of *England's Helicon: Fountains in Early Modern Literature and Culture* (2007) and *Shakespeare and Memory* (2013), as well as many articles and essays on Shakespeare and early modern literature. Her current project has the working title 'Textile Shakespeare'.

Courtney Lehmann is the Tully Knoles Professor of the Humanities and Professor of English and Film Studies at the University of the Pacific. She is an award-winning teacher and the author of *Shakespeare Remains: Theater to Film, Early Modern to Postmodern* (2002), *Screen Adaptations: Shakespeare's Romeo and Juliet* (2010), and co-author of *Great Shakespeareans: Welles, Kurosawa, Kozintsev, and Zeffirelli* (2013). She is the co-editor of several Shakespeare and film anthologies, as well as *The New Kittredge King John and Henry VIII*.

Rory Loughnane is Assistant Research Professor and Associate Editor of *The New Oxford Shakespeare* project at IUPUI. Recent and current book projects include *The Memory Arts in Renaissance England: A Critical Anthology* (2016) with William E. Engel and Grant Williams, *Staged Normality in Shakespeare's England* with Edel Semple, *Early Shakespeare* with Andrew J. Power, and a monograph entitled *Middleton Reading Shakespeare*. For the *Authorship Companion* to *The New Oxford Shakespeare* he is co-authoring, with Gary Taylor, a new essay about the 'Canon and Chronology' of Shakespeare's works.

Lynne Magnusson is a Professor of English at the University of Toronto, with research interests in Shakespeare's language and the social rhetoric of the early modern letter. The author of *Shakespeare and Social Dialogue: Dramatic Language and Elizabethan Letters,* she has recently edited Shakespeare's Sonnets for *The Norton Shakespeare* and is working on *Shakespeare and the Grammar of Possibility.*

Leah S. Marcus is Edwin Mims Professor of English at Vanderbilt University. She is the author of *Childhood and Cultural Despair* (1978), *The Politics of Mirth* (1986), *Puzzling Shakespeare* (1988), *Unediting the Renaissance* (1996), and has edited works of Queen Elizabeth I (2000 and 2003), John Webster's *Duchess of Malfi* (2009), *The Merchant of Venice*, and *As You Like It* (both in Norton Critical Editions, 2006 and 2011). She is currently finishing a book provisionally titled *How Shakespeare Became Colonial* and treating colonial survivals in our current texts of the plays.

Madhavi Menon is Professor of English at Ashoka University, editor of *Shakesqueer: A Queer Companion to The Complete Works of Shakespeare* (2011), and author of *Indifference: On Queer Universalism* (2015).

Alfredo Michel Modenessi is Professor of Comparative Studies at the National University of Mexico (UNAM), as well as stage translator and dramaturge. He has published extensively on Shakespeare, translation, and cinema, and translated over forty plays, including fifteen by Shakespeare. Currently, he is Deputy Director of UNAM's Centre for Mexican Studies at King's College London, and is preparing a book on the presence of Shakespeare in Mexican cinema.

Subha Mukherji is Senior Lecturer in English at Cambridge University. Her publications include *Law and Representation in Early Modern Drama* (2006); *Early Modern Tragicomedy* (co-ed., 2007); *Fictions of Knowledge: Fact, Evidence, Doubt* (co-ed., 2012); *Thinking on Thresholds: the Poetics of Transitive Spaces* (ed., 2011); and numerous articles on Shakespeare and early modern literature. She is leading the ERC-funded project, *Crossroads of Knowledge in Early Modern England: The Place of Literature* (2014-19), and writing on a monograph on *Questioning Knowledge in Early Modern Literature.*

Steven Mullaney is Professor of English at the University of Michigan in Ann Arbor. He is the author of *The Place of the Stage: License, Play, and Power in Renaissance England* (1988; 1994) and most recently, *The Reformation of Emotions in the Age of Shakespeare* (2015). Currently, he is a co-participant in a multi-disciplinary project, 'Early Modern Conversions: Religions, Cultures, Ecologies'.

Michael Neill is Professor in Early Modern Literature at the University of Kent and Emeritus Professor of English at the University of Auckland. He is the author of *Issues of Death* (1997) and *Putting History to the Question* (2000). He has edited a number of early modern plays, including *Anthony and Cleopatra* (1994) and *Othello* (2006) for the Oxford Shakespeare, and (most recently) *The Renegado* (2010) for Arden Early Modern Drama, as well as *The Spanish Tragedy* (2014) and *The Duchess of Malfi* (2015) for Norton Critical Editions.

Avraham Oz received his PhD from the University of Bristol. Professor of Theatre at the Academy of Performing Arts, Tel Aviv and Emeritus Professor at The University of Haifa, where he founded and chaired the Department of Theatre. He chaired the Department of Theatre, Tel Aviv University; taught at drama schools and The Hebrew University in Jerusalem; served as associate artistic director at The Cameri Theatre and dramaturg at the Haifa Theatre; presented TV and radio shows; founded magazines as *Assaph* and *JTD*, and published numerous books and articles on Shakespeare, Marlowe, political theatre, and Israeli theatre. His many Hebrew translations of plays and operas for the Hebrew stage include nine Shakespearean plays.

Gail Kern Paster is Director emerita of the Folger Shakespeare Library in Washington, DC and Editor of *Shakespeare Quarterly*. She is the author of numerous essays in the cultural history of the body and the emotions. Her books include *The Body Embarrassed: Drama and The Disciplines of Shame in Early Modern England* (1993) and *Humoring the Body: Emotions and the Shakespearean Stage* (2004). She has edited the Revels editions of Thomas Middleton's *Michaelmas Term* and is the textual editor of *Twelfth Night* for *The Norton Shakespeare* (2015).

Edward Pechter is Distinguished Professor Emeritus, Concordia University (Montreal), and Adjunct Profesor of English, University of Victoria (British Columbia). His recent work includes *Shakespeare Studies Today: Romanticism Lost* (2011) and a new Norton Critical Edition of *Othello* (2016).

Andrew J. Power is Lecturer of Shakespeare and Early Modern Drama in Saint Louis University—Madrid Campus. He is the editor of *Late Shakespeare, 1608-1613* with Rory Loughnane and of *The Yearbook of English Studies* 2014 (special issue on 'Caroline Literature' with Rory Loughnane and Peter Sillitoe). His forthcoming monograph is entitled *Stages of Madness: Sin, Sickness and Seneca in Shakespearean Drama*.

Margie Rauen (Margarida Gandara Rauen, Ph.D.) is a Professor in the Graduate Program of Education at UNICENTRO, Paraná, Brazil, with research on cultural studies and participatory poetics. She has published internationally, and directed performance works about postcolonial and women's topics, as well as forum theatre projects that were conceived for intervention at urban and community venues. A website is available at [www.margierauen.com].

Nathalie Rivère de Carles is Assistant Professor in Shakespearean Drama at the University of Toulouse. Her research covers material and theatre history and the representation of cultural and political exchanges in early modern plays. She authored a chapter on 'Performing Materiality: Curtains on the Modern Stage' in *Shakespeare's Theatres and the Effects of Performance* (Arden Shakespeare, 2013), and is the textual editor of *The Two Gentlemen of Verona* for *The Norton Shakespeare*, (3rd edn, 2015). Her books include *Early Modern Diplomacy, Soft Power and Theatre: the Making of Peace* (ed., 2016) and *Forms of Diplomacy* (co-ed, 2015), and her current project is a monograph on Diplomacy on the Shakespearean Stage.

Daniel Roux is Senior Lecturer in English at the University of Stellenbosch, where he specializes in Shakespeare, Postcolonial Literature, and South African Literature.

Katherine Rowe is Provost and Dean of the Faculty at Smith College, studies the history of reading, writing, and performance, from the Renaissance to the present. She is the author of *Dead Hands, Fictions of Agency Renaissance to Modern* (1999), co-author of *New Wave Shakespeare on Screen* (2007), and co-editor of *Reading the Early Modern Passions: Essays in the Cultural History of Emotion,* with Gail Kern Paster and Mary Floyd-Wilson (2004). A recipient of grants from the NEH, the Mellon Foundation, and the PA Department of Education that support her work in the digital humanities, Prof. Rowe is Associate General Editor of *The Cambridge Guide to the Worlds of Shakespeare* and served as a Trustee of the Shakespeare Association of America.

David Schalkwyk is currently Academic Director of Global Shakespeare, a joint venture between Queen Mary College, London and the University of Warwick. He was formerly Director of Research at the Folger Shakespeare Library in Washington DC and editor of *Shakespeare Quarterly.* Before that he was Professor of English at the University of Cape Town, where he held the positions of Head of Department and Deputy Dean in the faculty of the Humanities. His books include *Speech and Performance in Shakespeare's Sonnets and Plays* (2002), *Literature and the Touch of the Real* (2004), and *Shakespeare, Love and Service* (2008). His most recent book is *Hamlet's Dreams: The Robben Island Shakespeare,* published in 2013 by the Arden Shakespeare. He has just completed a monograph on love in Shakespeare.

Emma Smith is Professor of Shakespeare Studies at Hertford College, Oxford. She has published widely on Shakespeare and early modern drama including, most recently, *Shakespeare's First Folio: Four Centuries of an Iconic Book* (2016). Her current work is on early modern libraries and the history of the book.

Gay Smith, Theatre Historian and Dramaturg. Professor Emerita Wesleyan University, author *Lady Macbeth in America: From the Stage to the White House* (2010), *George Sand's Theatre Career* (1985); translator and adaptor *George Sand's Gabriel* (1992).

Ian Smith is Professor of English at Lafayette College. He is the author of *Race and Rhetoric in the Renaissance: Barbarian Errors* (2009), and his work on Shakespeare, race, and early modern drama has appeared in several anthologies and journals. He is currently preparing a book on Shakespeare's unique commitment to the politics of blackness titled *Black Shakespeare.*

Tiffany Stern is Professor of Early Modern Drama at Oxford University, and author of *Rehearsal from Shakespeare to Sheridan* (2000), *Making Shakespeare* (2004), *Shakespeare in Parts* (with Simon Palfrey, 2007), and *Documents of Performance in Early Modern England* (2009). She has co-edited a collection of essays with Farah Karim-Cooper, *Shakespeare's Theatres and the Effects of Performance* (2013), and has edited *King Leir* (2001), Sheridan's *The Rivals* (2004), Farquhar's *Recruiting Officer* (2010), and Brome's *Jovial Crew* (2014). She is a general editor of New Mermaids and Arden Shakespeare series 4.

Richard Sugg is Lecturer in English Studies at the University of Durham. He is the author of *John Donne* (2007); *Murder After Death* (2007); *Mummies, Cannibals and Vampires* (2011; 2nd edn 2015); *The Secret History of the Soul* (2013); *The Smoke of the Soul* (2013); and *A Century of Supernatural Stories* (2015). He has just completed *The Real Vampires,* and is researching a new book on poltergeist phenomena.

Poonam Trivedi was Associate Professor in English at University of Delhi. She has co-edited *Re-playing Shakespeare in Asia* (2010), *India's Shakespeare: Translation, Interpretation and Performance* (2005) and authored a CD-ROM 'King Lear *in India*' (2006). She has published articles on Shakespeare in India, performance and film versions of Shakespeare, on women in Shakespeare and on the theory and performance of Indian theatre. Her current project is a collection of essays on *Shakespeare and Indian Cinemas*. She is also the vice-chair of the Asian Shakespeare Association.

Nathalie Vienne-Guerrin is Professor in Shakespeare studies at the University Paul-Valéry Montpellier 3 and director of the 'Institut de Recherche sur la Renaissance, l'âge Classique et les Lumières' (IRCL, UMR 5186 CNRS). She is co-general editor of the international journal *Cahiers Élisabéthains* (Sage) and co-director (with Patricia Dorval) of the *Shakespeare on Screen in Francophonia Database* (shakscreen.org). She has published *The Unruly Tongue in Early Modern England, Three Treatises* (2012) and is the author of *Shakespeare's Insults: A Pragmatic Dictionary* (2016). She is co-editor, with Sarah Hatchuel, of the *Shakespeare on Screen* series.

Paul Werstine, at King's University College at Western, Canada, is co-editor, with Barbara A. Mowat, of the 42 volumes of the Folger Library Edition of Shakespeare (1992-2010). He is also general editor, with Richard Knowles and Eric Rasmussen, of the Modern Language Association's New Variorum Edition of Shakespeare. He's written *Early Modern Playhouse Manuscripts and the Editing of Shakespeare* (2013).

Michael Witmore is Director of the Folger Shakespeare Library, Washington, DC. His publications include *Landscapes of the Passing Strange: Reflections from Shakespeare* (2010, with Rosamond Purcell); *Shakespearean Metaphysics* (2008); *Pretty Creatures: Children and Fiction in the English Renaissance* (2007); and *Culture of Accidents: Unexpected Knowledges in Early Modern England* (2001). With Jonathan Hope (Strathclyde University, Glasgow), he is part of a major digital humanities project, funded by the Mellon Foundation, to develop tools and procedures for the linguistic analysis of texts across the period 1450-1800. Early work from this project is blogged at: winedarksea.org.

Tzachi Zamir is a philosopher and a literary critic (Associate Professor of English & Comparative Literature) and is currently Chair of Comparative Literature at the Hebrew University of Jerusalem. Zamir is the author of *Double Vision: Moral Philosophy and Shakespearean Drama* (2006), *Ethics and the Beast* (2007), and *Acts: Theater, Philosophy and the Performing Self* (2014).

PART I

GENRE

CHAPTER 1

....

WHAT IS SHAKESPEAREAN
TRAGEDY?

....

PAUL A. KOTTMAN

1

....

THE question 'What is Shakespearean Tragedy?' can understandably prompt one to start listing distinctive features of various plays by Shakespeare—as if a successful enumeration of its characteristics would amount to an understanding of the genre. To a certain extent, such inventories are probably unavoidable when talking about an entire body of work, about more than a particular scene or play. Moreover, many descriptions of what A. C. Bradley famously called the 'facts' of Shakespearean tragedy are undeniably true and useful. It is illuminating, for instance, to observe with Bradley that Shakespeare's tragedies present 'a story of exceptional calamity leading to the death of a man in high estate', where the protagonist 'always contributes in some measure to the disaster in which he perishes', and where this active 'contribution' means not just things done ''tween sleep and wake' but 'acts or omissions thoroughly expressive of the doer—characteristic deeds'.[1] Bradley's conclusions, like those of other perceptive commentators on Shakespeare, are important and worth discussing, and I will return to them.

However, rather than approach Shakespearean tragedy as the sum-total of certain features or 'facts', or as a generic object of study, I propose that we see Shakespearean tragedy as a discrete form of art—as the birth of a distinctive art form, the same way we think of 'painting on canvas' or 'symphonic music' as art forms that arrived on the world stage at a particular place and time.[2] Whereas a 'genre' purports to be a collection

---

[1] The centre of a Shakespearean tragedy, Bradley argues, 'may be said with equal truth to lie in action issuing from character, or in character issuing in action.' A. C. Bradley, *Shakespearean Tragedy* (New York: Penguin, 1991), 28–9.

[2] Having said this, I must quickly add that I am not concerned with establishing which play is the 'first' Shakespearean tragedy, any more than I would want to fix a precise date or origin for painting on canvas, or for orchestra music. Such matters are subject to debate, and we can change our minds about the particulars. The larger point is that every artistic medium emerges historically—it was not always 'there'—and unfolds through a certain historical development that can be examined. Which means the point of 'changing our mind' about the particulars, or dates, would be the new

of objects that share common, taxonomically graspable features or techniques, there is no exhaustive list of features that 'add up' to Shakespearean tragedy—since, for a start, it is up to us to discern, decide, or debate, what will even count as features of this art form. Moreover, if Shakespearean tragedies all shared certain inherent, generic characteristics, then it would be difficult to distinguish between *Macbeth* and *Hamlet* and *Othello*—but of course we all know that each of these is an entirely different play; each brings to light new features or expressive possibilities for Shakespearean tragedy, helping us to better discern the art form as such, to better see its purview or expressive task. Shakespearean tragedies show what they are, as an art form, in light of one another. For the same reason, though it is unconventional to say so, we should probably regard Shakespearean tragedy not just as a finite, canonical collection of plays by William Shakespeare (*Hamlet, Macbeth, Othello, King Lear*, and so forth) but as a novel, modern, artistic practice—instanced with special power in a range of works by Shakespeare, but still practicable by others afterwards. Shakespeare may have been the first, or the most successful or the most indispensable, to work in the medium of Shakespearean tragedy, but he was not the last.[3]

To see Shakespearean tragedy as an art form, then, is to see it as a practice that, having originated somewhere and sometime (with Shakespeare, in this instance), takes on a life of its own by generating new features, techniques, and characteristics—thereby resisting any final taxonomy, at least so long as the art form remains vital as a human practice. If to delimit a 'genre' is to circumscribe a domain of objects or experiences according to constitutive traits or attributes, then art forms or practices take it upon themselves to 'work through', or make sense of, their own socio-historical and material pre-conditions as if expressing a newly discovered need for such sense-making.

All this gets me to the question that I really want to raise in this brief essay: What does the art form of Shakespearean tragedy 'work through', respond to, and make sense of?

I will propose at least one answer to this: Shakespearean tragedy works through the loss of any 'given'—nature, or God, or 'fate'—that might explain human societies, histories, actions, destinies, relationships, and values. At the same time, Shakespearean tragedy works through the loss of social bonds on which we depend for the meaning and worth

---

historical-self-understanding such a change of mind would amount to (and not just a different chronology).

[3] By 'indispensable', I mean that we need Shakespeare's work, especially, in order to understand later developments in the 'art of Shakespearean tragedy'. Though I do not have the space here to discuss what might be called the history of Shakespearean tragedy since Shakespeare, I would note that Friedrich Schlegel and Goethe—like many German romantics—saw modern drama, the novel, and romantic literature as developments of Shakespearean drama; just as Jan Kott saw Beckett's work as traversing the terrain of *King Lear*; just as Stanley Cavell sees Hollywood comedies of remarriage as extending Shakespearean romance—a suggestion that is being developed by Sarah Beckwith in her recent work on *The Winter's Tale* and its inheritors. (To say nothing of the *New York Times*, in which one reads recently, 'Haven't you heard TV is the new Shakespeare?') My suggestion, at any rate, is that we regard Shakespearean tragedy as inaugurating an artistic form whose possibilities have been explored by other artists in Shakespeare's wake—from Ibsen and Beckett, to Sarah Kane and Pedro Almodovar and on and on—though obviously one can regard Shakespeare as a 'master' of the form. (See Charles Isherwood, *The New York Times*, 'Too Much Shakespeare? Be Not Cowed', 12 September 2013.)

of our lives together—showing those bonds to be, in spite of that dependence, fully dissolvable. In this way, Shakespearean tragedy helps us make sense of how we interact with one another—without the help of any Archimedean standpoint, with only the interactions themselves as sources of intelligibility and meaning. In Shakespearean tragedy, our actions (must) explain themselves.

By this point you will have realized that my ambitions for this essay are hopelessly lofty. Although these ambitions are probably not realizable in these few pages, I want to try to convince you that they are not misguided, and they at least set us in the right horizon when it comes to thinking about Shakespearean tragedy.

2

How, then, does Shakespearean tragedy 'work through' the loss of any givens that might explain our interactions—or that might explain what happens in a Shakespearean drama?

Consider that all artistic practices are ways that we try to evaluate and make sense of our lives, of our social-historical world and its demands, of the claims of nature upon us (whatever those are felt to be at a given place and time), and of what we do (or might do) and say with one another. Artistic practices are not the only way we do this, of course; there are also mythology, religion, education, science, and philosophy. Still, by defining art in this somewhat grandiose way, I mean to suggest that artistic practices are—like religion or philosophy—a fundamental way in which we find out who we are, and who we might become, in light of the material and social conditions we inherit.[4] To put it the way that many German philosophers would once have put it, art is a historical practice through which we come to understand ourselves both as 'objects'—as bodies in motion, as finite or mortal creatures, exposed to the claims of social norms, nature, and the laws of physics—and as 'subjects', capable of leading or directing our lives, and of reflecting on them as such.[5] At the same time, artistic practices can be distinguished from religion and philosophy, in that their sense-making potential is tied to the way they work with (or through) specific media—stone, paint, sound, or speech—and to the way in which artistic transformations of these media reflect socio-historical transformations in our overall self-understanding.[6]

---

[4] To avoid confusion, by the term 'we' I mean 'we creatures who undertake artistic practices that express and reflect their social-historical and material conditions'. Because those conditions are social and historical, this 'we' is a historically changing and revisable 'we'—not an ahistorical, uncritical 'we'. I see the formation of human collectives as a practical, social-historical matter—not as stemming from some metaphysical, natural, or theological given.

[5] Consider how many similar reflections can be found in Shakespearean tragedy. To take perhaps the most famous: is not Hamlet's 'to be or not to be …' an expression of *both* Hamlet's position as subject-agent directing his life, one who might 'take arms against a sea of troubles, and by opposing, end them', *and* as an object in the world, one who suffers 'the slings and arrows of outrageous fortune' and 'the thousand natural shocks the flesh is heir to'?

[6] For a discussion of the way in which early modern artistic practices presage and anticipate modern aesthetic philosophy, see the essays collected in *The Insistence of Art: Aesthetic Philosophy and Early Modernity*, ed. Paul A. Kottman (Bronx, NY: Fordham University Press, forthcoming).

Some readers will already have recognized that I am borrowing my terms for discussion from G. W. F. Hegel's discussion in his *Lectures on Fine Art*. Hegel's terms are useful in this context, I think, for two basic reasons. First, Hegel provides a way of talking about 'dramatic poetry', and about Shakespearean tragedy in particular, in terms of our 'need' for particular art forms at a given place and time. By 'need', I mean our need to carry out certain artistic practices in order to understand who we are, and what we might do together, in light of certain historical-material conditions.[7] In this sense, Hegel's approach has the virtue of helping us to understand Shakespearean tragedy within a broader history of concrete artistic practices and works, with its internal transformations and innovations—rather than in terms of ahistorical 'genres', or categorical 'features' of aesthetic experience. Second, Hegel is useful here because he himself struggled to articulate the distinctiveness of Shakespearean tragedy (which he thought of as emblematically 'modern') with respect to ancient tragedy, and above all with respect to his own powerful interpretations of Greek tragedies like *Antigone* or *Oedipus the King*. Towards the end of this chapter, while taking account of the usefulness of Hegel's interpretation of tragedy for understanding Shakespearean tragedy, I also want to show how Shakespearean tragedy productively challenges Hegel's own claims about tragedy, in ways that might help us to better see what Shakespearean tragedy is doing.[8]

For Hegel, the development of artistic practices—that is, of historically shifting, context-specific needs for different 'art forms' (e.g. the need for pyramids in Egypt, for classical sculpture in Greece, or for painting in Christian Europe, or for film in the twentieth century), as well as internal developments within those arts (from 'symbolic to classical to romantic', for example, or from epic to lyric to drama)—presents an ongoing and increasing de-naturalization or 'spiritualization' of our self-understanding. In other words, the more that we see ourselves as—or teach ourselves that we are—free and self-determining subjects, the less we are dependent upon, or needful of, artistic expressions that work with 'natural' media (stone, wood, clay) in order to understand ourselves, and our world. The twist in Hegel's story is that artistic practices *are* (or 'have been') a primary way we teach ourselves this lesson—because by transforming natural material in modes that we can regard as 'free' from material or instrumental needs, we express our own liberation and, in this way, *become* free. (Art, claims Hegel in at famous passage, allows a free human

---

[7] So, I mean what Hegel calls 'the deepest interests of mankind, and the most comprehensive truths of spirit [*Geist*].' G. W. F. Hegel, *Lectures on Fine Art*, trans. T. M. Knox, (Oxford: Clarendon University Press, 1975), 1: 7. This is not to preclude there being other 'needs' for Shakespearean tragedy. For instance, I think we continue to 'need' Shakespeare (or the theatre generally) to do important work for, and by, the imagination (what the Chorus in *Henry V* calls our 'imaginary forces'). I am thinking, especially, of the way in which reading of performing Shakespeare can, from a young age, 'educate the imagination' (to use Northrop Frye's felicitous phrase) or cultivate emotional sensibility to, and practical judgments about, intractably difficult human predicaments. This is a deeply important cultural need, surely, and one that Shakespeare and great literature meet better, probably, than any other human product.

[8] Quick aside: while Hegel's lectures may seem an arbitrary point of entry in light of the terms of much contemporary Shakespeare scholarship, they might appear more pertinent if we recall the debt owed to Hegel's account of Shakespeare and of dramatic poetry by many of our most influential commentaries on Shakespearean tragedy: Goethe, Nietzsche, Bradley, Lukacs, Benjamin, Wilson Knight, Kott, Frye, Cavell, and others.

being to 'strip the external world of its inflexible foreignness and to enjoy in the shape of things only an external realization of himself'.)[9] And once this lesson is absorbed—that is, once we see ourselves as increasingly liberated from the demands of nature, inasmuch as the terms of our self-understanding depend less upon, are less limited by, something 'out there' called 'Nature' or 'God' or the 'One' or whatever—we find ourselves less needful of artworks by which we 'taught ourselves' this lesson.

Furthermore, Hegel observes, this ongoing de-naturalization unfolds (or has unfolded) through an increased awareness *within* artistic practices *of* artistic practices as medium-specific. Classical Greek architecture, for instance, manifests a higher awareness of its own status as 'architecture'—of itself as a freestanding, artificial, material construction—than does earlier 'symbolic' architecture.[10] Similarly, as Robert Pippin has convincingly argued, the deepening self-reflexivity of modernist and abstract painting—paintings about painting as such—might be understood to fall within the purview of the overall narrative that Hegel offers.[11] And—to move closer to Shakespeare—thinking along these lines also led Hegel himself, at the end of his *Lectures on Fine Art*, to consider dramatic poetry as 'the highest stage of poetry and of art generally'—first, because 'in contrast to the other perceptible materials, stone, wood, color and notes, speech is alone the element worthy of the expression of spirit'.[12] If artistic practices are medium-specific modes of self-understanding, goes the thinking here, then what medium or form could be more adequate to our reflexive self-understanding than that which, so to speak, we know to be 'ours' from the get-go? Not just elements ripped from an indifferent domain of nature (sound, colour, hard materials like stone or marble)—but what Giambattista Vico described in terms of 'poetic wisdom:' elements of culture and history, words and deeds, social principles and passionate aims, conflicts between individual characters.[13] And—second—because such elements are the 'stuff' of dramatic poetry, to work in the dramatic arts entails a degree of self-awareness (as a historical being or 'people') that is probably missing, say, from most symbolic sculpture. Dramatic poetry is, in other words, inherently more self-reflexive than sculpture,

---

[9] Hegel, *Lectures on Fine Art*, 1: 31.

[10] 'The peculiarity of Greek architecture,' writes Hegel in a typical formulation, is that by fluting and other means 'it gives shape to ... supporting *as such* and therefore employs the column as the fundamental element in the purposiveness of architecture.' Ibid., 2: 666, my emphasis.

[11] I am, of course, skipping over a number of important questions—for example, those having to do with the differences between the fates of classical and romantic art in Hegel's account. But I think my overall point about denaturalization as self-reflexivity can stand, for the moment, without tackling those questions. See, Robert Pippin, 'What was Abstract Art? (From the Point of View of Hegel)', *Critical Inquiry* 29 (August 2002), 1–24; and *After the Beautiful: Hegel and the Philosophy of Pictoral Modernism* (Chicago: University of Chicago Press, 2013).

[12] G. W. F. Hegel, 'Dramatic Poetry' from *Philosophers on Shakespeare*, ed. Paul A. Kottman (Stanford: Stanford University Press, 2009), 57.

[13] If sculpture or painting must grapple with the 'given-ness' of stone or colour or some other material, then the self-reflexive character of Shakespearean drama cannot 'fall back' on any natural medium (colour, texture, sound) in order to thematize its own expressive material capacities. Shakespearean drama does not and cannot rely upon any givens to determine its artistic form— not even the fact of the actors' embodiment determines what unfolds (given the preponderance of ghosts, spirits, visions, or 'unnatural' sights and sounds that populate Shakespeare's plays). Again, one of the tasks of the art of Shakespearean tragedy is to 'work through' the fact that there is nothing 'given' by God or nature that govern or determine our interactions, our dramatic activity.

painting or architecture because its medium—namely, speech and action—is from the start 'spiritual', human, relatively de-naturalized.[14]

Hence—and this is the point I want to underscore for my discussion of Shakespearean tragedy—drama is already 'formally' freer from nature, from external determination, than the other arts and consequently freer when it comes to choosing its content.

To avoid confusion, I do not want to deny that Shakespearean tragedy required for its formal viability, at a minimum, the concrete, material resources of early modern performance spaces—the physical capacities of the playhouse or the court, the lungs of the actors, the 'imaginary forces' of an audience prepared to receive and appreciate what they are seeing and hearing, the sensorial experiences afforded by the spatial and temporal limits of such performances, certain economic-financial conditions and so on. But these requirements, I would argue, amount only to something like a prehistory for the art form of Shakespearean tragedy: its initial material, socio-historical conditions of possibility. For, while these elements allowed Shakespearean tragedy to come into the world, they have not amounted to ongoing limitations on, or exhaustive explanations for, the vitality of this art form and its expressive possibilities. Once brought to life, Shakespearean tragedy has proven capable of flourishing even in the absence of these initial material conditions: on celluloid, in classrooms, in the reflections of solitary readers, in a variety of foreign settings, in performance spaces that bear little or no resemblance to those Shakespeare himself knew and in many other ways. In short, because the material circumstances of the early modern world set up the conditions required for the 'formal' viability of Shakespearean tragedy—but without governing or determining the course the art form has taken, once made viable—these original material conditions cannot be taken to wholly explain what Shakespearean tragedy 'works with' or 'works through'.

Pushing this thought a bit further, I argue that the vitality of dramatic poetry as such is—when compared to, say, sculpture, painting, or music—less formally restricted by the sensuous conditions that make up its prehistory.[15] That is, the expressive life and creative

---

[14] Hegel's apparent emphasis on 'speech' here seems to place him close to a view prevalent in Jena Romanticism—found especially in the thought of Lessing and Friedrich Schlegel—according to which poetry holds a privileged place among the arts because its medium (speech, language) places fewer material constraints on the freedom of the imagination. However, although Hegel apparently analyses drama in the *Lectures on Fine Art* under the heading of poetry, he does not reduce drama to linguistic or poetic expression. Drama, he writes, 'also displays a complete action', and it is this centrality of *action* (not just of the poetic free imagination) that, for Hegel, permits and requires drama to suture subjective experience and objective reality more fully than the other arts. Hence, dramatic poetry is, for Hegel, more self-reflexive than sculpture, painting or architecture not only because both its 'medium' and its content—namely, speech and action—are from the start 'spiritual', human, de-naturalized; drama's self-reflexive potential is also tied to its resulting capacity to hold together both a first-person (subjective) and a third-person (objective) viewpoint. See Hegel, 'Dramatic Poetry', 57 and *passim*. For the romantic viewpoint, to which Hegel is responding, see Gottfried Ephraim Lessing, 'Laocoön: An Essay on the Limits of Painting and Poetry', trans. A. W. Steel; and Friedrich Schlegel, excerpts from 'Critical Fragments', '*Athenaeum* Fragments', 'Ideas', 'On Goethe's *Meister*', 'Letter about the Novel', and 'On Incomprehensibility', in J. M. Bernstein, ed., *Classic and Romantic German Aesthetics* (Cambridge: Cambridge University Press, 2003).

[15] This is not to say that drama or art is thereby dis-embodied or non-sensuous, but—as Hegel puts it—such art is 'not tied to sensuous presentation, as if that corresponded to it ... romantic art is the self-transcendence of art but within its own sphere and in the form of art itself' (Hegel, *Lectures on Fine Art*, 1: 80.

possibilities of dramatic poetry are less determined by the concrete, material conditions that, initially, allowed it to become viable. In this sense, dramatic poetry in general is 'freer', more modernist—capable of a more capacious, or less inhibited, expressivity—than the other arts. Drama can *contain* music without being reducible to a musical performance, can *contain* dance without being confused with an occasion to move one's body about, can *contain* spectacles of all sorts without being thereby reducible to mere show. Moreover, drama can purposefully *show* this containment—and, hence, supersession—of other media as essential to its *own* specifically expressive power. Hence, dramatic poetry enjoys a relatively broad formal freedom with respect to other artistic media. At the same time, this formal freedom that dramatic poetry enjoys with respect to other art forms is commensurate with its freedom to determine its own content. The vitality of dramatic poetry is tied—as is the vitality of all art forms—to the vitality of its content, to the vitality of what it is 'about', what it can take up and present to us. And the more that dramatic poetry decides *for itself* what it will or will not present, the greater its formal capacities for expressiveness, the less inhibited it is by this or that concrete-material prehistory.[16]

Think of it this way: once artworks no longer need (due to the restrictions of a particular social world's self-conception) to be about this or that content 'out there' (a material purpose, an animal quarry, a 'god', a creation myth, a moral lesson, 'epochal' historical events)—they are freed up to determine *for themselves* their own content.[17] And this 'freeing up' is perhaps most clearly manifested when artworks also start to be about themselves. Self-reflexive artworks and practices undeniably assert the autonomy of human artistry, of human activity. For all these reasons, Hegel not only ranks dramatic poetry as the highest (the freest, most prevalently 'spiritual') artistic practice; he also thought that among modern dramatists 'you will scarcely find any … who can be compared with Shakespeare'.[18] And so, although Hegel does not say so explicitly, we can nevertheless infer—from the perspective of my highly condensed account here—that Shakespeare's pre-eminence in Hegel's account of the history of human artistic development should have something to do with the heightened self-reflexivity of Shakespearean tragedy, and its corresponding achievement of a kind of 'formal' freedom.[19] And if this same kind of formal freedom is understood—as in Georg Lukàcs' *Theory of the Novel*—to belong especially to novelistic

---

[16] For more on these points, see my essays, 'These Charms Dissolve' in *Shakespeare and Continental Philosophy*, ed. Jennifer Bates (Edinburgh: Edinburgh University Press, 2014), and 'Duel' in *The Oxford Handbook to Early Modern Theatricality* (Oxford: Oxford University Press, 2014).

[17] Compare Hegel: In modern (romantic) art, 'the scope of the subject matter is therefore also infinitely *extended* … It opens out into a multiciplicity without bounds' (Hegel, *Lectures on Fine Art*, 1: 525).

[18] Hegel, *Lectures on Fine Art*, 2: 1228.

[19] Shakespeare's pre-eminence in Hegel's account—the fact, for instance, that Hegel's discussion of Shakespeare comes at the culmination of his *Lectures on Fine Art*—would, of course, require some qualification. Hegel also seems to claim that Greek art is more fulfilled *as art* than modern art, and his high regard for Sophocles seems of a piece with that view. 'There is,' as Robert Pippin notes, however, 'another sense in which he claims that the ethical life behind Shakespeare's presentation and the kind of self-awareness visible in Hamlet, say, does represent an advance or moment of progress.' Robert Pippin, *The Persistence of Subjectivity: On the Kantian Aftermath* (Cambridge: Cambridge University Press, 2005), 84 n. 12. See, further, the discussion of Hegel and Shakespeare in Henry and Anne Paolucci, *Hegelian Literary Perspectives* (Smyrna, DE: Griffon House (repr.), 2002).

writing, then we might remember Friedrich Schlegel's remark about Shakespeare's founding of the novel: 'there is so little contrast between drama and the novel that it is rather drama, treated thoroughly and historically, as for instance by Shakespeare, which is the true foundation of the novel.'[20]

This formal freedom is moreover evident in the fact that—as Johann Gottfried Herder observed, taking issue with neo-classical objections to Shakespeare—'classical' rules are of no help for understanding Shakespearean tragedy, an art form that has had to solve, with each new work (and with each new interpretation or performance) what it is and what it might become. Hence, for instance, the sense of ongoing revisions in Shakespeare—the feeling that *Cymbeline* and *The Winter's Tale* revisit *Othello* and *King Lear*, or that each new comedy is a self-critical vision of its predecessor. As Herder knew, at issue is not only Shakespeare's alleged lack of 'poetics'—for instance, his unravelling of 'plot' as a consequential separation of deed from recognition—but rather the way in which Shakespearean tragedy shows how the historical conditions of human activity (social, political, economic) have been wholly transformed, and must therefore be seen as transformable still. Which also means that our formal depictions of those activities must be seen as shifting and alterable. Think, for example, of the way that Hamlet's inability to furnish an answer to his own rhetorical question—'What is Hecuba to him, or he to her, that he should weep for her?'—necessitates and prompts Hamlet's reflection not on his or our connection to the events of the *Iliad*, but on the more self-reflexive question of how the sensuous performance of a mimetic action can (still) meaningfully grip a performer and an audience.

Along these lines, we should also recall the (often overlooked fact) that while earlier dramatic forms, like Greek and Roman theatre or English morality plays, were 'art forms' that were inextricable elements of essential social rituals—civic duties, liturgical practices, state-sponsored public entertainment, and so forth—Shakespearean tragedy cannot rely on (and thereby frees itself from) the essentiality of any such ritual culture. In this sense, Shakespearean tragedy shares the predicament of a great number of 'modernist' artistic practices: it must be self-justifying, self-legitimating since it does not accomplish any other universally recognized cultural (social, civic, religious) task. All of this is evidenced, as so many have noted, in the precarious and ambiguous status of the theatrical practices in Shakespeare's London (and in the years since then). Shakespearean tragedy is forged in the collapse of a dominant, unified culture that can fully sustain or justify its existence.

3

Corollary to this, Shakespearean tragedy cannot take for granted just what exactly it is supposed to depict or represent, and why. If Aeschylus and Sophocles had, at least, some

---

[20] Friedrich Schlegel, 'Dialogue on Poetry' in *German Romantic Criticism*, ed. A. Leslie Willson (New York: Continuum, 1982), 108. However—as Thomas Pavel has pointed out to me—Schlegel's observation might reveal his ignorance of the novelistic origins of Shakespeare's own drama (his debt to Italian *novelle*). Pavel's own history of the novel rightly shows how far back the history of the novel can be extended. See Thomas Pavel, *The Lives of the Novel* (Princeton: Princeton University Press, 2011).

sense of what the appropriate purview of tragedy was—the relation between family life and city life; or the struggle between ancient religious beliefs and (then) contemporary political values; or the choreography of protagonists and *polis* (or chorus)—then Shakespearean tragedy has far fewer productive limitations. So, even though Shakespeare of course continued to represent historically significant figures (Princes, Kings, Generals) as well as apparently 'universal' concerns (death, family life, sexual desire) he nevertheless leaves us with no sense that he could know, conclusively, just what exactly he was supposed to show us about any of these things. And by the same token this explains why we see Shakespeare as possessed (as *needing* to be possessed) of far more imaginative energy than, say, Sophocles. Indeed, Shakespeare continually expands his dramatic vision to include whores, merchants, beggars, children, spirits, and so on in a seemingly endless variety of worldly contexts—to the point where we (modern interpreters, directors, and actors) must also imaginatively *choose* how or where to present multifarious 'Shakespearean' works which seem suitable to so many domains and, hence, representative of no single, particular viewpoint on human life.

Recall that prior to Shakespeare, dramatic poetry by and large presented, or relied upon, a generic, standard, universalizing view of the connection between human actions and the natural, or social, or divine context for those actions and histories. That is, pre-Shakespearean drama worked with some vision of a natural or social (or divine, theological) horizon, against which human actions could be measured, weighed, determined.[21] There is, for instance, the 'moral-divine' horizon of English morality plays, whose given-ness is taken to govern the significance of human acts and consequently determines both the expressive form and the dramatic content of morality plays. In Shakespeare, by contrast, there is no such governing moral order, no transcendent horizon of good and evil in relation to which we can make sense of what happens in the plays—a fact which explains, among other things, the interpretive liberties that might be taken when it comes to approaching both the dramatic content of Shakespearean tragedy and its formal presentation.[22] Greek tragedy, too, presents a certain vision of the connection between human actions, human culture, and a set of natural facts, or 'divine-natural-fated' demands that challenge or limit human activity.[23] To compose the plot of a Greek tragedy meant, as

[21] This is obviously a sweeping statement, one that would require more defence and qualification than I can give here. Still, I think it is a basically defensible statement—useful in this context, I hope, for getting at the distinctiveness of Shakespearean tragedy.

[22] Samuel Johnson had it right when he wrote: 'Shakespeare does not write with any moral purpose.' Arthur Sherbo, ed., *Johnson on Shakespeare*, 23 vols. (New Haven: Yale University Press, 1958-77), 7: 71. This does not, of course, stop anyone from trying to impose a moral order onto the interpretation of Shakespeare. But such impositions invariably do little more than beg all the interesting questions about, say, Macbeth's fate, or Othello's, or Lear's.

[23] But what about Euripides, or Aristophanes—or, for that matter, Seneca or Terence—whose works have seemed to many (to Hegel and Nietzsche, for instance) to be more 'Shakespearean' or modern that Sophocles or Aeschylus? I do not have the space here to give proper consideration to these questions, but my suggestion would be that—leaving aside the 'proto-modern' individual-psychological complexity in Euripides, say—these ancient works still presuppose some way of connecting human actions, human history, to given 'facts of the matter' (whether natural, divine-given, or somehow fated). In Shakespeare, I am suggesting, there is no such way of suturing the purported 'facts' of nature (or God's command, or fate) and what human beings do to, or with, one another.

Aristotle suggested, grasping the 'unity' of an individual's time and place; it entailed supposing a view of the whole of someone's relation to the natural or social world of which he is a part. Sophocles, for instance, saw—*had* to see—that Oedipus' was *both* King of Thebes (hence, Jocasta's husband) *and* Jocasta's son (hence, Laius' murderer) in order to show how Oedipus himself was brought to 'see' the whole picture, by means of the reversals and recognitions of which Aristotle spoke. So, while Oedipus' view of things at the outset of Sophocles' play is partial and subjective—*he* thinks that he is Jocasta's husband, even as he is blind to the fact that he is also her son—events bring him to see the whole picture, to come to know everything that Sophocles (not to mention the audience, or the soothsayer Tiresias) already knows from the outset. And by finally seeing the entirety of his relation to his social world—the way, say, that ancient mythologies saw the cosmos as bounded by comprehensible horizons—Oedipus is brought to ruin, and the tragedy concludes. To compose a drama of this sort is thus to present a God's-eye, a-historical view on the spectacle of humans beings in action—a perspective that allows us all (playwright, protagonists, audience) to perceive such-and-such a situation by coming to know the relationship between (subjective) individuals and their (objective) world.

Shakespeare, by contrast, shows us how different situations look from the standpoint of particular individuals (Hamlet, for instance)—as well as from other standpoints *on* those individuals and that situation (Claudius, Gertrude, Polonius, Ophelia, Horatio, each of whom has a subjective world-view of their own)—without ever showing how or whether these individual points of view truly coincide in a panoptic whole. In fact, the action of a Shakespearean drama is invariably motivated by the non-coincidence of these multiple points of view—the sheer lack of an objective view of subjective stances. Think, for example, of the way that differing perspectives on Hamlet's behaviour drive much of what actually occurs in the play *Hamlet*. Or, of the way that what an audience perceives—about Macbeth's response at the banquet to the murder of Banquo, for instance—does not correspond to how others in the play see things. Or, of how the Friar's retelling of the lovers' actions at the end of *Romeo and Juliet* necessarily misses so much of what mattered to the audience—the balcony scene, the morning aubade and so on. Or of how Horatio's bald plot-summary at the close of *Hamlet* will hardly capture what we have just witnessed.

In this way, Shakespeare forces us to regard any perspective on human actions as deeply provisional, historically bounded, and contextually determined.[24] Which is to say that no character in Shakespeare—and no audience of a Shakespeare play—ever learns the 'whole truth', or gains a panoptic perspective on human actors in the world. Quite the contrary: in *King Lear*, for instance, Lear's or Gloucester's blindness to the standpoints of their respective children is never subsequently 'reversed' into insight by the unintended consequences of their deeds. Instead of moving from blindness to insight, we see how and with what implications an ongoing (and worsening) blindness can replace insight.[25] Even when events seem to be cleared up at the end of a Shakespearean drama—the way, for instance, that revelations come tumbling one after the other at the close of *Cymbeline*—we are left not with a sense of clarity and insight, but with more questions than ever. 'Nor the

---

[24] Shakespeare-the-playwright invariably seems to know more than what any individual protagonist *in* the play, or any particular audience, comes to know.

[25] See my chapter on *King Lear* in *Tragic Conditions in Shakespeare: Disinheriting the Globe* (Baltimore: Johns Hopkins University Press, 2009).

time nor place | Will serve our long inter'gatories', admits the baffled King Cymbeline at the play's close (5.5.391-2). Our sense of 'closure' at the conclusion of a Shakespeare play is, moreover, belied by our sense that the fate of one or more of the characters remains deeply unresolved, or unexplained, by the actions we have witnessed. Even our clarity about what is wrong or broken is diminished. Whereas in Greek tragedy, it matters tremendously— to the city that watches, above all—that at least the terms of the crises, if not of solutions, are clear, in Shakespeare we are denied even that clarity. Will Iago confess once back in Venice? What will become of the broken kingdom at the end of *King Lear*? Why, if Shakespeare meant to invoke a legend according to which Banquo was King James' ancestor, is Malcolm (and not Fleance) crowned at the conclusion of *Macbeth*? And what is the connection between, say, this broader history and Macduff's role as Macbeth's assassin? One could go on and on with questions such as these, since no perspective in Shakespeare's work—neither the author's, nor the audience's, nor that of any individual character—is capable of presenting the events as a unified whole.[26] In Shakespeare, subjective-individual and objective-worldly points of view never fully coincide.

4

Having said all this, we can now begin to see how Shakespearean tragedy responds to the loss of any 'given'—nature, or God, or 'fate'—that might explain human societies, histories, actions, destinies, relationships and values. Shakespeare challenges us to understand tragedies not as responding to given-ness of existential facts (desire, or mortality) or historical situations (Henry V's invasion of France, or the fate of the Roman republic), but as responding to the fact that there are no givens that govern our dramatic activity. To say it all at once: Shakespearean tragedy displays our provisional self-determination, as subjects in the world—while at the same time asking us to see our actions as intelligible, as somehow meaningful, as something more than the vanity of 'so-and-so' doing 'this-or-that'. The loss of 'givens' (the death of old gods, the devaluation of our highest values) that Shakespeare 'works through' does not, I propose, leave us with a desperate nihilism—but rather with the sense that it is precisely this loss of 'givens' that, finally, allows us to see ourselves as provisionally free in the world, and as reckoning with the implications of this new self-understanding.

This is why, in Shakespearean tragedy, subjective freedom comes to light through (or, in some cases, *as*) the dissolution of the social bonds on which we rely—kinship ties, civic relations, economic dependencies, or political allegiances. The ritual practices that had sustained prior, traditional forms of social life—funerary rites, the performance of 'noble' or 'honourable' deeds, military service, conventional modes of language, ritual ways of bequeathing the material world, formal modes of punishment or retribution—appear in

---

[26] Such questions might be further extended in order to reconsider traditional generic distinctions between comedy and tragedy. We might ask about *The Merchant of Venice*, for instance, whether Shylock is really 'content,' and whether he actually performs the acts he has pledged to perform. For a start in this direction, see my remarks on comedy and the comic in my Introduction to *Tragic Conditions in Shakespeare*, esp. 4–5, 18–24, 31–3.

Shakespearean tragedy as perverse, inadequate or even irrational. As a result, the meaning our actions cannot derive from their recognizable adherence to, or transgression of, this or that norm.[27] Macbeth welcomes Duncan 'as his kinsman and his subject ... and his host'—all of which should lead Macbeth to shut the door on any murderer, not bear the knife himself. And yet by killing Duncan, Macbeth becomes King! So, to what are we to attribute Macbeth's actions and their outcome? Is not 'ambition' a name or placeholder for the breakdown of any other, external motivation or ethical horizon? ('I have no spur | To prick the sides of my intent, but only | Vaulting ambition, which o'erleaps itself | And falls on the other' (*Macbeth* 7.1.25-8).) Shakespeare's protagonists (like us) have undergone the collapse of a motivating way of life, of an inheritable set of norms by means of which to make what we do intelligible or acceptable or meaningful to ourselves (and others). Yet it is not just that these older ways of life collapse or fail, or cease to be sufficiently motivating—leaving only particular, naked, imperfect individuals. Rather, these limited, imperfect human beings turn out to be the bearers of these collapsed values. How they bear up under the weight *completes* the collapse. 'Let Rome in Tiber melt and the wide arch | Of the rang'd empire fall!' cries Antony, as he embraces Cleopatra (*Antony and Cleopatra* 1.1.35-6).

Similarly, Hamlet's can be identified with any number of deeds, and yet no one knows exactly how to understand his actions in view of collective norms or 'reasons for acting'. What to make of his behaviour after his father's death, or of his treatment of Ophelia, or of his slaughter of Polonius, or of his subsequent refusal to treat Polonius' dead body with appropriate care? (Gertrude: 'O me, what hast thou done? | Hamlet: Nay, I know not ...' (*Hamlet* 3.4.25-6)). And whenever Hamlet seeks the meaning of his actions in the clarity of others' responses, his social world seems incapable of answering him—beyond expressing incomprehension, or sending him away. In a sense, Hamlet is disinherited not only by Claudius' election and the insufficiency of natural-matrilineal ties, but by the sheer vacuity of the social activities that remain open to him, such as revenge or life as a courtier. Hamlet's task, it seems, is not to figure out how best to carry out what is ostensibly being asked of him—revenge, filial love, loyalty to the court—but to try to lead his own life, under the realization that none of these social demands, each of which is incompatible with the others, can be sufficiently motivating. Our interpretation of the play will express our sense of whether Hamlet succeeds or fails in this.

In his *Lectures on Fine Art*, Hegel saw that Shakespearean tragedy 'takes for its proper subject matter .... the subjective inner life of the character who is not, as in classical tragedy, a purely individual embodiment of ethical powers'.[28] In other words, the interests, aims and actions of Shakespeare's characters are not fully absorbed or explained by those of the family, church, state, and so on—which is why even minor characters in Shakespeare stand out to us as individuals who might be 'played' by actors in radically diverse ways, with different ticks, passions, motivations, and so forth. But Hegel nonetheless wanted to hold to the belief that 'in human action a basis of specific ends drawn from the concrete spheres of family, state, church etc. is never missing'. For Hegel, our actions invariably throw us into the 'sphere of real world and its particular concerns'.[29] What Hegel means

---

[27] For a fuller defence of this, see my *Tragic Conditions in Shakespeare*.
[28] Hegel, 'Dramatic Poetry', 73.   [29] Ibid.

is that tragedies show how our actions invariably implicate us in a broader social world, and by the same token the fate of a social world itself unfolds through our actions. If there are no worldly consequences to our actions, then they do not appear as actions at all; if our worldly ties are not transformed by what particular human beings do, then no tragedy would be possible, and individual human agents would not come to light as such.

This left Hegel somewhat puzzled about Shakespearean tragedy, since in Shakespeare— as just observed—the relationship between the actions of individual characters and objective 'powers' (substantial social demands, inheritable forms of social life) is far from clear.[30] Here is Hegel confessing his bewilderment: the 'aims' of Shakespeare's characters, he writes, 'are broadly and variously particularized and in such detail that what is truly substantial can often glimmer through them in only a very dim way'.[31] This seems true, but also inadequate. After all, it seems impossible to account for—say—Regan or Goneril's attachment to Edmund as (even dimly) expressing anything 'truly substantial', as revealing anything beyond the contingency of *their* passionate attachment to him, or their jealousy of one another. Think also of how Shakespeare's frequent and diverse explorations of the vicissitudes of sexual love reveal attachments to which society is utterly blind, or by which social commitments cannot be explained. Desdemona's father openly declares, for instance, that he cannot see the legitimacy or meaning of his daughter's desire for Othello. And later, Desdemona's dying words will refute Othello's perception of himself as her murderer—challenging us to see her motivation as hers alone, as a form of self-expression: 'Nobody; I *myself. Farewell.*' So, too, because Romeo's and Juliet's aims are not immediately those of their families or of Verona, their tragic end cannot be seen as the consequence of their prior actions. This is why their suicides still need explaining, even when the consequences for the family or the city are clear ('Go hence and have more talk of these sad things' (5.3.306)).[32]

It is as if Shakespearean tragedy shows how we can (and do) *lose* any external ethical or cultural reason, or explanation, for our actions—without, however, losing all 'moral' motivation, where by 'moral' I mean not a transcendent set of orienting values but a lived experience of ourselves as not utterly worthless, base, expendable. As if we are perhaps capable of finding some other way of justifying ourselves to one another, some way of *being* or *becoming* that justification. As if, therefore, the moral stakes of our actions were best glimpsed when conventional, ethical justifications for acting fail—when we have no other 'reason' to offer one another but ourselves.[33]

---

[30] For an admirably clear and genuinely insightful exploration of the limits of Hegel's view of tragedy with respect to Shakespeare, see A. C. Bradley, 'Hegel's Theory of Tragedy' in *Oxford Lectures on Poetry* www.gutenberg.org/ebooks/36773.

[31] Ibid.

[32] For more, see my essay, 'Defying the Stars: Tragic Love as the Struggle for Freedom in *Romeo and Juliet*', *Shakespeare Quarterly* 63:1 (Spring 2012), and the chapters on *Romeo and Juliet* and *Othello* in my *Love as Human Freedom* (Stanford: Stanford University Press, forthcoming).

[33] This formulation sounds close to Montaigne's famous words about Étienne de La Boétie: 'Si on me presse, continue-t-il, de dire pourquoi je l'aimais, je sens que cela ne se peut exprimer qu'en répondant: parce que c'était lui; parce que c'était moi' ('If urged to tell wherefore I loved him, I feel it cannot be expressed but by answering: Because it was he, because it was myself'). However, in Shakespeare's beloved Montaigne there is not the same sense of broader 'ethical collapse'—the disappearance, that is, of other possible 'reasons'—that, I am arguing, is in Shakespeare. See Montaigne, *Essays* (New York: Penguin, 1993), bk.1, ch. 28.

5

Shakespeare offers, so says Hegel, 'the finest examples of firm and consistent characters who come to ruin simply because of this decisive adherence to themselves'.[34] Similarly Hegel's contemporary, the English critic William Hazlitt (1778-1830)—who, with his friend Samuel Coleridge, had been influenced by the German enthusiasm for Shakespeare—emphasized the importance of character-type in his *Characters of Shakespear's Plays* (1813). A. C. Bradley's 1904 lectures on Shakespeare offer the most sustained and influential elaboration: in Shakespeare's tragedies, Bradley writes, 'action is essentially the expression of character'. I understand Bradley's insight to be as follows: Shakespearean tragedy displays human beings not as representational figures acting on behalf of any way of life or 'value' greater than themselves—but as staging *themselves* as potentially valuable to us, as agents in the world *leading* their lives rather than just suffering whatever befalls them. Rather than ask us to grasp what Antony's fate means for Rome, or what Hamlet's fate means for Denmark, Shakespeare invites us to determine why (or if) Antony's and Hamlet's actions matter, without relying on any external values or norms to anchor that meaning. And if Othello's fate seems reflected in the fate of Venice, in the structure of the republic's 'way of life', then this is only because we also perceive Othello to be acting on his own when he lays his hands on Desdemona—only insofar as we witness Othello's subsequent failure to explain the murder in terms that bear essentially upon Venice.

All of which forces us to ask: can we matter to one another not only in virtue of what we might represent, but also with nothing to offer but ourselves, our self-expressive deeds? Can we recognize one another, as individual actors in the world, in our very ordinariness, as of extraordinary worth?

These issues coalesce with particular intensity in *King Lear*. No other Shakespearean tragedy opens with a more firmly established and secure social world; and yet none finishes with a more profound sense of worldly loss—where the viability of any intergenerational social life is in question. At the same time, by the play's end, our concern for the fate of the Kingdom has been replaced by our efforts to understand the state of the relationships in the play—and by the characters' attempts to understand one another.

At the opening, Lear strives to outlive the necessity of his natural death for the transmission of the Kingdom—in order to definitively separate the intergenerational life of his society from its mooring in a natural cycle of life and death, growth and decay. By denying the necessity of his own 'natural' death for the transmission of the Kingdom, he would denaturalize society, and free intergenerational devolution from the claims of nature. ('I will forget my nature' (1.5.33).)

But to what end?

By liberating society from nature's demands, Lear would freely bring about his own rebirth, his own re-entrance into the world. He would make clear that his presence among others is a self-determining social reality, not a natural fact. With sovereign autonomy, he would lay his natural life at the feet of others, for their approval or disapproval. For the sake of testing—*really* testing—his daughters' love, he strips himself of accommodation in

---

[34] Hegel, 'Dramatic Poetry', 79.

order to see if he will be accommodated. For the truest test of love will lie not in rhetorical demonstrations, but in whether or not his daughters—without being legally, ethically or ritually required to do so—will take his aging body into their homes, tolerate its inevitable failings, and let Lear crawl unburdened toward death.

In thinking to set his rest on Cordelia's kind nursery, Lear not only desired the chance to be loved as himself—rather than just as King or father—but he also wanted his desire to be seen in his otherwise puzzling action: his self-divestment as a demand for loving recognition. For Lear, the possibility of loving Cordelia, and of being loved by her is something that neither nature nor the Kingdom, with all its prerogatives and wealth, can furnish. And yet it is a possibility that might be achieved by Lear's letting go of the Kingdom—and *that* can only be achieved if, again, the Kingdom's *durée* is no longer tethered to the natural cycle of birth and death. Freeing the Kingdom from nature's authority would give Lear the chance to see how Cordelia responds to *him*, to his desire for *her* recognition.[35]

For this same reason, things go awry for Lear and Cordelia whenever they misguidedly turn to some external social or natural justification for their actions, for their demands of one another: *Because I am your father, a sovereign power, because 'I gave you all'* (2.4.252), or—on Cordelia's part—*Because I am your child, the fruit of your loins, because I know I am your 'joy'* (1.1.82). In thinking that they already have the 'right'—whether by natural or positive law—to be loved or respected or acknowledged, they set themselves up for the awakening that 'being loved' or 'acting on one's own' are not 'rights' to which one can be socially or naturally entitled. What they fail to see in such moments, therefore, is that they have nothing to offer one another, no 'reason'. except themselves—and that 'they themselves' count as meaningful offerings only by being received, loved and recognized as such.

That loving and being loved make our worldly rights and social entitlements worth having, not the reverse, is something that can perhaps only be learned through the sting of finding oneself unloved, rebuked, put down—or, conversely, through the remorse that comes from having injured a loved one. This is why, as soon as he feels himself unloved by Cordelia, Lear throws the Kingdom away. The world he was about to bestow was meaningful to him only so long as he thought that, by bequeathing it on his own terms, he might bring about the possibility of finally leading his own life with Cordelia, on their terms.

It is as if the worth of our shared world, of our lives together, were determined by our success or failure in being—or in somehow becoming—worthwhile for one another.

Success in this enterprise demands that we somehow inhabit others' lives, and imagine for ourselves what they would do, what they want from us, and why they act the way they do. Shakespearean tragedy responds to this demand.

SELECT BIBLIOGRAPHY

Auden, W. H., *The Dyer's Hand* (New York: Vintage, 1988).

Bradley, A. C., 'Hegel's Theory of Tragedy', in *Oxford Lectures on Poetry* (Project Gutenberg: www.gutenberg.org/ebooks/36773).

Bradley, A. C., *Shakespearean Tragedy* (New York: Penguin, 1991).

[35] Again, for a fuller reading of *King Lear*, see ch. 3 of my *Tragic Conditions in Shakespeare*.

Cavell, Stanley, *Disowning Knowledge in Seven Plays of Shakespeare* (Cambridge: Cambridge University Press, 2003).

Dollimore, Jonathan, *Radical Tragedy: Religion, Ideology, and Power in the Drama of Shakespeare and His Contemporaries* (2nd edn., Durham, NC: Duke University Press, 1993).

Freud, Sigmund, *Mourning and Melancholia* (London: Karnac, 2008).

Frye, Northrop, *Fools of Time: Studies in Shakespearean Tragedy* (Toronto: University of Toronto Press, 1991).

Hammond, Paul, *The Strangeness of Tragedy* (Oxford: Oxford University Press, 2008).

Hegel, G. W. F., 'Dramatic Poetry', from *Lectures on Fine Art*, in *Philosophers on Shakespeare*, ed. Paul A. Kottman (Stanford: Stanford University Press, 2009), 57–85.

Herder, J. G., 'Shakespeare', in *Philosophers on Shakespeare*, ed. Paul A. Kottman (Stanford: Stanford University Press, 2009), 21–38.

Knight, G. Wilson, *The Wheel of Fire: Interpretations of Shakespearean Tragedy* (London: Oxford University Press, 1930).

Kott, Jan, *Shakespeare Our Contemporary* (New York: Norton, 1964).

Kottman, Paul A., *Tragic Conditions in Shakespeare* (Baltimore: Johns Hopkins University Press, 2009).

Neill, Michael, *Issues of Death: Mortality and Identity in English Renaissance Tragedy* (Oxford: Clarendon, 1997).

Szondi, Peter, *An Essay on the Tragic* (Stanford: Stanford University Press, 2002).

CHAPTER 2

....

THE CLASSICAL
INHERITANCE

....

RICHARD HALPERN

WHAT distinguishes a tragedy from a sad story? For Aristotle, one of the criteria was *megethos*, which we may translate as greatness, amplitude, or stature.[1] Enduring the death of a parent or getting dumped by a romantic partner can be excruciatingly painful, but it is also excruciatingly ordinary, which for Aristotle would have barred it from the realm of the tragic. When the king of Thebes finds that he has brought a deadly plague upon the city he rules because he has unwittingly married his mother and killed his father, that sad story is extraordinary—it has tragic amplitude. Or when (to take a Shakespearean example) Marc Antony loses the Roman Empire because of his irresistible passion for an Egyptian Queen, that too has tragic *megethos*.

Similar considerations, I think, surround the question of Shakespearean tragedy and the classical tradition. Why care about this particular source of influence rather than others? Shakespeare was a voracious reworker of all kinds of materials, cannibalizing Tudor chronicles, contemporary drama, Italian novellas, medieval mystery and morality plays, and so forth. It would be difficult to claim that classical sources are more influential than any of these. And yet, for centuries, the question of classical influence has managed to set itself apart from others. Shakespeare's relation to a Sophocles or Euripides has a kind of *megethos* that his indebtedness to a Giraldi Cinthio or a Thomas Kyd does not. In part this has to do with the titanic stature of the writers involved, in part with the world-historical achievements of Greek and Roman culture, and in part with the sheer allure of a literary relation that stretches across a millennium. In a way, Shakespeare's relation to the classical world is itself tragic, at least by this one Aristotelian standard.

The question of 'amplitude' takes on quantitative as well as qualitative dimensions, moreover. In his own day, Shakespeare's relation to the classics seemed rather minor, limited by his 'small Latin and less Greek'. And yet if Shakespeare's direct knowledge of classical languages was relatively modest (by Ben Jonson's standards, not ours), his familiarity with classical letters via translations and the works of contemporaries who themselves read more widely than he did opens up a vista of potentially embarrassing magnitude. There

[1] Aristotle, *Poetics* 1449b 25.

is more than a little to say about Shakespeare and classical philosophy of several schools (Platonic, Aristotelian, sceptical, Stoic, atomist, etc.), about Shakespeare and classical history, rhetoric, medicine, law, astronomy, poetics, natural history, as well as literature in a wide array of forms (drama, epic, satire, lyric, elegy, romance, epyllion, pastoral, georgic, etc.). Trying to survey this landscape in a short essay would necessarily result in superficiality, incoherence, or both. I will therefore restrict the 'classical inheritance' to mean the inheritance of classical tragic *drama*—Shakespeare's relations with his fellow tragedians of antiquity. This (somewhat arbitrary) move limits the scope of the problem, but issues of many kinds remain, since the degree to which Shakespeare was influenced by classical playwrights has been extensively debated.[2] And of course, the question of Shakespeare's relation to the classical past has not historically been limited to empirical questions of influence and allusion. Antiquity has also offered an aesthetic standard compared to which Shakespeare was felt to excel or fall short, while for writers like Hegel and Freud it was a foil against which Shakespeare's essential modernity could be shown.

What Shakespeare inherits from the classical past is not an inert array of texts but rather a *tradition*. Tradition arises when the past is not simply 'there', a resource awaiting whatever the present wants to do with it. It is rather the past as already self-organized, already shot through with lines of development, emulation, and contestation that solicit and inform the inheriting author's engagement with them. A tradition is a past that can seduce and entangle, a past that utters its own hoots and cries. In tragic drama, of course, the demands of the past are often inexorable. Oedipus is chained to his own prior actions, Agamemnon to those of his ancestors. But classical tragedy's plots also come from the reserves of an antedeluvian, mythic history, which can be reshaped by the playwright but only within respectful limits (Euripides, admittedly, sometimes stretches the boundaries of respect). Both Greek and Roman comedy occupy the present-day world, and just as their protagonists get by on improvisation, luck, and irreverence, so their authors are required to invent scenarios out of whole cloth. Tragedy must recycle the old stories; hence the tug of tradition is strong within it. Comedy embodies freedom from the past, tragedy the weight of the past.[3]

And yet the temporality of tradition is more complex than this—not a negotiation between present and past alone, but one in which the future also plays a part. In the case of Shakespeare, it was readers of succeeding centuries who began to ponder his relation to the classics in any detail. By contrast, his contemporaries and near-contemporaries (Ben Jonson, John Dryden) were largely unimpressed with his classical learning.[4] For them, Shakespeare's classical inheritance was negligible both in extent and as a source of what was significant about his work. His relation to the classical past was largely

---

[2] On the history of critical debates concerning the degree of Seneca's influence on Shakespeare, see Robert S. Miola, *Shakespeare and Classical Tragedy: The Influence of Seneca* (Oxford: Oxford University Press, 1992), 3–7.

[3] This distinction is complicated by the fact that Shakespearean comedy does draw on Roman comedy and moreover sometimes tries to 'outdo' its Plautine models in the same way that Shakespearean tragedy aims to outdo its Senecan ones. But the question of classical inheritance never becomes a freighted critical issue for comedy in the way that it does for tragedy.

[4] An exception is John Aubrey, who declared around 1680 that Shakespeare 'understood Latine pretty well'. Quoted in John W. Velz, *Shakespeare and the Classical Tradition: A Critical Guide to Commentary, 1660–1960* (Minneapolis: University of Minnesota Press, 1968), 4.

a non-relation—a relation of ignorance, either blessed or blameworthy. True, Jonson compares Shakespeare's greatness to that of Aeschylus, Sophocles, and Euripides, and Dryden declares Shakespeare 'the *Homer*, or father of our dramatick Poets'.[5] But this is the bringing to bear of an aesthetic standard, not an examination of what Shakespeare *inherited* from the past. Indeed, Shakespeare's 'less Greek' supposedly rendered him incapable of reading the very playwrights to whom Jonson compares him. But already implicit in Dryden's assessment, if not quite fully in Jonson's, is a privileging of the Greek over the Roman—a sense that only the Greek poets offer a meaningful point of comparison. And this results in a peculiar divergence between assessment and influence. The Roman playwright Seneca was long held to be the one classical predecessor whom Shakespeare had clearly and unquestionably read—the sole theatrical medium of his classical dramatic inheritance (in tragedy, anyway. Shakespeare read Roman comic playwrights as well). Yet Seneca's own reputation waned after the early modern period. Hence it was comparisons with Sophocles, not with Seneca, which largely interested the eighteenth and nineteenth centuries. The point I am trying to make here is that Shakespeare's relation to the classical past is not something that solely he constructs. It is also something constructed for him by subsequent readers to answer their own interests and predilections. Tradition is something negotiated among Shakespeare's present, past, and future.

One result of Seneca's reduced stature was a growing tendency to locate parallels of plot and character between Shakespearean and Greek (particularly Sophoclean) drama. In *The Spectator* (No.44, 20 April 1711), Joseph Addison was among the first to point out Hamlet's resemblance to Sophocles' Orestes in the *Electra*.[6] Thomas Davies, in 1785, observed that Cordelia's filial piety is rivalled only by that of Antigone, and he also noted that Gloucester's blinding finds a precedent in that of Oedipus.[7] Of course, very general parallels such as these could also have been gleaned from Seneca. But he was no longer a sufficiently worthy ancestor. A kind of spiritual kinship, born of shared literary greatness, eclipsed mere empirical fact. Among German thinkers, in particular, the comparison of Shakespeare and the Greeks was elevated from tendency to law, since both parties were felt to bear a special spiritual kinship to German culture.[8]

In his *Lectures on Aesthetics*, Hegel invokes the parallels between Hamlet and Orestes in order to elaborate differences between the ethical orders of ancient and modern tragedy.[9] But the most famous—or notorious—connection between Shakespeare and Sophocles is drawn by Freud in *The Interpretation of Dreams*, where Hamlet's dilemma is compared,

---

[5] Jonson, 'To the Memory of my Beloved Master William Shakespeare, and What He Hath Left Us', lines 33–4. For Dryden, see Velz, *Shakespeare and the Classical Tradition*, 4.

[6] Velz, *Shakespeare and the Classical Tradition*, 285.   [7] Ibid., 297.

[8] On the habit of comparing Shakespeare and the Greeks on the part of German philosophers, see the Introduction to (and some of the excerpts in) Paul A Kottman, ed., *Philosophers on Shakespeare* (Stanford: Stanford University Press, 2009). See also Kristin Gjesdal, 'Literature, Prejudice, Historicity: The Philosophical Importance of Herder's Shakespeare Studies', in Michael Forster and Klaus Vieweg, eds., *Die Aktualität der Romantik* (Berlin: Lit, 2012), 137–60. On Shakespeare's reception in Germany more broadly, see Roger Paulin, *The Critical Reception of Shakespeare in Germany, 1682–1914* (Hildesheim, Zurich, and New York: Georg Olms Verlag, 2003).

[9] G. W. F. Hegel, *Aesthetic: Lectures on Fine Art*, vol. 2, trans. J. M. Knox (Oxford: Oxford University Press, 1975), 1224–5.

not to that of Orestes but—for the first time—to that of Oedipus.[10] Freud, like Hegel, is interested in drawing contrasts between ancient and modern drama. In Sophocles' *Oedipus the King*, composed at an early stage of the civilizing process, incestuous desires can still be directly acted out, whereas in *Hamlet* (written in a later and more repressed era), they emerge only as Hamlet's symptoms of suicidal melancholy and delay.

Both Hegel and Freud posit an historical development wherein dramatic protagonists become increasingly 'inward' over time. But in Freud's case a secondary, unstated motive is also at play, since Oedipus' detective work, through which he uncovers his own repressed past, offers an implicit parallel to the interpretive labours of the psychoanalyst. In this case, then, the parallel to Sophocles is justified, since Seneca's version of the Oedipus legend focuses much less on the process by which Oedipus slowly and painfully uncovers the truth. Here it is truly Sophocles, rather than Seneca, who offers the meaningful precedent—a precedent that Shakespeare could supposedly not have known directly and that therefore occupies something akin to the Freudian unconscious with respect to literary history.

The main lines of twentieth- and twenty-first- century Shakespeare scholarship undertook to 'set things right' by exploring Shakespeare's traceable relations to Seneca rather than his merely figurative ones to Sophocles—without quite managing to banish the residual fascination of what A. D. Nutall suggestively calls the 'action at a distance' between Shakespeare and the Greeks.[11] But a crucial minority of scholars has not been quite so ready to dismiss the possibility of direct Greek influence, and that minority has become more vocal and assured in recent years.[12] While it is true that Shakespeare probably could not have read Greek tragedies in Greek, and while the few translations into English were unlikely to have fallen into his hands, editions of Greek tragic playwrights with facing page translations into Latin—a language with which Shakespeare was more familiar— might well have entered his orbit.[13] Or he might have seen performances of plays based directly on Greek tragedies by playwrights more learned than he.[14] There are details of

[10] Sigmund Freud, 'The Interpretation of Dreams', in *The Standard Edition of the Complete Psychological Works of Sigmund Freud*, ed. James Strachey et al., 24 vols. (London: Hogarth Press, 1953–74), 4: 264.

[11] See A. D. Nuttall, 'Action at a Distance: Shakespeare and the Greeks', in *Shakespeare and the Classics*, ed. Charles Martindale and A. B. Taylor (Cambridge: Cambridge University Press, 2004), 209–22. In the same volume, see Michael Silk, 'Shakespeare and Greek Tragedy Strange Relationship', 241–57. See also Adrian Poole, *Tragedy: Shakespeare and the Greek Example* (London: Blackwell, 1987).

[12] See Emrys Jones, *The Origins of Shakespeare* (Oxford: Clarendon Press, 1977), 85–118; Douglas B. Wilson, 'Euripides' *Alcestis* and the Ending of Shakespeare's *The Winter's Tale*', *Iowa State Journal of Research* 58 (1984), 345–55. Louise Schleiner, 'Latinized Greek Drama in Shakespeare's Writing of *Hamlet*', *Shakespeare Quarterly* 41 (1990), 29–48; Sarah Dewar-Watson, 'The *Alcestis* and the Statue Scene in *The Winter's Tale*', *Shakespeare Quarterly* 60 (2009), 73–80; Tanya Pollard, 'What's Hecuba to Shakespeare?', *Shakespeare Quarterly* 65 (2012), 1060–93; Tanya Pollard, 'Greek Playbooks and Dramatic Forms in Early Modern England',in *Formal Matters: Reading the Materials of English Renaissance Literature*, ed. Allison K. Deutermann and András Kiséry (Manchester: Manchester University Press, 2013), 99–115; Susanne Wofford, 'Recognizing Euripides: The *Alcestis, Much Ado about Nothing* and *The Winter's Tale*' (unpublished manuscript).

[13] See Schleiner, 'Latinized Greek Drama'; Pollard, 'What's Hecuba to Shakespeare' and 'Greek Playbooks'.

[14] See Schleiner, 'Latinized Greek Drama', 34–7.

plot and character in Shakespeare for which possible sources can apparently be found in Greek tragic plays but not elsewhere. The whole question of Shakespeare and the Greeks is currently up for re-evaluation, while at the same time irrefutable proof of such influence remains difficult to pin down. The least one can say, however, is that the former certainty that Shakespeare had no access to Greek tragic drama looks much less solid than it once did.

Yet even the most optimistic reading of present evidence suggests that Shakespeare was unlikely to have encountered more than a very few Greek plays, and those few not what we today would regard as the greatest examples of Greek tragedy. No one has yet made a case that Shakespeare knew *Oedipus the King*, *Antigone* or *The Bacchae*, though a somewhat speculative argument has been proffered that he might have either read in translation or seen at the theater some version of the *Oresteia*.[15] Recent work on Shakespeare and the Greeks has focused largely on Euripides, thereby leaving the Shakespeare-Sophocles connection of which the eighteenth century dreamed still in shadow. Tanya Pollard, the most persuasive of the recent critics to claim Greek influence, holds for the most part that Greek tragedy affects Shakespeare by shifting the general conceptions of tragedy at work in early modern culture rather than by supplying specific source materials.[16] While it expands and enriches our sense of Shakespeare's engagement with the classical past, then, recent work on Greek tragedy does not yet significantly threaten the centrality of Seneca as dramatic influence. If Seneca was not Shakespeare's sole model of classical tragedy, he was still the predominant one.

While the assumption that Shakespeare had no knowledge of the Greeks may turn out to be a hoary myth, the persistent desire to connect Shakespeare to the Greeks may itself rely on an equally outdated premise: that Seneca is a crude, bombastic, and aesthetically inferior successor who offers an inadequate model for Shakespearean greatness. Recent criticism of Seneca, however has come to regard him as the practitioner of a 'baroque, post-classical' aesthetic that is of value in its own right, and not simply a failed attempt to emulate a Greek example. [17] Seneca is redeemed from having vulgarized the past by attaching him instead to a critical term—'baroque'—borrowed from the post-Shakespearean future. He is to the Augustan standards of Virgil and Horace as baroque drama of the seventeenth century is to the more classical aesthetics of the Renaissance. Of course, since seventeenth-century Trauerspiel is heavily influenced by Senecan tragedy, there is something potentially circular in this manoeuvre. But it is certainly true that Walter Benjamin's famous analysis of baroque Trauerspiel has retrospectively elucidated important aspects of Senecan drama.[18] Because the baroque dimensions of Seneca would not have been so clearly visible without Benjamin's work, replacing the somewhat speculative relation between Shakespeare and Greeks in favour of the more scholarly, 'responsible' account of

---

[15] See Schleiner, 'Latinized Greek Drama'.

[16] Pollard, 'What's Hecuba to Shakespeare' and 'Greek Playbooks'.

[17] A. J. Boyle, *Tragic Seneca: An Essay on the Theatrical Tradition* (New York: Routledge, 1997), 18. Thomas Rosenmeyer likewise observes that German baroque drama 'furnishes the closest parallels to Seneca's obsessive somatic particularity' in *Senecan Drama and Stoic Cosmology* (Berkeley: University of California Press, 1989), 123.

[18] See Julia Reinhard Lupton and Kenneth Reinhard, *After Oedipus: Shakespeare in Psychoanalysis* (Ithaca: Cornell University Press, 1993), 89–118.

his influence by Seneca does not entirely manage to restore a simple, normative relation between Shakespeare's present and his past. The temporal complexities of tradition, triangulated as they necessarily are among Shakespeare, the classics, and post-Shakespearean thinkers, is not banished by the substitution of Seneca for the Greeks.

In any case, the question of Shakespeare and the classical inheritance remains divided between scholarship and speculation—between, that is, Shakespeare's relation to Seneca, which has the advantages of being direct and demonstrable but perhaps somewhat dull, and his relation to the Greek playwrights, which is mediated at best but has captivated some of the great minds of recent centuries. I don't claim to be able to square this circle, and in fact, what follows will focus mainly on Shakespeare's reworking of Seneca. But I want to make a stronger case than is usually made for Shakespeare's encounter with the Greek playwrights *by way of* Seneca. Shakespeare, I claim, grasps and extends Seneca's ways of emulating the Greek playwrights. If he had actually read some of the Greeks as well, so much the better. But even if he hadn't, Seneca might provide instructions for 're-verse engineering' them. My approach entails a focus less on Senecan reference and citation than on vectors of development—in short, on a Senecan *tradition* that reaches back to the Greeks and forward to Shakespeare.

We can begin to situate Shakespeare with respect to Seneca by noting that the latter is already a 'Renaissance' playwright in the sense that he confronts a classical (Greek) tradition of intimidating prestige. 'Enslaved Greece enslaved her savage victor and brought | The arts to rustic Latium,' wrote Horace, leaving the Romans subject to an older, authoritative body of literature in a foreign tongue that they were forced to study, imitate and contend with.[19] Seneca would have encountered the works of Aeschylus, Sophocles, and Euripides in the same manner that Shakespeare first encountered Seneca—as school texts, not as living drama on a stage. And since early modern schooling was patterned largely on Roman models, Seneca would have served Shakespeare as the occasion for rhetorical, grammatical, and stylistic analysis of a kind comparable to that which Seneca himself would have performed on his Greek forebears. In Shakespeare's case, more than Seneca's, this academic training imparts an air of the schoolroom to the early plays. *Titus Andronicus* goes so far as to quote Seneca's *Thyestes* in Latin, lest anyone doubt that Shakespeare's years in grammar school had been well spent.

In what follows, I will trace the influence of some central Senecan motifs on Shakespearean tragedy, focusing on those that not only serve important functions within dramatic plot but also allow plays to reflect metadramatically on the concept of tradition. *Thyestes* and *Titus Andronicus* will provide a useful starting point, in part because Seneca's influence on Shakespeare is so clearly legible in this pairing, and in part because

---

[19]   Horace, *Epistles* 2.1.156–7, quoted in Boyle, *Tragic Seneca*, 3. Classicists will rightly regard any claim that Seneca contends primarily or solely with the Greeks as misleading. Boyle describes Seneca's plays as 'palimpsestic texts' beneath which are visible 'a host of subtexts—Greek and Roman, Attic, Hellenistic, republican, Augustan, and early imperial—clarifying and informing their discourse' (Boyle, *Tragic Seneca*, 89). In 1989, Thomas Rosenmeyer could speak of a 'consensus … that Seneca probably owes most to his immediate [Roman] predecessors'. Yet Rosenmeyer opines that 'Seneca's debt to the republican dramatists, and to the ancient Greeks, may currently be underestimated' (Rosenmeyer, *Senecan Drama*, 5). I don't mean to omit other possible influences in focusing on Seneca's relation to the Greeks.

Thyestes, along with plays such as *Medea* and *Agamemnon*, exerts a seminal influence on Renaissance revenge tragedy. Indeed, the essential logic of revenge tragedy is contained within Atreus' lines: 'scelera non ulcisceris | nisi uincis' (195-6), 'You do not avenge crimes unless you surpass them.'[20] In Atreus' view it is not enough to repay past wrongs; one must tip the balance in the opposite direction, a process that inevitably leads to grotesque excess. Hence Atreus avenges Thyestes' sin of adultery by killing and cooking his children and feeding them to him. Not justice but an insane disproportion of punishment is his aim.

Atreus' motto does not merely govern the action within the play, however; it also describes the play's relation to its Greek precursors.[21] Of course, no Greek plays about Thyestes and Atreus survive, though eight Greek playwrights, including Sophocles and Euripides, wrote lost versions, as did six other Roman playwrights.[22] Even in the absence of a direct antecedent, however, we can see Seneca's attempt to 'outdo' the Greeks by directly presenting Thyestes' feast—a scene that Sophocles would almost certainly have conveyed in narrative form, via a messenger. Horace's *Ars Poetica* (179-88) renews the Greek proscription against showing excessively bloody scenes on stage, so Seneca would have been aware of it. In violating the laws of Greek dramatic decorum, Seneca commits an aesthetic *scelus* or crime that is a counterpart to that of Atreus. Of course, if Seneca's plays were indeed closet dramas, the stakes here would be lower; but critical opinion now leans against this once widely-accepted view.[23]

Shakespeare's challenge in *Titus Andronicus* is thus to out-Seneca Seneca, as Seneca outdid the Greeks.[24] How to accomplish this is not immediately obvious, however. The feasting scene in *Thyestes* achieves a pitch of horror that would be difficult to equal, much less exceed. But then there is act three, scene one, of *Titus* in which Titus' hand is cut off, the decapitated heads of his two sons are brought to him, and Titus and his brother Marcus exit each carrying one of the decapitated heads while Lavinia, herself handless and tongueless, bears Titus' severed hand in her teeth. It is not just that the sheer number of lopped limbs exceeds that in Seneca; the scene is so grotesque that it generates a kind of black humour. Shakespeare outdoes Seneca, in other words, by pushing stage violence to

---

[20] All Latin quotations and English translations of the plays are taken from the Loeb edition, *Seneca VIII. Tragedies: Hercules, Trojan Women, Phoenician Women, Medea, Phaedra*, trans. and ed. John G. Fitch (Cambridge, MA: Harvard University Press, 2002) and *Seneca IX. Tragedies: Oedipus, Agamemnon, Thyestes, Hercules on Oeta, Octavia* trans. and ed. John G. Fitch (Cambridge: Harvard University Press, 2004).

[21] This metadramatic dimension would have been reinforced by the fact that Seneca's Atreus is himself a poet-figure. See Alessandro Schiesaro, *The Passions in Play:* Thyestes *and the Dynamics of Senecan Drama* (Cambridge: Cambridge University Press, 2003), 54 *et passim*.

[22] Thomas D. Kohn, *The Dramaturgy of Senecan Tragedy* (Ann Arbor: University of Michigan Press, 2013), 131.

[23] For recent arguments that Seneca's works were written to be presented in the theatre, not just read in silence or declaimed without being acted out, see Dan Ferrin Sutton, *Seneca on the Stage* (Leiden: E. J. Brill, 1986); George M. W. Harrison, ed., *Seneca in Performance* (London: Duckworth with The Classical Press of Wales, 2000); and Kohn, *The Dramaturgy of Senecan Tragedy*.

[24] It should be noted, of course, that Thyestes' feast is not the only scene in Seneca that violated Greek strictures against staged violence, and that Roman tragedy in general was bloodier than the Greek. But in the context of a play that thematizes the outdoing of violence, this theatrical practice takes on an added significance.

a point where it can no longer be taken entirely seriously. The result is something that can only be called Senecan camp. Shakespeare isn't the sole inventor of this mode, however. It can also be glimpsed at times in *The Spanish Tragedy*. And *Titus Andronicus* isn't the only early play where Shakespeare dabbles in it; *Richard III* offers a sometimes campy version of the Senecan tyrant. Campy excess is not a mode that is easily sustained over the course of a whole career; but the theatrical self-consciousness that undergirds it serves Shakespeare well in his later, definitive engagement with revenge tragedy: *Hamlet*.

Hamlet is less obviously indebted to *Thyestes* than is *Titus Andronicus*. Still, some intriguing parallels link them. *Hamlet* features a Senecan ghost (of which, more later), as well as adultery and vengeance between brothers. One of Hamlet's soliloquies (2.2.550 ff.) even echoes a speech of Atreus' in *Thyestes* (176–80).[25] Yet this allusion serves to emphasize differences rather than similarities between the two avengers. Atreus enjoys a complete absence of moral scruples while Hamlet is burdened by an excess of them. As a result, revenge is delicious for Atreus—a source of giddy pleasure—but distasteful, as is almost everything else, for Hamlet. When the Danish Prince's vengeance does finally occur, it is over in a flash, unlike Atreus's drawn-out feasting on his brother's agony. Apart from a few moments of fatal swordplay, *Hamlet* avoids violence, much less the grotesque bloodletting of plays like *Thyestes* and *Titus Andronicus*. If it attempts to surpass its Senecan predecessor, it clearly adopts a very different strategy for doing so.

Two of Hamlet's characteristic speech forms—the aside and the soliloquy—are already present in Seneca. As A. J. Boyle observes:

> Seneca's frequent use of [the aside] is a function of his drama's pervasive concern with psychological interiority—a concern most particularly and clearly exhibited in Seneca's predilection for self- presentational soliloquies or monologues, in which the focus is on the inner workings of the human mind, on the mind as locus of emotional conflict, vulnerability, self-deception, irrational guilt. The dramatization of the emotions seems to have been central to Roman tragedy in a way it was not to Greek.[26]

If it is difficult to read this passage without thinking of Hamlet, this is a sign of the degree to which Shakespeare develops tendencies already present in Seneca. Just as the Roman playwright exceeds the Greeks' interest in psychological interiority, Shakespeare will take this process one step further by making Hamlet a character who obsessively monitors his own interiority, reflects philosophically upon it, and converts this monitoring and reflection themselves into problems for further reflection. Hamlet is a hero who wades not in pools of blood but in pools of self-consciousness. In a related tactic, *Hamlet* takes the already considerable if implicit metadramatic self-consciousness of Senecan drama and renders it explicit via devices such as the wandering players and Hamlet's production of the Mousetrap.

As more than one critic as noted, the Renaissance soliloquy derives not only from the Senecan monologue but also from the Senecan chorus, and this is a fact of particular interest to *Hamlet*.[27] The Senecan chorus differs from the Greek in that it is entirely divorced from the dramatic action. Indeed, it often leaves the stage to the protagonists, while

---

[25] Miola, *Shakespeare and Classical Tragedy*, 38.   [26] Boyle, *Tragic Seneca*, 25.

[27] Boyle, *Tragic Seneca*, 156; Miola, *Shakespeare and Classical Tragedy*, 39.

the Greek chorus is always present in the orchestra. This detachment, in turn, frees the Senecan chorus to engage in philosophical reflection, often of a Stoic turn. The philosophically 'cool' observations of the chorus frequently offer a counterpoint to the 'hot', emotionally overwrought *Schreireden* of the protagonists.

The philosophical content of Hamlet's soliloquies makes this Senecan provenance especially vivid. Indeed, Hamlet's most famous soliloquy borrows generously from the chorus of Seneca's *Troades*:

> Verum est an timidos fabula decipit
> umbras corporibus vivere conditis
> cum coniunx oculis imposuit manum
> supremusque dies solibus obstitit
> et tristis cineres urna corecuit?
> non prodest animam tradere funeri,
> sed restat miseris vivere longius?
> an toti morimur nullaque pars manet
> nostri, cum profugo spiritus halitu
> immixtus nebulis cessit in aëra
> et nudum tetigit subdita fax latus?

(Seneca, *Troades* 371-81)

> Is it true, or a tale to deceive the fainthearted,
> that spirits live on after bodies are buried,
> when the spouse has placed a hand over the eyes,
> and the final day has blocked out future suns,
> and the grim urn has confined the ashes?
> Is nothing gained in yielding the soul to death?
> Are the wretched faced with further life?
> Or do we die wholly, and does no part of us
> survive, once the spirit carried on the fugitive breath
> has mingled with the mist and receded into the air,
> and the kindling torch has touched the naked flesh?

Hamlet's soliloquies do not merely echo the philosophical content and style of Senecan choruses; in rendering visible their derivation from choral song, they show Hamlet as speaking *from the place of the chorus*—that is, from a place fundamentally detached from dramatic action. To say that Hamlet's philosophizing renders him incapable of carrying out his revenge is in a sense to say that he finds himself trapped in the extra-dramatic position of the chorus. Ophelia's witty observation that Hamlet is 'as good as a chorus' (3.2.243) thus inadvertently captures his structural dilemma, occupying as he does a choral discursive space rife with philosophical reflection but in some sense cut off from possibilities of dramatic engagement.[28]

Hamlet's revisions of Seneca are, not surprisingly, more sophisticated than those of *Titus Andronicus*, and one might therefore be tempted to say that the latter play tries to outdo Seneca's most visceral elements while the former outdoes his most cerebral. But this dichotomy is a little too neat. Rendering Senecan violence campy, as *Titus Andronicus*

---

[28] Tanya Pollard advances a similar line of argument in 'What's Hecuba to Shakespeare', 1082–8. Here, however, I think that the Senecan chorus offers a more pertinent model than the Greek one.

does, is to intellectualize it. When Tamora does a thoroughly campy turn as Revenge in act 5, scene 2, we are no longer in a revenge tragedy but in a play that is self-consciously *about* revenge tragedy—one in which the generic conventions of revenge tragedy have become an intellectual problem.

Another Senecan element that appears in *Hamlet* as well as other Shakespearean tragedies is the figure of the revenge ghost derived from *Thyestes* and *Agamemnon* and taken up by Kyd among others. In demanding justice for past wrongs, the Senecan ghost stands for the uncanny power of the past itself, including the literary past. The ghost is thus another figure for tradition, a fact that would have been made plain for Shakespeare by the Senecan translator Jasper Heywood. To his 1560 translation of *Thyestes*, Heywood appended a dream vision in which the ghost of Seneca appears to him. This ghost, while a good deal less ominous than that of King Hamlet, nevertheless saddles the recipient of its visit with a burdensome task. Seneca asks Heywood to 'renew my name', a phrase that seems to condense the roles of translator and offspring, by turning his works into English.[29] Heywood objects that he is too young and inexperienced for this task, for which he recommends more seasoned scholars and poets, some by name. But the ghost, after rumbling about the wrongs done to him by printers, gets his way. Heywood's poem, its suggestive parallels to *Hamlet* aside, makes explicit the fact that the figure of the Senecan ghost is also always in some sense the ghost *of* Seneca, which imposes its cultural authority on the early modern playwright from afar.

Shakespeare's response to the Senecan ghost, like his response to Senecan revenge tragedy, is to problematize it, but this is no easy task, since the standing of the Senecan ghost is already rather complicated. Some of these ghosts are glimpsed in sleep, which renders their status as either spirit or dream unclear. In the *Troades*, the chorus reacts to the demands of Achilles' ghost (made manifest only indirectly, through an interpreting priest) with scepticism toward the very idea of the afterlife: 'After death is nothing, and death itself is nothing' (397). As if to push the whole concept towards the absurd, in the pseudo-Senecan *Octavia* the ghost of Agrippina is herself plagued by a ghost—that of her dead husband—demanding revenge.

Early modern translations of Seneca add further complexities. Jasper Heywood not only composes a dream-interview with the ghost of Seneca; to his translation of the *Troades* he adds a long speech, not present in Seneca, from the ghost of Achilles. This supplement undercuts the scepticism of the chorus, since in Heywood's version the defunct Achilles has already put in an impressive appearance before their denial (in line with Seneca's own philosophical position) that anything remains after death. More provocatively, perhaps, Heywood's Achilles is a 'ghost' character in a secondary, metadramatic sense—a revenant from the literary future projected back onto Seneca's text, where he has no proper place. He haunts not only the Greeks and Trojans in the play, but the play itself. And he thereby introduces the uncanny temporality of tradition into it.

In Shakespeare, the ambiguities of ghostly existence in Seneca are often amplified and made so systematic as to induce epistemological or even cosmological vertigo. A case in point is *Richard III*. In 5.3, a ghostly procession of Richard's victims appears to both Richard and Henry Richmond, cursing the former and comforting the latter, to whom

---

[29] Jasper Heywood, *The second tragedie of Seneca entituled Thyestes* (London, 1560), 6.

they predict victory in the coming day's battle. At the end of the procession, the stage direction '*Richard starteth up out of a dream*' raises the question of whether the ghosts were real or simply figures of his guilty imagination. That the ghosts appear simultaneously and in the same order to both Henry and Richard may tend to verify them. And yet the fact that Richard and Henry are supposedly in their respective camps yet lying mere feet from each other onstage (which is the only way the ghosts can deliver their messages) signals a striking departure from naturalistic staging and suggests that we have entered a symbolic rather than actual space. The ontological status of the ghosts in *Richard III* is thus strictly undecideable, with significant thematic implications. 'Real' ghosts would point to supernatural mechanisms at work in the play's world, shaping the destinies of its characters. Imaginary ones would suggest that natural causes rather prevail. Ghostly apparitions thus condense within themselves the larger and likewise undecided question of whether the historical 'world' of *Richard III* is providential or machiavellian—whether, that is, supernatural forces shape and constrain human endeavour or whether the world provides only a bare stage on which characters like Richard are free to do what they will, opposed solely by the likewise secular actions of others.[30]

In *Macbeth*, the ghost of Banquo, unseen by any of the guests at the banquet in 3.4 other than Macbeth himself, occupies a similar threshold between the supernatural and the hallucinatory, this one more disturbing still because it infects the waking world. While the presence of supernatural forces seems less disputable in *Macbeth* than in *Richard III*, this does not cancel out the possibility that the guilt-racked Macbeth merely imagines Banquo's presence at the feast. And then there is Macbeth's spectral dagger, which not even the audience can see. The phantasmagoric space of *Macbeth* somehow folds the psychological and the supernatural into one. It is no longer a question of trying to 'decide' between them—a task that is impossible but at least meaningful in *Richard III*. This is a play in which the boundary between the dead and the living has become entirely porous as well as one in which internal and external landscapes are confused. Seneca provides a precedent for all of this, but not to the degree seen in Shakespeare. My point here is not that ghosts in Shakespeare are themselves 'questionable shape[s]' (as Hamlet puts it) but that they throw into question the very constitution of the worlds of the plays.

In 4.1, Banquo reappears as the last of a series of apparitions conjured up by the weird sisters, standing at the head of a line of future kings. Now embroiled with the future as well as the past, the ghost occupies yet another liminal space, this one chronological. He thus embodies the temporality of tradition, with royal succession figuring poetic succession as well. The Senecan ghost is the ghost of Seneca, spawning poetic progeny into the indefinite future. Shakespearean ghosts typically engage with the future, whether through prophecy (*Julius Caesar*) or through blessings and curses (*Richard III*).

Compared to Shakespeare's other ghosts, that of King Hamlet is surprisingly straightforward in one respect: he is clearly a ghost and not a figment of Hamlet's imagination, since other characters in the play also see him. And yet, in perhaps the most notorious essay on *Hamlet* ever written, W. W. Gregg argues that Hamlet's interview with the ghost in act 1, scene 5 (which takes place out of the sight of others) is in fact a literary hallucination,

---

[30] I borrow the dichotomy of 'providential' and 'machiavellian' from Phyllis Rackin, *Stages of History: Shakespeare's English Chronicles* (Ithaca: Cornell University Press, 1990), 40–85.

derived by Hamlet's unconscious from the text of 'The Murder of Gonzago'.[31] It is fitting that the ghost in the most metadramatic of Shakespeare's plays might be a textual phantom. But this is also the ghost who, despite differences from the classic Senecan 'revenge ghost', is the most vividly Senecan spirit in Shakespeare.[32] King Hamlet bears an especially close relation to the ghost of Thyestes in Seneca's *Agamemnon*. Warped by his brother's sadistic torture, Thyestes impregnates his own daughter in order to spawn Aegisthus as an agent of revenge. The combined themes of fraternal wrong, incest, and filial vengeance that surround Thyestes resurface through King Hamlet, and they hardly provide a reassuring aura to this already ambiguous figure. It is not just that his Senecan background reinforces the suspicion that this ghost may be a demon impersonating Hamlet's father in order to damn him. More fundamentally, I think, the ghost raises the larger question of whether *Hamlet*'s cosmic order is Christian or Senecan (meaning, of course, that of Senecan tragedy, not that of the philosophical works).[33] Once again the figure of the Senecan ghost becomes a kind of hinge on which the world of the play turns. Only this time his blatant role as *Senecan* ghost, or rather his double role as Senecan/Christian ghost, confers this status. And of course, in a metadramatic register the influence of this possibly pagan spirit over Hamlet also figures the pagan influence of Senecan tragedy on the author of *Hamlet*.

The last Senecan motif I shall explore here (there are many others I am omitting) is *furor*: the madness, raving, or blinding anger that grips characters such as Atreus and Medea and drives them toward revenge. Unlike vengeance and the ghost, the other two motifs I have examined, *furor* is not directly a figure for tradition. Indeed, it seems the very opposite of this. Tradition is, in effect, relation—an ongoing enchainment of literary works and authors that propagates itself even as it accommodates constant change and revision. The essence of *furor*, by contrast, obliterates human relation. It is not as if others cease to exist entirely; but the erasure of mutuality deprives them of the power to exert any restraint on anger. The other becomes merely the stripped down, instrumentalized object of vengeance—something to be hurt, killed, punished beyond limit. At its extreme, in Seneca's *Hercules Furens*, it blinds the perpetrator and completely blots out the identities of his victims. The state of *furor* completes that walling off of the self, that dangerous isolation that marks many Senecan characters.[34]

The extreme state of *furor* is merely the final term of a non-relationality that infects relation in general in Senecan tragedy, triggering fatal consequences. To take up the other motifs I have explored here: the logic of vengeance as amplified, disproportional punishment for wrongdoing goes hand in hand with *furor*, since it denies all mutuality and abandons all restraint with respect to the hated villain. Likewise, the revenge ghost is always willing to sacrifice the avenger as well as the proposed victim to his own demands.

[31] W. W. Gregg, 'Hamlet's Hallucination', *The Modern Language Review* 12:4 (October 1917), 393–421.

[32] See Miola, *Shakespeare and Classical Tragedy*, 34–5, on differences between King Hamlet and the Senecan ghost.

[33] On Senecan tragedy as a counterpoint to his Stoicism rather than an illustration of it, see Miola, *Shakespeare and Classical Tragedy*, 43. A similar argument is made at greater length by Schiesaro, *The Passions in Play*, 6–7, 20–1.

[34] This view of the Senecan self is developed in Gordon Braden, *Renaissance Tragedy and the Senecan Tradition: Anger's Privilege* (New Haven: Yale University Press, 1985).

The ghost of Tantalus in *Thyestes* experiences the drive towards vengeance as hunger; he embodies the state of *furor* as pure bodily impulse, as upsurge of one's own *physis* that obliterates the moral reality of others. Its kinship with the Senecan figures for tradition therefore suggests that *furor* embodies a certain non-relationality within tradition itself—a hollowing out of the otherness of the works of the past in subordinating them to current literary purposes. Herculean *furor*, in which one literally fails to see the other, points to a potentially tragic non-relationality within the logic of tradition. Thus is tradition assimilated to the shape of tragedy more generally in Seneca.

The language of *Herculens Furens* echoes in the mouths of Macbeth and (improbably) Hamlet, and elements of the play surface in *Richard III*; but the figure of the Herculean *furens* is most recognizably embodied in Othello.[35] Not only is Othello (like Hercules) an imposing physical presence; his language, when he is fully convinced of Desdemona's infidelity, achieves a pitch of full Senecan intensity:

> Arise, black vengeance, from the hollow hell!
> … Oh, blood, blood, blood! …
>   Like to the Pontic Sea,
> Whose icy current and compulsive course
> Ne'er feels retiring ebb, but keeps due on
> To the Propontic and the Hellespont,
> Even so my bloody thoughts with violent pace
> Shall ne'er look back, ne'er ebb to humble love,
> Till that a capable and wide revenge
> Swallow them up.
>
>   (3.3.462, 467, 469-76)

What connects Othello's *furor* to that of Hercules in particular is an element of misapprehension within it. Seneca's other furious characters are angry for reasons that they grasp with precision, though their anger drives them to madly disproportionate responses. Hercules, by contrast, is blinded by the goddess Juno so that he mistakes his wife and children for his enemies and slaughters them. Awakening from the spell and confronted with his actions, Hercules is more a victim than a villain. Othello likewise is led by Iago to misapprehend Desdemona's true nature, though his senses are not taken possession of in quite the way that Hercules' are, and so he cannot avoid culpability for his deeds. Moreover, since Iago's spell is artificially and not divinely induced, Shakespeare is able to anatomize *furor* to a depth that Seneca does not.

Othello, moreover, is a tale of two furors: Othello's and Iago's. Despite his cold-blooded calculations, Iago is gripped by overwhelming feelings of betrayal, resentment, ambition, unrequited love (for Othello), and thwarted identification (likewise with Othello)—an overdetermined mixture of motives that is the very opposite of the 'motiveless malignity' assigned to him by Coleridge.[36] Iago does not engage in a Senecan rhetoric of *furor*, but the ethical structure of his anger strongly resembles that of Seneca's Medea. Her *furor*, unlike that of Hercules, is based on no misapprehension. She grasps, all too lucidly, the depth of

---

[35] Miola, *Shakespeare and Classical Tragedy*, 82–4 (*Richard III*); 43–4 (*Hamlet*); 113–14 (*Macbeth*); 125–43 (*Othello*); see also 165–71 on furor and *King Lear*.

[36] Samuel Taylor Coleridge, *Lectures 1808–1819. On Literature*, vol. 2, ed. R. A. Foakes (Princeton: Princeton University Press, 1987), 315.

the betrayal that Jason has perpetrated against her. Her madness consists, therefore, not so much in her wish to be avenged upon him but rather in her willingness to sacrifice her children, who are morally innocent, toward this end. The non-relationality of Medea's *furor* is displaced onto them, and the absurdity of this displacement is in part what constitutes her as mad.

Medea's (il)logic is, moreover, precisely Iago's. Like Medea, Iago has been spurned for another (Cassio), and while the context is professional rather than amorous, Iago also seems to harbour a suppressed passion for Othello. Iago's *furor* therefore consists not so much in his desire for vengeance as in his willingness to use an innocent party (Desdemona) as his instrument: to cancel relationality with respect to *her*.

Iago's plan is not simply to destroy Othello's peace of mind. Nor is it merely to make him believe or internalize the racist assumptions of Venice, to which Othello had previously been immune. It is also to infect Othello with Iago's own non-relationality, to make him treat the person he most loves in the world as a mere object, and indeed literally to reduce her to an object by smothering her in her bed. Iago takes what is most disturbingly singular about himself and tries to impose it onto the world in general and Othello in particular, so that non-relation is no longer the (Senecan) exception but the (Shakespearean) rule. While this vision of non-relation is morally horrifying, it also provides a glimpse of absolute, unfettered freedom that makes characters such as Iago and Medea irresistibly compelling.

Senecan *furor*, as I have already mentioned, suggests a potential for non-relationality within literary tradition. But its metapoetic import is greater still, since, as Alessandro Schiesaro has persuasively argued, it bears a connection to the *furor poeticus* theorized by Democritus and Plato and endorsed (somewhat ambivalently) by Seneca.[37] Thus Seneca's Atreus is, as Schiesaro shows, a figure for the poet as well as a murderous madman.[38] Of course, this connection works best for a sublime poetics of which one can certainly see traces in Seneca but which seems largely alien to Shakespeare. Whatever image we have of Shakespeare, it is probably *not* that of the oracular, sublime poet rapt in the *furor poeticus*. And yet, a different, milder form of non-relationality subsists in the negative capability that Keats famously assigned to Shakespeare.[39] His characters speak, but Shakespeare does not speak, either to them or to us.

One might argue that a certain kind of negative capability extends to Shakespeare's handling of the classical tradition. While it is clear that Shakespeare takes up and responds to elements in Seneca, for instance—not to mention elements of Ovid, Virgil, Plutarch, and a host of others not treated here—his engagement with the classics never pulls him toward the different forms of classic*ism* evident in a Ben Jonson, a Dryden, or a Racine. Shakespeare is by no means so absorbed by his relation to Greece and Rome that conforming to classical canons or mediating his relation to them becomes an engrossing end in itself. And this may be, paradoxically, one of the things that allows him to be ranged with the great authors of antiquity. If Shakespeare is modernity's Sophocles, this is in part because the question of Sophocles did not concern him overmuch.

---

[37] Schiesaro, *The Passions in Play*, 22–5.   [38] Schiesaro, *The Passions in Play*, 54.

[39] *Selected Letters of John Keats*, ed. Grant F. Scott (Cambridge: Harvard University Press, 1985; rev. edn., 2002), 60.

SELECT BIBLIOGRAPHY

Shakespeare and the Classics (in general)

Baldwin, T. W., *William Shakespeare's Small Latin and Less Greek* (Urbana: University of Illinois Press, 1944). (On Shakespeare's classical education in Latin grammar school.)

Martindale, Charles and Martindale, Michelle, *Shakespeare and the Use of Antiquity: An Introductory Essay* (London and New York: Routledge, 1990).

Martindale, Charles and Taylor, A. B., eds., *Shakespeare and the Classics* (Cambridge: Cambridge University Press, 2004).

Velz, John W., *Shakespeare and the Classical Tradition: A Critical Guide to Commentary, 1660–1960* (Minneapolis: University of Minnesota Press, 1968). (Critical compendium of references by later readers to Shakespeare's use of the classics.)

Walker, Lewis, *Shakespeare and the Classical Tradition: An Annotated Bibliography, 1961–1991* (New York and London: Routledge, 2002).

Shakespeare and Greek Tragedy

Nuttall, A. D., 'Action at a Distance: Shakespeare and the Greeks', in *Shakespeare and the Classics*, ed. Charles Martindale and A. B. Taylor (Cambridge: Cambridge University Press, 2004), 209–22.

Pollard, Tanya, 'What's Hecuba to Shakespeare?', *Shakespeare Quarterly* 65 (2012), 1060–93

Pollard, Tanya, 'Greek Playbooks and Dramatic Forms in Early Modern England', in *Formal Matters: Reading the Materials of English Renaissance Literature*, ed. Allison K. Deutermann and András Kiséry (Manchester: Manchester University Press, 2013), 99–115.

Schleiner, Louise, 'Latinized Greek Drama in Shakespeare's Writing of *Hamlet*', *Shakespeare Quarterly* 41 (1990), 29–48.

Silk, Michael, 'Shakespeare and Greek Tragedy: Strange Relationship', in *Shakespeare and the Classics*, ed. Charles Martindale and A. B. Taylor (Cambridge: Cambridge University Press, 2004), 241–57.

Shakespeare and Seneca

Braden, Gordon, *Renaissance Tragedy and the Senecan Tradition: Anger's Privilege* (New Haven: Yale University Press, 1985).

Hunter, G. K., 'Seneca and English Tragedy', in C.D.N. Costa, ed. *Seneca* (London and Boston: Routledge and Kegan Paul, 1974), 166–204.

Lupton, Julia Reinhard and Reinhard, Kenneth, '*Hamlet*'s Ursceneca', in Julia Reinhard Lupton and Kenneth Reinhard, *After Oedipus: Shakespeare in Psychoanalysis* (Ithaca: Cornell University Press, 1993), 89–118.

Miola, Robert S., *Shakespeare and Classical Tragedy: The Influence of Seneca* (Oxford: Oxford University Press, 1992).

Seneca

(Note: all volumes listed below include discussion of Shakespeare)

Boyle, A. J., *Tragic Seneca: An Essay on the Theatrical Tradition* (New York: Routledge, 1997).

Rosenmeyer, Thomas, *Senecan Drama and Stoic Cosmology* (Berkeley: University of California Press, 1989).

Staley, Gregory A., *Seneca and the Idea of Tragedy* (New York and Oxford: Oxford University Press, 2010).

CHAPTER 3

∙∙

THE MEDIEVAL
INHERITANCE

∙∙

RORY LOUGHNANE

Theseus

No epilogue, I pray you; for your play needs no excuse. Never excuse; for when
the players are all dead there need none to be blamed. Marry, if he that writ it had
played Pyramus and hanged himself in Thisbe's garter it would have been a fine
tragedy; and so it is, truly, and very notably discharged.

A Midsummer Night's Dream (5.1.349-54)[1]

FOLLOWING the absurd antics of 'Pyramus and Thisbie', Nick Bottom asks Duke Theseus
if he would like to 'see' an epilogue or 'hear' a bergamask dance. Theseus responds by
saying there is no need for an epilogue to 'excuse' the play, not least because there is
no character left alive to deliver the epilogue. He then insults the play's attempts at the
tragic genre by saying that if the playwright had also died 'it would have been a fine
tragedy', before sympathetically qualifying this by saying that it was indeed, 'truly' a
fine tragedy and 'very notably discharged'. Physical comedy and malapropisms aside,
much of the humour in the mechanicals' performance stems from its (unintentional)
parody of the hyperbolic excesses of stage tragedy, not least the prolonged death scenes
of the protagonists. But what is the concept of 'tragedy' that is being parodied, and
from where is it derived? I begin this chapter by describing how the English genre of
tragedy evolved. In the second half, I switch emphasis from the presence of tragedy in
the medieval period to the presence of the medieval period in tragedy, focusing on the
anxieties such a medieval presence might cause for contemporary audiences and readers
of Shakespeare's tragic plays.

---

[1] All citations to Shakespeare are taken from *William Shakespeare: The Complete Works*, ed.
Stanley Wells, Gary Taylor, John Jowett, and William Montgomery, 2nd edn. (Oxford: Clarendon
Press, 2005).

TRAGEDY AS A *MEDIEVAL* INHERITANCE

The version of tragedy first performed on the stages of the commercial theatres in late Tudor England is far removed from classical definitions of the genre. Writing in the mid-1560s, Roger Ascham lamented the poor quality of literary attempts at the genre in contemporary Europe. His standards were exacting, as he praised the 'proprietie of wordes ... forme of sentence, [and] handlyng of ... matter' in the classical works of Greek poets including Aristophanes and Sophocles and Roman poets such as Terence and Seneca.[2] Indeed, for Ascham, only two contemporary plays, both Latin tragedies, Thomas Watson's *Absalon* (*c.*1540) and George Buchanan's *Jephthes* (*c.*1542–3) were 'able to abyde the trew touch of *Aristotles* preceptes, and *Euripides* examples'.[3] He describes the 'many pleasant talkes' he enjoyed with Sir John Cheke and Thomas Watson when they compared 'the preceptes of *Aristotle* and *Horace*['s] *de Arte Poetica,* with the examples of *Euripides, Sophocles*, and *Seneca*'. With displeasure, he comments that

> Few men, in writyng of Tragedies in our dayes, haue shot at this marke.[4]

In his *An Apologie for Poetrie* (*The Defence of Poesie*), Sir Philip Sidney also rued the dramatic achievements of late Tudor English tragedians, commenting that now 'Playes be neither right Tragedies, nor right Comedies: mingling Kings & Clownes'.[5] In Sidney's account, 'high and excellent' tragedy should be that which

> openeth the greatest wounds, and sheweth forth the Ulcers, that are couered with Tissue: that maketh Kinges feare to be Tyrants, and Tyrants manifest their tiranicall humors: that with sturring the affects of admiration and commiseration, teacheth, the vncertainety of this world; and vpon howe weake foundations guilden roofes are builded.[6]

Similarly, George Puttenham, who sought to describe the difference between classical tragedy and classical comedy, writes that the former 'medled not with so base matters' as the latter, and instead 'set forth the dolefull falles of infortunate & afflicted Princes'.[7] Whereas Puttenham is attempting to write specifically about the classical tradition, Sidney's conception of tragedy is based only in part upon his reading of Aristotle, Seneca, and Horace as well as neo-classical continental commentators on these writers.[8] He also discusses contemporary performances. Like Puttenham, Sidney's understanding of what tragedy means is also influenced by a quite separate medieval conception of tragedy. In *Poetics*, Aristotle observed certain features of plot and characterization in tragedies: a (male) protagonist suffers a reversal in situation (*peripeteia*) from prosperity to misery. This reversal is caused by a mistake or failing or momentary error in judgement by the protagonist (*hamartia*—derived from the archery term for 'missing the mark'), and he is unwittingly culpable in the initiation of his own downfall. The reversal of situation for this

---

[2] Roger Ascham, *The Scholemaster* (London: 1570), R[r].   [3] Ibid.

[4] Ibid. Ascham is possibly punning on the etymological root of *hamartia* here ('missing the mark').

[5] Sir Philip Sidney, *An Apologie for Poetrie* (London: 1595), K2[r].   [6] Ibid., F3[v]–F4[r].

[7] George Puttenham, *The Arte of English Poesie* (London: 1589), E2[v].

[8] Sidney draws heavily on the commentaries of Minturno, Castelvetro, and Scaliger.

'great man' (in the sense of power and importance; he was neither purely good nor purely evil) was determined by a combination of fate, *hubris*, and the will of the gods. These are the basic parameters for the ancient dramatic genre that Ascham writes admiringly about; the standards he wants upheld. But the tragic plays and writings on tragedy of Antiquity were almost entirely unknown in late medieval England, and at this time another distinct notion of the literary genre emerged.

When Sidney writes of the 'weak foundations' of worldly success that might collapse at any moment—the 'vncertainety of this world'—and Puttenham describes 'miserable ends painted out in playes and pageants' to show 'the mutabilitie of fortune' they are both demonstrating their own inheritance of the medieval concept of tragedy.[9] To better understand the origins of this alternative interpretation of the word (and thus the early English literary genre that evolves) we must turn to Chaucer, who first translated and glossed the meaning of 'tragedy' in English.

Chaucer, who likely knew nothing of the ancient dramatic genre, writes two complementary definitions of tragedy. One is found in *Boece*, his translation of *The Consolation of Philosophy* by the sixth-century Roman statesman Boethius: 'Tragedie ys to seyne a ditee of a prosperite for a tyme that endeth in wretchednesse' (Book II, Prosa 2, 70-2).[10] Here Chaucer glosses the lines

> What other thynge bewaylen the cryinges of
> tragedyes but oonly the dedes of Fortune, that
> with an unwar strook overturneth the
> realmes of greet nobleye?
>
> (Book II, Prosa 2. 67-70)

Another is found at the conclusion to the prologue to 'The Monk's Tale' in his *Canterbury Tales*, where a 'tragedy' is a tale

> Of hym that stode in greet prosperitee,
> And is yfallen out of heigh degree
> Into myserie, and endeth wrecchedly.
>
> (VII 1975-7)

Chaucer's version of tragedy is accommodating. He observes that the genre's prominent feature is an unexpected reversal of fortune ending in misery for the protagonist. His understanding of the tragic 'high to low' trajectory is also informed by his reading of Boccaccio's *De Casibus Virorum Illustrium*. This is a prose collection of 56 biographies of famous historical figures, all of whom suffered misfortune at a time when they least expected it. Chaucer seems to have understood these stories to be 'tragedies', and in turn his reading influenced later writers as to the constituent parts of the literary genre; that is, that those of 'heigh degre' (i.e. nobility) who are initially prosperous suffer from a turn of events that ends 'wrecchedly'. Dame Fortune, or Fortuna, who brings about the reversal, is an allegorized personification rooted in classical philosophy, but Christianized in the

---

[9] Puttenham, *The Arte of English Poesie*, F2ʳ.

[10] All citations to Chaucer are taken from *The Riverside* Chaucer, gen. ed. Larry D. Benson, 3rd edn. (Boston: Houghton Mifflin, 1987). Chaucer's translation of Boethius drew on Jean De Meun's French translation of the work, as well as Nicholas Trivet's commentary.

writings of St Augustine, Boethius, and others, as a vehicle for God's divine will. Chaucer's Monk warns us that at any point, with a turn of Fortuna's wheel (*Rota Fortunae*), happiness can swiftly lead to misery:

> Thus kan Fortune hir wheel governe and gye,
> And out of joye brynge men to sorwe.
>
> (VII 2397–8)

The world the Monk depicts in his 17 'tragedies', ending with Croesus' premonition of his own execution, is bleak and unforgiving. But we should not forget that in the medieval Christianity of the Western Church such examples of tragedy are merely episodic within a providential divine plan; Lucifer's fall, the expulsion from Eden, the sacrifice of Isaac, and, even the death of Christ, etc., are tragic, in the sense of sorrowful events, but not tragedies, because they are all part of a greater prophesied eschatological destiny. The Monk prefaces his tragic exempla ('thise ensamples trewe and olde') by stating their lesson in prudence—'Let no man truste on blynd prosperitee' (VI 1998; 1997). The culpability of the protagonists is not necessarily in question because tragedy is 'noon oother maner thyng … but that Fortune alwey wole biwaillle' (VII 2761–3). With that said, many of the protagonists in 'The Monk's Tale' do help contribute to their own reversal in fortunes, either through personal sin (Lucifer, Adam, et al.) or overconfidence.[11] The sin of Pride, the Christianized version of *hubris*—'pride goeth before a fall' (*Proverbs* 16:18)—is especially prominent, as it would continue to be in later *De Casibus* literature. Of great importance too was the merging of classical pagan stoicism with its version in Boethian Christian philosophy. Chaucer, after all, translates Boethius' account where Lady Philosophy consoles the author against the ravages of Fortune. Neo-Stoicism emerged as an influential syncretic philosophical movement in Shakespeare's age; Hamlet's several famous meditations on suffering and providence, from life's 'slings and arrows' to the 'fall of a sparrow', resonate with contemporary debates about the acceptance of fate and/ or faith in God's plan.

Despite the widespread influence of Chaucer's writing, what tragedy means in the fourteenth and fifteenth century is hardly uniform. Sometimes, as Henry Ansgar Kelly observes, it seems to equate with 'disaster' and at other times it is mistakenly understood to simply mean 'book' or 'chapter'.[12] We turn below to dramatic writing of the period, but at this point let us simply observe that 'tragedy' as a recognisable dramatic genre did not exist in late medieval England. The English genre of stage tragedy was only to emerge much later. But narrative tales of downfall and capricious fortune, labelled in part as 'tragedies', were widely circulated in the period. The Benedictine monk John Lydgate's *The Fall of Princes* includes almost five hundred tales about famous figures, biblical and historical, who all suffer from a downturn in fortune, beginning with Adam and Eve being put out of paradise and ending with the capture of King Jean of France in 1356.[13] Lydgate's work, a massive nine-book vernacular poem, based on Laurent de Premierfait's French translation

---

[11] See Henry Ansgar Kelly, *Chaucerian Tragedy* (Cambridge: D. S. Brewer, 1997), 70–1.

[12] See Henry Ansgar Kelly, *Ideas and Forms of Tragedy from Aristotle to the Middle Ages* (Cambridge: Cambridge University Press, 1993), 170.

[13] Lydgate's work includes eleven of the seventeen 'tragedies' from 'The Monk's Tale'.

of Boccaccio's *De Casibus*, helped to establish the parameters for an anglicized version of this narrative genre:[14]

> Till that fortune with hir sharpe shoures
> Whan that he sat highest on his whele
> This blynde goddesse began him to assaile
> Hir frowarde malice he felt it full wele[15]

So, too, Lydgate's *Troy Book* defined 'Tragedye' as that which 'begynneth | in prosperyte And endeth euer | in aduersyte'.[16] In ways the 'tragic' works of Chaucer and Lydgate also contributed to the popular genre of romance, with its tales of chivalric quests and deeds. Helen Cooper, in describing the frequency of 'unhappy endings' in such works, observes that 'a surprising number [of romance tales] … finally opt for bleak fate over benevolent Providence'.[17] Just as conceptions of tragedy were unfixed in the period, so too some generic features of romance were adaptable. Romance was 'shaken loose' in Cooper's terms, and numerous works in this genre seemed to conclude by saying that 'God does not necessarily support the good, and an arbitrary or maleficent fate can appear to have at least as much control over what happens'. While romances more commonly ended happily, the genre's feature of episodic unexpected downfall bears an obvious influence of Christian negative exempla literature.

The advent of the printing press in late fifteenth-century England meant that these popular late medieval texts (*c.*30 manuscripts of *The Fall of Princes* survive) were more widely circulated than ever before. The sententious lessons of Lydgate's great work contributed to the continent-wide development of a sub-genre of *speculum* literature: 'advice to princes'.[18] In England this reached its apex with the bestselling and multi-edition *A myrroure for magistrates*, first printed in 1559. Although principally an advisory work for those in positions of power, the sin of Pride once more features prominently in the 'tragedyes' of *A myrroure*. Not least of which is an extraordinary digressive meditation on Pride's role in the tragic downfall of Thomas Mowbray, leading to Richard II's own fall. This passage influenced Shakespeare's own account in his history play:

> For pride is suche, yf it be kindely caught,
> As stroyeth good, and styrreth vp every nought.[19]

Here 'tragedy' is used repeatedly in the prose glosses of the historical narrative poems (e.g. 'After that this Tragedy was ended', 'Whan he had ended this so wofull a tragedy', 'Lord Sayes Tragedie', 'The Earles tragedy', 'this tragedy ended', etc.). Indeed in William

---

[14] See Nigel Mortimer, *John Lydgate's Fall of Princes Narrative Tragedy in its Literary and Political Contexts* (Oxford: Clarendon Press, 2005).

[15] John Lydgate, *Falle of princis* (London: 1594), E5ᵛ.

[16] John Lydgate, *The hystorye, sege and dystruccyon of Troye* (London: 1513), F2ᵛ.

[17] Helen Cooper, *The English Romance in Time: Transforming Motifs from Geoffrey of Monmouth to the Death of Shakespeare* (Oxford: Oxford University Press, 2004), 363.

[18] The *speculum* genre itself emerges from didactic religious writing. See Herbert Grabes, *The Mutable Glass: Mirror-imagery in the Titles and Texts of the Middle Ages and English Renaissance*, trans. Gordon Collier (Cambridge: Cambridge University Press, 1982).

[19] William Baldin et al., *A myrroure for magistrates* (London: 1559), D2ᵛ.

Baldwin's preface to the first edition, he writes: 'I purpose not to stand here vppon the particulers, because they be in part set furth in the tragedyes.'[20]

The effect of such varying uses of the term meant that 'tragedy' had a hybrid meaning in sixteenth-century writing. Broadly speaking, it could be used in the modern sense of 'a dreadful calamity or disaster', in the medieval sense of the narrative poems, and in the classical sense of the dramatic genre. The various meanings were already blurred and remained blurry in the period. We see this in the title-pages to several of Shakespeare's history plays in the 1590s (e.g. *The true tragedie of Richard Duke of Yorke*, the alternative version of Shakespeare's *3 Henry VI*, printed in octavo in 1595, and the first quarto of Shakespeare's *The tragedie of King Richard the second* in 1597). Indeed Frances Meres, in praising Shakespeare as a tragedian, lists 'Richard the 2. Richard the 3. Henry the 4. [and] King Iohn' as tragedies.[21] Of course at the same time other Shakespearean plays such as *Titus Andronicus* and *Romeo and Juliet* bore the same 'tragedy' description on their title-pages—named also as tragedies by Meres—and unlike the history plays, these took their place in the 'Tragedies' section of the 1623 Folio of Shakespeare's works. Slowly but surely 'tragedy' in dramatic literature came to be reserved for a specific genre of play, albeit one that has several sub-genres e.g. revenge, love, domestic, etc., and whose categorical features are not necessarily always clear (see Chapter 1 in the present volume). That *Cymbeline* is listed as a tragedy in the Folio should indicate that the dramatic genre was loosely defined.

That the classical dramatic genre of tragedy was largely unknown, or that 'tragedy' was otherwise interpreted until the early sixteenth century should not suggest that later English tragedy is wholly disconnected from the various other forms of theatrical performance that flourished in late medieval England. Rather, later tragedy, its conventions, motifs, and tropes, is deeply informed by its medieval inheritance of early religious community drama. While early seventeenth-century commentators could be dismissive of the imaginative achievements of pre-Reformation England—for example, William Camden describes a 'midle age ... ouercast with darke clouds, or rather thicke fogges of ignorance' and Henry Wotton observes that the 'good *Literature*' have been 'vnciuilized' by 'combustions and tumults of the *middle Age*'—the commercial drama that later emerged, the genre of tragedy included, bore many of the hallmarks of the earlier edifying Catholic drama.[22] This process was not without its tensions. The 'Dark Ages' may be an eighteenth-century coinage, but puritanical 'hot' or hardline Protestant contemporaries of Shakespeare would certainly have viewed with suspicion and contempt the religious rituals, 'popish' relics, and superstitious beliefs of England's recent past. The English state underwent three major religious transformations and four monarchs in the space of less than twenty years in the mid-sixteenth century, with the Church of England's split from the Roman Catholic Church in the reigns of Henry VIII and Edward VI, the Restoration of Catholicism as state religion under Mary I, and the consolidation of the split from Rome under Elizabeth I in 1558. This sequence of national traumas altered irrevocably the English population's understanding of, and relationship with, its own cultural inheritance, drama included.

---

[20] Ibid., ¶2ᵛ.   [21] Francis Meres, *Palladis tamia* (London: 1598), Oo2ʳ.
[22] William Camden, *Remaines of a greater worke, concerning Britaine* (London: 1605), a1ᵛ; Henry Wotton, *The elements of architecture* (London: 1624), ¶4ʳ.

Early English Drama and Tragedy

Pope Clement V established the feast of Corpus Christi in 1311, an annual early summer celebration of the doctrine of transubstantiation on the first Thursday after Trinity Sunday. From such ritualized festivities, several new types of community religious theatre emerged in England. One type consisted of a set of plays—'mysteries'—grouped together into a 'cycle', and performed consecutively over the Corpus Christi feast-day. Such vernacular cycles are extant from several towns including York, Chester, and Wakefield (Towneley), as well as the rural region of East Anglia (N-Town). The Bible, primarily the Latin Vulgate, was the principle but not the only source for plots. Plays might showcase typological interpretations of narratives from the Old Testament or episodes from the life of Christ such as the Passion and Resurrection. Unlike the Latin used in Church services, these plays were performed in English. And much license was taken in how the elements of the story were presented, with comic episodes frequently included. Other forms of religious drama also emerged in late medieval England, including hagiographical drama or 'saint's plays', but only a small number of this genre survive, including *Mary Magdalene* and *The Conversion of Saint Paul*. Emerging slightly later than the saints plays and mysteries are morality plays. These are homiletic plays expounding a Christian ideal, where personified abstractions (principally vice and virtue figures in various forms) microcosmically battle for the soul of eponymous figures such as 'everyman' or 'mankind'. As with saints and mystery plays, the morality plays' purpose is the edification of its listeners. They also helped to instruct a lay audience in some of the more abstract concepts of medieval Christian doctrine (for example, *The Castle of Perseverance* includes dramatized figures of the Seven Deadly Sins and Seven Virtues).

As such, late medieval English drama was religious drama; the plays were not tragedies, but there were potentially tragic consequences for not heeding their edifying theological lesson. The plays' exegetical conventions—audiences expected such plays to conclude with a sound interpretation, message, or moral—in part enabled the subversive elements of its comedy. Professional actors did not usually perform the plays, but that is not to dismiss the often high production value of these performances, especially as the Guilds became more involved in orchestrating urban productions. As Greg Walker observes, 'its cultural work was … *work in the world* rather than just work in the theatre'.[23] These were important productions, bridging the gap between the church and the laity, including the civic authorities; a public show of devotion that combined festival entertainment with solemn didacticism.

The first printing presses made widely available the ancient tragedies of Sophocles, Euripides, Aeschylus, and, perhaps most importantly for later English tragedy, Seneca. These texts were widely available for readers versed in Latin. But, more importantly, passages from classical works, Greek and Roman, became a regular feature of Latin lesson-work in English grammar school curricula, informing habits of writing and thinking. Thus, the dramatic genre of tragedy in the classical sense became more familiar to the

---

[23] Greg Walker, 'The Cultural Work of Early Drama', in *The Cambridge Companion to Medieval English Theatre*, ed. Richard Beadle and Alan J. Fletcher, 2nd edn. (Cambridge: Cambridge University Press, 2008), 76.

English reading public.[24] In his Latin-to-English dictionary, Thomas Elyot defines '*tragoedia*' as 'a tragedye, whiche is an enterlude [i.e. play], wherin the personages do represent somme hystorie or fable lamentable, for the crueltie and myserye therin expressed'.[25] In this humanist scholar's account, there is no mention of Dame Fortune or her wheel or the protagonist's downfall from prosperity to wretchedness. Tragedy is here specifically an interlude, or type of dramatic performance. It is certainly not tragedy as described in Aristotle's *Poetics*, but it is also removed from the Chaucer-Lydgate 'fall of princes' configuration of the genre.

Classical tragedy influenced the first English attempts at writing in this dramatic genre in closet, academic, and privately staged plays (see also Chapter 2 in this volume). It may be surprising to note that the earliest printed 'tragedy' in English is Jasper Heywood's translation of Seneca's *Troas* in 1559. The first attempt at an original English tragedy is Thomas Preston's *Cambises* (*c.*1560, printed 1570).[26] In its prologue, Preston refers to 'The sage and witty *Seneca*', but the play itself is a lamentable 'fall of princes' post-Marian account of bloody tyranny. The first original English tragedy about English subject matter is Thomas Sackville and Thomas Norton's *Gorboduc*, performed by the Gentlemen of the Inner Temple in the winter of 1561-2. George Gascoigne and Francis Kinwelmersche's *Jocasta* (Gray's Inn, 1566), is the first known English adaptation of Greek tragedy.[27] The 1581 publication of Thomas Newton's English translation of Seneca' *Tenne Tragedies* marks another obvious watershed, but there is widespread evidence of the popularity of classical tragedy throughout this period. For example, Seneca's tragedies were performed regularly at Cambridge in the early part of Elizabeth I's reign: *Troas* (Trinity, 1551-2), *Oedipus* (Trinity, 1559-60), *Troas* and *Medea* (Trinity, 1560-1), and *Thebias* (King's, 1561-2).[28] Several other tragedies from Elizabeth's reign, including Robert Wilmot et al.'s *Tancred and Gismund* (Inner Temple, 1567) and Thomas Hughes' *The Misfortunes of Arthur* (Gray's Inn, 1587) are clearly influenced by Seneca's oeuvre.

Of course, English tragedy also departed quite radically from the classical form, inviting the type of critical opprobrium we read earlier by Sidney and others. What is remarkable, however, is how early English tragedies such as Preston's *Cambises*, R[ichard] B[ower]'s *Apius and Virginia* (printed 1564), John Pickering's *Horestes* (printed 1567), combine elements of classical tragedy with the morally instructional form of earlier English religious drama. It would be a mistake, then, to overlook the residual influence of vernacular religious drama in the later dramatic genre of tragedy that evolved. In pre-Reformation Tudor plays, we can easily observe how drama is appropriated for disseminating partisan political ideology and/or contributing to theological debate. (See, for examples of this practice, the political allegories *Youth, Hickscorner, Respublica*, John Skelton's *Magnyfycence* (*c.*1519)

---

[24] See Robert Miola, *Shakespeare's Reading* (Oxford: Oxford University Press, 2000), esp. 2–4.

[25] Thomas Elyot, *The dictionary* (London: 1538), Dd1[r].

[26] Thomas Preston, *Cambises* (London: 1570), A2[v]. The tragedy is evidently familiar to Shakespeare: in *1 Henry IV*, Falstaff says that he will try to speak passionately 'in King Cambyses' vein' (2.5.390).

[27] Their translation was derived from Ludovico Dolce's Italian *Giocasta*, but also shows the influence of Senecan tragedy.

[28] For a further account of such performances, see Andrew J. Power, 'Early Elizabethan Seneca and the Religious Settlement', *Theta IX*, 129–48.

and John Ritwise's anti-Lutheran Latin play, performed before Henry VIII in 1527.) With the advent of the Reformation, as Pamela M. King suggests, earlier drama's 'pattern of innocence, temptation, fall and redemption was exploited … as an organ of political satire and religious propaganda'.[29] Prominent Protestant dramatists such as John Bale adapted the conventions of earlier religious drama to suit their needs, with new vice figures such as 'Hypocrisy' and 'False Doctrine' appearing on stages promulgating anti-Catholic vitriol. Bale's *Three Lawes* (1538) and *God's Promises* (1538) are particularly polemical works of this nature. However, Bale's plays are merely the most famous examples of a widespread use of drama to impart the Protestant ethos in Reformation England. Paul Whitfield White observes:

> Since the institutions responsible for producing drama remained firmly intact after the Reformation, the Crown, with its many loyal officials strategically placed throughout the realm, could exercise some measure of control over the stage and exploit it, along with the pulpit and the press, as a means of drawing the people away from residual Catholicism and winning broad support for its Reformation policy.[30]

As Bale's later exile following Mary I's accession suggests, this could be a perilous approach to dramatic composition. Elizabeth I's 1558 decree that religious matters should not be performed onstage contributed to the increased secularization of drama, and, thereafter, the formation of commercial theatres. But despite the state's wishes, all forms of religious theatre did not simply disappear overnight. Old habits die hard—as the quasi-morality structure of Marlowe's *Doctor Faustus* attests, and as we will see in readings of *Titus Andronicus* and *Hamlet* below. Indeed there is surviving evidence for performances of mystery cycles as late as 1575 (in Chester), almost fifty years after Henry VIII's first break with Rome. One year later, the first purpose-built theatre in London would begin operations, setting the stage, literally and figuratively, for the English version of dramatic tragedy to emerge.

SHAKESPEARE THE MEDIEVALIST

Until relatively recently scholarship on Shakespeare's medieval inheritance had a rehearsed, familiar feel: the drama of Shakespeare's age emerged from the twin impulses of a secular departure from didactic religious drama and a growing awareness of the ideas and forms of classical drama. Scholars aimed to extricate the medieval from the early modern, glossing references in Shakespeare's works that appeared to rely upon knowledge of, or gestured towards, the conventions and tropes of earlier drama. As such, much vital spadework was completed, observing in Shakespeare's plays, for example, medieval moral theory and homiletic rhetoric; the psychomachia of allegorized figures; neo-chivalric behaviours and courtly games; motifs such as

---

[29] Pamela King, 'Morality plays', *The Cambridge Companion to Medieval English Theatre*, ed. Richard Beadle and Alan J. Fletcher, 2nd edn. (Cambridge: Cambridge University Press, 2008), 260.
[30] Paul Whitfield White, 'Theater and Religious Culture' in *A New History of Early English Drama*, ed. John D. Cox and David Scott Kastan (New York: Columbia University Press, 1997), 135–6.

de casibus or 'fall of princes', *ubi sunt*, 'triumph of truth'; and the precepts of *ars moriendi* or the imagery of the 'dance of death'. Mid-twentieth-century commentators on the influence of medieval traditions on later drama, from Willard Farnham to David Bevington, generally sought to assert difference rather than commonality. That there was an inheritance of ideas, forms, and conventions was true, they argued, but later drama deployed its inheritance in a wholly original way. For example, David Bevington argues that

> One cannot account for these [early] plays by aesthetic laws of unity, correspondence, subordination, and the like, because they were not composed with such ideas in mind.[31]

And even within the last twenty-five years, Leah Scragg comments that 'It would be ludicrous to suggest that the crowds flocking into the Elizabethan-Jacobean playhouses regarded the plays of Shakespeare in the same light that their ancestors viewed the Mystery and Morality plays that directly inculcated the truths of their faith.'[32] Similarly, Robert Knapp proposes that 'where Shakespeare's predecessors were medieval, he is modern; mimetic where they were didactic, ... iconoclastic where they were enthralled to images of truth'.[33] That late medieval drama might require a distinct type of explication, Knapp suggests, is evidence of 'a forgotten semiotic'. While certainly there is an evolution of dramatic form, the disjunction proposed by Bevington, where later drama aims for a type of aesthetic not countenanced by earlier dramatists, or the disjunction proposed by Scragg and Knapp, where audience expectation and authorial intention are fundamentally different, may be misleadingly definitive.

While such ground-breaking work remains important, the underlying theory about a marked disjunction between early and late, medieval and early modern, has come increasingly under attack in a broader discussion of the value and validity of periodization in early European studies. In the work of cultural historians such as Eamon Duffy, David Aers, David Wallace, and James Simpson, the divide between the 'middle ages' or medieval and the Renaissance or early modern is argued to be arbitrary.[34] Moreover, this strand of criticism observes that the insistence on difference between early and late is itself a convention of polemical post-Reformation writing of the sixteenth and seventeenth century.[35] Such revised opinion about inheritance of the medieval in late

---

[31] David Bevington, *From Mankind to Marlowe: Growth and Structure in the Popular Drama of Tudor England* (Cambridge, MA.: Harvard University Press, 1962), 3.

[32] Leah Scragg, *Shakespeare's Mouldy Tales* (London and New York: Longman, 1992), 192.

[33] Robert S. Knapp, *Shakespeare: The Theater and the Book* (Princeton: Princeton University Press, 1989), 10.

[34] See Eamon Duffy, *The Stripping of the Altars* (New Haven: Yale University Press, 1992); David Aers 'A Whisper in the Ear of Early Modernists; or, Reflections on Literary Critics Writing the "History of the Subject"' in *Culture and History 1350-1600* (Hempstead: Harvester, 1992), 177–202; David Wallace, *Premodern Places: Calais to Surinam, Chaucer to Aphra Behn* (Oxford: Blackwell, 2004); James Simpson, *Reform and Cultural Revolution* (Oxford: Oxford University Press, 2002), and, co-edited with Brian Cummings, *Cultural Reformations: Medieval and Renaissance in Literary History* (Oxford: Oxford University Press, 2010).

[35] See e.g. Brian Stock, *Listening for the Text: On the Uses of the Past* (Baltimore, MD: Johns Hopkins University Press, 1990); Cathy Shrank, 'John Bale and Reconfiguring the 'Medieval' in Reformation England' in *Reading the Medieval*, 179–92.

Tudor culture has, perhaps naturally enough, produced a recent upswell of interest in Shakespeare's understanding of England's past. The publication of a flurry of monographs and important essay collections attest to this renewed interest in Shakespeare's deployment of apparently archaistic medievalism.[36] Thus, recent scholarship has aimed to quantify and qualify difference and sameness, while drawing attention to the assumptions of periodization.

Helping to elucidate such contrasting critical enterprises is Bruce R. Smith's recent categorization of ways to approach the topic of the 'middle ages' in Shakespeare's works.[37] Five of his categories are pertinent to our discussion. The first two are the preserve of the traditional approach: first, a play might be set in the 'middle ages' or medieval period. For example, we observe this setting in *Macbeth* and in any of the plays of the two history tetralogies. Second, the play might be based on medieval sources. One obvious example of such an approach would be to establish *Troilus and Cressida*'s relationship to Chaucer's *Troilus and Criseyde*, observing also Chaucer's own borrowings from Boccacio's *Il Filostrato*, while also noting the Scottish makar Robert Henryson's own fifteenth-century version of the tale, *The Testament of Cresseid*. Third is Shakespeare's engagement with the philosophical concerns of the thirteenth to fifteenth centuries. For example, Hamlet's apparent nod to Christian stoicism in his compliments to Horatio as a man unaltered either by fortune's buffets or rewards. Fourth are 'hold-overs' of 'dramatic devices' from medieval drama. In this category we might observe the use of dumb shows and morality play structures, the self-addressing vice-like characters of Richard III, Iago, or Edmund, the *Ubi Sunt* motif in *Hamlet*, or the 'fall of princes' motif in plays such as *Anthony and Cleopatra* and *Julius Caesar*. Finally, in the fifth category, Smith observes 'regimes of watching and listening, protocols for making sense of dramatic action, that belong to an earlier aesthetic'.

In concluding this chapter, I too want to eschew a critical path that emphasizes Shakespeare's early modernity alone, and focus on what is inherited and retained rather than discarded. The play's message in early drama, whether liturgical (mystery and miracle) or homiletic (in the *psychomachia* of morality plays), is typically reinforced and singular. That later theatre is not didactic in the same way as earlier drama is true. But contrasting didactic with mimetic to mark a significant departure point in drama's evolution is to dismiss the vital presence of the earlier edifying form still found in later drama. In this light Smith's fifth category seems particularly important because it identifies neither processes of continuity nor disjunction, but rather a deployment of the medieval that directs audiences to recognize how the past remains a residual presence and to how it is being consciously adopted in the present. In readings from *Titus Andronicus* and *Hamlet*, we will now see how such recognition of the past may have created its own anxieties for early audiences.

---

[36] See e.g. *Reading the Medieval in Early Modern England*, ed. Gordon McMullan and David Matthews (Cambridge: Cambridge University Press, 2009); *Shakespeare and the Middle Ages*, ed. Curtis Perry and John Watkins (Oxford: Oxford University Press, 2009); and *Medieval Shakespeare: Pasts and Presents*, ed. Ruth Morse, Helen Cooper, and Peter Holland (Cambridge: Cambridge University Press, 2013).

[37] Bruce R. Smith, 'Shakespeare's Middle Ages', in *Medieval Shakespeare*, 37–52, esp. 24–7.

'... would I were a devil'

Titus Andronicus grants a strong insight into how two early modern dramatists deploy an inheritance from earlier drama. Studies in attribution have established that the revenge tragedy was co-authored by Shakespeare and George Peele. If we focus on the character of Aaron, who appears in different scenes written by both dramatists, and who has long been identified as a borrowing from the stage villains of late medieval drama, we are able to compare how Shakespeare and Peele use their dramatic inheritance.[38] H. T. Price's observation helped to begin the trend for such readings of the Moor:

> Aaron may owe something to Seneca, but he is still more a child of English stage-tradition. He is black, like the devil, the villain of the old mysteries. His character is a hash of all the blood-curdling traits which go to make up the Elizabethan stage bogey-man.[39]

Bernard Spivack further qualified this reading by describing Aaron as a 'hybrid', both 'older stage image' (or 'old morality role') and 'Aaron the Moor'.[40] Several recent studies have sought to focus on Aaron's distinctiveness in terms of race, but the association of the Moor with the allegorical figure of Vice, or stage devils of earlier drama, remains marked. Indeed, recently, Thomas Betteridge writes that Aaron is a 'vice dedicated to mischief and mayhem'. [41] Of course, in pre-Reformation drama vice figures and stage devils were often indistinguishable, and it is only in Tudor drama that the defined role of 'Vice' or 'Vice-derived human beings' appears.[42] But why should Shakespeare and Peele draw on such a dramatic inheritance, and do they both characterize Aaron in the same way?

Aaron is onstage but silent for most of Peele's long opening scene at the Capitol in *Titus Andronicus*. Only when the rest of the stage is cleared—incorrectly designated as an act-break in most modern editions—do we hear him first speak. Here we find Aaron in a familiar Vice-like posture as he delivers his self-addressing soliloquy plotting his next move. Following the arrival onstage of the 'braving' Chiron and Demetrius, disputing the

---

[38] Peele is certainly the primary author of the long opening scene 1.1 (roughly the first 650 lines of the play, usually, following the division in the First Folio, divided into 1.1. and 2.1 in editions; in the 1594 first quarto the opening scene is continuous). See Brian Vickers, *Shakespeare, Co-author* (Oxford: Oxford University Press, 2002), esp. 148–243. Peele's authorship of 4.1, once suspected, is now disputed, and the scene is attributed to Shakespeare. See William Weber, 'Shakespeare After All? The Authorship of *Titus Andronicus* 4.1 Reconsidered', *Shakespeare Survey* 67 (2014), 69–84, and Anna Pruitt, 'Refining the LION Collocation Test: A Comparative Study of Authorship Test Results for *Titus Andronicus* 4.1', in *Shakespearean Authorship: A Companion to the New Oxford Shakespeare*, ed. Gary Taylor and Gabriel Egan (Oxford University Press, forthcoming).

[39] H. T. Price, 'The Authorship of *Titus Andronicus*', JEGP 41 (1943), 58 (55–81).

[40] Bernard Spivack, *Shakespeare and the Allegory of Evil* (New York: Columbia University Press, 1958), 380–1. Spivack argues that Aaron is less of an allegorical figure in certain scenes, including 'his first soliloquy, his vicious counsel to Chiron and Demetrius, his relations with Tamora and with his child' (380).

[41] Thomas Betteridge, 'The Most Lamentable Roman Tragedy of *Titus Andronicus*', *The Oxford Handbook of Tudor Drama*, ed. Thomas Betteridge and Greg Walker (Oxford: Oxford University Press, 2012), 661 (653–68).

[42] See John D. Cox, *The Devil and the Sacred in English Drama, 1350–1642* (Cambridge: Cambridge University Press, 2000), 3.

rights to Lavinia (who is already betrothed to Bassianus), Aaron proposes that they find a simple solution to their conflict: they should both rape her, taking their 'turns' to 'serve [their] lust'. This Aaron is full of ideas for plots and schemes, cunning, cruel and without compassion. But his motives are not entirely clear. He wants riches, of course, to 'shine in pearl and gold', and he lusts after Tamora, but there seems to be no overall personal objective beyond satisfying his destructive will:

> to wanton with this queen,
>
> ...
>
> This siren that will charm Rome's Saturnine
> And see his shipwreck and his commonweal's.

As Emily C. Bartels smartly observes, in this scene (and, for Bartels, throughout the play) Aaron's 'purposelessness ... makes his villainy all the more insidious'.[43]

Compare this character with the Aaron we discover in 4.2, where he defends his child, and 5.1, where, now captured by the Goth soldiers—perhaps tellingly near another remnant of the medieval past, a 'ruinous monastery' (see below)—he pleads to Lucius for his son's life, saying that if the child is saved he will 'show [i.e. tell them] wondrous things | That highly may advantage [Lucius] to hear'. Lucius commands him to speak on, swearing that: '*if* it please me which thou speak'st | Thy child shall live' (5.1.59-60, my emphasis). The Moor does so and much more, naming Tamora as the child's mother, disclosing his earlier role in Bassianus' murder, and then revealing his culpability in a litany of crimes, stretching from the horrific to the improbable, including murder, rape, arson, grave-digging, and corpse mutilation. He says he wishes he could 'do ten thousand more' evil deeds, and his final lines in the play are:

> If there be devils, would I were a devil,
> To live and burn in everlasting fire,
> So I might have your company in hell
> But to torment you with my bitter tongue.

> (5.1.147-50)

There is nothing particularly original in noting Aaron's sudden alteration in character, or in pointing out that Aaron seems to be the most concerned parent figure in the play—the 'twist' that critics often write of—but now we know that this alteration occurs in Shakespeare's final scenes. My purpose here is not to rehabilitate Aaron's character—after all, he murders his child's nurse in 4.2, comparing her dying exclamations to those of a pig being killed for a spit—but to note that the defence of his child and confession reveals another dimension to the identification of Aaron as stage devil or Vice. While in *all* scenes by either Peele or Shakespeare he is all too easily identifiable as an allegorical figure of evil, that identification is overly reductive. In the later Shakespearean scenes Aaron diverges perceptibly from the path of destructive villainy; we are now given a reason for why he would say he has done such 'abominable deeds': if the confession satisfies Lucius, Aaron's

---

[43] Emily C. Bartels, 'Making more of the Moor: Aaron, Othello, and Renaissance Refashionings of Race', *Shakespeare Quarterly* 41:4 (Winter, 1990), 445 (433-54). Aaron continues to play this part well in the first scenes Shakespeare writes; in 2.3 (2.2), for example, Aaron appears again alone onstage bearing a bag of gold, and talking of a 'very excellent piece of villainy' to be 'cunningly effected'. And in an aside in 3.1 Aaron states 'O how this villainy/Doth fat me with the very thoughts of it'.

child lives. In this sense, the character of Aaron, who wishes he 'were a devil', is only recognizable as a stock medieval figure in the final scenes because he is actively playing up to the audience expectations of that convention. But by doing so, of course, Aaron is revealed as more fully developed than any abstract allegory. His imitative practice, his self-conscious performance of a convention, rejects the limits supposed and imposed by the traditional figuration of an abstract concept of evil or an incarnation of a devil from a pageant cycle.

Of course, it is not enough to observe that a character like Aaron owes something to earlier theatre, without considering exactly how such an inheritance is deployed. Indeed we need only look at the very next scene in *Titus Andronicus* (5.2, also written by Shakespeare) to explicate this point further. Here Tamora, Demetrius, and Chiron all adopt the guises of allegorical figures—'Revenge', 'Murder', and 'Rape' respectively—believing that their impersonations convince 'mad' Titus. But Titus 'knew them all', recognizing the persons capable of the deed they personify. Unlike Aaron's exaggerated impersonation of evil that reveals his humanity, the Goths' impersonation of allegorical figures only serves to emphasize the horror of their past and present actions. The division of labour between Peele and Shakespeare enables us to discern two distinct ways in which medieval allegory informs Aaron's character, one that is bluntly imitative, and one that, as with the Goths in 5.2, meta-theatrically directs attention to the tradition being imitated within the performance itself.

This seems one important distinction to observe in discussing Shakespeare's medieval dramatic inheritance: that what we perceive as an inheritance from early English religious drama could actually be a way of marking a discontinuity between the earlier and later form. But in evoking the past, if only to reject it, audiences must recognize the earlier form's residual presence in the later to observe the difference between the two. It is the presence of the medieval in tragedy that I wish to explore in the final section; that is, not simply the continuity of forms and modes derived from medieval drama, but representations of the period itself and the cultural anxieties its presence evokes. In *Hamlet* this tension between past and present is explored more fully.

'*A flourish of trumpets …*'

For hardline reformers to remember the none-too-distant pre-Reformation past was to remember a time of irrationality; a time of subservience to a Church that had lost its way and that mediated the word of God incorrectly to an ignorant collective. But for the wider public such a rejection of the past was fraught with its own existential anxieties, because that same collective, their ancestors, were only removed by one or two generations. The disconnect between those dead and alive, the past and the present, was further exacerbated by changes made to practices of remembrance for the dead in the Anglican Church. With the abolition of purgatory and its accompanying intercessionary and supplicatory services (obits, trentals, month-minds, chantry prayers, etc.), the duty and consolation of still benefiting the dead was removed and the connection between this world and the next was severed.[44]

---

[44] For an in-depth discussion of the broader cultural impact of the abolition of purgatory, see Julian Litten, *The English Way of Death: The Common Funeral since 1450* (London: Robert Hale,

While the faithful hoped that such a separation would be temporary, this doctrinal shift, with its jettisoning of the penitential middle pathway, made the horrors of *not* being part of the elect, of God's predetermined chosen few (in the Calvinist configuration), totalizing and final. In the face of such potential eternal damnation, over which the individual had no control, it is hardly surprising that neo-Stoic philosophy gained in popularity in this period. The moment of death, the beginning of a journey from whose path there was no chance of deviation, was also commonly analogized with the stage tragedies first performed on public stages. So Thomas Dekker, playwright and committed Protestant, observes in a plague pamphlet that 'The terriblest Tragedie is that, of the Soule, fighting to get off (well,) from the Body'.[45] And, in the conclusion to his work on 'preparation for death', John Rogers, the vicar of Chacombe, implored his readers to know that

> when iniquity hath played her part vpon the Theater of this sinfull world ... the Comedy is short, but the Tragedy is ouer-long, bloudy and bitter.[46]

Scholars widely regard *Hamlet* as a tragedy that reflects such contemporary cultural concerns about the afterlife, observing the play's detailing of practices of memorialization and remembrance, private and public, and the protagonist's own obsessive concerns with the efficacy of memory. Historiography in the early modern sense, the literal 'writing of history'—that is, its recording, re-telling, remembering (*OED*, n. 1)—is seen as one of the central concerns of the play, from Hamlet's tables to the enactment of 'The Mousetrap'. Indeed, Horatio's final duty in the play is to promise to reiterate the tale the audience has just seen—'to tell [Hamlet's] story'. The past is recorded and remembered to help stave off the crumbling deterioration of memory, personal and cultural. However we should observe that the past haunts the present, sometimes quite literally, in no other Shakespearean play so much as *Hamlet*. The ability to *forget* the past, personally and culturally, is also persistently in question, from Hamlet's 'Must I remember?' to Claudius' opening court speech that effectively dispenses with the troublesome memories of his accession. The ghost's provenance in *Hamlet* has been long debated (purgatory, hell, or somewhere else), but its very *presence* bridges the gap between past and present, death and life, that the reformed faith firmly denied; here the medieval haunts and confronts the modern, concurrent rather than simply disjunctive, exaggerating those cultural anxieties manifested by a crisis surrounding commemoration of and negotiation with the past.

Indeed Hamlet's question has a reflexive quality in Reformation England, where the residual remnants of its Catholic medieval past were still evident for all to see. While the split with Rome brought with it processes of effacement, such as the whitewashing of church walls, and of destruction, as with the dissolution of the monasteries, evidence of England's recent Catholic past and its medieval inheritance were still conspicuous. We

---

1992), esp. 143–61 and Peter Marshall, *Beliefs and the Dead in Reformation England* (Oxford: Oxford University Press, 2002); for its impact on early modern drama, see Michael Neill, *Issues of Death: Mortality and Identity in English Renaissance Tragedy* (Oxford: Clarendon Press, 1997), Stephen Greenblatt, *Hamlet in Purgatory* (Princeton: Princeton University Press, 2001), and Andrew Gordon and Thomas Rist, eds. *The Arts of Remembrance in Early Modern England: Memorial Cultures of the Post Reformation* (Farnham, Surrey and Burlington, VT: Ashgate, 2013), esp. chs. 10–13.

45   Thomas Dekker, *The blacke rod, and the white rod* (London: 1630), A3[r].

46   John Rogers, *A discourse of Christian watchfulnesse* (London: 1620), Aa8[r-v].

find an echo of this in *Titus*, when Aaron is captured in a 'ruinous monastery', discovered after a Goth soldier had 'strayed' from the troops to 'gaze … earnestly … upon the wasted building'. Audiences could not help but be aware of state-wide practices of re-signification (e.g. the meaning of the properties at communion), adaptation (e.g. church vestments) and repurposing (e.g. monasteries as private homes; church lands in ownership) for the residual vestiges of the traditional faith. Many practices associated with the earlier faith and the medieval past simply acquired new meaning, thus simultaneously signifying its present meaning while also evoking its alternate past. One small episode in *Hamlet*, often overlooked, helps to illustrate the tensions around such residual practices and properties, multiplied in meaning, bridging past and present.

As Hamlet, Horatio, and Marcellus await the ghost on the battlements of Elsinore, '*A flourish of trumpets and two pieces goes off*' (1.4.7.1-2).[47] Although Claudius' celebrations are promised in the first court scene, these offstage sounds anger Hamlet and startle Horatio. We might imagine that such an unexpected noise often unsettles audiences as well as characters. Hamlet explains that it is a long-held Danish custom to toast successes by drinking alcohol and then sounding 'kettledrum and trumpet'. In upholding this custom, Claudius communicates his success(es) publicly to the hinterland of Elsinore. As Bruce Johnson rightly observes, this interjection of sound creates 'an intensely dramatic effect, an acoustic shock through which is proclaimed a stepfather's tasteless usurpation, a King's debauchery, and a state's decline'.[48] But Hamlet's subsequent disapproval also directs our attention to the normalcy of this celebration:

> But to my mind, though I am a native here
> And to the manner born, it is a custom
> More honoured in the breach than the observance.
>
> (1.4.14-16)[49]

This means, of course, that Hamlet's father also communicated his successes publicly in this manner, and that for the Danish subjects to interpret the sound's meaning correctly is for them to recall the association of success for such aural cues. For Claudius it is a means of acoustically rejecting the discordant elements of his accession by connecting past successes with the present; a public denial that Denmark is 'disjoint and out of frame' (1.2.20). For Hamlet, as listening subject—physically and figuratively peripheral, at this moment, to the court's centre—his liminality is made explicit via these sounds. But, of course, the sounds also troublesomely connect the reigns of both father and uncle for the

[47] This stage direction is unique to Q2. Q1 includes 'Sound Trumpets', while no stage direction is included in the Folio. The requirement for offstage music is made explicit by the line 'The kettledrum and trumpet *thus* bray out' (1.4.11 my emphasis) which is present in all three texts. In the Folio, where such a musical cue should be is at a page break between formes (Nn6v to Oo1). Compositor I set both pages, but not sequentially. He may have omitted the direction from Nn6v because it falls between pages. Or he may have cast off inaccurately, forcing him to omit the direction from the crowded Oo1. The 1986 *Oxford Shakespeare* adopts the Folio as its control-text, but inserts the Q2 direction. See Stanley Wells, Gary Taylor, John Jowett, and William Montgomery, *William Shakespeare: A Textual Companion* (Oxford: Clarendon Press, 1987), 404.
[48] Bruce Johnson, '*Hamlet*: Voice, Music, Sound', *Popular Music* 24:2 (2005), 261 (257–67).
[49] Hamlet's lengthy speech is found only in Q2 (1.4.13-37). In both Q1 and F, the ghost enters after Hamlet says 'more honoured in the breach than in the observance'.

prince. Hamlet expresses his concern that the signs may be misinterpreted—they 'clepe us drunkards'—but the very meaningfulness of the sound evokes a consoling past while at the same time confirming a painful separation.

It is the *presence* of these cues that provides the keenest contextual insight. In a tragedy set in medieval Denmark yet heralded for its early modernity, the cues simultaneously recall the past while also insisting upon the present. This semiotic crux would have been familiar to early audiences of the play. Recalling Knapp's argument, it seems to me that the identification of a 'forgotten semiotic' necessary to explicate earlier drama is also required for the later plays. We can overstate the power of severance between periods, regimes, past and present, but we should not overlook the pain involved in recognizing remnants of the past in a present that all the while asserts its own separation from that past. Early English performances certainly relied on a familiar stock of tropes, motifs, resonances, and recognitions. It was not so very different in the later plays, but the evocation of the past itself, of medieval pre-Reformation England, was a process of memorialization that evidently summoned up its own anxieties. The nervous figures on the battlements in *Hamlet*, listening to Claudius' celebrations while awaiting the ghost, evoke the tensions inherent in the period's own recognition and recollection of its recent past, an analogy of isolation and insecurity within regime change.

SELECT BIBLIOGRAPHY

Aers, David, 'A Whisper in the Ear of Early Modernists; or, Reflections on Literary Critics Writing the "History of the Subject"' in *Culture and History 1350–1600* (Hempstead: Harvester, 1992), 177–202.

Ascham, Roger, *The scholemaster* (London: 1570).

Baldin, William et al., *A myrroure for magistrates* (London: 1559).

Bartels, Emily C., 'Making More of the Moor: Aaron, Othello, and Renaissance Refashionings of Race', *Shakespeare Quarterly* 41:4 (Winter, 1990), 433–54.

Betteridge, Thomas, 'The Most Lamentable Roman Tragedy of *Titus Andronicus*' in Thomas Betteridge and Greg Walker, eds. *The Oxford Handbook of Tudor Drama* (Oxford: Oxford University Press, 2012), 653–68.

Bevington, David, *From Mankind to Marlowe: Growth and Structure in the Popular Drama of Tudor England* (Cambridge, MA.: Harvard University Press, 1962).

Camden, William, *Remaines of a greater worke, concerning Britaine* (London: 1605).

Chaucer, Geoffrey, *The Riverside Chaucer*, gen. ed. Larry D. Benson, 3rd edn. (Boston: Houghton Mifflin, 1987).

Cooper, Helen, *The English romance in time: transforming motifs from Geoffrey of Monmouth to the death of Shakespeare* (Oxford: Oxford University Press, 2004).

Cox, John D., *The Devil and the Sacred in English Drama, 1350–1642* (Cambridge: Cambridge University Press, 2000).

Dekker, Thomas, *The blacke rod, and the white rod* (London: 1630).

Duffy, Eamon, *The Stripping of the Altars* (New Haven: Yale University Press, 1992).

Elyot, Thomas, *The dictionary* (London: 1538).

Gordon, Andrew and Thomas Rist, eds., *The Arts of Remembrance in Early Modern England: Memorial Cultures of the Post Reformation* (Farnham, Surrey and Burlington, VT: Ashgate, 2013).

Grabes, Herbert, *The Mutable Glass: Mirror-Imagery in the Titles and Texts of the Middle Ages and English Renaissance*, trans. Gordon Collier (Cambridge: Cambridge University Press, 1982).

Greenblatt, Stephen, *Hamlet in Purgatory* (Princeton: Princeton University Press, 2001).

Johnson, Bruce, '*Hamlet*: Voice, Music, Sound', *Popular Music* 24:2 (2005), 257–67.

Kelly, Henry Ansgar, *Ideas and Forms of Tragedy from Aristotle to the Middle Ages* (Cambridge: Cambridge University Press, 1993).

Kelly, Henry Ansgar, *Chaucerian Tragedy* (Cambridge: D. S. Brewer, 1997).

King, Pamela, 'Morality Plays', *The Cambridge Companion to Medieval English Theatre*, ed. Richard Beadle and Alan J. Fletcher, 2nd edn. (Cambridge: Cambridge University Press, 2008).

Knapp, Robert S., *Shakespeare: The Theater and the Book* (Princeton: Princeton University Press, 1989).

Litten, Julian, *The English Way of Death: The Common Funeral since 1450* (London: Robert Hale, 1992).

Lydgate, John, *Falle of princis* (London: 1594).

Lydgate, John, *The hystorye, sege and dystruccyon of Troye* (London: 1513).

Marshall, Peter, *Beliefs and the Dead in Reformation England* (Oxford: Oxford University Press, 2002).

McMullan, Gordon, and David Matthews, eds., *Reading the Medieval in Early Modern England* (Cambridge: Cambridge University Press, 2009).

Meres, Francis, *Palladis tamia* (London: 1598), O02[r].

Miola, Robert, *Shakespeare's Reading* (Oxford: Oxford University Press, 2000).

Morse, Ruth, Helen Cooper, and Peter Holland, eds., *Medieval Shakespeare: Pasts and Presents* (Cambridge: Cambridge University Press, 2013).

Mortimer, Nigel, *John Lydgate's Fall of Princes Narrative Tragedy in its Literary and Political Contexts* (Oxford: Clarendon Press, 2005).

Neill, Michael, *Issues of Death: Mortality and Identity in English Renaissance Tragedy* (Oxford: Clarendon Press, 1997).

Perry, Curtis and John Watkins, eds., *Shakespeare and the Middle Ages*, (Oxford: Oxford University Press, 2009).

Power, Andrew J., 'Early Elizabethan Seneca and the Religious Settlement', *Theta IX*, 129–48.

Preston, Thomas, *Cambises* (London: 1570).

Price, H. T., 'The Authorship of *Titus Andronicus*', *JEGP* 41 (1943), 55–81.

Pruitt, Anna, 'Refining the LION Collocation Test: A Comparative Study of Authorship Test Results for *Titus Andronicus* 4.1', in *Shakespearean Authorship: A Companion to the New Oxford Shakespeare*, ed. Gary Taylor and Gabriel Egan (Oxford University Press, forthcoming).

Puttenham, George, *The arte of English poesie* (London: 1589).

Rogers, John, *A discourse of Christian watchfulnesse* (London: 1620).

Scragg, Leah, *Shakespeare's Mouldy Tales* (London and New York: Longman, 1992).

Shakespeare, William, *William Shakespeare: The Complete Works*, ed. Stanley Wells, Gary Taylor, John Jowett, and William Montgomery, 2nd edn. (Oxford: Clarendon Press, 2005).

Shrank, Cathy, 'John Bale and Reconfiguring the 'Medieval' in Reformation England' in Gordon McMullan and David Matthews, eds., *Reading the Medieval in Early Modern England* (Cambridge: Cambridge University Press, 2009), 179–92.

Sidney, Sir Philip, *An apologie for poetrie* (London: 1595).

Simpson, James and Brian Cummings, eds., *Cultural Reformations: Medieval and Renaissance in Literary History* (Oxford: Oxford University Press, 2010).

Simpson, James, *Reform and Cultural Revolution* (Oxford: Oxford University Press, 2002).

Smith, Bruce R., 'Shakespeare's Middle Ages', in *Medieval Shakespeare: Pasts and Presents* (Cambridge: Cambridge University Press, 2013), 37–52.

Spivack, Bernard, *Shakespeare and the Allegory of Evil: The History of a Metaphor in Relation to his Major Villains* (New York: Columbia University Press, 1958).

Stock, Brian, *Listening for the Text: On the Uses of the Past* (Baltimore: Johns Hopkins University Press, 1990).

Vickers, Brian, *Shakespeare, Co-author* (Oxford: Oxford University Press, 2002).

Walker, Greg, 'The Cultural Work of Early Drama' in *The Cambridge Companion to Medieval English Theatre*, ed. Richard Beadle and Alan J. Fletcher, 2nd edn. (Cambridge: Cambridge University Press, 2008).

Wallace, David, *Premodern Places: Calais to Surinam, Chaucer to Aphra Behn* (Oxford: Blackwell, 2004).

Weber, William, 'Shakespeare After All?: The Authorship of *Titus Andronicus* 4.1 Reconsidered', *Shakespeare Survey* 67 (2014), 69–84.

Wells, Stanley, Gary Taylor, John Jowett, and William Montgomery, *William Shakespeare: A Textual Companion* (Oxford: Clarendon Press, 1987).

White, Paul Whitfield, 'Theater and Religious Culture' in *A New History of Early English Drama*, eds. John D. Cox and David Scott Kastan (New York: Columbia University Press, 1997).

Wotton, Henry, *The elements of architecture* (London: 1624).

CHAPTER 4

....

THE ROMANTIC
INHERITANCE

....

EDWARD PECHTER

IT is a truth universally acknowledged that our engagements with Shakespearean tragedy have
been shaped by romanticism. Beyond this, however, agreement is hard to come by. The problem is partly in romanticism itself; its meaning and value have long been debated. I'm applying
the term loosely to writers mostly in late eighteenth- and early nineteenth-century England
and Germany, for whom Shakespeare was supremely important. This approach allows me to
admit two outliers, Goethe and Hegel, to the centre of discussion, and with 'mostly' to embrace later figures like A. C. Bradley and Harold Bloom. Another part of the problem is that
the romantics didn't say much about Shakespearean tragedy as such. I'll try to account for
their reticence, but the upshot is that we need to include romantic commentaries generally
on Shakespeare, even on literature and drama independently of Shakespeare, to see how they
nourish our understanding of Shakespearean tragedy in particular. One final complication: if
'the study of romanticism' is 'necessarily part of a study of assumptions governing *current*
literary-critical and theoretical practices', we find ourselves trying to 'inquire into the grounds
and initial elaboration of "our" literary-critical and theoretical concerns'.[1] This doesn't look
like a foundation for detached analysis: how can we get outside of what's inside us?

1

....

For English romantics, Shakespeare was the focus of boundless esteem. According to
Coleridge, 'our *myriad-minded* Shakspear' is the 'greatest genius, that perhaps human
nature has yet produced' (1815).[2] People would not 'cry him up to the skies', Hazlitt says

---

[1] Philip Barnard and Cheryl Lester, 'The Presentation of Romantic Literature', in Philippe
Lacoue-Labarthe and Jean-Luc Nancy, *The Literary Absolute: The Theory of Literature in German
Romanticism* (Albany: State University of New York Press, 1988), p. viii.
[2] James Engell and Walter Jackson Bate, eds., *Biographia Literaria or Biographical Sketches of
My Literary Life and Opinions. Collected Works of Samuel Taylor Coleridge* (Princeton: Princeton
University Press, 1980), vol. 7, Part 2, 19.

about Shakespeare, 'if he had not first raised them there' (1826).[3] Among German critics, who first articulated the beliefs of what we now call romanticism, Bardolatry is even more extravagant. In *Wilhelm Meister's Apprenticeship* (1795-6), Goethe's protagonist describes the prodigious effect of his first encounter with this 'most extraordinary and most marvelous of writers'. After reading 'but a few of the plays', he 'had to stop because they affected him so deeply'.

> I cannot remember a book, a person, or an event that has affected me as deeply as these wonderful plays. They seem to be the work of some spirit from heaven that comes down to men and gently makes them more acquainted with themselves.... Presentiments that I have had from youth on, without being aware of them, about human beings and their destinies, all these I have found confirmed and enlarged in Shakespeare's plays. He seems to reveal all the mysteries without our being able to point to the magic word that unlocked the secret.[4]

The scales fall from Wilhelm's eyes, as from Paul's on the road to Damascus. Goethe sometimes treats his protagonist ironically, but his own first encounter with Shakespeare resonates equally with the excitement of religious renewal. 'The first page of Shakespeare that I read made me aware that he and I were one.... I had been as one born blind who first sees the light.... In the face of Shakespeare I acknowledge that I am a poor sinner, while he prophesies through the pure force of nature.'[5]

The romantics are drawn especially to the tragedies. Herder's *Shakespeare* (1773) limits sustained discussion to *Hamlet, Othello, Lear*, and *Macbeth*. John Kinnaird remarks on the 'overriding concern with tragedy' in Hazlitt's *Characters of Shakespear's Plays*, where 'only three of the book's first fourteen essays deal with non-tragic plays'.[6] Six of Coleridge's eight single-play lectures are devoted to the tragedies. Three of these are on *Hamlet*, evidently his play of choice, to whose protagonist he feels a special proximity ('I have a smack of Hamlet myself'; 1827), as do Hazlitt ('It is *we* who are Hamlet'; 1817, 4: 232) and Keats ('Hamlet's heart is full of such Misery as mine is'; 1820).[7] Here as elsewhere, the Germans anticipate the English. When Wilhelm transfers his Shakespearean interests into theatrical production, Hamlet is the role he chooses to perform. Friedrich Schlegel, rifling tradition for examples of writing to serve the interests of a radically new modernity, turns to Shakespeare—'especially *Hamlet*', whose protagonist, conceived as 'a development of Goethe's in the direction of Coleridge's philosophical prince', reinforces Schlegel's conviction 'that only the German critics have understood Shakespeare and that he is particularly theirs'.[8] The identification reaches a crescendo in 1844, with Ferdinand Freiligrath's proclamation that '*Deutschland ist Hamlet*'.[9]

[3] P. P. Howe, ed., *Complete Works of William Hazlitt* (London and Toronto: J. M. Dent, 1930), 12: 187. Subsequent references interpolated.

[4] Ed. and trans. Eric A. Blackall and Victor Lange (New York: Suhrkamp, 1989), 112.

[5] Quoted in Oscar James Campbell, ed., *The Reader's Encyclopedia of Shakespeare* (New York: Crowell, 1966), 259.

[6] *William Hazlitt: Critic of Power* (New York: Columbia University Press, 1978), 174.

[7] See Coleridge, in Carl Woodring, ed., *Table Talk*, in *Collected Coleridge*, vol. 14, Part 1, 76 and n. 22; and Keats, in Grant F. Scott, ed., *Selected Letters of John Keats* (Cambridge, MA and London: Harvard University Press, 2002), 458.

[8] René Wellek, *A History of Modern Criticism, 1750–1950* (London: Jonathan Cape, 1955), 2: 27 and 28.

[9] See H. H. Furness, ed., *Hamlet* (1877; repr. New York: Dover, 1963), 2: 376.

All this makes it unsurprising that the romantics have a lot to say about Shakespeare's tragedies, especially *Hamlet*. That they have so little to say about Shakespearean tragedy as such, though, is harder to explain. According to Kinnaird, 'almost any of [Hazlitt's] general comments on tragedy' illustrates 'the central importance of the genre for his literary theory';[10] but except for a few passing remarks, Hazlitt makes no general comments on tragedy. In this respect, he departs from classical tradition. Aristotle declares at the beginning of the *Poetics* that 'the natural order' for treating 'Poetry itself' is to 'begin at the beginning', distinguishing among its 'various kinds' and then determining 'the essential quality of each'. For Hazlitt, though, the effects 'derived from tragic poetry' depend less on 'any thing peculiar to it as poetry' than on 'the common love of strong excitement' (1818; 5: 7). From this position, determining the special properties of tragedy will not seem particularly worthwhile.

Where Hazlitt is indifferent to generic distinctions, Coleridge is antipathetic:

> If the Tragedies of Sophocles are in the strict sense of the word Tragedies, and the Comedies of Aristophanes Comedies, we must emancipate ourselves of a false association arising from misapplied names—& find a new word for the Plays of Shakespear—they are in the ancient sense neither Tragedies nor Comedies, ~~but~~ nor both in one—but a different genus, diverse in kind not merely different in Degree.[11] (1812)

Coleridge's position is not altogether new. Samuel Johnson's *Preface to Shakespeare*, a repository of the classical values romanticism sought to displace, develops a similar argument. Acknowledging that 'the ancient poets' established 'the two modes of imitation known by the names of tragedy and comedy', and that Shakespeare's plays are 'not in the rigorous and critical sense either tragedies or comedies, but compositions of a distinct kind', Johnson nonetheless defends Shakespearean practice. There's 'always an appeal open from criticism to nature', and if 'the end of poetry is to instruct by pleasing', it 'cannot be denied' that 'the mingled drama' of Shakespeare 'may convey all the instruction of tragedy or comedy' in their purer forms.[12]

But Johnson and Coleridge are saying different things. Johnson makes room for Shakespeare's exceptional genius to snatch graces beyond the reach of art, but 'the exception', Johnson argues, 'only confirms the rule' (85). Generic distinction, sustained over a long history, remains a useful principle. Established tradition retains its normative force. Even as Shakespeare violates a particular prohibition, he obeys the spirit of the law, deferring to the universal authority of a knowable moral order, according to which 'it is always a writer's duty to make the world better' (71). Against the continuity of Johnson's 'always', Coleridge asserts difference. Where Latin was characterized 'by the simple attraction of homogeneous parts', the 'Northern tongues' are now 'more rich, more expressive, & various' (1: 466). Coleridge unpacks the consequences of this distinction for anyone 'who would intelligently study the works either of the Athenian Dramatists or of Shakespeare— that the very essence of the former consists in the sternest separation of the diverse in

---

[10]   Kinnaird, *Hazlitt*, 174.

[11]   R. A. Foakes, ed., *Lectures 1808–1819: On Literature, Collected Coleridge*, vol. 5, Part 1, 466. Subsequent references interpolated.

[12]   Arthur Sherbo, ed., *Preface to Shakespeare* (1765), in *Yale Edition of the Works of Samuel Johnson* (New Haven and London: Yale University Press, 1968), 7: 66–7. Subsequent references interpolated.

kind and the disparate in the degree, whilst the later delights in interlacing by a rainbow-like transfusion of hues the one with the other' (1: 467). For Coleridge, the principle of generic distinction is essentially incommensurable with a Shakespearean practice that succeeds not in spite of the fact that it mingles kinds, but precisely because it does so. It's not enough, like Johnson, to apply the rules flexibly; we have to jettison them altogether. Shakespeare's 'different genus' transports us into an undiscovered country where we need 'a new word'—a whole new vocabulary—to tell us where we are.

Coleridge would have found support for this position among the Germans. Historical difference is central to Herder ('how far we are from Greece!'), who links it with the idea of cultural specificity (as Sophocles 'teaches and moves and cultivates *Greeks*', so 'Shakespeare teaches, moves, and cultivates *northern men*').[13] But if 'the very essence, virtue, and perfection of the latter reside in the fact that it is not the former', what 'manner of fool would now compare and even condemn the two things because the latter was not the former?' (27). Herder answers by mocking his contemporary Gerstenberg's claim 'that the series of "-als" and "-cals" [Polonius] spouts should be taken seriously as the basis of classification for all of Shakespeare's plays'. Gerstenberg is tone deaf in 'making the childish Polonius the poet's Aristotle' (60); but Aristotle himself, Herder believes, would be inadequate when it comes to Shakespeare.

If 'Not a single one of Shakespeare's plays would be a Greek Tragedy', what are they? Herder anticipates Coleridge's problem, finding 'a new word' to 'emancipate ourselves' from the 'misapplied names' of an exhausted tradition. Herder's suggestion, 'Each play is History in the broadest sense' (62), hardly delivers definitive specificity, and his amplification, 'a complete *enactment of a world event, of a human destiny possessed of grandeur*' (63), produces no greater clarity. As Paul Kottman says, 'formal rules and inherited categories are of no help at all' to Herder because the kind of drama he is trying to account for 'has to solve for itself, again and again with each new play and performance, what it means to be dramatic'.[14] Language fails Herder as he tries to describe the experience of engaging Shakespeare's plays. 'If only I had the words to describe the one main feeling that prevails in each drama and courses through it like a world soul'; 'if only it were possible to capture all this in words, how it is all a vital and profound part of a single world, a single event' (47).

Coleridge himself is not altogether bereft of a 'new word' for Shakespeare: 'I have named the true genuine modern Poetry the romantic—& the works of Shakspere are romantic Poetry revealing itself in the Drama' (1812; 1: 466). Again, the Germans are in the background. 'Romantic Poetry' summons up *'romantische Poesie'*, the culminating idea in Friedrich Schlegel's thought. Schlegel derives *romantische* from the French *roman*, but if its etymological meaning is *novelistic*, Schlegel emphatically disconnects the term from any determinate textual kind. His 'Letter about the Novel' (1799) stipulates that 'the Romantic' is an essential 'element of poetry' rather than 'a literary genre'; it 'must be clear' from this why 'all poetry should be Romantic and why I detest the novel as far as it wants to be a separate genre'.[15] *Roman*, Hans Eichner remarks, 'could be applied to any work of

---

[13] Johann Gottfried Herder, *Shakespeare*, ed. and trans. Gregory Moore (Princeton: Princeton University Press), 26 and 32. Subsequent references interpolated.

[14] *Tragic Conditions in Shakespeare* (Baltimore: Johns Hopkins University Press, 2009), 10–11. Subsequent references interpolated.

[15] Kathleen M. Wheeler, ed., *German Aesthetic and Literary Criticism: The Romantic Ironists and Goethe* (Cambridge: Cambridge University Press, 1984), 78.

fiction that did not belong to any of the three classical genres', including 'plays such as those of Shakespeare, whose form was radically un-Aristotelian'.[16] But Shakespeare does more than just illustrate undifferentiated textuality; he embodies its supreme achievement, becoming the writer in whom Schlegel 'would like to fix the actual centre, the core of the Romantic imagination'.[17]

Hobbes's response to Davenant's *Gondibert* (1650) allows us to identify the larger implications of these romantic claims. Hobbes begins with genre, like Aristotle, but doesn't end there. He maps textual categories onto their corresponding geographical and cosmological coordinates: 'as philosophers have divided the universe ... into three regions, *celestial, aerial,* and *terrestrial;* so the poets ... have lodged themselves in the three regions of mankind, *court, city,* and *country'.* He then differentiates the inhabitants of these domains in rhetorical, social, and political terms, working down from the 'princes, and men of conspicuous power, anciently called *heroes',* who radiate 'a lustre and influence upon the rest of men, resembling that of the heavens', to the busy dwellers of 'populous cities', and finally to the 'rural people' who are of 'the earth they labour' earthy.[18] For Hobbes, the literary kinds are nested within a universal order constituted by hierarchically fixed categories.

From this perspective, the romantic dismissal of generic distinction abandons more than the rules governing literary composition. Schlegel's Athenaeum Fragment 116 (1798) makes explicit what's at stake. 'As "a progressive, universal poetry", the "aim" of *romantische Poesie* "isn't merely to reunite all the separate species of poetry and put poetry in touch with philosophy and rhetoric", but to "fuse poetry and prose, inspiration and criticism, the poetry of art and the poetry of nature; and [to] make poetry lively and sociable, and life and society poetical"'.[19] For Schlegel, collapsing literary distinctions is bound up with transforming the social order. The revolution in France, which could not have been absent from Schlegel's mind and which might be described as an attempt to make 'life and society poetical', must have rendered unintelligible Hobbes's confidence in centring authority in the court. Given the secularizing trajectory of Enlightenment, even the 'celestial' domain is subject to reconception: finding a 'new word' for the 'true genuine modern poetry' means looking for new heaven as well as new earth.

For Schlegel, the possibilities opened up by romantic Poetry generate excited expectation, but the mission is daunting, and here the romantic investment in *Hamlet* becomes clearer. The ghost's revelation produces (or reinforces) in Hamlet a scepticism encompassing 'all trivial fond records, | All saws of books, all forms, all pressures past | That youth and observation copied there'. His first instinct is to 'wipe away' this accumulated detritus from 'the table of my memory';[20] but instead of emptying his mind Hamlet keeps

[16] Hans Eichner, *Friedrich Schlegel* (New York: Twayne, 1970), 53.
[17] 'Letter about the Novel', in Wheeler, *German Aesthetic and Literary Criticism,* 77.
[18] 'Answer to Sir William Davenant's Preface before *Gondibert',* in William Molesworth, ed., *The English Works of Thomas Hobbes of Malmesbury* (Aalen: Scientia, 1962), 4: 443–4.
[19] Peter Furchow, ed. and trans., *Friedrich Schlegel's 'Lucinde' and the Fragments* (Minneapolis: University of Minnesota Press, 1971), 175–6. Subsequent references interpolated.
[20] Stanley Wells, Gary Taylor, et al., eds., *William Shakespeare: The Complete Works* (Oxford: Oxford University Press, 1988), 1.5.99–101. Subsequent references interpolated.

it open, not only to the inert platitudes of tradition, but to sentiments of a radically unconventional kind. This adventurous sensibility exacts a terrible cost. Since the vast array of
phenomena welcomed into Hamlet's consciousness cannot be organized into a coherent
structure of belief, they register as disconnected fragments, loading yet more mass onto
the already unbearable burden he had hoped to jettison at the beginning. For Bradley,
'There were no old truths for Hamlet',[21] but in another sense there are only old truths for
Hamlet. Either proposition accounts for *Hamlet*'s privileged position among the romantics. Weighed down by an exhausted tradition, energized by the prospect of renewal they
glimpsed in Shakespeare, but also overwhelmed by the magnitude of the task in front of
them, the romantics must have found the play an uncanny embodiment of their most
exuberant hopes and darkest fears.

If the broader context helps explain why the romantics made *Hamlet* their tragedy of
choice, it also accounts more fully for their indifference to tragedy as such. More is involved
than antipathy to genre. The tragic mode seems minimally to require two elements: the
conviction of a transcendent power giving value to human action, and a heroic protagonist, whose sacrifice elevates us into harmony with the absolute. This rehash of Tragedy 101
is meant to introduce George Steiner's argument in *The Death of Tragedy*—that the level-
ling and secularizing tendencies of romanticism undermine tragic effects. As a 'liberation
of the individual from predetermined hierarchies of social station and caste', romanticism
diminishes the charismatic authority required for the protagonist to perform a purgative
function. If romanticism's 'radical critique of the notion of guilt' effectively 'closes the
doors of hell', then the 'intolerable burden of God's presence … no longer falls upon us as
it fell on Agamemnon or Macbeth or Athalie'. Steiner is struck by Schiller's subtitle for *The
Maid of Orleans, Eine romantische Tragödie*: 'this is, I believe, the first time the antithetical
terms "romanticism" and "tragedy" were conjoined. They cannot honestly go together.'[22]

Steiner's argument, though powerful, strains credulity. He assumes not just secular
tendencies but radical discontinuity: a religious sensibility broad enough to sustain conviction across a range of cultures from ancient Greece to seventeenth-century France
abruptly ceases to matter with romanticism. I'll come back to this assumption, but for now
it's enough to note that *The Death of Tragedy* leads to implausible conclusions. If romanticism and tragedy are inherently incompatible, why do the romantics situate Shakespeare's
tragedies at the centre of their interests? Shakespeare's tragedies matter to them in new
ways, of course, and their departures from tradition make it uncertain whether they were
developing 'a new version of tragedy or an alternative view to it'.[23] Both, presumably; the
romantics were at once recuperating and repudiating tragic traditions, as complementary
strategies in a complex project of cultural renewal.

Hegel's *Aesthetics* is a good place to see how this works out, since it pivots on the difference between ancient and 'modern, or romantic' modes of tragedy.[24] For Hegel, Greek

---

[21] A. C. Bradley, *Shakespearean Tragedy* (1904; Houndmills: Palgrave Macmillan, 2007), 83.
Subsequent references interpolated.

[22] George Steiner, *The Death of Tragedy* (New York: Knopf, 1961), 124, 127, 353, and 135.

[23] Jeffrey N. Cox, 'Romantic Tragic Drama and its Eighteenth-Century Precursors: Remaking
British Tragedy', in Rebecca Bushnell, ed., *A Companion to Tragedy* (Malden: Blackwell, 2005), 413.

[24] G. W. F. Hegel, *Aesthetics: Lectures on Fine Art*, trans. T. M. Knox (c.1820; Oxford: Clarendon,
1975), 2: 1206. Subsequent references interpolated.

tragedy centres on 'the ethical substance of the ethical order' (1230), manifested in 'the authority of a higher world-governor, whether Providence or fate' (1208). Everything is subordinated to this overarching perspective, including the dramatic characters, who interest us less as 'particular and personal' individuals than as 'representatives' of 'the essential powers that rule human life' (1206). Tragedy proceeds from a collision between the fragments of a fractured ethical substance (Antigone's familial piety vs. Creon's political allegiance, say), and it ends when these fragments are synthesized into the 'undisturbed harmony' of a reunified ethical substance. 'Only in that case', Hegel declares, 'can the necessity of what happens to the individuals appear as absolute rationality, and only then can our hearts be morally at peace: shattered by the fate of the heroes but reconciled fundamentally' (1215).

Modern tragedy, as Hegel describes it, abandons (or is abandoned by) the 'world-governing authority' of the Greeks, but even as it loses the sense of a transcendent 'ethical substance', modern tragedy gains in its capacity to represent 'the greatness of the characters' and the 'depth of [their] feeling'. In both these achievements, Shakespeare 'stands at an almost unapproachable height'. His dramatis personae 'display the full wealth of their heart, and their elevation over their situations', in actions seemingly 'produced on the spur of the moment' from out of their own inner resources. By endowing his creations with self-consciousness, the capacity to 'contemplate and see themselves objectively like a work of art', Shakespeare 'makes them free artists of their own selves' (1206-7, 1227-8).

To witness the full range of this achievement, Hegel says, we need pay 'direct attention only to Shakespeare's Hamlet' (1225), thereby providing another way to account for *Hamlet*'s special claim on romantic imaginations. With 'that within which passeth show' (1.2.85), Hamlet provokes an irresistible desire to pluck out the heart of his mystery, not just in his on-stage company but in those who 'are but mutes or audience' to the performance (5.2.287). Engagements with *Hamlet* have long been driven by the felt need to gain access to the protagonist's interiority beyond the fleeting and contradictory impressions available to us on stage or in the text. It is much debated when this desire first becomes decisive, but if the romantics did not invent it out of nothing, they intensified an interest in Hamlet's subjectivity to an extent that has dominated subsequent analysis. Its effects are immediately evident in the dramatic tragedies of Coleridge, Wordsworth, Byron, Shelley, and others, where the 'inward turn of the romantic hero is perhaps the best known feature' in works which 'operate as psychological case studies under, as it were, the sign of Hamlet'.[25] A century later, *Shakespearean Tragedy* positions *Hamlet* in the same context: 'the psychological point of view' is 'the centre of the tragedy', Bradley says,

> and to omit from consideration or to underrate its intensity is to make Shakespeare's story unintelligible.... this is the reason why, in the great ideal movement which began towards the close of the eighteenth century, this tragedy acquired a position unique among Shakespeare's dramas ... *Hamlet* most brings home to us at once the sense of the soul's infinity, and the sense of doom which not only circumscribes that infinity but appears to be its offspring (*Shakespearean Tragedy*, 92-3).

---

[25] Cox, 'Romantic Tragic Drama', 424.

To judge from the astounding reprint history of *Shakespearean Tragedy*, a large audience shares Bradley's interest in trying to plumb the depths of Hamlet's infinite soul. This audience does not include most professional Shakespeareans, with the notable exception of Harold Bloom who, declaring that 'the representation of human character and personality remains always the supreme literary value', marches under the banner of 'Romantic criticism, from Hazlitt through Pater and A. C. Bradley'. Bloom appropriates Hegel's 'free artist of the self' as the signature for Shakespearean interiority, manifested above all in Hamlet's preternaturally developed capacity to listen to his own words and thoughts, and to produce new words and thoughts—new versions of himself—accordingly.[26]

When Hegel identified a new centre for modern tragedy, he saw that it needed a new kind of resolution as well: 'what presses for satisfaction' now is not 'the *substantial* nature' for whose larger interests characters are acting, but 'the *subjectivity*' of the protagonists themselves, 'their heart and mind and the privacy of their own character' (1225). Rather than contributing to a restored ethical substance, 'the individuals must have shown themselves inwardly reconciled to their own particular fate' (1231). Hegel had doubts whether this inward reconciliation adequately replaced the numinous aura that allowed Greek tragedy to close with a restored ethical substance. Nonetheless, he celebrates modernity (the teleological impetus of the dialectic requires it), and over time, his reservations recede from prominence. In 'Hegel's Theory of Tragedy', Bradley argues that Hegel's 'enthusiasm for the affirmative' in Greek tragedy prevented him from fully registering the differently affirmative feeling produced by the protagonist-centred denouements in the romantic mode—'something like [the] exultation' resonating above all 'at the close of *Hamlet, Othello*, and *King Lear*'.

> This exultation appears to be connected with our sense that the hero has never shown himself so great or noble as in the death which seals his failure. A rush of passionate admiration, and a glory in the greatness of the soul, mingle with our grief; and the coming of death, so far from destroying these feelings, appears to leave them untouched, or even to be entirely in harmony with them.... He dies, and our hearts die with him; and yet his death matters nothing to us, or we even exult. He is dead; and he has no more to do with death than the power which killed him and with which he is one.[27]

In summing up romantic ideas about Shakespearean tragedy, Bradley serves as the culminating figure in the development described here. In *Hamlet's Perfection*, William Kerrigan sketches a version of the same story, beginning with Schlegel, whose reconfiguration of *Hamlet* into 'the first and greatest of the *psychologische Romane*' breaks 'with Aristotelian tragedy by giving character priority over action', a 'notion' which 'Hegel adopts' and 'passes on to A. C. Bradley', from whom it descends to the great variety of Bradley's readers and finally to us.[28] If we approach Shakespearean tragedy focused less on a 'conflict

[26] Harold Bloom, *Shakespeare: The Invention of the Human* (London: Fourth Estate, 1999), 3–4, and 1. For the Hegel tag, see 56, 268, 275, 408, 583, and 693.

[27] A. C. Bradley, 'Hegel's Theory of Tragedy', in *Oxford Lectures on Poetry* (1901; repr. Bloomington: Indiana University Press, 1961), 83, 84, and 91.

[28] William Kerrigan, *Hamlet's Perfection* (Baltimore and London: Johns Hopkins University Press), 7.

of principles or abstract universals' than on the 'individual relationships whose personal conflicts, crises, and failure bear the full weight of the drama's meaning' (Kottman, *Tragic Conditions in Shakespeare*, 14-15), this is because, even today, we carry romanticism with us into the experience.

This is a good story (how else could it have become the standard account?), but it needs fine tuning, chiefly to determine where it begins. Character was a main focus in Shakespearean commentary going back through Maurice Morgann, William Richardson, and Elizabeth Montagu to Alexander Pope. 'His *characters*' are 'Nature her self', Pope declared; 'every single character in *Shakespear* is as much an Individual as those in Life itself'. Since this comment comes from Pope's 1725 edition (pp. ii–iii), long before romanticism was a visionary gleam in anyone's eye, it can't be claimed that the primacy of character was a romantic invention. We need to ask exactly how romantic engagements with Shakespeare's characters differ from earlier engagements.

Kottman's reflections on Bradley suggest an answer. 'Departing from the Aristotelian inheritance, Bradley notes that Shakespeare's protagonists are not compelling because of their moral righteousness', so that 'our "moral" judgement of the protagonists' actions ends up being detached, or detachable, from our affective response' (7). This coincides with the Bradley I've described, endorsing the Shakespearean emphasis on interiority over the larger moral order in the Greeks, but something deeper is involved. A shift from one topic (ethical substance) to another (subjectivity) is a horizontal move (both topics are aligned within the same critical orientation), but Kottman's Bradley negotiates a shift of orientation itself. He exchanges a mimetic focus on the ideas or subject matter for an approach keyed to tragic effects and the interpretive actions with which we register these effects.

Bradley's 'attention to our affective response' may be his 'greatest virtue',[29] but it does not originate with him; again, he sums up a story that began earlier on. In departing from Aristotelian tradition, he is (and understands himself to be) extending the tradition of such departures initiated in 'the great ideal movement which began towards the close of the eighteenth century'. He recapitulates the action by which the romantics, suspending the normative morality with which earlier critics understood Shakespeare's characters as models for conduct, freed themselves to explore new kinds of engagement centred in affect.

Keats's 'camelion Poet', taking 'as much delight in conceiving an Iago or an Imogen',[30] is perhaps the best-known example of this new kind of engagement; but many others resonate in Bradley as well. In his insistence that 'we should feel' the 'weight' of Creon's demands, even if they seem 'morally wrong', and that we 'do feel it', and that 'we still feel' it through to the denouement,[31] Bradley's percussive reiteration echoes an emphasis in Coleridge: 'let the Reader *feel*' Iago's 'disappointed Passion & Envy', Coleridge enjoins us, because the effect, like 'music on an inattentive auditor, *swelling* the thoughts which prevented him from listening to it', allows entry into an

---

[29] Paul Kottman, Introduction, in Kottman, ed., *Philosophers on Shakespeare* (Stanford: Stanford University Press, 2009), 11.
[30] Scott, *Letters*, 195.   [31] 'Hegel's Theory of Tragedy', 73.

area of sensibility which ethical standards render off limits (1819; 2.313-14). An *unwill-ing* suspension of disbelief, we might call this, the delight of the camelion reader, and again the story has a German foundation. According to Herder, guiding our counter-intuitively self-abandoning response to the brutalities in *Macbeth*: 'if then, my dear reader, you were too timid to give yourself over to the feeling of setting and place in any scene, then woe betide Shakespeare and the withered page in your hand' (42). Imaginative sympathy is crucial for Herder, a way into otherwise inaccessibly remote forms of cultural expression. The idea was without precedent in the German critical lexicon of his day, and he had to invent a new word for it: *Einfühlung*—empathy, as it is now routinely rendered.[32]

We risk misapprehension here, as if romantic endorsements of affect rejected ana-lytical cognition. Romantic suspicions are familiar ('we murder to dissect', 'philosophy can clip an angel's wings'); but they were directed less against analysis per se than against Enlightenment tendencies to make scientific method the only path to knowl-edge. In contesting this rationality-or-nothing position, the romantics did not mean to limit themselves to the affective register. Schlegel, who yields to nobody in breath-less enthusiasm, nonetheless dismisses those 'mystical lovers of art who consider all criticism dissection and every dissection a destruction of enjoyment', as if ' "I'll be damned!" would be the best judgment on the greatest work'.[33] Hazlitt disparages do-mestic tragedy precisely because it 'appeals almost exclusively' to 'our sensibility'. By contrast, he remarks in one of those rare 'general comments' Kinnaird mentions, 'the tragedy of Shakespeare, which is true poetry', engages 'the moral and intellectual part of our nature, as well as the sensitive' and 'rouses the whole man within us' (1820; 5: 6). For Coleridge, feeling is not a substitute for thinking but its complement; hence his symmetrical emphasis on Shakespeare's unique power to make us '*think* ourselves in to the Thoughts and Feelings of Beings in circumstances wholly and strangely different from our own'.[34]

Affect-vs.-analysis is not the issue; the issue is effort. As the romantics transfer interest from formal properties to interpretive engagement, they emphasize the sustained exer-tion such engagement entails. The exalted value Schlegel attributes to fragments derives precisely from this emphasis. 'Other kinds of poetry are finished and are now capable of being fully analyzed', he declares in Athenaeum Fragment 116, but the 'romantic kind of poetry ... should forever be becoming and never be perfected' (Furchow, *Schlegel's 'Lucinde'*, 175). So, too, should the romantic kind of criticism: it is not exactly that Schlegel 'wants us to take the fragment and make of it a whole' (Furchow, 18); he wants us to *try* to make it whole. There will always be a 'vast discrepancy between the claim and the ac-complishment', as Walter Benjamin says of romantic criticism, but if interpretive action delights more in process than achievement, then failure, as long as it generates further effort, constitutes success: 'under the name of criticism, the Romantics at the same time confessed the inescapable insufficiency of their efforts' and 'sought to designate this

---

[32] See Hans W. Frei, *The Eclipse of Biblical Narrative: A Study in Eighteenth and Nineteenth Century Hermeneutics* (New Haven: Yale University Press, 1974), 184.

[33] Quoted by Wellek, 'Friedrich Schlegel', 10.

[34] *Biographia*, in Engell and Bate, *Collected Coleridge*, part 2, 27 n. 2.

insufficiency as necessary'—the 'necessary "incompleteness of infallibility," as it might be called'.[35]

Schlegel's spirit migrates into England, taking up residence in Wordsworth and Coleridge. Crossing the Alps proves to be a dispiriting anticlimax in the *Prelude*, but even as Wordsworth grieves 'To have a soulless image on the eye | Which had usurped upon a living thought', his material disappointments become the basis on which imaginative exertion generates new and more idealized expectations:

> the light of sense
> Goes out, but with a flash that has revealed
> The invisible world ...
> Our destiny, our being's heart and home,
> Is with infinitude, and only there;
> With hope it is, hope that can never die,
> Effort, and expectation, and desire,
> And something evermore about to be.

(1850; 6. 527–8 and 601–9)

Coleridge enacts a similar process. His analysis of the 'thousand outward images' proliferating in *Venus and Adonis* morphs into the consequences when 'a mind thus roused and awakened' and 'forced into too much action' tries to take possession of these effects.[36] *Tries* is again the key word; possession remains unachieved and evidently undesirable, as when Coleridge remarks on the 'effort in the mind' provoked by a passage in *Romeo and Juliet* that 'would describe what it cannot satisfy itself with the description of', and on the 'strong working of the mind' generated by Milton's description of Death, 'still producing what it still repels & again calling forth what it again negatives' (1811; 1: 311). Coleridge explores the consequence of withheld closure—an interpretive concentration that can, theoretically, sustain itself indefinitely.

In 'Poetry for Poetry's Sake' (1901), Bradley describes 'an actual poem' as 'the succession of experiences—sounds, images, thoughts, emotions—through which we pass when we are reading as poetically as we can'.[37] In one sentence, Bradley recapitulates the whole process of romantic thought, from textual properties to interpretive response to the intense and ongoing effort required in this response. The initial shift, from objective form to subjective experience, is consequential: it produces the protagonist at the centre of romantic interest in Shakespearean tragedy. But personality and interiority by themselves fail to account for the powerful tradition culminating in *Shakespearean Tragedy*. It's the last step, *reading as poetically as we can*, that drives the process. When Bradley gives pride of place to *Hamlet*, he celebrates the unlimited depths of the protagonist but even more the limitless opportunities the play 'brings home to us' to try to penetrate those depths. Our efforts to possess 'the soul's infinity' are 'circumscribed' by the 'sense of doom' inextricably bound up with 'that infinity', but for the romantics Shakespearean tragedy was never about possession. As Browning's Andrea del Sarto puts it in another late romantic synopsis, 'a man's reach should exceed his grasp, | Or what's a heaven for?'.

---

[35] *The Concept of Criticism in German Romanticism* (1920), in Marcus Bullock and Michael W. Jennings, eds., *Walter Benjamin, Selected Writings* (Cambridge, MA: Harvard University Press, 1996), 1: 143.

[36] See Engell and Bate, *Biographia*, Part 2, 22.

[37] In *Oxford Lectures on Poetry* (1901; repr. Bloomington: Indiana University Press, 1961), 4.

2

In his 1976 study, *Shakespeare, Seven Tragedies: The Dramatist's Manipulation of Response*, E. A. J. Honigmann helps to suggest the magnitude of current indebtedness to romanticism. Reflecting on the issue identified in his subtitle, Honigmann remarks that, 'Although there are signs of a new "movement" in literary and dramatic criticism, it has not so far made much progress. More and more books now touch on the reader's or theatre-goer's response, yet even those who believe that we should pursue this new critical interest draw back, all too often, when they consider the dangers.'[38] In the years since Honigmann wrote, a proliferation of initiatives along the lines he sketched out have established themselves at the centre of Shakespeare and literary studies where, performing under titles like 'The Beholder's Share', 'Reader Response Criticism', and 'Affective Stylistics', they exhibit none of the tentativeness Honigmann described. If we want to account for such a rapidly achieved prominence, the preceding pages suggest one factor: this new movement is not really new. In transferring attention from textual objects to interpreting subjects, we are recapitulating the shift of interest negotiated by romantic critics more than two centuries ago.

But there are aspects of romanticism from which we are bound to feel remote, and in shifting my argument to these divergences now, I am imagining a different kind of audience as well. Readers who have been concerned chiefly to get a handle on romantic assumptions and values may find the following discussion less immediately relevant to their interests. Professional Shakespeareans, on the other hand, or those training to be so, will wish to sharpen their red pencils.

Current departures from romanticism can be summed up in a single word—religion. Romantic interpretive strategies develop out of biblical hermeneutics. When Schlegel describes criticism as the attempt to 'spy on' the 'secret intentions' that 'genius' wants 'to hide from our sight',[39] he extends a long history of commentary focused on the efforts required to tease out meanings concealed in Scripture. The continuity is evident in Herder, whose injunction to 'give yourself over to the feeling' of Shakespeare replicates his approach to the Hebrew Bible: 'place yourself in the circumstances of the ancient herdsmen' to get 'back something of the original sounds of the words, and of the original feeling'.[40] The connection goes beyond strategy to overall purpose. Self-abandonment to Shakespeare can, no less than to the Bible, produce an intuition of the unity of things: 'individual impressions' of 'independently acting' beings 'come together', like the 'dark little symbols' of 'a divine theodicy', to 'form a single, whole dramatic image' of 'what we are in the hands of the Creator' (32-3). As Moore remarks, Herder's *Shakespeare* 'is not just—perhaps not even primarily—literary criticism: the justification of God is at the heart of Herder's project'.[41]

Though self-declared theodicies are rare, romantic projects regularly direct themselves toward intimations of transcendence and are in that sense motivated by religious values.

---

[38] (London and Basingstoke: Macmillan, 1976), 1.
[39] Quoted by Wellek, *History of Modern Criticism*, 1: 8–9.
[40] *The Spirit of Hebrew Poetry* (1782–3; Burlington, Vermont: Edward Smith, 1833), 36.
[41] Introduction, p. xxxiv.

Schlegel's 'On Incomprehensibility' (1800) begins by observing that 'some subjects of human thought stimulate us to ever deeper thought': 'the more we are stimulated and lose ourselves in these subjects, the more do they become a Single Subject'; as we 'withdraw into holy seclusion', this 'subject of subjects' emerges into the form 'we designate the Nature of Things or the Destiny of Man'.[42] Coleridge represents poetic engagement as a spiritual quest. 'We take the purest parts & combine it with our own minds, with our own hopes, with our own inward yearnings after perfection … poetry results from that instinct[,] the effort of perfecting ourselves' (1811; 1: 224). (The Sermon on the Mount, 'Be ye therefore perfect', seems to hover in the background here.) Keats describes poetic engagement as a form of 'Soul-making' or 'Spirit-creation', a 'grander system of salvation' than the 'misguided and superstitious' notions of 'the chrystiain religion', in which 'we are to be redeemed by a certain arbitrary interposition of God and taken to Heaven'.[43] Keats's tone is of a piece with the irritated dismissals of Aristotelian values elsewhere (like received critical language, the old theological and doctrinal words no longer sustain belief), and here too the repudiation of exhausted tradition serves a reconstructive purpose. As M. H. Abrams puts it, the romantics sought not 'the deletion and replacement of religious ideas but rather the assimilation and reinterpretation of religious ideas, as constitutive elements in a world view founded on secular premises'.[44]

Abrams's recuperative continuity is more persuasive than Steiner's decisive rupture, at least for representing romanticism's relation to its own past; but switch from what went into romanticism to what came out of it, and Steiner's position looks more convincing. Religious values have become attenuated in commentary on Shakespearean tragedy, and are now sometimes treated with implicit hostility. Consider the witheringly sceptical revisions of the romantic *Hamlet* in current work. The 'innatist tradition', preoccupied 'with inspecting the contents' of Hamlet's 'private self', have, we are told, 'mistaken' Hamlet's 'that within which passeth show' to affirm his 'own inner gaze'. The misreading is based on anachronism: 'we read back from the present' to project inappropriate meanings onto the past; in this case, an interior domain unavailable until 'the auroral breakthrough of 1800', when the romantics invented and then 'fixed on' the protagonist's uniquely 'personal' investments as the main objects of interpretive interest. Properly contextualized, Hamlet's problem is not really particular to him. He is dispossessed of his legitimate inheritance, and his grievance is what any normal sixteenth-century eldest son would feel. Attempts to explain his situation in terms of a mysterious interiority are not only mistaken ('a 200-year-old critical tradition has been built on an oversight'), but futile. Since at 'the centre of Hamlet, in the interior of his mystery, there is, in short, nothing', the 'successive generations' of 'especially Romantic and post-Romantic' critics who have attempted 'to fill the vacuum' are on a wild goose chase. 'The quest is, of course, endless, because the object of it is not there'.[45]

---

[42] In Wheeler, *German Aesthetic and Literary Criticism*, 32.   [43] Scott, *Letters*, 290–1.

[44] *Natural Supernaturalism: Tradition and Revolution in Romantic Literature* (New York: Norton, 1971), 13.

[45] For these quotations, see Paul A. Cefalu, '"Damnèd Custom … Habits Devil": Shakespeare's *Hamlet*, Anti-Dualism, and the Early Modern Philosophy of Mind', *ELH* 67:2 (2000), 400; Francis Barker, *The Tremulous Private Body: Essays on Subjection* (London and New York: Methuen, 1984), 30; Margreta de Grazia, *'Hamlet' Without Hamlet* (Cambridge: Cambridge University Press, 2007),

The critics lumped together here do not have identical agendas, but the consequences of their arguments for romantic versions of Hamlet are the same. Where a 'sense of the soul's infinity' produced interpretive efforts commensurate with the object of their own wonder, acknowledging the emptiness of this illusory object now discredits any such endeavour. If romanticism 'has driven critical inquiry deep into Hamlet's psyche where it has discovered an inexhaustible hermeneutic resource', then the drive needs to be reversed and the resource renounced: instead of speculating endlessly about Hamlet's 'intransitive and unfathomable depth', we should focus on the tangible evidence of 'his worldliness'. [46] Worldliness here is conceived as the determining factor in a play that does not merely include, but centres on the specific political and legal practices that defined inheritance and dispossession for the sixteenth-century aristocracy. We've come a long way from Herder's *Einfühlung* and Coleridge's 'inward yearnings after perfection', but whatever the attraction of such an austere historicism, it no longer monopolizes critical practice. Thanks in part to a religious turn in literary studies, some Shakespeareans now embrace the power they find in *Hamlet* to figure forth meanings and feelings unrestricted to the material realities of its own moment.[47] Nonetheless, anti-romantic *Hamlet*s remain the norm. As Adam Phillips remarks, reviewing a 2013 study of *The Hamlet Doctrine*, the 'yearning for reconciliation between the individual and the cosmic order' has been largely absent from 'Shakespeare criticism for some time. For many readers and critics of Shakespeare redemption is not what it used to be'.[48]

'If only I had the words', Herder laments; 'if only it were possible to capture all this in words.' Small wonder we have turned away from such expressions. The romantics themselves acknowledged a vagueness in their intimations of transcendence. Wilhelm's inability 'to point to the magic word' that might name the intuition of primal unity 'confirmed and enlarged in Shakespeare' is just the first of many such confessions recorded in the preceding pages. Problematic in their own day, these undocumented assertions of 'something far more deeply interfused' have not aged well. To an authentically professional audience raised on Larkin's 'less deceived', they sound like New Age psychobabble—or jokes: asked about 'the Ultimate Question of Life, the Universe and Everything' in *The Hitchhiker's Guide to the Galaxy*, Deep Thought responds '42'. Ask a silly question, you get a silly answer.

The world has changed since Herder, and we can't just repeat the words that nourished cultural practice centuries ago. Herder himself made the point. Greek Antiquity was different from the northern Renaissance, and if Shakespeare had followed Aristotelian norms, he would have been making mouths at invisible events. To be like Sophocles—that is, speak to the needs of his own world—Shakespeare had to be unlike Sophocles. So, too, the current *Hamlet* needs to differentiate itself from the romantic version. Out with the old *Hamlet*, in with the new.

4–5, and 5; Barker, *Private Body*, 37; and Catherine Belsey, *The Subject of Tragedy: Identity and Difference in Renaissance Drama* (London and New York: Methuen, 1985), 41.

[46] De Grazia, '*Hamlet*', 5.

[47] See the *Hamlet* chapters in Paul A. Kottman, *A Politics of the* Scene (Stanford: Stanford University Press, 2008), 139–65, and Julia Reinhard Lupton, *Thinking with Shakespeare: Essays on Politics and Life* (Chicago: University of Chicago Press, 2011), 69–95.

[48] See 'To Be or Knot to Be', *London Review of Books* 35:19 (10 October 2013), 11.

Making it new, though, is no simple matter. Karen Newman gets at some of the complications, remarking that 'the political *Hamlet* de Grazia claims only now to have finally observed' was anticipated by Dover Wilson and Honigmann in the earlier part of the last century, and then assimilated into the mainstream. 'As a graduate student ... in the 70s', Newman recalls, 'we were taught precisely that the psychological' approach 'ignored the importance of the play's political dimension, Hamlet's thwarted claim to the throne of Denmark'.[49] It's not just the political dimension and de Grazia that are anticipated in early twentieth-century work. When current critics repudiate the 'innatist tradition' behind the romantic *Hamlet*, they follow along the lines mapped out by L. C. Knights, whose hugely influential 'How Many Children Had Lady Macbeth?' (1933) mounted a take-no-prisoners assault against the then-dominant practice of character criticism, for which Knights held romanticism and Bradley to blame. A remark of Empson's, that Knights's attack was part of 'the antihumanist movement of Ezra Pound, Wyndham Lewis, and T. S. Eliot',[50] allows us to identify a fundamental continuity between the critique of the 'innatist tradition' underlying the current *Hamlet* and the dismissal of psychology underlying the *Hamlet* of a generation or two ago: the postmodern interrogation of the subject recapitulates the High Modernist repudiation of the human. Today's tough-minded materialism carries on the unillusioned anti-romanticism with which Eliot, dismissing *Hamlet* as an 'artistic failure' and Othello's last speech as '*bovarysme*', reduced Bardolatry and heroism to self-deluding bombast.

That current versions of *Hamlet* fail to deliver on their innovating promises is not particularly noteworthy. Any post-Pound-era claim to Make It New is inevitably compromised by merely repeating the slogan High Modernism installed at the centre of cultural practice a century ago. What makes the situation more interesting is that the installation antedates High Modernism. In *The Tradition of the New*, Harold Rosenberg traces the 'famous "modern break with tradition"' back beyond Wyndham Lewis et al. to Baudelaire in the middle of the nineteenth century[51]; but if the tradition of breaking with tradition originates even earlier than this, with the romantics discussed here, then the anti-romanticism underlying current work is a self-cancelling position: the more aggressively we claim to break with the outmoded values of romantic tradition, the more inextricably we find ourselves implicated in the modes of thought on which those values are founded.

All this suggests an answer to the question at the beginning, 'how can we get out of what's inside us?': *we can't*. Except that we can and do, more or less easily, all the time. A radical disconnection with the past is inconceivable, so there will always be repetition, but repetition isn't identity, so there will always be difference as well. Any understanding of historical process, such as determining what current versions of Shakespearean tragedy owe to romanticism, needs both Abrams and Steiner, since elements of both continuity and discontinuity are bound to be involved. The hard thing is figuring out the right proportions, for which I have no Bright Ideas beyond passing on Herder's canny reflections on the matter at the end of *Shakespeare*.

---

[49] *Shakespeare Studies* 39 (2011), 224 and 222.
[50] 'L. C. Knights on A. C. Bradley', in John Haffenden, ed., *The Strengths of Shakespeare's Shrew: Essays, Memoirs and Reviews* (Sheffield: Sheffield Academic Press, 1996), 109.
[51] (London: Thames and Hudson, 1962), 9.

In the last words of his penultimate paragraph, Herder declares that 'each play remains and must remain *what it is: History! A heroic drama bringing to life the fortunes of a nation during Middle Ages!*' (63). As a climactic celebration of Shakespearean transcendence, these words could end the book; but the following paragraph shifts abruptly from heroic fulfilment to irretrievable loss. 'Sadder and more important is the thought that this great creator of history and the world soul grows older every day', and that 'soon ... even his drama ... will become the dilapidated remains of a colossus, of a pyramid, which all gaze upon with wonder and none understands' (64-5). Before we can assimilate this stunning reversal, Herder shifts perspective yet again, superimposing onto Shakespearean ruins the image of a triumphant Goethe who, recreating the (only apparently terminated) mode of epic nation-building, 'will erect a monument to him in our degenerate land, *drawn from our own age of chivalry* and written in our language' (64). *Götz von Berlichingen*, the monument referred to, seems inadequate compensation for the imminent loss of *Hamlet*, and Goethe, years away from the masterpieces that will make him the Sage of Weimar, is not an obvious choice as Shakespeare's heir apparent. Perhaps aware of the problem, Herder tones down the hyperbole, looking ahead beyond Goethe's putative triumph to the certainty of his death. Herder is not totally downbeat: 'your work will endure', he tells Goethe, and the book's last sentence summons up 'a faithful successor', who 'will seek out your grave and write with devoted hand the words ... *Voluit! quiescit!*' [he struggled, he rests] (65). This anonymous figure may be meant to suggest continuity and renewal, but the last word of the book means death, and it's not 'written in our language' but in the language of a moribund Antiquity.

I'm not sure which of these ironies are intentional, but the one that precipitates all the others is surely not. Herder takes it for granted that he inhabits 'the last days of an age' (64) when Shakespeare is a living force. Wrong. Shakespeare's power to generate interpretive interest, not least in the tragedies, extends now to the round earth's imagined corners, in accents yet unknown and technologies undreamed of in Herder's day. Maybe we should reconsider—for now, anyway—Jonson's uncharacteristically proto-romantic appreciation of Shakespeare's myriad-minded genius: 'He was not of an age, but for all time.'

Select Bibliography

Babcock, Robert Witbeck, *The Genesis of Shakespeare Idolatry, 1766–1799: A Study in English Criticism of the Late Eighteenth Century* (1931; repr. New York: Russell & Russell, 1964).

Bate, Jonathan, *Shakespeare and the English Romantic Imagination* (Oxford: Clarendon, 1989).

Bate, Jonathan, *Shakespearean Constitutions: Politics, Theatre, Criticism 1730–1830* (Oxford: Clarendon, 1989).

Bate, Jonathan, 'Shakespeare and Original Genius', in P. Murray, ed., *Genius: The History of an Idea* (Oxford: Blackwell, 1992), 76–97.

Bate, Jonathan, *The Genius of Shakespeare* (New York: Oxford University Press, 1998).

Bate, Jonathan, ed., *The Romantics on Shakespeare* (London: Penguin, 1992).

Benjamin, Walter, *Origin of German Tragic Drama*, trans. John Osborne (London: New Left Books, 1977).

Bernstein, J. M., ed., *Classic and Romantic German Aesthetics* (Cambridge: Cambridge University Press), 2003.

Bilgrami, Akeel, 'The Political Possibilities in the Long Romantic Period', *Studies in Romanticism* 49:3 (Winter 2010), 533–52.

Booth, Stephen, *'King Lear', 'Macbeth', Indefinition, and Tragedy* (New Haven and London: Yale University Press, 1983).

Booth, Stephen, 'On the Value of *Hamlet*', in Norman Rabkin, ed., *Reinterpretations of Elizabethan Drama* (New York: Columbia University Press, 1969), 137–76.

Bowie, Andrew, *From Romanticism to Critical Theory: The Philosophy of German Literary Theory* (London and New York: Routledge, 1997).

Coldwell, Joan, ed., *Charles Lamb on Shakespeare* (Gerrards Cross: Colin Smythe, 1978).

Cutrofello, Andrew, 'Kant's Debate with Herder about the Philosophical Significance of the Genius of Shakespeare', *Philosophy Compass* 3:1 (January 2008), 66–82.

Dávidházi, Péter, *The Romantic Cult of Shakespeare: Literary Reception in Anthropological Perspective* (Houndmills, Basingstoke: Macmillan; New York: St. Martin's Press, 1998).

Ferris, David, ed., *Walter Benjamin on Romanticism, Studies in Romanticism* 31:4 (Winter 1992).

Foakes, R. A., ed., *Coleridge's Criticism of Shakespeare: A Selection* (London: Athlone, 1989).

Gjesdal, Kristin, 'Reading Shakespeare—Reading Modernity', *Angelaki: Journal of the Theoretical Humanities* 9:3 (July 2004), 17–31.

Gjesdal, Kristin, 'Shakespeare's Hermeneutic Legacy: Herder on Modern Drama and the Challenge of Cultural Prejudice', *Shakespeare Quarterly* 64:1 (Spring 2013), 60–9.

Habicht, Werner, 'Shakespeare and the German Imagination', International Shakespeare Association Occasional Paper 5 (Hertford: Stephen Austin and Sons, 1994).

Nisbet, H. B., ed., *German Aesthetic and Literary Criticism: Winckelmann, Lessing, Hamann, Herder, Schiller, Goethe* (Cambridge: Cambridge University Press, 1985).

Ortiz, Joseph M., ed., *Shakespeare and the Culture of Romanticism* (Farnham and Burlington: Ashgate, 2013).

Paoloucci, Anne and Henry Paoloucci, eds., *Hegel on Tragedy* (New York: Harper, 1962).

Parker, Reeve, *Romantic Tragedies: The Dark Employments of Wordsworth, Coleridge, and Shelley* (Cambridge: Cambridge University Press, 2011).

Tuveson, Ernest Lee, *The Imagination as a Means of Grace: Locke and the Aesthetics of Romanticism* (Berkeley, University of California Press, 1960).

White, R. S., ed., *Hazlitt's Criticism of Shakespeare: A Selection* (Lewiston, Queenston, and Lampeter: Edwin Mellen, 1996).

Young, Edward, *Conjectures on Original Composition*, ed. Edith Julia Morley (1759; repr. Manchester: Manchester University Press, 1918).

CHAPTER 5

....

ETHICS AND
SHAKESPEAREAN TRAGEDY

....

TZACHI ZAMIR

ANYONE attempting to address the relationship between ethics and Shakespeare's tragedies must come to terms with an apparent contradiction between two claims. The first is that Shakespeare's tragedies should not be reduced to pleasurable vehicles for moral instruction. The second is that as one reads, performs, or watches Shakespeare, one is somehow *growing* in an important way as a human being, and that such growth often consists of elements which seem somehow related to morality. It is said, for example, that tragedy sharpens one's interpretative capacities regarding complex actions and situations; that one's sensitivities are deepened by discovering fresh linguistic articulations for them; that one's relationship with language is revitalized by responding to its energy and becoming alert to a vocabulary's capacity to restrict or enable freedom. It is claimed that one often grasps something novel regarding who and what one values as well as the conceptual structure and psychological layering of such valuing, a structure that surfaces particularly when—as in tragedy—whoever and whatever bears these values is lost. Emotional, conceptual and experiential constituents of one's attachments—of being a father, a citizen, a friend, a lover, a son, a sibling—are newly understood. It is said that tragedy enables insights into important notions such as love, honour, knowledge, or the dignity of human life—all revealingly interrogated or contextualized. Virtues such as these, dutifully mentioned when serious study of Shakespeare is advocated or defended, are all aspects of morality: the attempt to live well by understanding one's values, or the attempt to avoid superficiality when thinking comprehensively about multifaceted human situations.

The challenge undertaken in this chapter is to relax this apparent tension between regarding Shakespearean tragedy as enabling moral growth and the refusal to reduce an aesthetic text to an edifying lesson. I begin by presenting two ways in which ethics and Shakespeare's tragedies should *not* be interrelated (§§ 1-2). I then dismiss the objection that reading a work for its moral rewards necessarily instrumentalizes and debases an aesthetic creation (§ 3). Three kinds of connection between Shakespearean tragedy and ethics are then proposed. The first includes ways whereby particular rewards of reading the tragedies uniquely contribute to *existing* objectives within ethics (§§ 4-5). The second suggests how the tragedies may add (rather than merely respond to) the familiar repertoire of questions which ethics typically discusses (§§ 6-7). The third initially accepts an account that argues for an opposition between tragedy and morality, and then suggests that this account relies upon an overly restrictive sense of morality, and that the non-moral values it argues for can and should be moralized (§ 8). Attempts to relate the tragedies to moral value undertaken in this chapter will not be presented merely as defendable readings. I hope to show, rather, that explicating such connections with ethics is interpretively fruitful precisely because the distinct moral attainments being argued for can partly account for the attribution of aesthetic merit to the plays: what makes these tragedies stand out as literary works is often an implied moral reward.

1 AGAINST ABSTRACTIONS

The philosophy of tragedy has repeatedly articulated a 'moral perspective' or 'a tragic point of view' (which tragedy either invokes or undermines). For thinkers such as Schopenhauer or Nietzsche tragedy aggravates the felt rift between the purposeful world of human beings and the purposeless reality in which they are embedded. For Schopenhauer the moral value of such experience is that it leads to resignation and release from the vexing demands of the will. For Nietzsche, the value inheres in enabling the audience to bond with destructive aspects of reality, a response triggered by the death of the powerful protagonist. For a more contemporary philosopher, tragedy is supposed to reveal 'that life is aporetic, that life is not unconditionally or self-sufficiently rational, consistent, orderly, lovable, intelligible, safe, lawful, or moral'. Tragedy 'brings into view what the triumphs of civilization—what philosophy rationally celebrates—have sought to repress, dominate, discount, deauthorize, and empty. Tragedy is a return of the repressed.'[1]

Forcing such schemes onto Shakespeare's tragedies is strained, overly abstract, and unpersuasive. Shakespeare was not really weaving his plays around conflicting principles, such as the conflict between 'law' and 'love' that Hegel imposed on *Antigone*, or such as the one between 'necessity' and 'freedom' that Schelling read into *Oedipus Rex*. His tragedies do not prompt Schopenhauerian resignation. Nor do they lend themselves to analysis in accordance with the Dyonisian-Apollonian dualism. As with many other great literary works, something in Shakespeare's plays altogether resists the vocabulary of philosophical extrapolations. Whatever is repressed does not return, and—in Shakespeare at least—one's trust in rationality is not even initially raised in order to be later undermined. Shakespeare was not attempting to convey some tragic view. If he were, he failed abysmally, since given the intense scrutiny to which his plays have been subjected, one would expect critics to be

---

[1] For Schopenhauer's position, see Alex Neill, 'Schopenhauer on Tragedy and Value', in *Art and Morality*, ed. Jose Bermudez and Sebastian Gardner (New York: Routledge, 2003), 204–17. For the positions of Hegel and Schelling, see the relevant chapters in Peter Szondi's *An Essay on the Tragic*, trans. Paul Fleming (California: Stanford University Press, 2002). Nietzsche's claims regarding tragedy as bonding with the destructive are found in *Twilight of the Idols*, 'What I owe to the ancients', section 5. For discussion and overview of Nietzsche's position, see Oliver Conolly, 'Pity, Tragedy and the Pathos of Distance', *European Journal of Philosophy* 6:3 (1998), 277–96. The citation is from J. M. Bernstein, 'Tragedy', *The Oxford Handbook of Philosophy and Literature*, ed. Richard Eldridge (New York: Oxford University Press, 2009), 71–94 (72).

in accord at least regarding the rough outlines of such a central unifying view purportedly underlying his tragedies. No such consensus exists.

But to resist the idea of reading the tragedies against a single sweeping abstraction or 'tragic view' need not entail a categorical ban on any thematic statement.[2] Avoiding some broader reflective considerations regarding the plays in favour of an unflinching commitment to particularism is ultimately impossible: any act of sustained understanding and interpretation is conducted in relation to concepts and themes. Such avoidance is no less artificial than the generalist's desire to regard the tragedies as interchangeable instances of some tragic view. George Harris, for example, has recently suggested that a tragic view of life encapsulates a fourfold perspective from which (a) the world is understood as hostile; (b) values are understood as elements that may potentially conflict in powerful irreconcilable ways; (c) when such values conflict they cannot be compared and rationally weighed against some shared criteria; and (d) nothing is of unqualified value (d).[3] No single Shakespearean tragedy exemplifies all four elements. But Lear certainly discovers that nothing possesses unqualified value when he runs up against the disappointing limits of filial duty and Antony is surely torn between the conflicting, incommensurable, and (for him) irreconcilable values of happiness, on the one hand, and the value of self-preserving political prudence on the other.

Note though, that even in cases such as these, where such abstractions are appropriate, they are merely the scaffolding upon which Shakespeare erects his dramatic edifice. They cannot *account* for the achieved distinctive aesthetic merit. This is because these abstract features existed before, in the undistinguished source plays that Shakespeare adapted (*The True Chronicle Historie of King Leir*), or in the anodyne alternative versions of the same stories that were composed by Shakespeare's contemporaries (Garnier-Pembroke's *The Tragedie of Antonie*, or Samuel Daniel's *The Tragedy of Cleopatra*). Accordingly, the effect of such abstractions is either nonexistent (since they are simply correlated—rather than causally related—with other independent underlying features of Shakespeare's art), or parasitical upon these other elements (in the sense that such tragic abstractions achieve their full aesthetic force *because* they are woven into a fabric that enables them to

---

[2] Peter Lamarque—'Tragedy and Moral Value', *Australasian Journal of Philosophy* 73:2 (1995), 239–49—usefully distinguishes between the fictive, literary, and moral dimensions of a tragic work. The 'fictive' dimension is our awareness that the tragedy does not present actual events, releasing in us a form of imaginative response. Because such response differs from the one used in relation to non-fictional events, we can suspend judgement and thereby achieve a broader scope of sympathetic understanding (we can, for example, cultivate immoral identification which we would avoid in life). The 'literary' dimension is an attempt to unify or illuminate the text in relation to overarching themes or ideals. It is here that a literary work—tragedies in our case—may suggest several conflicting moral readings. The 'moral' dimension consists of the attempt to relate the moral themes that emerge from the literary dimension of the tragedy to some independently held moral principles, holding that the tragedy supports, illuminates or undermines such principles. Lamarque's typology is helpful in many ways, one of which is pinpointing the logical gap between opposing the use of thematic statements of whatever kind (an opposition I find both impossible and implausible), and opposing the attempt to relate tragedies to overarching principles or moral views (a position I share).

[3] *Reason's Grief: An Essay on Tragedy and Value* (New York: Cambridge University Press, 2006), 29. Harris's objective—it should be pointed out—is *not* to argue that this fourfold view is conveyed or implied by *literary* tragedies.

meaningfully touch the reader/audience due to altogether independent merits). In both cases, generalizations like (a)–(d), even when at work, are secondary.[4]

In practice, this means that such abstractions should not be imposed on the plays, but be derived by the interpreter in a bottom-up manner. As features of a literary work rather than a philosophical treatise, the force of these abstractions should be understood not in terms of the truth value of what they themselves independently assert, but primarily in their interrelations with poetic, psychological, and rhetorical details. Such details and these abstractions should mutually reinforce and inform each other in order to establish a unified effect. As a result, the audience/reader will absorb the lived underside of an abstraction not primarily via fact or argument, but because of an experience they undergo.

Detailed analysis of the idea of experiential knowledge cannot be undertaken here. But since it is assumed by much of what follows, here is the gist of what such knowledge means. The underlying conviction is that art and literature are centrally about the creation of an experience, so the uniqueness of the illumination they provide (when they provide it) is rooted in the interplay between what they say and the experience undergone by the recipient. As experiences, such states cannot be fully conveyed through paraphrase or description: one must actually undergo them in order to access the unique quality which the knowledge-claim receives from the work. The terminological construction 'knowledge claim' (rather than 'truth' or 'knowledge') is designed to capture the idea that in many domains in life (literary criticism being one of these), a proposition can be put forth for someone else's consideration without presenting it as an asserted truth.[5] Thus, what we relate to as a 'deepening' of understanding in relation to some central concepts may refer not to acquiring more truths, but either to a proliferation of possible understandings (knowledge-claims) regarding the concept, or to an experience undergone in relation to a familiar claim, one which anchors the claim in a significant response.

2 AGAINST BETTERMENT

There are three kinds of ethical theories: act-oriented theories, agent-oriented theories and what we may call 'contact-oriented' theories. For act-oriented theories (consequentialism, deontologism, and contracterianism) ethical thinking should focus on individual *actions*. Such theories propose and then defend some procedure that can determine the right conduct. Agent-oriented theories (varieties of virtue ethics) assert that the right conduct is likely to be performed by individuals who have cultivated the morally desirable

---

[4] The resistance to philosophical extrapolation is not unique to Shakespeare. As Peter Larmarque claims, when looking for the moral value that might reside in depictions of human suffering 'it is not sufficient to locate this value in an independently statable metaphysical view of the place of man in nature even if there are characteristic themes in tragic drama which reinforce some such general vision. For what gets left out of account is the specific means by which this vision, or these themes, are represented in literary works and the special achievement of this mode of presentation' (Lamarque, 'Tragedy and Moral Value', 241,).

[5] The distinction was introduced by Peter Lamarque and Stein Haugom Olsen, in their *Truth, Fiction and Literature: A Philosophical Perspective* (Oxford: Clarendon Press, 1994), 328.

character, which means a character endowed with the right virtues. Contact-oriented theories (Buber, Levinas, Cavell), postulate that right conduct results from a capacity to foster *meaningful contact* among individuals, from perceiving others non-instrumentally and fully acknowledging them as fellow individuals.

Shakespeare's tragedies are unrelated to ethics in any of these ways. Reading or watching them will not enable you to know where your more binding obligation truly lies, or what to do in cases of conflict among duties. You will not improve your capacity to weigh the consequences of alternative courses of actions. You will not develop new virtues or cultivate the virtues you already have. If you have a tendency to instrumentalize others, there is no substantial reason to suppose that immersing yourself in Shakespeare's tragedies will make you less cold in your dealings with others. While many characters in Shakespeare misuse others, the tragedies do not present or suggest a method through which such disregard can be remedied. Reading or watching these tragedies will not make you a morally better human being. If it did, my fellow Shakespeareans would be morally superior to others. They would be kinder, or more prudent, or more virtuous, or clearer about their moral duties, or less obtuse, or more perceptive regarding morally relevant features of situations. Nothing in my experience suggests to me that this is so.

More disturbingly, the tragedies may even be *skewing* our moral perceptions rather than improving them. Take, for example, the glaringly disproportionate attention we bestow on titular heroes when compared with our relative indifference to the disasters of other characters. Often the protagonist's entire country is lost. Egypt is overtaken by Rome (*Antony and Cleopatra*), Rome is almost demolished by the Volscians (*Coriolanus*), Denmark is invaded by Norway (*Hamlet*), Scotland is destroyed by civil war by the end of *Macbeth*, England is conquered by France (*King Lear*). How is it that such overwhelming consequences are regarded as mere background echoes to the main event? Shakespeare sometimes seems to be intentionally showing us these seemingly insignificant victims: the vault scene at the end of *Romeo and Juliet* is, for example, peppered with reminders of casualties who got caught in the tragic unfolding of the events. But we are not invited to think about collateral damage: about characters such as Polonius; Cornwall's servant, defying his lord; Eros—Antony's servant—killing himself rather than his master; Iras and Charmian (the first dying accidentally because of Cleopatra's poisoned lips, the second committing suicide); about Cinna the poet, about Mutius, the Macduffs, Emilia, Roderigo and so many others. Even if we momentarily sympathize with them, our attention immediately shifts to more important occurrences. Such marginalization implies that instead of moral edification, tragedy cultivates a selective and, thus, a potentially damaging form of moral attention.

Dubious moral responses elicited by tragedy can take other forms. An audience member who is dismayed by Desdemona being strangled by Othello when she did not commit the adultery for which she is accused, misses the manner whereby the tragedy problematically naturalizes the outrageous linkage between infidelity and a capital crime. Desdemona's adultery, had it actually occurred, would not have led Elizabethans or a contemporary audience to condone her husband killing her in her bed as the appropriate measure. From such a perspective, instead of moral betterment, responding deeply to the tragedies causes us to withdraw from—rather than sharpen—the moral capacities we already possess.

Shakespeare's tragedies will not, on their own, turn their readers into better human beings. But betterment should not be confused with moral growth. One can grow morally—in the ways catalogued at the beginning of this chapter and explained in greater detail in later sections—without becoming a morally better human being. Students who, for example, take an ethics course may consistently regard themselves as growing morally because of their studies—they attain greater clarity in moral reasoning, and a more comprehensive understanding of the considerations relevant for a thorough moral analysis—without necessarily judging themselves to thereby becoming morally better. The professional ethicist teaching them might experience the same discrepancy felt by her students. Her training provides her a greater scope for understanding by utilizing a broader spectrum of morally relevant critical procedures that are unfamiliar to her upright next-door neighbour. But such breadth is unconnected to the real world of better conduct. Moral growth in this sense facilitates but does not necessitate betterment. Moreover, it might even be the case that moral growth undermines betterment, that betterment is sometimes dependent upon a simplification and a narrowing of one's moral understanding, and that moral growth (in the sense of, for example, greater awareness of the culturally determined nature of one's moral intuitions, or a deeper capacity to empathize with others, including those who perform immoral acts) enfeebles one's past convictions into unsure preferences. But I will regard as uncontroversial the idea that although growth and betterment may conflict, they can also reinforce each other when they are yoked together. It is *this* latter merging between the two—rather than some simple-minded, docile, good conduct that happens to be commendable merely because it has not been sufficiently challenged or reflectively refined—that we wish for ourselves and for others.

3   AGAINST AESTHETICISM

'Moralists' versus 'aesthetes'. These are supposed to be the feuding camps in the debate over the desirability of establishing a dialogue between a literary work and moral sensitivities. The moralists are often cast as morbid prudes who force a work to conform to a moral vision that they are likely to hold anyway, independently of the literary work, and which they then support through the authority they and their readers attribute to the work. Aesthetes, on the other hand, resist this move, upholding an interest in art for art's sake, in which one examines the formal properties of works, holding their content—moral or other—as being no more than raw material for the artist. An excellent literary work may exhibit immoral sentiments. It may consistently be praised for its aesthetic merits and criticized for its moral flaws. Alternatively, an inferior work will not improve as literature if it happens to exhibits a laudable morality.[6]

Oversimplified mapping of this kind—at least five distinct positions are being reduced into two—is responsible for severe distortions of the actual debate and for overlooking important interconnections between moral and non-moral features in a literary work.

---

[6] For such a presentation of the debate over ethical criticism and aesthetics, see Richard Posner, *Law and Literature* (Cambridge: Harvard University Press, 2000), ch. 9.

A more careful cartography distinguishes between moralists, moderate moralists, immoralists, radical autonomists, and moderate autonomists. Moralists hold that moral flaws/merits of the work (Shakespeare's tragedies in our case) *are* aesthetic flaws/merits. Moderate moralists hold that *some* moral flaws/merits constitute aesthetic flaws/merits. Immoralists suggest that immoral aspects of works can sometimes *enhance* aesthetic values rather than detract from them. Autonomists believe that moral flaws/merits are never aesthetically relevant, either because it is simply a category mistake to describe works of literature in moral terms ('radical autonomism') or because, while literature or its experience can be described morally for various purposes, such description is irrelevant to its aesthetic merit ('moderate autonomism').[7] Without entering the debates themselves, one can readily recognize how three distinct positions—moralism, moderate moralism, and immoralism—are being run together in the simplified 'aesthetes' versus 'moralists' division with which we began.

Once the terrain of genuine theoretical options is presented in this way, a highly plausible and uncontroversial view suggests itself: a combination of moderate moralism and immoralism. Moderate moralists believe that all things being (in some undefined sense) equal, a work is better as literature if it is morally insightful, if it enriches our moral perception, if it illuminates the non-obvious subtleties of morally complex situations, if it awakens morally relevant feelings such as compassion or moral outrage or empathy to another's suffering (particularly types of suffering that tend to be left unacknowledged or simplified). Immoralists add that in some cases, a work is better as literature if, all things being equal, it invites us to imaginatively cultivate impermissible possibilities. Both positions also accept merits of the work that have nothing to do with morality, thus absorbing much of what the autonomists wish to say. They also resist the idea that any moral merit is necessarily an aesthetic merit or that such merits can by themselves redeem an otherwise flawed work. They thus avoid the cruder didactic stance adopted by moralists. These positions are also consistent. There is no contradiction in holding that some morally relevant features of a work make it aesthetically meritorious, and also that a work's capacity to undermine existing norms can, by virtue of that fact, acquire aesthetic value.

One can, then, easily enough relate to the tragedies as engaging with one's moral perspective without instrumentalizing or distorting aesthetic values and without appealing to some linear and rigid process in which reading the plays leads to moral betterment. Having thus removed the more obvious obstacles that may induce resistance to bringing together Shakespeare's tragedy and ethics, I will now specify three groups of such connections. The first group will consist of existing objectives within ethics which Shakespeare's tragedies can enhance. The second will consist of ways whereby the tragedies broaden the range of questions and concerns taken up by ethics. The third will show that the particular merits of Shakespeare's work—specifically the intensity of his language—may be understood as a moral merit. In all three, the idea is that such connections are implicitly responsible for the high value repeatedly attributed to these works. Aesthetic value is thus explained rather than debased by suggesting that it is underpinned by moral growth. A serious pursuit of

---

[7] I am here following the third chapter in Berys Gaut's *Art, Emotions and Ethics* (Oxford: Oxford University Press, 2007). Gaut offers a further breakdown of these classifications, ultimately proposing to replace them with another typology. This further argument need not concern us here.

literature and a deep response to it is thereby revealed as being tied up with broader existential pursuits.

4 CLARIFYING VALUES

Tragedy is the process whereby values and the meanings that constitute them are sharpened and crystallized through loss. Through what characters discover as they suffer, readers and audience access non-obvious dimensions of the values they themselves hold, dimensions that are ordinarily taken for granted or superficially experienced. The epistemic conviction underlying tragedy—a 'tragic epistemology' if one wishes to call it that—is that beyond the fictional events we behold on stage, the real, non-fictional, underlying tragedy concerns our restricted understanding: for human beings, central, life-defining values are fully grasped only when they are being taken away.

Loss is a useful entry point into Shakespearean tragedy in particular. While characterizing tragedy is a notoriously difficult matter, and situating Shakespeare's tragedies within existing accounts of tragedy is even more awkward (not least because of Shakespeare's own loose adherence to genre), serious loss and lament over such loss features in all of Shakespeare's tragedies, and makes up one of the features (if not the salient feature) that infuses them with their distinct tragic quality. Comedy too, negotiates and presents substantial loss, but in his comedies Shakespeare sticks to forms of loss that are usually of a more psychological nature: the collapse of an over-commending self-image, the underestimation of one's weakness, the breakdown of an illusion of control. In his tragedies, the psychological processes are the same, but the loss is of a different order. Death of the protagonist and others is presented. Recovery—available to comic sufferers—is not an option. The tragic protagonist learns important lessons, but—unlike the hope for greater maturity implied in comic humbling—will be unable to put them to use.

Our capacity to relate to the tragic protagonists' loss as touching *our* values stems from the respect and admiration they elicit. Note again their difference from comic heroes. Shakespeare's greatest comic characters (Rosalind, Viola, Falstaff, Berowne) do not occasion admiration. We delight in their inventiveness, their humour, intelligence, and boundless energy. We do not, however, look up to them. Tragic protagonists, by contrast, even when they are haughty (Coriolanus), ostentatious (Antony and Cleopatra), hyperbolic (Romeo), gloomy (Hamlet), vicious (Macbeth), over-zealous (Titus), or rash (Othello and Lear), stand out in some way. Defying conventions, running up against common wisdom, attempting to reinvent themselves by resisting the givens of their situation, such characters do not draw our sympathy or love, but (and here Aristotle's analysis of tragedy is certainly applicable to Shakespeare) our respect. Admiration is a precondition for being moved, since it means that errors these characters make are possible for us too: Lear overvalues words and ignores subtext, Antony is too confident in his power and belittles the effects of his age on his ability, Coriolanus' naïve meritocratic philosophy leads him to underestimate the effectiveness of those he justifiably regards as inferior to him, Othello is over-trusting in his self-control, and Titus places too much faith in the justice of the system he serves. All are errors that we can see ourselves making too. Such a structure of learning by an example to which one looks up, explains why watching tragedy is an uplifting experience (often confused with 'pleasure'[8]): we allow what admirable characters discover to shed light upon our own values and attachments.

Such illumination often occurs through responding to the character's grief. A damaging misconception identifies grief with speechlessness and a resistance to language.[9] The mistake is that such speechlessness, when alluded to by grievers (and it is undeniable that the discrepancy between words and pain is powerfully experienced in situations of devastating loss), is immediately overwhelmed by words, by the griever's greater desire *not* to remain silent, but to provide a linguistic shape to pain.[10] The point of this reappropriation of language is not some cathartic unburdening. Grief—in tragedy and in life—is an unfolding of attachment performed when attaining unique clarity regarding what one values. By articulation in words, grief registers the surfacing of toned down qualities interlacing the existence of someone else. When Cleopatra grieves over Antony, she experiences a world becoming colourless ('the odds is gone, and there is nothing left remarkable beneath the visiting moon'). Romeo takes in Juliet's beauty for the last time. Without his wife, Macbeth's reality fades into an empty, noisy, meaningless spectacle, and Lear cries out that Cordelia will no longer appear to him ('thou'lt come no more'). Our response to these episodes is not one of empathy, pity, or fear (Aristotelian catharsis is a virtually useless concept in the context of Shakespeare). We are, rather, primarily gripped and guided by the *inventive* and *precise* use of language and what these reveal. Both components require explanation.

Inventiveness in a fictional character's use of language is more than a testimony to the author's creative power. Considered as a piece of characterization, as suggesting something about a character whose language becomes inventive in a particular context, such inventiveness means that the character's mind is momentarily released from the tyranny of stock expressive patterns. In responding to the powerful event, the speaker is distanced from his words, enabling fresh selection and release from familiar expressive unites into which his

[8] For an excellent argument against the reductive coordinates that give rise to the 'Why does tragedy give pleasure?' puzzle, see Neill, 'Schopenhauer on Tragedy and Value'. Neill claims that what he calls 'the hedonic theory of motivation'—the theory that we act merely to acquire pleasure and to avoid pain—is too easily assumed by the question above. Values other than pleasure can be reasons for action.

[9] Reflecting on Lear's howl, William Desmond writes that 'Lear's Howl is a transconceptual voice in the "conversation of mankind" that not only ruptures all logical systems but threatens the very basis of that civilized conversation ... when one hears that Howl a crushing night descends wherein the mind is threatened with blacking out or going blank. The mind shudders, as if a dark abyss had opened and swallowed all sense. Rational mind undergoes a liquefaction in which all intelligibility seems to be reclaimed by a malign formlessness.' He later writes that 'Tragedy brings a knowing that shatters every naïve faith in the intelligibility and worth of being and saying.' Desmond is right to identify a receding from language in grief. But he misses how this withdrawal is not only momentary, but also that it gives rise to an energized return into language, a desire to speak and provide precise articulation to the value emerging through the loss ('Being at a Loss: Reflections on Philosophy and the Tragic', in *Tragedy and Philosophy*, ed. N. Georgopoulos (New York: St. Martin's Press, 1993), 154–86 (155; 159)).

[10] Derrida repeatedly alludes to this contradictory state—being both disconnected from speech and, at the same time, being unable to remain silent—in his *The Work of Mourning* (Chicago: Chicago University Press, 2001).

thoughts are typically cast. Inventiveness means, then, that the speaker achieves a momentary *relationship* with words, rather than maintaining the state of being driven by them—a state which is at once a symptom of and an opportunity for discovery and insight. *Precision* means that, in such moments, language picks out with clarity the features of that which will no longer be experienced, but is now withering into a mere memory: a remarkable and interesting world, a loved daughter appearing, a life that possesses fullness of meaning, an arrestingly beautiful face. In all these examples, language captures not the abstract, discursive dimensions of the value of that which recedes, but perceptual subtleties that are revealed as composite parts of these values. *Looking* at the world was a different experience when the lost person was still alive.

Aesthetic value in such examples is clearly constituted by moral insight. By virtue of their grandness, tragic protagonists invite us into their perception as their world is being destroyed. They are thus able to reacquaint us with what we too see, yet fail to take in.[11]

5 Eudaimistic Failures

Tragedy and ethics have also been significantly interrelated through moral approaches that begin with the question: 'How should one live?'.[12] Aristotle is the fountainhead for such discussions, explicating the happy (flourishing) life as one that realizes a significant collection of intrinsically valuable goods (that is, objectives such as friendship, love, health or pleasure that are not desired as means for some other end). Aristotle recognized that it is possible to err in relation to one's happiness (call such errors 'eudaimonistic failures'). Such failures include mistaking means for ends, overlooking ends that ought to be pursued, instrumentalizing ends instead of seeing them for what they are, or failing to strike a balance between the pursuit of several distinct, valuable ends.

Perceiving such eudaimonistic failures underlies the powerful response Shakespeare's tragedies often generate. I will discuss four such failures. First, and most obviously, the tragedies present characters who miss what is important. Secondly, they present characters who are unable to experience meaning. Thirdly, they show characters who undermine their own happiness. Fourthly, they present characters who mistake the contingent nature of self-defining arrangements for independently existing entities.

I have already discussed the first of these in relation to clarifying values, but it is relevant in the context of eudaimonistic failures as well. Lear loves Cordelia at the beginning of the play. He loves her at its end too. But the nature and meaning of such love metamorphoses. Described as little more than a form of playful joy to begin with, his love for her turns into

---

[11] 'Clarificationism', an approach within contemporary ethical criticism that has been developed by Noël Carroll, is a position that explains literature's contribution to knowledge as consisting of clarifying our existing beliefs. The position is probably extendible to the clarifying of values in the manner suggested above.

[12] Martha Nussbaum links literature and moral philosophy through this question in her *Love's Knowledge: Essays on Philosophy and Literature* (New York: Oxford University Press, 1990), and specifically with tragedy in her *The Fragility of Goodness* (New York: Cambridge University Press, 1986).

startling realizations regarding the meaning of proximity in loving a child, of time spent together, of the importance of seeing her. Titus is introduced as a man who regards his children as interchangeable pieces of actual or potential sacrifice through which he may manifest his loyalty to Rome. In the course of the play he transforms into a diligent mouth-piece for Lavinia, silently attempting to decipher her particular language. In both examples, an intrinsically valued end is believed to have been mastered and acquired, when in fact it is valued for the wrong reasons. It is therefore casually risked or instrumentalized.

Often though, Shakespeare is preoccupied less with direct loss, and more with characters who are unable to experience meaning. Macbeth and Hamlet come to mind—both highly limited in this capacity. In Macbeth's case, this lack is underscored via the central contrast with Macduff: movingly responding to the destruction of his family, Macduff conveys a warmth and direct attachment that was missing from Macbeth's world all along. In Hamlet's case, the distance from meaning qualitatively marks his words. His cold eloquence, so exquisitely able to describe value (of life, human beings, his own impotence, the greatness of his father), unfailingly suggests an inner distance from these values as they are being described. Life's energies are brilliantly noted and articulated. But they are not lived. It is precisely this gap between words and inner resonance that renders his beautiful rhetoric artificial. He glorifies his father to excess, turning him into a mythical god rather than a loved presence of flesh and blood. Even his famous contemplation of suicide is suspect. Would genuinely suicidal thoughts latch themselves onto the general unfairness of life? A similar distance from meaning is felt when Macbeth describes the honours he has lately received. Robes, external trappings of identity are all they are—rather than constitutional parts of what one is. It is also present in Othello's strikingly morbid language when he is happily reunited with Desdemona, joyfully kissing her while speaking of chaos and death. All appear to lack a vital and direct experience of that which they know they should treasure. Contrast these examples with the fullness with which Antony describes his friendship to Caesar, Portia tells her Brutus that he has withdrawn from her, Juliet attempts to extract Romeo's answer regarding marriage from the Nurse, Capulet's rage at Juliet's disobedience, Cleopatra's jealousy or Enobarbus' shame. In such episodes, a value—of friendship, of marital companionship, of parental authority, of love, of loyalty—is readily and immediately experienced by the character. Shakespeare is able to show continuity of expression with felt meanings, and also to highlight discontinuity between these, as a central characteristic of some of his tragic heroes.

Another eudaimonistic failure Shakespeare builds into his tragic protagonists is their tendency to sabotage their own existing or potential happiness. Romeo's 'rash' killing of Tybalt, Coriolanus' inability to control his scorn, Othello's implausibly uncritical acceptance of Iago's slanders, Macbeth's killing of Duncan, Lear's banishing of Cordelia and Kent—are all forms of self-undermining. Dismissing such errors as indicative of a mere a lack of judgement is undercut by the esteem these characters evoke. Such mistakes seem to be an outcome of something deeper: the manner whereby admirable human beings participate in their own foreseeable disaster. Even when metaphysical forces are mobilized against the protagonists (as is the case for Macbeth, and for Romeo and Juliet, the star-crossed lovers), the characters preserve a degree of choice and are able to subvert the course of events: Macbeth could have waited for fate to crown him; Hamlet could have killed Claudius rather than wait for a better opportunity; Romeo could have anticipated the Friar's plan, attempting to use his love to make peace with the Capulets (he should have certainly avoided fighting Tybalt);

Coriolanus could have resisted the temptation to antagonize the plebeians; Lear could have listened to Kent; Antony could have fought on land as his loyal soldiers begged him to.

Another way in which Shakespeare's tragedies may contribute to an examined life by exposing errors relating to one's happiness, relates to what tragedy manages to de-naturalize for us. Paul Kottman recently suggested that as they are removed from home, family, or some other feature that was considered natural and permanent, tragic protagonists live through the discovery of the contingency of formative arrangements.[13] De-automating certainties, tragedy invites the audience to reflect on various links and ties not as givens, but as entities that demand repeated, conscious, active sustaining.[14] Language tends to misleadingly objectify these ties. We think of a 'home' as a demarcated space, of 'family' as a group of individuals, of 'status' as a possession that we have. In all, the mistake consists of regarding that which needs to be repeatedly remade as if it possesses some independent existence. Tragedy is the process whereby an impressive mind discovers that central notions such as home, family, and status are actually made up of intentions, willpower, rituals, decisions, gestures, and more importantly, that *all* of these can abruptly change.

This process is reflected in the tragedies through an agonizing suspicion regarding some dubious disconnection between words and reference. Shakespeare's tragic heroes are often beset by an alarming discrepancy between vocabulary and intention. Lear senses it (and Othello suspects it) in relation to love, deflated from meaningful experience to mere talk. Hamlet hears it in the word 'father' when he perceives his family turned by his mother into an arrangement of replaceable parts (think of me 'as of a father', says Claudius to him in a casual remark that sends Hamlet off to consider suicide). Coriolanus feels it as a gulf separating the discourse of praise from truly honourable action. In all, that which should genuinely animate the vocabulary of love, honor, and family, is usurped by something other, and prized notions are cheapened into mere signifiers. Perhaps—as Falstaff suggests in a different context—such notions always were nothing more than words ('What is honour? A word. What is in that word honour? What is honour? Air.'). [15] But part of the beauty of tragic protagonists is that they are less cynical and more optimistic than Falstaff, holding words to be much more than air. It is such seriousness that endows their experience with a tragic quality, since they are compelled to undergo the process whereby meanings fade into hollow gestures.

What aggravates the tragic nature of such demotion is that the depletion of self-constituting attachments results from rather ordinary circumstances. In *Hamlet* it is the wish of a mother to remarry, in *Lear* it is the overturning of relations of dependency with one's daughters, and in *Coriolanus* it consists of posing a political danger to someone else. There is nothing extraordinary about such changes. Indeed, part of the dramatic

---

[13] Paul Kottman, *Tragic Conditions in Shakespeare: Disinheriting the Globe* (Baltimore: The Johns Hopkins University Press, 2009).

[14] A previous formulation of this idea is implied in A. M. Quinton—'Tragedy', *Proceedings of the Aristotelian Society, Supplementary Volumes* 34 (1960), 145–64—though he regrettably casts it as part of a tragic view of life, the central theme of which 'is the contingency of value. Whatever is of value in the world … is due to men. Not merely in the sense that without human purposes and satisfactions nothing would be of value at all … but rather that the achievement and maintenance of value in the world can only be brought about by the efforts of men' (162).

[15] *The First Part of King Henry IV*, 5.2.132–4.

effectiveness consists of touching rather mundane events and what these may reveal regarding the ephemeral nature of self-defining ties and attachments. Impermanence haunts central dimensions of one's life, and tragedy is the aesthetic medium that will not allow this awareness to be suppressed.

Recognizing the contingent nature of such notions informs the ethicist's concern with the question how to live. It spotlights the typically overlooked *background* in which goals and objectives are set (if family, home and citizenship can be justifiably called 'background'), and how maintaining such a background is itself an end in an examined life. There are forms of moral failure that relate to a withdrawal from spending the energy that sustains personal, familial, cultural and political relations, an energy which renders them substantial and real. Other failures consist of taking such relations for granted by underestimating the way in which they can be radically transformed by someone else. Common to both errors is that dynamic, affectively determined attachments are mistaken for independently existing entities.

6 THOUGHTS VERSUS THINKERS

The directions pursued in sections 4 and 5 link particular forms of illumination acquired through Shakespeare's tragedies with independently existing goals within ethics. Other connections of this kind can be added (e.g. the familiar idea of enhancing one's empathy by noting how tragedies voice distinct forms of pain). But Shakespeare's tragedies can also reorient moral attention in a way that is not merely contained within existing ethics, but adds something important to its existing questions and objectives.

The typical tasks that fall under ethics include prioritizing conflicting judgements, determining right conduct in particular cases, exploring virtues that make up moral character, distinguishing between superior and inferior ways of tackling specific moral issues, investigating the structure of moral language as such, proposing orientation in relation to living well, as well as attempting to understand the basis and merit of one's existing moral intuitions. Shakespeare's tragedies can add to this repertoire the interest in the *relationship* between adopted philosophy and the life in which it is embedded. In Plato's earlier and middle dialogues—to repeat a common observation of his critics—philosophical positions were typically presented as interlocking with other sensitivities, aspirations, hidden agendas, and existential predilections. Often, these other dimensions needed to be exposed and understood by Socrates before a philosophical position could be meaningfully interrogated. Although the dialogue form was repeatedly adopted in later philosophy, this particular attention to ties between philosophy and other aspects of existence was largely abandoned.

Shakespeare's tragedies are especially potent in this regard. By focusing on crisis, on the inability to maintain who and what one is, the tragedies focalize moments of philosophizing that are situated in complex personal circumstances. By understanding such philosophizing as feeding off these events, we note how an abstract position may constitute an insight or, alternatively, an evasion. Hamlet, for example, usually turns to the abstract in order to avoid the pressingly personal. He will not confront the painful and conflicting thoughts he has about Ophelia, but will begin discoursing about women in general. He will not consider suicide in personal terms, but will philosophize about the value of existence as such. This is (partly) why his assault on Gertrude, in which this pattern is finally broken, constitutes the most moving episode in the play. But it is also (partly) why he is a bad philosopher. Philosophy for him is *used* for some other end. He becomes philosophically interesting only when his philosophical digressions are related to a broader personal agenda. Other characters, by contrast, arrive at genuine philosophical insights. Macbeth dispiritedly discovers the empty theatricality of existence as soon as he hears that his wife is dead. Lear accesses the tactile feel of poverty and the moral obligations of the powerful in the storm. These explicit insights are rare, since Shakespeare was (fortunately) not disposed to issue forth sententious statements regarding life's meaning in his plays. What one repeatedly notes, however, is a carefully worked out personal and circumstantial context that gives rise to forms of justification and self-vindication when complex decisions are being made or abstract positions are momentarily held. Of particular import here, is the withdrawal from previously held capacities under some circumstances. Romeo's withdrawal from the wit that characterized him in the past (for which he is accused by Mercutio) is linked with love. Antony's receding from martial prudence should not be considered apart from his age and his desire to reassert his virility. Hamlet's resistance to action is not the outcome of a built-in impotence, but results from an avoidance of agency that is somehow triggered by his experience of his father's death.

Ethics is routinely concerned with cataloguing the constituents of a fully integrated moral thinking. Shakespeare's tragedies can suggest where and how such thinking is suspended, as well as how non-moral factors affect the kind of considerations that will be privileged by a particular mind. For the moral philosopher, they thus help shape a different kind of moral attunement, sensitive not merely to the coherence and defensibility of a moral position, but to its embeddedness within a particular life undergoing distinct experiences. This is not to relativize ethics, but to contextualize and broaden the range of what moral thinking should include. For the literary reader, the point is that sometimes the *literary* merit of an episode consists of non-obvious connections drawn between endorsing abstract thoughts and undergoing particular experiences. Do not look for the literary merit of Macbeth's 'signifying nothing' speech by attending to its content—life's meaninglessness—but by responding to the relationship between the surfacing of an experience of life as noisy, inferior theatricality and losing the only person that Macbeth seems to have loved. Do not glorify the philosophical content of Hamlet's lines regarding the beauty of man, situated between angels and animals. Instead, note how Hamlet's frustration of relating to the beauty his sees around him is an outcropping of a degree of grief in which one's experiential coordinates have been removed.

7 ON GOODNESS

Shakespeare's tragedies contribute to ethics in another way that is not simply continuous with ethics' existing objectives: how they treat good characters. Wicked and flawed characters are the ones to whom the audience is no doubt drawn. But subtle yet significant effects emerge from the presentation of the relative vulnerability of goodness. In the tragedies, such goodness—'goodness' need not denote simple or saintly, but merely the exemplifying of a normative outlook, as opposed to characters who question it explicitly—is typically synonymous with fidelity and unquestioning loyalty. It consists of never doubting where one's obligations lie. Characters such as Cordelia, Emilia, Kent, Edgar, Horatio, Ophelia, Gloucester, Macduff, Mercutio, or Lavinia, all share a lack of shrewdness that turns them into easy prey for forces that lie beyond their comprehension. Yet such characters are not silly, naïve, or even unambiguously moral.[16] They appear simply to embody normative, ordinary agency unprepared to confront something that falls outside its interpretative horizons. One should look for this effect of such characters less on the page than on the stage. Such effect is felt in moments in which these characters are perplexed, or fail to harmonize a bewildering dissonance by casting something alien into a form they understand.

Ophelia's inability to understand Hamlet, Macduff's stammering when Ross tells him that his family has been massacred, Gloucester's taking insult from the plucking of his beard moments before he is blinded, Emilia's dumbfounded 'My husband?', Lear's no/yes exchange with the stocked Kent, are textual examples of processes one often notes in the non-verbal acting of these roles on stage: a mind equipped with sound moral expectations confronting something alien to norms and inherited explanatory schemes. It is part of Shakespeare's characterization of these good characters: being unprepared and taking some things for granted constitutes the lack of complexity we actually look for in goodness. Implied in this is that someone who is simply able to take in various forms of counter-normativity is already somehow tainted. An Edgar cannot be prepared for the appearance of an Edmund, Emilia cannot suspect that Iago is who he is, a Gloucester cannot grasp that Lear's daughters can manifest utter heartlessness. Shakespeare is associating goodness with a restricted world-view, which renders it vulnerable but also infuses it with a particular dignity. The moral point is (arguably) that the tragic outcome in these plays should not necessarily prompt us to expand our awareness of possible deception, but, rather, to cultivate respect for being a particular kind of victim.

8 BEYOND ETHICS?

Sebastian Gardner argues that there is an essential antagonism between morality and tragedy:

> Macbeth discovers that he is not 'annulled' by his evil: there is in him a dimension of value which is immune to moral criticism, which morality cannot subtract from. Tragic value thus eclipses or overshadows moral value, rendering the negative and affirmative moments of tragedy symmetrical: tragic value, like tragic loss and suffering, represents itself as possessing greater depth than moral value.[17]

---

[16] While some of these good characters have their darker moral sides, to blame them for the actions of the villains of the plays, as does Berger, seems to me excessive. For Berger's argument, see Harry Berger Jr., *Making Triffles of Terrors: Redistributing Complicities in Shakespeare* (California: Stanford University Press, 1997), 300.

[17] 'Tragedy, Morality and Metaphysics', in *Art and Morality*, ed. Sebastian Gardner and José Luis Bemúdez (London & New York: Routledge, 2003), 218–59 (p. 238).

For Gardner, subordinating the effects of tragedy or the insights it contains to morality distorts an essential non-moral dimension it possesses. Tragedy is not concerned with demonstrating what Martha Nussbaum calls 'the fragility of goodness'. Nor is it primarily attempting to present a fuller reaffirming of values that are initially superficially held. Tragedy unburdens human life of its contingent contents, showing us life's *form*. It is this content-less form of life, unconnected to deeds or virtues, that possesses value: 'as he [Macbeth] is morally stripped, something else shines through his moral negativity' (247).

The idea of tragedy as a presentation of a form of life stripped of its content is somewhat unclear and seems limited in application. But the emphasis on a response to amoral value is an intuition I would like to respect and integrate into this discussion of ethics and Shakespearean tragedy. For while I have attempted to show various ways in which tragedy's experience either significantly contributes to ethics' existing aims or adds to its objectives, features, and concerns, there is an obvious sense in which Shakespeare's tragedy appeals to a range of central experiences that appear to be wholly discontinuous with ethics.

Instead of the idea of a life stripped of content, exposing its bare form, I suggest that the non-moral merit Gardner is attempting to pinpoint is, again, the creative intensity that erupts from these characters because of (or as part of) their predicament. As I claimed above, such creativity consists of a release of the mind from platitudes and familiar discursive articulations. Romeo's leap from the clichés he issues forth in relation to Rosaline ('cold fire, sick health'), to strikingly original combinations when he beholds Juliet ('Oh she doth teach the torches to burn brighter')—a release of mind that is ignited in both lovers in their first exchange when they spontaneously and jointly compose a sonnet—exemplifies such creativity. But this quality is everywhere in the tragedies, effortlessly pouring out of the mouths of the protagonists as they sink deeper into their predicaments. The non-moral merit we respond to is this exploratory dimension of their language. Discovering anew their situation and its subtleties and managing to articulate it reveals a lived experience—'lived' in the sense of achieving friction with language rather than servile subordination to it. We perceive it in Macbeth's deliberations before murdering Duncan, in Titus' apprehension of the muted and mutilated Lavinia, in Othello's pseudo-judicial language when he pauses above Desdemona's bed, in Lear's rage and in Hamlet's despair.

We undoubtedly encounter this quality in comedy too, since such intensity is an aspect of Shakespeare's poetic art, regardless of genre. But particular to the tragedies is the manner in which the admiration for the character and the magnitude of the events, coupled with the impending or present suffering and death, infuse the liberated, unpredictable nature of language with a special kind of attraction unrelated to moral value. Tamora in seducing Aaron, Edmund in calling out to nature, Lady Macbeth in conjuring the spirits to unsex her, Claudius in attempting to pray, exemplify Gardner's point: how a villain can manifest the quality of being alive in and to one's moment, of being able to process it in categories and terms that are discovered rather than applied. This sense of living in and with language is valuable in a sense that need not overlap with moral value and that elicits our most immediate and deepest response to the tragedies.

Life is that which is in tension with conventions, with known linguistic formulations, with established institutions and familiar expectations. *Life* is that which re-invents its relationship with these, and *life* is what Shakespeare's heroes and villains show in abundance. By opposition, the 'humdrum'—to borrow Richard Shusterman's terminology—is that which is boringly governed by the familiar.[18] This existential energy is what we respond to in the language of the tragedies. It is this vibrant quality which actors treasure and convey to their audience, since it enables them to unite with a force unleashed by the words themselves rather than depending solely on their capacity to create subtexts. It is precisely this potency of words that we refuse to subsume under moral categories.

But even here the ethicist has the final word. For what is this intensity but a call, an invitation to achieve lived freedom in language in opposition to the lukewarm subservience to given schemes? And is not such existential guidance itself a part of ethics when the category is extended to encompass more than good and evil?

To repeat, this chapter has not attempted to merely defend the interpretative viability of formulating moral insights as part of a response to Shakespeare's tragedies—setting such readings up as yet another legitimate critical modality amongst many—but to more ambitiously claim that, sometimes, experiences in which moral perception occurs are precisely the merits that constitute the work's aesthetic value. The various moral insights sketched in previous sections are not some paraphrasable content that can be formulated out of the context of the work. Rather, these surface through a close engagement with the play's literary textures; they form part of its experience. As interpretative suggestions, they offer guidance with regard to what one should be sensitive to when absorbing the play as a rewarding literary experience. Often, they are the reason why we are moved, and, when explicitly articulated by an illuminating interpretation, enhance and empower the work's effect even further. To care for literature as autonomous from extraneous matter, to be an aesthete and hold that art is for art only, to be fixated on nothing but aesthetic effect frequently means attending the ways whereby literature uniquely facilitates moral growth.

Select Bibliography

Cavell, S., *Disowning Knowledge: In Seven Plays of Shakespeare* (Cambridge: Cambridge University Press, 2003).

Gjesdal, Kristin, 'Reading Shakespeare—Reading Modernity', *Memoria di Shakespeare. A Journal of Shakespearean Studies* 1 (2014), 57–82.

Goldman, Michael, *Acting and Action in Shakespearean Tragedy* (Princeton: Princeton University Press, 1985).

Hammond, P., *The Strangeness of Tragedy* (Oxford: Oxford University Press, 2009).

Hillman, David '"If It Be Love Indeed": Transference, Love, and Antony and Cleopatra', *Shakespeare Quarterly* 64:3 (2013), 301–33.

Kottman, P. A., *Tragic Conditions in Shakespeare: Disinheriting the Globe* (Baltimore: Johns Hopkins University Press, 2009).

Lupton, J. R., *Thinking with Shakespeare: Essays on Politics and Life* (Chicago: University of Chicago Press, 2011).

---

[18] *Surface and Depth: Dialectics of Criticism and Culture* (Ithaca: Cornell University Press, 2002), 234.

Nussbaum, Martha C., ' "Romans, Countrymen, and Lovers": Political Love and the Rule of Law in Julius Caesar', in *Shakespeare and the Law: A Conversation among Disciplines and Professions*, ed. Bradin Cormack, Martha C. Nussbaum, and Richard Strier (Chicago: University of Chicago Press, 2013), 256–81.

Schalkwyk, David, *Shakespeare, Love and Service* (Cambridge: Cambridge University Press, 2008).

Schmidt, Erik W., 'Sucking the Sweets of Sweet Philosophy: Shakespeare's Dramatic Use of Philosophy', *Memoria di Shakespeare. A Journal of Shakespearean Studies* 1 (2014), 299–326.

Zamir, Tzachi, ed., *Hamlet, Philosophy, and Literature*, gen. ed. Richard T. Eldridge (Oxford: Oxford University Press, forthcoming).

CHAPTER 6

CHARACTER IN SHAKESPEAREAN TRAGEDY

EMMA SMITH

'THAT WITHIN' (*HAMLET*, 1.2.85)[1]

WE all know where to begin: the perennial locus of discussion about Shakespearean tragedy and character is the prince's first extended speech in *Hamlet*. Responding to his mother's exhortations to cease mourning his father, Hamlet counters her casual use of the word 'seems':

> Seems, madam? Nay it is: I know not seems.
> 'Tis not alone my inky cloak, good-mother,
> Nor customary suits of solemn black,
> Nor windy suspiration of forced breath,
> No, nor the fruitful river in the eye,
> Nor the dejected haviour of the visage,
> Together with all forms, moods, shows of grief
> That can denote me truly. These indeed 'seem',
> For they are actions that a man might play;
> But I have that within which passeth show—
> These but the trappings and the suits of woe.
>
> (1.2.77–86)

Hamlet's claim is famously paradoxical: he argues not that there is a difference between how he appears to others and how he truly feels, but rather that these are radically continuous. His sombre clothes and his melancholy countenance look as if he is in mourning, but even beyond these 'trappings' he really is in mourning. Hamlet simultaneously suggests the possibility of a disparity between exterior and interior—a man's actions may be deceptive or inauthentic ('might play')—but then denies that this is the case. 'That within' seems both identical to, and in inaccessible excess of, external signifiers of grief. These signifiers have themselves been ironized by the recognition that they might be merely social

---

[1] All references to Shakespeare are to John Jowett, William Montgomery, Gary Taylor, and Stanley Wells, eds., *William Shakespeare: The Complete Works* (Oxford: Oxford University Press, 2005).

performance. And, of course, we are in an actual play: even 'authenticity' is personation. This paradox of acted and authentic emotion anticipates the crisis produced in Hamlet by the Player's speech about Pyrrhus: 'What would he do | Had he the motive and the cue for passion | That I have? He would drown the stage with tears' (2.2.562–4).

The prince's claim to have 'that within which passeth show' has thus been at the epicentre of debates both about fictional character and about early modern subjectivity. It focuses a contested binary between inner and outer and between essence and performance that has become the test case for theatrical, psychoanalytical, historical, political, textual, and philosophical interpretations both of Hamlet and of the very idea of character. Critics variously invested in character as autonomy, as privacy, as property or as embodiment share an understanding of the speech as significant, but disagree about the precise nature of that significance. For Bart van Es, focusing on Shakespeare's acting company as crucial agents in the formation of his plays, Hamlet's speech was 'penned in full knowledge of the capacities of the person for whom it was meant'. Van Es argues that the Chamberlain's leading actor Richard Burbage had the unique skill of 'unprecedented emotional contact with the character he embodies', enabling him to pull off the idea 'that Hamlet's emotions are more real than those that are performed around him'.[2] Hamlet's interior is a product of Burbage's impersonatory skills: it is because the actor Burbage is so good at playing that the fiction of Hamlet's unactable core is so compelling. Romantic critics also propped up Hamlet's fictional selfhood with that of living people, preferring to see Hamlet embodied in themselves rather than in the unsubtle histrionics of actors: 'we do not like to see our author's plays acted', wrote Hazlitt, 'and least of all *Hamlet*.'[3] Hazlitt understood the character's speeches to be 'as real as our own thoughts. Their reality is in the reader's mind. It is we who are Hamlet'. Coleridge's claim to have a 'smack of Hamlet' epitomized this Romantic identification: Schlegel designated the play 'a tragedy of thought' and Hegel recognized Hamlet's 'beautiful inner soul' and his 'withdrawn inner life'.[4] For A. C. Bradley, often seen as the Romantics' final critical heir, the 'character of the hero' alone saves *Hamlet*'s melodramatic revenge plot inherited from the imagined savagery of its putative source, the *ur*-Hamlet, from being 'sensational and horrible'.[5] Marvin Rosenberg extends the play's characterological generosity, arguing, from his survey of performances, that 'all *Hamlet*'s characters have *that within which passes show*'.[6] Harold Bloom locates in *Hamlet* 'the internalization of the self [that] is one of Shakespeare's greatest inventions, particularly because it came before anyone else was ready for it'.[7]

If more recent critics have revised claims about transcendent character, they too have tended to articulate their arguments around *Hamlet* (or often Hamlet: as Margreta de Grazia observes, since the eighteenth century, 'the play has been seen as a mere pretext for the main character').[8] Francis Barker asserts that Hamlet's claim to inwardness remains

---

[2] Bart van Es, *Shakespeare in Company* (Oxford: Oxford University Press, 2013), 238, 241, 239.

[3] William Hazlitt, *The Selected Writings of William Hazlitt*, ed. Duncan Wu (London: Pickering & Chatto, 1998), 1: 148.

[4] Jonathan Bate, ed., *The Romantics on Shakespeare* (Harmondsworth: Penguin, 1997), 2, 307; G. W. F. Hegel, *Aesthetics: Lectures on Fine Art*, ed. T. M. Knox (Oxford: Clarendon Press, 1988), 1: 584.

[5] A. C. Bradley, *Shakespearean Tragedy* (Basingstoke: Macmillan, 1985), 70.

[6] Marvin Rosenberg, *The Masks of Hamlet* (Newark: University of Delaware Press, 1992), 68.

[7] Harold Bloom, *Shakespeare: The Invention of the Human* (Fourth Estate: London, 1999), 409.

[8] Margreta de Grazia, *'Hamlet' without Hamlet* (Cambridge: Cambridge University Press, 2007), 3.

'gestural' because of its 'historical prematurity': 'at the centre of Hamlet, in the interior of his mystery, there is, in short, nothing', and into this interpretative and personal void 'successive generations of criticism—especially Romantic and post-Romantic variants have poured their bourgeois attempts at self-recognition'.[9] For David Hillman the interior here suggests 'a realm of specifically *corporeal* interiority contrasted with mere outward signs'.[10] Katharine Maus, recuperating a historicized idea of character, uses Hamlet's speech as the prompt for her nuanced exploration of 'the afflictions and satisfactions that attend upon the difference between an unexpressed interior and a theatricalized exterior: the epistemological anxieties that gap generates, the social practices that are devised to manage it, and the sociopolitical purposes it serves'.[11]

This focus on *Hamlet* and on Hamlet is, as is often noted, an interestingly belated response to the play, part of what R. A. Foakes identifies as 'that shift towards an emphasis on subjectivity that began in the late eighteenth century and flowered with the Romantics'.[12] In its own time the play's greatest impact seems not to have been the reflective character of Hamlet himself, but rather its compelling representation of zany or histrionic madness within the revenge plot. Hamlet's immediate early modern heirs—Henry Chettle's Hoffman (in *The Tragedy of Hoffman, or, The Revenge for a Father*, 1602), the augmented Hieronimo in post-1602 editions of Kyd's play *The Spanish Tragedy*, and Marston's stoic revenger Antonio (*Antonio's Revenge*, 1600), as well as, a little later, Middleton's Vindice (*The Revenger's Tragedy*, 1606)—all respond more obviously to the play's bloodthirsty scenario and language than to any new notion of interior characterization. Post-*Hamlet* editions of Kyd's play, for example, bear the additional subtitle 'Hieronimo is mad again', suggesting, rather like the reference to 'mad Hamlet' in Antony Scoloker's *Diaphantus* (1604) or the throwaway observation to a footman who enters once, 'in haste', 'Sfoote Hamlet, are you madde?' in *Eastward Ho* (1605), that what registered most with contemporaries was the externalized performance of insanity rather than the quiet insistence on the inscrutable interior.[13] The primacy of Hamlet's inner self is a later invention, and, significantly, an invention of a sensibility that enjoyed its Shakespeare as a poetry of the interior rather than the highly theatrical drama enjoyed in the early modern playhouse. It is clear that the robustly social personality of the fat knight Falstaff was the Shakespeare creation who was most urgent to his first audiences. Falstaff notably displays little if any of that torment, introspection, and fear of mortality which might gesture to a modern internalized subjectivity. He, however, achieved the fiction of personal autonomy independent of his play long before the Romantics identified Hamlet as the shorthand for

[9] Francis Barker, *The Tremulous Private Body: Essays on Subjection* (London: Methuen, 1984), 36–7.

[10] David Hillman, 'Visceral Knowledge: Shakespeare, Skepticism, and the Interior of the Early Modern Body', in David Hillman and Carla Mazzio, eds., *The Body in Parts: Fantasies of Corporeality in Early Modern England* (New York and London: Routledge, 1997), 91.

[11] Katharine Eisaman Maus, *Inwardness and Theater in the English Renaissance* (Chicago: University of Chicago Press, 1995), 2.

[12] R. A. Foakes, *'Hamlet' versus 'Lear': Cultural Politics and Shakespeare's Art* (Cambridge: Cambridge University Press, 1993), 14.

[13] Anthony Scoloker, *Diaphantus, or the passions of love Comicall to reade, but tragicall to act* (London: 1604), sig.E4v; George Chapman, Ben Jonson, and John Marston, *Eastward Hoe* (London: 1605), sig D3.

character itself. Early modern people saw Falstaffs around them in a way they did not apparently see Hamlets.[14]

So far, then, it is clear that character criticism and its procedures of identification and empathy have had a particular focus and a particular history, and that both the focus and the range of methods postdate the play by at least two centuries. *Hamlet*'s priority unites discussions of characterization from otherwise incompatible critical or philosophical standpoints, and has become a discourse that is literally self-perpetuating. The self that is thus perpetuated is attractively reflective, mordant, interrogative and intelligent (hence its appeal to poets and critics), but it is also crucially defined by its violent misogyny and solipsism (perhaps ditto): Hamlet has become 'a free-floating signifier, taking on the subjectivity of the critic, and typically reflecting his anxieties'.[15] The critical discourse taking *Hamlet* as the high-point of Shakespeare's development of tragic character is both over-determined and self-limiting, not least since one consequence of a focus on Hamlet's interiority has meant a separation between the plot—'tragedy'—and the person—'character'.

In what follows, I try to move away from this powerful narrative of character criticism. Instead, I propose that the genre of tragedy itself, and an understanding of the embodied character in early modern thought and on the stage, can develop a more material understanding of character as action. Thinking further about characters within their tragic plots helps to reexamine assumptions about individual agency and primacy within the plays; gathering the implications of characters within an epistemology of the human in which the psychological and the physiological were not firmly differentiated inverts Hamlet's habitual suspicion of the body's deceptive potential. Finally, a reading of *Coriolanus* tries to recentre critical debate about character as a theme of that late tragedy: Coriolanus and his play are engaged in an explicit struggle to define and display his character, putting particular pressure on the personal name as the locus of individuality.

'PLOTS HAVE I LAID' (*RICHARD III*, 1.1.32)

The understanding of tragedy and character as inseparable comes in part from a reading of Aristotle. For Aristotle, the first essential of tragedy is *mythos*—plot: 'tragedy is not a representation of men but a piece of action, of life, of happiness and unhappiness, which come under the head of action, and the end aimed at is the representation not of qualities of character but of some action'. 'It follows that the incidents and plot are the end at which tragedy aims': the plot is 'the *soul* of tragedy' (emphasis added). By anthropomorphizing tragedy, Aristotle can help us to see an idea of characterization that is not trapped in a one-to-one correspondence with the persons of the play. Aristotle's plot elements of reversal, discovery, and calamity can seem similarly anthropomorphized but again he refers to them as properties of the plot rather than of character—we can think of them as things that happen to the play rather than its individuals. Aristotle makes clear that characters are always in the

---

[14] C. M. Ingleby, L. Toulmin Smith, F. J. Furnivall, *The Shakspere Allusion-Book: A Collection of Allusions to Shakspere from 1591–1700* (London: Chatto & Windus, 1909), 1: 88.

[15] Foakes, '*Hamlet*' versus '*Lear*', 15.

service of the plot: 'in character-drawing ... one should always seek what is inevitable or probable, so as to make it inevitable or probable that such and such a person should say or do such' (1454a). Tragic characters are acted upon by their plots rather than being complete or primary agents of those plots. Tragedy writes character rather than vice versa. Analyses of Shakespeare's tragedies have been somewhat reluctant to accept the implications of this precedence. Perhaps it has been more reassuring to practitioners of the secular discipline of literary criticism to find human agency at the centre of tragedy, since it emphasizes, however perversely, that humans control their world. 'What we do feel strongly as a tragedy advances to its close,' writes Bradley, 'is that the calamities and catastrophe follow inevitably from the deeds of men, and that the main source of these deeds is character.'[16]

But this fantasy of human agency is itself one of the dynamics that tragedy interrogates. Because, as Renaissance genre theory by Donatus and Evanthus prescribed, comedies tend to draw on fiction and tragedies on history, tragic events have an overdetermined logic. Characters cannot avert the fates that are already intrinsic to their realization: Romeo and Juliet are trapped by the tragic contours of their pre-existence in Shakespeare's source, Brooke's *Romeus and Juliet* (and, in the quarto texts, by the Prologue's pre-emptive outline), just as Richard III cannot survive his historical nemesis Richmond. Inevitability is itself inevitable, a generic necessity in plots where the tragedy has always already happened in its source. Because this rule has been insistently established by earlier plays, the ending of one obvious exception, *King Lear*, gains the momentum of horrified surprise: Cordelia's death is contrary to all Shakespeare's chronicle, dramatic, and folkloric sources. Comic plots turn on what Susan Snyder has called 'a kind of "evitability" principle' where human ingenuity (Portia's knowledge of loopholes in Venetian law) or chance (the overhearing of Borachio's boasting by the Watch in *Much Ado About Nothing*) dominate; in tragic plots that 'causal chain unwinds inexorably towards destruction'.[17] In *Othello*, for instance, we see how Iago, himself a version of the stock Plautine comic servant, rewrites a comedy of marriage into a tragedy by redeploying its generic elements. Human cleverness is here harnessed to precipitating rather than averting tragedy. Instances of chance and accident, such as the unscripted entrance of Bianca into 4.1 and the scene of Othello's 'ocular proof' (3.3.365), are ruthlessly repurposed from their comic origins, just as the comic trope of personal fulfilment in marriage is twisted to reveal Othello's fatally incomplete vulnerability.

Character in this play can be understood as a product of genre, as the play moves through potential or pre-emptive comedy into tragedy, redirecting its characters in the process. Desdemona is crucial to this process. In turning from the outspoken comic heroine besting the classic comic blocking figure Brabantio, into the passive tragic accessory of the final act in which she absolves all of responsibility ('who hath done this deed? | Nobody, I myself' 5.2.132-3), she is an embodiment of the play's shifting generic affiliations. What has happened to her during the course of the play is less the psychologically plausible assumption of the timid pose of abused wife and more the dramatically necessary preparation for the tragic conclusion. Peter Stallybrass identifies the play's 'two Desdemonas', arguing that 'Desdemona's subservience, enforced by her death, has

[16] Bradley, *Shakespearean Tragedy*, 7.

[17] Susan Snyder, 'The genres of Shakespeare's plays', in Margreta de Grazia and Stanley Wells, *The Cambridge Companion to Shakespeare* (Cambridge: Cambridge University Press, 2001), 83–98 (85).

already been enforced by the play's structure': seeing Desdemona's inconsistency as necessary generic symptom rather than individual pathology reorients the play as a dissection of plot-as-agent.[18]

We might develop this suggestion in relation to Coleridge's famous idea of Iago's 'motiveless malignity'.[19] The actor David Suchet, describing his performance of Iago in Terry Hands's 1985 production of the play, gives an overview of the possible psychological readings of his character, including familiar narratives such as Iago's repressed homosexuality or the comparison with the modern category of psychopath. In the end, Suchet finds the idea of jealousy most useful for his interpretation, and adduces more general experience to corroborate this: 'Human beings are given to finding justifications for deeds or actions to make those deeds allowable: in their own minds even though they are not always valid justifications. And so it is with Iago.'[20] The syntactical logic is significant here: Suchet knows how humans behave and uses this to corroborate a psychological basis for Iago's actions. Our shared human subjectivity, that's to say, is evidence for Iago's. Hazlitt suggested that tragedy 'gives us a high and permanent interest, beyond ourselves, in humanity as such', but 'humanity as such' tends rather towards narcissism: it is we who are the real characters in the tragedies we consume, and we prop up their claims to psychological verisimilitude with our own human experience.[21] For the actor, as for the character critic, motivation is key; Suchet's is a play in which human agency is nastily sovereign. But perhaps what we actually see in *Othello* is the tragic plot personified, and hence the search for Iago's motivation is misplaced. Iago's plotting manipulates and distorts character: he thus functions as a dramatic device to make visible the defining primacy of genre over characterization. Bradley's summary that 'Iago's plot is Iago's character in action' needs to be flipped: Iago's character is his plot in action.[22] His soliloquies in the play confirm that their role is less of self-disclosure and more of self-presentation: they punctuate his plotting rather than his interiority. The axiomatic impenetrability of his own motivations is therefore appropriately strategic, since his primary purpose is to subject character to his own relentless plot, and thus to undermine any possible critical privileging of character over plot. When Iago shuts off Othello's question 'why'? (5.2.308) with 'what you know, you know' (5.2.309), he denies—and thus forever encourages—a characterological interpretation of the play's actions.

If *Othello* gives us a play in which characters are written by the plot rather than vice versa, elsewhere Shakespeare's tragedies are similarly sceptical about the notion of human self-direction. The verb 'to do' resounds throughout *Macbeth*: the First Witch's chilling 'I'll do, I'll do, and I'll do' (1.3.9); Macbeth's 'If it were done when 'tis done, then 'twere well | It were done quickly' (1.7.1-2); Lady Macbeth's 'what's done cannot be undone' (5.1.65). These repetitions propose a compromised syntax of agency that enacts in miniature the play's larger questions of who, or what, controls our actions. The play's opening sequence neatly compromises clear lines of cause and effect: the witches know they will 'meet with

[18] Peter Stallybrass, 'Patriarchal Territories: The Body Enclosed', in Margaret W. Ferguson, Maureen Quilligan, and Nancy J. Vickers, eds., *Rewriting the Renaissance: The Discourse of Sexual Difference in Early Modern Europe* (Chicago: University of Chicago Press, 1986), 123–42 (141).

[19] Bate, *Romantics on Shakespeare*, 485.

[20] David Suchet, 'Iago', in Russell Jackson and Robert Smallwood, eds., *Players of Shakespeare 2* (Cambridge: Cambridge University Press, 1988), 179–99 (182).

[21] Hazlitt, *Selected Writings*, 1: 112.   [22] Bradley, *Shakespearean Tragedy*, 145.

Macbeth' in the first lines, and, when they do, they pronounce him Thane of Cawdor. This promotion is immediately realized: as we know and Macbeth doesn't, in the intervening scene the king has stripped the traitor Cawdor of his title and pronounced the military hero Macbeth Cawdor in his place. Do the witches simply share the audience's ability to overhear scenes and superintend the unfolding of the plot, or are they agents of that plot? Productions of *Macbeth*, as Bernice Kliman has identified, can be classified around the way in which they answer this question of agency, from productions in which the psychologies of Macbeth and Lady Macbeth predominate and the witches are merely the catalyst, to those in which 'a controlling supernatural sphere' or a shaping social context seem to pre-empt the characters' room for manoeuvre.[23] *Macbeth*'s insistent structural questioning of whether humans are actors or acted upon seems rather to be the point: as in *Othello*, the issue of the relationship between tragedy and character is internal to the drama.

'EVEN SUCH A BODY'
(*ANTONY AND CLEOPATRA*, 4.15.13)

Shakespeare's tragic characters, then, can be read as subject to their plots: they are a product of genre. They are also constructed via their language. Although Hamlet's speech asserting his inaccessible interior is not a soliloquy, it is often read alongside that play's particular reliance on solo speech. In this critical model, soliloquy becomes the privileged moment of interior access to character. The audience is cued to expect further revelations of 'that within' when the rest of the characters leave Hamlet alone on stage, and, indeed, Hamlet responds by breaking into passionate self-disclosure and wishing that 'the Everlasting had not fixed | His canon 'gainst self-slaughter' (1.2.131-2). His recognition that 'break, my heart, for I must hold my tongue' (1.2.159) at the entrance of Horatio and the guards confirms the play's formal establishment of soliloquy as the audience's particular and favoured intimacy. The focus on soliloquy in *Hamlet* has often distorted the role of this device elsewhere in Shakespeare's tragedies. In no other play is soliloquy so prominent, and, further, in plays which use soliloquies, these often serve to reorient the focus of our attention away from the eponymous character. So, while King Lear and Othello rarely use soliloquy, both Edmund and Iago do, and often they use the same structure as the example from *Hamlet* 1.2: these characters remain on stage after others have left and deliver themselves of their true assessment or intentions. Soliloquizing is here a symptom less of the inalienable privacy of the human subject but rather of the specific, and often devious, relation of these characters to the others in their plays. Edmund despises 'legitimate Edgar' (1.2.16) and plots against him; Iago does 'hate the Moor' (1.3.378). What is revealed by soliloquy is theatrical duplicity rather than interiority.

It's a useful commonplace to point out that the word 'character' in this period, and as used by Shakespeare, denotes writing or inscription. When, for example, Claudius exclaims ''tis Hamlet's character' (4.7.50), he is not contributing to the vast literature on his

---

[23] Bernice W. Kliman, *Macbeth: Shakespeare in Performance* (Manchester: Manchester University Press, 1992), xii-xvi.

nephew's personality, but rather referring to the handwriting in his letter. In his famously titled essay of 1933 'How Many Children had Lady Macbeth?', L. C. Knights censured that 'most fruitful of irrelevancies' in critical discourse: 'the assumption that Shakespeare was pre-eminently a great "creator of characters"'.[24] For Knights, 'a Shakespeare play is a dramatic poem', in which everything—character, plot, rhythm, construction—'is brought into being by written or spoken words'.[25] A focus on character, he writes, is a simplification deriving from a reluctance to master 'the words of the play' and a 'readiness to abstract a character and treat him (because he is more manageable that way) as a human being'.[26] For Knights, Lady Macbeth, herself mere words, did not and could not have any children, although she may well have fostered some metaphors and been surrogate to some images along the way. Discussing the lines in which the apparently childless Lady Macbeth claims to 'have given suck, and know | How tender 'tis to love the babe that milks me' (1.7.54–5), Nicholas Brooke agrees, proposing that this baby is a metaphor which 'takes its place, with Macbeth's naked new-born babe, and all the other babes of the play, in a dimension well beyond the reach of the characters'. Brooke adds helpfully that he does 'not believe that that example need be any special problem to the actress',[27] although the tradition of performance, particularly as it is captured in discussions in the later twentieth and twenty-first centuries, does not bear this out.[28] Plays in performance always give us embodied persons in which the real presence of the actor physicalizes more conceptual or verbal understandings of character: it is hard to act in a poem.

That character might be understood as embodied—physiological rather than psychological—offers another way of historicizing ideas of subjectivity. The understanding of the humoral body as governing individual temperament and behaviour registers the early modern relationship between the body and the self as indivisible.[29] Early modern emotions were often understood somatically: a division between the psychological or inner, and the physiological or outer, had not solidified, although as Hillman argues, this barrier was one of the great inventions of the Renaissance and a necessary fiction on which 'the new disembodied and psychologized interiority of the modern subject is founded'.[30] Early modern ideas of subjectivity were, that is to say, thoroughly material: bodily matters. And actors who embodied these bodily characters were closely identified with them. The elegy for the tragic actor Richard Burbage makes explicit the physiological connection between character and player, and also understands character as physical performance of body—a leap 'suiting the person'—and face—'so true an eye':

> Young Hamlet, old Hieronimo,
> Kind Lear, the grieved Moor, and more beside,
> That liv'd in him, have now forever died.

[24] L. C. Knights, 'How Many Children had Lady Macbeth?' in L. C. Knights, *Explorations: Essays in Criticism Mainly on the Literature of the Seventeenth Century* (London: Chatto & Windus, 1946), 13.

[25] Ibid., 16.   [26] Ibid., 26.

[27] Nicholas Brooke, ed., *The Tragedy of Macbeth* (Oxford: Oxford University Press, 1990), 14.

[28] I discuss this in more detail in *Macbeth: Language and Writing* (London: Bloomsbury, 2013), 150–6.

[29] See Gail Kern Paster, Ch. 13 in this volume.

[30] David Hillman, *Shakespeare's Entrails: Belief, Scepticism and the Interior of the Body* (Basingstoke: Palgrave Macmillan, 1997), 4.

> Oft have I seen him leap into the grave,
> Suiting the person, which he seem'd to have,
> Of a sad lover, with so true an eye
> That there I would have sworn he meant to die.[31]

Burbage's real death is here in ironic juxtaposition with the many staged deaths he has repeatedly performed. Only now that their animating body is dead are the characters of Lear, Hamlet and Othello truly lifeless: before, they were simply performing death under the view of spectators trying to spot signs of their breathing.

The destruction of the tragic body is the ultimate end, both as conclusion and as purpose, of Shakespearean tragedy. Extended dying speeches focus final attention on the dying hero: Hamlet speaks thirty lines across eight speeches after Laertes has delivered the fatal swipe with the poisoned rapier; Othello's speech of self-exculpation before his suicide stills the busy stage to allow him his own epitaph. The absence of the dead body at the end of *Timon of Athens* is one measure of that play's thoroughgoing challenge to tragic norms. Timon produces his own epitaph which, within a few lines, has already become obscure: the 'character' of his tombstone has to be read by a skilled interpreter (5.4.4), to produce the bathetic 'Here lies a wretched corpse, | Of wretched soul bereft. | Seek not my name' (5.5.71-3). Elsewhere, the tragic downfall is, finally, physical, written—charactered—on the body. *Antony and Cleopatra* offers us the most extensive analysis of this form of spectacular, histrionic and corporeal tragic character. Not only does this tragedy double its tragic focus but it also extends the physical enactment of both its tragic deaths. This carnal pair of lovers live and die publicly and physically: their characters are histrionically constructed and then gloriously deconstructed as display, in a play which has almost entirely abandoned notions of soliloquy and privacy. After the disastrous battle of Actium, Antony's recognition that 'Here I am Antony, | Yet cannot hold this visible shape' (4.15.13-14) shows his exoskeletal reliance on his armour:

> The seven-fold shield of Ajax cannot keep
> The battery from my heart. O, cleave, my sides!
> Heart, once be stronger than thy continent;
> Crack thy frail case.

> (4.15.38-41)

This speech recapitulates Philo's description of the effects of Antony's 'dotage' in the play's opening speech: 'His captain's heart, | Which in the scuffles of great fights hath burst | The buckles on his breast, reneges all temper' (1.1.6-8). Antony's emotion on hearing the death—feigned—of Cleopatra cannot be separated from somatic response: the suffering self is experienced in the body's organs. His painfully extended death focuses attention on the physical body: he tells his guard—who number '4 or 5' in the stage direction—to 'carry me now, good friends' (4.15.137), and the word 'heave' in the stage direction as he

---

[31] Glynne Wickham, Herbert Berry, and William Ingram, *English Professional Theatre 1530-1660* (Cambridge: Cambridge University Press, 2000), 182. On Shakespeare's dramaturgy as 'an arena where the art of physiognomy is put to the test', see Michael Neill, '"A Book Where One May Read Strange Matters": En-visaging Character and Emotion on the Shakespearian Stage', *Shakespeare Survey* 66 (2013), 246-64 (251).

is raised to Cleopatra's monument, followed by the exclamation 'a heavy sight' (4.16.42) stresses his dense corporeality. For Cleopatra, death is a more choreographed but still bodily performance: 'Give me my robe. Put on my crown' (5.2.275). These are characters understood as bodies rather than essences, and this recognition makes a different sense of Cleopatra's much-quoted fear that 'Some squeaking Cleopatra boy my greatness | I'th' posture of a whore.' (5.2.215-16). This self-reflexive allusion to and by the young male actor at this advanced stage of the tragedy serves to reify her character as ultimately and ineluctably embodied.

'AUTHOR OF HIMSELF' (*CORIOLANUS* 5.3.36)

At a similar point in his play, Coriolanus also acknowledges himself as a player: 'like a dull actor now | I have forgot my part' (5.3.40-1). Perhaps only T. S. Eliot has experienced this play as 'Shakespeare's most assured artistic success': no-one, to my knowledge, has claimed a smack of Coriolanus, although for Eliot it was better than *Hamlet*.[32] But reading this rebarbative late play can offer some different methodological contours for a discussion of tragedy and character than those parameters of interiority established by the focus on *Hamlet*. As an alternative locus for a discussion of tragedy and character, *Coriolanus* reveals itself to be preoccupied with problematizing this very issue. Shakespeare's final tragedy performs that inscrutability Hamlet talks about, debating and deferring the notion and location of personality and individual agency. Bradley, who omitted it from his discussion in *Shakespearean Tragedy*, returned to it in a lecture in 1912. Describing Coriolanus as 'totally ignorant of himself', he finds him 'what we call an "impossible" person'.[33] Bradley's adjective suggests exasperation: the OED offers 'impossible to deal with ... to get on with, to tolerate, to recognize; utterly unsuitable or impracticable'. It is an interesting judgement that the play itself shares. The repeated word 'strange' when the Volscian servingmen try to identify the muffled stranger who is attempting to access Aufidius does something of the same interpretative shrug as does Bradley's 'impossible': their forty lines of fruitless interrogation seem to identify an unreadability that is in excess of the immediate dramatic situation (4.5.20, 36).

This unreadability starts with the play's opening. *Coriolanus* begins with an ominous gathering. The Folio stage direction gives us *'Enter a Company of Mutinous Citizens with Staves, Clubs, and other weapons'*. Their leader offers the rallying cry 'rather to die than to famish' (1.1.4-5), but the insurrection is immediately diverted into a discussion of the 'chief enemy to the people' (7-8), Caius Martius. The citizens argue over Martius's conduct: he is both 'a very dog to the commonalty' (27) but also one who has done 'services' for his country (28). Opinions vary: 'Though soft-conscienced men can be content to say it was for his country, he did it to please his mother and to be partly proud' (35-7). Martius is described as 'not covetous' but full of 'faults with surplus' (41, 43). 'What he cannot help

---

[32] T. S. Eliot, *The Sacred Wood: Essays on Poetry and Criticism* [1920] (London: Faber and Faber Ltd, 1997), 84.
[33] A. C. Bradley, *The British Academy Second Annual Shakespeare Lecture: Coriolanus* (London: British Academy, 1912), 13, 9.

in his nature you account a vice in him' (39–40). That the revolt over grain prices quickly becomes a debate about the character of the play's eponymous figure sets the tone for the tragedy. In *Coriolanus* political events can seem merely the occasion for the anatomizing of the central character: this is a play in which inner conflict is compulsively externalized, and in which from the very outset the nature of Coriolanus himself remains a source and symptom of dissent.

Again and again the play attempts to get to know Coriolanus and is rebuffed. The soliloquies we might expect as indications of inner reflection are fractured into acerbically public asides. Of all the tragedies, this play has the fewest lines of soliloquy; Coriolanus' lengthiest speeches, at least in Rome, are rather vituperative admonition of the citizens. His interlocutors find it increasingly hard to describe his 'singularity' (1.1.273): 'he had, sir, a kind of face, methought—I cannot tell how to term it'; 'I thought there was more in him than I could think' (4.5.157–61); Cominius finds 'a kind of nothing, titleless' (5.1.14). The word 'thing' is often used of Coriolanus: to Cominius he is 'a thing of blood' (2.2.109); to Aufidius 'a noble thing' (4.5.11); it is reported 'he leads them like a thing | Made by some other deity than nature' (4.6.94–5); implacable, 'he sits in his state, as a thing made for Alexander' (5.4 .21–2). Coriolanus uses the word of himself to express his greater affinity with his enemy Aufidius than with the people of Rome: 'were I any thing but what I am, | I would wish me only he' (1.1.231–2). In some readings this repeated use registers Coriolanus's inhumanity, as echoed in G. Wilson Knight's description of him as 'a blind mechanic, metallic thing of pride'.[34] But perhaps it is rather a lexical equivalent of the play's conceptual difficulty in defining its hero. The play is 'contemptuous of its audiences' just as Coriolanus is of the citizens: when he refuses to 'put on the gown, stand naked and entreat' the citizens (2.2.137), Martius is simultaneously rejecting attempts by audiences or readers to understand his character.[35] Even the famous stage direction when he responds to Volumnia's passionate petition to spare Rome—'*Holds her by the hand silent*' (5.3.183sd)—invites and rebuffs any attempt to read his inner, inscrutable emotion. Coriolanus breaks the silence by reflecting attention back to his mother: 'O mother, mother! | What have you done?', and referring to himself only in the third person as 'your son' (5.3.183–8).

The first scenes in *Coriolanus* introduce us serially to the playworld's groups of characters: to the citizens first, then Menenius and Martius, to Sicinius, Brutus, Cominius, Lartius and the senators, to Aufidius and the senators of Corioles, and to Virgilia and Volumnia. The dramaturgy of character is thus social: individuals emerge through and within dialogue and through reciprocal interaction. It is also diachronic—existing through time—rather than synchronic—gathered in a single moment. As with all the other plays published in the Folio, and, indeed, in common with all editions of Shakespeare's plays before 1637, there is no list of characters to precede the play.[36] Margreta de Grazia and Peter Stallybrass note that, in contrast to modern editions where a character-list suggests that 'characters preexist their speeches', early 'readers had to arbitrate for themselves the

---

[34] G. Wilson Knight, *The Imperial Theme* (London: Methuen & Co Ltd, 1965), 161.

[35] Peter Holland, ed., *Coriolanus: Oxford World's Classics* (Oxford: Oxford University Press, 1994), 1.

[36] Seven plays have character-lists *after* the texts in the Folio: see my essay 'The Canonization of Shakespeare in Print, 1623', in M. J. Kidnie and Sonia Massai, eds., *Shakespeare and Textual Studies* (Cambridge: Cambridge University Press, 2015), 134-46.

boundaries of identity, constructing (or failing to construct or refusing to construct) "in-dividual" characters in the process of reading'.[37] Character, like plot, is established gradu-ally through the act of reading, rather than being discovered by it. The entrance of Caius Martius following Menenius' diversionary discussion with the citizens is thus the reader's first acquaintance with him: he is shaped both by the debates in the opening lines about him and by the stage space which is established for his entrance by that discussion, and only then by his own uncompromising first speech:

> Thanks.—What's the matter, you dissentious rogues
> That, rubbing the poor itch of your opinion,
> Make yourselves scabs?

> (1.1.162–4)

But if Shakespeare's Coriolanus does not precede his own speeches in the experience of read-ing the Folio text, multiple versions of this character do pre-exist the play. All Shakespeare's tragic characters, save perhaps Titus, have a life before their play: Romeo and Juliet in Arthur Brooke's poem, Antony, Cleopatra, and Brutus in North's translation of Plutarch, Lear in Holinshed and in the anonymous *King Leir*, Macbeth, Richard II and III in Holinshed, Hamlet in the supposed ur-*Hamlet*. Similarly, the figure of Coriolanus was an available ex-emplar in a number of texts before Shakespeare's play, and is mentioned in English versions of Cicero, Agrippa, Livy, Bodin, Peter Martyr, Augustine of Hippo, and Seneca.

Two factors were current and accepted in the circulation of Coriolanus' name in early modern print culture: his exile from Rome and his obedience to his mother. For Peter Martyr, Coriolanus' death was an example of the inevitable end of fugitives;[38] in Francis Meres' commonplace book his welcome among the Volscians was counter to the current of negative images of banishment.[39] Robert Allott mentions Coriolanus at three points in his commonplace *Wits theater of the little world* under the headings 'Of Clemencie', 'Countrey or Commonwealth', and 'Of Sorrow';[40] in Bodenham's *Bel-vedere, or The Garden of the Muses*, he appears at the end 'Of Griefe &c' and 'Of Teares &c'.[41] He is cited as a model for filial piety in the section 'A Glasse for disobedient Sonnes to looke in' of W. Averill's *A dyall for dainty darlings*.[42] Shakespeare himself draws on this commonplace or exem-plary Coriolanus in a simile in his earlier tragedy *Titus Andronicus*. Bringing news to the emperor Saturninus that Lucius Andronicus is marching on Rome at the head of a Goth army, Emillius warns that he 'threats in course of this revenge to do | As much as ever Coriolanus did' (4.4.65–6). Coriolanus, that is to say, enters his own play with baggage, and with baggage that does not lend itself to characterological nuance or development. His character is already fixed, written as a series of commonplaces—rather as the contempora-neous Theophrastan character-studies of Joseph Hall and Sir Thomas Overbury presented

---

[37] Margreta de Grazia and Peter Stallybrass, 'The Materiality of the Shakespearean Text', *Shakespeare Quarterly* 44 (1993), 255–83 (267).

[38] *The Common places of the most famous and renowmed divine Doctor Peter Martyr* (London: 1583), 294.

[39] Francis Meres, *Palladis Tamia* (London: 1598), 236.

[40] Robert Allott, *Wits theater of the little world* (London: 1599), 45, 87, 118.

[41] John Bodenham, *Bel-vedere, or The Garden of the Muses* (London: 1600), 144, 190.

[42] W. Averill, *A dyall for dainty darlings* (London: 1584), sig. D3.

their popular social types. The implacability of Coriolanus in the play can be read inter-
textually as well as psychologically. The received Coriolanus is briefly and repeatedly cited
as an illustration of a particular quality or situation. He thus already possesses something
of that 'notorious identity' discussed by Linda Charnes as 'a pathological form of fame'.[43]

Perhaps to stave off this restrictive familiarity, the play withholds the name of the hero in
a way no other Shakespeare tragedy does. Titus names himself at his entrance in 1.1; Romeo
enters first just after his mother and Benvolio have been discussing him, and his name is
quickly used twice in the dialogue twice; Juliet enters in response to the nurse calling her
name; Macbeth is named three times by the witches almost as soon as he enters; in *Hamlet*,
appropriately, the name of the prince overlaps with references to his late father: three of the
first four uses of the name refer to the king, but when Hamlet is on stage in his first scene he
is addressed by name four times; Othello is significantly established as the nameless 'Moor'
of Shakespeare's source in the play's first scene but is named by the duke as he tells the story
of his marriage before the senators in 1.3; Antony and Cleopatra address each other by name
several times in 1.1. In all these instances, readers of the play have particular advance notice,
because the name of the title character is pre-introduced in their stage direction entrances
and speech prefixes. In *Coriolanus* the presentation is rather different. The play takes its
name from the honorific given to Martius in recognition of his exceptional bravery at the
Volscian town of Corioles at the end of Act 1. His grateful soldiers '*all cry Martius, Martius*',
and Cominius declares him 'Coriolanus' (1.10.64). The Folio text, however, continues to
label the reluctant hero Martius in speech prefixes throughout the remainder of the scene.
It is not until his triumphant entry as Coriolanus, '*crown'd with an Oaken Garland*' in 2.1,
that the play's apparatus gives us the eponymous tragic character *Coriol*.

The proper name, therefore, as a symbol of personal autonomy and individuality is
withheld in this play. Although other of Shakespeare's heroes undergo status or name
changes during the course of the play, none adopts the name of the play as his new name.
Coriolanus' tragic agnomen, and with it his identification as the play's tragic figure, is belated. Moreover, the new name Coriolanus serves to upset, rather than confirm, Martius'
previous designation. In the Folio Cominius names his general '*Marcus Caius Coriolanus*',
a formula repeated by '*Omnes*'. Many editors, from Nicholas Rowe onwards, have corrected the names to the more usual 'Caius Martius'.[44] In Shakespeare's source, Thomas
North's translation of Plutarch, Coriolanus' new name prompts a digression, with numerous examples, to explain how Roman names work: 'and thereby it appeareth, that
the first name the Romaines have, as *Caius:* was our Christian name now. The second, as
Martius: was the name of the house and familie they came of. The third, was some addition geven, either for some acte or notable service, or for some marke on their face, or of
some shape of their bodie, or else for some special vertue they had'.[45] So it is odd to see
the Folio commit a double mistake—both inverting the order of the names, and changing
'Martius' into 'Marcus'. The footnote to the play's most recent edition does nothing to clarify: 'F's order for the name is repeated later and hence is unlikely to be an error … it places

---

[43] Linda Charnes, *Notorious Identity: Materializing the Subject in Shakespeare* (Cambridge, MA
and London: Harvard University Press, 1993), 3.

[44] H. H. Furness, ed., *The Tragedie of Coriolanus* (Philadelphia; London: J. B. Lippincott, 1928), 160.

[45] Thomas North, *The lives of the noble Grecians and Romanes compared together by that grave
learned philosopher and historiographer, Plutarke of Chaeronea* (London: 1579), 242.

the emphasis on the character of *Martius*, the man who belongs to the god of war Mars', omitting the fact that the name is actually mistakenly given as 'Marcus'.[46] The effect of these muddles mean that the Folio text of the play inadvertently forgets Coriolanus' name in the act of bestowing it. Norman Rabkin notes that 'In accepting the name Coriolanus, Martius accepts public recognition for what he has done, and necessarily compromises himself';[47] we can see the anticipation of that destructive compromise verbally enacted in the play's onomastic mistake. And this seems somehow more than an accidental or trivial error because it is followed within a couple of moments by the play's more significant and willed name amnesia. Cominius, moved by Martius' description of a poor Corioles man who 'used me kindly' (1.10.82), orders him to be freed, but Martius cannot remember his name. In North's Plutarch no name is given of this 'olde friend and hoste of mine, an honest wealthie man', but there is no suggestion that Coriolanus does not know his name.[48] The general whose own names are in post-traumatic flux forgets the name of his host, in a moment which is itself important for different views of Coriolanus' character: is habitual disdain, or momentary frailty, the explanation for his amnesia?

North's description of the way Roman names are allocated offers a map for different models of personal identity: the second name identifies the individual as a product of their family, while the third can be given either for deeds or for some particular intrinsic quality. These associations indicate some of the many ways in which the play refuses to sanction the desire for individual autonomy. The scene of Virgilia and Volumnia's embassy to the exiled Coriolanus in Antium is a good example, in which Coriolanus' vain wish that 'man were author of himself' (5.3.36) is sabotaged. The desire 'to please his mother' (1.1.37) which the citizens adduced as the motivation for his military success in the play's opening moments returns as the site of Coriolanus' greatest vulnerability. When Volumnia prevails with him not to sack Rome, he acknowledges that the peace is 'most mortal to him': 'Mother, mother! | What have you done?' (5.3.190; 183–4). Volumnia taunts him with naming: 'To his surname 'Coriolanus' 'longs more pride | Than pity to our prayers' (5.3.171–2). What Coriolanus is called becomes increasingly fractious in his final interview with Aufidius, when the names 'Martius'—'Dost thou think | I'll grace the with that robbery, thy stol'n name, | 'Coriolanus', in Corioles'?' (5.6.9–2)—and 'boy' (103) anticipate and authorize Coriolanus' death.

At every point in *Coriolanus* where dramatic identity might be secured—through family, through social position, through soliloquy, through naming, through contrast with the other, through consistent action, through self-knowledge—the play instead subjects the notion of character itself to sustained, ironic analysis. Even at the end, Coriolanus is subject to multiple interpretations: he is attacked physically by a mob in a parallel with that verbal dissection of his character with which the play began. The Volscian people turn on him: 'Kill, kill, kill, kill, kill him' (5.6.30), and the stage direction reads: *Draw both the Conspirators, and kils Martius, who falls, Auffidius stands on him.* Coriolanus is denied life, name, dignity, and singularity in this tableau. Michael Goldman writes, drawing on his analysis of *Coriolanus*, that 'perhaps this is what tragedy is about—that there is such a thing as human character.

---

[46] Holland, *Coriolanus*, 210.

[47] Norman Rabkin, '*Coriolanus*: The Tragedy of Politics', *Shakespeare Quarterly* 17 (1966), 195–212 (203).

[48] North (*Plutarch*), 242.

Perhaps it is only in tragedy that we feel that character as a personal possession really exists, in spite of the contradictions which surround it as a philosophical conception.[49] Perhaps. Or perhaps we can understand this tragedy, and Shakespearean tragedy more generally, as interrogating and problematizing ideas of character. These questions are within the plays, rather than external to them. Supplementing Romantic engagement with Hamlet's interiority with ideas of character as written—by plot and by the body—gives us a more material form of subjectivity. Taking our cues not from the Shakespearean character who most compels our fascination—Hamlet—but from the one who repeatedly professes himself utterly contemptuous of us—Coriolanus—challenges some of the terms of the debate. The ultimate *subject* of Shakespearean tragedy emerges as less those individual eponyms of the plays but rather the contingent, mobile, and evasive notion of 'character' itself.

SELECT BIBLIOGRAPHY

Bradley, A. C., *Shakespearean Tragedy* (1904; Basingstoke: Macmillan, 1985).

Craig, Hugh, ' "Speak, That I May See Thee": Shakespeare Characters and Common Words', *Shakespeare Survey* 61 (2008), 281–8.

Desmet, Christy, 'Character', *The Oxford Handbook of Shakespeare*, ed. Arthur F. Kinney (Oxford: Oxford University Press, 2011), 536–53.

Hillman, David, *Shakespeare's Entrails: Belief, Scepticism and the Interior of the Body* (Basingstoke: Palgrave Macmillan, 1997).

Maus, Katharine Eisaman, *Inwardness and Theater in the English Renaissance* (Chicago: University of Chicago Press, 1995).

Neill, Michael, ' "A Book Where One May Read Strange Matters": En-visaging Character and Emotion on the Shakespearian Stage', *Shakespeare Survey* 66 (2013), 246–64.

Yachnin, Paul and Jessica Slights, eds., *Shakespeare and Character: Theory, History, Performance, and Theatrical Persons* (Basingstoke: Palgrave Macmillan, 2009).

---

[49] Michael Goldman, *Acting and Action in Shakespearean Tragedy* (Princeton: Princeton University Press, 1985), 163.

CHAPTER 7

....

PREPOSTEROUS NATURE IN SHAKESPEARE'S TRAGEDIES

....

PHILIP ARMSTRONG

A few years ago, on a cold spring night, I found myself huddled on a temporary seating stand to see an outdoor performance of *Macbeth*. The playing-area appeared to be laid out in a post-apocalyptic style: collapsed walls, twisted stairways, broken pallets, pools of rusty water, piles of debris and concrete dust. The audience could be heard admiring the set, but in fact the designers didn't have much to do with it. A couple of months earlier the local theatre had been declared unsafe following a sequence of severe earthquakes, so the producers opted to stage the play in the open, amid the ruins of three buildings demolished after the quakes. It was Nature, then, in the form of seismic activity, who set this stage.[1]

From 2010 to 2012, the city of Christchurch in New Zealand experienced thousands of earthquakes, including several that measured higher than six on the Richter magnitude scale. In the most destructive quake 185 people died, and half the high-rise buildings in the central city were damaged beyond repair, along with the majority of heritage structures and over ten thousand suburban houses. In September 2011, when I attended the outdoor *Macbeth*, aftershocks were still occurring most days; even as we waited for the play to start, a tremor rattled the seating stand and made us shift uneasily.

In such a context, the most resonant line in the performance was inevitably the one spoken by Lennox following Duncan's murder: '[s]ome say the earth | Was feverous and did shake' (2.3.59–60). Hearing those words, the audience murmured ruefully. But more than that, we couldn't help notice the play's pervasive references to the restiveness and inconstancy of the natural world: 'Stones have been known to move' (3.4.122); 'the earth hath bubbles, as the water does' (1.3.77); 'The multiplying villanies of nature' (1.2.10). Such phrases assumed a new significance because local events had already forced us to think of nature as far more active, capricious, and treacherous than we, as prosperous citizens of a modern society, had previously tended to assume.

---

[1] *Macbeth,* directed by Mike Friend, The Loons Theatre Company, Lyttelton, New Zealand, August–September 2011.

I begin with this experience because it exemplifies a challenge to some of the fundamental assumptions about what we like to call 'the natural world', and about our relationship to it. In her recent book *Vibrant Matter* (2010), Jane Bennett ascribes to modern
thought the 'habit of parsing the world into dull matter (it, things) and vibrant life (us,
beings)'.[2] We're shaken out of this habit, at least for a while, by events like earthquakes, but
Bennett's project is to ask how differently we might see and treat the world if, rather than
waiting for such an extreme example of nature's power, we were systematically to replace
our view of 'matter as passive stuff, as raw, brute or inert' with a notion of *vibrant matter*
or *vital materiality*. By these phrases Bennett means 'the capacity of things—edibles, commodities, storms, metals—not only to impede or block the designs of humans but also to
act as quasi agents or forces with trajectories, propensities or tendencies of their own'.[3]

Bennett draws on Bruno Latour's contention that the dominant forms of knowledge
in modern cultures have been organized by what he calls the 'Modern Constitution', a
structure that relies on two fundamental divisions. The 'first dichotomy' creates 'two entirely distinct ontological zones': that of non-humans and nature on one hand, and that
of humans and culture on the other.[4] Nature—the non-human material world—is perceived as mindless, passive, mechanistic, and devoid of agency: a resource or instrument
for humans to use and control. The human world, by contrast, becomes the sole location
of mind, action, deliberation, intention, and agency. For Latour, this opposition is an illusion, a kind of false consciousness, reliant on a 'second dichotomy', which erects a screen
or safety barrier between the oppositional first dichotomy and all the phenomena, events
and practices that transgress it—that is, the continuing incidence and necessary production of networks and mixtures, 'hybrids of nature and culture'.[5] Modernity cannot do
without such hybrids—indeed it is committed to the production of new ones—but it behaves as if the first dichotomy were reality; as if nature and culture were separate; as if the
non-human and the human were two distinct realms.

Latour locates the emergence of the Modern Constitution in the seventeenth century,
so if his schema has validity we should expect to find in Shakespeare's works, on the cusp
of the early modern transition, something very different. And we do: precisely those kinds
of vigorous and constitutive interaction between nature and culture, between non-human
matter and human being, which the Modern Constitution will obscure and discredit, are
in Shakespeare's works still visibly, volubly, and vibrantly centre-stage.

In Shakespeare's tragedies the most recurrent, potent, and complex instances of such
assemblages are provided by storms. In three of the four major tragedies, severe climatic
conditions assume the agentive force of antagonists; they are not merely atmospheric expressions of, but causative contributors to, the turmoil of human interactions. In particular, extreme weather functions as a splitting agent, separating characters in ways that
set in train the tragic conflicts that follow. In *Macbeth*, the disrupted weather provides a
first and immediate sign of something badly awry; it features as a precipitating motive

---

[2] Jane Bennett, *Vibrant Matter: A Political Ecology of Things* (Durham and London: Duke
University Press, 2010), p. vii.

[3] Ibid., p. viii.

[4] Bruno Latour, *We Have Never Been Modern*, trans. Catherine Porter (Cambridge, MA: Harvard
University Press, 1993), 10–11.

[5] Ibid., 11.

for those, including Macduff, who decide to place themselves beyond the usurper's reach. The day after Duncan's murder, Ross greets Macduff, 'How goes the world, sir, now?' and receives the reply, 'Why, see you not?' (2.4.5-6). The evident disorder of a climate in which 'the heavens, as troubled with man's act, | Threatens his bloody stage' provides sufficient warning for Macduff to avoid Macbeth's investiture and escape, first to Fife and then to England, from where he will eventually return to help overthrow the tyrant (2.4.21). In *Othello*, in a comparable fashion, Shakespeare makes use of a vividly evoked sea-storm to delay his protagonist while allowing both Cassio's ship and the one carrying Desdemona and Iago through. 'Tempests themselves, high seas and howling winds, | The guttered rocks and congregated sands ... do omit | Their mortal natures, letting go safely by | The divine Desdemona' (2.1.67-73). These lines describe the storm not as a single phenomenon but as a congeries of anthropomorphized agencies, each in turn made up of plural materials (seas, winds, rocks, sands). Again, the congregation of elements represented by storm weather has agentive power: it creates the opportunity for Iago to observe and encourage flirtation between Desdemona and Cassio without Othello present, which behaviour he can then use to provoke Roderigo's attack on Cassio, the first thread in the 'net | That shall enmesh them all' (2.3.52-3). Yet another storm, this time in *King Lear*, impacts potently both on plot and on the behaviour of (other) characters. Its imminent arrival prompts Regan to forbid Lear's knights because 'This house is little. The old man and his people | Cannot be well bestowed.' (2.2.461-2).[6] It is this peremptory dismissal of his knights that finally turns Lear against his daughters, turns his mind and turns him out in fury—into the storm: 'In such a night | To shut me out? Pour on, I will endure. | In such a night as this! O Regan, Goneril, | Your old kind father, whose frank heart gave all—O, that way madness lies' (3.4.17-21).

At which point we might ask: why does this sense of radical inconstancy, aberrance, and hostility in nature prove so ubiquitous in the tragedies? For in each of these cases, as well as using a storm as a kind of non-human cast member, Shakespeare evokes weather so extreme that young and old alike attest to its unprecedented violence. In *Lear*, witnessing the growing fury of the tempest, Kent declares: 'Such sheets of fire, such bursts of horrid thunder, | Such groans of roaring wind and rain I ne'er | Remember to have heard' (3.2.46-8). Similarly, when Macbeth replies dismissively to Lennox's description of the wild storm that follows Duncan's assassination—''Twas a rough night', he grunts—Lennox assures him that 'My young remembrance cannot parallel | A fellow to it' (2.3.62-4). Nor, it turns out, can more venerable remembrance: in the next scene the Old Man tells Ross: 'Threescore and ten I can remember well, | Within the volume of which time I have seen | Hours dreadful and things strange, but this sore night | Hath trifled former knowings' (2.4.1-4). And in *Othello*, the gentleman who describes the sea-storm from the Cypriot shoreline insists he 'never did like molestation view | Of the enchafèd flood' (2.1.16-17).

If we continue to work within the Modern Constitution, according to which effective agency is the sole prerogative of human society, such moments will be merely dramatic reflections of a tumult whose source and centre resides in the social and political shifts

---

[6] Unless otherwise stated, quotations from *King Lear* are from the 1623 Folio text, as it appears under the title *The Tragedy of King Lear* in the Oxford *Complete Works*, ed. Stanley Wells et al. (Oxford: Clarendon Press, 1988). Quotations from the 1608 Quarto are distinguished by the title given to that version in the same volume: *The History of King Lear*.

of early modern Europe: stormy weather, in other words, allegorizes a stormy period in human history. If, on the other hand, we take seriously Shakespeare's engagement with the extra-human material world, we must wonder whether his recurrent and detailed evocations of unprecedented storm activity derived from climatic realities present in his actual environment.[7] And there is growing evidence that they did.

Climate historians agree that the 'Medieval Warm Period'—a time of generally mild and settled climate in Europe from the tenth to the thirteenth centuries—began to give way to extensive cooling during the 1300s, a 'Little Ice Age' that continued until the next warming period, the one we now inhabit, began in the mid-1900s. Within this 600 years of colder and stormier weather, more specific regional fluctuations can be identified. 'The temperatures which we derive from sixteenth-century material available for England', writes H. H. Lamb, 'point to generally rather warmer conditions between about 1500 and 1550 than in the previous century'.[8] This relatively temperate half-century, however, gave way to 'a remarkably sharp change' in the middle of the sixteenth century.[9] During Elizabeth's reign and Shakespeare's lifetime, the whole European climate became significantly colder and more unpredictable. 'Storm activity increased by 85 per cent in the second half of the sixteenth century', writes Brian Fagan, and he cites the pastor of Stendhal in the Prussian Alps, who wrote in 1595 that '[t]here is no real, constant sunshine, neither a steady winter nor summer; the earth's crops and produce do not ripen ... The fruitfulness of all creatures and of the world as a whole is receding; fields and grounds have tired from bearing fruits'.[10] Similarly, in England, surveys of wheat harvests show runs of ruinously bad years in the 1550s, the 1560s, and 1594–7.[11]

The sharpness of this contrast between the climate of Elizabeth's reign and that of her father's means that Shakespeare would have grown to maturity surrounded by a generational sense that a previously fecund, temperate, and reliable natural environment had been replaced by freezing temperatures, blighted harvests, and sudden, wild storms. For example, at the age of 24 he would have been absorbed, like all his compatriots, by the drama of the impending Spanish invasion, whose defeat was achieved not primarily by naval defences but by climatic caprice. 'The great gales of August 1588', writes Fagan, 'destroyed more of the Spanish Armada than the combined guns of English warships.'[12] And no wonder: climate historians have found that combining meteorological analysis of reports from ships in the Armada with concurrent observations by Danish astronomer Tycho Brahe reveals 'wind storms over this part of the Atlantic exceeding the severity of most of the worst storms of modern times'.[13] Fifteen years later, Shakespeare adds to his

---

[7] For a compelling discussion of Shakespeare's dramatization of the 'environmental fear' evoked by 'an eminently unpredictable natural world', see Simon C. Estok's *Ecocriticism and Shakespeare: Reading Ecophobia* (New York: Palgrave Macmillan, 2011), 19, 32; also Gabriel Egan, *Green Shakespeare: From Ecopolitics to Ecocriticism* (London and New York: Routledge, 2006), 132–47.

[8] H. H. Lamb, *Climate, History and the Modern World*, second edition (London and New York: Routledge, 1995), 211.

[9] Ibid., 212.

[10] Brian Fagan, *The Little Ice Age: How Climate Made History, 1300–1850* (New York: Basic Books, 2000), 90–1, citing Christian Pfister and Rudolf Brázdil, 'Climatic variability in Sixteenth-Century Europe and its Social Dimension: A Synthesis', *Climatic Change* 43:1 (1999), 5–53 (44).

[11] Lamb, *Climate*, 228.   [12] Fagan, *The Little Ice Age*, p. xvi.   [13] Lamb, *Climate*, 218.

version of the Othello story the sea-storm already mentioned, in which the Turkish fleet is 'so banged' by the 'desperate tempest ... | That their designment halts' (2.1.21–2).[14]

Meanwhile, in the real world, things were getting worse: the 1590s were the coldest decade of the sixteenth century; out of the entire second millennium the coldest century was the seventeenth; its coldest year was 1601[15]—a year in which audiences at the Globe heard Shakespeare compare freezing air to a sharp-toothed animal: 'The air bites shrewdly, it is very cold', says Horatio, to which Hamlet responds, 'It is a nipping and an eager air' (1.4.1–2). As Sergio Fava notes, however, 'the real problem' of the new climatic conditions, 'more than the cold, was the unpredictable sharp variability of the weather.'[16] It is precisely this sense of lability that dominates Shakespeare's tragedies. The storm language in *King Lear, Macbeth*, and *Othello* repeatedly evokes the possibility that nature's elemental agencies might suddenly overflow their proper locations and usurp each other's places, and even tear apart the constitution of the natural world at its foundations. During the sea-storm in *Othello*, 'The chidden billow seems to pelt the clouds, | The wind-shaked surge with high and monstrous mane | Seems to cast water on the burning Bear | And quench the guards of the'ever-fixéd Pole' (2.1.12–15). Lear calls on the winds to blow till they have cracked their cheeks, the lightning to cleave the oaks, and the 'all-shaking thunder' to 'Strike flat the thick rotundity o'th' world, | Crack nature's moulds, all germans spill at once | That makes ingrateful man' (3.2.1, 5–9). Macbeth, similarly, demands that the witches answer him even though 'the yeasty waves | Confound and swallow navigation up, | Though bladed corn be lodged and trees blown down, ... | though the treasure | Of nature's germens tumble all together | Even till destruction sicken' (4.1.69–76).

This same conviction, that an ordered and harmonious nature has been disrupted by a climate of unprecedented unruliness, pervades the tragedies' portrayal of the internal worlds of their characters. Which comes as no surprise given that, as Gail Kern Paster has compellingly argued, Shakespeare and his contemporaries perceived the continuities between human nature (what we now call human biology) and the larger non-human natural world (plants, animals, lands, waters, weather, and so on) to be literal and material, rather than merely rhetorical as we have (from our modern perspective) too often assumed. The 'analogical structure [in which] ordinary microcosmic man's flesh is earth and his passions are the seas', writes Paster, was authoritative not merely because of its rhetorical force but 'because the body itself' was believed to be, in its actual substance, 'a vessel of liquids':

> the passions—thanks to their close functional relation to the four bodily humors of blood, choler, black bile, and phlegm—had a more than analogical relation to liquid states and forces of nature. In an important sense, the passions actually *were* liquid forces of nature,

---

[14] As Michael Neill notes, the addition of the storm 'involves a significant alteration to Giraldi's story [that is, the play's source], in which the Moor and Disdemona cross to Cyprus "with a sea of utmost tranquillity"': see Michael Neill, ed., *William Shakespeare: Othello, the Moor of Venice* (Oxford: Oxford University Press, 2006), 240. For an extended ecocritical analysis of the storm see Steven Mentz, *At the Bottom of Shakespeare's Ocean* (London and New York: Continuum, 2009), 19–32.

[15] Sergio Fava, *Environmental Apocalypse in Science and Art: Designing Nightmares* (New York: Routledge, 2013), 11.

[16] Ibid.

because, in this cosmology, the stuff of the outside world and the stuff of the body were composed of the same elemental materials.[17]

Shakespeare draws on this interconnected (or hybrid, as Latour would call it) quality of human and non-human nature everywhere in the tragedies, but nowhere more explicitly than in the storm scene in *King Lear*, where his language insists that tempestuous weather and emotional turmoil are not merely comparable but consubstantial. When he seeks Lear, Kent is told the king is

> Contending with the fretful element;
> Bids the wind blow the earth into the sea
> Or swell the curlèd waters 'bove the main,
> That things might change or cease; tears his white hair,
> Which the impetuous blasts, with eyeless rage,
> Catch in their fury and make nothing of;
> Strives in his little world of man to outstorm
> The to-and-fro-conflicting wind and rain.
>
> (*History of King Lear*, 8.2–10)

These lines portray an intimate dialogue between Lear's passions and those of the elements. Like speaks to like: Lear's voice bids and the wind blows; he tears his hair and the blasts catch at it; he 'strives in his little world of man' as wind and rain are 'to-and-fro conflicting'. Meanwhile, emotionally charged epithets transfer from Lear to the storm and back again: his fretfulness, impetuousness, rage, and fury are attributed to the blasting winds, while the contentiousness of wind and rain—even the very storminess of the storm—are Lear's. Man and weather are made of the same stuff, behaving in the same ways.

Such passages confirm Paster's assertion that we need to understand Shakespeare's portrayal of 'the passions and the body that houses them in ecological terms—that is, in terms of that body's reciprocal relation to the world … the passions of the early modern subject … are the winds and waves of the body, producing internal changes that the subject suffers as if they came from the outside.'[18] In his *Treatise of Melancholie* (1586), Timothie Bright refers to 'the stormy weather of internall discontentment', which is 'more troublesome, and boisterous to our nature, than all the blustering windes of the Ocean sea'.[19] Nor is it hard to think of other Shakespearean examples: Lear, 'mad as the vexed sea' (4.3.2); Hamlet, 'Mad as the sea and wind, when both contend | Which is the mightier' (4.1.6–7); Romeo, 'With tears augmenting the fresh morning's dew, | Adding to clouds more clouds with his deep sighs' (1.1.129–30). Moreover, if external nature is envisaged as coterminous with human passions and behaviour, while at the same time (as described above) the climate has within living memory become radically more unstable, it would seem inevitable that the early modern body's 'particular, historically specific relation to its immediate environment' should be, as Paster describes it, 'characterized not only by its physical openness but also by its emotional

---

[17] Gail Kern Paster, *Humoring the Body: Emotions and the Shakespearean Stage* (Chicago: University of Chicago Press, 2004), 4 (emphasis in original). For an excellent ecocritical application of Paster's work, to which I am much indebted, see Egan's *Green Shakespeare*, 97ff.

[18] Paster, *Humoring*, 18–19.

[19] Timothie Bright, *A Treatise of Melancholie* (London: Thomas Vautrollier, 1586), 96.

instability and volatility, by an internal microclimate knowable, like climates in the outer world, more for changeability than for stasis'.[20]

Thus Shakespeare's characters continually express their location within what Paster terms 'an ecology of the passions peculiar to the psychological materialism of early modern thought, which recognizes the influence of environment on the passions and the effect of human passions on the objective world outside self'.[21] Such a paradigm renders impossible two of the default dualisms characteristic of modern thought. First, for the early moderns it makes no sense to distinguish sharply between the mental (or psychological) and the physical (or physiological). For example the emotional state of melancholy, so vital to understanding several of Shakespeare's tragic heroes (including Romeo, Hamlet, and Macbeth) is not analogous to, or even a symptom of, the material presence in the body of black bile; rather, '[m]elancholia *is* black bile ... Black bile doesn't just cause melancholy; melancholy somehow resides in it'.[22] Second, the oppositional distinction between humans and nature, so fundamental to Latour's Modern Constitution, cannot apply if both comprise the same substance and are subject to the same processes—if the human world and the natural world are not just analogically correlated but materially cognate.

One further implication of this 'psychophysiology', as Paster calls it,[23] is that the nucleus of modern individualism familiar to us today—particularly the notion of the rational, consistent, self-contained, and self-determining will—cannot hold. Instead of deriving from a coherent motive located deep within the self, the behaviours, intentions, and actions of Shakespeare's characters are dispersed across a network of interrelating impulses, passions, drives, and influences, some deriving from the embodied mind and some from its exterior environment. To achieve anything, these characters must manage not only their fellow characters, but also the disparate collection of agencies both within their own bodies and in the external non-human environment. This is the intense struggle evoked by Lady Macbeth:

> Come, you spirits
> That tend on mortal thoughts, unsex me here,
> And fill me from the crown to the toe top-full
> Of direst cruelty. Make thick my blood,
> Stop up th'access and passage to remorse,
> That no compunctious visitings of nature
> Shake my fell purpose, nor keep peace between
> Th'effect and it. Come to my woman's breasts
> And take my milk for gall, you murd'ring ministers,
> Wherever, in your sightless substances
> You wait on nature's mischief. Come, thick night,
> And pall thee in the dunnest smoke of hell,
> That my keen knife see not the wound it makes,
> Nor heaven peep through the blanket of the dark
> To cry, 'Hold, hold!'

(1.4.39–53)

---

[20] Paster, *Humoring*, 19.   [21] Ibid., 42.
[22] Charles Taylor, *Sources of the Self: The Making of the Modern Identity* (Cambridge, MA.: Harvard University Press, 1989), 188–9 (emphasis added); cited in Paster, *Humoring*, 5.
[23] Paster, *Humoring*, 12.

In this speech two forms of nature are explicitly in conflict. Lady Macbeth vehemently rejects a model of orderly, harmonious nature when she demands freedom from the 'compunctious visitings of nature'—that is, her own supposedly endemic feminine nature, whose material substance is the breast-milk she wishes replaced with yellow bile or choler (gall), the humoral incarnation of ruthlessness. Repudiating the maternal place prepared for her in the naturalized social order, she invokes instead the disorderly form of natural agency that she names 'nature's mischief': a darkness that operates not as a mere absence of light but as a palpable matter that actively suppresses human senses: 'sightless substances', 'thick night', 'the dunnest smoke of Hell', 'the blanket of the dark'. As the play proceeds, this dark matter becomes increasingly pervasive and vigorous. 'By th'clock 'tis day, | And yet dark night strangles the travelling lamp', observes Ross after Duncan's death (2.4.6–7), while Macbeth, contemplating his next assassination, invokes an even more violently muscular natural mischief: 'Come, seeling night, | Scarf up the tender eye of pitiful day, | And with thy bloody and invisible hand | Cancel and tear to pieces that great bond | Which keeps me pale' (3.3.47–51). Night, here, has greater efficacy than day because it is more substantial and massy; indeed it is not just tangible but itself capable of taction—it can strangle, stifle, grasp, and tear asunder.

Lady Macbeth's invitation to the dark substances of external nature corresponds to her request that her body's internal environment be suffocated by congealed matter: 'Make thick my blood, | Stop up th'access and passage to remorse'. As Nicholas Brooke explains, in early modern psychophysiology, '[h]ealthy blood is clear, permitting the passage of "natural spirits" (in this case pity and fear) to the brain; "thick" blood obstructs their passage.'[24] When Lady Macbeth summons the 'spirits | That tend on mortal thoughts' she therefore refers not only, and perhaps not predominantly, to immaterial or demonic presences. In the context of the emphatic materialism of the entire speech, Shakespeare's contemporaries would just as readily take 'spirits' here to allude to another of the bodily substances that they understood to constitute and affect human emotions, senses and actions. 'As J. B. Bamborough suggests, "many Elizabethans had difficulty in thinking of an immaterial substance." Thus they posited the existence of animal spirits—bodily substance in its most rarefied form—moving in the neural pathways along the sinews …'.[25] Like Shakespeare's other tragic protagonists, both Macbeths are keenly attuned to—and make themselves subject to—the material agency of animal spirits. Macbeth ultimately overcomes his own irresolution by an interchange between his own bodily constituents and the external atmosphere surrounding him. Pausing just before Duncan's murder, he experiences a hallucination:

> Is this a dagger which I see before me,
> The handle toward my hand? Come, let me clutch thee.
> I have thee not, and yet I see thee still.
> Art thou not, fatal vision, sensible
> To feeling as to sight? Or art thou but
> A dagger of the mind, a false creation

[24] Nicholas Brooke, ed., *William Shakespeare: The Tragedy of Macbeth* (Oxford: Oxford University Press, 1990), 113.

[25] Paster, *Humoring*, 12; citing J. B. Bamborough, *The Little World of Man* (London: Longmans, Green, 1952), 30.

> Proceeding from the heat-oppressèd brain?
> I see thee yet, in form as palpable
> As this which now I draw.
> Thou marshall'st me the way that I was going,
> And such an instrument I was to use.
> Mine eyes are made the fools o'th' other senses,
> Or else worth all the rest. I see thee still,
> And on thy blade and dudgeon gouts of blood,
> Which was not so before. There's no such thing.
> It is the bloody business which informs
> Thus to mine eyes.
>
> (2.1.33–49)

These lines employ with precision the Galenic model according to which dreams, day-dreams, and visual delusions arise from an imbalance of humours. According to Bright, persons afflicted by melancholy are liable to 'phantasticall apparitions' caused 'not of absence of light only, but by a presence of a substantiall obscurity, which is possessed with an actuall power of operation'.[26] Reginald Scot's *Discoverie of Witchcraft* (1594) describes how the eye operates as a transfer-point between such external visions and internal humoral imbalances: vision occurs when

> the lightest and finest spirits, ascending into the highest parts of the head, doo fall into the eies, and so are from thence sent foorth, as being of all other parts of the bodie the most clear, and fullest of veines and pores, and with the verie spirit or vapor proceeding thence, is conveied out as it were bye beames and streames a certeine fierie force.[27]

In the case of the distempered person, therefore, 'the poison and disease in the eie infecteth the aire next unto it, and the same proceedeth further, carrieng with it the vapor and infection of the corrupted bloud'.[28] Bright's and Scot's accounts exactly match Macbeth's description of the dagger as a 'false creation | Proceeding from the heat-oppressèd brain'.

Macbeth's dagger, then, occurs because the very air into which his eyes are gazing becomes infected with his melancholic humour and its congealed fantasies. Such moments conform exactly to Paster's notion of an early modern 'ecology of the passions'; they 'disperse agency from the body out into the environment and back', in such a way that 'agency is vividly produced and just as vividly decentred'.[29] Macbeth alternates between interpreting the dagger as a phenomenon projected outwards from his brain, and as an invitation or command from the external environment. The distempered fluids in his body correspond to 'the bloody business' ahead of him, 'which informs | Thus to mine eyes' as if the murder were demanding to be carried out; the vision of the bloody dagger actively incites him to employ the metal knife 'which now I draw. | Thou marshall'st me the way that I was going, | And such an instrument I was to use'.

For both Macbeth and Lady Macbeth, the execution of their murderous and tyrannous intentions involves a struggle to command both their own natural agencies (the animal

---

[26] Bright, *Treatise* (1586), 103.

[27] Reginald Scot, *The Discoverie of Witchcraft* (1594), ed. Brinsley Nicholson (London: Elliot Stock, 1886), 41, 409.

[28] Ibid., 409.   [29] Paster, *Humoring*, 42.

spirits, blood, bile, gall and other substances that govern their minds and bodies) and the equivalents of those agencies in the non-human environment: 'Stars, hide your fires; | Let not light see my black and deep desires'; 'Thou sure and firm-set earth, | Hear not my steps, which way they walk, for fear | Thy very stones prate of my whereabout' (1.4.5–1; 2.1.56–8). The ungovernability of their own bodies, and of external nature, belongs to an epistemology of nature in which order, harmony, and health are just as likely—more than likely, in the tragedies—to give way to rebellion, disunity, and disequilibrium: as Bright puts it,

> while the body is in health, the humors beare no sway of private action, but it being once altered, and they evill disposed, and breaking from that regiment whereunto they should be subject, are so far from subjection to the disposition of our bodies, and strength of our partes, that they oppresse them, and ... despise that government, wherto by natures law they stand bound.[30]

This sense of rebellious forces at work within the body's own microcosmic ecology permeates the other tragedies as well. In *Othello*, for instance, Brabanzio portrays the passion felt by his daughter, a young Venetian maiden, for an older Moorish general as an affront to the set pattern that he believes should regulate nature and culture alike: Desdemona's desire occurs 'in spite of nature, | Of years, of country, credit, everything ... | Against all rules of nature ' (1.3.96–101). 'For nature so preposterously to err,' Brabanzio tells the Duke, 'Sans witchcraft could not' (1.3.62–4). Glossing *preposterously*, Michael Neill notes that '[t]he literal sense of the word is arsey-versey';[31] derived from the Latin *prae* (pre-) and *posterus* (later), it means 'before-afterish'. Neill offers the synonyms 'monstrously, perversely, contrary to the order of nature';[32] contrary, that is, to the supposedly stable order of nature-and-society invoked by patriarchs like Brabanzio and repudiated by the likes of Lady Macbeth. In *Othello*, as in *Macbeth*, another kind of nature predominates. Later in the same scene, Iago describes human 'nature' as inherently inclined to the preposterous: 'If the beam of our lives had not one scale of reason to peise another of sensuality, the blood and baseness of our natures would conduct us to most preposterous conclusions' (1.3.326–9). 'Preposterous' nature (here, opposed to reason and supposedly balanced by it) represents the tendency for nature to swerve in unexpected directions; to err, stray or drift from its course; to reverse, invert or disrupt its supposedly conventional order.

Thinking about the relationship between characters and their environments 'ecologically', as Paster suggests, allows us to perceive the Shakespearean stage as a network of engagements amongst a diverse and ever-changing set of agents. In so doing, of course, we respect the constitutively theatrical structure of Shakespeare's imagination. When Shakespeare's characters, as they often do, compare themselves explicitly to actors in a play, they draw attention to their placement within an ensemble of players of all kinds, wherein each role depends upon and responds to the unpredictable performances of all the others. By focusing on agency in this sense we also eschew the temptation to impose a modern, post-Romantic or post-Freudian psychology of personality on Shakespeare's characters, and we do a better job of responding to the psychophysiological epistemology

---

[30] Bright, *Treatise*, 92.   [31] Neill, *Othello*, 219.   [32] Ibid.

of the time, within which all kinds of agents were in operation, sometimes in collaboration and sometimes in conflict, both within and outside the human body.

Shakespeare himself sometimes uses the word 'agent' in just this way—especially when a character is working strenuously to try and impose his or her will upon a complex field of scattered action: for example when Macbeth resolves to marshal his jittery passions, organs, limbs, and humours in the service of his wife's plan: 'I am settled and bend up | Each corporal agent to this terrible feat' (1.7.79–80); or when he calls on the power of the various elements and organisms of external nature to assist in his next murder: 'Light thickens, and the crow | Makes wing to th' rooky wood. | Good things of day begin to droop and drowse, | Whiles night's black agents to their preys do rouse' (3.2.51–4). In both of these cases *agent* conforms to the primary meaning of the word in the *OED*—that is, '[a] person who or thing which acts upon someone or something; one who or that which exerts power; the doer of an action'—rather than the secondary sense of '[a] person who acts as a substitute for another'.[33] These usages also correspond to the conceptualization of agency in the Actor Network Theory espoused by Latour and deployed by Bennett, in which the word *agent* (used more or less interchangeably with *actant* or *actor*) signifies 'a source of action that can be either human or non-human; … that which has efficacy, can *do* things, has sufficient coherence to make a difference, produce effects, alter the course of events'.[34]

Like Latour's networks, Shakespeare's plays are motivated by the interaction of multiple agencies of many kinds: some are human and some intra-human (humours, organs, limbs, animal spirits); some are artefacts (weapons, letters, drugs, poisons, alcohol, and at least one handkerchief), some are non-human organisms (trees, plants, snakes) and some are non-human inorganic elements (brooks, seas, storms, stars, planets, darkness, light). Often, events turn on the agency of some component of nature that proves highly ambivalent, unpredictable, or even treacherous.

The most obvious candidates for rebellious natural agency, apart from humans and their bodily parts and properties, are of course non-human animals. Yet actual animals— as distinct from allusions to animals, which are very common—feature very rarely on Shakespeare's stage. *Macbeth* contains a great many references to animals, which do indeed contribute to the play's overall sense of nature as a field of wildly unruly agencies,[35] but they are made present to the audience only imaginatively, via descriptive rhetoric: the 'temple-haunting martlet' that misleads Banquo and Duncan about the benign nature of Dunsinane (1.6.1–6), the raven croaking himself hoarse on Lady Macbeth's battlements (1.5.37–9), the bat in its 'cloistered flight' and the 'shard-borne beetle' summoned by Macbeth to create the kind of atmosphere sympathetic to his intentions (3.2.43–5), the witches' ingredient-list of anxiogenic animals, which includes toad, fenny snake, newt, frog, bat, dog, adder, blind-worm, lizard, owlet, dragon, wolf, shark, goat, tiger, baboon (4.1.1–38).

Only on one occasion does a (supposedly) live animal appear onstage in Shakespeare's tragedies: the asp in *Anthony and Cleopatra*. Imagery of serpents, of course, features

---

[33] *OED*, 'agent, n.', 1a and 2a.   [34] Bennett, *Vibrant Matter*, p. viii.
[35] For an enlightening discussion of animals in *Macbeth* see Richard Kerridge, 'An Ecocritic's *Macbeth*', in *Ecocritical Shakespeare*, ed. Lynne Bruckner and Dan Brayton (Farnham: Ashgate, 2011), 193–210.

importantly in that play well before the final scene—most strikingly in Anthony's description of that 'strange serpent', the crocodile: 'It is shaped, sir, like itself, and it is as broad
as it has breadth. It is just so high as it is, and moves with it own organs' (2.7.41–7). Neill
reads these lines as a tautological parody of the play's 'Roman' philosophy, whereby identity requires 'absolute self consistency and singleness of being', which he contrasts with the
'Egyptian' paradox 'by which opposites flourish in mysterious complementarity'.[36] This
'Egyptian' mode is another manifestation of the kind of preposterous natural agency discussed above—as exemplified when the asp arrives onstage in the final scene. Here the
snake embodies all the animate, protean, slippery, and contrary tendencies of non-human
nature. Shakespeare has the asp brought to the queen by a rustic clown, whose foolish language emphasizes the self-contradictory nature of the animal in his basket. '[H]is biting is
immortal', he asserts; 'those that die of it do seldom or never recover' (5.2.246–7). Although
there could hardly be an animal more freighted with symbolic associations (Biblical, erotic,
maternal, and sepulchral)[37] the snake here also functions as a material agent, whose effects leave corporeal and environmental traces for the Romans to discover after Cleopatra's
death: the 'vent of blood, and something blown' on the queen's breast and arm, and the trail
of slime left on the fig-leaves (5.2.346–51). In opposition to the 'Roman' model of self-contained and singular identity, the asp emerges from a rich compost of literary and cultural
traditions, just as (according to the early modern natural history utilised by Shakespeare)
it is generated out of the fertile mud left by the seasonal flooding of 'the ambivalent river
Nile, whose "mud" and "slime" are at once the signs of mortal corruption and the philopro-
genitive source of spontaneous life'.[38] Its primary quality as a natural agent, moreover, is its
unpredictability. '[T]his is most falliable', the clown warns Cleopatra: 'the worm's an odd
worm' (5.2.256). In Shakespeare's usage 'odd' most often means 'eccentric, peculiar', but it
carries connotations of chance and of enmity or disagreement.[39] When Cleopatra seeks further reassurance 'that the worm will do his kind'—that is, act according to its nature—the
clown responds, 'Look you, the worm is not to be trusted but in the keeping of wise people'
(5.2.258–61).

Cleopatra's asp is also odd in that most of the active non-human organic agents in
Shakespearean tragedy are not animals, but plants or their derivatives. An obvious example is provided by the narcotic herbal distillation supplied by Friar Laurence in *Romeo and
Juliet*, which, in conjunction with a second non-human organic agent, the 'infectious pes-
tilence' that prevents Brother John from leaving for Mantua with the explanatory letter to
Romeo (5.2.5–16), provides the catalyst for the tragic events of the final scene: Juliet's feigned
death, Romeo's suicide (itself accomplished by another herbal distillation, poisonous this

---

[36] Michael Neill, ed., *William Shakespeare: Anthony and Cleopatra* (Oxford: Oxford University
Press, 1994), 102.

[37] See Neill's discussion of these symbolic meanings of the asp: Ibid., 124–5; also Egan, *Green
Shakespeare*, 108–19.

[38] Neill, *Anthony and Cleopatra*, 125 n. 1. For an extended discussion of the association of both
the Nile and the asp with the potent fecundity of nature, see Edward J. Geisweidt, ' "The Nobleness
of Life": Spontaneous Generation and Excremental Life in *Antony and Cleopatra*', in *Ecocritical
Shakespeare*, 89–103.

[39] David Crystal and Ben Crystal, *Shakespeare's Words: A Glossary and Language Companion*
(London: Penguin, 2002), 303.

time), Juliet's suicide. Friar Laurence of all people should have anticipated the potential for nature's agents to act so capriciously. He first appears in the play gathering herbs at dawn, and explains at length the opposing vices and virtues endemic to all 'plants, herbs, stones, and their true qualities': brandishing an example, he concludes, 'Within the rind of this weak flower | Poison hath residence and medicine power' (2.2.16, 23–4).

Many kinds of vegetal agency play crucial roles in Shakespeare's tragic action. The flowers and herbs worn and carried by King Lear and Ophelia operate (to use another term of Latour's) as 'quasi-subjects'; they do not possess subjectivity, yet they have the non-human equivalent of a speaking role. As she distributes her flowers, Ophelia begins by spelling out their significance, but after the first couple she merely names them and allows them to speak for themselves: 'There's rosemary, that's for remembrance.... There's fennel for you ... There's rue for you; and here's some for me ... There's a daisy. I would give you violets, but they withered all when my father died' (Hamlet 4.5.175–84). For Shakespeare's audience, the impact of this distribution would not be merely or even primarily symbolic; accepting the complex interactions between external nature (including plants and their extracts) and the internal ecology of the body, they would perceive the flowers as embodiments and effectors of emotional states rather than just metaphors for them. Rebecca Laroche suggests John Gerard's *Herball* (1597) as an index to the popularly-accepted potencies of Ophelia's bouquets.[40] There we find that the flowers of rosemary 'quicken the senses and memory'; fennel 'openeth the obstructions or stoppings' of various organs including the liver,[41] understood to be the source of powerful emotions;[42] daisies 'purgeth the head mightilie of foule and filthie slimie humours'; violets 'sofeneth the bellie, and purgeth choler'; and rue, amongst a host of medicinal qualities, 'is good for the mother'[43]— that condition of emotional prostration experienced by King Lear as it 'swells up toward [his] heart! | *Hysterica passio*' (2.2.231–2).

Ophelia's flowers, then, are a collection of powerful calmatives, supposedly capable of mitigating dangerous passions and pernicious humoral imbalances. Accordingly their presence onstage—where they remain, of course, after Ophelia and Gertrude exit, and while Laertes and Claudius plan Hamlet's death—is bitterly ironic: Ophelia's madness continues, and shortly results in her death, upon which Laertes' vengeful rage redoubles, while Claudius' murderous nature remains unaffected. Once again, the idealized vision of a harmonious and ordered nature, according to which plant remedies should counterbalance the virulent passions at work in human society, proves far less potent than the kind of preposterous and errant nature represented by other kinds of vegetal properties: those plants, and their derivatives, that instead have the power to cause imbalances, disorders and lethal effects in the ecologies of the body and society. Examples of such herbal miscreants include the 'cursèd hebenon' that Claudius pours in his brother's ear, 'whose effect | Holds such an enmity with blood of man' that 'it does posset | And curd ... | The thin and wholesome blood' (1.5.62–70); the 'unction' with which Laertes anoints his sword, more powerful than any 'cataplasm' (remedy) made from medicinal herbs (4.7.114–119); and the 'mixture rank of midnight weeds collected' by Lucianus, which possesses a 'natural magic

---

[40] Rebecca Laroche, 'Ophelia's Flowers and the Death of Violets', in *Ecocritical Shakespeare*, 216–17.
[41] John Gerard, *The Herball or Generall Historie of Plantes* (London: John Norton, 1597), 1110, 878.
[42] Paster, *Humoring*, 26–7.   [43] Gerard, *Herball*, 512, 702, 1072.

and dire property' capable of usurping 'wholesome life' (3.2.245–8).[44] In *Macbeth*, similarly, the witches' cauldron includes 'Root of hemlock digged i'the' dark' and the 'slips of
yew | Slivered in the moon's eclipse' (4.1.25, 27–8).[45]

Not only plant derivatives but also plants themselves play decisive roles in *Hamlet*. In
Gertrude's description of Ophelia's death, a tree, or more particularly one of its branches,
is the precipitating agent:

> There is a willow grows aslant a brook
> That shows his hoar leaves in the glassy stream.
> Therewith fantastic garlands did she make
> Of crow-flowers, nettles, daisies, and long purples …
> There on the pendant boughs her coronet weeds
> Clamb'ring to hang, an envious sliver broke,
> When down her weedy trophies and herself
> Fell in the weeping brook. Her clothes spread wide;
> And, mermaid-like, awhile they bore her up;
> Which time she chanted snatches of old tunes,
> As one incapable of her own distress,
> Or like a creature native and endued
> Unto that element. But long it could not be
> Till that her garments, heavy with their drink,
> Pull'd the poor wretch from her melodious lay
> To muddy death.

(4.7.138–55)

The weeping willow's strong and flexible branches have long supplied the material for
garlands, while the tree's growth habit associates it with sorrow.[46] Both of these material
aspects of the tree draw the grieving Ophelia to it, and position her over the river: the first
two lines of Gertrude's speech emphasize the fatal inclination of the tree in the direction
of the water. The other ingredients of Ophelia's 'fantastic garland' also contribute to her
destiny: 'crow-flowers', according to Gerard, 'are not used either in medicine or in nourishment: but they serve for garlands and crowns'.[47] In place of the healing herbs she preferred previously, Ophelia now seeks flowers associated with the decorative impulse that
will be the death of her. The lines that follow persistently shift agency from the human to
the non-human elements: in the crucial phrase, the subject of the main clause is the 'envious sliver' that breaks, while the dependent clauses before and after emphasize Ophelia's
'crownet weeds', whose hanging from the 'pendent boughs' motivates her 'clamb'ring' up
the tree in the first place, and those same 'weedy trophies', whose downward fall into the
stream she (represented only by the object pronoun 'herself') merely accompanies. From
that point, the agents of Ophelia's death are the water itself and her clothes, which eventually weigh her down. In Gertrude's account, then, the drowning results from the coopera-
tion of agencies closely interrelated by shared qualities and propensities: weeping willow,
flowery wreaths, pendant boughs, hanging weeds, broken branch, fallen weeds, weeping

---

[44] See Paster's superb exegesis of these lines in *Humoring*, 55.
[45] 'The Yew tree, as Galen reporteth, is of a venomous qualitie, and against mans nature' (Gerard,
Herball, 1188).
[46] G. R. Hibbard, ed.,*William Shakespeare: Hamlet* (Oxford: Oxford University Press, 1987), 318.
[47] Gerard, *Herball*, 481.

brook, waterlogged garments, clinging mud. Ophelia is utterly immersed in this network of natural agents, 'like a creature native and endued | Unto that element';[48] thereby her capacity for separate human agency, her ability to remove herself from what the environment does to her, is diluted virtually to nothing: she drifts passively, first carried by the stream and then taken down by it, 'incapable of her own distress'.

Just as in *Macbeth* Shakespeare follows Duncan's murder with the comic Porter's drunken disquisition on the effects of alcohol upon the body's capacity to act, in *Hamlet* he follows the news of Ophelia's death with an extended comic litigation of agency, as two rustic clowns debate whether or not she should be entitled to a Christian burial. This of course depends on whether or not she intentionally committed suicide. The First Clown, who is digging her grave, spells out the issue in a parody of legal language:

> if I drown myself wittingly, it argues an act; and an act hath three branches: it is to act, to do, and to perform. Argal she drowned herself wittingly ... If the man go to this water and drown himself, it is, will he nill he, he goes. Mark you that. But if the water come to him and drown him, he drowns not himself; argal he that is not guilty of his own death shortens not his own life. (5.1.1–20)

In spite of the gravedigger's scepticism, the redundancy of his language (*act, do,* and *perform* are actually synonyms here) emphasizes precisely the overwhelming impression created by Gertrude's account—that it is not primarily Ophelia who makes the drowning occur. Accordingly the coroner, as the Second Clown attests, has found that Ophelia's death was not suicide—a verdict that identifies her as the passive recipient of agencies at work in her body (the disrupted passions that comprise her madness) and outside of it: broken willow-branch, brook, drenched garments. As John Kerrigan suggests, *Hamlet* as a whole 'revolves around the question, what might action be? Everybody in the play seems to have a different answer, whether it is the prince, the first gravedigger (dividing "an act" into "three branches"), or those men who make acting their profession, the troupe of travelling players.[49] Shakespeare's attentiveness to the decisive roles played by natural matter in its myriad forms invites bodies other than just human ones to suggest their own answers to this question.

Plants and trees, then, in Shakespeare's tragedies, become witnesses to the unpredictability of nature. Who would expect a branch of the willow, a tree whose 'woode is white, tough, and hard to be broken',[50] 'envious[ly]' (a word that in Shakespeare usually means 'spitefully')[51] to betray the weight of a young woman? The tragedies insist, over and over, that nothing in nature can be taken for granted; that nature will always generate unpredictable effects.

To attend to the multiple kinds of agency at work in Shakespeare's tragedies, then, is to read his theatre as the kind of environmental field, simultaneously natural and cultural, envisaged by Bennett, in which '[a]ll forces and flows (materialities) are or can become lively, affective, and signaling. And so an affective, speaking human body is not *radically*

---

[48] In Shakespearean usage 'endued' could mean both *endowed* or *supplied with* and *led into*: see Crystal and Crystal, *Shakespeare's Words*, 238.

[49] John Kerrigan, *Revenge Tragedy: Aeschylus to Armageddon* (Oxford: Oxford University Press, 1998), 4.

[50] Gerard, *Herball*, 1202.   [51] Crystal and Crystal, *Shakespeare's Words*, 154.

different from the affective, signaling non-humans with which it coexists'.[52] This is not to say, of course, that no distinctions at all can be made amongst the various vibrant actors or the parts they enact. But, while portions of the field 'congeal into bodies' (or onstage, into characters), these are never the sole source of agency: '[t]he source of effects is, rather, always an ontologically diverse assemblage of energies and bodies, of the physical and the physiological.'[53]

Reconsidering Shakespeare's embodiment of the natural world thus allows us to step outside the confines imposed by the Modern Constitution, and to consider how differently we might conceive the agencies and relationships that constitute our own experience of 'nature' today. In this respect, by seeking imaginatively to inhabit Shakespeare's nature, if only for the few hours of a performance, we can hope to offset some of the shortcomings of our own young remembrance—the tendency for each generation to assume the conditions of its world comprise the perpetual and the necessary state of things.

Select Bibliography

Boehrer, Bruce, *Shakespeare Among the Animals* (Houndmills: Palgrave, 2006).

Brayton, Dan, *Shakespeare's Ocean: An Ecocritical Exploration* (Charlottesville and London: University of Virginia Press, 2012).

Bruckner, Lynne, and Brayton, Dan (eds.) *Ecocritical Shakespeare* (Farnham: Ashgate, 2011).

Egan, Gabriel, *Green Shakespeare: From Ecopolitics to Ecocriticism* (London and New York: Routledge, 2006).

Estok, Simon C., *Ecocriticism and Shakespeare: Reading Ecophobia* (New York: Palgrave Macmillan, 2011).

Feerick, Jean E., 'Economies of Nature in Shakespeare', *Shakespeare Studies* 39 (2011), 32–42.

Fudge, Erica, 'Renaissance Animal Things', *New Formations* 76 (2012), 86–100.

Höfele, Andreas, *Stage, Stake and Scaffold: Humans and Animals in Shakespeare's Theatre* (Oxford: Oxford University Press, 2011).

Markley, Robert, ' "Summer's Lease': Shakespeare (and Others) in the Little Ice Age', in *Early Modern Ecostudies from the Florentine Codex to Shakespeare*, ed. Ivo Kamps et al. (New York: Palgrave Macmillan), 131–42.

Mentz, Stephen, *At the Bottom of Shakespeare's Ocean* (London: Continuum, 2009).

Paster, Gail Kern, *Humoring the Body: Emotions and the Shakespearean Stage* (Chicago: University of Chicago Press, 2004).

Robertson, Jean Addison, *The Shakespearean Wild: Geography, Genus, and Gender* (University of Nebraska Press, 1991).

Shannon, Laurie, *The Accommodated Animal: Cosmopolity in Shakespearean Locales* (Chicago: University of Chicago Press, 2013).

[52] Bennett, *Vibrant Matter*, 117 (emphasis in original).

[53] Ibid.

CHAPTER 8

···

SHAKESPEAREAN TRAGEDY
AND THE LANGUAGE
OF LAMENT

···

LYNNE MAGNUSSON

MANY have claimed that 'the life of Shakespeare's plays is in the language' and its fullest expression is in the tragedies.[1] The creation of a highly individuated voice for each tragic hero and the development of the solitary and inward-turned speech form of the soliloquy are the achievements most usually associated with the language of Shakespearean tragedy. This essay proposes a different emphasis. It begins not with claims about unique individual voices and solitary speech but instead suggests that two apparently opposed kinds of social discourse need attention as mainstays of Shakespearean tragedy. One is not individual speech but dialogic exchanges, the complex speech dynamics of verbal encounters (sometimes highly fraught, sometimes quiet and subtle) that rehearse in microcosm the plays' distinctive tragic situations or conflicts. The second is the passionate speech of woeful lament, the grieving rhetoric that, in one kind or other, invariably attends the suffering of tragedy. Exemplifying the first case, we might consider the speech dynamic of an interaction like Caesar's 'Forget not … | To touch Calpurnia' and Antony's reply, 'I shall remember: | When Caesar says 'Do this', it is performed'; or look at the patterning of Kent's initial confrontation with Lear or Iago's seductive conversations with Othello.[2] Exemplifying the second case, Titus Andronicus, for instance, exclaims, 'My tears are now prevailing orators!'; or the Queens in *The Tragedy of Richard III*, who are 'copious in exclaims', bemoan 'Ah, who hath any cause to mourn but we?'; or Lear calls upon 'thou all-shaking thunder' to 'Smite flat the thick rotundity of the world'; or Cleopatra grieves, 'O see, my women, | The crown o'th' earth doth melt'; or Hamlet laments his incapacity to

---

[1] Frank Kermode, *Shakespeare's Language* (London: Penguin Books, 2000), 4.

[2] For a dialogic approach emphasizing the social life of language, see Lynne Magnusson, *Shakespeare and Social Dialogue: Dramatic Language and Elizabethan Letters* (Cambridge: Cambridge University Press, 1999), 141–53 and 163–82. For dialogue in relation to the changing vernacular, see Sylvia Adamson, 'Questions of Identity in Renaissance Drama: New Historicism Meets Old Philology', *Shakespeare Quarterly* 61:1 (Spring 2010), 5–77.

grieve.[3] These laments fill and reverberate throughout the tragic theatre, not just as inert expressions of woe but as eloquent performances and as petitions demanding response.

These two cases are of equal importance to an understanding of the language of tragedy, but it is the second I will focus on in this essay. In this first case, we can see Shakespeare's genius at observing and assimilating the potential of the quickly changing vernacular and the complexity and interest of the social life in the everyday conversations happening all around him. In the second case, Shakespeare initially took materials not directly from life but from a developing Elizabethan dramatic tradition and, above all, from a widely shared Renaissance rhetorical culture and the Elizabethan schoolroom's lessons in the classical arts of language—that is, in oratory, grammar, and poetic imitation, all applied to the Latin language. I focus on the tragic rhetoric of grief by addressing five aspects or modes of the passionate lament: the lament as set speech, in copious variation, as situated interaction, as imitated passion, and, most important, as a transaction with the audience.

THE LAMENT AS SET SPEECH

Extensive as the criticism on Shakespeare's tragic soliloquies has been (especially as they are invested in arguments about the invention of subjectivity), there are simply too few of them to consider soliloquies the most prevalent form of tragic expression. If we ask what speech form Shakespeare's own plays and those of his contemporaries most consistently identify with tragedy, the passionate lament moves centre-stage. *The Most Lamentable Romaine Tragedie of Titus Andronicus* is what appears on the title-page of Shakespeare's first tragedy, printed in 1594. In *A Midsummer Night's Dream*, the humour of Peter Quince's genre-confusing '*The Most Lamentable Comedy and Most Cruel Death of Pyramus and Thisbe*' (1.2.11–12) relies on the hearers' recognition of a stereotype for tragedy, as does the parody in *Romeo and Juliet* of lament—'O lamentable day!' | 'O woeful time!' (4.4.57)—when the Nurse discovers Juliet's apparent death. Indeed, Giorgio Valla, the first Renaissance humanist to translate Aristotle's *Poetics* into Latin, wrote that 'the aim of tragedy is to produce or reproduce tears and lamentations'.[4] The parodic references in Shakespeare to stereotypical forms of lament, it needs to be emphasized, should not prevent us from recognizing the serious engagement throughout Shakespeare's tragedies with the rhetoric of grief.

Consensus on how to define Renaissance tragedy, or specifically Shakespearean tragedy, beyond emphasis on its dire ending, is hard to come by, but what none of Shakespeare's great tragedies exclude is the copious improvisation and eloquent voicing of grief. However

---

[3] *Julius Caesar* 1.2.8–12; *Titus Andronicus* 3.1.26; *The Tragedy of King Richard III* 4.4.135, 34; *The History of King Lear* (The Quarto Text), scene 9 [3.2].6–7; *Antony and Cleopatra* 4.16.64–5; Shakespeare's plays are quoted from William Shakespeare, *The Complete Plays*, 2nd edn., gen. eds. Stanley Wells and Gary Taylor (Oxford: Clarendon Press, 2005); henceforth cited parenthetically in the text.

[4] Quoted from Timothy J. Reiss, 'Renaissance Theatre and the Theory of Tragedy', *The Cambridge History of Literary Criticism*, vol. 3: *The Renaissance*, ed. Glyn P. Norton (Cambridge: Cambridge University Press, 1999), 237.

specific the situations in Shakespeare's tragedies that call this forth, the demand for language to lament touches upon a communal need that no audience member can disavow, the shared recurring dilemma of how to find words for our woes and how to respond in the paralysing presence of others' grief. The rhetorical predicament Albany puts so simply at the end of *King Lear* (Quarto Text), 'The weight of this sad time we must obey, | Speak what we feel, not what we ought to say' (scene 24 [5.3].318–19), is our own dilemma, whether past or future. Our twenty-first-century schools and universities, unlike those of the sixteenth century, offer no explicit place in the curriculum for lessons in the language of impassioned grief. One central argument of this essay will concern what lessons in passionate lament Shakespeare's schooling offered the potential tragedian and how he explored and improvised on this instruction in his tragic language.

Wolfgang Clemen is especially interesting in recognizing the importance of the 'formal set-speech lament'. He traced the artificial conventions of this form in sixteenth-century English tragedy preceding Shakespeare, identifying its classical and especially Senecan inheritance and characterizing it as 'the *locus classicus*' in these plays 'for diction heightened by rhetorical adornment'.[5] The characteristic tropes he spells out in these hyperbolic emotional set pieces are readily illustrated in Shakespeare's plays, whether in their most obvious forms and abundant accumulation in early tragedies like *Titus Andronicus* and *Richard III* or varied and adapted in the still-hyperbolic woes of later tragedies like *King Lear* or *Antony and Cleopatra*. Apostrophe and appeal, whether to gods, to fortune, to grief itself, or to the elements is a foundational trope of lament,[6] as in Titus' vocative 'O earth, I will befriend thee more with rain' (3.1.16) or Lear's famous address to the storm:

> Blow, wind, and crack your cheeks! Rage, blow,
> You cataracts and hurricanoes, spout
> Till you have drenched the steeples, drowned the cocks!
> You sulphurous and thought-executing fires,
> Vaunt-couriers to oak-cleaving thunderbolts,
> Singe my white head; and thou all-shaking thunder,
> Smite flat the thick rotundity of the world,
> Crack nature's mould, all germens spill at once
> That make ingrateful man.
>
>   (scene 9 [3.2].1–9)

Clemen emphasizes apostrophe as adorned diction, but one can readily see how this mode of speech can evoke at once a speaker's powerlessness and frustrated will to power. In this, in insisting on the limits of human agency, Shakespearean tragedies are true to their classical originals. Related to apostrophe, the call or petition for annihilation or universal extinction exhibited in Lear's speech is another commonplace formula.[7] What seems most evidently to imprint a Shakespearean accent upon this exploitation of the formulaic *topos* in Lear's grandiloquent lament, in the minds of many critics, is the play of contrastive registers that is so often noted as a mark of his tragic diction: lines of monosyllables stretched taut set against polysyllabic word rhythms and compound epithets. Sylvia Adamson has

---

[5] Wolfgang Clemen, *English Tragedy Before Shakespeare: The Development of Dramatic Speech*, trans. T. S. Dorsch (London: Methuen & Co. Ltd., 1961), 213, 214.

[6] Clemen, *English Tragedy*, 226, 233.   [7] Clemen, *English Tragedy*, 246–52.

commented that 'interweav[ing] latinate and Saxon' is, by mid-sixteenth century, 'the norm for the grand style',[8] and, so, perhaps as much a sign of Shakespeare's mastery of a prescribed style for tragedy as a distinguishing mark.

Another basic syntactic form Clemen identifies as characteristic of lament set-speeches is the rhetorical question, or a repetitive battery of questions. This form serves as a foundation-piece of the Queens' lamentations in *Richard III*: 'Wilt thou, O God, fly from such gentle lambs | And throw them in the entrails of the wolf?' (Queen Elizabeth, 4.4.22–3). The rhetorical question can become a malleable vehicle not only for the interrogation of the personal suffering by the helpless speaker but also for framing the larger, Job-like questions of existence: 'Why should a dog, a horse, a rat have life, | And thou no breath at all?' (*Lear*, scene 24 [5.3].301–2). Clemen also shows how the lamenter's thought and questions readily turn to the paradoxically common refrain of extreme suffering—that no one apart from the speaker has suffered like woes: 'Ah, who hath any cause to mourn but we?' (*Richard III*, Queen Elizabeth, 4.4.34). He elaborates on the *'plange mecum'* topos in pre-Shakespearean tragedy, where grief seeks relief in company. We find Shakespeare exploiting it in Queen Margaret's directive to the assembled Queens, 'If sorrow can admit society, | Tell o'er your woes again by viewing mine' (4.4.38–9); in Edgar's self-consoling 'grief hath mates, and bearing fellowship' (*Lear*, scene 13 [3.6].100); in Titus' plea to stones rather than tribunes to receive his tears ('A stone is soft as wax, tribunes more hard than stones', 3.1.44). Nonetheless, when the speaker's woes are set in relation to those of others, it is generally their singularity that is highlighted, amplified by means of another characteristic formula, the 'outbidding topos'. Clemen's thoroughgoing survey of the Renaissance set-speech of lament also details how it draws upon classical types—Hecuba, Priam, and Niobe—as ultimate patterns and precedents for the mourner.[9] As we shall discuss later, it is this lament *topos* that is in the background of Hamlet's meditation on the skilful play-actor's tears, 'What's Hecuba to him, or he to Hecuba, | That he should weep for her?' (2.2.561–2).

For all the care Clemen takes to delineate the available linguistic resources for the Elizabethan dramatic lament, he asks, however, 'whether the smoke-screen of commonplaces and rhetorical devices laid over the expression of grief … is so thick as entirely to cloak all personal feeling'. Language occludes emotion, he concludes: 'the emotional speech remains a derivative product, a linguistic structure organized by the intellect, and not a spontaneous expression of the feelings.'[10] Given Shakespeare's evident exploitation of these conventional resources to frame the passionate expression of extreme suffering, both in his early and his mature tragedies, one might wonder if his verbal inventiveness, what is original and significant in his tragic utterance, must be sought elsewhere. This would be a mistake. Two important reasons immediately come to mind. First, the critical importance within the rhetorical culture that fostered Shakespeare's linguistic achievements of eloquence and of what Erasmus calls *copia*, stands quite at odds with Clemen's derogation of artifice and of the commonplace. Second, Shakespeare's engagement with passionate lament as a fully situated rhetorical speech act or an interaction genre with a pragmatic function lies at the heart of tragedy: it is not merely a type of expressive set-speech.

---

[8] Sylvia Adamson, 'Literary Language', in *The Cambridge History of the English Language*, vol. 3, *1476-776*, ed. Roger Lass (Cambridge: Cambridge University Press, 1999), 539–653 (574).

[9] Clemen, *English Tragedy*, 23–1.   [10] Clemen, *English Tragedy*, 215, 257.

THE LAMENT AND *COPIA*

Rhetorical instruction called for a grand style as the requisite decorum of tragedy, motivating the unembarrassed exploitation of language at its fullest stretch. And it was precisely the abundant repetition and variation of commonplace expressions that was cultivated and valued in the language arts so central to Tudor rhetorical culture and grammarschool education. The most important humanist work adapting classical oratorical training to the Renaissance schoolroom was Desiderius Erasmus' 'Copia: Foundations of the Abundant Style' (*De duplici copia verborum ac rerum commentarii duo*), intended to guide the daily rhetorical practice of schoolboys. Erasmus drew upon the authority of Cicero and Quintilian in elevating to central place the value of a copious style or eloquence built upon amplification: 'The speech of a man is a magnificent and impressive thing when it surges along like a golden river, with thoughts and words pouring out in rich abundance.'[11] As Cicero claimed in *De oratore*, 'the highest distinction of eloquence consists in amplification ... which can be used to make one's speech not only increase the importance of a subject but raise it to the highest level'.[12] To illustrate the practices he recommended, Erasmus drew commonplace expressions from everyday life ('Your letter mightily pleased me' and, addressed to his friend Thomas More, 'Always, as long as I live, I shall remember you') and demonstrated his rhetorical virtuosity by repeating and varying their expression in hundreds of ways.[13] In the expression of grief recurrently demanded by scenes of suffering in tragedy, Shakespeare might be said to have discovered a commonplace rhetorical situation or theme to serve as a performance space for his fertile powers of inventive variation. Indeed, in *King Lear*, Edgar alludes directly to technical terms from classical rhetoric related to copious variation—*amplificatio* and *periodos*—when he characterizes the expression requisite to the situation's extremities of suffering, commenting on how one pitiful speech, occasioned by Gloucester's death 'would have seemed a period | To such as love not sorrow; but another' [occasioned by Kent's 'piteous tale of Lear and him'], | To amplify too much would make much more, | And top extremity' (scene 24 [5.3].201–4, 211).

In tragedies like *Titus Andronicus* and *Richard III* at the outset of his career, Shakespeare developed and improvised upon the grand style and his schoolroom's lessons in copious oratory as the means to 'produce' and 'reproduce tears and lamentations'.[14] He afterward played variations throughout his tragic career on these inventions, repeating, improvising, restraining, and varying these first experiments. In what follows I look at how this basic tragic speech act of passionate lament in Shakespeare's plays is built upon the historically specific values, practices, and affects inculcated in the Elizabethan schoolroom and then how Shakespeare's improvisations, adaptations, and startling variations turn such lessons (both the schools' direct and inadvertent forms of instruction) into the most prized tragic art. *Titus*, with its grotesquely excessive violence and its over-the-top

---

[11] Desiderius Erasmus, 'Copia: Foundations of the Abundant Style' (*De duplici copia verborum ac rerum commentarii duo*), trans. Betty I. Knott, in *Collected Works of* Erasmus, vol. 24, ed. Craig R. Thompson (Toronto: University of Toronto Press, 1978), 279–659 (295).

[12] Cicero, *De oratore*, trans. H. Rackham, Loeb Classical Library 348 and 349 (Cambridge, MA: Harvard University Press, 1942), 3.26.104.

[13] Erasmus, 'Copia', 349, 354.   [14] Valla, from Reiss, 'Renaissance Theatre', 237.

match between a heightened and ornamental style and dire horrors, hardly strikes one as a model for effective tragic utterance, yet it can fruitfully be read as apprentice work in which Shakespeare tests out the linguistic resources acquired through his schooling. This does not simply involve the ornamental amplification of passionate set-speeches. It involves a highly self-conscious exploration of the rhetorical situation of passionate utterance.

THE LAMENT AND INTERACTION

As a backdrop to effects explored in its passionate orations, *Titus Andronicus* draws on a classical ideal of the orator as the guarantor of civic discourse. Few books or writers are explicitly named in Shakespeare's plays, but this tragedy refers directly to 'Tully's *Orator*' (4.1.14), cueing the reader to its engagement with foundational ideals concerning the power of oratory and the persuasive force of eloquent language. Cicero's much-loved book identified the power of speech and the eloquence of the orator as what creates and sustains social communities, political states, and their judicial underpinnings:

> there is to my mind no more excellent thing than the power, by means of oratory, to get a hold on assemblies of men, win their good will, direct their inclinations wherever the speaker wishes, or divert them from whatever he wishes…. For the one point in which we have our very greatest advantage over the brute creation is that we hold converse one with another…. To come … to the highest achievements of eloquence, what other power could have been strong enough either to gather scattered humanity into one place, or to lead it out of its brutish existence in the wilderness up to our present condition of civilization as men and as citizens, or, after the establishment of social communities, to give shape to laws, tribunals, and civic rights?[15]

At the end of *Titus*, even as 'floods of tears' threaten to 'drown' the Roman lords' 'oratory | And break [their] utt'rance', Titus's brother Marcus echoes Cicero's vision as he seeks to reassert the cohesive power of eloquence: 'O, let me teach you how to knit again | This scattered corn into one mutual sheaf, | These broken limbs again into one body' (5.3.89–90, 69–71). My point here is that within this rhetorical culture, a carefully wrought speech (for example, any one of Titus' passionate laments) is not imagined or judged by its capacity to represent or express a state of mind or emotional situation. An oration is, first and foremost, oriented to an audience: it addresses a listener, it presses its designs and purposes upon its hearers. It is as pragmatic as it is expressive. A passionate oration is oriented more specifically in its persuasive strategies to *pathos*—to securing the sympathetic identification of the speaker's interlocutors in order to affect their emotions, change their minds, reorient their actions.

One paradigmatic speech situation repeatedly modelled in the Elizabethan schoolroom's ancient rhetoric texts was that of the forensic orator, the lawyer pleading before his client's judges. This is an oddity not always noted in accounts of rhetoric as a centrepiece in the Tudor schoolroom, the orientation of the most-used classical textbooks (like the *Rhetorica*

---

[15] Cicero, *De oratore*, 1.8.30–3.

Ad Herennium) to judicial oratory.[16] This may account in part for Shakespeare's casting of Titus' climactic scene of lamentation (3.1) not as solitary emoting but as motivated address, and, specifically, failed persuasion of his sons' judges. The hero's performance of grief, his eloquent pleading, begins by seeking to establish his rhetorical *ethos*, the legitimation of his speech in terms of his personal authority: 'Hear me, grave fathers; noble Tribunes, stay. | For pity of mine age, whose youth was spent | In dangerous wars whilst you securely slept; | … Be pitiful to my condemnèd sons' (3.1.1–3, 8). Shakespeare's theatrical instinct in developing this situation of pathos is to motivate the conventional poetic lament's artifice of apostrophe, address to the elements ('O earth, I will befriend thee'—3.1.16), speech to nobody, as responsive to the judges' withdrawal and refusal of response:

> O reverend Tribunes, O gentle, agèd men,
> Unbind my sons, reverse the doom of death,
> And let me say, that never wept before,
> My tears are now prevailing orators!
> LUCIUS   O noble father, you lament in vain.
> The Tribunes hear you not. No man is by,
> And you recount your sorrows to a stone.
> . . . .
> TITUS   Why, 'tis no matter, man. If they did hear,
> They would not mark me; if they did mark,
> They would not pity me; yet plead I must.
> Therefore I tell my sorrows to the stones,
> Who, though they cannot answer my distress,
> Yet in some sort they are better than the Tribunes
> For that they will not intercept my tale.
>
> (3.1.23–39)

In *Titus*, Shakespeare intensifies speeches of tragic woe by situating them as interactions, their speakers as un-'prevailing orators'. Passionate utterance here is being posited as potentially transformative speech action rather than as mere representation or expression. David Schalkwyk has distinguished 'transformative performatives' or speech acts (such as promises), whether transacted in real life or represented in Shakespeare's poems and plays, from rhetorical acts. The former, as instances of J. L. Austin's illocutionary acts, are 'carried out *in* [their] utterance'; the latter 'are calculated to have a force on a listener or reader, but that force is incalculable or unpredictable'.[17] Stanley Cavell, in his essay on 'Performative and Passionate Utterance', has tried to go beyond Austin's limited focus on the illocutionary act to offer a fuller understanding of speech acts that can encompass 'the passional side of speech', which he relates to the perlocutionary acts undertaken to produce effects *by means of* speech.[18] It is almost as if Shakespeare's innovative word use in early

---

[16]   Recent books like Quentin Skinner, *Forensic Shakespeare* (Oxford: Oxford University Press, 2014) and Lorna Hutson, *The Invention of Suspicion: Law and Mimesis in Shakespeare and Renaissance Drama* (Oxford: Oxford University Press, 2007) are bringing the importance of this branch of rhetoric within Renaissance culture more fully into view.

[17]   David Schalkwyk, 'Poetry and Performance', *The Cambridge Companion to Shakespeare's Poetry*, ed. Patrick Cheney (Cambridge: Cambridge University Press, 2007), 241–59 (242).

[18]   Stanley Cavell, 'Performative and Passionate Utterance', in *Philosophy the Day After Tomorrow* (Cambridge: Belknap Press of Harvard University Press, 2005), 155–91 (170).

plays like *Titus Andronicus* is oriented to a similar aim. The playwright uses words like 'passion' and 'passionate' as active verbs, as verbs of doing. In *Two Gentlemen of Verona*, Julia, disguised as a boy, tells Silvia of how she performed 'a lamentable part' in an entertainment: ''twas Ariadne, *passioning* | For Theseus' perjury and unjust flight' (4.4.163–5, emphasis added). Titus remarks to his brother that he and Lavinia 'cannot *passionate* our tenfold grief' (3.2.6, emphasis added). Just as 'passion' and 'passionate' are herein cast as verbal actions, so, by a suggestive conversion of the noun 'compassion' to a verb, does the tragedy aim to 'calculate' or 'predict' a comparable action in the hearer as its projected (although frustrated) effect: 'O heavens, can you hear a good man groan | And not relent, or not *compassion* him?' (4.1.122–3, emphasis added). Cavell's aim in positing 'passionate utterance' as 'performative' action is not always as clear as it might be, but his aim at 'some fragment of a view of expression, of recognizing language as everywhere revealing desire', he claims, is 'meant in service of something I want from moral theory, namely a systematic recognition of speech as confrontation, as demanding, as owed, … each instance of which directs, and risks, if not costs, blood' (186). As he imagines it, 'passionate utterance' risks and confronts; it makes the speaker 'vulnerable to your rebuke, thus staking our future' (185). For Cicero's vision of the efficacy of orator's speech as pragmatic action that can create community, sustain the *polis*, to be anything but a fantasy, its passionate appeals must negotiate this vulnerability and risk, must stake the future on some answerable action in the hearers. In *Titus Andronicus*, the onstage refusals of pity repeatedly deliver 'passion' in the speaker without answering 'compassion' in the listener. As the play draws to its conclusion, the Roman orators continue to declare their standing, to stake the future on 'utt'rance' that 'should move ye' (the Roman people) 'to commiseration' and 'knit … These broken limbs again into one body' (5.3.90–1, 69–71). As the play ends, the audience is still being pressed, by the echoing word 'pity' in the concluding lines—'Her life was beastly and devoid of pity, | And being dead, let birds on her take pity' (5.3.198–9). The demand still rings in the auditor's ears, a question about what is owed, a challenge to 'compassionate'.

The extent of Shakespeare's knowledge, even at second or third hand, of Aristotle's definition of tragedy with its complex evocation of the 'arousing' and 'catharsis' of pity and fear as integral to the tragic effect, is unclear.[19] And yet, the play's persistent emphasis is on woeful speeches aimed at arousing pity, as the drama enacts and re-enacts scenes of dysfunctional persuasion: first in Tamora's plea for Titus to pity and preserve her eldest son, next in Lavinia's pleas to hold off ravishment, finally in Titus's unanswered pleas. The apprentice dramatist presses against the persuasive limits of eloquent lament, in speech situations where the characters not only bewail their own woes but also struggle with the complex politics of speaking for the suffering of a silenced character, the tongueless ravished Lavinia. As interactions of orator and judge, of 'passioner' and potential 'compassioner', the tearful orations repeatedly test out the idealistic premise of the social and political efficaciousness of Ciceronian oratory. The theatre audience cannot escape the position of listener or shadow addressee, and with it the burden and responsibility of membership (or its refusal) in an imagined community premised on sympathetic identification, on pity. In the play's repeated demands for the hearers' pity and its dialogics of grief,

---

[19] Aristotle, 'Poetics' (*De poetica*), in *The Basic Works of Aristotle*, ed. Richard McKeon (New York: Random House, 1941), 1455–87, 1449.6.28–9.

it is hard not to hear in *Titus* a meta-discursive reflection on the language of tragedy and the role of tragic lament in staking futures, seeding pity.

Titus is only the beginning of an inquiry into 'pity' as a calculated or desired effect of tragic lament. Perhaps Shakespearean tragedy could be said to always appeal to and never fully deliver on the action of pity, but Shakespeare certainly keeps constantly in play the imaginative possibility of a moral, community-building dialogue of lamenting plea and answering efficacious pity. Nowhere does he evoke it more powerfully than in the metaphoric language of Macbeth, who is shaken by his own vivid imagination of a virtuous plea, 'trumpet-tongued', summoning against his murderous infliction of suffering the countervailing action of 'pity, like a naked new-born babe, | Striding the blast', its fragile potency supported by a host of 'heaven's cherubin' (1.7.19–22).

IMITATION AND PASSIONATE LAMENT

If Ciceronian oratory inspires Shakespeare's experiments with masculine lamentation in *Titus*, it is surprising and more than a little counter-intuitive to discover not only rhetoric but once again forensic oratory inspiring feminine lamentation in *Richard III*. In a play where the titular hero is a villain who, when touched by affliction, finds no way to legitimate a call for pity, 'Since that I myself | Find in myself no pity to myself' (5.5.156–7), the tragic idiom of lament is distributed among the wronged female characters. The women's grief is by no means 'tongue-tied' (4.4.132), and the primary associations of their fullness of speech are not, as one might expect, with derogated blabbing female tongues or inchoate passion. Instead, the principles of Ciceronian eloquence and Erasmian copia remain on abundant display, highlighted by self-reflexive comments on how these values govern the invention and accumulation of woeful words. 'Be copious in exclaims' (4.4.135), the women urge one another. 'Why should calamity be full of words?' (4.4.126) inquires the Duchess of York. The Duchess's question triggers this astonishing characterization by Queen Elizabeth of the women's eloquent words: 'Windy attorneys to their client woes, | Airy recorders of intestate joys, | Poor breathing orators of miseries. | Let them have scope' (4.4.127–30). The startling metaphors developed here evoke, once again, the branch of forensic oratory in which Cicero specialized. They make it apparent how the linguistic capital motivated in Ciceronian oratory by the requirements of Roman attorneys pleading their clients' causes is being imitated, repurposed, translated from a remote culture and a highly specialized context, to supply the passionate rhetoric of the noblewomen's laments. The idea that male writers of the Renaissance imitated the speeches of classical heroines to ventriloquize female emotion is a familiar one; the conception of female passion ventriloquized through the voices of Roman lawyers is more surprising and inventive.

For Shakespeare, the meaningful models for grief were not primarily the stammering or inarticulate performances to which we are made privy by a media with global reach, one that disparages articulate speech and constantly purports to take us 'inside' the personal stories and deliver the emotions of real people in the throes of disaster. The concern of Shakespearean tragedy is not with raw spectacle, but with a representation of tragic action, an *imitation* of suffering: gesture and spectacle play a role but Shakespeare's theatre is a primarily a theatre of words, and its imitated emotion for the most part is emotion mediated and performed in articulate speech. As I mentioned at the outset of this chapter, Renaissance schools offered lessons in voicing passion in order to appeal to pity, and they were, specifically, lessons in classical imitation. For a 'passionate speech', Shakespeare and his contemporaries had readily available for emulation those classical examples whose grammar and rhetoric they had parsed, analysed, translated into English, retranslated into Latin, and recited as schoolboys. And, very often, strangely, the portraits of grief they described or the voices they ventriloquized in the classroom were those of grief-stricken female characters, as in the example mentioned of 'a lamentable part' that Julia, disguised as a boy in *The Two Gentlemen of Verona*, claims once to have enacted in a pageant: 'Ariadne, passioning | For Theseus' perjury and unjust flight' (4.4.164–5). Nor did schoolroom instruction in these practices of imitating the passion of classical characters await a boy's advanced study of Ovid or Virgil or Seneca. Recent historians of schoolroom rhetoric like Lynn Enterline have emphasized how these imitative practices were inculcated in daily classroom practice by means of introductory drills in rhetorical composition and oratorical declamation set forth in school-texts like Lorich's edition of Apthonius' *Progymnasmata*, a text in which 'all but two of his eleven exemplary speeches' modelling what a well-known character *might* have said in a particular situation 'are uttered by women in highly emotional states'.[20] In these early exercises in rhetoric, the passionate appeal in frequent rehearsal in Renaissance schoolrooms encompassed not only first-person lament but also highly elaborated descriptions or narrations of a classical figure's grief or disaster. What I am emphasizing is not Shakespeare's slavish imitation of classical models but instead how absolutely engrained imitation was within Renaissance rhetorical culture and Shakespearean poetics as the foundational basis for original improvisation and invention. Clemen worried that emotional speech in the Renaissance set-speech of lament 'remain[ed] a derivative product' and 'not a spontaneous expression of the feelings',[21] but this judgment seriously underestimates the imitative character of *all* expression: as M. M. Bakhtin's work made clear, 'in the everyday speech of any person living in society, no less than half ... of all the words uttered by him will be someone else's words': the 'ideological becoming of a human being ... is the process of selectively assimilating the words of others'.[22]

By indirection, studying the artificial rhetoric of lament and descriptions of grief, we arrive back at the topic we left aside at the outset of this chapter: that is, Shakespeare's original invention of 'subjectivity effects' in tragic soliloquys. Lynn Enterline has offered a brilliant explanation of Hamlet's famous soliloquy of self-interrogation ('O, what a rogue and peasant slave am I!', 2.2.552), a soliloquy responsive to the player's tearful performance of a 'passionate speech' (2.2.435 and 452ff.) that Hamlet himself has internalized in memory and claims so to have loved, a speech articulating Aeneas's piteous tale to Dido of Priam's death and Hecuba's grief ('What's Hecuba to him?', 2.2.561). The soliloquy, she

---

[20] Lynn Enterline, *Shakespeare's Schoolroom: Rhetoric, Discipline, Emotion* (Philadelphia: University of Pennsylvania Press, 2012), 137.

[21] Clemen, *English Tragedy*, 257.

[22] M. M. Bakhtin, 'Discourse in the Novel', in *The Dialogic Imagination: Four Essays*, ed. Michael Holquist, trans. Caryl Emerson and Michael Holquist (Austin: University of Texas Press, 1981), 259–422 (339, 341).

explains, achieves 'the effect of inwardness, of intense personal feeling' through a 'medita-tion on the technique and possible effects of imitating *someone else's* passion'.[23] Here, of course, Shakespeare's art does not consist merely in the faithful reproduction or in the demonstrated mastery of the schoolroom's lessons in rhetorical imitation of passion. His improvisation upon these lessons takes fully on board the alternative perspective: that powerful emotional affect may elude polished verbal articulation, that highly mediated linguistic invention may entirely miss the heart of the matter. Indeed, that discovery helps to make Hamlet's voice original, individuated. But the traditional imitation of passion here becomes Shakespeare's discovery tool to construct the complexity of what Hamlet 'has within': it includes both anticipation of the inculcated piteous response to the 'passionate speech' of which he is part performer, part audience; and a self-conscious acknowledge-ment of its misfire, its lack. If the unhearing judges in *Titus Andronicus* and the empathetic Edgar in *King Lear* offer onstage surrogates for the audience's potential 'answer words' to the pitiful tragic appeals, Hamlet's complex reflection on hearing speeches of another person's passion not only constructs his seeming inwardness but also mirrors the auditor's potential re-purposing of another person's (Hamlet's) passion as his or her own. In both cases, Shakespeare's implicit meta-discourse enlists the auditors as potential participants in the linguistic transaction of tragic grief, exploring the dialogic possibilities it raises, however fragile, for the discovery of community and the invention of selfhood. And no-where do we see this more clearly than in *King Lear*.

TRANSACTING GRIEF IN THE QUARTO TEXT OF *KING LEAR*

Inarticulate passion, woe beyond words, it is true, often appears to be an important con-stituent of Shakespearean tragedy; it needs to be emphasized, however, that its effects are characteristically achieved either (as in *Hamlet*) in relation to meta-discursive interroga-tion of the Renaissance cult of eloquence or (as in *King Lear*) in a choreographed inter-play between artifice and 'clamour' (scene 24 [5.3].205). This interplay as a key element of Shakespeare's improvisation of passion in *King Lear* can be illustrated if we focus on lam-entation in the concluding movement of the 1608 First Quarto. Even though the Quarto, printed by Nicholas Okes, is full of errors, it is generally thought to have been printed from Shakespeare's rough draft of the play and to represent 'the play as Shakespeare originally wrote it'.[24] Scholars constructing revision hypotheses concerning the 'two texts' of *King Lear*, the Quarto and the 1623 First Folio, have pored over the multitude of small differ-ences and the approximately 300 lines of the Quarto text omitted from the Folio. They pos-tulate transformations in character, plot structure, and thematic focus, but one of the most striking differences is to be found in the Quarto's treatment of passionate speeches of grief and lamentation. The Quarto text may show us Shakespeare workshopping the language

---

[23] Enterline, *Shakespeare's Schoolroom*, 122.
[24] Shakespeare, *The Complete Plays*, 2nd edn., gen. eds., Stanley Wells and Gary Taylor, Introduction to *The History of King Lear*, 909.

of grief, and comparison with changes made to the Folio text, perhaps oriented to theatrical needs, helps bring into focus what was striking and unexpected in Shakespeare's original composition. What it reveals is a language of grief in the Quarto that pulls in two seemingly contradictory directions: on the one hand, Lear's lamenting over Cordelia's death is raw, expressed in disconnected syntax, in repeated words that register as or merge into visceral and inarticulate sounds, becoming cries, howls, groans. On the other hand, eloquent and artful speeches of passion recount Cordelia's 'demonstratio[n] of griefe' on reading letters about Lear's distress and self-conscious rhetorical amplification embellishes Edgar's narration of 'the most piteous tale' of Kent and Lear.[25] As if smoothing over and effacing this curious contradiction, the Folio text regularizes the language of Lear's raw suffering and cuts out altogether the polished descriptions of Cordelia's and Kent's distress. But what might Shakespeare have aimed at through the incongruous interplay of these seemingly opposite modes?

No one hearing or reading the ending of the Quarto *Lear* could maintain that Shakespeare never breaks with the articulate rhetoric of lament:

> LEAR And my poore foole is hangd, no, no life, why should a dog, a
> horse, a rat of life and thou no breath at all, O thou wilt come no
> more, neuer, neuer, neuer, pray you vndo this button, thanke you
> sir, O, o, o, o.
>
> (Q1, lines 2967–70)

The Folio revision adds to this a dubious form of artifice. Here, where broken verse and repetitive word-like sounds virtually merge into emotive wordlessness, the Folio inserts words in the repeated series ('no, no, no life?' and an extra 'neuer') to regularize the pentameter line length. It also excises the breaking off into the groaning 'O, o, o, o'.[26] In addition to adding metrical polish and regularity, the Folio also rounds off the lament with a facile consolation that suggests Lear dies believing Cordelia may be alive:

> LEAR: And my poore Foole is hang'd: no, no, no life?
> Why should a Dog, a Horse, a Rat haue life,
> And thou[ ]no breath at all? Thou'lt come no more,
> Neuer, neuer, neuer, neuer, neuer.
> Pray you vndo this Button. Thanke you Sir,
> Do you see this, looke on her? Looke her lips,
> Looke there, looke there. *He dies.*
>
> (F1, lines 3277–83)

In the First Quarto version, the rawness of the lines remains in evidence even where a modernized edition punctuates, emends textual error, and introduces verse lineation:

> And my poor fool is hanged. No, no life.
> Why should a dog, a horse, a rat have life,

---

[25] Here and in the next paragraph I quote the unmodernized Quarto text from William Shakespeare, *The Parallel* King Lear *1608—1623*, ed. Michael Warren (Berkeley: University of California Press, 1989), lines 2104 and 2874.

[26] R. A. Foakes, ed., *King Lear*, Arden Shakespeare, 3rd Series (Walton-on-Thames: Thomas Nelson and Sons Ltd, 1997), notes that Q1's 'O, o, o, o' is 'a conventional representation of a dying groan' (391).

> And thou no breath at all? O, thou wilt come no more,
> Never, never, never.—Pray you, undo
> This button. Thank you, sir. O, O, O, O!

(scene 24 [5.3].300–4)

The uncompromising painfulness is in keeping with the progress of a play in which characters like Edgar have tested out and then been confronted with the inadequacy of a range of consolations for suffering. And yet, while representing, as the innovative expression of *King Lear* so often has done, the motions of Lear's confused mind by means of a disjunctive syntactic sequence and shifting direction of address, each constitutive part of the speech resonates with contexts and connections the play has built up, so that the speech is very far from incoherent in its effect. The brief but complete narration, establishing the situation and motive for grief—'And my poor fool is hanged'—famously conflates the identity of two missing loved ones. The repeated 'no's resonate with Cordelia's initial answer, 'nothing', with Lear's echoing 'Nothing can come of nothing', with the Fool's iteration and criticism of Lear's words, and with Kent's determined 'no's as antidotes to the flattery of Lear's 'ay'-saying lords. The 'why should?' question encapsulates the broadest interrogation of meaning raised by grief in a form that coheres both with the high formality of lament and with the untutored simplicity of a small child's questioning. The painful exclamation and direct address of 'O, thou wilt come no more' is moving as Lear's register in loss of how love can be recognized in the most commonplace actions. Tapping into one of the most basic cognitive metaphors that grounds human identity and association in terms of spatial movement, his utterance cannot help but move audience members to identification with the mourner's common experience of expecting the lost one to 'come' and, then, painfully having to self-correct, 'O, thou wilt come no more'. Here it is the trigger for the terrible extra-metrical 'Never, never, never' of Lear's lament. The small polite request (whether to undo his own button or Cordelia's) with the correspondingly humble register of thankfulness is a gracious transaction of service. It reprises the play's rich interrogation of the abuses and uses of courteous speech, recovering a use and value for everyday forms of civility. It marks Lear's tacit acknowledgement that, in even the simplest relationship, something is owed to, as well as owed by, others. In these tragic speeches, the most basic forms of language come together with what an actor's embodied voice and breath can make of the textual representations in repeated vowels ('O, O, O, O!') and wordlike sounds ('Never', 'Howl') of a body's involuntary somatic expression to create a kind of moving lament nowhere forecast in the lessons of rhetoric.

I would suggest that the Folio's efforts to polish the rough edges of Lear's lament are not improvements. This is not, however, to argue that Shakespeare abandoned the artificial rhetoric of grief and rejected its value in his great tragedy. If Lear's raw grief over Cordelia's death does without the heightening of pathos through *copia* and eloquence in its immediate expression, we still need to ask why the Quarto text so strongly foregrounds rhetorically polished cameos, self-conscious 'demonstration[s]' of how represented grief may be expected to affect a reader, viewer, or auditor. If the revision of Q's language of grief was the work of a single writer, he may have added artifice to Lear's lament but he had no patience for the Gentleman's embellished account of how letters about Lear's suffering 'moved' Cordelia:

> [FIRST] GENTLEMAN … Patience and sorrow strove
> Who should express her goodliest. You have seen
> Sunshine and rain at once; her smiles and tears
> Were like, a better way. Those happy smilets
> That played on her ripe lip seemed not to know
> What guests were in her eyes, which parted thence
> As pearls from diamonds dropped….
> KENT   Made she no verbal question?
> [FIRST] GENTLEMAN
> Faith, once or twice she heaved the name of 'father'
> Pantingly forth as if it pressed her heart,
> Cried 'Sisters, sisters, shame of ladies, sisters,
> Kent, father, sisters, what, i'th'storm, i'th'night,
> Let [pity] not be believed!' There she shook
> The holy water from her heavenly eyes
> And clamour [moistened her]. Then away she started
> To deal with grief alone.[27]

Strangely, here, this eloquent speech makes Cordelia's grief out to be as inarticulate as Lear's, her words not persuasive eloquence but clamorous and broken sounds hardly distinguishable from her bodily heaving and panting. The endeavour of art here is to reflect on and illustrate an ethical response to the show of tragic suffering. It is so stylized and idealized a portrayal that it may not be credible as a model for the play's own auditors, but the virtuous 'pity' that Cordelia is moved to by the tale of Lear's woe and her loving care for Lear in the later scenes of their meeting are not undermined, or shown as illusory, as with so many of the play's proffered consolations. The Quarto text does not offer just this single idealized 'demonstration of grief' but instead prepares its audience for the lamenting outcry of Lear's ending with repeated illustrations of how on-stage auditors respond to heart-piercing tales or speeches of grief. Edgar's tale of Gloucester's 'flawed heart … 'Twixt two extremes of passion, joy and grief, | Burst[ing] smilingly' (scene 24 [5.3].193–6) draws from Edmund, quite extraordinarily, this testimony of its rhetorical action upon him: 'This speech of yours hath moved me, | And shall perchance do good' (196–7). Edmund even urges Edgar to 'speak you on—', drawing forth Edgar's self-conscious reference to practices of rhetorical *copia* or amplification as he sets forth the account of the meeting with Kent, where 'the strings of life | Began to crack' (213–14).

King Lear is, famously, the tragedy that uncompromisingly withdraws all consolations or rationale for virtue. Albany's promise of poetic justice, for example—that 'All friends shall taste | The wages of their virtue, and all foes | The cup of their deservings' (scene 24 [5.3].297–9)—is immediately undermined by Lear's death, preceded by Cordelia's and to be followed by Kent's. But Shakespeare's repeated anticipatory modelling of the language of grief as a potentially transformative speech act for its auditors leaves something important open in its ending—the critical question of whether 'This speech of [his]' will move us his auditors, whether it 'shall perchance do good'.

---

[27] Scene 17 [4.3].17–33. Here, as elsewhere, I quote the Oxford text of the Quarto, but I have retained the Quarto's words 'pitie' and 'moystened her' instead of the editor's emendations, 'piety' and 'mastered'.

Select Bibliography

Adamson, Sylvia, 'Literary Language', in *The Cambridge History of the English Language*, vol. 3, *1476-1776*, ed. Roger Lass (Cambridge: Cambridge University Press, 1999), 539–653.

Adamson, Sylvia, 'Questions of Identity in Renaissance Drama: New Historicism Meets Old Philology', *Shakespeare Quarterly* 61:1 (Spring 2010), 56–77.

Aristotle, 'Poetics' (*De poetica*), in *The Basic Works of Aristotle*, ed. Richard McKeon (New York: Random House, 1941), 1455–87.

Bakhtin, M. M., 'Discourse in the Novel', in *The Dialogic Imagination: Four Essays*, ed. Michael Holquist, trans. Caryl Emerson and Michael Holquist (Austin: University of Texas Press, 1981), 259–422.

Cavell, Stanley, 'Performative and Passionate Utterance', in *Philosophy the Day After Tomorrow* (Cambridge: Belknap Press of Harvard University Press, 2005), 155–91.

Cicero, *De oratore*, trans. H. Rackham, Loeb Classical Library 348 and 349 (Cambridge: Harvard University Press, 1942).

Clemen, Wolfgang, *English Tragedy Before Shakespeare: The Development of Dramatic Speech*, trans. T. S. Dorsch (London: Methuen & Co. Ltd., 1961).

Enterline, Lynn, *Shakespeare's Schoolroom: Rhetoric, Discipline, Emotion* (Philadelphia: University of Pennsylvania Press, 2012).

Erasmus, Desiderius, 'Copia: Foundations of the Abundant Style' (*De duplici copia verborum ac rerum commentarii duo*), trans. Betty I. Knott, in *Collected Works of* Erasmus, vol. 24, ed. Craig R. Thompson (Toronto: University of Toronto Press, 1978), 279–659.

Hutson, Lorna, *The Invention of Suspicion: Law and Mimesis in Shakespeare and Renaissance Drama* (Oxford: Oxford University Press, 2007).

Kermode, Frank, *Shakespeare's Language* (London: Penguin Books, 2000).

Magnusson, Lynne, *Shakespeare and Social Dialogue: Dramatic Language and Elizabethan Letters* (Cambridge: Cambridge University Press, 1999).

Reiss, Timothy J., 'Renaissance Theatre and the Theory of Tragedy', *The Cambridge History of Literary Criticism*, vol. 3: *The Renaissance*, ed. Glyn P. Norton (Cambridge: Cambridge University Press, 1999), 229–47.

Schalkwyk, David, 'Poetry and Performance', *The Cambridge Companion to Shakespeare's Poetry*, ed. Patrick Cheney (Cambridge: Cambridge University Press, 2007), 241–59.

Skinner, Quentin, *Forensic Shakespeare* (Oxford: Oxford University Press, 2014).

Shakespeare, William, *The Complete Plays*, 2nd edn., gen. eds., Stanley Wells and Gary Taylor (Oxford: Clarendon Press, 2005).

Shakespeare, William, *The Parallel* King Lear *1608-1623*, ed. Michael Warren (Berkeley: University of California Press, 1989).

CHAPTER 9

··

THE PITY OF IT
Shakespearean Tragedy and Affect

··

DAVID HILLMAN

'The purpose of your contribution to the volume is simple: to offer an informed
account of the place of affect/emotion in Shakespearean tragedy.'

(David Schalkwyk, email to the author, 21 Jan. 2012)

SIMPLE it is not. If it is the case that tragedy is the genre par excellence that resists attempts
at generalization,[1] it is no less true that trying to define affect (and its relation to cognate
ideas such as emotion, feeling, or passion)[2] and to put this definition to analytic use is a
thankless task. How much more so, then, attempting to characterize the relations *between*

---

[1] On which see in particular Stephen Booth, *King Lear, Macbeth, Indefinition, and Tragedy*
(New Haven: Yale University Press, 1983), and Andrew Bennett and Nicholas Royle, *Introduction to
Literature, Criticism and Theory* (Edinburgh: Pearson Education, 1995), 99–101.

[2] I do not intend to enter the debate about the precise differences and relations between these various
terms, beyond noting that 'passion' was the standard term in the early modern period to denote 'any
strong, controlling, or overpowering emotion, as desire, hate, fear, etc.; an intense feeling or impulse'
(*OED* II.6.a). 'Affect(ion)' was used in similar senses (minus the Christian connotations) from the
fourteenth century on (*OED*, 'affection' I.1.a and b). 'Emotion' was just coming into use in the sixteenth
century and beginning to displace these other terms by the late seventeenth century, having previously
denoted either a public commotion or movement per se. *OED*'s first citation of the word to denote
'an excited mental state … any strong mental or instinctive feeling' is from 1602 (*OED*, 'emotion', 1.a
and b. and 3.a and b.); Cotgrave's *Dictionary of the French and English Tongues* (1611) has 'An emotion,
commotion, sudden, or turbulent stirring; an agitation of the spirit, violent motion of the thoughts,
vehement inclination of the mind'. Until the end of the sixteenth century, 'motion' seems to have been the
more usual term (see Michael Neill, '"A book where one may read strange matters": en-visaging character
and emotion on the Shakespearian stage', *Shakespeare Survey*, 66 (2013): *Working with Shakespeare*,
246–64 (246–7)). It is worth noting that unlike 'emotion', 'affect' (from the Latin *afficere*, to produce a
physical effect on, to influence) more often than not has an object(ive)—something desired or aspired to,
an inclination or desire, or something that is having a strong effect on the subject; it is also in this period
often close to the sense 'infect'—as in *Troilus and Cressida*, 2.2.59–60: 'the will dotes that is attributive/To
what infectiously itself affects'), so that it is implicitly more relational and active than 'emotion' or 'passion'.
Like 'emotion', 'affect(ion)' has (in the early modern period) almost indistinguishably corporeal and
psychological meanings.

tragedy and affect; as Samuel Goldwyn is said to have declared: it's absolutely impossible; but it has possibilities.

Affects, in nearly all their human variations, are the very stuff of tragedy.[3] Horace Walpole's famous dictum—'The world is a tragedy to those who feel, but a comedy to those who think'[4] comes in a long tradition of agreeing that, as Giordano Bruno put it in the sixteenth century, 'tragic harmonies give rise to more passions than comic ones'.[5] When one contemplates Shakespeare's tragedies alongside those of his contemporaries— beside, say, Kyd's heavily ironized brand of tragic pity, or Marlowe's strident tone and sense of come-uppance in the debacle, or Middleton's dry (and dry-eyed), sardonic, knowing, partially self-parodic species of tragedy, or Jonson's weighty, largely (if not homogeneously) moralizing figurations, or Webster's savage and lurid steeping in the powers of horror—we can see that Shakespeare, more than anyone else, plumbs the emotional depths—and concomitantly reaches the affective heights—afforded by the tragic form. Over and over, his plays show their protagonists in the grip of raw emotions, 'too rash, too unadvised, too sudden' (*Romeo and Juliet*, 2.1.260)[6]—emotions that are existentially threatening: the stirring up in itself leaves the characters vulnerable and can feel far more dangerous than the particular circumstances in which he or she is placed. Indeed, the exact emotion often seems less significant than the very existence of strong passion.

'Affection! Thy intention stabs the centre' (*The Winter's Tale*, 1.2.137): Leontes' *cri de coeur* makes vivid the fact that affect (or 'affection', which here appears to mean 'passion', whether that of Hermione's desire or of Leontes' jealousy) reaches to the 'centre' of his being—as well as the centre of the world—and that it is excruciating in its intensity: 'affection' causes Leontes to imagine 'crack[ing] his gorge, his sides, | With violent hefts' (2.1.44–5). Hamlet's passion, says Ophelia, 'did seem to shatter all his bulk | And end his being' (2.1.92–3); Othello's 'shadowing passion … shakes [him] thus' (4.1.40–2), bringing on a quasi-epileptic fit. Strong emotion can be experienced as a wounding of the very 'centre' of one's body, or in Cynthia Marshall's term, a shattering of the self.[7] In Shakespearean tragedy, it tends to shatter a whole society, so that the entire world can feel like a torture device—'the rack of this tough world' (*King Lear*, 5.3.309) which it is a relief

---

[3] It may be for this reason that tragedy has traditionally been considered the 'highest' genre. In the view of Gilles Deleuze and Felix Guattari, it is the role of the greatest art to illuminate—indeed, to create—hitherto-unfamiliar emotional vectors: 'A great novelist is above all an artist who invents unknown or unrecognized affects and brings them to light as the becoming of his characters', they write: Gilles Deleuze and Felix Guattari, *What Is Philosophy?* trans. Hugh Tomlinson and Graham Burchell (New York: Columbia University Press, 1994), 174.

[4] Horace Walpole—from a letter to Anne, Countess of Ossory, on 16 August 1776. The original, fuller version appeared in a letter to Sir Horace Mann on 31 December 1769: 'I have often said, and oftener think, that this world is a comedy to those that think, a tragedy to those that feel—a solution of why Democritus laughed and Heraclitus wept'. *Horace Walpole's Correspondence*, ed. W. S. Lewis (New Haven: Yale University Press, 1983), 23: 163–6.

[5] Bruno, *Theses de Magia* (1588), XV, vol. 3: 433, trans. by and cited in Ioan P. Culianu, *Eros and Magic in the Renaissance* (Chicago: University of Chicago Press, 1987), 91.

[6] All quotations from Shakespeare are from *The Oxford Shakespeare*, ed. John Jowett et al., 2nd edn. (Oxford: Clarendon Press, 2005).

[7] See Cynthia Marshall, *The Shattering of the Self: Violence, Subjectivity and Early Modern Texts* (Baltimore: Johns Hopkins University Press, 2002).

to leave behind, a 'harsh world' in which even the mere act of 'draw[ing] breath' entails being 'in pain' (*Hamlet*, 5.2.300).

But it is not just the ostensibly 'negative' emotions such as anger or jealousy that cause this kind of pain: any powerful emotion, even a supposedly 'positive' one, shakes the core of the embodied self—for better and for worse. As Leontes has said a few lines earlier in the same scene: 'I have *tremor cordis* on me: my heart dances, | But not for joy, not joy' (1.2.109–10); on the face of it, a dancing heart sounds like something one might welcome. His self-diagnosis allows for the possibility that joy might have brought on his attack.[8] (And we can be sceptical about the disavowal of joy here: the Shakespearean tragic hero seems often enough to experience a kind of Nietzschean destructive *jouissance* along-side the pain—something one intuits at times with, say, Othello's embrace of his 'capable and wide revenge' (3.3.520), or Hamlet's rage ('Now could I drink hot blood…', 3.2.422). Hamlet's madness is, in Polonius' view,

> the very ecstasy of love
> Whose violent property fordoes itself
> And leads the will to desperate undertakings
> As oft as any passion under heaven
> That does afflict our natures.
>
> (2.1.99–103)

Hamlet's Player King puts it succinctly:

> The violence of either grief or joy
> Their own enactures with themselves destroy.
>
> (3.2.190–1)

Gloucester's heart ''Twixt two extremes of passion, joy and grief, | Burst smilingly' (5.3.197–8), and the repeated cry of the Shakespearean tragic hero is of a near-unbear-able pain felt as threatening the integrity of the bodily interior: Hamlet's 'Hold, hold, my heart' (*Hamlet*, 1.5.92), or Lear's 'O sides, you are too tough! | Will you yet hold?' (*King Lear*, 2.2.386–7), or Antony's 'O, cleave my sides! | Heart, once be stronger than thy continent, | Crack thy frail case!' (*Antony and Cleopatra*, 4.15.39–41) or Cleopatra's perhaps–ironic 'It cannot be thus long, the sides of nature | Will not sustain it' (1.3.16–17). Macbeth, early on, speaks of 'that suggestion whose horrid image doth …make my seated heart knock at my ribs | Against the use of nature' (1.3.134–7). The blame may be directed outside, towards someone else's 'suggestion' or temptation, but the emotion is felt as a commotion within; or rather, affections can shatter the distinction between inner and outer: as the physician Edward Jorden writes: 'seeing we are not maisters of our owne affections, wee are like battered Citties without walles, or shippes tossed in the Sea, ex-posed to all maner of assaults and daungers, even to the overthrow of our owne bodies.'[9]

---

[8] On the tendency of Shakespeare's tragic protagonists to take flight from the sheer intensity of emotion by giving it a 'medical' diagnosis (*tremor cordis, hysterica passio*), see my *Shakespeare's Entrails: Belief, Scepticism and the Interior of the Body* (Basingstoke: Palgrave Macmillan, 2007), 157.

[9] Edward Jorden, *A Briefe Discourse of a Disease Called the Suffocation of the Mother* (London: John Windet, 1603), G3v, cited from Michael MacDonald's edition in *Witchcraft and Hysteria in Elizabethan England: Edward Jorden and the Mary Glover Case* (London: Tavistock/Routledge, 1991).

So on the one hand, violent emotion is excessive, painful, destructive; but on the other, the tragic heroes' lack of restraint in embracing their passions is precisely what these tragedies offer us as admirable, as pictures of the greatness of the human spirit, or of what Racine calls 'that majestic sadness which constitutes the whole pleasure of tragedy'.[10] Emotions in Shakespearean tragedy take on a grandeur that comes close to the heart of the sense of wonder these plays engender.

Shakespeare's tragic heroes struggle to hold on to a sense of self and the time-honoured heroic virtue of constancy. Their impassioned natures render them almost literally beside themselves, ec-static, mad. And yet paradoxically enough, it often seems that these primal emotions constitute precisely the core around which the protagonist's heroic subjectivity is formed. Their anguished *jouissance* both makes and unmakes them. Affects have profoundly transformative power; they can put any stable sense of self radically at risk— even as they offer rich rewards: as Thomas Wright puts it in his widely-read treatise, *The Passions of the Minde* (1601): 'By this alteration which the Passions work in the Wit and the Will we may understand the admirable Metamorphosis and change of a man from himself.'[11] For the Shakespearean tragic hero, the transformation is 'admirable' in the sense that we wonder at it, but also in the sense that at some level we extol it. The way in which 'intense states of emotion' lead to radical transformation is, as Eugene Waith has suggested, perhaps the main reason for Shakespeare's lifelong fascination with Ovid—with the way metamorphosis in the earlier writer is an expression of, indeed a result of, such emotional intensity; and this is true in the comedies as in the tragedies.[12] In the former, however, emotion generally functions to release the characters from societal shackles, offering an avenue of temporary liberation. Temporary—because Shakespeare's comedies eventually work to re-bind tragic potentialities in formalized, communal arrangements. His tragedies, on the other hand, repeatedly depict the breakdown of such ritualized, ceremonial public structures and rites of passage whose function it is to contain and redistribute emotion—funerals, weddings, investitures, laws. One could say that private emotion overwhelms these public structures, or that it bursts the bounds of the civic formations (precariously) maintained in the comedies (so that figures such as Coriolanus, Lear, Hamlet, Timon, or Romeo find themselves banished or self-banished beyond the pales of their societies). This is why the structure of the tragic drama itself must step in to contain the threatened overflow of emotion.

Though affects are never static, the dramatic *ordering* of emotions gives pattern to their flux, 'a kind of ritualistic form' to contain them.[13] Attempts have been made to describe the typical affective rhythm of Shakespeare's tragedies. Kenneth Burke, for example, has labelled the fourth act—'this station of a Shakespearean tragedy'—the "pity" act'.[14] In a play, emotions develop in relation to a formal dramatic orchestration; and it is in part this

[10]   Jean Racine, Preface to *Bérénice* (1668), in *Oeuvres Complètes*, vol. 1 (Paris: Gallimard 'Pleiade', 1950), 466 (my translation).

[11]   Thomas Wright, *The Passions of the Minde in Generall* (London, 1601), 133–4.

[12]   Eugene Waith, 'The Metamorphosis of Violence in *Titus Andronicus*', *Shakespeare Survey* 10 (1957), 39–49 (41–2).

[13]   Kenneth Burke, *Kenneth Burke on Shakespeare*, ed. Scott Newstock (West Lafayette, IN: Parlor Press, 2007), 74.

[14]   Ibid., 73.

unfolding tragic rhythm that balances out the typical speed and intensity of the onset of extreme emotion in these plays (heightened by the frequently foreshortened time-spans (with respect to the sources)). It is this rhythm, again, that counterbalances the almost literally heart-rending affective dimension of these plays, imparting a sense of the 'poetic rightness' of the representation—'the vision of life as accomplished … the sense of ful-filment' in Susanne Langer's words.[15] But it is only *through* the shattering experience of emotion that the sense of completeness can be experienced. Ruth Nevo has done as much as anyone to try to characterize the distinctive cadence of a Shakespearean tragedy.[16] But here again we are always in the realm of complexity, a blend of emotions at every point. At the close of *Romeo and Juliet*, for example, we feel, as Nevo writes, a 'reconcilement with the pity and fear we have experienced' through 'the resources of tenderness, desire, and gaiety, freedom and self-possession' which the protagonists achieve in and through their deaths, in and through the poetic intensity of their passion.[17] Equally, Hamlet's final mo-ments appear to be marked by rage, exultation, grief, equanimity, as well as a good dose of cool-headed pragmatism (indeed, similar things can be said of him throughout the play). Though one particular mood may dominate a scene, every turn in a Shakespearean tragedy is characterized by and evokes a mixture of emotions. There is a constant tension between the broad trajectory and the local complexity of affect in these plays.

One can go about labelling the various emotions which Shakespearean tragedy ex-presses and to which it gives rise—love, desire, guilt, shame, jealousy, anger, disgust, devotion, doubt, resentment, sadness, pity, fear, joy (though whether all of these are precisely affects is a moot point). It may even be possible to point to a predominant af-fective thrust (or 'feeling state', in Sianne Ngai's recent coinage)[18] presiding over each of the plays, as Lily B. Campbell did nearly a century ago in her once-influential book on Shakespearean tragedy: '*Hamlet*: A Tragedy of Grief'; '*Othello*: A Tragedy of Jealousy'; '*King Lear*: A Tragedy of Wrath in Old Age'; '*Macbeth*: A Study in Fear' are the titles of her chapters on Shakespeare.[19] But is *King Lear*, for example, really a tragedy of wrath? Is it not also a 'bitter-sweet' (Keats's characterization) tragedy of love, of envy, of terror and of despair?[20] Clearly, every tragedy puts its characters, actors, and audiences through a wide spectrum of emotions, some of them ostensibly contradictory. It takes no Sigmund come from the grave to show us that emotions such as love and hate, or love and jealousy, are at some level inseparable; that one emotion can be used as a cover story for another; and that irrationality and confusion undo any simple attribution of emotion to a given situation.

[15] Susanne K. Langer, *Feeling and Form: A Theory of Art Developed from Philosophy in a New Key* (London: Routledge & Kegan Paul, 1953), 327.

[16] Ruth Nevo, *Tragic Form in Shakespeare* (Princeton: Princeton University Press, 1972).

[17] Ibid., 57–8.

[18] See Sianne Ngai, *Ugly Feelings* (Cambridge, MA.: Harvard University Press, 2005).

[19] See Lily B. Campbell, *Shakespeare's Tragic Heroes: Slaves of Passion* (London: Methuen, 1970).

[20] John Keats, 'On Sitting Down to Read *King Lear* Once Again', l. 8 in *John Keats: Complete Poems*, ed. Jack Stillinger (Cambridge, MA: Belknap Press of Harvard University Press, 1991). Reactions to the play's denouement have ranged from Dr Johnson's shock to the point of unendurability to A. C. Bradley's finding in Lear's final moments a vision of 'unbearable joy': Samuel Johnson, *Samuel Johnson on Shakespeare*, ed. H. R. Woudhuysen (1989), 222; A. C. Bradley, *Shakespearean Tragedy* (London: Macmillan, 1904), 284–5.

Classification of the emotions is an age-old enterprise, dating back at least to Aristotle's *Rhetoric* and the Greek Stoics, taking in Cicero's four fundamental passions (distress, pleasure, fear, and desire), Aquinas' eleven basic affects (the six 'concupiscible' emotions of love and hate, desire and aversion, delight and distress; and the five 'irascible' emotions of hope and despair, confidence and fear, and anger—a schema often reiterated in the seventeenth century), and on into our own times, with systematizing attempts such as those of Antonio Damasio and Silvan Tomkins, who have promoted 'primary' or 'basic' emotions paradigms.[21] But again, it is highly questionable whether one can ever clearly distinguish between the infinite variety of possible affects. At the end of his detailed, careful categorization of affective states in *The Ethics*, published a few decades after Shakespeare's death, Spinoza notes that 'the emotions may be compounded one with another in so many ways, and so many variations may arise therefrom, as to exceed all possibility of computation'.[22] The chain-gang on the well-known frontispiece to Jean-François Senault's *The Use of the Passions* (1641), while showing the 'correct' subordination of the eleven Aquinian passions to the sovereignty of reason, may also be taken to show how interlinked these passions are. Just as there can be no single definition of Shakespearean tragedy, so too emotion refuses to be pinned down, closed off, categorized: its power derives from its propensity to spill over, to be excessive (just as any particular Shakespearean tragedy far exceeds any definition of tragedy). Affect's protean ability to evade analysis inexhaustibly is exactly why there is a concomitant temptation to become programmatic in discussing affects (just as there is in trying to pin down the genre of tragedy). Hamlet tells the Players that in enacting their 'passion' they 'must acquire or beget a temperance that may give it smoothness' (3.1.6–7): he sounds here like something we might find in one of the many faculty psychology treatises and religious manuals on the passions in this period—all those 'drie discourses of affections' (in Wright's words).[23] From Pierre de le Primaudaye, Edward Reynolds, and Thomas Wright in the sixteenth century to Descartes and Spinoza in the seventeenth, these popular anatomies of the passions manifest an impulse to control and direct the passions, partly through their classification. But Hamlet also chides himself for not acquiring or begetting the 'gall | To make oppression bitter' (2.2.512–13), and he opens the play's final scene with a paean to 'rashness' and 'indiscretion' (5.2.6–9).

The complexity and fluidity of affects become all the more obvious when we place emotions in an early modern context. Over the past two decades, scholarship has been

---

[21] See Peter King, 'Emotions' in *The Oxford Handbook of Aquinas*, ed. Brian Davies and Eleonore Stump (Oxford: Oxford University Press, 2012), 209–26; Antonio Damasio, *The Feeling of What Happens: Body, Emotion and the Making of Consciousness* (New York: Vintage, 2000); Silvan S. Tomkins, *Exploring Affect: The Selected Writings of Silvan S. Tomkins*, ed. E. Virginia Demos (Cambridge: Cambridge University Press, 1995). For a helpful summary of ancient and Renaissance classificatory systems, see Susan James, *Passion and Action: The Emotions in Seventeenth-Century Philosophy* (Oxford: Oxford University Press, 1997); and of modern positions, see Ruth Leys, 'The Turn to Affect: A Critique', *Critical Inquiry* 37:3 (Spring 2011), 434–72. Tomkins's influential account promotes a view of basic affects which can combine and produce an infinite range of emotions; Damasio outlines six primary emotions: happiness, sadness, fear, anger, surprise, disgust (*The Feeling of What Happens*, 50).

[22] Benedict de Spinoza, *The Ethics*, trans. R. H. M. Elwes (New York: Dover Publications, 1955), III, Prop. LIX, 172.

[23] Wright, *Passions*, 193.

paying increasing attention to the cultural constructedness and the historicity of concepts of affect; Clifford Geertz's dictum—'Not only ideas, but emotions too, are cultural arte-facts in man'[24]—has almost become a critical maxim. The affective realm, it is now said, is historically conditioned—by linguistic norms, psycho-physiological assumptions about selfhood, social and political attitudes and needs, and so on. If it is the case that tragedy 'drags the unconscious into the public place',[25] it is also true that there is no such thing as fully private emotion (or entirely public spaces)—there is a publicness to all emotion (it has a history, a context, even a politics) and a privacy to the public space (nobody is ever fully subsumed into this space). Recent research on early modern theories of emotions has underlined, on the one hand, the profoundly embodied character of affective states, and, on the other, the intersubjective and environmental nature of these ideas as the men and women of this period conceived of them. These may at first glance appear to us as pulling in opposite directions—somatically inward and inchoately outward at once—but in fact the normative depiction of the body as porous and in constant interanimation with the environment in early modern writing meant that the inner and the outer were experi-enced as far less separate than we tend to imagine today. As Gail Kern Paster explains: 'By using the terms of Renaissance behavioural thought to reconceptualize the tragic self as a permeable and hence changeable one, we are able to see Shakespeare's tragic heroes moved, and even transformed, by passions understood as "psycho-physiological" events embedded in an environment both natural and cultural.'[26]

In some respects, the wheel has come full circle—present–day understandings of emo-tion increasingly highlight the material basis of all feeling in and through the body as well as the intersubjectivity of affects.[27] Brian Massumi, for example, summarizing the work of Deleuze and Guattari, asserts that affects are 'irreducibly bodily and autonomic'; Teresa Brennan has argued that current study of affect reveals that there is 'no secure distinction between the individual and the "environment"'.[28] Though we still know little about the mechanisms of transmission, there can be little doubt that affect does make its way insidiously and assiduously across interpersonal boundaries. The work of Paster among others has helped us see how literally we should be taking many of the references

[24] Clifford Geertz, *The Interpretation of Cultures* (New York: Basic Books, 1973), 81.

[25] Howard Barker, *Arguments for a Theatre* (London: John Calder, 1989), 13.

[26] Gail Kern Paster, 'The Tragic Subject and Its Passions', in *The Cambridge Companion to Shakespearean Tragedy*, ed. Claire McEachern (Cambridge: Cambridge University Press, 2002), 142–59 (154). Compare her contention that 'the psychophysiology of early modern thought means that embodiment is everywhere assumed in affective discourse, just as bodily references always assume an affective context or consequence': Gail Kern Paster, *Humoring the Body: Emotions and the Shakespearean Stage* (Chicago: University of Chicago Press, 2004), 85. For a more recent set of views on the relations between embodiment, the self and the passions, see Brian Cummings and Freya Sierhuis, eds., *Passions and Subjectivity in Early Modern Culture* (Farnham: Ashgate, 2013).

[27] See e.g. David Schalkwyk's very helpful summary of the terrain in his essay 'Is Love an Emotion? Shakespeare's *Twelfth Night* and *Antony and Cleopatra*', *Symploke* 18:1–2 (2011), 99–130.

[28] Brian Massumi, *Parables for the Virtual: Movement, Affect, Sensation* (Durham, NC: Duke University Press, 2002), 28; Teresa Brennan, *The Transmission of Affect* (Ithaca: Cornell University Press, 2004), 6. As Leys summarizes: 'For both the new affect theorists and the neuroscientists from whom they variously borrow—and transcending differences of philosophical background, approach, and orientation—affect is a matter of autonomic responses that are held to occur below the threshold of consciousness and cognition and to be rooted in the body' (443).

to what might seem to post-Enlightenment ears metaphoric evocations of emotion in early modern writing. Certainly, in this context, we need to be cautious in disentangling the physiology of the body from its psychological workings, or internal humoral events from the surroundings—geography, weather, landscape, food, occasion.

It came naturally to early modern writers (notwithstanding the pathetic fallacy) to image the turmoil of the emotions—what Hamlet refers to as 'the very torrent, tempest, and, as I may say, the whirlwind of your passion' (3.2.5–6)—through natural phenomena, especially (in Shakespeare's tragedies) through the storms that punctuate these plays, the cosmic correlatives of the protagonists' passions.[29] These are not just metaphoric externalizations of internal affective states, or symbolic correlates of micro– and macrocosmic realms: they become more or less concrete manifestations of emotions that overflow the self and take over the world (and vice versa). (Here again, we can see the connections between Shakespeare's interest in Ovid and the interweaving of the human and natural worlds in the earlier writer's work.) The storms in Shakespeare conjure up the fluidity and disorientation felt by the plays' protagonists at the high point of affective instability in these plays—the *processus turbarum*. In the early modern world, psychological emotion and physical (com)motion are closely aligned—both etymologically and dramatically—meaning (among other things) that plot and character are necessarily intertwined.

The implications of such a material and environmental understanding for reading Shakespeare's tragic passions are multiple, ranging from reconsidering the relations between players and audiences[30] to rendering the self (tragic or otherwise) radically unstable, forever battling to keep the labile affective realm under control in the face of a multitude of outside influences—and vice versa: often struggling to either effect or prevent the transmission of one's 'own' affects into or onto others. (The rhetoricians, both ancient and early modern, taught the best ways of influencing listeners' (or readers') emotions.) Tragedy has always been one place where the relation between internal and external agency is searchingly interrogated; Greek tragic writers frequently represented strong affects as uncertainly poised between something that wells up within the hero and something the gods have instilled in him or her. Shakespearean tragedy for the most part leaves the gods out of the picture, but nevertheless finds ways of radically unsettling our sense of the sources of emotion. To what extent is, for example, Macbeth's ambition (or should we think of his dominant affect as closer to envy, or fear, perhaps even love?) attributable to the witches' influence, or to that of his wife—or is it a product of his own 'strange and self-abuse' (3.4.143)? What role does the environment—the 'fog and filthy air' (1.1.11) in which *Macbeth* opens—play in muddying his passions? Is the tragic hero merely 'passion's slave' (*Hamlet*, 3.2.68) or are these passions largely volitional? These possibilities correlate to a degree with a somatic and a more purely mental understanding of the origins of emotions. It seems to me crucial to Shakespearean tragedy to see the material understanding of the world not as a fixed one, but rather as in flux—shifting between a world-view that sees the individual as deeply embedded in his or her cultural and natural environment and one

---

[29] On this, see esp. Gail Kern Paster, Ch. 13 in this volume.

[30] See esp. Katharine A. Craik and Tanya Pollard's work on early modern audiences' sympathetic receptiveness to staged emotion in *Shakespearean Sensations: Experiencing Literature in Early Modern England* (Cambridge: Cambridge University Press, 2013); and Joseph R. Roach, *The Player's Passion: Studies in the Science of Acting* (Newark: University of Delaware Press, 1985).

approaching more 'enlightenment' assumptions of the individual psyche in relative isolation (from the body and from the environment). For it is in part through the disjunction
between these differing comprehensions that problems of choice and free will—so crucial
to tragedy—come sharply into view.

Some of Shakespeare's protagonists openly embrace the intensity of emotion—Lear, for
instance, seems all too willing to erupt into states of vehement rage. But then it is hard to
avoid sensing that the eruption is also a displacement, a channelling of more complex affects into something that feels manageable; he has, doubtless, much to be angry about, but
there are many other emotions that get swept up in his 'great rage' (4.7.78). Indeed, Lear
is at one point quite explicit about this mechanism: 'Touch me with noble anger, | And let
not women's weapons, water-drops, | Stain my man's cheeks' (2.4.276–8), he implores the
heavens. (Here again, the issue of authenticity comes up: Lear's 'noble anger' also hints at
a tradition that promotes the value of *furor*.)[31] In Stanley Cavell's view, this is a disowning of emotion, or rather of a particular emotion (in this case, in Cavell's view, of love) by
covering it up with a more manageable affective drive.[32] We could say something similar
about most of Shakespeare's tragic protagonists. Their way of dealing with the turbulent,
layered, at times irreconcilable nature of the emotions is often enough to bring their emotional focus to one sharp point—say, jealousy in Othello's case, revenge in Titus', hatred
or contempt in Timon's, and so on. (Hence the temptation to follow Lily Campbell's route
of pigeonholing each tragedy according to one dominant passion.) An argument could be
made that in general in these plays, anger, contempt or hatred—projective or projectile
mechanisms (epitomized in Coriolanus' 'I banish you!', 3.3.122)—tends to replace a more
vulnerable inward–facing affect—above all, love. Here again we can see the relation between interior and exterior being interrogated.

Others amongst Shakespeare's tragic characters attempt to banish emotion altogether.
Macbeth's attempt to extinguish his own thought-processes ends with a devastating dull-
ing of feeling, of any affective attachment to the world ('I have lived long enough. My
way of life | Is fall'n into the sere'—*Macbeth*, 5.3.24–5). Lady Macbeth's prayer to 'Make
thick my blood. | Stop up th'access and passage to remorse' (1.4.42–3) only seemingly suc-
ceeds in steeling her, or only steels her for so long. Titus aims to adhere to Roman stoical
ideals and traditional tenets of piousness, but ends up a single-mindedly vengeful, 'frantic wretch' (5.3.63); Brutus intellectualizes, fatally suppressing one side of his feelings for
Julius Caesar; Othello 'stone[s his] heart' (*Othello*, 5.2.68), repressing his love and desire
for Desdemona; Coriolanus tries to make himself into an inhuman killing machine before
succumbing to the emotional hold of his family. All are eventually overcome by passion.
The most controlled, self-abnegating characters in Shakespeare either leave one cold or
are revealed to be no less passionate than anyone else, moved by affections and desires
beyond the delusion of self-discipline. These heroes are in the grip of emotions over which
they have barely any grasp, and the roots of which they are only ever dimly aware of
at best. The Shakespearean tragic hero lives out this truth to the full. And it is in this
sense, I suggest, that these characters become scapegoats: not in a moral sense (of taking

---

[31] See e.g. John Kerrigan, *Revenge Tragedy: Aeschylus to Armageddon* (Oxford: Clarendon Press,
1996), esp. 137–41.

[32] See Stanley Cavell, 'The Avoidance of Love: A Reading of *King Lear*', in *Disowning
Knowledge: In Seven Plays of Shakespeare*, 2nd edn. (Cambridge: Cambridge University Press, 2008).

the ethical blame) but in the psychological sense of taking upon themselves (though the term is too volitional) the extremes of emotion we—the hoi polloi of the passions—generally prefer to keep at bay. *We* may attempt at least partially to 'Smooth every passion | That in the nature of their lords rebel' (*Lear*, 2.2.66–7); *they* do not.

The affects, or passions, had a mixed reception in early modern England. On the one side, there was an acceptance of a longstanding anti-passional bias in the West—a combination of classical (Platonic and Stoic) and Christian emphases on the importance of patience and moderation. These converged, and were widely recognized, in the Renaissance, where we can find numberless voices piously upholding the value of reason and self-control. Michael Schoenfeldt has suggested that the disciplining of emotion was constitutive of early modern subjectivity (in the face of the uncertainty and flux of the humoral body in particular).[33] On the other side, Susan James, among others, has amply demonstrated the ambivalence characterizing the period's relation to the passions, and, as Richard Strier has recently argued, this disciplinary regime was very far from all-encompassing: writers like Petrarch, Erasmus, and Montaigne found value in the passions, as did many Christian thinkers, often following St Augustine in conceiving of the passions as subject to either benign or malignant use, but in any case accepting their vital role in helping to shape our lives. When Bishop Edward Reynolds suggests that 'the *Passions* of *Christ* were like the shaking of pure Water in a cleane Vessell, which though it be thereby *troubled*, yet it is not *fouled* at all',[34] he is relying upon a traditional distinction between a (positive) emotional troubling and a (negative) emotional fouling. Shakespeare's Sonnet 94, which opens with the apparent praise of those 'who moving others are themselves as stone, | Unmoved, cold, and to temptation slow' (3–4), can also be taken as an exposé of the inhumanity of emotional control. As Strier points out, Shakespeare's plays and sonnets more often than not tend to embrace the passions.[35] 'Anger', in Kent's words, 'hath a privilege' (*King Lear*, 2.2.68). Indeed, it is precisely when most suppressed—in speaking the language of stoicism and extolling the virtue of self-control—that the actions of the characters tend to display passions at their most violent and uncontrolled. Over and over in Shakespeare's tragedies, the counterweight of emotion (stoicism, patience, calm, control) is not allowed to hold sway as an ideal: the height of stoicism is not the height of humanity, and the 'men of stones' surrounding King Lear (5.3.255) cannot achieve anything approaching his stature. 'Gentlemen by blood, and Noblemen by birth', as Wright puts it, can be 'so appassionate in affections that their company [is] to most men intollerable'.[36] While for most of the other characters, the extremes of emotion are unbearable, the protagonists are fully 'appassionate in affections'; their exceptionality may

---

[33] James, *Passion and Action*; Michael Schoenfeldt, *Bodies and Selves in Early Modern England: Physiology and Inwardness in Spenser, Shakespeare, Herbert and Milton* (Cambridge: Cambridge University Press, 1999), 15–16.

[34] Bishop Edward Reynolds, *A Treatise of the Passions and Faculties of the Soule of Man*, ed. Margaret Lee Wiley (Gainesville, FL: Scholars' Facsimiles and Reprints, 1971), 49 (1640) cit. Paster, *Humoring the Body*, 1.

[35] Richard Strier, *The Unrepentant Renaissance* (Chicago: University of Chicago Press, 2011); as Katherine Rowe has written, 'Shakespeare's interest in tragic emotions is as often anti-Stoic as Stoic': 'Minds in Company: Shakespearean Tragic Emotions', in *A Companion to Shakespeare's Works*, vol. 1: *The Tragedies*, ed. Richard Dutton and Jean E. Howard (Oxford: Blackwell, 2003), 47–72 (47).

[36] Wright, *Passions*, 6.

be 'intollerable', but it inspires something in us. For these tragic heroes are heroic in, among other things, their refusal of patience, their rejection of emotional temperance. They are all 'great of heart' (*Othello*, 5.2.360), by which is meant, I take it, not just that they are noble or courageous, but that their hearts have a capaciousness, a capacity to feel (grief or rage or joy or any other emotion) beyond that of those around them—the very same capacity that threatens to burst the confines of their bodies. 'His captain's heart, | Which in the scuffles of great fights hath burst | The buckles on his breast, reneges all temper' is how Philo admiringly describes the warlike Antony (1.1.6–8).

These issues of agency and volition intersect with yet another uncertainty that emerges in Shakespeare's tragedies' representation and evocation of affect: the problem of 'authenticity' and 'theatricality', of whether affects simply exist, welling up like forces of nature, autonomically and automatically, or whether they can be 'put on', like clothes; and the quality of the relation between these two possibilities. Likewise, the plays leave unanswered the question of how far the emotions can (or should) be controlled: do we acquire or do we beget our temperance? Lear's injunction (to himself? To the gods? To nature?), 'Touch me with noble anger' (2.4.276–8), could make us question something about the authenticity of his wrath; and yet there is no doubting the fact that he *is* angry. Timon appears to make a deliberate choice to embrace wrath: 'The gods ... grant, as Timon grows, his hate may grow, | To the whole race of mankind' (4.1.37–40); at the same time, his enraged state seems to reach the core of his being. Though a character may protest, like Hamlet, that he has 'that within which passes show'—in contradistinction to the 'trappings and the suits of woe', the 'forms, moods, shapes of grief' that are mere 'actions that a man might play' (1.2.82–5)—the standing possibility that even the strongest emotions are always already (at least partly) theatricalized can never be excluded. Hamlet's 'whirlwind of passion' refers to the Players' enactment of a role, and he himself seems to envy the First Player's capacity to 'force his soul [and not, we should note, 'merely' his body] so to his own conceit' (2.2.487) as to generate powerful emotions. Where then is the precise line between 'real' passion and a performed 'dream of passion' (l.488)?[37] The old question of whether Hamlet's madness is 'real' or 'feigned' may be 'something musty', but it can serve to remind us of the uncertainty about these issues coursing through many of Shakespeare's plays. By the time we reach *Antony and Cleopatra*, the distinction between 'real' emotion and that which is performed or fake has become radically eroded, so that it is undecideable in this play whether love is an emotion, an enactment, or a 'mere' performance (and what the relation between these may be).[38] Emotions, as Eve Kosofsky Sedgwick has argued, have an inherently performative dimension, and for performance to be effective—to affect others—it must adhere to certain conventions.[39] Indeed the word 'affect' catches something of this complexity in its combination of meanings—'powerful emotion' on the one hand, 'that which is feigned or

---

[37] On the way performance can produce in the actor a 'real' emotion, see e.g. Neill '"A book where one may read strange matters"'.

[38] For two recent views of the indeterminacy of the (in)authenticity of emotion in *Antony and Cleopatra*, see Schalkwyk, 'Is Love an Emotion', and David Hillman, '"If it be love indeed": Transference, Love, and *Anthony and Cleopatra*', *Shakespeare Quarterly* 64:3 (Fall 2013), 301–33.

[39] See Eve Kosofsky Sedgwick, *Touching Feeling: Affect, Pedagogy, Performativity* (Durham, NC: Duke University Press, 2003).

put on—*affected*' on the other. Hence, when the Countess of Roussillon warns Helena to rein in her sorrow 'lest it be rather thought you affect a sorrow' (*All's Well*, 1.1.50), Helen's response—'I do affect a sorrow indeed, but I have it too' (51)—nicely walks the tightrope between 'real' and performed emotion.

What, then, do *we* feel when watching a Shakespearean tragedy? Tragedy gives us access to affective realms beyond those of everyday experience—though not, Freud would say, beyond the realms of the everyday unconscious: from a psychoanalytic point of view, it is precisely because these emotions are so close to our most repressed core that tragedy speaks to us with such overwhelming force; we can hardly help but identify ambivalently with its protagonists. One could argue, then, that Shakespeare's tragic heroes go through the extremes of emotion *for* us; the intensity with which they feel both gives us and spares us the experience, allowing us to have these passions at one remove, so to speak. We feel for them because they feel for us; we partake, or participate, not only without the consequences in our lives but also without the full blast of affective heat. No need for *us* to be, like Othello, 'eaten up with passion' (3.3.446)—though it is worth contemplating the fact that even Othello seems at times to be both inside and outside the experience of tragedy, commenting upon it even as he goes through it: 'But yet the pity of it, Iago!' (4.1.214–15).

It is as if there is a kind of emotional chiaroscuro at work here: while the events represented in tragedy (and the normative staging of early modern tragedies) are often described as black[40]—the audiences watching are typically depicted as turning white (e.g. 'to turn white and sound [=swoon] at tragic shows'—*A Lover's Complaint* (308), or Hamlet's 'you that look pale and tremble at this chance, | That are but mutes or audience to this act' (5.2.286–7). We are literally appalled at the darkness before us. Thus, when Cassius describes Casca's reaction to 'this dreadful night', he could easily be describing a prototypical audience at a tragedy: 'You look pale, and gaze, | And put on fear, and cast yourself in wonder' (*Julius Caesar*, 1.3.57–72). The purposive dimension of 'put on' and 'cast yourself' may serve to remind us that audiences go to the theatre actively desiring to experience the emotions—the fear and wonder—engendered by tragedy. As Goethe writes in his brief essay on tragedy: 'Whoever is in pursuit of truly moral education of the mind knows and will concede that tragedy and tragic novels do not soothe the spirit, but rather unsettle the emotions and what we call the heart.'[41] Why this should be so has of course been the subject of endless debate. The main lines of response have suggested one of two possibilities: that the emotions experienced by the audience are in some sense unreal, aestheticized and at one remove from the representation (compare for example Timothy Reiss's severe dictum: 'Our dismay and pity inspired by the majestic suffering … are the result of the "machine" of tragedy: our emotions are not to be confused with that machine');[42] or that our emotions *are* real and somehow worked upon—either beneficially, if we follow Aristotle's cathartic hypothesis, or to the detriment of

---

[40] See, for example, the 'bitter, black and tragical' events of *Richard III* (4.4.7), or *Lucrece's* 'Black stage for tragedies' (766), or the reference to the 'blacke visag'd showes' of 'a sullen Tragicke Sceane' in John Marston, *Antonio's Revenge: The History of Antonio and Mellida* (W. Sheares: London, 1633), Prologue, ll. 20 and 7.

[41] Johann Wolfgang von Goethe, 'On Interpreting Aristotle's *Poetics*' (1827), in *Essays on Art and Literature*, ed. John Gearey, trans. Ellen von Nardoff and Ernest von Nardoff (New York: Suhrkamp Publishers, 1986), 199.

[42] Timothy J. Reiss, *Tragedy and Truth: Studies in the Development of a Renaissance and Neoclassical Discourse* (New Haven and London: Yale University Press, 1980), 10.

the common weal, if we follow a Platonic line of reasoning; for it is above all this ability to stir us up—the sheer pathos of tragedy—that troubled Plato and his followers.[43]

But, as we have already seen, there is no reason to have to choose between 'real' and somehow detached emotions: in fact, it seems to me intuitively right to think of Shakespearean tragedy as *both* providing access to powerful emotions in the audience *and* protecting it from their shattering intensity.[44] It is essential to the experience of tragedy that the audience should feel the impulse to turn away in the face of the intolerability of the emotions evoked—and also that it should remain and bear witness, participating in the *almost* literally heart-rending experience. The endings of these tragedies at times openly thematize this ambivalent impulse at once to engage and disengage. It is epitomized in Lodovico's 'Look on the tragic loading of this bed…. The object poisons sight. | Let it be hid' (*Othello*, 5.2.373–4). Again, Timon's self-authored epitaphs at once invite attention and turn the onlookers away: 'Pass by and curse thy fill, but pass | And stay not here' (*Timon*, 5.5.77–8).

It is in *King Lear* that this ambivalent impulse is most sustainedly and intensively interrogated. Watching the titanic emotions released onstage in this play, we are also exposed to a range of potential responses. At one extreme lies the active, interventionist impulse, epitomized by Cornwall's nameless servant who steps in to stop his master from torturing Gloucester—a response for which we surely feel grateful, and also one which we are thankfully spared from having to take on ourselves. Edmund's 'This speech of yours hath moved me, | And shall perchance do good' (5.3.195–6) partakes of this impulse, though the unreliability of the transition from emotion to action may be glimpsed in the long, possibly fatal and barely explicable gap between this statement and his eventual 'Some good I mean to do … Quickly send …' (239–40). At the other extreme lies Lear's vision of himself and Cordelia as incarcerated observers of the court scene (5.3.8–19)—rising above the realm of emotion as they look down, 'As if we were God's spies', at the 'ebb and flow' of 'great ones' (the subject, after all, of so much tragedy). It is an impossible fantasy of superhuman detachment, of transcending the conditions of weeping (an imagination of using one's eyes, Cavell might say, to observe or know while forgetting their function of expressing emotion or acknowledging). It is precisely *not* the position we should be in when watching a tragedy. Our identification with the characters in Shakespeare's tragedies—perpetrators and victims, insofar as they are separable—entails a wrenching emotional experience. Equally, though, it is clear that though we may feel deeply, our hearts do not burst and we do not die: like Albany, we may be 'almost ready to dissolve, | Hearing of this' (5.3.199–200)—but that 'almost' is essential ('dissolve' here may simply mean 'weep', but it may also mean something closer to 'lose oneself'—'As water is in water', in Antony's words, unable to 'hold this visible shape' any longer (*Antony and Cleopatra*, 4.15.10–14)). Though we may 'weep [Lear's] fortune', we cannot 'take [his] eyes' (4.5.165). Kenneth Burke's suggestion that the

---

[43] See esp. Aristotle's *Poetics* 1449b21–28, and Plato's *Republic* bks. 2 and 10; also A. D. Nuttall, *Why Does Tragedy Give Pleasure?* (Oxford: Clarendon Press, 1996), 1–28, and Terry Eagleton, *Sweet Violence: The idea of the tragic* (Oxford: Blackwell, 2003), 153–77.

[44] On this balance between spectatorial distance and engagement, see esp. Maynard Mack, 'Engagement and Detachment in Shakespeare's Plays', in *Essays on Shakespeare and Elizabethan Drama in Honor of Hardin Craig*, ed. Richard Hosley (Columbia: University of Missouri Press, 1962), 275–96; and Kent Cartwright, *Shakespearean Tragedy and Its Double: The Rhythms of Audience Response* (University Park, PA: The Pennsylvania State University Press, 1991).

fifth act of a Shakespearean tragedy 'permits us the great privilege of being present at our own funeral' brilliantly pinpoints the mixed emotions felt by the audience, the way we find ourselves emotionally both inside and outside the representation, 'transform[ing] the passion into an assertion'.[45]

That watching a tragedy entails a balance or tension between identification and distance is already implicit in Aristotle's linking of pity and fear as the desired effect of tragedy. St Augustine takes a similar line in his rejection of tragic drama, in the process offering an insight into the relation between tragedy and affect; as he narrates in the *Confessions*, in going to view 'doleful and tragic scenes'

> a man is more affected by these actions the more he is spuriously involved in these affections. Now, if he should suffer them in his own person, it is the custom to call this 'misery.' But when he suffers with another, then it is called 'compassion.' But what kind of compassion is it that arises from viewing fictitious and unreal sufferings? ... This is the reason for my love of [staged] griefs: that they would not probe into me too deeply (for I did not love to suffer in myself such things as I loved to look at), and they were the sort of grief which came from hearing those fictions, which affected only the surface of my emotion.[46]

Watching a tragedy, Augustine suggests, we desire a delicate balance between feeling too much and feeling not enough. We want to be 'deeply touched' (as he puts it),[47] but not '*too deeply*', so that the representation, in Augustine's striking words, 'affected only the surface of my emotion'. Here again, the question of the relation between inner and outer arises sharply: for where exactly do we place 'the surface of my emotion'?

The protagonists must feel the passion in all its brute, painful force, but we, the spectators, want only to feel '*com*passion': *doloroso, ma non troppo*. Over the past four hundred years, this, more or less, has been the dominant view of the reason we experience tragic affects as pleasurable. Montaigne, writing shortly before Shakespeare's career began, expresses a similar view of the pleasure of tragedy:

> Yet seeke we evidently to know in shadowes, and understand by fabulous representations upon Theaters, to shew of the tragicke revolutions of humane fortune. It is not with out compassion of that wee heare, but wee please our selves to rowze up our displeasure, by the rarenesse of these pitifull events. *Nothing tickles, that pincheth not.*[48]

---

[45]   Burke, *Burke on Shakespeare*, 76–7.

[46]   St Augustine, *The Confessions of St. Augustine*, trans. Albert C. Outler (Mineola, NY: Dover Publications, 2002), Book III, chap. 2, 32.

[47]   Ibid.

[48]   Michel de Montaigne, *The Essayes*, trans. John Florio (London, 1603), bk. II, 12 ('Of Physiognomy'), 589. The French [1595 edition] has: 'Si cherchons nous evidemment de recognoistre en ombre mesme, et en la fable des Theatres, la montre des jeux tragiques de l'humaine fortune. Ce n'est pas sans compassion de ce que nous oyons: mais nous nous plaisons d'esveiller nostre desplaisir, par la rareté de ces pitoyables evenements. Rien ne chatouille, qui ne pince' (Montaigne, *Les Essais*, ed. Jean Balsamo et al. (Paris: Gallimard, 2007), 1092). As Hume says in his essay on tragedy (which, like Montaigne, speculates about the relation between pain and tickling): 'No matter what the passion is: Let it be disagreeable, afflicting, melancholy, disordered; it is still better than that insipid languor, which arises from perfect tranquility and repose': David Hume, 'Of Tragedy' (1757), in Hume, *Essays, moral, political, and literary*, ed. and intro. James Fieser (Bristol: Thoemmes, 2002).

No pain, no gain: not too much emotion, but also, crucially not too little—'wee please our selves to rowze up our displeasure'. What we get from watching a tragedy is a kind of knowledge 'in shadows', a mimetic representation whose remove from 'these pitifull events' is crucial to our ability to experience them 'not with out compassion'. Like Miranda watching the ship go down, we too 'Have comfort', for (as Prospero tells her):

> The direful spectacle of the wrack, which touched
> The very virtue of compassion in thee,
> I have with such provision in mine art
> So safely ordered that there is no soul—
> No, not so much perdition as an hair,
> Betid to any creature in the vessel
> Which thou heard'st cry, which thou saw'st sink.
>
> (*The Tempest*, 1.2.31–40)

If we do not either intervene or die in the face of the tragic affect represented in Shakespeare's 'art', it is because we are held—held together, as well as held in our places—by something we could variously identify as form, ordering structure, poetic rightness, the eloquence of the language (as Hume thought) or even its very metre (as Wordsworth suggested). The affective and the aesthetic realms are held in tension. Thus Walter Kaufmann's claim, that what is tragic about tragedy is 'the emotions it evokes in the spectator', does not seem quite right: it is always these emotions plus something else, something which protects us from them.[49] As Nietzsche saw, the essence of tragedy is the counterpoising of the Dionysian and the Apollonian, which we can perhaps here gloss as the forces of extreme affect and the powers of containment. Miranda's 'O, I have suffered | With those that I saw suffer' (*The Tempest*, 1.2.5–6) tells only half the story: for the spectator at a tragedy, as for Miranda, what is seen and heard may 'knock | Against my very heart' (8–9), but the direction of the knocking—from the outside in (unlike Macbeth's heart knocking at his ribs)—means that we are protected from the uttermost emotion. Our hearts do not break, and we know that we *can also* 'Tell [our] piteous heart[s] | There's no harm done' (14–15), as Prospero tells his daughter.

Lear's 'I should ev'n die with pity | To see another thus' (4.6.50–1) may or may not contain (in that 'should') an ethical imperative, but it does at the very least put pressure on the question of the proper response to tragedy, of what we *should* do when faced with 'a sight most pitiful' (4.5.194). The play's enigmatic closing injunction—'Speak what we feel, not what we ought to say' (5.3.319)—in unbalancing the delicate equilibrium between the affective and the self-protective, nudges us away from the latter (though 'ought' here is as opaque as Lear's 'should'). For, whatever else it does, Shakespearean tragedy reminds us that, though we may be tempted to become 'men of stones' (5.3.253), we should not yield to the temptation.

Note: I thank Jessa Leff, John Kerrigan, Joe Moshenska, Adam Phillips, and Adrian Poole for their generous and helpful comments on drafts of this chapter.

---

[49] Walter Kaufmann, *Tragedy and Philosophy* (Garden City, NY: Doubleday, 1968), 59, cited in Reiss, *Tragedy and Truth*, 12.

SELECT BIBLIOGRAPHY

Campbell, Lily B., *Shakespeare's Tragic Heroes: Slaves of Passion* (London: Methuen, 1970).

Craik, Katharine A. and Tanya Pollard, eds., *Shakespearean Sensations: Experiencing Literature in Early Modern England* (Cambridge: Cambridge University Press, 2013).

Cummings, Brian and Freya Sierhuis, eds., *Passions and Subjectivity in Early Modern Culture* (Farnham: Ashgate, 2013).

Enterline, Lynn, *Shakespeare's Schoolroom: Rhetoric, Discipline, Emotion* (Philadelphia: University of Pennsylvania Press, 2011).

James, Susan, *Passion and Action: The Emotions in Seventeenth-Century Philosophy* (Oxford: Oxford University Press, 1997).

Kerrigan, John, *Revenge Tragedy: Aeschylus to Armageddon* (Oxford: Oxford University Press, 1996).

Maus, Katharine Eisaman, *Inwardness and Theater in the English Renaissance* (Chicago: University of Chicago Press, 1995).

Neill, Michael, '"A book where one may read strange matters": En-visaging Character and Emotion on the Shakespearian Stage', *Shakespeare Survey* 66 (2013), *Working with Shakespeare*, 246–64.

Nevo, Ruth, *Tragic Form in Shakespeare* (Princeton: Princeton University Press, 1972).

Nuttall, A. D., *Why Does Tragedy Give Pleasure?* (Oxford: Clarendon Press, 1996).

Paster, Gail Kern, Katherine Rowe, and Mary Floyd-Wilson, eds., *Reading the Early Modern Passions: Essays in the Cultural History of Emotion* (Philadelphia: University of Pennsylvania Press, 2004).

Paster, Gail Kern, 'The Tragic Subject and Its Passions', in *The Cambridge Companion to Shakespearean Tragedy*, ed. Claire McEachern (Cambridge: Cambridge University Press, 2002), 142–59.

Roach, Joseph, *The Player's Passion: Studies in the Science of Acting* (Ann Arbor: University of Michigan Press, 1993).

Rowe, Katherine, 'Minds in Company: Shakespearean Tragic Emotions', in *A Companion to Shakespeare's Works* vol. 1: *The Tragedies*, ed. Richard Dutton and Jean E. Howard (Oxford: Blackwell, 2003), 47–72.

Schalkwyk, David, 'Is Love an Emotion? Shakespeare's *Twelfth Night* and *Antony and Cleopatra*', *Symploke* 18:1–2 (2011), 99–130.

Strier, Richard, *The Unrepentant Renaissance* (Chicago: University of Chicago Press, 2011).

CHAPTER 10

'DO YOU SEE THIS?' THE POLITICS OF ATTENTION IN SHAKESPEAREAN TRAGEDY

STEVEN MULLANEY

1

NORMAN Rabkin once suggested that there was something to learn about the politics of Shakespearean drama despite the absence of critical consensus about those politics.[1] The conservative, royalist Shakespeare of one generation and the radical, sceptical, ambiguous Shakespeare of the next generation were not merely mutually exclusive but also mutually necessary, in all their contradictions. The politics of a play like *Henry V*, he argued, looked more like a gestalt drawing than an Elizabethan World Picture or a product of the School of Night. He turned, for his gestalt example, to the well-known drawing of a rabbit and/or a duck. At first, the viewer sees a crudely-drawn rabbit; a second later, a crudely-drawn duck. The oscillation from one to the other is prompted not by a shift in visual point-of-view—such as that required by an anamorphic painting like Holbein's *Ambassadors*—but rather a shift in conceptual point-of-view.[2] Two different animals occupy the same lines of the same drawing seen from the same perspective, but only one can be perceived at any given moment. In another gestalt example, one 'sees' a simple drawing of a vase which abruptly becomes two heads facing one another, nose to nose. Foreground and background change places. One image is no more real or plausible than the other and no more obvious or apparent. The same material object—the same pencil or charcoal lines on a page—represents two entirely different entities. The fact that they cannot both be perceived at the same time suggests that they coexist on a time-space continuum that exceeds the viewer's perceptual and conceptual capacities.

---

[1] See Norman Rabkin, 'Rabbits, Ducks, and *Henry V*', *Shakespeare Quarterly* 28:3 (1977), 279–96.

[2] The painting is in The National Gallery, London UK. A smear runs across the lower portion of the portrait of two wealthy merchants; viewed from the side, through a viewing hole in the frame, the smear resolves itself into a human skull. The resolution is produced by a corresponding shift in the viewer's spatial perspective on the painting. It is a positional rather than a conceptual conceit.

It is an elegant analogy, in part because it is so contained, so binary, so either-or, and so easily demonstrable with gestalt figures. The ambivalence becomes more problematic, of course, when it shifts from the visual to the dramaturgical, especially when the gestalt phenomenon is a Shakespearean play, performed before a large and heterogeneous audience. The range of conceptual points of view would be wide in Reformation England, and for a modern critic, this raises the unwelcome spectre of an extreme and unregulated pluralism of interpretations—'anything goes'—or a radical, subjective indeterminacy—'as you like it.' The methodological, analytical, and theoretical cadres of literary criticism are properly skeptical of unbridled pluralisms or *mise en abyme* indeterminacies.[3] Granted, the trade has often recognized rhetorical and theatrical tropes of conceptual incongruity like paradox, contradiction, ambiguity, ambivalence, and so forth. New Criticism spoke this language like a native, but the final aesthetic achievement of New Critical ambiguity was a well-wrought urn; like a Balinese cockfight viewed with the help of 'thick description' also becomes aesthetic whole, albeit a messy, noisy, and bloody one.[4]

But a Shakespearean audience was not composed of twentieth- or twenty-first-century literary critics and cultural anthropologists, and was most likely not concerned with the issues that occupy professors and students of theatre. They did not venture out to The Theatre or across the Thames to the Rose or the Globe in search of cohesive literary meaning or aesthetic integrity—a qualification so obvious that it should perhaps be said out loud every so often. Rabkin's gestalt metaphor doesn't describe what can be found on stage or on the page but rather in the audience, where many different conceptual perspectives would be found. Shifts, conflicts, and incongruities in conceptual perspective are not binary but manifold in early modern drama, especially once 'the audience' is included in the picture. The oscillations an audience can embody, in all of its singularities, make the two dimensions of a gestalt image look flat, for lack of a better word. Shakespeare's audiences were remarkably heterogeneous in terms of class, disposable income, gender, education, citizenship and, among other key and incompatible differences, in terms of religion. Each member of any Elizabethan theatrical audience would occupy his or her own historical, ontological, and social moment, in shared and different and conflicting ways. But the common ground itself was in crisis, due in large part to the affective and cognitive upheavals and after-shocks of the English Reformation(s).[5] Each member of Shakespeare's

[3] I refer to interpretive and ideological pluralism rather than to (multi)cultural pluralism. For the latter, see Mark Eaton, 'The Cultural Capital of Imaginary versus Pedagogical Canons,' *Pedagogy* 1:2 (2001), 305–15; Stefanie Stiles, 'From "Representative" to Relatable: Constructing Pedagogical Canons Based on Student Ethical Engagement', *Pedagogy* 13:3 (2013), 487–50; and John Guillory, *Cultural Capital: The Problem of Literary Canon Formation* (Chicago: University of Chicago Press, 1993), who summarizes and develops the lively debates over canonical and cultural pluralism of the 1980s. In its translation from Derrida to J. Hillis Miller, American deconstruction largely became a celebration of semantic indeterminacy as opposed to a critical analysis of overdetermination and the mystified structures of power it fosters.

[4] See Cleanth Brooks, *The Well-Wrought Urn: Studies in the Structure of Poetry* (New York: Harcourt Brace, 1947) and Clifford Geertz, 'Deep Play: Notes on the Balinese Cockfight', in *The Interpretation of Cultures: Selected Essays* (New York: Basic Books, 1973), 412–54.

[5] Christopher Haigh suggested that the English Reformation was neither singular nor settled in *Reformations: Religion, Politics, and Society under the Tudors* (Oxford: Oxford University Press, 1993).

audiences would be rooted in the gaps and fissures that had been produced in the social landscape—and were still being produced—by those Reformations. Each would have brought his or her own version of the 'trauma of reform', as Huston Diehl characterized it, with them to the playhouse. It was this felt condition of the times, this rooted uprootedness, that produced a corresponding 'drama of reform' whose conceptual points of view could be as contradictory, as oscillating, as unfriendly to consensus or binary modes of thought, as the Elizabethan popular theatre that Diehl and Rabkin had in mind.[6]

For any audience, the phenomenology of theatrical performance is synaptic as well as synthetic, a series of flashpoints which do not necessarily or ultimately cohere in an aesthetic whole. In addition to and sometimes in place of any shared or aesthetic illumination, the audience feels the lack of its own consensus at such points; audience members are variously struck and differently respond—moment by moment, trigger point by trigger point—by the play they nonetheless share. In this, audiences are all alike—but each in its own way—and some are more disquietful than others. In this sense, early modern, public, amphitheatre drama was not only a drama of crisis but also a drama of critical attention, dialectical in its relation to its audience in contrast to other, more didactic examples of theatre.[7] It emerged within a new symbiosis of the public and the private that developed in sixteenth-century England. Moreover, theatrical performance played a role in the development of that symbiosis: in the formation of what social historians have begun to call, with due caution and qualification, an early modern public sphere.

If tragedy is politics, as Napoleon is thought to have said, it is not only because, and perhaps not primarily because, of what is represented and performed on stage. In the case of early modern popular tragedy, the open-ended dialectical engagement I have in mind—between collective and individual, public and private selves—was a dynamic that took place in the audience and not merely in the characters or themes of the play. It was not a process of interpellation, as Louis Althusser characterized the irresistible siren song of ideology, or a didactic message or lesson disguised as a play, but a process of critical social thought and feeling.[8] It can be found in surprisingly small moments of Shakespearean tragedy as well as major crises and turning points, as I hope to show in what follows, turning first to the last moments of *King Lear*.

2

....

Lear sometimes welcomes madness as if it could be a refuge from hard truths—'I am a man more sinned against than sinning'—and sometimes he fears it, as if it might embody the shattered acknowledgement of his own role in the ruin of a family and a kingdom.

---

[6] For these phrases, see Huston Diehl, *Staging Reform, Reforming the Stage: Protestantism and Popular Theater in Early Modern England* (Ithaca, NY: Cornell University Press, 1997).

[7] For a fuller examination of the relation between early modern popular drama and the crises and traumas of the Reformation, see Steven Mullaney, *The Reformation of Emotions in the Age of Shakespeare* (Chicago: University of Chicago Press, 2015).

[8] See Louis Althusser, *Lenin and Philosophy and Other Essays*, trans. Ben Brewster (New York: Monthly Review Press, 1971), 171–5.

Long before the promised end, the audience has repeatedly 'suffered' through the king's ambivalence, self-pity, and shame. His final words, another self-comforting delusion, come as no surprise but they are all the more marked, made all the more possibly significant, by the familiarity of the delusion:

> Do you see this? Look on her: look, her lips,
> Look there, look there!

$$(5.3.308-9)^9$$

Are we glad that Lear dies in false hope rather than despair, even if it allows him, once again, to escape the sharp hook of a just reckoning? The affective and ethical choices of the audience are notably stark in the play's final moments, when the king oscillates between Cordelia alive, a reality which would redeem all sorrows, and Cordelia dead and never to return, 'Never, never, never, never, never.' A moment earlier, a line later, and all is changed. Lear cycles between hope and despair with increasing frequency in the final moments of the play, producing an arrhythmic beat that has become, in this final scene, as inevitable as dying. Back and forth, forth and back, in unpredictable spasms of redemption and damnation in their arbitrary and never eternal return. Will he die redeemed or damned, in hope or in despair? That is the question raised by the irregular and sporadic beating of Lear's heart. Edgar was wrong: in this example of Shakespearean tragedy, at least, it is the banality of timing and not the ripeness that is all.

'Tragedy', as Rita Felski has remarked, 'is good to think with.'[10] The kind of thinking it does—or rather, the kind of thinking we can do with it—has been recognized as a 'mode of critical reflection' with political, ethical, moral, and affective dimensions.[11] In some of its major instantiations, particularly in fifth-century Athens and sixteenth-century England, tragedy has proved acutely sensitive to epistemic conflicts whose effects are also felt and suffered at the level of everyday life. According to Jean-Pierre Vernant, tragedy first emerged as a distinct genre precisely at such a moment of cultural crisis. A 'gap' had developed in what he called 'the heart of social experience':

> It [the gap] is wide enough for the oppositions between legal and political thought on the one hand and the mythical and heroic traditions on the other to stand out quite clearly. Yet it is narrow enough for the conflict in values still to be a painful one and for the clash to continue to take place ... The particular domain of tragedy lies in this border zone ... [and] involves a particular moment.[12]

For Shakespeare and his contemporaries—playwrights, actors, and audiences alike—the opposition was not mythical or heroic but historical, political, social, and religious. The gaps that had opened in social experience were felt at the personal and the familial level

---

[9] All quotations from the play are from *King Lear*, ed. R. A. Foakes (London: The Arden Shakespeare, 2006).

[10] Rita Felski, 'Introduction,' in *Rethinking Tragedy*, ed. Rita Felski (Baltimore: The Johns Hopkins University Press, 2008), 12.

[11] David Scott, 'Tragedy's Time,' in *Rethinking Tragedy*, ed. Rita Felski (Baltimore: Johns Hopkins University Press, 2008), 209.

[12] Jean-Pierre Vernant, 'The Historical Moment of Tragedy in Greece: Some of the Social and Psychological Conditions,' in Jean-Pierre Vernant and Pierre Vidal-Naquet (eds.), *Myth and Tragedy in Ancient Greece*, trans. Janet Lloyd (New York: Zone 1988), 27.

as well as those of state and church governance. They were felt by everyone who had lived through the seismic and unsettling turmoils of the English Reformation,[13] and they were also keenly yet differently felt by the next generation, born as it was into the contested stabilization of English Protestantism and Tudor monarchy.[14] In post-Reformation England, the conflict in values was indeed still painful and the clash of mutually exclusive worlds, still ongoing.

Lear's dying is a private, subjective, and even intimate moment in the play, hardly 'political' in any accustomed sense of the word. But it is also a public moment, taking place in the midst of a number of nested audiences and their worlds, virtual as well as actual, on stage and off. The offstage audience, that singular heterogeneity, can (or must) choose one of a number of ways of thinking and feeling at such moments, and its conflicting and cohering points of view are fundamental to the politics of the play itself. Whether any given individual pities or condemns Lear—he or she might not even care how he dies, as long as he is finally gone—that individual judges him all the same and she does so in an open and public social space, surrounded by a broad sampling of contemporaries of almost every social rank. Whether our responses cleave together or apart, they will at once embody and obscure a complex set of social and political relations. We judge the king, which is a matter of the heart as well as the head, and we reveal ourselves in the process—in all of 'our' post-Reformation contradictions, conjunctions, differences, and communalities. The political in Shakespearean tragedy and tragic drama—what makes tragedy good to think with—grows from moments such as these, I would suggest. It is the product, in other words, of the affective agency of the audience.

'The public stage', write Peter Lake and Stephen Pincus, 'played a crucial role in the creation of the [early modern] public sphere.'[15] It joined in this creation with other, more commonly recognized social forces and media, as Lake and Pincus have noted:

> Print, the pulpit, performance, and circulating manuscripts were all used to address promiscuously uncontrollable, socially heterogeneous, and, in some sense, popular audiences. Such activity implied the existence of, and indeed notionally at least called into being, an adjudicating public or publics able to judge or determine the truth of the matter in hand on the basis of the information and argument placed before them. (276-7)[16]

It is important to recognize, as Lake and Pincus do here, that early modern theatre was a powerful social and discursive force in and of itself. In contemporary discussions of early modern media such as print, manuscript, and forms of orality, we sometimes forget that theatrical 'publication'—the performance of plays on a stage, before a

---

[13] See Mullaney, *The Reformation of Emotions*.

[14] See especially Patrick Collinson, *Elizabethans* (New York: Hambledon and London, 2003); Norman Jones, *The Birth of the Elizabethan Age: England in the 1560's* (London: Wiley-Blackwell, 1995); and Peter Marshall, *Beliefs and the Dead in Reformation England* (Oxford: Oxford University Press, 2002).

[15] Peter Lake and Stephen Pincus, 'Rethinking the Public Sphere in Early Modern England', in *The Politics of the Public Sphere in Early Modern England*, ed. Lake and Pincus (Manchester: Manchester University Press, 2007), 25 n. 23. See also Peter Lake and Michael C. Questier, *The Antichrist's Lewd Hat: Protestants, Papists and Players in Post-Reformation England* (New Haven: Yale University Press, 2002), esp. ch. 14.

[16] Lake and Pincus, 'Rethinking the Public Sphere', 6.

public audience—played the phenomenal role that it did, making public, to thousands of Londoners on a daily basis, a wide range of issues, ideas, and histories.[17] However, I would qualify the closing phrase of their otherwise succinct description above. To my ear, an 'argument placed before them' suggests a more didactic form of theatrical performance than we typically find in the amphitheatre drama of early modern London, one that emphasizes the rhetorical or polemical relation of a performance to an audience at the expense of their dramaturgical and performative relation. Many contemporary discussions of the public sphere share this bias toward direct and ratiocinative debate about public issues, but this emphasis on literal debate and argument asks the wrong question of many forms of art. Shakespeare's tragedies, at any rate, are not pamphlets in disguise or arguments dressed up in a theatrical costume. In its own element, as a form of 'theatrical publication' distinct—especially in this time and place—from oral, scribal, and written forms of publication, theater can produce a powerful way of thinking about social issues that other means and media cannot necessarily address. The arguments produced by Shakespeare's theatre were the ones 'drafted' by his public audience, if you will; each member of that audience exercised an agency that was affective as well as cognitive and not as strictly ratiocinative as Lake and Pincus seem to have in mind.[18]

Such affective agency is not unique to early modern popular audiences, of course. Historical context is everything: here the context includes not only the ongoing 'trauma of reform' but also the surprising emergence of a limited, religiously grounded form of popular sovereignty (such as that which Lake, Questier, Pincus, and others have proposed).[19] In the tragic 'drama of reform,' the limited sovereignty of the audience, a congeries of public or potentially public individuals, was exercised in and produced by the affective thinking that tragedy enables. Sympathy, empathy, pity, and related forms of tragic engagement are social emotions at heart—they are 'embodied thoughts', as Michelle Rosaldo once defined them. They are not merely absorptive or expressive. Rather, they are forms of action in and of themselves, modes of active participation with the world. Affective agency in post-Reformation tragedy creates an inseparable social conjunction of emotion and cognition, 'steeped with the apprehension that "I am involved"' (143).[20]

The social and generic hierarchies of rank and blood are observed in Shakespearean tragedy—these are plays of kings and queens and dukes and earls—yet these hierarchies are

[17] For a fuller exegesis of 'theatrical publication', see Steven Mullaney, *The Reformation of Emotions in the Age of Shakespeare* (Chicago: University of Chicago Press, 2016). See also Andrew Gurr, 'The Shakespearean Stage', in *The Norton Shakespeare*, ed. Stephen Greenblatt et al., 2nd edn. (New York: W. W. Norton & Company, Inc., 2008), 79–99.

[18] Michael Warner also suggests that publics are 'called' or 'addressed' into being. See *Publics and CounterPublics* (Cambridge, MA: Zone Books, 2005), 71. For a fuller critique of such a view, see Steven Mullaney, 'What's Hamlet to Habermas? Spatial Literacy, Theatrical Publication, and the Publics of the Early Modern Public Stage', in *Making Space Public in Early Modern Europe: Performance, Geography, Privacy*, ed. Angela Vanhaelen and Joseph P. Ward (Routledge, 2013), 17–40.

[19] G. R. Elton proposed the development of a form 'national sovereignty' in *England under the Tudors* (London: Routledge, 1991), 160.

[20] Michelle Z. Rosaldo, 'Toward an Anthropology of Self and Feeling', in *Culture Theory: Essays on Mind, Self, and Emotion*, ed. Richard Shweder and Robert Levine (Cambridge: Cambridge University Press, 1984), 137–57 (143).

also in a state of perpetual oscillation with the domestic, the private and, most important, the common. Once we recognize Reformation popular drama as one of the contributors to an early modern public sphere, Shakespearean tragedy comes into focus as a venue and catalyst for thinking about the inherent contradictions as well as the hegemonic structures of hierarchical authority. Elizabethan theatre was not, as Jürgen Habermas misconceived it, a mirror that reproduced and disseminated the princely or 'representative publicity' of the state.[21] Shakespearean tragedy displaces the *res publica* (matters of state accessible only through privileged *arcanae imperii*) into public things, accessible to anyone with a heart, a mind, and the price of admission to the Globe. The public stage expanded, as it were, to include the stage of majesty, as if the former contained and produced the latter.

Shakespeare's tragedies and tragic histories seem particularly intent on discovering difference in addition to, and sometimes instead of, communality. Empathy for the heavy head that wears the crown can mystify princely power and authority, as many have argued in the history of twentieth-century interpretation, and probably did so for many members of Shakespeare's original audiences. But on the early modern public stage in general, and Shakespeare's tragedies in particular, sympathy or empathy can also clarify and hold up for judgement, ironize, and 'derogate' that authority.[22] Empathy on the early modern public stage involved a complex and paradoxical enfolding of public and private spheres. Ever wary of 'empathy' in the theatre of his own times and devoted to its alienation, Brecht nonetheless embraced its Shakespearean embodiments:

> Take the element of conflict in Elizabethan plays, complex, shifting, largely impersonal, never soluble, and then see what has been made of it today, whether in contemporary plays or in contemporary renderings of the Elizabethans. Compare the part played by empathy then and now. What a contradictory, complicated and intermittent operation it was in Shakespeare's theatre![23]

Brecht's enthusiasm is remarkable, considering how sceptical he could be about many if not all forms of emotional immersion in the world on stage. This is an empathy of conflict rather than immersion, insoluble rather than self-consuming.

'To see the world feelingly,' as Lear counsels Gloucester, one needs ears and hearts as well as the mind's eyes. To see it feelingly was also to see it politically: to see it and rethink it from the perspective of a more self-interpellated public individual.[24] The fault-lines that had opened up in the social, religious, and political landscape of the period were typically not performed or represented on Shakespeare's stage in any direct or explicit sense. They

[21] See Jürgen Habermas, *The Structural Transformation of the Public Sphere: An Inquiry into a Category of Bourgeois Society*, trans. Thomas Burger (Cambridge, MA: MIT Press, 1989), 38.

[22] See David Scott Kastan, 'Proud Majesty made a subject: Shakespeare and the Spectacle of Rule', *Shakespeare Quarterly* 37:4 (1986), 459–75; Robert Weimann, 'Bifold Authority in Shakespeare's Theatre', *Shakespeare Quarterly* 39:4 (1988), 401–17.

[23] Berthold Brecht, *Brecht on Theatre: The Development of an Aesthetic*, ed. and trans. John Willett (New York: Hill and Wang, 1964), 161.

[24] For further discussion of this aspect of publics and counter-publics, see Craig Calhoun, 'Imagining Solidarity: Cosmopolitanism, Constitutional Patriotism, and the Public Sphere', *Public Culture* 14:1 (2002), 152.

did not have to be. They were always and already there, incarnated in the fractured collective identity of its 'post-Reformation' audience.

3

Is tragedy a *genre* of theatre, with rules or expected features that playwright and audience can anticipate? Or is it a *mode* of critical social thought? The question is falsely framed, of course. These are not mutually exclusive categories but different ways of approaching the same object of inquiry. Shakespeare was notoriously unconcerned with generic consistency, to the disdain of Restoration critics like Dryden or Nahum Tate, who corrected him by rewriting his plays as well as chiding him for them. Given the range of Shakespeare's treatment of protagonist, structure, time, place, and so forth, it is clear that tragedy's potential for experiment and discovery fascinated him. From early to late experiments with the genre, his interest in tragedy as a mode of critical social thought remains keen as well as consistent. Shakespearean tragedy, then and in a number of modern productions, can operate brilliantly as a vehicle for political, social, and historical thinking.

But thinking by whom? And thinking about what? The question of agency in classical tragedy is not neatly answered by the question of fate. Greek tragedy has been characterized as 'an uncanny unraveling of the distinction between agency and fate'.[25] Jean-Pierre Vernant and Pierre Vidal-Naquet observed that 'the same character appears now as an agent, the cause and source of his actions, and now as acted upon, engulfed in a force that is beyond him and sweeps him away'.[26] Athenian tragedy viewed the relationship between the two roles, first as a subject with agency and then again as object of fate, as an oscillation rather than an opposition, a preliminary grappling with the 'tensions and ambiguities' that remained in the city, outside the bounds of the Theatre of Dionysos. These were tensions and ambiguities of the present rather than the past, questions of the *polis* and the practices of everyday life within it rather than the *mythos* alone.

Shakespeare's tragedies were written for a generation whose 'official' beliefs left little room for human agency in any ultimate or cosmological sense, although many actually existing Calvinists found ways of making the doctrine of predestination more malleable.[27] Moreover, they were written for a generation whose affective as well as doctrinal ties to the past had been under attack for nearly sixty years. The English Reformation sought 'to sever the relationship between the dead and the living,' in Keith Thomas's terms, and to create a new generation that would be 'indifferent to the spiritual fate of its predecessors'.[28] Indifferent, in other words, about whether your mother or father, beloved grandmother or grandfather, were in hell or in heaven. Tragedy is a genre of memory and mourning, of grief and its unsettled relations with the past, the dead, and the losses that can't be forgotten or left behind.[29] The Protestant 'rage against the dead' in England has been well documented in

---

[25] Felski, *Rethinking Tragedy*, 11.   [26] Vernant and Vidal-Naquet, *Myth and Tragedy*, 77.
[27] See Jones, *The Birth of the Elizabethan Age*.
[28] Keith Thomas, *Religion and the Decline of Magic: Studies in Popular Beliefs in Sixteenth- and Seventeenth-Century England* (New York: Scribner's, 1971), 603.
[29] Tragedy as a genre of mourning is more directly developed by Walter Benjamin, *The Origin of German Tragic Drama* (London: Verso Books, 1977).

both its doctrinal and its popular aspects.[30] In general, it amounted to a massive attempt at social, emotional, and spiritual reprogramming. The elimination of Purgatory from all past, present, and future existence, the declaration that it had never been anything but a papist lie, had staggering effects on historical consciousness and domestic, familial, and generational identities. England had been a public, performative culture long before the Reformation or the emergence of the popular stages of Shakespeare's lifetime. Tragedy had been missing from its public performances, however, throughout the medieval period. It has sometimes been suggested that tragedy is not possible in a faith as redemptive in shape and theological form as Christianity, but the Protestant Reformation in England would seem to reveal the absurdity of such speculation. In a public, performative, and sometimes radically Christian culture like Reformation England, tragedy seems to have been a collateral necessity, providing one way to address the fault-lines that had perforce opened up in collective memory and private feeling.

The politics of faith in the late Middle Ages, unlike that fostered or attempted by Protestant reformers, included an embodied affective consciousness of the past, deeply rooted and localized in the dead. In Natalie Davis's wry phrase, the dead were one of the core 'age groups' of early modern society.[31] The place of the dead in the social body was challenged on a number of fronts by the Reformation; their presence, in the actual, everyday landscapes of memory like churchyards and ossuaries, was uprooted and eliminated in literal as well as symbolic ways. Tragedy as a mode of social thought seems purposebuilt for traumas of reform such as these. It is historical consciousness in performance, as it were.

It is odd but illuminating that revenge tragedy was one of the most popular genres of the Elizabethan stage. Odd, because the revenge stories enacted on the popular stage were, for the most part, imported from abroad, and because England was not, as Spain and Italy were, a revenge culture in the historical or anthropological sense of the term. Revenge tragedy becomes English, as it were, local and immediately compelling, once we place it in its proper, immediate relation to the Protestant 'rage against the dead'. It 'spoke to the anxieties produced by this painful transformation in relations with the dead'.

> Revenge tragedy, at the deepest level, is less about the ethics of vendetta that it is about murderous legacies of the past and the terrible power of memory. If English Renaissance tragedy played out society's effort to reach a new accommodation with death, the drama of revenge showed how that must be contingent on the struggle to accommodate the dead themselves.... [The revenger] is the agent of that remembrance upon which a restored social order is felt to depend; but he has ceased to be a social man, for in his willed surrender to the claims of the dead he invariably 'loses' or 'forgets' himself. [32]

The unsettled status of the dead in Reformation England haunted the affective landscape. In a Calvinist state, intent on a massive reconfiguration of historical and eschatological consciousness, graves and ossuaries were also, always and already, political issues.

---

[30] J. Weever, *Ancient Funerall Monuments* (1631), 50–1; cited in Marshall, *Beliefs and the Dead in Reformation England*, 93.

[31] Natalie Zemon Davis, 'Ghosts, Kin, and Progeny: Some Features of Family Life in Early Modern France,' *Daedalus* 106:2 (1977), 92.

[32] Neill, 'Accommodating the Dead', 244, 252.

4

By indirections, as Claudius says in *Hamlet*, we find directions out. His comment is a more precise articulation of the politics and poetics of Shakespearean tragedy than Hamlet's more often cited talk of mirrors held up to nature. As a political device in the right hands, indirection provides recourse to varied forms of tactical subterfuge and is represented as such in the actions of revenge protagonists like Hamlet as well as villains like Claudius. As a theatrical device, however, indirection also provides a kind of methodology for thinking about 'political Shakespeare'. Shakespeare's histories, sometimes published as tragedies, represent the Catholic past of England but with regular echoes and intrusions of Reformation thought, beliefs, and concerns; they work not by analogy, allegory, topicality, or teleology but through structures of what Peter Womack has called 'constructed anachronisms'.[33] Revenge tragedy offered a different mode of social and cultural refraction. Drawn from stories told by other cultures, often in prose fictions and histories, it 'translated' or conveyed these stories to a society whose everyday and irresolvable concerns had little or nothing to do with the ethics of revenge but everything to do with the political, religious, social, and historical contradictions of Reformation England. The contemporaneous relevance of revenge tragedies like *Titus Andronicus, Romeo and Juliet, Hamlet*, and *Othello* lies not in their social relevance but in their social irrelevance, so to speak. They are about societies that are broken and cannot fix themselves by traditional means such as courts of law; they are about the dead, who need to be remembered but cannot be properly heard; and most important, they are about disrupted relations between the world of the living and the worlds of the past.

There is every reason to think that Shakespeare's audiences welcomed the oblique and indirect modes of political and social thought with which he challenged them. The demographics of attendance alone suggest that they were. For more direct and satiric dealings with the lesser dilemmas of early modern life, playgoers went elsewhere, to city comedies in intramural theatres. They delighted in decoding sometimes subtle, sometimes caricatured topical allusions to actual citizens—in the case of Jonson, Chapman, and Marston's *Eastward Ho!*, the sitting monarch himself.[34] At the amphitheatres outside the city walls, where tragedy flourished, playgoers went to see and hear plays that demanded a different kind of investment, attention, and performative literacy.

5

'I am Richard II,' Elizabeth exclaimed in August of 1601, 'know ye not that?' According to William Lambarde, she was referring to a play that had been commissioned by friends

---

[33] Peter Womack, 'Imagining Communities: Theatres and the English Nation in the Sixteenth Century,' in *Culture and History 1350–1600: Essays on English Communities, Identities, and Writing*, ed. David Aers (Detroit, MI: Wayne State University Press, 1992), 99.

[34] On topicality, see Leah Marcus, *Puzzling Shakespeare: Local Reading and Its Discontents* (Berkeley: University of California Press, 1988).

of Robert Devereaux, the Earl of Essex, to be performed at The Globe on the eve of the abortive Essex rebellion in 1601.[35] We do not know if it was Shakespeare's *The Tragedie of Richard the Second*, as the venue and company might intimate. But the possibility that it was, that the 'tragedy [that] was played 40tie times in open streets and houses' was Shakespeare's play, has made this passage from Lambarde 'arguably the most widely cited "historical evidence" in discussions relating to Elizabethan theatre and society'.[36]

It was Elizabeth's recognition scene that prompted Jonathan Dollimore to ask, 'can "tragedy" be a strictly literary term when the Queen's own life is endangered by the play?'[37] Revisionist historians and critics have challenged the authenticity of the 'evidence', most aggressively Jonathan Bate in his biography of Shakespeare, *The Soul of an Age* (2009). Counter-revisionists have countered, some of them quite convincingly.[38] What we can say for certain is that the queen's purported reaction—taking it both personally and politically—is entirely credible in historical terms. It provides a vivid account of how a play becomes political. It tells us nothing about the politics of the play as written, however, and it tells us nothing about the way in which it was performed on any given occasion, providing no clue as to props, style of acting, tone, blocking, interpretive cuts and inclusions, and so forth. What it does tell us, or remind us of, is the fact that tragedy (like politics) is always local, always contextual, and always the judgement of a specific, adjudicating public individual.[39] Imagine a commoner in the queen's place, surrounded by other commoners instead of courtiers, and the same is true with one qualification. Elizabeth was already a public individual and had been one for her entire life, while the commoner became him or herself as such—a public individual—at the moment she or he reached a similar conclusion about the politics of the play in performance, on the night in question.

By 1601, regular playgoers at The Globe or The Swan or any of the other venues for popular drama on the outskirts of early modern London would have been well-versed in such metamorphoses of private and public identities. A kind of 'professional' public audience, as it were, had developed in conjunction with a newly professional kind of public theatre. Playgoers paid for admission, of course, which is not just an economic transaction but also a choice, a discretionary or elective decision to attend. And they had also become 'professional' in another and more important sense of the word. They had become a skilled or fully-apprenticed audience. The playgoers were literate, in other words, in a theatrical or performative sense. Not uniformly so, of course. Some brought a finer attention and a better ear to the theatre, without a doubt, but the economic success of amphitheatre drama alone bears witness to the audience's definitive capability to experience and enjoy a

---

[35] See James Scott-Warren, 'Was Elizabeth I Richard II? The Authenticity of Lambarde's "Conversations"', *The Review of English Studies* 64:264 (2012), 208–30.

[36] James Siemon, *Word against Word: Shakespearean Utterance* (Amherst: University of Massachusetts Press, 2002), 101.

[37] Jonathan Dollimore and Alan Sinfield, *Political Shakespeare: new essays in cultural materialism* (Ithaca, NY: Cornell University Press, 1985), 8.

[38] See Scott-Warren, 'Was Elizabeth Richard II?'

[39] Elizabeth's purported words also remind us that Shakespeare's *Richard II* was a tragedy (as opposed to a history play) in the critical, theatrical, historical, and political worlds of 1601. It would continue to be regarded as such until the *Folio* of 1623, where it appears among the history plays with the less provocative title, *The Life and Death of King Richard the Second*.

repertoire of drama in verse that was extraordinarily rich, dense, complex, and, for them as for us, demanding.

One individual might register the anachronisms of *Titus Andronicus* while another might be oblivious to the 'popish tricks and ceremonies' Aaron claims to have observed and the 'ruinous monasteries' that dot the landscape of a classical Rome that shares peculiar landmarks with Reformation England. Lucas Erne has argued that such anomalies would have been noticed by some and that, when noticed, they would have established what he calls 'the Reformation context in *Titus Andronicus*'.[40] I would agree entirely. However, Erne assumes there would be a single probable signification to such religious anachronisms, once noticed. They were 'innocuous enough for the inattentive, yet meaningful for the insider'—and 'the insider,' in Erne's argument, is a Catholic who, being in the know, would be attentive enough to hear the playwright when whispering his own sympathies in his or her ear. This seems fanciful, remotely possible—Erne himself demonstrates that such an association can be made, since he has made it—but it is largely counter-intuitive. Wouldn't attentive playhouse papists be more likely to take offence at the play or author when 'popish tricks and ceremonies' are discovered in an ancient Rome whose 'cruel irreligious piety' encompasses human sacrifice and cannibalism? Jean de Lery was not the only early modern Protestant to wryly regard the doctrine of transubstantiation as a theological endorsement of cannibalism, even cruder than that practised by Titus or the Tupinamba of Brazil. 'They wanted not only to eat the flesh of Jesus Christ grossly rather than spiritually,' as he commented on those who believed in either tran- or consubstantiation, 'but what was worse, like the savages named *Ouetaca* … they wanted to chew and swallow it raw.'[41]

My point is not to replace one veiled declaration of authorial belief with another; rather, it is to suggest that anachronism, incongruity, contradiction, and other signatures of Shakespearean tragedy should not be approached as semiotic codes at the expense of the phenomenological experience of the audience. Brief phrases and moments of incongruity are easily let go as unnoticed or insignificant, but once noticed, they can be arresting in a quasi-Brechtian sense. Fresh from his Protestant education in Wittenberg, Hamlet meets the spirit of his murdered father, who has himself arrived that night from a Catholic purgatory that, from the perspective of Wittenberg (the home of Luther), has never existed and never will—yet the ghost must return to it at the sound of the cock. I have no idea how an Elizabethan audience member might react to the scene in terms of his or her own beliefs, but I do think it would be safe to say that Catholic and Protestant would not react the same.[42]

Matters of religion are not the only provocations to thought. When Henry V rouses his troops with the prophetic promise that their deeds at Agincourt will be hallowed and remembered every year on St Crispin's day, it is an inspiring moment for his men. For his

[40] Lucas Christian Erne, ' "Popish Tricks" and "a Ruinous Monastery": *Titus Andronicus* and the Question of Shakespeare's Catholicism', in Lucas Erne and Guillemette Bolens, *The Limits of Textuality* (Tübingen: Université de Genève, 2000), 135–55.

[41] Jean de Léry, *History of a Voyage to the Land of Brazil, Otherwise Called America*, trans. Janet (Berkeley: University of California Press, 1990), 41.

[42] For an extensive meditation on this moment, see Stephen Greenblatt, *Hamlet in Purgatory* (Princeton: Princeton University Press, 2002).

larger, offstage audience, however, the effect might have been less celebratory. St Crispin's Day, a Catholic holy day, had not been observed for most of Elizabeth's reign, as any Londoner in the audience would certainly have known. The soldiers' hope and inspiration, produced by the proto-nationalistic invocation of England, is framed by the dramatic irony of history. The paid-forward anachronism is there for anyone to hear, everyone to ignore. The entire audience might cheer with the soldiers, proud of being English men and women too, but knowing as they do what the soldiers can't know—that the prophecy is false, that the promise of lasting, national, and collective commemoration will prove a lie—their cheer might hollow out at the end, leaving them with something to think about once the play is over.

Audience members might not know much about English history, in terms of what they brought with them to the theatre, especially the majority who could not read and had little or no schooling. Knowledge is power, it is often said.[43] Among the powers that historical knowledge confers is the realization that alternative political, social, cultural, and religious worlds are possible and have existed. As popular audiences attended to a play like *Richard II*, they acquired a body of accurate and distorted facts about the past and they also, more important, made public judgements about public things like the motives and shortcomings of kings, the justifications for rising up against an anointed king, and the thought that there are many kinds of uprising, including various kinds of indirection, as Bolingbroke demonstrates. They might side with Bolingbroke or the king in one scene but change their hearts and minds in the next, making different cognitive and affective decisions than those around them and for different reasons. All the while, by direct and indirect means, they were made well aware of the fractures that remained unset and poorly healed in their individual and collective identities.

If early modern audience members were becoming participants in 'an adjudicating public or publics' as they experienced and responded to a play in process, this does not mean that 'the audience' judged or responded as a whole, on cue, or even necessarily in accord. It takes a lot of work and craft to catalyse such moments of affective communality on stage, then and now, as any actor, author, or director can testify. Like the word that designates it, or them, an audience *in situ* is at once a singular plurality and a plural *individuum* of singularities—and the relation between these states of being is highly unstable. Situated as it was in the midst of a radically heterogeneous and conflicted post-Reformation society, Shakespearean tragedy seems to have played to its strengths: the heterogeneity of its audience, the embodied conflicts and differences that tragedy confronted, literally, spatially, and conceptually. Day-lit, thrust into the midst of the auditors and spectators in the yard, nested within all the uncertainties of belief of the Reformation, the theatrical and cultural architectonics of amphitheater drama meant that no one in the audience could view the action on stage without also seeing other audience members in the immediate background or periphery. The awareness was audible as well as visual. Frowns, smiles, quizzical brows, and other registers of embodied thought would betray, in the climate of the Elizabethan compromise, identities and ideas that might otherwise be kept close and secret. Any serious issue could be a trigger for the church papists, the Anabaptists, the strict Calvinists, the Anglicans, and so forth, to disapprove or embrace.

---

[43] Most memorably, for most of us, by Michel Foucault.

The same action or words might bring sadness to one but joy to another. The fault-lines of the social, religious, and political landscape of the period were not merely performed or alluded to onstage. They were also, immediately and viscerally, embodied in the fractured collective identity of its 'post-Reformation' audience.

According to Aristotle, Athenian tragedy brought the social back into association with itself by means of 'catharsis', in a purgative, cleansing, and quasi-ritual resolution. Tragedy only achieves the tragic, in a sense, when it finally forgets itself, ceases to behave like theatre and shifts instead into ritual. The city becomes healthy and whole again through a sublated ceremony of the pharmakos. The theatre of Dionysus coheres the community, once again. Whether this is what Aristotle meant or not—this understanding of *catharsis*—is debatable among classicists, who draw a more distinct line between ritual and theatre. Was Aristotle correct, that the function of tragedy was ultimately to restore the city to health and wholeness? Some prominent classicists have disagreed. 'The tragic universe is everything but a replica of the city,' Nicole Loraux has recently cautioned, 'which Vidal-Naquet characterizes as being "in its very structure an anti-tragic machine".'[44]

The history of twentieth-century Shakespearean criticism is similarly divided, as a brief return to *King Lear* might clarify. When Albany invokes divine assistance, he joins the many other characters who have also invoked the gods, always with the same result—no one home—but Albany's effort receives an enhanced and ironic dramatic emphasis:

> ALBANY: The gods defend her. Bear him hence awhile.
> *[Enter Lear with Cordelia in his arms]*
>
> (5.3.254-SD)[45]

The play is peopled by individuals who keep doing the same thing over and over again and keep expecting different results.[46] For a generation of religiously-minded scholars in the mid-twentieth-century, however, the existential bleakness of *Lear* was understood as a prompt and reminder of the need for Christian redemption. In this view, the play took its audience to the brink of despair in order to produce a countervailing embrace of a Christian god and a stable, providential, and hierarchical order.[47] Cordelia becomes a paradoxical prefiguration of Christ, from such an interpretive perspective. In *King Lear and the Gods*, however, William R. Elton instead aligned the play's political scepticism with potentially radical strands of Reformation thinking, an avenue later explored by J. M. Lever and Jonathan Dollimore.[48] Many today would say that Elton, Lever, and Dollimore

---

[44] Nicole Loraux, *The Mourning Voice: An Essay on Greek Tragedy* (Ithaca: Cornell University Press, 2000), 20.

[45] The stage direction appears in both quarto and folio.

[46] Offered as a definition of insanity, the saying has been attributed to figures as various as Albert Einstein and Benjamin Franklin.

[47] For a representative sampling of such work, see Roy Wesley Battenhouse, ed., *Shakespeare's Christian Dimension: An Anthology of Commentary* (Bloomington: Indiana University Press, 1994).

[48] William R. Elton, *King Lear and the gods* (San Marino, CA: Huntington Library, 1966); J. W. Lever, *The Tragedy of State* (London: Methuen, 1971); Jonathan Dollimore, *Radical Tragedy: Religion, Ideology, and Power in the Drama of Shakespeare and his Contemporaries* (Chicago: University of Chicago Press, 1984).

captured the social, political, religious, and tragic dimensions of the play most fully and that earlier, redemptive views were self-revealing projections of the critic onto the play. Such wishful thinking, from this point of view, was precisely what the play had been deconstructing, from start to finish.

And that's true, too. Gloucester's devastating affirmation of Edgar's penultimate philosophy of endurance rather than hope—that 'ripeness is all'—captures the radical pluralism of Shakespearean tragedy quite well. Does the overt nihilism of a play like *King Lear* produce a contrary if not paradoxical need for everything that is not in the play—a world where god or gods do answer prayers, who could and would have defended Cordelia? Could such a response have occurred in 1604? All is not lost if the speculative answer is in the positive. The clash between mutually exclusive points of view, whether in journals of English literature or among an audience at The Globe, is not necessarily the sign of an unhealthy interpretative community. In fact, such possibilities for tension may be more accurate registers of the way tragic thought takes place in the theatre than the supposition that contradiction and ambiguity are meant to resolve themselves into a well-wrought aesthetic or ideological urn.

As a mode of critical social thought, dialectical rather than didactic, Shakespeare's tragedies were diagnostic in nature and not always or necessarily therapeutic. From any perspective or any level of attention, there would always be something overlooked by one but not by another, appalling to one but comforting or reassuring to another, sometimes unsettling to all but in starkly different ways. Shakespearean tragedy might be best described in terms of an open-ended dialectical engagement with the audience, an engagement that might be resolved at the level of genre—on stage or on the page, tragedy must also have a stop—but not as a mode of critical social thought. Theatre is a social art in phenomenological as well as thematic or mimetic terms, and in times of social crisis—which are, after all, the times when tragedy tends to emerge—resolution is not necessarily the goal. The poetics as well as the politics of early modern popular tragedy were radically heterodyne: it had been custom-built for an audience that was well-practised, because well-rehearsed, in the art of making different and contradictory senses out of the rabbits and ducks it paid to see and hear on a daily basis.

SELECT BIBLIOGRAPHY

Collinson, Patrick, *The Birthpangs of Protestant England: Religious and Cultural Change in the Sixteenth and Seventeenth Centuries* (Basingstoke: Macmillan, 1988).

Diehl, Huston, *Staging Reform, Reforming the Stage: Protestantism and Popular Theater in Early Modern England* (Ithaca, NY: Cornell University Press, 1997).

Eiland, Howard, 'Reception in Distraction', *boundary* 2, 30:1 (2003), 51–66.

Felski, Rita, ed., *Rethinking Tragedy* (Baltimore: Johns Hopkins University Press, 2008).

Garner, Stanton, *Bodied Spaces: Phenomenology and Performance in Contemporary Drama* (Ithaca, NY: Cornell University Press, 1994).

Greenblatt, Stephen, *Hamlet in Purgatory* (Princeton: Princeton University Press, 2001).

Lake, Peter and Stephen Pincus, 'Rethinking the Public Sphere in Early Modern England', in *The Politics of the Public Sphere in Early Modern England*, ed. Lake and Pincus (Manchester: Manchester University Press, 2007), 1–30.

Marshall, Peter, *Beliefs and the Dead in Reformation England* (Oxford: Oxford University Press, 2002).

Mullaney, Steven, *The Reformation of Emotions in the Age of Shakespeare* (Chicago: University of Chicago Press, 2015).

Neill, Michael, *Putting History to the Question; Interrogation, Torture, Truth* (New York: Columbia University Press, 2000).

Vanhaelen, Angela and Joseph P. Ward, eds., *Making Space Public in Early Modern Europe: Performance, Geography, Privacy* (Routledge, 2013).

CHAPTER 11

....

TRAGEDY AND RELIGION
Religion and Revenge in Titus Andronicus
and Hamlet

....

PETER LAKE

1

....

MURDER was conceived in the early modern period as the primal crime and sin. Not only did it cry to heaven for justice, it created a rent in the social and moral fabric that demanded retributive and compensatory action if social peace and moral consensus were to be restored. Revenge could be conceived as a means to achieve both those ends, doing God's work by bringing the culprit to a just end, while performing the compensatory, as well as punitive, work necessary to restore the human community to some sort of equilibrium. If revenge can be conceived as a form of justice, justice can also be conceived as a form of revenge.

While justice is public, revenge is private. In the early modern period no less than today, whereas judicial punishment might retain many of the lineaments of revenge—and perhaps even perform some of the same social, symbolic and emotional work—the official ideologies of both church and state sought to distinguish sharply between them. On one view a means to see justice done, and reparation made, as an extra-legal, private act, revenge also almost always led to another crime being committed and could thus itself easily become the source not of social peace but of continuing, indeed heightened, conflict. Unconstrained, the dynamic of action and reaction inherent in revenge, the mutually defining and confirming identities and enmities of revenger and revengee, could all too easily become perpetuated, almost institutionalized, in the feud. In the most extreme situations, when the deeds involved took in the highest levels of social and political power, this was a process of escalation that could culminate not only in civil war but even in the complete breakdown of both moral and political order.[1] That, of course, was the nightmare world that Shakespeare conjured in the *Henry VI* plays.

---

[1] See the discussion in Michael Neill, 'English Revenge Tragedy', in Rebecca Busnell, ed., *Revenge, a Companion* (Oxford: Blackwell, 2005); Fredson Bowers, *Elizabethan Revenge Tragedy* (Princeton: Princeton University Press, 1940).

Historians of medieval and early modern Europe have been much concerned with the ways in which contemporaries, for the most part agents of the church and state, sought to constrain, contain, and redirect the energies and impulses released by revenge and instantiated in, and sustained by, the feud. While of long standing, such efforts were both accelerated and transformed by the two defining events of the early modern period. For when clerics and lawyers, formed by the definitions of obedience, order, and true Christianity produced by the Renaissance and Reformation |s, looked at the sort of peace produced by the feud, and at the animosities and tensions that it was the *raison d'être* of late medieval Christianity to contain within the ritual and social instantiations of charity and community, they—unlike many anthropologically informed modern historians—tended to see nothing but sin and irreligion, disorder and conflict.[2] The results were intermittently systematic and cumulatively incremental attempts to extend the jurisdiction of both the secular and ecclesiastical courts, and, with that, the reach of various forms of (coactive and internalized) spiritual discipline over areas of life hitherto controlled by more local, unofficial and collectively consensual—if not always consensus-producing—systems of arbitration, dispute resolution, and justice. Of course, as historians of crime, like Cynthia Herrup, have long insisted, the supposedly impersonal and objective workings of the royal courts continued to be mitigated by communal norms and local knowledge,[3] but, over the *longue durée,* the direction of change was clear enough.[4] In post-Reformation England, the dominant ideal was expressed in a somewhat idealized vision of the ways in which divine and human justice, the workings of the courts and of divine providence, the efforts of the ministers of God's word and of secular magistrates, worked together in the doing of justice, the maintenance of social peace and reaffirmation of the moral norms of the Christian community.

The central belief was that, as the most dreadful of crimes, murder (even when committed in secret, by the most powerful or well-connected of people) must and would out. If all else failed, and the flimsy, hand to mouth investigative powers of the authorities failed to reveal the truth of the matter, it was widely assumed or asserted that the demands of divine justice and workings of divine providence would ensure that, if necessary by miraculous means, even the most successfully hidden of crimes would eventually be revealed, along with the identity of the perpetrators.

Once the crime and its perpetrators had been discovered, it was the task of public justice to bring the culprits to judgement, condemnation and execution, leaving their souls, first, to the tender ministrations of the clergy and ultimately to the both perfectly just and perfectly merciful judgement of God. On this account, the secular authorities showed mercy, and

---

[2] See e.g. John Bossy, *Christianity in the West, 1400-1800* (Oxford: Oxford University Press, 1985).

[3] Cynthjia Herrup, *The Common Peace* (Cambridge: Cambridge University Press, 1987).

[4] John Bossy, ed., *Disputes and Settlements: Law and Human Relations in the West* (Cambridge: Cambridge University Press, 1983); Bossy, *Christianity in the West*; Keith Brown, *Bloodfeud in Scotland 1573-1625: Violence, Justice and Politics in an Early Modern Society* (Edinburgh: John Donald, 1986); Mervyn James, *Society, Politics and Culture; Studies in Early Modern England* (Cambridge: Cambridge University Press 1986); Lawrence Stone, *The Crisis of the Aristocracy, 1558-1641* (Oxford: Oxford Univeristy Press 1965). Out of a vast literature, for the earlier period see Paul Hyams, *Rancour and Reconciliation in Medieval England (Conjunctions of Religion and Power in the Medieval Past)* (Ithaca, NY; Cornell University Press, 2003).

discharged their spiritual obligations towards God and man, only when they ensured that condemned felons died the death, in the process denying them any prospect of reprieve or pardon, so that, facing the imminent judgement of God, they could be induced or enabled, not only to admit their guilt—and hence acknowledge the justice of the verdict—but also to confront the dreadful reality of their current spiritual condition. Then, and only then, through the ministrations of the godly clergy, might they be brought to a potentially saving repentance. [5]

Over the *longue durée*, when dealing with the questions outlined above, historians have tended to tell a series of success stories about the inexorable spread of state power and the equally inexorable dissemination of various ideals of civility and piety. However, in the last third of the sixteenth century the interaction between confessional, aristocratic and dynastic politics, consequent upon the reformation, seemed to many observers to be not merely reversing these trends but actually plunging parts of western Europe into moral and political chaos and even dissolution. The paradigmatic case was provided by the French wars of religion, in the course of which a variety of different forms of religious violence and confessional conflict were added to the already violent and unstable course of aristocratic feud and dynastic civil war. [6]

It was, of course, one of the great claims made in defence of the Elizabethan regime that the moderation and good government of the queen had protected England from such a fate. And it was true that, with the possible exception of the revolt of the northern earls, and the sad farce of the Essex rebellion, Elizabeth's reign saw no major aristocratic risings, no (successful) dynastic coups. However, the reign also featured a succession of conspiracies and projected revolts, involving the planned assassination of the queen, and, through various combinations of native rising and foreign invasion, the transfer of the crown from Elizabeth to some suitably Catholic claimant, more often than not Mary Stuart. Moreover, Mary's execution only settled the succession to the extent that it definitively removed Mary herself as a possible successor and thus, as recent research has revealed, even after her death in 1587 the issue of the succession continued to be a source of instability, anxiety, and speculation. [7]

In addition, while England did not experience the outbreaks of religious violence that occurred in France, Elizabeth's reign was punctuated with outbreaks of annihilating state violence visited upon the bodies of certain English Catholics, usually priests. Admittedly, the state went out of its way to deny that what was involved was any species of religious violence. Rather its Catholic victims were being punished for the secular offences of disobedience and treason, not for their religious beliefs. But the Catholics on the receiving end

[5] Peter Lake and Michael Questier, *The Antichrist's Lewd Hat; Protestants, Papists and Players in Post Reformation England* (London and New Haven: Yalue University Press, 2002), section one; Malcolm Gaskill, *Crime and mentalities in early modern England* (Cambridge: Cambridge University Press, 2000).

[6] Natalie Zemon Davies, 'The rites of violence' reprinted in her *Society and Culture in Early Modern France: Eight Essays* (Stanford, CA.; Stanford University Press 1975). Also see G. Murdoch, P. Roberts, and A. Spicer, eds., *Ritual and Violence: Natalie Zemon Davies and Early Modern France, Past and Present Supplements*, no. 7 (Oxford, 2012).

[7] Susan Doran and Paulina Kewes, *Doubtful and Dangerous: The Question of Succession in Late Elizabethan England* (Manchester: Manchester Univesity Press, 2014).

of these policies vigorously denied such claims, maintaining that those doing the dying were martyrs for their faith, and therefore that those doing the killing were by definition persecutors.[8]

Moreover, 'revenge', conceived as some sort of religiously sanctioned, either providentially or papally sponsored, doing-of-justice, had a central role to play. For at least some English Catholics, as the offspring of the adulterous and allegedly incestuous union between Henry VIII and Ann Boleyn, Elizabeth I had always been a usurper and thus a tyrant twice over, rendered such both by her illegal seizure of the throne and by her subsequent persecution of Catholic subjects, and latterly by her judicial murder of Mary Stuart. Such crimes positively demanded punishment, not only at the hands of God in the next life, but also (perhaps) at the hands of her subjects in this.[9]

Conversely, by the early 1570s, many of the English political elite believed that Mary Stuart was already guilty of crimes against the queen and realm that deserved death. From 1584 onwards, having taken the bond of association, a good part of the political nation was committed, in the event of Elizabeth's assassination, to take summary 'revenge'—the word features prominently in the bond—not merely on the queen's killers, but also on anyone likely to benefit from the queen's death, i.e. on Mary Stuart and quite possibly her son, James VI.[10]

Very often the dynastic and confessional politics of the period turned or seemed about to turn on assassination, both successful and attempted. Given the political dynamics of the age, there was a pressing need to cast or recast allegedly private acts of revenge as inherently legitimate acts of resistance: public acts of justice, committed in the name of some combination of 'the people' or 'the commonwealth', or of true religion, against variously heretical, tyrannical or persecuting rulers.[11] Thus revenge as resistance and resistance as revenge always remained intensely controversial and souls were always at stake. Indeed, on some views of the matter, even if the object of the revenger or regicide's attentions were a genuine tyrant and his or her death therefore represented a providential judgement, the act of killing a monarch remained a sin so dreadful as virtually to assure that the killer would be accompanying his victim to hell. In this scenario, God would be using the sin of one individual to punish that of another before throwing them both onto the fires of eternal judgement.[12]

---

[8] Lake and Questier, *The Antichrist's Lewd Hat*, ch. 7.

[9] The strongest statements of this view of the queen are to be found in William Allen, *An admonition to the nobility and people of England* (1588) and Nicholas Sander, *De origine ac progressu schismatis Anglicani* (1585).

[10] Helen Gardner, 'The Historical Approach to Hamlet', in J. Jump, ed., *Shakespeare; Hamlet, a Casebook*, (Nashville: Aurora Publishers, 1970, 1968), 137–50 (138). Also see Stuart M. Kurland, 'Hamlet and the Scottish Succession', *Studies in English Literature, 1500-1900* 34 (1994), 282.

[11] Both George Buchanan, *De iure regni apud Scotos* and Robert Parsons, *Conference about the next succession*, make this point, the first using the rhetoric of 'the people', the second that of 'the commonwealth'. Cf. my article, 'The King (the Queen) and the Jesuit: James Stuart's *True law of free monarchies* in context |s', *Transactions of the Royal Historical Society* 6th ser., 14 (2004), 243–60.

[12] Such, for instance, is the logic of James VI's *The true law of free monarchies*, which argues that tyrants will almost inevitably come to a bad end in this world as well as the next, but which also affirms that any form of resistance to a regnant monarch is an extremely grave sin.

2

....

In what remains, I want to suggest that in his two revenge tragedies, *Titus Andronicus* and *Hamlet,* Shakespeare addresses the nexus of theoretical, practical, political, and religious concerns outlined above. In *Titus* he examines the relationship between religion and revenge and between revenge, resistance and an (emergently Christian) sense of justice. In *Hamlet* he plumbs the depths of the soteriological politics of revenge and resistance. In both cases he was arguably using the temporal and geographical distance afforded him by setting *Titus* in a remote, wholly pagan, and entirely made-up Rome, and *Hamlet* in an entirely foreign and temporally remote—albeit also remarkably contemporary—Denmark in order to address questions that in the context of a play about recent English history might have proven a little too close to home.

Apart from both being 'revenge tragedies' the two plays have a good deal in common. Both are set in elective monarchies. Both chart the course of events after a seemingly successful exercise in regime change. In both, the central protagonists, who could, or, in a strictly hereditary monarchy, would, have been kings, are confronted by dreadful deeds, the precise nature and perpetrators of which are not immediately apparent. In both, those protagonists go 'mad', and in both cases, the precise status of their 'madness' is unclear. Seemingly genuinely distracted, their distraction also serves as a mask behind which they can find out what really happened, identify and threaten the guilty parties, while they decide precisely what form their revenge should take. In both, the denouement sees plots to undo the revenger turned back upon the plotters themselves. In both, the successful realization of revenge serves a political as well as a moral purpose, with a purging regime-change effected by invading forces from the north, led by generals who thereupon take power, their legitimacy affirmed in each case by essentially the same mixture of hereditary right, the workings of elective monarchy and the punishing and |or publishing of the dark deeds which have undone their tyrannical and usurping predecessors. Indeed, in many ways, *Hamlet* can legitimately be seen as the reworking, in an explicitly Christian setting, of many of the central elements of *Titus.*

In *Titus*, the cycle of revenge starts with a religious act, Titus' sacrifice of Tamora's son Alarbus. This is not 'revenge', but rather the discharge of a religious obligation towards the shades of his sons killed in the war against the Goths. Other than that, Titus shows no ill will towards Tamora or her sons, in particular, or the Goths in general. He willingly gives his captives to the emperor, is perfectly happy to see them freed and even takes comfort from Tamora's marriage to Saturninus, believing that she will look kindly upon him as the cause of her sudden elevation.

What could be thought to be Titus' piety and restraint, is (unsurprisingly) not received as such by Tamora, who determines not merely to destroy the Andronici, root and branch, but to inflict precisely the same sort of abjection and anguish on Titus that he has inflicted on her. What ensues has nothing to do with 'religion' or even some rudimentary notion of retributory justice and everything to do with revenge. The Andronici are being persecuted neither because of their religious beliefs or practices, nor because of the sort of god- or ancestor- satisfying considerations that prompted Titus to sacrifice Alarbus. Rather they are being killed to satisfy Tamora's atavistic urge to be revenged and Saturninus' desire to undo and humiliate someone he regards as a threat to his rule as emperor.

However the play insists on talking about the sufferings imposed on the Andronici, and, in particular on the horribly mutilated Lavinia, in the determinedly religious terms of 'martyrdom'. Both Lucius and Titus ask Lavinia 'who hath martyred thee?' (3.1.82, 108). Later in the same scene Titus laments that his daughter has no tongue 'to tell me who hath martyred thee' (3.1.108). Later Titus refers to her mute and disfigured body as so many 'martyred signs' (3.1.36).

The right reading of the martyred signs or wounds of those consigned by the Elizabethan regime to a traitor's death was a subject of bitter contemporary controversy. For the Protestant regime and its supporters, the quartered limbs and eviscerated bodies of the state's Catholic victims spoke for themselves, proclaiming them traitors by virtue of their having died the peculiarly terrible death reserved by English law for traitors. For Catholics, however, those same wounds were proof positive that these people were martyrs indeed, innocent victims of a persecuting state.[13]

For all that this is a revenge tragedy—and at various points Titus does indeed talk the language of revenge,—'which way shall I find revenge's cave?' (3.1.271)—the play draws a stark contrast between revenge Titus- and Tamora-style. Even in the depths of his madness, Titus rushes neither to judgement nor to action. He rather waits until he has discovered the precise nature of Lavinia's fate and the identity of her tormentors. For all his anguish and madness, there is something measured, judicious, even judicial, about Titus' approach to revenge and resistance. Christopher Crosbie has even argued that Titus's search for revenge can be seen as an exercise in rectificatory justice, creating as he puts it 'proportionate exchange, an equivalent return, even in his method of revenge'.[14]

Moreover, because of the identity and status of its objects, Titus' powerful private impulse to revenge himself becomes coterminous with his public duty to save the state from tyranny and destruction at the hands of Saturninus, Tamora, and Aaron. As Coppélia Kahn observes, 'a political over-plot—the assault on Rome to unseat Saturninus … is paralleled and interwoven with the revenge plot against Tamora'.[15] At this point, 'revenge' and the service of the Roman state, private revenge and resistance in the public interest, together with Titus' personae as both a revenging and a Roman hero, the vindicator of the honour of the Andronici and the servant of the Roman state, all come back into alignment—the one incorporating the other in a coherent plan of action and a unitary sense of both moral and political identity and purpose. The consequent shift back from the 'feminine' emotional incontinence, the excess of human sympathy, that Titus has exhibited during his madness in the central sections of the play, to an inhuman, quintessentially masculine and Roman, self-control is figured by Titus' coldly premediated and carefully staged slaughter of Lavinia, the very person whose 'martyred signs' had provoked in him such an unwonted excess of emotion in the first place.

---

[13] Lake and Questier, *The Antichrist's Lewd Hat*, ch. 7.

[14] Christopher Crosbie, 'Fixing Moderation: *Titus Andronicus* and the Aristotelian Determination of Value', *Shakespeare Quarterly* 58, (2007), 147–73 (163, 170).

[15] Coppélia Kahn, *Roman Shakespeare: Warriors, Wounds and Women* (London: Routledge 1997), 71.

Perhaps even more than the episode with the pie, it is this that calls into radical question the claims of the Andronici to either political virtue or true piety. Indeed, while Crosbie can discern a 'substructure of moderation', a finely judged 'proportionality and Aristotelian temperance of anger' 'beneath the grotesque appearance of Titus's revenge', Gary Kuchar claims that far from 'advocating an Aristotelian ethics, the play performs a *reductio ad absurdum* of it'.[16] At the very least, it is hard to avoid agreeing with Tamora's verdict, handed down at the start of the play, that Titus' is a 'false and irreligious piety'.

Indeed, the play shows that while the Andronici constantly strive to find 'a pattern, precedent and lively warrant' for their actions in some of the core texts of *romanitas*, Titus, in particular, constantly misconstrues the key texts, lapsing all too often into disastrously over-literal, indeed frankly idolatrous, misapplications. Thus Titus cites the conduct of Marcus Junius Brutus and Virginius as precedents for his own slaughter of Lavinia, but his conduct corresponds to neither example. Far from killing Lucrece, Brutus had reassured her that, though her body was violated, she herself was innocent. In marked contrast to Lavinia, Lucrece's decision to take her own life had been entirely her own, taken both to save herself and her family from dishonour and to provoke her male kin into taking revenge on Tarquin, thereby saving the Roman state from tyranny. Virginius had killed his daughter to save her from a fate worse than death, himself from dishonour and Rome from the depredations of the tyrannous regime of the *decemvirs*. He hadn't murdered her in cold blood to demonstrate his own Roman virtue. In so doing, Titus is here reverting to type, sacrificing Lavinia, reduced once more to the role of her father's (necessarily) silently dutiful daughter, on the altar of his family's honour, just as he had earlier sacrificed Alarbus and Mutius.[17]

Indeed the child-killing propensities of Titus represent the moral crux of the matter. The play opens with Titus killing someone else's child. It ends with him killing one of his own, having slain another, Mutius, in between. If the play is conceived as a contest to see who can kill more of Titus' progeny the result is a two-all draw between Titus and Tamora. While Tamora ends up a failed infanticide, foiled in her plot to murder her own baby by the finer feelings of its father, Aaron the Moor, Titus has succeeded in committing that most unnatural of crimes twice over.

But then 'cruel and irreligious' as it is, the piety of the Andronici is the only form of piety on offer in the play. The Andronici may fail properly to interpret and apply the canonical texts of *romanitas* to their situation, but at least they consistently try to do so. Their opponents neither know nor care about such things. Aaron knows the key texts well enough—unlike Tamora's idiot sons, he immediately gets the threat implicit in Titus' citation of Horace—but he uses that knowledge merely to facilitate his own murderous plans. He applies the story of Tereus and Philomela entirely appropriately to his immediate circumstances but only as a blueprint for the rape of Lavinia.

[16] Gary Kuchar, 'Decorum and the Politics of ceremony in Shakespeare's *Titus Andronicus*', in Ken Jackson and Arthur Marotti, eds., *Shakespeare and Religion* (Notre Dame, IN: Notre Dame University Press, 2011), 46–78, (75 n.16).

[17] Peter Culhane, 'Livy and *Titus Andronicus*', *English* 55 (2006): 1–13; Vernon Guy Dickson, '"A pattern, precedent and lively warrant": Emulation, Rhetoric and Cruel Propriety in *Titus Andronicus*', *Renaissance Quarterly* 62 (2009), 376–409; Danielle St Hilaire, 'Allusion and Sacrifice in *Titus Andronicus*', *Studies in English literature, 1500-1900* 49 (2009) 311-31.

The play thus presents us with a stark choice between the malignity, the practical (and in Aaron's case the badly stated) atheism of their enemies and the deeply flawed Roman piety and virtue of the Andronici. After all, it is through the efforts of Titus, Marcus, and Lucius that a form of justice is done, both revenger and revengee punished, regime change managed and a form of order restored to the state.

Moreover, the fact that order is restored by the election of Lucius as emperor—the very man who has just killed Saturninus with his own hands—implies not merely the justice but also the legitimacy of tyrannicide. But Lucius' elevation also contains within it a gesture towards a different sort of religion and rule. For as a number of critics have pointed out, not only was Lucius the name of the mythical king who introduced Christianity to ancient Britain,[18] the Lucius of the play is the only character who, when offered the opportunity for a vengeful or sacrificial murder of a child, holds his hand.[19] The child in question is Aaron's bastard son conceived with Tamora, to save whose life Aaron offers to expose his own and his accomplices' villainy. Aaron demands that Lucius take an oath that he will keep his side of the bargain, only to be asked in disgust what business Aaron can possibly have with oaths, given that he is an atheist. Aaron does not deny that charge, but merely observes that 'I know thou art religious | And hast a thing within called conscience, | With twenty popish tricks and ceremonies | Which I have seen thee careful to observe', (5.1.73-83), and then insists that he swear to spare his son.

Here is 'religion', dismissed as superstition and popery by the atheist Aaron, triumphing, for the one and only time in the play, over the impulse to take revenge. It may have taken the perverse atheistical logic of Aaron to do it, but, alone amongst the central characters in the play, Lucius has been saved by the force of religion and the demands of conscience from his own atavistic impulse toward revenge; an impulse that, up to that point, had been leading him inexorably towards what was—for a Christian Elizabethan audience, if not for the pagan Romans of the play—that most monstrous of crimes, the slaughter of an innocent child.

Lucius is certainly not saved from baby killing by any feelings of compunction or natural sympathy of his own; that is to say, by any either residual or emergent belief that killing babies is wrong. What holds his hand is the oath that Aaron has induced him to take. Lucius' 'religious' instincts thus continue to take the cold, legalistic forms that have thus far characterized his father's, and indeed his own, conduct. When bound by certain obligations towards the gods, the Andronici discharge those obligations, whatever the human cost, with a chilling absence of affect. In the opening act religious duty had led them to slaughter in cold blood one of Tamora's children, Alarbus. Here, once bound by his oath, it leads Lucius to spare the life of another. The difference between the two outcomes has no sympathetic or affective content or cause; it is purely a function of differently structured obligations towards the gods.

---

[18] Klause, 'Politics, Heresy and Martyrdom', 228; Jonathan Bate, ed., *Titus Andronicus*, The Arden Shakespeare (London, 1995), 21. Andreas Höfele reads the horrific violence staged in the play against the real violence staged on the contemporary scaffold, making particular reference to martyrdom, albeit only that inflicted by Catholics on Protestants and heretics described by John Foxe. See his *Stage, Stake and Scaffold* (Oxford: Oxford University Press, 2011), esp. ch. 4, 'Cannibal-Animal: Figurations of the (In)human in Montaigne, Foxe and Shakespearean Revenge Tragedy'.

[19] St Hilaire, 'Allusion and Sacrifice in *Titus Andronicus*', 325.

If there is an element of human sympathy, of moral compunction, in operation here it does not come from Lucius but from the atheist, Aaron, in whom a natural, as we might say, instinctive, impulse to save his son has precisely not prompted any wider awakening of conscience, moral sense, or human sympathy. As his almost instant murder of the midwife shows, whatever finer feelings his ties to his newborn son may provoke in Aaron, neither a heightened respect for human life nor a repentant propensity to resist the ruthless promptings of 'policy' are amongst them. But it is precisely because Aaron lacks a 'conscience', and is therefore free from the legalistic structures of religious obligation that constrain the Andronici, that he is vulnerable to the feelings that bind a father to his child—a basic impulse that Titus' and Lucius' austere Roman *pietas*, their idolatrous religious rigourism and literalism (described here tellingly as a form of 'popery') has all but entirely suppressed in them. Thus if Aaron lacks even a spark of the sort of conscience that animates both Titus and Lucius, they are similarly devoid of the sort of instinctual human sympathies or bonds that have prevented even Aaron from killing his own son.

On the one hand, we might see in these exchanges a basic human bond or instinct saving a rigidly legalistic religious system from its own worst excesses and effects. On the other, we might see a defective notion of conscience—a determination to obey the dictates of a 'cruel and irreligious piety'—being mitigated by the most basic of human sympathies. Unattached to notions of conscience, as they clearly were in Aaron's case, the very intensity and particularity of the bond between parent and child was likely to produce actions and reactions quite as immoral and violent as those taken by Aaron to preserve the life of his son. But when such sentiments were connected to a sense of conscience, an acknowledgement of a wider obligation to obey the promptings and demands of divine authority—of the sort that Aaron discerns in Lucius, but entirely lacks himself—the basis of a more general set of constraints and solidarities might emerge.

Something of what is going on here can be captured in the ambiguities inherent in the word 'piety'. Its primary referent would seem to be Roman *pietas*, the austerely patriarchal bonds of loyalty and obedience that tied Roman citizens both to the honour of their lineage and to the Roman state and its gods; in other words, the value system that prompted Tritus to slaughter not only Alarbus, but also Mutius and Lavinia. In the thought world of the Elizabethan audience, however, the English word 'piety' conjured an altogether different set of 'Christian' connotations, a view of religion in which, as Tamora of all people explains, 'being merciful' is the defining characteristic, not only of 'the gods' but also of the properly pious (1.1.120-1). Certainly, Lucius's sparing of Aaron's bastard child is the only 'merciful' act in the entire play.

While the play locates the iron age in which it is set in a pagan, pre-Christian version of *romanitas*, at several points—in its famous reference to ruined monastery, in Aaron's ridicule of Lucius' religious scruples as 'popish', in the clown who introduces the Christianized street speech of Elizabethan London into the midst of pagan Rome—the play's invented Roman past is collapsed into the post-Reformation English present. Moreover, if, as some critics have suggested, the trumped-up charges behind the peremptory, and, to an Elizabethan audience, entirely illegal,execution of Titus' sons[20] and the martyred signs

---

[20] Lorna Hutson, 'Rethinking the "Spectacle of the Scaffold": Juridical Epistemologies and English Revenge Tragedy', *Representations* 89 (2005), 30–58.

visited upon Lavinia do indeed recall the sufferings of certain English Catholics at the hands of the Elizabethan regime, then it might be thought that the Christian England of Elizabeth was quite as much in need of the moral example provided by Lucius' sparing of Aaron's black, bastard child, as was the brutally pagan, pre-Christian, Rome evoked in the play.[21]

The play stages a number of events and outcomes—a tongueless mute speaking, a monstrous birth—which would normally lend themselves to miraculously providential explanation, and then moves to explain them through a series of aggressively secular, as we might say, 'natural', causes. Lavinia can 'speak' because of the device of the stick and the reference to Ovid. Aaron's child is 'monstrous' or prodigious because it is black and it is black simply because its father is a Moor. The play appropriates providential elements and motifs central to many a murder pamphlet, but only as part of the entirely fraudulent case that Aaron and Tamora use to falsely incriminate and slaughter Titus's two sons. Indeed, the crucial sentiment that 'murder will out' is put into the mouth of Tamora—'O wondrous thing! | How easily is murder discovered', (2.2.286–7)—as she responds (apparently spontaneously) to the planted evidence used to convict Titus' two innocent sons of murder. Later, the personified figures of Murder and Revenge, used in other revenge plays to heighten the sense that providence was intervening to reveal enormity and punish sin, actually appear on stage, but only as part of a ludicrous attempt by Tamora and her idiot sons to play on the supposed madness of Titus, who simply turns their own scheme against them by playing along, in order to further his own meticulously planned (and entirely un-miraculous) revenge.

For the complex series of manoeuvres with which the play ends are precisely not presented either as accidents or as the work of providence. Rather, they are carefully choreographed by Titus, to discharge all of the carefully calibrated moral and narrative functions usually attributed in such plays to the action of providence. Thus, having killed Lavinia, Titus reveals the full extent of Tamora's crime, not to mention the providentially fitting contents of the pies that she has just consumed. He then kills Tamora but makes no move against Saturninus, thus ceding to the emperor an opportunity to react to his wife's crimes with shock, revulsion, or even repentance. Predictably enough, this is an opportunity that Saturninus can refuse and he reacts instead by killing Titus, thus providing Titus with the opportunity finally to sacrifice himself (rather than his children) on the altar of loyalty to Rome and her emperor. It is thus left to Lucius to kill Saturninus, whose tyranny has now been established beyond doubt by his entirely unrepentant and vengeful reaction to the revelation of the crimes committed by his wife and her lover. This leaves the king-killer Lucius to claim the throne.

Here we might think that the play was merely being faithful to its utterly pagan, pre-Christian, setting. After all, if the whole point was to construct the moral argument of the play out of basic human drives and impulses, untainted by the impact of revealed religion, then such patently Christian providential motifs would have to be suppressed. But the

---

[21] Nicholas Moschovakis, '"Irreligious Piety" and Christian History; Persecution as Pagan Anachronism in *Titus Andronicus*', *Shakespeare Quarterly* 53 (2002), 460–86. This chapter is particularly indebted to Moshovakis' argument, central elements of which it appropriates for its own, slightly divergent, purposes. On the Catholic issue also see John Klause, 'Politics, Heresy and Martyrdom in Shakespeare's Sonnet 124 and *Titus Andronicus*', in James Schiffer, ed., *Shakespeare's Sonnets: Critical Essays* (New York: Garland Publishing, 2000), 219–40.

play does not merely avoid or omit providentialist interpretation, it rather positively resists, parodies, and even derides it, in ways that seem designed to invade the hermeneutic universe inhabited by the play's Elizabethan Christian audiences, to whom such interpretative moves by now came as second nature. This matters because, *sans* providence, the morally and politically appropriate outcomes achieved at play's end can only be attributed to the efforts of the characters themselves. It is the political virtue and ingenuity of the Andronici that have saved the day and the state. And when we recall that the means used to achieve those much-to-be-desired consummations have included conspiracy and sedition, regicide and foreign invasion, then the potentially subversive meaning of the play becomes clear.

3

Very similar issues and materials are handled very differently in *Hamlet*. For there the basic contours and dilemmas of revenge, and indeed of resistance, are played out within a recognizably Christian, if confessionally ambiguous, setting. In *Hamlet* the workings and dictates of 'conscience' are put front and centre. In a series of soliloquies Hamlet defines 'conscience' as a supervening concern with the effect of actions taken in this life on outcomes in the next. Hamlet thus identifies 'conscience' as a check on his capacity to fulfil an otherwise clear-cut obligation to act against Claudius and proceeds to excoriate it under the rubric of 'cowardice'. He then invokes the purely secular, this-worldly demands of 'honour', 'passion', and 'revenge' to force himself to act. In Elizabethan terms he is talking like an 'atheist'—even as, in his refusal to act, he is actually behaving more like a Christian.

Since his father was a king, and he the hereditary successor to the throne—someone who in a monarchy not elective but hereditary would now be king himself—and since his father's murderer, Claudius, is now the prince, the revelations of the ghost have plunged Hamlet into a quintessentially political quandary. Thus for him, as much as for Titus, revenge is also a form of resistance. For the justice that he is about to mete out is not merely some private matter, the consequence of an intense but largely personal impulse to vindicate his family honour: it also concerns the public interest. The moral and political condition of the state and the consequences of the 'cess of majesty' likely to follow any action he might take against the reigning king are both most definitely in question. And yet, having, just like Titus, under cover of his own madness, gone to considerable lengths to ascertain the truth of the matter, Hamlet, unlike Titus, then eschews all and every political means to achieve his goal.

When trying to screw himself up to do the deed, he may at times excoriate himself for 'thinking too precisely upon th' event' (Q2 4.4.40), but the events about whose outcome he is obsessing, are not political ones. At no point can Hamlet be found plotting, calculating the odds, setting the stage for his revenge, or planning to take power. On the contrary, the only 'events' upon which he is shown thinking too closely concern the consequences in the next life of his and others people's actions in this one.

The play drives this point home through a running comparison between Hamlet and Laertes. Placed in a situation precisely parallel to Hamlet's, Laertes takes the sort of explicitly political action that Hamlet does not merely eschew but never even seems to consider. In so doing, he decides his fate. Using his considerable following with the people, a following of just the kind that, Claudius informs us, Hamlet also enjoys, Laertes goes public, mobilizing the sympathies and suspicions aroused by the death of his father to raise an insurrection and confront the king. Thereafter he becomes embroiled in precisely the sort of conspiracy to kill Hamlet that Hamlet had never even considered adopting in order to kill Claudius.

Of course, Hamlet had conspired with Horatio and the players, not to kill the king, but merely to establish his guilt. The audience might expect this to be, and Hamlet himself might talk as though this was, merely a preliminary to killing Claudius, but that is not, in fact, what he does. (Critics have, in general, tended to pay rather too much attention to what Hamlet says and not enough to what he does. In a play rather than a treatise, what happens matters.) Hamlet's immediate response to his now certain knowledge that Claudius has killed his father is not an attempt to kill the king—indeed the play shows us Hamlet self-consciously deciding not to do so (albeit for the worst of reasons)—but rather a desperate attempt to bring his mother to repentance. Where Hamlet has sworn desperate oaths and uttered dreadful revenge-fuelled imprecations, but failed to act, Laertes explicitly dares 'damnation', and expresses a willingness 'to cut his throat i' th' church', (Q2, 4.5.129–35; F, 4.1.128–134; Q2, 4.7.124; F, 4.3.99), which is something that Hamlet self-consciously refuses to do when he comes upon Claudius at prayer. Thereafter Laertes not only falls in with Claudius' desperate plot to murder Hamlet in secret with his scheme for the poisoned blade, he materially improves upon it. However honourable or just his initial impulse to revenge the death of his father may have been, Laertes has now been seduced into the most damnable means to achieve it. Employing arguments that closely parallel those used to Hamlet by the ghost and, as Catherine Belsey points out (Ch. 24 in this volume), others that Hamlet has used on himself, the positively diabolic Claudius succeeds in doing to Laertes what the ghost has, by this point, utterly failed to do to Hamlet.

Not, of course, that Hamlet fails to act. *Pace* the strain of critical convention that sees Hamlet's 'delay' as the central crux of the play, [22] from the moment he conceives of *The Murder of Gonzago* as the thing with which he can catch the conscience of the king, Hamlet takes precipitate, heedless, indeed desperate action, but not in the realm of politics, nor even that of revenge, but rather of 'conscience'. He emerges from the play-within-the-play obsessed, as ever, with the consequences in the next life of actions taken in this, and now certain of his capacity to consign Claudius to hell, while sending his mother to heaven. The contrast with both Laertes and Claudius is patent.

Of course, all of Hamlet's frenetic activity in this mode proves fruitless. This is inevitable, since his actions constitute a blasphemous attempt to usurp the prerogatives of God. Hamlet is trying to decide the fate of sinful humanity in the next life, and, accordingly, his efforts end in disaster, producing a situation in which revenge is unachieved; Claudius is still on the throne; his mother has been confirmed in her conviction that Hamlet is 'mad' and thus left blissfully unaware both of Claudius' guilt and of her own

---

[22] For a brilliant discussion of the critical obsession with 'delay' see Margreta de Grazia, *Hamlet without Hamlet* (Cambridge: Cambridge University Press, 2007), ch. 6.

desperately dangerous situation. As for Hamlet, having accidentally-on-purpose killed Polonius, he is now guilty of murder, and about to be packed off to seemingly certain death in England.

Hamlet is rescued from this predicament by a series of contingencies so bizarre and un-likely that the reigning conventions of pamphlet writing and theatre going, not to mention of sermonic commentary on both biblical and contemporary events, virtually demanded that they be regarded as the work of 'providence'. Of course, these same events could be organized under the rubric of 'fortune', with Hamlet's actions aboard ship attributed to his capacity to seize the opportunity it offers. But that is precisely not how Hamlet chooses to view the matter. His comment that 'even in that was heaven ordinant' (Q2, 5.2.48–50; F, 5.2.48–50) and his general conclusion that his deliverance proves that 'there's a divin-ity that shapes our ends, | Rough-hew them how we will' (Q2, 5.2.4–11; F, 5.2.4–11), both presage his later claim that 'there is a special providence in the fall of a sparrow' (Q2, 5.2.190–202; F, 5.2.160–171). (Perhaps tellingly, Q1 has 'there's a predestinate providence in the fall of a sparrow'(Q1, sc. 17.45–6)). Taken together these *aperçus* look back to the insight vouchsafed him by his murder of Polonius: ' heaven hath pleased it so, | To punish me with this, and this with me, | That I must be their scourge and minister. | I will bestow him and will answer well | The death I gave him' (Q2, 3.4.170–5; F, 3.4.156–61).

That speech served to move the world of the play from that of a revenge tragedy to that of a murder pamphlet, alerting, as it did so, both the audience and Hamlet himself to the dual roles as 'minister' and 'scourge' that he has already either been playing, or at least trying to play, since the ghost first broke the news of his father's murder. Despite his best intentions to the contrary, to this point Hamlet has succeeded only in fulfilling the function of God's minister. For, first in the play-within-the-play and later in the scene in his mother's closet, he has successfully, albeit not effectually, called both Claudius and Gertrude to a saving repentance.

Of course, what remained was his role as scourge, that is to say, as the instrument of God's judgement in this life—a function fulfilled in the murder pamphlets by the secu-lar magistrate and his agent, the hangman. It was, of course, also the role to which he had been called by the ghost; one which, despite his insistently blood-curdling injunc-tions to himself to 'revenge', Hamlet had thus far not so much failed, as refused, to fulfil. Admittedly, in the last act of the play, armed with certain (written) evidence of Claudius' guilt, and with his own reasons to be revenged, Hamlet does finally embrace the need to plan Claudius' death. As he tells Horatio, the time might be short, but 'the interim's mine. | And a man's life's no more than to say "one"' (F, 5.2.73–4).

But even now providence intervenes to save him from the role of political conspira-tor and |or premeditated murderer that he has himself thus far avoided with such suc-cess. No sooner has Hamlet (once again, just in case we haven't noticed) acknowledged the supervening sovereignty of divine providence, admitting that 'if it be now, 'tis not to come; if it be not to come, it will be now', and admonishing Horatio to stop fussing and 'let be' (Q2, 5.2.190–202; F, 5.2.160–71), he is plunged, entirely unknowing—indeed while intending to reconcile with Laertes—into the midst of the plot designed by Laertes and Claudius to destroy him. There, through a mixture of 'accident'—Gertrude drink-ing the poisoned cup—and the operation of 'conscience'—in this instance that of Laertes, who confesses to his and Claudius' malign intentions—Hamlet is literally forced into a series of entirely spontaneous reactions—reactions that effect precisely the sort of highly structured denouement with which *Titus* had ended, and that the conventions of revenge tragedy demanded.

But while in *Titus* that outcome is shown to have been the result of the careful plotting and coordinated action of the Andronici (not to mention the invading Goths), the very opposite is true in *Hamlet*.

Hamlet acts on the spur of the moment: were he not dying as he does the deed, one might almost say that he acts in self-defence. His mother is killed, but he has nothing to do with that. The man he kills has (albeit accidentally) killed his mother and (rather more on purpose) murdered his father and in effect (with the poisoned sword he has placed in Laertes' hand for exactly that purpose) just killed him.

On the one hand, this is as close to contemporary rationalizations ('killing no murder') as it is possible to get: a tyrant may end up dead, but Hamlet is scarcely guilty of tyrannicide. On the other hand, Hamlet succeeds in inflicting on Claudius precisely the sort of death that he had wished for him when he had stopped himself from dispatching the king while at prayer. Claudius has indeed been killed in the midst of dreadful and damning sins—not drunk, swearing, but while attempting to commit the most treacherous of premeditated murders. In his last words—'Oh, yet defend me friends, I am but hurt' (Q2, 5.2.308; F, 5.2.278)—there is no trace of repentance, but rather a futile attempt to keep up appearances to the end. Had Hamlet killed Claudius while he prayed, he might not have sent the king to heaven, but he would almost certainly have consigned himself to the other place. Hamlet had avoided that fate, but only for the worst of reasons. Yet avoid it he had. Now he gets his wish, with, as it were, no blame attached, except, of course, that, by this point, it is no longer his wish or intention, but rather providence's judgement. Thus has Hamlet been able to escape what Michael Neill terms the 'ironies that force the revenger to imitate the methods of the very adversary he seeks to destroy' even as he has also enacted them.[23] As Peter Ure puts it, Hamlet 'is able to achieve the act of revenge without ever really becoming a revenger' because providence, or the storyteller, 'has ... abolished the role'.[24] We are left then with providence's judgement upon the unrepentant Claudius rather than Hamlet's revenge upon his uncle. The moral and political effects of revenge, resistance and tyrannicide, of the doing of both private and public justice, have all been collapsed into one another and triumphantly achieved, all without Hamlet having, self-consciously or purposefully, played any of those roles.

If we want to plumb the political meanings of the play once again we must return to Hamlet's abiding concern throughout, that is to say, to the question of salvation, in this instance, to the question of *his* salvation. Famously, Horatio consigns Hamlet's soul to heaven, but the play itself leaves more than an element of ambiguity around the issue of Hamlet's salvation. While in Q1 Hamlet's final words—'farewell Horatio, heaven receive my soul' (Q1, sc. 17.111)—do indeed seem to insist that, at the last, Hamlet's thoughts have turned to heaven and that he is therefore saved, his last words in Q2 and the Folio— 'the rest is silence' (Q2, 5.2.342; F, 5.2.312)—do not. Of course, they do not insist upon

---

[23] Neill, 'Revenge Tragedy', 336.

[24] Peter Ure, *Elizabethan and Jacobean Drama:Critical Essays*, ed. J. C. Maxwell (Liverpool; Liverpool University Press, 1974), 40, 42.

the opposite conclusion either, but rather leave the question open, for the audience to decide.

If the audience takes Hamlet to be damned, then the play becomes merely a restatement of one of the central orthodoxies of late Elizabethan and Jacobean political theology. For if Hamlet is damned, the play is merely staging the inevitable consequence of usurpation and tyranny in revolt and regicide, while reminding us, through the fate of Hamlet, both in this world and the next, that the wages of those particular sins remain (both temporal and spiritual) death.

Only if Hamlet is saved does the play become something rather more contentious, with the killer of a regnant prince being shown on stage ascending to a heavenly reward. Admittedly, even on the most optimistic view, the aperture opened by the play for 'resistance' is very narrow indeed. When Hamlet kills Claudius he is certain that he himself is dying. In this state, and for the first time in the play, there can be no chance that he could gain politically from the death of Claudius. About to pass from the world, he kills the king and then, with his dying breath, elects Fortinbras to the empty throne. Whatever else this is, it is as close to a politically selfless act as it is possible to get.

Here, then, is an act of resistance that is not really resistance, of regicide that is not really regicide. As such, it sends a murderous tyrant and usurper to a deserved fate and—if we decide that Hamlet is indeed saved—his killer to heaven, while conferring the crown on a claimant of unimpeachable legitimacy, all this without causing the least popular disorder or even widespread political conflict, let alone civil war. Read politically, then, and, if 'flights of angels' really do 'sing' Hamlet 'to his rest', spiritually too, as the resolution of a peculiarly knotty religio-political case of conscience, *Hamlet* is a play with a really rather happy ending.

4

I have argued, then, that for a variety of reasons—some rooted in the long-term history of the Christian West, others in the more immediate political and religious circumstances of the post-Reformation—'revenge' and 'religion', and the concomitant concepts of 'justice' and 'resistance', were all integrally linked. I have also argued that in a series of plays, some, most notably *Titus Andronicus* and *Julius Caesar*, located in carefully delineated pagan Roman contexts, others, most notably *Richard III* and *Hamlet*, in decidedly Christian, albeit confessionally ambiguous, settings, Shakespeare set out to examine the relations between these concepts. In so doing he mobilized energies and expectations drawn not merely from the emergent genre of the revenge tragedy, of which, admittedly, *Titus* represents something of a paradigmatic example, but also from the history play, the murder pamphlet, and the soteriologically charged case of conscience, a genre only just establishing itself in the circulating manuscript and print culture of the Elizabethan *fin de siècle*.

The point of the analysis has not been to attribute to Shakespeare settled ideological positions, or coherent sets of either secular or religious belief; still less, to decide whether or not he was a 'Protestant' or a 'Catholic', a 'Calvinist' or an 'Arminian', a believer in resistance theory or in passive disobedience, in elective monarchy or in indefeasible hereditary right.[25] These plays circle around those categories and questions. They raise, and might even be thought rather pointedly to have posed to their first audiences, some of the issues (both theoretical and practical) that defined and divided those ideologies and groups. But they can scarcely be said to offer definitive answers to any of those questions. Indeed, given the explosive nature of the issues concerned, to have done so could only have invited trouble.

Indeterminacy, a refusal either to achieve or to offer final closure, to settle on any coherent ideological message, to broadcast any readily identifiable soundbite, except of the most banal, killing-babies-is-wrong sort, was the necessary price of—the enabling occasion for—these plays' capacity to address directly some of the most pressing religio-political questions of the age. It has been the purpose of this chapter to illustrate the complex, multifaceted nature of that address, while casting at least some light on the relation between revenge tragedy and religion, at least in the plays of Shakespeare.

SELECT BIBLIOGRAPHY

Armstrong, Robert G., *Shakespeare and the Mysteries of God's Judgment* (Athens, OH: Georgia University Press , 1976).

Bossy, John, *Christianity in the West, 1400–1800* (Oxford: Oxford University Press, 1985).

Brown, Keith, *Bloodfeud in Scotland 1573–1625: Violence, Justice and Politics in an Early Modern Society* (Edinburgh: John Donald, 1986).

Crosbie, Christopher, 'Fixing Moderation: *Titus Andronicus* and the Aristotelian Determination of Value', *Shakespeare Quarterly* 58, (2007), 147–73.

de Grazia, Margreta, *Hamlet without Hamlet* (Cambridge: Cambridge University Press, 2007).

Dickson, Vernon Guy, ' "A pattern, precedent and lively warrant": Emulation, Rhetoric and Cruel Propriety in *Titus Andronicus*', *Renaissance Quarterly* 62 (2009), 376–409.

Doran, Susan, and Paulina Kewes, eds., *Doubtful and Dangerous: The Question of Succession in Late Elizabethan England* (Manchester; Manchester University Press, 2014).

Lake, Peter, and Michael Questier, *The Antichrist's Lewd Hat; Protestants, Papists and Players in Post- Reformation England* (London and New Haven: Yale University Press, 2002).

[25] Religious, and indeed explicitly confessional, issues are raised both by the ghost's (quintessentially Catholic) claim to be a spirit on night release from purgatory and by the play's close engagement, not merely with the doctrine of providence but also with that of predestination. Religious despair, demonic possession, and suicide were all topics linked both to predestinarian soteriological crisis and to the doubt and apostasy that could attend movement from one confessional identity to another. In explicitly raising those issues, and drawing a great deal of its emotional energy from their resolution, *Hamlet* certainly seems to move definitively from an intercessory, purgatory- and lineage-centred style of religion to a far more individualistic, providence- and predestination-centred view, But whether that involved a move from Catholicism to Protestantism, or whether the view of predestination encoded in the play is a Calvinist or proto-Arminian one are questions that are left to be decided. I do not have space to pursue either of those themes in this chapter. I hope to do so elsewhere. On the abolition of purgatory and intercession for the dead, see Stephen Greenblatt, *Hamlet in Purgatory* (Princeton: Princeton University Press, 2001) and Michael Neill *Issues of Death* Oxford: Oxford University Press, 1997), ch. 7. On predestination, see Robert G. Armstrong, *Shakespeare and the Mysteries of God's Judgment* (Athens, 1976).

Gaskill, Malcolm, *Crime and Mentalities in Early Modern England* (Cambridge: Cambridge University Press, 2000).

Hofele, Andreas, *Stage, Stake and Scaffold* (Oxford: Oxford University Press, 2011).

Hutson, Lorna, 'Rethinking the "Spectacle of the Scaffold": Juridical Epistemologies and English Revenge Tragedy', *Representations* 89 (2005), 30–58.

Kahn, Coppélia, *Roman Shakespeare: Warriors, Wounds and Women* (London, Routledge, 1997).

Moschovakis, Nicholas, ' "Irreligious Piety" and Christian History; Persecution as Pagan Anachronism in *Titus Andronicus*', *Shakespeare Quarterly* 53 (2002), 460–86.

St Hilaire, Danielle, 'Allusion and Sacrifice in *Titus Andronicus*', *Studies in English literature, 1500–1900* 49 (2009), 311–31.

CHAPTER 12

SHAKESPEARE'S ANATOMIES OF DEATH

RICHARD SUGG

THERE are many contenders for most famous or most iconic moment in Shakespeare's plays. Yet it is hard to think of any that are so peculiarly universal and transferable as those in *Hamlet*. People who have never read or seen a Shakespeare play can nonetheless recognize instantly the image of a young man in black, holding a skull. The same is true of Hamlet's third soliloquy. If a person can accurately quote just a single line from Shakespeare's drama, 'To be or not to be; that is the question', is by far the most likely choice. Again, both moments are not only transferable (the skull scene played as comic skit or parody; 'To shop or not to shop'; 'To drink or not to drink') but for many, the original scene or speech flashes through the parody with effortless speed and recognizability.

A rather different kind of duality applies to what is arguably the play's third most iconic moment: the death of Ophelia. For many of us, Gertrude's original description of this offstage drowning now takes second place to John Everett Millais's mid-nineteenth-century painting (despite the fact that in the painting Ophelia is still alive). Jostling with Ophelia for third place, we have the ghost of Hamlet's murdered father. *Hamlet*, then, covers almost all of the major dramatic possibilities surrounding death. Of these, I will focus on the following in *Hamlet, Romeo and Juliet, Othello, Antony and Cleopatra, Macbeth*, and *King Lear*: suicide; images and aestheticization of death; and responses to bereavement.

Certain broad patterns span the different scenes in question. Perhaps most obviously, female deaths are primarily a matter of image, whilst male deaths or responses to death are more likely to involve ideas—about honour or reputation, or the nature of death itself. Working against this tendency to give focus, form, and shape, however, is an opposing force: a recurrent sense of the unknowable or unspeakable. In such moments, very often dramatised through male reactions to death, there is a refusal to conceptualise mortality, and in particular sudden, personal bereavement.

SUICIDE

In *Hamlet*, we have a famous contemplation of suicide, and one seemingly actual suicide.

Enter Hamlet
To be, or not to be; that is the question:
Whether 'tis nobler in the mind to suffer
The slings and arrows of outrageous fortune,
Or to take arms against a sea of troubles
And, by opposing, end them. To die, to sleep—
No more, and by a sleep to say we end
The heartache and the thousand natural shocks
That flesh is heir to—'tis a consummation
Devoutly to be wish'd. To die, to sleep,
To sleep, perchance to dream. Ay, there's the rub,
For in that sleep of death what dreams may come
When we have shuffled off this mortal coil
Must give us pause. There's the respect
That makes calamity of so long life,
For who would bear the whips and scorns of time,
Th'oppressor's wrong, the proud man's contumely,
The pangs of disprized love, the law's delay,
The insolence of office, and the spurns
That patient merit of th'unworthy takes,
When he himself might his quietus make
With a bare bodkin? who would fardels bear,
To grunt and sweat under a weary life,
But that the dread of something after death,
The undiscovered country from whose bourn
No traveller returns, puzzles the will,
And makes us rather bear those ills we have
Than fly to others that we know not of?
Thus conscience does make cowards of us all;
And thus the native hue of resolution
Is sicklied o'er with the pale cast of thought,
And enterprises of great pith and moment
With this regard their currents turn awry,
And lose the name of action.—Soft you, now,
The fair Ophelia!—Nymph, in thy orisons
Be all my sins remembered.[1]

QUEEN GERTRUDE   One woe doth tread upon another's heel,
So fast they follow. Your sister's drowned, Laertes.
LAERTES   Drowned? O, where?
QUEEN GERTRUDE   There is a willow grows aslant a brook,
That shows his hoar leaves in the glassy stream.
Therewith fantastic garlands did she make
Of crow-flowers, nettles, daisies, and long purples,
That liberal shepherds give a grosser name,
But our cold maids do dead men's fingers call them.
There on the pendent boughs her crownet weeds

---

[1] *Hamlet*, 3.1.58-92, in *The Oxford Shakespeare: The Complete Works*, gen. eds. Stanley Wells and Gary Taylor (Oxford: Clarendon Press, 1998). Unless otherwise stated, all references to Shakespeare are to this edition.

Clambering to hang, an envious sliver broke;
When down her weedy trophies and herself
Fell in the weeping brook. Her clothes spread wide,
And, mermaid-like, awhile they bore her up;
Which time she chanted snatches of old tunes,
As one incapable of her own distress,
Or like a creature native and indued
Unto that element. But long it could not be
Till that her garments, heavy with their drink,
Pulled the poor wretch from her melodious lay
To muddy death.

(4.7.135-55)

These two passages raise three central questions: why do people kill themselves? Why do some want to, but fail? And how do certain people kill themselves, or imagine doing so? In his novel *Prater Violet*, Christopher Isherwood asked: 'What makes you go on living? Why don't you kill yourself? Why is all this bearable? What makes you bear it?' before answering: 'I supposed, vaguely, that it was a kind of balance, a complex of tensions. You did whatever was next on the list. A meal to be eaten. Chapter eleven to be written'.[2]

This modern analysis may well look familiar to any present-day agnostics or atheists who have ever contemplated suicide: the complex of tensions—probably including family and friends—webs us tightly into the living world, pulling us back even at moments when life seems temporarily intolerable. This of course also matches Durkheim's classic analysis of suicides, as people who lack sufficient connection to others and to society.[3] But this restraining web or complex is not what restrains Hamlet. By contrast, what he says about life ('th'oppressor's wrong, the proud man's contumely') is part of his reason for *wanting* death.

A second thing which probably restrains many potential suicides is the strange power of human consciousness. 'To be' human is to refuse to accept that you and the world are actually separate, and separable, entities. Our consciousness depends on the world; but the world does not depend on our consciousness. Does this potential obliteration of the mind trouble the suicidal Hamlet? It seems to later, when he prepares to clasp and address that famous skull. Yet in his third soliloquy, it does not seem to be fear of losing his consciousness which tugs Hamlet back from the brink. When he talks about 'the dread of something after death, | The undiscovered country' he implies that he is restrained, not by fear of mental and physical obliteration, but precisely by the fear of being preserved, mentally and physically (at least come the resurrection), in some kind of afterlife.

And when he concludes with 'Thus conscience does make cowards of us all', he is almost certainly using 'conscience' to mean both ethical or Christian conscience and 'consciousness'. Part of what stops Hamlet from thrusting the bare bodkin is thinking too much about his thoughts in the afterlife. He had begun, after all, by trying to lullaby himself to death:

  [2] *Prater Violet* (London: Vintage, 2012), 117.
  [3] See: Emile Durkheim, *Suicide: a Study in Sociology*, ed. G. Simpson (London: Routledge and Kegan Paul, 1951).

> To die, to sleep—
> No more ...
> . . . .
>
> To die, to sleep,
> To sleep, perchance to dream. Ay, there's the rub,
> For in that sleep of death what dreams may come ...

From the hard dental to the murmurous sibilant, the sliding rhythm drifts on until the sleeper is woken with a jolt by those dreams which imply thought. To fully understand this 'rude awakening' of the slumbrous dead we need to know something about the strange interval between one person's death and the general resurrection in Shakespeare's time. For many members of his original audiences, these lines prompted unresolved questions. Were the dead actually *conscious* in the time prior to the general resurrection? Hamlet seems to hope not, but is unsure. Donne, by contrast, often seemed to wish to retain his consciousness, but to simultaneously fear the limbo of disembodied, disconnected thought.

Such uncertainties remind us that 'sleep', around four hundred years ago, was rarely the woolly euphemism of Victorian gravestones. Rather, it could mean quite precisely that the *soul* slept until the general resurrection. For some Christians, it was literally unconscious, dormant, and thoughtless, until it was re-embodied. This belief was either part of, or at least closely associated with, the doctrine known as mortalism. Although nominally heretics, all mortalists were Christians (and included both Luther and Milton in their ranks). The most radical mortalists held that the soul was permanently annihilated at death; less extreme ones, that it died but was restored at the resurrection; and the 'soul sleepers' that it snoozed in a state of blissful (and presumably dreamless) unconsciousness until the Day of Judgement.[4]

How does Ophelia's actual end compare to these dark musings? If Hamlet thinks too much to die, Ophelia feels too much to live. Packed to bursting point with feelings she cannot fully express or realize (in the sense of a consummated sexual love), she first dissolves into the musical realm of song, before lullabying herself to death in the willowy brook. This fluid dissolution of both language and self reminds us of the strange ambiguity enfolding Ophelia's end. Does she kill herself or not? It perhaps seems more accurate to say that she merely fails to let herself live. She had allegedly fallen into the brook by accident when a small branch broke, rather than deliberately filling her pockets with stones and immediately thrusting her head underwater.

Ironically, then, Hamlet seems more active in what he merely talks about, than Ophelia in what she does (or fails to do). Even when imagining, he is ready to 'take arms against a sea of troubles', and to enact the plosive double thrust of the 'bare bodkin'. As so often, John Berger's pithy summary of traditional gender roles applies here: 'Men *act* and women *appear*.'[5] Despite being, for much of the play, one of the least active of Shakespeare's protagonists, Hamlet is at least relatively vigorous by comparison with the oppressed and paralysed Ophelia. One of his greatest moments is highly verbal, whilst hers (even before Millais) is intensely visual. To this we can add one more famous gender distinction: the fact that female suicide is typically achieved by poison or drowning, in a kind of fluid, passive

---

[4] See Richard Sugg, *The Smoke of the Soul: Medicine, Physiology and Religion in Early Modern England* (Basingstoke: Palgrave, 2013), 206–33.

[5] John Berger, *Ways of Seeing* (New York: Penguin, 1977), 47.

blurring of life into death; whilst male suicides are more likely to die in one violent, more or less definite moment, by gunshot, stabbing, hanging, or fatal plunge.[6] When Hamlet finally does die, it is in action and in pursuit of active aims; unlike Ophelia, who does indeed seem to drift softly down into the water, 'like a creature native and indued | Unto that element'. It is not just, in fact, that we cannot easily say when she dies; but also that, visualizing this in whatever form we might, we cannot easily say where the female ends and nature begins.

This vision clearly appealed to Millais, and despite the painting's initially mixed reception, his rendering ultimately became the patent Ophelia. As implied above, the particular mode of Ophelia's death seems to follow the internally consistent psychology of her oppression, marginalization, and madness. But from another angle, this famous death by water looks distinctly odd. After all, Gertrude must be describing what she *saw*. She could have inferred most details after the event; but to know that Ophelia was singing, she had to be there—standing on the bank, and doing nothing to help. This point is important, because its dramatic implausibility suggests that the vision also appealed to Shakespeare. He *wanted* us to see it, despite the tricky questions this might raise about Gertrude's watching passivity.

Towards the close of *Macbeth*, hearing that 'the Queen, my lord, is dead' (5.5.15), audiences coming to the play first time around would not know about her alleged suicide. For this they had to wait until the very final speech, alluding to

> ... this dead butcher and his fiend-like queen,
> Who, as 'tis thought, by self and violent hands
> Took off her life;
>
> (5.11, 35-7)

And so, if there is any space or breath for reflection on Lady Macbeth's end as the heat and noise of battle explodes in Act 5, Scene 7, viewers might in this interval have some sense of that great anti-heroine as merely fading to a natural close, through madness and the intermediate space of her sleepwalkings. Even as the curtain drops, we are not certain that she committed suicide, nor how she achieved it. For all that, it seems fair to add that the death of this anti-icon could hardly have been allowed the kind of aestheticization given to Ophelia, Juliet, or Desdemona.

Turning to Cleopatra, we find a female suicide which partly matches the death of Ophelia, but also strongly contrasts. Shakespeare's Cleopatra is the epitome of glittering image. (Let us not forget that the Richard Burton and Elizabeth Taylor film *Cleopatra* remains, allowing for inflation, the most expensive screen production of all time.[7]) And she is also the epitome of feminine fluidity. Enobarbus' famous description of Cleopatra places her on water, and images of fluid change dominate a tragedy in which Antony is seen to lose his hard Roman outline as he sinks into the sensuous currents of Egypt. The pithily balanced, 'Let Rome in Tiber melt, and the wide arch | Of the ranged empire fall' (1.1.35-6) is only the most obvious glance at this erotic and exotic undermining of Roman male honour.

It is perhaps no accident, then, that Antony botches his attempted Roman death, being forced to appeal vainly to several bystanders to end him. Briefly outliving him, Cleopatra

---

[6] See: Diane G. Denning, Yeates Conwell, Chris Cox, 'Method Choice, Intent, and Gender in Completed Suicide', *Suicide and Life-Threatening Behaviour* 30:3 (2000): 282–8.

[7] *Cleopatra*, dir. Joseph L. Mankiewicz (1963), cost $60 million, 1960s valuation.

dies with a perfectly well-preserved sense of her spectacular powers. Horrified at the notion that she might otherwise be bundled into an undignified spectacle of someone else's power (namely, Caesar's triumphal procession) she stages her own death with great artistry and control. And yet, whilst she is accorded vastly greater agency than Ophelia or Lady Macbeth, her end is again notably feminized. Her death (with asp at her breast) is a dramatic spectacle, and has left a potent visual spectacle: one as likely to come to mind at the name 'Cleopatra' as does Yorick's skull at the mention of 'Hamlet'. Not only that, but her final words do not publicly commend her deeds or honour to posterity in the way of dying male heroes. Instead, she again lullabies herself to death: first with the almost darkly comic: 'Dost thou not see my baby at my breast, | That sucks the nurse asleep?' and then with the warm drift of: 'As sweet as balm, as soft as air, as gentle', before breathing, 'O Antony!' (5.2.303-4, 306) one last time. It is also worth reminding ourselves that Cleopatra went to some trouble to achieve an eminently smooth and painless death:

> ... for her physician tells me
> She hath pursued conclusions infinite
> Of easy ways to die
>
> (5.2.348-50)

remarks Caesar in the play's final lines.

Like Cleopatra, Juliet achieves a good measure of efficient control over her death, stabbing herself decisively when she suspects that poisoned lips may not be enough to overcome her. Here the contrast with the poisoned Romeo is notable, but not especially strong. What is more interesting is the repeated desire to conjure an image of sensuously feminized death:

> ... O my love, my wife!
> Death, that hath sucked the honey of thy breath,
> Hath had no power yet upon thy beauty.
> Thou art not conquered. Beauty's ensign yet
> Is crimson in thy lips and in thy cheeks,
> And death's pale flag is not advancèd there.
> . . . .
> ... Ah, dear Juliet,
> Why art thou yet so fair? shall I believe
> That unsubstantial death is amorous,
> And that the lean abhorrèd monster keeps
> Thee here in dark to be his paramour?
>
> (5.3.91-105)

It would probably be going too far to say that Romeo secretly envies the necrophiliac pleasures which he conjures here. But this speech again shows us how Shakespeare's women often slide uncertainly across the line between life and death. And, as they do so, they retain a kind of aesthetic completeness. Seemingly breathless as she may be in Romeo's eyes, Juliet can be granted an eerie life just because her most essentially female quality—her beauty—remains intact. For Romeo, and for some early modern male viewers, this conveniently idealized, unblemished simulacrum may well have been more attractive than a living woman, far too likely to interfere with or disappoint one's ideals.

So it is with Desdemona too, in the final moments before Othello smothers her. As he leans over her sleeping form in the hushed candlelit intimacy of Act 5, Scene 2, the Moor delivers a speech which is at once dramatically realistic in its staccato indecision, and all too familiar in its fusion of love, death, and femininity:

> *Enter Othello*
>
> It is the cause, it is the cause, my soul.
> Let me not name it to you, you chaste stars.
> It is the cause. Yet I'll not shed her blood,
> Nor scar that whiter skin of hers than snow,
> And smooth as monumental alabaster.
> Yet she must die, else she'll betray more men.
> Put out the light, and then put out the light.
> If I quench thee, thou flaming minister,
> I can again thy former light restore
> Should I repent me; but once put out thy light,
> Thou cunning'st pattern of excelling nature,
> I know not where is that Promethean heat
> That can thy light relume. When I have pluck'd the rose,
> I cannot give it vital growth again.
> It must needs wither: I'll smell thee on the tree.
>   [*He kisses her*]
> O balmy breath, that dost almost persuade
> Justice to break her sword! One more, one more.
> Be thus when thou art dead, and I will kill thee
> And love thee after. One more, and that's the last.
>   *He kisses her*

(5.2.1–19)

Most arresting here, at first glance, is the sense that for Othello his sleeping wife is already dead. Her skin has not only the whiteness of snow but (as opposed to, say, milk) its chill, and the unyielding immobility of an alabaster statue which, in the circumstances, can plausibly be imagined as a tomb monument. Yet after this, Othello enacts a peculiarly ironic and godlike reversal of what he is about to do. Probably leaning closer to Desdemona as his lines progress, he first gives this cold statue the heat and light of flame (very often, in this period, synonymous with the soul) before moving through the typically feminized life of the rose, the sensualized evocation of Desdemona's smell, and on to kisses which could well be seen as a miniature parody of the enlivening breath of God himself. We might indeed extend this parallel by reminding ourselves of how that newly animated creature then takes on a thankless and unpredictable life of its own: the previously silent and idealized Desdemona now arguing against Othello's mistaken beliefs, until her unwelcome voice is quite literally smothered out of existence.

Turning from the realm of female suicide and the aesthetics of feminine death, we have one final image of male self-cancellation from Othello himself:

> Soft you; a word or two before you go.
> I have done the state some service, and they know't.
> No more of that. I pray you, in your letters,
> When you shall these unlucky deeds relate,

> Speak of me as I am. Nothing extenuate,
> Nor set down aught in malice. Then must you speak
> Of one that loved not wisely but too well,
> Of one not easily jealous but, being wrought,
> Perplex'd in the extreme; of one whose hand,
> Like the base Indian, threw a pearl away
> Richer than all his tribe; of one whose subdued eyes,
> Albeit unusèd to the melting mood,
> Drops tears as fast as the Arabian trees
> Their medicinal gum. Set you down this,
> And say besides that in Aleppo once,
> Where a malignant and a turbaned Turk
> Beat a Venetian and traduced the state,
> I took by the throat the circumcisèd dog,
> And smote him thus.
> *He stabs himself*

(5.2.347–65)

Having realized the folly of his supposedly 'honourable murder' (5.2.300) Othello now offers a typically articulate version of himself for the living to disseminate after his death. The self-portrait, for all its lingering exoticization ('Indian pearl', 'Arabian trees') is in many ways well rounded. It evokes the military public service which arguably made Othello an honorary Christian, via his battles against the heathen Turks, and balances this with his self-criticism and genuine grief. Yet in its final words it shifts into paradox. In Syrian Aleppo, notably farther east than Cyprus, the Christianized Othello should indeed have been an especially valuable defence against Turkish malice or insolence. But as he recollects this incident, he also strangely skews it by his partial re-enactment. The thrust which killed the Turk now kills himself. Relatively positive as the tragedy is about Othello's race, we seem here to meet a suicide which is motivated by more than just the hero's personal agonies. It is hard to confidently gloss this densely entangled mesh of the valorised past and ruined present. One reading, though, would be that Othello's final blow actually cancels his past achievements in defence of Christendom, implying by association that such a figure had ultimately crossed too many boundaries to survive intact in the militant world of early modern Christianity.[8]

BEREAVEMENT

In Shakespeare's tragedies, responses to bereavement span a broad range.[9] My chief interest, however, is in the tragedies' implicit debate about the 'correct' response to bereavement. The most famous example of this debate is found in the first onstage encounter

---

[8] E. A. J. Honigmann, arguing that 'Othello, stabbing himself, also identifies himself with the Turk' arguably plays up Othello's otherness at the expense of his 'mask-like' Christianity; by contrast his 'when we shall meet at compt' (5.2.271) suggests a thoroughly internalized faith (*Othello*, ed. E. A. J. Honigmann (Arden Shakespeare, 2006), 22–3 (331)).

[9] See e.g. the quasi-tribal revenge or rebalancing at the opening of *Titus Andronicus* (1.1.96–156).

between Hamlet and Claudius. Following Gertrude's lines about the common inevitability of death, her son replies:

> Ay, madam, it is common.
> QUEEN GERTRUDE If it be,
> Why seems it so particular with thee?
> HAMLET Seems, madam? Nay, it *is*. I know not 'seems'.
> 'Tis not alone my inky cloak, good-mother,
> Nor customary suits of solemn black,
> Nor windy suspiration of forced breath,
> No, nor the fruitful river in the eye,
> Nor the dejected haviour of the visage,
> Together with all forms, moods, shows of grief
> That can denote me truly. These indeed 'seem',
> For they are actions that a man might play;
> But I have that within which passeth show—
> These but the trappings and the suits of woe.
> CLAUDIUS 'Tis sweet and commendable in your nature, Hamlet,
> To give these mourning duties to your father;
> But you must know your father lost a father;
> That father lost, lost his; and the survivor bound
> In filial obligation for some term
> To do obsequious sorrow. But to persever
> In obstinate condolement is a course
> Of impious stubbornness, 'tis unmanly grief,
> It shows a will most incorrect to heaven,
> A heart unfortified, a mind impatient,
> An understanding simple and unschooled;
> . . . .
> Fie, 'tis a fault to heaven,
> A fault against the dead, a fault to nature,
> To reason most absurd, whose common theme
> Is death of fathers, and who still hath cried,
> From the first corse till he that died to-day,
> 'This must be so'.

(1.2.68–105)

For modern audiences, Claudius here is very likely to establish himself at once as a glib, oily and disingenuous villain. Not only he is obviously insincere about a death which he himself caused, but he stoops even to humiliating public insults about the bereaved son's 'simple' nature and 'unmanly grief'. If this modern response is in many ways understandable, it nevertheless blinds us to how that scene may have been received circa 1601. First, Hamlet does not at this stage suspect Claudius as murderer, and nor would first-time audiences necessarily do so. Secondly, both Gertrude and Hamlet evoke the stability of the state of Denmark ('look like a friend on Denmark'; 'You are the most immediate to our throne'). Even Claudius' request that Hamlet should 'think of us | As of a father' could easily be heard as a strategic political plea, far more concerned with monarchical succession than with personal family harmony. This dimension of the scene would have made good sense to any politically astute or worldly viewer of the early modern era—and especially to Elizabethans, who, circa 1601, might reasonably expect the death of their childless queen at any time. That kind of attitude also needs to be meshed with questions of drama and performance. For a dramatist such as Shakespeare, a flatly villainous Claudius would be far too dull. If there is to be some real dramatic tension, his speech needs to have at least some edge of genuine persuasion to it.

Thirdly, we have Hamlet's response to Gertrude. Just what *is* he saying? Again, our post-Romantic ears might easily jump to the conclusion that he simply opposes surface ritual and outward expressions of grief to its deeper, more genuine, finally ineffable feeling. But the speech is too enigmatic to be easily and finally taken in that sense. Hamlet may have something within which passeth show, or he may just be good at persuading us to believe in it, spinning round a hollow centre his supple nets of words. Even assuming that he *does* have this something within him, there is good reason to think that he himself does not know what it is.

The fourth point is focused most sharply in Claudius'

> ... Fie, 'tis a fault to heaven,
> A fault against the dead, a fault to nature,
> To reason most absurd,

In Shakespeare's time, it could indeed seem a fault to nature or reason to very strongly resent death: born during a Stratford plague, the Bard himself may well have only narrowly survived the recurrent scourge that, in 1592-3, carried off around 20,000 Londoners.[10] It was also a fault against the dead to lament them very greatly, given that their real and full life had now truly begun. As Donne put it in 1612,

> ... this to thy soul allow,
> Think thy shell broke, think thy soul hatched but now.[11]

This not only echoed a conceit from Sir John Davies' immensely popular poem, *Nosce Teipsum*, but occurred in an elegy for a girl who had died just two years before, at the age of 14.[12] And if that should not seem close enough to Donne's own heart, we might hear him, in 1616, warning his mother against that 'fault to heaven' which Claudius sees in Hamlet:

> I hope, therefore, my most dear mother, that your experience of the calamities of this life ... your wisdom to distinguish the value of this world from the next, and your religious fear of offending our merciful God by repining at anything which He doeth, will preserve you from any inordinate and dangerous sorrow for the loss of my most beloved sister.[13]

This referred to Anne, Donne's sister by blood, and the bereavement meant that he was now the sole child of his surprisingly long-lived mother. Such sentiments were probably not atypical: they were, rather, the natural response to losses which were all overseen and ordained by an omnipotent, omniscient, and somehow beneficent God.[14]

---

[10] See Park Honan, *Shakespeare: A Life* (Oxford: Oxford University Press, 1998), 15, 17–18.

[11] 'Of the Progress of the Soul', in *John Donne: the Complete English Poems*, ed. A. J. Smith (Harmondsworth: Penguin, 1996), 292.

[12] See R. C. Bald, *John Donne: A Life* (Oxford: Clarendon Press, 1970), 197–8; Sir John Davies, *Nosce Teipsum* (1599), 99.

[13] Edmund Gosse, *The Life and Letters of John Donne*, 2 vols. (London: William Heinemann, 1899), 2: 260–1, 2: 89.

[14] Another example comes from Ben Jonson's 'On my first son', with its very clear sense that the death of the 7-year-old child was just and divinely fated (*Works* (1616), 780–1).

We know enough about Donne to know that he was less unfeeling than many of his peers. And what we know of the French thinker Michel de Montaigne also suggests that he was hardly callous. For all that, Montaigne could vaguely remark, 'I have lost two or three children'.[15] Whilst we know far less about Shakespeare, it has been plausibly claimed that the death of his son, Hamnet, aged just 11, had a powerful effect on him, and may indeed have coloured or shaped some of his evocations of grief after August 1596.[16]

This brings us to the other, more emotional, side of the debate. How do tragic characters respond to the first news of personal bereavement? At times, they can seem yet more unfeeling than Donne, Montaigne, or the duplicitous Danish king. Consider Siward, in the midst of battle against the forces of Macbeth:

> ROSS   Your son, my lord, has paid a soldier's debt.
> He only lived but till he was a man,
> The which no sooner had his prowess confirmed
> In the unshrinking station where he fought,
> But like a man he died.
> SIWARD   Then he is dead?
> ROSS   Ay, and brought off the field. Your cause of sorrow
> Must not be measured by his worth, for then
> It hath no end.
> SIWARD   Had he his hurts before?
> ROSS   Ay, on the front.
> SIWARD   Why then, God's soldier be he.
> Had I as many sons as I have hairs
> I would not wish them to a fairer death;
> And so, his knell is knoll'd.
> MALCOLM   He's worth more sorrow,
> And that I'll spend for him.
> SIWARD   He's worth no more.
> They say he parted well, and paid his score,
> And so, God be with him. Here comes newer comfort.

(5.11.5-19)

At first glance or hearing, Siward's second question is so peculiarly coded to the norms of early modern male honour that it is probably incomprehensible to many of us. Following lines make us realise that 'before' indeed means, as Ross confirms, 'on the front'. Satisfied, now, that his son died fighting, not fleeing, Siward more or less rejoices. By way of comparison, it is worth trying to recall a modern war film in which a soldier responds in any similar way to the death of a comrade or friend, let alone close relative. Admittedly, Malcolm's 'he's worth more sorrow' at least invites audience members to take sides here. But there is little space for reflection, given that seconds later one death cancels another—the 'newer comfort' being, of course, Macbeth's severed (and probably dripping) head.

Immediate reactions to Ophelia's death come a little closer to modern notions of grief.

> LAERTES: Alas, then, she is drowned?
> QUEEN GERTRUDE   Drowned, drowned.

---

[15] Quoted in Lawrence Stone, *The Family, Sex and Marriage in England 1500–1800* (Harmondsworth: Penguin, 1979), 82.

[16] Peter Holland, 'William Shakespeare', *Oxford Dictionary of National Biography*.

> LAERTES   Too much of water hast thou, poor Ophelia,
> And therefore I forbid my tears. But yet
> It is our trick; nature her custom holds,
> Let shame say what it will.
>   *He weeps*
> When these are gone,
> The woman will be out. Adieu, my lord.
> I have a speech of fire that fain would blaze,
> But that this folly douts it.[17]

First, we have the realistic impression of shock, with the stupefied Laertes repeating a question which Gertrude has answered at some length; whilst the Queen herself could also deliver the double knell of 'Drowned, drowned' in a state of numb automatism, as one who is trying to make the impossible word sink in. Next, when Laertes sheds tears for his sister, there is a sense of genuine inner feeling breaking out, despite the period's rules about male behaviour. This kind of spontaneous reaction is repeated in Act 5, when Laertes leaps into Ophelia's open grave, proposing to clasp her body once more (and, in some productions, actually doing so). But it is also notable that Laertes quite quickly goes on to transform his grief into far more typical male aggression, when grappling violently with the supposedly culpable Hamlet a few seconds later. Moving out a little further, we have the more general frame of Christian orthodoxy, which sternly refuses the alleged suicide full rites of burial.

In two other famous cases of tragic loss, violent emotion calls for plain language. First, we have Macduff. Seemingly fated to be the chief bringer of bad news, Ross tells him:

> Your castle is surprised, your wife and babes
> Savagely slaughtered. To relate the manner
> Were on the quarry of these murdered deer
> To add the death of you.

Macduff's immediate response is eminently dramatic, needing to be staged for full effect; readers, by contrast, can gauge it only from Malcolm's succeeding

> Merciful heaven!
> (*To Macduff*) What, man, ne'er pull your hat upon your brows.
> Give sorrow words. The grief that does not speak
> Whispers the o'erfraught heart and bids it break,

alerting them to the fact that Macduff is temporarily speechless.

> MACDUFF   My children too?
> ROSS   Wife, children, servants, all
> That could be found.
> MACDUFF   And I must be from thence!
> My wife killed too?
> ROSS   I have said.
> MALCOLM   Be comforted.
> Let's make us medicines of our great revenge
> To cure this deadly grief.

---

[17] *Hamlet*, 4.7.183–91. I have here used Philip Edwards's edition, which gives Laertes' 'she is drowned' as question, not statement (*Hamlet, Prince of Denmark*, ed. Philip Edwards (Cambridge: Cambridge University Press, 2003)).

MACDUFF   He has no children. All my pretty ones?
Did you say all? O hell-kite! All?
What, all my pretty chickens and their dam
At one fell swoop?
MALCOLM   Dispute it like a man.
MACDUFF   I shall do so,
But I must also feel it as a man.
I cannot but remember such things were,
That were most precious to me.

(4.3.205–25)

Aside from the repeated evocation of someone stunned, stranded between their well-established past and their inconceivable present ('My wife killed too? … Did you say all?'), the most power-ful evidence of grief comes from those poignant phrases, 'my pretty ones', and 'my pretty chick-ens'. These feminine terms are strikingly unlike the public speech of early modern men. Given that it would seem improbable for Macduff to suddenly coin them on the spur of the moment, we must assume either that he borrows them from the mouth of his dead wife, or that he now publicly uses terms he had once used only in the intimate and private spaces of his family.

But this is as much private, spontaneous emotion as can be allowed for the loss of all Macduff's young children and his wife. Having asked, 'Did heaven look on | And would not take their part?', he immediately regains control of his Christian identity, rebuking himself in a way that broadly recalls both Claudius and the bereaved Donne:

… Sinful Macduff,
They were all struck for thee. Naught that I am,
Not for their own demerits but for mine
Fell slaughter on their souls. Heaven rest them now.

(4.3.225–9)

For all that, the power of those plain and poignant words is confirmed, elsewhere in the play, by Macbeth's deviously staged response to the murder of Duncan. Having framed Duncan's servants for his murder, and slain them for convenience, Macbeth justifies this alleged violence to Macduff:

MACBETH … Here lay Duncan,
His silver skin laced with his golden blood,
And his gashed stabs looked like a breach in nature
For ruin's wasteful entrance; there the murderers,
Steeped in the colours of their trade, their daggers
Unmannerly breeched with gore: who could refrain,
That had a heart to love, and in that heart
Courage to make 's love known?

(2.3.106–18)

The line which rings most glaringly false here is, 'His silver skin laced with his golden blood'. The image is far too elevated, far too artificial for its context (even, indeed, for an age when 'artificial' was usually a positive term), a world away from the homely immediacy of Macduff's 'pretty chickens'.[18]

---

[18] Whilst it is true that, in the era of routine phlebotomy, different constituents or states of blood offered a wide colour spectrum (the surgeon John Browne, for example, talks of the 'chestnut' hue

Turning to Lear, we find the now famous stage direction, *Enter King Lear, with Queen Cordelia in his arms, [followed by the Gentleman]*

> Howl, howl, howl, howl! O, you are men of stones.
> Had I your tongues and eyes, I'd use them so
> That heaven's vault should crack. She's gone for ever.
> I know when one is dead, and when one lives.
> She's dead as earth.
> [*He lays her down*]
> Lend me a looking-glass.
> If that her breath will mist or stain the stone,
> Why, then she lives.

$$(5.3.232-7)$$

This is now so well known that it is, again, useful to try and imagine seeing it for the first time. In the Globe theatre circa 1607, Cordelia's fate remained unknown—or, indeed, perhaps tilted toward the happy ending of the earlier *True Chronicle History of King Leir*, which many viewers would have known. The question, accordingly, was which part of Lear's wildly oscillating speech one should believe. For a few moments, he at least believes the better part of it:

> This feather stirs. She lives! If it be so,
> It is a chance which does redeem all sorrows
> That ever I have felt.

$$(5.3.240-2)$$

As the scene continues, Lear occasionally falls silent for some moments, leaving an actor with some difficult decisions about how to behave until, finally, the thread of pathos spins to its finest limit and breaks:

> And my poor fool is hanged. No, no, no life?
> Why should a dog, a horse, a rat, have life,
> And thou no breath at all? Thou'lt come no more.
> Never, never, never, never, never.
> [*To Kent*] Pray you, undo this button. Thank you, sir.
> Do you see this? Look on her. Look, her lips.
> Look there, look there! *He dies*[19]

That extraordinary central line reminds us that much of Shakespeare's best dramatic language fuses music with meaning. Like some startlingly unexpected and unrepeated phrase in a symphony or string quartet, that brutally plain trochaic line derives much of its force from the fact that it is so atypical (albeit anticipated, in part, by the similarly plain, 'Howl, howl, howl, howl!'). And even circa 1607, long before his canonization, Shakespeare's audiences must have been the more struck by such plainness, from a writer already known for his poetic artifice, dexterity, and seemingly effortless ability to coin words and mint phrases.

After such a primal crescendo, there is no other option but a sudden change of key. And so, with poignant realism, we shift to the homely 'Pray you, undo this button'—a different

---

of coagulated blood (*Adenochoiradelogia* (1684), 116)) the opposition with 'silver' seems to rule out Shakespeare's 'golden' as an empirically realistic term.

[19]   5.3. 281–7. All quotations are from the Oxford *Tragedy of King Lear*.

kind of plainness, and one which might almost seem to be delivered by a different speaker, were it not for the hint of the now intolerable emotional pressure that prompts the request.

In Act 5, Scene 5 of *Macbeth*, the protagonist's response to his wife's death offers us a far more ambiguous and enigmatic elegy. Potentially forewarned by the initial 'cry of women' offstage, Macbeth first states:

> I have almost forgot the taste of fears.
> . . . .
> I have supped full with horrors.
> Direness, familiar to my slaughterous thoughts,
> Cannot once start me.

On Seyton's re-entry, he then asks:

> MACBETH   Wherefore was that cry?
> SEYTON   The Queen, my lord, is dead.
> MACBETH   She should have died hereafter.
> There would have been a time for such a word.
> Tomorrow, and tomorrow, and tomorrow,
> Creeps in this petty pace from day to day
> To the last syllable of recorded time,
> And all our yesterdays have lighted fools
> The way to dusty death. Out, out, brief candle.
> Life's but a walking shadow, a poor player
> That struts and frets his hour upon the stage,
> And then is heard no more. It is a tale
> Told by an idiot, full of sound and fury,
> Signifying nothing.
>
> (5.5.9-27)

We seem, here, to be at the limits of human emotion, and at the limits of poetry. Macbeth's speech hovers between the flatness of indifference, and the flatness of someone whose very capacity for feeling has been all but exhausted. Certainly, there is no repeated question, as with Laertes or Macduff; nor the half-crazed denials of Lear. On the surface, there is no particular trace of Lady Macbeth after that brief, relatively impersonal 'she'—itself occurring in lines which could indeed suggest her death as something of an ill-planned inconvenience.

And yet, if Macbeth does use his wife's death as the cue for a generalized lament on mortality, he produces one of Shakespeare's finest poetic moments in the process. It begins with that strangely dislocating implication of a death that was not carefully booked into Macbeth's schedule (recall Samuel Beckett: 'death has not required us to keep a day free'), and the seemingly no less strange reduction of death to 'such a word'.[20] A *word*—not an event? As the speech winds us further into a disorienting labyrinth of past and present, personal and general ('*our* yesterdays have lighted [*other*] fools the way to dusty death') we hear this apparent attempt at linguistic control of death break down. 'the last syllable of recorded time' might at first imply a prewritten, divinely authored teleology (prompting us to wonder about the significance of *extra* syllables in certain of these lines, especially the numbing 'Tomorrow, and tomorrow …'). But in those final lines the stage curtain is

---

[20] Samuel Beckett, *Proust and Three Dialogues with Georges Duthuit* (London: Calder and Boyars, 1965), 17.

whipped back, and where we may have hoped to see a sage and controlling God in some ultimate platonic library, we meet, instead,

> a tale
> Told by an idiot, full of sound and fury,
> Signifying nothing.

How trustworthy is our speaker as a guide to human life and death? We might well remind ourselves that those last lines are in part a sharply demystifying inversion of the earlier sense of prophetic, pre-written destiny. But at the same time, the speech sounds a little too much like the hard-won knowledge of the blinded Gloucester—'As flies to wanton boys, are we to th' gods; | They kill us for their sport'—to entirely write off as the desperate personal nihilism of one errant character (*Tragedy of King Lear*, 4.1.37–8). Moreover, the extraordinary irreducibility of this speech alone takes it beyond the particular demands of one dramatic moment. Ultimately, glosses and interpretations falter hopelessly: the best we can say is that in listening we peer inside a human mind, as it in turn squints up and down the spiral stairway of past, future, and eternity, lighted by one frail and faltering candle.

Turning from this generalized meditation on life and death, I will close with a yet more famous one, in which the revolutions of past, present and future are also powerfully evoked. The graveyard scene of Hamlet is best known for the moment when the hero, told that a freshly unearthed skull 'was Yorick's skull, the King's jester', responds:

> Let me see.
> *He takes the skull*
> Alas, poor Yorick. I knew him, Horatio—a fellow of
> Infinite jest, of most excellent fancy. He hath borne me
> On his back a thousand times; and now, how abhorred
> My imagination is! my gorge rises at it. Here hung
> Those lips that I have kissed I know
> not how oft. Where be your gibes now, your
> gambols, your songs, your flashes of merriment,
> that were wont to set the table on a roar? ...
> Now get you to my lady's chamber
> and tell her, let her paint an inch thick, to this favour
> she must come. Make her laugh at that.

> (5.2.176–90)

It is hard, finally, to say why this moment has become so iconic. It may have done so, in part, because it shows a freer attitude toward death and bodily decay than later periods would allow themselves. What this scene certainly can do is remind us why other iconic moments gained their enduring status. The reason was the language which flowed through them. Scenes of Titus serving up a cannibal pie, or of Macbeth's severed head failed to gain such status just because their language does not reach the kind of peaks we have seen in these pages.

Amongst Hamlet's deathly musings, the sheer ephemerality of the human body is one key element, as when, having thrown Yorick's skull down, he states:

> Alexander died, Alexander was buried, Alexander
> returneth into dust, the dust is earth, of earth we make
> loam, and why of that loam whereto he was converted,
> might they not stop a beer-barrel?

Perhaps Donne had this in mind when, in a sermon preached some years later, he asked: 'who knows the revolutions of dust? Dust upon the King's high-way, and dust upon the King's grave, are both, or neither, dust royal, and may change places; who knows the revolutions of dust?'[21]

But for both Donne and Shakespeare, there was something yet more chilling than the promiscuous revolutions of dust. What seems to have sobered them most of all was the loss of language. Hence Donne's reflection that, just as 'the ashes of an oak in the chimney, are no epitaph of that oak, to tell me how high or how large that was', so 'the dust of great persons' graves is speechless too, it says nothing, it distinguishes nothing'; hence too his impressively macabre imagining of 'that brain that produced means to becalm gusts at council tables, storms in parliaments, tempests in popular commotions, now produc[ing] nothing but swarms of worms, and no proclamation to disperse them'.[22]

Similarly, as he watches the various skulls rudely tossed about by the gravedigger, Hamlet is moved to imagine how these may have once cradled the brains of a courtier and a lawyer—both now long speechless and wordless. Here is 'fine revolution' indeed: a deathly silence echoed when Hamlet laments Yorick's lost 'gibes ... songs' and 'flashes of merriment'. Almost in the same breath, the Prince seems to try and divide the surface changes of death from the more abstract loss of speech and language. For, though he holds a man's skull, he yet warns some courtly lady that, 'let her paint an inch thick, to this favour she must come'.

Nevertheless, if this seems to valorize the highest achievements of language as peculiarly male, Hamlet's relation to that famous skull is also both personal and partly sensuous. He has, after all, seen two skulls cast out of the dirt before he troubles to pick up the third. And he does so precisely because he *knew* its sometime owner.[23] Not only that, but when he recalls having once kissed Yorick's lips, his 'gorge rises at it'. This strikingly immediate reaction to a dry skull suggests that, for a brief instant, he *is* kissing Yorick again—that he momentarily loses himself in a past which he has reanimated. It is just possible, then, that between Hamlet's ruminations on vapoured speech, humbled dust, lost language and perished lips, we are invited to remould all of these into that peculiarly human, peculiarly dramatic, and once most frail of all entities: the personal speaking voice.

Ultimately, death in Shakespeare is a typically multiple play of forces in opposition. Much of the texture of a given scene depends on the demands of the particular play or particular characters. In the cases of Juliet, Ophelia and Desdemona, female deaths are figured with a kind of wholeness, and a fluidity, which suggest a desire to thereby bridge the divide between life and death. But the famous images which these women offer (along with, differently, Cleopatra) are countered by that recurrent sense of blankness, of the failure of language in the face, especially, of bereavement. If anything adequate can be said in such cases, it must be said plainly—often through disjointed monosyllables or mere repetition. And it is in such cases, of course, that the speaking voice is all—this being that medium that shows, as much as says, in moments of crisis.

---

[21] *The Complete Sermons of John Donne*, ed. George R. Potter and Evelyn M. Simpson, 10 vols. (Berkeley and Los Angeles: California University Press, 1953-62), 3: 105–6.
[22] *Sermons*, 4.333.
[23] This itself leads us to wonder how the gravedigger could ever identify the 23-year-old skull: our best guess must be via positioning, perhaps combined with professional obsessiveness.

It is perhaps worth reminding ourselves, on this note, that centuries of arduous scholarship have given us no idea of what Shakespeare's own voice sounded like, for all the limitless ventriloquising he has left us.

SELECT BIBLIOGRAPHY

Ariès, Philippe, *The Hour of Our Death*, trans. Helen Weaver (London: Lane, 1981).

Belsey, Catherine, *Why Shakespeare?* (Basingstoke: Palgrave, 2007).

Kermode, Frank, *Shakespeare's Language* (London: Penguin, 2001).

Neill, Michael, *Issues of Death: Mortality and Identity in English Renaissance Tragedy* (Oxford: Clarendon, 1997).

Schalkwyk, David, *Speech and Performance in Shakespeare's Sonnets and Plays* (Cambridge: Cambridge University Press, 2002).

Sugg, Richard, *John Donne* (Basingstoke: Palgrave, 2007).

CHAPTER 13

••

MINDED LIKE THE WEATHER

The Tragic Body and its Passions

••

GAIL KERN PASTER

No weather be ill if the wind be still.

(Elizabethan proverb)[1]

THE early modern body—marked by porousness, humoural instability, and the extreme volatility of its passions—was in continual reciprocal interaction with its environment, at times taking that environment into itself, at times spilling out of its own boundaries.[2] What this means is that such a body cannot be understood apart from its environment, as Steve Mentz has argued in a lovely insight: 'a fundamental task of literary narratives is representing how human bodies interact with the natural world.'[3] It follows as the night the day that a fundamental task for scholarship of the body in Shakespeare is to give narratives of bodies and their environments historical particularity. It is with such an aim that I will focus this essay—narrowly but intensely—on a single body in Shakespearean tragedy which is strongly marked by its relation to a particular environment and which is iconically representative of tragic bodies elsewhere in the canon. The body in question belongs to King Lear, who rushes furiously out into an oncoming storm preferring to contend 'with the fretful elements' (3.1.4) rather than face the escalating cruelty being visited upon him by his daughters.[4]

In the course of that storm, Lear directly addresses the four elements of fire, air, earth, and water that comprised early modern nature. In doing so, he articulates a variety of

---

[1] Morris Palmer Tilley, ed., *A Dictionary of Proverbs in England in the Sixteenth and Seventeenth Centuries* (Ann Arbor: University of Michigan Press, 1960).

[2] Mary Floyd-Wilson and Garrett A. Sullivan, Jr., 'Introduction', *Environment and Embodiment in Early Modern England* (Basingstoke, UK: Palgrave Macmillan, 2007), 2.

[3] Steve Mentz, 'Strange Weather in *King Lear*', *Shakespeare* 6:1–4 (Routledge: 2010). 139. This chapter owes much to Mentz's insights but his major interest is in how understanding weather in *King Lear* helps reorient current eco-criticism rather than in the storm as way of understanding cruelty.

[4] Quotations follow the New Cambridge Shakespeare's edition of the Folio text, *The Tragedy of King Lear*, ed. Jay L. Halio (Cambridge University Press, 1992). I have chosen not to retain Halio's spelling Gonerill, preferring the more conventional Goneril. Differences between the Q and F texts will be noted where appropriate.

possible human relations to the natural world, relations characterized by paradox, self-pity, alienation, and contradiction:

> I tax not you, you elements, with unkindness.
> I never gave you kingdom, called you children.
> You owe me no subscription. Then let fall
> Your horrible pleasure. Here I stand your slave,
> A poor, infirm, weak, and despised old man;
> But yet I call you servile ministers,
> That will with two pernicious daughters join
> Your high-engendered battles 'gainst a head
> So old and white as this.
>
> (3.2.15–23)

Lear begins by absolving the four elements of blame for his suffering, telling 'rain, wind, thunder, fire' (13) they are not his daughters. But, by speech's end, he has changed his mind, not exactly equating the storm with his daughters but finding the elements nevertheless actively leagued with the daughters in hostilities against him—being, in his word, unkind.

The movement of this speech from portraying the weather first as entirely separate from, then subservient to the conduct of human affairs bespeaks more than the incipient confusion in Lear's mind or his own internal debate—suggested by the moral braggadocio of 'I am a man | More sinned against than sinning' (3.2.57–8)—over whom to blame for his plight. Clearly, for a modern reader, Lear's absolution of the weather makes thematic sense mostly as a reminder of several kinds of sharp distinctions relevant both to the action of the play and to the real world that we inhabit outside it—distinctions between physical and mental suffering, between natural and human agency, and between the accidental and the deliberate infliction of pain. The wind and rain manifestly cause Lear discomfort but, unlike Goneril and Regan, the storm does not mean to and the Fool's poignant presence onstage here demonstrates that it is not singling the king out for abjection. Lear draws a sharp line between a social sphere of reciprocal obligation and a natural world devoid of it: the weather owes Lear no gifts, having received none; it owes him no service ('subscription') since he cannot do it any benefit. His word 'kingdom,' adds to the implied differences between the social and natural spheres: 'the rain it raineth every day,' sings the wet, windblown Fool a few minutes later (3.2.75). Falling on all alike, the weather makes no distinctions among the world's kingdoms because failing to respect boundaries is to not recognize their existence.

But the oddity to modern ears of this moral absolution of the weather should alert us to the possibility that, for the early moderns listening to it, Lear's language here has a more than tautological significance. After all, to state that one is forbearing to do something is to imply that one might have chosen to do otherwise—that it might be reasonable for Lear to blame weather for 'unkindness' or that in such a blame game the social and natural spheres might not be so easily disentangled. Then as now, the words 'kind' and 'unkind' referred to ethically and morally opposite human traits and behaviours, but in earlier usage 'kind' and 'unkind' also referred more neutrally to a whole set of traits and behaviours ranged around larger notions of the natural and unnatural.[5] In early modern

---

[5] See *OED*, *unkind*, 2 a, b, c.

English it was usual to describe very cold winters, east winds, high fevers, hot furnaces, and many other phenomena as 'unkind'—meaning unusual, excessive, unpleasant, severe, causing hardship to man and beast. And so, after making sharp distinctions between human and natural spheres, Lear goes on—with increasing bitterness against the formerly forgiven elements—to merge those spheres and indeed to reverse the customary cosmological order of things by subsuming the natural within the human. He first endows the elements with an appetite for general destruction—falling oxymoronically with 'horrible pleasure'—but then he pointedly arranges them in a hierarchy of hostile forces in which he, a 'slave' at the bottom, serves their will by suffering just as they, being intermediate causal forces, serve the will of pernicious daughters by turning their 'high-engendered' battles with each other upon him.[6]

Lear's self-destructive narcissism is nowhere more clearly represented than in this speech, oscillating as it does between contradictory self-images, first grandiosely in a dialogue of equals with the four elements of creation and then self-pityingly as their hapless earthly target. But the speech is founded upon a more basic contradiction: if Lear's absolution of the weather for being weather is not merely tautological or insane, there must be terms in early modern thought to blame the natural for being unnatural, to blame the elements for being 'unkind.'[7] And in Western natural philosophy beginning with Aristotle's foundational weather text, *Meteorologica*, such had been a possible ethical framework for explanations of meteorological events, for wondering—as Vladimir Jankovic puts it neatly—'whether meteors participated in the world's order or not'.[8] Unusual meteorological events were classed with other prodigious phenomena such as monstrous births of human or animal babies, sudden sinkholes, and miraculous fasts.[9] The difficulty was understood to be objective—to lie with causal ambiguities in the meteorological phenomena themselves, not with the mind contemplating them.[10] Thus the Roman poet Lucretius finds a progressive narrative in meteorological events akin to battles, epidemics, and dramas; the early moderns debated vigorously whether or not weather had providential significance. Elizabethan mathematician Robert Recorde insists, 'So was there never any great change in the world but God by signs of heaven did premonish men thereof.'[11] As a result of such thinking, the early modern discourse of meteorology has significant lexical overlap with ethical discourses of heart and mind, as when natural philosopher John Maplet in 1567 writes of 'the coldnesse or other affection of the aire'.[12] In the general context of quizzing the natural order about its purposes, the storm provides a resonant, apt, and even portentous background for what may be termed the central question of the play, when Lear wonders what 'breeds' about Regan's heart and asks, not at all rhetorically,

---

[6] For a helpful presentation of Renaissance meteorology, see Craig Martin, *Renaissance Meteorology: Pomponazzi to Descartes* (Baltimore: Johns Hopkins UPress, 2011), esp. 7–9.

[7] For an elegant recent meditation on contested meanings of the early modern natural, see Laurie Shannon, 'Lear's Queer Cosmos', in *Shakesqueer: A Queer Companion to the Works of Shakespeare*, ed. Madhavi Menon (Durham, NC: Duke University Press, 2011), 171–8. She is responding to such classic critical treatments as that of John F. Danby, *Shakespeare and the Doctrine of Nature: A Study of 'King Lear'* (London: Faber & Faber, 1949).

[8] Vladimir Jankovic, *Reading the Skies: A Cultural History of English Weather, 1650–1820* (Chicago: University of Chicago Press, 2000), 19.

[9] Ibid., 37.   [10] Ibid., 19.   [11] Quoted ibid., 37.

[12] John Maplet, *A Greene Forest* (London, 1567), cited in *OED*, sub. *affection* 11.

'is there any cause in nature that makes these hard-hearts?' (3.6.34-5). Such a question—asked about the violence of the heavens—was central to Renaissance meteorology too.

In this chapter I want to pursue two related arguments about the body in *King Lear*—the complex matter of what, for the early moderns, did go into the natural making of hard hearts and how to link such making to Lear's embodied emotions in the storm. In other words, I intend to suggest the relation between the ethical implications of early modern cosmology and the play's representation of embodied emotions, especially the dark social emotions bred by choler that give rise to the evil characters' manifest competition in cruelty—their hard-heartedness. The cruelty visited upon Lear by the sisters and the pain inflicted upon him by the storm will become part of the play's representation of elemental nature, as that nature is reflected in human emotions, human behaviour, and the tempestuous physical world. And in the play's representation of elemental nature Lear's body becomes a representative tragic body.

It is a truism of *Lear* criticism that the huge storm in Act 3 is a reflection in the macrocosm of human disorder—the political disorder that Lear has wreaked on his kingdom and the emotional turmoil he has incurred for himself by turning over that kingdom so heedlessly to his daughters and their husbands.[13] The storm, as we have seen, is a key cause of the physical suffering experienced by Lear, the Fool, and Poor Tom before they are taken to shelter in a hovel. Using the approach that I and others have called 'the ecology of the passions', I believe that the early moderns would have understood the storm's contentiousness first as synonymous with weather generally and, second, as a trait shared literally between meteorological events and their own embodied passions. That such traits were thought to be shared is precisely why study of early modern emotions has to be ecological—using that term with deliberate reference to its etymological roots in *oikos,* the ancient Greek word for home—in order to situate the human body within its environment and define environment broadly as biological *and* social, natural *and* human. To note the physical analogy between the trajectory of Lear's fury and the action of the storm is to recognize the storm as a heuristic of similarity for early modern emotions generally and thus as part of the play's bleak answer to Lear's question about the natural making of hard hearts. As I began to suggest above and will amplify below, the explanation for 'kind' being naturally 'unkind' lies within the constituent elements of nature itself of which human nature is seamlessly and inextricably a part.

In early modern English, the link between emotions and the weather comes first of all etymologically. As Jankovic explains, the ancient Greek word *meteoros* derives from the passive verb form of *meteorizo,* to rise to a height. Its cognate forms could refer to physical things rising (smoke, dust, water, or vapour rising up into the air, wind rising in the stomach) or immaterial qualities such as the lofty or abstruse character of thought and speech. A doubtful or excited mind might be *meteoros.*[14] Thus in 3.1, Lear's Gentleman describes himself meteorologically—'minded like the weather, most unquietly' (2). Here,

[13] Coppélia Kahn, for example, describes the storm as a 'metaphor for his internal emotional process.' See 'The Absent Mother in *King Lear*', in *Rewriting the Renaissance: The Discourses of Sexual Difference in Early Modern Europe,* ed. Margaret W. Ferguson, Maureen Quilligan, and Nancy Vickers (Chicago: University of Chicago Press, 1986), 33–49.

[14] Jankovic, *Reading the Skies,* 15. See also S. K. Heninger, Jr., *A Handbook of Renaissance Meteorology* (Durham: Duke University Press, 1960), 5.

as elsewhere, etymology is testimony of cosmology. The traditional link between emotions and weather was neatly summarized in the early seventeenth century by the French natural philosopher Bishop Nicolas Coeffeteau in these terms: 'as there were foure chiefe winds which excite diuers stormes, be it at land or sea; so there are four principall *Passions* which trouble our *Soules*, and which stir vp diuers tempests by their irregular motions, that is to say, *Pleasure, Paine, Hope* & *Feare*.'[15] Gertrude employs a similar comparison in describing Hamlet to Claudius after the closet scene: he is 'Mad as the sea and wind when both contend which is mightier' (4.1.7-8). Examples from within the Shakespeare canon and works outside it might be multiplied indefinitely, being motivated in part by the commonplace comparisons of various emotions to the wind and seas in the emblem tradition. In *King Lear*, Lear's Gentleman describes the king as 'contending with the fearful elements' (3.1.4). The word 'contending'—to which I will return—suggests the lexical field co-habited by the embodied self and its environment, because in English usage then and now 'contend' refers to the 'strife of natural forces, feelings, passions, etc.'[16] Emotions contend in the embodied self just as the elements contend in heaven and earth, though the casual progression in the *OED*'s definition here from natural forces to human feelings belies the profound conceptual division between the body's feelings and natural forces that we moderns have inherited from René Descartes and his followers.[17] Clearly all commonplace comparisons such as Coeffeteau's between the winds and the passions derive from the overarching analogy between the macrocosm and the microcosm.[18] For the ancients and early moderns alike, this analogy was part of a divine order with that artful construct—'man'—at its centre.

But the analogy itself can also function for us as another potent reminder that early modern emotions belonged fully and seamlessly to the natural order. As I have noted elsewhere, the human body like the rest of the created world was composed of the four elements of air, fire, earth, and water (which Lear itemizes in the storm). The body's actions—again like those of the rest of creation—were governed by the four qualities of hot, cold, wet, and dry. The four humours of blood, phlegm, bile, and melancholy flowed through the bloodstream to deliver characteristic forms of nourishment to all the parts. But the humours also determined the operative behaviours of plants, minerals, and animals. The bodily humours were closely allied with the embodied passions: 'Passions ingender Humours, and humours breed Passions,' the philosopher Thomas Wright pointed out, using the reproductive discourse of breeding as Lear did to describe bodily processes.[19] Desire (and its opposite, aversion) was not only present in the bodies of humans and animals but was also distributed in chains of sympathy and antipathy throughout the cosmos. Reporting on an emotion—whether experienced in oneself or witnessed in another—was to describe an

---

[15] Nicolas Coeffeteau, *A Table of Humaine Passions*, trans. Edward Grimston (London, 1621).

[16] See the *OED* here for *contend*, 2b.

[17] On this aspect of modernity, see Charles Taylor, *Sources of the Self: The Making of the Modern Identity* (Cambridge, MA: Harvard University Press, 1989), 189.

[18] There is a wonderful chapter on ancient beliefs about wind, many of them inherited by the early moderns, in Shigehisa Kuriyama, *The Expressiveness of the Body and the Divergence of Greek and Chinese Medicine* (New York: Zone, 1999), 233-70.

[19] Thomas Wright, *The Passions of the Minde in Generall*, ed. Thomas O. Sloan (Urbana: University of Illinois Press, 1971), 64.

event occurring in nature and understandable in natural terms. Emotions became a key feature of the body's internal climate corresponding to key features of climate in the world outside. Emotions were a body's weather—its winds, its waves, its storms—as it contended with itself and the world.[20]

We need to have a holistic image of the selfhood that results from so thorough a suturing in the cosmological chain. That selfhood has been aptly described by Timothy Reiss in a Latinate term, 'passibility'. Passibility denotes 'experiences of being whose common denominator was a sense of being *embedded in and acted on*' by a set of circles—material world, society, family, animal being, rational mind, spiritual or divine life. These all-encompassing circles, says Reiss, '*preceded* the person, which acted as *subjected to* forces working in complicated ways from "outside"'. Because of the embedding, that '"outside" was manifest in all aspects and elements of "inside"—of *being* a person'.[21] In early modern English, being *passible* denoted the capacity to suffer or to receive impressions, physical and mental. In being opposed to *impassible*—a quality imputed to God—passibility was synonymous with being human.[22] The experience of Lear out in a 'contentious' storm is emblematic of passibility in Reiss's sense, when the symbolically central figure of an absolute monarch—one who has reconfigured the map of his kingdom, the members of his court, and family—depicts himself subjected to elemental forces construed as both social and natural. Reiss's notion of an all-encompassing passibility, furthermore, has significant overlap with the historically specific habitus of the early modern body which I described at the beginning of this chapter as porous and exquisitely sensitive to atmospheric change.[23] For Levinas Lemnius, 'the Ayre, that compasseth, and on each side environeth us, ... being either extremely hot or dry, or overmuch moist or cold, causeth and enforceth a manifest alteration in the state of the whole body.'[24] The English physician Helkiah Crooke notes, 'For the matter of mans body, it is soft, pliable, and temperate, readie to follow the Workeman in every thing.'[25] In a 1623 Lenten sermon, John Donne lugubriously declares, 'every man is a spunge, and but a spunge filled with teares.'[26] The storm 'invades us to the skin,' Lear tells Kent before accepting shelter (3.4.7). It is the fraught relation between outside and inside—the environment and the body, the weather

---

[20] For a fuller exposition, see Gail Kern Paster, *Humoring the Body: Emotions on the Shakespearean Stage* (Chicago: University of Chicago Press, 2004), 7–11.

[21] Timothy J. Reiss, *Mirages of the Selfe: Patterns of Personhood in Ancient and Early Modern Europe* (Palo Alto: Stanford University Press, 2003), 2. In aligning myself with Reiss here, I take issue with David Hillman's thesis that *King Lear* is marked by 'the sense of an increasingly impenetrable boundary between the inside and the outside of the body'. As Hillman's reading at other points makes clear, it is the chaotic relations between inside and outside that the play enacts. See *Shakespeare's Entrails: Belief, Skepticism and the Interior of the Body* (Basingstoke: Palgrave Macmillan, 2007), 119.

[22] See *OED*, *s.v. passible* 1, where William Caxton in 1491 describes Christ's transformation in these terms: 'he was made man passyble & mortall: whiche was Immortall & Impassyble.'

[23] See Gail Kern Paster, *The Body Embarrassed: Drama and the Disciplines of Shame in Early Modern England* (Ithaca: Cornell University Press, 1993), 8–10.

[24] Levinas Lemnius, *The Touchstone of Complexions* (London, 1633), G1r. I am grateful to Darryl Chalk of the University of Queensland for this citation.

[25] Helkiah Crooke, *Microcosmographia: A Description of the Body of Man* (London, 1615), 5.

[26] John Donne, *The Sermons of John Donne*, ed. George R. Potter and Evelyn M. Simpson, vol. 4 (Berkeley: University of California Press, 1959), 337. The line is cited in the *OED*, *s.v. sponge*.

and the embodied passions—to which the storm in *King Lear* and the self it invades so theatrically call our attention.

These assumptions—of an early modern self thoroughly embedded within a natural order constituted holistically as biological, social, and familial—provide a framework for how I want to consider the embodied self exemplified by Lear and his passions in Shakespeare's bleakest tragedy. It is a play preoccupied by the contents of hearts, the texture of flesh, and a storm of contending passions composed of cruelty, anger, ingratitude, and filial love. The image of the cosmos and the passible self at its centre are never distant from the action of *King Lear* because, from its inception, the question of how the cosmological bonds of sympathy and antipathy, desire and aversion, express themselves socially preoccupies everyone. In substituting strife where love should be, in explicitly authorizing rhetorical competition as a means of familial restructuring and lawful inheritance, the love contest is a social act with cosmological import. But even before the love contest begins, the conversation between Gloucester and Kent shows cosmological traces when the two courtiers imagine the disposition of land and affection as a function of comparing the 'qualities' of men. Gloucester says that, despite the king's apparent preference for Albany over Cornwall, the 'qualities' of the two sons-in-law 'are so weighed that curiosity in neither can make choice of either's moiety' (1.1.5–6). His term, *qualities*, refers both to personal traits and behaviours and to traits in the world writ large: by definition, the cold, hot, wet, or dry qualities of all created things include within their compass the natural character and behaviour of dukes. Elemental imagery continues to attach to the two men: later in the play, Goneril will chide Albany for his 'milky gentleness' (1.4.295) while Gloucester tries to excuse Cornwall's refusal to see Lear by citing 'the fiery quality of the duke, | How unremovable and fixed he is | In his own course' (2.4.85–7). That the difference in the 'qualities' of the two men has not mattered in Lear's division of the kingdom surprises the courtiers perhaps because they imagined that the qualities thus weighed should be reflected in the distribution of land.[27] But Gloucester, too, by declaring his two socially unequal sons equally dear 'in his account' (16) may violate the hierarchical ordering of the cosmos since his affectionate promotion of the illegitimate son seems to contravene rather than affirm sympathetic, mirroring links between the social and the natural orders.

The more serious offence against the natural bonds of sympathy, of course, arises from the bogus competition Lear creates for his land and affections. Preparing us to think deeply about the making of hard hearts, the play presents the false and true sisters as different in bodily equipment, contents, and textures. By substituting love as strife for love as bond, Lear causes Goneril and Regan to manufacture or at least give voice to feelings they do not have and Cordelia to silence the ones she does. As the three sisters respond, the capacity for truthful or false speaking registers as a difference in bodily regime and ways of inhabiting the natural world. The idea is not unique to *King Lear*: flatterers—the role to which the sisters accede—were frequently described in terms of bodily abjection and extreme porousness to the court world. In *Sejanus*, Jonson describes flatterers as men with 'shift of faces', 'cleft tongues', and 'soft and glutinous bodies' (1.1.7–8). Such men

---

[27] For a discussion of weight imagery in the play, see Mary Thomas Crane, 'The Physics of *King Lear*: Cognition in a Void', in *Shakespearean International Yearbook*, 4 (2004), 3–23.

Laugh, when their patron laughs; sweat, when he sweats;
Be hot, and cold with him; change every mood,
Habit, and garb as often as he varies.

$$(1.1.33-5)^{28}$$

The flatterers will themselves into an extreme of bodily responsiveness: their bodies—and, in Elizabethan terms, their dispositions—have ceased to be their own, uniting with their patron's as his mirroring instrument. In John Webster's *The Duchess of Malfi*, Duke Ferdinand is astonished when his courtiers take a break from responding to his will and have the temerity to laugh before he does: 'Methinks you that are my courtiers should be my touchwood, take fire when I give fire; that is, laugh when I laugh' (1.2.43-4). In this volatile environment, it is for him alone to spark laughter and motivate speech. In *King Lear*, Kent contemptuously describes Oswald in similar terms as one of those who

Smooth every passion
That in the natures of their lords rebel,
Bring oil to fire, snow to the colder moods,
Renege, affirm, and turn their halcyon beaks
With every gall and vary of their masters,
Knowing naught, like dogs, but following.

$$(2.2.66-71)$$

I would describe all of this as satiric imagery of court ecology, the relations between bodies construed in the elemental terms of hot, cold, wet, and dry and the behaviour of court bodies judged morally in terms of their independent firmness, or its lack. The lord's embodied self constitutes an all-encompassing environment, its changes of atmosphere carefully monitored by servile courtiers in order to recalibrate their own. Kent implies that an ideal courtier, properly motivated to regulate a lord's passionateness and ameliorate the courtly environment, would look to balance rather than encourage it—as we have already seen him try to do in objecting to Cordelia's banishment.[29]

In the love contest, it is symptomatic of the injury that Lear inflicts on the passible self and its entire environment—the relations in a given space between and within bodies—that familial love not only entails a competition between sisters (as proxies for their husbands) but also dysfunctional strife within the self between the embodied emotion of love and other bodily faculties. Like the flatterers in the speeches quoted above, the sisters affirm the subsumption of their bodies—within and without, faculties and flesh—to the will of their father. Goneril describes her love for Lear as 'dearer than eyesight', 'a love that makes breath poor, and speech unable' (1.1.51, 55).[30] Regan pronounces herself oddly as of

---

[28] Quotations from *Sejanus* follow *The Complete Plays of Ben Jonson*, ed G. A. Wilkes, vol. 2 (Oxford: Clarendon Press).

[29] In *The Passions of the Minde in Generall*, Wright, glancing at the doctrine of sympathies, writes that 'all likelinesse causeth loue; … if thou wilt please thy master or friend, thou must apparell thy selfe with his affections, and loue where he loueth, and hate where he hateth: … as this meane fostereth flatterie, if it be abused, so it nourisheth charitie, if it be well vsed' (97).

[30] John Gillies describes Goneril's notion of eyesight as 'the luxurious overlordship of the eye.' But her flattery ridiculously implies that she prefers her father to a faculty as precious and necessary as

one flesh with Goneril, 'made of that self-mettle as my sister'—*mettle* referring equally to body and mind.[31] In even more self-destructive and obscure terms, she professes herself 'an enemy to all other joys | Which the most precious square of sense possesses, | And find I am alone felicitate | In your dear highness' love' (68–71). It is a speech against common sense in several ways, since Regan is presenting herself as an enemy to the wholeness of her own appetites and sensations—her 'square of sense' perhaps being the appetites which guaranteed the self's basic instincts for preservation.[32] In early modern theories of the passions, the senses and passions like joy were allied, as Thomas Wright points out: 'for all the time of our infancy and child-hood, our senses were ioint-friends in such sort with Passions, that whateuer was hurtfull to the one, was an enemy to the other' (9).

The sisters' apparent willingness to declare themselves enemies to the self-governing appetites and faculties of their own bodies is a physical impossibility, and establishes their essential falseness. Such impossible willingness also provides an essential context for understanding Cordelia's refusal to comply with Lear's demand, a refusal which not only affirms the self-evidence and cosmological propriety of the familial bond but also her own bodily wholeness which—as we have seen—is equivalent to emotional integrity. She presents the compliance that speaking would represent as physically impossible: 'I cannot heave | My heart into my mouth' (1.1.86–7). She uses 'heart' metonymically to stand for the feelings generated there but the image is literally one of bodily self-violence, with the heaving of disgust at its core, the larger organ thrust up and shoved impossibly into the smaller. For the early moderns, as Robert Erickson has reminded us, the heart was imagined as a container of blood and the feelings carried literally in the blood:

> the heart was the center of all vital functions, the sources of one's inmost thoughts and secret feelings or one's inmost being, the seat of courage and the emotions generally, the essential, innermost, or central part of anything, the source of desire, volition, truth, understanding, intellect, ethics, spirit. *It was the single most important word referring both to the body and to the mind.*[33]

This understanding of the heart is why Cordelia experiences the production of speech against her will as a violent extrusion of bodily contents, the violation of her heart as the bodily container of her inmost feelings by an unwelcome external demand. Kent's dark comment—'Nor are those empty-hearted whose low sounds | Reverb no hollowness' (147–8)—extends the imagery of the sisters' behaviour. Goneril and Regan may be surprised by Lear's demand but, in the early modern logic of embodied feeling, they

---

vision. See 'Introduction: Elizabethan Drama and the Cartographizations of Space', in *Playing the Globe: Genre and Geography in English Renaissance Drama*, ed. Virginia Mason Vaughan and John Gillies (Madison, NJ: Fairleigh Dickinson University Press, 1998), 33.

[31] Jay Halio glosses this line as 'spirit' and 'substance', noting that Shakespeare uses the spellings *metal* and *mettle* interchangeably; see ed., note to 1.1.64. On *metal* and *mettle* as synonymous, see Gail Kern Paster, *Humoring the Body*, 36–7; and Mary Floyd-Wilson, 'English Mettle', in *Reading the Early Modern Passions*, ed. Gail Kern Paster, Katherine Rowe, and Mary Floyd-Wilson (Philadelphia: University of Pennsylvania Press, 2004), 131–2.

[32] Coeffeteau, *Humaine Passions*, describes the appetites as 'that which nature hath given the creature to preserve his life' (22).

[33] Robert A. Erickson, *The Language of the Heart, 1600–1750* (Philadelphia: University of Pennsylvania Press, 1997), 11.

are able rhetorically to shape their bodies to their father's will because their hearts are empty containers, lacking Cordelia's plenitude of feeling. But Lear perversely misreads Cordelia's unresponsiveness not as fullness of heart but as a hard-heartedness unnatural in a youthful female body: 'Goes thy heart with this?' 'So young and so untender?' (99, 100).

Literal interpretation of bodily textures, I have argued elsewhere, is required by the physical naturalness of early modern emotions and the bodily places where they are generated.[34] As Katharine Park has noted, the physical model for the organic soul was 'based on a clear localisation of psychological function by organ or system of organs'.[35] The imagery of hearts here—full or empty of feeling, hard or soft in texture—is literal and metaphorical, biological and social. It prepares not only for the anatomical imagery in Lear's coming tirades against his daughters and his depiction of 'climbing sorrow' as the rising up of feeling from below but also for the central question of natural hard-heartedness in 3.6.[36] Lear's explosive response to Cordelia's rebuff, moreover, sets the terms for understanding the deep analogy between his emotions and the storm. As long as Lear possesses both the reality and the symbolic accoutrements of power, his wrath has a scope virtually meteorological in its destructiveness. Coeffeteau's translator Edward Grimston describes the sway of kings as meteorological: 'For no more doth Sun and Wind exhale and blow uppe past temper, Vapors, and Tempests, then the graces and amplifications of Kings; cause aestures & uprores of affection and *Passion*' (A3v). This power provides a stark display of the social sway and dangerousness of passions when they are supported by power. This is why, in disclaiming Cordelia, it makes cosmological sense for Lear to call upon the 'sacred radiance of the sun, | The mysteries of Hecate and the night, | By all the operation of the orbs | From whom we do exist and cease to be' (1.1.103-6). He is able in an instant to transform the distribution of property, redraw the map of his kingdom, and re-form the human contents of his family and court. But by abdicating, he not only cedes control over the physical and social elements of his kingdom but he also authoritatively sets in motion the growth of a hard new social environment of increasing 'unkindness,' in the modern sense of that keyword.

The massiveness of Lear's error in authorizing untruth, ceding power to his false daughters, and banishing his true one is never in doubt. But it is important to my argument here that the sisters' astonishing capacity for cruelty should be understood less as the narrative unfolding of what was already concealed in their natures than as the result of a new environment and the competition in cruelty afforded by it. This is why, I think, Kent refers to the sisters' hearts as hollow, as bodily places where feelings like cruelty, implanted by nature, have yet to grow. Perhaps this is also why Shakespeare has Cordelia forbear to name her sisters' faults: 'I know you what you are, | And like a sister am most loath to call |

---

[34] See Gail Kern Paster, 'Nervous Tension: Networks of Blood and Spirit in the Early Modern Body', in *The Body In Parts: Fantasies of Corporeality in Early Modern Europe,* ed. David Hillman and Carla Mazzio (London: Routledge, 1997), 110–11.

[35] See Katharine Park, 'The Organic Soul', in *The Cambridge History of Natural Philosophy,* ed. Charles B. Schmitt et al. (Cambridge: Cambridge University Press, 1988), 469.

[36] On Lear's famous image of the *mother* or emotion swelling from the womb, see Kaara L. Peterson, '*Historica Passio:* Early Modern Medicine, *King Lear,* and Editorial Practice', *Shakespeare Quarterly* 57 (2006), 1–22.

Your faults as they are named' (263-5). Once it is clear that Lear intends to sojourn with his entourage in their households, all that Goneril and Regan agree on is to 'do something, and i' th'heat' (298)—the temperature word referring here as always to qualities of mind and body in action. By transferring dominion to his daughters, Lear also transfers to them whatever power to create an environment which rulers may be said to have. Social power has an entailment in the body: it grants Goneril and Regan the environmental affordance to 'breed' their hard hearts, to nurture within themselves the cruel emotions to which their natural dispositions already incline them. In early modern terms, the social privilege of such self-perpetuating emotional sway is called feeding one's humour.[37]

Not surprisingly in a world where 'Passions ingender Humours, and humours breed Passions', that affordance becomes systematic and contentious. The regime that results is one of ever greater physical and mental cruelty towards Lear himself, an increasing indifference to the physical suffering of others, and apparent delight in the infliction of pain and torture.[38] The upward trajectory of cruelty is clear, from Goneril's instructions to her servant Oswald to 'put on what weary negligence you please' (1.3.13); to stocking the disguised Kent overnight; to denying Lear the maintenance of his entourage and with-drawing shelter from the old man and his Fool in the face of the oncoming storm; to the horrific blinding of Gloucester when his support of the king becomes known to Regan and Cornwall.

It is true, as Lars Engle notes, that cruelty does not name a sin in early modern Christianity and that—generally speaking—Elizabethans seem to have been hardened to the infliction of pain on people and animals in ways that seem callous to modern sen-sibilities.[39] Even so, the early moderns clearly had the conceptual vocabulary to under-stand cruelty in subtle and sophisticated terms—to understand cruel behaviour as the manifestation of both nature and culture, as a product of individual temperament and innate disposition which could be encouraged or discouraged by a whole set of social and environmental factors like Lear's transfer of the means of power and the unleashing of a regime of vicious appetites. This too is entailed by a broad understanding of forces govern-ing the self's *passibility*.

Engle suggests that Shakespeare may well have shared Montaigne's belief in inborn dispositions to cruelty or kindness.[40] The doctrine of sympathy and antipathy would help to explain why. Referring to 'the inclinations toward goodness that are born in us', Montaigne says, 'Souls naturally regulated and wellborn follow the same path, and show the same countenance in their actions, as virtuous ones.'[41] It follows that souls of the cruel, born with a native inclination to evil, would be naturally ill- or unregulated. Coeffeteau proposes that 'the wicked haue bad feares, wicked desires, & bad ioyes, whereas the good

---

[37] See *OED*, sub. *humour*, 6b: 'An inclination or disposition for some specified action, etc.; a fancy (to do something); a mood or state of mind characterized by such inclination.' On feeding one's humour, see Paster, *Humoring the Body*, 234–5.

[38] With Lars Engle here, I would define cruelty as the deliberate 'infliction of physical pain on other sentient beings who are helpless to prevent it'. See Lars Engle, 'Sovereign Cruelty in Montaigne and *King Lear*', *The Shakespearean International Yearbook*, 6 (2006), 120.

[39] Ibid., 121.   [40] Ibid., 128.

[41] Michel de Montaigne, 'Of Cruelty', in *The Complete Essays of Montaigne*, ed. Donald M. Frame (Stanford: Stanford University Press, 1965), 306. I use Frame here for accuracy rather than the 1603 Florio translation that Shakespeare would have known.

haue none but good feares, good desires, and good ioyes, for that the branches do alwaies participate of the nature of the roote' (55). Montaigne was well known for his soft-heartedness in the face of suffering, but he denies that such soft-heartedness is a matter of principle or conditioning. It is instead a matter of native disposition: 'What good I have in me I have ... by the chance of my birth. I have gotten it neither from law, nor from precept, nor from any other apprenticeship' (313). What Montaigne instructs us to recognize in Goneril and Regan is therefore a native inclination to vicious appetites and cruel behaviour, an inclination untutored in goodness and released by Lear's abdication from the social constraints of law, precept, or apprenticeship. But no less dismaying is that the sisters become instructors in cruelty. They make it a matter of tutorial precept and policy, encouraging cruelty in their inferiors and competing with each other in the arts of discipline and torture. Their vicious appetites flourish reciprocally in the new and hard environment they compete to create 'I'th'heat.'

Shakespeare structures the escalation of Lear's humiliation by his daughters to emphasize the new disparity between his rage and his powerlessness, between the emotional intensity of his language and the growing ineffectuality of his means—between inside and outside, self and environment. Rather than confronting Lear privately with her complaints about the behaviour of his entourage, Goneril provocatively creates an environment of socially nullifying disrespect for her father. 'Put on what weary negligence you please,' she instructs Oswald, 'You and your fellows: I'd have it come to question' (1.4.13-14). It is part of Lear's first humiliation that it comes from someone like Oswald so far below him in the social order and that his daughter's rebuke of him occurs before the shameful witness of her servant, her husband, and his own followers. The result for Lear himself is what he describes as a shift or restructuring of his own emotional contents—a diminution of his capacity for love and an increase in his capacity for bitterness and anger, what he names 'gall':

> O most small fault,
> How ugly didst thou in Cordelia show!
> Which, like an engine, wrenched my frame of nature
> From the fixed place, drew from my heart all love,
> And added to the gall.
>
> (1.4.221-5)

This image of the embodied self—the '*frame* of nature' (emphasis added)—responding to the action of external forces here is complexly architectural, environmental, and physiological, as we would expect in the discourse of passibility. Lear imagines his body as a structure once fixed in place, its social power and emotional contents secure, but—in the new climate created by the forceful 'engine' of Cordelia's wrenching denial—which has been suddenly displaced and reconstituted. His body's store of love was drawn out and replaced by gall, creating a new environment of the self within and without.

But humiliation comes in stages here, escalating from the psychological to the material. Lear—storming offstage—soon discovers that Goneril has vowed to dismiss half his entourage on precisely the ground that they exist to 'enguard his dotage with their powers', and act on his desires, 'each buzz, each fancy, each complaint, dislike' (1.4.279-80). The ironic futility of Lear's tirade against Goneril—his desire that she not bear children at all contending with his desire that she give birth to a 'child of spleen, that it may live | And

be a thwart disnatured torment to her' (1.4.237-8)—juxtaposes his own continuing inclination for psychological cruelty with his inability to refashion this harsh new world. He
would have her tormented by a splenetic child of bad nature and evil disposition as she—
his own splenetic offspring—is tormenting him.

But the idea of cruelty as a competitive drive—inborn yet susceptible to environmental
encouragement—emerges fully when Regan and Cornwall decide how to punish Kent for
his boorish behaviour to Oswald.[42] Regan, warming easily to the idea of stocking Kent, asks
her husband to prolong the harsh sentence: 'Till noon? Till night, my lord, and all night too'
(2.2.123). Not only will Regan urge her husband to greater cruelty but, in doing so, she also
outdoes her sister in disrespect for her father, as Gloucester points out: 'The king his master
needs must take it ill | That he, so slightly valued in his messenger, | Should have him thus
restrained' (2.2.129-31). It is in this competitive spirit that Regan and Goneril systematically
dismantle Lear of his followers—'What need you five and twenty? ten? or five?' 'What need
one?' (2.4.254, 256). And it is demonstrably in this spirit as well that Regan and Cornwall
decide to put out Gloucester's eyes, one at a time: 'One side will mock another,' Regan declares gratuitously to a husband who needed no such encouragement, 'th'other, too' (3.7.70).
Her image—of the sighted eye mockingly vaunting its advantage over the other's injury
and blindness—reveals a view of the world deeply committed to the idea of contention and
'thwart disnature'. Her view imagines a natural competition between bodily organs of sense
that function naturally together, the pair of eyes producing a whole image of the world by
seeing it together.

The idea of human cruelty here, climactically manifested in the blinding, is of a compounded cruelty—born of a natural disposition, empowered by abdication, nurtured by
contention and imitation, and escalating in an unjust social environment. Such a picture
of cruelty serves as essential backdrop for Lear's anguished question: 'Is there any cause
in nature that makes these hard-hearts?' Cruelty also serves as background for the huge
storm that erupts in Act 3. Shakespeare's insertion of the storm here seems designed to
highlight the contrast between human malevolence and natural adversity and to reveal
the many kinds of cruelty and suffering. But it is also designed to highlight a deep resemblance between passions warring for expression in Lear and contending forces in the
natural world. Lear's choice to run out furiously into the tempest may be a symptom of
incipient madness, but the spontaneous behaviour is also clearly in the old man's choleric
character, of a piece with the impulsiveness and recklessness, the 'unconstant starts' and
'infirmity of age' (1.2.295, 288) that seem to predate the play and set it in motion. And
the collective decision by Cornwall and the sisters to deny the landless king their shelter
is, once again, presented as an escalating cruelty—from Regan's pretended concern over
Gloucester's house as fit shelter for so many people to Goneril's smug wish to impose dis-
cipline ''tis his own blame; |Hath put himself from rest | And must needs taste his folly'
[2.4.283-4]), to Cornwall's decisive command, 'Shut up your doors, my lord' (472).

As we have seen, Lear first experiences the storm as indifferent, then as its victim. But at
moments he is also its co-agent because Lear's passions and the storm share a lexical terrain
of *contention* and *fret* equally descriptive in early modern usage of inner states and outer

    [42] Michael Goldman anticipates me here in describing *Lear* as a 'play of competitions', specifically
the daughters' habit of 'competing in bloody-mindedness'. See *Shakespeare and the Energies of
Drama* (Princeton: Princeton University Press, 1972).

actions—material motions of the embodied mind, of wind and water alike. The Gentleman's description of Lear 'contending with the fretful elements' (3.1.20) neatly captures the imagined complexity and energy of human and natural forces here, Lear's action of contending matched by the contentiousness of the elements themselves—fretting, consuming, devouring, rubbing against each other. Contention is internal to the storm in relation to itself, external as it pummels the king, just as Lear is in contention both with himself and it. States of mind are rendered here as material contention, so that likeness between Lear's emotional state and the action of the storm is underwritten and naturalized here as a function of language itself. Lear contends *against* the elements as they buffet him and make him suffer as his daughters have done, but—in Lear's violent call for a general annihilation—he contends intransitively *as part of them*. He engages rhetorically with the storm, lending it figuration as a cartographical wind-blower, particularizing its features: 'Blow, winds, and crack your cheeks! Rage, blow, | You cataracts and hurricanoes' (3.2.1-2). Apposition—'rage, blow'— points the analogy between the workings of passion in the mind and out in the cosmos. Lear did not cause the storm nor, despite the analogy, is the storm susceptible to royal fiat. Yet the violence of its destructiveness matches the violence of his will to destroy the external world and lose himself in destruction, and it matches the violence of the will of his daughters. This is why he can see the storm as their servile minister, doing their horrible pleasure. This contention of inside and outside, of macrocosm and microcosm, is captured neatly by theatrical reality: in the conditions of the early modern theatre where a violent storm could only be represented by the rattling of tin sheets backstage, Lear's body functions as the lexical and material site of the storm, the place where fretful elements locate and signify their universal contention. The stage image of Lear in the storm—virtually iconic of the play—is emblematic of what Reiss means by declaring that, in the cosmological embedding of the passible self, forces inside and outside conjoin.

It is in this sense that the storm in *King Lear* is a reflection in the macrocosm of the microcosm which is the embodied self. Lear's defiant invocations to the storm are not the misapplied commands of madness and delirium but what Coeffeteau calls 'the contrary motions & desires' (7) of the passions. For Elizabethans, violent weather was a manifestation not so much of natural *disorder* as of a contention natural to the elements and characteristic of their behaviour. Like the 'unconstant starts' of the old king himself ('unconstant' here meaning changeable), the weather's elements were always more or less fretful, being conceived as an agonistic struggle between the forces of hot, cold, wet, and dry. 'No weather be ill if the wind be still,' ran an Elizabethan proverb quoted as epigraph to this chapter. Thunder was the noise resulting from a collision of wind and cloud, air and water; lightning was the burning of an ejected wind.[43] As we have seen in Coeffeteau's four winds quoted above, the contention of the four qualities constituted the heart of weather's resemblance to the passions. And like the violence of the storm, the material violence of Lear's rage consumes itself and is spent.

It was the *meaning* of destructive storms that the early moderns hotly debated, whether storms represented a direct expression of divine will or whether—as Francis Bacon believed—unusual weather was valuable to human beings because the true nature of an event manifested itself more clearly in its most extreme form.[44] This is the contemporary

---

[43] Jankovic, *Reading the Skies*, 17–18.   [44] Jankovic, *Reading the Skies*, 4.

debate glanced at in Gloucester's dour interpretation of 'these late eclipses of the sun and moon' which 'portend no good to us' (1.2.91-2) and in Edmund's sturdy rejection of prognostication: 'This is the excellent foppery of the world, that when we are sick in fortune … we make guilty of our disasters the sun, the moon, and stars' (1.2.104-6). And Edmund goes on—perhaps scandalously, perhaps futuristically—to deny the very classical terms of embedded passibility itself. 'I should have been that I am had the maidenliest star in the firmament twinkled on my bastardising' (1.2.115-16), he declares in his famous apostrophe to Nature.

The play does not support such a rejection, such a statement of radical individualism and apartness from the cosmos, even if it offers no comforting assurances in its place other than the equivalent naturalness of good and evil. Given the cruelty of the action and the wrenching pain of the denouement, it is not surprising that *King Lear* should raise a question about the causes of hard hearts with far more urgency than the equally relevant question about the causes of soft ones, the sources of loyalty, goodness, and pity so evident—if unavailing—in the behaviour of Cordelia, Edgar, Kent, Gloucester, and Cornwall's servant. Recalling Montaigne's notion of the inborn inclination to goodness or cruelty is helpful here. But the central image of Lear out in the storm—he representing the scope of human passionateness, the elements representing their predilection for strife—offers a telling, if oblique response to the meteorological debate and to the spectacle of cruelty unleashed by Lear's abdication. While Lear himself offers us the self-pitying and hence not altogether credible moral judgment that he is a 'man | More sinned against than sinning' (3.2.57-8), the scenes in the storm reveal, powerfully and impartially, a key underlying natural fact of the early modern cosmos: that there was an undeniable affinity between the passions of the embodied self and the passions of the air, between rage and wind, apostrophe and thunder, and thus—by an intellectually difficult extension of the circles of our common embedding—between inborn inclinations to human cruelty or human kindness, and the elemental framework of the natural order.

What cause in nature makes hard hearts may be taken as a large question for Shakespearean tragedy generally. The storm in *King Lear* offers a powerful answer to Lear's anguished question about the making of his daughters' hard hearts and the moral question about the source of human suffering posed more generally in many of Shakespeare's tragedies. But the answer, embodied in the image of King Lear out in the violence of the storm, makes the question itself tautological. It is the same set of causes—the familial, social, biological circles of our common embedding—that also makes softer, kinder hearts and puts them into fretful contention.

SELECT BIBLIOGRAPHY

Crane, Mary Thomas, *Shakespeare's Brain: Reading with Cognitive Theory* (Princeton: Princeton University Press, 2001).

Cummings, Brian and Freya Sierhuis, eds., *Passions and Subjectivity in Early Modern Culture* (Farnham, Surrey and Burlington, VT: Ashgate, 2013).

Daniel, Drew, *The Melancholy Assemblage: Affect and Epistemology in the English Renaissance* (New York: Fordham University Press, 2013).

Floyd-Wilson, Mary, *English Ethnicity and Race in Early Modern England* (Cambridge: Cambridge University Press, 2003).

Floyd-Wilson, Mary and Garrett Sullivan, eds., *Environment and Embodiment in Early Modern England* (Houndsmills, Basingstoke: Palgrave Macmillan, 2007).

Hobgood, Allison P., *Passionate Playgoing in Early Modern England* (Cambridge: Cambridge University Press, 2014).

James, Susan, *Passion and Action: The Emotions in Seventeenth-Century Philosophy* (Oxford: Clarendon Press, 1997).

Kuriyama, Shigehisa *The Expressiveness of the Body and the Divergence of Greek and Chinese Medicine* (New York: Zone, 1999).

Paster, Gail Kern, *Humoring the Body: Emotions and the Shakespearean Stage* (Chicago and London: University of Chicago Press, 2004).

Paster, Gail Kern, Katherine Rowe, and Mary Floyd-Wilson, eds., *Reading the Early Modern Passions: Essays in the Cultural History of Emotion* (Philadelphia: University of Pennsylvania Press, 2004).

Shannon, Laurie, *The Accommodated Animal: Cosmopolity in Shakespearean Locales* (Chicago and London: U niversity of Chicago Press, 2013).

Sullivan, Garrett A., Jr., *Sleep, Romance and Human Embodiment Vitality from Spenser to Milton* (Cambridge: Cambridge University Press, 2012).

Sutton, John. 'Porous Memory and the Cognitive Life of Things', in *Prefiguring Cyberculture: An Intellectual History*, ed. Darren Tofts, Annemarie Jonson, and Alessio Cavallaro (Cambridge, MA.: MIT Press, 2003), 130–9.

CHAPTER 14

SHAKESPEARE'S TRAGEDY AND ENGLISH HISTORY

ANDREW HADFIELD

SHAKESPEARE'S plays represent great swathes of English history. They cover virtually the whole of the later Middle Ages before the advent of the Tudors, delving back even further into the twelfth century (*King John*) before, at the very end of his career, he explores more recent events (*Henry VIII*). Of course, many of these works are history plays, not necessarily tragedies, but the genre of the history play, as Paulina Kewes has cogently argued, is always mixed and impure.[1] The first folio classified British plays as tragedies—*King Lear* and *Cymbeline*—and the English histories as a separate category, but many quartos were clear that English history contained its fair share of tragedy. Hence, what became *The Second Part of King Henry The Sixth* was first published as *The First Part of the Contention Betwixt the Two Famous Houses of Yorke and Lancaster, with the death of the good Duke Humphrey: And the banishment and death of the Duke of Suffolke, and the Tragicall end of the proud Cardinall of Winchester, with the notable Rebellion of Iacke Cade* (1594). What became part three was first published in octavo as *The True Tragedie of Richard Duke of York, and the Death of Good King Henrie the Sixt, with the Whole Contention Betweene the Two Houses Lancaster and Yorke* (1595), advertising the link between the two plays as tragic stories of English history. *Richard III* was a history in the folio but it was first published in quarto as *The Tragedy of Richard III* (1597), as was *Richard II*, published in the same year.

The fact that English history could be read as a tragedy indicates that we should also imagine Shakespeare's plays in other ways. Shakespeare did not just think of English history as material to use in a tragedy; his plays were often written as ways of understanding English history as a tragedy that had unfolded before and might all too easily be repeated. Of course there is a significant difference between tragedy as a complex generic form and a reading of history that emphasizes its destructive effects on the population. Even so, the historical imagination in late Elizabethan and early Jacobean England was predominantly

---

[1] Paulina Kewes, 'The Elizabethan History Play: A True Genre?', in Richard Dutton and Jean E. Howard, eds., *A Companion to Shakespeare's Works*, vol. 2, *The Histories* (Oxford: Blackwell, 2003), 170–93.

tragic in nature, suggesting that those in the present needed to learn from the past in order to escape its malign effects, while realizing that they were doomed to repeat many of the mistakes made by their ancestors. English history was often represented as material for tragedy and this understanding of events then characterized the variety of historical narratives produced in works such as *A Mirror for Magistrates* and Samuel Daniel's *Civil Wars*. Moreover, as plays were printed in ever larger numbers in the 1590s the impact of drama became more significant for a wider understanding of history, and it is likely that history plays—many of which were either tragedies or contained many tragic elements— had as great an impact as formal historical works on the public understanding of the English past.[2]

The Wars of the Roses (1455-87) had devastated the social fabric of England, as a series of bitterly contested claims to the throne led to brutal and protracted civil war, including the Battle of Towton (1461), the bloodiest battle ever fought on English soil. The triumph of Henry VII at the Battle of Bosworth (1485) had inaugurated the Tudor dynasty, a period of relative stability during which England emerged as a Protestant nation with a state church, the Church of England; a fledgling central bureaucracy; a powerful capital; and, largely thanks to the printing press, a common language. But by 1590 it was clear that it was only a matter of time before the dynasty ended as Elizabeth, Henry's grand-daughter, was going to die childless. Her death, so her contemporaries feared, would probably lead to a succession crisis, a further series of disputes between parties with equally problematic claims—James VI of Scotland, The Spanish Infanta, Arbella Stuart, Lord Ferdinando Stanley, fifth earl of Derby—perhaps stretching into the future for over a hundred years, as had happened after the murder of Richard II in 1399.[3] The fact that the accession of James VI and I, a married monarch with an heir and a spare, was achieved with so little fuss in 1603 has often led to commentators to underestimate the extent of the fear generated in the 1590s. Far from being a 'Golden Age' of post-Armada triumphalism this was a period of intense anxiety as the English waited to see what powers would emerge to shape their uncertain future.

The first half of Shakespeare's writing career took place in a time of acute awareness that history might well repeat itself. Not only did he write a series of plays which told the story of English history from the reign of Richard II to the triumph of Henry VII, but many other tragedies were clearly written with the past in mind. It can surely be no accident that *Hamlet* and *Julius Caesar*, plays written around the year 1600, so among the first staged at the large Globe Theatre, centre on a contested succession, conspiracy theories, assassination, and civil war.[4] Theatre companies had to attract an audience, especially when they had just moved to more capacious and more expensive premises, so would not put on plays unless they were certain that they would strike a chord with the theatre-going public.[5] Clearly such plays had a topical appeal, just as *Macbeth* was designed to attract an audience who

---

[2] Peter Blayney, 'The Publication of Playbooks', in John D. Cox and David Scott Kastan, eds., *A New History of Early English Drama* (New York: Columbia University Press, 1997), 383–422.

[3] See Susan Doran, *Monarchy and Matriarchy: the Courtships of Elizabeth I* (London: Routledge, 1996).

[4] Stuart M. Kurland, '*Hamlet* and the Scottish Succession?', *SEL* 34 (1994), 279–300; Andrew Hadfield, *Shakespeare and Republicanism* (Cambridge: Cambridge University Press, 2005), 167–83.

[5] James Shapiro, *1599: A Year in the Life of William Shakespeare* (London: Faber, 2005), Ch. 1.

lived in a country ruled by a Scottish king and *King Lear* reflects on the break-up of Britain when the same monarch was attempting to unite the different kingdoms. Furthermore, it is worth noting that both of these plays derived from the same historical sources as the English history plays of the 1590s and *Lear* was classified as a history in the first quarto. English|British history shaped what Shakespeare wrote whether he was writing directly about it or not.

In thinking about tragedy critics often turn to classical sources, in particular Aristotle. It is also important to remember that there was a much more obviously demotic understanding of tragedy that shaped Shakespeare's imaginative engagement with history and helps to explain why his history plays can often be read in similar ways to many of his tragedies. The term 'tragedy' could be used to refer to any story of the fall of a noble person due to some inherent flaw, the story serving to warn readers of the perils of over-ambition—a definition which informs such widely read late medieval works as John Lydgate's *The Fall of Princes*.[6] Lydgate's verse histories were the most extensive English collection of *de casibus* stories, named after Boccaccio's *De Casibus Virorum Illustrium* (About the falls of famous men), which used history to tell moral tales. Shakespeare's history plays, while not directly indebted to Lydgate, have an obvious relationship to this tradition, an easily understood notion of popular tragedy that provided a shape and purpose to the fledgling genre of the history play.

Shakespeare probably acquired his history from two main sources: Holinshed's *Chronicles* (1577, 1587) and *A Mirror for Magistrates* (probably the expanded 1587 version, edited by John Higgins), the sixteenth-century work that owed most to the *de casibus* tradition. As Jonathan Bate has argued, Shakespeare's plays suggest that he had access to a relatively small number of books—certainly compared to his learned contemporary Ben Jonson who pointedly referred to his 'small Latin and less Greek'—a selection which he used intensively throughout his career.[7] Holinshed and the *Mirror* would have been among those most frequently used.[8] Holinshed's *Chronicles* covered the history of the British Isles from earliest times to the reign of Elizabeth, providing surveys of each reign. Written by a number of diverse hands, the work functions as a chronicle in that it provides miscellaneous perspectives on English history rather than a coherent narrative throughout.[9] Indeed, the *Chronicles* has been seen as a liberal work because it contains an early version of the debates and disputes that eventually created the public sphere.[10] A similar case can be made for *A Mirror*, another work by miscellaneous authors that contained verse tragedies of history linked together by prose discussions. In the earliest version, edited by William Baldwin in Edward VI's reign, the

  [6] John Lydgate, *The Fall of Princes*, ed. Henry Bergen, 4 vols. (London: Early English Text Society, 1923–7).
  [7] Jonathan Bate, *Soul of the Age: The Life, Mind and World of William Shakespeare* (London: Viking, 2008), ch. 9.
  [8] Stuart Gillespie, *Shakespeare's Books: A Dictionary of Shakespeare's Sources* (London: Athlone, 2001), 240–51, 336–41; Allardyce and Josephine Nicoll, *Holinshed's Chronicle, as Used in Shakespeare's Plays* (London: Dent, 1955, repr. of 1927).
  [9] Paulina Kewes, Ian W. Archer, and Felicity Heal, eds., *The Oxford Handbook of Holinshed's Chronicles* (Oxford: Oxford University Press, 2012).
  [10] Annabel Patterson, *Reading Holinshed's 'Chronicles'* (Chicago: Chicago University Press, 1994).

tragedies were all stories told by the ghosts of the mighty who had fallen, complaints that warned readers not to follow the paths into vice that had led to their own downfall. *A Mirror* was so successful that it was reprinted and adapted numerous times (1563, 1574, 1578, 1587), in the process changing its emphasis so that it became a storehouse of historical tales.[11]

Although it has had a reputation as a dreary work that simply upholds the status quo, *A Mirror* was designed to warn the powerful that they needed to take account of those beneath them in the social hierarchy. Kings had to learn how to govern properly and listen to useful advice. Richard II provides readers with a stark warning of the consequences of failing to govern justly with consent, his ghost urging Baldwin to tell the truth so that others may learn to avoid the deadly pitfalls that destroyed Richard and caused so much suffering in England:

> Beholde my hap, see how the sely route
> Do gase vpon me, and eche to other saye:
> Se where he lieth for whome none late might route,
> Loe howe the power, the pride, and rich aray
> Of myghty rulers lightly fade away.
> The Kyng whych erst kept all the realme in doubte,
> The veryest rascall now dare checke and lowte:
> What moulde be Knyges made of, but carayn clay?
> Beholde his woundes, howe blew they be about,
>
> Whych whyle he lived, thought neuer to decay.
> Me thinke I heare the people thus deuise:
> And therfore Baldwin sith thou wilt declare
> How princes fell, to make the liuing wise,
> My vicious story in no poynt see thou spare,
> But paynt it out, that rulers may beware
> Good counsayle, lawe, or vertue to despyse.
> For realmes haue rules, and rulers haue a syse,
> Which if they kepe not, doubtles say I dare
> That eythers gryefes the other shall agrise
> Till one be lost, the other brought to care.[12]

The lines can be read as an old-fashioned plea for the monarch to listen to the counsel of his subjects.[13] But there is also an explicit warning that monarchs who fail to heed counsel, who overrule the country's laws to indulge in their own vices, and who do not care whether they behave virtuously, will reap their just reward. Read another way this is a stark warning that it does not take long for a king to become a tyrant, someone who cannot govern himself let alone govern a realm. The Bible was full of examples of tyrants, such as Holofernes and Ahab, as were classical history and literature (e.g. the Tarquins),

---

[11] For analysis see Scott C. Lucas, '*A Mirror for Magistrates' and the Politics of the English Reformation* (Amherst: University of Massachusetts Press, 2009); Jessica Winston, '*A Mirror for Magistrates* and Public Political Discourse in Elizabethan England', *Studies in Philology* 101 (2004), 381–400.

[12] *The Mirror for Magistrates*, ed. Lily B. Campbell (Cambridge: Cambridge University Press, 1938), 112–13.

[13] L. K. Born, 'The Perfect Prince: A Study in Thirteenth- and Fourteenth-Century Ideals', *Speculum* 3 (1928), 470–504.

all frequent subjects of later art and literature.[14] Probably the most important political debate in the sixteenth century, inspired by the religious divisions inaugurated by the Reformation, was whether it was ever permissible to depose a tyrant, or whether one simply had to accept any existing ruler as a gift or punishment from God.[15] A Mirror does not tell its readers what to do, but it certainly forces them to ask whether Richard could be seen as a tyrant and, if so, whether his deposition and murder were justified. Richard draws attention to the wounds that killed him (the prose link asks Baldwin to imagine that Richard is seen 'al to be mangled, with blew wounds, lying pale and wanne al naked vpon the cold stones in Paules church' (111)), and asks for nothing to be spared from the tragic narrative of his justified fall. He is also concerned to point out the terrible effects that his reign had on the people who were constantly left 'in doubte' [fear] as a result of his disastrous government. Richard continues that he was 'a king that ruled al by lust' (30), trusting in 'false Flatterers' (32), who enabled his vices to grow and his virtues to disappear. As he admits his story is 'vicious' [characterized by an addiction to vice].

Shakespeare's tragedy follows the moral outlined in A Mirror, and so surely poses the question of whether Richard's murder was justified. When Elizabeth acknowledged to William Lambarde that she was commonly represented as Richard, the sad underlying message was that her subjects were waiting for her to die, perhaps even thinking about accelerating the process.[16] The topical message of A Mirror, warning rulers that they needed to scour the historical record in order to understand the present, and that it would tell them to think carefully about the opposition they would encounter, had certainly hit home. The striking omission of the 'deposition scene' in the quarto of Richard II suggests that such connections were generally made.[17]

Shakespeare's play reads like an expansion of the narrative of Richard's ghost in A Mirror. Holinshed's Chronicles is, perhaps not surprisingly, a bit less pointed than A Mirror, criticizing Richard as a man 'seemelie of shape and fauor, & of nature good inough, if the wickednesse & naghtie demeanor of such as were about him had not altered it', and emphasizing that, while his murder should be condemned, Richard 'was lawfullie deposed from his roiall dignitie' by parliament.[18] Shakespeare elaborates significant details from the historical records available to him to create a plausible drama of the traumatic disaster of Richard's reign. The one figure who is prepared to offer the king proper and helpful criticism is his uncle, the dying John of Gaunt. York warns Gaunt to temper his criticism of the king because he is immature: 'For young hot colts, being raged, do rage the more' (2.1.70).[19]

[14] Rebecca Bushnell, Tragedies of Tyrants: Political Thought and Theater in the English Renaissance (Ithaca, NY: Cornell University Press, 1990).

[15] Robert M. Kingdon, 'Calvinism and Resistance Theory, 1550-1580', in J. H. Burns and Mark Goldie, eds., The Cambridge History of Political Thought, 1450-1700 (Cambridge: Cambridge University Press, 1991), 193–218.

[16] For recent analysis, see Jason Scott-Warren, 'Was Elizabeth I Richard II? The Authenticity of Lambarde's "Conversation"', RES 64 (2013), 208–30.

[17] William Shakespeare, Richard II, ed. Charles Forker (London: Thomson, 2002), introd. 33–8. Subsequent references to this edition in parentheses in the text.

[18] Nicoll and Nicoll, Holinshed's Chronicle, 51, 43. See also the comparison of the two narratives of Richard's deposition in Holinshed's Chronicles (1577, 1587): The Holinshed Project (http://www.cems. ox.ac.uk|holinshed|extracts4.shtml) (accessed 29.11.13).

[19] All references to the Arden editions, series 3 when available, throughout.

The scene takes an immediate turn for the worse when Richard flippantly addresses the peer: 'How is't with aged Gaunt' (72) and he gives the foolish young upstart a piece of his mind, quibbling on his own name to drive the point home:

> O, how that name befits my composition!
> Old Gaunt indeed, and gaunt in being old.
> Within me Grief hath kept a tedious fast,
> And who abstains from meat that is not gaunt?
> For sleeping England long time hath I watched;
> Watching breeds leanness, leanness is all gaunt.
> The pleasure that some fathers feed upon
> Is my strict fast—I mean my children's looks,
> And therein fasting hast thou made me gaunt.
> Gaunt am I for the grave, gaunt as a grave,
> Whose hollow womb inherits naught but bones.
>
> (2.1.73-83)

Gaunt's lines are designed to advise the young king, to make him stop his current profligate rule, think, and save England so that the old can worry less about the future for their children. England is not working, but sleeping when it is not partying, lost in a time of carnival that will be followed by a period of Lenten fasting. The young will start to feel like Gaunt, emaciated, sad, and exhausted, perhaps even worn into a premature death, whereas they should be looking towards a happy future. With its incantatory repetitions and insistent word-play, driving to a powerfully crafted conclusion which employs the familiar 'womb|tomb' motif, Gaunt's advice is meant to seem powerful and striking. The 'hollow womb' filled with bones points forward to Richard's realization that within the 'hollow crown | That rounds the mortal temples of a king | Keeps death his court' (3.2.160-2)—an unacknowledged recognition of Gaunt's forceful warning that life and death are not as easy to prize apart as the young king thinks.

For all its impressiveness, however, Gaunt's speech is a disastrously conceived failure which merely encourages Richard to continue on his destructive way. This is largely Richard's fault, of course, for Gaunt, following the goals of rhetoric, casts his speech as he does in part because he wants to shock the king into reforming himself. It is a desperate move because Gaunt has no more time and this will be his only encounter with Richard in the play. Warned to humour and temper the king, he has been too blunt and direct and has not heeded York's advice, with the result that Richard then refuses to heed his. The quick-fire punning of Gaunt's speech plays into Richard's foolish hands:

> RICH   Can sick men play so nicely with their names?
> GAUNT   No, misery makes sport to mock itself.
> Since thou dost seek to kill my name in me,
> I mock my name, great king, to flatter thee.
> RICH   Should dying men flatter with those that live?
> GAUNT   No, no, men living flatter those that die.
> RICH   Thou, now a-dying, sayest thou flatterest me.
> GAUNT   O no, thou diest, though I the sicker be.
>
> (2.1.84-91)

Gaunt hopes to introduce a moment of sober reflection in arguing that he is flattering the king in mocking his own name, a sarcastic ploy designed to shock Richard into realizing that he is ignoring the wise counsel of the elderly who will not be around to help him for long. But he enables Richard to sidestep the issue as the two men indulge in a self-regarding and self-sealed repartee based on the word 'flatter', verbal pyrotechnics which change nothing. Richard uses 'Flatter' to mean trying to please: Gaunt responds with the quibble that the living flatter the dying to cheer them up and, in doing so, ensures that the point of his speech has been lost.

The issue of flattery, probably the most significant element in the historical record of Richard's sad downfall, is repeated later, and no play in the Shakespeare canon has more references to the word. Gaunt provides yet another startling image of the 'hollow crown': 'A thousand flatterers sit within thy crown, | Whose compass is not bigger than thy head' (100-1); and Northumberland soon makes a similar point: 'The King is not himself, but basely led | By flatterers' (241-2). The exchange between Richard and Gaunt is a spectacular failure of counsel, with a king unwilling to seek proper advice, blocking out unwelcome comment, and a powerful subject who fails to understand how best to tailor his message to suit his audience, one of the most basic principles of rhetoric.[20] Shakespeare has expanded and adapted his sources to develop the basic moral of the story of Richard's reign. The tragedy is not simply that of the monarch. The mighty feel that they are oppressed under a 'slavish yoke' and need to make 'high majesty look like itself' (2.2.291, 295). Northumberland's words express the alienation, so dangerous for Richard, of the king-making class, and contain the threat that if the current monarch cannot be made to look like a king then someone else must fulfil the role.[21] The play shows that England is a garden out of control, while Bolingbroke, the future Henry IV, argues that the chief flatterers, Bushy and Bagot are 'The caterpillars of the commonwealth' (2.3.166) who need to be removed, a judgement supported in the 'garden scene' after the King has been captured. The gardener reflects on the king's failures:

> O, what pity it is
> That he had not so trimmed and dressed his land
> As we this garden! We at time of year
> Do wound the bark, the skin of our fruit trees,
> Lest, being over-proud in sap and blood,
> With too much riches it confound itself.
> Had he done so to great and growing men,
> They might have lived to bear and he to taste
> Their fruits of duty. Superfluous branches
> We lop away that bearing boughs may live.
> Had he done so, himself had borne the crown,
> Which waste of idle hours hath quite thrown down
>
> (3.4.55-66)

There is, of course, no source for this scene, but the gardener reveals the extent of Richard's ignorance of his kingdom and the effects that his behaviour is having on the land he fails

---

[20] Jennifer Richards, *Rhetoric and Courtliness in Early Modern Literature* (Cambridge: Cambridge University Press, 2003), ch. 1; John Guy, 'The Rhetoric of Counsel in Early Modern England', in Dale Hoak, ed., *Tudor Political Culture* (Cambridge: Cambridge University Press, 1995), 292–310.

[21] In Holinshed Northumberland lures Richard to Conway Castle where he is captured. Shakespeare omits this detail so that Richard is more blameworthy in his dealings with the nobles.

to rule as they are outlined in Holinshed's *Chronicles* and *A Mirror*. The commonly understood 'waste' of Richard's reign is finally recognized by the king in his great soliloquy as he waits for the end in Pomfret Castle: 'I wasted time, and now doth Time waste me' (5.5.49).

Holinshed's *Chronicle* makes it clear that Richard's throne is in danger when he travels to Ireland to subdue the 'wild Irish [who] dailie wasted and destroied the townes and villages within the English pale.'[22] In some ways Richard is damned if he does and damned if he doesn't, given the role that Ireland frequently played in developing rebellion against the English crown.[23] The real problem, however, is Richard's choice of unpopular governors in his absence and his unreasonable taxation demands whereby blank charters are circulated in which 'the kings officers wrote in ... what they liked, as well for charging the parties with paiment of monie, as otherwise'.[24] The *Chronicles* declare that the king is 'maruellouslie amazed' when he learns how many of his subjects favour the Duke of Lancaster's rebellion.[25] Shakespeare further dramatizes the extent of Richard's ignorance of his plight. Landing at Barkloughly Castle in Wales, Richard declares that he has been 'wand'ring with the Antipodes' but now he has returned Bolingbroke will repent of his actions because 'Not all the water in the rough rude sea | Can wash the balm off from an anointed king' (3.2.49, 54-5). The lines show that Richard has no understanding of the multiple kingdoms he rules. Even after a campaign in Ireland he thinks that the island, granted to the English king in the Laudabiliter (1155), is a strange, exotic place which has little to do with him. As Peter Saccio has pointed out, 'Richard certainly held a theory of the kingly dignity and power more exalted than that of his predecessors', a fact of which Shakespeare was well aware.[26] The unfortunate journey across the Irish Sea, the last by an English Head of State until Oliver Cromwell in 1649, two hundred and fifty years later, helps to wash Richard's sacred monarchical balm away, and opposition builds in his absence. Richard's rhetoric is memorable, just as John of Gaunt's was earlier, but misconceived and ineffective. Shakespeare's play skilfully develops its historical sources to create a powerfully tragic moment, as we witness in the disintegration of an inadequate ruler, supported by an ideology of divine right, the prelude to an unbridled outbreak of destructive competition between over-mighty subjects.

Shakespeare adapts, develops and changes historical sources for other plays in order to make them into tragedies. The moral of Richard II's fall, derived from verse tragedy, is clear, even if the ways of responding to it may not be. Richard III's reign asks fewer interpretative questions, forcing the dramatist to work hard to prevent the play from lapsing into a series of clichés about the reign of tyrants. The tragedy of Richard's life represented in *A Mirror* tells a straightforward story of an over-ambitious noble who rises through dastardly deeds until 'fawning Fortune began ... to frowne', opposition becomes too intense and he gets his just deserts as his ghost concludes

> Ah cursed caytive why did I clymbe so hye,
> Which was the cause of this my baleful thrall.

[22] Nicoll and Nicoll, *Holinshed's Chronicle*, 29.
[23] The Duke of York launches his campaign for the crown in Ireland in *Henry VI, Part Two*, stirring up the rebellion of Jack Cade, a Kentish man who has served in Ireland.
[24] Nicoll and Nicoll, *Holinshed's Chronicle*, 30.
[25] Nicoll and Nicoll, *Holinshed's Chronicle*, 37.
[26] Peter Saccio, *Shakespeare's English Kings: History, Chronicle, and Drama*, 2nd. edn (Oxford: Oxford University Press, 2000), 23.

> For styll I thyrsted for the regal dignitie,
> But hasty rising threatneth sodayn fall,
> Content your selves with your estates all.
> And seeke not right by wrong to suppresse,
> For God hath promist eche wrong to redresse.
>
> See here the fine and fatall fall of me,
> And guerdon due for this my wretched deede,
> Whych to all prynces a myrrour nowe may be
> That shal this tragicall story after reede,
> Wyshyng them all by me to take heede,
> And suffer ryght to rule as it is reason,
> For Time trieth out both truth and also treason.[27]

It is hard to see readers feeling particularly challenged by this story which advises everyone to accept their station in life and not to question the status quo. The tragedies of those who lived in Richard's reign are much more interesting, especially that of the poet Collingborne, executed for his satirical beast fable, 'The Cat, the Rat, and Lovel the Dog, | Do Rule all England, under a hog', a tale that asks complicated questions about the nature of poetry and politics.[28] The account in Holinshed provides a wealth of further detail and supplies the underlying structure of Shakespeare's play, as well as Thomas More's history of Richard III and the anonymous *True Tragedie of Richard III* (1594), a far more obviously didactic work than Shakespeare's play.[29] Holinshed contains brief accounts of incidents that correspond to Shakespeare's representations of Richard's life and reign, such as the drowning of Clarence in a butt of Malmsey and Richard's dream before the Battle of Bosworth (although this Richard sees 'terrible diuels, which puled and haled him' not the ghosts of those he has murdered).[30] The *True Tragedie* is a narrative history that takes its moral bearings from an account such as that in *A Mirror*. Richard first appears in the second scene, where he is left on stage for his opening soliloquy after his loyal supporter, Sir William Catsby, has expressed his desire that Richard, the Lord Protector, govern well in the young prince's name. Richard's ambitions are more self-centred:

> Ah yoong Prince, and why not I?
> Or who shall inherit Plantagines but his sonne?
> And who the King deceased, but his brother?
> Shall law bridle nature, or authoritie hinder inheritance?
> No, I say no: Principalitie brookes no equalitie,
> Much less superioritie,
> And the title of a King, is next under the degree of a God,
> For if he be worthie to be called valiant,
> That in his life winnes honour, and by his sword winnes riches,
> Why now I with renowne of a soldier, which is never sold but

---

[27] *Mirror for Magistrates*, ed. Campbell, 370.

[28] *Mirror for Magistrates*, ed. Campbell, 349. For comment see Andrew Hadfield, *Literature, Politics and National Identity: Reformation to Renaissance* (Cambridge: Cambridge University Press, 1994), 102–7.

[29] For analysis see Geoffrey Bullough, ed., *Narrative and Dramatic Sources of Shakespeare*, 8 vols. (London: Routledge, 2002), 3: 233–8, 317–45.

[30] Nicoll and Nicoll, *Holinshed's Chronicle*, 169.

> By wraight, nor chaged but by losse of life,
> I reapt not the gaine but the glorie, and since it becommeth
> A sone to maintain the honor of his deceased father,
> Why should I not hazard his dignitie by his brothers sonnes?[31]

This is a cleverly designed speech which shows Richard twisting and turning arguments to suit his ambitions. He starts by imagining himself superior to others, the fair reward for an honourable man of accomplishment, which justifies his claim to the throne. This argument resembles the claim of his father Richard, Duke of York, in *Henry VI, Part Two*, suggesting that history plays probably borrowed from each other as well as from prose histories.[32] He then bases his argument on family honour with the spurious claim that he is seeking the throne for the glory of his dead father, providing more evidence of a link to Shakespeare's earlier play. An audience would have had little trouble in understanding the limitations and confusions of Richard's opportunistic reasoning: the crown was not simply a reward or a desirable job, but a burden that someone had to undertake on behalf of everyone else; and, if one believed in hereditary monarchy then there had to be a succession, not a dangerous competition for power.

Similar representations of Richard and his faulty reasoning and self-delusion can be found in Shakespeare's play.[33] But what is remarkable about *Richard III* is the way in which it transforms the familiar story of a tyrant by trying to show how and why Richard might have succeeded. To achieve this Shakespeare represents Richard as a self-conscious stage villain, intimate with the audience with whom he colludes as he undermines and destroys the rest of the characters. It is important that Richard is shown to be charismatic and funny, not just a plausible figure in the world created on the stage. To achieve this, to make the audience understand the lure of Richard, Shakespeare has him address them directly throughout the first half of the play. The wooing of Lady Anne has no obvious historical source but is crucial to our comprehension of Richard as an energetic and appealing villain, as are his pronouncements before and after his success. Richard announces his plans with a breathtaking and hilarious insouciance: 'What though I killed her husband and her father? | The readiest way to make the wench amends | Is to become her husband and her father' (1.1.154-5). We see Richard set himself the most difficult seduction task in history, as he has already recognized that he is 'rudely stamped' and lacks 'love's majesty | To strut before a wanton ambling nymph' (16-17), has no love for Anne, admits that he killed her husband, Prince Edward, and her father-in-law, the king, whose corpse lies in the room where the wooing takes place. Having succeeded, Richard turns to the audience to revel in his triumph:

> Was ever woman in this humour wooed?
> Was ever woman in this humour won?
> I'll have her, but I will not keep her long.
> What? I that killed her husband and his father,
> To take her in her heart's extremest hate,
> With curses in her mouth, tears in her eyes,

---

[31] Bullough, ed., *Narrative and Dramatic Sources*, III, 318.

[32] For comment see Nicholas Grene, *Shakespeare's Serial History Plays* (Cambridge: Cambridge University Press, 2002), 104–8.

[33] See Andrew Hadfield, *Shakespeare and Renaissance Politics* (London: Thomson, 2004), ch. 1.

> The bleeding witness of my hatred by,
> Having God, her conscience and these bars against me,
> And I, no friends to my suit withal
> But the plain devil and dissembling looks?
>
> (1.2.230–9).

Admiration for Richard's triumph depends on our detaching what he is doing from the historical record so that his actions are imagined dramatically rather than in terms of the accepted facts. In order to work as tragic drama the history play has to abandon its fidelity to history, a paradox that has always characterized this problematic genre, as it does the historical novel.[34]

Shakespeare falsifies the historical record in order to increase the dramatic significance of his tragedy. He keeps Queen Margaret, the ferocious widow of Henry VI, alive into Richard's reign so that she can provide a historical memory—the truth that Prince Edward wants to live on?—a link to the destructive past that Richard in part caused and which enabled him to become king.[35] Margaret is the one figure at court who can stand up to Richard and who has his measure. In a long scene at the end of Act IV the three *grand dames* who have survived the wars, Margaret, The Duchess of York, mother of Richard, Edward IV, and Clarence, and Queen Elizabeth, widow of Edward IV, parade their suffering and loss, in laments that turn into a litany of names of unremembered and interchangeable dead before Margaret reminds those present of the spectacular difference of the present king:

> MARG.   I had an Edward, till a Richard killed him;
> I had a husband, till a Richard killed him.
> Thou hadst an Edward, till a Richard killed him.
> Thou hadst a Richard, till a Richard killed him.
> DUCH.   I had a Richard too, and thou didst kill him;
> I had a Rutland too; thou holps'st to kill him.
> MARG.   Thou hadst a Clarence too, and Richard killed him.
> From forth the kennel of thy womb hath crept
> A hell-hound that doth hunt us all to death:
> That dog, that had his teeth before his eyes,
> To worry lambs and lap their gentle blood;
> That excellent grand tyrant of the earth,
> That reigns in galled eyes of weeping souls[.]
>
> (4.4.40–52)

There is a grim humour to this neat, rhetorical patterning, as well as a series of ironies. English history has been reduced to a series of names, one figure substituting for another. What neither widow nor bereaved mother is prepared to admit is that many of these figures killed each other and their speaking as if it were simply the fault of the other family empties the Wars of the Roses of all significance. Margaret wants to blame the rise of Richard on the Duchess of York, as though she were responsible for producing a monster from out

---

[34] See Jerome De Groot, *The Historical Novel* (London: Routledge, 2009).

[35] On Queen Margaret, see Helen Castor, *She Wolves: The Women Who Ruled England Before Elizabeth* (London: Faber, 2010), 321–403. Margaret died in 1482; Richard's reign began on 26 June 1483.

of her body. Her description of Richard emphasizes his inappropriate maturity, emerging from his mother's womb almost fully grown and so ready to work his black magic from birth. But the argument works against itself too: parents are not necessarily responsible for all the ways in which their children develop. The audience—especially those who have seen the *Henry VI* plays—know that Richard was only able to rise to power because he was the last man standing. This brutal fact bedevils his reign in Shakespeare's play when Richard is shown to be vicious and ineffective as a ruler, uncertain how to govern and deluded in believing that the talents that helped him obtain the throne will sustain him in government. The culture of reciprocal violence that the two women articulate explains why England has fallen to its knees in a conflict that has engulfed far more than the dead protagonists listed here. Richard is indeed a monster—and Shakespeare is doing no more than repeating how Thomas More described Richard in his history, an account that found its way into the chronicles:

> Richard ... was in wit and courage the equal of them [Edward IV and Richard, Duke of York], in body and prowess far under them both: little of stature, ill-featured of limbs, crook-backed, his left shoulder much higher than his right, hard favored of visage [i.e. ugly], and such as is in states called warly [warlike] ... He was malicious, wrathful, envious, and from afore his birth, ever froward ... his mother had so much ado in her travail, that she could not be delivered of him uncut, and that he came into the world feet forward, as men be borne outward, and (as the fame runneth) also not untoothed[.][36]

In representing Richard as he was envisaged by the historians Shakespeare was following his sources. However, the play cannot be read simply as a reminder that Richard was an undesirable king who was replaced by the glorious reign of the Tudors. Rather, *Richard III* show us how such a monster was able to gain power: through the failure of any monarch to establish legitimacy after the murder of Richard II; the lack of a strong central authority after the death of Henry V; and the murderous competition for power which saw statesmen degenerating into warlords.[37] There may be no source for the conversation of the widows, but their exchange shows us how Shakespeare imagined history and how he pointed to the morals that his audience ought to understand, especially with regime change imminent.

The Life and Death of King John opens the section of history plays in the folio and, as the play survives only in this text, it is clear that it was never published as a tragedy, unlike *Richard II* and *Richard III*. Nevertheless, like those two plays, *King John* was often read as a tragic play. William Hazlitt recognized the tragic nature of the events represented in the play even as he worried about the complicated relationship between history and tragedy:

> That the treachery of King John, the death of Arthur, the grief of Constance, had a real truth in history, sharpens the sense of pain, while it hangs a leaden weight on the heart and the

---

[36] Thomas More, *The History of King Richard III and Selections from the English and Latin Poems* (New Haven: Yale University Press, 1976), 8.

[37] Graham Holderness points out how nostalgic Richard is 'for the loss of a heroic past, a warrior nostalgia that laments the passing of war' (*Shakespeare: The Histories* (Basingstoke: Macmillan, 2000), 81).

imagination … still we think that the actual truth of the particular events, in proportion as we are conscious of it, is a drawback on the pleasure as well as the dignity of tragedy.[38]

Hazlitt wrestles with the familiar question of whether the historical record can provide material for tragedy and what is at stake when history itself is tragedy. If the events of John's reign are tragic then what is the play actually doing, and how are we to experience its tragic nature if we are denied the pleasure of admiring the forces that shaped the drama?

Hazlitt, working within a familiar tradition that saw tragedy as fictional, is establishing a problematic dichotomy in separating the play and the historical narrative, as if one were simply a given and the other shaped by its creator. Shakespeare, as in all his history plays, transforms a narrative for the stage in a way that works both with and against the grain of its origins, a story that was already conceived in terms of literary genres such as verse tragedy. Shakespeare's *King John* is an inconclusive play, the plot structured around a series of carefully balanced national and personal oppositions: England against France; individual nations against the authority of Christendom; John against Philip of France; Eleanor of Aquitaine (mother of King John), against Constance (mother of Arthur); martial might against diplomatic values; weakness against strength; rightful inheritance against pragmatic expediency. In many ways the play looks forward to the experimental works of Shakespeare's last phase, especially *Cymbeline*, an equally balanced and ambiguous play with a shadowy king at the centre. King John, now known principally as a cowardly and spineless monarch overshadowed by his heroic older brother, Richard the Lionheart, had a rather better reputation in the sixteenth century, and was championed by the Protestant hagiographers, John Bale and John Foxe, as a monarch who stood up for an independent England against the illegal demands of the Papacy.[39] The anonymous play, *The Troublesome Reign of King John* concludes with John poisoned by treacherous friars, loyal to the Pope not the king, and with his son, Henry III, promising to establish a free, independent England that, united, can resist whatever the world throws at it: 'Let *England* live but true within it selfe, | And all the world can never wrong her State.'[40]

Shakespeare's *King John* concludes with similar lines, but they are spoken by the character with the most lines in the play, the Bastard, illegitimate son of Richard the Lionheart, who has been an aggressive warrior loyal to England throughout, casting aside his claim to his family estate to serve John whom he always urges on to fight the French to claim his rights. When John's courage falters in Act 5 as French forces seem overwhelming, the Bastard reminds his uncle that he is the king:

> But wherefore do you droop? Why look you sad?
> Be great in act as you have been in thought;
> Let not the world see fear and sad distrust
> Govern the motion of a kingly eye! …
> Away, and glister like the god of war
> When he intendeth to become the field:
> Show boldness and aspiring confidence![41]

---

[38] William Hazlitt, *Liber Amoris and Dramatic Criticisms*, ed. Charles Morgan (London: Peter Nevill, 1948), 347.

[39] Bullough, ed., *Narrative and Dramatic Sources*, 4: 1–151; Saccio, *Shakespeare's English Kings*, ch. 8.

[40] Bullough, ed., *Narrative and Dramatic Sources*, 4: 151.

[41] William Shakespeare, *King John*, ed. E. A. J. Honigmann (London: Methuen, 1954), 5.1.44–7, 54–6.

Henry III in the *Troublesome Reign* looks to end conflict and restore peace; the Bastard in *King John* wants to claim ancient rights in a world that grants him none, and continue the conflict. While the anonymous play suggests there is resolution, Shakespeare is conscious that the Bastard's concluding couplet, 'And we shall shock them! Nought shall make us rue | If England to itself do rest but true!' (5.1.117-18) points to a violent future. The play, like the three *Henry VI* plays, has shown the audience enough bloodshed and suffering for there to be no possibility of misunderstanding, most notably in the belated realisation of Constance that the actions of the rival factions have led to the 'odiferous stench' and 'sound rottenness' (2.3.26) that have spread through France. Henry III's reign was characterized by two bitter civil wars with his barons, which saw the king imprisoned by Simon De Montfort, as well as further conflict with France. He died with further rebellion threatening the stability of the realm.[42]

The most obvious focus for tragic pathos in *King John* is Prince Arthur, a reluctant pawn with no particular ambition for high office. His sad life hovers between tragedy and farce. His mother tries to realize his strong claim for the throne, despite Arthur's clear reticence. John, understanding the threat that Arthur poses to his security, entices his loyal follower, Hubert, to murder the boy he holds secure in a castle supposedly for his own protection. John's wheedling supplication to Hubert contrasts strongly to the desperate self-defensive denial of his intentions later:

> Good Hubert, Hubert, Hubert, throw thine eye
> On yon young boy; I'll tell thee what, my friend,
> He is a very serpent in my way;
> And whereso'er this foot of mine doth tread,
> He lies before me: dost thou understand me?
> Thou art his keeper.
>
> (3.2.69-74)

Hubert loyally follows his king, although he claims to Arthur that he means only to put out his eyes with hot irons. It is clear that a bond has developed between the jailer and his prisoner, and Hubert is aware that he will struggle to carry out John's wishes: 'If I talk to him, with his innocent prate | He will awake my mercy, which lies dead: | Therefore I will be sudden and dispatch' (4.1.25-7). Inevitably, Arthur's beguiling innocence prevents Hubert from carrying out the deed, a pointed contrast to the ruthlessness of Richard, Duke of Gloucester. Arthur pleads eloquently for his eyes, flattering his persecutor: 'O, spare mine eyes, | Though to no use but still to look on you' (101-2), and Hubert relents, keeping his failure to kill the boy secret. When the rumour of Arthur's death escapes, opposition to John grows and the weak king pretends that he never intended his death. Hubert reveals that Arthur was not murdered, but any relief that a crime has not been committed is short-lived, before matters are fortunately resolved. Arthur dies attempting to escape from prison. The opposition to John grows, but is ebbing as the fevered king dies, possibly the victim of poison, and peace is concluded.

King John follows the messy and chaotic nature of the historical record, but changes the manner of Arthur's sad death from 'sorrow and grief' in prison to his bungled

---

[42] John Paul Davies, *The Gothic King: A Biography of Henry III* (London: Peter Owen, 2013).

escape attempt.[43] The play emphasizes the chaos and contingency of history: John is not an admirable, or even a neutral figure, as he is in other accounts of his reign, but, as elsewhere, he is the victim of conspiracies which do not have the best interests of England at heart. The play shows how sad, comic, ridiculous and tragic human life can be, especially when the actors are caught up by forces too powerful for them to comprehend, let alone resist. Accordingly, the tragic vision of *King John* is not as far removed from that of *King Lear* or *Hamlet* as is habitually assumed. However he may have transformed the material at his disposal, Shakespeare's history plays are often tragic in nature just because English history contained so many narratives that could be read as tragic, and which had indeed been already represented as 'tragedy' before the dramatist got to work on them.

SELECT BIBLIOGRAPHY

Bullough, Geoffrey, ed., *Narrative and Dramatic Sources of Shakespeare*, 8 vols. (London: Routledge, 2002).

Bushnell, Rebecca, *Tragedies of Tyrants: Political Thought and Theater in the English Renaissance* (Ithaca, NY: Cornell University Press, 1990).

Castor, Helen, *She Wolves: The Women Who Ruled England Before Elizabeth* (London: Faber, 2010).

Doran, Susan, *Monarchy and Matriarchy: the Courtships of Elizabeth I* (London: Routledge, 1996).

Gillespie, Stuart, *Shakespeare's Books: A Dictionary of Shakespeare's Sources* (London: Athlone, 2001).

Grene, Nicholas, *Shakespeare's Serial History Play.* (Cambridge: Cambridge University Press, 2002).

Guy, John, 'The Rhetoric of Counsel in Early Modern England', in Dale Hoak, ed., *Tudor Political Culture* (Cambridge: Cambridge University Press, 1995), 292–310.

Hadfield, Andrew, *Shakespeare and Renaissance Politics* (London: Thomson, 2004).

Hadfield, Andrew, *Shakespeare and Republicanism* (Cambridge: Cambridge University Press, 2005).

Holderness, Graham, *Shakespeare: The Histories* (Basingstoke: Macmillan, 2000).

Kewes, Paulina, 'The Elizabethan History Play: A True Genre?', in Richard Dutton and Jean E. Howard, eds., *A Companion to Shakespeare's Works*, vol. 2 *The Histories* (Oxford: Blackwell, 2003), 170–93.

Kewes, Paulina, Ian W. Archer, and Felicity Heal, eds., *The Oxford Handbook of Holinshed's Chronicles* (Oxford: Oxford University Press, 2012).

Kingdon, Robert M., 'Calvinism and Resistance Theory, 155–1580', in J. H. Burns and Mark Goldie, eds., *The Cambridge History of Political Thought, 145–1700* (Cambridge: Cambridge University Press, 1991), 193–218.

The Mirror for Magistrates, ed. Lily B. Campbell (Cambridge: Cambridge University Press, 1938).

---

[43] Nicoll and Nicoll, *Holinshed's Chronicle*, 9.

Nicoll, Allardyce and Josephine Nicoll, *Holinshed's Chronicle, as Used in Shakespeare's Plays* (London: Dent, 1955; repr. of 1927).

Patterson, Annabel, *Reading Holinshed's 'Chronicles'* (Chicago: Chicago University Press, 1994).

Rossiter, A. P., *Angel With Horns: Fifteen Lectures on Shakespeare* (London: Longman, 1961).

Saccio, Peter, *Shakespeare's English Kings: History, Chronicle, and Drama*, 2nd. edn. (Oxford: Oxford University Press, 2000).

Scott-Warren, Jason, 'Was Elizabeth I Richard II?: The Authenticity of Lambarde's "Conversation"', *RES* 64 (2013), 208–30.

Shapiro, James, *1599: A Year in the Life of William Shakespeare* (London: Faber, 2005).

CHAPTER 15

....

SHAKESPEARE'S TRAGEDY
AND ROMAN HISTORY

....

TOM BISHOP

> Haply you think, but bootless are your thoughts,
> That this is fabulously counterfeit
> And that we do as all tragedians do:
> To die today, for fashioning our scene,
> The death of Ajax, or some Roman peer,
> And in a minute starting up again
> Revive to please tomorrow's audience.
>
> (Kyd, *The Spanish Tragedy*, 4.4.76–82)

STANDING among the corpses at the end of *The Spanish Tragedy*, Hieronimo invites his audience to consider his 'fabulously counterfeit' scene. The startling self-consciousness of the lines rehearses both Hieronimo's performance and that of the actor playing him—the one of tragic revenge, the other of a tragic play. For both of them, a quintessentially tragic action is indexed by the gesture towards Roman history. 'Some Roman peer', the formulation surprisingly casual, might almost be any Roman peer, the history of Rome an extended pageant of aristocratic slaughter, a reservoir of monstrosities at once outlandish and familiar.[1]

Hieronimo's lines suggest why an understanding of Renaissance English tragedy needs to grasp the deep integration of Rome and its history into early modern intellectual and emotional life. Awareness of Roman matters was not just a habit cultivated by the learned, though it formed the ground of almost all learning. Daniel Woolf argues for the emergence in England across this period of a 'more or less coherent—which does not mean "uncontested"—historical sense of a *national* past', a sense of 'the place of England, and eventually Britain, within a world history that includes the classical and pre-classical eras'.[2] To this

---

[1] Tragic characters even in non-Roman plays are often 'Romanized': Suffolk in Shakespeare's *2 Henry VI*, Marlowe's Tamburlaine, and Chapman's Bussy. Even non-tragic characters turn to Rome to fulfil a tragic idea of their fate. Horatio, reaching for poison to show his love for the dying Hamlet, declares himself 'more an antique Roman than a Dane' (5.2.293). See Clifford Ronan, *'Antique Roman': Power Symbology and the Roman Play in Early Modern England* (Athens: University of Georgia Press, 1995), 156–63.

[2] Daniel Woolf, *The Social Circulation of the Past: English Historical Culture 1500–1750* (Oxford: Oxford University Press, 2003), 12.

sense, English history was also a part of Roman history, just as Britannia Magna, 'Great Britain', had been a part of the Roman Empire: the first certainly dated event in English history was Julius Caesar's invasion of 55 BC.[3] At the same time, a counter-current sought to distinguish 'British' and 'Roman' strands in the early tangled history of the two.[4] For an Elizabethan, Roman history was at once 'mine own and not mine own' and it is between these alternatives that its tragic staging plays out.[5]

We can see this mixture of familiarity and strangeness—this 'uncanny' Rome, in Freud's sense[6]—even in small encounters. In 1576, the antiquarian chronicler, John Stow, attended an excavation in Spitalfield, north-east of the City of London, where interest was greatly excited by the discovery of a cemetery even older than the twelfth-century priory formerly nearby. In the field, Stow reported:

> many earthen pots called *Urnae* were found full of ashes and burnt bones of men, to wit, of the Romans that inhabited here.... Every of these pots had in them, with the ashes of the dead, one piece of copper money with the inscription of the Emperor then reigning... Besides those *Urnas*, many other pots were there found made of a white earth, with long necks and handles, like to our stone jugs ... I myself have reserved, amongst divers of those antiquities there, one *Urna*, with the ashes and bones, and one pot of white earth very small ... made in shape of a hare squatted upon her legs, and between her ears is the mouth of the pot.[7]

Stow displays towards these Roman remains a characteristic mix of wonder and pathos. He goes on to consider whether some nearby skeletons were those of men murdered with the large nails adjacent, a hypothesis joining these old bones with terrible violence. Stow demurs—since 'a smaller nail would more aptly serve to so bad a purpose, and a more secret place would lightly be employed for their burial'—but the debate confirms a certain expectation about antique corpses. For Stow, *Romanitas*, in all its ambivalence, is both immediate and evocative; its residue can be held in a modern hand, a tangible part of

---

[3] Earlier accounts of Britain survived in fragments from Pytheas' voyages of the late fourth century BCE in later writings of Strabo, Pliny, and others, but these are ethnographic and geographic rather than historical.

[4] *Cymbeline* (c.1610) stages part of the Roman invasion of Britain and even includes scenes in 'Rome'. Though printed as a Tragedy in the 1623 Folio, the play will not be considered here, being more a tragicomedy, or indeed an example of Polonius's chimerical 'tragical-comical-historical-pastoral'. *Cymbeline*'s Rome is largely a Renaissance Italian city of erotic intrigue; what historical character it has comes from non-Roman sources. For legal and constitutional issues in its historiography, see J. Clinton Crumley, 'Questioning History in *Cymbeline*', *Studies in English Literature* 41:2 (Spring, 2001), 297–315.

[5] Compare Robert S. Miola's description of Rome as both *alia* and *eadem*—other and the same—in 'Shakespeare's Ancient Rome: Difference and Identity,' in Michael Hattaway ed., *The Cambridge Companion to Shakespeare's History Plays* (Cambridge, Cambridge University Press, 2002), 193–213.

[6] Freud notes how, in German, the 'unheimlich' or 'uncanny' is entangled with the 'heimlich' or 'homely'. For him, the essence of an 'uncanny' feeling is the revelation of what has been concealed or repressed in the familiar. See Sigmund Freud, 'The Uncanny' [1919] trans. Alix Strachey, repr. in Benjamin Nelson ed., *On Creativity and the Unconscious* (New York: Harper Torchbooks, 1958), 122–61. For an 'uncanny' Rome in Shakespeare, and Shakespeare's Rome as 'uncanny' for later readers, see Marjorie Garber, *Shakespeare's Ghost Writers* (London: Methuen, 1987), esp. ch. 3.

[7] John Stow, *A Survey of London; reprinted from the text of 1603*, C. L Kingsford, ed., 1908. Text modernized from online publication accessed 11 August 2013 at http://www.british-history.ac.uk/report.aspx?compid=60033#n2.

English history. It can open its mouth and pour out the past. For him, as for antiquarians like Camden and Speed and also for their readers, the ground underfoot, the landscape around, the coinage in their purses,[8] the words they spoke, the institutions they lived within were all deeply shaped by a Rome towards which they felt a complex mix of admiration, pity, and fear—the very stuff of tragic emotion.[9]

No audience in Shakespeare's London could escape Rome. London's walls, its foundations, and many of its major landmarks were known, or taken, to be Roman. Looking on London's Tower, the new young King in Shakespeare's *Richard III* speaks openly of this:

> PRINCE EDWARD   Did Julius Caesar build that place, my lord?
> BUCKINGHAM   He did, my gracious lord, begin that place,
> Which since succeeding ages have re-edified.
> PRINCE EDWARD   Is it upon record, or else reported
> Successively from age to age, he built it?
> BUCKINGHAM   Upon record, my gracious liege.
> PRINCE EDWARD   But say, my lord, it were not register'd,
> Methinks the truth should live from age to age,
> As 'twere retail'd to all posterity
> Even to the general all-ending day.
>
> (3.1.69–78)[10]

The deeds of Rome provide a framework for modern action and ambition, for the very definition of heroic English enterprise a future history is to record:

> PRINCE EDWARD   That Julius Caesar was a famous man:
> With what his valour did t'enrich his wit,
> His wit set down to make his valour live.
> Death makes no conquest of this conqueror,
> For now he lives in fame though not in life.
> I'll tell you what, my cousin Buckingham.
> BUCKINGHAM   What, my good lord?
> PRINCE EDWARD   An if I live until I be a man,
> I'll win our ancient right in France again,
> Or die a soldier, as I lived a king.
>
> (3.1.84–93)

For the Elizabethan audience, both the promise and the pathos of the young King are measured in the shadow of Julius Caesar's 'Tower', visible just south of the theatre where these words were spoken.[11]

---

[8] Each of the biographies in the Elizabethan editions of North's Plutarch featured a medallion image, and coinage was, for the early modern period, essentially a Roman technology. See Sean Keilen, *Vulgar Eloquence* (New Haven: Yale University Press, 2005), 79–83.

[9] The early modern assumption that Rome was the fountain of heroic pasts explains the belief that Romans built Stonehenge. See e.g. the architect Inigo Jones's posthumous (1655) book discussed in Caroline Van Eck, *Inigo Jones on Stonehenge* (Amsterdam: Architectura & Natura, 2010).

[10] 'Julius Cesar's ill-erected tower' reappears as tragic icon and harbinger in *Richard II* (5.1.2). All quotations from Shakespeare are taken from Stanley Wells and Gary Taylor, eds., *William Shakespeare: The Complete Works*, 2nd edn. (Oxford: Clarendon Press, 2005).

[11] Assuming *Richard III* was performed at the 'Theatre' just north of London. On consciousness of Roman history underlying local history outside London, see Sheila Christie, 'When in Rome: Shifting Conceptions of the Chester Cycle's Roman References in Pre- and Post-Reformation

Roman history for Elizabethan writers was 'mine own' in another sense too. Histories of Rome and of England had been entangled for many decades, and a dramatist of the end of the century had contact with Roman history both as matter and as manner, directly through the availability of Roman histories in Latin and in English as potential stage actions, and indirectly through the influence of Roman writing on the content and shaping of English histories themselves.[12] Nor did the influence run only one way, from the printed source to the stage. All through the two plus decades of Shakespeare's career, Roman history, English history, and dramatic versions of both engaged in a complex conversation of mutual influence and instruction. To understand Shakespeare's deployment of Roman history in tragedy, it is helpful to be aware of how this conversation had already influenced and been influenced by his work.

A simple instance is again given by *Richard III*. Shakespeare took the main outlines of his narrative from various chronicle histories, especially Holinshed. But those sources themselves had already assimilated the earlier account of Richard by Thomas More, which was in turn shaped by More's reading of Roman history-writing, so that Shakespeare, whether he knew it or not, incorporated aspects of Roman historiography already transmuted into English from generations earlier.

This is a fairly simple case, but relations between prose and dramatic history could also be more complex, as in the case of histories of Henry IV and V. Shakespeare's work on this material stretches over several years and joins a broad contemporary interest in early fifteenth-century English history, where stage histories provided one impetus for the development of English historical prose. John Hayward's history of the reign of King Henry IV, for instance, published in 1599, was influenced in shape and temper by the Roman historian Tacitus. But so too was it by Shakespeare's own earlier work on the subject, with its powerfully-composed speeches and its sustained and compelling trajectory, which contrasts sharply with Holinshed's looseness.[13] Roman history, English history, and English historical drama were complexly intertwined in the years before Shakespeare turned directly to staging tragic Rome. Both the appeal and, in some sort, the dangers of these interconnections are epitomized by the Chorus in *Henry V* as he knots together Henry's victories in France, Roman conquest, and Elizabethan imperial politics, to imagine:

> In the quick forge and working-house of thought,
> How London doth pour out her citizens.
> The mayor and all his brethren, in best sort,
> Like to the senators of th'antique Rome
> With the plebeians swarming at their heels,
> Go forth and fetch their conqu'ring Caesar in—

England', in Jessica Dell, David Klausner and Helen Ostovich, eds., *The Chester Cycle in Context: Religion, Drama and the Impact of Change* (Farnham, Surrey: Ashgate, 2012), 149–60.

[12] Roman history was not only available in historians proper, but in other genres as well. The career of Julius Caesar, for instance, appears in Virgil and Ovid and in Lucan's poem *Pharsalia*. Octavius's victory at Actium was portrayed memorably, if briefly, by both Virgil in the *Aeneid* (bk. 8) and Horace in his 'Cleopatra Ode' (1.37). Against these portrayals, even more than against Plutarch, Shakespeare's development of Cleopatra is especially radical.

[13] See F. J. Levy, *Tudor Historical Thought* (Toronto: University of Toronto Press, 1967), ch. 6, and James Shapiro, *1599—A Year in the Life of William Shakespeare* (London; Faber and Faber, 2005), ch. 7.

As, by a lower but high-loving likelihood,
Were now the General of our gracious Empress—
As in good time he may—from Ireland coming,
Bringing rebellion broachèd on his sword,
How many would the peaceful city quit
To welcome him!

(5.0.23–34)

The tensions in this triangle of relations speak much to the complexity of Roman history for a contemporary audience, not the least element of which is an awareness of the shadow of tragedy alike over Caesar, Henry, and, prophetically, Essex.

If such connections show some of the ways in which Roman history for an Elizabethan reader was 'mine own', there are important checks that set it off as in crucial ways 'not mine own'. Chief among these was the stark fact of religious difference: Romans were not Christians. As pagans, the shape of their world, the structure and force of their beliefs, the bent of their emotional and imaginative commitments, and even the events that could count as historically plausible (the god Hercules abandoning Mark Antony, for instance) were strikingly different. And through such differences, antiquity offered a field of exploration in some ways richer and more plastic than recent, English, Christian history. All the major orientation points through which tragedy was articulated—heroism, love, destiny, sacrifice—look radically different in a pagan world committed to Mars not Christ, Venus not Charity, Fate not Providence, Elysium not Heaven. The culture of antiquity was, in this respect, a rich 'non-identical twin' to its converted successor.

And then there was the no less clear fact of the relative remoteness of Roman historical matters from English priorities and investments, despite the fashionable doctrine of the *translatio imperii* which imagined Elizabeth as 'our gracious empress'. This is partly a matter of there being no overwhelming and directly active inheritance of any strand of Rome in contemporary life—no Holy *Roman* Empire, no *Roman* Catholicism. That is, as G. K. Hunter put it, there was no envelope of historical destiny that contained both Roman and English experience in one embrace.[14] The ideas, habits and actions of Shakespeare's Romans unfold to a greater extent within their own horizon than those of Richard III, whose actions are directly linked to a national order and set of commitments still in contention. Like the disjoining fact of pagan religion, this gives the Roman example a separateness that allows certain complexions of events and currents of political experience to be examined with a dispassion that English history plays cannot hope to achieve. Roman history, for all its ghostly survival, is also, crucially, *finished*. Its whole course can be plotted, its junctures more objectively identified, its lessons more certainly drawn, and the actions of its agents seen in a longer, cooler perspective.

Titus Andronicus, the first 'Roman' play now associated with Shakespeare, follows the prevailing fashion of 'blood and thunder' tragedies of the late 1580s and early 1590s, a pattern set by Marlowe in *Tamburlaine* and followed by many seeking to emulate his popular success. Recent discussion has argued that the play was written collaboratively, probably with George Peele, and this would fit with both its date and a plausible narrative of Shakespeare's

---

[14] G. K. Hunter, *English Drama 1586–1642: The Age of Shakespeare* (Oxford: Oxford University Press, 1997), 449–50, and also 86–92, 449–60, 466–73.

career.[15] The strand of bravura Marlovian villainy in it can be traced in Aaron the Moor, a thoroughly anomalous figure in a supposedly Roman scene. But along with its marketable adoptions of Marlowe's rhetoric of charismatic violence and of the bereaved revenger from Kyd's *Spanish Tragedy*, the play offers a kind of anatomy of *Romanitas* in general as an imaginative presence in the late sixteenth century.

This pressure of Rome as a poetic subject is the more urgently registered in that the play makes a complete nonsense of actual Roman history, jumbling in its omnium-gatherum plot the patricians of the Republic, the corruptions of imperial tyranny, and the convulsions of the 'barbarian invasions'. Such a hodge-podge of Rome is best understood not as history but as a kind of fantasia on Roman themes, bearing the same relation to Rome as *Sweeney Todd* does to Victorian London. The play's invocation of Rome as a general subject, its entertainment of the city's whole destiny, is implicit from Titus' first appearance:

> CAPTAIN   Romans, make way. The good Andronicus,
> Patron of virtue, Rome's best champion,
> Successful in the battles that he fights,
> With honour and with fortune is returned
> From where he circumscribèd with his sword
> And brought to yoke the enemies of Rome.
>
> *Sound drums and trumpets, and then enter Martius and Mutius, two of Titus' sons, and then two men bearing a coffin covered with black, then Lucius and Quintus, two other sons; then Titus Andronicus [in his chariot] and then Tamora the Queen of Goths and her sons Alarbus, Chiron and Demetrius, with Aaron the Moor and others as many as can be. Then set down the coffin, and Titus speaks*
>
> TITUS   Hail, Rome, victorious in thy mourning weeds!
> Lo, as the bark that hath discharged his fraught,
> Returns with precious lading to the bay
> From whence at first she weighed her anchorage,
> Cometh Andronicus, bound with laurel bows,
> To re-salute his country with his tears,
> Tears of true joy for his return to Rome.
>
> (1.1.64–76)[16]

This greeting to Rome could hardly be more evocative of the 'precious lading' of the tragic. Its chiastic structure makes the point: Rome, tears, tears, Rome: Rome is as full of tears as the coffin is of death. To engage with Rome is to enter a commerce in death, to voyage to extremity and return in victorious grief. Titus invokes the audience collectively as 'Rome' so that Rome's 'fraught' is ours. In bringing home the coffin, Titus is bringing the matter of Rome— its freight of death—forward on the stage for our inspection, perhaps for our destruction. The end of his triumphing, tragic journey is also the start of a 'return to Rome' for us.

---

[15] See Brian Vickers, *Shakespeare, Co-Author: A Historical Study of Five Collaborative Plays* (Oxford: Oxford University Press, 2002), ch. 3.

[16] The Oxford edition emends to two coffins; early texts indicate one, as here. Oxford also emends 'fraught' to 'freight', but here too I have restored the original, since our overtone of promise or menace is recorded from 1576.

The play allows the grief and strife of John Stow's Spitalfield encounter to flourish with a direct and vivid dramatic energy, a testimony to the sheer *force* of the subject for the Elizabethan stage. A series of powerful wills work in equally powerful language to wrench the currents of Roman history to their benefit, in gestures of interminable blood-shed and retribution. The remorseless titanism that made Tamburlaine so charismatic is transplanted from an Eastern exoticism to the fatal convulsions of an entire Roman heroic culture which is also, alarmingly, one of the precursors of English modernity. In *Titus Andronicus*, Roman history is a nightmare from which even Elizabethans have yet to awake.

As an enduring mythic presence rather than a site of determinate historical action, the Rome of *Titus* unfolds in a series of dramatic emblems—a corpse borne in triumph, a woman terribly maimed, a madman shooting arrows at the gods, a mother eating her children—culminating in its perfect realization as a stage filled with bodies. Though staged in a kind of comic masquerade, which Titus at once sees through, the incarnation of Revenge, Rape and Murder directly in the streets in the persons of Tamora and her sons is a way of affirming how Rome is a place of allegorical extremity for the Elizabethan audience. Historical and mythic events appear at the same level of reality, a commerce emblematized when the mangled Lavinia searches a schoolboy's textbook for a way of communicating, of *reading* her sufferings:

> TITUS   Lucius, what book is that she tosseth so?
> YOUNG LUCIUS   Grandsire, 'tis Ovid's *Metamorphoses*.
> My mother gave it me.
> MARCUS   For love of her that's gone,
> Perhaps she cull'd it from among the rest.
> TITUS   Soft, so busily she turns the leaves.
> Help her. What would she find? Lavinia, shall I read?
> This is the tragic tale of Philomel,
> And treats of Tereus' treason and his rape,
> And rape, I fear, was root of thine annoy.
> MARCUS   See, brother, see. Note how she quotes the leaves.
>
> (4.1.41–50)

The action of 'quoting the leaves'—intently studying as well as citing them—of Ovid, and of Seneca and others throughout the play, suggests how *Titus Andronicus* is less about Roman history proper than about the impact of the fact and idea of Roman power, in-cluding the imaginative power of Latin on Renaissance inheritors like Shakespeare. As Jonathan Bate has suggested, Lavinia is in part a figure for Latin literature itself, traduced and violated by barbarian outsiders. But Sean Keilin counters that the relationship is also strangely reversed, with 'England and English writing the fortunate victims of a Roman conquest'.[17] An interchange of ideas of power is figured in various kinds of violation, em-bedded in a language and narrative that freely depart from any obligation to literal histori-cal accuracy. 'Quoting the leaves', Shakespeare assembles his play as a sort of Thyestean banquet of horrors, where Livy, Ovid and Seneca have equal claims. The world of *Titus* is

---

[17] See Jonathan Bate, *Shakespeare and Ovid* (Oxford: Oxford University Press, 1993), 83–117 and Keilen, *Vulgar Eloquence*, 91–3.

one of violent struggle not only in its action but in its very construction for the Elizabethan imagination.[18]

Ten years or so later, when Shakespeare takes up the history of Rome once more in *Julius Caesar* (1599), things look very different. Tamburlaine's charismatic violence has been thoroughly assimilated, embedded in questions of wider action and couched in a more detailed and capacious historiography aimed at producing a more sober, though not less tragic, account of the process of Roman history. The choice of Plutarch as source is determining here, but it also points to what Shakespeare brings to his renewed staging of Roman history that is original as much in what he does *not* do with Plutarch as in what he does.[19]

Plutarch is not a Roman historian, but a Greek rhetorician and biographer constructing parallels between major figures of Greek and Roman history in order to make a point about their comparability, and their, as it were, counterpart enactments of individual moral destinies.[20] But Shakespeare is not particularly interested in Plutarch's large moral and philosophical scheme of providing 'models of lives [*paradeigmata biōn*]'.[21] He treats the whole subject of the 'Lives of the Most Noble Grecians and Romans' quite differently from the great majority of readers, including dramatists, who tended to assimilate the fortunes of ancient characters to exemplarizing moral traditions like 'Fortune's Wheel' and the 'Mirror for Magistrates'.[22] Instead he approaches Plutarch as a highly accomplished and detailed biographer, a recorder of the particular style and force of a personality.[23] Plundering Plutarch's vividness of biographical narrative, at times directly versifying North's translation, recomposing it and combining it with other sources, Shakespeare poses a series of intimate and searching questions about the relation of Plutarch's enterprise

---

[18] Julie Taymor's 1999 film of the play responds to Shakespeare's play by compiling a landscape of Romes, including ancient ruins, Fascist architecture, and the 'Popemobile', jumbled together, and framed by the aggressive and terrified fantasy life of a boy.

[19] North's Plutarch, first published in 1579, was a bestseller, mostly not taken up by dramatists. Shakespeare is unusual in choosing it—Lodge used Ammianus for his *Wounds of Civil War* (pub. 1594), while later Roman plays following Jonson's *Sejanus* (perf. 1603; pub. 1605) built a line of 'tyrant plays' on Tacitus and Suetonius. For Roman matters as *topoi* in the drama of the period see Ronan, and also Hunter.

[20] On Plutarch, see D. A. Russell, *Plutarch* (London: Duckworth, 1973). Russell's comment on Plutarch's biographical project is helpful: '*Bion graphein*, "to write a life", carries connotations alien to modern concepts of biography. The differences are important if we are to understand what Plutarch intended. *Bios* means, roughly, "way of life", whether in an individual or a society ... It also has some connotations of *ordinary* life, and is associated with the realism of comedy rather than the grand topics of epic or, for that matter, history.' And again: 'the question which is being answered all along is the rather unsophisticated "What sort of man was he?" that could almost find adequate answer in a series of descriptive adjectives' (101–3).

[21] Plutarch's Antony exemplifies 'the corruptions of *erōs* and the effects of flattery [*kolakeia*]' (Russell, 135). As an account of Shakespeare's Antony, this would be grossly inadequate.

[22] For a detailed discussion of an exemplarizing tradition in relation to *Julius Caesar*, see Timothy Hampton, *Writing from History: The Rhetoric of Exemplarity in Renaissance Literature* (Ithaca, NY: Cornell University Press, 1990), ch. 5.

[23] Curiously, given the artistry with which Shakespeare shaped Plutarch's material as a biographer, there is no reference to this attention in the recent volume edited by Kevin Sharpe and Steven N. Zwicker, *Writing Lives: Biography and Textuality, Identity and Representation in Early Modern England* (Oxford: Oxford University Press, 2008).

to that of historians such as Tacitus—the relation of action and personality to the variable or compelling currents of circumstance.[24]

It is this combination of Plutarch's fine-grained and vivid detail with the scope and directedness of historical drama learned in his work on English history that makes Shakespeare's later Roman plays so original and so striking. And it may be just this confluence of his interests at once in the smaller movements of personality and in the framework of events in which that personality unfolds itself that led Shakespeare to select from Plutarch for dramatic treatment the particular lives he did—those around Julius Caesar, Marcus Antonius, and Gaius Martius Coriolanus. For each of these choices explores the exigencies of personality in relation to a key juncture of the history of Roman political organization and institutions. In *Julius Caesar* we are shown the collapse of the Roman Republic, with its patriciate senatorial constitution of collective government, in the face of steady and remorseless pressure from individual and factional self-aggrandizement, first in Caesar and later jointly (and incompletely) in Antony and Octavius. In *Antony and Cleopatra* this scenario is then developed further and more largely, to encompass the final extinction of factional politics itself with the emergence of the solitary principate under Octavius, later Augustus, Caesar, a transformation with the very largest implications. In *Coriolanus*, finally, Shakespeare returns to a key event in the construction of the Roman Republic whose demise he has already treated: the violent but necessary subjugation of heroic masculine individualism on the Homeric model to an emerging constitution of political parties and negotiations, where the key event is the creation of the tribunate of the people depicted in the opening movement of the play.

Shakespeare did not really derive from either Plutarch or from other Roman historians this strategy of analysing key junctures in the constitutional history of the Roman Republic as the product of acts and failures by particular figures. If modern English readers think of Plutarch this way, it is because of Shakespeare's revision. Nor was this combination really a foregrounded enterprise of his English history plays, though its genesis probably lies there.[25] Though the later of these works—those depicting the career of Hal as prince and then king—trace a concerted development in their central figure's understanding of his role, they do not present any fundamental change in the institutions and procedures of the English 'constitution'. At best, one could point to a few places in these plays where some such interest seems to show itself. Richmond's language at the end of *Richard III* suggests a shift away from dynastic faction and towards a reframing of politics in ideologies of mutual love ('Fellows in arms and my most loving friends', 5.2.1) and quasi-sacramental unity ('And then—as we have ta'en the sacrament— | We will unite the white rose and the red', 5.8.18–19). But his rhetoric indicates how this is conceived less as novelty than as the

---

[24] For a digest of North's Plutarch as used by Shakespeare, see T. J. B. Spencer, ed., *Shakespeare's Plutarch: The Lives of Julius Caesar, Brutus, Marcus Antonius and Coriolanus in the Translation of Sir Thomas North* (Harmondsworth: Penguin, 1964). The convenience of Spencer's collocations, however, obscures the synthetic labour Shakespeare subjected Plutarch to and the extent of his reading throughout the volume, borrowing details from lives not directly employed, even from marginalia.

[25] See the discussion of *2 Henry 6* by Dermot Cavanagh, 'Sovereignty and Commonwealth in Shakespeare's *Henry VI, Part 2*', in Thomas Betteridge and Greg Walker, eds., *The Oxford Handbook of Tudor Drama* (Oxford: Oxford University Press, 2012), 619–34.

resetting of a political world disturbed by aberration: 'England hath long been mad and scarred herself' (5.8.23). A more suggestive example occurs in *Richard II*, where the failure of sacramental monarchy effectively to defend itself releases a novelty of opportunity that one character describes as 'this new world' (4.1.69). The temper of politics in the play warps just here, parodying its earlier ceremonial rhythm in hectic challenges and counter-challenges amidst a blizzard of flying gauntlets. But such local instances of historic shifts remain subordinated to a project fundamentally confirming a stable legacy of English enterprise to its Elizabethan audience. The embedding of Plutarch's moral biographies in a framework of historical and political change running from the formation to the death-agonies of the Roman Republic is quite differently conceived.[26]

Something of the difference can be seen at once in the vigour and concentration of the opening of *Julius Caesar*, where every element is deployed to several functions. It would be hard to overemphasize how original this action is. Its constructs with great economy a focus at once on the structure of Roman politics and on the range of personalities of its patrician inhabitants. In the first scene, a brisk confrontation between Flavius and Murellus and a pair of tradesmen outlines the threat of Caesar's personal dominance, as his critics see it, to the settled order and interest of the Roman state.[27] Here, the standard comic word-play of the servant-clown points the patricians' frustration at how signs and circumstances are slipping from their control:

> MURELLUS …You, sir, what trade are you?
> COBBLER   Truly, sir, in respect of a fine workman, I am but, as you would say, a cobbler.
> MURELLUS But what trade art thou? Answer me directly.
> COBBLER   A trade, sir, that I hope I may use with a safe conscience, which is indeed, sir, a mender of bad soles.
> FLAVIUS   What trade, thou knave? Thou naughty knave, what trade?
> COBBLER   Nay, I beseech you, sir, be not out with me. Yet, if you be out, sir, I can mend you.
> MURELLUS What mean'st thou by that? Mend me, thou saucy fellow!
> COBBLER   Why, sir, cobble you.
> FLAVIUS   Thou art a cobbler, art thou?
> COBBLER   Truly, sir, all that I live by is with the awl.
>
> (1.1.9–20)

The second scene, with its processional crossings and offstage crowd noise punctuating the conversation in which Cassius draws out Brutus's disposition to conspiracy, gives a sense of the turbulent rush of events requiring an equal rapidity and decisiveness of individual characters, a sense sustained through the following scene of storm and

---

[26] A forerunner is Shakespeare's narrative poem, *Lucrece* (pub. 1594 and retitled *The Rape of Lucrece* from 1616). Here Lucrece's suicide immediately motivates the expulsion of the Tarquins and the invention of the Roman republic. The choice of this moment for narrative treatment suggests how Shakespeare's response to Roman history from an early date placed individual fates in relation to historical crises.

[27] Usually tagged as tribunes in modern editions, Flavius and Murellus (or Marullus), are not so identified in the play, and their actions here attach them to the patrician/republican party opposing Caesar. Casca later reports that they have been 'put to silence'—we are not told how or by whom—for 'pulling scarves off Caesar's images' (1.2.285-6).

subornation.[28] The economy with which Casca is delineated is exemplary of Shakespeare's method: in Caesar's presence he is bluntly fawning ('Peace ho! Caesar speaks.' 1.2.2), but once gone, he 'after his sour fashion' as Cassius says, affects an indifference of spirit ('I can as well be hanged as tell the manner of it. It was mere foolery, I did not mark it.' 1.2.236–7). Such detailing, carefully assembled from Plutarch's more scattered remarks, outlines a network of mutual observation and assessment whose cross-linked tensions define Roman republican politics, as when we watch Caesar discuss Cassius with Antony, while Cassius himself asks Casca for news of Cicero.[29] And in the background, we are kept aware of the turbulence of popular opinion, expressed in shouts and crowds and, eventually, riots.

Tragedy here is not a matter of the old machinery of Fortune, of Roman *virtus* or of Christian Virtue, but rather the new, Machiavellian concept of *virtù*—the force, courage or luck that a given personality has to rule or fail in mutable circumstances. Caesar's decision to attend the Senate at the end of Act Two is exemplary. He intends to go and defies auguries, but a magnanimous consideration for Calpurnia's welfare—already displayed in Act One—persuades him otherwise (not, he insists, her fears themselves) until, again, the able flattery of Decius Brutus ('I can o'ersway him') changes his mind again. It is important that Decius does this job and not Brutus or Cassius—the network of tragic relations is, we might say, 'highly distributed'. That is what makes it so original, and that is the mark of Shakespeare's particular responsiveness to the density of Plutarch as historical reportage.

The handling of Plutarch, however, is shaped by a vision of historical action not found anywhere in Roman sources, and which can only be called, despite the risks of the term, 'modern'. Whether or not Shakespeare was directly aware of Machiavelli's work (and it seems unlikely), the latter's sense of the contingency and lability of historical action and of political institutions under pressure of that action is fully expressed in the plays' account of Roman history, as indeed it was in Machiavelli's response to Livy.[30] In Shakespeare, this sense of the force of individual agency in shaping events is registered even in small details of style and personal choice. When Brutus refuses to approve the murder of Antony because he prefers to imagine Caesar as 'a dish fit for the gods' and his assassination as the work of 'sacrificers, but not butchers' (2.1.173, 166), Cassius, having invested his own probity in the suasiveness of Brutus's unimpeached honour, cannot safely challenge the choice of metaphor with a more pragmatic political calculus. Likewise later, the two having made up the long bitter quarrel between them (4.2), Cassius cannot overrule Brutus's disastrous decision to march on their opponents at Philippi.[31] This is not so much a case of 'if Cleopatra's nose had been shorter' as it is a way of measuring how the final destruction of the Roman republic is as entangled with the necessities of friendship as with the fortunes of war.[32]

---

[28] For excellent discussion of how the shape of these scenes develops 'scenic forms' from earlier plays, including by other writers, see Emrys Jones, *Scenic Form in Shakespeare* (Oxford: Clarendon Press, 1971), 18–23, 106–113. Jones later discusses *Antony and Cleopatra* in relation to *Henry V*.

[29] Brutus even remembers Casca at school (1.2.296)!

[30] From the vast literature on Machiavelli, see especially J. G. A. Pocock, *The Machiavellian Moment* (Princeton: Princeton University Press, 1975).

[31] This is surely the structural justification for the length and intensity of the quarrel on stage—the resulting exhaustion and fragility underpin the fatal mistake.

[32] Pascal's famous maxim is 'Had Cleopatra's nose been shorter, the whole face of the world would have changed' ('Le nez de Cléopatre: s'il eût été plus court, toute la face de la terre aurait changé,' *Pensées*, 162).

What goes for these small details of decision also applies to ways of speaking. Throughout the play, the characters' various rhetorics are not merely media of expression (as with Tamburlaine) but also chosen strategies of action deployed by agents in historical circumstances to do or avoid doing certain kinds of things, strategies whose results the action carefully weighs. The value and consequence of these rhetorics are central to the tragic character of the action both for the actors and for the larger fate of the Republic in its moment of crisis. Speaking to Caesar's assassination in the Forum, Brutus chooses a rhetoric of balance, order, and rationality, couched for us in the cool medium of prose. He wants to seem above all deliberate in action and commitment whereas Antony's 'Asiatic' declamation following seeks to capture and manage political momentum by extreme emotive means.[33] On such personal choices, it emerges, the fate of the Republic turns.

A notable sense of climax and transformation at the end of *Julius Caesar* underscores its particular conception of historical tragedy: Cassius is 'the last of all the Romans' (5.3.98), Brutus 'the noblest Roman of them all' (5.5.67), registering not merely individual fates, but also how a definite climacteric has passed. The Republic cannot now be the thing it was, and the deaths of Brutus and Cassius tell also against the institutions in whose name and for whose interests they acted.

Shakespeare's second Plutarchan play, *Antony and Cleopatra* (ca. 1606), traces a similar enterprise in an even larger framework, one that touches the modern world directly through its reminder that Octavius's rule will coincide with the birth of Jesus ('The time of universal peace is near.' 4.6.4). The extraordinary evocative power of this play lies partly in the sense, as carefully cultivated in the title characters' visions of one another as in other characters'—even Caesar's—visions of them, that an alternative line of development for the history of the world is abruptly closed off after the Battle of Actium. Nowhere does Shakespeare explore antiquity as disclosing alternative worlds more than here. Nowhere is the sense of a radically different way of thinking about human possibility more plangent and more beckoning than in the failure of this play's protagonists.

This sense of the giant imaginative shapes of antiquity, present in Cassius's momentary and bitter evocation of a Caesar who 'doth bestride the narrow world | Like a Colossus' (1.2.136–7) is a pervasive feature of the world of *Antony and Cleopatra*. Cleopatra at Cydnus is a stunning mythographic self-coronation 'O'er-picturing that Venus where we see | The fancy outwork Nature' (2.2.207–8), Antony in Cleopatra's vision has kept 'realms and islands' like loose change in his pocket (5.2.90–1). The horizons of human aspiration and of mutual imaginative creation retreat under this pressure in the direction of 'new heaven, new earth', an apocalypse radically different from anything a coming Christian era could tolerate. Even Caesar, though it also benefits him, acknowledges in death the attraction of Cleopatra's 'strong toil of grace' (5.2.342) and the last word is loaded with a counter-Christian charge of value.

This is not to say that the lovers' failure is not also carefully placed, and even explained by the play. Caesar is a study in success, and his success, for all its cool precision, is not to be sneered at. He is a kind of Prince Hal writ in world-historical letters, just as Antony

---

[33] 'Asiatic' rhetoric, a classical style of speaking, was marked by highly emotive presentation, and was contrasted by Cicero and others with a sparer, more pointed 'Attic' style. The terms encode Hellenistic and Roman ideologies of national character. See M. L. Clarke, *Rhetoric at Rome*, 3rd edn., rev. D. H. Berry (London: Routledge, 1996). The same contrast in rhetorical styles is apparent in Antony and Octavius in *Antony and Cleopatra*, though that play is less interested in *public* rhetoric.

is Falstaff-as-Hercules. The balance of forces when the play begins is calculated to throw into relief how their contrasting styles push at the crucial moment. The differences are mapped out schematically, and with a Machiavellian analytic deliberateness, in a pair of short scenes immediately before the Battle of Actium:

> 3.8 *Enter Caesar with his army, marching, and Taurus*
> CAESAR Taurus!
> TAURUS My lord?
> CAESAR Strike not by land. Keep whole. Provoke not battle
> Till we have done at sea. (*Giving a scroll*) Do not exceed
> The prescript of this scroll. Our fortune lies
> Upon this jump.
> *Exit Caesar and his army at one door, Taurus at another*
>
> 3.9 *Enter Antony and Enobarbus*
> ANTONY Set we our squadrons on yon side o'th'hill
> In eye of Caesar's battle, from which place
> We may the number of the ships behold,
> And so proceed accordingly. *Exeunt*

Antony proceeds by charismatic improvisatory response to local conditions; Caesar by careful and deliberate preparation. In Machiavelli's terms, Antony is the lion, Caesar the fox.[34] Antony here fails, and the failure is his ruin, but the strategy had served a younger self well in the forum scene of *Julius Caesar*. Charisma and calculation circle one another warily throughout the play, from the opening speech in which the Romanizing Philo calls on his interlocutors (including the audience) to 'Behold and see' Antony's degradation (1.1.13).[35] He may think the two verbs reduce to the same thing, but the play's design, especially its investment in structural paradox, refuses to endorse this view, and the contrast between them as modes of response becomes a central principle or fault-line. Enobarbus, the blunt soldier, assesses Antony as in decline and leaves him in Act Four. But his betrayal earns him a heart 'dried with grief', and he collapses in quasi-erotic longing ('O Antony! O Antony!' 4.10.22) in what must be the strangest death in Shakespeare—to be echoed by the spontaneous collapse of Iras before her mistress in the final scene.

The tragic character of this pivotal moment of Roman history for the play is perhaps best caught in a single image, as Antony in defeat struggles to understand how the power of his imaginative apprehension of himself has failed to deliver a viable historical destiny:

> ANTONY Sometimes we see a cloud that's dragonish;
> A vapour sometime like a bear or lion,
> A tower'd citadel, a pendent rock,
> A forked mountain, or blue promontory
> With trees upon't, that nod unto the world,
> And mock our eyes with air: thou hast seen these signs;

---

[34] See Machiavelli's remarks in *The Prince*, ch. 18. He calls on rulers to use both beast *personae*, but by chapter 25 has to concede that changing circumstances will eventually exhaust any ruler's flexibility, a concession which marks the collapse of the book's central project. An English text of *The Prince* (trans. W. K. Marriot) can be found at http://www.gutenberg.org/files/1232/1232-h/1232-h.htm#link2HCH0018 and an Italian text at http://it.wikisource.org/wiki/Il_Principe.

[35] Philo is a Greek name, so a 'Roman' assessment is not the exclusive property of actual Romans.

They are black vesper's pageants.
EROS   Ay, my lord,
ANTONY   That which is now a horse, even with a thought
The rack dislimns, and makes it indistinct,
As water is in water.
EROS   It does, my lord.
ANTONY   My good knave Eros, now thy captain is
Even such a body: here I am Antony:
Yet cannot hold this visible shape, my knave.

(4.15.2–14)

Antony may see himself as such a cloud, with all the rich pathos of the mutable that such images accrue in Shakespeare, but Octavius is the wind, which has no need to worry over its identity.

Shakespeare's final play based on Roman history, *Coriolanus* (ca. 1608), marks a sharp contraction of horizons after *Antony and Cleopatra*, the world it treats not the juggernaut of Roman imperial arms, but the card-house of the early Republic, threatened with both internal strife and external foes. It is a fierce and unyielding play, like its protagonist, a play as though expertly cast in iron, with a concentration of execution and effect that wastes nothing. Again, it stages a crisis in Roman history, demonstrating the necessity of mutual accommodations for the survival of the republican order whose politics it anatomizes. Coriolanus, that engine of martial excess, remains for most of the play impervious to this necessity, and his inflexibility—or, at best, his late enlightenment at the hand of that necessity—finally destroys him.[36]

The mould of the action is set soon after the play's opening. The door is already closed in the very first scene, when popular agitation at crippling food-shortage among the populace leads the patricians to concede the establishment of 'Five tribunes to defend their vulgar wisdoms | Of their own choice' (1.1.213–14). It is Martius himself, as yet without the cognomen 'Coriolanus' he will earn for his deeds in war, who announces this in disgust, its full bitterness of import for himself, of course, as yet invisible. What follows, in one way, merely works out in detail the implications of this constitutional innovation—what it closes off or narrows in the way of options for the citizenship of Rome. Coriolanus' inflexibility and steadfast commitment to his own purity of self-validating excellence cannot finally be accommodated within a reformed republic that includes the new calculation of ambitiously factional popular tribunes. The pervasive taut feeling that the action of the play is already caught in a trap—its bitterness and recrimination like a fox gnawing its own leg off—stems from this choice of design. And in this sense, Coriolanus as an historical agent differs from Brutus and even from Antony. His options are fatally foreclosed, and in ways he cannot see, almost before he begins. It is not surprising that the play floats in him, claustrophobically, the fantasy of a 'world elsewhere' (3.3.139). But, unlike in *Antony and Cleopatra*, the imaginative disclosure of such a world is never made viable or convincing. Escape from Romans to Volsces only reveals a twin world, enclosing the same pattern of faction and intrigue, and equally intolerant of Coriolanus' infuriating excellences. No matter what one makes of the tribunes—and the play is not complimentary—the political fact of them is determining from the start.

---

[36] For an account of these failed transitions in a world dominated by oath, contract, fidelity and compromise, see John Kerrigan, 'Coriolanus Fidiussed', *Essays in Criticism* 62:4 (2012), 319–53.

Whether Shakespeare himself had definite opinions about the gains and losses involved in the history of the Roman Republic is difficult to say. Some, such as Andrew Hadfield, have discerned in him republican sympathy; others, Warren Chernaik for instance, have denied this, seeing him as constructing his dramas from a variety of positions, *in utramque partem* with respect to his characters, neither endorsing nor denying, simply tracing the interplay of character, history and circumstance.[37] What one can say is that his deep responsiveness to Roman history as an arena of tragedy is of a piece with a central preoccupation throughout his career with dramatizing the experience of *change* as both a personal and a public matter. In Jonson's Roman plays, powerfully influential as they were, nothing changes, things are merely confirmed more solidly as what they were before. Change may threaten but is resisted, whether as Catiline's or Sejanus's conspiracies against the state, and whether resistance is Cicero's republican activation of the *pater patriae* or Tiberius's grim confirmation of imperial rigor. In Shakespeare's versions of Roman history, however, something crucial has altered between the beginning and the end of the play, some viable historical option has gone out of the Roman world in the character of the dead protagonist, and something new emerged in the texture of final arrangements. Roman history provided Shakespeare with an unusually dense focus at once of striking historical events and crisply delineated personalities shaping and being shaped. This combination of sweeping force with resonant detail in a political culture at once ancestral and remote to his own proved a potent attraction to his tragic imagination.

Select Bibliography

Armitage, David, Conal Condren, and Andrew Fitzmaurice, eds., *Shakespeare and Early Modern Political Thought* (Cambridge: Cambridge University Press, 2009).

Burrow, Colin, *Shakespeare and Classical Antiquity* (Oxford: Oxford University Press, 2013).

Cantor, Paul A., *Shakespeare's Rome: Republic and Empire* (Ithaca, NY: Cornell University Press, 1976).

Chernaik, Warren, *The Myth of Rome in Shakespeare and his Contemporaries* (Cambridge: Cambridge University Press, 2011).

Garber, Marjorie, *Shakespeare's Ghost Writers* (London: Methuen, 1987).

Garbero, Maria Del Sapio, ed., *Identity, Otherness and Empire in Shakespeare's Rome* (Farnham, Surrey: Ashgate, 2009).

Hadfield, Andrew, *Shakespeare and Republicanism* (Cambridge: Cambridge University Press, 2005).

Hampton, Timothy, *Writing from History: The Rhetoric of Exemplarity in Renaissance Literature* (Ithaca, NY: Cornell University Press, 1990).

Jones, Emrys, *Scenic Form in Shakespeare* (Oxford: Clarendon Press, 1971).

---

[37] See Andrew Hadfield, *Shakespeare and Republicanism* (Cambridge: Cambridge University Press, 2005), and, contra, Warren Chernaik, *The Myth of Rome in Shakespeare and his Contemporaries* (Cambridge: Cambridge University Press, 2011), esp. 244–8, also the various essays in David Armitage, Conal Condren, and Andrew Fitzmaurice, eds., *Shakespeare and Early Modern Political Thought* (Cambridge: Cambridge University Press, 2009).

Kahn, Coppelia, 'Shakespeare's Classical Tragedies', in Claire McEachern, ed., *Cambridge Companion to Shakespearean Tragedy*, 2nd edn., (Cambridge: Cambridge University Press, 2013), 218–39.

Kahn, Coppelia, *Roman Shakespeare: Warriors, Wounds and Women* (New York: Routledge, 1997).

Keilen, Sean, *Vulgar Eloquence* (New Haven: Yale University Press, 2005).

Kerrigan, John, 'Coriolanus Fidiussed', *Essays in Criticism* 62:4 (2012), 319–53.

Kewes, Paulina, 'Roman History and Early Stuart Drama: Thomas Heywood's *The Rape of Lucrece*', *English Literary Renaissance* 32:2 (2002), 239–67.

Levy, F. J., *Tudor Historical Thought* (Toronto: University of Toronto Press, 1967).

Maxwell, J. C., 'Shakespeare's Roman Plays: 1900–1956', *Shakespeare Survey* 10 (1957), 1–11.

Miles, Gary B., 'How Roman are Shakespeare's "Romans"?', *Shakespeare Quarterly* 40:3 (Autumn, 1989), 257–83.

Miles, Geoffrey, *Shakespeare and the Constant Romans* (Oxford: Oxford University Press, 1996).

Miola, Robert S., 'Shakespeare's Ancient Religions', *Shakespeare Survey* 54 (2001), 31–45.

Miola, Robert S., *Shakespeare's Rome* (Cambridge: Cambridge University Press, 2004).

Miola, Robert S., 'Shakespeare's Ancient Rome: Difference and Identity', in Michael Hattaway, ed., *The Cambridge Companion to Shakespeare's History Plays* (Cambridge: Cambridge University Press, 2002), 193–213.

Pocock, J. G. A., *The Machiavellian Moment* (Princeton: Princeton University Press, 1975).

Ronan, Clifford, '*Antique Roman*': Power Symbology and the Roman Play in Early Modern England* (Athens: University of Georgia Press, 1995).

Russell, D. A., *Plutarch* (London: Duckworth, 1973).

Shapiro, James, *1599—A Year in the Life of William Shakespeare* (London; Faber and Faber, 2005).

Siegel, Paul N., *Shakespeare's English and Roman History Plays: A Marxist Approach* (Cranbury, NJ and London: Associated University Presses, 1986).

Spencer, T. J. B., 'Shakespeare and the Elizabethan Romans', *Shakespeare Survey* 10 (1957), 27–38.

Woolf, Daniel, *The Social Circulation of the Past: English Historical Culture 1500–1750* (Oxford: Oxford University Press, 2003).

CHAPTER 16

··

TRAGEDY AND THE
SATIRIC VOICE

··

HESTER LEES-JEFFRIES

AT the beginning of *The second part of the return from Parnassus*, a Christmas entertainment performed in 1601 or 1602 by students at St John's College, Cambridge, Ingenioso enters '*with Iuuenall in his hand*':

> *Difficile est, Satyram non scribere, nam quis iniquae*
> *Tam patiens vrbis, tam furens ut teneat se?*[1]
> I, Iuuenall: thy ierking [scourging] hand is good,
> Not gently laying on, but fetching bloud.
> So surgean-like thou dost with cutting heale.

'It is difficult not to write satire', protests the speaker near the beginning of the first satire by the Roman writer Juvenal, going on to list the many irksome provocations of his day and age. Ingenioso, an ambitious recent graduate, strikes a standard pose for such a young man around the turn of the seventeenth century. The 'Parnassus plays' are now best known for their allusions to Shakespeare, as the characters and writers show off their familiarity with the London literary scene, and Ingenioso is in the thick of these often strikingly modern metatextual moments. These young men read Sidney, Spenser, and Shakespeare (Ingenioso's potential patron Gullio sleeps with *Venus and Adonis* under his pillow), they write sonnets and epyllia, and they are regulars in the playhouses, but it's Juvenal's satire that opens the play. Ingenioso and his friends aspire to imitate its savage energy and its world-weary pose. To be a young man with literary pretensions around 1600, on this evidence, is to read satire and go to plays.

In the classical tradition—the major (although not the sole) influence on writers of satire in early modern England—satire combined censure of folly and dissuasion from vice, with, on occasion, a positive encouragement to virtue. It could be written as a diatribe—a rant—or as a dialogue; the satirist speaks for himself or adopts a persona.

---

[1] 'difficile est saturam non scribere. nam quis iniquae | tam patiens Vrbis, tam ferreus, ut teneat se ...' ('[given all these provocations], it is hard *not* to write satire. After all, who is so tolerant of the injustices of Rome ["the City"], who is so hardened, that they can contain themselves ...') (Susanna Morton Braund, ed., *Juvenal and Persius* (Cambridge, MA: Harvard University Press, 2004), 1: 30-1).

Juvenal (Decius Junius Juvenalis), who wrote in the late first/early second century AD, wrote his sixteen *Satires* in verse: his particular targets include women, effeminate men, Greeks, and hypocrites. Horace (Quintus Horatius Flaccus, first century BC) wrote satire in a number of forms; while still severe, his works (*Satires, Epistles, Epodes*) were generally less savage than Juvenal's. Other classical writers of satire whose works were influential in Renaissance England included the Romans Martial and Persius, and Lucian, who wrote in Greek. Lucian's dialogues had been translated by Thomas More and Desiderius Erasmus, whose *Utopia* and *Praise of Folly* respectively remain the best-known works of Tudor satire. Writing in Latin, they drew on the medieval traditions exemplified by Chaucer's anti-clerical writings in the *Canterbury Tales*, but their work can also be described as 'Menippean satire', named for the Greek satirist Menippus (whose works are all lost), which was characterized by *spoudogeloioi*, or 'serious laughter'.

Satire deals in extremes: it exaggerates that which it criticizes, sometimes to the point of parody, adopting a world-weary tone. But whereas parody leaves the criticism of its targets largely implicit, satire both exposes and censures, sometimes also suggesting possible correctives. The satirist often sees himself (and it does always seem to be a him) as a 'voice of reason'; and in the classical tradition in particular, satire had its roots in Stoic and, especially, Cynic philosophy. The former emphasized reason and self-control, especially over the emotions; the latter, more extreme, cultivated indifference to all the values of human society (the desire for wealth or possessions, adherence to laws or social conventions), promoting a simple life lived in accordance with nature; the Cynics were apparently so called in part because they lived on the streets like dogs (Greek *kynos*), and also because of their tendency to 'bite'. It is the cynical tradition—exemplified by Juvenal—that can most easily be discerned as an influence on English satire of the sixteenth and seventeenth centuries: it is railing, iconoclastic, dark, and angry. Shakespeare's satirists, as will be seen, are often identified (not least by themselves) with dogs.

Ironically, it would be difficult for Ingenioso to write (or at least publish) satire, for satire was a banned form, proscribed by the 'Bishops' Ban' promulgated in the summer of 1599 by John Whitgift, archbishop of Canterbury, and Richard Bancroft, bishop of London. The ban named some books (by Marston, Hall, and others); and a number were publically burned. It ordered the censorship of many kinds of texts, but was mostly seen as an attempt to curb the printing of satire. The banning of satire was evidence of its popularity at the time: it had indeed been the form favoured by ambitious young men, often law students at the Inns of Court. John Donne wrote at least some of his five Satires while at Lincoln's Inn in the early 1590s; his targets include idle students, the law, and the court, and his great third satire on religion combines vitriol, scepticism, and profound theological seriousness. Joseph Hall was based in Cambridge rather than London; he published the first part of his *Virgidemiarum* (which he termed 'Tooth-lesse Satyrs') in 1597, the first English satires on the Latinate model to be printed, and the second ('Byting Satyrs') in 1598. (In later life, Hall's satires, written when he was in his early twenties, became a source of embarrassment to him, not least when he became bishop of Exeter in 1627 and of Norwich in 1641.) Everard Guilpin, of whom little else is known, published *Skialetheia, or, A Shadowe of Truth* in 1598: its seven constituent satires include attacks on hypocrisy, vanity, women who wear make-up, and poetry itself. John Marston, now best known as a dramatist, had been a law student at the Middle Temple, but made no secret of his distaste for legal studies; he published his *Scourge of Villanie* in 1598, when he was 22, pursued a long-running feud with Hall, and was invoked in the second part of *The returne from Parnassus* as 'Monsier Kinsayder ['dog-castrator'], lifting vp your legge and pissing against the world' (B2–B2v). His later plays (such as *The Malcontent*, *c*.1603) continued to reflect his satirical skills; he was one of the main participants in the so-called 'war of the theatres', with Jonson, Dekker, and others, with which Shakespeare's *Troilus and Cressida* is sometimes linked.

Historically, satire's connection with drama, and with tragic drama in particular, has not been uncontroversial. A resilient false etymology derived 'satire' from the 'satyr' plays which accompanied Greek tragedy with their scenes of rustic, ribald comedy (featuring satyrs, the half-man half-goat woodland creatures of ancient mythology)—this despite the fact that the classicist Isaac Casaubon definitively demonstrated in *De satyrica Graecorum poesi et Romanorum satira libri duo* (Paris, 1605) that there were no historical or etymological connections between the satyr-plays of Ancient Greece and the writings of Roman satirists. An imaginative connection between satire and tragedy persisted, however, evident in its frequent spelling with a 'y'; and, as Ingenioso demonstrates, the more savage Juvenalian style characterized English satire at the end of the sixteenth century. Where Horatian satire mocks the follies of the age (for example, in the comedies of Ben Jonson), Juvenalian satire is severe, denouncing rather than merely ridiculing, concerned with the wicked and utterly depraved rather than with mere fools and those who seek to gull them.[2] Juvenalian satire is therefore more akin to tragedy than to comedy, its world largely without hope or redeeming features, to be railed at with pessimism rather than optimistically encouraged to reform.

In *The Art of English Poesy* (1589), George Puttenham identified tragedy as the form in which 'the evil and outrageous behaviours of princes were reprehended', while satire was 'most bitter invective against vice and vicious men',[3] and Puttenham was not the only early modern critic to note the connections between tragedy and satire: in *The Defence of Poesy*, Philip Sidney described both forms in strikingly similar terms. For Sidney, 'tragedy … openeth the greatest wounds, and showeth forth the ulcers that are covered with tissue' whereas 'bitter but wholesome [satire] rubs the galled mind in making shame the trumpet of villainy, with bold and open crying out against naughtiness'.[4] Both satire and tragedy are typically conceived by early modern writers in such corporeal, medical, or even surgical terms, as forms that will both expose vice and purge it: the satirist is to be cutting and biting in his invective. *Hamlet* draws considerably on this vocabulary and idiom, as will be seen.

Another etymology derives 'satire' from *satura*, a medley or mixture, an idea especially germane to a discussion of the plays to be considered here. *Troilus and Cressida* and *Timon of Athens* are generically mixed, pushing the boundaries of form and genre and questioning categories more generally; like *Hamlet*, they are also textually difficult, their texts

---

[2] On this distinction, see the introduction in Raman Selden, *English Verse Satire 1590–1765* (London: George Allen and Unwin, 1978).

[3] George Puttenham, *The Art of English Poesy* (1589), in Gavin Alexander, ed., *Sidney's 'The Defence of Poesy' and Selected Renaissance Literary Criticism* (London: Penguin, 2004), 82–3, 85.

[4] 'Tissue' here means 'rich fabric' rather than 'membrane'. Here Sidney in fact uses the term 'iambic' to distinguish Juvenalian satire from Horatian, which he terms 'satiric'. Alexander, ed., *Sidney's 'The Defence of Poesy'*, 26, 27–8, 337 n. 127.

apparently corrupt or extant in more than one version. At the end of *Julius Caesar*, the conflicted Brutus can be praised in defeat by Antony as one whose 'life was gentle, and the elements | So mixed in him that nature might stand up | And say to all the world "This was a man"' (5.5.72-4), yet such balance seems always to elude Hamlet. One of the ways in which satire and tragedy inform one another in Shakespeare's middle period is in the probing of the question of what it is to be a man (and in particular a good man). Both tragedy and satire are also crucially engaged with the perennial early modern debates over the moral status of theatre and of literature more generally. The plays which form the basis of discussion here, *Hamlet* (*c*.1600), *Troilus and Cressida* (1601–2), and *Timon of Athens* (1605–7) all contribute different perspectives on these questions, even as they complicate possible answers.

HAMLET

> *Enter Prince Hamlet, madly attired, reading on a book ...*
> POLONIUS   What do you read, my lord? ...
> HAMLET   Slanders, sir; for the satirical slave says here that old men have
>   grey beards, that their faces are wrinkled, their eyes purging thick amber,
>   or plum-tree gum, and that they have a plentiful lack of wit, together with
>   most weak hams ...
>
> (2.2.1SD, 193-4, 199-203)

Exactly what Hamlet is reading is unclear but, at least since the mid-eighteenth century, his book has sometimes been identified as Juvenal's *Satires*, with its savage reflections on the miseries of old age (10.190–5).[5] Significant here is less any borrowing or even any marked resemblance between the texts than the expectation that this is what Hamlet *should* be reading. Like Ingenioso, Hamlet is a 'university man', albeit from Wittenberg rather than Cambridge; satire is what he is expected to read, just as he is also familiar with the 'tragedians of the city'. *Hamlet* is a political and psychological drama, but it is also a young man's play, about the condition of being an exceptional young man with all its conflicts and frustrations. The Wittenberg of Luther, Faustus, and Hamlet might as well be the Cambridge of Nashe and Hall, or the Inns of Court of Donne and Marston.

Raman Selden notes the way in which the 'melancholy pessimist's voice' found in satire becomes a hallmark of the Jacobean tragic hero: 'A corrupt and diseased world is described in a language which is densely metaphoric, gross (even salacious), declamatory and subjectively intense'.[6] To see Hamlet as a satirist, or at least as a character shaped by, and speaking to, the tropes of contemporary satirical writing is to suggest a subtly altered

---

[5] This suggestion seems first to have been made by William Warburton in his 1747 edition; see 2.2.196LN in Harold Jenkins's Arden 2 edition. 'Satirical rogue' is the Q2 reading; in F the author is a 'satirical slave', and in Q1 a 'satirical satyr' ['Satyricall Satyre'].

[6] Selden, *English Verse Satire*, 72.

perspective on some aspects of his character. When he is plotting the device of the play to expose Claudius's guilt, Hamlet promises that he will 'tent him to the quick' (2.2.593), that is, probe the wound, discover the truth; and he later invokes 'th'impostume [abscess] of much wealth and peace, | That inward breaks, and shows no cause without | Why the man dies' (4.4.27–9). His language in the closet scene in particular draws on such corporeal and medical conceits, the vocabulary of disease and its cure, as when he beseeches Gertrude:

> Lay not a flattering unction to your soul
> That not your trespass but my madness speaks.
> It will but skin and film the ulcerous place
> Whilst rank corruption, mining all within,
> Infects unseen ...

> (3.4.136–9)

This is the language of tragedy but, even more, it is the language of satire: as Kernan notes, 'The traditional metaphorical tools employed ... by the satirist, the surgical probe and caustic medicine, blend readily with the actual tools of the revenger, the sword and cup of poison'.[7] (Syphilis in particular is characterized by ulcers and, in its later stages, lesions of the skin and bones; it is frequently the disease invoked, directly or indirectly, by the satirist, pathologizing as it does the connection between the physical and the moral, between sexual licence and bodily decay).[8] Hamlet is to be physician and surgeon; his diagnosis and its terminology reflect not simply his own 'psychology' but the literary and moral pathology of the day.

To see Hamlet as a satirist also contextualizes his misogynist railing, even if it does not excuse it. In the closet scene, his revulsion at his mother's sexuality is Juvenalian in its bitterness, but he also describes himself as a 'scourge', 'cruel only to be kind', 3.4.159, 162). When he berates Ophelia in the nunnery scene, his excoriation of women's dissembling ('I have heard of your paintings, too, well enough, God hath given you one face and you make yourselves another', 3.1.145–7) both anticipates his later meditation on mortality with the skull ('Now get you to my lady's chamber and tell her, let her paint an inch thick', 5.1.188–9) and recalls Juvenal's Sixth Satire, with its vicious mockery of Roman women.

Yet Hamlet cannot simply be a satirist any more than he can simply be a student. Even as he rails against Ophelia and Gertrude, in all the bitter pain of his invective, even as he promises to search the wound, expose the crime, and purge the rottenness of court and country, the audience is reminded that he is more than a railing, satirical malcontent. Ophelia's first response to Hamlet's abuse is a bewildered lament:

> O what a noble mind is here o'erthrown!
> The courtier's, soldier's, scholar's eye, tongue, sword,
> Th'expectancy and rose of the fair state,
> The glass of fashion and the mould of form,
> Th'observed of all observers, quite, quite, down! ...
> Now see that noble and most sovereign reason
> Like sweet bells jangled out of tune and harsh ...

> (3.1.153–7, 160–1)

---

[7] Alvin Kernan, *The Cankered Muse: Satire of the English Renaissance* (New Haven: Yale University Press, 1959), 220.

[8] See Greg W. Bentley, *Shakespeare and the New Disease: the Dramatic Function of Syphilis in Troilus and Cressida, Measure for Measure, and Timon of Athens* (New York: Peter Lang, 1989).

Hamlet's railing is a symptom as much as a diagnosis; it is aberrant and apparently out of character. As he explains to his student companions Rosencrantz and Guildenstern, he has 'of late—but wherefore I know not—lost all my mirth, forgone all custom of exercise' (2.2.297–8). To see Hamlet as satirist enables a more nuanced consideration of Hamlet the tragic hero: the mirror that he later exhorts the players to 'hold ... up to nature ... show[ing] virtue her own feature, scorn her own image, and the very age and body of the time his form and pressure' (3.2.22–4) has a range of mimetic and didactic possibilities that encompasses the satirical as much as the tragic.

Reuben Brower suggests that Shakespeare may have been influenced in his conception of the hero, at around the time he was writing *Hamlet*, by George Chapman's *Seauen bookes of the Iliades of Homere* (1598). In Chapman's translation of Homer's *Iliad*, according to Brower, there is a tendency 'to replace physical with moral heroism, to make the great battle the inner one of the soul or of reason against passion', and he describes 'the increased self-consciousness of Chapman's heroes as compared with Homer's, [and] their penchant for reflection and meditative analysis [as] equally typical of the heroes of Shakespeare...'.[9] Hamlet's reaction to the player ('O, what a rogue and peasant slave am I!', 2.2.552) is a frustrated and lengthy meditation not simply on his inaction and apparent inability to feel, but also his tendency to over-analyse. The presence of Troy in the scene with the players, via Hecuba and the 'Pyrrhus' speech, suggests the possibility of considering Hamlet in a Homeric light, and specifically in the light of Chapman's particular emphasis on the *Iliad*'s heroes' tendency to over-think. In Kernan's terms,

> both satirist and tragic hero suffer an agonized compulsion to appraise the ills of the world and cure them by naming them. Every tragic hero has pronounced satiric tendencies, but he also has additional dimensions; chief among these [is] his ability to ponder and to change.[10]

The tragic hero who thinks too much, the obsessive who persists in unpacking his heart with words even as he mocks his own apparent inability to *do* rather than merely to *say*, has much in common with the satirist. And *Hamlet* suggests, perhaps, that the condition of the satirist is inherently a tragic one, not least when, despite ever-more precise definitions of its cues and motives, the capacity to change seems lost.

TROILUS AND CRESSIDA

Hamlet looks a little different when the play is put in conversation with *Troilus and Cressida*.[11] *Troilus* might well be the kind of work envisaged in Polonius' catalogue of ever-more-diffuse generic categories ('tragical-historical, tragical-comical-historical-pastoral,

---

[9] Reuben A. Brower, *Hero and Saint: Shakespeare and the Graeco-Roman Heroic Tradition* (Oxford: Oxford University Press, 1971), 80.

[10] Kernan, *Cankered Muse*, 21.

[11] The Pyrrhus (2.2) speech is evidence that Shakespeare was already thinking about Trojan material while writing *Hamlet*.

scene individable or poem unlimited', 2.2.400–1), especially were 'pastoral' to be replaced with 'satirical' (a term notably lacking from Polonius' list). The play's generic difficulties, its resistance to categorization, may be an obvious place to begin a discussion of the play. Unsurprisingly, for such a notoriously recondite work, the textual history of *Troilus and Cressida* is complicated. The 1609 quarto exists in two distinct states, one of which includes a title-page that calls it a 'Famous Historie', as well as a preface that describes it as 'passing full of the palm comical'; but in the 1623 Folio it became a 'Tragedie'. It was influentially termed a 'comical satire' by Oscar Campbell, and he discussed it in relation to Jonson's *Poetaster, Every Man Out of His Humour, Cynthia's Revels*, Marston's plays and late Elizabethan satire more generally.[12] Yet it might prove more interesting to consider it as a satirical *tragedy*,[13] or a satire *on* tragedy.

Troilus criticism often notes the possibility that the play was written for an Inns of Court audience, young men whose talents and tastes had fostered the *fin de siècle* vogue for satire, and whose preoccupations often shaped the agenda for the London stage. Far more than *Hamlet, Troilus and Cressida* is firmly located in its context in early seventeenth-century London, especially by Pandarus' epilogue. The play can be seen as a satire of Troy both old and new ('Troynovant' was still sometimes used as a title for London, despite the debunking of the Trojan origin myth), and in particular of Troy's (and Homer's) high cultural status. Here are the heroes of the Western canon, clay-footed and cut down to size, their rhetoric hollow, their lofty conceits soured with the tropes of satire: disease, deformity, excess, and waste. Satire is a crucial ingredient in the play's often dizzying intertextuality. The characters comment on themselves and each other as individuals with pasts and futures that are not personal so much as literary. Its characters, notably Thersites, rail, but one of the play's most compelling aspects is that its satire is disseminated in a *mise en abîme* of self-referentiality, even self-disgust. Its satire cannot simply be located in or confined to the role most easily characterized as that of 'the satirist'.

The play's metatheatricality is a key part of its satire, yet some of the ways in which it has been discussed can have the effect of closing down a more throughgoing consideration of the play. Much can be done, for example, with the Prologue. That the Prologue enters '*armed*' recalls the similarly armed prologue of Ben Jonson's *Poetaster* (1601), which may echo the armed Epilogue of John Marston's *Antonio and Mellida* (1599–1600), often cited as evidence for *Troilus*'s participation in the 'war of the theatres', the professional rivalry between the Admiral's Men and the Lord Chamberlain's Men, as well as with the children's companies (*Hamlet*'s 'little eyases'; the children's companies specialized in satirical plays) and their associated playwrights.[14] A long critical tradition identifies Ajax as a satirical portrait of Ben Jonson, who was sometimes mocked both for his bulky physique and his

---

[12]   Oscar J. Campbell, *Comicall Satyre and Shakespeare's Troilus and Cressida* (San Marino: Huntington Library Publications, 1959).

[13]   See Kenneth Muir, 'The Fusing of Themes' (1953), in Priscilla Martin, ed., *Shakespeare: Troilus and Cressida: A Selection of Critical Essays* (London: Macmillan, 1976), and Harold Brooks, '*Troilus and Cressida*: its Dramatic Unity and Genre', in *'Fanned and Winnowed Opinions': Shakespearean Essays Presented to Harold Jenkins* (London and New York: Methuen, 1987).

[14]   *Hamlet* 2.2.335–63 (a passage only found in the Folio). See James P. Bednarz, *Shakespeare and the Poets' War* (New York: Columbia University Press, 2001).

relative slowness as a writer; Thersites has sometimes been identified with John Marston. Yet this alluring *à clef* specificity can obscure other things. One of the most striking qualities of the prologue is its unevenness of tone, its weary, off-key gestures at the tropes of epic (the catalogue, the opening *in medias res*), and its bathos. The prologue satirizes itself; it is an exercise in deflation as it collapses the elevated diction of the opening lines ('the princes orgulous', 'their crownets regal', Troy's 'strong immures', 2, 6, 8) into a 'quarrel' (10). The play doesn't need to wait for Thersites' pithier observation that 'all the argument is a whore and a cuckold' (2.3.71) to make its bathetic point. Like the play, with its promiscuous intermingling of war plot and love plot, the prologue is a mixture; it signals the play's interest in its own nature as historical-satirical-comical-tragical, as a mixed thing.

Having declared in his first line that 'In Troy there lies the scene' (1), the Prologue announces that the ensuing action will be confined 'To what may be digested in a play' (29), and this metatheatricality is not confined to prologue and epilogue. Achilles is first introduced into the play in the context of satirical drama, as Ulysses describes the ways in which he is passing the time:

> ...[he] in his tent
> Lies mocking our designs. With him Patroclus
> Upon a lazy bed the livelong day
> Breaks scurrile jests
> And, with ridiculous and awkward action
> Which, slanderer, he 'imitation' calls,
> He pageants us...
>   And at this sport
> Sir Valour dies, cries, 'O enough, Patroclus!
> Or give me ribs of steel. I shall split all
> In pleasure of my spleen.'
>
> (1.3.145–51, 175–8)

Idiotic Ajax is now doing the same; he

> rails on our state of war
> Bold as an oracle, and sets Thersites,
> A slave whose gall coins slanders like a mint,
> To match us in comparisons with dirt...
>
> (1.3.191–4)

Thersites' voice is most consistently that of the satirist, as he rails his way through the play. In his first scene with Ajax, his vivid, extended riff on rashes is characteristic:

> Agamemnon—how if he had boils, full, all over, generally? ... And those boils did run? Say so, did not the General run then? Were not that a botchy core? ... Then there would come some matter from him.
>
> (2.1.2–9)

When Ajax beats and berates him ('Dog ... Thou bitch-wolf's son ... thou unsifted leaven ... Toad's stool ... Porcupine', 2.1.7–27), he continues in the same vein:

> I would thou didst itch from head to foot. An I had the scratching of thee, I would make thee the loathsomest scab in Greece
>
> (2.1.28–30)

That even block-headed Ajax addresses Thersites as 'dog' and 'porcupine' attests to how squarely Thersites can be located in the tradition of railing Juvenalian satire. 'Dog' is a reminder of the Cynic tradition, and of the satirist as one who barks and bites. Furthermore, Joseph Hall asserts that 'The *Satyre* should be like the *Porcupine*, | That shoots sharp quilles out in each angry line',[15] and Gregory Bredbeck has suggested that 'it is probably not too farfetched to label Thersites as a personification of satire'.[16] His 'mastic jaws' (1.3.72) are telling: *mastic* is the resinous gum of a tree, sometimes used medicinally, but it also suggests *to masticate*, to chew or grind to pulp, and, above all, *-mastix*, the Latin suffix (Greek μάστιξ) meaning a whip or scourge, a severe critic, a satirist or satire.[17] This semantic mixture, the way in which a single word can be both sticky and fragmented, a source of both injury and cure, is as important as the straightforward 'satirical' resonance.

Thersites' railing is so extreme that at times it seems like parody, or a satire on satire. No-one escapes, although Ajax and Patroclus get the worst of it: Ajax is mocked for his stupidity ('[He] wears his wit in his belly and his guts in his head', 2.1.75–6) and Patroclus mostly for his apparent effeminacy: Thersites addresses him as 'Achilles' brach' (2.1.115),[18] and in 5.1 outdoes himself in a great crescendo of invective from standard homophobic insults ('male varlet', 'masculine whore', 5.1.15, 17), via a grotesque catalogue of (venereal) diseases, to baroque mockery of Patroclus' delicacy:

> Now the rotten diseases of the south, the guts-griping, ruptures, catarrhs, loads o' gravel in the back, lethargies, cold palsies, raw eyes, dirt-rotten livers, wheezing lungs, bladders full of impostume, sciaticas, lime-kilns i'th' palm, incurable bone-ache, and the rivelled fee-simple of the tetter, take and take again such preposterous discoveries ... Why art thou then exasperate? Thou idle immaterial skein of sleave-silk, thou green sarsenet flap for a sore eye, thou tassel of a prodigal's purse, thou! Ah, how the poor world is pestered with such waterflies!
>
> (5.1.17–30)[19]

In the 1990 Royal Shakespeare Company production directed by Sam Mendes, Simon Russell Beale's Thersites wore surgical gloves that looked like discoloured and blistered skin—a neatly modern materialization of the character's (and the play's) preoccupation with disease, troped on so obsessively by satirists.

Troilus and Cressida is not only mixed, but also crammed and bloated; it is satire as something over-full, *saturated*. Hazlitt put it elegantly, describing Shakespeare himself as 'full, even to o'erflowing. He gave heaped measure, running over. This was his greatest

---

[15] Joseph Hall, *Virgidemiarum* (London, 1598), F3v. 'Satyre' means both 'satirist' and 'satire'.

[16] Gregory W. Bredbeck, *Sodomy and Interpretation: Marlowe to Milton* (Ithaca and London: Cornell University Press, 1991), 37.

[17] Thomas Dekker's *Satiromastix*, satirizing poets (probably Ben Jonson in particular) was performed in 1601 (printed 1602); Marston's *Histriomastix* (performed c.1598, printed 1610) mocked actors.

[18] A 'brach' is a bitch-hound, suggesting whore or catamite. Q and F have 'brooch'; the emendation is standard.

[19] The disease catalogue is quoted from Q. Bevington comments that the 'preposterous discoveries' are 'revelations of practices that are "arsy-versy" ... perverted, unnatural, backside foremost, sodomitical' (5.1.23 n.). Hamlet calls Osric 'water-fly' (5.2.84).

fault',[20] but this seems almost wilfully to overlook the degree to which the play repeatedly goes too far, whether it is in the queasiness of Troilus' erotic anticipation ('... give me swift transportation to those fields | Where I may wallow in the lily beds', 3.2.1–11) or the windy rhetoric of the Greek generals. Thersites' railing is part of this overflowing excess, not an antidote to it or even a proper diagnosis; and, as Russell Beale has pointed out, 'Thersites is not necessarily to be trusted. If he is trusted without question, then the play becomes complacently reductive'.[21] Thersites may sometimes look like a chorus, but he does not speak for the play any more than does the Prologue or Pandarus's bitter epilogue.

Thersites makes only a handful of appearances in the first four acts of the play, but in the fifth he is hardly offstage: Russell Beale suggests that '[i]t is as if his vision of the world has finally come to light'.[22] Not simply in his railing, but in his apparent inability to know when to stop, he provides a vital frame for the strange, 'tragic' denouements of both the love plot (as Cressida betrays Troilus with Diomedes in 5.2) and the war plot, when Hector is murdered in cold blood by Achilles and his Myrmidons after the death of Patroclus (5.9). If the play has a tragic hero, it is probably Hector. Heather James points out that '[r]eaders no longer assume that the play is tragic and that we are supposed to identify with Troilus as a hero...',[23] but the play's intellectual fascination and its real psychological power derives from the way in which the fates of Troilus, Hector, Achilles, Cressida, and the rest cannot be separated from Thersites and Pandarus, disease and disgust. They cannot be set in contradistinction to the language used to describe them; they do not rise above it, and the 'so *strained* a purity' in which Troilus protests he loves Cressida must be at once perfectly refined, tightly bound, and distorted beyond its proper form. For *Troilus* doesn't know when to stop, as its series of abortive endings attests. Agamemnon manages a martial conclusion that recalls other tragedies: 'If in [Hector's] death the gods have us befriended, | Great Troy is ours, and our sharp wars are ended' (5.10.8–9); and Troilus attempts a similarly formal exit line as he tells the others of Hector's death: 'But march away. | Hector is dead; there is no more to say' (5.11.21–2). Nevertheless he can't stop: 'Stay yet...' (23) until he reaches another couplet: 'To Troy with comfort go: | Hope of revenge shall hide our inward woe' (30–1). Thus Troilus twice tries to end 'his' tragedy, but in the Quarto he must speak a third rhyming couplet, this time to introduce Pandarus' festering epilogue: 'Hence, broker-lackey! Ignomy and shame | Pursue thy life, and live aye with thy name'. Despite his best efforts, the play doesn't conclude so much as stop, with Pandarus's final, excessive, feminine rhyme on 'eases/diseases'. Shakespeare's play is indeed satire as something mixed and overflowing, as well as being characterized by Thersites' satirical invective, his mastic jaws chewing over what might be digested in a play and, all too often, spitting it out in disgust.

[20] William Hazlitt, 'Characters of Shakespear's Plays', in Martin, *Troilus and Cressida*, 35–6.

[21] Simon Russell Beale, 'Thersites in *Troilus and Cressida*', in Russell Jackson and Robert Smallwood, eds., *Players of Shakespeare 3* (Cambridge: Cambridge University Press, 1993), 162.

[22] In the first four acts he speaks fewer than 180 lines (2.1, 2.3, 3.3); in act 5 he speaks over 100 lines (5.1, 5.2, 5.4, 5.8). Russell Beale, 'Thersites', 171.

[23] Heather James, *Shakespeare's Troy: Drama, Politics, and the Translation of Empire* (Cambridge: Cambridge University Press, 1997), 241 n.20.

Can such a distorted tragedy, a satirical tragedy or a satire on tragedy, still be tragic? This question might briefly be explored in relation to the fate of Robert Devereux, earl of Essex. An Essexian context has often been suggested for *Troilus and Cressida*:[24] Chapman had dedicated his 1598 translation of the *Iliad* 'To the Most Honored now living of the Achilleian vertues eternized by divine Homere, the Earle of ESSEXE',[25] yet readers accustomed to Achilles as the (flawed) hero of the *Iliad*, the greatest exemplar of Homeric renown, would have been shocked by Shakespeare's Achilles, who is indolent and cynical. In Hector and Achilles, the play scrutinizes, and satirizes, the different modes of honour and heroism that Essex failed to reconcile. Essex was fiercely jealous of his personal honour. As a soldier he was charismatic, with an eye for the grand gesture but little understanding of either long-term strategy or political pragmatism. On the morning of his 'rebellion', 8 February 1601, when Essex walked through the City of London with around 300 followers, they wore no armour and had almost no weapons beyond their swords. He was tried, and executed for treason on 25 February (and so were many of his followers: Shakespeare's patron Henry Wriothesley, earl of Southampton, was sentenced to death but imprisoned instead). There was little room for honour and renown in the brutal, pragmatic world of *fin de siècle* politics.

And none on Shakespeare's Phrygian plain, either. Yet Hector's defeat is not really a triumph for Achilles and the 'Achillean virtues' (whatever they might be in this play). Ulysses has warned Achilles that 'beauty, wit, | High birth, vigour of bone, desert in service, | Love, friendship, charity, are subjects all | To envious and calumniating time' (3.3.165–8): the play is obsessed with time and the inevitability of its depredations, but its association here is not simply with the passive neglect of oblivion but with far more active envy and calumny. These are not identical with satire, but they are not ethically or tonally unrelated to it either: even Thersites would be hard-pressed to define where one ends and the other begins in Shakespeare's bitter play of love and war, disease and desire. Perhaps the true tragedy of the play lay without the walls of Troy, its last act played out on a scaffold in the Tower of London. Essex remains one of a small number of early modern historical figures whose fate is typically described as a 'fall'. If he was not the model for (Shakespeare's) Achilles he was not his Hector either, but both characters at times satirize their own literary antecedents in ways which glance at the earl. Notoriously, Hector dies because he has pursued 'one in sumptuous armour' as a trophy, addressing the body as 'Most putrefièd core, so fair without' (5.9.1). But this is too easy a metaphor for the play. As a satire (or a satirical tragedy) it exposes the rottenness within, but (to anticipate that great satirist, and translator of Homer, Alexander Pope) it is less concerned with the falls of great men than with what might be termed their sinking.[26]

TIMON OF ATHENS

At the beginning of Act 5 of *Timon of Athens*, the Poet tells the Painter that he is thinking over what he will tell Timon he would like to dedicate to him next:

[24] See James, *Shakespeare's Troy*, 91.
[25] George Chapman, *Seauen bookes of the Iliades of Homere* (London, 1598), A3.
[26] In *The Art of Sinking in Poetry* (1727), Pope introduced *bathos* to English criticism to describe (and ridicule) failed attempts at the high style or sublime, or more general anti-climax and deflation.

> It must be a personating of himself, a satire against the softness of
> prosperity, with a discovery of the infinite flatteries that follow youth and
> opulency.
> TIMON [aside   Must thou needs stand for a villain in thine own work? Wilt
> thou whip thine own faults in other men?

(5.1.33–8)

The Poet and the Painter are characters without names, whose only other appearance has been in the opening scene of the play; their smooth, slick prose is urban(e) and contemporary and they make no attempt to disguise their self-interest. But although the Poet proclaims himself a satirist, it is Timon who employs the satirist's conceit of the scourge. There is a kind of satirical *mise en abîme* at work here, in satirizing the proposal to write satire; and like *Troilus and Cressida*, the play is at times almost too self-aware, and less playfully so. Kernan draws a pointed contrast between the two plays, and Timon and Thersites in particular:

> Where Thersites is simply a given, a dark energy who has no final explanation, Timon the
> satirist is a mutation, a distortion of a nature which was originally one of love and generos-
> ity. The play is the most penetrating analysis ever made of the satiric sense of life.[27]

Despite its focus on its title character, the play resists categorization (in the Folio it is a 'Life' rather than a tragedy). Like *Troilus*, therefore, it provides useful and provocative grounds for scrutinizing both tragedy and satire, and for considering the claims and limitations of such categories more generally.

The play's hybridity can be linked most obviously to its co-authorship by Shakespeare and Thomas Middleton. Middleton was the author of satires (his *Microcynicon: six snarling satires* was publicly burned as a result of the Bishops' Ban); his city comedies such as *Michaelmas Term* (1604), *A mad world, my masters* (1605), and *A trick to catch the old one* (1605) are filled with characters who are feckless, venal, on the make. He was London-centric in his concerns,[28] and at the height of his career also wrote civic pageants and court entertainments; in 1620 he was appointed as city 'chronologer', official historian. *Timon* is a play of urban elites, concerned with magnates and politicians rather than with the tapsters, drawers, and hostesses of Eastcheap or even 'Vienna'. Its prostitutes are the (notionally) 'high-class' Phrynia and Timandra, rather than 'Kate Keepdown' and 'Doll Tearsheet' (or Common).[29] The language of mercantilism so characteristic of *Troilus* has a 'real', hard currency here. If *Timon* is a tragedy, it is an urban one, its values those of a city that is London rather than Plutarch's Athens, and more Middleton's London than Shakespeare's.

How might a case be made for Timon's story as a tragedy? The urban setting is central to the play's satire, and urban tragedy, like domestic tragedy, is qualitatively different to the tragedy of the court or noble household, for example in its sharp eye for financial considerations. Timon's tragedy is partly a social one. He is a character utterly without relationships: alone among Shakespeare's (tragic) protagonists, Timon has no family. Flavius

---

[27] Kernan, *Cankered Muse*, 198.
[28] Notable exceptions include *The Revenger's Tragedy* (1606) and *The Changeling* (1622).
[29] Prostitutes in *Measure for Measure*, *2 Henry IV*, and Jonson's *The Alchemist* respectively.

is a faithful servant, not a friend, and the whole point of his various 'friendships' in the play is that they are none. *Timon* pushes to extremes something that characterizes all of Shakespeare's mid-period tragedies: an intense interest in the nature of friendship and the centrality of friendship to notions of selfhood and social identity. Friendship is fundamental to Shakespeare's tragic dramaturgy. Richard II protests that 'I live with bread, like you; | feel want, | Taste grief, need friends' (3.2.171–2). The rich exploration of friendship in the two parts of *Henry IV* lays the groundwork for the isolation of the king in *Henry V*, prepared to send his friends to execution (Scrope in 2.2; Bardolph in 3.6). '*Et tu, Bruté?*' (*Julius Caesar*, 3.1.76) goes without saying, and Hamlet, too, becomes a friend-killer when he leaves Rosencrantz and Guildenstern to their fate (5.2.57–9). And when Macbeth contemplates his isolation and mortality, it is friendship which is prominent:

> My way of life
> Is fall'n into the sere, the yellow leaf,
> And that which should accompany old age,
> As honour, love, obedience, troops of friends,
> I must not look to have, but in their stead
> Curses, not loud but deep, mouth-honour, breath…

(5.3.24–9)

'Troops of friends'? Macbeth has become a friend-killer, yet at the play's denouement, it is friendship for which he yearns, not wife or crown.

Macbeth's 'mouth-honour' speaks to *Timon*. For its protagonist, the loss of friendship is a slow agony, and the revelation of the self-interested hypocrisy of those thought of as friends a protracted crisis no less acute than Macbeth's. The falseness of Timon's friends is early apparent to Apemantus, as he rejects Timon's invitation to join the banquet:

> O you gods, what a number of men eats Timon, and he sees 'em not! It grieves me to see so many dip their meat in one man's blood; and all the madness is, he cheers them up, too.
> I wonder men dare trust themselves with men.
> Methinks they should invite them without knives:
> Good for their meat, and safer for their lives…

(1.2.38–43)

Albeit that, being Apemantus, he generalizes from this to all humanity, it is an early instance of the play's scrutiny of friendship. Here is a protagonist, a potential tragic hero, who is surrounded by friends and yet has none, who is rejected by or rejects every other character in the play, in a kind of *reductio ad absurdam* of the great tragedies of friendship.

More obviously, though, *Timon* is a play that abounds in railing—not confined to a single character, but rather dispersed, largely shared by Apemantus and, latterly, Timon. Apemantus, compared so often to a dog and even introduced in the Dramatis Personae as 'a churlish philosopher', is performatively excessive in his bitterness during the first half of the play. But by the time Timon takes over, there is almost no room for the railing voice to develop further. The first occasion on which Timon lets rip is, admittedly, striking:

> May you a better feast never behold,
> You knot of mouth-friends. Smoke and lukewarm water
> Is your perfection. This is Timon's last …

(3.7.87–9)

The problem is, however, that he keeps going—for another twenty lines in this passage alone. Only a few moments of stage-time later, when he has left Athens,[30] he begins again:

> Let me look back upon thee. O thou wall
> That girdles in those wolves, dive in the earth,
> And fence not Athens! Matrons, turn incontinent!
> Obedience fail in children!

and so on, for forty lines without pause, until (having cursed Athens with the customary range of diseases) he arrives at his peroration:

> The gods confound—hear me you good gods all—
> Th'Athenians, both within and out that wall;
> And grant, as Timon grows, his hate may grow
> To the whole race of mankind, high and low.
> Amen

(4.1.1–4, 37–41)

The 'Amen' acknowledges the speech's excess, and often gets a laugh in the theatre. But when the play's protagonist removes himself from its defining location to sneer and castigate, the ethical vacuum which results is also a dramatic one; there is little sense of what this railing might be *for*, other than the entertainment of a cynical audience who are to be fleetingly amused, or appalled, by extended passages of superior invective. Invective is theatrical, but it is not necessarily *dramatic*: as Kernan remarks, 'the most striking quality of satire is the absence of plot ... constant movement without change forms the basis of satire',[31] and in this respect, satire is inherently undramatic. Hence a play characterized above all by invective, especially in its latter stages, is also difficult to conceive as tragic: this is, perhaps, what *Troilus and Cressida* would look like if we were to take Thersites at his word, ignoring the admirable, if flawed, aspirations of Hector and the transient, misguided idealism of the lovers.

The play's invective reaches a climax in 4.3. As Timon digs for roots (only to find gold) he issues a global curse:

> Therefore be abhorred
> All feasts, societies, and throngs of men.
> His semblable, yea, himself, Timon disdains.
> Destruction fang mankind...

(4.3.20–3)

'Fang' suggests both 'seize', as if destruction were the dog, and 'give fangs to', as if mankind were; everything is cursed as both biter and bitten. When Alcibiades greets him, Timon rails:

> ALCIBIADES   What is thy name? Is man so hateful to thee
> That art thyself a man?
> TIMON   I am misanthropos, and hate mankind.

(4.3.51–3)

In this, the play's longest scene, he curses Alcibiades (whom he wants to attack Athens), the prostitutes Phrynia and Timandra (whom he wants to spread venereal disease), and

---

[30] Although it makes for a long first half, this is a logical place for an interval, partly because it breaks up Timon's speeches.
[31] Kernan, *Cankered Muse*, 30, 33.

has a long, ill-tempered debate with Apemantus as to which of them is more entitled to rail, ending in simple name-calling:

> TIMON   Away, thou tedious rogue!
> I am sorry I shall lose a stone by thee.
> APEMANTUS   Beast!
> TIMON   Slave!
> APEMANTUS   Toad!
> TIMON   Rogue, rogue, rogue!
>
> (4.3.372–7)

This exchange has little aesthetic weight or ethical force: the language and characters of the play, the play itself, have nowhere to go. And they continue going nowhere, as Timon sees off the 'Banditti', abuses the Poet and the Painter, rejects his faithful steward Flavius (twice) and the Senators who accompany him, announces that he is shortly to die, and makes his final speech.

Recent critical work has focused attention on the tragedy of 'over-living',[32] of the tragic protagonist who should die and yet suffers on. Such a principle can also be discerned in plays which carry on beyond any point of resolution, continually promising and then deferring an end: *King Lear* is the greatest example, but it is there in the over-full *Troilus* too. It might also be a way of thinking about *Timon*'s excesses, which are linguistic and dramaturgical as well as material. Like *Troilus*, only more so, *Timon* depicts not growth and change in a positive sense, but mutation, empty proliferation, metastasis. Both tragedy and satire are formally interested in the definition of kinds of wrongness; both satirist and tragic hero have a function which is diagnostic and, sometimes, curative, and the tragic protagonist is sometimes the diseased limb that must ultimately be cut away for the health of the body. This is often the protagonist's tragedy but, surgery completed, in tragedy there does usually seem to be (at least gestured at) the possibility of something better. The satirist bites on, his impotence inseparable from his fury as his invective does nothing at all.

KING LEAR

Where Timon *persists*, Lear *endures*,[33] and (if it is not too glib) that may be why the latter is a tragedy while the former remains undefinable. In conclusion I will explore some ways in which *King Lear* clarifies the intersections between tragedy and satire. The Fool's voice is often that of the satirist, mocking Lear (and his daughters) to his face, being addressed by Lear as 'pestilent gall', 'bitter fool' (1.4.113, 134), and perennially threatened with whipping. As Poor Tom and Lear take over the Fool's fooling, so Lear in particular inherits the Fool's propensity to rail in a more biting way, while at the same time demonstrating, again, that such invective makes nothing happen, but all too easily becomes absurd, (the word which

---

[32] See Emily R. Wilson, *Mocked with Death: Tragic Overliving from Sophocles to Milton* (Baltimore: Johns Hopkins University Press, 2004).

[33] '[Timon's] situation and speeches often resemble Lear's, but where Lear passes through satiric outrage with the world to tragic perception, Timon persists in his unyielding hatred. He is offered chances for redemption but rejects them' (Kernan, *Cankered Muse*, 203).

has so characterized modern discussion of *King Lear*). Much of the violence and disgust of satire is directed by Lear against himself, and it is also appallingly literalized. Lear may curse Regan as 'a disease that's in my flesh, | Which I must needs call mine. Thou art a boil, | A plague-sore or embossèd carbuncle…' (2.2.395–7) and propose 'anatomiz[ing]' her, (3.6.34), but the satiric impulse to strip and whip, expose and punish, is also repeatedly *staged*.

Edmond begins the play, like Ingenioso or even Hamlet, commenting on 'the excellent foppery of the world' (1.2.116) and adopting the railing voice and 'outsider' pose of the satirist. Yet he is also prepared to act, though not in any sense restoratively or curatively. When Lear, eventually, perceives with awful clarity the depths of human suffering and the wrongness of the world, he also sees the slender possibility of forgiveness and restoration. But for Edmond, weakness or injustice is simply to be exploited for gain. He is not a Thersites or a Timon, railing impotently from the sidelines, but a ruthless machiavel prepared to turn his own blade against himself for effect (2.1), and to lie, cheat, connive at torture, and kill. There is an irrefutable logic to Edgar's words to Edmond, about their father Gloucester:

> The gods are just, and of our pleasant vices
> Make instruments to plague us.
> The dark and vicious place where thee he got
> Cost him his eyes…
>
> (5.3.161–4)

There *is* a kind of justice in Gloucester's fate. It is an extreme and distressing outworking of the satiric impulse, literalized and performed by human agents. When Edgar observes that 'The worst is not | So long as we can say "This is the worst"' (4.1.27–8), one way of reading his remark might be to note that while there's satire, there's hope.[34] But by the end of the play, everything is as bad as it could possibly be, and there is no need of the satirist to point it out. *Difficile est*, indeed.

SELECT BIBLIOGRAPHY

(Juvenal's satires are widely available in modern translations: in addition to the Loeb edition, cited here (which includes the Latin text) see e.g. the Oxford World's Classics edition, trans. Niall Rudd, ed. William Barr (2008).)

Barton, Anne, *Ben Jonson, Dramatist* (Cambridge: Cambridge University Press, 1984).
Bednarz, James P., *Shakespeare and the Poets' War* (New York: Columbia University Press, 2001).
Bentley, Greg W., *Shakespeare and the New Disease: The Dramatic Function of Syphilis in Troilus and Cressida, Measure for Measure, and Timon of Athens* (New York: Peter Lang, 1989).
Bredbeck, Gregory W., *Sodomy and Interpretation: Marlowe to Milton* (Ithaca and London: Cornell University Press, 1991).

---

[34] '[*Troilus and Cressida* and *Hamlet* are] explorations of "the troubled mind", of consciousness discovering, in Frost's wry phrase, "that life really is as terrible as we sometimes think it is"' (Brower, *Hero and Saint*, 239); *Timon* and *Lear* could surely be adduced.

Brower, Reuben A., *Hero and Saint: Shakespeare and the Graeco-Roman Heroic Tradition* (Oxford: Oxford University Press, 1971).

Burrow, Colin, *Shakespeare and Classical Antiquity* (Oxford: Oxford University Press, 2013).

Campbell, Oscar J., *Comicall Satyre and Shakespeare's Troilus and Cressida* (San Marino: Huntington Library Publications, 1959).

Goldberg, Jonathan, *James I and the Politics of Literature: Jonson, Shakespeare, Donne and their Contemporaries* (Baltimore: Johns Hopkins University Press, 1983).

James, Heather, *Shakespeare's Troy: Drama, Politics, and the Translation of Empire* (Cambridge: Cambridge University Press, 1997).

Kernan, Alvin, *The Cankered Muse: Satire of the English Renaissance* (New Haven: Yale University Press, 1959).

Martin, Priscilla, ed., *Shakespeare: Troilus and Cressida: A Selection of Critical Essays* (London: Macmillan, 1976).

Miller, Paul Allen, ed., *Latin Verse Satire: An Anthology and Reader* (New York: Routledge, 2005).

Quintero, Ruben, ed., *A Companion to Satire: Ancient and Modern* (Malden, MA: Wiley-Blackwell, 2011).

Selden, Raman, *English verse satire 1590–1765* (London: George Allen and Unwin, 1978).

Soellner, Rolf, *Timon of Athens: Shakespeare's Pessimistic Tragedy* (Columbus: Ohio State University Press, 1979).

Taylor, Gary, and John Lavagnino, eds., *Thomas Middleton and Early Modern Textual Culture: A Companion to the Collected Works* (Oxford: Oxford University Press, 2007).

Wharton, T. F., ed., *The Drama of John Marston* (Cambridge: Cambridge University Press, 2000).

CHAPTER 17

'THE ACTION OF MY LIFE'
Tragedy, Tragicomedy, and Shakespeare's Mimetic Experiments

SUBHA MUKHERJI

IN the middle of that high comedy of desire and badinage, *Much Ado about Nothing*, as Benedick protests his love to Beatrice and asks her to 'bid [him] to do anything for [her]', Beatrice comes sharply back: 'Kill Claudio'. Staggered at this challenge to kill his best friend, Benedick exclaims, 'Ha, not for the wide world', but Beatrice replies, 'You kill me to deny it' (4.1.289-91). Hero has only been given out to be dead—like so many tragicomic heroines—and this Benedick and Beatrice know, as do the audience. So Beatrice's command may sound disproportionate. But its logic is precise. For Claudio has indeed killed Hero, emotionally. Beatrice's demand, however, is more than a call for exact justice or revenge: Benedick will only prove himself worthy of her if he can understand its affective seriousness. And the audience can only tune in if they are jolted out of the complacency of knowing that this is a false death. What could have been a purely formal move from comedy into tragicomedy is pushed, through a brush with tragic terror, to evoke the unpredictable directions of human agency, and the teetering of living moments between opposite possibilities. Giambattista Guarini, the influential Renaissance theorist of tragicomedy, characterized the genre as one that deploys the danger, but not the death, of tragedy—'*il pericolo, non la morte*':[1] that, to him, was an absolute distinction that made the form safe as well as marvellous. Shakespeare, in this scene, provocatively blurs the distinction between the two.

The use of an affective interjection as an impulse towards comedic self-checking is most striking at the end of *Love's Labours Lost*. Not only does 'the scene [begin] to cloud' with Monsieur Marcade bringing the news of the Princess's father's death (5.2.714); the consequent deferral of the expected marriage is premised on explicitly affective conditions. For none is it so pointed as for the central couple. Rosaline challenges Biron, addicted to witty wordplay, sometimes at the expense of others, to spend a year making 'the speechless sick' and 'painèd impotent' smile:

---

[1] Giambattista Guarini, *A Compendium of Tragicomic Poetry*, in Allan Gilbert, *Literary Criticism: Plato to Dryden* (Detroit: Wayne State University Press, 1962), 504–33 (511).

> A jest's prosperity lies in the ear
> Of him that hears it, never in the tongue
> Of him that makes it.
>
> (5.2.847–9)

In making reception and empathy the conditions of legitimate jest, Rosaline aborts the 'comedy' the play's 'sport' could have produced (862). For Biron, a year's wait is 'too long for a play' (860). For the young dramatist, not untouched by the self-delighting facility of linguistic craft, this is a disciplining of his play (and playing); a stepping out of self-enclosed artifice into a dialogue with lived time, pain and intersubjective sympathy—normally tragic attributes.

This chapter will put pressure on moments at generic thresholds—in particular, those between tragicomedy and tragedy—to understand the stakes of Shakespeare's interrogation of genre, and its implications for representation and response. But if the opening examples suggest that comedy is the form associated with an aesthetic refusal of natural reality, Shakespeare's formal explorations show how the opposite may be equally true— how tragedy can offer solaces that belong more to art than to life. Broadly speaking, the product of these experiments is Shakespearean tragicomedy—the peculiarly mixed mode that characterizes so much of his drama. Though the Folio's non-coordinate classifications do not even feature it as a separate category, Shakespeare was, as Yeats said, always a writer of tragicomedy, and Elizabethan England was clearly registering tragicomic mingling well before the publication of Guarini's *Compendio della poesia tragicomica* (1509-1601)—the first systematic theory of the genre—alongside his play *Il Pastor Fido*. After the explicit acknowledgement and adaptation of Guarini in Fletcher's *The Faithful Shepherdess* (1608-9), Shakespeare collaborated with Fletcher around 1613 on at least two tragicomedies, *Two Noble Kinsmen* and *Cardenio*. So, did 'tragicomedy' come to mean anything distinct from comedy to Shakespeare, as he played around with generic components, and as its shape and nature began to be formally defined on the Continent? Do his late pastoral tragicomedies offer any clues? The boundaries of his tragedies are no less problematic than those of his comedies: witness the grotesquerie of *Titus Andronicus*, the acerbic wit and the grim hilarity of *Hamlet*, the comedy of the porter-scene in *Macbeth*, or the familiar comic domesticity and littleness of Cinthio's sub-tragic world of handkerchiefs and whispers in *Othello*. How does the notion of tragicomedy trouble these edges further?

But it is neither tragedy nor tragicomedy alone that effects Shakespeare's ethical and affective questioning of his art. As his career progresses, each helps the other sharpen its own claims on mimetic responsibility. A consideration of his tragic art in relation to tragicomedy—both his consciously mixed-genre plays and his inscription of moments from an apparently incompatible generic world within a dominant tragic genre— illuminate the urgency of these experiments.

ANTECEDENTS, MODELS, AND DRAMATIC THEORY

Heinrich Heine captured the flamboyant generic elusiveness of *Troilus and Cressida*—in content, mood, and even its printing history—when he wrote that it presents Melpomene, the Tragic Muse, '[acting] the clown ... dancing the *cancan* at a ball of *grisettes*, with shameless laughter on her pallid lips, and with death in her heart'.[2] In the classicist literary theory of the playwright's own time, though, mixtures were illegitimate: witness Sidney's famous denigration of 'mongrel tragicomedy'; or Whetstone's lament of the 'gross indecorum' of making a clown companion to a king 'to make mirth'.[3] Where, then does Shakespeare find a model for his indecorous mixtures?

Even the most introspective of Shakespeare's tragedies spring out of the same hybrid ground as the tragedies of the 1580s. Mingling foolery with serious drama, kings with clowns, was a feature of medieval moralities, inherited and developed by the Elizabethan stage. Nor was the continuity merely literary: both Elizabeth and James had their court fools. Besides, Shakespeare was a professional playwright working with a company, and had to find roles for the comic actor, Robert Armin, as well as for the usual actor of the great tragic roles, Richard Burbage. Nahum Tate's *History of King Lear* (1681) got rid of the Fool; Tate found the mixing of tragedy with 'unseasonable jests' abhorrent, and it wasn't till 1838 that the Fool reappeared on stage. Ironically, Tate thought he was purifying the play, though he gave it a 'tragicomic' happy ending; he failed to see, as the Jacobeans did, that the Fool 'labours to outjest | | [Lear's] heart-struck injuries' (3.1.8-9).[4]

But Shakespeare's was a period obsessed with classical dramatic precedents. And we must remember that the main body of theoretical writing on classical drama available to sixteenth-century playwrights—largely via Latin new comedy—was about comic, not tragic plots. But 'tragicomedia' was also part of the mental terrain of Elizabethan playwrights, thanks to Mercury's arch promise in the prologue to Plautus' *Amphitryo*:

> faciam ut commixta sit: sit tragicomoedia
> nam me perpetuo facere ut sit comoedia,
> reges quo veniant et di, non par arbitror.[5]

I will make it a mixture; let it be a tragicomedia. I don't think it would be appropriate to make it consistently a comedy, when there are kings and gods in it.

Though the feel of the play is very different to that of Shakespeare's tragicomedies, it shares the motif of a loved one lost and recovered, while the perceptual errors shaping its love-plot morph into a basis for tragedy in Shakespearian drama, as Colin Burrow notes.[6] Another equally popular classical influence—theatrical in style and conception but narrative in form—was Heliodorus' *Aethiopica*—a major vehicle of romance plots, a mediator of Aristotelian ideas in fictional practice, precursor of English tragicomedy, and

---

[2] Quoted in Harold Hillebrand and T. W. Baldwin, *Troilus and Cressida*, New Variorum edition (1953), 523.

[3] From George Whetstone's 'Epistle Dedicatory to *Promos and Cassandra*', in Michael Sidnell, ed., *Sources of Dramatic Theory: vol 1: Plato to Congreve* (Cambridge: Cambridge University Press, 1991, 1994), 166.

[4] All references to *Lear* are to René Weis, ed., *King Lear: A Parallel Text Edition* (London: Longman, 1993); citations refer to the Folio unless otherwise specified.

[5] Plautus Titus Maccius, *Amphitryo* (c.204-184 BC), Prologue, ll. 59–61.

[6] Colin Burrow, 'What is a Shakespearean Tragedy?', in Claire McEachern, ed., *The Cambridge Companion to Shakespeare's Tragedy* (Cambridge: Cambridge University Press, 2013). 1–22 (12).

a transmission route of Euripidean concepts about happy-ending-tragedies. So it is not hard to see how, without access to a systematic theory of tragedy, Elizabethan tragedians might have gravitated towards tragicomedy as a form closer to tragedy than pure comedy, but with familiar classical referents. Indeed, tragicomedy was often regarded as a subgenre of tragedy. Giraldi Cinthio's notion of *tragedia di fin lieto*, justified in Aristotelian terms, proved influential in sixteenth-century Italy, as did his nine posthumously published tragedies (1583), seven of which shared plots with his prose work *Gli Hecatommithi* (1565) which, like Boccaccio and Bandello's *novellae*, provided dramatic plots for Shakespeare. Meanwhile, though the paradoxical classicism of Guarini's mixed genre has been illuminatingly demonstrated by Tanya Pollard,[7] the internal aesthetic and aestheticist implications of his theory for Shakespeare and his contemporaries merit attention, not least because they bring into sharper relief his final conceptualizations of tragedy.

And then there was Seneca, whose tragedies of blood, widely read in grammar schools, and available in Thomas Newton's translation, *Tenne Tragedies of Seneca* from 1581, were probably the greatest classical influence on early modern tragedy till at least the turn of the century. Though Lydgate's *Fall of Princes* provided the dominant tragic model in the vernacular, Seneca loomed larger in the dramatic context. Sidney praised *Gorboduc* (1565)— arguably the first English tragedy—for 'climbing to the height of Seneca's style'.[8] Even more than that majesty of style, it is the coexistence of aesthetic and formal control on the one hand, and huge, unruly passions on the other, that is relevant for my purpose. Seneca seems to have been self-divided across his own genres. As A. D. Nuttall points out, Seneca's moral essays treat the passions as objects for expulsion, but his tragedies explore characters not only swayed but dignified by uncontrollable passions; this maps on to the distinction between Stoicism as *apatheia* and a dynamic model of Stoicism which needed passions as material for moral conquest.[9] Shakespeare's tragic texts make this coexistence dialogic in more ways than one. In his early poem *Lucrece*, the raped Lucrece, initially a 'lamenting Philomel', '[gushes] pure streams' of 'well-tuned warble', like the metamorphosed bird of the Ovidian myth (ll. 1077-80). But then, as she begins to vacillate between copious lament and choked silence—'Sometimes her grief is dumb and hath no words; | Sometimes 'tis mad and too much talk affords'—she identifies with the pre-metamorphic raped and gagged woman of the Ovidian myth (ll. 1105-6, 1128). All she ends up writing to her husband is 'a short schedule', lest her *copia* should misrepresent her feelings. Two models meet in *Lucrece*— Ovid who treats rape after rape with effortless elegance, and Seneca, who vivifies obtruded horror. Seneca was the source of the familiar tag, 'Curae leves loquuntur, ingentes stupent' (light griefs speak, huge griefs are silent) (*Phaedra*, 607). Thus, he complicates Shakespeare's early Ovidianism and helps him fashion a poetic of obtrusion as a counter to facile, misleading, or perverse eloquence. But he also complicates late Shakespearean generic mixture where this rhetorically focused duality widens into a dialogue between Seneca and Guarini around formal representations of pain; Ovid lingers, transformed. This process gleams into

---

    [7] Tanya Pollard, 'Tragicomedy', in Patrick Cheney and Philip Hardie, eds, *The Oxford History of Classical Reception in English Literature*, vol 2: *1558-1660* (Oxford: Oxford University Press, 2015), 419-32.
    [8] Sir Philip Sidney, *An Apology for Poetry*, ed. Geoffrey Shepherd (Manchester: Manchester University Press, 1973), 133-4.
    [9] A. D. Nuttall, 'The Stoic in Love', in *The Stoic in Love* (Savage, MD: Barnes & Noble, 1989), 56-67.

light most fully in the play that embodies Shakespeare's most self-conscious manipulation of the tragic form. For in *Lear*, the Guarinian and the Senecan are set against one another to define generic difference, as well as to draw on the innate tension within the Senecan tragic example. Such acts of generic sharpening in the tragedies occur in direct negotiation with an evolving idea of tragicomedy.

The Aesthetic of Mixing, Middle to Late

The sudden tragic twists of the early comedies give way, in Shakespeare's middle phase, to mixed-mode plays where comedy and tragedy are sharply juxtaposed: as across 3.2 and 4.1 in *Measure for Measure*:

> DUKE … Craft against vice I must apply:
> With Angelo to-night shall lie
> His old betrothed but despised;
> So disguise shall, by the disguised,
> Pay with falsehood false exacting,
> And perform an old contracting.
> *Exit*
>
> 4.1
> *Mariana [discovered] with a Boy singing*
> BOY Take, O, take those lips away,
> That so sweetly were forsworn;
> And those eyes, the break of day,
> Lights that do mislead the morn:
> But my kisses bring again, bring again;
> Seals of love, but sealed in vain, sealed in vain.
> …
> [*Enter Duke*]
> …
> MARIANA … I have sat here all day.
>
> (3.2.533–4.1.20)

Vincentio's speech smacks of phonetic revenge—eye for eye and tooth for tooth—and hence of comedic ordering. What immediately follows is the stilled pathos of the dilatory song about what is lost, what has been betrayed. Time has stood still in Mariana's world—while in the Duke's, it has been moving swiftly, patly, tritely. The end-stopped rhymes enact the fantasy of end-stopped grief, just as the over-neatness of the resolutions of this play push the comic mode to cracking point. The ending is thick with 'an orgy of clemency',[10] and multiple weddings are proposed oftener as punishment than reward, unwelcome to all except Claudio and Juliet, the one pair genuinely in love, though condemned to die at the play's start for their supposed fornication. By not giving Isabella any lines at all in response to the Duke's final proposal—his third in this scene—Shakespeare leaves the actor/director with the gift of an

---

[10] A. D. Nuttall, 'Measure for Measure: Quid pro Quo?', *Shakespeare Studies* 4 (1968), 231–51 (239).

open silence. Trevor Nunn's 1991 production at the Young Vic had 'Isabella' (Clare Skinner) stop dead for two minutes and stare at the Duke. Then, suddenly, the lights went on, bells jingled, and Isabella became a giggly, girly confetti-covered bride, taking the Duke's hand and tripping away with the other couples into a Hollywood-Jane Austen-double-wedding-type bliss. She had stepped into genre, and the audience were aghast—there were gasps of horror. The director exploited the play's own use of a hyper-comedic mode to invoke potential tragedy, by showing the cost at which personhood yields to generic formula.

Troilus, written a year or so earlier, also works through ironic juxtapositions. Each of its proto-endings offers a different generic possibility. When Troilus declares, 'But march away; | Hector is dead, there is no more to say' (5.11.21-2), the play is on the brink of a sonorous tragic ending. But he says more—'Stay yet'! (22)—and ends his speech like a revenge-play hero: 'Strike a free March to Troy, with comfort go: | Hope of revenge shall hide our inward woe' (30-1). But then Pandarus steps in—by now neither a comic nor a tragic 'fool' but a version of the scabby Thersites—and bequeaths his diseases in illustrative 'verse' very different from Troilus' decisive couplets, ending the play on an inconclusive 'feminine' rhyme.[11] The offer of bodily contamination clinches a *contaminatio* of sources and genres: a 'fountain stirr'd' (3.3.306), most directly through Thersites and Pandarus, mediators and detractors of myth, heroism, and the entire matter of Troy which was itself a cumulative mish-mash of textual traditions: testimonial, epic, romance, poetic, salutary, and satiric; Greek, French, Italian, and English.

While the jostling of genres places *Troilus*'s mixing in the middle period, its intuition of the relation between form and subjecthood anticipates the blending of the late tragicomedies. In the Greek camp, as Cressida is passed around for a kiss, a textually vexed exchange follows:

> ULYSSES   May I, sweet lady, beg a kiss of you?
> CRESSIDA   You may.
> ULYSSES   I do desire it.
> CRESSIDA   Why, beg then.

(4.5.47-8)

Dr Johnson amended the Quarto's 'Why begge then' and the Folio's 'Why begge then?'— between them already opening up diverse tonal and performative options—into 'Why, beg two.' Joseph Ritson followed: 'Why, beg too.' These editors were mending the rhyme, but in the process losing the effect of the break of rhyme—Cressida's refusal to play the bantering game of the Greeks, and/or her loss of grip over the moment. Formal control usually speaks of anti-tragic, if not comic, agency in the mixed-mode plays: Cressida is no Vincentio. Her vulnerability is like that of Isabella, betrayed by her own metaphoricity as Angelo '[arrests] her at her word' when she refuses sex by talking eloquently about 'keen whips and rubies', and then protesting in panic that women are frail (2.4.99-130; 134). The medium is an extension of the voice and the self, and registers their struggles, triumphs and surrenders. The play exacts its linguistic revenge on the woman who has

---

[11] References to *Troilus* are from Anthony Dawson's New Cambridge edition, as I concur with him (and other editors) that Pandarus' Epilogue, present in both early texts, was an intended part of the play, and disagree with Taylor's speculative reasons for cutting it.

tried to control her relations to men through verbal wit, when the Greeks announce together, 'The Trojans' trumpet'—aurally identical to 'the Trojans' strumpet'—as if to affirm Ulysses' presentation of her as a text that 'wide unclasps the tables of [its] thoughts | To every ticklish reader' (60-1). It is at the interface with this obstacle that her subjecthood glimmers. Yet, the next time we see her, she is flirting with Diomed, and Ulysses seems to have been right. When her letter to Troilus is shredded, unread, as 'Words, words, mere words, no matter from the heart', the play keeps alive the tension between tragic subjectivity and its doomed formal pre-inscription (5.3.107). Her earlier construction of unknowability as a shield against the power of men to empty her out (1.1.250-5) rebounds tragically on her now—manifesting in her inability to be 'read'—while at the same time allowing us a glimpse of that within her, beyond Ulysses' bawdy blazon. The play, unlike Cressid, never succumbs to a longing for its 'kind of self' (3.2.128) to be known, but remains an ongoing commentary on knowability itself. But in another key, Cressida becomes a generic microcosm of the play—its confusion a mimetic register for a human nature whose plurality Troilus cannot brook: 'This is, and is not, Cressid' (5.2.145). The purity of tragic crisis remains a fantasy of integrity that is untrue to the realities of the psyche. It was those realities that Dryden pre-empted by replacing the camp scene with a report by Pandarus. An indeterminate Cressida, theatrically seized upon by Shakespeare, would have unsettled Dryden's project of turning the play into a tragedy.

In the last plays, these moments of inter-generic off-setting give way to a Guarinian 'third sort', which brings with it its own aesthetic. In *The Tempest*, Ferdinand wakes up to the sweet music of the island where he has been washed ashore after a shipwreck. Ariel sings of the supposed death of the Duke, Ferdinand's father, by drowning, while Ferdinand 'weeps':

> Fall fadom five thy father lies;
> Of his bones are coral made;
> Those are pearls that were his eyes:
> Nothing of him that doth fade,
> But doth suffer a sea-change
> Into something rich and strange.

> (1.2.399-405)

Ariel's song seems to encapsulate the process of romance transformation itself. It describes and effects the transmutation of a dead body into non-human artefacts, rendering the macabre expensive and artificial—'rich and strange'. The function of art in transforming death, sorrow and loss into aesthetic objects is an old preoccupation with Shakespeare. In his earliest poem, *Venus and Adonis*, the tears in Venus' affrighted eyes were 'like pearls in glass' (l. 980), while her final possession of Adonis turned him into a pretty trinket cradled in her bosom—'love's flower'—white and purple as blood trickling down his fair flank from the fatal goring of a boar (l. 1188)!

But in the late romances, artifice is specifically connected with tragicomic art. In *Cymbeline*, the subtle villain Iachimo sneaks into Innogen's bedchamber to obtain a token that will convince her husband, Posthumus, of her infidelity. Transforming a virtual rape-scene, he peruses the sleeping Innogen like an art connoisseur lovingly collecting priceless miniatures 't'enrich [his] inventory': her lips, 'rubies unparagon'd', and the mole on her breast, 'like the crimson drops | I'th' bottom of a cowslip', are translated into the same order of preciousness as the bracelet he takes off her arm (2.2.30, 38-9). In the last scene, this pleasure in the exquisite culminates in Iachimo's zestful, erotic recounting of the act of stealth he supposedly repents, and which has cost Innogen all her pain.

The potential perversity of this can only be sanctioned by a form that guarantees a happy ending but contains tragic experience—so that the painful can be dwelt on in an artistic way. Iachimo's ravishing *enargeia* crops up effortlessly at moments of suspense or anticipated knowledge, bringing artful but agonising deferral in its wake. For Guarini, the wonder of the resolution is proportional to the danger of the action: 'the more firmly knotted' the story, the 'more delightful' the end (528). The justification is the assurance, in the artificer's mind, that it is 'tragic in possibility but not in fact' (522). This is what allows for Paulina's relentless protraction of Leontes' penance over sixteen years in *The Winter's Tale*, and Hermione's exile in a garden shed with packed lunches, in pretence that she is dead: the art that 'resurrects' her 'statue' seems the more ingenious for the tortuous wait.

In mood and style, Guarini's 'tragicomedy' takes from tragedy its 'pleasure, but not its sadness', and from comedy its 'feigned difficulty' and 'laughter that is not excessive' (511). With this hybrid material, it sets to work towards an avoidance of excess—either of 'tragic melancholy' or of 'comic relaxation' (512). Each has its 'texture' 'pleasingly ... [tempered]' (526). Redefining Aristotelian 'purgation' in relation to tragicomedy, Guarini describes it as reducing extreme emotions and humours to a just and profitable measure (interestingly, contrasting this with total removal of the 'affections' 'in Stoic fashion', 516). This tempering of affective content sits comfortably with Guarini's main points about the differentia of tragicomic style:

> The normal and chief style of tragicomedy is the magnificent, which, when accompanied with the grave, becomes the norm of tragedy, but when mingled with the *polished*, makes the combination fitting to tragicomic poetry. ... [I]t abandons the grave and employs the *sweet*'. (525)

The potential preciousness of the aesthetic of the late plays—their 'pearls in glass' moments—are a function of tragicomic logic and aesthetic. Such artistic transformation of the grotesque can take the form not only of the tempering of the tragic but its diminution; a refining away of life's intractables. Shakespeare's recognition of this potential to set tragedy apart from tragicomic pleasures is nowhere put to such piercing use as in *The Tragedy of King Lear* (1623).

'WITHIN A FOOT OF THE EXTREME VERGE': TRAGICOMIC PRECIPICE AND TRAGIC ABYSS

A Quarto-specific passage in *Lear* has gone relatively unremarked: Kent's exchange with the 'Gentleman' in 4.3 describing Cordelia's reaction on receiving the letter from England. Kent asks, 'Did your letters pierce the Queen to any demonstration of grief?' (4.3.10), and the Gentleman responds:

> And now and then an ample tear trilled down
> Her delicate cheek. It seemed she was a queen
> Over her passion who, most rebel-like,
> Sought to be king o'er her.

'O, then it moved her', Kent infers from the dainty alliterations and containing occlusions of stop consonants. This scene, staged, might ironically recall the tragic fallibility of inferences from '[demonstrations]' in the love-trial, except that here we have a comment on the response to tragic news, rather than the response itself. Crafting that distance, the Gentleman elaborates:

> Not to a rage. Patience and sorrow strove
> Who should express her goodliest. You have seen
> Sunshine and rain at once; her smiles and tears
> Were like, a better way. Those happy smilets
> That played on her ripe lip seem not to know
> What guests were in her eyes, which parted thence
> As pearls from diamonds dropped. In brief,
> Sorrow would be a rarity most beloved
> If all could so become it.
> …
> Faith, once or twice she heaved the name of 'Father'
> Pantingly forth, as if it pressed her heart.
> Cried, 'Sisters, sisters, shame of ladies, sisters …'
>
> (4.3.11-27)

The sentimentalized image of the grieving Cordelia is premised on defining poignancy and authenticity of response by a conflict of rebellious passions and an attempt to hold them in; a tragicomic 'tempering' that lays claim to the perception of a Stoic mean. The Gentleman's aestheticization of 'strife' at once expands on this and trivializes the idea of strife itself, against the savage pain that takes over the play. Art's pretty images of grief are mocked on the one hand by the art-defying breaking of bounds that at once surrounds and places such neat, exquisite descriptions; and on the other, by the authentic failures of expression that the play presents. These 'pearls in diamonds'—fruits of the narrative indulgence that makes sorrow a 'rarity', polished and sweet, crossing over from the preciousness of early Ovidian and late Guarinian modes—sit uneasily in the 'Tragedy' that the Folio *Lear* becomes, when Shakespeare rewrites it. Excising this scene may well have been part of the honing of tragic form that John Jones persuasively shows Shakespeare doing in the Folio text.[12] But it is also a lost opportunity for pitting the play's own representation of sorrow against that of inset commentators who inhabit a tragicomic world, expecting a lasting union between father and daughter, the throne and its legitimate heir. Elsewhere, precisely such opportunities are seized, with negative evocations of 'the promis'd end' of romance (through a succession of false endings or providentialist thanksgivings), undercut by irredeemable pain and injustice. The delicacy of speculation in 'as if it pressed her heart' calls up, by contrast, all the breaking and cracking hearts in this play. The point, surely, is that they fail to crack and break physically. When characters talk of cracking hearts, they are using a particular mood, a particular range of verbs, indicating either an imperative or a wish. '*Let* sorrow split my heart', says Albany. 'O that my heart *would* burst', says Edgar. What Lynn Magnusson calls the 'optative mode', following the classifications of 'moods' in William Lily's popular *Grammar* (1523), pervades *King Lear*: 'wissheth or

---

[12] I premise my argument on John Jones's widely accepted thesis that Shakespeare revised *Lear* around the time he was writing the late romances: see *Shakespeare at Work* (Clarendon: Oxford, 1995), ch. 4.

desireth' is how Lily defined this mood.[13] But while Magnusson focuses on modal auxiliaries to explore 'the playwright's invention of possible worlds and crafting of dramatic plots' in *Titus* and *Richard III* (70), the grammar of possibility is connected in the mature tragedies, especially *Lear*, with the *im*possibility of congruence between the desired and the attainable.

Colin Burrow comments acutely on the gap between action and desire in Seneca, indicated through modal verbs, as in Atreus' self-berating speech in *Thyestes* (176-84) which finds a route into *Hamlet*'s 'O what a rogue and peasant slave am I' (albeit with a performative twist).[14] He also notes the transformed echo of Seneca's Hippolytus' speech in Lear's address to the gods on the heath: 'Lear's speech turns Hippolytus' cry of guilt upside-down … calling down destruction not on himself but on others. The storm and thunderbolts—which in Hippolytus are only wished for but are pointedly *not* happening—are realized onstage.'[15] Burrow is, here, tapping into the Stoic idea of a sympathetic correlation between the individual's rage and cosmic chaos, once personal control cracks. But even that correlation can surely be a fantasy of agency? While the storms may happen on stage, the coincidence between 'the tempest in [Lear's] mind' and the deluge out there may be just that—coincidental (3.4.12). Indeed, Burrow himself intimates this possibility at the conclusion to his chapter on Seneca elsewhere: 'Lear orders the elements to rage with him and for criminals to cower. Do the wretches tremble with fear rather than just with cold?'[16] But there is a further irony yet. In *The Tragedy of King Lear*, the Senecan 'space between speaking and doing' that Burrow identifies in *Hamlet*,[17] or the falling short of the Senecan Medea in Lady Macbeth, get translated, I propose, into a gap between feeling and form, for both the characters and the play. Aesthetic form becomes an analogue for the body, or its extension, as Shakespeare converts Seneca's hypothetical excesses into ruminations on the futility of correspondence. The energy inheres in a fretful inversion of the comfort of an apparently Senecan poise between craft and violence: Stoicism, after all, was both a philosophy and an aesthetic. But Senecan control is already a world apart from Guarini's middle way: Shakespeare's tragedies draw, and put pressure, on a deeper, more dynamic Senecan tussle between *tranquillitas* and *furor* in the life of the individual, by making matter chafe against containment. There are recurrent images of the *rightness* of physical limits bursting, the mortal frame being racked. When Lear, on seeing Kent in stocks, cries, 'Oh sides, you are too tough | Will you yet hold?', he is exclaiming at the failure of his bounds to dissolve, as they should; raging against the obstinacy of form in the face of such suffering. This tragic strife is set against the tragicomic impulse to craft and contain. When, half-crazed, Lear asks Kent, 'Wilt break my heart?', Kent says 'I had rather break my own' (3.4.5). And in the Folio ending, looking upon the old deluded Lear dying at the point of a possibly false recognition, Kent is given the lines that belong to Lear in Quarto: 'Break heart, I prithee break'. But he lives on, of course, to say, almost to pray, 'O let him pass. He hates him | That would upon the rack of this tough world | Stretch him out

[13] Lynn Magnusson, 'A Play of Modals: Grammar and Potential Action in Early Shakespeare', *Shakespeare Survey* 62 (Cambridge: Cambridge University Press, Nov. 2009), 69–80 (71).

[14] Burrow, 'Shakespearean Tragedy', 15–16.   [15] Ibid., 15.

[16] Colin Burrow, *Shakespeare and Classical Antiquity* (Oxford: Oxford University Press, 2013), ch. 5 (201).

[17] 'Shakespearean Tragedy', 16.

longer', as he watches Lear live on too, if only for minutes. After all, the first time the heart was mentioned in *Lear* was when Cordelia said 'I cannot heave my heart into my mouth' (F, 1.1.90–1). All subsequent abortions of commensurate expression of what is within, be it through words or the body, are corollaries of this tragic non-congruence. The repeated wishes for a synergy between that within and its outward register are but a fantasy of expressivity, a dream of what Seneca or Stoic cosmology would have called *sumpatheia*.[18] Only, it extends beyond individual emotion or its connection with nature, to a further link with the aesthetic medium's relation to its experiential content. The Folio's paring away of the Quarto's mock-trial perhaps sharpens this modified focus, though in fact there is a continuum between its fantasy of judicial agency and the failure of control and correspondence by which the play is haunted.[19] The play's own claim to mimesis lies not only in its self-differentiation from tragicomedy but in its refusal, ultimately, of the conventional pleasure even of tragedy—Aristotle's *megethos*—and the artifice it entails, as it wrestles to forge a form that acknowledges the inadequacy of 'tragic' aesthetics in the face of extremity. The King does not command his own heart to break as in the Quarto; we do not have the satisfaction of a momentous recognition brought about by art, and language breaks down rather than ascending to formal magnitude: 'Howl, howl, howl'; 'Never, never, never, never, never' (F, 5.3.231, 282). The play ends on the verge of a different kind of tragedy—one that locates the potential of its expressive medium in the difficulty of negotiating its limits, in the ability to look the abyss in the face.

Edgar, meanwhile, gathers up many of the tragicomic traits that stand opposed to such rough strife. Not only does the Folio cut the Gentleman's prettified descriptions of grief; it also excises Edgar's report of how Kent was overcome by grief as he

> Told the most piteous tale of Lear and him
> That ever ear received, which in recounting
> His grief grew puissant and the strings of life
> Began to crack.
>
> (Q, 5.3.208–11)

Perhaps his preceding description of Gloucester's broken heart that "Twixt two extremes of passion, joy and grief, | Burst smilingly' (F, 192) was just about enough elegance to retain as another glimpse of the tragicomic narrative impulse, and not to let it compromise the Folio's generic distinctiveness; for here, 'side-piercing [sights]' (4.5.85) replace delicate descriptions of how letters pierce a grieving queen with decorous moderation (Q, 4.3.16). Shakespeare's scepticism about the fetishizing of measure stretches back to his early tragedies. When Marcus asks Titus 'not [to] break into these deep extremes', Titus replies: 'Is not my sorrows deep, having no bottom? | Then be my passions bottomless with them'. As Marcus preaches autarchy—'let reason govern thy lament'—Titus retaliates: 'If there were reason for these miseries, | Then into limits would I bind my woes' (*Titus*, 3.1.214–20).

---

[18] On *sumpatheia*, see Thomas G. Rosenmeyer, *Senecan Drama and Stoic Cosmology* (Berkeley, Los Angeles, and London: University of California Press, 1989), 107–12. See also Seneca, *Thyestes*, 106–11, for an example of the *sumpatheia* of nature.

[19] If its removal in F was due to censorship—a widely held critical assumption, there may not have been a conceptual reason for the cut in the first instance.

Edgar also embodies the tragicomic impulse in another sense: using art to shape, control or interpret life. Pretending to be poor Tom, he stands on even ground with his freshly blinded and already grief-crazed father, taking his time in an ekphrastic speech to create the vertigo effect of a sheer precipice (*Lear*, 4.5.11-24). Edging Gloucester closer and closer to the temptation of leaping off the edge of the supposed cliff, Edgar suggests: 'You are now within a foot | Of th'extreme verge' (ll. 25-6). And so Gloucester takes the 'suicidal' leap and falls on flat ground. 'Thy life's a miracle', Edgar informs him (l. 55), with the smugness of the tragicomic artificer who, like Hal in *Henry IV* 1.1, gathers clouds so that the sun may shine the brighter when it comes through (1.2.197-203)—'the worst' not only 'returns to laughter' but helps fulfil the tragicomic promise of the miraculous (*Lear*, 4.1.6). Bewildered, Gloucester asks, 'Have I fall'n or no?' (4.5.56). If this is farcical, the audience's sense of comedy shares the bizarre humour of Edgar's charade. He has himself articulated, earlier, a sense of the indecorum of such jest: 'Bad is the trade that must play fool to sorrow' (4.1.39). Edgar's aside tells us: 'Why I do trifle thus with his despair | Is done to cure it' (4.5.33-4). This sanctimonious self-justification smacks of the righteousness of dramatic characters who try other people from a high moral ground, backed by the knowledge that the suffering they are putting someone else through will be revealed, eventually, to be causeless; and may even prove to be morally edifying. Remember Paulina to Leontes at the end of sixteen years' penance and on the verge of bliss: 'I could afflict you further' (5.3.75).

But this does not stand alone. Looking at level surface and imagining the chalky cliffs of Dover, Shakespeare's audiences, like Gloucester, would have had little reason not to believe Edgar; and even then a playgoer might easily take the aside to refer to Edgar's concealment of his identity rather than to his little salutary drama. So if the joke is at Gloucester's expense, it is at the playgoer's too, as they have not only dwelt on the thrilling verge of tragicomic suspense but also leapt off it with him. And if, having been drawn through this game, they think they now know better, why should they not believe—when Lear sees the feather stir near the (dead) Cordelia's lips—that she lives, as the actor's breath makes it flutter? The play's manipulation of the non-naturalistic theatre works through a sharpening of tragic edge against the whetstone of tragicomic 'esperance' (an Edgar word in the Folio, 4.1.4).

Such inset plots, however, make for brilliant drama, even where the audience have enfranchised knowledge—as when another old, blind father is led on by his son, Lanceleot Gobbo who '[tries] confusions on him' and tells him that his son is dead.[20] The fictive impulse that feeds such plot-making, comic or tragic—whether it is Edgar's, or Vincentio's, or Malcolm's false trial of Macduff—often creates a generic wobble, working as it tends to do through asymmetrical knowledges. Its ancestry goes back to the returned Odysseus in Homer, spinning tales about his identity not only to Athene, the Swine-herd and Penelope, but also '[trying] an experiment' with his old father, telling him that he (Odysseus) is dead.[21] Cariclea, heroine of *Aethiopica*, is also addicted to this habit of testing people. By the sixteenth century, such trying gets associated with tragicomedy—a genre affined to trials, working through signs to disclose truths of action, relation and identity. Founded on the idea of *felix culpa*—'happier

---

[20] *The Merchant of Venice*, 2.2.1-92 (28-9).
[21] Homer, *The Odyssey*, trans. F.V. Rieu (Pengiun: Harmondsworth, 1955), 24.356.

much by [...] affliction made'—it licenses torment and trial.[22] When it is inscribed within a tragedy, it signals and positions the ambivalence of a particular generic impulse.

Cognitive plots are a hallmark of Shakespeare's plays, capitalising on the innate drama of uncertainty and disclosure. Following up on Lorna Hutson's work on circumstances and suspicion, Colin Burrow suggests that it was the contemporary legal 'processes of inference and conjecture' that theatrical audiences were interested in, and that Shakespeare's tragedies were 'dramas of knowledge' rather than 'dramas of emotion' (as Bradley would have it).[23] While I, too, have written on the productive uses of uncertainty and speculation in the theatre of the time, I propose that the cognitive drama was brought into direct dialogue with affective matter, and uncertainty was precisely deployed to raise questions about the ethics of emotion. Shakespeare's tool for this interrogation is a pushing of moments of generic artifice till they yield intimations of tragic subjectivities. While he uses tragicomic components to hone his idea of tragedy, his tragicomedies go on their own mimetic journey, using moments of alienating emplotment to put pressure on the mimesis that Guarini identifies but fails to flesh out.

'THE ART ITSELF IS NATURE': THE PARADOX OF TRAGICOMIC MIMESIS

When Iachimo plays a game of knowledge with Innogen, using hints and insinuations to plant doubts in her mind about her absent husband, and tightening of suspense with relish, the British princess explodes:

> You do seem to know
> Something of me, or what concerns me; pray you,
> Since doubting things go ill often hurts more
> Than to be sure they do—for certainties
> Either are past remedies; or timely knowing,
> The remedy then born—discover to me
> What both you spur and stop.

> (*Cymbeline*, 1.6.94-100)

Spurring and stopping are the Italian narrator-villain's stock in trade—manifest in his dealings with Posthumus too, and, most clearly, in the final scene of dilatory disclosure. But Innogen's interjection checks the play's complicity with the temptation of ingenious plotting, making it impossible for the audience to disregard its emotional cost, the

---

[22] On false trials in Renaissance drama, see Subha Mukherji, 'False trials in Shakespeare, Massinger and Ford', *Essays in Criticism* 56:3 (2006), 219–40; and 'False trials and the Impulse to Try in Shakespeare and his Contemporaries', in *Thinking With Shakespeare: Comparative and Interdisciplinary Essays*, ed. William Poole and Richard Scholar (London: Legenda, 2007), 53–72.

[23] 'Shakespearean Tragedy', 4. On the appeal of forensic drama, see Lorna Hutson, *The Invention of Suspicion: Law and Mimesis in Shakespeare and Renaissance Drama* (Oxford: Oxford University Press, 2007), and Subha Mukherji, *Law and Representation in Early Modern Drama* (Cambridge: Cambridge University Press, 2006).

experiential reality of what Guarini dismisses as mere 'danger'. Innogen wakes up in the Welsh forest and laments, in surreally anguished poetry, over what she thinks is her husband's headless body, while the audience titter to see that it is only his gross double, the very Cloten she has scorned to look on (4.2.293-334). If, like Geraldine James in Peter Hall's 1988 production, an actor plays the speech straight, the bizarre dissonance of this moment comes alive and makes the audience's titter an uncomfortable one. The 'rassomiglianza del terribile' on which the form turns, is a simulacrum only to the plot-maker; but to the characters affected, the terror is far from unreal: no wonder Guarini theorizes the 'fictive terror of someone else' as an affect of tragicomedy.[24] Nowhere are the implications more sharply highlighted than in the last scene of *Cymbeline*—itself an extended joke on over-explication. Posthumus' striking of Innogen dressed as a page with the words, 'There lie thy part' (5.6.228), usually triggers smug giggles in the audience who are in on the secret (as they are not in *The Winter's Tale*—which shifts the epistemic counters). It is a knowing, tragic-comic joke, which excises the affective reality of the gesture within the dramatic fiction as we savour our privileged knowledge that this is a boy playing the part of a girl playing the part of a boy: this recognition is what absorbs our wit. But after another five minutes of playing time, when the visual abjection of this misrecognition has faded as 'recognition' piles upon 'recognition', Innogen comes right back at Posthumus: 'Why did you throw your wedded lady from you? | Think that you are upon a rock; and now | Throw me again' (261-3).[25] The gutting emotional directness of her question is a rebuke to the tragicomic habit of dicing with danger, and to humour that feeds off such epistemic variance across the fourth wall. Posthumus' moving reply draws us wholly into the mimetic reality of the moment: 'Hang there like fruit, my soul, | Till the tree die' (263-4); it gives us a chance to experience recognition as felt reality, even as Posthumus re-cognizes. When, later, Posthumus (Leonatus), unable to 'make any collection' of the suddenly remembered oracle (432-4), challenges the soothsayer to 'show his skill in the construction', the soothsayer's laboriously 'apt construction' of 'the letter of the oracle' (445, 451) feels redundant, as its text has already been 'collected' and absorbed into the play's embodied language through the embrace: 'When as a lion's whelp shall, to himself unknown, without seeking find, and be embrac'd by a piece of tender air' (436-8). Earlier, when Pisanio presented Innogen with his plan to tuck her away and let Posthumus believe her dead, she had replied,

> Why, good fellow
> What shall I do the while? Where bide? How live?
> Or in my life what comfort, when I am
> Dead to my husband?
>
> (3.4.128-31

If Hermione had asked these questions, she could not have been turned into a 'meaner moveable' of Paulina's tragi-comic plot. In *The Winter's Tale*, Shakespeare points up the

---

[24] Guarini, *Il Verato ovvero difesa di quanto ha scritto M. Giason Denores di quanto ha egli ditto in un suo discorso delle tragicomedie, e delli pastorali* (Ferrara, 1588), in *Delle Opere del cavalier Battista Guarini* (Turin: UTET, 1971), 2:259.

[25] 'Recognition' is the Aristotelian criterion for a good plot identified by Guarini as being common to both tragedy and tragicomedy.

human cost of genre through Hermione's wrinkles, and maintains his own separateness from Paulina's plot-making. In *Cymbeline*, Innogen herself resists being assimilated into the romance plot, and transmutes all perception into a thing 'not imagined, felt' (4.2.309). From the hilarious longueur and orgy of artifice that is the final scene, presented tongue-in cheek as 'this fierce abridgement' (5.5.383), Innogen, like the play, gathers up the meaning of subjective emotional lives which refuse to be alienated in spite of the excesses of art.

And yet, Hazlitt was not entirely right when he called her 'the most artless' of all Shakespeare's women.[26] For Innogen is a bit of an image-maker herself. She 'would' fain-have said 'pretty things', 'set' a parting kiss 'betwixt two charming words', like a precious stone in the locket, freezing the moment of her parting from her husband into something exquisite, had it not been for her father's entry like 'the tyrannous breathing of the North' to shake the buds about to take shape out of imaginative indulgence (1.3.26-38). In describing what could not happen she almost writes a valedictory poem. Yet her subjunctives do not make her an aesthete, for she is articulating, even here, a sense of life; intuiting a hiatus between consciousness and its representations, the gap between the imagined valediction and the actual, inadequate parting. Posthumus' response to his dream also expresses a heightened 'sense of real things',[27] but it is arrived at through a feeling of *likeness* to actual experience. His awakening from his strange dream to find it true—'the action of my life is like it, which | I'll keep, if but for sympathy' (5.5.243-4)—nonetheless recalls and echoes Innogen's, after *her* dream—'The dream's here still: even when I wake it is | Without me, as within me' (4.2.308-9). An aesthetic complicatedness as well as a feeling of strangeness enter the sense of life rather than effecting estrangement, as real feelings rub shoulders with the artificial and the surreal: 'life's nonsense pierces us with strange relation', as Wallace Stevens says of 'supreme fiction'.[28] The stranger things get in this play, the truer they feel—while in *The Winter's Tale* life itself is made to feel so strange as to be a miracle.

Indeed, the wider, if peculiar, realism of the late romances has gone largely unnoticed. The inscribed art-object in *Winter's Tale*, Hermione's 'statue', turns out to be a lie, even as foregrounded artifice is overtaken by 'dear life'. It has to be comprehended, finally, through a domestic image—'If this be magic, let it be an art lawful as eating' (5.3.103, 110-11). In *Pericles*, Marina, presumed dead, is restored to her father like an apparition, as though by magic, yet really through human means—'mortally brought forth' (21.93). Pericles' queen Thaisa, 'supposèd dead and drowned' (22.57), is *almost* miraculously revived—'is not this strange'? 'most rare' (12.104)—and restored to Pericles in Diana's temple to the sound of music. But she, too, is recovered, no matter how ceremonially, with the warmth of a fire and the physician Cerimon's restoratives. Think once again of Ariel's song: it too is about a natural process, which appears to be magical because of its strangeness; a human body petrifying into pearls and coral is but an effect of the sea transforming matter into richer forms, but emblematic of the characteristic romance action of dying into life. Guarini's boldest claim for tragicomedy is its mimetic fidelity. But in laying down the rules, as it were, he ends up focusing on the art more than its relation to life. Shakespeare begins with the prescriptions, but then uses them as a lever to question the genre's relation to

---

[26] William Hazlitt, *The Round Table: The Characters of Shakespeare's Plays* (J. M. Dent: London, 1944), 180.
[27] John Keats, 'Sleep and Poetry', l. 157.
[28] Wallace Stevens, 'Notes Towards a Supreme Fiction', l. 71.

lived reality. His final tragicomedies are not what Florio in 1598 labelled the genre—'half a tragedie, and half a comedie' (*Worlde of Wordes*). The tragic and comic elements coupled in the early and middle plays transmute themselves into the compound that Guarini advocates, and not the double plots that he unfortunately uses as his examples. The 'problem plays', with their sharp, cerebral awareness of the limits and expenses of the comic form or of generic homogeneity, make us see through artifice. His late tragicomedies offer a knowing, yet all-containing vision of what life and art can do for each other, and thereby make us see, and feel, beyond artifice. Shakespeare's primary concern, here, remains with the nature of the theatrical experience, but always in relation to how we live, have lived and would like to relive our ordinary and extraordinary lives.

CURIOUS PERSPECTIVES

Tragedy and (tragi)comedy, then, become, for Shakespeare, counters that can be moved around and set off against each other, to explore the meaning of genre itself, and the scope of a sympathetic engagement between subjectivity and experience in the interrelation of art and life. Empathy and attuned response are key to his exploration the legitimacy of artifice. Yet his work is acutely perspectival, never losing sight of its own existence in aesthetic media, encompassing both body and language. I will end with three examples to indicate how he deploys dislocations of generic effects to point up the limits of empathy and the necessity of distance in our response both to grief and to art. This, in turn, generates an altogether different order of tragicomic devices that *place* extremity of grief, and mimetic art's attempt to respond with affective rather than aesthetic decorum.

In his earliest tragedy, *Titus*, Shakespeare opposes the horror of tonguelessness to the eloquence of poetry, as Marcus addresses his freshly ravished, muted, and maimed niece Lavinia in forty-six lines of rhetorically consummate, allusive, aestheticizing poetry (2.4.11-57). Titus' own response is a contrast—he relates to his daughter through identification and action, not through similes. Yet when, in his extreme sorrow, he explodes at Marcus for killing a fly, the temptation towards an eco-critical reading of an empathetic continuum between human and animal worlds is always checked, in performance, by the ludicrous disproportion of Titus' railing:

> MARCUS   Alas, my lord, I have but kill'd a fly.
> TITUS   'But'? How if that fly had a father and mother?
> How would he hang his slender gilded wings,
> And buzz lamenting doings in the air!
> Poor harmless fly,
> That, with his pretty buzzing melody,
> Came here to make us merry, and thou hast kill'd him.
>
> (3.2.59-65)

It is significant that Shakespeare's mistrust of indulgent, prettifying imagination is harnessed here to the reaction of an unquestionably grief-consumed character.

The same play offers the most theatrical glimpse of an alternative perspective when Aaron the Moor, recounting his evil deeds with amoral glee, pauses on a scene we have already witnessed: the heightened tragedy of Titus, Marcus, and Lucius competing over whose hand should be sent to the Emperor, followed closely by their being re-warded for Titus' hand with his sons' heads; followed in turn by ritual mourning and resolve to avenge (3.1.150-91; and 234 ff.). 'Prying' at the scene 'through the crevice of a hole', Aaron says, he 'almost broke [his] heart with extreme laughter' (5.1.113-14). The twinning of an extreme 'tragic' affect, heartbreak, with extreme laughter dislocates our perspective as we suddenly see the high-minded heroic ethic of the big boys of Rome from the view-point (literally) of a cultural outsider. This is as effective as Titus' own absurd laugher: 'Ha, ha, ha' (3.1.265). When Marcus remonstrates that laugher 'fits not with this hour'—recalling Guarini's dictum that laughter '[destroys]' 'the tragic form' (521)—Titus offers a radical rationale that sends up any residual notion of generic decorum: that he has 'not another tear to shed' (265-6).

In *Lucrece*, written around the same time as *Titus*, the raped Lucrece finds 'a sym-pathy of woes' in a tapestry depicting the siege of Troy—specifically, with the figure of Hecuba, who has 'so much grief and not a tongue'. Echoing Marcus' words to the dumb Lavinia, 'shall I speak for thee?' (*Titus*, 2.4. 33), Lucrece offers to 'tune' Hecuba's pain with her own 'lamenting tongue' (ll. 1464-5). Yet she is qualified to speak for Hecuba as Marcus is not for Lavinia. Identity of grief creates an extreme collaboration: 'She lends them words, and she their looks doth borrow' (l. 1498). But an uncritical identification is shown to have destructive results too—Lucrece ends up tearing the work apart, in her fit of 'passion' against the 'perjured' Sinon (instrumental in the massacre of Troy, and Hecuba's grief), 'comparing him to that unhappy guest | Whose deed hath made herself herself detest' (ll. 1565-6). In one sense, this is Lucrece refusing to play the game of art. But there is also something faintly ridiculous, even hysterical, about the enraged Lucrece—'she tears the senseless Sinon with her nails'. Even her own response, in its sudden shift, registers this:

> At last she smilingly with this gives o'er;
> 'Fool, fool', quoth she, 'his wounds will not be sore'.
>
> (ll. 1567-8)

The tapestry scene is an ambiguous comment on the relation between pain, its represen-tation and its reader. Do we have to be a Marcus in order for art to retain its status as art and for us to remain its consumers? Where, in the middle ground, do we find the right distance between tragic art and its interpreter, the tale and its teller?

SELECT BIBLIOGRAPHY

Burrow, Colin, 'What is a Shakespearean Tragedy?', in Claire McEachern, ed., *The Cambridge Companion to Shakespeare's Tragedy* (Cambridge: Cambridge University Press, 2013), 1–22.

Guarini, Giambattista, *A Compendium of Tragicomic Poetry*, in Allan Gilbert, *Literary Criticism: Plato to Dryden* (Detroit: Wayne State University Press, 1962), 504–33.

Guarini, Giambattista, *Il Verato ovvero difesa di quanto ha scritto M. Giason Denores di quanto ha egli ditto in un suo discorso delle tragicomedie, e delli pastorali* (Ferrara, 1588), in *Delle Opere del cavalier Battista Guarini* (Turin: UTET, 1971).

Jones, John, *Shakespeare at Work* (Oxford: Clarendon, 1995).

Magnusson, Lynn, 'A Play of Modals: Grammar and Potential Action in Early Shakespeare', *Shakespeare Survey* 62 (Cambridge: Cambridge University Press, Nov. 2009), 69–80.

Mukherji, Subha, 'False Trials and the Impulse to Try in Shakespeare and his Contemporaries', in *Thinking With Shakespeare: Comparative and Interdisciplinary Essays*, ed. William Poole and Richard Scholar (London: Legenda, 2007), 53–72.

Nuttall, A. D., 'The Stoic in Love', in *The Stoic in Love* (Savage, Maryland: Barnes & Noble, 1989), 56–67.

CHAPTER 18

QUEER TRAGEDY, OR TWO MEDITATIONS ON CAUSE

LEE EDELMAN AND MADHAVI MENON

1

In approaching the notion of queer tragedy, one should not begin with the supposition that Shakespeare's tragedies have a connection to queerness that his other works do not. The experience defined as 'Shakespeare' springs in no small part from the queerness he unveils in our efforts to construct a relational universe (socially, politically, romantically) through the medium of a language irreducible to the collective understandings that we tend to think of relation as allowing us to achieve. Such queerness should not be understood, then, in terms of 'sexual orientations' at odds with the reigning sexual norm, but more generally as the persistent undoings of relational legibility occasioned by the libidinal charge (whether positively or negatively inflected) with which enjoyment, the radical aim of the drive in its movement beyond the pleasure principle, occasions an encounter with ourselves as inseparable from what we or our culture would abject. Enjoyment, to put this another way, exposes the subject as always divided between the subject of desire (the subject who thinks it can articulate and pursue its pleasures and aims) and the subject of the drive (the subject in the grip of unconscious attachments propelling it to actions at odds with the desires it consciously avows and leading it to encounters with unpleasure, repetition, and compulsion). It follows that enjoyment will frequently entail an experience of anxiety, frustration, or pain as the subject approaches what it is driven to enjoy against, as it were, its desire—or against, at least, its conscious desire and in obedience to a far more inflexible attachment that defines the being of the subject as always in excess of its meaning and so in excess of anything *meant* by the pleasures in which it takes ready joy. Like the excess that prohibits language from resolving into the meaning it continues to promise, this queerness inhabits the madness let loose by the fairies of *A Midsummer Night's Dream* as much as it does the mania unleashed in *Hamlet* or *King Lear*.

But if comedy and tragedy alike engage the queerness of unbridled enjoyment, tragedy more fully acknowledges enjoyment's threat to sociality. Comedy mocks or marginalizes its figures of excess and abjection, punishing or redeeming them (or punishing *and* redeeming them) the better to affirm society's ability to incorporate their energy and revitalize the norm. Malvolio and Jaques may never fit into the order of social harmony but their externality to it gives it coherent shape. Tragedy, by contrast, reads such enjoyment as incompatible with social survival. It mounts the spectacle of enjoyment's threat to the logic of social relation and answers that threat of destruction with a destructiveness of its own. Recognizing the negativity of enjoyment as the ground, however negated, of all law, of all rational order, tragedy responds by performing the queerness that defines the law of its genre: the queerness of unleashing the law's negativity against the negativity of enjoyment in order to posit the law's positivity (its status as something *meant* to be) against enjoyment's undoing of meaning as the social order's ground. The law, in other words, can enjoy the fantasy of embodying what is *meant*, but only insofar as seems not to 'mean' the enjoyment it performs. To the extent that this locates enjoyment as the unconscious of the law, it might seem to make the tension between enjoyment and law, between queerness and order, the very cause of tragedy. But Shakespeare's tragedies take this one step further by exploring how queerness questions the concept of 'cause' itself.

Before approaching an account of *Othello* as a play that enacts and articulates the complex relations among tragedy, queerness, and cause, it might be useful to establish a larger context in which the question of causality can be situated. In Seminar 11, *The Four Fundamental Concepts of Psychoanalysis,* Jacques Lacan, the French psychoanalytic theorist, notes that the philosopher Immanuel Kant comes close to declaring 'cause' 'unanalysable' as a concept because of what Lacan, referring to Kant's use of the term, evokes as a 'gap' in its function.[1] Lacan has in mind what scientific notions of causality fail to account for: the framework or structure that shapes the logic with which we 'account' for cause. 'Cause,' he writes, 'is to be distinguished from that which is determinate in a chain, in other words the *law*' (*The Four Fundamental Concepts*, 22). Though referring, in the first instance, to laws like those of physics or biology ('the law of action and reaction' or the knowledge that 'miasmas are the cause of fever', to cite two examples offered up by Lacan), this positioning of cause in opposition to law will have serious consequences for the notion of law more broadly. It will establish from the outset the relation of cause to the violence of the *indeterminate* and thus to what resists determination within any signifying chain, which is to say, within any sequence of signifiers (such as words in a sentence) presumed to give access to signification. Central to Lacan's understanding of cause is its retroactive positing in order to construct an explanation for something that fails to make sense: 'in short, there is cause only in something that doesn't work' (ibid.). Thus, to take a pertinent example, a culture may look for the 'cause' of non-heterosexual orientations without feeling compelled to seek explanations for what it assumes as the norm.

This focus on what doesn't work as inextricable from the concept of cause speaks to Lacan's insistence on the 'gap' or 'hole' in the logical order, the order of law and of signification that he describes as the Symbolic. Situating 'the Freudian unconscious at that point, where, between cause and that which it affects, there is always something wrong' (ibid.), Lacan refutes the misconception that 'the unconscious determines neurosis,' maintaining instead that 'what the unconscious does is to show us the gap through which neurosis joins up with a real that may well not be determined' (ibid., translation modified). The

---

[1] Jacques Lacan, *The Four Fundamental Concepts of Psychoanalysis (Seminar 11)*, ed. Jacques-Alain Miller, trans. Alan Sheridan (New York: Norton, 1981), 21.

unconscious, in other words, indicates the hole in the order of reason or law. Such a hole or gap inheres in that order and brings it into association with the indeterminacy, the resistance to Symbolic meaning, that Lacan describes as the Real, by which he names what escapes every naming in a signifying chain and what, therefore, always registers only as a traumatizing disturbance of the order that reason and logic seem to sustain. In this sense the order of reason itself is structured by what it excludes so that, as Lacan will suggest in 'The Instance of the Letter, or Reason since Freud', the sense-making function never escapes the kernel of nonsense or madness that it also can never comprehend. Barbara Johnson sheds light on the relationship between such gaps and the concept of cause when, talking about what Herman Melville, in his novella *Billy Budd*, calls 'the deadly space between', she writes: 'The cognitive spaces marked out by these eclipses of meaning are important not because they mark the limits of interpretation but because they function as its cause.'[2] Here too causality functions not as a putative explanation for actions whose meaning may be unclear, but rather as the gap that calls forth explanations to dissimulate it in the first place.

In this sense the cause resists every effort to contain it in a signifier because the cause is itself the signifier's failure to name what eludes or exceeds it. As a gap in signification, then, the cause, as Lacan invokes it, opens onto something unaccomplished. Rather than suggesting potentiality, though, the prospect of something awaiting its eventual realization, its proper signifier or name, the cause denotes the site of an encounter with the inherent impossibility that haunts the signifying chain. In its relation to the unconscious, the cause unleashes a violent disturbance of the normative order of things that expresses itself in Lacan's own text by reference to abortion and the ghosts of those consigned to limbo as a result of it. 'It is part of the analyst's role,' Lacan writes, 'to be besieged—I mean *really*—by those in whom he has invoked this world of shades' (*The Four Fundamental Concepts*, 23). Like good Symbolic subjects, the second or third generation of analysts, according to Lacan, were intent on 'stitching up this gap' and so on keeping the traumatic encounter with those shades, with the Real, at bay. But for Lacan, however fraught it might be, the task of the analyst required encountering the gap of the cause, not evading it, even though to do so might have what he calls a 'harmful effect'. Perhaps it is not insignificant, then, that in the letter with which, at the end of his life, Lacan dissolved his school, he established, with the explicit understanding that it would only endure for a time, a para-school intended to exist through his mailbox and the post. The name he gave it? 'La Cause freudienne'.

All this suggests that the cause, for Lacan, to the extent that it pertains to the Real, operates like the figure of speech that rhetoricians call anacoluthon. This latter term designates uses of language that join two different syntactical structures across a gap in which meaning gets lost. Something in the signifying chain falls out; what follows in time doesn't follow in logic and the break can be read as enjoyment's intrusion into the order of what is meant. This essay may soon encounter such a disjunctive break itself as its first part gives way to the second across a divide that may rupture its sense. *Othello*, moreover, which will serve to exemplify queer tragedy as a function of the cause, includes several

---

[2] Barbara Johnson, *The Critical Difference: Essays in the Contemporary Rhetoric of Reading* (Baltimore: Johns Hopkins University Press, 1985), 94.

instances of anacoluthon that figure the queerness of such a division, of 'nature, erring from itself' (3.3.231).³ In fact, when Othello utters this phrase in response to the doubts about Desdemona that Iago has been encouraging, the latter responds immediately, interrupting Othello with an utterance that itself is interrupted by an instance of anacoluthon:

> Ay, there's the point! As—to be bold with you—
> Not to affect many proposèd matches
> Of her own clime, complexion, and degree,
> Whereto we see in all things nature tends—
> Foh! One may smell in such a will most rank,
> Foul disproportions, thoughts unnatural—

(3.3.232–7)

Appropriating Othello's words in order to fill them with a meaning of his own, Iago alleges Desdemona's deviation from the norm to which 'nature tends' in a syntax that deviates from its straightforward path with the dash that follows his reference to the natural tendency of 'all things'. Desdemona's failure to 'affect' the more appropriate 'matches' that were proposed, 'erring' instead by virtue of the desire she felt for Othello, is matched by Iago's failure to match the component parts of his syntax. Such 'disproportion,' such 'unnatural' tendencies, mark anacoluthon's relation to the queerness associated with cause: a queerness that overthrows logic and makes the putative cause the retroactive effect of its effects. That's what Emilia will explain to Desdemona when the latter, before the suggestion of her husband's jealousy, cries, 'Alas the day, I never gave him cause' (3.4.153). Dismissing such logic, Emilia responds: 'But jealous souls will not be answered so. | They are not ever jealous for the cause, | But jealous for they're jealous' (3.4.154–6).

That jealousy itself causes jealousy might seem merely tautological. But tautology here covers a lack: the Symbolic's inability to articulate the Real, the dimension whose pressure on the Subject divides it forever between truth and knowledge. Lacan positions the subject's truth over and against the scientific elaboration of what can be known. In the essay titled 'Science and Truth,' he figures that division with a metaphor drawn from printing: 'an inscription does not etch into the same side of the parchment when it comes from the printing-press of truth and when it comes from that of knowledge.' ⁴ But knowledge nonetheless rests on this division from the truth, where truth is to be understood as the gap of the Real as cause. 'Nothing ever gets spoken,' Lacan asserts, 'without leaning on the cause' (*Écrits*,734); for insofar as 'the unconscious is language' (ibid. 736), 'truth speaks' (ibid. 737). But this means, as he is quick to point out, that 'there is no … metalanguage,' no knowledge of language from the outside, 'no language … able to speak the truth about truth' (ibid. 737). Only the 'unconscious … tells the truth about truth' (ibid. 737) and it does so by way of the lack that disrupts the signifying chain.

Othello proliferates figures for this break between science or law and cause, the break that both expresses and constitutes the subject of enjoyment. Anacoluthon is one such figure; the sort of repetition Emilia produces in accounting for jealousy is another. Othello provides a powerful example of the latter before killing Desdemona, famously intoning

---

³ All references to *Othello* are from Michael Neill, ed., *The Oxford Shakespeare: Othello* (Oxford: Oxford University Press, 2006).

⁴ Jacques Lacan, *Écrits*, trans. Bruce Fink (New York: Norton, 2006), 734.

the words 'Put out the light, and then put out the light' (5.2.7), but that act of putting out the light, that undoing of enlightenment and reason, has been visible in the epileptic fits that constitute lapses of consciousness standing in for the effect that demands, and so causes, the production of some explanatory cause. Such fits speak to something that doesn't fit, syntactically, logically, lawfully, within the order of social relations and that can never comport with disciplines of knowledge or regulatory regimes. They stand, that is, for the queerness that Shakespeare's tragedies enact in their recurrent encounter with, to borrow Othello's phrase, 'nature, erring from itself'—which we might understand instead as the insistence of Shakespeare's lost cause.

2

What is tragedy? For Plato, tragedy is an essential ingredient in the education of the 'Philosopher Rulers,' one that needs to be recognized and celebrated in as pure a form as possible. To this end, Books 2 and 3 of The Republic criticize the current crop of poets for being too weak and encouraging excessive emotion, for actively ignoring the realm of pure reason which alone is conducive to producing the good. This criticism is couched under four major headings. First, tragedies are created by poets not through understanding or reason but by inspiration; second, poetry arouses emotions in a way that is not in accord with rationality; and third, poetry is ignorant and dangerous to the soul, since it produces the wrong emotions. His fourth criticism of art is exclusive to representational poetry or drama—he notes with disapproval that theatre creates many roles and encourages people to occupy different personas when 'a man cannot play many parts as well as he can one'.[5] Plato loved the poets of his time—Homer was a favourite—but he disliked what poetry and drama did to the audience; it made them scared of death and the afterlife, it encouraged belief in the pusillanimity of the gods, it did not offer a rational cause for its actions, and it modelled the performance of multiple selves. The inspiration that is clearly in excess of reason produces emotions that are not harnessed by the rational faculty. In the case of tragedy, the inappropriate emotions aroused in spectators are pity and fear when all that the philosophers should be learning are rationality and temperance. The experience of pity is pleasurable and *therefore* inappropriate. The education of future philosopher-kings needs to be undertaken more carefully.

Plato's objections to poetry thus pivot on the idea that poets do not compose within the bounds of reason. This lack of reason is to be guarded against since it creates sub-optimal emotions in the characters of narrative poetry and drama, and in turn encourages wrong emotions in the audience—'the thrill of terror [that plays] cause will make our guardians more nervous and less tough than they should be' (142). Even more, drama is so far removed from the real that it cannot be taken seriously. This Platonic Real—the realm of the unseen and therefore idealized Forms—is not the Lacanian Real of the trauma that shapes reality. Instead, Plato's Real has no truck with the imitations that invoke its name; Plato argues that poetry is ignorant about what it teaches since it has no access to the ideal,

---

[5] Plato, *The Republic*, trans. Desmond Lee, 2nd edn. (London: Penguin, 1987), 153.

and thus it encourages wrong emotions like fear and cowardice. A representational poet is 'like a portrait painter whose portraits bear no resemblance to their originals' (132). Poetry is a mimesis at two removes from the real—it imitates the object that is itself an imitation of an Ideal version of itself. Every degree of distance from the Ideal Form implies a recession also from the realm of rationality. Poetry panders to the irrational side of the human psyche, fleeing from temperance and causality, and therefore needs to be banned from the ideal *polis*:

> So if we are visited in our state by someone who has the skill to transform himself into all sorts of characters and represent all sorts of things, and he wants to show off himself and his poems to us, we shall treat him with all the reverence due to a priest and giver of rare pleasure, but shall tell him that he and his kind have no place in our city, their presence being forbidden by our code ... we shall for our own good employ story-tellers and poets who are severe rather than amusing, who portray the style of the good man and in their works abide by the principles we laid down for them. (157)

It is not poetry per se that is being banished from the state, then, but only poetry that proves harmful in its deviation from rationality and the Platonic 'code'. Such poetry and drama—Plato mentions both tragedy and comedy—imparts 'rare pleasure' and must be shunned precisely for causing that effect in us. The more we enjoy a play, the more it needs to be banned.

Plato's student, Aristotle, argues against such a masochistic understanding of pleasure by refuting the Platonic understanding of drama. In both his *Poetics* and *Nicomachean Ethics*, Aristotle counters Plato by insisting that poetry is a skill governed by rational rules. Poetry can be learned, and has rules comprehensible by reason. Even more, poetry represents universals; it may not have direct access to the Forms, but by presenting a poetic version of them, the poet presents what is unchanging in the realm of ethics and politics. Poetry presents the truth by focusing on what is universal rather than what is incidental or particular, thus laying down the ideal way of life for all regardless of circumstance or qualification. Aristotle's final intervention is to defend poetry from the charge of excessive and inappropriate emotion that Plato has levelled against it. He has already started doing this by asserting that poetry follows rational rules in its composition. But then he adds that poetry arouses the emotions in such a way as to increase our ability to control them. This *katharsis* is necessary for purging an excess of emotion and purifying us so that we can be more receptive to the universal lessons that poetry imparts. Despite defending poetry, however, Aristotle does not change the terms of the debate within which Plato has already condemned it. Instead of arguing that rationality might not be the best yardstick by which to measure poetry, Aristotle instead claims that poetry is rational rather than irrational, thus keeping intact the valorization of the idea of rationality. Good poetry, then, and poetry that conduces to the good in human beings, must be rational—Plato wants to dismiss poetry that is not rational (by which he means most poetry) while Aristotle wants to keep all poetry precisely because it is governed by rational rules.

Such an assumption about poetry—that is it is good only when governed by reason—zeroes in on causality as one of the indicators of the good. Thus Plato is able to conclude his defence of the purity and morality of the gods by saying that '*God is the cause, not of all things, but only of good*' (135). Causality is crucial to determining the difference between moral turpitude and fortitude; only good causes can be attributed for good effects, and even if the effects seem bad, so long as the cause is good the chain of actions must itself be deemed good. Indeed, this becomes one of Plato's central axioms:

> we must forbid anyone who writes a play about the sufferings of Niobe ... or the house of Pelops, or the Trojan war, or any similar topic, to say they are acts of god; or if he does he must produce the sort of interpretation we are now demanding, and say that god's acts were good and just, and that the sufferers were benefited by being punished. (135)

This formula for good poetry pivots crucially on the idea that (a) every action has an originary cause, and (b) the things for which the gods provide a cause are always good. God is the cause of all good things. Or to put it another way, that which is good always has a (good) cause. Might we extrapolate from this a third axiom: only that which has a cause can be considered good? The intertwining of causality and goodness is the hallmark in Plato of the very idea of the rational. Removing either causality or goodness from a play also removes it from the realm of the rational. Effects without causes, and bad effects in general that cannot be explained by good causes, do not conduce to good drama. The ideal ruler/philosopher/dramatist is the one who is rational, who shuns everything that is irrational, emotional, and not conducing to the good. Even though it seems clear that bad drama too can subscribe to the register of causality, for Plato, so long as there is causality, there is rationality. And so long as there is rationality, we are in the realm of the good.

Such a conviction automatically assumes that all tragedy must have a rational cause, or rather, that cause is the marker of the rational which in turn is the sign of a good tragedy. Aristotle, often known as the Philosopher of Cause, takes even further this emphasis on the importance of cause, specifically in relation to tragedy. For him, the fact of mimesis is itself the cause of pleasure—by means of imitation, the dramatist is able to convert painful experiences into pleasurable ones. Equally, the specific cause of tragedy in any individual play is *hamartia*, commonly translated as a 'tragic flaw' or an 'error in judgement'. For Aristotle, not only does the mimesis of drama cause pleasure in a tragedy, but also the painful events in a tragedy have a clear cause that can be located and then held up as a warning to the audience. Quite apart from his observations on cause in relation to Physics, Aristotle is clear about the importance of cause in relation to tragedy.[6]

Even more than Plato, who is not specific enough about the relation between cause and tragic drama, Aristotle lays out two fundamental principles for that link: first, there is a causal relation between mimesis and the pleasure of tragedy, and second, the cause of tragedy must be located squarely in the tragic flaw of an otherwise noble protagonist. Aristotle's definition of tragedy makes this link clear:

> Tragedy, then, is an imitation of an action that is serious, complete, and of a certain magnitude; in language embellished with each kind of artistic ornament, the several kinds being found in separate parts of the play; in the form of action, not of narrative; with incidents arousing pity and fear, wherewith to accomplish its catharsis of such emotions.[7]

---

[6] Aristotle argues that causality can be divided into four categories: the material cause, which is the material out of which a substance is made; the formal cause, which refers to the form or shape of an object; the efficient cause, or that which causes movement in an object; and the final cause, the completion or end at which an object arrives.

[7] http://www2.cnr.edu/home/bmcmanus/poetics.html.

Cause is thus crucial to a tragedy on two fronts. The first register of causality—mimesis—is definitionally central to drama; without mimesis there can be no drama. And the second cause—the tragic flaw or error in judgment—is necessary for Aristotle since he cannot theorize tragedy without such a cause. We must remember that contrary to Plato, Aristotle has pointed to the importance of the emotions that well up in response to good poetry. But despite his seeming endorsement of excessive emotion, he adds that they should be expressed only to be purged more effectively. The emphasis, then, is always on containing the repercussions of the non-rational sphere. As one of the most important members of this sphere, causality is a marker of the rationality towards which all drama—Platonic and Aristotelian—aspires. But what happens to a play that does not have or cannot present a cause in this second register? What happens to a play that does not ascribe causality to the flaws of its protagonists? Does it not qualify as a play? For both Plato and Aristotle, if cause maketh a tragedy, then a tragedy without cause doth not make a good drama.

Yet another way of stating the problem is to suggest that a lack of cause makes a tragedy queer. This is not to argue that flouting Platonic or Aristotelian rules is of necessity queer. If anything, the liberal sprinkling of man-boy love in several treatises by these philosophers might qualify *them* rather than their opponents as being queer. But if we think about queerness not only as being synonymous with the truth or otherwise of bodily desire, then queer tragedy points to that which in tragedy—all tragedy—is unsupportive of the classical prescriptions for good drama. If tragedy enacts horrific deeds but refuses to explain them (away), then that lack of an explanation is queer. The excess of deeds and the paucity of causes echoes what Jacques Lacan sees as the excess that always attaches to sexual desire. Even more, the text's inability or unwillingness to explain itself is not in the service of a greater good. Rather, by thwarting it, the text lays bare the scaffolding of our desire to have every effect explained by a cause. This is a scaffolding on which we all build our lives. The queerness of tragedy is that it shows us unbearable effects but it does not contain them in the cocoon of a cause. It does not explain and therefore control the overflow of emotion. Such an overflow is not only difficult (if pleasurable) to experience, but it also impossible to live with. Equally, because this excess is impossible to live with, the queerness of tragedy is the thing we avoid in order to be able to live.

'I never gave you cause' Let us take the case of cause in *Othello*. Immediately before murdering Desdemona, Othello enters the stage with the following speech:

> It is the cause, it is the cause, my soul;
> Let me not name it to you, you chaste stars!
> It is the cause. Yet I'll not shed her blood,
> Nor scar that whiter skin of hers than snow,
> And smooth as monumental alabaster.
> Yet she must die, else she'll betray more men.

> (5.2.1-6)

Given that this speech comes at the end of the play, Othello assumes that the audience knows whereof he speaks. This is why he is able to repeat 'cause' three times without specifying what it is; the speech assumes that we all know the referent of the 'it'. Othello assumes it which is why he does not spell it out; we assume it which is why for generations we have blamed Othello's jealousy as the cause of his downfall; the play assumes it which is why it leads us into Desdemona's murder with a triple announcement of causality.

But even as *Othello* might seem to be the perfect Aristotelian tragedy—complete with the tragic flaw in an otherwise noble protagonist—the play begins its end by bringing centre-stage the question of cause without specifying an answer to it. Indeed, even before Othello comes on stage to murder Desdemona, the play has made a persistent point of asking questions about causality and denying us answers. Instead, cause is presented as being retrospective: when Cassio has given her Desdemona's handkerchief to copy the work, Bianca exclaims, 'O, Cassio, whence came this? | This is some token from a newer friend. | To the felt absence now I feel a cause' (3.4.175-7). Or it is perplexing: Cassio, when he learns at the end of the play that Othello has colluded in the plan to murder him, says 'Dear general, I never gave you cause' (5.2.297). The text repeatedly tries to understand the cause of actions, the motive for passions, and the reason for disasters. And each time it comes up with nothing. Even so seemingly straightforward a plot device as the attack by the Turks early in the play is repeatedly removed from both cause and course—we are given conflicting reports about the number of their ships and the destination of their trajectory. Yet the more the Venetian senators are faced with this uncertainty, the more pompously they exclaim, "Tis certain, then' (1.3.44). This search for a certain cause, so prevalent in the play, is again thwarted at the end when Iago refuses to explain the cause of his actions: 'Demand me nothing: what you know, you know; | From this time forth I never will speak word' (5.2.301-2).

Indeed, Iago is the prime generator of absent causes in this play, especially when he tries to explain his animosity towards Othello ('I do hate him as I do hell pains', 1.1.153). First, in conversation with Roderigo, he refers to the fact of Cassio having been promoted to the rank of lieutenant over him; then he simply repeats to Roderigo: 'I have told thee often, and I re-tell thee again and again, I hate the Moor' (1.3.356-8). And then he lies about lying: 'I hate the Moor, | And it is thought abroad that 'twixt my sheets | He's done my office. I know not if 't be true | But I, for mere suspicion in that kind, | Will do as if for surety' (1.3.375-9). This situation of multiple causes is at odds with the one in Shakespeare's supposed source, Cinthio's *Gli Hecatommithi*, in which the Iago character lusts after Desdemona and his plan to bring down both the Moor and Desdemona stems from her rejection of his advances. In Cinthio, Iago has a cause and effect relation to desire—Desdemona spurns his desire and therefore he desires to have her dead. In Shakespeare's play, none of the causes adduced by Iago is the whole truth because in the play causality is hard to find.

In each of these instances, not knowing the cause—indeed, wondering if there ever can be a cause—is of paramount importance. So much so that even Iago's attempts at communicating the cause of his hatred of Othello have drawn flak from his critics, prime among them Samuel Taylor Coleridge. Commenting on the unclear relationship between (Iago's) cause and action, Coleridge says that Iago is Shakespeare's only presentation of 'utter monstrosity,' because it 'depends on the ... absence of causes'. But that in itself is insufficient reason to dislike Iago; rather he is to be disliked because he performs the 'motive-hunting of motiveless malignity ... [i]n itself fiendish'.[8] Instead of faulting Iago for *being* motivelessly malignant (as is commonly understood), Coleridge blames him *for* hunting after motives, for seeking causes where none might exist; in other words, for not sufficiently accepting the motivelessness of his malignity. According to Coleridge, Iago's malignity

---

[8] Sylvan Barnet, 'Coleridge on Shakespeare's Villains', *Shakespeare Quarterly* 7:1 (Winter 1956), 9–20 (19).

cannot be explained and it cannot be contained by a cause. Iago should embrace motive-less malignity, not look to cure it, because his particular brand of malignity can only ever *be* motiveless.

Othello thus ends with causeless questions that have remained unanswered through-out the play: why does Iago hate Othello? Why does Othello believe Iago's lies? Why does Desdemona allow herself to be killed? Why would Iago want Desdemona dead? Why does Emilia desire to please Iago despite disliking him intensely? Why does Iago hate Othello so much? The cause has vanished in *Othello*, not because characters do not ascribe causes to their actions, but because the play does not support those ascriptions. Or the text comes up with so many causes that no single one can be considered originary. The final scene in *Othello* is agonizing because the play repeatedly refuses to give us a cause for it: the cause of the final scene's agony is the causelessness of the final scene. Or rather, the final scene presents a queer cause that removes causality from the realm of ontological certainty—a progenitor that explains its offspring—or logical explanation—if *x*, then *y*—and propels us instead into an excess that is queer.

Too many causes, then, and not a single sufficient one. We are convinced that Othello's jealousy is his tragic flaw, the cause that leads to the effect that is the murder of Desdemona. But what causes that jealousy? What makes him believe Iago? Iago lies to Othello because he wants revenge, but why does he want revenge? Desdemona sees that Othello is jealous, but why does she do nothing to protect herself from the force of his fury? Every one of these questions calls forth multiple causes—patriarchy, obedience, ambition, love—but the fact remains that each of them points back to another question about cause rather than forward to the reason for an effect. Desdemona and Othello's desire for each other—coded from the very beginning as overstepping the bounds of class and race—marks the entire text as being excessive. This excessiveness lacks causality; the tragedy of *Othello* is queer because it removes itself from the realm of the causal. We know as little about why Desdemona desires Othello as we do about why Othello kills Desdemona. Several causes are adduced for both effects, but none of them is definitive. Desire instead introduces a sense of sense-lessness into the play; it resolutely refuses to satisfy Aristotle's requirement for tragedy. Yet we would much rather *presume* a cause that can explain things rather than acknowledge a lack of causality. This is why Othello can mention 'cause' three times with-out elaborating upon it, and also why in the final scene, the audience thinks it *knows* the cause—surely something that has been repeated thrice must have some foundation? But what we know only is our desire for a cause of desire. What is the cause is the inevitable question we ask of a tragedy. Yet it is also unanswerable, and that is what makes tragedy *tragic*. The cause of tragedy is that it does not have a cause. Yet it is to avoid this causeless-ness that we subscribe to the inevitability of cause—Othello *must* have a fatal flaw that makes him murder Desdemona. If not, then how will we keep at bay the Othello in us all?

Shakespeare warns us against this desire for security in several of his tragedies. In *Macbeth*, for instance, what kills Macbeth is not only Macduff, but rather Macbeth's own desire for complete control over events—'His hopes 'bove wisdom, grace and fear: | And you all know, security | Is mortals' chiefest enemy' (3.5.31-3).[9] And even in the face of impossible

---

[9] All references to plays other than *Othello* are from Stephen Greenblatt, et al., eds. *The Norton Shakespeare* based on the Oxford Edition (New York: W. W. Norton, 1997); quotations from *King Lear* are from the Folio *Tragedy of King Lear*.

tragedy, Shakespeare underscores the impossibility of cause. *King Lear* is perhaps the most relentless example of this impossibility; everything that can go wrong, does, and then it goes wrong some more. Nothing can explain Lear's misery in the play; at the very end his youngest daughter too is dead and he voices perhaps the most poignant statement about non-causality—'And my poor fool is hang'd! No, no, no life! | Why should a dog, a horse, a rat, have life, | And thou no breath at all? Thou'lt come no more, | Never, never, never, never, never' (5.3.304-7). Why indeed?

Cause has a rich history in *King Lear* inasmuch as it does what it is best at doing—frustrating the demand for an explanation to which it has itself given rise. Interestingly, this rich vein of causality is mined fully only after Act 3, once madness and chaos have set in and both the text and its protagonist cast about for answers and explanations. 'Is there any cause in nature that makes these hard-hearts?' (3.6.32), asks Lear. Like all the other questions about cause, this one too does not elicit an answer; indeed, Lear does not even pause for one. The unremitting tragedy of *Lear* lies not in its inability to provide us with hope or rationality or plausibility. Rather, it insists in its lack of interest in doing so. The excessiveness of despair in the play is what makes it a queer tragedy; it is a despair that the play embraces without trying to explain away.

Stephen Greenblatt implies that we can see in *Lear* the tragedy of the political as such, the tragedy that obliged us to confront injustice without the possibility of 'striking a blow for a different, more ethically adequate political system' (*NYRB*, letter, 31 May 2007). Such a tragedy remains bound up with the insistence of enjoyment as figured by the father. No relation to that father, whether embodied in Lear or in the tyrant who dominates the primal horde, can escape the stain of enjoyment and therefore the father's obscenity, like enjoyment itself, can neither be renounced, passed on to another, or destroyed. It drives social relations in excess of any recognized reason or cause. Lear, so fatally invested in quantification and rational measurement, encounters the fictionality of the causal determinations he values so highly. Confronting Goneril's limitation of his retinue, he calls down on her the curse by which he feels afflicted himself, praying that whatever child she produce be 'a thwart disnatured torment to her ... That she may feel | How sharper than a serpent's tooth it is | To have a thankless child' (1.4.245, 250-2). The 'thwart,' that is, the perverse or the queer, would then be the effect of her own perversion in thwarting her father's will and occasion in her the tears Lear will shed in the face of the arbitrary, irrational conjunction of power and enjoyment. Anticipating Gloucester's fate, which serves as the occasion for Greenblatt's reading, Lear cries out, 'Old fond eyes, | Beweep this cause again, I'll pluck ye out, | And cast you, with the waters that you lose, | To temper clay' (1.4.264-7). When he finds that Regan is no more willing to accommodate his own enjoyment than Goneril, he moves beyond beweeping 'this cause' insisting that though he 'has full cause of weeping,' his 'heart | Shall break into a hundred thousand flaws | Or ere I'll weep' (2.2.449-50). Cause in these cases signifies Lear's sense that his demands and his outrage are warranted; he constantly appeals to a higher power to perceive the injustice in his treatment by others, if not in his treatment of them. Later, however, in losing his reason Lear will discover that reason, like cause, was always already lost; he has already maintained that rationality cannot explain his need, or indeed, need itself ('O, reason not the need', 2.2.430). This most stentorian of tragic figures now seeks to find out, from one disguised as a fool, 'What is the cause of thunder' (3.4.138). But the answer proposed by the play has nothing to do with a knowledge of science. Thunder, like all explosions of power, expresses the senselessness of enjoyment;

in Gloucester's well-known words, 'As flies to wanton boys, are we to th' gods. | They kill us for their sport' (4.1.37–8). Only Cordelia, knowingly or not, can speak the truth. When Lear acknowledges, near the end of the play, that she, unlike her sisters, has 'some cause' to do him wrong, she mirrors the negativity of her refusal to measure her love against promise of land by murmuring in response the words that resonate beyond her intention: 'No cause, no cause' (4.6.69).

Like *King Lear*, *Othello* suggests its tragedy has multiple causes, but none of them is explanatory. Indeed, the queerness of this excess undermines the rationality sought by causality. Far from allowing for a healthy purge of emotions, Shakespearean tragedy seems to wallow in the inescapability of the tragic. It disrupts the causal explanation demanded of tragedies, and gives us instead a plethora of questions—too many—without answers. As Kenneth Burke points out in his brilliant essay on *Othello* and the idea of catharsis, 'The Greek word *hubris*, often used to designate the hero's "tragic flaw", is in many contexts translated [as] "excess".'[10]

What makes this excess queer? *Hubris*, that which is supposed to identify the cause of tragedy by locating a flaw in its protagonist, simultaneously and always exists in excess of that supposition. We *want* to find a scapegoat, we *want* to pinpoint a flaw, we *want* to find a cause. But in the grip of that desire to contain, we can no longer control the course of the text. Instead we are overwhelmed by a queerness that threatens to undo Aristotle's prescription for the good of the social order. By refusing to blame his heroes, and by refusing to allow his villains explanations for their motives; by limning the contours of a dangerous desire, and by sketching the manifold effects of unleashing it onto the world of his plays, Shakespeare theorizes the queerness that makes tragic villains of us all. It is *we* who would murder and bribe and stab and steal; it is *our* lives that are tragic inasmuch as they are drenched in an excess that we try to control. It is we who resist tragedy, then, and we do that by looking for and identifying a cause (Burke would say a scapegoat) that can be localized in the play and preferably in the person of one of its characters. The tragedy of excess is so intense that it needs to be recuperated as a play abiding by the strict rules of aesthetic composition. It is testimony to the terrifying reach of a queer excess that we make every attempt to steer clear of its ambit.

Not only does this queerness resist the imperative to work for the collective good of society—it does not purge, it does not allow us to scapegoat someone else's flaw—but it also places itself firmly in the realm of tragedy. *Othello*, like *King Lear*, *Hamlet*, and *Macbeth*, deals with a desire that turns the social order upside down. Kings get murdered, women grow beards, daughters turn unnatural, sons are bastards, mothers are incestuous, white women turn to black. We might not describe any of these plays as a tragedy *about* queerness but every one of them is a queer tragedy. Each of them is unable to explain away the tragic effects of desire because none of them can pinpoint the cause. From regicide to possible infanticide, murder, incest, and madness, queer tragedy names the impossibility of escaping from the effects of excess. No longer can we blame the tragic flaw of an otherwise noble hero, no longer are we able to distinguish hero from villain (is Macbeth a villain? Why does the villainous Iago get the best lines in his play?), no longer are we able

---

[10] Kenneth Burke, '*Othello*: An Essay to Illustrate a Method', *The Hudson Review* 4:2 (Summer 1951), 165–203 (199).

to predict the course taken by a cause-less desire. And when I say 'we' cannot do any of this, I mean that the text resists our most valiant efforts to do them. Queer tragedy does not describe a tragedy that is queer. It points instead to an excess in a tragedy that cannot be recuperated by a reading. Tragedy is queer not only because it ends badly (a more conventional understanding of tragedy) but also because it resists prescriptions for the good, including the good that will result from limiting effect to cause. Queer tragedy is tragedy without cause, a world without end or explanation.

Select Bibliography

Barnet, Sylvan, 'Coleridge on Shakespeare's Villains', *Shakespeare Quarterly* 7:1 (Winter 1956), 9–20.

Benjamin, Walter, *The Origin of German Tragic Drama*, trans. John Osborne (London: Verso, 1985).

Burke, Kenneth, '*Othello*: An Essay to Illustrate a Method', *The Hudson Review* 4:2 (Summer 1951), 165–203.

Dollimore, Jonathan, *Radical Tragedy: Religion, Ideology and Power in the Drama of Shakespeare and his Contemporaries*, (New York: Palgrave Macmillan, 2010).

Drakakis, John and Naomi Liebler, eds., *Tragedy* (New York: Routledge, 2013).

Edelman, Lee, *No Future: Queer Theory and the Death Drive* (Durham: Duke UniversityPress, 2004).

Greenblatt, Stephen, et al., eds., *The Norton Shakespeare* based on the Oxford Edition (New York: W. W. Norton, 1997).

Johnson, Barbara, *The Critical Difference: Essays in the Contemporary Rhetoric of Reading* (Baltimore: Johns Hopkins University Press, 1985).

Lacan, Jacques, *The Four Fundamental Concepts of Psychoanalysis (Seminar 11)*, ed. Jacques-Alain Miller, trans. Alan Sheridan (New York: Norton, 1981).

Lacan, Jacques, *Écrits*, trans. Bruce Fink (New York: Norton, 2006).

Neill, Michael, ed. *The Oxford Shakespeare: Othello* (Oxford: Oxford University Press, 2006).

Plato, *The Republic*, trans. Desmond Lee, 2nd edn. (London: Penguin, 1987).

Schmitt, Carl, *Hamlet or Hecuba: The Intrusion of Time into the Play*, trans. David Pan and Jennifer R. Rust (New York: Telos, 2009).

PART II

TEXTUAL ISSUES

CHAPTER 19

···

AUTHORIAL REVISION
IN THE TRAGEDIES

···

PAUL WERSTINE

IN 1987 Gary Taylor wrote that 'although all previous editions have been based on the unexamined belief that Shakespeare did *not* revise his work, all future editions should be, and I believe will be, based on the recognition that he habitually did'.[1] More recent writing, though, has called attention to the long history of editorial consideration of the possibility of Shakespearean revision of the tragedies. For example, Jonathan Bate, co-editor with Eric Rasmussen of the 2007 *RSC Shakespeare: Complete Works*,[2] notes the comments on Shakespearean revision by a number of editors—Charles Knight, Charlotte Porter, and Helen A. Clarke—who, like Taylor, favour the Folio texts of *King Lear, Hamlet,* and *Othello* over the earlier quartos.[3] Evidence of a great deal more editorial consideration of revision lies unregarded in the pages of H. H. Furness's New Variorum editions of *Hamlet, Lear, Romeo and Juliet,* and *Othello*.[4] More recent arguments for Shakespeare's revision sometimes resemble and sometimes differ from the arguments collected in the Furness variorum editions; some of these novel recent arguments embed the hypothesis of revision in inferentially constructed authorial manuscripts, and others go even further in an attempt to ground dramatists' allegedly habitual revisions of their plays on surviving play manuscripts. Whether from the eighteenth, nineteenth, late twentieth, or early twenty-first century, such arguments have largely failed to stand up to scrutiny. The sheer volume and the bewildering variety of difference between Quarto and Folio versions of some of the tragedies presents an enduring challenge to editors that is unlikely to be resolved any time soon. Nonetheless, future examination of the revision hypothesis has a vast field to survey as it looks to a long past when belief in Shakespeare's revising of his plays flourished.

---

[1] Gary Taylor, 'Revising Shakespeare', *TEXT: Transactions of the Society for Textual Scholarship* 3 (1987), 303.

[2] Jonathan Bate and Eric Rasmussen, eds., *The RSC Shakespeare: Complete Works* (New York: Modern Library, 2007).

[3] 'The Case for the Folio' www.modernlibrary.com/files/2010/09/TheCaseForTheFolio.pdf.

[4] Horace Howard Furness, ed., *Hamlet*, A New Variorum Edition of Shakespeare, 2 vols. (Philadelphia: Lippincott, 1877); *King Lear*, 1880; *Romeo and Juliet*, 1871; *Othello*, 1886.

Attention to the possibility of authorial revision as the source of at least some of the difference between early printed texts is practically coeval with the Shakespeare editorial tradition. The first editor who tried to distinguish between Shakespeare's revision and others' interference is just the second Shakespeare editor whose name we know—Alexander Pope, in his 1725 edition. Pope had copies of the 1597 and 1599 Quarto printings of *Romeo and Juliet*, the 1597 text being only about two-thirds the length of the 1599 one, which serves as the basis of almost all subsequent texts. At first Pope seems to reject authorial revision as a possible cause of the difference between printings, the plot of the play not varying much from the one to the other, but the dialogue differing greatly: 'in the old editions of *Romeo and Juliet* there is no hint of a great number of the mean conceits and ribaldries now to be found therein'. He suggests that these 'had been added ... by the actors, or had [been] stolen from their mouths into the written parts'.[5] Nevertheless, no sooner does he start to edit the play but he re-examines his belief that it was the actors and not Shakespeare who added to the 1597 text. On the third page of his *Romeo and Juliet* edition, commenting on the beginning of what is now 1.1, Pope writes *'Much of this Scene is added since the first edition; but probably by* Shakespear, *since we find it in that of the year* 1599'.[6] Thus Pope, like so many editors after him, as we shall see, is divided against himself in speculating about the agency behind the variants he finds in the early printed texts and sets himself the Herculean task of distinguishing what he judges to be authorial revision from what he consigns to theatrical interpolation and adaptation.

A great many of Pope's eighteenth- and nineteenth-century editorial successors were more comfortable than he in the belief that variants between the two earliest printed texts of *Romeo and Juliet* arise exclusively from Shakespeare's revision of his earlier work. Although most editions of the play preserve in full only the later and fuller printed version, George Steevens provides two texts, the 1597 and the 1609 (a reprint of the 1599).[7] His explanation for doing so takes for granted that Shakespeare alone is responsible for both versions:

> Of some [plays] I have printed more than one copy; as there are many persons, who not contented with the possession of a finished picture of some great master, are desirous to procure the first sketch that was made for it, that they may have the pleasure of tracing the progress of the artist from the first light colouring to the finishing stroke. To such the earlier [version] of ... ROMEO AND JULIET, will, I apprehend, not be unwelcome; since in [this] we may discern as much as will be found in the hasty outlines of the pencil, with a fair prospect of that perfection to which He brought every performance He took the pains to retouch.[8]

Steevens was a prolific editor of Shakespeare, publishing (often in collaboration first with Samuel Johnson and then with Isaac Reed) four variorum editions of 1773, 1778, 1785, and 1793; he generously lards his commentary on *Romeo and Juliet* with extensive quotation from the 1597 text and with invitations to his readers to compare them to their counterparts in the fuller text so as to experience Shakespeare as reviser.

---

[5] Alexander Pope, ed., *The Works of Shakespear*, 6 vols. (London, 1725), 1: xvi.
[6] Ibid., 6: 247.
[7] George Steevens, ed., *Twenty of the Plays of Shakespeare*, 4 vols. (London, 1766), 4: sigs. A1-M3.
[8] Ibid., 1: 7.

Steevens was followed in this belief at least to some extent even by the great Edmond Malone, who calls the 1597 *Romeo* text a 'sketch', although an 'imperfect' one.[9] Also in line with Steevens was Charles Knight, a Shakespeare editor seven times over from the 1830s to the 1870s, whose editions were often reprinted. For Knight, 'the [printer's] copy, both of the [1597] first edition and the [1599] second, was derived from [Shakespeare]', and Knight delights in what he takes to be Shakespeare's 'exceeding judgment [and] marvellous tact' in transforming one into the other.[10] Following Steevens and Knight were Henry Hudson (with editions in the 1850s, the 1870s, and the 1880s), Howard Staunton (who edited his Shakespeare in 1858-60), Richard Grant White (whose editions of 1857-66 and 1883 argue that Shakespeare collaborated on the 1597 text), James Orchard Halliwell-Phillipps (editor of a 1853-65 Shakespeare), and Alexander Dyce (in his editions of 1857, 1864-7, and 1875-6).[11] These editors and their revision theory dominate the nineteenth century every bit as much as Steevens and Malone command the later eighteenth century. Resistance to the revision narrative was left to John Payne Collier in his editions of 1842-4, 1858, and 1875-8, and to the influential editors of the Cambridge Edition (1863-6), William George Clark and William Aldis Wright.[12] Worthy of note, though, is the gentleness of Collier's rejection of the revision hypothesis—a rejection that does not even wholly reject the theory: 'We do not of course go the length of contending that Shakespeare did not alter and improve the play, subsequent to its earliest production on the stage, but merely that the quarto, 1597, does not contain the tragedy as it was originally represented'.[13]

When a previously unknown 1603 quarto of *Hamlet*, the earliest printing of any version of that play, came to light in 1823, it became a another magnet for editors of the revisionist persuasion. It is little more than half the length of the familiar text, and some of the characters have different names, Polonius appearing as Corambis and Reynaldo as Montano. According to Thomas Caldecott, editor of an 1832 *Hamlet*, this 1603 Quarto supplies 'the first conception, and comparatively feeble expression of a great mind'.[14] Knight's bardolatry is again on display as he glories, during what he calls 'a careful study of this original edition ... as a sketch of the perfect *Hamlet*', in 'the opportunity which [the 1603 Quarto] affords of studying the growth, not only of the great poet's command over language,—not only his dramatic skill.—but of the higher qualities of his intellect,—his profound philosophy, his wonderful penetration into what is most hidden and obscure in men's characters and motives'.[15] Knight in his turn was followed by Staunton and Dyce, as well as by the German editor Nicolas Deilus,[16] with editions of 1854-61, 1864, and 1872. However, Knight's followers were rather more inclined than he to allow for the operation of extra-Shakespearean agency in the production of the 1603 Quarto and for considerable distortion of Shakespeare's alleged early draft as a consequence. Once again opposition to such accounts of revision was at first led by Collier, who was later seconded by others, including White and Clark and Wright.[17]

Belief in the 1597 text of *Romeo and Juliet* and the 1603 of *Hamlet* as the basis of Shakespeare's revisions was still going strong early in the twentieth century during the

[9] Edmond Malone and James Boswell, eds., *The Plays and Poems*, 21 vols. (London, 1821), 1: 207 n.

[10] Furness, ed., *Romeo and Juliet*, 1871, 416.   [11] Ibid., 417-22.   [12] Ibid., 416-17, 422-3.

[13] John Payne Collier, ed., *The Works of Shakespeare*, 8 vols. (London, 1842-4), 6: 368.

[14] Furness, ed. *Hamlet*, 1877, 2: 14.   [15] Ibid., 2: 14-15.   [16] Ibid., 2: 21-3.

[17] Ibid., 2:24-5, 26-33.

rise of the New Bibliography, as is evident in the narrative of the genesis of these texts elaborated by the two New Bibliographers, A. W. Pollard and J. Dover Wilson, the latter soon to be editor of the radically innovative and controversial New Shakespeare edition published by Cambridge University Press. According to Pollard and Wilson, versions of both *Hamlet* and *Romeo* already had a place in the repertory of the Lord Chamberlain's company before Shakespeare turned to their subjects. Shakespeare began revising these pre-existing plays on an occasion not long before some of his fellow actors were about to leave London to tour in the provinces in 1593. One of the plays performed in the course of the tour was an abridged version of what *Romeo and Juliet* had become after Shakespeare had begun to overhaul it, but before he had progressed to the end of what is now the second act. Hence the much closer verbal resemblance of most of the first two acts in the 1597 Quarto to their counterparts in the 1599 Quarto than of the last three acts of the two Quartos; hence also what appear, when it is compared with 1599 version, to be cuts in the 1597 edition. Once the actors came back to London, Shakespeare had finished his revision, much superior to what these actors had been performing, and, with their text now of so little value, one of them made a futile attempt to bring it more in line with the Shakespeare play, relying on memory of 1596 performances, and submitted what he had concocted to a stationer to be published.[18] Also, according to Wilson, in the early 1590s Shakespeare had revised the first act of *Hamlet* but had got no farther into the second than the verbal report of Valtemand and Cornelius to Claudius (2.2.60-79). After abridgement of this version of *Hamlet*, followed by its subsequent alteration in the light of Shakespeare's later revisions, this play too got into print in 1603. Again Wilson's story explains why the early part of the play is sometimes (but not always) so close in its language to that of the fuller version published later, but his account, just like the account of *Romeo and Juliet* that he and Pollard dreamed up, has nothing more to recommend it, conjured as it is out of thin air.[19]

Meanwhile, though, the New Bibliography was paying comparatively less attention to authorial revision and ever greater attention to the difference that might be made to texts in the course of their transmission into print. (Of course, attention to extra-authorial agency had been anticipated by eighteenth- and nineteenth-century editors opposing the authorial-revision hypothesis.) As the twentieth century wore on, actors' incomplete and inaccurate memorial reconstruction of Shakespeare's single writings of both *Romeo and Juliet* (as published in 1599) and *Hamlet* (as published in 1604-5 and again in 1623) would come to be the prevailing explanations for the origins of the 1597 *Romeo and Juliet* and the 1603 *Hamlet*.[20] Then in turn memorial reconstruction would itself come under skeptical scrutiny, so that it would be concluded that such imagined reconstruction by actors could give no convincing demonstration whatsoever of how the 1597 *Romeo and Juliet* came to be, and, while impossible to dismiss altogether in

---

[18] J. Dover Wilson and A. W. Pollard, 'The "Stolne and Surreptitious" Shakespearian Texts: *Romeo and Juliet*, 1597', *TLS*, 14 August 1919, 434.

[19] J. Dover Wilson, 'The Copy for "Hamlet," 1603' and 'The "Hamlet" Transcript, 1593', *The Library*, 3rd ser., 35 and 36 (July and October, 1918), 151–85, 217–47.

[20] W. W. Greg, *The Shakespeare First Folio: Its Bibliographical and Textual History* (Oxford: Clarendon Press, 1955), 225–8, 299–307.

connection with the 1603 *Hamlet*, such reconstruction could not account for the origin of very much of it.[21]

Nonetheless, it has become clear that the 1597 *Romeo* and 1603 *Hamlet* did not anticipate the fuller versions, but instead derived somehow from them. The derivative nature of the 1597 *Romeo* is evident, for example, in its faulty reproduction of Capulet's farewell to the maskers, to whom he has been so faultlessly courteous, but whom he suddenly selfishly blames for keeping him from his bed by their not knowing when to leave:

> Nay gentlemen prepare not to be gone,
> We haue a trifling foolish banquet towards.
>   *They whisper in his eare.*
> I pray you let me intreat you. Is it so?
> Well then *I* thanke you honest Gentlemen,
> I promise you but for your company,
> I would haue bin a bed an houre agoe:
> Light to my chamber hoe.
>
>   (sig. C4ʳ)

In the 1599 version, Capulet exhibits no comparable churlishness:

> Nay gentlemen prepare not to be gone,
> We haue a trifling foolish banquet towards:
> Is it ene so? why then I thanke you all.
> I thanke you honest gentlemen, good night:
> More torches here, come on, then lets to bed.
> Ah sirrah, by my faie it waxes late,
> Ile to my rest.
>
>   (sig. C4ᵛ, 1.5.120–6)

Here the 1597 text has assimilated this passage from 1.5 with a passage early in 3.4 in which Capulet is trying to get away from Paris after that persistent suitor has intruded on the Capulets when they are grieving the loss of Tybalt, thus making Capulet's impatience with guests explicable. There in the 1599 text Capulet tells Paris "I promise you, but for your companie, | I would haue bene a bed an houre ago" (sig. H2, 3.4.6–7)—the very lines that 1597 inappropriately gives Capulet in 1.5. Yet the presence of these lines in 1.5 of 1597 testifies to their existence in the script that lies behind the 1599 Quarto and therefore to the existence of that version prior to the construction of the 1597 text, which omits the lines in question from its 3.4, where it fails to complete Capulet's speech.

In an analogous way, the 1603 *Hamlet* also betrays its derivation from the fuller text when suddenly, upon the entrance of particular characters early in the play, its dialogue swells to virtually replicate complete speeches from the later version, even though before the entrances and after the exits of these characters, the 1603 text remains a shrunken representation of the play as we know it. For example, before the entrance of the ambassadors Valtemand and Cornelius in 1.2, 1603 has nothing of the first two dozen or so lines of the scene (1.2.1–26), but when the ambassadors enter, then the dialogue swells to nearly

---

[21] Laurie Maguire, *Shakespearean Suspect Texts: The 'Bad' Quartos and Their Contexts* (Cambridge University Press, 1996), 256, 302; Paul Werstine, 'A Century of "Bad" Quartos', *Shakespeare Quarterly* 50:3 (Fall, 1999), 317–23, 326–7.

the size of that in the fuller text, and there is a high level of verbal resemblance between 1603, on the one hand, and the 1604-5/1623 text, on the other (1.2.27-42). With the exit of the ambassadors (1.2.41.0), the 1603 dialogue shrinks to half the size of its counterparts'; the verbal resemblance between the texts also diminishes (1.2.43-159). However, with the entrance of Marcellus and his companions later in the scene, the 1603 text again assumes the size of the later texts, its words now closely matching theirs (1.2.16-257). Such evidence is used to support the theory of memorial construction of 1603 by actors playing Marcellus and Valtemand in the fuller version, and while there is merit to this argument, the theory cannot be extended beyond the early part of the play as an account of the genesis of 1603. Nonetheless, the appearance in 1603 of parts of the fuller version of the play that will later be printed demonstrates that this fuller version was already in existence by the time the 1603 text was created, indicating that the latter must derive from, rather than predate the fuller version. Authorial revision is therefore beside the point when the 1603 *Hamlet* and the 1597 *Romeo and Juliet* are in question. The idea of revision can be revived only by those with an implicit faith, as strong as the nineteenth-century Charles Knight's, that the only person who could make a difference between printed texts of Shakespeare was Shakespeare: 'The only canonizer and constituter of Shakespeare's texts, in all their infinitely revisable variety, is Shakespeare himself.'[22] Stanley Wells and Gary Taylor, principal editors of the 1986 Oxford University Press *William Shakespeare: The Complete Works*, which did so much to bring the revision hypothesis back to the notice of Shakespeareans, had no truck with the notions that the 1597 *Romeo* and 1603 *Hamlet* provide us with Shakespeare's first versions of these plays.

Rather more challenging to advocates for revision and their opponents are the variations among printings of the longer versions of the tragedies *Hamlet* (1604-5 and 1623), *Othello* (1622 and 1623), and *King Lear* (1608 and 1623). The chief differences between such printings are the appearance of many lines in one version that do not show up in the other: *Othello* 1622 lacks some 160 lines to be found in the 1623 printing, while preserving only about dozen lines or part-lines not in 1623; *Hamlet* 1623 lacks some 200 lines present in 1604-5 but prints about eighty-five or so lines not in 1604-5; and, finally, 1623 *King Lear* goes without about 300 lines that are in 1608 but supplies over one hundred lines not to be seen in 1608. Since these are plays, and since the theatre of Shakespeare's time, just like that of our own, cuts plays, the simplest explanation of these massive differences between these texts is that they have been cut in the playhouse and, in the case of *King Lear* and *Hamlet*, perhaps cut in different ways. As will be demonstrated later, the theatre of Shakespeare's time needed no author on hand in order to cut a play, and so again authorial revision seems beside the point, although, as we will also see, many throughout history have differed from this judgement. There are also hundreds of verbal differences between the printings of these plays, many more than can be charged to their typesetters and proofreaders. However, some scribes associated with the playhouses in the early seventeenth century have left evidence of the considerable difference scribes could make to the texts of the plays they copied.[23] Brian Vickers has recently brought new attention to

---

[22] Grace Ioppolo, *Revising Shakespeare* (Cambridge, MA: Harvard University Press, 1991), 132.
[23] Paul Werstine, *Early Modern Playhouse Manuscripts and the Editing of Shakespeare* (Cambridge: Cambridge University Press, 2012), 80–9, 91–7.

instances collected by H. S. Bennett and Leo Kirschbaum of Shakespeare's contemporaries complaining about the deleterious effects of scribes—'unskilfull pen men' whose 'merce- narie hand', and 'frequent transcription … still run forward in corruption'.[24] In sum, then, from a viewpoint informed by surviving documentary evidence, the readiest explanation for variation between Quarto and Folio versions of Shakespeare's tragedies is that the plays were cut for performance, sometimes in different ways, and that, before and/or after they were cut, they were transcribed, perhaps more than once.[25] While close attention to such documentary evidence began in the twentieth century, nonetheless the opinion itself can be found in earlier writers too. Here, for example, is Nicolaus Delius, writing in 1875:

> 'Is it at all probable, that Shakespeare, even granting that he revised the text [of *King Lear*] would have undertaken such superfluous trouble, as, we cannot say to improve, but merely to change the text in these innumerable, and minute, and insignificant particulars; and for no conceivable reason withal, instead of taking in hand some real incisive improve- ment? Or is it not more likely that a simple transcriber, attaching but slight importance to Shakespeare's words as such, in the hurry of his work substituted heedlessly or purposely, any phrase that occurred to him for another, one particle for another, one mood or number for another?'

As for the omissions from the Folio, Delius thought these '"were made by the players, for the purpose of shortening the time of representation"'.[26]

Many early editors, though, as I noted earlier, championed authorial revision, as is evi- dent from their discussion of *King Lear*. Although in the preface to his edition as a whole, Pope undertakes to identify for his readers 'the Alterations or Additions which *Shakespear* himself made',[27] he does not specify any in *King Lear*. It was left to Samuel Johnson in his 1765 edition to declare 'I believe the folio [1623 *King Lear*] is printed from *Shakespeare*'s last revision, carelessly and hastily performed, with more thought of shortening the scenes, than of continuing the action'.[28] Johnson's view made its way into the nineteenth century, quoted in variorum editions of 1803, 1813, and 1821. Even Edward Capell, the best of the eighteenth-century editors, thought occasional alterations in the 1623 text the result of Shakespearean revision, although other variants were, for him, errors of transmission or editorial interference.[29] Charles Knight, predictably, opted for Shakespearean revision as the origin of differences between 1608 and 1623 *Lears*.[30] However, Staunton expressed some reservations: he was unwilling to attribute to Shakespeare the 1623 cuts, doubting that all 1623 substitutions for individual 1608 words were authorial, even though confident that 1623's additional passages had come from Shakespeare.[31] (Staunton's refusal to subsume all the ways in which 1623 varies from 1608 under Shakespeare revision is evident elsewhere among nineteenth-century editors; and see Capell's account above.) Even Delius—in spite of his dismissal of the revision hypothesis in 1875—had previously subscribed to the

---

[24] Brian Vickers, *Shakespeare, Co-Author* (Oxford: Oxford University Press, 2002), 520.
[25] Paul Werstine, 'The Textual Mystery of *Hamlet*', *Shakespeare Quarterly* 39:1 (Spring, 1988), 1–26.
[26] Furness, ed., *King Lear*, 1880, 362–3.   [27] Pope, ed., *Works of Shakespear*, 1: xxii.
[28] Samuel Johnson, ed., *The Plays of William Shakespeare*, 8 vols. (London, 1765), 6: 116.
[29] Edward Capell, *Notes and Various Readings to Shakespeare*, 3 vols. (London, 1783), 1.2: 147, 151–2.
[30] Charles Knight, ed., *Comedies, Histories, Tragedies, & Poems*. Pictorial Ed., 55 parts (London, 1838-43), part 18, 393.
[31] Furness, ed., *King Lear*, 1880, 361.

hypothesis in his 1854 edition.[32] As a theory of the *Lear* texts, authorial revision made its way into the twentieth century in, for example, the 1906 edition by W. A. Neilson, who says that the 1623 text is 'cut down in some instances for stage presentation, but in other cases competently revised, perhaps by Shakespeare himself'.[33] Indeed by far the most detailed case for Shakespeare's revision of the play belongs to the twentieth century—Madeleine Doran's *The Text of* King Lear.[34]

The revision thesis was equally popular, although by no means universally accepted, across the eighteenth and nineteenth centuries as an explanation for the variants between the 1604-5 and 1623 *Hamlet*s and the 1622 and 1623 *Othello*s. Writers as temporally far removed from each other as Samuel Johnson,[35] on the one hand, and Charles and Mary Cowden Clarke,[36] on the other, simply take for granted that they share with their readership an understanding that the 1623 *Hamlet* is Shakespeare's own rehandling of his 1604-5 version. And Benjamin Heath in his 1765 *A revisal of Shakespear's text*[37] and William J. Rolfe in his 1879 edition of *Othello*[38] make the same assumption about the 1622 and 1623 texts of that play.

In spite of this demonstrably widespread editorial entertainment of the idea of Shakespeare as reviser of his tragedies, the differences between edited texts of *King Lear*, *Hamlet*, and *Othello* presented by those editors advocating revision and those resisting it did not become sizeable until the 1980s. Only then did there arise an expectation in some quarters that an editor inclined to regard authorial revision as possible or likely was obliged to remove from the edited text of these tragedies all, or almost all, the passages in them that are missing from their 1623 versions. This expectation is made explicit, for example, in MacDonald P. Jackson's review of Philip Edwards's New Cambridge Shakespeare edition of *Hamlet, Prince of Denmark*.[39] It is to be noted that Jackson is anything but an objective reviewer, for he collaborated with the editors of the 1986 Oxford University Press *William Shakespeare: The Complete Works*,[40] and these editors chose to relegate to an appendix many passages unique to the 1604-5 *Hamlet*. Jackson wrote in his review of Edwards's edition,

> although convinced that many [1623] F[olio] cuts [from the 1604-5 Second Quarto (Q2) version] are authorial, Edwards, perhaps under pressure from his publishers, shuns the logical editorial course of relegating to the commentary or an appendix the Q2 passages

[32] Nicolaus Delius, ed., *Shakspere's Werke*. 7 vols. (Elberfeld: Friderichs, 1854-61), 1: I-II.

[33] W. A. Neilson, ed., *The complete dramatic and poetic works of William Shakespeare: edited from the text of the early quartos and the first folio* (Cambridge, MA: Riverside, 1906), 3.

[34] Madeleine Doran, *The Text of* King Lear. Stanford Studies in Language and Literature 4.2 (Stanford University Press, 1931).

[35] Johnson, ed., *Hamlet*, 8: 282.

[36] Charles and Mary Cowden Clarke, eds., *The Plays of William Shakespeare*, 3 vols. (London: Cassell Petter & Galpin, 1864-9), 3: 376.

[37] Benjamin Heath, *A revisal of Shakespear's text* (London, 1765), 559.

[38] Furness ed., *Othello*, 1886, 173.

[39] Philip Edwards, ed., *Hamlet, Prince of Denmark* (Cambridge: Cambridge University Press, 1985).

[40] See Stanley Wells, Gary Taylor, et al., *William Shakespeare: A Textual Companion* (Oxford: Clarendon Press, 1987), 560, where the editing of *Pericles* for the Oxford Shakespeare is said to be the joint work of Gary Taylor and MacDonald P. Jackson.

that Shakespeare supposedly planned to discard. Instead he places passages unique to Q2 within square brackets, which we may ignore with all the insouciance that he imputes to the Q2 compositors [in their alleged overlooking of Shakespeare's marks of deletion in their supposedly autograph printer's copy]. He regrets that 'it is not always possible … to have the courage of one's convictions' (p. 32).[41]

It is unfortunate that Edwards resorted to the inexactness of a cliché ('the courage of one's convictions') in characterizing the relation between his theory of the early printed *Hamlet* texts and his editorial practice because, like many editors before him who entertained the possibility that Shakespeare may have revised *Hamlet*, the strength of Edwards's conviction corresponded fairly precisely with his practice. That is, he prudently refrained from putting into practice the rather hesitant belief in the likelihood of revision that is evident in the careful language with which he weighed that possibility. According to Edwards, 'A number of cuts made in the Folio version of Hamlet's speeches to Gertrude in Act 3, Scene 4 … *may* reflect Shakespeare's own tightening of his dialogue', the subjunctive indicating Edwards's recognition that by their very nature cuts do not reveal who made them.[42] Edwards's doubts are rational, and so is his decision not to impose on his readers by insisting on an editorial policy that cannot be grounded in evidence.

Such care for the reader is also widely evident earlier in the editorial tradition, for example, in the writing of Charles Knight, the nineteenth century's leading advocate of revision. While Knight prizes the 1623 texts as Shakespeare's final versions, he does not discount the earlier quartos, which, he says, 'warrant us receiving them as authentic copies … entitled to a very high respect in the settlement of the author's text'. He believes, though, that 'the author's posthumous copies in manuscript [which Knight assumes were used to print the Folio] were distinguished from the printed copies [i.e., the quartos] by verbal alterations, by additions, by omissions not arbitrarily made, by a more correct metrical arrangement'. For Knight, these alterations, additions, and omissions are 'in numerous cases, the minute but most effective touches of the skilful artist, … sufficient to satisfy us of the jealous care with which Shakespeare watched over the more important of these productions, so as to leave with his "fellows" more complete and accurate copies than had been preserved by the press'. In spite of the specificity of this claim, however, Knight, couches his characterization of particular Folio texts in language as careful as Edwards's: according to Knight, there was only '*probably* a dramatic reason' for Folio cuts from the 1604-5 Quarto text of *Hamlet*—lines 'which we should indeed be sorry to lose'. Before he winds up his evaluation of Quarto and Folio texts, he is willing to claim only that the Folio alterations 'are in many cases either the corrections of the author, or the corrections of those who represented the plays [that is, the actors]'. This summative judgement, which is scrupulous in acknowledging the limits of our knowledge, warrants his editorial decision 'to preserve even what the author, *we may believe*, advisedly rejected; and, in preserving it, to furnish materials for a just appreciation of the judgement with which he retrenched as well as added. Where there are omissions in the folio of passages found in the Quartos, such omissions not being superseded by an extended or a condensed passage of a similar character, we give them a place

---

[41] MacDonald P. Jackson, 'The Year's Contributions to Shakespearian Study: Editions and Textual Studies', *Shakespeare Survey* 39 (1987), 245–6.

[42] Edwards, ed., *Hamlet*, 12. Cf. also pp. 13, 15: 'Here *we can imagine* Shakespeare stopping himself after running on too far' and 'Shakespeare himself *may* have removed both speeches'(italics mine).

in the text'.[43] Bate, echoing Jackson's review of Edwards, says that 'On this and several other occasions, Knight did not quite have the courage of his Folio convictions'.[44] But it seems, as in Edwards's case, that Knight's practice of including Quarto-only passages in his editions is logically consistent with his stated uncertainty about whether the Folio's variations are 'the corrections of the author, or the corrections of those who represented the plays,' and that Knight's courage accords with his conviction or, more precisely, lack of it.

Knight's editorial successors, both in the strength of their belief in the Folio texts of *Othello, King Lear*, and *Hamlet*, and the practice, nevertheless, of preserving Quarto-only passages, were Charlotte Porter and Helen A. Clarke. Bate quotes from their 1903 Pembroke Edition a statement illustrating their extravagant devotion to the Folio: 'The First Folio remains, as a matter of fact, the text nearest to Shakespeare's stage, to Shakespeare's ownership, to Shakespeare's authority.'[45] Yet as Porter and Clarke assess the variants between the early printed texts of particular tragedies, they are as conscious as Knight of their inability to identify precisely the agents responsible for these differences. Of the 1604-5 and 1623 texts of *Hamlet* they write, 'Both texts have apparently been derived from stage manuscripts cut somewhat differently. The Folio text seems to be printed from an independent manuscript, with the latest revision or additions and changes *made by Shakespeare or his fellows*, and it therefore presents what is most nearly an authoritative text.'[46] Porter and Clarke's characterization of the 1608 and 1623 texts of *King Lear* is much the same:

> Whether the abridging of the Folio text is Shakespeare's or not, is matter of conjecture. The additions are unquestioned. Knight regards many of the omissions from the Folio ... [as] made for dramatic effect, the parts cut out being description rather than action.... It is to be remembered, however, that Shakespeare as actor or 'fellow' in the Globe Company *is likelier* to have been aware of cuts, and to authorize them, than dramatists less acquainted with the stage side of playcraft.[47]

Not knowing if the Folio cuts are Shakespeare's, Porter and Clarke do not make these cuts in their edition.

In contrast, the editors of the 1986 Oxford Shakespeare do make most of the Folio cuts from *Hamlet* and regard the 1608 and 1623 *King Lears* as two distinct Shakespearean versions of the play. These editors offer more than one rationale for their practice; sometimes they claim that Shakespeare himself is responsible for the cuts as well as for most of the other differences between early printed texts;[48] but sometimes in providing their rationale, they appear to echo the writings of Knight and Porter and Clarke, although in terms peculiar to the 1980s. These two rationales sit in uneasy relation to each other. The first is influenced by E. A. J. Honigmann's *The Stability of Shakespeare's Text*,[49] in which Shakespeare's playwriting is conceived by analogy to the composition and revision of their poetry by Keats and Burns. Honigmann was chiefly responsible for reviving the dormant revision

---

[43] Charles Knight, *Old Lamps, or New? A Plea for the Original Editions of the Text of Shakespeare* (London: Knight, 1853), xv-vii, italics mine.

[44] Bate, 'The Case for the Folio'.

[45] Bate, 'The Case for the Folio'.

[46] Charlotte Porter and Helen A. Clarke, eds., *The Tragedie of Hamlet, Prince of Denmarke*. The First Folio Edition (New York: Crowell, 1905), 179, italics mine.

[47] Ibid., 146, italics mine.   [48] Taylor, 'Revising Shakespeare', 299. See also n. 52.

[49] E. A. J. Honigmann, *The Stability of Shakespeare's Text* (London: Arnold, 1965).

hypothesis in the later twentieth century, and Wells acknowledges his debt to Honigmann in a Hilda Hulme Lecture.[50] As the Oxford editors follow Honigmann, he followed W. W. Greg. According to Greg, Shakespeare turned over his plays to his company in a manuscript form too untidy for use by the company, which therefore was required to have the authorial manuscripts copied. Rather than investigating extant playhouse manuscripts to verify or falsify Greg's teaching, Honigmann adapted it to a theory of Shakespeare revision according to which Shakespeare himself copied his original untidy manuscript to provide one suitable to the company, and in the course of copying revised. In Honigmann's view, the original Shakespeare manuscript served as printer's copy for such quartos as 1604-5 *Hamlet,* and the revised authorial copies underlie Folio texts. As a copyist, Shakespeare, for Honigmann, was the image of such Romantic poets as Keats and Burns who, as copyists, introduced into their poems many of the same kinds of changes that can be found in the work of scribes and compositors. Thus, for Honigmann and for the Oxford editors (to the extent that they follow him), Shakespeare—alone—generated most of the variants evident in the early printings of his tragedies, not including errors of transmission. In line with Honigmann, Wells suggests we regard the 1608 and 1623 printings of *King Lear* as being like Wordsworth's two versions of *The Prelude* (1805, 1850).[51] However, now that surviving playhouse manuscripts have been examined in detail, it has been discovered that there are no grounds for Greg's and Honigmann's belief that dramatists provided unsuitable copy to acting companies; some manuscript plays in their dramatists' hands were actually used by the companies, which did not require such neat and tidy manuscripts as Greg imagines.[52] Therefore there was no occasion for Shakespeare to recopy and, in the course of transcription, revise his work to satisfy his company.

The other rationale proposed by the Oxford editors for following the 1623 *Hamlet,* cuts and all, and for printing both a Folio and a Quarto *King Lear,* is one that will now be familiar to readers from this chapter's review of the editorial tradition, even though the terms in which it is expressed are new. The Oxford editors announce their preference for 'a socialized text, one which has been communally prepared for communication to a wider public'. They explain that 'Shakespeare ... devoted his life to the theatre, and dramatic texts are necessarily the most socialized of all literary forms. Where matters of verbal and theatrical substance are involved, we have therefore chosen ... to prefer ... the text closer to the prompt-book [an anachronistic term for an Early Modern theatrical manuscript] of Shakespeare's company'.[53] For this conception of the 'socialized text', the Oxford editors properly reference Jerome McGann's *A Critique of Modern Textual Criticism.*[54] There McGann argues for an acceptance by editors that certain authors produce literary work in a social (rather than, according to, say, Honigmann, a solitary) context of 'institutional conditions—which vary with period and place—and whose impact upon

---

[50] Stanley Wells, 'Shakespeare and Revision', The Hilda Hulme Lecture, 3 December 1987 (University of London), 8-10.

[51] Stanley Wells, 'Introduction: The Once and Future *King Lear*', in *The Division of the Kingdoms: Shakespeare's Two Versions of* King Lear, ed. Gary Taylor and Michael Warren (Oxford: Clarendon Press, 1983), 1-2.

[52] Werstine, *Early Modern Playhouse Manuscripts*, throughout.

[53] Wells, Taylor, et al., *Textual Companion*, 15.

[54] Jerome McGann, *A Critique of Modern Textual Criticism* (1983; 2nd edn., Charlottesville: University Press of Virginia, 1992).

the author's work in the literary production is by no means always an alien or contaminating influence'. Indeed, according to McGann, an author like Thomas Wolfe depends for the success of his literary production 'upon the editorial assistance of the publishing house'.[55] Shakespeare, in his turn, depends, for the Oxford editors, on the playhouse and the assistance of his fellow actors. While, like Porter and Clarke, the Oxford editors gesture towards Shakespeare's presence in the theatre—'it seems reasonable to suppose that Shakespeare personally suggested many or most of the alterations made in rehearsal, and that he acquiesced in others'[56]—by invoking the conception of the social text, the Oxford editors lift from themselves the intolerable burden of having to distinguish between Shakespeare's revisions and his company's, just as did Knight (for whom the Folio contains 'either the corrections of the author, or the corrections of those who represented the plays') and Porter and Clarke (for whom the Folio offers 'additions and changes made by Shakespeare or his fellows').

A question therefore arises: if the Oxford editors' theory regarding revision is, in their second rationale, no different from that of their predecessors, why is their practice of following Folio cuts so different? One answer to this question reflects the climate of Shakespeare criticism in the 1970s and 1980s, when the Oxford edition was in progress— a climate that has since changed. As Lukas Erne observes, this climate was shaped by writing of John Styan and Herbert Coursen, with 'the call for a stage-centred study of Shakespeare'[57] and with, in Erne's words, 'more dogmatic claims ... about the importance of performance for our understanding of Shakespeare's plays'.[58] As examples of such dogmatism, Erne quotes Styan's assertion that 'the stage expanding before an audience is the source of all valid discovery'[59] and Coursen's 'a play has to be seen and heard in order to be understood'.[60] A similar claim is evident in Wells's 'Introduction' to *The Division of the Kingdoms*: 'plays written for performance are not fully realized until they reach the stage, and critics who treat such plays purely as literature are choosing to work in blinkers'.[61] (In *The Struggle for Shakespeare's Text*, Gabriel Egan gives an account of Wells's training and background in stage-centred criticism.[62]) From this perspective Shakespeare's plays' exclusive ontological status is as performance, and it seems to be this conception of plays, rather than a belief, distinctly old-fashioned by 1986, in Shakespearean revision, that impels the Oxford editors to follow the Folio in its cuts. Even if these cuts cannot be known to be Shakespeare's, they may reasonably be inferred to be theatrical.

There are some twenty-one texts (all of which may date from before the closing of the playhouses in 1642) that show theatrical mark-up of one kind or another and that

[55] McGann, *Critique*, 103, 79.   [56] Wells, Taylor, et al., *Textual Companion*, 19.

[57] John Styan, *The Shakespeare Revolution: Criticism and Performance in the Twentieth Century* (Cambridge: Cambridge University Press, 1977), 6.

[58] Lukas Erne, *Shakespeare as Literary Dramatist* (Cambridge: Cambridge University Press, 2003), 22.

[59] Styan, *Revolution*, 235.

[60] Herbert Coursen, *Reading Shakespeare on Stage* (Newark: University of Delaware Press, 1995), 46.

[61] Wells, 'Introduction', in *Division*, 1.

[62] Gabriel Egan, *The Struggle for Shakespeare's Text* (Cambridge: Cambridge University Press, 2010), 167.

thereby identify themselves as texts used in the playhouses.[63] All but a single one of these contains passages marked for deletion.[64] Of course, passages are also deleted from manuscripts that bear no theatrical mark-up, such as *The Faithful Friends* (Victoria and Albert Museum: Dyce 25. F. 10), which is heavily cut. Nonetheless, there is a high correlation in extant documents between cutting and mark-up for production, and that correlation is the basis for ascribing to the playhouse the cuts found in the 1623 *King Lear* and *Hamlet* and the 1622 *Othello*. While documentary evidence warrants this association of cutting with the playhouse, the surviving documents cannot support the view that playwrights usually participate in the cutting and shaping of their plays for the stage, as must be assumed by advocates of revision. There is only a single one of these playhouse texts that shows good evidence of an author joining with the playhouse functionary, the book-keeper, whose task it was to cut a play and otherwise to prepare it or supervise its preparation for production. This single playhouse text, a scribal transcript of Henry Glapthorne's *The Lady Mother*, is peripheral to Shakespearean interests, written as it was for the King's Revels Company of 1635, a peculiar company consisting of more boys than men, and employing a style of production not to be found in the public playhouses of earlier decades.[65] Nonetheless, the manuscript is highly useful in providing an example of how a playhouse text would look if a playwright actually worked with a bookkeeper to cut it; its example of these processes establishes that they are unique to this document. Glapthorne himself made most of the cuts including the most extensive ones; however, one of these extensive cuts was subsequently reversed by the book-keeper's writing 'stet' four times in the margins opposite the authorial cut. The Malone Society editor of this transcript, Arthur Brown, nicely captures in his syntax the indeterminacy concerning the agent who made the decision to keep the passage: 'Later it was apparently decided to allow this passage to stand.' Thus even when we have a manuscript of a play we may face to some extent the same problem of identifying the source of its alteration that we face with the different printings of particular Shakespeare's plays. Furthermore, since Glapthorne's rehandling of his play, in Brown's words, 'chiefly concerned the cancellation of scenes and passages',[66] rather than any extensive additional writing, this playwright's revision lacks a key element of what advocates of revision imagine Shakespeare sometimes to have done in adding around a hundred lines to a tragedy in supposedly converting it from its earlier Quarto to its later Folio form.

Writers intent on gauging the popularity of the revision hypothesis judge the revision craze of the 1980s, centred on *King Lear*, to have passed. The swing away from it is explicitly marked in the difference between the editions of René Weis's *King Lear: A Parallel Text Edition*, the 1993 edition featuring parallel texts (each edited on its own terms in deference to the idea of 'Shakespeare's Two Versions of *King Lear*', to quote part of the title of the then-influential 1983 Taylor and Warren collection of essays) and the 2010 edition, prefaced by an essay entitled 'The Integral *King Lear*: its War and Variants of Convergence', arguing for the derivation of both the 1608 and the 1623 texts from a single Shakespearean version and the new edition frequently

---

[63] Werstine, *Early Modern Playhouse Manuscripts*, 245–357.   [64] Ibid., 243.

[65] Ibid., 201, 211–16.

[66] Arthur Brown, ed., *The Lady Mother by Henry Glapthorne*, Malone Society Reprint (London: Malone Society, 1959), x, xii.

emending the 1608 with reference to the 1623.[67] Ron Rosenbaum largely credits Richard Knowles, editor of the soon to be forthcoming New Variorum Edition of *King Lear*, with calming the revision craze:

> for some time Knowles was, it seems to me, quite the loner; if not a complete outsider, certainly a lonely dissident going against the tide of Reviser thought that seems to have swept the field of Shakespeare studies in the eighties and nineties…. Nonetheless, in a relatively short time Knowles, firing off powerfully argued polemics, has almost single-handedly stemmed, if not reversed … the rush to divide and distinguish the two versions of *Lear*…. When I first spoke to him … in 2001, he'd seemed to me to represent a resistance that was receding into the past. But by the time I spoke to him for the second time, four years later, the tide seemed to be shifting to his side of the battle, largely through his persistence.[68]

Rosenbaum has the disadvantage of being no Shakespeare scholar but, in terms of the likely objectivity of his assessment, that disadvantage also constitutes a significant advantage.

SELECT BIBLIOGRAPHY

Bate, Jonathan, 'The Case for the Folio', www.modernlibrary.com/files/2010/09/TheCaseForTheFolio.pdf.

Doran, Madeleine, *The Text of* King Lear. Stanford Studies in Language and Literature 4.2 (Stanford: Stanford University Press, 1931).

Furness, Horace Howard, ed., *Hamlet*. A New Variorum Edition of Shakespeare. 2 vols. (Philadelphia: Lippincott, 1877; *King Lear*, 1880; *Othello*, 1886; *Romeo and Juliet*, 1871).

Honigmann, E. A. J., *The Stability of Shakespeare's Text* (London: Arnold, 1965).

Johnson, Samuel, ed., *The Plays of William Shakespeare*, 8 vols. (London, 1765).

Knight, Charles, *Old Lamps, or New? A plea for the Original Editions of the Text of Shakespeare* (London: Knight, 1853).

Knowles, Richard, 'Two *Lears*? By Shakespeare?', in James Ogden and Arthur H. Scouten, eds., *Lear From Study to Stage; Essays in Criticism* (Madison: Fairleigh Dickinson University Press; London: Associated University Presses, 1997, 57–78).

Knowles, Richard, 'The Evolution of the Texts of *Lear*', in Jeffrey Kahan, ed., *King Lear: New Critical Essays* (New York: Routledge, 2008), 124–54.

Pope, Alexander, ed., *The Works of Shakespear*, 6 vols. (London, 1725).

---

[67] René Weis, ed., *King Lear: A Parallel Text Edition* (1993; 2nd edn., London: Longman, 2010), 36–72 (71).

[68] *The Shakespeare Wars: Clashing Scholars, Public Fiascoes, Palace Coups* (New York: Random House, 2006), 140. See Richard Knowles, 'Revision Awry in Folio *Lear* 3.1', *Shakespeare Quarterly* 46:1 (Spring 1995), 32–46; 'Two *Lears*? By Shakespeare?', in James Ogden and Arthur H. Scouten, eds., *Lear From Study to Stage; Essays in Criticism* (Madison: Fairleigh Dickinson University Press; London: Associated University Presses, 1997), 57–78; 'Merging the Kingdoms: *King Lear*', *Shakespeare International Yearbook* 1 (1999), 266–86; 'Cordelia's Return', *Shakespeare Quarterly* 50:1 (Spring, 1999), 33–50; 'The Evolution of the Texts of *Lear*', in Jeffrey Kahan, ed., *King Lear: New Critical Essays* (New York: Routledge, 2008), 124–54.

Taylor, Gary and Michael Warren, eds., *The Division of the Kingdoms: Shakespeare's Two Versions of* King Lear (Oxford: Clarendon Press, 1983).

Urkowitz, Steven, *Shakespeare's Revision of* King Lear (Princeton: Princeton University Press, 1980).

Wells, Stanley, Gary Taylor, et al., *William Shakespeare: A Textual Companion* (Oxford Clarendon Press, 1987).

Werstine, Paul, 'The Textual Mystery of *Hamlet*', *Shakespeare Quarterly* 39:1 (Spring, 1988), 1–26.

CHAPTER 20

....

DIGITAL APPROACHES
TO THE LANGUAGE OF
SHAKESPEAREAN TRAGEDY

....

MICHAEL WITMORE, JONATHAN HOPE,
AND MICHAEL GLEICHER

WE are living through a revolution in our ability to study Early Modern literature and culture. In January 2015, the Text Creation Partnership (TCP) released around 25,000 texts drawn from Early English Books Online (EEBO) into the public domain. In the past, these texts have been available as page images to subscriber institutions only. Now anyone can download these as fully searchable text files, and with further releases planned, we can look forward to a situation when every person with an internet connection will be able to download and search something close to the entire corpus of surviving Early Modern printed books.[1]

Access to such corpora gives us the chance to consider questions across larger numbers of documents than has been the norm in literary studies. However, investigating at scale necessarily requires different approaches to scholarship: it clearly is not practical to close-read the entirety of a corpus of 25,000 texts. The challenge is twofold: to engage literary specialists whose specialist knowledge of the field is essential to the interpretation of results; and to frame new research questions. To make the most of these new resources, we must integrate traditional literary scholarship with new approaches.[2]

---

[1] For the TCP project, see http://www.textcreationpartnership.org/tcp-eebo/ (accessed 4.5.2015). EEBO–TCP Phase I contains 25,363 texts, manually keyed to allow full text searching. EEBO–TCP Phase II aims to similarly transcribe a further 45,000 texts from EEBO. Files can be downloaded from https://github.com/textcreationpartnership (accessed 4.5.2015), and a master list of all TCP files is at https://github.com/textcreationpartnership/Texts/blob/master/TCP.csv (accessed 4.5.2015). EEBO–TCP seeks to cover as much as possible of the surviving corpus of Early Modern Print, but we should remember that a large number of texts have been lost (see n. 18)—and the process of transcription is continuing, with new files regularly added to the corpus.

[2] The authors of this paper are involved with the Mellon-funded Visualizing English Print project, which is developing tools and methods for analysing EEBO–TCP (and any large corpus of texts). See the project website http://vep.cs.wisc.edu (accessed 4.5.2015) and project members' blog http://winedarksea.org (accessed 4.5.2015).

This chapter aims to give an example of such a combined approach. Specifically, we consider the language of a corpus of 554 printed plays from the Early Modern period.[3] We explore two research questions, each requiring the consideration of a large collection of plays:

(a) is there a distinct 'language of tragedy'?
(b) is there a distinctively Shakespearean language of tragedy?

These are questions that could be considered using traditional literary-critical methods of extensive reading followed by selective quotation and rhetorically-based argument. Our goal is to show how computational and traditional literary techniques can be combined to give better-grounded answers to these questions: computational techniques allow us to compare the language of *all* 554 plays, reliably establishing the groupings of linguistic features which together characterize the language of genres and authors.

As this chapter is focused on showing the potential of our approach, we present our results first, and defer detailed discussion of the methods until later. However an initial outline of our methodology is important, especially for literary scholars intending to make their own use of EEBO–TCP. Briefly, there are four phases to any computational text study such as this:

(1) a corpus of texts is curated: for this study, we assembled a corpus of 554 texts (as described in note 3), removed any language not spoken on stage (such as speech prefixes, stage directions, and so on), and used an automatic spelling modernizer to normalize spelling

(2) some form of measurement of the content of the documents is made: here, we used software to count the frequency of 113 linguistic features in each play

(3) the measurements taken in phase 2 are analysed: in this study we chose to apply standard statistical methodologies which combine the frequency counts of the linguistic features in ways that allow us to 'see' patterns in the occurrence of those features among the documents by plotting them on a two-dimensional chart

---

[3] Our corpus of dramatic texts comes from the EEBO–TCP transcriptions, and was originally selected and supplied to us by Martin Mueller, for which we are very grateful. Subsequently, in order to ensure that the entire corpus was processed in the same way, we re-selected and re-processed EEBO–TCP texts. Texts went through three stages of processing: (i) we performed automatic clean-up to remove certain characters introduced during transcription (for example, the pipe character < | > frequently appears where hyphens have triggered an incorrect word division in the transcription); (ii) we modernized texts automatically, using VARD (http://ucrel.lancs.ac.uk/vard/about/ - accessed 8.5.2015); (iii) we stripped texts of all non-spoken elements (stage directions, act and scene numbers, speaker designations) using XML codes. Genre labels were assigned by Jonathan Hope, drawing on metadata supplied with some of the texts, titles and title pages, and labels given in the Database of Early English Playbooks (DEEP - http://deep.sas.upenn.edu - accessed 4.5.2015). The metadata originally associated with the play texts, and included in the file TCP.csv (downloadable from the address given in n. 1) has been checked, corrected and extensively expanded by Beth Ralston as part of the VEP project. This new metadata, a list of all the plays in the corpus, their genre labels, and the frequency scores used in this study, can be found in a new spreadsheet which we are making available along with the stripped, VARDed.txt files and tagged HTML files of the corpus play texts. For details of this material, see http://winedarksea.org/?p=2013 (accessed 12.5.2015). See note 6 for further comment on the texts and our method of referencing.

(4) we return to individual texts to examine examples of the broader linguistic patterns *in situ* so that we can attempt to explain their presence using traditional literary reading

Each phase is important, and all must be completed carefully in order to obtain valid results. It is also crucial to remember that we could have made many different choices at phases two and three: choices of what to count, and how to analyse the results. Each choice brings with it a different set of merits and drawbacks, and as more work is done in this new field we will discover more about the best things to count, and the best statistical methods to analyse the results.

Figure 20.1 shows an initial result from the first three phases of our analysis. Each play is represented by a dot, with tragedies picked-out in black. The dots are positioned such that plays that are linguistically similar to each other are placed next to each other, while plays that are dissimilar are further apart. The statistical method we used to determine similarity and difference is called Principal Components Analysis (PCA), and is designed to summarize as much of the variation in the linguistic measurements we made for each play as is possible in a two-dimensional chart. We have chosen to use PCA in this study as it is a standard approach for summarizing such complex data, and allows for visual presentation, but there are many other ways in which we could investigate and visualize our measurements.

Turning to Figure 20.1, we can see that the tragedies are not evenly distributed amongst the plays: they tend to be more to the left of the graph, and to be more towards the top. Since the process of positioning was 'blind' to the generic labelling of individual plays,

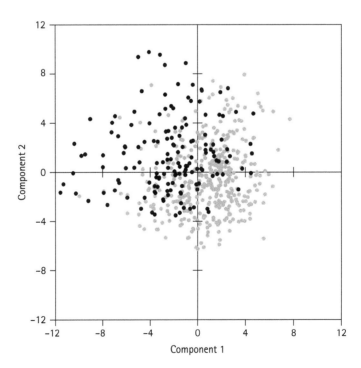

FIG. 20.1 The 554-play Early Modern Drama corpus with tragedies highlighted in black.

the fact that the tragedies differ from the total corpus in this way implies that there are differences between them and the other plays in terms of what *was* considered for the positioning, namely the frequencies of the linguistic features we counted. In brief, Figure 20.1 suggests that there is indeed a 'language of tragedy': a group of linguistic features whose use correlates with a play being a tragedy (statistical tests confirm that these differences are not likely to be due to chance).

We can contrast this with Figure 20.2, where the comedies have been marked in black. Again, the marked plays tend to occupy a specific region of the graph, however comedies occupy a different region to tragedies: they tend to be more to the right, and lower. This result suggests strongly that tragedy and comedy differ in their use of linguistic features— and it invites further exploration. What are the features each genre uses? *Why* do genres use different types of language? Are the plays from each genre on the 'wrong' side of the dividing line experiments, or mixed-genre texts? Do certain writers predictably write 'close to' or 'over' the line? There is not space here to do more than begin to consider some of these questions: they indicate the extent of work for the future.

We can also say that there are areas that each genre avoids strongly: tragedies are virtually absent from the bottom right-hand quadrant of the graph, while comedies are very rare in the opposite, top left quadrant. This oppositional patterning tells us that there is an 'anti-signature' for each genre: that is, a set of linguistic features that each genre avoids, but which is present in many of the plays in the other genre. This ability to identify absence as readily as presence is one of the strengths of quantitative-digital work, and one of the things it does that traditional human readers are less good at.

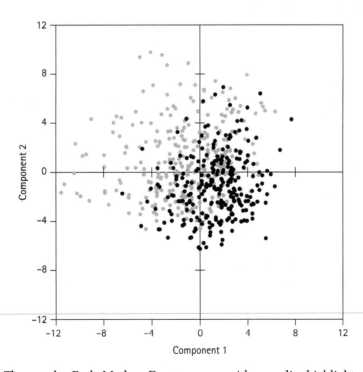

FIG. 20.2 The 554-play Early Modern Drama corpus with comedies highlighted in black.

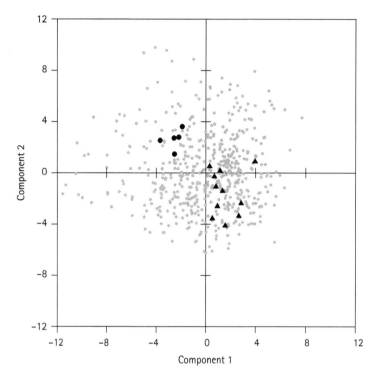

FIG. 20.3 George Chapman's plays in the Early Modern drama corpus (tragedies = black circles; comedies = black triangles).

So what are the characteristic languages of tragedy and comedy in the Early Modern drama corpus? What differences in linguistic practice are reflected in these separations in the space of the graph? On analysis, it turns out that tragedies (perhaps not surprisingly) favour a set of linguistic features used to communicate negative emotion and affect, while comedies, less predictably, favour a set associated with the representation of rapid, highly interactive speech, including first and second person pronouns, questions, discourse markers, words for social roles and relationships, and imperatives. We term these groups the 'negative' and 'oral' groups.

To show these linguistic styles in context, we will use the work of George Chapman, who emerges from this study as a generically exemplary writer. The plays in our Chapman corpus are as given in Table 20.1 (eleven comedies first, followed by five tragedies).[4] Chapman's plays are visualized in Figure 20.3, with his tragedies picked out as black circles, and his comedies as black triangles. This graph repeats the pattern of generic separation between tragedy and comedy observed in Figures 20.1 and 20.2: Chapman's tragedies all group to the upper left, in the quadrant which has mainly tragedies, and very few comedies (and which we can term the 'core' tragedy space). Chapman's comedies, although slightly less tightly grouped than his tragedies, all lie to the right and lower, and almost all are in the quadrant of the graph which has many comedies and almost no tragedies (the 'core' comedy space).

---

[4] Note that dates and ascriptions are from our corrected metadata referenced in n. 3, but many dates and ascriptions in the corpus are conjectural and subject to change in the light of future scholarship.

Table 20.1 The plays in our Chapman corpus (11 comedies first, followed by 5 tragedies)

TCP number	Title
A09134	*Fedele and Fortunia* (1585)
A18402	*The Blind Beggar of Alexandria* (1596)
A18419	*An Humorous Day's Mirth* (1597)
A18400	*All Fools* (1601)
A01911	*Sir Giles Goosecap* (1602)
A18413	*The Gentleman Usher* (1602)
A18415	*May Day* (1602)
A18426	*The Widow's Tears* (1604)
A69093	*Monsieur D'Olive* (1605)
A18407	*Eastward Ho* (1605)
A18423	*Two Wise Men and All the Rest Fools* (1619)
A18403	*Bussy D'Ambois* (1604)
A18425	*Caesar and Pompey (Wars of Caesar and Pompey)* (1605)
A18404	*The Conspiracy of Charles Duke of Byron* (1608)
A18404	*The Tragedy of Charles Duke of Byron* (1608)
A18421	*The Revenge of Bussy D'Ambois* (1610)

Before we give textual illustrations of these contrasting strategies, a caveat. Traditionally, literary criticism has worked by building arguments around exemplary quotations, chosen for their rhetorical force. The quotations represent the key moment, or the height of the author's performance. The argument stands or falls on the aptness and quality of the supporting quotations. Russ McDonald's essay on the language of tragedy is an outstandingly good example of this (in both senses: it is a good example, and it is an excellent essay).[5] McDonald uses skilfully chosen quotations to make his points, working from the particular to the exceptional. What we are doing here is something very different. We are counting at scale (554 plays), and we are not looking for unusual, stand-out passages, but for large-scale patterns that assert themselves repeatedly over many plays. We are comparing large groups of plays on the basis of what is similar between them—and the differences we identify are similarly at scale. Things that happen only once, or only a few times, do not register in our analysis: they are drowned out by the force of numbers. When we present you with quotations from plays, they are intended to be representative of what goes on across very large amounts of text: they are not 'plums' plucked from a literary pie, but are the stodge that makes up the vast majority of what is going

---

[5] Russ McDonald, 'The Language of Tragedy', in Claire McEachern, ed., *The Cambridge Companion to Shakespearean Tragedy*, 2nd edn (Cambridge: Cambridge University Press, 2006), 23–49.

on in the text. This is an unfamiliar way of thinking about literary practice, and one of the challenges for literary studies in the coming years is to come to terms with it as a method.

Here is a passage from Chapman's tragedy *Bussy D'Ambois* with negative group features in bold:[6]

> will she but disclose
> Who was the **hateful** minister of her love,
> And through what maze he served it, we are friends.
> It is **a damned** work to pursue those secrets,
> That would op more **sin**, and prove springs of **slaughter**;
> Nor is it a path for Christian feet to touch;
> But out of all way to the health of souls,
> A **sin impossible to be** forgiven:
> Which he that dares commit;
> Good father cease:
> Tempt not a man **distracted**; I am apt
> To **outrages** that I shall ever rue:
> I will not pass the verge that bounds a Christian,
> Nor **break the** limits of a man nor husband.
> Then God inspire ye both with thoughts and deeds
> Worthy his high respect, and your own souls.
> Who shall remove the mountain from my heart,
> Op the seuentimes-heat furnace of my thoughts,
> And set fit outcries for a soul **in hell**?
> O now it nothing fits my cares to speak,
> But thunder, or to take into my throat
> The trump of Heaven; with whose determinate **blasts**
> **The** winds shall burst, and the **enraged** seas
> Be drunk up in his sounds; that my hot woes
> (**Vented** enough) I might convert to vapour,
> Ascending from my **infamy** unseen;
>
>   (George Chapman, *Bussy D'Ambois* TCP A18403)

And here, by contrast, is a passage from the comedy *An Humorous Day's Mirth* with oral group features in bold (see also Table 20.3):

> Honour to my good lord, and his fair **young lady**.
> Now **Monsieur** Satan, **you are** come to tempt and prove at full the spirit of **my wife**.

---

[6] See also Table 20.2. We quote directly from the EEBO–TCP texts as processed according to the procedure outlined in note 3. This means that there are no speech prefixes or stage directions. For each text we give a TCP number, which identifies the TCP text file containing the text (if, as with plays from Shakespeare's First Folio, the play comes from a collected volume, transcribed as a single textfile in TCP, we give a 'playfile' number, with a numerical suffix distinguishing the play). These texts are not 'edited' or 'good' texts in the senses literary scholars are used to. TCP transcribers were told to leave blanks where they could not read the images they worked from, so there are gaps in the text (though none in these examples). Our automatic modernization process does not get everything right ('doe' = 'do' for example, is left untreated on the mistaken assumption that it is 'doe' = female deer). It is possible to train VARD, so that errors are reduced, but for this exploratory study we decided to use the basic VARD settings so that all texts went through the same, replicable, process. We are working at scale here, and our belief is that the frequencies of the items we are counting means that 'dirt' in the data does not affect the overall result. Scholars undertaking a more focused study might want to fine-tune the modernization process.

I am **my lord**, but vainly **I** suppose.
You see she dares put on this brave attire fit with the fashion, which **you think** serves
    much to lead a **woman** into light desires.
My lord I see it: and the sight thereof doth half dismay **me** to make further proof.
Nay prove her, prove her **sir**, and spare not: **what** doth the witty **minion** of our **King**
    think any dame in France will say him nay? but prove her, prove her, see and spare not.
Well **sir**, though half discouraged in **my** comming, yet Isle go forward: **lady**, by your leave.
Now **sir, your** cunning in a Ladyesproofe.
Madam, in proving **you** I find no proof against **your** piercing glancings, but swear
    I am shot thorough **with your** love.
I do believe **you**: who will swear he loves, to get the thing he loves not? if he love,
    what needs more perfect trial?
Most true rare **lady**.

(George Chapman, An Humorous Day's Mirth TCP A18419)

Clearly these are very different discourse situations: the conventions of the genres, and the demands of the different narrative structures they set up, encourage the use, and avoidance, of the associated features. Tragedies favour relatively formal speech situations, typically with longer speeches, fewer exchanges, and with declarative, rather than interactive, tendencies. Comedies favour informal situations, with rapid shifts of speaker, and the use of features to mark turn-taking, attention-getting, contradiction, agreement, and so-on. Now, a reader not well-disposed to quantitative work might observe that it is not surprising to find that tragedies favour language about death, sorrow, and nasty things in general, and that we hardly need computers and advanced statistical analysis to point this out to ourselves—and we would have to agree. But there is something, if only relief, in new techniques that produce results that make sense to domain-specialists. This, at the very least, can give us some confidence that the linguistic software is counting things that do have a role in producing recognizable literary effects.

We can also say that quantitative methods add several things to our understanding we could not otherwise arrive at. For one thing, we now know that these differences are visible across the whole range of Early Modern drama: the human cultural categories of tragedy and comedy are mapped by consistent differences in the use of a range of quantifiable, small-scale linguistic features. We have linked high-level, rather abstract conceptions (genre categories) with low-level linguistic forms. The statistics link these in a correlation (high use of negative features correlates with plays which have been termed tragedies), and human researchers can offer plausible explanations for why there might be an association.

It is important to note that simply establishing a statistical correlation between a group of texts and a set of linguistic features does not guarantee that we have found something that is significant in a literary sense. Statistical significance does not equate to literary significance or interest. The statistics simply form the basis for literary investigation and interpretation: they are a starting point, and a way to return to the texts with a new perspective, but there are many correlations in our data that we do not find 'interesting' in a literary sense.

Furthermore, we can note that quantitative methods allow us to be specific about what tragedies are *not* in a way traditional literary analysis would find much harder. This is important, because Figure 20.1 shows tragedies spread across a large area of the graph, implying that there is a large amount of linguistic variation within the genre. Tragedies plotted in the upper right of the graph will have a different linguistic make-up to those in the lower left—and tragedies close to the centre of the graph will differ from those in the outlier cloud. So what characterizes tragedies is not simply the shared *presence* of a set of features (the negative ones listed in Table 20.2), but also the shared relative *absence* of a second group (the oral features displayed in Table 20.3).

A further strength of quantitative methods is that they can often present us with results that are counter-intuitive and which open up avenues for further research. In the course of this study, for example, we identified a third set of associated features with a role in patterning the placement of the texts, whose distribution raises some fascinating literary questions. Features in this group share a function in representing the self, as shown in Table 20.4.

Counter-intuitively, to us at least, this 'self' group is generally more characteristic of comedies than tragedies: use of this group of features tends to pull plays into the lower right-hand side of the graph. We find this counter-intuitive because of literary accounts of tragedy as the locus for Renaissance investigation, even creation, of the self: if these

Table 20.2 Linguistic features or Language Action Types (LATs, using the terminology employed by our linguistic software, Docuscope) of the 'negative' group

Standards Negative	words and phrases indicating standards or values most people would treat negatively: e.g. *disease, unworthy, oppressed, malady, shame, the poor, unkind, envy, treason.*
Fear	words and phrases referencing or evoking fear: e.g. *fear, threatening, anxiety, terror, apprehension, dangerously.*
Negative Relation	words and phrases used to represent relationships between people which are either negatively viewed or unstable: e.g. *at war with, has been offensive, broke his heart, the rift between, draw blood.*
Anger	words and phrases referencing or evoking anger: e.g. *angry, vengeance, slaughter, contempt, rage, cannot forgive, coward, reproach, indignant, cruel.*
Negativity	words and phrases indicating negativity and negative emotions: e.g. *gloom, distrust, abhor, wretched, disappointment, warning, death, ugly, villain.*

Table 20.3 Linguistic features (LATs) of the 'oral' group

Direct Address	pronouns and discourse markers aimed at an interlocutor: e.g. *you, you are, prithee, thy, thou, yourself, my Lord.*
First Person	bare first person pronouns: e.g. *I, me, mine, myself.*
Question	*wh-* question words and punctuation implying questions: e.g. *Who? What? Why?*
Oral Cues	discourse markers typical of flowing speech: e.g. *nay, well, good morrow, ho, yea, ha.*
Person Property	words and phrases designating occupational and social roles: e.g. *brother, bondsman, mother, generals, men, sir, fellow, attendants, wife, women.*
Imperative	this feature identifies imperatives by looking for the base form of a verb occurring immediately after a full stop: e.g. *'. Speak,' '. Go,' '. Let,' '. Give,' '. Swear'.*

Table 20.4 Linguistic features (LATs) of the 'self' group

Self-Disclosure	first person pronouns occurring with verbs expressing thought or consciousness (e.g. *I think, I am, I feel, I believe, I confess*) and certain pronoun-preposition combinations that function similarly (e.g. *to me, for me*).
Autobiography	first person pronouns occurring with verbs expressing thought or consciousness (e.g. *I think, I am, I feel, I believe, I confess*) and certain pronoun-preposition combinations that function similarly (e.g. *to me, for me*). first person pronouns used with a certain set of verbs, often past-tense, and a set of nouns that indicate past or familial relationships, in an attempt to capture self-revelation that is rooted in a sense of the past: e.g. *I have been, I was, when I, my name, my daughter.*
Metadiscourse	explicit signposts from a speaker or writer to guide the audience through a piece of language: e.g. *too, we shall, but there is, either, further, moreover, aforesaid, as it were*. In our analysis, this LAT patterns with the 'self' features because it includes phrases such as 'I come', 'we come', 'I shall', 'we shall', 'I will consider', 'I will do'.

were correct, we might expect 'self' features to be a characteristic of tragedy, or at least of Shakespearean tragedy. As we will see, however, this is not the case. We do not have space in this overview of the corpus to investigate this finding fully, but we will discuss it further in relation to Shakespeare below, and we invite other scholars to test our finding.[7]

To sum-up the first part of our study. The 'negative'/'oral' opposition is the key distinction between the language found in tragedies and that found in comedies. Of course, both genres use features from both groups: tragedies use first person pronouns, and comedies use negative language. But what digital analysis can show us are the consistent differences in rates of use: overall, tragedies consistently use more negative language, and less oral language, than comedies. Look, like a human, at any one speech, and features from both groups are likely to be present; look, like a computer, at 554 plays at once, and small but consistent differences in frequency combine to produce clear tendencies.

We now move on to consider Shakespeare. Figure 20.4 once again shows the entire Early Modern drama corpus, this time with Shakespeare's tragedies picked out as black circles, and his comedies as black triangles. Figure 20.4 makes an interesting comparison with Figure 20.3: where Chapman's tragedies and comedies divided neatly into the tragedy and comedy quadrants, Shakespeare's plays are not so well-behaved.

The most striking difference between Figures 20.3 and 20.4 is the lack of clear generic separation between Shakespeare's tragedies and comedies. Where Chapman's tragedies and comedies grouped by genre in different parts of the graph, Shakespeare's plays all occupy broadly the same space. Additionally, both genres tend to lie slightly away from their 'core' quadrants as identified in the corpus-wide analysis. This is particularly clear for tragedy, pulled lower and to the left of the core tragedy space, and slightly less clear for comedy. This is a suggestive finding: on the one hand, Shakespeare's plays are all within the central space of Early Modern drama, so his linguistic choices are not extreme, but on the other, his

---

[7] It may be that our 'self' features are missing some crucial marker which the tragedies associated with the 'self' in literary-critical work use to effect its linguistic representation. In which case, its identification is a job for literary criticism.

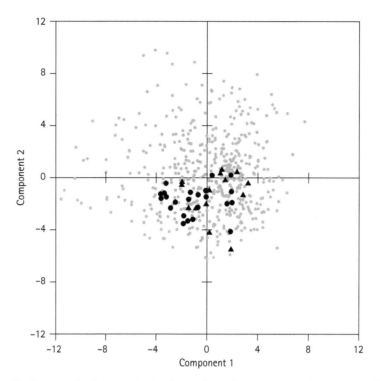

FIG. 20.4 Shakespeare's plays in the Early Modern drama corpus (tragedies = black circles; comedies = black triangles).

linguistic choices map slightly to the margins of the core, with less clear generic distinction than we find in some writers (e.g. Chapman). This suggests a mixing of features in general, though it is important not to forget that Shakespeare's plays do still show usage of the typical genre-features at rates comparable to those of other 'core' writers (if this were not the case, his plays would lie in the outer regions of the graph).[8]

If we look at Shakespeare's tragedies, and ask what sends them to the lower left, we can say that this is primarily due to the presence of three groups of language-features. First, Shakespeare's tragedies have the expected higher rates of the 'negative' group features. Here, as an example, is a passage of 'negative' language from *Titus*:

> Art thou not **sorry for** these **heinous** deeds?
> I, that I had not done a thousand more:
> Even now I **curse the** day, and yet I think
> Few come within few compass of my **curse**,
> Wherein I did not some **Notorious ill**,
> As **kill** a man, or else devise his **death**,

---

[8] It is also important to point out the effect of corpus size on what we can 'see' in this type of analysis. In the context of 554 plays, the differences between Shakespeare's genres are not big enough to separate them: the similarities are more significant, and all of his plays group together. Reduce the corpus size, for example to just Shakespeare, as in our early work, and the generic differences become visible. No view is 'truer' than any other: but different perspectives allow you to see different aspects of the data.

Ravish a Maid, or plot the way to do it,
Accuse some Innocent, and **forswear** my self,
Set **deadly Enmity** between two Friends,
Make **poor** men's Cattle **break their necks**,
Set **fire on** Barnes and Haystackes in the night,
And bid the Owners quench them with the **tears**:
Oft have I dug up **dead men** from their graves,
And set them upright at their dear Friends door,
Even when their **sorrows** almost was **forgot**,
And on their skins, as on the Bark of Trees,
Have with my knife carved in Romaine Letters,
Let not your **sorrow** die, though I am **dead**.

(William Shakespeare, *Titus Andronicus*
TCP A11954_27)

In addition to this, however, Shakespeare's tragedies are pulled down into the lower part of the graph because they use two sets of features more than those tragedies plotted in the mid-point, and upper right of the graph. The first set is the 'oral' group (primarily associated with comedies). Here is the opening of *Julius Caesar*, which has a large amount of 'oral' language:

HEnce: home **you** idle Creatures, **get you** home:
Is this a Holiday? What, know **you** not
(Being Mechanical) you ought not walk
Upon a labouring day, without the sign
Of **your** Profession? Speak, what Trade art **thou?**
Why Sir, a Carpenter.
Where is thy Leather Apron, and **thy** Rule?
What dost **thou** with **thy** best Apparel on?
You sir, what Trade are **you?**
Truly Sir, in respect of a fine Workman, **I am** but as you would say, a Cobbler.
But what Trade art **thou?** Answer **me** directly.
A Trade Sir, that **I hope I** may use, with a safe Conscience, which is indeed Sir,
    a Mender of bad souls.
What Trade **thou** knave? **Thou** naughty knave, what Trade?
Nay I beseech **you** Sir, be not out with me: yet if **you be** out Sir, I can mend **you.**
What mean **thou** by that? Mend **me, thou** saucy Fellow?
Why sir, Cobble **you.**
Thou art a Cobbler, art **thou?**

(William Shakespeare, *Julius Caesar*
TCP A11954_30)

Admittedly this is an extreme example, but the presence of all of Shakespeare's tragedies below the horizontal axis of the graph shows that this increased use of 'oral' features (relative to tragedies plotted above and to the right) is consistent.

The second set of features pulling Shakespeare's tragedies away from the core tragedy space is an additional group termed the 'world-space' group (see Table 20.5). The linguistic items in this group are concerned with describing things in the visible world, and mapping the spaces in which objects and people exist. One implication of the location of Shakespeare's tragedies in the lower left of the graph is that they are more concerned with representing the 'real' physical world than many other Early Modern tragedies (especially those in the upper right of the graph).

Table 20.5 Linguistic features (LATs) of the world–space group.

Sense Objects	concrete nouns: e.g. lump, the fruit, forest, pawn, tongue.
Sense Property	properties of nouns: e.g. the appearance of, loud, hollow, round, old, voice of, sweet, hungry.
Spatial Relation	words and phrases indicating location in space: e.g. alcove, next door to, with whom, in the country, above, at the, dwell, alone.
Motions	language indicating motion: e.g. knocking, convulsions, unloose, till the, bowing, rising from, tremble, walk into the. Much of this has a figurative emotional sense (e.g. shudder, moved).

Here is an example of the 'world-space' group from *King Lear*:

> Thou were better **in a Grave**, then to answer with thy uncovered **body**, this **extremity of the Skies**. Is man no more then this? Consider him well. Thou ow'st the **Worm** no **Silk**; the Beast, no Hide; **the Sheep**, no **Wool**; **the Cat**, no **perfume**. Ha? Here's three on's are sophisticated. Thou art the thing it self; unaccommodated man is no more but such a poor, **bare**, **forked** Animal as thou art. Off, off you Landings: Come, unbutton **here**.
>
> Prithee Nunckle be contented, it is a naughty night to **swim** in. Now a **little fire** in a wild **Field**, were like an **old** Lechers **heart**, a **small spark**, all the rest on's **body**, **cold**: Look, here comes a **walking fire**.
>
> (William Shakespeare, King Lear TCP A11954_33)

There are two surprising findings here. First, Shakespeare's tragic language has an increased focus on the external, physical world compared to the language of most other Early Modern tragedies. Second, Shakespeare's tragedies show an *avoidance* of the 'self' group. High use of the 'self' group would have pulled Shakespeare's tragedies up and to the right, but they are located diagonally opposite, low and to the left—so within tragedies as a whole, Shakespeare's plays use these features less than the average.

Figure 20.4 shows that while there is generally not a very clear generic separation at this scale between Shakespeare's comedies and tragedies, there is a clear tendency for only comedies to have positive values on the horizontal axis: out of the Shakespeare corpus, only comedies appear on the right hand side of the graph. This means that Shakespeare uses 'self' language relatively more in comedy than in tragedy (though there are some comedies which do not use it very much). Here is an example of 'self' language from *The Winter's Tale*, as Autolycus slyly misrepresents himself.

> Doest lack any money? **I have** a little money for thee.
>
> No, good sweet sir: no, I beseech you sir: **I have** a Kinsman not past three quarters of a mile hence, unto whom **I was** going: **I shall** there have money, or any thing **I want**: Offer me no money I pray you, that kills **my heart**.
>
> What manner of Fellow was hee that robbed you?
>
> A fellow (sir) that **I have known** to go about with Troll-my-dames: **I knew** him once a servant of the Prince
>
> (William Shakespeare, The Winter's Tale TCP A11954_14)

And here is an example of 'self' language in the Shakespeare tragedy that lies closest to the right hand side of the graph: *Julius Caesar*. This comes from Brutus' reply to the conspirators, employing 'Self Disclosure' ('I am', 'I have', 'I would') and 'Metadiscourse' ('I shall', 'I will consider'):

> That you do love me, **I am** nothing jealous:
> What you would work me too, **I have** some aim:
> How **I have** thought of this, and of these times
> **I shall** recount hereafter. For this present,
> **I would** not so (with love I might entreat you)
> Be any further moved: What you have said,
> **I will consider**:
>
> (William Shakespeare, *Julius Caesar*
> TCP A11954_30)

There is of course much more to explore in these relationships. What we have provided here is the beginning of an outline of a space mapped out using one set of criteria.[9] This space can be investigated much more thoroughly—and other spaces can be created by counting different features in the same set of plays. In the following section we provide more detail of our methodology, a discussion of some of the implications for literary study, and a summary of findings and further questions.

Method

We use Docuscope, a rhetorical analysis package, to count linguistic features in a corpus of Early Modern drama. Computationally, Docuscope is a very simple string-matching program. It searches text files for strings of characters (made up of single words, phrases, and in some cases punctuation marks) which it recognizes from its dictionaries (which are simply lists of words and phrases). Each word or phrase that is recognized is tagged as belonging to a 'Language Action Type', or LAT. This is where Docuscope becomes more sophisticated: the LATs are rhetorical-linguistic categories, constructed and populated by the human designers of Docuscope. The LATs attempt to capture words and phrases that have predictable effects on the reader of a text: that create different experiences when reading.[10] We could have characterized the differences between genre with less developed categories—counting, for example, all of the prepositions in the plays and using these as discriminating features. We find, however, that the Docuscope categories are more 'interpretable' because they are functionally driven (and human-crafted).

---

[9] A reminder that our results, though we present them as being 'about' Early Modern drama, are restricted by (a) what Docuscope counts; and (b) our corpus. In the future, Docuscope will be adaptable by users so that what it counts can be adjusted, or changed completely—and of course, other text analysis tools are available. The Early Modern drama corpus will be refined over time, in terms of the plays it contains, the quality of the texts of those plays (as correction projects are funded), and the quality of the metadata.

[10] The language theory underpinning Docuscope, and the categories it sets up, are detailed in David Kaufer, Suguru Ishizaki, Brian Butler, Jeff Collins, *The Power of Words: Unveiling the Speaker and Writer's Hidden Craft*, London, Routledge, 2004. A number of studies illustrating its use in the classroom, and authorship work are listed at http://wiki.mla.org/index.php/Docuscope (accessed 8.5.2015).

For example, the LAT 'First Person' tags first person pronouns ('I', 'me', and so on): a text high in 'First Person' is likely to be presenting a relatively straightforward set of self-references. This may seem a rather obvious and crude example, but some of the subtlety of Docuscope's categories (and one of the drawbacks in its method of operation) can be seen by comparing 'First Person' with three other LATs, 'Self Disclosure', 'Self-Reluctance', and 'Autobiography' (see Table 20.4). These three LATs attempt to tag more complex forms of self-representation. 'Self-Disclosure' tags first person pronouns in combination with verbs associated with self-revelation, or prepositions doing a similar job ('I am', 'I think', '"I feel', 'I believe', 'I confess', 'to me', 'for me')—here, a more complex, more conscious, self-representation is effected. 'Self-Reluctance' tags first person pronouns in combination with verbs of resistance or disagreement ('"I regret that', 'I am forced to', 'I had to', 'against my will')—again attempting to capture a more nuanced self-representation. 'Autobiography' tags first person pronouns combining with verbs, nouns, or conjunctions in self-representations which reflect back in time on a personal past ('I have been', 'I was', 'when I', 'my name', 'my daughter'). This gives some sense of the distinctions the designers of Docuscope were seeking to be able to make in textual effects. It also demonstrates one of the restrictions on Docuscope's counting: no character string can be tagged more than once, and each character string is included in the longest string Docuscope can find. So any first person pronoun tagged as 'Autobiography' is not available to be tagged as 'First Person'. The same is true for all character strings: Docuscope behaves as if all elements of language contribute once only, and in only one way, to the effect of a passage. This makes counting simpler, but it certainly runs against what we know of language.

The version of Docuscope used in this study has 113 categories into which it places strings: for each text it counts, it produces a tagged version of the text (viewable in a text-viewer), and a spreadsheet-readable file (as 'csv' or comma-separated variable file). The csv file gives the normalized frequency of each of the 113 LATs for each of the texts in the analysed corpus (in our case 554 plays).[11] We discard any LATs where the frequency is zero, or close to zero. In this study, our results are based on a spreadsheet with 554 rows and 72 active columns.[12] Once we have passed our play corpus through Docuscope, we have effectively compared 554 plays on the basis of 72 points of comparison—giving us 39,888 data points. At this point, we come up against the limitations of human attention and cognition. We could try and 'read' the 39,888 cells of the spreadsheet, looking for patterns of similarity and difference, perhaps including extra columns of metadata (author, date, genre, and so on). Of course, we would not get very far: humans are bad at reading large tables of numbers, and in any case, a lot of the information in the spreadsheet is not very

---

[11] Normalization means that the raw totals for each LAT in each play are adjusted to show frequency per a set amount of words. This allows us to compare LAT frequencies between plays of different lengths.

[12] The 41 LATs excluded from our study are as follows: Attack_Citation; Authoritative_Citation; CommunicatorRole; ConfirmExperience;; ConfirmedThought; Confront; Consequence; Contested_Citation; Definition; DialogCues; DirectReasoning; Example; Feedback; FollowUp; Future_in_Past; In_Media; Innovations; MatureProcess; MoveBody; NegFeedback; Neg_Citation; Negative_Attribution; PosFeedback; Positive_Attribution; Precedent_Defending; Precedent_Setting; PriorKnowledge; Procedures; Promise; Quotation; ReceivedPOV; Reinforce; Repair_Citation; Request; Responsibility; SelfReluctance; Self_Promise; Speculative_Citation; Substitution; Support; TimeDate.

interesting: all the plays may be more or less the same on a particular LAT, or the variations in frequency between them might have no pattern.

So what we need to do is reduce the complexity of the information, and present it in a
way that will enable us to see patterns of similarity and difference that are interesting to
us. This is the basis of almost all statistical analysis and visualization: *reduction* in information, and then presentation in a form humans can cope with cognitively.

In fact, put like this, what we are doing is pretty similar to what literary critics have
tended to do in the past: they reduce the complexity of the information by focussing on a
few attributes of the texts they study, and they make a huge body of material cognitively
accessible to humans by citing just a few quotations in evidence. And the ultimate aim
can be cast in similar terms too: both approaches seek to say 'look at this text—it is similar to this text for these reasons, and different to those texts for these reasons'. This is a
simplification of several hundred years of literary criticism of course, but it is not a gross
misrepresentation.

How much of a simplification we make to our data during the analysis will become clear
as we look more closely at what we have done by counting 72 LATs in each of our plays.
What we effectively did was to plot all 554 plays in a space defined by the total linguistic
variation between all the LATs in the corpus. Each play is located at a unique point in that
space—and each point is fixed by a set of co-ordinates made up by all of the frequencies
for each LAT in the play. Because we counted 72 LATs, each play has 72 co-ordinates: and
the space representing the linguistic variation in the Early Modern drama corpus is made
up of 72 dimensions.

Once again, we are beyond the limits of human brains. We can easily imagine a one
dimensional space: that is a line. We can plot all 554 plays along a line using the frequency
results from any one of the LATs, running from lowest to highest. This would be a useful
visualization, as it would quickly show us the relationships between plays for this single
LAT. We can also easily imagine a two dimensional space: this is a graph with each axis
representing the results from a different LAT. Each play would have a position in the space
of the graph produced by the two values. Again, this is a useful visualization—perhaps
even more useful—as it shows us the relationship between two LATs: plays high on both
will be at the top right of the graph; plays low on both at bottom left. And we can also
imagine a three-dimensional visualization, adding a third axis, and LAT, to our graph, so
the plays are arranged in a cuboid space.

At this point, while our brains give up, mathematics does not. We can carry on adding
LATs and axes until we have 72 dimensions, with our plays arranged within the resulting, unimaginable, but mathematically describable, space. What we now need is a means
of seeing the 72-dimensional space in a form humans can process: a way of reducing the
dimensionality. There are various standard ways of doing this statistically, and in this
study we have used Principal Components Analysis.[13] This is a common technique for
reducing the dimensionality of complex data sets, and revealing patterns of association

[13] We give a fuller account of PCA in Anupam Basu, Jonathan Hope, and Michael Witmore,
forthcoming, 'The Professional and Linguistic Communities of Early Modern Dramatists' in
Roger D. Sell, Anthony W. Johnson, and Helen Wilcox eds., *Community-Making in Early Stuart
Theatres: Stage and Audience* (Ashgate). Most standard statistics textbooks cover PCA (and Factor
Analysis, to which it is closely related). We have found Andy Field, *Discovering Statistics Using IBM*

within high-dimensional space. Like all statistical techniques, it is simply one way of slicing through the data: it does not give the only possible view of a data set, and there may be other approaches that will show other things about the data. We have used PCA here because we think the results are interesting—and we have attempted to support them from non-PCA techniques[14]—but once again, readers should treat this study and these results as experimental and exploratory. There is much more to be investigated in this data set, and many other approaches to be tried.

The graph shown in Figures 20.1-4 is a two-dimensional representation of the 72-dimensional data space. The axes of the graph are two 'principal components', or PCs. These are derived from a mathematical reduction of the relationships between the 72 LATs in Principal Components Analysis space (PCA Space). Each PC is an attempt to represent as much of the variation in the 72-dimensional data space as possible: the 72 coordinates fixing each play in PCA space are reduced to two, one on each PC, which reduce and summarize the much more complex high-dimensional space. If we imagine the 72-dimensional space as a graph with 72 axes, all pointing in different directions, then the PCs are attempts to draw axes which 'summarize' as many as possible of the 72 axes, re-orienting the data around a smaller number of axes that capture the most variation. Together, the two PCs we have extracted from this data set account for just over 26 per cent of the total variation in the drama corpus. This means that we have thrown out about 74 per cent of the information! The reward for doing this, we hope, is that we can now see relationships and patterns in the data that are impossible to visualize at 72 dimensions: but we need to remember that this is a *reduction*—a simplification—and that other views and representations of the data set are possible.

CONCLUDING DISCUSSION

Digital tools and resources (such as EEBO–TCP) allow literary scholars to approach their object of study in new ways. In many respects, we continue to do the same thing: we read texts and compare them, making links and contrasts. We associate certain texts, and we separate others. Traditionally, literary criticism has made these associations and separations using notions such as 'genre', 'influence', and 'period'. The evidence for links and distinctions has been gleaned by close reading, and is constituted by quotation, and summary of plot, theme and technique. Although not always the case, it is generally true that literary criticism has sought out the exceptional above the typical: a tragedy is discussed

---

SPSS Statistics: And Sex and Drugs and Rock and Roll (London: 2013, 4th ed.) useful. Literary scholars will probably get most out of Mick Alt, *Exploring Hyperspace: A Non-Mathematical Explanation of Multivariate Analysis* (London: 1990), which is a brief and very clear conceptual account of what the statistical procedures are trying to achieve.

[14] PCA is designed to extract patterns from very complex data sets. One consequence of this is that the patterns it extracts can themselves be very complex, and difficult for human interpreters to make sense of because they consist of multiple relationships between variables—or LATs in this case. In this study, we have checked the individual distributions of the LATs we focus on in tragedies against their distribution in the drama as a whole. The box plots for this can be seen at http://winedarksea.org/?p=2013 (accessed 8.5.2015).

as such because of an explicit, or implicit, claim that it is an outstandingly good tragedy, or is unusual in some important way. Plays considered to be 'average' or 'typical' examples of their genre may be referenced as such, but are unlikely to be the focus of sustained examination.

As Ted Underwood has suggested, the dominant model in literary study is one of exceptionalism and fracture: the narratives literary scholars construct stress the turning point, the break with the past: major writers are points of sudden change, after which nothing is the same.[15] While digital methods allow us to continue comparing and making claims about similarity and difference, the fact that they allow us to do these operations at scales, and with a consistency not possible for single human readers, shifts the nature of literary study as individual texts are read through the lens of much larger groups. Further, as Underwood has argued, the nature of the evidence digital studies present for use in constructing literary arguments, and the stories that evidence tends to tell, reorients the history of literary study itself: digital evidence, high in frequency, stressing the average and the mean, rather than the exceptional outliers, running over timescales and including volumes of text impossible for single human readers, tends to emphasize gradual change and continuity rather than sudden fracture. The differences it detects tend to be relative rather than absolute.

Digital methods can detect things human readers find impossible or very difficult: shifts in the frequency of very common features;[16] absences rather than presences. And these offer new ways of approaching familiar texts—new ways of contextualizing them. Digital methods also offer an opening up of the canon: with large corpora, each text is treated equally by the software—associations between canonical texts and those less, or hardly ever studied, are possible. Texts previously available only in research libraries, or subscription-only web resources, and hardly mentioned in accounts of literary history, or on undergraduate survey courses, will pop up next to canonical texts in visualizations: students will be able to access them, and will have a reason to do so.

However, we should note that there are downsides to this apparently bright prospect. In digital work we are constrained by other things than the limits of human attention spans and cognition—though it is easy to forget those constraints as we conjure multi-coloured three-dimensional graphs from our software. We are constrained first of all by what *can* be counted: at a base level this is strings of characters, or, slightly more sophisticated, tags in a text file. When we claim to be counting rhetorical features, or influence, or style, we are really counting something we have identified as a proxy for those things: something that can, ultimately, be reduced to a set of character codes a program can recognize. Our results will only be as good as the relationship of the proxy to whatever it is we think

---

[15] Ted Underwood, *Why Literary Periods Mattered: Historical Contrast and the Prestige of English Studies* (Stanford: Stanford University Press, 2013)—especially ch. 6, 'Digital Humanities and the Future of Literary History', 157-75—on the strange commitment to discontinuity in literary studies, and the tendency of digital/at scale work to dissolve this into a picture of gradualism. Underwood notes the extent to which this is a Romantic and post-Romantic mind-set: Classical and Renaissance approaches to literary history were very different, generally assuming genres to be trans-historical, with 'good' writers fulfilling, rather than revolutionizing, generic expectations.

[16] See e.g. on the frequency of 'the' in *Macbeth*, Jonathan Hope and Michael Witmore, 'The Language of *Macbeth*', in *Macbeth: The State of Play*, ed. Ann Thompson, Arden (London: Bloomsbury, 2014), 183-208.

we are studying: identifying and describing the proxy is a job for literary specialists, as Underwood has argued—and often the process of identifying such proxies prompts fundamental questions about the object of study: what is 'influence'? what is 'style'? These questions are outside the remit of digital methods; they belong squarely back in 'traditional' literary theory.[17]

Even assuming some ideal situation where we identify a perfect, countable, proxy for whatever it is we wish to study, we are also constrained by what we have to count *in*. The impressive size of digital data sets offers an illusion of completeness: EEBO–TCP offers us 'every' printed text in English between certain dates. But of course, this is 'really' the set of *surviving* printed texts from the period[18]—and, while an impressively extensive collection, it is not *complete* even of those printed texts we know to have survived—'new' texts are still being added to EEBO. The huge body of surviving Early Modern manuscript material is absent—which is significant for this chapter given the number of manuscript plays we know about in the period (and even more so for those who wish to use EEBO–TCP for cultural and linguistic history).

Even within the texts we have, we must remember that no data set is perfect: EEBO–TCP texts are human artefacts: keyed transcriptions of microfilm; microfilms which are themselves imperfect representations of imperfectly printed texts. The EEBO–TCP text files have many gaps, marked by the transcribers, where they simply could not read what was in front of them (this is especially the case for black letter texts). We can hope that these gaps are (more or less) evenly distributed through the corpus, and that the counts we perform are on features so frequent that the losses due to miss- or missing transcription are negligible—that the data is 'good enough', in a telling statistical phrase likely to strike literary, and especially textual scholars, as chilling—but we must always be prepared to accept that our results may be affected by such gaps.

SUMMARY OF FINDINGS AND FURTHER QUESTIONS

1. It is possible to identify linguistic signatures for tragedy and comedy: compared to the corpus of Early Modern drama as a whole, tragedies are characterized by increased use of language involved with the communication of negativity, and reduced use of language involved in representing oral exchange. (Comedies show the reverse pattern.)
   Further questions: (a) Why do writers follow these linguistic patterns when writing in these two genres? Is there something about the dramatic situations the genres

---

[17] For a discussion of 'influence', see 'What is Influence?' http://winedarksea.org/?p=1629 with comments from Matt Jockers and Ted Underwood (accessed 8.5.2015), and Bill Benzon's detailed reading of Jockers' *Macroanalysis*, the full version of which can be downloaded from this URL: http://papers.ssrn.com/sol3/papers.cfm?abstract_id=2491205 (accessed 8.5.2015).

[18] Alan Farmer is currently working on estimates of the number of texts and editions we have lost. Although we can never know for sure how much material has not survived, it will be important for future users of EEBO–TCP to remind themselves that, however large the digitized corpus, it is always incomplete.

create that favour the use of certain types of language over others? (b) Which plays or writers go against these general trends to produce tragedies which are mapped onto the 'comic' half of the graph?

2. Shakespeare's tragic language, while falling in the central 'core' of linguistic practice, can be characterized in relation to the tragedy corpus as a whole as using more language associated with real-world description, and the representation of oral exchange. Perhaps surprisingly, given the history of critical comment on Shakespeare, it does not show an increase in the use of language associated with self-revelation.

   Further questions: (a) Why does Shakespeare move towards real-world reference and orality? (b) Is our surprising finding regarding 'self' language robust? Are we counting the right features? What constitutes 'self' in language and can it be counted? (c) If our finding that Shakespeare fits within the common core of writers in terms of linguistic practice is right, what makes him 'better' than other writers who share his linguistic practices?

3. Taken as a whole, the corpus of Early Modern drama is characterized by a central core group of plays with a broadly similar linguistic makeup.

   Further questions: (a) Is this core group made up of particular types of plays, authors or genres—for example, are professional playwrights/major companies located here?

4. Outside this core group, outlier plays are found in only certain parts of the possible linguistic space (on the left-hand side of a diagonal line drawn across the graph).

   Further questions: (a) Is the outlier cloud made up of particular types of plays, authors or genres? (b) Why do no plays have the linguistic makeup that would put them on the right-hand side of the diagonal?

5. There are many practical issues to be faced as we develop this hybrid approach to exploring literary texts. Notably in this paper we have come up against the problem of referencing within the processed TCP texts we have used for our analysis. Scholars will need to address this if we are to be able to move through the TCP text set easily: especially as we move from working on the relatively well-known drama texts to the rest of the corpus.

SELECT BIBLIOGRAPHY

Alt, Mick, *Exploring Hyperspace: A Non-Mathematical Explanation of Multivariate Analysis* (London: McGraw Hill, 1990).

Hope, Jonathan and Witmore, Michael, 'The Language of *Macbeth*', in *Macbeth: The State of Play*, ed. Ann Thompson, Arden (London: Bloomsbury, 2014), 183–208.

McDonald, Russ, 'The Language of Tragedy', in Claire McEachern, ed., *The Cambridge Companion to Shakespearean Tragedy*, 2nd edn. (Cambridge: Cambridge University Press, 2006), 23–49.

PART III

READING
THE TRAGEDIES

CHAPTER 21

··

'ROMAINE TRAGEDIE'
The Designs of Titus Andronicus

··

MICHAEL NEILL

There is no document of civilization, which is not at the same time a document of barbarism.

(Walter Benjamin)[1]

WRITING to a friend in 1947, the novelist Malcolm Lowry described his recent hospital experience: 'I reread *Titus Andronicus* … after the operation—in fact while it was still going on, for the doctor had forgotten something on the operating table and had to pursue me, needle and claw bar in hand, to the ward itself. It isn't really such a bad play after all. That is, there seems to be nothing wrong with it, save the writing and sundry little details like that.'[2] The black comedy of the surgeon's pursuit, tailored to resemble the *grand guignol* of the play itself, is of a piece with Lowry's ironic mockery of Shakespeare's earliest tragedy,[3] and symptomatic of the patronizing disdain in which *Titus* was held for three centuries.[4]

Titus was, however, among the most successful plays of its own day: frequently revived, and twice reprinted after its initial publication in 1594, it could still attract the scornful envy of Ben Jonson in his Induction to *Bartholomew Fair* (1614), more than twenty years after its first performance. But the play's reputation did not survive the critical and theatrical revolution of the mid-seventeenth century, which found in its accumulation of atrocities and black-comic grotesquerie a barbaric abuse of tragic decorum—making it *'the most incorrect and indigested piece in all [its author's] Works … rather a heap of Rubbish then a Structure'*,

---

[1] *Theses on the Philosophy of History* (1940), VII.

[2] Letter to Earle Birney, 26 March, 1949, cited from *The Selected Letters of Malcom Lowry,* ed. Harvey Breit and Margerie Bonner Lowry (London: Penguin, 1985), 176.

[3] The play's first recorded performance was by Sussex's Men at the Rose playhouse on 23 January 1594—the year of its initial publication. It was then described as a 'new' play; but there are reasons for thinking that it may have been written before the prolonged plague-closure of London theatres in June 1592, and it might even belong to the late 1580s. The claim of novelty may simply have referred to the addition of 3.2, which did not appear in print until the 1623 Folio.

[4] For discussion of Aaron as a re-imagined and a partially humanized version of the diabolic medieval Vice, see Rory Loughnane, Ch. 3 in this volume, 46–8.

as its Restoration reviser famously complained.[5] Rejected by Hazlitt as a mere 'accumulation of vulgar physical horrors', and by T. S. Eliot as 'one of the stupidest and most uninspired plays ever written',[6] it has attracted the odium even of the bardolatrous Harold Bloom, who dismisses it as 'a poetic atrocity'.[7] On the stage—though briefly revived in Victorian times by the great African-American actor, Ira Aldridge, who transformed Shakespeare's villainous Moor, Aaron, into 'a noble and lofty character'[8]—*Titus* was allowed to languish in almost complete obscurity until the second half of the twentieth century, when a powerful revival by Peter Brook at Stratford-upon-Avon (1955) awakened new interest in its vision of civilizational collapse, finding there a disturbing mirror for the post-war world.

Brook's revival stimulated an immediate critical response, beginning with a groundbreaking lecture by Eugene Waith:[9] where Brook discovered a theatrical language for the play by matching the conscious artificiality of its language with shows of stylized violence, Waith sought to redeem *Titus*' literary reputation by exploring the dark wit with which its melodramatic action is counterpointed by ingenious reworkings of episodes and motifs from Ovid's *Metamorphoses*. Subsequent studies have helped to amplify Waith's account of *Titus*'s formal strengths by tracing the elaborate patterns of imagery and symbolism that are used to set city against wilderness, Roman against Goth.[10] In the wake of this work, critical responses to the play have become increasingly sympathetic. Yet this emerging consensus has paradoxically coincided with a gradual acceptance that *Titus* was not—as its earliest attributions seemed to indicate—the unaided work of Shakespeare.[11]

The notion that another playwright was involved has a long history: Ravenscroft sought to justify his own refurbishment by dissociating *Titus* as much as he could from Shakespeare's genius, declaring that 'I have been told by some anciently conversant with the Stage, that it was not Originally his, but brought by a private Author to be Acted, and he only gave some Master-touches to one or two of the Principal Parts or Characters.'[12] This claim was widely accepted throughout the eighteenth century, and ultimately provided the foundation for the disintegrationist arguments, first advanced by J. M. Robertson,[13] that dominated much twentieth-century criticism of the play. Whilst some scholars have continued to argue for Shakespeare's sole authorship, the overwhelming balance of opinion

---

[5] Edward Ravenscroft, 'To the Reader', *Titus Andronicus, or the Rape of Lavinia* (London, 1687), Sig. A2. Oddly enough, given this exhibition of disdain, Ravenscroft's adaptation is, by Restoration standards, unusually faithful to the original.

[6] William Hazlitt, *Characters of Shakespear's Plays & Lectures on the English Poets* (London, 1818), 316; T. S. Eliot, *Selected Essays, 1917-1932* (London: Faber, 1951), 82.

[7] Harold Bloom, *Shakespeare: The Invention of the Human* (New York: Riverhead Books, 1998), 77–86.

[8] Anonymous review in *The Era*, 26 April, 1857, 10. For a useful account of Aldridge's version see Jonathan Bate's introduction to his Arden edition (London: Routledge, 1995), 54–9.

[9] Later published as 'The Metamorphosis of Violence in *Titus Andronicus*', *Shakespeare Survey* 10 (1957), 26–35.

[10] Alan Summers, 'Wilderness of Tigers: Structure and Symbolism in *Titus Andronicus*', *Essays in Criticism* 10 (1960), 275–89; A. C. Hamilton, '*Titus Andronicus*: The Form of Shakespearean Tragedy', *Shakespeare Quarterly* 14 (1963), 201–13.

[11] Although the original quarto (1594) was published anonymously, *Titus* was listed among Shakespeare's works as early as 1598 by Francis Meres in *Palladis Tamia*, and was among the tragedies included in the First Folio (1623).

[12] Ravenscroft, 'To the Reader', Sig. A2.

[13] J. M Robertson, *Did Shakespeare Write 'Titus Andronicus'?* (London: Watts & Co., 1905); and *An Introduction to the Study of Shakespeare Canon* (London: Routledge, 1924).

now inclines to the view that it is indeed a collaborative work, and that George Peele was responsible for the whole of Act 1, as well as for Act 2, Scene 1, probably for Act 2, Scene 2, and perhaps for Act 4, Scene 1—in all approximately one-third of the entire play.[14] What becomes abundantly clear, however—both from the play's dramaturgical coherence and from the consistency of its linguistic and theatrical detail—is that the two dramatists must have collaborated very closely, repeatedly exchanging ideas and perhaps even editing or revising one another's material.[15]

The play's more recent performance history—including Deborah Warner's superb RSC production (1987-8), and Julie Taymor's remarkable cinematic version (1999)—has amply demonstrated the theatrical power of what Shakespeare and Peele achieved. But its real originality has been obscured by what even many of its admirers, looking at it through the prism of Shakespeare's mature tragedies, have seen as the play's wooden characterization and melodramatic action. In this context, it is worth remembering that on the popular stages of Elizabethan London, tragedy was itself a relative novelty; and that, in composing this play, the two playwrights were helping to reinvent a genre that had effectively ceased to exist for more than a thousand years.[16] London's first permanent playhouse, James Burbage's The Theatre, had been erected in 1576; and in the next twenty years it was followed by three similar buildings. Yet surprisingly few plays denominated as tragedies survive from this initial period, and all are from its second decade: what is most striking about these pioneering works is their extraordinarily various, experimental character—as if their authors were conscious of working in a dramatic form for which there were no secure guidelines: thus the terms 'tragedy' and 'tragical' could encompass anything from Kyd's neo-Senecan revenge drama, *The Spanish Tragedy*, to the dark satire of Marlowe's *Jew of Malta* and the revamped morality drama of his *Dr Faustus*; from the domestic melodrama of the anonymous *Arden of Faversham*, to the sequence of rhetorical joustings and bloodthirsty tableaux that make up the two parts of Marlowe's *Tamburlaine*. By self-consciously reaching back to the classical past to create what its first edition called *The Most Lamentable Romaine Tragedie of Titus Andronicus*,[17] Shakespeare and Peele struck out in their own new direction.

The designation 'Romaine Tragedie', like Burbage's choice of the classical name 'Theatre' in place of the more familiar 'playhouse', constituted a claim to cultural legitimacy,[18] one

---

[14] For a detailed summary of the evidence, see Brian Vickers, *Shakespeare, Co-Author: A Historical Study of Five Collaborative Plays* (Oxford: Oxford University Press, 2002).

[15] For evidence see Colin Burrow, *Shakespeare and Classical Antiquity* (Oxford: Oxford University Press, 2013), 113–14.

[16] See Rory Loughnane, Ch. 3 in this volume, 36–43.

[17] The long title may have been devised by its publisher Edward White; but his emphasis on the play's 'Roman' character was anticipated by the printer John Danter, whose entry in the Stationers' Register (6 February 1594) includes 'a booke intituled a Noble Roman Historye of Tytus Andronicus'. For further discussion of the play's deliberate Romanness, see Ronald Broude, 'Roman and Goth in *Titus Andronicus*', *Shakespeare Studies* 6 (1970), 27–34; Gail Kern Paster, *The Idea of the City in the Age of Shakespeare* (Athens: University of Georgia Press, 1986), 58–61, 65–6, 82–4; Robert S. Miola, *Shakespeare's Rome* (Cambridge: Cambridge University Press, 1983), 42–75; Heather James, 'Cultural Disintegration in *Titus Andronicus*: Mutilating Titus, Vergil, and Rome', in *Violence in Drama: Themes in Drama* 13 (1991), 123–40; Bate, Introd., 16–21; and Tom Bishop, Ch. 15 in this volume, 238–41.

[18] Compare Thomas Heywood's justification for the establishment of London theatres: '*Rome* was a *metropolis* … so is *London* … being to receiue all Estates, all Princes, all Nations … to affoord them all choice of sports, pastimes, and Recreations', *An Apology for Actors* (1612), C2.

that enhanced the classical credentials of 'tragedy' with the declaration that this was drama of a distinctively 'Roman' kind. Unusually for Shakespeare, moreover, the plot that he and Peele devised seems to have been a largely invented one;[19] so it can hardly be a coincidence that its protagonist should share a name with the playwright remembered as 'the first that writ any *Roman* tragedy',[20] Lucius Livius Andronicus (c. 280 | 26—c. 200 BC).[21] *Titus*, after all, was amongst the first plays to bring ancient Rome onto the London stage;[22] and if we can judge from the costumes in Henry Peacham's famous Longleat drawing,[23] the players were equally determined to emphasize the play's 'Romaine' pretensions: although its pair of anonymous guards appear (with the cavalier anachronism usual to early modern theatres) in sixteenth-century armour, the sketch centres on the figure of Titus himself, arrayed in the military tunic, toga-like sash, and triumphal garland of a Roman general; before him kneels Tamora, clad in what is perhaps meant to be 'Gothic' costume,[24] accompanied by her sons and Aaron, all three in Roman tunics. The prominence of these sartorial details is pointed up by the lines that Peacham transcribed like an extended caption to his drawing: 'Stay, Roman bretheren, gracious conqueror … Sufficeth not that we are brought to Rome … Captive to thee and to thy Roman yoke?' (1.1.104-11).[25] The incantatory repetition is characteristic: indeed the words 'Rome' and 'Roman' recur no fewer than 127 times—more often than in any other of Shakespeare's plays[26]—44 times in Peele's opening act, and as many as 15 times in Shakespeare's much shorter final scene.

The effect of self-conscious Romanness is most obviously enhanced by the Latin tags with which speakers ornament their rhetoric[27]—as well as by the complex patterns of allusion to Roman poetry, especially Ovid's *Metamorphoses* and Virgil's *Aeneid*, that critics have explored.[28] Like Aeneas, the hero of Virgil's epic, Titus is 'surnamèd Pius' (1.1.23), whilst his daughter takes her name from the Latin princess, Lavinia, with whom this Trojan refugee cemented his bond to Italy. Saturninus' proposal to make Lavinia 'my

[19] Whilst Eugene Waith's Oxford edition supposes that the play was based on a prose 'History' of Titus (which, however survives only in an eighteenth-century chapbook), more recent opinion, as represented by Bate's New Arden , inclines the view that, like the ballad 'Titus Andronicus' Complaint', the history derived from the play.

[20] Heywood, *Apology,* D1v.

[21] The Roman dramatist may also have given his cognomen to Lucius, Titus' surviving son who remains to 'tell the tale' at the play's end (5.3.93).

[22] The public theatre records list only three earlier dramatizations of Roman subjects—all now lost: Stephen Gosson's *Catiline's Conspiracies* (1576-79), the anonymous *Caesar and Pompey* (1576-82) and *Titus and Vespasian* (1592).

[23] The drawing is reproduced in Waith's Oxford edition, 21.

[24] *OED*'s earliest use of 'Gothic' to denote a medieval style is from John Evelyn's *Diary* (1641), but Evelyn's confident phrasing suggests that the meaning was already current.

[25] All citations of *Titus* are from Eugene Waith's edition (Oxford: Oxford University Press (1984). Citations of other plays are from the Stanley Wells and Gary Taylor, eds., *William Shakespeare: The Complete Works* (Oxford University Press, 1986).

[26] Of Shakespeare's other Roman plays, *Coriolanus* (119) comes closest, followed by *Julius Caesar* (74), *Anthony and Cleopatra* (42), and *Cymbeline* (37). As Burrow points out, 'barbarous', the antonym of 'Roman' also occurs more frequently than in any other play (*Shakespeare and Classical Antiquity*, 113).

[27] These include quotations from Seneca (2.1.136; 4.1.80-1), Horace (4.2.20-1), and Ovid (4.3.4).

[28] See e.g. Waith, 'Metamorphosis', Burrow, *Shakespeare and Classical Antiquity*, 75. 105–17; and Peter Lake, Ch. 11 in the present volume, 173–6.

FIG. 21.1 Map made as adjunct to Elizabeth's campaign against the Earl of Tyrone, portraying the Norman conqueror of Ulster, Sir John de Courcy in the costume of a Roman general.

Used by permission of the National Maritime Museum, P/49 (25).

empress, Rome's royal mistress' (1.1.240-1), at first promises to repeat this foundational union; but the emperor's subsequent alliance with the Gothic queen, Tamora, together with Lavinia's violation by the empress's barbarous sons, reconfigures the play's beginning as a violent reversal of Aeneas' nuptial conquest; at the same time, a series of comparisons linking Lavinia to the most celebrated rape victim in Roman legend suggest that the play's events will enact the end rather than the beginning of a royal line: in *The Rape of Lucrece*, the narrative poem that Shakespeare published in the year that *Titus* was printed, he drew on versions of the story in Ovid's *Fasti* and Livy's *History of Rome*, to retrace the events that were supposed to have brought down the Tarquin monarchy and led to the establishment of the Roman Republic.[29]

The play's classical flourishes are not simply designed to flatter the self-esteem of educated playgoers, or to assert the theatre's pride in what the playwright Thomas Heywood would call its 'ancient Dignitie'.[30] By entangling two foundational legends within a narrative that belongs to the end of empire, *Titus*, in Jonathan Bate's words, 'collapses the whole of Roman history ... into a single action',[31] thereby making of itself a political fable whose exemplary character depends on the symbolic meaning of 'Rome' for the early modern imagination as the archetypal representative of what we now call 'civilization'. For Shakespeare's contemporaries, as Trevor Nunn observed, introducing his production of *The Romans* for the Royal Shakespeare Company, it was impossible to discuss the idea of 'civilization' in the abstract, since the word did not yet exist: Rome was 'the only example of the thing itself'.[32] Thus in *Titus* the opposition between Roman and Goth is initially imagined (though the action will progressively confuse this simple dichotomy) as a contest between civilization and barbarism: to be truly Roman, as Marcus Andronicus reminds his brother, is precisely to be defined as 'not barbarous' (1.1.378).

But Rome was more than a vanished example of a cultural ideal. The doctrine of *translatio imperii*, which encouraged European monarchs to see themselves as heirs to Rome's imperial mantle, is echoed in *Henry V*, for example, where Elizabeth becomes 'our gracious Empress', while the Chorus envisages Essex's return from Ireland like 'conqu'ring Caesar' to 'th'antique Rome' (5.0.26-30).[33] The doctrine was given a local accent by the carefully concocted legend of Brut, which made Britain another Rome, founded by another Trojan refugee, the great-grandson of Aeneas. So when *Titus*'s characters remember 'The wand'ring prince' Aeneas (2.3.22-4) and see in the destruction of 'Priam's Troy' a mirror for the 'civil wound' that threatens 'our Troy, our Rome' (5.3.79-86), the audience were clearly meant to feel Marcus' possessive pronouns as their own, since London was the reincarnation of both great cities.[34] Furthermore, the influence of antiquarians like Camden and Stowe had encouraged a sense of the island's Roman history as a physical

---

[29] It was surely the play's recollections of Lucrece that encouraged Ravenscroft to subtitle his revision of the play *The Rape of Lavinia*.

[30] Heywood, *An Apology for Actors* (1612), sig.D1.

[31] Bate, Introd., 17. See also Tom Bishop, Ch. 15 in this volume, 239–41.

[32] Trevor Nunn, Programme note for *The Romans* (*Coriolanus, Julius Caesar, Antony and Cleopatra*, and *Titus Andronicus*), Stratford-upon-Avon, 1972.

[33] It is precisely as such a Caesar, clad in the armour and parade helmet of a Roman general, that a contemporary map, made as adjunct to Elizabeth's final Irish campaign, portrays the Norman conqueror of Ulster, Sir John de Courcy [National Maritime Museum, P | 49 (25)]—see Figure 21.1.

[34] See also 1.1.136, 3.1.69, 3.2.28-9, 4.1.20-1.

presence[35]—one made visible a few years later in that magnificent display of cartographic nationalism, John Speed's significantly named *The Theatre of the Empire of Great Britain*. Speed's title-page displays 'A Romane', among the five ancestors of the modern British people (Figure 21.2), while a number of his maps are ornamented with images of surviving Roman monuments (Figure 21.3).

In Shakespeare's *Richard III* (3.1.69-78) and again in *Richard II* (5.1.2), the Tower of London is imagined as one such monument; while *Cymbeline* maps Roman invasion onto Milford Haven, Richmond's landing-place in *Richard III*, as if to identify the Tudors with a new instauration of imperial power. In constructing a 'Romaine Tragedie', therefore, Shakespeare and Peele were in some ways extending the historical project begun in the three parts of *Henry VI*: if those plays had exploited more recent English history to demonstrate the terrible fragility of social and political order, *Titus*, as Jonathan Bate remarks, was 'interrogating Rome, asking what kind of example it provide[d] for Elizabethan England'.[36]

Even the Ovidian allusions that seem designed to anchor the play to the literature of the classical past could be used to animate its connection with the present. Thus in his quest for retribution Titus, like Hieronimo in Kyd's *The Spanish Tragedy* (3.14.138-9), invokes the Roman goddess of justice, last of the immortals to leave the earth at the end of Saturn's Golden Age; and in both plays her departure symbolically justifies the protagonist's turn to private revenge; unlike Kyd, however, Shakespeare complicates the reference by quoting the goddess's name, reminding the audience of Queen Elizabeth's most famous sobriquet, Astraea: '*Terras Astraea reliquit*; be you remembered, Marcus, | She's gone, she's fled' (4.3.4-5). In the *Metamorphoses*, moreover, Astraea is transformed into the constellation Virgo: thus when Titus' petition for divine justice is imagined to land 'in Virgo's lap' (l. 64), it is as if his hopeless appeal were directed to the Virgin Queen herself.

The dramatists' invitation to see in Rome's crisis a political mirror for late Tudor England is especially conspicuous in Peele's opening scene. To sixteenth-century eyes, at least, the very 'form' of London playhouses resembled 'Roman work';[37] and *Titus* further capitalises on the structural resemblance between the two-level Elizabethan stage and the triumphal arches built for great state occasions to create a peculiarly 'Roman' spectacle. First 'the Tribunes and Senators [enter] aloft', while the rival factions of Saturninus

---

[35] See Tom Bishop, Ch. 15 in this volume, 234-6; and Michael Neill, '"The Exact Map or Discovery of Human Affairs": Shakespeare and the Plotting of History', in *Putting History to the Question* (New York: Columbia University Press, 2000), 373-97 (38-6).

[36] Bate, Introd. Cf. Heywood, *Apology*, sig. F3v: 'If we present a forreigne History, the subiect is so intended, that in the liues of *Romans* … either the vertues of our Country-men are extolled, or their vices reproued.' Cf. Tom Bishop's suggestion that *Titus* presents 'Roman history as a nightmare from which even Elizabethans may not yet have escaped' (Ch. 15, 240).

[37] See Johannes de Witt's famous description of the Swan, cited in Andrew Gurr, *The Shakespearean Stage, 1574-1642*, 2nd edn. (Cambridge: Cambridge University Press, 1980), 122. Heywood's lengthy description of the architecture of Greek and Roman theatres (*Apology*, sig. D2-D3) is clearly designed to make them appear as similar as possible to the playhouses for which he himself wrote.

Labels within the engraving: A BRITAINE, A ROMANE, A SAXON, A DANE, A NORMAN, BRITANNIA

THE
THEATRE
OF THE EMPIRE
OF GREAT
BRITAINE:
Preſenting
AN EXACT GEOGRAPHY
of the Kingdomes of ENGLAND,
SCOTLAND, IRELAND,
and the ILES adioyning:
with
The *Shires, Hundreds, Cities* and
Shire-townes, within ƴ Kingdome
of ENGLAND, divided and
deſcribed
By
IOHN SPEED.

IMPRINTED AT LONDON

Anno
Cum Privilegio
1614.

And are to be ſolde by Iohn Sudbury & Georg
Humble, in Popes-head alley at ƴ ſigne of ƴ white Horſe.

FIG. 21.2 Title-page engraving, *John Speed, The Theatre of the Empire of Great Britaine* (1611).
Used by permission of the Folger Shakespeare Library

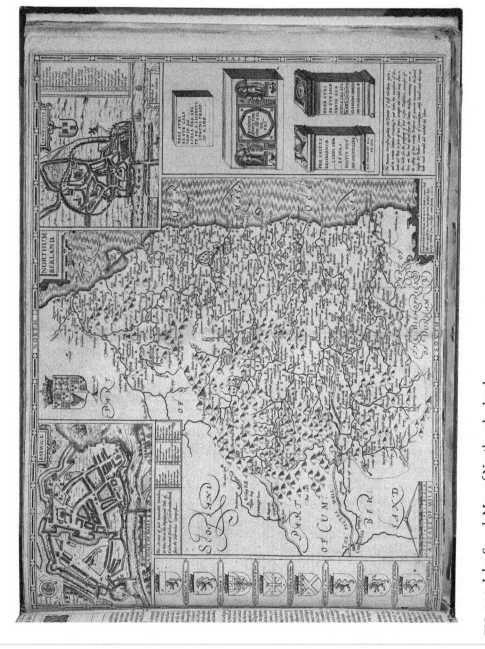

FIG. 21.3 John Speed, Map of Northumberland.

and Bassianus 'with Drum & Colours' confront one another below, until their dispute is interrupted by the entry of Titus and his army, celebrating their victory over the Goths:

> Sound drums and trumpet, and then enter two of Titus's sons … and then two men bearing a coffin covered with black; then two other sons … Titus Andronicus [in a chariot], and then Tamora, the Queen of the Goths and her three sons … with Aaron the Moor, and others as many as can be.

1.1.69.1-7

The stage direction calls on the actors to muster all their resources to present what the language of the scene identifies as a formal 'triumph'—both one of the ceremonies accorded to successful Roman generals (l. 110), and a funeral rite for the latest of Titus's twenty-one sons to be sacrificed in battle:[38] 'But safer triumph is this funeral pomp | That … triumphs over chance in honour's bed' (ll. 176-8).

This visual display of *romanitas* is matched in the language of the play. It begins with a confrontation between Saturninus and Bassianus who are vying to succeed their father (1.1.1-15). Their symmetrical appeals to the citizenry of Rome, marked by Latinate phrasing ('successive title', 'to virtue consecrate'), by repetitions of 'Rome' and 'Roman', by emblematic reminders of 'imperial' power, and by invocation of traditionally Roman qualities—continence (*continentia*), nobility (*nobilitas*), and above all 'virtue' (*virtus*) and 'justice' (*iustitia*)—serve to underline the importance of the play's 'scene'.[39] 'Virtue', in particular, stands for the Roman ideal of manhood supposedly incarnate in Titus himself, who is announced as the 'Patron of virtue, Rome's best champion' (1.1.65); while Saturninus' flattering address to the 'patricians' as 'patrons' of his cause, set against Bassianus' more general appeal to the 'Romans, friends, followers' whom he urges to 'fight for freedom in your choice', echoes the language of dispute between aristocratic and popular factions that had so frequently divided republican Rome. In Shakespeare's day the word 'patrician' had yet to acquire any significant currency outside the translation of classical texts; so rather than loosely referring to the noble status of his listeners, it locates them quite precisely in the hierarchic order of ancient Rome. 'Patron' had a more familiar ring; but, juxtaposed with 'patrician', it necessarily recalls the system of patron-client dependence that governed so much of Roman social relations. In addition, the alliterative and assonantal link between the two words (weakened by the modern pronunciation of 'patron'), plays on their common root in Latin *pater* (father), as a reminder that the senators whom he addresses were formally known as *patres conscripti*—a mark of the sternly patriarchal ideology for which the protagonist himself will come to stand.[40]

Yet even as language and spectacle measure *Titus*'s historical distance from its audience, the play's dramaturgical method serves to collapse that distance: deliberately eschewing the expository advantage of the formal prologues with which contemporaries

---

[38] For early moderns, funerals, like 'coronation[s] … [royal] marriages, entry of cities … [and] progresses' were among the forms of 'triumph … first invented and practised by the Romans'—see Sir William Segar, *Honor Military, and Civill* (London, 1602), 138. The triumphal character of the scene is extended through the coronation of Saturninus (ll. 220-33), and the wedding processions of Saturninus and Bassianus (ll. 398.1-5).

[39] For other examples of the play's self-conscious Latinisms, see Burrow, *Shakespeare and Classical Antiquity*, 113.

[40] On patriarchal ideology in early modern England, see Neill, 'Massinger's Patriarchy: The Social Vision of Massinger's *A New Way to Pay Old Debts*', in *Putting History to the Question*, 72-97 (esp. 76-8).

like Kyd and Marlowe chose to introduce their tragedies, it not only plunges its viewers *in medias res*, but makes them silent participants in the drama. Reaching back to the
conventions of medieval religious theatre (where onlookers were regularly incorporated
into the action of crowd scenes), the brothers' rivalrous appeals extend beyond the stage,
inviting the audience to lean now towards one faction, now towards another. Seated in
the gallery or standing in the pit, they become the 'Patricians and plebeians' called upon
to acclaim Saturninus as 'Rome's great emperor' (ll. 230-3)—just as they will become the
'heavy people' before whom Titus makes his vow of vengeance (3.1.275), and the 'gracious
auditory' of 'gentle Romans', 'sad-faced men, people and sons of Rome', hailed by Marcus
and Lucius when, in the final scene, they seek to reunite the city (5.3.66, 95, 146).

The play's Rome, then, is also England—or at least it is so at certain dramatically strategic moments; and in so far as it seems to pit Roman civilisation 'against the barbarous
Goths' (1.1.28), it appeals to the nascent imperialism that presented the nation's Irish wars,
like its colonizing ventures in Virginia, as attempts to subdue the savage other, bringing
civil order to the chaotic wilderness. But if the audience are invited to see themselves as
latter-day Romans, they are also reminded of their Gothic antecedents as the descendants
of invading Germanic barbarians.[41] At the beginning of the play, Tamora and her sons
appear as representatives of the barbarous hordes whose invasion would usher in Europe's
Dark Ages; but when the exiled Lucius returns at the head of another Gothic army to
purge the city of its corrupt rulers, Shakespeare draws on an alternative historiographic
tradition in which the Goths embodied ideals of primitive simplicity, courage, and loyalty;
and their victory conveniently anticipates a second undoing of Roman decadence by the
instigators of Protestant Reformation.[42]

This ambivalence towards things Roman is reflected in the very device that seems to
declare the tragedy's authentic Romanness—its insistent allusions to Latin literature.
By their aestheticizing self-consciousness, these can produce a kind of alienation-effect,
which not only controls the play's impulse towards melodrama, but forces the audience
into a more detached view of the action[43]—as, for example, when the spectacle of Lavinia's
mutilation is greeted by her uncle's elaborately rhetorical lament, with its repeated invocations of Ovid's Philomela story;

> Speak, gentle niece, what stern ungentle hands
> Hath lopped and hewed and made thy body bare
> Of her two branches, those sweet ornaments ...
> Alas, a crimson river of warm blood,
> Like to a bubbling fountain stirred with wind,
> Doth rise and fall between thy rosèd lips,
> Coming and going with thy honey breath.
> But sure some Tereus hath deflowered thee ....
> Fair Philomela, why she but lost her tongue,

[41] Ronald Broude, 'Roman and Goth in *Titus Andronicus*', *Shakespeare Studies* 6 (1970), 27–34.

[42] See Bate, Introd., 2–1. It is perhaps their common barbarism that accounts for Tamora's
unexplained alliance with the 'barbarous Moor', Aaron, the seemingly anomalous native of
Barbary, the barber whose sanguinary 'trimming' the play's quibbling language identifies as the
quintessential mark of barbarity (5.1.94-6).

[43] Richard Halpern notes a similar effect in the way that *Titus* turns from 'a revenge tragedy [into]
a play that is self-consciously *about* revenge tragedy' (Ch. 2 in this volume, 28).

> And in a tedious sampler sewed her mind …
> A craftier Tereus, cousin, has thou met,
> And he hath cut thy fingers off,
> That could have better sewed than Philomel.
>
> (2.4.16-44)

The strangely contrived wit of Marcus' similes enacts a series of Ovidian metamorphoses, thereby pointing up what Burrow describes as a 'tragic lack of connection between the words used and the pain felt by a violated woman';[44] like Ovid's rape victim Arethusa, Lavinia is transformed into a sanguinary spring, 'a crimson river … a bubbling fountain', or 'a conduit with three issuing spouts' (l. 30); and just as Ovid's Daphne was metamorphosed into a laurel, so Lavinia becomes a dismembered tree 'bare of her two branches', whose 'lily hands | Tremble like aspen leaves' (ll. 44-5)—a figure brutally deconstructed in Julie Taymor's film, where Lavinia's amputated hands are replaced by clusters of claw-like twigs.

The ambivalent effect of such episodes is made even more apparent by the play's imagined topography. As numerous critics have recognized, the conflict between Roman and Goth is mirrored in the contrast between the city and the wild forest beyond its walls, 'Fitted by kind for rape and villainy' (2.1.117). 'The Emperor's court', declares Aaron, 'is like the house of fame | The palace full of tongues, of eyes and ears,' whereas 'The woods are ruthless, dreadful, deaf, and dull' (2.1.128-9). But the play will progressively confuse that apparently straightforward opposition;[45] and it does so in part through the conspicuous use of another alienation device, archly reminding the audience that on the bare Elizabethan stage 'landscape' is simply a function of their own imagination. Thus in Act 2 the action moves from Rome to the wilderness, only for Titus (2.1.1-6), and then Tamora, to present it as a place of paradisial innocence:

> The birds chant melody on every bush,
> The snake lies rolled in the cheerful sun,
> The green leaves quiver with the cooling wind,
> And make a chequered shadow on the ground.
> Under their sweet shade, Aaron let us sit …
>
> (2.3.12-16)

In less than a hundred lines, however, Aaron's 'hellish tale' (l. 105) will transform it to a deathly fallen landscape once again:

> A barren detested vale you see it is;
> The trees, though summer, yet forlorn and lean,
> Overcome with moss and baleful mistletoe.
> Here never shines the sun, here nothing breeds,
> Unless the nightly owl or fatal raven;

---

[44] Burrow, *Shakespeare and Classical Antiquity*, 112.

[45] Even here the traditional iconography of Fame can appear slightly sinister, as it does in the celebrated Rainbow Portrait of Queen Elizabeth, whose embroidered ears and eyes clearly represent the royal power of surveillance –see Michael Neill, 'Broken English and Broken Irish: Language, Nation and the Optic of Power in Shakespeare's Histories', in *Putting History to the Question*, 339–72 (369–71).

And when they showed me this abhorrèd pit,
They told me here at dead time of the night
A thousand fiends, a thousand hissing snakes,
Ten thousand swelling toads, as many urchins,
Would make such fearful and confusèd cries
As any mortal body hearing it,
Should straight fall mad, or else die suddenly.

(2.3.94-104)

This contradiction mirrors the play's pervasive topographic confusion. The emblematic heart of the city is to be found in the 'sacred' tomb of the Andronici, the 500-year-old 'monument' that Titus identifies as the hallowed repository of Roman values, a 'Sweet cell of virtue and nobility', where 'none but soldiers and Rome's servitors | Repose in fame' (1.1.93; 352-3). It has its savage counterpart at the core of the wilderness, in the 'unhallowed and bloodstainèd hole' over which Tamora presides, and into whose 'swallowing womb' the murdered body of Bassianus is cast (2.3.210, 239). But if the two are imagined as symbolic opposites, they are, of course, represented by the same device—the trapdoor placed at the centre of the Elizabethan stage—and both language and action insist upon their fundamental resemblance. If the hole, where Aaron once 'espied the panther' (l. 194), is the lair of wild beasts, it also becomes 'poor Bassianus' grave', illuminated by a ring 'Which, like a taper in some *monument*, | Doth shine upon the dead man's earthy cheeks, | And shows the ragged entrails of this pit' (ll. 240, 228-30; emphasis added). In retrospect, moreover, the Andronicus mausoleum appears as hungry for bodies as Martius' 'detested, dark, blood-drinking pit' (l. 224): like that 'gaping hollow of the earth', it too is an 'earthy prison' filled with the bones of Titus's sons (1.1.99); and both become places of blood sacrifice—the one a gruesome altar where the entrails of the Gothic prince Alarbus 'feed the sacrificing fire' (1.1.143-4), and before which Titus even sacrifices his own son, the defiant Mutius; the other a 'devouring receptacle' (2.3.235) in which two more of Titus' sons, Quintus and Martius, are trapped alongside the butchered corpse of Bassianus. The insistent metaphors of consumption that link the scene of Roman piety to the place of butchery look forward to a denouement in which extreme savagery and civilized ceremonial are compacted together: here, in Titus' meticulously prepared banquet, the 'ravenous tiger' Tamora (5.3.5) is made to feed on the dismembered bodies of her surviving sons so that she may 'Like to the earth swallow her own increase' (5.2.191). But scarcely has she performed this unwitting atrocity than Titus outdoes her by killing his own daughter in an action that appalls even Saturninus as 'unnatural and unkind', l. 48).

The terms of the emperor's denunciation recall the ways in which the contrast between civilization and barbarism has been compromised almost from the beginning by the accusations hurled at Titus—first by Tamora and Chiron in response to the sacrifice of Alarbus ('O cruel, irreligious piety! | Was never Scythia half so barbarous', 1.1.130-1), and then by Marcus, when Titus refuses burial to the son he himself has murdered: 'My lord this is impiety in you ... Thou art a Roman; be not barbarous' (ll. 355, 378). The values of Roman civilization are anchored in 'piety', the virtue that binds citizens to the city, and individuals to their ancestors, just as it ties child to parent, and—especially, in this patriarchal dispensation—son to father. Wishing to marry his daughter to the Emperor, Titus is outraged by the 'dishonour' inflicted upon him by his sons' defiance (l. 295)—a violation of filial *pietas* that, by calling in question his status as *paterfamilias*, provokes the killing of Mutius. By the same token, it is not so much this murder—'unjust' though Lucius calls it (l. 292)—that produces accusations of

impiety and barbarity, but rather Titus's refusal to allow the proper interment that will symbolically restore the murdered child's bond to his family.

The impulsive violence with which the old man responds to Mutius ('Barr'st me my way
in Rome? ... *Kills him*' l. 291) contrasts as starkly as possible with Tamora's maternal grief
for her own son, and her eloquent insistence upon the parental love that should hold up a
sympathetic mirror to her captor:

> Victorious Titus, rue the tears I shed,
> A mother's tears in passion for her son;
> And if thy sons were ever dear to thee,
> O, think my son to be as dear to me ...
>
> (1.1.105-8)

The mother's 'passion for her son' and her pleas for 'mercy' fleetingly recall a very different
display of maternal grief—the Virgin Mother's *pietà*; and (remembering the common root
of the two words) we might be tempted into imagining a contrast here between maternal
pity and patriarchal piety. Titus' patriarchal role is repeatedly underlined: not only is he the
biological father of 25 sons, he is also saluted by Saturninus as 'father of my life' (l. 253), and
by Bassianus as nothing less than 'A father and a friend ... to Rome' herself (l. 422). Rome,
moreover, is about to fall into the hands of an emperor who takes his name from Saturn.
A complex irony is involved here: in Ovid Saturn was the deity who presided over the
Golden Age—the symbolic opposite of Saturninus's Rome—when human beings lived in
perfect harmony with nature and with one another; but Saturn was also the type of extreme
savagery—a father who devoured his own children. Titus, in effect, does the same: having
willingly sacrificed 21 sons in wars against the Goths, he not only murders another to defend
his sense of paternal honour, but finally kills his daughter to cancel out the 'shame' of a rape
that he defines simply as the source of his own sorrow and dishonour (5.3.45-6).

On closer inspection, however, the apparent contrast between maternal pity and patriarchal piety does not survive the first act: Tamora has barely married Saturninus than she
is shown seducing Aaron, whose desires are governed by a Saturn whom he identifies as
the god of melancholy (2.3.31-3). It is the saturnine Aaron who promptly instructs her in
the barbaric revenge she and her sons will take upon Bassianus and Lavinia, leaving the
latter to plead in vain for 'a woman's pity' (l. 147). No wonder then that the proto-Freudian
imagery of the scene should identify the tigress's 'blood-drinking pit' with the female body,
whose 'devouring ... misty mouth' and 'swallowing womb' (ll. 224, 235-6, 239) uncannily
prefigure Tamora's feeding upon her own sons at the end of the play, when 'like to the earth,
[she] swallow[s] her own increase' (5.2.191): it is not Saturninus but his empress whom Titus
forces to mimic Saturn's crime of devouring his own offspring. Titus, by contrast, is forced
to assume the role of weeping parental suppliant that once belonged to Tamora, begging the
'grave fathers' of the Roman state to 'Be pitiful to my condemned sons' (3.1.1, 8). These ironies are compounded by the way in which the pitiless and sardonic Aaron becomes another
unexpected exemplar of paternal concern, a fearless protector of his own 'flesh and blood'
(4.2.84). Denouncing Chiron and Demetrius for their readiness to kill their own brother (l.
88), Aaron is willing to sacrifice himself, if only Lucius will 'vow ... to save my boy' (5.1.81-4).

In the wake of the concluding holocaust, Lucius orders the bodies of Titus and Lavinia
to be 'closèd in our household monument' (5.3.193), an honour that Roman piety requires

for the emperor too ('give him burial in his father's grave', l. 191); Tamora and Aaron, by contrast, are consigned to the barbarous wilderness to feed what Titus once called 'the earth's dry appetite' (3.1.14)—Aaron 'fastened in the earth' to starve (l. 182), while Tamora becomes food for 'beasts and birds [of] prey' (l. 197). But in a city that has itself become, in Titus' words, 'a wilderness of tigers' (3.1.54), the absolute difference that these sentences are meant to enforce is once again erased.

It should be apparent that more is at stake here than the bloodthirsty symmetry through which revenge tragedy typically renders the revenger indistinguishable from the vicious objects of his revenge. Critics of the play often complain that, compared with the protagonists of later Shakespearean tragedies, Titus is a somewhat wooden figure, whose emotional lurches answer to the demands of plot, but show nothing resembling the painful psychological progress of a Lear, or even the self-tormenting degeneration of a Macbeth. That, however, is to miss the point of a tragedy that is less concerned with exploring the drama of individual consciousness than with dramatizing abstract ideas about the ideology of social and political institutions, and with showing the ways in which such institutions shape and distort the fundamentals of 'nature' and 'kind'. We can understand this most clearly, perhaps, by looking at the way in which the play regards the human body.

In the marvellous simplicities of *King Lear*'s restoration scene, where the old king awakes in confusion from the sleep that is meant to 'Cure this great gap in his abusèd nature' (4.6.15), Lear slowly comes to himself by rediscovering the physical realities first of his own body ('I will not swear these are my hands. Let's see; | I feel this pin prick. Would I were assured | Of my condition', ll. 48–50), and then of Cordelia's ('Be your tears wet? Yes, faith. I pray weep not', l. 64). Bodies here give evidence for (or are simply inseparable from) the characters' inward 'condition', the selfhood that Lear seeks to recover in himself even as he struggles to recognize it in his daughter. It is quite otherwise in *Titus*. In no play of Shakespeare's is the physical vulnerability of the body made more brutally apparent; but the insult to which human flesh is exposed is saved from mere sensational extravagance by the way in which the play frames its understanding of the body as an emblem for the state itself—an imaginary Leviathan in which even Tamora can declare herself 'incorporate' (1.1.462). So, in the opening scene, when Marcus urges his brother to assume the imperial headship of 'headless Rome', Titus refuses in words that appear to render his own parts interchangeable with those of the mutilated body politic: 'A better head her glorious body fits | Than his that shakes for age and feebleness' (1.1.187–8). Marcus will return to this venerable conceit after the butchery of the final scene: 'O, let me teach you how to knit again | This scattered corn into one mutual sheaf, | These broken limbs again into one body'(5.3.69–71). But, in the wake of Titus' cannibal feast, any conviction that this will prevent Rome from doing 'shameful execution on herself' is undermined by the metaphorical confusion that makes the city a source of food as well as a mutilated human body.

Framed in this way, the 'lopp[ing] and hew[ing]' of Lavinia's, Alarbus', and Titus' limbs, together with the beheading of Quintus and Martius, and the final dismemberment of Chiron and Demetrius, ask to be read as dramatic *imprese* or emblems—allegorical figures, whose grotesque extravagance is intended, in the fashion approved by Ciceronian rhetoricians,[46] to impress the horror of political disintegration upon the viewers' minds.

---

[46] See Cicero, *Ad Herennium*, 3.22. For further comment on the play's emblematic technique, see Bishop, Ch. 15 in this volume, 40.

Thus Marcus' undertaking to 'knit … these broken limbs into one body' is prefigured in the weird spectacle orchestrated by Titus towards the end of Act 3, Scene 1:

> Come, brother, take a head,
> And in this hand the other will I bear;
> And, Lavinia, thou shalt be employed in this;
> Bear thou my hand, sweet wench, between thy teeth
>
> (3.1.278–81)

Here, however, the sight of a handless Lavinia clenching her father's severed hand in her tongueless mouth, grotesquely complicates the emblematic significance of the scene;[47] for not only does it look forward to Tamora's anthropophagy, but, in its brutal conjunction of hand and mouth, it insists upon the semiotic kinship of these organs of action and speech.

At first sight the two seem to represent opposed qualities: the mouth is the vehicle of language, the hand an instrument of action. The loss of her tongue renders Lavinia a 'speechless complainer' in Titus's oxymoron (3.2.39), severing her from the world of language; and language, as Aristotle's *Politics* famously argued, is the defining faculty of humankind, fundamental to the order that defines the *polis* against the chaos of barbarism. The hand, by contrast, appears to belong to the world of inarticulate violence: with 'Vengeance in my heart, death in my hand' Aaron swears that he and Tamora will revenge themselves on the Andronici (2.3.38); and they do so through the 'stern ungentle hands' of Chiron and Demetrius (2.4.16). But the hand—as Titus's appeal to the precedent of 'rash Virginius' suggests—is also symbolically essential to the Roman civilisation for which he stands: not only is it the paternal hand of blessing to which Lavinia kneels (1.1.163), as well as the vehicle that binds Marcus and Lucius, when, 'hand in hand' they submit to the judgement of the Roman people (5.3.131, 135); it is also is the 'victorious' hand with which Titus has slaughtered the Goths, the 'warlike hand' whose function is 'to do Rome service' (1.1.163; 3.1.234, 80), and the instrument of patriarchal authority with which he punishes Mutius's filial disobedience (1.1. 418) and finally purges his daughter's shame (5.3.36–8).

Moreover, if Roman and barbarian turn out to be equally implicated in violence of the hand, the opposition of hand and mouth itself proves to be radically confused: as Tamora gorges herself upon the pie in which her sons are baked, the mouth is exposed as a vehicle of the savagery prefigured in the 'unhallowed and bloodstainèd hole' into which Bassianus' corpse is thrown, the 'devouring receptacle' that Martius compares to the mouth of hell (2.3.210, 235–6). Conversely, when Marcus remembers his brother's hands 'Writing destruction on the enemy's castle' (3.1.169), he turns manual violence into a kind of scripture. The hand indeed is persistently identified as an instrument of language, gestural as well as written—becoming a site of meaning secondary only to the tongue. '[H]ow can I grace my talk,' demands Titus, 'Wanting a hand to give it action' (5.2.17–18). 'Action' here has nothing to do with the hand as an instrument of physical force, it is simply *actio*—the Latin word for the vocabulary of gesture essential to the arts of oratory and theatrical performance. According to the seventeenth-century theorist of manual rhetoric, John Bulwer, the hand, after the confusion of languages at Babel, itself became 'the *Tongue and general language of*

---

[47] For an account of this episode as 'Senecan camp', see Halpern, Ch. 2 in this volume, 27–8.

Human Nature.[48] Lavinia's hands are amputated not only to prevent her from writing ('See how with signs and tokens she can scrawl', (2.1.5) but to deny her the eloquence of gesture. If the hands of Chiron and Demetrius are 'stern ungentle' weapons of abuse, Lavinia's 'lily hands' were once (in a phrase that recalls the terms of rhetoric) 'sweet ornaments' of speech (2.4.16-18, 44). Titus is the man who remembers his daughter reading 'Tully's orator'—an ironic recollection, since his own condition mirrors that of its author, Cicero, whose right hand, 'instrument of his divine Eloquence' was notoriously severed by Mark Antony—just as, according to Cassius Dio, his tongue—like Lavinia's—was sadistically torn out by Mark Antony's wife, Fulvia.[49] In this context, literate playgoers were no doubt expected to remember that, if Andronicus' name recalls that of the pioneer of Roman tragedy, it was also that of a Greek actor famous for his gestural eloquence, as well as, fittingly enough, of a Byzantine emperor whose hand was hacked off by an insurrectionary mob.[50]

In the vein of cruel, self-lacerating humour with which he responds to his daughter's mutilation, Titus suggests that the Andronici should 'cut away our hands like thine [.] | Or ... bite our tongues, and in dumb shows | Pass the remainder of our hateful days' (3.1.130-3). Calling Lavinia a 'map of woe, that thus dost talk in signs' (3.2.12), he speaks as if her frantic, handless gestures constituted precisely such a 'dumb-show' for which he serves as the lucid presenter—

> Mark, Marcus, mark. I understand her signs;
> Had she a tongue to speak, now would she say
> That to her brother which I said to thee.
>
> (3.1.143-5)

> I can interpret all her martyred signs—
> She says she drinks no other drink but tears,
> Brewed with her sorrow, mashed upon her cheeks.
>
> (3.2.36-8)

—only for him to confess that hers is a dialect of *actio* that he has yet to master:

> Speechless complainer, I will learn thy thought;
> In thy dumb action will I be as perfect
> As begging hermits in their holy prayers.
> Thou shalt not sigh, nor hold thy stumps to heaven,
> Nor wink, nor nod, nor kneel, nor make a sign,
> But I of these will wrest an alphabet,
> And still by practice learn to know thy meaning.
>
> (ll. 39-45)

---

[48] John Bulwer, *Chirologia: or, the Natural Language of the Hand* (London, 1644)

[49] See John Bulwer, *Chironomia: or, the Art of Manual Rhetoric* (London, 1644), 17; and cf. Plutarch's lives of Marcus Tullius Cicero and Mark Antony (trans. Sir Thomas North), in Geoffrey Bullough, ed., *Narrative and Dramatic Sources of Shakespeare*, 5 vols. (London: Routledge, 1964), 5: 140, 269); Cassius Dio, *Roman History*, 47.8.4. See my 'Amphitheaters in the Body', 188, for a suggestion that Titus' sacrifice of his own hand was also inspired by the Roman hero Gaius Mucius Scaevola, who seems to have given his name to Mutius, and whose story, recorded by Livy, was to be spectacularly dramatized in Heywood's *Rape of Lucrece* (1607).

[50] The title-page engraving of Bulwer's *Chironomia* shows the orators Cicero and Demosthenes taking instruction from the actors Andronicus and Roscius. The fate of the emperor Andronicus Commenus is cited as a possible source by J. C Maxwell in his Arden edn.

Here, as in Kyd's *Spanish Tragedy*, social crisis is figured as linguistic breakdown: Kyd's re-venger, himself a judge, but cheated of justice, expresses his frustration in three displays of *actio*: first wildly digging in the earth with his dagger to the bafflement of the king ('What means this outrage?' 3.12.79); then, in a berserk gesture, tearing an appellant's legal papers with his teeth (3.13.123 SD); and finally biting out his own tongue (4.4.191 SD), repudiating language altogether in a show of extreme defiance ('What lesser liberty can kings afford than harmless silence ... never shalt thou force me to reveal | The thing which I have vowed inviolate', 4.4.180, 187-8). For Titus, by contrast, as he struggles to 'wrest an alphabet' from Lavinia's demented gesticulation, it is as though language has to be patiently reinvented. Instead of stabbing the earth, he instructs Lavinia to use its 'sandy plot' as a 'plain' (clear; easily deciphered) surface on which, with a staff clutched between tongueless mouth and handless arms, she can write to 'discover' her abusers 'Without the help of any hand at all' (4.1.67-73). This is the plot with whose sanguinary scripture he confronts Tamora in 5.2:

> You are deceived, for what I mean to do
> See here in bloody lines I have set down
> And what is written shall be executed.
>
> (5.2.13-15)

Titus, though he 'want[s] a hand to give it action', is now the master of language, in a world where 'what is written' seems endowed with scriptural unavoidability. Chiron and Demetrius, by contrast, are to be cut off from speech as decisively as their victim: prepar-ing to butcher them, Titus orders his followers to 'Stop close their mouths; let them not speak a word' (l. 164), whilst he translates his own 'fearful words' into brutal action: 'Hark, wretches, how I mean to martyr you: | This one hand yet is left to cut your throats' (ll. 180-1). *Actio* and action, speech and performance, inscription and execution have all, in a hideous fashion become one.

Titus Andronicus does not challenge comparison with the tragedies of Shakespeare's ma-turity. There is even something a little jejune about its self-conscious displays of learning, its flourishes of wit, and the black-comic extravagance with which it treats its displays of violence. It has moments of remarkable emotional power, such as the protagonist's lament over his mutilated child, 'If there were reason ... ' (3.1.218-32); but even here the moving simplicity of Titus's 'I am the sea ... She is the weeping welkin, I the earth' cannot entirely escape a knowing glance at Ovidian metamorphosis; and (unlike, say, Lear's explosion of grief for Cordelia) the speech belongs to no psychologically coherent attempt to map the progress or plumb the depths of human experience. There is a wonderful unexpectedness about Aaron's sudden emergence as the voice of paternal tenderness, but it comes with no properly motivated sense of revelation—like Tamora's initial appearance as the grieving mother, it is a local effect, designed for purely theatrical purposes. To labour such com-plaints, however, is to ignore the play's real strengths: its exceptional dramatic flair and, above all, the ruthlessly schematic way in which it sets about dismantling the most treas-ured piety of what we have come to call 'the Renaissance': the aspirational belief that the rediscovery of the classical past enabled by humanist learning would open the doors to a brave new world—a Rome magnificently reborn. Contemplating the monument of Roman civilization that dominates the tragedy's opening and closing scenes, it is impossible not to recognize in *Titus Andronicus* a formidable demonstration of the famous aphorism by Walter Benjamin with which I began this essay; and if this 'Romaine Tragedy' flatters its audience with the idea of England as a new Rome, it also implicitly reminds them of the need to make Rome new—and therefore, perhaps, to take tragedy itself in new directions.

Select Bibliography

Broude, Ronald, 'Roman and Goth in *Titus Andronicus*', *Sh. Stud.* 6 (1970), 27–34.

Brucher, Richard, '"Tragedy Laugh On": Comic Violence in *Titus Andronicus*', *RenD* NS10 (1979), 71–92.

Burrow, Colin, *Shakespeare and Classical Antiquity* (Oxford: Oxford University Press, 2013).

Charney, Maurice, *Titus Andronicus* (Brighton: Harvester, 1990).

Gibbons, Brian, 'The Human Body in *Titus Andronicus* and Other Early Shakespeare Plays', *Shakespeare Jahrbuch* (1989), 209–22.

Green, Douglas, 'Interpreting "her martyr'd signs": Gender and Tragedy in *Titus Andronicus*', *SQ* 40 (1989), 317–26.

Hamilton, A.C., '*Titus Andronicus*: The Form of Shakespearean Tragedy', *SQ* 14 (1963), 201–13.

Hunter, G. K. 'Shakespeare's Earliest Tragedies: *Titus Andronicus* & *Romeo and Juliet*', *ShSur* 27 (1974), 1–9.

Joplin, Patricia Kleindienst, 'Ritual Work on Human Flesh: Livy's Lucretia and the Rape of the Body Politic', *Helios* 17 (1990), 51–70.

Kahn, Coppélia, 'The Daughter's Seduction in *Titus Andronicus*, or Writing is the Best Revenge', *Roman Shakespeare: Warriors, Wounds, and Weapons* (London: Routledge, 1997), 46–76.

Kendall, Gillian M., '"Lend me thy hand": Metaphor and Mayhem in *Titus Andronicus*', *SQ* 40 (1989), 299–316.

Kolin, Philip C., '*Titus Andronicus: Critical Essays* (New York: Garland, 1995).

Liebler, Naomi Conn, 'Getting It All Right: *Titus Andronicus* and Roman History', *SQ* 45 (1994), 263–78.

Miola, Robert S., *Shakespeare's Rome* (Cambridge: Cambridge University Press, 1983).

Miola, Robert S., '*Titus Andronicus* and the Mythos of Shakespeare's Rome', *SStud* 14 (1981), 85–98.

Rowe, Katherine R., 'Dismembering and Forgetting in *Titus Andronicus*', *SQ* 45 (1994), 279–303.

Royster, Francesca T., 'White-limed Walls: Whiteness and Gothic Extremism in *Titus Andronicus*', *SQ* 51 (2000), 432–55.

Somers, Alan, '"Wilderness of Tigers": Structure and Symbol in *Titus Andronicus*', *ECrit* 10 (1960), 275–89.

Taylor, Neil, and Loughrey, Bryan, eds., *Shakespeare's Early Tragedies* (Basingstoke: Macmillan, 1990).

Tricomi, Albert H., 'The Mutilated Garden in *Titus Andronicus*', *Sh. Stud.* 9 (1976), 89–105.

Waith, Eugene, 'The Metamorphosis of Violence in *Titus Andronicus*', *Sh. Sur.* 10 (1957), 39–49.

Willbern, David, 'Rape and Revenge in *Titus Andronicus*', *ELR* 8 (1978), 123–40.

CHAPTER 22

....

ROMEO AND JULIET
AS EVENT

....

CRYSTAL BARTOLOVICH

Romeo and Juliet depicts love as an *event*, which is perhaps why it remains so compelling to readers and viewers.[1] Two young people meet unexpectedly and their lives are utterly transformed. 'Did my heart love till now?' Romeo asks, so subjectively disrupted by the first sight of Juliet that he speaks it aloud.[2] The play intriguingly links this rupturing love to the equally powerful disruptive possibilities of art by having Romeo first address Juliet with what turns out to be the opening quatrain of a sonnet:

> If I profane with my unworthiest hand
> This holy shrine, the gentle sin is this:
> My lips, two blushing pilgrims ready stand
> To smooth that rough touch with a tender kiss.
>
> (1.5.92–5)

Juliet—arrestingly, playfully—responds in kind:

> Good pilgrim, you do wrong your hand too much,
> Which mannerly devotion shows in this,
> For saints have hands that pilgrims' hands do touch,
> And palm to palm is holy palmers' kiss.
>
> (1.5.96–9)

We might be tempted to see these lines solely as formal containment of love's unruliness: what could be more structured than a sonnet?[3] More subordinated to rules? More

---

[1] Alain Badiou, 'Affirmative Dialectics: from Logic to Anthropology', *International Journal of Badiou Studies* 2:1 (2013): 1–13, describes the event as an encounter that 'interrupts the law, the rules, the structure of the situation, and creates a new possibility' (3).

[2] Rene Weis, ed., *Romeo and Juliet* (London: Arden Shakespeare, 2012), 1.5.51 (Hereafter 'Weis, *RJ*'). All subsequent quotations from the play will be noted parenthetically in the body of this essay. It is worth underscoring that Romeo's speech when he first sees Juliet is not a soliloquy. Tybalt *overhears* it and recognizes a 'Montague' voice. The audience is thus meant to appreciate that the words slip out of him, despite the surrounding danger, because of the overwhelming power of the encounter.

[3] See Joel Fineman, *Shakespeare's Perjured Eye: The Invention of Poetic Subjectivity in the Sonnets* (Berkeley: University of California Press, 1986) on the dialectic of repetition and rupture in prescribed poetic form that gives rise to both exhaustion and invention.

familiar (and spiritualizing) than the figuration of love as religion? And, yet: the scene as performed nonetheless signals to us that something disruptive is occurring. To be sure, Romeo, as numerous other English sonnet writers before him, starts things off with Petrarchan figures that were a farthing a hundred in the 1590s, and, obviously, the form itself is not new; nonetheless, *this* specific poem—like *this* love—*is* new. The lovers do not simply rehearse well-known lines borrowed from miscellanies; their emergent love generates a sonnet. Sixteenth-century fantasies of aristocratic *sprezzatura* notwithstanding, spontaneous generation of sonnets is not commonplace. The poem thus figures Romeo's and Juliet's encounter *as* extraordinary—an event in which art and love are allied.

The poem's novelty is in fact underscored because its atypical enacted co-authorship inserts mutuality—as well as dialectical dynamism by way of embodied carnality—into the familiar figures of love as worship in sonnets.[4] Romeo's plaintive question—'Have not saints lips and holy palmers too?' (1.5.100)—alongside Juliet's teasing retort—'Ay, pilgrim, lips that they must use in prayer' (1.5.101)—cannot but call attention to the hands and lips of the young people on the stage (or screen) before us in performance, however spiritualizing the language. When Romeo persists against Juliet's second coy rebuff, elaborating the bodily figure—'O, then, dear saint, let lips do what hands do— | They pray; grant thou, lest faith turn to despair' (1.5.102–3)—we see love being produced as the effect of two active embodied subjects who bring a sonnet into the world as love's vehicle. After the sonnet form has been introduced, Juliet's next line, 'Saints do not move, though grant for prayer's sake', (1.5.104) is an invitation to Romeo's 'Then move not while my prayer's effect I take' (1.5.105). The shared final couplet produces a kiss of rhymes (which pass through lips) that serve as prologue to a physical kiss.

Until this couplet emerges, we don't know for sure that they will have produced a sonnet, but when they *do*, they demonstrate that love, like a poem, is composed. If Romeo and Juliet had determined never to see each other again after they learn each other's names, the love event would have dwindled into a mere missed opportunity. Love builds over time as a mutual construction to which the lovers must remain faithful or the whole edifice collapses. A sonnet is an apt vehicle for this ongoing exchange because love and sonnets are related not only thematically but also in what we might call their serial specificity: no matter how many 14-line lyrics of intricately rhymed iambic pentameter appear, each is, as art, still a singular instance of the general form: 'eternal love in love's fresh case' as Shakespeare's sonnet 107 puts it. A jaded Prospero might comment wearily ''tis new to thee', but he would be missing the point. However many billions of times love is repeated, it is always an event for those immediately involved. Similarly, *Romeo and Juliet* may have become 'the normative love story of our time', as Marjorie Garber puts it, banalized in sitcoms and advertisements, but to the degree it retains art's power, it can still rub against the grain of normativity—though only if we open ourselves to its provocation as fully as its eponymous lovers open themselves to each other.[5]

Sustained faithfulness to such opening is rare. This is why neither love nor art necessarily disrupts. The openings that love and art produce are far more common than any transformation, since rupturing possibilities are typically captured and tamed by the

---

[4] See David Schalkwyk, *Speech and Performance in Shakespeare's Sonnets and Plays* (Cambridge: Cambridge University Press, 2002), ch. 4. See also Gayle Whittier, 'The Sonnet's Body and the Body Sonnetized in *Romeo and Juliet*', *Shakespeare Quarterly* 40.1 (1989): 27–41.

[5] Marjorie Garber, *Shakespeare and Modern Culture* (New York: Pantheon, 2008), 34.

conventionality that social orders impose on dangers to the status quo. Institutions of containment (schools, theatres, museums, etc.) integrate art with the actually existing social order. Marriage, the family, as well as norms of expression and behaviour, rein in love, rendering it mere repetition rather than rupture. *Romeo and Juliet* makes the possibility of rupture with social order manifest by having the young lovers compose their sonnet in public, though they address only each other. As editors and directors note, the feast scene 'poses a major problem of choreography' in performance.[6] That is: how—*in a crowded room full of people*—do Romeo and Juliet manage their intimate exchange—and kiss—twice—without the nurse or any other supervising adults intervening? In his cinematic version, Baz Luhrmann (1996) has the couple retreat behind a large pillar while the rest of the guests are distracted by spectacle or each other (a tactic borrowed from Zeffirelli[7]); he then resorts to an extreme close up on the lovers as they compose the pilgrim sonnet together, a technical solution, only possible in film, where the camera can consign the surrounding crush of guests to an out of focus blur.

Luhrman's stratagems underscore the intriguing problem posed by this scene for directors committed to 'realistic' representation. Of course late sixteenth-century audiences, who readily accepted asides, iambic pentameter speeches, boys in dresses as adult women, actors announcing their characters to be 'invisible' when they were still quite visible, and the like, could well have understood the scene, as I am suggesting, figuratively rather than literally. The crucial point is: the young lovers exchange their intimate lines *as if* they inhabit a 'pretty room' outside of social norms and constraints while in actuality their families, the feud (Tybalt has just stormed out menacingly), social hierarchy and expectations *manifestly swirl all around them*.[8] The scene thus visually encapsulates in microcosm a predicament explored by the play as a whole: that individuals cannot simply extricate themselves from the social order by individual acts of will or attempted transcendence, artistic, amatory, or any other, however keenly they may inhabit—and generate for readers and even viewers—the illusion that they have done so. Nevertheless, love opens the possibility of a new mode of existence for the lovers, affirmatively at odds with their previous lives. By situating this opening to transformation in the thick of a feast, an 'old accustomed' Capulet ritual (1.2.19) that attempts to anchor participants in the continuous, expected, and normative, the play demonstrates emphatically that the disruption love—like art—offers is not just to the young couple but also, potentially, to the world that they inhabit.

The feast scene not only brilliantly captures the first flush of young love, then, but also lends support to Theodor Adorno's later theorization of lyric. Adorno argues that lyrics *appear* to be the least social of literary forms, the most 'individual', but they are, for all of that, like all uses of language and conventional poetic modes, nonetheless saturated by

[6] Weis, *RJ*, 173.

[7] Zeffirelli increases the privacy of the scene by having the couple move fully behind an arras into a separate room where the refreshments are laid out. Romeo nonetheless looks around anxiously before kissing Juliet.

[8] The convention of love and poetry each offering a respite from the pressures of the world are ubiquitous. 'Pretty room' comes from Donne's 'Canonization', where lovers create a poetic and amatory space of their own. *Romeo and Juliet* underscores the fragility of such fantasies of autonomy.

the social.[9] For Adorno, art says 'no' to the status quo in a specific way; aesthetic capture of the social gives 'form to the crucial contradictions in real existence' instead of covering over or suturing them as myth or ideology do. Art can thus make manifest the injustices of the social order from which it emerges and in which it participates. It does so even—in fact especially—if the artist does not intend to produce social criticism. Because language is irreducibly social, the concentrating and structuring of language in aesthetic form irreducibly bears within it the trace of the society in which it is produced—and in which it continues to have life—as art.

Most immediately, the clash of social forces represented by the feud enters the feast scene as dramatic irony because the audience watches a Capulet and Montague—unbeknownst to each other—fall into interdicted love, but it also enters the pilgrim sonnet immanently, private as it may appear. Romeo at once acknowledges and enacts a social contradiction, using sacred terms to describe worldly existence in his first line, 'If I profane with my unworthiest hand'. This spiritualization of love, commonplace though it may be, emerges in a Verona where 'civil blood' is making 'civil *hands* unclean' (as we have learned from the Prologue) and in which the Prince has already described the feuders as 'profaners' with 'bloody hands' (1.1.80-4). Without ever mentioning the feud, then, the pilgrim sonnet echoes specific tensions between general and particular, collective and individual, as well as sacred and profane that previous scenes already laid before us. Furthermore, the figuration of the lovers' relation to each other in terms of plural 'saints' and 'pilgrims' inserts their 'individual' encounter into larger social terms of group relations, indicating the inextricability of the two levels. Thus the ostensible spirituality of love is not only belied by the embodied carnal embrace of the young lovers, but also the transcendence of individuals (and sonnets) is belied by allusions to the particular threatening situation into which love and the sonnet alike emerge in the play. *The old situation, inevitably, remains inside the new possibility.* The play as a whole will suggest, as we shall see, that the old situation must thus be confronted collectively to be superseded.

Hence Alain Badiou, though he adamantly defends the transformative capacity of love in the face of centuries of philosophical scepticism of it, carefully distinguishes love from *politics*, which is always—and irreducibly—a 'collective' project. For 'love' to have political efficacy, it cannot remain an individual or interpersonal disruption alone.[10] *Romeo and Juliet* already recognizes this distinction, I would suggest, by carefully inserting the lovers into a total social situation depicted as constraining and destructive to them, but also to numerous others ('all are punished' (5.3.295), as the Prince puts it at the end of the play—an observation which extends further than he seems to recognize). The tension between individual and collective in *Romeo and Juliet* not only foregrounds the tragic constraint that the latter imposes on the former, then, but also points to the less recognized but equally important constraints that the existing social order imposes universally—constraints that can only be overcome by collective total transformation of the status quo.

In what follows, then, I draw attention to the Friar's attempt to direct the potential effects of the transformative potential unleashed by Romeo's and Juliet's love towards

⁹ Theodor Adorno, 'On Lyric Poetry and Society', *Notes to Literature*, vol. 1, trans. Shierry Weber Nicholson (New York: Columbia University Press, 1991), 37–54.

¹⁰ Alain Badiou, *In Praise of Love*, trans. Peter Bush (London: Serpent's Tail, 2012), esp. ch. 5.

properly *political* uses. I also underscore, however, that the feud is an insufficient, patently limited, characterization of politics in the play, as can readily be seen when we consider why seemingly superfluous figures, such as the play's many servants, appear so frequently. *Romeo and Juliet*'s depiction of a broad array of social contradictions beyond the feud provokes the scandalous recognition that the Friar's intervention would not have produced a 'happy ending' even if the play concluded with the Romeo and Juliet setting up housekeeping. Art's role—as art—is precisely to push us beyond such easy and comforting assumptions, I suggest. To understand why this is so, though, we first need to understand a bit more about the Friar's political role.

22.1 Love and Politics

The Friar is *Romeo and Juliet*'s most purposefully socially destabilizing character. Not only does his role as the primary agent furthering the lovers' goals unsettle any attempt to reduce the play to a simple generational conflict between youth and age, but, more interestingly, as an authority figure, he is extremely ambiguous. He readily dispenses with the Ten Commandments, social convention, and political imperatives in order to help Romeo and Juliet. Although he marries the couple, institutionally sanctioning their union in the eyes of church and state, he is well aware that neither family would approve; easily defying the norms and power structure of the status quo, he dissembles—indeed, lies outright—to the Capulets when they believe Juliet dead; and he assists the exiled Romeo in extending his stay in Verona against the Prince's direct decree. His stated rationale for such dissident behaviour is, as he observes to Romeo, 'To turn your households' rancor to pure love' (2.3.88). Crucially, then, he sees Romeo and Juliet's 'love' as—at least potentially—participating in a larger social transformation. The feast scene has already foregrounded for the audience the larger social relations in which the lovers are so awkwardly positioned, but the Friar sets in motion an explicit agenda to transform the situation in which the lovers find themselves. To the end of promoting this expansive 'love', he does not hesitate to conspire and connive against the current arrangements of family and state, encouraging Romeo and Juliet to do so as well. In short, he alone recognizes and acts upon a specifically political opportunity—a collective adjustment of existing power relations—that love opens up.

He is positioned to do so because while, institutionally, the Friar represents a third great pillar of European early modern social order—the church—alongside family and state, his knowledge renders him potentially independent of entrenched social interests. In social terms, he is thus better understood as a philosopher than a cleric. In a commonplace at least as old as Plato's *Republic*, 'philosophers' are at odds with the interests of existing elites in the struggle for a just commonwealth because (in theory, at least) they have the pursuit of truth and the collective good as their goals rather than the preservation of their own power.[11] In the case of *Romeo and Juliet*, the Friar's embodiment of this tension is partly obscured because one powerful social institution—the family—is pitted against

---

[11] I discuss the social role of 'intellectuals' (and what this anachronistic term means when applied to earlier periods) in 'Utopia and its New Enemies', *Journal for Early Modern Cultural Studies* 13:3 (2013), 33–65.

another—the state—given that the Prince demands an end to the feud just as emphatically as Romeo and Juliet desire the disappearance of impediments to their love. In such a context, the Friar can appear to support authority by furthering the wishes of the young lovers against their families even though in practice he is also dissident with respect to the state (as well as the letter of the Ten Commandments).

In short, the Friar embodies the contradictions of a social order in which struggles are underway among competing interests and not everyone is positioned equally favourably in these conflicted social relations. He is comparable to Romeo and Juliet in this respect, but takes a far broader temporal, spatial and social view than either of them (or anyone else in the play). While for Romeo 'there is no world without Verona's walls', so long as Juliet is within those walls, for the Friar, 'the world is broad and wide' (3.3.16-17). The implication of his expansive view is that while Romeo and Juliet attempt a retreat from the feud into love, the Friar, conversely, seeks to 'use' the unsettling space of possibility opened by this 'love' politically. Provoked by the accident of Romeo and Juliet's love into recognition of an alternative to the current unhappy social relations in Verona, the Friar struggles against entrenched interests to realize the possibilities opened by individual love in collective terms.

The contrast between the balcony scene and the Friar's first speech underscores this distinction in scale. Romeo only overhears Juliet's private musings on his name because he has 'leapt' (2.1.5) over the Capulet wall into the family's enclosed orchard, which becomes the whole universe in the figures of the lovers, as Romeo compares Juliet to celestial bodies ('Juliet is the sun', 2.2.3) and Juliet insists on the transfer of emphasis from the moon to his *self* when Romeo swears his faithfulness to her by the moon (2.2.113). Enacting a commonplace of love lyrics, the lovers withdraw into the substitute universe of each other, in what is at once a literary convention (the *hortus conclusus* of the Song of Songs) and a response to an immediate threat (Juliet worryingly points out, it is 'death' (2.2.64) for Romeo to trespass on the Capulet orchard). This situation echoes—and inverts—Shakespeare's sonnet 137, where the poet laments that his beloved, who should be his exclusive private property ('a several plot') is actually 'the wide world's common place'. Romeo and Juliet are successfully privatized, in this sense, but also socially constrained—enclosure in their case cuts both ways. No longer oblivious to the dangerous social situation they inhabit, as they had been at the feast, they whisper so as not to arouse the suspicion of Juliet's nurse, who is alarmingly nearby, or the rest of the Capulet household ('bondage is hoarse and may not speak aloud', 2.2.160), increasing our sense that they are *enclosed*. Remarkably, they even characterize their own love in terms evocative of their constrained condition, with Romeo tied by a 'silken thread' to Juliet in her own figure, as if he were a pet bird (2.2.180). When the 'bondage' is understood in concretely social terms, rather than as the ahistorical longing for death often underscored in psychoanalytic readings,[12] we can see that the couple is attempting to turn necessity into a virtue: constraint is a *given* for them in the historical situation into which they were born. They respond to the perils in which they find themselves by enacting the conventional lovers' reduction of the world to themselves, as if their love can elude the social constraints imposed by their names, which, of

---

[12] Psychoanalytic interpretations of the play, following Julia Kristeva, have tended to emphasize the love-death (*liebestod*) tradition. See *Tales of Love*, trans. Leon S. Roudiez. (New York: Columbia University Press, 1987).

course, they learn is not the case—at least not without social changes beyond the level of the couple: political transformation.

The Friar mediates their love quite differently. Introduced immediately following the balcony scene, the Friar is provoked by the dawn to an extended philosophical specula-tion, which is crucial to establishing his character. He speaks in couplets, drawing atten-tion to the relation of his lines to those of Romeo and Juliet in the previous scene, but his couplets point to a larger world than those of the young couple, who understandably attempt to enclose themselves in their love in response to the dangers of the feud. While the balcony scene urges denial of society if it would get in the way of love ('refuse thy name', 2.2.34)—the Friar, conversely, aspires to *transform* social situations. The first thing we learn about him is that he is awake early in order to gather medicinal herbs—'baleful weeds and precious-juiced flowers'—to cure worldly ills (2.3.4). He is explicitly at work for socially useful purposes. And while the Capulets' orchard is private (enclosed) property, the Friar refers to even his basket as 'ours' (2.3.3) emphasizing the communal property of the order as well as the collective purposes to which the herbs are directed. These are not only character attributes but also figurations of potential alternatives to the status quo of petty feuds, social hierarchy and unequal distribution of property.

The Friar not only draws attention to the sociality of resources by telling us the uses to which he will put them, but makes clear that use is an effect of human choice—though not, of course, entirely free choice—which is always liable to bad purposes as well as good:

> For naught so vile that on the earth doth live
> But to the earth some special good doth give,
> Nor aught so good but strain'd from that fair *use*
> Revolts from true birth, stumbling on abuse:
> Virtue itself turns vice, being misapplied,
> And vice sometime's by action dignified

(2.3.135–18, emphasis added)

What's interesting about the Friar's characterization of 'use', here, is its conditionality. Human 'action' can swerve the effects of earthly creation from 'fair use' to 'abuse', from 'virtue' to 'vice.'[13] The 'vile' can be made to do 'good' and vice versa. The conversion of one into the other is always a possibility—though not only the 'will' of agents, but the con-straints of situation impact on outcomes, as demonstrated by the Friar's inverted double in Mantua, the apothecary, who sells poison to Romeo, prompted by 'poverty' rather than 'will' (5.1.75). The point is: change for the better is possible, despite constraints, even in the case of seemingly intractable situations like the feud.

Later the Friar will elaborate this point about proper 'use', emphatically associat-ing it with choice, when Romeo laments his exile and threatens to kill himself. The Friar points out that Romeo is seeing the situation the wrong way around, and that

---

[13] Julia Lupton and C. J. Gordon, 'Shakespeare by Design', *English Studies* 94:3 (2013), 259-77 (265), similarly emphasize the Friar's insistence on the right 'use' of objects, linking this view to Aristotelian ethics. See also Victoria Kahn's discussion of the influence of Aristotle on early modern understanding of 'judgement', in *Rhetoric, Prudence and Skepticism in the Renaissance* (Ithaca, NY: Cornell University Press, 1985). Extended treatment of the Friar is relatively rare, but see James C. Bryant, 'The Problematic Friar in Romeo and Juliet', *English Studies* 55 (1974), 340-50, and Gerry Brenner, 'Shakespeare's Politically ambitious Friar', *Shakespeare Studies* 13 (1980), 47-58.

he requires 'adversity's sweet milk, philosophy' (3.3.55) in order to view the world aright, instead of 'like a usurer' who 'abound'st in all, | And usest none in that true *use*' (3.3.122-3, emphasis added). Similarly, in an earlier speech, the Friar compares the potential effects of human 'use' (and 'abuse') of nature to the historical choices humans make in response to their own desires and each other, figuring these options in vegetation metaphors, but not in order to close historical choices down (by implying that people are naturally either good or bad and always act accordingly), but rather to open history to the multiple possibilities that he has just shown that nature offers us. Whether the 'worser' or better is 'predominant' in our actions—and therefore in our selves—is up to us:

> Within the infant rind of this weak flower
> Poison hath residence and medicine power,
> . . . .
> Two such opposed kings encamp them still
> In man as well as herbs, grace and rude will,
> And where the worser is predominant,
> Full soon canker death eats up the plant

(2.3.19-26)

This earlier speech establishes a context for the Friar's later castigation of Romeo as he rolls around on the ground in senseless lamentation at his situation. Just as the same 'flower' used well can be a medicine and used ill can assist a murder, so too is it with people, who can, like Romeo, misconstrue his situation as a 'userer' misuses money and defies the collective good—the definition of a userer—or act wisely and well—that is, unlike a userer.

Each *choice* works to effect the balance of 'grace' and 'rude will' that are 'encamp[ed]' in each subject and in the world. The availability of choices does not, of course, mean that the choices available are limitless or just. Indeed, the Friar's words resonate particularly strongly because Shakespeare's two lovers inhabit a world in which we know that 'two ... opposèd kings' are not only 'in' themselves (and everyone else), as the Friar muses here, but are—as the prologue sonnet underscores with its reference to the 'two foes' when it summarizes the plot—in Verona, where the conflict between the Montagues and the Capulets constrains the lovers' choices. Furthermore, the individual and structural levels are distinct, albeit imbricated, in social action: when Romeo and Juliet choose to be faithful to 'love' and each other rather than to the demands imposed by the situation into which they were born, the ramifications are, of necessity, socially limited, so long as they remain at the level of their faithfulness to each other alone—liberating and lovely as their mutual devotion may be. Such a view implies no blame: their love *is* portrayed as a disruption—*potentially* progressive in social as well as individual terms.

Friar Lawrence thus serves a situating and scale-shifting function, emphasizing the *collective use* of Romeo's and Juliet's individual love for each other in the broader world in which the lovers are, willy nilly, placed. *His* mode of fidelity to *their* love attempts to translate it from the individual to the collective, as he purposefully attempts to make it politically transformative. And yet he fails to produce a comic ending for the couple, or their world, which, I will suggest, shifts the responsibility for change to *us*. Before we can recognize this (living) provocation of the play to the audience, however, we must first see how thoroughly *Romeo and Juliet,* as art, depicts a whole social world demanding collective transformative agency.

22.2 How We Read Now?

How we read books *and* the world is important to *Romeo and Juliet.* Mercutio disparages Tybalt's fencing skills as so mechanical and unpractised that they seem to have been learned out of a 'book of arithmetic' (3.1.104). Similarly, Juliet teases Romeo for 'kiss[ing] by th' book' in the feast scene (1.5.109). Both comments distinguish between theory and practice, reading and doing, and suggest that what ultimately matters about a 'book' is your response to it—how you *use* it in the world—which requires perspicacious and relevant experience of a specific world in all its lived particularity. Thus the Friar suggests to Romeo that Rosalind saw through his 'love' that 'could not spell' but merely 'read by rote', modelling itself on courtly love conventions without putting them into conscious, *critical* dialectic with their particular amatory (and social) situation (2.3.84). As we have seen, the sonnet Romeo and Juliet produce at the feast uses these conventions quite differently—indeed, transformatively, in marking the emergence of love in its specificity. Their dissident 'reading' of love codes manifests in the transformative singularity of their collaborative composition. Such moments in the play put an emphasis on reading as an active process, an engagement with a *world* in which to read is to act, more or less well, in a specific historical situation. From this perspective, we *all* kiss by the book (social codes)—there is no escaping social meaning making—but these irreducible conditions can be interrupted, opening the possibility that such 'books' might be better written.

From this perspective, what might we make of the anonymous 'servingman' *accidentally* encountered in Act 1, a man whose illiteracy offers the occasion for Romeo to learn about the Capulet feast? Ordered by Old Capulet to 'trudge about | Through fair Verona' to invite guests named on a written list, the servant comments ruefully:

> Find them out whose names are written here? It is written that the
> shoemaker should meddle with his yard and the tailor with his last, the
> fisher with his pencil and the painter with his nets, but I am sent to find
> those persons whose names are here writ, and can never find what names
> the writing person hath here writ. I must to the learned.

(1.2.33–43)

In the late sixteenth century, many in the audience would have recognized these lines as a garbled quotation from one of the most influential books of the period, John Lyly's *Euphues,* but even audience members not in on that joke can appreciate their assertion that literacy is not merely an individual condition but a social relation, in which status is maintained through privileged access to knowledge that will later be called 'cultural capital'.[14]

---

[14] Pierre Bourdieu and Jean-Claude Passeron, *Reproduction in Education, Society and Culture,* trans. Richard Nice, 2nd edn (London: Sage, 1990). On the integration of this term into Early

A social relation is specified not only in the servant's recognition of dependency ('I must to the learned'), but also in his specific exchange with Romeo. In response to the query 'Can you read?', lovelorn Romeo responds, narcissistically, '*mine* own fortune in *my* misery', to which his interlocutor remarks, 'Perhaps you have learnt it without book' (1.2.56-8, emphasis added). This brief colloquy underscores that Romeo is socially positioned to have both the leisure and the entitlement to pay attention only to himself, while the servingman is not. Belonging to a group whose literacy was often viewed with suspicion in the period, the servingman is depicted as dependent on 'learned' persons, while the 'individual' preoccupations of the sons of elite families, such as Romeo, were cultivated in households dependent for their functioning on the labours of numerous servants.[15] Though the social roles are underwritten by unequal property and power, the original distributions of social roles by birth are as *accidental* as the encounter of Romeo and the servant in the street. Romeo and Juliet were unluckily born into feuding families—what reader or viewer of the play fails to recognize that? But from a broader view, servants and masters, poor and rich, are *also* accidentally born into their situations; the play, I suggest, would have us recognize *all* these accidents of birth, which is why it troubles itself to depict a rich, diverse, and broad array of social relations, far in excess of the sources.

In order to draw out the broader social situation of Romeo's role along these lines, Bertolt Brecht composed an exercise scene for actors (not meant for performance, but to tease out the social contradictions of character in the play).[16] In it, Romeo is depicted having an exchange with a tenant, who he has decided to evict in order to sell land to buy a parting gift for Rosalind now that he has transferred his affections to Juliet. Brecht's point is not to suggest that Romeo is a bad person; to the contrary, in the exercise, Romeo is depicted as embarrassed and conflicted about turning the tenant out, though distracted by the demands of his passion. Brecht's point is *social*: actual people are positioned unequally in relation to each other because of their relation to property, with material consequences far more substantial than any internal disagreements within the ruling class (i.e. the feud). By indicating the hierarchical web of social relations in which Romeo and the tenant—were they real persons—would be embedded, Brecht calls attention to a different set of oppressions than are ordinarily seen to be at work in the play, so that they can be seen at work in the world. The patriarchal constraints and the impact of the feud on the young lovers are affectively evident to viewers and readers. Brecht's point is not that these depredations are irrelevant, but rather that the risks that Romeo and Juliet take to whisper words of love to each other in the garden, or to transact and consummate their marriage, do not render them any less Veronese elites who also issue orders to servants and are freed from labours that servants perform on stage (and off) by an accident of birth more lastingly consequential in their society than the family feud. Brecht wants us to think about

Modern Studies, see Henry Turner, ed., *The Culture of Capital: Property, Cities and Knowledge in Early Modern England* (New York: Routledge, 2002).

[15] I am purposefully resisting here the recent trend toward treating service as 'volitional' or a 'love' relation (when examined from the perspective of 'individuals') in order to keep the focus squarely on the material social relations that underwrite all inequality. For the counter view, see David Schalkwyk, *Shakespeare, Love and Service* (Cambridge: Cambridge University Press, 2008) and David Evett, *Discourses of Service in Shakespeare's England* (Palgrave, 2005).

[16] Bertolt Brecht, 'The Servants', *The Drama Review* 12:1 (1967), 108–11.

the class dimensions of the play immanent to it, though he supplements the text to draw them out.

The classed implications of Romeo's encounter with the illiterate servant, for example, are underscored by its allusion to the dedication to Sir William West ('my very good lord and master'), in Lyly's *Euphues*, as I suggested earlier. Lyly writes: 'the shoemaker must not go above his latchet nor the hedger meddle with anything but his bill. It is unseemly for the painter to feather a shaft, or a fletcher to handle a pencil. All which things make most against me in that a fool hath intruded himself to discourse of wit.'[17] For Lyly, any aspiration of a craftsman 'above his latchet' is so ludicrous that he can raise it only to mock it in the course of his own (effectively ironic) apology for his ostensible lack of wit in a book that was received from the start as the most witty book of its time—*the* fiction bestseller of the period. The lines are particularly pointed, given Lyly's own increasingly desperate quest for court preferment, a quest that draws attention to the dependence of artists and intellectuals without independent means—the ones forced to sell their cultural capital of 'wit'—on aristocratic and royal patrons, as well as on the literary marketplace in this period of transition when 'Feudal' preferment and market forces were both impinging on intellectual laborers. Indeed, *Euphues* and 'Euphuism' become one of the principle signifiers of cultural capital in late sixteenth-century London, when the book became a sort of self-help manual for the upwardly aspirant.[18] An intellectual chaffing at his dependence on patrons is figured by Lyly in comic contrast to a shoemaker's dreams of upward mobility, exposing tensions in the social hierarchy at the same time as supporting it. Lyly's strategy of exceptionalism (let *me* rise even if no one else does, because I am special!) attempts to evade the structural with the immediate, the collective with the individual, the material with the discursive, but cannot displace social relations even if it succeeds in a singular case. From *this* point of view, a 'happy ending' for Romeo and Juliet (or Lyly) would not necessarily imply social justice. Exceptions that prove the rule tend, rather, to reinforce oppressive social relations.

The garbling of lines from *Euphues* in *Romeo and Juliet*, where the servingman misattributes the tools of trades, assigning pencils to fishermen and lasts to tailors, might seem to argue that the play depicts him as rightly excluded from social aspiration. And yet: there is an interesting shift between *Euphues* and the play that opens it to other, more provocative, interpretations. Whereas Lyly's construction is negative and prohibitive ('must not'), declaring 'unseemly' any deviation from one's place (except Lyly's own), Shakespeare's servingman recasts the statement affirmatively. He also misquotes while appealing to authority ('it is written') indicating how authorial control over meaning is tenuous. Indeed, *Euphues* can be seen to 'travel' and be transformed simply by issuing from the mouth of a very different sort of speaker than Lyly's persona, just as Arthur Brooke's *Romeus and Juliet* (the poem on which Shakespeare's play largely is based) transforms Italian stories, and Shakespeare transforms Brooke (who does not include this 'servingman' at all). Given the shift in standpoint, we might even read the servingman's comment straight—as an appeal to a world in which fisherman and tailors would be free to make use of more than their own particular tools—that is, a world in which a fisherman '*should* meddle ... with

[17] John Lyly, *Collected Works* (Clarendon, 1902), 1: 180.
[18] For a recent overview of Euphuism, see Katherine Wilson, *Fictions of Authorship in Late Elizabethan Narratives: Euphues in Arcadia* (Oxford: Oxford University Press, 2006).

his pencil' *as well as* his nets—that is, not be bound to a rigidly defined social role. From this perspective, the passage is an interruption of a world in which writers are one kind of people and servants another, without any possibility of convergence. It asks: why is it *not* possible to grow food in the morning, sew in the afternoon, and philosophize in the evening rather than be restricted in our social roles by unequal access to cultural and economic capital?[19]

This question is raised all the more pressingly by the play because the list the servant cannot read is of names, to which servants and masters alike attach significance. Yet names—we learn from Romeo's and Juliet's predicament—are bound up in *accidents* of birth. Might we not extend our concern for such accidents to servants whose names are not deemed significant enough to record or know? Why include so many scenelets in which servants carry wood and provisions, dishes, or messages if not to call attention to the whole set of social relations on which the plight of Romeo and Juliet is situated?[20] Doesn't the (ideological) conviction that the social constraints on Romeo's and Juliet's choices are lamentable, but that we need not concern ourselves with the constraints on the servingman, repeat Capulet's indifference and authorize the current forms of such indifference? What if Romeo and Juliet are not 'everything we care about'.[21]

22.3 RESPONDING TO DEATH: SACRIFICE AND WASTE

How, then, to read otherwise? We *do* care about the deaths of Romeo and Juliet of course. But they do not exhaust the play's concerns. Thus, the prologue sonnet, as is often remarked, inserts the eponymous lovers into a larger social situation:

> Two households, both alike in dignity,
> In fair Verona, where we lay our scene,
> From ancient grudge break to new mutiny,
> Where civil blood makes civil hands unclean.

[19] At the end of *Cultural Capital* (Chicago: University of Chicago Press, 1993), John Guillory affirmatively points to the 'thought experiment' in the *German Ideology* where Marx speculates on the future world in which there would be no special social role of 'painters' because everyone would have the education and leisure to paint. Earlier, in the *Ideology*, Marx explodes the division of labour even more radically, when he proposes that in communist society it would be 'possible for me to do one thing today and another tomorrow, to hunt in the morning, fish in the afternoon, rear cattle in the evening, criticise after dinner ... without ever becoming hunter, fisherman, herdsman or critic'. His purpose here is critical rather than predictive: he seeks to expose the lack of human freedom under conditions of labor that are hierarchical, exploitative and rigid.

[20] All the more so because these scenelets—1.5.1-15, for example—are 'cut in most performances' (Weis, *RJ*, 166). For gesturing toward a whole social world into which the Montagues and Capulets are situated, however, they are necessary.

[21] Paul Kottman, 'Defying the Stars: Tragic Love as the Struggle for Freedom in *Romeo and Juliet*', *Shakespeare Quarterly* 63:1 (2012), 1–38, belongs to the recent trend of focusing on the 'individual' in Shakespeare's plays, in his case through the Hegelian concept of 'freedom', which Kottman sees *Romeo and Juliet* demonstrating through the struggle for mutual recognition of the eponymous

> From forth the fatal loins of these two foes
> A pair of star-crossed lovers take their life,
> Whose misadventured piteous overthrows
> Doth with their death bury their parents' strife.
> The fearful passage of their death-marked love,
> And the continuance of their parents' rage,
> Which but their children's end naught could remove,
> Is now the two hours' traffic of our stage;
> The which, if you with patient ears attend,
> What here shall miss, our toil shall strive to mend.

Though critics have been less attentive to this aspect of it, the sonnet inserts not only Romeo and Juliet into history, but audiences as well by orienting them in time on two distinct levels. First of all, the sonnet summarizes the plot, carefully situating the deaths of the lovers in a much longer diegetic historical trajectory, one in which an 'ancient grudge' is brought to an end by these deaths. But the prologue also draws attention to a specific 'now' of performance, one in which the audience is addressed directly in its serial specificity. Each successive set of players promises that they will try to 'mend' what might 'miss' in the script they are about to perform: a necessarily extra-diegetic (external to the story's narrative) gesture—one that calls attention to the work of art as a whole in an ever changing now. This task is transferred to the audience by the end of the play when, diegetically, the possibility of love transforming into politics is foreclosed.

I dissent, then, from the many readings of the play that take it as a given that Romeo and Juliet's love *is* transformed into politics by the end of the feud. My alternative reading proposes that the opportunity opened by love *fails* to translate into politics; the play thus returns us to the challenge of art to provoke politics rather than simply to depict it. The relation of the play to sonnets in general and Shakespeare's in particular can help us tease out more clearly the play's take on the relation of art to politics. *Romeo and Juliet* continually folds into its fabric themes not only from the prologue sonnet and the pilgrim sonnet, but from Shakespeare's whole sonnet oeuvre—most notably, I propose, in a shared concern with 'waste', as when Romeo refers to Rosalind's refusal to return his love in terms that directly echo the procreation sonnets.[22] Asked if Rosalind has determined to 'live chaste', Romeo responds:

> She hath, and in that sparing makes huge waste,
> For beauty starved with her severity,
> Cuts beauty off from all posterity

> (1.1.216–18)

This thematic of 'waste' takes on a more general significance in the play as a whole, since even though Juliet does reciprocate Romeo's advances, their lives are cut short before

characters, a struggle that, in his reading, effectively renders the rest of the cast subordinated, and, in the case of the servants, superfluous—an understanding of the play that my essay resists emphatically.

22   Jonathan Goldberg, '*Romeo and Juliet*'s Open R's', *Queering the Renaissance* (Durham: Duke University Press, 1993), also notes the shared thematic of waste in *Romeo and Juliet* and the sonnets.

'posterity' can inherit their beauty—at least in the form of children. Though Romeo and Juliet do not produce children, however, they do—as we have seen—compose a sonnet together. Just as the sonnet crystalizes the lovers' attempt to move beyond the social order that interdicts their love, the play as a whole elicits audience desire for a mode of existence in which such utopian aspiration is not crushed.

This point brings me to a second observation about the prologue sonnet: its narrative draws particular attention to death ('fatal loins', 'take their life', 'death', 'death-marked love', 'children's end') but also to the social response to the death in its (repeated) assertion that the deaths of the children 'bury their parents' strife'. It foretells the patriarchs' embrace at the end of the play when they declare the deaths of their children 'sacrifices', an attempt on their part to provide social meaning to deaths that would otherwise be a waste: necessarily gesturing towards a political dimension for the deaths (5.3.304). To pursue this political dimension does *not* imply that the putative reconciliation of the families is 'worth the price' of Romeo's and Juliet's deaths, as Paul Kottman worries.[23] The point rather is a distinction between a world in which Romeo and Juliet (as individuals) can believe they are happy (a happiness plausible even in Verona as depicted, with a few tweaks in parental attitude) and one in which love is *structurally* encouraged in its best and strongest forms for everyone (not just a special dispensation made for two individuals). Even the most profound individual disruption of the status quo can effect no permanent social transformation, as Badiou reminds us, until it is translated into a *political*—necessarily *collective*—and structural form.

Romeo and Juliet do not inhabit a world in which their love can thrive, as their deaths testify. However, a world in which nothing changed *except* a happy ending for them—a world in which their love would be an *exception* (like Lyly's attempt to social climb while keeping the rest of the social hierarchy intact)—would not be satisfactory either from the point of view of social justice, since the social hierarchies and inequalities that give rise to oppression would remain unchanged. A world in which love in general might thrive would demand social transformation—a 'mend[ing]' of the whole social script, to borrow the language of the prologue sonnet. This brings me to a third point about the prologue sonnet: it underscores the efforts of actors—'*our* toil'—as *collective* 'mend[ing]'. Art in this sense is a possible cure, like the Friar's herbs, if used well, but if used poorly, it is at best a soporific, perhaps the apothecary's poison.

From the perspective of collective 'mend[ing]', the Friar's intervention, too, is limited. His goal might be broader than Romeo's and Juliet's, but is nevertheless not broad enough, since it ultimately fails to stretch to encompass the structural conditions that render it so difficult for love and freedom to thrive in the world in which he and the young lovers move. Furthermore, he acts, almost exclusively, as an atomized individual agent. This is why *art*—not the Friar's intervention—is the most promising resource conjured up by the play to provoke action at the structural level—if it is *collectively* well used. Thus the work of the play, as art, I would suggest, is to transfer this responsibility to the audience as actors in the world, given that the characters in the play all fail.

---

[23] Kottman, 'Stars', 4.

When the patriarchs seek to transform the death of the lovers into 'sacrifices' they promise to build a physical monument to them. This, however, is a gesture that the sonnets repeatedly dismiss as futile, or, at the very least, inferior to art, as in sonnet 55:

> Not marble, nor the gilded monuments
> Of princes, shall outlive this powerful rhyme;
> But you shall shine more bright in these contents
> Than unswept stone, besmear'd with sluttish time.

The divergence of the patriarchs' response to death from the overt argument of the sonnets is, I think, meant to suggest that their gesture is insufficient given the play's overt entanglement with sonnet content and form. Indeed, the Patriarchs' declaration of the deaths of their children to be 'sacrifices' seeks to contain the potential social disruption of the couple's dissident refusal of the status quo. That is, by limiting the meaning of the deaths to family repercussions (the end of the feud), they narrow it: the implications of disobedience to family, state, and church, after all, would be potentially far more dangerous, if it were to escalate into collective agitation for structural transformation.

The patriarchs cannot transform waste into 'sacrifice' merely by erecting a physical monument.[24] Countless lyrics tell us so. But *we* –collectively, each audience on its own now—have a chance to remake historical waste into sacrifice by transforming the world in ways that give the suffering of the past meaning by finally overturning the oppressive structures that cause suffering, as Walter Benjamin, who influenced Adorno so profoundly, insisted.[25] The ending of *Romeo and Juliet is* 'unsatisfying'—but not because the play privileges individual freedom over the social as Kottman suggests.[26] Rather, the conclusion draws attention to the insufficiency of *all* the 'solutions' the play offers diegetically, each being partial—*including* Romeo and Juliet's love, if it remains merely individual—an exception. The ending thus 'opens' the play by putting the onus on us, *now*, to mend the world and create 'an association in which the free development of each is the condition for the free development of all'.[27] There is no meaningful freedom for individuals otherwise, however pretty it is to think so.

SELECT BIBLIOGRAPHY

Fitter, Chris, 'The Quarrel Is between our Masters and us their Men: *Romeo and Juliet*, Dearth and the London Riots', *English Literary Renaissance* 30 (2000), 154–83.
Kahn, Coppelia, 'Coming of Age in Verona', in *The Woman's Part*, ed. Carolyn Lenz et al. (Urbana: University of Illinois Press, 1983), 171-93.

[24] Hugh Grady's reading of *Romeo and Juliet* in *Impure Aesthetics* (Cambridge: Cambridge University Press, 2009) also emphasizes the importance of art, but suggests that the monument the fathers promise would *be* art, whereas I suggest that the play (and the sonnets) suggest otherwise.

[25] This is the 'weak messianic power' through which we resist the triumphal march of cultural treasures that renders them the tools of oppressors. See Walter Benjamin, 'On the Concept of History', *Selected Writings*, vol. 4, ed. Howard Eiland and Michael W. Jennings (Cambridge, MA: Harvard University Press, 2006).

[26] Kottman, 'Defying', 4, rightly describes the ending of the play as 'unsatisfying', but I am pointing to very different reasons for thinking so than he does.

[27] Karl Marx and Fredric Engels, *The Communist Manifesto*, trans. Samuel Moore (London: Penguin, 2002), 244.

Menon, Madhavi, *Wanton Words: Rhetoric and Sexuality in English Renaissance Drama* (Toronto: University of Toronto Press, 2004).

Nevo, Ruth, 'Tragic Form in Romeo and Juliet', *Studies in English Literature* 9 (1969), 241–58.

Roberts, Sasha, 'Reading Shakespeare's Tragedies of Love: *Romeo and Juliet, Othello* and *Anthony and Cleopatra* in Early Modern England', in Richard Dutton and Jean E. Howard, eds., *A Companion to Shakespeare's Works*, vol. 1, *The Tragedies* (Blackwell, 2005), 108-33.

Snyder, Susan, 'Ideology and the Feud in Romeo and Juliet', *Shakespeare Survey* 49 (1996), 87–96.

Tanselle, G. Thomas, 'Time in Romeo and Juliet', *Shakespeare Quarterly* 15:4 (1964), 349–61.

Wall, Wendy, 'De-generation: Editions, Offspring and Romeo and Juliet', in *From Performance to Print in Shakespeare's England*, ed. Peter Holland and Steven Orgel (Basingstoke: Palgrave, 2006), 152–70.

Wells, Stanley, *Shakespeare, Sex and Love* (Oxford: Oxford University Press, 2010).

White, R. S., ed., *Romeo and Juliet: Critical Essays* (Basingstoke: Palgrave, 2001).

CHAPTER 23

···

JULIUS CAESAR
Making History

···

EMILY C. BARTELS

No introduction to Shakespeare's *Julius Caesar* (performed and probably written in 1599) would be complete without some reference to its primary source, Thomas North's translation of Plutarch's *Lives of the Noble Grecians and Romans* (1579, 1595). As scholars and editors take on the problem that preoccupies the leading characters—is or isn't Caesar (or by extension, the conspiracy) good for Rome?—they turn to the historical narrative for clues. There we can find some answers, despite the fact that this history offers multiple, sometimes divergent accounts of characters and events. In North, Caesar is named a 'perpetual dictator' 'never to be afraid to be deposed' (1426) and is condemned for his 'covetous desire' to 'be called king'.[1] Brutus appears 'rightly made and framed into virtue' (1843)—being one who 'always did incline to that which was good' (1849) and who got the credit 'if there were any noble attempt done in all this conspiracy' (1843).[2] Antonius is characterized by 'great follies', 'vain expenses', and reprobate acquaintances (1660); his 'Asiatic' eloquence is 'full of ostentation, foolish bravery, and vain ambition' 'much like to his manners and life' (1660), and his 'noble presence', 'authority and power' are all undone by the 'thousand other faults he had' (1661).[3] In North as well, the nameless Roman people get their indelible reputation as 'a fickle and inconstant multitude' (1867).[4] Whether we find such assessments also in Shakespeare's play, track its departure from them, or forage for other illuminating historical details, the source appears to provide a window onto the political controversy that surrounds Caesar's rise and fall.[5]

---

[1] Plutarch, 'The Life of Julius Caesar,' in *The Lives of the Noble Grecians and Romans*, vol. 2, trans. Sir Thomas North (New York: Heritage Press, 1941); page numbers appear in the text. These parts of North are excerpted in the Signet edition, a popular teaching text, which implicitly encourages students to read the play through these judgements: see William Shakespeare, *Julius Caesar*, ed. William and Barbara Rosen (New York: Penguin, 1998), 108–51.

[2] Plutarch, 'The Life of Marcus Brutus,' in *Lives*.

[3] Plutarch, 'The Life of Marcus Antonius,' in *Lives*.

[4] Plutarch, 'The Life of Marcus Brutus', in *Lives*.

[5] On one extreme, as the editor of the Oxford Shakespeare, Arthur Humphreys, includes excerpts from North, he asserts that these show 'how closely ... Shakespeare followed his source'; William Shakespeare, *Julius Caesar*, ed. Arthur Humphreys (Oxford: Oxford University Press, 1984; reissued 2008), 233.

Shakespeare's later Roman tragedies—*Antony and Cleopatra* (1606-7) and *Coriolanus* (1607-8)—which also take their bearings from North's Plutarch, are less likely to send us scurrying to an historical source.[6] Though, like Shakespeare's English histories, they are stories of state, in them politics are overrun by exotic personalities, history by theatre, fact by fiction and elaborate fiction-making. In *Antony and Cleopatra*, for example, the Roman Philo inaugurates the play by asking spectators to 'behold and see' 'the triple pillar of the world transformed | Into a strumpet's fool' (1.1.12-13).[7] In what follows, the allure is not the political fortune and legacy of that 'triple pillar' Mark Antony, left hanging at the end of *Julius Caesar*, but the testy erotics of the Egyptian Cleopatra, whose theatrically multiplex persona seems to 'beggar all description' (2.2.204), her 'to-be-looked-at-ness' drawing us in and creating 'a gap in nature' (2.2.224).[8] Because theatricality is so obviously central here (as in *Coriolanus*), the drama itself, apart from the historical evidence that surrounds it, seems adequate as our crucial point of reference.

Not so in the case of *Julius Caesar*, which persistently calls for its supplementation. More history than tragedy, this early Roman play is primarily a story of state—ostensibly of a declining republic whose leader, the controversial Julius Caesar, is the target of those who think he has become (Cassius), is becoming (Marullus and Flavius), or will become (Brutus) too big for his political breeches.[9] Yet the play provides virtually no evidence of Caesar's political inclinations or merit—in fact, virtually no evidence of Caesar himself. The character appears just three times: at the games of Lupercal, surveying those around him; at home, accommodating and then dismissing his wife Calpurnia's portentous dream, warning him not to go out on the Ides of March; and, finally, at the Senate House, hearing and rejecting an appeal from Metallus Cimber for the 'enfranchisement' of his banished brother Publius (3.1.57).[10] Though this last provides an instance—in fact, the only instance—of rule, it is not one we can evaluate: the play offers no explanation of when or why the decree was first imposed and no evidence as to whether Cimber really 'should be banished', as Caesar contends (3.1.172). Before we can see more, the conspirators kneel submissively before him, only to rise up and 'kill him in the shell' (2.1.34). Though we might make the case, as some have, that 'the spirit of Caesar dominates' past his death, the rest is silence (from Caesar) and hearsay (from those, including Mark Antony, who would supplant him).[11]

In North, the breaking point of Caesar's career comes at the end of the games, when Antonius repeatedly offers Caesar a laurel crown and 'unaware' sets the leader up for a fall (1673).[12] Each time Caesar refuses the offer, and each time the crowd 'rejoice[s] at it'

    [6] Compare Tom Bishop, 'Tragedy and Roman History', Ch. 15 in this volume.
    [7] Unless otherwise noted, quotations from Shakespeare are from *The Norton Shakespeare*, ed. Stephen Greenblatt et al. (New York: Norton, 1997), which uses the Oxford texts. I take the dating of the plays from *The Riverside Shakespeare*, ed. G. Blakemore Evans et al. (Boston: Houghton Mifflin, 1974).
    [8] Laura Mulvey, 'Visual Pleasure and Narrative Cinema,' *Screen* 16:3 (1975), 6–18.
    [9] See Annabel Patterson, *Shakespeare and the Popular Voice* (Oxford: Basil Blackwell, 1989), 11, 126, who characterizes the republic as 'decaying'.
    [10] Humphreys, *Julius Caesar*. References to *Julius Caesar* in this chapter are to this edn.
    [11] R. A. Yoder, 'History and the Histories in *Julius Caesar*', *Shakespeare Quarterly* 24:3 (1973), 309–27 (310).
    [12] Plutarch, 'The Life of Marcus Antonius,' in *Lives*.

(1674). This, according to the 'Life of Marcus Antonius', 'was a wonderful thing'—that the people who 'suffered all things subjects should do by commandment of their kings' 'could not abide the name of a king, detesting it as the utter destruction of their liberty' (1674). Caesar is enraged, and when a tribune afterwards removes the laurel from 'one of Caesar's statues or images' where it had been put, Caesar 'turn[s] them out of their offices for it' (1674). 'This was a good encouragement for Brutus and Cassius to conspire his death' (1674), translates North, Antony's good-will gesture giving 'Caesar's enemies just occasion and color to do as they did' (1673). A prompt for action and interpretation, the faux crowning exposes Caesar's 'covetous desire' 'to be called king' and, in turn, provides a rationale for the conspiracy.

In Shakespeare, Brutus uses a similar allegation to justify the assassination: Caesar 'would be crowned. | How that might change his nature, there's the question…. | Crown him that, | And then, I grant, we put a sting in him | That at his will he may do danger with' (2.1.12-13, 15-17). Strikingly, however, neither Brutus nor the catalysing Cassius—nor we—witness this crowning moment, which begs for theatrical representation but is not staged. We hear only the 'general shout[s]' and 'applauses' (1.2.132-3) which sound from offstage while on stage Cassius attempts to lure Brutus into the conspiracy. Brutus projects his own changing anxieties onto the sounds, surmising that 'the people' are about to 'choose Caesar for their king' (ll. 79-80) and, slightly differently, that 'new honours' are being 'heaped on Caesar' (l. 134). Though Caesar and his train make no reference to the crowning when they appear, Brutus reads unsettled reactions—the 'angry spot' on 'Caesar's brow', paleness in Calpurnia's 'cheek', and 'fiery', ferret-like 'looks' of Cicero (ll. 183, 185-6)—into their faces. Only when Casca, who has seen the events, arrives to report that Caesar has thrice refused the crown does the play fill in the gaps, and not exactly as Brutus has. Even then, because Casca puts multiple spins on the story (and I will return to these), we are made aware that almost everything we know about Caesar's ambitions comes to us with conspicuous indirection from narratives his opponents construct and that we have nothing solid by which to assess his politics. No wonder we need North.

Or do we? As Cassius, Brutus, and Antony use their impressive rhetorical powers to persuade themselves and others that their actions serve the 'general good' of Rome, it is tempting to follow their leads (1.2.85). But how can we determine whose right is right in the face of such limited evidence? Theatrical productions have bypassed this dilemma by taking a definitive stand, casting Caesar as 'a dictatorial monster of modern times'— Mussolini (1937), Hitler (1953), Fidel Castro (1986), Margaret Thatcher (1993)—as well as something less.[13] In a 2012 production, for example, the title character becomes 'an ailing war hero' in Africa, 'fed pep-up pills by Calpurnia', 'who must puff himself up to assert his questionable authority'.[14] Literary criticism too has tended to fill in the gaps and make a choice one way or another, supporting Caesar against the conspirators, the conspirators against Caesar. Even in the mid-twentieth century, when critics emphasized the play's ambiguity and status as a 'problem play', their approach was based on the problematic of taking sides: in refusing to privilege either faction, the play demonstrated the limits of

---

[13] See John Ripley, Julius Caesar *on Stage in England & America, 1599-1973* (Cambridge: Cambridge University Press, 1980).

[14] Patrick Carnegy, 'Friends, Romans, Africans', *The Spectator* 16 June 2012, 58. See also Samuel Crow, *Shakespeare and Film: A Norton Guide* (New York: Norton, 2008), 138-40.

human knowledge, perspective, or psychology, or followed early modern rhetorical training, which required the production of competing arguments.[15] Under these circumstances, the best that critics could do was to find solace in Cicero's dictum, taken as the guiding idea of this rhetorically driven play, that 'men may construe things after their fashion, | Clean from the purpose of the things themselves' (1.3.34-5).

But suppose that, instead of asking us to evaluate the competitors, the play directs our attention to the process of evaluation itself, exposing *how* history—instead of *what* history—is made. For as the play, with all its gaps, prompts us to look to North, it simultaneously rejects rather than supports the sort of clarifying master narrative we expect such histories to supply (whether or not they actually do). Instead, *Julius Caesar*—which is as theatrically oriented as the later Roman plays—locates its history in a nexus of local interactions, improvised by characters who cannot see (beyond) themselves and their moment in time.[16] Taking on a case of cataclysmic political upheaval, it shows historical motivations, actions, and outcomes not to be omnisciently crafted, connected, and coherent, but to be disorganized, disjointed, and uncontrolled. Ultimately, what falls with Caesar and the conspiracy is not simply the illusion of historical agency: the idea that, for better or worse, great men (and in this play it is 'men') autonomously make or break the day. What falls as well is the reliability of historical narratives, which impose an unforeseeable meaning on the past, apart from the messy contingencies of the present.

THEN FALL, CAESAR

Julius Caesar has all the trappings of a political thriller: a nervous power-broker at the height of his game, worried about thin men with 'lean and hungry look[s]' who 'thin[k] too much' (1.2.194-5); a conspiracy that goes viral against him, turning his closest friends into his most powerful foes; secret meetings, deceptive letters; a spectacular gang-stabbing with mass mutiny in the aftermath; and the rise of a ruthless new regime—all accompanied by omens, prophecies, a Soothsayer, shrieking owls, and visions of 'men, all in fire' and 'a hundred ghastly women | Transformed by their fear' (1.3.24-5). Yet while such a trailer promises chills and thrills, the play takes the punch out of the plot by putting more emphasis on reactions than it does on actions—to the point that in some instances (such as the crowning of Caesar) narrative reporting takes the place of dramatization of signal events. Drama and characterization are, of course, constituted by the dynamic interplay of action and reaction, and while every action in some way at once cues and is reaction, in any given moment there is an implicit cause (action) and effect (reaction) which will in turn become the cause of a new effect. Yet *Julius Caesar* habitually obscures or eclipses that primary act or cause, with the result that characters seem to be caught up in contingencies, fielding more than they are setting the terms of action.

---

[15] See Ernest Schanzer, 'The Problem of *Julius Caesar*', *Shakespeare Quarterly* 6:3 (1955), 297-308; Jeffrey J. Yu, '*Julius Caesar*, Erasmus's *De Copia* and Sentential Ambiguity', *Comparative Drama* 41:1. (2007): 79-106 (80).

[16] Compare Oliver Arnold, *The Third Citizen: Shakespeare's Theater and the Early Modern House of Commons* (Baltimore: Johns Hopkins University Press, 2007), 140-78, esp. 140-4.

The opening scene establishes this pattern as it introduces two tribunes, Marullus and Flavius, who are sidelined from direct commemoration of—or resistance to—Caesar's ascendancy and are tasked rather with closing down the celebrations of the plebeians. Instead of staging Caesar's celebratory parade, the play presents the tribunes' reactions to the plebeians' reactions to Caesar, redacted through the plebeians' alleged reactions to Pompey. Castigating the plebeians, Marullus recalls the time when they 'climbed up to walls and battlements, | To towers and windows, yea, to chimney-tops, | ... To see great Pompey pass the streets of Rome' (ll. 38-40). How can they now 'strew flowers in his way | That comes in triumph over Pompey's blood'? (ll. 50-1). We can take away from the exchange what many do: the idea that the tribunes, though the putative representatives of the people, are notably at odds with them, at least with regard to Caesar. The emphasis, however, is not on the tribunes' agency, attitudes, or authority but on their remoteness from the procession of Caesar, which neither they nor we see. Indeed, neither tribune has a part in the conspiracy: their role begins and ends with the regulation of public response. After the crowd exits at the end of the scene, Flavius voices his fear that, unless 'growing feathers' are 'plucked from Caesar's wing,' he will otherwise 'soar above the view of men, | And keep us all in servile fearfulness' (ll. 72, 74-5). The next we hear (from Casca in the following scene), Marullus and Flavius 'are put to silence' 'for pulling scarfs off Caesar's images', a reactive undoing that ultimately undoes them (1.2.281-3).[17]

We may not be surprised to find tribunes reacting rather than acting, since they are on a low rung of the ladder of rule—beneath the senators and Caesar. But the same kind of reactiveness also marks the characterization of Caesar, who is repeatedly blasted for his actual and potential domination of the Roman state. There is some reason to believe, with North, Cassius, and eventually Brutus, that Caesar strides over the people of Rome like a Colossus, imposing his voice, will, and third-person powered pre-eminence on the 'underlings', whose freedoms are crushed beneath his feet (1.2.142). Limited though it is, his speech is marked by commands ('Set him before me', 1.2.20); third-person absolutes ('Caesar shall forth', 2.2.10); as well as combinations of the two ('Know, Caesar doth not wrong', 3.1.47). Yet that apparent puissance emerges not as an autonomous gesture but as a symptomatic response to others' prompts. After all, one of Caesar's and the play's most memorable lines is his deer-in-the-headlights response to the surprise attack of the conspirators: 'Et tu, Brute' (3.1.77). In the second half of his line, 'Then fall, Caesar', Caesar's imperative claim to agency is defined, and undermined, by the action—Caesar falling at the hands of others. That too is paradigmatic of a figure who, like Marullus and Flavius, reacts more than he acts and whose identity is a product of the words and actions that embed him. I'm not talking simply about the hearsay that surrounds and supplants Caesar's characterization, though there is an unusually large amount of it. Nor am I talking about those moments (relevant too) when Caesar is being directly swayed by others—for example, by Calpurnia and Decius Brutus over what to do on the Ides of March. I'm talking rather about those instances when Caesar appears to be most commanding and most controversial, and so, most himself.

---

[17] In his editorial comments on this essay, Michael Neill has called this line 'one of the most sinisterly enigmatic lines in Shakespeare'.

Consider his initial appearance—at a celebration which technically *should* be about Caesar but isn't. Shakespeare compresses the historical timeline, collapsing Caesar's defeat of Pompey (which happened in October) into the feast of Lupercalia (15 February) as well as the Ides of March (15 March). Neither a Colossus nor a pepped-up has-been at the centre of events, Caesar is positioned first in the margins of a fertility festival, vying to get the attention of those around him but encumbered by his inability to be heard as well as to hear. He shouts to his wife Calpurnia (twice) and then to his second-in-command Mark Antony, arranging for Antony to touch her 'barren' body in the day's race and remove her 'sterile curse' (1.2.8, 9). Meanwhile Casca tries (needs?) to alert the crowd that 'Caesar speaks' (1.2.2), his line finishing Caesar's, and directs undesignated others to 'bid every noise be still' (l. 14). Set Caesar beside Richard of Gloucester who inaugurates *Richard III* with an unforgettable soliloquy: 'Now is the winter of our discontent' (1.1.1); or beside King Lear, who, almost without warning at the start of 'his' play, demands that his daughters earn their part of a divided kingdom by proving on the spot 'which of you shall we say doth love us most' (1.1.49); or beside Prince Hal in *Henry IV, Part One*, who first appears within a disreputable tavern world of 'riot and dishonour' (1.1.84) only to reject it and display his integrity by casting aside the 'base contagious clouds' who would 'smother up his beauty from the world' (1.2.176-7). Even Hamlet's initial retort, 'I am too much i' th' sun' (1.2.67), to his step-father-uncle-king interrupts Claudius' show of kingly and fatherly power, requiring that Claudius adjust his terms and bring forth some thirty lines of precedents and platitudes to dissuade Hamlet from mourning his real father. When these heroes first speak, their words define or generate action; when Caesar first speaks, very few even hear.

What resonates instead is the Soothsayer's warning 'Beware the Ides of March' (1.2.18), which rivals 'Et tu, Brute', 'To be or not to be', 'What's in a name?' as best-in-show Shakespearean memorabilia. The exchange between Caesar and the Soothsayer provides an obvious foreshadowing of Caesar's soon-to-be-realized future (some would say 'fate'). But equally important is how it casts Caesar in the present, in a receiving position to another's intervention. In lines superfluous to both plot and portent, the scene emphasizes how embedded Caesar is in the unfolding moment by emphasizing his difficulty in getting the story straight, determining who has spoken—('Who calls?' 'Who is it in the press that calls on me?' 'What man is that?' 1.2.13, 15, 18) and what he has said. Even after Brutus recites the line 'A soothsayer bids you beware the ides of March' (l. 19), Caesar orders the Soothsayer to repeat his words: 'What sayst thou to me now? Speak once again' (l. 22). Although Caesar does not follow the Soothsayer's advice, he clearly follows the figure's lead, deciding only whether to accept or reject what he has finally heard: 'He is a dreamer. Let us leave him. Pass' (l. 24). We miss the point if we read this exchange solely in terms of what it prognosticates. To do so is to take the play's incorporation of prophetic signs as truth rather than to interrogatethem as an object of critique. It is also to confuse Caesar's lack of foresight, evident only later, with Caesar's lack of initiative, which resonates here and now, and to privilege an omniscient arc of 'history' over the unfolding of a short-sighted dramatic exchange.

Even in those signal moments when Caesar distinguishes himself as a self-constituted subject—an 'I' who is 'always' 'Caesar', 'constant as the Northern star' (1.2.213; 3.1.60)—his locutions are time-bound responses rather than timeless proclamations. On the early modern stage, the production of an 'I am' is both distinctive and rare, appearing usually once per play, usually at crucial turning point.[18] Hamlet, for example, declares 'This is I, Hamlet the Dane' when he returns to Danish soil after exile in England, finally ready to confront Claudius (*Ham.* 5.2.241-2). In John Webster's *Duchess of Malfi*, the lead defiantly asserts 'I am Duchess of Malfi still' at the very moment the fiendish Bosola is about to murder her (4.2.139).[19] Such statements often emerge when the character is on the brink of losing all. But however ironic or transient they may prove to be, the 'I' stands out against the odds in the moment of its articulation, a self-propelled and self-authorizing pronouncement. Though *we* may worry that Hamlet's or the Duchess's 'I' will not resonate for long, the characters themselves do not.

Caesar speaks similarly, as if only he is setting the terms of his identity. But his self-glorifications come in response to contrastingly petty challenges to his authority. When he appears after the faux crowning, for example, he attempts without success to provoke in Mark Antony suspicion of the 'lean and hungry' looking Cassius, whom Caesar presents as 'dangerous' (2.1.194-5). Antony (I think not innocently) offers an insinuating rebuff, 'Fear him not, Caesar, he's not dangerous' (l. 196). Denying that fear, Caesar continues to insist that Cassius—who 'reads much', 'looks quite through the deeds of men', 'loves no plays', 'hears no music', and so on—is to be feared (1.2.201-4). He then circles back to repudiate Antony's suggestion that he is afraid, announcing: 'I rather tell thee what is to be feared | Than what I fear; for always I am Caesar' (ll. 211-12). Put in its place by the subordinating conjunction, 'always I am Caesar' appears not as the point of Caesar's discourse but as the after-effect of an exchange that is not going his way; instead of indicating what Caesar is, it indicates only what he isn't, in a conversation that is primarily about Cassius. Caesar himself seems to put little stock or staying power in his self-pronouncement. After making the claim, he orders Antony to move to his other side, since one 'ear is deaf' (ll. 213), and to tell him 'truly' what he thinks of Cassius (ll. 214). So much for Caesar.

The most imposing of Caesar's self-promotions comes in the Senate just before his assassination, when he addresses Metellus Cimber's plea for pardon for his brother. Within this political context, the stakes are higher and Caesar's rhetoric is grander. But instead of being in control of the session, as Lear is when he first convenes the court and sets the terms of state, Caesar is yet again in a reactive position: his self-production derives from a seemingly innocuous gesture, the 'couchings and lowly courtesies' (3.1.36) that Cimber and the conspirators perform as they address the 'most high, most mighty, and most puissant Caesar' (ll. 33, 36). Before Cimber can begin to make his case, Caesar interrupts him, objecting to what he underscores as 'sweet words, | Low-crooked curtsies, and base spaniel fawning' (ll. 42-4). Following Cimber's lead, Brutus and Cassius also kneel, perhaps in order to unsettle Caesar further (which they do) and set him up for the kill—with Brutus kissing Caesar's hand and Cassius drawing attention to the fact that he is falling 'as low as to [Caesar's] foot' (ll. 57). Caesar himself does not see what is coming and insists on his inimitable constancy to counter only these fawnings: 'If I could pray to move, | prayers would move me, | But I am constant as the northern star, | Of whose true-fixed

[18] See Catherine Belsey, *The Subject of Tragedy: Identity and Difference in Renaissance Drama* (London: Methuen, 1985), 93–125.

[19] John Webster, *The Duchess of Malfi*, ed. Elizabeth M. Brennan (1993; London: A & C Black, reprt 1998).

and resting quality | There is no fellow in the firmament' (ll. 59-62). The 'but' exposes this self-assertion as a mere appendage of another thought. Although Caesar subsequently tries to make his claims relevant to the looming political issue, that transfer is clearly an after-thought. 'That I am he', that one and only northern star, he announces, 'let me a little show it, *even in this—* | That I was constant Cimber should be banished, | And constant do remain to keep him so' (ll. 70-3; emphasis added). When Cinna and Decius Brutus then kneel, putting an exasperated Caesar on the defensive ('Hence! Wilt thou lift up Olympus?'; 'Doth not Brutus bootless kneel?', ll. 74-5) and cueing the assassination, the illusion that Caesar's identity is autonomously conceived and contained shatters along with the fiction of his unassailability.

This is not Hamlet, or the Duchess of Malfi, or Lear. This is Julius Caesar linking his 'I' to an ever constant 'always Caesar' because Mark Antony accuses him of fear and to a northern star because the conspirators kneel against his will. In exposing Caesar as a figure defined by the interventions of others, I do not mean to return to the age-old, Cassius-like conclusion that he is somehow weak, a term that is always judgemental and, in Cassius' discourse, obviously self-serving. The point is rather that Caesar's articulations of a distinguishing political identity are not self-generated actions but rather are re-actions to others' prompts. Remove them, the small, almost random acts that seem more like rudeness than resistance, and there is no almighty Caesar. We can't then impose a narrative on Caesar, as North's Plutarch does, that takes him out of context and assigns his moves and pronouncements a sustained motive, politics, or self-regard—a 'covetous desire' to 'be called king'. Rather we must read him as a figure whose political self-constitution, even and especially at its most puissant, evolves dramatically on the sidelines of plot, as improvised responses to small and local cues. No wonder we need Shakespeare.

ET TU, BRUTE

'Had you rather Caesar were living, and die all slaves, than that Caesar were dead, to live all free men?' (3.2.22-3). This is the question Brutus poses to the audience at Caesar's funeral— as if the choice to live under Caesar or to live free within some kind of 'commonwealth', as Oliver Arnold provocatively suggests, were still in play (3.2.41).[20] Critics typically interpret the play as a study of a waning republic which is threatened by Caesar's potential as a dictator, monarch, or tyrant—a study particularly relevant to the Elizabethans, whose parliament was increasingly vocal in its claims to represent the people and the state.[21] These kinds of political tensions certainly do play out in Shakespeare—with Caesar representing one-man rule, undone by those who worry that his power has grown too great, who are in turn undone by a temporary triumvirate and a new Caesar. But in this case of political conspiracy and revolution, the action evolves locally and disjunctively, and not according

---

[20] See Arnold, *The Third Citizen*, 170-1.

[21] Arnold, *The Third Citizen*; see also Rita Banerjee, 'The Common Good and the Necessity of War: Republican Ideals in Shakespeare's *Henry V* and *Coriolanus*', *Comparative Drama* 40:1 (2006), 29–49.

to some clear-cut master plan.[22] If we are looking to the representation of the conspirators to find the historical clarity that the representation of Caesar and the tribunes challenges, we will not find it here.

Strikingly, in what is touted as a dramatic representation of the decline of the Roman republic, there is no explicit mention of the republic. Brutus makes a passing reference to the 'commonwealth' in his funeral oration, advocating that Mark Antony, 'though he had no hand in [Caesar's] death', have 'a place in the commonwealth' (3.2.41-2). A commonwealth, however, is not necessarily a republic. The Oxford edition glosses the term 'with all the rights of a free Roman', noting that Brutus is vague about what those rights are; (the editor declares those rights: 'perhaps a vague … "citizenship in the republic"', inserting 'republic' where the play does not).[23] Moreover, almost every edition identifies the conspirators as 'conspirators' without regard to their political titles. In the list of *dramatic personae* (not available to early modern spectators, but relevant to us), characters outside their immediate circle are designated as 'senators' (e.g. Cicero) and 'tribunes' (Marullus and Flavius), while figures within the circle, such as Cassius (historically a senator) and Casca (a tribune), are simply labelled 'conspirators', sometimes along with Brutus (a praetor, i.e. a judge at the top of the political hierarchy). Nor does the play itself emphasize, or in some cases even identify, those characters' official posts. In remarks about Brutus, Cassius references 'the praetor's chair' (1.3.143) but otherwise explains the conspiracy's 'great need' of Brutus only in abstract terms of 'worth' (1.3.161). While Casca presumes to know what's 'in all the people's hearts' (1.3.157), he is never identified as a tribune and never associated with the designated tribunes Flavius and Marullus, except when he conveys the news of their executions. Conspirators all, these figures are defined therefore not by their place in or allegiance to a republican state but by their involvement in a single action: the ousting of Julius Caesar. Obsessed with eradicating him, they represent an opposition, not an alternative.

But an opposition to what? Tyranny? Dictatorship? Monarchy? On everyone's mind, of course, is the fear that Caesar is too overbearing or ambitious for the 'general good' of Rome. But Cassius only once declares Caesar a 'tyrant' (1.3.103), and then only to Casca. Otherwise the charges against Caesar are politically formless, and we have no access to their origins since the staging of the conspiracy begins *in medias res*, with Cassisus' recruitment of Brutus, the final, not first, stage of Cassius' operations. In the subsequent scene, Cinna reports to Cassius that he, along with Decius Brutus, Trebonius, and 'all but Metellus Cimber', are waiting for word and action, hoping that Cassius will be successful in 'win[ning] the noble Brutus to our party' (1.3.149, 141). But at what point has anxiety necessitated action? What has turned agitation into conspiracy? What has been the tipping point that has transformed disliking Caesar into destroying him? North's 'Life of Marcus Brutus' explains that the 'first cause of Cassius's malice against Caesar' was that Caesar appointed Brutus first praetor and not he (1851). In Shakespeare, there is no representation of a first cause. We enter in the middle of a work-in-progress, which congeals in fragments around characters who stand and speak at a notable remove from each other and the organizing subjects of Caesar and Rome.

---

[22] On the play's approach to political history, compare Rebecca Bushnell, '*Julius Caesar*', in *A Companion to Shakespeare's Works*, vol. 1, *The Tragedies*, ed. Richard Dutton and Jean E. Howard (Malden, MA: Blackwell Publishing, 2003), 339–56.

[23] In the note to 3.2.42.

Take Cassius' approach to Brutus, which is our introduction to the conspiracy's rationale. Cassius makes his case through a set of persuasions clearly calculated to what he imagines Brutus, who declares himself already 'vexèd' by 'passions of some difference' (1.2.39, 40), wants to hear. When Brutus objects to Cassius' initial insinuation that 'many of the best respect in Rome' want him to undo 'this age's yoke' (ll. 58-60), Cassius changes course. He not only produces two conflicting images of Caesar—first a man 'feeble temper' who almost drowns, has fevers and shaking fits, and, when that fails to capture Brutus' attention, 'a colossus' who 'doth bestride the narrow world' (ll. 135-6), while 'petty men' (like Brutus and Cassius) must 'walk under his huge legs' (ll. 136-7).[24] Emphasizing the idea that Rome's 'wide walks' are currently 'encompassed' by 'one man', 'but one man', 'but only one man' (ll. 153, 155, 157), he simultaneously stokes any anti-monarchical fears and any monarchical ambitions that Brutus, who could 'be Caesar' (l. 50), might have. Ironically, the play's only invocation of Rome's republican past appears as part of that bipolar stoking, in Cassius' reminder that 'there was a Brutus once that would have brooked | Th' eternal devil to keep his state in Rome | As easily as a king' (ll. 158-61).[25] Cassius presents Junius Brutus—who overthrew a Roman tyrant (Tarquin), transformed Rome's monarchy into a republic, and established himself as first consul—as a republican hero who sees king's rule as devil's work. He also dangles before Brutus the premise 'as easily as a king', which is detached from its referent (devil) as from its implied subject and verb (he would have) within a semantically messy line, bringing the name of Brutus into uneasy proximity with both devil and king. At what might otherwise be a big moment of historical truth, we get mixed messages instead of the articulation of cause, the head conspirator covering all the bases, appealing to whatever politics might reach an ostensibly unreachable peer.

In Brutus' case history is no clearer, not in Shakespeare's play. To be sure, Brutus emerges as the spokesman for the 'general good'—one whom Antony, making his own play for power, will tout posthumously as the only conspirator who did what he did not 'in envy of great Caesar' but 'in a general honest thought | And common good to all' (5.5.71-3). We may be tempted to believe that, right or wrong, Brutus stands on solid, if abstract, ground. Throughout the play, however, he stands at one remove from Caesar, from the conspirators, and from us, 'vexèd' by those unarticulated 'passions' ' which he admits concealing from Cassius as 'conceptions only proper to myself' (1.2.41). It's hard to tell, in fact, how much he attends to Cassius' opening advances. In closing off the interaction, he explicitly addresses only Cassius' professed fears, voiced a hundred lines earlier,that he would be 'jealous'—that is, untrusting--of Cassius' 'love' (1.2.161). Although he promises to consider '*what* [Cassius] ha[s] said' and 'with patience' to hear '*what* [Cassius] ha[s] to say' (ll. 167-8; emphasis added), he reduces Cassius' persuasions to an emphatically reiterated 'what' and turns attention to his own premeditations, 'how I have thought of this, and these times' (l. 164). Inviting Cassius to 'chew upon this', 'Brutus had rather be a villager | Than to repute himself a son of Rome | Under these hard conditions as this time | Is like to lay upon us' (ll. 171-5), his focus is not the oppressive present which Cassius has depicted

---

[24] Shakespeare will recycle the image in *Antony and Cleopatra*, having Cleopatra (who had a fling and a son with Julius Caesar) present the now dead Antony one whose 'legs bestrid the ocean' (5.2.81), and so, retrospectively, turning that image into something of a great man's cliché.

[25] See also Ronald Berman, 'A Note on the Motives of Marcus Brutus', *Shakespeare Quarterly* 23:2 (1972), 197-200.

but a future of 'hard conditions' which he himself fears will come. I think we might raise an eyebrow or two when Cassius says he is 'glad | That [his] weak words have struck but thus much show | Of fire from Brutus' (1.2.176-8).[26] If Cassius' arguments lead Brutus anywhere, they lead him in a direction that he already has been going, much as the vision of daggers leads Macbeth.

It is that 'already been going' that at once defines—and muddies our view of—Brutus' involvement in the conspiracy. His admission of pre-formed 'passions' as well as his insistence that he 'spurn[s] at' Caesar for a 'general', not 'personal', cause (2.1.11) create the illusion that he is guided by a consistent politics and interior and acts above and beyond the kinds of contingencies, manipulations, and theatrics that characters such as Cassius, Caesar, and Antony seem to be subject to. Yet his signal soliloquy on the problem of Caesar is riven by discontinuities, making us question not only how much we can know him but also how much he knows himself. Strikingly, Brutus is the first to explicitly translate ousting Caesar into killing him: Cassius speaks only of planning to 'shake' him (1.2.319). Brutus' logic is chronologically ajar. His defining soliloquy starts with the idea that 'it must be by his death' (2.1.1) and ends with the imperative action of 'kill[ing]' Caesar 'in the shell' (l.34)—as if the end (death) justifies and precedes the means (killing). It may be stretching the point to see an anticipation of Macbeth, who leaps at the chance to kill the Scottish king Duncan because three Weird Sisters have forecast that Macbeth himself will 'be King hereafter' (*Macbeth* 1.3.48). Yet Brutus too leaps over alternatives (and realities) as he chooses murder as the only way to address 'hard conditions' which he has forecast quite apart from any definitive starting or turning point. Moreover, he never says what exactly 'must be by' the unnamed Caesar's 'death'. When Othello is about to murder his wife, he defers to an evasive 'it' to avoid speaking of an unspeakable cause: 'It is the cause, it is the cause, my soul: | Let me not name it to you, you chaste stars. | It is the cause' (*Oth.* 5.1.1-3). If there we have seen enough to have some idea of what 'it' signifies (sexual infidelity), in *Julius Caesar* we have not: Brutus' invocation of 'it' points to a desired outcome, which appears unspoken, not unspeakable.

What he does speak and specify stands at odd with other facts. Brutus emphasizes that Caesar 'would be crowned' (l. 12), even though he has just heard from Casca that, in the face of the crowd's resistance, Caesar has repeatedly *refused* the crown. Tellingly too, Brutus makes no mention of the crowning when he justifies the assassination at Caesar's funeral, before a crowd who have likely witnessed the refusal. When he takes on the question of Caesar's ambition privately and publicly, his objections shift: from the worries that Caesar will sting in the light of day, will 'scorn the base degrees | By which he did ascend', or will 'grow mischievous' (2.1. 25-7, 33), to the worry that Caesar will turn the people into slaves ('Had you rather Caesar were living, and die all slaves than that Caesar were dead, to live all free men?' 3.2.22-3). As for the 'general', Brutus first mentions the 'general good' only to get the cagey Cassius to declare his intent, asserting: 'If it [what Cassius plans] be for the general good, | Set honour in one eye, and death i'th' other, | And I will look on both indifferently' (1.2.86-7). He then immediately equivocates, insisting that he 'love[s] the name of honour more than [he] fear[s] death' (ll. 88-9). Editors who struggle to 'amend' this apparent 'inconsistency' miss the point, that from the start Brutus'

---

[26] Oxford editor Arthur Humphreys takes the line as 'dubious' (see the note to 1.2.175-7), arguing that it is unclear whether Cassius is pleased or disappointed with Brutus' response.

representation of the relation between honour, death, and the 'general good' is confused.[27] Even if we give him some allowance for playing to his audiences, for 'fashion[ing]' the best persuasions for the times (2.1.30), what holds his case together is the illusion—which he himself produces—that he knows, has come into the play knowing, what he is after. But if we take that illusion for truth, we have to take it on faith, apart from all that Brutus leaves significantly unsaid.

At every point, then, the play stresses not only our distance from the characters but also their distance from the history they would make. Where Cassius is too much in the moment to produce a larger view, Brutus is too far from it, and we never know what they think must or will be by Caesar's death. Though the anarchy that erupts after the assassination has been read as 'consequences defeat[ing] intentions', the problem is finally that the conspirators seem to have no intentions, no alternatives beyond the elimination of Caesar.[28] When the wheel comes full circle after the assassination, we're back to where we started, a dramatic world in which action is coded as reaction. In the play's second half, Brutus and Cassius take name and definition not as the progenitors of a new political order, recreating Rome, but as generals, attempting to defend themselves against the rise of a regime led by Antony and Octavius. Even that, the play emphasizes, is remarkably short-sighted. Octavius comes to Rome under summons from Julius Caesar, and Antony attempts to cut him off at the pass by presenting the state, after Caesar's murder, as too 'dangerous' for the 'young' leader (3.1.228, 296). When that effort fails, Antony joins with Octavius (and momentarily Lepidus), and while Octavius has the last word (literally) at the end of the play, it is not without some competition from Antony, who, through his valorization of Brutus, the 'noblest Roman of them all', seems to establish himself as spokesman for the 'common good' (5.5.73). As Octavius enjoins all to leave and 'part the glories of the happy day' (l.82), it is hard to predict, without clues from North, what will come next for Rome.

Writing on the relation between tragedy and Roman history, Tom Bishop argues: 'In *Julius Caesar* we are shown the collapse of the Roman republic in the face of steady and remorseless pressure from individual and factional self-aggrandizement' (Ch. 15 in this volume, 234–49). But in this play, if tragedy and its investment in self trump history and its investment in state, tragedy also constitutes history. There is no representation of a republic, of individual or faction, outside the interactions of the characters, who make history from within a given moment, without the kind of omniscience and control that 'history' would impart. In the end, the point is not simply that the key figures cannot see the forest for the trees; it is finally that the forest is all trees.

THE RAG-TAG PEOPLE

People, rag-tag people, men, countrymen, poor men, tradesmen, citizens, friends, Romans, honest neighbours, idle creatures, blocks, stones, worse than senseless things, common

---

[27] See the note to 1.2.86–9 in the Oxford edition.
[28] Humphreys, 'Introduction', *Julius Caesar*, 7.

herd, commoners: these are the terms that designate the plebeians within the text and paratexts of *Julius Caesar*. From the opening scene where Flavius and Marullus put them down, to the crowning and funeral of Caesar, these are the subjects that everyone needs to woo and loves to hate. Thanks to North, they are known, more than anything else, as that 'fickle and inconstant multitude'. By now no reading of the play probably seems complete without some jab at this motley crew, almost always treated en masse as a collective and not particularly enlightened or enlightening voice.[29] In its representation of 'the people', however, *Julius Caesar* challenges us most to rethink the assumptions we bring to both history and drama, looking for the generalizations that will turn a single moment into a paradigm or prognostication, a diverse many into a representative one.

Though critics, editors, and readers tend to lump 'the people' into one category, the play, in fact, does not. Nor does it demean them as easily manipulated. The opening scene makes a distinction among the 'certain commoners' who first appear, represented synecdochally by a carpenter and a cobbler, and one or two others (1.1. SD). When pressured by the tribunes to identify their trades, the carpenter responds directly ('Why, sir, a carpenter', l. 6), while the cobbler indulges in a circumlocution that puns on his ability to 'mend' 'bad soles' | souls (l. 14) and draws the irritation from the tribunes for his 'saucy' and 'naughty' demeanour (l. 18, 15). A third group is speechless—but not necessarily compliant. Flavius and Marullus try different tactics in order to disband the pro-Caesar celebrations, acting as if the people require strategic handling: Marullus insults the 'cruel men of Rome' as 'you blocks, you stones, you worse than senseless things' while Flavius urges the 'good countrymen' to go their ways (ll. 35-6, 56). The outcome is not success. According to the First Folio (1623), which includes the earliest and most authoritative version of the play, once the crowd exits Flavius directs Marullus to 'see *where* their basest mettle be not mou'd' (109; emphasis added). Most modern editions replace 'where' with a form of whether, (usually 'whe'er'), and so transform Flavius' observation that the plebeians have *not* been moved to a request that Marullus discover *whether* they've been moved (ll. 61).[30] In so doing these editions turn a potentially recalcitrant group of people into a swayable one, flying in the face of the First Folio, perhaps to follow North.

The play almost predicts, even provokes, this kind of move in its representation of Casca, that would-have-been tribune, who turns the people's voices against them to reflect his own grumbling biases. In his reports to Brutus and Cassius on Caesar's crowning, he starts gingerly, with the bare bones—that Caesar 'put ... by' an offered crown and 'the people fell a-shouting' (1.2.221-2)—perhaps uncertain of the interests of his listeners.[31] But as they continue to ask for more information about the crowning, Casca adds details. In the second rendition, he admits that 'to [his] thinking' Caesar indeed 'wound fain have had'

[29] As Bushnell comments: 'Commentators on *Julius Caesar* tend to agree that it does not present a favorable view of Rome's people, who are fickle in their allegiance to their leaders and easily roused to violence' ('*Julius Caesar*', 348). Despite nuanced readings of the populace in *Coriolanus*, Patterson passes *Caesar*'s people by almost entirely; see esp. *Shakespeare and the Popular Voice*, 129. Even Arnold, who (in *The Third Citizen*) pays careful attention to the matter of representation in the play, assumes that they are a single, not terribly attractive, people.

[30] For example, the Oxford, Longman, and Riverside editions of the play do so. The Signet uses 'whe'r', another variant of 'whether'.

[31] Arnold makes the interesting case that Brutus is preoccupied with saving face here, after misreading what the shouts actually mean; see 148-9.

the rejected crown, but the real centre of his narrative is the 'rabblement', who 'hooted, and clapped their chopped hands, and threw up their sweaty nightcaps, and uttered such a deal of stinking breath because Caesar refused the crown that it had almost choked Caesar' (ll. 238-45). Crucial but unclear is whether the clapping crowd supports Caesar or not. But no matter: part of Casca's point is that the 'rag-tag people' would 'clap … and hiss' Caesar 'according as he pleased and displeased them, as they use to do the players in the theatre' (ll. 256-8). Only in a final accounting does Casca make clear that 'the common herd was glad [Caesar] refused the crown', but again his point is their malleability. He concludes, superfluously, by noting that the 'three or four wenches' who 'forgave him with all their hearts' would have supported Caesar even if he 'had stabbed their mothers' (ll. 268-72).

That it is Casca—whom Brutus and Cassius critique as a 'blunt fellow' whose 'rudeness is a sauce to his good wit' (1.2.292, 297)—who so defames the people might deter us from doing the same. I am probably the only one on the planet who believes that the plebeians' initial responses to Brutus' and Antony's funeral orations show neither fickleness nor collective ignorance, but discrete, potentially reasonable takes; but the text bears me out. Though the scene starts with a shared plebeian voice ('We will be satisfied! Let us be satisfied!' 3.2.1), the group splits in two, with some staying to hear Brutus and others going off to hear Cassius, including one, the 'second plebeian', who means to 'compare their reasons, | When severally we hear them rendered' (ll. 9-10). Editions that inscribe one continuous set of speech prefixes across the scene obscure the split, tagging both the plebeian who goes off with Cassius and the plebeian among Brutus' group who speaks second as the 'second plebeian'. And though after Brutus' oration the plebeians are persuaded to his side, their ideas for the next step differ: one wants to bring Brutus 'with triumph home unto his house' (ll. 48, 52); another, to 'give him a statue with his ancestors' (l. 49), another, to 'let him be Caesar' (l. 50), and another, more sceptical about Caesar, to let 'Caesar's better parts' 'be crowned in Brutus' (ll.50-1). In response to Antony's opening line ('For Brutus's sake I am beholden to you', l. 65), two are ready to declare Caesar a tyrant, including the one who suggested, before his fellow's emendation (could it have affected him?), that Brutus be Caesar. After Antony's extended eulogy, the plebeians begin to change sides, but they do seem to be working to a new consensus: when one suggests 'there is much reason in [Antony's] sayings', one agrees that 'considered rightly' 'Caesar had great wrong' (using an oxymoronic rhetorical twist, from 'rightly' to 'wrong'), while another is sceptical: 'Has he, masters? | I fear there will a worse come in his place' (ll. 108-11). Another challenges that scepticism, bringing up Caesar's refusal to take the crown as evidence that 'he was not ambitious', with another thinking forward to the consequences ('if it be found so, some will dear abide it'), before two others shift the focus back to Antony, who is gearing up for a second round of rhetoric (ll. 113-14).

The more Antony speaks, of course, the more the plebeians speak as one. But what we see, instead of a once and for all rag-tag embrace of whoever is speaking at the moment, is a shift in grounds from reason to emotion. Stirred finally by Antony's production of the bloody mantle, the plebeians offer a series of emotionally coded apostrophes—'O piteous spectacle!' 'O noble Caesar!' 'O woeful day!' 'O traitors! Villains!' 'O most bloody sight!' (ll.195-9)—each slightly different from the others, and the whole quite different in tenor from the responses which preceded. It is at this point, when voice is emotion more than thought, that the plebeians agree on a course of action, what Antony calls and they embrace as 'mutiny' (ll. 223, 224). Even then, there is some reason within the madness: one suggests that they burn Caesar's body 'in the holy place' before they 'fire the traitors' houses' (ll. 247–8).

Obviously, these are secondary characters who would be played as parts to represent a fuller whole: as the prologue to *Henry V* reminds us, on the stage 'a crookèd figure may | Attest in little place a million' (1.1.15–16). Still, there is enough differentiation between these voices to give us pause: if it were not for Casca, the tribunes, and North, and the long tradition of responses that have taken their words for truth, would we gloss so quickly over a people who are not sure quite what to believe in the face of a Caesar and a conspiracy that no one, including ourselves, can ever fully see? If it is true that the leads are inventing themselves, their histories, and their politics in reaction to what emerges unpredictably around them, are we right to condemn the crowd for a single-minded fickleness and inconstancy—especially since we arguably are they, the audience whom Shakespeare's players must ultimately woo? That readers routinely do so testifies to the appeal of historical narrative and omniscience. That the play at once provokes and rebuts such readings exposes its power to unsettle the most settled historical truths.

Julius Caesar is clearly not *Waiting for Godot*. But neither is it a no-fear Shakespeare that matches the scripts we bring to it from 'sources' such as North. Indeed, with all the unknowables at its centre, it may be one of Shakespeare's most dramatically, if not also historically, challenging plays, one that it refuses to distil into recognizably noble or ignoble causes the messy, sometimes petty particulars that might, without design, change the face of nations. Analysing the unfathomable representation of kingship in *Henry V*, Stephen Greenblatt has argued that 'prodded by constant reminders of a gap between real and ideal, facts and values, the spectators are induced to make up the difference'.[32] But if the gaps in *Julius Caesar* tempt us to 'make up the difference', they also show us how history is made—by characters who are never in control of its facts. In this dramatic world, where political action is presented as reaction, we can neither extract nor extrapolate a master narrative that would hold character and climaxes in place, for the play's productions of self and state take their meanings not from context, but only in. In the end, history appears at the disjointed intersection of short-sighted interactions, which not only alter but *are* the course of events.[33]

Select Bibliography

Arnold, Oliver, *The Third Citizen: Shakespeare's Theater and the Early Modern House of Commons* (Baltimore: Johns Hopkins University Press, 2007), 140–78.

Bathory, Dennis, 'With Himself at War: Shakespeare's Roman Hero and the Republican Tradition', in *Shakespeare's Political Pageant: Essays in Literature and Politics*, ed. Joseph Alulis and Vickie B. Sullivan (Lanham, MD: Rowman & Littlefield, 1996), 237–61.

Bono, Barbara J., 'The Birth of Tragedy: Tragic Action in *Julius Caesar*', *English Literary Renaissance* 24 (1994), 449–70.

---

[32] Stephen Greenblatt, 'Invisible bullets: Renaissance Authority and its Subversion in *Henry IV* and *Henry V*', in *Political Shakespeare: New essays in cultural materialism*, ed. Jonathan Dollimore and Alan Sinfield (Ithaca, NY: Cornell University Press, 1985), 43.

[33] I am grateful to Claudia L. Johnson for many conversations about this essay and the play.

Bushnell, Rebecca, '*Julius Caesar*', in *A Companion to Shakespeare's Works*, vol. 1, *The Tragedies*, ed. Richard Dutton and Jean E. Howard (Malden, MA: Blackwell Publishing, 2003), 339–56.

Hadfield, Andrew, *Shakespeare and Republicanism* (Cambridge: Cambridge University Press, 2008), 154–83.

Leggatt, Alexander, *Shakespeare's Political Drama: The History Plays and the Roman Plays* (London: Routledge, 1989), 141–62.

Lucking, David, 'Brutus's Reasons: *Julius Caesar* and the Mystery of Motive', *English Studies* 91:2 (2010), 119–32.

McCutcheon, Robert, 'The Call of Vocation in *Julius Caesar* and *Coriolanus*', *English Literary Renaissance* 41:2 (2011), 332–74.

Patterson, Annabel, *Shakespeare and the Popular Voice* (Oxford: Blackwell, 1989).

Ripley, John, Julius Caesar *on State in England & America, 1599-1973* (Cambridge: Cambridge University Press, 1980).

Rose, Mark, 'Conjuring Caesar: Ceremony, History, and Authority in 1599', in *True Rites and Maimed Rites: Ritual and Anti-Ritual in Shakespeare and His Age*, ed. Linda Woodbridge and Edward Berry (Urbana: University of Illinois Press, 1992), 256–69.

Spotswood, Jerald W., ' "We are undone already": Disarming the Multitude in *Julius Caesar* and *Coriolanus*', *Texas Studies in Literature and Language* 42:1 (2000), 61–79.

Wills, Garry, *Rome and Rhetoric: Shakespeare's* Julius Caesar (New Haven: Yale University Press, 2011).

Yu, Jeffrey J., '*Julius Caesar*, Erasmus's *De Copia* and Sentential Ambiguity', *Comparative Drama* 41:1 (2007), 79–106.

CHAPTER 24

....

THE QUESTION OF *HAMLET*

....

CATHERINE BELSEY

DOUBTS

....

AT the dead of night a ghost appears in the person of the late king. He was murdered by his brother, he declares; his son must take revenge.

But should he? The Ghost claims that he was killed in his sleep: Claudius poured poison in his ears, before marrying his widow and seizing the throne. In the heat of the moment Hamlet, who loved his father and has had his suspicions of his uncle, promises never to forget the injunction but in the cold light of day the way forward is not quite so clear. His source is an apparition; can it be trusted? Is the demand of a self-proclaimed spirit a sound basis for assassinating a king who is also his uncle (and who wants to take the place of his father)? If Claudius stands accused of a crime against monarchy and the family, the Ghost's call for vengeance asks Hamlet to repeat the offence. Would it be right to obey? And what are the likely consequences for the regicide (and perhaps parricide)? Death, surely, even if the assassin succeeds in finding the king unattended, followed by the likelihood of punishment in the next life. What is the noble course? Hamlet puzzles over what he ought to do. It is not clear that he ever finally settles the question in his mind, although he comes close.

Hamlet, Prince of Denmark is probably the best known of all Shakespeare's plays. People who have never seen or read it can place the image of a man in black with a skull in his hands; 'To be or not to be' is widely cited, sometimes in unlikely contexts; so familiar are parts of the text that on the stage the play can sound like a patchwork of quotations. *Hamlet* has attracted international attention way beyond the theatre or the critical institution. Sigmund Freud, for example, claimed to be the first person to make real sense of the play: in his view, Hamlet fails to act out of guilt because he recognizes an element of himself in Claudius; he too would be glad to take his father's place with his mother.[1] Encouraged by Freud, Ernest Jones went into more detail in *Hamlet and Oedipus*, while

---

[1] Sigmund Freud, 'Psychopathic Characters on the Stage', *Art and Literature*, ed. Albert Dickson (London: Penguin, 1985), 119–27, 126; *The Interpretation of Dreams*, ed. Angela Richards (London: Penguin, 1976), 366–8.

Freud's successor, Jacques Lacan, described a hero who loses his drive when he renounces his desire for Ophelia.[2] Among philosophers Hegel, Nietzsche, and Walter Benjamin all found in Shakespeare's tragedy food for thought of their own,[3] while the Young Germany movement of the mid-nineteenth century identified a whole nation with the undecided prince. Arguably, the play owes its sustained popularity across the centuries to Hamlet's doubts. Perhaps audiences like to be left to reflect on an unresolved question: what ought Hamlet to have done? What would *they* have done? Henrik Ibsen, George Bernard Shaw, and Berthold Brecht all enlisted audiences by posing moral questions. Or perhaps play-goers just enjoy watching a man wrestle intensely, passionately, with an ethical and political issue.

Critics, however, have been reluctant to admit to uncertainties of their own. The history of *Hamlet* criticism has been a story of answers, and most commonly of explanations by reference to Hamlet's character: from this perspective his indecision is an effect of personality, not the conflict of values involved in doing the right thing. Nineteenth-century commentators, for example, were very sure what Hamlet should do: living or dead, fathers were to be obeyed; anyone who hesitated to fulfil this obligation was a weakling or a ditherer. A. C. Bradley's reading, which triumphantly turned Shakespeare's tragedies into Victorian novels, allows for no reservations on this score: 'we are meant in the play to assume that he *ought* to have obeyed the Ghost'.[4] In this view, Hamlet's problem is a state of paralysing clinical depression ('melancholy') brought on by the shock of his mother's rapid second marriage. In such a condition, no wonder he just talks and talks—and does nothing. Or, rather, not *nothing*: he kills Polonius and his old school friends without a second thought—and Bradley comes close to diagnosing, ahead of Freud himself, the psychoanalytic death drive, suicidal but capable of turning outwards as aggression.

If Bradley's reading crystallized the novelistic view that prevailed in the years leading up to 1904, his book continues to exert an influence more than 100 years on. Stephen Greenblatt's biography of Shakespeare, published, as luck would have it, exactly a century later, reproduces the main thrust of Bradley's case: the play's central focus is Hamlet's 'profound depression', the 'soul sickness' that will not let him act.[5] And, like these critics, self-certified 'outsiders' Simon Critchley and Jamieson Webster sustain the nineteenth-century opinion, this time updated by a Nietzschean version of psychoanalysis: Hamlet suffers from 'morbid inhibition' that confines him to 'chattering and punning endlessly' while he surveys with disgust the wreckage of the world.[6] From this angle, the doubts the play raises are not ethical or political but psychological; as Harold Bloom puts it, 'The question of *Hamlet* always must be Hamlet himself.'[7] To Bloom the revenge plot is no more than a pretext, since the task of killing Claudius is too petty to engage Hamlet's towering intellect. Conversely, more conventional character readings find the hero incapable of the sustaining

[2] Jacques Lacan, 'Desire and the Interpretation of Desire in *Hamlet*', in *Literature and Psychoanalysis*, ed. Shoshana Felman (Baltimore: Johns Hopkins University Press, 1982), 11–52.

[3] Simon Critchley and Jamieson Webster, *The Hamlet Doctrine* (London: Verso, 2013).

[4] A. C. Bradley, *Shakespearean Tragedy* (Basingstoke: Palgrave Macmillan, 2007), 72.

[5] Stephen Greenblatt, *Will in the World: How Shakespeare Became Shakespeare* (London: Cape, 2004), 306–7.

[6] Critchley and Webster, *The Hamlet Doctrine*, 3, 9, 11, 92.

[7] Harold Bloom, *Shakespeare: The Invention of the Human* (London: Fourth Estate, 1999), 387.

the obligation placed on his frail shoulders. Many of these interpretations adopt variants of Goethe's account, ascribed in a vivid image to his creation Wilhelm Meister, of a sensitive prince unfit for violent action: 'There is an oak-tree planted in a costly jar, which should have borne only pleasant flowers in its bosom; the roots expand, the jar is shivered.'[8]

This wealth of subsequent commentary on the tragedy, which often discloses more about its own time than Shakespeare's, may obscure *Hamlet's* historical location as a work in the first instance of 1601. The best way to come to terms with the play as it might have seemed to early modern theatregoers must be to look closely at the words, which are all that survive of the first performances. Much that audiences would have seen by way of action, interaction, and stage business is irretrievably lost; stage directions are generally minimal where detail might have clarified the issues. Who overhears what, for example, in this world of spies? J. Dover Wilson was convinced that the only way to make sense of the hero's cruelty to Ophelia was to assume that Hamlet must have eavesdropped on the plan to eavesdrop on him in 3.1.[9] Because the play presents so many uncertainties, what remains to us deserves our closest attention.

How, then, in the light of his encounter with the Ghost, does Hamlet himself see his position? He admits to melancholy but that doesn't seem to him to go to the heart of the problem:

> The spirit that I have seen
> May be a devil, and the devil hath power
> T'assume a pleasing shape; yea, and perhaps,
> Out of my weakness and my melancholy—
> As he is very potent with such spirits—
> Abuses me to damn me.
>
> (2.2.600-5)

This is not the first time he has raised the issue of the Ghost's credentials. In his astonishment at the apparition on the battlements, he resolves to speak to it whatever its nature,

> Be thou a spirit of health or goblin damned,
> Bring with thee airs from heaven or blasts from hell,
> Be thy intents wicked or charitable.
>
> (1.4.21-3)

Nor will it be the last. The play-within-the play will test the veracity of the dead king's tale and, if Claudius does not betray his guilt, 'It is a damned ghost that we have seen' (3.2.80). The question the spectre prompts is its origin and its designs in walking. Are its intentions good or evil? Can it be relied on to have told the truth?

Ghosts

Doctrinally, Hamlet is wise to raise the question. The figure that takes his father's shape might be a good angel; it is more likely to be the devil in disguise. According to Reformation

---

[8] David Farley-Hills, ed., *Critical Responses to 'Hamlet' 1600-1900*, 3 vols. (New York: AMS Press, 1996), 2: 25.

[9] J. Dover Wilson, *What Happens in Hamlet* (Cambridge: Cambridge University Press, 1951), 101–36.

orthodoxy, the one thing it cannot be is a ghost. The Christian church regularly changed its mind about ghosts. Among its most influential founding fathers, St Augustine denied their existence on the grounds that the ghost stories told by the Romans were an instance of the pagan superstition Christianity was to drive out. God, Augustine maintained, would not let the dead return; they had no further business on earth. The evidence indicates, however, that theological doctrine exerted very little influence on the storytellers of medieval Europe, who continued to thrill and appal their audiences with tales of revenants. Eventually the Catholic Church bowed to popular conviction and devised Purgatory to rehabilitate the walking dead. But the Protestant Reformers of the sixteenth century reiterated St Augustine's rejection of superstition in a new context. This time, the target was Catholicism. On Augustine's authority they reviled Purgatory, along with the ghosts who solicited money to buy masses for the dead. As before, however, ghost stories lived on by winter firesides while, despite the protestations of intellectual sceptics, many people continued to regard graveyards as places of terror after dark. Reluctantly, Christianity made a minor concession to popular beliefs: there were no ghosts but devils might impersonate them to win us to our harm.

Hamlet takes proper account of the prevailing Protestant opinion but this is a drama, not a religious tract. Although certain subjects had to be handled with caution, early modern fiction was evidently not accountable in every particular to the religious authorities and the popular option also remains fully in play. At the dead of night 'churchyards yawn', as Hamlet puts it (3.2.378), disgorging their corpses, just as the vernacular tradition had long maintained. One minute, the spirit that appears on the castle walls as the clock strikes one may be a devil pretending to be a ghost; the next, he is perceived as a dead father, cast up by the tomb to disfigure the night and stretch credulity 'With thoughts beyond the reaches of our souls' (1.4.26-37). Moreover, the Ghost itself deepens its bloodcurdling appeal to an audience familiar with the fireside tales when it claims to spend its days amid the flames of the repudiated Catholic Purgatory (1.5.11-13). As fiction allows, the status of this Ghost hovers undecidably between two religious dogmas, as well as between orthodoxy and an old wives' tale. *Hamlet* is theatre, not theology.

REVENGE

Are critics right when they assume that Hamlet's duty is to obey the Ghost? Are its intents in practice wicked or charitable? If recourse to church doctrine does not resolve the question, perhaps its behaviour will. We have Hamlet's word for it that the late monarch was altogether noble, a man on whom 'every god did seem to set his seal' (3.4.60), 'So excellent a king', 'so loving to my mother' that the bereft prince laments the divine interdiction against suicide when he rehearses his mother's perfidy in remarrying so soon and within the prohibited degrees of kinship (1.2.129-59). Is there something incongruous in the fact that this virtuous, majestic monarch walks to demand his brother's death, appealing to a filial piety he must know he can count on? The Ghost leaves as dawn breaks with 'Remember me' (1.5.91). There is no possibility that Hamlet will forget but his immediate response, passionate, committed, determined to remember nothing else, also embraces the option that will in due course deter unthinking obedience: 'O all you host of heaven! O earth! What else? | And shall I couple hell?' (1.5.92-3).

It is easy to take the prince's subsequent self-reproaches at face value: Hamlet is ashamed of his own inaction; action, then, must be his duty. But the terms in which he castigates himself give an indication of what revenge entails: 'ere this | I should 'a' fatted all the region kites | With this slave's offal' (2.2.580-2). Revenge would scatter the king's entrails as carrion for birds of prey. This is an explicitly bloodthirsty ethic: 'Now could I drink hot blood', cries the prince, once the performance of *The Mousetrap* has confirmed the king's guilt (3.2.379). Moreover, if vengeance is prompted by hell as well as heaven (2.2.587), the impulse is not satisfied with death but seeks the eternal damnation of the victim (3.3.93-5). The corollary of Hamlet's continuing love for his dead father is to be a hatred of his uncle that also reaches beyond the grave.

In all these respects vengeance differs from justice. The recurrence of revenge as a theme of tragedy at this time marks it out as a matter of concern in a period when the state was making efforts, with varying degrees of conviction and success, to take control of private quarrels and bring them to public judgement in the law courts. In principle, at least, justice is blind, impartial, and impersonal; it is designed to reinforce social cohesion as the community combines to condemn crime and a judicial system parts warring individuals to adjudicate between them. Revenge, on the other hand, is passionate, personal, divisive. In the drama at least, it is also a last resort, a reluctant response to the unreliability of juridical practice. One of Shakespeare's earlier protagonists remains 'so just that he will not revenge' (*Titus Andronicus*, 4.1.127) until despair at imperial duplicity drives him to violence on his own account. In an abiding image from Thomas Kyd's *The Spanish Tragedy* some ten years before *Hamlet*, Hieronimo digs in the earth for justice with his dagger, maddened by official indifference to his son's murder.[10]

Revenge exceeds justice, however. Hieronimo's vengeance is literally spectacular, as the deaths in the play he puts on for the king turn out to be real. Once possessed by the spirit of revenge, Titus bakes the heads of the empress's sons in a pie and feeds them to their mother. On the basis of the genre, early modern audiences might well understand the Ghost to be asking Hamlet for an invention to match these, and in the source story Amleth burns down the hall with the entire court inside. Hamlet's eventual revenge, if that is what it is, falls well short of this: no one is cooked or incinerated; the play he stages for the king is no more than a test of Claudius' guilt. In the end, the main contenders will die before our eyes but the final spectacle is not of Hamlet's choosing.

Commenting in the eighteenth century on the prince's deliberations when he finds Claudius alone in prayer, Samuel Johnson registered in the sharpest terms the exorbitant character of revenge. 'This speech, in which Hamlet, represented as a virtuous character, is not content with taking blood for blood, but contrives damnation for the man that he would punish, is too horrible to be read or uttered.'[11] Hamlet himself is clear about the distinction between due punishment and vengeance:

> A villain kills my father, and for that
> I, his sole son, do this same villain send

[10] Thomas Kyd, *The Spanish Tragedy*, ed. Philip Edwards (London: Methuen, 1959), 3.12.71SD.
[11] Arthur Sherbo ed., *Johnson on Shakespeare*, 2 vols. (New Haven: Yale University Press) 2: 990.

To heaven
O, this is hire and salary, not revenge!

(3.3.76-9)

How could the purpose of sending Claudius to hell be reconciled with the theory of revenge as a moral requirement? Proponents of the view that Hamlet ought to kill Claudius
find a way out of the dilemma: self-evidently, Hamlet doesn't mean it: 'That this again is
an unconscious excuse for delay is now pretty generally agreed,' Bradley notes serenely.[12]
The same goes for the 'To be or not to be' speech, and his doubts about the origins of the
Ghost: Hamlet talks to avoid action; what he says is no more than a pretext for inertia. Is
there something unsatisfactory in a reading that is obliged to discount such a substantial
proportion of the text?

SCRUPLES

If the play leaves the duty of the prince in doubt, criticism ironically reproduces the ambivalence in its assessment of Hamlet himself. Perhaps astutely, writers and critics of the
nineteenth century, although they were generally convinced that Hamlet's duty was to kill
his uncle, often admired him, nevertheless, for reflecting before he did so. While the period
continued to insist that violence was the proper, manly way to right a wrong, many of its
intellectuals also saw Hamlet the poet and thinker as a role model. Ineffectual though he
might be, his mind confronted the major questions of life and death and in the process
legitimated their own recoil from the public obligations of nineteenth-century manhood.
Paradoxically, the irresolute Hamlet was also a genius and 'I have a smack of Hamlet myself,
if I may say so', Coleridge the poet and thinker was happy to allow.[13]

While 'What a piece of work is a man' (2.2.305-10) rated highly in their estimation, the
strongest instance of Hamlet's intellectual powers was thought to be the soliloquy beginning 'To be, or not to be' (3.1.58-92). Opinions varied on the theme of the speech but it was
widely regarded as addressing the great existential issues. Character critics, then and now,
tend to read it as Hamlet's contemplation of suicide.[14] He is depressed; naturally, then, they
conclude, his mind reverts to killing himself: 'For who would bear the whips and scorns of
time, | ... | When he himself might his quietus make | With a bare bodkin?' Dr Johnson,
however, took a different view: the soliloquy was about whether opposition or endurance
was the nobler course for an injured man.[15] Here at the heart of the play, in Hamlet's
own most explicit formulation of his problem, lies a speech that continues to provoke
debate not just on matters of detail but about its main concern. 'To be, or not to be; that
is the question'. The third Arden edition of 2006 encompasses the collective irresolution

[12] Bradley, *Shakespearean Tragedy*, 98.
[13] Samuel Taylor Coleridge, *Table Talk, Collected Works* 14, ed. Carl Woodring, 2 vols.
(Princeton: Princeton University Press, 1990) 2: 61.
[14] See e.g. Bradley, *Shakespearean Tragedy*, 96; Greenblatt, *Will in the World*, 307, 311; Critchley
and Webster, *The Hamlet Doctrine*, 6.
[15] Sherbo ed., *Johnson on Shakespeare*, 980-1.

in its note on this line: 'editors and critics still disagree as to whether *the question* for Hamlet is (a) whether life in general is worth living, (b) whether he should take his own life, (c) whether he should act against the king'.[16]

That critics and editors cannot agree is no reason to give up on the issue. On the contrary. What does the prince say? As he formulates it, the question is 'Whether 'tis nobler in the mind to suffer | The slings and arrows of outrageous fortune, | Or to take arms against a sea of troubles'. Is it nobler to suffer, to bear affliction, or to take arms against adversity (even if opposition is as hopeless as fighting the sea)? But how could it be noble to tolerate injustice? Kyd's Hieronimo, confronting the same problem, begins, '*Vindicta mihi!*', vengeance is mine (*The Spanish Tragedy*, 3.13.1). Hieronimo is quoting the New Testament: 'Dearly beloved, avenge not yourselves, but rather give place unto wrath: for it is written, Vengeance is mine; I will repay, saith the Lord' (Romans 12:19). 'Ay', Hieronimo continues, 'heaven will be reveng'd of every ill | Nor will they suffer murder unrepaid' (2–3).

There is some evidence that in *Hamlet* Shakespeare was rewriting an old tragedy. Incidental allusions by Thomas Lodge and Thomas Nashe suggest that such a play was popular over a decade before Shakespeare's version, and that it was written by Kyd. It is possible that Kyd's Hamlet rehearsed some of the same doubts as Hieronimo displays here. Is Shakespeare's hero momentarily retracing the same path? Either way, the biblical tag was a commonplace of moral and political debate. Although it allotted punishment to God, it was quoted in support of efforts to deter private retribution and bring personal injury under the control of the courts. As Francis Bacon would go on to declare, the initial crime offends the law 'but the revenge of that wrong putteth the law out of office'. A lawyer himself, Bacon was against personal vengeance but he might have sympathized, even so, with Hamlet's predicament: 'The most tolerable sort of revenge is for those wrongs which there is no law to remedy.'[17] In medieval Denmark there is no court to appeal to, no police force to invoke: Claudius holds all the power. Eventually, Hamlet will defer to divine providence (5.2.165–6) but only after he has pondered further the question of right action.

Nothing in the first four lines of the soliloquy suggests suicide. The puzzle comes with the next line: 'And, by opposing, end them. To die'. Dr Johnson, who found the ideas in the speech connected 'rather in the speaker's mind, than on his tongue' glossed 'To die' as the likely outcome of opposition to the king. Assassination would surely not go unpunished in its turn. Since we have no access to the speaker's mind but only his elliptical words, it might be helpful to look outside the text for illumination, turning again to other extant revenge plays. Hieronimo goes on to juxtapose Christian patience with action. What, after all, is there to fear? 'Death's the worst of resolution' (3.13.9). In the end Hieronimo kills himself, but not before his retaliation is complete. Antonio and his accomplices survive in John Marston's play *Antonio's Revenge* but retreat from the world into a monastery. In most other contemporary instances of the genre murder is punished either by the authorities or by the perpetrator himself as an admission of guilt. Although in the medieval

---

[16] William Shakespeare, *Hamlet*, ed. Ann Thompson and Neil Taylor (London: Thomson Learning, 2006), note on 3.1.55.

[17] Francis Bacon, 'Of Revenge', *The Essayes or Counsels, Civill and Morall*, ed. Michael Kiernan (Oxford: Clarendon Press, 2000), 16–17 (16).

Danish source story Amleth is crowned after killing his uncle, this ending might not entirely satisfy an audience in Elizabethan England[18] where, as Shakespeare's *Richard II* indicates, sovereignty was conditional on obedience to the law. Richard loses his crown when he violates legality to seize Bolingbroke's lands. Lawbreakers do not generally flourish in the plays. At the end of *The Revenger's Tragedy*, printed in 1607, Vindice and Hippolito are despatched to immediate execution by the new Duke the vengeance they publicize has helped to install: 'You that would murder him would murder me,' Antonio explains succinctly.[19] Killers are dangerous; sovereignty based on crime is unstable. Shakespeare's Bolingbroke lives on uneasily to see his old allies turn on the king who has secretly assassinated Richard.

The remaining sequence of ideas in Hamlet's speech is more straightforward: 'To die, to sleep—No more, and by a sleep to say we end | The heartache and the thousand natural shocks | That flesh is heir to.' If death were no more than the sleep it resembles, it would be a welcome release from the troubles of this life. But 'To sleep, perchance to dream. Ay, there's the rub'. There may, in other words, be more to come, although even this is not certain, 'something after death', a *something* that would deter a killer who faced the fear of damnation. The thought of hell is never far away in *Hamlet* but this is not the realm of demons and physical tortures so vividly imagined in medieval iconography. On the contrary, the next world is represented as unknown, a perhaps more unnerving 'undiscovered country', and the one traveller who might be thought to have returned speaks of terrifying secrets that must not be disclosed to the living (1.5.13–22).[20] 'There's the respect | That makes calamity of so long life', the consideration that makes us bear troubles for so long, rather than 'fly to others that we know not of'. 'Thus conscience does make cowards of us all, | And thus the native hue of resolution' (red, angry, bloodthirsty) 'Is sicklied o'er with the pale cast of thought'. In this way Hamlet puts forward a provisional answer to his earlier question, 'Am I a coward?' (2.2.573)—and his reluctance to surrender an enterprise 'of great pith and moment' is registered in the image of ill health. The self-examination of the second soliloquy concerned physical cowardice: 'Who calls me villain, breaks my pate across' with impunity (574)? No one, evidently, and yet Hamlet does not act against Claudius. The third soliloquy shows why. If it is timid to hesitate before incurring the possibility of retribution in the next life, then timidity is what conscience requires.

[18] Once again an exception is *Antonio's Revenge*, where the senators welcome the assassination of Piero, against whom other evidence of corruption has come to light independently. For an argument that private vengeance was seen as honourable and a critique of prevailing injustices, see Linda Woodbridge, *English Revenge Drama: Money, Resistance, Equality* (Cambridge: Cambridge University Press, 2010).

[19] Cyril Tourneur, *The Revenger's Tragedy*, ed. R. A. Foakes (London: Methuen, 1966), 5.3.105. This play, almost certainly written within a year or two of the publication of *Hamlet*, opens with Vindice contemplating a skull. Incidental textual parallels confirm a link but *The Revenger's Tragedy*, with its riot of sworn revenges, corrupted justice, and inventive retribution, might also be seen as the antithesis of Shakespeare's play. Ironically, Antonio himself had presided over an oath of revenge for his wife's rape but the project is forestalled.

[20] It is possible to find an inconsistency between the appearance of the Ghost and Hamlet's affirmation that 'no traveller returns' from death. Can he have forgotten? Hardly. Perhaps, then, such fleeting visitations are distinguishable from taking up residence again.

CONSCIENCE

The soliloquy ends with Hamlet's conscience triumphant but the play's reflections on right action are not over. Laertes will have far less trouble with *his* conscience when he breaks down the door to demand vengeance for the murder of *his* father. Laertes is enraged: 'That drop of blood that's calm proclaims me bastard' (4.5.116); he is ready for any sacrilege to appease his bloodlust (4.7.99); without hesitation, he is prepared to poison the sword he will use to fence with Hamlet. Laertes, no coward but the true revenger, unwittingly throws into relief the workings of Hamlet's conscience by contrast with his own:

> To hell, allegiance! Vows to the blackest devil!
> Conscience and grace to the profoundest pit!
> I dare damnation. To this point I stand,
> That both the worlds I give to negligence,
> Let come what comes. Only I'll be revenged
> Most throughly for my father.
>
> (4.5.129-34)

Since at this point he blames Claudius for his father's death, the parallel and contrast are exact. Laertes is ready to repudiate his sworn allegiance to the king in favour of regicide; he willingly consigns his conscience to hell; he cares nothing for the prospect of damnation in the cause of vengeance. It is hard to find any indication in this speech that revenge could ever be a moral duty. And, after a lapse of time only long enough to arrange the duel, even Laertes experiences a moment of doubt. Determined to wound Hamlet with the poisoned sword, he nevertheless hesitates: 'And yet'tis almost 'gainst my conscience' (5.2.250). Laertes is, after all, a 'noble' youth (5.1.218), if not quite noble enough to yield to his scruples. While revenge exceeds justice, conscience is incompatible with revenge.

Hamlet's own conscience is less active, it seems, when it comes to Rosencrantz and Guildenstern, set on to conduct him to execution in England. Perhaps their deaths were hire and salary? Certainly, they enjoyed their work: 'Why, man, they did make love to this employment. | They are not near my conscience' (5.2.58-9). But the faculty is still operative in relation to Claudius, even if the terms of the debate have changed. By now Hamlet is in possession of more facts: Claudius has not only killed his father, as he learns from the play scene (3.2.274-8), but also devised a trick to rid himself of Hamlet too. Horatio's brief exclamation puts the question the prince faces in a new light: 'Why, what a king is this!' (5.2.63). Perhaps it is no longer so much a matter of avenging a murder as of removing a tyrant?

> Does it not, think thee, stand me now upon—
> He that hath killed my king and whored my mother,
> Popped in between th'election and my hopes,
> Thrown out his angle for my proper life,
> And with such coz'nage—is't not perfect conscience
> To quit him with this arm? And is't not to be damned
> To let this canker of our nature come
> In further evil?
>
> (5.2.64-71)

The moral counters, conscience, and damnation, are familiar but they have changed places. If the issue is explicitly political, doesn't conscience now urge action? But, as so often in this play, the question is not definitively answered: the legitimacy of assassinating an anointed king, however tyrannical, was itself debated. Could it be 'perfect conscience'?

PASSION

Since the reasons to hesitate are so clearly spelt out in the play, why have so many commentators assumed that Hamlet ought simply to obey the Ghost and kill Claudius? Because Hamlet says so. There's the respect that makes controversy of so long life. Moreover, he says so repeatedly, prompting those who treat fictional figures as real people to puzzle over his psychological state. Tell me what happened, he urges the Ghost, 'that [I] with wings as swift | As meditation or the thoughts of love | May sweep to my revenge' (1.5.29–31). The impulse is natural: 'If thou hast nature in thee, bear it not' (81). At the end of Act 2, however, Hamlet has not acted, even though, as he passionately declares, this seems to prove him impassive. And according to one version of the text, he is still castigating himself for his inertia on the eve of his enforced departure for England as he reacts to the entry of Fortinbras with his army.

This fourth soliloquy, beginning 'How all occasions do inform against me', presents critics with yet another kind of question. Textual differences are not the least of the problems *Hamlet* leaves unresolved. The first quarto version of the play, roughly the size of a modern paperback, appeared in print in 1603 (Q1). Q1 is short and relatively racy, covering much of the same ground as subsequent versions where the plot is concerned, although it adds a meeting between Horatio and Gertrude that aligns his mother more firmly with the prince after the closet scene. Some stage directions may illuminate the more familiar versions: at its final appearance the Ghost enters in a night-gown. Q1 pays far less attention to conscience: Laertes is not reproached by his; Hamlet's does not engage with the question of tyranny. And Q1 does not include the fourth soliloquy.

The 1603 text, then, presents a less irresolute Hamlet. How much authority should we ascribe to its version of the play? On this, as on so much else, there is no consensus. Was Q1 Shakespeare's first draft of *Hamlet*? Alternatively, was it an abridged version of Shakespeare's fully formed play, cut down for the actors to take on tour or, indeed, to perform at the Globe itself? Or was it, as an earlier generation of editors assumed, a reconstruction of the play by one or more of the actors, recited to the printer with as much accuracy as they could muster, or instead a short-hand version of an actual performance?[21]

The following year another quarto of the play appeared (Q2). While it reproduces much of Q1, this version is very nearly twice as long and the language and versification seem more careful in some places—although not in others. Q2 has traditionally been seen as closest to the play Shakespeare actually wrote. Was it issued to correct the 'bad' Q1? On the other hand, performance at four hours or more seems too long to fit the 'two-hours' traffic

---

[21] See Tiffany Stern, 'Sermons, Plays and Note-Takers: *Hamlet Q1 as a 'Noted' Text*,' *Shakespeare Survey* 66 (2013), 1–23.

of our stage' referred to in the Prologue to *Romeo and Juliet*, however loosely we interpret that poetic timing. Why would Shakespeare, who knew the theatre he worked in, write more than his colleagues could reasonably expect to perform? Was Q2 a reading version, then?[22] Some people were evidently buying these texts, perhaps with a view to annotating them, or transcribing their favourite passages into their commonplace books.[23] Q2 was more reflective, more lyrical, perhaps designed for this distinct context.

Q2 breaks off the discussion of conscience and tyranny in mid-sentence (at 5.2.68) but it includes the fourth soliloquy, the one that implies a static, inert prince who by Act 4 has not detectably advanced beyond the self-reproach of 2.2.551-90. This is the Hamlet whose symptoms so fascinate Bradley. Further quartos were derived from Q2 with minor variants but the next substantial edition of the tragedy appeared in 1623 when, after his death, Shakespeare's colleagues produced a large memorial volume of his collected plays. The First Folio *Hamlet* (F) is shorter by over 200 lines than Q2, though not nearly as short as Q1.[24] Was it closest to the version performed by the Shakespeare company, adapted and abridged as it made its way through the repertoire in the years following 1601? And is that why F does not reproduce the crucial fourth soliloquy, on the grounds that the self-castigation for cowardice, although it now takes a new and more philosophic turn, duplicates the concerns of the second soliloquy in Act 2? Alternatively, do the differences owe more to accidents of transcription than deliberate selection?[25]

Most old editions reproduced the fourth soliloquy. These were Shakespeare's precious words; they introduced the notion of honour as the motive for action (4.4.47), and they confirmed the puzzle of Hamlet's delay:

> Now whether it be
> Bestial oblivion, or some craven scruple
> Of thinking too precisely on th'event—
> A thought which, quartered, hath but one part wisdom
> And ever three parts coward—I do not know
> Why yet I live to say 'This thing's to do',
> Sith I have cause, and will, and strength, and means,
> To do't.
>
> (4.4.30-7)

Hamlet doesn't know why he doesn't act, but subsequent commentators were ready with explanations, and the rest is history.

---

[22] See Lukas Erne, *Shakespeare as Literary Dramatist* (Cambridge: Cambridge University Press, 2013). For a counter-argument see Michael J. Hirrel, 'Duration of Performances and Lengths of Plays: How Shall We Beguile the Lazy Time?', *Shakespeare Quarterly* 61 (2010), 159–82.

[23] See Zachary Lesser and Peter Stallybrass, 'The First Literary *Hamlet* and the Commonplacing of Professional Plays', *Shakespeare Quarterly* 59 (2008), 371–420.

[24] The Oxford text is based on F. The additional lines from Q2, including the fourth soliloquy, are printed at the end of the text (716–18). For a text based on Q2 see *Hamlet*, ed. Thompson and Taylor and for a modernized Q1 see their *Hamlet: The Texts of 1603 and 1623* (London: Thomson Learning, 2006).

[25] For a detailed account of the differences between the three texts and the difficulties in the way of a master-theory that would explain them, see Paul Werstine, '"The Cause of this Defect": *Hamlet's* Editors', in *Hamlet: New Critical Essays*, ed. Arthur F. Kinney (New York: Routledge, 2002), 115–33.

Whether we take Q2 as authoritative or follow the Folio's cut will influence our view of Hamlet and our attitude to his hesitation. But the choice need not be decisive. Either way, the play insists on a conflict of imperatives. Hamlet was devoted to his father. This is made clear at his first appearance in mourning while the rest of the court celebrates his mother's remarriage, and it is the basis of the Ghost's appeal for action:

> GHOST   If thou didst ever thy dear father love—
> HAMLET   Oh God!
> GHOST   Revenge his foul and most unnatural murder.
>
> (1.5.23-5)

There is no need to labour the matter: 'I find thee apt', the Ghost acknowledges (31). The same point is pressed home, however, when it comes to the revenge of Laertes, since Claudius has a motive for keeping him up to the mark. 'Laertes, was your father dear to you?' The words are almost identical to the Ghost's, but the villainous king does not stop there: 'or are you like the painting of a sorrow, | A face without a heart?' (4.7.90-2). And he goes on to raise the stakes still further:

> Not that I think you did not love your father,
> But that I know love is begun by time,
> And that I see, in passages of proof,
> Time qualifies the spark and fire of it.
> Hamlet comes back. What would you undertake
> To show yourself your father's son in deed
> More than in words?
>
> (4.7.93-9)

Here the king summarizes the issues that also preoccupy Hamlet: words are not enough when vengeance calls for deeds (cf. 2.2.585-90); time blunts purposes, allowing passion to lapse (cf. 3.4.97-101); by taking action the revenger proves himself a loving son (cf. 2.2.572, 586). Claudius is not an impartial observer, however; his synopsis takes care to avoid the hesitation conscience exacts, dwelling instead on the passion that deflects thought.

'Is it not monstrous', Hamlet asks, that the performance of a fictional emotion, 'a dream of passion', should so engage the player's own feelings? 'What would he do | Had he the motive and the cue for passion | That I have?' (2.2.553-64). Filial affection makes Hamlet follow the Ghost, whatever the dangers; intensity prompts 'wild and whirling words' in the aftermath of the encounter (1.5.137); emotion dominates the second soliloquy; love for his father drives the interview with Gertrude in her closet. *Hamlet* is neither an ethical treatise nor a case study but a play, and passion is dramatic. It is the passion in the player's manner that impresses even Polonius (2.2.522-3) and moves Hamlet; how to present passion on the stage is Hamlet's first concern in his advice to the players (3.2.1-14). Passion is theatrical; revenge is passionate; passion is sympathetic.

At the same time, the theatre has its own economy. A revenge play with the passionate Laertes as its hero would presumably come to an abrupt end in the second act. Meanwhile, by contrast, the 'just' Horatio is not 'passion's slave'; in suffering (enduring) whatever comes, he suffers nothing (preserves his equanimity) (3.2.52, 70, 64). A revenge play with Horatio as its hero would never get underway. The conflict between stoicism and filial love, prompting the question whether it is nobler to suffer or take arms, sustains the tragedy for more than the length of most plays of its epoch.

In the event, it is hard not to feel relieved that Hamlet finally succeeds in killing the king whose villainy is now plain to see. But he does so with the weapon prepared by a revenger. Although justice conventionally wields a sword, it is not a poisoned one.

THE ANTIC DISPOSITION

If intensity is theatrical, so is comedy. Hamlets on the modern stage are generally livelier and wittier than their Victorian predecessors, exploiting the opportunities offered by the antic disposition the hero says he may put on (1.5.173). Indeed, by the time he makes this declaration it seems he has already adopted a comic mask, when he darts from one part of the stage to another as the Ghost loses his horror to become 'this fellow in the cellarage', and 'old mole' (153, 164). Feigned madness justifies Hamlet in inviting Rosencrantz and Guildenstern to play hide and seek (4.2.29-30) as well as to tease Polonius remorselessly, until even he begins to see that 'there is method in't' (2.2.207-8). Performed with energy, delivered with relish, the clowning alternates reflection with a far less brooding, less depressive prince.

But the antic disposition also brings its own difficulties for the critic. Where does it begin and end? It is evidently at work when Hamlet baffles the King on whereabouts of the dead body:

> KING   Now, Hamlet, where's Polonius?
> HAMLET   At supper.
> KING   At supper? Where?
> HAMLET   Not where he eats, but where a is eaten. A certain convocation of politic
> worms are e'en at him.
>
> (4.3.17-21)

And it is equally clearly discarded in conversation with Horatio, or in greeting the players, where Hamlet justifies Ophelia's comments on what from her perspective he once was, 'Th' expectancy and rose of the fair state' (3.1.155). But it is just this perspective that cuts across the distinction. Is Hamlet's unkindness to Ophelia assumed or felt?

There is no reason to doubt her account. He loved her once (1.3.99-114); he confirms it (3.1.117)—and then retracts his confirmation (121). Are the antics of the nunnery scene for her benefit and that of any likely eavesdroppers, or is this Hamlet out of control, no longer the 'courtier' he once was (3.1.154), gratuitously cruel? On the one hand, his appearance in her chamber, pale, ungartered, unbraced, 'As if he had been loosed out of hell' (2.1.84) mimics the conventional suitor mad for love. On the other hand, there is pathos in Ophelia's account of the sigh, 'so piteous and profound | That it did seem to shatter all his bulk' (2.1.95-6). Does this after all register the genuine pain of renunciation? There is no place for courtship in the programme of the revenger: revenge is conventionally obsessive; Hamlet has sworn that the Ghost's command alone will concern him (1.5.98-104). Romance would be a distraction, marriage and children a forlorn hope. Is bitterness at this loss enough to account for the innuendoes of the play scene, or are they purely for public consumption? Perhaps. Hamlet breaks off his confidential exchanges with Horatio: 'They are coming to the play. I must be idle' (3.2.88). At the same time, Ophelia innocently represents the option Hamlet has yet to choose: she obeys her father (1.3.136). In consequence, there is never any possibility that Hamlet can count on her as his confidant. However unwittingly, however reluctantly, Ophelia is complicit with the enemy.

The most enigmatic moment comes at her burial. Laertes, almost crazed with grief, leaps into the grave. A stage direction in Q1 and an elegy for Richard Burbage, who first played the part, indicate that Hamlet leaps in after him, prompting a struggle. Hamlet insists, 'I loved Ophelia. Forty thousand brothers | Could not, with all their quantity of love, | Make up my sum' (5.1.266–8). The bystanders assume that this is madness and so it seems, as Hamlet promises to outdo in mourning whatever Laertes proposes: 'Nay, an thou'lt mouth, | I'll rant as well as thou' (5.1.280–1). But he goes on to tell Horatio otherwise, regretting 'That to Laertes I forgot myself'; 'the bravery of his grief did put me | Into a tow'ring passion' (5.2.77, 80–1).

Our difficulty in telling an antic disposition from a towering passion ensures that *Hamlet* keeps some of its secrets. Perhaps in the end the only serious wrong we can do the play is to claim that we have mastered them.

AFTERLIVES

Hamlet has been popular on the stage from the beginning in a record interrupted only by the closure of the theatres in 1642-60.[26] Its treatment on screen is discussed elsewhere in this volume. The play has also enjoyed a rich afterlife in painting and sculpture: Hamlet and Ophelia were both favoured subjects in the nineteenth century.[27]

In addition, there is just space to mention the most prominent of its fictional reappearances in English. Early instances made comedy out of what was officially treated with unremitting solemnity but the laughter is not at the expense of the play. Henry Fielding, for example, immortalized David Garrick's performance in a visit to the theatre recorded in *Tom Jones* (1749). Partridge, most naïve of spectators, refuses to praise Garrick's acting: anyone, facing a ghost, would have behaved just as he did.[28] By contrast, Charles Dickens, no doubt with a glance at his predecessor, introduces a thoroughly inept Hamlet in Mr Wopsle of *Great Expectations* (1861). This production arouses the derision of the audience to the point where 'on the question whether 'twas nobler in the mind to suffer, some roared yes, and some no, and some inclining to both opinions said "toss up for it"'.[29]

---

[26] See Anthony B. Dawson, Hamlet, *Shakespeare in Performance* (Manchester: Manchester University Press, 1995).

[27] See Catherine Belsey, '"Was Hamlet a Man or a Woman?": The Prince in the Graveyard, 1800-1920', in *Hamlet: New Critical Essays*, ed. Kinney, 135–58; Stuart Sillars, *Shakespeare, Time and the Victorians: A Pictorial Exploration* (Cambridge: Cambridge University Press, 2012), 71–4, 95–9.

[28] Henry Fielding, *Tom Jones*, bk. 16, ch. 5.

[29] Charles Dickens, *Great Expectations*, chap. 31.

Mark Twain's travelling player rehearses the same speech from inadequate memory in *Huckleberry Finn* (1884), concluding, 'But soft you, the fair Ophelia: | Ope not thy ponderous and marble jaws, | But get thee to a nunnery—go!'[30]

Hamlet plays a major part in the structure of Herman Melville's *Pierre* (1852), as well as James Joyce's *Ulysses* (1922), where the 'Scylla and Charybdis' episode includes a discussion of the tragedy.[31] Iris Murdoch gives it a critical role in *The Black Prince* (1973), naming her narrator Bradley. Other modern works reinscribe the play from the point of view of less central characters, in Tom Stoppard's *Rosencrantz and Guildenstern are Dead* (1966) or John Updike's ironic prequel, *Gertrude and Claudius* (2000). Although I fear the texts would not support this, it would be gratifying to believe that this reluctance to let the play rest is prompted at some profound level by the central question it raises, whether violence is the best way to counter violence. That issue remains pressing—and equally unresolved—more than four centuries on.

SELECT BIBLIOGRAPHY

Belsey, Catherine, 'Shakespeare's Sad Tale for Winter: *Hamlet* and the Tradition of Fireside Ghost Stories', *Shakespeare Quarterly* 61 (2010), 1–27.

de Grazia, Margreta, Hamlet *without Hamlet* (Cambridge: Cambridge University Press, 2007).

Erne, Lukas, *Shakespeare as Literary Dramatist* (Cambridge: Cambridge University Press, 2013).

Kermode, Frank, *Shakespeare's Language* (London: Penguin, 2000).

Kinney, Arthur F., ed., Hamlet: *New Critical Essays* (New York: Routledge, 2002).

Neill, Michael, *Issues of Death: Mortality and Identity in English Renaissance Tragedy* (Oxford: Clarendon Press, 1997), esp. 216–61.

Weimann, Robert, *Author's Pen and Actor's Voice: Playing and Writing in Shakespeare's Theatre* (Cambridge: Cambridge University Press, 2000), esp. 18–28.

[30] Mark Twain, *The Adventures of Huckleberry Finn*, chap. 21.

[31] James Joyce, *Ulysses*, ed. Jeri Johnson (Oxford: Oxford University Press, 1993), 176–201. For further instances, see *Hamlet*, ed. Thompson and Taylor, 126–37.

CHAPTER 25

SEEING BLACKNESS
Reading Race in Othello

IAN SMITH

(UN) RELIABLE SIGHT

FOR an early modern play that locates a black man at the centre of the dramatic action, we should probably not be surprised by the frequent references to sight in *Othello* (1604). Sight is interlaced in every aspect of the language and action—famously, even jealousy, a potentially destructive emotion, is construed as 'the green-eyed monster' (3.3.169).[1] In the play's ocularcentric universe Othello is a sight to behold, his spectacular difference identified repeatedly as in Emilia's colour-sensitive wish for her mistress, 'I would you had never seen him' (4.3.16). At the turning point in Othello's self-awareness, he admits to what others have already assigned hermeneutic value: 'I am black' (3.3.265). While Othello is a Moor, as the play's full title announces, the term 'black' was sufficiently capacious to be employed strategically to nominate outsiders whose difference from the majority culture was to be marked.[2] Still, 'black' worked most often as an effective synonym for a person of African origin. Desdemona's claim that she saw 'Othello's visage in his mind' (1.3.250) asserts what today we might describe as a politics of colour blindness, but for others Othello's blackness is hardly a negligible or neutral fact. This chapter follows the play's interest in sight and seeing, investigating Shakespeare's investment in *seeing blackness* and the consequence of such an investment for reading and interpretive practices.

In the Western cultural tradition, sight has long been identified as superior among the senses, since it offers a seemingly indispensable means by which information about the external world is relayed in a reliable fashion to the viewer. Plato in the *Timaeus* declares that, 'sight in my opinion is the source of the greatest benefit to us', for observation of the natural universe with its constant change produces the concept of time from which 'we have derived philosophy'.[3] His exaltation of sight as providing 'the clearest

---

[1] Steven Baker, 'Sight and a Sight in *Othello*', *Iowa State Journal of Research* 61:3 (1987), 302.

[2] On Moors and blackness, see Ania Loomba, *Shakespeare, Race, and Colonialism* (Oxford: Oxford University Press, 2002), 45–9.

[3] Plato, *Timaeus*, 47a-b, in Edith Hamilton and Huntington Cairns, eds., *The Collected Dialogues of Plato* (Princeton: Princeton University Press, 1961). See also the *Republic*, 507b-511d.

knowledge of the natural world' is thereby coupled with 'the sustaining principles of order and harmony'.[4] In his *Metaphysics*, Aristotle establishes the firm connection between sight and knowledge in the text's famous opening and, guided by his fundamental belief in the relation between sensation and thought, Aristotle extols sight as the sense that allows the mind to make fine discriminations and distinctions: sight 'most of all the senses, makes us know and brings to light many differences between things'.[5] Together, these two major classical statements by Plato and Aristotle have shaped the tradition surrounding sight, emphasizing access to the natural world as the basis of human knowledge and thought.[6] The derivation of 'idea' from the Greek *idein*, meaning 'to see', sustains this intersection of sight and insight, vision and contemplation, viewing and reflection. Or as Chris Jenks writes, the 'lexical etymology reminds us that the way we think about the way that we think in Western culture is guided by a visual paradigm'.[7]

The actual physiological process of seeing as theorized by Aristotle assumed greater importance in the early modern period over its Galenic rival that followed Plato.[8] In Galen, 'the eye emits a "visual pneuma" that transforms the air into an optical instrument, illuminating the object of vision with the eye's sensory power'.[9] Stuart Clark offers a summary of the Aristotelian process as documented in the period's medical, moral, and psychological literature: 'objects in the world gave off resemblances or replicas of themselves (*species*) which then travelled to the eyes and, via the eyes and the optic nerves, into the various ventricles of the brain to be evaluated and processed.'[10] A linear, logical pattern governs Aristotle's system of visual cognition. The conversion of external *species* into internal matter or *phantasms* that then pass into the brain represents an entirely rational system that underwrites the secure and grounded relation between the viewer and the world.[11] Such an epistemology of sight suggests a consistency between inside and outside where the material world of objects has a reliable representation in the mind, thus confirming the

---

[4] David Summers, *The Judgment of Sense: Renaissance Naturalism and the Rise of Aesthetics* (Cambridge: Cambridge University Press, 1990), 32.

[5] Aristotle, *Metaphysics*, 980a, trans. W. D. Ross, in Richard McKeon, ed., *Introduction to Aristotle* (New York: Random House, 1947).

[6] See also 'The Noblest of the Senses: Vision from Plato to Descartes', in Martin Jay, *Downcast Eyes: The Denigration of Vision in Twentieth-Century French Thought* (Berkeley: University of California Press, 1994), 21–82. Despite some disagreement from important figures like Lucien Febvre and Robert Mandrou, who rearrange the hierarchy of senses in the late medieval and early modern periods, Jay argues that their contention rests on marginal evidence (34–5).

[7] Chris Jenks, 'The Centrality of the Eye in Western Culture: An Introduction', in Jenks, ed., *Visual Culture* (New York: Routledge, 1995), 1.

[8] Sergei Lobanov-Rostovsky, 'Taming the Basilisk', in David Hillman and Carla Mazzio, eds., *The Body in Parts: Fantasies of Corporeality in Early Modern Europe* (New York: Routledge, 1997), 199. On the importance of Aristotle's theories of sight, knowledge, and memory for the early modern period, see Arthur F. Kinney, *Shakespeare and Cognition: Aristotle's Legacy and Shakespeare's Drama* (New York: Routledge, 2006).

[9] Lobanov-Rostovsky, 'Taming the Basilisk', 198.

[10] Stuart Clark, *Vanities of the Eye: Vision in Early Modern European Culture* (Oxford: Oxford University Press, 2007), 2.

[11] See Clark, *Vanities of the Eye*, 15 and 39–77 for a more detailed description of the process of seeing that includes the role of phantasms.

equation between objective truth and sight as well as sight's veridical status.[12] 'Not only is sight reason-like,' avers David Summers, 'but reason is sight-like.'[13]

But Clark's fundamental thesis in *Vanities of the Eye* is that for the early modern period, 'several important developments unique to the cultural history of Europe over roughly two and a half centuries worked to undermine this inherited confidence and disrupted the relationship between human beings and what they observed'.[14] Among these developments were the Protestant Reformation and the visual complications inherent in the distrust of icons and idolatry; the revival of Greek scepticism rooted in doubt that challenged the validity of sensory evidence, especially data deriving from the eyes; and the fascination with demonology that prompted disturbing questions about vision and the real. In a chapter titled, 'Ocular Proof in the Age of Reform', Huston Diehl, arriving at a similar conclusion about the impact of Protestant reform, notes the 'epistemological crisis created by the reformers when they deny the magical efficacy of images and relics and yet assert the power of visible signs'.[15] 'In one context after another', Clark contends, 'vision came to be characterized by uncertainty and unreliability, such that access to visual reality could no longer be normally guaranteed. It was as though European intellectuals lost their optical nerve.'[16]

In this chapter I extend the premise of this inquiry concerning the disruption of stable conventions of sight into the domain of race, examining by way of *Othello* how seeing blackness raises questions of unreliability not just of sight and knowledge, but of related intellectual engagements: reflection, reading, and interpretation. As Jenks observes, 'it is critical that vision should be realigned with interpretation rather than with mere perception.'[17] At the same time, the notion that perception (sight or vision as a physiological experience) is influenced by culture is now a critical norm. Subsequently, the counter-intuitive and unexpected finding, that sight might not be comprehensively trustworthy, turns out to be particularly compelling when it comes to seeing and reflecting on race. Employing the analytical premise that blackness is the biological datum that is read and interpreted according to the prevailing social paradigm (that is, blackness is to race as sex is to gender), this chapter engages *Othello* further to raise questions about seeing blackness in relation to the racial faultlines of our current critical and reading practices.

THE PANOPTIC REGIME OF WHITENESS

Othello's demand for 'ocular proof' (3.3.362) of Desdemona's purported infidelity is consistent with the conventional notion that what one sees constitutes infallible knowledge that,

---

[12] Jenks notes that 'philosophy's project became dedicated to the "rigorous" and "scientific" divination of the accurate and most appropriate transportation of the "outside" into the "inside". The conventional highway for this transport has been the senses, but primarily "sight"' ('The Centrality of the Eye', 3).

[13] Summers, *The Judgment of Sense*, 40.   [14] Clark, *Vanities of the Eye*, 2.

[15] Huston Diehl, *Staging Reform, Reforming the Stage: Protestantism and Popular Theater in Early Modern England* (Ithaca, NY: Cornell University Press, 1997), 134.

[16] Clark, *Vanities of the Eye*, 2.   [17] Jenks, 'The Centrality of the Eye', 4.

in turn, serves as the basis for accurate interpretation. Since 'to be once in doubt | Is once to be resolved' (3.3.182-3), Othello tells Iago, 'I'll see before I doubt; when I doubt, prove' (3.3.193). When doubt does enter Othello's mind, the predicted outcome ensues: 'What sense had I in her stolen hours of lust? | I saw't not, thought it not—it harm'd not me' (3.3.340-1), confirming the seemingly logical connection between seeing and knowing. Launched unalterably on the path toward conviction, Othello confronts Desdemona, the handkerchief becoming the chief, material proof: 'Fetch't, let me see't' (3.4.84). Of course, proof ascertained by firsthand or eyewitness experience, it turns out, is not as foolproof as it might at first appear, and the play's tragic unfolding rests on this counterintuitive recognition exemplified in the cognitive confusion caused by a visible, peripatetic hand-kerchief. Proffered as the ultimate instance of 'ocular proof', the handkerchief fails, in the end, to deliver the truth or knowledge Othello imagines. Moreover, while sight is invoked as a credo of certainty to counter Othello's rising doubt, the dramatic irony of the request cannot be overstated: the Moor and black man, whose alien presence in Venice is defined by his corporal visibility, demands proof of the visible kind, thereby surrendering to the very optical system within which his racial tragedy is enshrined. For if sight is conducive to certainty and contemplation, Othello runs the risk of supporting the idea that his black-ness is sufficient to justify the claims made and conclusions drawn according to the law of visible proof.

Notions of blackness saturate the play, turning a physiological fact into a racial idea expressing the collective cultural thinking. As a useful comparison, most readers are aware of the Prince of Morocco's colour-conscious appeal in *The Merchant of Venice* (1596): 'Mislike me not for my complexion, | The shadowed livery of the burnished sun, | To whom I am a neighbour and near bred' (2.1.1-3). [18] The anxious suitor's apology repre-sents more than the rhetoric of competitive advantage. Rather, given Morocco's position as the object of scrutiny, it signals his clear recognition of the Venetian social aversion directed squarely at skin colour, thereby confirming that seeing blackness is never just a neutral sensory experience but *a fortiori* an ideologically encoded act. In this regard, vision relays the defining collective institutional practices and ideas that inform and produce the structural homogeneity essential for the community's white power elite. It encapsulates the Venetian *habitus*, in Pierre Bourdieu's sense of the term, in which an intersection of social and cultural factors gives shape to a way of life and thought. [19] Immediately upon the prince's entry, therefore, Morocco's skin tone triggers an opposi-tional orchestration of ideas and values through the complex racializing mechanism of the Venetian optical system.

Othello likewise represents the alienating power of the Venetian system in which, to adapt Bourdieu's language, the black man is effectively pitted against the 'cognitive and motivating structures' whose task it is to 'reproduce the regularities immanent in' the self-identified white society. [20] Brabantio complains before the full senate that without the

[18] On the useful intersection of meanings located in 'complexion' as a concept from humoral theory, see Roxann Wheeler, *The Complexion of Race: Categories of Difference in Eighteenth-Century British Culture* (Philadelphia: University of Pennsylvania Press, 2000).

[19] On the 'habitus' and 'homogeneity', see Pierre Bourdieu, *Outline of a Theory of Practice*, trans. Richard Nice (Cambridge: Cambridge University Press, 1977), 80-3.

[20] Bourdieu, *Outline of a Theory of Practice*, 78.

intervention of witchcraft, evoked as an alien practice to further indict Othello's black-ness, Desdemona would not have found Othello desirable. 'For nature so preposterously to err— | Being not deficient, blind, or lame of sense' (1.3.63-4) is, for the angry senator-father, unthinkable. Brabantio's argument rests on the appeal to 'nature', making it clear that whiteness is the natural order that resists the disorder and perversity endemic to racial mingling. Iago also invalidates the interracial match, making an appeal to 'nature' to contend that sameness is the organizing cultural principle that legitimizes racial exclu-sion. Desdemona, he claims, made the error in rejecting white men 'Of her own clime, complexion, and degree, | Whereto we see in all things nature tends' (3.3.234-5). While Brabantio and Iago may be the most vocal defenders of the normative order of whiteness (one should also include Emilia), the language used makes it clear that theirs is not an isolated view. Desdemona's behaviour in shunning 'The wealthy curled darlings of our nation' (1.2.68) for Othello's 'sooty bosom' (1.2.70), Brabantio states, would 'incur a gen-eral mock' (1.2.69), implying a broadly shared set of values. Such aberrant behaviour on Desdemona's part constitutes a reckless disregard for the natural ordination of whiteness and nation as the presumed order of things. These arguments, grounded in the principle of sameness, effectively theorize the 'cognitive and motivating structures' of the Venetian cultural system.

Difference is not only subjected to heavy scrutiny within a similar corporal system, but Othello's black features also elicit fear among Venice's viewing subjects. Brabantio can only conceive of Othello as a 'thing ... to fear, not to delight' (1.2.71), and, concerning Desdemona, Iago questions, 'what delight shall she have to look on the devil' (2.1.220-1), exploiting the commonly held association between devils and blackness. While the con-sternation caused by Jonson's royal women all painted black in *The Masque of Blackness* (1605) is well known, other texts perpetuate this propensity for black panic.[21] In William Rowley's *All's Lost by Lust* (c.1622), the widely shared notion that a black person's face has the power to terrify is adduced several times. For example, Alonso, relies on this funda-mental premise in declaring that the Moors 'have not yet, unless with grim aspects | So much as frighted this my tender daughter' (2.2.17-18).[22] Rejecting Mully Mumen's offer of love, Jacinta states bluntly, 'Th'art frightfull to me' (5.5.2) to the Moor of whom Julianus demands, 'Set the black character of death upon me, | Give me a sentence horrid as thy selfe art' (5.5.35-6). In their representation of black fear, Rowley and Shakespeare register an aspect of contemporary English life conveyed in the annual mayoral pageants that unfolded in London's streets, incorporating citizens in the drama of social construction and cognitive alignment with the civic attitudes expressed. Written for the Grocers' Company, Middleton's *The Triumphs of Truth* (1613) features among its dichotomous drama of good versus evil, error versus truth, the arrival of a small group of Moors whose 'black' appearance generates the trepidation evident in 'the faces | Of these white people' (415, 411-12). Again, in Middleton's *The Triumphs of Honour and Virtue* (1622), written for the same livery company, the Indian Queen's colour—'this black is but my native dye' (54)—requires justification among London's white citizenry. In the case of

---

[21] Ian Smith, 'White Skin, Black Masks: Racial Cross-Dressing on the Early Modern Stage', *Renaissance Drama* 32 (2003): 44–5.

[22] William Rowley, *All's Lost by Lust and A Shoemaker, A Gentleman* (Philadelphia: University of Pennsylvania, 1910); all citations are taken from this edition.

both pageants, blackness stands as a sign of distrust and fear until these aliens, the Moors and the Black Queen, confess to Christian conversion through the intervention of enterprising English merchants who serve London's corporate culture's investment in growing overseas commerce. Yet blackness carried such an indelible and predetermined negative meaning that white viewers repeatedly experienced visual and cognitive dissonance, unable to reconcile outward appearance with the symbolic internal whiteness of conversion.

Seeing blackness, therefore, often produced fear and paranoid fantasies, the sign of multiple tactical reactions to the black presence within Europe. First, visual paranoia did not only serve the destructive purposes of stereotyping and racial rejection; it also enabled the construction of a powerful and, as history has shown, long-lasting invention of whiteness. The historian Kate Lowe has argued that the influx of African slaves into Europe in the early modern period (for a century and a half starting in the 1440s), with the resulting transition from white slavery to predominantly black slavery, initiated 'a momentous time of white, European self-definition'.[23] Othello and Morocco are not slaves (both, in fact, have royal lineage), but even their racial presence in Europe is sufficiently disruptive for Shakespeare to dramatize the increasing historical pressures of proximity. The will to preserve whiteness acted as the defensive counterpart to the perceived necessity to contain and discredit the expansive presence of blackness. Fear, understood from an early modern English perspective as a proactive response, is a symptom of the desire to manage the cultural integrity of whiteness.

The visual response to blackness as a source of fear reinforced the damaging negative stereotypes that transformed a physical fact into a racial idea. Even Iago's seemingly innocuous but patently disjunctive reference to 'black Othello' (2.3.29) affirms Othello's colour as anomalous and marginalizing within the demographic norm of the republic. While advances in anatomy confirmed Aristotelian theories of vision in the early modern period, the tendency to hold onto Platonic (later Galenic) models revealed a desire to explain vision and, by extension the agency of the viewer, in gendered terms. For Aristotle, the human eye functioned as a passive 'matrix in which light implants its substance', whereas for Galen, the emission of pneuma implied a masculine agency.[24] An allusion to Galen's theory of extramission can be identified in the Black Queen's appeal for Englishmen to see past her colour: 'But view me with an intellectual eye, | As wise men shoot their beams forth, you'll then find | A change in the complexion of the mind' (35-7). Notably, therefore, Sergei Lobanov-Rostovsky concludes that the persistence of the Platonic model served a particular political purpose: 'what replaced the emission of Platonic "fire" as a cultural model of the masculine's eye power was ideology in its purest form: the gaze'.[25] I would argue further that the coalescence of sight, fear, and blackness in early modern texts is not only informed by gender, but reproduces the masculine for the purposes of installing the objectifying power of the racial gaze. In demanding 'ocular proof', therefore, Othello has unwittingly surrendered to the racial gaze, cultivated within the Venetian panoptic regime, which would turn colour into the totality of his character.

---

[23] Kate Lowe, 'The Stereotyping of Black Africans in Renaissance Europe', in T. F. Earle and K. J. P. Lowe, eds., *Black Africans in Renaissance Europe* (Cambridge: Cambridge University Press, 2005), 17.
[24] Lobanov-Rostovsky, 'Taming the Basilisk', 199.   [25] Ibid.

RACISM'S MENTAL DEFORMITY

The play's concern with sight centers most prominently on the dramatic action surrounding Othello's request for visible evidence as well as Iago's verbal repertoire of tricks to satisfy that demand. Othello is insistent, declaring mere verbal challenge or accusation insufficient—"'Tis not to make me jealous | To say my wife is fair, feeds well, loves company' (3.3.186-7)—and demanding instead incontrovertible visible proof: 'Make me to see't' (3.3.366). The distinction Othello makes between words and sight is noteworthy, for its importance lies not in its accuracy or validity, but in the attention it brings to the verbal tools and strategies employed by Iago. Rather than accuse Desdemona directly in the beginning, Iago is hesitant, repeating Othello's own words or using half-formed sentiments, leaving Othello to observe: 'these stops of thine fright me the more' (3.3.124). Iago uses aposiopesis, described in the *Ad Herennium* as occurring 'when something is said and then the rest of what the speaker had begun to say is left unfinished'; it continues to explain the rhetorical impact, providing an excellent gloss on Iago's tactics: 'Here a suspicion, unexpressed, becomes more telling than a detailed explanation would have been'.[26] The ultimate effect of aposiopesis used by Iago is to make Othello an intellectual collaborator who finishes up the half-stated ideas himself to give the 'worst of thoughts | The worst of words' (3.3.136-7). In the worst-case scenario, Othello imagines himself a generator of ideas, becoming the first to actually indict his wife by name following Iago's spurious hints about cuckoldry and jealousy. Gradually, the accumulation of rhetorical silences, stops, and starts takes its toll, sucking Othello into a vortex of suspicion and doubt from which he will not escape.

While Iago's rhetorical strategies throughout produce his desired fatal outcome for Othello and Desdemona, they reveal in the 'temptation scene' a certain racial mentality Shakespeare foregrounds for the audience's attention. At a crucial moment, Iago's hesitant but deliberate repetitions prompt Othello to exclaim, 'By heaven, thou echo'st me, | As if there were some monster in thy thought | Too hideous to be shown' (3.3.109-11), followed by Othello's logical request for those thoughts to be unfolded: 'Show me thy thought' (3.3.119). Yet early in the play, at the conclusion of the senate scene, Iago, in a soliloquy, formulates a plot to ensnare and destroy Othello using this same language of monstrosity: 'It is engendered: Hell and Night | Must bring this monstrous birth to the world's light' (1.3.391-3). Thus Othello's initial reading of Iago's verbal hesitations as possibly concealing a monstrous and 'horrible conceit' (3.3.118) is correct and linguistically consistent with Iago's stated long-term plan. Indeed, something dreadful is 'shut up in [Iago's] brain' (3.3.117), something that is both 'monstrous' and 'hideous', commonplace but powerful terms used to designate black Africans.

Monsters have been discussed in the context of miscegenation and cross-species mixing, the deformed progeny being incorporated into European cultural and political

---

[26] *Ad Herennium*, trans. Harry Caplan, Loeb Classical Library (Cambridge: Harvard University Press, 1981), 4.30.41. See also George Puttenham, *The Art of English Poesy*, ed. Frank Whigham and Wayne A. Rebhorn (Ithaca, NY: Cornell University Press, 2007), 250: 'when we begin to speak a thing and break off in the middle way, as if either it needed no further to be spoken of, or that we were ashamed or afraid to speak it out'.

discourse to create in-group classifications, establish normative practices, contain in-stability, and justify hierarchies of difference.[27] Additionally, and supremely relevant for this play, in the early modern 'popular imagination, of course, the association of African races with monsters supposed to inhabit their continent made it easy for blackness to be imagined as a symptom of the monstrous'.[28] Thus, for example, William Cunningham, from a survey of classical and contemporary sources about black Africans, concludes: 'The people [are] blacke, Savage, Monstrous, & rude.'[29] Johannes Boemus writes of Africans in Ethiopia: 'There be in it dyuers peoples of sondry phisonomy and shape, monstruous and of hugly shewe.'[30] This emphasis on size implicit in notions of the monstrous is extended to blacks' prodigious physical endowments often the source of scandalized commentary; some 'early cartographers ornamented maps with representations of naked black men bearing enormous sexual organs'.[31] At the same time, 'horrible', meaning 'extremely re-pulsive to the senses or feelings; dreadful, hideous, shocking, frightful' (OED), recalls the equally well documented optical power of black faces to inspire fear and dread.

The play, therefore, does not simply achieve a deft and insightful reversal, relocating the monstrous and the hideous in Iago while teasing out the repeated early modern English associations of Africans, blackness, and monstrosity. More important is the exposure of a way of thinking and state of mind, identified with trafficking in stereotypes of blackness, that is justly characterized as 'monstrous'.[32] In the margins of his 1581 text, *Doom Warning All Men to the Judgment*, Stephen Bateman makes the notation, 'Black Monsters', while delivering moral warnings about divine judgement exemplified in 'the sundry strange and deformed men and women' in Africa.[33] In contrast to the catalogue of physical deformi-ties attending blacks, Shakespeare reveals Iago's mental deformity, consciously coded as a monstrosity to alert us to its frightening power. Iago, having rejected an idealist or religious philosophy, affirmed that it is 'in ourselves that we are thus or thus' (1.3.315-16), espousing a secular, existentialist declaration that posits ownership of his hideous mind. Iago refers not just to a set of desperate actions that he will undertake, but with 'monstrous' as a proxy

---

[27] On monsters and monstrosity in the early modern period, see Mark Thornton Burnett, *Constructing 'Monsters' in Shakespearean Drama and Early Modern Culture* (New York: Palgrave Macmillan, 2002); Patricia Parker, *Shakespeare from the Margins: Language, Culture, Context* (Chicago: University of Chicago Press, 1996), 231-72; and Karen Newman, ' "And Wash the Ethiop White": Femininity and the Monstrous in *Othello*', in Jean E. Howard and Marion F. O'Connor, eds., *Shakespeare Reproduced: The Text in History and Ideology* (New York: Methuen, 1987), 143-62.

[28] Michael Neill, 'Unproper Beds: Race, Adultery, and the Hideous in *Othello*', *Shakespeare Quarterly* 40: 4 (1989), 409; on the popular association of monsters and black Africans, see James R. Aubrey, 'Race and the Spectacle of the Monstrous in *Othello*', *Clio* 22:3 (1993), 221-38.

[29] Quoted in Alden Vaughan and Virginia Mason Vaughan, 'Before *Othello*: Elizabethan Representations of Sub-Saharan Africans', *William and Mary Quarterly* 54:1 (1997), 24.

[30] Johannes Boemus, *The Fardle of Facions* (London: John Kingston and Henry Sutton, 1555), sig. C2r.

[31] Newman, ' "And Wash the Ethiop White" ', 148.

[32] Burnett, *Constructing 'Monsters'*, 122, suggests: '*Othello* aims to suggest, in fact, that the "monster" that has been produced is not Desdemona's death, still less the "monstrous" behaviour of Othello, but the "monstrous" mystery of Iago's inner compulsions.' Although I agree with Burnett's notion of Iago's 'inner compulsions', I want to also emphasize the role of the mind and its relation to thinking and seeing.

[33] Quoted in Aubrey, 'Race and Spectacle', 229.

for blackness, he identifies specific deeds as 'black', revealing a racialized mindset even as he surrenders to those behaviours himself, and thereby links blackness and danger—that is, blackness and criminality—as part of the Venetian racial mythos. Accused of being a devil at play's end (5.2.284-5), Iago emblematizes blackness in his monstrous diabolism.

Othello's destiny is to be caught in the maelstrom of innuendo and monstrous thinking, internalize its worst imaginings, and project onto the handkerchief his fears while holding onto it as a totem of truth. Rather than prove the truth of Desdemona's supposed infidelity, the handkerchief comes to embody the full 'compliment extern' (1.1.63) of machinations conceived in Iago's mind. The handkerchief—especially a black handkerchief, given the period's repeated associations of blackness and the monstrous—becomes a visible, material manifestation of Iago's mental monstrosity unpacked, one might say, for the audience to see.[34] Iago has notoriously and fiercely guarded his private thoughts, secret agenda, and true allegiance, vowing never to 'wear my heart upon my sleeve' (1.1.64). While 'hideous' hints at the hidden, secret nature of Iago's thoughts, 'monstrous', with a pun on *monstrare*, from Latin meaning 'to show', points to the exorbitant grotesque that cannot be completely concealed from sight, and that, once revealed, creates visions of horror.[35] The key words 'monster', 'hideous', and 'show' tap into the play's visual episteme to capture the dynamic tension of seeing and hiding, revelation and occlusion, concealment and disclosure, here aptly directed at Iago's mental programme—an example, in contemporary terms, of racist thinking masking itself from view. The audience, however, as the sole witness to Iago's earlier pledge of 'monstrous birth' recognizes its uncanny diabolical delivery in the form of the black handkerchief, the objective correlative of the 'horrible conceit' Othello rightly feared. While Othello remains blinded to the full truth of his own initial suspicions, Shakespeare has set firmly in place a debate about 'horrible' and 'monstrous' ideas privately held or unacknowledged and the possibility that they can be rendered visible through unintended or indirect means.

THE AUDIENCE'S MIND'S EYE

Further attention to Iago's rhetorical strategies in the 'temptation scene' reveals that in response to Othello's demand for 'ocular proof', he offers first a detailed account of Cassio's purportedly sexual dream. At first seemingly a mere stalling tactic, the narrative description has an intrinsic value, remaining true to the play's visual focus as an example of *enargeia*, defined by classical and early modern rhetoricians as the strikingly vivid quality of a description that brings a scene before the mind's eye. As a distinctive feature of the larger category of description (*ekphrasis*), *enargeia* often achieves amplification through the accumulation of striking narrative details.[36]

One of the most widely used classical rhetorics in the Renaissance provides a definition of *enargeia* that echoes Shakespeare's famous phrase ('ocular proof'): 'It is Ocular

---

[34] Ian Smith, 'Othello's Black Handkerchief', *Shakespeare Quarterly* 64:1 (2013), 1–25.

[35] Burnett, *Constructing 'Monsters'*, 2–3; Burnett also considers the importance of the visual dimension of 'monster'.

[36] On the history and distinction between the terms, see Graham Zanker, 'Enargeia in the Ancient Criticism of Poetry', *Rheinisches Museum für Philologie* 124 (1981), 297–311.

Demonstration when an event is so described in words that the business seems to be enacted and the subject to pass before our eyes.'[37] Other writers elucidate several points embedded in this compact statement. Quintilian calls attention to the forensic value of vivid description (*evidentia* in Latin) in persuading a judge, insisting that the goal is not simply to narrate but to display the facts 'in their living truth to the eyes of the mind'.[38] What is uniquely fitting for Iago's purposes, however, is that the use of language Quintilian envisions approximates eyewitness content created with another's words (seeing as if with one's own eyes). Henry Peacham explains the effect in *The Garden of Eloquence*: the listener's mind is, 'therby so drawen to an earnest and stedfast contemplation of the thing described, that he rather thinketh he seeth it then heareth it'.[39] Thanks to Iago, Othello's imagination is inflamed with vivid narrative details, the result of the phenomenon of seeing with words that turns 'listeners [or readers] into spectators'.[40] Importantly, the concept of *enargeia* from the discipline of rhetoric brings the notion of audience, and the audience's mind, to the fore in early modern theories of sight. The conjunction of rhetoric, sight, and audience finds its most clear statement in Erasmus' evocation of *enargeia*'s performative effect in painting a powerful verbal picture 'so that at length it draws the hearer or reader outside himself as in the theatre'.[41]

Iago clearly has a prominent role in the deployment of vivid description that 'convince[s] Othello of the epistemological priority of visual experience over any less-sensible evidence'.[42] Othello, too, uses *enargeia* in his defense in the senate, loaded with ethnographic details of strange people and foreign lands as well as biographical data about 'hair-breadth scapes i'th'imminent deadly breach, | Of being taken by the insolent foe | And sold to slavery' (1.3.136-8). Othello's history of the handkerchief is similarly rich in the particulars of its manufacture and the mysteries of its provenance (3.4.54-74). In both instances, the choice to paint a densely delineated portrait that becomes cemented in the hearers' minds is joined to the need to produce exculpatory evidence: establishing Othello's innocence against charges of illicit magic, in one instance, and verifying the handkerchief as legitimate and valid proof, in the other. The legal framework identified in Quintilian's explication of vivid description resonates with the demand for evidentiary proof that concerns Othello on diverse fronts.[43]

---

[37] *Ad Herennium*, 4.55.68.

[38] Quintilian, *Institutio Oratoria*, 4 vols., trans. H. E. Butler, Loeb Classical Library (Cambridge: Harvard University Press, 1986), 8.3.62.

[39] Henry Peacham, *The Garden of Eloquence* (London: H. Jackson, 1593), 134.

[40] Heinrich F. Plett, *Enargeia in Classical Antiquity and the Early Modern Age: The Aesthetics of Evidence* (Leiden: Brill, 2012), 27. The quotation is from the *Progymnasmata* of Nikolaos of Myra.

[41] Desiderius Erasmus, *On Copia of Words and Ideas*, trans. Donald B. King and H. David Hix (Milwaukee: Marquette University Press, 1963), 47; see also Joel B. Altman, '"Preposterous Conclusions": Eros, *Enargeia*, and Composition in *Othello*', in his *The Improbability of 'Othello': Rhetorical Anthropology and Shakespearean Selfhood* (Chicago: University of Chicago Press, 2010), where he examines *enargeia* in relation to the theatre but for very different purposes from the ones argued here.

[42] James Knapp, '"Ocular Proof": Archival Revelations and Aesthetic Response', *Poetics Today* 24:4 (2003), 712.

[43] For an engaging account of the law and the jury system in relation to *Othello*, see Katharine Eisaman Maus, *Inwardness and Theater in the English Renaissance* (Chicago: University of Chicago Press, 1995), 104-27.

The play's most important moments of striking description, at least for the purposes of this essay, occur in the two opening nighttime scenes (Act 1.1-2). I return to these well-known scenes for what they can help us understand about sight and the audience's mind. With Brabantio presenting himself at an upper window, Iago has an audience whom he wants to convince of Othello's guilt in stealing the senator's daughter. In effect, Othello is being charged with blackness; that is, he is being accused *in absentia* of violating the Venetian cultural code of whiteness. Iago's deliberate ploy is to present the evidence of proof to Brabantio in such a graphic way that the father's mind is shocked by the explicit images that lay bare the acts of seeming sexual transgression. The passages are well known, a consequence of the rhetorical impact being discussed, so one example will suffice: 'Even now, now, very now, an old black ram | Is tupping your white ewe' (1.1.88-9). Here, Iago punctuates the verbal illusion of a live event that, Heinrich Plett argues, is one of the effects of using *enargeia*: 'the event described seems to be happening *hic et nunc* before the inner eye of the recipient.'[44] And as the first scene unfolds, Roderigo piles on narrative details in a lengthy speech that indicts Othello by injecting life into popular racial stereotypes about 'the gross clasps of a lascivious Moor', the 'extravagant and wheeling stranger, | Of here and everywhere' (1.1.125, 135-6).

Erasmus' analysis, that the picture created through words 'draws the hearer or reader outside himself as in the theatre', shifts the lexicon around *enargeia* sufficiently for us to grasp the metatheatrical construction of the opening scene where the audience in the theatre functions as a prime interlocutor engaged. Othello's absence, in conjunction with the racially charged information brought forward, puts the audience in the position of having to use its mind's eye. The audience's resulting mental image of the Moor is the product of social and ideological conditioning of the time. Elizabeth Spiller argues that in the sixteenth century, 'written texts and paper images' were essential technologies that facilitated English encounter with foreigners.[45] The names Sir John Mandeville, Johannes Boemus, Sebastian Munster, Peter Heylyn, and Hakluyt figure significantly in this tradition of cross-cultural print encounter.[46] Starting in the mid-1550s, the introduction of Africans in English society, the result of capture, led to an appreciable growth of the black presence by the turn of the century, a largely shadow community 'disliked but valued, politically debarred but quietly retained, legally non-existent but historically permanent.'[47] But for the audience attending a performance of *Othello*, the encounters in reading and in the social environment of London notwithstanding, the stage tradition of presenting Moors must have played a significant educational role for those who had seen Muly in Peele's *Battle of Alcazar* (1588), Aaron in Shakespeare's own *Titus Andronicus* (1592), or Eleazer in *Lust's Dominion* (1600).

The congruence of these factors—textual, historical, and dramatic—can be seen, for example, in the way Heylyn's description of blacks operates as a template for several dramatic personae. Africans, he claims, are 'much given to lying, treacherous, very full of

---

[44] Plett, *Enargeia*, 9.

[45] Elizabeth Spiller, *Reading and the History of Race in the Renaissance* (Cambridge: Cambridge University Press, 2011), 16.

[46] On the non-literary sources of images of blackness, see Elliot H. Tokson, *The Popular Image of the Black Man in English Drama, 1550-1688* (Boston: G. K. Hall, 1982), 1-19.

[47] Imtiaz Habib, *Black Lives in the English Archives, 1500-1677: Imprints of the Invisible* (Burlington: Ashgate, 2008), 118.

talk, excessively venerous, and extream jealous', all of which attach to Othello at some point.[48] Though the non-literary and social data might mitigate the portraits of Moors in some instances, the theatrical evidence was unrelenting in its dogmatic denigration of blackness.[49] 'Moor', substituting for the absent Othello, is not just a blank, empty category label. The audience reacts to the deliberately unnamed and unseen Moor by testing, and most likely confirming, its portable knowledge about blackness against Iago and Roderigo's accusations while simultaneously filling in the blanks about the absent, as yet unknown black man (what I call the 'Othello blind spot') with a mind conditioned by cultural information gathered from the available non-literary texts, real life encounters, and accumulated knowledge from past theatrical performances. The theatre, to follow Erasmus' thinking, is the ultimate instantiation of *enargeia*, for as the 'seeing place' (from the Greek *theatron*), its images of blacks, past and present, come alive in full, animated degradation to be impressed on the audience's mind's eye.

The audience experience I am trying to theorize can be explored more fully by way of Norman Bryson's essay 'The Gaze in the Expanded Field' in which he writes: 'For human beings collectively to orchestrate their visual experience together it is required that each submit his or her retinal experience to the socially agreed description(s) of an intelligible world.'[50] The cultural conditioning that influenced how audiences saw, conceptualized, and thought about blackness in the early modern period is the product of 'socially agreed description(s)' that confirm vision as 'socialized'.[51] However, when the audience finally sees the anonymous Othello in the play's second scene, Shakespeare inserts dramaturgic details—a nighttime scene, men with torches arriving to arrest Othello, his refusal to hide, Othello's famous utterance, 'Keep up your bright swords, for the dew will rust them' (1.2.59)—that recall Jesus in Gethsemane at the moment of Judas' betrayal (John 18: 1–11) to dispel the negative stereotypes imputed previously to Othello. The audience experiences a visual shock; everything the strategically unnamed 'Moor' left to the audience's imagination to fill in earlier is instantly undermined. The earlier image of the violent social intruder and sexual predator is countered by Shakespeare's evocation of a man, like Jesus, calm and morally exemplary, who is the racial target of political jealousy. Shakespeare deviates from the prevailing 'social construction of visual reality', that is, the prevailing stereotypes of blackness, to produce an intellectual and 'visual disturbance'.[52]

Bryson invites us to see that the cultural or ideological conditioning that colours vision is, in an important sense, the source of blindness.

> Between the subject and the world is inserted the entire sum of discourses which make up visuality, that cultural construct, and make visuality different from vision, the notion of unmediated visual experience. Between retina and world is inserted a *screen*

[48] Quoted in Tokson, *The Popular Image of the Black Man*, 17–18.

[49] In the visual arts, a range of perspectives covering the African as slave, ambassador, and duke is documented in Joaneath Spicer, ed., *Revealing the African Presence in Renaissance Europe* (Baltimore: The Walters Art Museum, 2012).

[50] Norman Bryson, 'The Gaze in the Expanded Field', in Hal Foster, ed., *Vision and Visuality* (Seattle: Bay Press, 1988), 91.

[51] Ibid., 91.   [52] Ibid., 91.

of signs, a screen consisting of all the multiple discourses on vision built into the social arena.[53]

The notion of vision as unimpeded retinal access to the world is revised to explain how sight is always compromised by 'multiple discourses', and that 'screen of signs' blocks the view and *'casts a shadow'*.[54] That is, in the case of race, prejudicial and broadly shared stereotypes distort vision in ways that misrecognize blackness and make us poor readers of humanity. This is the audience recognition that Shakespeare brilliantly dramatizes in the opening pair of scenes in *Othello*. Moreover, the effect of such distortions is a kind of blindness or, according to Lacan, 'a scotoma'[55] (from Greek meaning 'darkness')—a blind spot, which is 'the area of the retina where the optic nerve exits the eye'.[56] The shadow cast by the multiple discourses that racialize blackness mimics the obstruction of vision that occurs in the ocular blind spot to explicate the full impact of racial conditioning and stereotype on the audience: critical and intellectual blindness that produces supremely unreliable readers. The play's legal language makes it entirely just to observe that Othello, as a black man, is put on trial in the Venetian setting, due in no small part to racial stereotyping. Equally important, in *Othello*'s framing pair of opening scenes, Shakespeare challenges the audience's ability to *see* clearly and places the reading and interpretation of blackness on trial.

READING AND WHITE PREFERENCE

Shakespeare's interrogation of seeing, reading, and interpretation has an important qualification: he is addressing, in the context of the early modern theatre, the issue of cross-racial reading. Shakespeare investigates an audience from a majority white culture that, due to multiple factors, sees and thinks from within racial stereotypes that the playwright, in turn, makes visible and available for conscious reflection. Iago's contention that Othello is handicapped as a reader of the Venetian scene because of racial and cultural differences is instrumental in Othello's gradual mental transformation. About the women, Iago claims: 'I know our country disposition well: | In Venice they do let God see the pranks | They dare not show their husbands' (3.3.204-6), to which Othello replies incredulously, 'Dost thou say so?' (3.3.208). Unlike Iago who challenges Othello's ability to read white culture, Shakespeare makes the dramatic departure to question the majority white culture's ability and willingness to read blackness. I would like to iterate the continuing relevance of that particular Shakespearean inquiry today.

In their recent study *Blindspot: Hidden Biases of Good People*, social psychologists Mahzarin Banaji and Anthony Greenwald examine hidden racial bias and its social effects. Developing their thesis by way of analogy with retinal scotoma, they argue that in American society subjects are unaware of and blind to their own racial biases. The issues

---

[53] Ibid., 91–2.   [54] Ibid., 92.   [55] Ibid., 92.

[56] Kinney, *Shakespeare and Cognition*, 19. On the distinction between the natural blind spot and artificial scotomas, see V. S. Ramachandran, 'Filling in Gaps in Perception', *Current Directions in Psychological Science* 2, no. 2 (1993): 56–7.

examined earlier in the context of early modern texts and culture—the panoptic order of whiteness, the imperative of cultural sameness, and hidden or unacknowledged racial bias—are found to operate in modern society but are subject in this instance to the evaluative scrutiny of experimental science. Rather than use explicit testing measures, such as direct response to questions which carries a greater risk of subject interference, Banaji and Greenwald used another method, the Implicit Association Test (IAT) and developed the first Race IAT to 'measure one of our society's most significant and emotion-laden types of attitudes—the attitude toward a racial group'.[57] The researchers focused especially on black and white racial groups. Years of testing, now confirmed by other researchers, have produced the following findings.[58] First, they conclude 'that automatic White preference is pervasive in American society' with 75per cent of those tested showing that preference: 'This is a surprisingly high figure.'[59] This preference holds true even when subjects subscribe consciously to different, non-biased outlooks.[60] Second, 'the automatic White preference expressed on the Race IAT is now established as signaling discriminatory behavior'.[61] Additional research into the reliability of eyewitness accounts elaborates the issue of cross-racial reading. Specifically, tests reveal that, 'With respect to false identifications, White participants exhibited a larger own-race bias than did Black participants; the size of the own-race bias was comparable for White and Black participants with respect to correct identifications.'[62] These findings speak to unconsciously held attitudes, but their material and social costs in all areas of African Americans' lives, from housing discrimination, job discrimination, healthcare, to the criminal justice system, are all too real.[63]

As contemporary readers, especially within the discipline of English studies, we cannot be immune to the implications of these findings that suggest, as Shakespeare has before us, that our ability to see and read blackness might be severely impaired by unconscious biases that have been socially and culturally conditioned. The impact of these claims in the experimental sciences has an immediate practical value for legal studies and critical race theory and should have an equally practical and imperative claim in literary studies regarding how we read and reflect on race.[64] While automatic white preference may result

[57] Mahzarin R. Banaji and Anthony G. Greenwald, *Blindspot: Hidden Biases of Good People* (New York: Delacorte Press, 2013), 41.

[58] Christian A Meissner and John C. Brigham, 'Thirty Years of Investigating the Own-Race Bias in Memory for Faces: A Meta-Analytic Review', *Psychology, Public Policy, and Law* 7:1 (2001), 3–35. A meta-analysis synthesizes the available data in a particular research area to provide 'greater statistical power'; see Brian Cutler, ed., *Expert Testimony on the Psychology of Eyewitness Identification* (Oxford: Oxford University Press, 2009), 15; and Kurt Hugenberg and Galen V. Bodenhausen, 'Facing Prejudice: Implicit Prejudice and the Perception of facial Threat', *Psychological Science* 14:6 (2003), 640–3.

[59] Banaji and Greenwald, *Blindspot*, 47.

[60] This is the effect of cognitive dissonance; see Banaji and Greenwald, *Blindspot*, 54–61.

[61] Banaji and Greenwald, *Blindspot*, 47.

[62] Brian Cutler and Margaret Bull Kovera, *Evaluating Eyewitness Identification* (Oxford: Oxford University Press, 2010), 39.

[63] Banaji and Greenwald, *Blindspot*, 189–209; see also Max H. Bazerman and Ann E. Tenbrunsel, *Blind Spots: Why We Fail to Do What's Right and What to Do about It* (Princeton: Princeton University Press, 2011), 43–8.

[64] Marianne Novy expresses a brief interest in experiments covering weapons and the propensity for racial misrecognition, but she turns her attention to whether works 'can be free from being read as exemplifying racist ideology'. *Shakespeare and Outsiders* (Oxford: Oxford University Press, 2013), 103.

from conditioned behaviour, Shakespeare's use of the play's second scene stands as an example of the importance of conscious intervention to disrupt oppressive racial orthodoxy and destabilize the sedimentation of convention. Seeing blackness, as examined in this chapter, helps us understand that race is the reading and interpretation of a physiological sign of colour, with the attendant attitudes and responses on the part of the reading subjects informed by an own-race bias. This definition is as true in the early modern period as it is today and helps to challenge the recurring scepticism about race as a viable early modern category and bypasses the too narrow insistence on post-Enlightenment taxonomies and the role of colonialism.[65] Again, the evidence of persistent racial discrimination that has emerged from the research examined counters the naïve presumptions of proponents of post-racial theory who would like to table race altogether as an issue that has been addressed and whose influence has been nullified. Such a move also guarantees the abrogation of responsibility. Given the factual data, '[o]ne would have to suffer from a very deep form of blindness to ignore the continuing presence of racism in the world today'.[66] A post-racial premise, moreover, would have a curbing effect on early modern race studies. In the end, the inference to be drawn from the collectible data is that white-bias significantly affects the casual, daily routine of seeing, thinking, and reflecting; so this essay asks, by way of *Othello*, how such bias influences acts of reading and interpretation within a profession whose scholars are, to use a memorable formulation, ideologically conditioned or 'positioned as white'.[67]

Select Bibliography

Baker, Steven, 'Sight and a Sight in *Othello*', *Iowa State Journal of Research* 61:3 (1987), 301–9.

Banaji, Mahzarin R. and Anthony G. Greenwald, *Blindspot: Hidden Biases of Good People* (New York: Delacorte Press, 2013).

Bryson, Norman, 'The Gaze in the Expanded Field', in Hal Foster, ed., *Vision and Visuality* (Seattle: Bay Press, 1988).

Clark, Stuart *Vanities of the Eye: Vision in Early Modern European Culture* (Oxford: Oxford University Press, 2007).

Cutler, Brian, ed., *Expert Testimony on the Psychology of Eyewitness Identification* (Oxford: Oxford University Press, 2009).

Hugenberg, Kurt, and Galen V. Bodenhausen, 'Facing Prejudice: Implicit Prejudice and the Perception of facial Threat', *Psychological Science* 14:6 (2003), 640–43.

Jenks, Chris, 'The Centrality of the Eye in Western Culture: An Introduction', in Jenks, ed., *Visual Culture* (New York: Routledge, 1995).

Kinney, Arthur F., *Shakespeare and Cognition: Aristotle's Legacy and Shakespeare's Drama* (New York: Routledge, 2006).

Knapp, James A., '"Ocular Proof": Archival Revelations and Aesthetic Response', *Poetics Today* 24:4 (2003), 695–727.

---

[65] This debate is the central concern for Ania Loomba and Jonathan Burton, eds., 'Introduction', in *Race in Early Modern England: A Documentary Companion* (New York: Palgrave, 2007), 1–36.

[66] W. J. T. Mitchell, *Seeing Through Race* (Cambridge: Harvard University Press, 2012), p. xi.

[67] Toni Morrison, *Playing in the Dark: Whiteness and the Literary Imagination* (Cambridge: Harvard University Press, 1992), p. viii.

Lobanov-Rostovsky, Sergei, 'Taming the Basilisk', in David Hillman and Carla Mazzio, eds., *The Body in Parts: Fantasies of Corporeality in Early Modern Europe* (New York: Routledge, 1997).

Martin, Jay, 'The Noblest of the Senses: Vision from Plato to Descartes', in Martin Jay, *Downcast Eyes: The Denigration of Vision in Twentieth-Century French Thought* (Berkeley: University of California Press, 1994).

Meissner, Christian A. and John C. Brigham, 'Thirty Years of Investigating the Own-Race Bias in Memory for Faces: A Meta-Analytic Review', *Psychology, Public Policy, and Law* 7:1 (2001), 3–35.

Mitchell, W. J. T., *Seeing Through Race* (Cambridge, MA: Harvard University Press, 2012).

Ryden, Wendy and Ian Marshall, *Reading, Writing, and the Rhetorics of Whiteness* (New York: Routledge, 2014).

CHAPTER 26

···

KING LEAR AND THE DEATH
OF THE WORLD

···

LEAH S. MARCUS

> Force, Force, everywhere Force, we ourselves a mysterious Force in the Centre
> of that. There is not a leaf rotting on the highway but has Force in it; how else
> could it rot? ... this huge illimitable whirlwind of Force, which envelops us here;
> never-resting whirlwind, high as Immensity, old as Eternity.
>
> Thomas Carlyle, *On Heroes, Hero-Worship and the Heroic in History* (1841)

KING Lear has frequently been considered Shakespeare's greatest play: William Hazlitt pronounced it so; A. C. Bradley acknowledged that it has 'again and again been described as Shakespeare's greatest work' though Bradley himself, for reasons to which we shall return, pronounced it 'Shakespeare's greatest achievement' but '*not* his best play.'[1] In the late twentieth century, R. A. Foakes argued, the play was consistently labelled Shakespeare's finest, beating out its usual competitor *Hamlet*, because its extreme bleakness resonated so strongly with a world haunted by the apocalyptic spectre of nuclear destruction.[2] Centring on a storm of epic proportions that prefigures the catastrophic civil war in which it concludes, the play is indeed vast, encompassing a range of characters from a king down to a rabble of beggars, two daughters whose viciousness comes close to the motiveless malignancy of Iago, and another daughter whose goodness almost overwhelms their vice. It is the only Shakespearean tragedy with a fully developed subplot (that of Gloucester and his sons), which parallels and comments upon the fate of the protagonist himself. It is also the only Shakespearean tragedy so proliferative and poetically fecund that recent editors have frequently felt compelled to offer it to readers not only in a single, composite text but also in two separate and distinct versions. These are based upon the 'Pied Bull' quarto of 1608 and the folio version of 1623, the quarto containing some 300 lines that are not in the folio,

---

[1] William Hazlitt, *The Characters of Shakespeare's Plays*, 3rd edn (London: John Templeman, 1836), 26; A. C. Bradley, *Shakespearean Tragedy: Hamlet, Othello, King Lear, Macbeth* (1904; New York: Fawcett World Library, 1965), 20–1.

[2] R. A. Foakes, *Hamlet versus Lear: Cultural Politics and Shakespeare's Art* (Cambridge: Cambridge University Press, 1993), 3–4.

and the folio a hundred-odd lines that are not in the quarto. There are also many smaller textual differences.[3]

We will concern ourselves here with both texts, but our central focus will be upon yet another way in which *King Lear* is unique among Shakespearean tragedies—its complex, repeated evocation of a mysterious 'Nature' throughout the play—a teeming world of shrubs, trees, barren heath, rats, dogs, pond-slime, thunder, whirlwinds and other elemental forces swirling about the humans—a presence that is so palpable to its characters that it almost deserves the status of an additional member of the cast. At least four characters—Lear, Edmund, Cordelia, and Edgar—address elements of nature directly and with more sustained, colloquial vigour than the brief and formulaic apostrophes to Night, Sun, or Moon characteristic of early Shakespeare (cf. Romeo's 'O blessèd, blessèd night!' in *Romeo and Juliet* 2.1.181). *Timon of Athens* is perhaps closest to *Lear* in its protagonist's direct addresses to elements of nature, and it is often placed contiguously to *Lear* in terms of date of composition. But *King Lear* is the only tragedy in which characters make a habit of conversing both with nature herself and with elements of the natural world, and in which that world, on occasion, may be said to talk back to them. Indeed, the word 'Nature' is almost always capitalized in the folio text as though to signal its unique status in this particular play.

It is largely because of the near omnipresence of a mysterious, brooding 'Nature' that *King Lear* has often been pronounced unplayable. Charles Lamb had nothing but scorn for the 'contemptible machinery' used to mimic the terrible storm at the centre of the play, though the version he saw was still Nahum Tate's, not Shakespeare's, which was not restored to the stage until 1838. On stage, according to Lamb, 'we see nothing but corporal infirmities and weakness' but reading the play 'we are Lear,—we are in his mind, we are sustained by a grandeur which baffles the malice of daughters and storms'.[4] Bradley agreed that the play was a dramatic failure, immense in scope, 'too huge for the stage' (*Shakespearean Tragedy*, 203), though not for the perceptive reader alive to Shakespeare's imaginative power. Most of us will disagree with Bradley's assertion that the play cannot be staged successfully: paradoxically, the barer the stage the more freedom the audience has to engage with the pervasive fluidity of 'Nature' evoked through the language of its characters.[5] Here, however, I will concentrate on the printed text and argue that *King Lear*

    [3] See in particular *William Shakespeare: The Complete Works*, ed. Stanley Wells, Gary Taylor, et al. (Oxford: Clarendon Press, 1986). All Shakespeare citations below, except those to early facsimile texts, are to this edition and indicated by act, scene, and line number (for the folio or F) and scene and line number (for the quarto or Q) in the text. For other editions that print both Q and F, see the second edition of the *Norton Shakespeare*, ed. Stephen Greenblatt et al. (New York and London: W. W. Norton, 2008), which is based on the Oxford text; and *King Lear (the Quarto and Folio Texts)* in the Pelican Shakespeare, ed. Stephen Orgel and A. R. Braunmuller (New York and London: Penguin, 2000). For an account of the controversy surrounding the two texts of the play, see *The Division of the Kingdoms: Shakespeare's Two Versions of King Lear*, ed. Gary Taylor and Michael Warren (Oxford: Clarendon, 1983); and Steven Urkowitz, *Shakespeare's Revision of King Lear* (Princeton: Princeton University Press, 1980). It is now generally accepted by scholars in the field that the two constitute distinct versions of the play.

    [4] Charles Lamb, 'On the Tragedies of Shakespeare', in *The Works of Charles Lamb in Two Volumes* (London: for C. and J. Ollier, 1818), 2: 24–5.

    [5] See esp. Jan Kott, *Shakespeare Our Contemporary*, trans. Boleslaw Taborski (1964; repr. New York: W. W. Norton, 1974), 127–68; and the stage histories of J. S. Bratton, *Plays in Performance: King Lear* (Bristol: Bristol Classical Press, 1987); and Alexander Leggatt, *Shakespeare in Performance: King Lear* (Manchester and New York: Manchester University Press, 1991).

is steeped in early modern vitalism, which we will define as a belief in some type of invisible, immanent force or network of forces, whether material or immaterial, that operates within and between things, linking them and determining their relations with each other. Indeed, the play may fruitfully be considered an investigation of vitalism—of the connections among things, the energy surging through things and people alike, thereby creating complex networks of sympathy and causality that can both sustain and destroy. I will argue that the modern resurgence of vitalist philosophy in the writings of Henri Bergson, Gilles Deleuze, Bruno Latour, and, most recently, Jane Bennett has allowed us renewed access to the pre-Cartesian sensibility of a play in which the hidden connections among things are made palpable through the power of language and in which the loss of a sense of vibrant connection among things is experienced as nothing less than the death of the world.[6]

Gail Kern Paster takes an approach that is in many ways similar to mine: she is interested in connections between human passions and larger phenomena like the storm at the centre of the play, which she interprets in terms of settled beliefs of the period—Galenic humoral theory and analogies between microcosm and macrocosm—that are played out in Lear's connections with a 'natural order constituted holistically as biological, social, and familial' (Ch. 13 in this volume, 202–17). By explicating the play in terms of one set of commonly held theories, she arrives at a reading that must surely resemble the way it was received by many of Shakespeare's contemporaries. My essay takes several steps back from humoral theory to interrogate a central question behind it and other competing medical models of the period: what does it mean to say that the natural world is alive, and what does that suggest about its relation with human beings? In contrast to Paster, I concentrate on the differences between quarto and folio *King Lear*, demonstrating that the passages that treat connections between humans and the natural world are among the most fluid and volatile of the play.

The varieties of modern vitalism are as diverse as the different schools of vitalist philosophy and physiology that coexisted in early modern England. Jane Bennett defines 'vitality' in her recent study *Vibrant Matter* as 'the capacity of things—edibles, commodities, storms, metals—not only to impede or block the will and designs of humans but also to act as quasi agents or forces with trajectories, propensities, or tendencies of their own' (p. viii). For Bennett and other modern vitalist materialists, Descartes marks the great divide between earlier vitalist beliefs and their more modern post-Cartesian rehabilitation, beginning in the late seventeenth and eighteenth centuries. The dualist mechanism of Descartes separated matter off from spirit and exalted the human in solitary eminence over all other life forms by positing the capacity for thought and reflection as uniquely human attributes. And this philosophical move, in the view of many modern vitalists, created a fissure in human experience from which we are still struggling to recover. For

---

[6] See Jane Bennett, *Vibrant Matter: A Political Ecology of Things* (Durham and London: Duke University Press, 2010); *The Crisis in Modernism: Bergson and the Vitalist* Controversy, ed. Frederick Burwick and Paul Douglass (Cambridge: Cambridge University Press, 1992); John Marks, *Gilles Deleuze: Vitalism and Multiplicity* (London: Pluto Press, 1998); Bruno Latour, *Reassembling the Social: An Introduction to Actor-Network-Theory* (Oxford: Oxford University Press, 2005); Latour, *Politics of Nature: How to Bring the Sciences into Democracy* (Cambridge, MA and London: Harvard University Press, 2004); and *Inventive Life: Approaches to the New Vitalism*, ed. Mariam Fraser, Sarah Kember and Celia Lury (London: Sage, 2006).

Bennett, 'Materiality is a rubric that tends to horizontalize the relations between humans, biota, and abiota. It draws human attention sideways, away from an ontologically ranked Great Chain of Being and toward a greater appreciation of the complex entanglements of humans and nonhumans. Here, the implicit moral imperative of Western thought—"Thou shall identify and defend what is special about Man"—loses some of its salience' (112). Much of this statement sounds uncannily like what King Lear experiences during his ordeal on the stormy heath at the centre of the play.

Early modern vitalism was pervasive and took many cultural forms, none of them particularly methodical: the 'entelechy' of Aristotle and 'vital spirits' of Galen, the 'Archeus' or vital force of Paracelsus, the world soul of Hermetic philosophy, and some strains of Christian ontology that argued for the pervasiveness and immanence of the divine, as in Cabbalistic teachings and Thomas Vaughan's '*Light* of *Nature* ... the *Secret Candle* of God'.[7] Many early modern vitalists held that objects could experience emotions and sympathies, and that these ties could connect them even across considerable distances, as in the ties of bodies posited in alchemical and astrological proto-scientific thought. Even the celebrated physician and researcher William Harvey, who discovered the circulation of the blood, believed that a wound could be cured without physical intervention through ameliorating remedies to the weapon that caused it: this was not magical thinking on Harvey's part (though it may appear so to us), but a vitalist belief in the power of sympathies among proximate and related entities. Similarly, the 'doctrine of signatures' by which plants and other earthly things were believed to contain hidden signs of their curative powers was not occult magic but standard vitalist thinking, in that the 'sympathies' of plants or minerals could vary depending on the properties of other bodies that were close at hand.[8] Vitalist thinking became a bit more methodized in the aftermath of Cartesianism in the later seventeenth century, when even the physicist (and devotee of the *Corpus Hermeticum*) Isaac Newton could argue for a 'subtle Spirit which pervades and lies hidden in all gross

---

[7] [Thomas Vaughan], *Lumen de Lumine: or, a new Magicall Light, discovered and Illuminated to the World* (London: for H. Blunden, 1651), 41 (Sig. E1r). For general studies, see Walter Pagel, *Paracelsus: An Introduction to Philosophical Medicine in the Era of the Renaissance* (Basel and New York: S. Karger, 1958); Allen G. Debus, *The English Paracelsians* (New York: Franklin Watts, 1966); G. Lloyd Jones, *The Discovery of Hebrew in Tudor England: A Third Language* (Manchester: Manchester University Press, 1983); and Allison P. Coudert, *The Impact of Kabbalah in the Seventeenth Century: The Life and Thought of Francis Mercury van Helmont, 1614–1698* (Leyden: Brill, 1998). Although van Helmont was obviously too late for Shakespeare, many ideas similar to his circulated in England well before his work was published, as documented in Pagel and Debus above. For vitalism and the plant world, see, among many other studies, Matthew Wood, *Vitalism: The History of Herbalism, Homeopathy, and Flower Essences* (1992; rpt. Berkeley, CA: North Atlantic Books, 2005).

[8] On Harvey, see Leo M. Zimmerman, 'Surgery', in *Medicine in Seventeenth Century England* ed. Allen G. Debus (Berkeley: University of California Press, 1974), 49–69, esp. 55–8; on the 'doctrine of signatures' more generally, see Wood, *Vitalism*. For these ideas and vitalism in early modern literature, I am indebted to John Rogers on the vitalist materialism of John Milton in *The Matter of Revolution: Science, Poetry, and Politics in the Age of Milton*. Ithaca and London: Cornell University Press, 1996); Gail Kern Paster, *Humoring the Body: Emotions and the Shakespearean Stage* (Chicago: University of Chicago Press, 2004); and Garrett A. Sullivan, Jr., *Sleep, Romance and Human Embodiment: Vitality from Spenser to Milton* (Cambridge: Cambridge University Press, 2012).

bodies'.[9] The sceptical early chemist Robert Boyle defined one 'vulgarly received notion' of nature as 'the Principle of all Motions and operations in Bodies', acknowledging that this common usage left open the questions of whether the principle in question was 'Immaterial or Corporeal', 'without Knowledge or else indowed with Understanding', and whether it applied only to animate or even to inanimate bodies, as in the attractive properties of magnets and the 'Medical Virtues of Gems and other Mineral Bodies, whether Consistent or Fluid'.[10] Boyle's retrospective definition of a received concept of nature will be our focus. What are the 'Motions' of nature and how durable are they? How are they expressed within a given being and what kinds of agency do they have? How, if at all, do they relate to an imagined realm governed by law and moral principles? These questions are asked in a variety of registers in *King Lear*.

The most arresting case of conversation with nature in *King Lear* is Lear's furious address to the storm in 3.2 (cited here from the folio version):

> Blow, winds, and crack your cheeks! Rage, blow,
> You cataracts and hurricanoes, spout
> Till you have drenched our steeples, drowned the cocks!
> You sulph'rous and thought-executing fires,
> Vaunt-couriers of oak-cleaving thunderbolts,
> Singe my white head; and thou all-shaking thunder,
> Strike flat the thick rotundity o'th' world,
> Crack nature's moulds, all germens spill at once
> That makes ingrateful man.
>
> (F 3.2.1–9)

In this tremendous speech, Lear calls upon various elements of the storm to injure him, 'Singe my white head'; to blast elements of civilized life, steeples and weathercocks; but also to assault the earth itself, striking its 'rotundity' 'flat'; and even to erase the possibility of its future continuance, spilling out the 'moulds' nature uses to shape generations to come. Lear's rage and the storm are seemingly inseparable: in F Lear's 'O, reason not the need!' speech is interrupted by the stage direction '*Storm and tempest*' just at the point at which Lear feels the onset of madness:

> You think I'll weep.
> No, I'll not weep. I have full cause of weeping,
>   *Storm and tempest.*
> But this heart shall break into a hundred thousand flaws
> Or ere I'll weep.—O Fool, I shall go mad!
>
> (F 2.2.456–9)

Which came first, Lear's madness or the storm, and how are the two related? The folio text emphasizes the connections by repeating the stage direction '*Storm still*' no fewer than five times at intervals through the ensuing scenes of Lear's madness (F 3.1.0, 3.2.0, 3.4.58, 3.4.95, 3.4.152). In *The Elizabethan World Picture* (1942) E. M. W. Tillyard used Lear to illustrate

---

[9] Cited from Newton's General Scholium, *Principia* (2nd edn, 1713), in Catherine Packham, *Eighteenth-Century Vitalism: Bodies, Culture, Politics* (Houndmills, Basingstoke: Palgrave Macmillan, 2012), 1.

[10] R[obert] B[oyle], *A Free Enquiry Into the Vulgarly Receiv'd Notion of Nature* (London: for John Taylor, 1685), 349, 367–9.

early modern belief in correspondences between macrocosm and microcosm and an invariably hierarchical view of order conflated with the 'Great Chain of Being'. It is not coincidental that Tillyard's highly schematic book was written during World War II, when the idea of order and stasis was particularly appealing. For us now, however, particularly in the light of our reawakened interest in early modern vitalism, his 'Picture' appears contrived and overly rigid.[11] The traditional understanding of Lear's relation to the storm emphasizes the correspondences between them—as one of the Gentlemen comments, Lear

> Strives in his little world of man to outstorm
> The too-and-fro-conflicting wind and rain.
> This night, wherein the cub-drawn bear would couch,
> The lion and the belly-pinchèd wolf
> Keep their fur dry, unbonneted he runs,
> And bids what will take all.
>
> (Oxford Q, Sc. 8, 9–14)

Tillyard's schematic understanding of this 'Picture' would reassure the reader that the Elizabethans believed in correspondences between the 'little world' of an individual human and the cosmos such that upheavals in one could be reflected in another. But this understanding of the play congeals its action to the stasis of a homily on order and reduces its mad scenes to a troubling chaos from which the play must recover as quickly as possible. The Gentleman's words linking the storm and the 'little world' of man exist in the quarto version of the play only; the Gentleman's speech in F stops several lines earlier. The play's evocations of relations between humans and the natural world are among its most fluid, frequently varying between Q and F and, I would contend, expressing a similar fluidity in early modern vitalist understanding of the links among things, which are not invariant but in a constant state of flux. From a vitalist perspective, King Lear's madness and the contest of the elements are best understood as a fragile, temporary mutually reinforcing system of vibrating sympathies: the king rages along with the storm and the storm rages along with the king; they are communicating with each other. Both registers of anger appear related to the undutiful behaviour of Goneril, Regan and perhaps also Edmund. But to state that possible causal relation is not to provide an answer but to pose a problem: what are the hidden ties between humans, especially members of the same family, and elements of the natural world? Recovering a vitalist understanding of the ties between bodies allows us to approach the play as a series of questions about possibly frail and temporary associations among things rather than as a tableau of moral platitudes about the importance of family harmony in larger schemes of order.

  There are many ways in which the play's characters struggle for language to express the idea of connections among disparate things. Kent refers early on to Goneril's steward Oswald as a breaker of links: 'Such smiling rogues as these, | Like rats, oft bite the holy cords a-twain | Which are too intrince t'unloose' (F 2.2.73–5). The 'cords' are 'holy' and so

---

[11] Recent ecocritics have begun to recuperate elements of the 'Great Chain of Being' by emphasizing its horizontal functioning and its similarities to the more recently recognized correspondences among levels in holograms and fractals. See in particular Robert N. Watson, 'The Ecology of Self in *Midsummer Night's Dream*'; and Gabriel Egan, 'Gaia and the Great Chain of Being', both in Lynne Bruckner and Dan Brayton, eds., *Ecocritical Shakespeare* (Farnham, Surrey: Ashgate, 2011), 33–56 and 57–70.

immanent ('ntrench' in Q, 'intrince' in F) within things that they can't be disentangled from them;[12] they can, however, be gnawed apart by a rat, whether of the animal or human variety. Kent's speech expresses both the indissoluble nature of the hidden links among things and their vulnerability, via natural means, to being broken. Human relations often operate this way in the play: Lear assumes that family ties are 'too intrince t'unloose', but his daughters, whom in F he calls his very 'breath and blood' (F 2.2.275), part of a single organism, sever the 'holy cords' through their disobedience. Later in the play, Albany similarly speculates in a Q-only passage that if Goneril persists in her alienation from her roots, she must perforce wither and die: 'That nature which contemns it origin | Cannot be bordered certain in itself. | She that herself will sliver and disbranch | From her material sap perforce must wither, | And come to deadly use' (Q Sc. 16, 32–6). Gloucester, too, complains in both Q and F of the 'bond cracked 'twixt son and father', but he attributes this breach to cosmic influence—recent 'eclipses in the sun and moon'. Only in F does he go on to generalize more broadly: 'This villain of mine comes under the prediction: there's son against father. The King falls from bias of nature: there's father against child. We have seen the best of our time. Machinations, hollowness, treachery, and all ruinous disorders follow us disquietly to our graves' (F 1.2.101–12).

Gloucester is, of course, contradicted by his bastard son Edmund, who flatly and (for us) convincingly denies that the stars determine human destinies. Here, as in King Lear's ranting against the heavens, the relationship between nature and human action is a question rather than an answer. In both texts Edmund, a bastard and therefore in the vocabulary of the period a 'natural' child, famously hails 'nature' as his 'goddess. To thy law | My services are bound' (F 1.2.1–2). But it becomes clear as the action progresses that his concept of natural 'law' is not generalizable to everyone else in the play: it is an idiosyncratic assemblage based on connections with others who are attracted by his dynamism and his jaunty dismissal of his father's stodgy moral platitudes. Edmund dies repudiating what he had earlier defined as natural 'law', affiliating himself with a different network of feeling and striving to undo his order for the execution of Lear and Cordelia: 'Some good I mean to do | Despite of mine own nature' (F 5.3.218–19). Like Edmund, King Lear address a personified Nature early in the play, calling upon his 'dear goddess' to 'hear' the horrific series of curses by which he seeks to blast his daughter's fertility: 'Into her womb convey sterility. | Dry up in her the organs of increase, | And from her derogate body never spring | A babe to honour her' (F 1.4.254–60). As Robert N. Watson has perceptively noted of the play, 'every definition of nature produces an equal and opposite one.'[13] These striking opening salvos by Edmund and Lear establish 'nature' as an important principle in the play, but as the action proceeds their oversimplifying personifications erode in favour of a conception of nature as a more immanent and fluid force. As in the standard seventeenth-century definition dismissively cited after the Restoration by Robert Boyle, nature in King Lear in its most fundamental meaning is no detachable goddess but 'the Principle of all

---

[12] Q and F readings are cited in original spelling from the useful facsimile parallel texts in The Complete King Lear, 1608–1623 ed. Michael Warren (Berkeley and London: University of California Press, 1989).

[13] Robert N. Watson, Back to Nature: The Green and the Real in the Late Renaissance (Philadelphia: University of Pennsylvania Press, 2006), 52.

Motions and operations in Bodies'—often, but not necessarily, nurturing and sometimes as savagely destructive as the human language with which it vibrates in sympathy.

In *The Accommodated Animal: Cosmopolity in Shakespearean Locales* Laurie Shannon invites us to reimagine a pre-Cartesian world in which animals had not yet been firmly defined as the not-human and thereby excluded from being thought along with the human and sharing various obligations and entitlements with humans. She sees this vision as strongly operative at the centre of *King Lear*, among many other Renaissance texts, when the king gradually discovers his kinship with a previously unrecognized world of animals, all of whom are better provided against the fury of the storm than he is. Shannon's list of the marvellous diversity of animals mentioned in *King Lear* runs to half a page of densely packed lines. For Shannon, the 'happy beast' tradition lies at the heart of *King Lear*, but in its most searingly negative form as a condemnation of human claims to special privilege.[14] Lear methodically strips humans of all their pretenses to special status and is left with a mere 'bare, forked animal' (F 3.4.101)—what Shannon terms a 'solitarily unhappy beast' who 'lacks a visible claim on the cosmos by which to make himself at home' (173). Early modern vitalism enables a less pessimistic view of the centre of the play: if Lear is severed from the privileged position he held in the opening scene, in which he stood as the apex of a community, that community began to dissolve the moment he prompted his daughters to put its network of obligations into language. On the heath he becomes attached to a different sort of community—an odd grouping in which interaction takes place through and among humans, animals, and even inanimate things. This is particularly true of the quarto version of the play, which contains a greatly amplified version of the seemingly nonsensical exchange among Edgar disguised as Tom O'Bedlam, the Fool, Lear, and Kent that is usually referred to as the 'mock trial scene'. The scene can also be described as the articulation of a new set of vibrant connections among beings and even things: what modern vitalists would call an 'assemblage'—a network of 'affective bodies' in which agency is horizontally distributed rather than hierarchical and in which interaction does not necessarily take place in its most customary and easily measurable forms (Bennett, *Vibrant Matter*, 23–4). 'Conversation' in the hovel is a series of seeming non sequiturs, that nevertheless convey mutual sympathy and even something resembling understanding.[15]

The exchange begins with Edgar's mutterings about 'Frateretto' and 'Nero' as 'an angler in the lake of darkness. Pray, innocent; beware the foul fiend.' The Fool takes up the idea of prayer and also Edgar's (feigned) madness: 'Prithee [pray thee], nuncle, tell me whether a madman be a gentleman or a yeoman.' To which Lear answers, picking up both the idea of madness and the Fool's reference to a yeoman, 'A king, a king! To have a thousand [yeomen] | With red burning spits come hissing in upon them!' He is confessing his own madness and imagining a possible revenge on his daughters, but Edgar (who is more appealing in his vulnerable role of mad beggar than he is in his own person as legitimate heir to Gloucester) feels the 'burning spits' and the paternal hatred that motivates them

---

[14] Laurie Shannon, *The Accommodated Animal: Cosmopolity in Shakespearean Locales* (Chicago and London: University of Chicago Press, 2013), 127–73.

[15] In several celebrated recent stagings, most notably the National Theatre's 2014 production directed by Sam Mendes, King Lear shockingly kills the Fool at the end of the hovel scene: obviously the degree to which the assembled characters can be seen as a mutually supportive community will depend a great deal on production details.

as though directed at him personally: 'The foul fiend bites my back.' To which the Fool replies, continuing Lear's speculations about possible revenge, 'He's mad that trusts in the tameness of a wolf, a horse's health, a boy's love, or a whore's oath.' Lear immediately picks up on the idea of whores swearing oaths, 'It shall be done. I will arraign them straight' and goes on to empanel 'justices' for the trial of his daughters (Q Sc. 13, 6–16). The characters are talking past one another in language that eerily resembles our modern psychoanalytic concept of the free association of ideas, but they are still managing to converse. As they set up for the trial, the assemblage of participating interlocutors expands to include, apparently, two joint-stools who stand in for Lear's hard-hearted daughters and play their parts fittingly for such inhumane creatures, showing 'warped looks' (48) and kicking the king (who has apparently stumbled against one of them). These objects are not precisely agents in this scene; they are more properly considered 'actants' in the modern vitalist understanding of the term (Bennett, *Vibrant Matter*, p. viii): they exert force and contribute along with a variety of other distributed agents to its outcome by interrupting the mock trial and sending Lear's musings in another direction. Immediately afterwards in Q, in one of the scene's most touching moments (which is also included in F, after the folio's omission of the mock trial), Lear brings in the animal kingdom as well: he imagines himself in interaction with little dogs, 'Tray, Blanch, and Sweetheart' who presumably stand in for his three estranged daughters, barking at him as at a hostile intruder. Poor Tom responds to Lear by conjuring up a veritable catalogue of mad 'curs' he wards off to protect the king (F 3.6.21–31). At this precise point, Lear proposes to undertake his 'anatomy': 'let them anatomize Regan; see what breeds about her heart. Is there any cause in nature that makes this hardness?' or in the folio version, 'these hard-hearts?' (Q Sc. 13, 70–2; 3.6.36).

In an influential article, Valerie Traub has pointed to this key speech as linking *King Lear* with an emerging discourse of anatomical and geographic 'norms' that anticipates later scientific discourses of the 'normal' as a measurable, statistical category.[16] She is right that the play is steeped in the language of contemporary science: many of the most prolific and articulate early modern vitalists, like William Harvey and the English Paracelsians, were engaged in what then passed for medical research as they scrutinized human, animal, and mineral bodies for the principles of life that infused them. To me, what is most striking about Lear's desire to 'anatomize' his still-living daughter is its purpose: he wants to find out the 'cause': the links, the elements of nature, that can transform a heart from a warm, pulsating organ to something solid, implacable, immovable.[17] It is in the midst of the unusual network of beings in the hovel—imaginary dogs, comically robed justices, madmen, and joint-stools—that Lear proposes his anatomy of the living to search for 'the Principle of all Motions and operations in Bodies' that can precipitate hardness of heart.

I have been suggesting that the core of *King Lear*, the scenes of madness at its centre, is simultaneously the most intense locus for the play's inquiry into the nature of the world

---

[16] Valerie Traub, 'The Nature of Norms in Early Modern England: Anatomy, Cartography, *King Lear*', *South Central Review* 26 (2009), 42–81.

[17] See Packham, *Eighteenth-Century Vitalism*, 210–13. She and other historians of medicine tend to see Lear's type of anatomy—devoted to a discovery of the causes of physiological change rather than to a simple analysis of structures—as coming to the fore only in the late seventeenth century and after. Lear does not actually conduct his 'anatomy' of causes, but he is clearly able to imagine its usefulness.

and the possible hidden connections among its seemingly disarticulated parts. In effect, I have turned Tillyard's view of the play inside out, contending, along with previous critics who have emphasized Lear's awakening to sympathy along with the onset of his madness, that the horizontally linked network of the centre of the play is also at the centre of its vision, which is to a significant degree vitalist in its view of ties among bodies and their effects. In his madness, Lear displays both an intense interest in how things connect and transform one another in theory and an ability to 'converse' and interact with a range of beings outside the limits of rational, logical thought and preconceived beliefs. Eventually he falls into a deep sleep that Kent hopes in a Q-only speech will balm 'thy broken sinews'; at the end of the scene, in a speech that is also Q-only, Edgar suggests that he himself has found comfort from the odd fellowship of the hovel: 'How light and portable my pain seems now, | When that which makes me bend, makes the King bow' (Q Sc. 13, 91, 101–2). There is an equivalent, but more interestingly expressed, sentiment in the F-only lines at the beginning of 4.1, when Edgar next appears on stage, addressing an element of nature by greeting the open air: 'Welcome, then, | Thou unsubstantial air that I embrace. | The wretch that thou hast blown unto the worst | Owes nothing to thy blasts' (F 4.1.6–9).

During the action that follows, the vitalist intelligence of the play is increasingly focused around the figure of Cordelia, who embodies through her solicitude for the fallen king the quasi-medical power of love and sympathy, according to the theory of the time. In Q we get a foretaste of her effect on Lear in her evident compassion on reading the letters about Lear's situation. As though to suggest a change of climate for the play, the Gentleman who delivers them describes her response as divided between joy and grief and carrying meteorological overtones, moving her 'Not to a rage. Patience and sorrow strove | Who should express her goodliest. You have seen | Sunshine and rain at once; her smiles and tears | Were like, a better way' (Q Sc. 17, 17–20). When we actually see her on stage in 4.3, she consults with a 'Doctor' ('Gentleman' in F) about her father's cure, but addresses the earth itself, imploring it to lend its plants and minerals, along with her own tears, to aid him: 'All blest secrets, | All you unpublished virtues of the earth, | Spring with my tears, be aidant and remediate | In the good man's distress!' (F 4.3.15–18). The remedies are 'unpublished' in the sense of 'not widely known': Cordelia shows herself here to be acquainted with early modern medicine and its doctrine of 'signatures', based on the idea of hidden sympathies among things, by which a plant or mineral might offer some physical indicator of the disease against which it was potent. But her version goes even further, suggesting that her tears and the healing substances of the earth may 'Spring' forth together and as part of the same network of sympathy.

When Cordelia and King Lear are finally reunited in 4.6, we see him surrounded in proper vitalist medical fashion with elements designed to cure the 'great breach in his abusèd nature' (13) by communicating positive energies to which his own nature will, it is hoped, respond in kind. The vitalist dimensions of the scene are particularly prominent in Q, where Lear's treatment is presided over by a 'Doctor' as opposed to F's 'Gentleman' and where the doctor prescribes 'music' (Q Sc. 21, 23) along with other 'simples' to restore him. The music is not mentioned in F; nor are the doctor's specific instructions to Cordelia not to remind the patient of the traumas of his recent past—'it is danger | To make him even o'er the time he has lost' (Sc. 21, 77–8)—presumably because such memories could disable his ability to receive and respond to the healing sympathies of the sickroom. In F, in the absence of the medical accoutrements of Q, Cordelia becomes a more central 'cause' of Lear's recovery. Surrounded with music, medical assistance in the form of 'virtues of the earth', 'Fair daylight' (50) and Cordelia's love, Lear gradually adapts to the new set of conditions and his great rage, however productive it may have been on some other levels, is cured. The same vibrant connectivity that linked Lear at earlier points to the storm and to the fellowship of madmen now restores him to his youngest daughter and to something resembling tranquility of mind.

Even after they are captured, Lear and Cordelia can imagine a future together in prison, where they will while away their time with observation of the vicissitudes of the world. But with Cordelia's death, all of Lear's hard-won capacity to attune himself to the sympathies of things is lost, as though to suggest that her death shatters the fragile sustaining network that has surrounded him since his recovery He enters at 5.3 howling like an animal and echoing his madness on the heath, but also repeating the zeal for the investigation of 'anatomy' and the inner workings of nature that followed upon his madness on the heath, as he closely scrutinizes Cordelia's body for any tenuous physical sign of her revival. The difference between the two similar sequences of action is that while he was on the heath, he was surrounded by a group with whom he was able to communicate in rudimentary fashion and from whom he was able to draw sympathy; now, even though he is surrounded by well-wishers whose hearts are bleeding at his plight, he calls them 'men of stones' (F 5.3.232)—perceives them as incapable, like the hard-hearted Goneril and Regan he had earlier proposed to 'anatomize', of participating in his affliction. He is utterly alone, unable to recognize that Kent was his trusty servant Caius or that Goneril and Regan are dead. His world has contracted to Cordelia and everything hinges on her: If she lives 'It is a chance which does redeem all sorrows | That ever I have felt' (F 5.3.241–2). And if she is dead, then everything else is dead as well. Earlier in the play, Cordelia had appealed directly to the earth to offer its healing remedies for her father's cure. But now, for Lear, Cordelia appears to be 'dead as earth' (236): the whole assemblage of earth and its principles of motion lives or falls together.

For many readers, beginning at least as early as Samuel Johnson, the death of Cordelia is unbearable: Johnson reported that 'I was many years ago so shocked by *Cordelia*'s death that I know not whether I ever endured to read again the last scenes of the play till I undertook to revise them as an editor.' It wasn't only the death of Cordelia he was mourning; he mourned the fact that something larger than Cordelia also perished along with her: '*Shakespeare* has suffered the virtue of *Cordelia* to perish in a just cause, contrary to the natural ideas of Justice, to the hope of the reader, and, what is yet more strange, to the faith of chronicles', since in earlier tellings of the story, including the old play of *King Leir* that was one of Shakespeare's chief sources, Cordelia was allowed to live. As Johnson goes on to note, even on stage in the popular and long-lived adaptation of Tate, Cordelia was crowned with 'success and happiness' at the end of the play.[18] Since he couples 'natural' with 'Justice', Johnson is understandably shocked by the idea that Shakespeare would brutally allow virtue to perish in a just cause. The play Shakespeare wrote was considerably darker than the one Johnson wanted to read, in that Shakespeare does not imbue the force

---

[18] *The Plays of William Shakespeare*, ed. Samuel Johnson, vol. 6 (London: J. and R. Tonson et al., 1765), 159.

of nature in any consistent way with divine or even with moral principles. This, I would contend, is one of the most interesting ways in which vitalism works in the play. As in the teaching of many early modern proponents of the theory, there is no necessary connection between the imminent life force that operates within and among bodies on the one hand and ethics or divine law on the other.

As we have seen, in his inquiry into vulgar errors about nature, Robert Boyle noted the number of forms a basically vitalist interpretation of nature could take in his own time: the subtle spirits that existed within and coterminously with bodies could be material or immaterial, endowed with understanding or not, present within inanimate bodies as well as animate or only in the latter. Because Boyle himself defined the vital spirits in bodies as identical with God (and was therefore also a vitalist in the broadest understanding of the term), he did not include on his list of variable attributes another important difference in the understanding of vital spirits that was very much in play during earlier parts of the century and in his own time: how (if at all) did vitalism relate to received Christian understandings of the soul, of divine grace, of beliefs in divine immanence? Some vitalists held that the innate spirits in bodies were entirely separate from divine revelation while others argued for various forms of connection or, like Boyle himself, for their identity. This basic question of the relationship between religion, ethics, and nature is asked again and again in *King Lear*, but without any clear answer. Over the course of the play, the moral connotations of 'nature' are so variously and incommensurately described by its various characters that any sense of its innate connection with ethical ideas is obliterated. To the extent that they are invoked during the play, *King Lear*'s deities are always plural— either Graeco-Roman or the pre-Christian gods of ancient Britain. To be sure, some of the play's imagery is strikingly Christian, or at least seems so to Christian readers and viewers: Lear's donning of a crown of thorns and 'furrow-weeds' out on the heath (4.3.3); the 'pietà' of Lear cradling Cordelia's body, as the positioning of the two is sometimes performed in the final scene. It is part of the enduring power of *King Lear* across centuries and through transformations in the climate of belief that Shakespeare presents a world of vital sympathies and potential connections among things, without making clear their links with any specific religious or ethical tradition.

As we have already noted, Reginald Foakes saw the ending of the play as capable of evoking the universal annihilation of nuclear holocaust. This view is also very evident in Jan Kott, for whom the play enacts nothing less than 'the disintegration of the world': although in acts 4 and 5 such characters as have managed to survive gradually resume the customs and rituals of life, the play is empty for us because for Lear and Gloucester, the world 'has ceased to exist' (Kott, *Shakespeare Our Contemporary*, 364–5). Stephen Greenblatt, following Kott, sees the play as systematically evacuating religion and its various consolations: 'haunted by a sense of rituals and beliefs that are no longer efficacious, that have been *emptied out*' so that the 'theatrical means that might have made something magical out of this moment' of Cordelia's death 'are abjured'.[19] It is a shrewd insight: Shakespeare withdraws his most powerful poetry from the play after the death

---

[19] Stephen Greenblatt, 'Shakespeare and the Exorcists', in *After Strange Texts: The Role of Theory in the Study of Literature*, ed. Gregory S. Jay and David L. Miller (University, AL: University of Alabama Press, 1985), 101–23 (115, 120).

of Lear and Cordelia. The play's *élan vital*, its power to express the connections among things, requires Shakespeare's poetry to communicate itself to readers. When they die, the poetry and the play's vital energies die along with them.

John Danby came close to expressing this idea when he suggested that by the end of *King Lear*, we are no longer observing individual characters: 'all we can see is stricken Humanity holding murdered Nature in its arms.'[20] His gendering of nature in the play is, by now, seriously dated: for most of us, Cordelia does not symbolize 'Nature' in any direct way, though she is associated with curative plants and also with another of the play's 'naturals,' the Fool. As I have tried to suggest above, the gendering of nature as a goddess may be prominent in several of the play's early speeches, but as the action proceeds the idea of an autonomous goddess capable of agency in the world gives way to a more subtle, intrinsic portrayal of nature as a vital, ungendered principle of motion and transformation within and among bodies. It is this nature that dies at the end of the play, bringing with it the death of the world in the sense that the vitalist vision of sympathy among bodies dies for us, its readers, along with the death of King Lear, who had earlier made the play's vitalist connections palpable to us. Several of the characters in the final scene seem to equate what they are witnessing with the 'end' of the Apocalypse or some other horrific cataclysm:

> KENT   Is this the promised end?
> EDGAR   Or image of that horror?
> ALBANY   Fall and cease.
>
> (5.3.238–9)

The 'promised end' could be the Christian apocalypse and therefore represent yet another Christian element of the play. But in Christian teachings, the Apocalypse is not so much an event of horror as a cataclysm yielding new life and new beginnings. In *King Lear*, unlike *Macbeth* and even *Hamlet*, there are no hints of a new beginning at the end of the play. After Lear's death, either Edgar or Albany, depending on whether we read the folio or the quarto, associates the passing of Lear with not only the end of an era but, more broadly, with the end of a way of apprehending the world: 'We that are young | Shall never see so much, nor live so long' (F 5.3.301–2).

As I have argued throughout this chapter, there is considerable instability not only within the play but also between the different early texts in terms of their flickering evocations of an immanent force within bodies and of sympathetic energies between them. Indeed, our sense of the degree to which the play's desolate ending is imbued with anything resembling hope will very much depend on whether we read the quarto or the folio version of the final scene. The two are largely similar until Lear's final speech in F, which is followed immediately, according to the stage direction in F, by his death:

> And my poor fool is hanged. No, no, no life?
> Why should a dog, a horse, a rat have life,
> And thou no breath at all? Thou'lt come no more.
> Never, never, never, never, never.

---

[20] John F. Danby, *Shakespeare's Doctrine of Nature: A Study of King Lear* (London: Faber and Faber, 1948), 175.

[*To Kent*] Pray you, undo this button. Thank you, sir.
Do you see this? Look on her. Look, her lips.
Look there, look there.   *He dies.*

(F 5.3.281–7)

There are, of course, many ways in which this scene can be performed. But Lear's language suggests that he may well die in the belief that Cordelia is alive. He has been scrutinizing her body for any sign of life and seems to see on her lips a trace of breath, which he exultantly invites those present to confirm. The 'button' he asks Kent to undo could be on his own clothing, which would take us back to the heath where he attempted to strip himself of his superfluous 'lendings'. But it is more likely a button on Cordelia's costume, assuming that she is still in the military garb that would have been appropriate to the battle a few scenes earlier: in this reading, Lear is trying to give his reviving daughter more room to breathe. If Lear dies in the belief that Cordelia is alive, then perhaps, on some level, he dies feeling 'redeemed', or freed, of 'all sorrows | That ever I have felt' (F 5.3.241–2). It is a delusion, but a joyous one, at least in some performances. Q's ending is considerably darker, in that the faint glimmer of hope represented in Lear's final observations of Cordelia is denied him and us. His last speech in full in Q is:

And my poor fool is hanged. No, no life.
Why should a dog, a horse, a rat have life,
And thou no breath at all? O thou wilt come no more.
Never, never, ever—Pray you, undo
This button. Thank you, sir. O, O, O, O!

(Q Sc. 24, 300–4)

The 'O's are presumably groans, as elsewhere in Shakespeare, and Lear has only one more line to utter: 'Break heart, I prithee break' (Q 306), which in F is given to Kent and is spoken as a reaction to Lear's death rather than by Lear himself. In Q, then, Lear dies not 'redeemed' but broken hearted. There is no stage direction signalling the precise moment of his death as there is in F, but his final words suggest a radically different state of mind. Most readers who have found the end of the play unbearable have found it so on the basis of reading the folio version, since that is the one adopted in most conflated editions of the play. But the quarto is even darker, if that is possible. To return to Kott's observations, the characters who are left seem like automata, bereft of life and poetry as the world is bereft of life, acting out a series of echoes of life rather than life itself, since the indwelling principle of motion is gone. 'A brother throws over his shoulder the body of the brother he has killed. This is all there is. There will not be another king. The stage remains empty. Like the world.' (*Shakespeare Our Contemporary*, 365).

Select Bibliography

Bennett, Jane, *Vibrant Matter: A Political Ecology of Things* (Durham and London: Duke University Press, 2010).

B[oyle], R[obert], *A Free Enquiry Into the Vulgarly Receiv'd Notion of Nature* (London: for John Taylor, 1685).

Bradley, A. C., *Shakespearean Tragedy: Hamlet, Othello, King Lear, Macbeth* (1904; New York: Fawcett World Library, 1965).

Bratton, J. S., *Plays in Performance: King Lear* (Bristol: Bristol Classical Press, 1987).

Bruckner, Lynne, and Dan Brayton, eds., *Ecocritical Shakespeare* (Farnham, Surrey: Ashgate, 2011).

Burwick, Frederick, and Paul Douglass, eds., *The Crisis in Modernism: Bergson and the Vitalist Controversy* (Cambridge: Cambridge University Press, 1992).

Carlyle, Thomas, *On Heroes, Hero Worship and the Heroic in History* (1841; rpt. E-book Classics), 13–14. 3 January 2014. http://site.ebrary.com.

Coudert, Allison P., *The Impact of Kabbalah in the Seventeenth Century: The Life and Thought of Francis Mercury van Helmont, 1614–1698* (Leyden: Brill, 1998).

Danby, John F., *Shakespeare's Doctrine of Nature: A Study of King Lear* (London: Faber and Faber, 1948).

Debus, Allen G., *The English Paracelsians* (New York: Franklin Watts, 1966).

Debus, Allen G., ed., *Medicine in Seventeenth Century England* (Berkeley: University of California Press, 1974).

Egan, Gabriel, 'Gaia and the Great Chain of Being' in Bruckner and Brayton, 57–70.

Foakes, R. A., *Hamlet versus Lear: Cultural Politics and Shakespeare's Art* (Cambridge: Cambridge University Press, 1993).

Fraser, Mariam, Sarah Kember and Celia Lury, eds., *Inventive Life: Approaches to the New Vitalism* (London: Sage, 2006).

Greenblatt, Stephen, et al., eds., *Norton Shakespeare* (New York and London: W. W. Norton, 2008).

Greenblatt, Stephen, 'Shakespeare and the Exorcists', in *After Strange Texts: The Role of Theory in the Study of Literature*, ed. Gregory S. Jay and David L. Miller (University, AL: University of Alabama Press, 1985), 101-23.

Hazlitt, William, *The Characters of Shakespeare's Plays*, 3rd edn. (London: John Templeman, 1836).

Johnson, Samuel, ed., *The Plays of William Shakespeare* vol. 6 (London: J. and R. Tonson et al., 1765).

Jones, G. Lloyd, *The Discovery of Hebrew in Tudor England: A Third Language* (Manchester: Manchester University Press, 1983).

Kott, Jan, *Shakespeare Our Contemporary*, trans. Boleslaw Taborski (1964; repr. New York: W. W. Norton, 1974).

Lamb, Charles, 'On the Tragedies of Shakespeare', in *The Works of Charles Lamb in Two Volumes* (London: for C. and J. Ollier, 1818), 2: 1-36.

Latour, Bruno, *Politics of Nature: How to Bring the Sciences into Democracy* (Cambridge, MA and London: Harvard University Press, 2004).

Latour, Bruno, *Reassembling the Social: An Introduction to Actor-Network-Theory* (Oxford: Oxford University Press, 2005).

Leggatt, Alexander, *Shakespeare in Performance: King Lear* (Manchester and New York: Manchester University Press, 1991).

Marks, John, *Gilles Deleuze: Vitalism and Multiplicity* (London: Pluto Press, 1998).

Orgel, Stephen, and A. R. Braunmuller, eds., *King Lear (the Quarto and Folio Texts)*, Pelican Shakespeare (New York and London: Penguin, 2000).

Packham, Catherine, *Eighteenth-Century Vitalism: Bodies, Culture, Politics* (Houndmills, Basingstoke: Palgrave Macmillan, 2012).

Pagel, Walter, *Paracelsus: An Introduction to Philosophical Medicine in the Era of the Renaissance* (Basel and New York: S. Karger, 1958).

Paster, Gail Kern, *Humoring the Body: Emotions and the Shakespearean Stage* (Chicago: University of Chicago Press, 2004).

Rogers, John, *The Matter of Revolution: Science, Poetry, and Politics in the Age of Milton* (Ithaca, NY, and London: Cornell University Press, 1996).

Shannon, Laurie, *The Accommodated Animal: Cosmopolity in Shakespearean Locales* (Chicago and London: University of Chicago Press, 2013).

Sullivan, Garrett A., Jr., *Sleep, Romance and Human Embodiment: Vitality from Spenser to Milton* (Cambridge: Cambridge University Press, 2012).

Taylor, Gary, and Michael Warren, ed., *The Division of the Kingdoms: Shakespeare's Two Versions of King Lear* (Oxford: Clarendon Press, 1983).

Tillyard, E. M. W., *The Elizabethan World Picture* (1942; repr. New York: Vintage Books, 1959).

Traub, Valerie, 'The Nature of Norms in Early Modern England: Anatomy, Cartography, *King Lear*', *South Central Review* 26 (2009), 42–81.

Urkowitz, Steven, *Shakespeare's Revision of King Lear* (Princeton: Princeton University Press, 1980).

[Vaughan, Thomas], *Lumen de Lumine: or, a new Magicall Light, discovered and Illuminated to the World* {London: for H. Blunden, 1651).

Warren, Michael, ed., *The Complete King Lear, 1608-1623* (Berkeley and London: University of California Press, 1989).

Watson, Robert N., *Back to Nature: The Green and the Real in the Late Renaissance* (Philadelphia: University of Pennsylvania Press, 2006).

Wells, Stanley, Gary Taylor, et al. eds., *William Shakespeare: The Complete Works*, (Oxford: Clarendon Press, 1986).

Wood, Matthew, *Vitalism: The History of Herbalism, Homeopathy, and Flower Essences* (1992; rpt. Berkeley, CA: North Atlantic Books, 2005).

Zimmerman, Leo M., 'Surgery', in Debus, ed., *Medicine in Seventeenth Century England*, 49–69.

CHAPTER 27

....

O HORROR! HORROR! HORROR!
Macbeth *and Fear*

....

ANDREW J. POWER

In discussing the peculiar type of pleasure involved in watching or reading tragedy, and in particular Shakespeare's *Macbeth*, Marjorie Garber turns to Freud's *Beyond the Pleasure Principle* (1920) and finds that

> A tragedy is like an unpleasurable memory—or rather a displacement of that repressed memory into theatrical performance. This compulsion to repeat, this 'perpetual recurrence of the same thing' that strikes us as uncanniness in life and as structure in art, is one of the functions performed in Shakespeare's plays by the figure of the ghost.[1]

A ghost is only one of the many structural tools that Shakespeare repeatedly deploys in *Macbeth* to arouse the sensation of horror in its audience. In the play the allusive powers of contemporary and traditional horror motifs (like the appearance of a ghost) are augmented by a persistent pattern of visual, aural, and rhetorical signals that constantly direct the playgoer to the experience of fear.

In this chapter I will examine some of the cultural and literary influences that helped to shape the original play, looking at several of the ways that Shakespeare uses intertexts to help generate a horrific atmosphere. I will then consider some of the influences that *Macbeth* has had on the Gothic genre and finally review some of the ways that recent stage directors have attempted to re-imagine the horror of the play for modern audiences. By examining the particulars of one production of the play, in which Dominic Goold uses motifs from modern horror, I will explore the similarly horrifying intertextual resonances that the play must have created for its original audiences. Horror is not necessarily universal but is

Note: I have used *The Oxford Shakespeare* throughout the body of my essay, and which would read for the chapter title (2.3.62) 'O horror, horror, horror!'; in my title, however, it is quoted from Kenneth Muir's edition of *Macbeth*, The Arden Shakespeare, Second Series (London: Methuen, 1951; 1984). Muir's editorial intervention is illuminating, the added exclamation marks helping to capture the theme of my essay, if not the play.

[1] Marjorie Garber, *Shakespeare's Ghost Writers: Literature as Uncanny Causality* (London and New York: Methuen, 1987), 14.

rather bound to contemporary anxieties. However, *Macbeth* calls attention to the processes and effects of fear so insistently that appropriations of the play and modern productions are forced to engage Shakespeare's text in creative ways. They reconfigure its treatment of the phenomenon of horror to realize the experience of fear for contemporary audiences. A detailed examination of the play's sources, its adaptations and modern productions, can help us to understand how horror is generated and regenerated for succeeding generations.

MACBETH, AS HORROR

The first scene brings a powerfully visual apparition to Shakespeare's stage in the form of three Witches, second only to the ghost in *Hamlet* as a fearsome opening move.[2] The second scene includes a bloody battle narrative so gruesome that it elicits the question 'Dismayed not this our noble captains' (1.2.34). By the third scene, when we eventually see Macbeth upon the stage, he is indeed startled in a way that he does not seem to have been during the gory battle described in the previous scene: 'Good sir, why do you start and seem to fear' (1.3.49)? It helps to highlight the fearful mood created by the Witches that Macbeth 'Nothing afeard of what [him]self did[] make, | Strange images of death' 1.3.94-5, is struck dumb with fear by his encounter with the Weird Sisters, or at least by the 'horrible imaginings' (1.3.137) that they inspire in him.[3] Indeed, when their first 'prophetic greeting' (1.3.76) that he will be Thane of Cawdor proves to be true, Macbeth paints a vivid portrait of what it is to be truly terrified:

> ... why do I yield to that suggestion
> Whose horrid image doth unfix my hair
> And make my seated heart knock at my ribs
> Against the use of nature?
>
> (1.3.133-6)

This 'horrid image', planted in Macbeth's mind by the Witches, 'Shakes so [his] single state of man that function | Is smothered' in him (1.3.139-40). He cannot move for fear.

In spite of his apparent immunity to violence and brutality in the first half of the play, Macbeth is rarely onstage in any state other than fear. He himself becomes part of what he calls the 'present horror [of] the time' (2.1.59), but for an audience it is his emotional state that matters as their experience of the play is for the most part mediated by him. The play has a set of stage effects that help to generate this fearful tension. Although it would originally have been staged in the outdoor Globe theatre during daylight hours, the play mostly takes place at night and it is pervaded by a sinisterly darkened atmosphere: 'There's husbandry in heaven, | Their candles are all out' (2.1.4-5). It is not simply that it is night.

---

[2] Though never actually referred to as 'witches' in the spoken text they would have been immediately recognizable as this popular (if unnerving) stage figure to a contemporary audience. They have also correctly been connected to figures as diverse as the Nordic Fates (or Wyrdes) (see Laura Annawyn Shamas, *"We Three": The Mythology of Shakespeare's Weird Sisters*, New York: Peter Lang, 2007, 10) and the classical Furies (Arthur Magee, 'Macbeth' and the Furies', *Shakespeare Survey* 19 (1966), 55–6).

[3] Banquo may draw attention to Macbeth's unlikely fear a second time when he says to the Witches, 'Speak then to me, who neither beg nor *fear* | Your favours nor your hate' (58–9).

There is also a hint of caution or maybe even fatalism in the 'husbandry' that causes the unspecified deities of the heavens to leave the world below in darkness. And even in the daytime scenes of the play 'dark night strangles the travelling lamp' and 'darkness does the face of earth entomb | When living light should kiss it' (2.4.7-10). The 'travelling lamp' (the sun) is not just out, it is murdered and the earth too is buried before its time.

In the soundscape of the play too there are haunting effects: thunder (1.1.1SD, 1.3.1SD, 3.5.1SD, 4.1.1SD, 84SD, 92SD, 102SD), drums (1.3.27SD), knocking (2.2.8, 63SD, 67SD, 71SD and throughout 2.3), bells (2.1.61SD, 2.3.80SD), 'A cry ... of women' (5.5.7SD), the eerie haut-boys (1.6.1SD, 1.7.1SD, 4.1.121SD), as well as perhaps a croaking raven (1.5.37-8), a scream-ing owl, and crying crickets (2.2.15).[4] This atmosphere is all a part of the nightmare world that the central characters come to inhabit. We hear of 'wicked dreams [that] abuse | The curtained sleep' (2.1.50-1), and are told that Macbeth 'hath murdered sleep' (2.2.40) so that 'terrible dreams | ... shake [him] nightly' (3.2.20-1) and he 'lack[s] the season of all natures, sleep' (3.4.140). Late in the play (5.1), his wife's madness and eerie somnambulism suggest that the barriers between nightmare and the waking world have broken down entirely.

The spiritual, perhaps cosmic, magnitude of the Macbeths' crime should not be under-estimated. Macduff describes the killing of Duncan as a 'sacrilegious murder [which] hath broke ope | The Lord's anointed temple and stole thence | The life o'th'building' (2.3.66-8).[5] As Michael Hattaway observes, 'Regicide was akin to deicide: both crimes were of a differ-ent order to homicide.'[6] It is thus no wonder that it is at this moment that the most pecu-liar image of horror is uttered, one that, to a modern auditor more familiar with popular culture, is likely to resonate with contemporary cinematic and television versions of the undead (*48 Days Later, World War Z, The Walking Dead*):

> Up, up, and see
> The great doom's image. Malcolm, Banquo,
> As from your graves rise up, and walk like sprites
> To countenance this horror.
>
> (2.3.77-80)

Here, Shakespeare is evoking a traditional horror motif from his own age. The vision of the walking dead evokes 1 *Corinthians*, which foresees doomsday when the dead will rise from their graves and walk again to judgement.

> Behold, I shew you a mystery; We shall not all sleep, but we shall all be changed, In a moment, in the twinkling of an eye, at the last trump: for the trumpet shall sound, and the dead shall be raised incorruptible, and we shall be changed. (KJV, 1 *Corinthians* 15: 51-2)

There are further scriptural parallels in Macbeth's assertion that Duncan's 'virtues | Will plead like angels, trumpet-tongued, against | The deep damnation' of his murder (1.7.18-20).[7] In

---

[4] David L. Kranz explores the formal poetic patterning, the sounds and echoes that make up the 'tune' of the play ('The Sounds of Supernatural Soliciting in *Macbeth*', *Studies in Philology* 100:3 (Summer, 2003), 346–83).

[5] This echoes Duncan's conceit of the 'temple-haunting' martlet (1.6.4) that seemed to him to indicate a healthy atmosphere in Macbeth's castle at his first arrival.

[6] Michael Hattaway, 'Tragedy and Political Authority', in Claire McEachern, ed., *The Cambridge Companion to Shakespearean Tragedy* (Cambridge: Cambridge University Press, 2002, 2004), 101–22 (106).

[7] See esp. *Revelations* 8-11. See Naseeb Shaheen, *Biblical References in Shakespeare's Plays* (London and Cranbury, NJ: Associated University Press), 1999, 626–7.

pre-Reformation England, church walls all across the land would have depicted such scenes as a reminder to the faithful to keep in mind that promised day of Doom. One such painting had adorned the Guild Chapel in Stratford-upon-Avon; and although Shakespeare was not yet born when his father, as Chamberlain of the town, was charged with removing such relics of Papist superstition, he will surely have known of the image.[8] It is tempting to see a particularly personal terror for Shakespeare in Lady Macbeth's line, ''Tis the eye of childhood | That fears a painted devil' (2.2.52–3) but Judgement of this kind for any Christian of this era must have been an ominous prospect, potent with the horror of damnation.

HELL-CASTLE AND ITS DOOR KEEPER

Preoccupation with the Judgement ensured that images of hell castle and of the mouth of hell were popular motifs of horror in late medieval English religious art.[9] They were often found in church wall painting, typically located on God's left at the bottom of the great Doom paintings that took pride of place above the chancel arch. It is to this tradition in its dramatic form that the Porter alludes when he says, 'If a man were porter of hell-gate he should have old turning the key' (2.3.1–2). 'Who's there, i'th' name of Beelzebub?' he asks, and we might be tempted to look above to the chancel arch for 'a farmer that hanged himself on th'expectation of plenty', for 'an equivocator, … [who] could not equivocate to heaven', or for 'an English tailor come hither for stealing out of a French hose'; for in the old Dooms you will indeed find 'some of all professions that go the primrose way to th'everlasting bonfire' (2.3.3–18). While the Porter scene is certainly comic, its imagery sustains the horrific allusions to the Doom and, even in its comedy, intensifies the detail of the image by inviting us in to view its tortured sinners one by one. Glynne Wickham linked the hell-castle of this scene to the Harrowing of Hell plays of the medieval mystery cycles, with the knocking at the gate reminiscent of the knocking that heralds Christ's arrival at the gate of hell.[10] While the defeat of these devils by Christ was staged as comic knockabout on one level, mystery plays, like church paintings, were primarily a devotional tool and a reminder of the genuinely terrifying pre-reformation (or Catholic) belief in devils. By generating this particular nexus of associated imagery, the comic Porter is made to evoke the theological horror of everlasting hellfire immediately after the tragic protagonist has committed a deed that will ensure his eternal damnation.

[8] Although the Catholic-leaning John Shakespeare took payment for his work, rather than defacing the walls and removing the stained glass (which also should have been taken out), he gave a simple whitewash and left it at that—as others did in churches all across England. In 1571 the stained glass was finally removed. See Anthony Holden, *William Shakespeare* (London: Little Brown, 1999), 28–9.

[9] The television series, *Buffy the Vampire Slayer* (1997–2003) recycled the idea for popular modern Gothic. The town of Sunnydale, which was the setting for the show, turned out to be built on a 'hellmouth'.

[10] Glynne Wickham, 'Hell-Castle and its Door-keeper', in Kenneth Muir and Philip Edwards, eds., *Aspects of Macbeth: Articles Reprinted from Shakespeare Survey* (Cambridge: Cambridge University Press, 1977), 42.

GHOSTS

When the ghost of Banquo appears at the banquet (3.4.37SD) he does so as only the most recent of a line of stage ghosts that goes back to the Roman tragedian Seneca and beyond.[11] This tradition informed the stage ghosts of Elizabethan England, from the appearance of the ghost of Gorlois in Thomas Hughes's *The Misfortunes of Arthur* (1587) to the opening scene of Shakespeare's own *Hamlet*.[12] In Seneca, there are ghosts who prophesy the deaths of tyrants and murderers and who foretell their torture in the underworld in *Octavia* (619-23), *Thyestes* (83-6, 101ff.), and *Agamemnon* (39-52).[13] Macbeth's description of Banquo's 'gory locks' may even borrow a detail from Hector's Ghost who appeared to Andromanche in *Troas*, and whose face was 'masked by filthy hair' as he 'shook his head and spoke' (*Troas*, 450-1).[14] Laius too cuts a grisly figure, as 'He stands caked in the blood that poured over his body, with his hair covered in squalid filth' (*Oedipus*, 624-5). Banquo's ghost does not have to speak in order to evoke the same impression, since Macbeth's response gives us all that we need: 'Thou canst not say I did it. Never shake | Thy gory locks at me' (3.4.49-50). The appearance of the ghost is accompanied by a rhetorical pattern that completes the classical allusion to this type of stage figure. It begins in the fourth scene when Macbeth meditates his passage to the crown:

> Stars, hide your fires,
> Let not light see my black and deep desires;
> The eye wink at the hand; yet let that be,
> Which the eye fears, when it is done, to see

(1.4.50-3)

Appeals to the heavens to close their eyes to sinful action, and for darkness or the forces of darkness to hide sinful deeds are a common feature in the Senecan tradition and indeed in the classically styled English tragedies of the Elizabethan period.[15] In Seneca's *Thyestes*, here translated by Cambridge scholar Jasper Heywood (1560), there is a similar passage:

> The Heavens be hid, about the Pole
> when shine the stars on high,
> And flames with wonted beams of light
> do deck the painted sky.

---

[11] All references to Seneca, except where an Elizabethan translator is specified, are taken from Seneca, *Tragedies*, 2 vols. ed. and trans. John G. Fitch. Loeb Classical Library (London and Cambridge MA: Harvard University Press, 2002-4).

[12] I have outlined this tradition in more detail and specifically in relation to the trapdoor (perhaps the Elizabethan equivalent of the lift in modern horror) in 'What the Hell is Under the Stage: Trapdoor Use in the English Senecan Tradition', *English* 60:231 (2011), 276-96.

[13] After Banquo's ghost has departed Macbeth echoes a line from this passage of *Agamemnon* ('Soon now the house will swim in blood answering blood', 44) ruminating, 'It will have blood, they say. Blood will have blood' (3.4.121).

[14] Talthybius relates the appearance of Achilles' ghost to the Trojans at the beginning of this play, demanding the sacrifice of Polyxena (*Troas*, 195-6).

[15] See e.g. *Jocasta* (1.4.32-5, 2.3.36-9) and *The Spanish Tragedy* (2.4.3, 16-19).

>   Let darkest night be made, and let
>   the day the heavens forsake
>
>   (95-102).[16]

In Shakespeare's play, Duncan (not having heard Macbeth's aside) continues his speech with a network of imagery that connects Macbeth to the cannibalistic feast of Thyestes: 'in his commendations I am fed. | It is a banquet to me' (1.4.55-6). In *Thyestes* the title character is fed his own children by his brother at a bloody banquet, supposedly held in his honour. The crime is so horrifying to the gods that they hide their celestial light from the world so as not to see it. In the context of these allusions, the darkness that engulfs the realm of Shakespeare's play, the wine and blood-soaked grooms of Duncan's chamber, and even the bizarre end of Duncan's horses (who 'ate each other', 2.4.18) take on a slightly different significance. The bloody banquet motif had developed in the period from its Senecan original into something of a horrifying set piece. So, for instance, Shakespeare's own *Titus Andronicus* (*c*.1590) climaxes in a cannibal feast orchestrated by its eponymous hero who enters '*like a cook*' to feed the empress Tamora with the heads of her sons 'both baked in [a] pie' (5.3.25SD, 59)); while in George Peele's *The Battel of Alcazar* (1588-9), the Presenter introduces a dumb show at the beginning of the fourth Act that has very little bearing on the play proper, in which 'a bloudie banket' is brought in for Sebastian 'and his noble peeres' (4.1.1063-70). The props called for in the marginal notes include 'Dead mans heads [in dishes, ...] Bones, [and] Blood'.[17]

The entry of Banquo's ghost to haunt Macbeth at the banquet fits neatly into this tradition, but he is associated with the image of the Thyestean feast even earlier, when he discusses his movements with his newly crowned king and queen. There is a fixation on the future banquet here that must augur ill for him. Macbeth greets him as 'our chief guest', and Lady Macbeth adds 'If he had been forgotten | It had been as a gap in our great feast, | And all-thing unbecoming' (3.1.11-13). Banquo is the one potential obstruction to Macbeth's ambitions. There is to be a 'solemn supper' (3.1.14) that evening, Macbeth reiterates, and, as with the banquet promised to Duncan in the earlier scene, 'chief guest' becomes a euphemism

---

[16] Jasper Heywood (trans.), *Thyestes*, by Seneca, in A. K. McIlwraith (ed.), *Five Elizabethan Tragedies*, The World's Classics (London: Oxford University Press, 1938). I have dealt with this motif in greater detail in Andrew J. Power, '"Why should I play the Roman fool, and die | On mine own sword?": The Senecan Tradition in *Macbeth*', in Willy Maley and Rory Loughnane, eds., *Celtic Shakespeare: The Bard and the Borderers*, (Aldershot: Ashgate, 2013), 139-56, 142-3. Compare also *Hamlet*, "Tis now the very witching time of night, | When churchyards yawn, and hell itself breathes out | Contagion to this world. Now could I drink hot blood, | And do such bitter business as the day | Would quake to look on' (3.2.377-381). In this image too Shakespeare links the image of the Doom (hell-mouth and all) with the more classical suggestion that the sun (or Phoebus) should be afraid or too disgusted to look down on the crimes taking place in the world.

[17] See Chris Meads, *Banquets Set Forth: Banqueting in English Renaissance Drama*, The Revels Plays Companion Library (Manchester: Manchester University Press, 2001), 81. These details are not recorded in the Malone Society edition, W. W. Greg, ed., *The Battle of Alcazar* 1594, The Malone Society Reprints (Chiswick: Malone Society, 1907). For Chris Meads the banquet provides Peele with 'a metaphor of the war, deceit, and death which follow it in the play' (*Banquets*, 81). See also Andrew J. Power, 'Lady Macbeth and Othello: Convention and Transgression in Early Modern Tragedy', in Rory Loughnane and Edel Semple, eds., *Staged Transgression* (London: Palgrave Macmillan, 2013), 224-38 (231-2).

for victim.[18] When Banquo explains that his journey cannot be delayed, Macbeth feigns disappointment but concludes 'we'll take tomorrow' (3.1.22).[19] The immediate meaning is that he will take his counsel tomorrow instead, but there is also a suggestion, in the context of the prophecy regarding Banquo's issue, that Macbeth, knowing when Banquo will be on the road, can grasp control of the future, i.e. 'take tomorrow'. Even Banquo himself responds to the question of how far he rides in terms of the proposed banquet, 'As far, my Lord as will fill up the time | 'Twixt this and supper' (3.1.25-6). All of this food imagery, taken in the context of its beginnings in the allusion to Thyestes, is meant to remind us of those classically styled English tragedies in which we would expect a bloody banquet. Senecan convention will lead the audience to expect that Banquo and Fleance will make up the food of the feast; and at the end of the next scene Macbeth closes his equally Senecan invocation of night with an image that indeed makes them the metaphorical food of his blood lust, 'Good things of day begin to droop and drowse, | Whiles night's black agents to their *preys* do rouse. | … | Things bad begun make strong themselves by ill' (3.2.53-4, 56). As he imagines Banquo and his son becoming the 'prey' of his 'black agents', he closes this second invocation of night with what is another Senecan parallel, perhaps specifically echoing John Studley's translation of *Agamemnon* (1566), 'The safest path to mischiefe is by mischiefe open still'.[20]

By the end of the play Macbeth has himself become the horror that earlier made him jump and fear and tremble more than any other character in the play. A shriek offstage makes him acknowledge as much in one final cannibalistic image of the horror that he has become:

> I have almost forgot the taste of fears.
> The time has been my senses would have cooled
> To hear a night-shriek, and my fell of hair
> Would at a dismal treatise rouse and stir
> As life were in't. I have supped full with horrors.
> Direness, familiar to my slaughterous thoughts,
> Cannot once start me.

> (5.5.9-15)

The bloody banquet motif, so popular in late Elizabethan tragedy from the opening scene of *The Misfortunes of Arthur* to the closing scene of *Titus Andronicus*, has been long since forgotten by popular audiences, as indeed are its origins in *Thyestes'* fatal banquet. The same is true of Salome's similarly bloody banquet (in which she demanded the head of John the Baptist from Herod Antipas as payment of his drunken promise to give her anything she wanted), or the Slaughter of the Innocents (committed by Herod the Great, and father of Herod Antipas) both of which, like the Harrowing of Hell discussed above,

---

[18] There are also resonances here with the Last Supper that link Macbeth and Lady Macbeth to Judas' great betrayal. The suggestion of cannibalism then also hints at the controversy over Catholic transubstantiation of which the murders of Duncan and Banquo become, in a way, travesties.

[19] I have retained 'take' from the Folio. Wells accepts Malone's emendation to 'talk'. This simplifies the meaning, but unnecessarily, I think, stripping away the playful rhetoric of the possession of time.

[20] John Studley, trans., *Agamemnon*, in Thomas Newton (ed.), *Seneca: His Tenne Tragedies* [1581], 2 vols., intro. T. S. Eliot, The Tudor Translations Series, 2nd ser. 11 (London: Constable and Co., 1927), 2: 106. Another line that may contribute here is 'The thing he feares he doth augment who heapeth sinne to sinne' (108).

were staged in the biblical pageant sequences of medieval drama. Macbeth's embarrassing behaviour at the banquet may owe something to Herod Antipas, as his slaughter of the children of Macduff certainly aligns him with Herod the Great. In their own time, these scenes must have evoked some of the most horrific and terrifying episodes both from the Bible (and biblical pageants) and from classical tragedy (and its popular Elizabethan adaptations). However, it is more difficult to account for the continued efficacy of these tropes when these cultural referents are lost to history. One of the tasks that traditional scholarship has undertaken has been to unearth these sources to help readers understand what lies behind the plays, not just to match up one text with another older one, but to help understand what a contemporary audience or reader might have thought or felt on hearing an echo of some older horrifying source.

SHAKESPEARE AND GOTHIC

Writing specifically about *Macbeth*, but also clearly thinking about Shakespeare's corpus more generally, Muriel C. Bradbrook writes,

> The repetitions, echoes and restatements which are to be detected in Shakespeare offer more than mere opportunity for pedantic correlation; they are alternative statements, varied embodiments of those deep-seated and permanent impulses which underlie all his work and make it, in spite of its variety, a vast and comprehensive whole—a single structure, though of Gothic design.[21]

The haunting analogy that she pursues tells us something about the play whose historical sources she endeavours to outline and about the way it affects those who read it and watch it. Digging deep into the chronicles that underlie the play, she attempts to unravel its mysterious and distant past. At the same time her Gothic conceit acts as a reminder of Shakespeare's own enormous influence on the Gothic genre in which we regularly find the ghosts of Shakespeare's characters.

For example, Ann Radcliffe—whose favourite tragedy was reported to be *Macbeth*—[22] uses a quotation from the play as the epigraph for Book 2 Chapter 9 of her great Gothic novel, *The Italian* (1797): 'I am settled, and bend up | Each corporal agent to this terrible feat' (1.7.79–80).[23] Indeed this chapter is indebted on many levels to the scene in *Macbeth* from which Radcliffe excerpts these two lines of *Macbeth*. A sinister monk named Schedoni proceeds (in a castle) towards the murder of the innocent protagonist Ellena. His own vacillations, and his argument with his reluctant henchman, Spalatro, repeatedly echo the argument between the Macbeths

---

[21] Muriel C. Bradbrook, 'The Sources of *Macbeth*', *Shakespeare Survey* 4 (1951) 35–48 (35).

[22] See Charles Bucke, *On the Beauties, Harmonies and Sublimities of Nature* (new edn.; 3 vols.; London: T. Tegg and Sons, 1837), 2: 123, cit. Rictor Norton, 'Ann Radcliffe, "The Shakespeare of Romance Writers"' in Christy Desmet and Anne Williams, eds., *Shakespearean Gothic* (Cardiff: University of Wales Press, 2009), 37–59 (58n.).

[23] Ann Radcliffe, *The Italian*, ed. Frederick Garber, notes and intro. E. J. Clery (Oxford: Oxford University Press, 1968, 1998), 225. This is one particular instance of the infectious horror that *Macbeth* has lent to the Gothic genre, but as Christy Desmet and Anne Williams observe: 'In *Hamlet* and *Macbeth*, in particular, Gothic writers found irregularity, irrationality and a sublime ignorance of

before the murder of Duncan. But the chapter also contains resonances of other moments surrounding the murder of this 'most sainted king' (4.3.110): noises off startle and suspend the two villains in their progress; a floating and bloody hand invisible to one (like Macbeth's 'air-drawn dagger', 3.4.61) beckons the other on to murder; a candle, cups of wine, and a dagger are passed back and forth like leftover stage props from a recent production of the play; and Spalatro is given a vision of a former victim who seems included to remind us of the appearance of Banquo's ghost. Radcliffe's most overt debt to Shakespeare's tragedy, however, is in the way that the horrified emotion produced by the murderers' advance involves sympathy not (in spite of the innocent and slumbering protagonist) for the person who is to be murdered, but for those who would commit that 'more than bloody deed' (2.4.22); our experience as readers is almost entirely mediated through Schedoni's experience in the same way that our experience of Shakespeare's play is mediated through the Macbeths. It is their fear of discovery, fear of the supernatural, and fear of repercussions that arrest us as audience and readers.[24]

In modern instances of the Gothic genre Shakespeare's influence is also evident. In the sixth and seventh chapters of Stephanie Meyer's (improbably) popular novel *Twilight*—entitled respectively 'Scary Stories' and 'Nightmare'—Bella's discovery and acceptance of the vampire Edward Cullen's true nature is framed within her own study of Shakespeare's *Macbeth* at high-school. Her difficulty in writing a paper about the play coincides with her discovery of Edward's true nature; this horrific realization proving only slightly more difficult for Bella than her efforts at interpreting Shakespeare's play.[25] The terrifying energies of *Macbeth* have long attracted writers of Gothic and horror who have drawn on its allusive potential. But if the play has encouraged others, including Radcliffe and Meyer, to tell scary stories, producers and directors of the play have borrowed in turn from the modern genre of horror.

HORROR AND SHAKESPEARE ON STAGE

Rupert Goold's production of *Macbeth* at the Chichester Festival Theatre in 2007 was an enormous critical success.[26] It made use of several recognizable motifs from modern horror, and this innovation caught the attention of several reviewers. Ben Brantley, writing in *The*

"the rules". They revelled in a promiscuous mixing of literary modes, of fiction and history, of the real and the supernatural, of the medieval and the barbarous. Readers of Shakespeare and writers of the Gothic began to see that "Nature" was a more capacious category than hitherto had been recognized. In producing "the Gothic" in and through "Shakespeare", critics and novelists alike began to redefine "nature", and particularly "human nature" ' (Desmet and Williams, *Shakespearean Gothic*, 3).

[24] For David Bevington, Macbeth 'is a man of poetic sensitivity and extraordinary insight into his own emotional drives. We are invited to sympathize with him, even in his torments of guilt, and to see things through his eyes' (Bevington, 'Tragedy in Shakespeare's Career', 65).

[25] See Yvette Kisor, 'Narrative Layering and "High-Culture" Romance', in Amy M. Clarke and Marijane Osborn, eds., *The Twilight Mystique: Critical Essays on the Novels and Films* (Jefferson, NC: McFarland, 2010), 35–59 (38–40).

[26] Ben Brantley, 'Something Wicked This Way Comes', *New York Times*, 15 February 2008. The production was subsequently played in The Gielgud Theatre, Brooklyn Academy of Music and on Broadway before being adapted and transferred to the small screen in 2010 for the Great Performances Series on BBC.

New York Times, declared it 'chilling', and noted that it contained 'enough flash [sic], blood and mutilated bodies to satisfy a Wes Craven fan'.[27] It began, unconventionally, with the battle narrative of the 'bloody man' (1.2.7–42, 1) redeployed from the second scene, a speech that gives us much of the blood and gore that Brantley describes and is, once its compliments to 'brave Macbeth' (1.2.16) are removed, horrific enough. We hear of Macbeth's 'brandished steel | Which smoked with bloody execution, | [and how he] ... | Carved out his passage till he faced the slave, | Which ne'er shook hands nor bade farewell to him | Till he unseamed him from the nave to th' chops, | And fixed his head upon our battlements' (1.2.17–23). In the specific context of medieval Scottish warfare, this is predictably 'brave', but we should not disregard the gleefully fulsome description of such butchery. We hear that Macbeth and Banquo fear nothing and seem to want to 'bathe in reeking wounds' (39). To the supposedly 'saintly' Duncan these words 'smack of honour' (44), but it is hard to imagine that to an audience they will smack of anything other than brutality. As Catherine Belsey astutely observes, 'The difference between this and the murder of Duncan, apart from the fact that this is more bloodthirsty, is that the battle is legitimate.'[28] Belsey compares the violence of one act with another in the play and ponders (for an academic readership) the difference in terms of legitimacy. Brantley (writing in a different genre) seeks to find a recognizable popular referent to convey a similar observation about the violence highlighted by a particular production. For Brantley's purposes it would be redundant to observe that the graphic descriptions of blood and violence in this type of battle narrative are a common feature of the Senecan styled English plays of the Elizabethan period.[29] Similarly, a modern director of the play must find a more recognizable set of referents to convey the horror of the play.

Goold set the play in some version of 1940s Russia, with TV screens around the stage showing clips of era-appropriate war footage. Before and between clips the screens displayed 'static', or 'noise', borrowing an unsettling effect from modern horror to use alongside the Witches' first speeches (after the battle narrative of 1.2). The use of static in horror may originally owe something to the opening titles of the 1960s TV series *The Outer Limits* (1963–5; 1995–9) which claimed to have wrested complete control of the viewer's TV sets from them. It warned its audience that they were about to experience the great adventure 'which reaches from the inner mind to the outer limits' (opening monologue). In recent years this same sense of drawing the viewer into the world of the horror movie has been used to great effect in films like *The Ring* (Gore Verbinski, 2002) and its sequel (Hideo Nakata, 2005), as well as, in a slightly different way, in the 'found footage' subgenre that includes films like *The Blair Witch Project* (Eduardo Sánchez and Daniel Myrick, 1999) and the *Paranormal Activity* (Oren Peli, 2007) series.

In Goold's set there were hanging light bulbs that flickered intermittently, gesturing towards some supernatural design, while in the opening scene the dank basement feel to the stage hinted at a hospital morgue). Such a set design recalls the creepy basement settings of Adrian Lyne's *Jacob's Ladder* (1990) or James Wan's *Saw* (2004), and, perhaps,

---

[27] The peril that the play's rhetoric discovers in falling asleep (see above) is perhaps what led Brantley to think of Craven's oeuvre, including the successful *Nightmare on Elm Street* series.

[28] Catherine Belsey, 'Gender and Family', in Claire McEachern, ed., *The Cambridge Companion to Shakespearean Tragedy* (Cambridge: Cambridge University Press, 2003), 121–41 (135).

[29] See e.g. George Gascoigne's *Jocasta* (5.2.37–200), Thomas Hughes's *The Misfortunes of Arthur* (2.1.1–76), and Thomas Kyd's *The Spanish Tragedy* (1.2.47–54).

the deserted and haunted childrens' hospital of Jaume Balaguero's *Fragile* (2005). The three witches, cast as sinister maids, waitresses, or nurses rounded out this unsettling effect. The efficacy of these allusive innovations is evident in the responses of newspaper reviewers. To Brantley the 'grimy, institutional sterility' of the set 'serv[ing] as a battlefield, a dining hall, a kitchen and an interrogation room, … always [felt] like a charnel house' (Brantley, 'Something Wicked'). And Nicholas de Jongh, similarly, called it a 'bewitching revelation' that generates 'shock, suspense and revulsion … confined within a windowless basement kitchen, perhaps a few tiers above hell' in a set that 'opens up to horrors'.[30] Two particularly resonant features of the set (that at first glance might seem extraordinarily mundane) merit further explication, as they were reminiscent, not of the horror of biblical judgement and apocalypse or of Senecan *scelus*, but of modern cinematic horror: an elevator and a kitchen.

THE ELEVATOR AND THE KITCHEN

In a later review of the same production at the Gielgud Theatre de Jongh again paid close attention to the set: 'This is a hell's kitchen to which the only entrance is an industrial lift that clanks up and down, bearing its human and ghostly cargo.'[31] Elevators and kitchens, as we will see, have become common sites of haunting in the modern horror genre: the elevator is a sort of inversion of Jacob's Ladder, described in *Genesis* (28:10-19). The 'Ladder of Salvation' which evolved from this tradition was a commonplace image in medieval art. Such images depicted ladders that extend upwards towards heaven, but also depicted demons, vices, and tempters trying to distract those on their journey from their upward course.[32] Typically, at the base of the ladder a dragon awaited the fallen, his jaws open. The implicit suggestion was that as much as providing a means of climbing virtuously to heaven the ladder also descends to hell. The elevator in modern horror films offers a similarly symbolic portal, through which dark forces can ascend, whether they be evil spirits from the foundations of a building or devils from the underworld itself.

Stanley Kubrick's *The Shining* (1980) includes perhaps the most famous use of this motif. In repeated mental flashes, Danny and his father, Jack Torrance, see the doors of the elevator open, pouring a flood of blood out into the corridor towards them. This image seems to represent both the dark and murderous history of the hotel and a promise of future bloodshed. The Dutch horror film by Dick Maas, *De Lift* (1983) gave an evil and angry human brain to its elevator. There is another chilling elevator scene in David Moreau and Xavier Palud's *The Eye* (2008). And, in John Erick Dowdle's *Devil* (2010) a group of sinners are trapped in a lift with the devil himself; he proceeds to wring confessions from each of his captives before killing them off one by one. A twist on this motif is found in the Coen Brothers' *Barton Fink* (1991) where John Goodman's cheerful and rather sweaty devil is ominously delivered via the lift to tempt and torment the title character. A set of episodes in *Angel* (1999-2004),

---

[30] Nicholas de Jongh, '*Macbeth* in hell's kitchen', *Evening Standard*, 4 June 2007.

[31] Nicholas de Jongh, 'The *Macbeth* of a Lifetime', *Evening Standard*, 27 September 2007.

[32] *Macbeth* may allude to this idea, alongside the coursing image inscribed in his 'vaulting ambition', when he says 'that is a step | On which I must fall down' (1.4.48-9). Appropriately, however, his ladder leads to a crown and not to heaven.

a spin off series from *Buffy the Vampire Slayer*, brought devils up from hell in a lift. It also provided the title character with the means to descend to the underworld. The joke in the end was that when he arrived at hell the elevator delivered him out into Los Angeles. Like Faustus, he discovered to his horror that hell is a state of mind: 'Why, this is hell, nor am I out of it' (1.3.76).[33] Recalling the location of the 'heavens' above a Shakespearean stage and the 'hell' beneath its trapdoor, Goold's use of an industrial elevator as the rear of stage entrance for Witches, Murderers, and a Ghost brought a set of horrific referents to his production, though modernized for a contemporary audience.

Goold's use of a large modern kitchen, where Macbeth delivered his solitary pre-banquet meditations, and where he later prepared a sandwich with a large kitchen knife while ordering Banquo's murder, was a similar innovation. The sink also doubled as the place where Lady Macbeth attempted to wash the blood from her hands. This clever mechanism for drawing together the preparation for slaughter and the clean-up in the aftermath also drew on a very common horror motif in which the domestic heart of the home becomes the most potent site of haunting. So for instance in *Gremlins* (1984) the mother of the house has to reclaim the kitchen from a group of the comical but frightening creatures. More recently, a chilling effect was achieved in *Sixth Sense* (M. Night Shyamalan, 1999) when the invisible spectral inhabitants of the home opened every cupboard and drawer in a matter of seconds—a trick that was redeployed with greater speed and perhaps shock value in *Paranormal Activity 2* (Tod Williams, 2010).

Kitchens can contain dangerous appliances, of course. But it seems likely that there is something of the essence of Freud's definition of the *unheimlich* or 'the uncanny' going on here; the German word literally translates as 'unhomely'. Freud describes the phenomenon as 'undoubtedly related to what is frightening—to what arouses dread and horror' but explains that it is not easy to define. Part of this difficulty resides in the fact that the word itself is Janus-faced, 'the uncanny is that class of the frightening which leads back to what is known of old and long familiar'.[34] That is, that the 'unheimlich', the 'uncanny', is in a way both homely—or 'long familiar'—and at the same time belongs to the frightening unknown. Macbeth puzzles out a similar difficulty for himself,

> He's here in double trust:
> First, as I am his kinsman and his subject,
> Strong both against the deed; then, as his host,
> Who should against his murderer shut the door,
> Not bear the knife myself.
>
> (1.7.12–16)

The ancient bonds of hospitality invoked by Macbeth have their equivalent in the expectation of warmth and safety associated with the kitchen space in modern family life.[35] When these bonds or expectations are broken the effect is terrifying (for Macbeth himself as for

---

[33] Christopher Marlowe, *Doctor Faustus*, in *The Complete Plays*, ed. J. B. Steane (London: Penguin, 1969, 1976).

[34] Sigmund Freud, 'The "Uncanny"' (1919), trans. Alix Strachey in *The Standard Edition of the Complete Psychological Works*, ed. and trans. James Strachey, vol. 17 (1917-19) (London: Hogarth Press, 1955), 218–52 (220).

[35] On another level Macbeth's duties are historically localized and fixed in the medieval world of the play.

the viewer of modern horror). Writing about Patrick Stewart's performance as Macbeth in the *Evening Standard*, Charles Spencer asserted, 'So charismatic is Stewart as an actor, that he can make the simple act of preparing a ham sandwich one of the scariest things you've ever seen.'[36] Stewart's Macbeth here also recalls the final Thyestean feast scene in Julie Taymor's *Titus* (1999) which gave Anthony Hopkins (playing the title role), in full chef regalia, the opportunity to playfully evoke his own Hannibal Lector persona, from *The Silence of the Lambs* (1991) series, as he prepared and then presented the flesh of Tamora's children for her to eat. In Goold's *Macbeth*, the result may be like an echo of the original performance effect. Indeed de Jongh went so far in his second review of the production as to write, 'It manages … freshly to convey the elemental sense of surprise, shock and supernatural horror that must have attended the tragedy's early 17th century performances and has long since been lost' (de Jongh, 27 September 2007). Goold's borrowings evoke modern horror in recognizable motifs that enhance the sense of horror already inherent in the play and replace some of the lost contemporary horrors (hell mouths and bloody banquets) with updated versions of the same (in the elevator and the kitchen).

CONCLUSION

Roman Polanski's film version of *Macbeth* (1971) has been embraced by critics and anthologists of horror and the play seems to do well when translated into this idiom.[37] However, to suggest that *Macbeth* is a horror fiction, in our modern sense, is anachronistic. Kenneth Branagh and Rob Ashford's more recent production of the play took a slightly different approach.[38] It was positively compared to 'elaborately detailed, thoroughly researched historical movies'; and the 'rain-soaked battle scene to rival anything seen in the movies' that opens the play was seen as a successful reimagining of the bloody captain's battle narrative. All this suggests that Branagh and Ashford think of the play as a history. But the same reviewer concludes, unfortunately, that audiences 'might do better to just go out and rent a copy of Branagh's *Henry V* instead'.[39] The review is harsh in its appraisal; but Branagh's success with Shakespeare's history plays may have influenced his treatment of *Macbeth*—even though Hemminges and Condell clearly decided not to place it among the Histories of the First Folio (1623). Another reviewer, who noted the 'thrills' of the production—'Hell's flames blaze through grilles. Daggers uncannily hover in mid air … and, on press night, sparks showered into the front row'—nevertheless concluded 'the overall effect is curiously dull'.[40] If the excitement of its battle scenes lent some

[36] Charles Spencer, 'The best Macbeth I have seen', *The Daily Telegraph*, 27 September 2007. http://www.telegraph.co.uk/culture/3668183/The-best-Macbeth-I-have-seen.html.

[37] Hutchings, 'Shakespeare and the Horror Film', 161.

[38] In the deconsecrated church of St Peter's, Ancoats in Manchester, 2013.

[39] Yoshi Makashima, 'Branagh's *Macbeth* leaves something to be desired', *Daily Collegian*, 22 October 2013. http://dailycollegian.com/2013/10/22/branagh's-'macbeth'-leaves-something-to-be-desired/.

[40] Kate Bassett, 'Kenneth Branagh's spot of bother at the Manchester International Festival', *Independent*, 6 July 2013. http://www.independent.co.uk/arts-entertainment/theatre-dance/reviews/theatre-review-macbeth--kenneth-branaghs-spot-of-bother-at-the-manchester-international-festival-8692542.html.

of the thrill of the regular skirmishes in the history plays to this production, it seems to have lost something else in the process.

It may be that the play itself resists any attempt to treat it as history, particularly following the advent of the modern horror genre. For it is a tragedy that repeatedly speaks of fear and of what it is to be afraid: from the opening horrors of the witches and the narrative of bloody battle that follows, we watch Macbeth afraid of his own 'thought' and 'imaginings' (1.3.137-8), afraid of his 'desire[s]' (1.7.41), of failure (1.7.59), and of the 'deep damnation' of eternal judgement (1.7.20). We then see him afraid 'to think what [he has] done' (2.2.49); we watch him afraid of Banquo (3.1.50) and Banquo foolishly 'dauntless' (53) when he, like Duncan, should have been afraid; we watch Macbeth and his wife live their lives in fear, 'eat … in fear' and sleep in nightmare (3.2.19-21); and we, the audience, are also terrified by certain effects in the play which are there to make us fearful. What would have made people living in Stuart England afraid is not necessarily the same as what frightens people reading nineteenth-century Gothic fiction or watching new productions of the play. Superstition surrounding the number three, for example, has lost much of its resonance for a modern audience.[41] But *Macbeth*, with its constant talk of fear, nonetheless has the potential and the adaptability to be made horrific for any audience. It is a tale about the downfall of a powerful man who lives in almost constant terror, 'supp[s] full with horrors' (5.5.13), and becomes, like a 'Hell-hound' (5.10.3), the thing of which to be most 'fearful' (5.7.10).

SELECT BIBLIOGRAPHY

Bradbrook, Muriel C., 'The Sources of *Macbeth*', *Shakespeare Survey* 4 (1951), 35–48.

Desmet, Christy, and Anne Williams, *Shakespearean Gothic* (Cardiff: University of Wales Press, 2009).

Doleman, James, *King James I and the Religious Culture of England*, Studies in Renaissance Literature (Suffolk: D. S. Brewer, 2000).

Kranz, David L., 'The Sounds of Supernatural Soliciting in *Macbeth*', *Studies in Philology* 100:3 (Summer, 2003), 346–83.

McEachern, Claire, ed., *The Cambridge Companion to Shakespearean Tragedy* (Cambridge: Cambridge University Press, 2003).

Magee, Arthur R., 'Macbeth and the Furies', *Shakespeare Survey* 19 (1966), 56–67.

Meads, Chris, *Banquets Set Forth: Banqueting in English Renaissance Drama*, The Revels Plays Companion Library (Manchester: Manchester University Press, 2001).

Power, Andrew J., 'What the Hell is Under the Stage: Trapdoor Use in the English Senecan Tradition', *English* 60:231 (2011), 276–96.

Power, Andrew J., 'Lady Macbeth and Othello: Convention and Transgression in Early Modern Tragedy', in Rory Loughnane and Edel Semple, eds., *Staged Transgression in Shakespeare's England* (London: Palgrave Macmillan, 2013), 224–38.

---

[41]   See Laura Annawyn Shamas's treatment of the significance of the number three in the play in *"We Three": The Mythology of Shakespeare's Weird Sisters*, New York: Peter Lang, 2007.

Power, Andrew J., '"Why should I play the Roman fool, and die | On mine own sword?":: The Senecan Tradition in *Macbeth*', in Willy Maley and Rory Loughnane, eds., *Celtic Shakespeare: The Bard and the Borderers* (Aldershot: Ashgate, 2013), 139–56.

Shaheen, Naseeb, *Biblical References in Shakespeare's Plays* (London and Cranbury, NJ: Associated University Press, 1999).

Wickham, Glynne, 'Hell-Castle and its Door-keeper', *Shakespeare Survey* 19 (1966), 68–74.

CHAPTER 28

....

ANTONY AND CLEOPATRA

....

BERNHARD KLEIN

PURELY as a dramatic exercise in hyperbole, Shakespeare's third Roman tragedy rarely fails to dazzle its audience. The play's love rhetoric scales the intoxicating heights of pathos, and its bold cosmic imagery evokes in equal measure the vastness of the spaces covered by the plot and the magnitude of Rome's imperial ambition. The action ranges over wide tracts of the ancient world, encompassing the eastern Mediterranean, the Aegean and Black Seas, the shorelines of North Africa, Asia Minor, and the modern Near East, and extends further into Asia by referencing ancient kingdoms and regions such as Syria, Parthia, and Media. Characters travel to and from Rome, Egypt, and places in between; they march through primeval landscapes, crossing the Alps or 'spurring' through Mesopotamia; they command armies and navies that move around land and sea like mobile entities on a giant map, clashing in mighty battles. The action is propelled forward at a rapid, breathless pace through more than forty scenes and changes in location, creating a kaleidoscopic panorama of the expanding empire.

The word 'world' alone is used over forty times in the play and spatial hyperbole shapes the characters' speech in every act. The affective centre of the play's cosmic fantasies is the god-like 'demi-Atlas' (1.5.23[1]) Antony, who towers over ordinary humans like a colossus, standing with 'legs [that] bestrid the ocean' and a 'reared arm [that] | Crested the world' (5.2.82-3). Cleopatra, who speaks these lines, is perhaps most given to the mythic exaltation of Antony, in whose face she sees the heavens, with sun and moon as eyes, and a voice 'propertied | As all the tuned spheres' (5.2.83-4), though other characters similarly project images of exaggerated greatness onto this singular 'man of men' (1.5.72): for Philo, his eyes glow 'like plated Mars' (1.1.4), for Enobarbus, he is a 'mine of bounty' (4.6.31), while for Agrippa, '[a] rarer spirit never | Did steer humanity' (5.1.31-2).

Yet such elevated speech dangerously 'courts the perils of anticlimax',[2] emphasizing the huge gap that the play exposes between talk and fact, between the rhetorical and the real. Hyperbole risks the descent into bathos when the characters fail to live up to their magnificent billing. This disconnect has been a recognized issue with stage productions of

---

[1] All quotations from the play are taken from William Shakespeare, *Anthony and Cleopatra*, ed. Michael Neill (Oxford: Oxford University Press, 1994). I have changed Neill's spelling of 'Anthony' to 'Antony' throughout.

[2] Michael Neill, 'Introduction', Shakespeare, *Anthony and Cleopatra*, ed. Neill, 1–130 (68).

the play,[3] which often disappoint, but is also the constituent feature of a text in which the dizzying poetry promises plenitude only to deepen a sense of emptiness and loss. Thus, while Antony attracts hymnic praise, he remains, despite his frequent onstage appearances, an 'absent object of desire',[4] perhaps even more so than Cleopatra, who occupies that position in Enobarbus' famous Cydnus speech (2.2.197-233). So many images in that speech—the burning water, the golden poop, the purple sails, the love-sick winds, the strange perfume which 'hits the sense'—foreground the sensual immediacy of Cleopatra's Egypt, its colours, forms, and smells, including their attendant effects on the viewer, that is never matched by any of the major characters' eloquent yearnings for Antony. The heroic, star-like Antony remains an abstract idea—disembodied, elusive, unattainable.

Octavius,[5] Cleopatra, even Enobarbus, often address Antony directly while he is not on stage, currently at the other end of the world, or even already dead (see 1.4.56-7; 1.5.25-6; 4.9.21-6; 5.1.35; 5.2.286, 311).[6] Throughout the play his heroic masculinity serves as the gold standard of an ideal *romanitas* which none of the male characters, let alone himself, can ever hope to emulate. Antony may still be able to win battles, even after Actium (as against Agrippa in 4.8), and the mere prospect of his return to Rome persuades a worried Pompey to agree to a truce. But already at the very beginning of the play Antony is less the glorified hero than a projection of anxiety and loss. '[S]ometimes', says Philo,

> ... he is not Antony,
> He comes too short of that great property
> Which still should go with Antony.

> (1.1.58-60)

Later, shortly before his botched suicide, he stands helpless in the face of his own legend: 'here I am Antony, | Yet cannot hold this visible shape' (4.15.13-14). As Cleopatra knows, the vision of Antony who keeps kings as servants and islands in his pockets is the stuff of dreams, an image predicated on the absence of the hero:

> CLEOPATRA   Think you there was, or might be such a man
>   As this I dreamt of?
> DOLABELLA   Gentle Madam, no.

> (5.2.93-4)

Here, the cosmic hyperbole focused on Antony is simply emptied out or denied, not reduced to bathos or ironized in a figure of anticlimax, with characters resigned to accept nostalgia as no more than a soothing illusion.

---

[3] See ibid., 68-73. A more recent overview of the play's stage history in the anglophone world is provided by Sara Munson Deats, 'Shakespeare's Anamorphic Drama: A Survey of *Antony and Cleopatra* in Criticism, on Stage, and on Screen', in Deats (ed.), *Antony and Cleopatra. New Critical Essays* (New York and London: Routledge, 2006), 1-93.

[4] Janet Adelman, 'Making Defect Perfection', *Suffocating Mothers: Fantasies of Maternal Origin in Shakespeare's Plays, Hamlet to The Tempest* (New York: Routledge, Chapman and Hall, 1992), 176-92 (177).

[5] In order to avoid confusion with Julius Caesar, I will refer to Octavius Caesar as Octavius throughout this chapter.

[6] Adelman, 'Making Defect Perfection', 177.

Janet Adelman has emphasized the important dramatic function of Cleopatra's dream vision in providing a counter model to the thoroughly Romanized soldier described by Octavius in 1.4. Once, driven from the site of a lost battle at Modena, Antony braved hunger, cold, and snow by surviving on horsepiss, berries, and the barks of trees (1.4.55-71), a perversely minimal anti-diet that is a far cry from the eight wild boars that are reputedly consumed at a breakfast for twelve in Egypt (2.2.186). This reduced, self-sufficient version of Antony stands in direct contrast to the excessive vitality projected on him by others. The Antony that Cleopatra recalls never finds himself in such a barren landscape: 'For his bounty, | There was no winter in't' (5.2.86-7). But winter is eternal in Octavius' Rome, where ideal masculinity is achieved through austerity and self-denial. In this male world of scarcity, which Antony renounces in favour of Cleopatra's Egypt, 'there are virtually no women',[7] apart from Octavia, who suffers the ignominious fate of getting married off to Antony for the short-lived prospect of a stable alliance between the two dominant men in her life, husband and brother. Alexandria, by contrast, is a female world of abundance, excess, and luxury, which features almost no men at all. From the perspective of Rome the only men in Alexandria are eunuchs, or, like Antony, effeminized pleasure boys, 'the bellows and the fan | To cool a gipsy's lust' (1.1.9-10).

The play feeds on contrasts like these between male and female, Rome and Egypt, duty and pleasure. Such polarities do not describe neutral circumstances, however, but biassed perceptions. They are also essentially unstable, prone to collapsing when challenged. Polarities are constructed through enforced juxtaposition, not objective comparison: Rome and Egypt appear as irreconcilable antagonisms because we only ever see the one through the perspective of the other. Jonathan Gil Harris has emphasized the importance of the Narcissus motif in the play's dramatization of inflected perception, arguing that its great polarities 'are less ones of opposition than of *specularity*',[8] a neologism derived from 'specular', 'having the reflecting property of a mirror' (*OED*). The play nowhere offers a midway position between the competing views expressed by the characters; instead it is built around multiple perspectives, anticlimax, sudden shifts, and hard contrasts, all of which are used as dramatic techniques to orchestrate the frequent leaps between positions, attitudes, opinions, and perceptions, not only from scene to scene but often from speech to speech or even within the same speech.

It is possible to see in these abrupt swings, shifts, or jumps the dramatic *mise-en-scène* of the idea of Fortune, prevailing symbol of the contingency of life, which forces opposites into close proximity and turnovers into an arbitrary sequence.[9] 'Our fortune lies upon this jump' (3.8.4), Octavius concludes his order to fight at sea in Actium, relegating the decision over the battle's outcome to Fortune's oldest domain. But in this play Shakespeare also follows his historical sources closely—Coleridge even thought, more closely than in any of his other plays[10]—and as in the rest of the histories he couples a focus on the divine

---

    [7] Ibid., 176.

    [8] Jonathan Gil Harris, '"Narcissus in thy face": Roman Desire and the Difference It Fakes in *Antony and Cleopatra*', *Shakespeare Quarterly* 45:4 (1994), 408–25 (410, my emphasis).

    [9] See Klaus Reichert, 'Formen des Launischen: *Antony and Cleopatra*', *Der fremde Shakespeare* (Munich: Hanser, 1998), 134–56.

    [10] See John Russell Brown, ed., *Shakespeare*: Antony and Cleopatra. *A Casebook* (London: Macmillan, 1968), 29.

meddling in human affairs with an interest in the 'defects of judgement' (2.2.59), or human inadequacy.

The conflict between Octavius and Antony, which is partly generational—'scarce-bearded Caesar' (1.1.22) versus Antony's 'grizzled head' (3.13.17)—is not in itself necessary or insurmountable, even though the play implies an impossible clash of opposing temperaments throughout. Pitted against the 'overflowing' Antony, Octavius is a cold and pragmatic ruler, an unkind literalist and spoil-sport, who is dubbed 'paltry' (5.2.2) by Cleopatra and who feels he has to remind everyone having fun at Pompey's feast that 'our graver business | Frowns at this levity' (2.7.119-20). A soothsayer warns Antony early on that he should avoid Octavius and '[m]ake space enough between' them (2.3.22), and his later defeat is owed, at least in Octavius' retrospective view, to a lack of space in a limited world: 'We could not stall together | In the whole world' (5.1.39-40). But actually Antony is less Octavius' opponent than his 'competitor' (1.4.3; 2.7.71; 5.1.42; the word is used in the old sense of 'ally' or 'partner', not 'rival') in the same political project. He even agrees to marry the sister of his 'mate in empire' (5.1.43), which at least temporarily suspends all political differences. Perhaps their united stand against Pompey was only a final glimmer of hope, the short-lived but doomed revival of a partnership that could never work, but it is more likely that the Roman political spectrum can accommodate the conflicting views even of such heavyweights, at least in principle.[11]

What it cannot so easily accommodate is the threat that Antony's actions in Egypt poses to the newly centralized empire rising from the ashes of the Roman republic. In the final act of Shakespeare's previous Roman play, *Julius Caesar*, Antony, Octavius, and Lepidus fought off the republican forces headed by Cassius and Brutus, the assassins of Julius Caesar. After their decisive victory at the Battle of Philippi, the 'three world-sharers' (2.7.71) formed the second triumvirate through which Antony ruled the East, Octavius the West, and Lepidus a smaller share in Northern Africa, from where Rome imported most of its grain. The ten-year political history covered in *Antony and Cleopatra* chronicles the break-up of this temporary political alliance and the establishment of a *pax Romana* under a single emperor.[12] Octavius Caesar, who was historically the first of the Roman emperors, reigned for over 44 years post-Actium over the largest empire Rome had ever seen, inaugurated a political system that remained stable for 250 years, and was later awarded the honorary title Augustus or 'the elevated one', which alongside Caesar became part of the Roman imperial titulature. In contrast to the joyless leader portrayed by Shakespeare, the historical Octavius possessed a formidable tactical and

---

[11] See Leonard Tennenhouse, *Power on Display. The Politics of Shakespeare's Genres* (London: Methuen, 1986), 142–6.

[12] For a reading of the play in terms of Jacobean republican thought see Andrew Hadfield, *Shakespeare and Republicanism* (Cambridge: Cambridge University Press, 2005), 220–9. On the contemporary reception of Rome in relation to the play see Warren Chernaik, *The Myth of Rome in Shakespeare and His Contemporaries* (Cambridge: Cambridge University Press, 2011), 135–64. Readings that approach the play as allegories of events in Jacobean England include, amongst others, H. Neville Davies, 'Jacobean *Antony and Cleopatra*', *Shakespeare Studies* 17 (1985), 123–58; Paul Yachnin, ' "Courtiers of Beauteous Freedom": *Antony and Cleopatra* in Its Time', *Renaissance and Reformation* 15 (1991), 1–20; and Lisa Hopkins, 'Cleopatra and the Myth of Scota', in Deats (ed.), *Antony and Cleopatra*, 231–42.

military brain, ran a highly efficient administration, and thrived on his reputation as the 'witty emperor'[13] who could easily take a joke at his own expense.

In the play Octavius stakes out his claim to 'a new age of imperialist consolida-tion'[14] most directly when he announces before the final battle that '[t]he time of uni-versal peace is near' (4.6.5). The sentence is prophetic, since Octavius' reign (31 BC to AD 14) overlapped with the arrival of Christ, but it is also a thinly veiled challenge to Antony's alternative vision of empire. The historical Antony took Alexander as his model, fostered a concept of empire as a union of equals rather than a collection of vassal states, and threatened through his relation with Cleopatra the ethnic hier-archies of the Roman world.[15] The danger is seen clearly by Octavius, who in Act 3 denounces the public ceremony in Alexandria during which Antony and Cleopatra handed out a whole raft of eastern kingdoms to Cleopatra's son Caesarion (reputedly fathered by Julius Caesar) and to 'all the unlawful issue that their lust | Since then hath made between them' (3.6.7-8). Plutarch considered the ceremony, in Thomas North's translation of Antony's biography that Shakespeare used as his main source, 'too ar-rogant and insolent a part, and done (as a man would say) in derision and contempt of the *Romanes*',[16] which goes some way towards explaining Octavius' conviction that Antony's 'rioting in Alexandria' (2.2.77) was not simply an instance of moral depravity but also a serious political threat.

That perceived threat is reinforced by the complex contemporary image of Egypt.[17] The biblical land of bondage was understood in early modern Europe as a place of grotesque fecundity, where the 'slime and ooze' (2.7.22) of the Nile spawned monsters and swarms of 'flies and gnats' (3.13.171).[18] But Egypt also stood as a cradle of ancient learning, especially in astronomy and mathematics, and was site of the pyramids, known as 'one of the seuen wonders of the world, being mightie huge buildings, erected of exceeding height, for the magnificence of their founders'.[19] Commercial links with England were forged in the six-teenth century with the establishment of the Levant Company, which in 1583 had a consul

---

[13] Ray Laurence and Jeremy Paterson, 'Power and Laughter: Imperial *Dicta*', *Papers of the British School at Rome* 67 (1999), 183–97 (192).

[14] Jonathan Dollimore, *Radical Tragedy. Religion, Ideology and Power in the Drama of Shakespeare and His Contemporaries* (Brighton: Harvester Wheatsheaf, 1984), 206.

[15] John Gillies, *Shakespeare and the Geography of Difference* (Cambridge: Cambridge University Press, 1994), 113.

[16] Plutarch, 'The Life of Marcus Antonius', *The Lives of the Noble Grecians and Romanes*, trans. Thomas North (London: Thomas Vautroullier and Iohn Wight, 1579), 970–1010 (996).

[17] For more extended discussions of contemporary notions of Egypt in relation to Shakespeare's play, see Gillies, *Geography of Difference*, 118–22; Geraldo de Sousa, 'Habitat, Race, and Culture in *Antony and Cleopatra*', *Shakespeare's Cross-Cultural Encounters* (Basingstoke: Palgrave, 1999), 129–58; John Michael Archer, 'Antiquity and Degeneration: The Representation of Egypt and Shakespeare's *Antony and Cleopatra*', *Old Worlds. Egypt, Southwest Asia, India, and Russia in Early Modern English Writing* (Stanford: Stanford University Press, 2001), 23–62; and Ania Loomba, 'The Imperial Romance of *Antony and Cleopatra*', *Shakespeare, Race and Colonialism* (Oxford: Oxford University Press, 2002), 112–34 (114–16).

[18] See Janet Adelman, *The Common Liar. An Essay on* Antony and Cleopatra (New Haven and London: Yale University Press, 1973), 66.

[19] George Abbott, *A Briefe Description of the Whole World* (London: T. Iudson for Iohn Browne, 1599), sig. E3r.

appointed 'in Cayro, Alexandria, Egypt, and other parts adiacent'.[20] Some English traders took a particular interest in Egyptian mummies whose embalmed body parts were used for pharmaceutical purposes, as George Abbott reported in 1605.[21]

Most importantly for the play, the Greek historian Herodotus, translated into English in 1584, framed Egypt as an exotic land of marvels. Located at the southern borders of the habitable world, he described the country in terms of opposition and difference as a *mundus inversus*, with an 'antipodean geography ... recapitulated in a carnivalesque society':[22] 'The Ægyptians therefore', the Elizabethan translation runs, 'as in the temperature of the ayre, and the nature of the riuer, they dissent from all other: euen so in their lawes and customes they are vnlike and disagreeing with all men.'[23] Women trade in the market while men weave at home; women carry goods on their shoulders, the men on their heads; '[w]omen make water standing, men crouching downe and cowring to the ground.'[24] Cleopatra's female-dominated court, her world of luxury, decadence, and sensuality, is both a theatrical reflection of this inverted social order and a wholesale negation of key Roman values.

Feminist approaches since the 1970s have analysed the gender dynamics implicit in such tropes of inversion,[25] while historicist and postcolonial inquiries have more recently focused on issues like the signifier 'Egypt' or the ethnic identity of the play's female protagonist.[26]

---

[20] Richard Hakluyt, *The Second Volvme of the principall Nauigations, Voyages, Traffiques, and Discoueries of the English nation*, part 1 (London: George Bishop et al., 1599), 171. On the Levant Company see Alfred C. Wood, *A History of the Levant Company* (London: Oxford University Press, 1935).

[21] Abbott, *Briefe Description*, 1605 ed., sig. K3r. On the mummy trade see Philip Schwyzer, '"Mummy Is Become Merchandise": Cannibals and Commodities in the Seventeenth Century', *Archaeologies of English Renaissance Literature* (Oxford: Oxford University Press, 2007), 151–74.

[22] Gillies, *Geography of Difference*, 120.

[23] Herodotus, *The Famous Hystory of Herodotus*, trans. B.R. [Barnaby Riche?] (London: Thomas Marshe, 1584), book 2, fo. 78r-v. The translation covered only the first two of the nine books that make up the whole of Herodotus' histories.

[24] Ibid., fo. 78v.

[25] Select feminist readings of the play include Anne Barton, '*Nature's piece 'gainst fancy': The Divided Catastrophe in* Antony and Cleopatra, *an Inaugural Lecture* (Bedford College: University of London, 1973); Linda T. Fitz [Linda Woodbridge], 'Egyptian Queens and Male Reviewers: Sexist Attitudes in "Antony and Cleopatra" Criticism' [1977], in John Drakakis (ed.), *New Casebooks: Antony and Cleopatra. Contemporary Critical Essays* (London: Macmillan, 1994), 182–211; Carol Thomas Neely, 'Gender and Genre in *Antony and Cleopatra*', *Broken Nuptials in Shakespeare's Plays* (New Haven: Yale University Press, 1985), 136–65; Peter Erickson, 'Identification with the Maternal in *Antony and Cleopatra*', *Patriarchal Structures in Shakespeare's Drama* (Berkeley: University of California Press, 1985), 123–47; Adelman, 'Making Defect Perfection'; Juliet Dusinberre, 'Squeaking Cleopatras: Gender and Performance in *Antony and Cleopatra*', in James C. Bulman (ed.), *Shakespeare, Theory and Performance* (London: Routledge, 1996), 46–67; Coppélia Kahn, 'Antony's Wound', *Roman Shakespeare. Warriors, Wounds and Women* (London: Routledge, 1997), 11–43; and Carol Chillington Rutter, 'Shadowing Cleopatra: Making Whiteness Strange', *Enter the Body. Women and Representation on Shakespeare's Stage* (New York: Routledge, 2001), 57–103.

[26] See Adelman, *Common Liar*, 184–8; Mary Nyquist, '"Profuse, Proud Cleopatra": "Barbarism" and Female Rule in Early Modern English Republicanism', *Women's Studies* 24:1-2 (1994), 85–13; Kim F. Hall, *Things of Darkness. Economies of Race and Gender in Early Modern England* (Ithaca, NY: Cornell University Press, 1995), 153–60; Joyce Green MacDonald, 'Sex, Race, and Empire in Shakespeare's *Antony and Cleopatra*', *Literature & History* 5:1 (1996), 6–77; de Sousa, 'Habitat, Race, and Culture'; Archer, 'Antiquity and Degeneration', 43–4; Rutter, 'Shadowing Cleopatra'; Arthur

The historical Cleopatra was Greek by origin and born into the Macedonian dynasty of the Ptolemys; one of her ancestors was an officer under Alexander the Great. She was not, technically, Egyptian, though she learned to speak Egyptian, officially represented herself as the Egyptian deity Isis, and was Egypt's last female pharaoh, ruling the country under Roman dispensation until her death in 30 BC. In the play, no one calls Cleopatra Greek while all the characters consider her Egyptian, and she herself and several others say so explicitly on more than twenty occasions.[27] She is also once called 'tawny' (1.1.6) by Philo and 'black' by herself, attributing that blackness metaphorically to the erotic advances of the god of the sun: 'Think on me | That am with amorous Phoebus' pinches black' (1.5.28-9).

The geographical theory that explained black skin colour as a result of excessive exposure to the heat of the sun in or near the torrid zone had existed since ancient times, but most early modern commentators rejected that opinion, for the simple reason that the evidence did not add up: as Abraham Ortelius pointed out in a much-quoted passage of his 1570 world atlas, the Spaniards and Italians have white skin, while the inhabitants of the Cape of Good Hope are black, even though all of them live at the same distance from the equator.[28] Some critics have taken Cleopatra's reference to her figurative sunburn as evidence that Shakespeare thought of her as black,[29] yet most English writers in the period shared Philo's view and described the Egyptians as tawny or brown, basing their accounts on the intelligence brought back by contemporary voyagers and merchants. George Abbott, for example, applied just these terms to Cleopatra in an updated edition of his 1599 *Briefe Description of the Whole World*, appearing in 1605, only a year or two before Shakespeare wrote the play: 'the inhabitants there [Egypt] are not blacke, but rather dunne [greyish brown], or tawnie. Of which colour *Cleopatra* was obserued to be.'[30]

In Shakespeare's play, the problem of establishing the colour of Cleopatra's skin is compounded by the absence of anything like a description of her actual appearance. Even

Little Jr., '(Re)Posing with Cleopatra', *Shakespeare Jungle Fever. National Re-Visions of Race, Rape, and Sacrifice* (Stanford: Stanford University Press, 2000), 143-56; Loomba, 'Imperial Romance'; and Sarah Hatchuel, *Shakespeare and the Cleopatra/Caesar Intertext. Sequel, Conflation, Remake* (Madison: Fairleigh Dickinson University Press, 2011), 19-24.

[27] Instances in which Cleopatra is either called 'Egyptian' or explicitly associated with 'Egypt' occur at 1.1.31; 1.2.116; 1.3.78; 1.5.34 and 43; 2.1.37; 2.2.225; 2.6.125; 2.7.25; 3.6.9; 3.10.10; 3.11.50 and 55; 3.13.165; 4.13.10 and 25; 4.15.15; 4.16.20 and 73; 5.2.9, 19, 112, and 115.

[28] See Abraham Ortelius, *Theatrum Orbis Terrarum* (Antwerp: A. C. Diesth, 1570), prefatory material to the section on Africa.

[29] See MacDonald, 'Sex, Race, and Empire', 60; Rutter, 'Shadowing Cleopatra', 62; Little Jr., *Shakespeare Jungle Fever*, 24; Loomba, 'Imperial Romance', 112-14; Celia Daileader, *Racism, Misogyny, and the Othello Myth* (Cambridge: Cambridge University Press, 2005), 28-31, and 'The Cleopatra Complex: White Actresses on the Interracial "Classic" Stage', in Ayanna Thomson (ed.), *Colorblind Shakespeare: New Perspectives on Race and Performance* (New York: Routledge, 2006), 205-20 (208); Anton Bosman, '"Best Play with Mardian": Eunuch and Blackamoor as Imperial Culturegram', *Shakespeare Studies* 34 (2006), 123-57 (139).

[30] Abbott, *Briefe Description*, 1605 edn., sig. K4r-v. The 1599 and 1600 editions of Abbott's *Briefe Description* did not contain this passage. In his revisions, Abbott made a point of adding a reference to English merchants coming back from the Levant, presumably the source of his knowledge. Peter Heylyn repeated the description in *Microcosmvs. Or, A Little Description of the Great World* (Oxford: Iohn Lichfield and Iames Short, 1621): 'The inhabitants … [of Egypt] are not blacke, but tawnie and browne' (387).

Enobarbus does not tell us what she looked like in his celebrated Cydnus speech; he simply says she 'beggared all description' (2.2.208). The signs of difference are instead discussed in various other, often subtle ways. One of the most strikingly unusual responses to the manifestations of Egyptian otherness is Antony's circular insistence on the impossibility of describing the crocodile, the reptile associated with the Nile and known as a defining emblem of Egypt (as well as of Cleopatra):

> LEPIDUS   What manner o' thing is your crocodile?
> ANTONY   It is shaped, sir, like itself, and it is as broad as it hath breadth. It is just so high as it is, and moves with it own organs. It lives by that which nourisheth it, and the elements once out of it, it transmigrates.
> LEPIDUS   What colour is it of?
> ANTONY   Of it own colour too.
>
> (2.7.41–6)

Ethnographic description of the kind practised by Herodotus would have made the crocodile intelligible through comparison, analogy, and approximation to a known quantity. 'By withholding analogy', John Gillies has argued, 'Antony is denying the possibility of "translation", linguistic appropriation, even knowledge itself,'[31] suggesting the futility of encompassing the 'other' ethnographically, politically, or in any other way, without first adopting cultural parameters that are not available in one's own society. Cleopatra's reptilian self-description as 'wrinkled deep in time' (1.5.30), an echo of Antony's address to her as 'serpent of old Nile' (1.5.26), amplifies the symbolic congruence between the crocodile and the Egyptian queen, and broadens the tautological sneer at Lepidus' drunken naivety into a stance of resistance against cultural appropriation (of Egypt by Rome).

In this sense, Cleopatra's refusal to be defined on Octavius' Roman terms, which motivates her suicide in Act 5, is as much a final act of defiance as a variation on the theme of her unrepresentability ('For her own person, | It beggared all description', 2.2.207–8). It is precisely the danger of having her own existence, both real and imagined, expressed through the imperial code of the conqueror, which Cleopatra aims to defy in this last desperate moment of self-assertion, her monumentally orchestrated suicide.[32] That suicide allows her to avoid the fate she fears most, being led around Rome in triumph ('her life in Rome | Would be eternal in our triumph', 5.2.65–6), although she knows that a posterity given to theatrical spectacle will distort and savage her memory in other ways:

> The quick comedians
> Extemporally will stage us and present
> Our Alexandrian revels; Antony
> Shall be brought drunken forth; and I shall see
> Some squeaking Cleopatra boy my greatness
> I'th' posture of a whore.
>
> (5.2.216–21)

---

[31] Gillies, *Geography of Difference*, 121.

[32] For an extended reading of that suicide, see Michael Neill, '*Finis coronat opus*: The Monumental Ending of *Anthony and Cleopatra*', *Issues of Death. Mortality and Identity in English Renaissance Tragedy* (Oxford: Clarendon Press, 1997), 305–27.

These lines are deeply ironic, coming towards the end of a stage play that presented a version of just these Alexandrian revels to an early seventeenth-century London audience, with a boy actor 'squeaking' the lines of the queen. The irony works in other ways too, because the term 'boy', strangely used as a verb here, is otherwise reserved for Octavius in the play ('The boy Caesar', 3.13.17; 'He calls me boy', 4.1.1; 'the young Roman boy', 4.13.48), suggesting a gender reversal of an unexpected kind, with Octavius suddenly visible, if only fleetingly, in the guise of the queen. On another level these lines are not ironic at all but deeply reflective, asking us to take a view on the detraction wrought by Augustan propaganda (Cleopatra as 'whore') on what she sees as her real self.

The accusation of sexual license echoes the Roman belief that the affair between the two most famous lovers of antiquity is nothing but the sad example of a formerly illustrious warrior ensnared by a wily temptress. Most Roman characters in the play would share Philo's view that Antony's love is mere 'dotage' (1.1.1), not a sublime exaltation of the self, which is how he prefers to see it: 'The nobleness of life | Is to do thus' (1.1.37-8). Yet the uncertainty whether this love is really genuine is fuelled even by Antony, who implies elsewhere that he is enthralled to the pleasure principle: 'I'th' East my pleasure lies' (2.3.39). Love has been among the most widely investigated themes in the play, largely because of the gigantic claims made by both lovers about the depth of their passion.[33] According to them, their love spans the globe, transcends life, cannot 'be reckoned' (1.1.15) in any human way or form. To curtail Antony, Cleopatra needs to 'find out new heaven, new earth' (1.1.17; a straight quotation from Revelations 21:1), while only the copious East is a match for Antony's expansive being: 'Here is my space!' (1.1.35) What seems certain about their passion is that it challenges received norms of gender identity. Antony's 'overflowing' self, of which Philo accuses him (1.1.2), thus linking him to the 'o'erflowing Nilus' (1.2.51), the symbol of Egypt's excessive fertility, 'is as much a sign of feminized instability as of heroic excess',[34] rendering any uncomplicated notions of Roman masculinity wholly inadequate as an explanatory framework for the gender dynamic in this play. Cleopatra's report of her and Antony's cross-dressing games:

> I drunk him to his bed—
> Then put my tires and mantles on him, whilst
> I wore his sword Philippan
>
> (2.5.21-3)

which ties in with Herodotus' description of an upside down Egyptian society, further extends the trope of gender reversal, as does Octavius' impression that Antony

> ... is not more manlike
> Than Cleopatra, nor the queen of Ptolemy
> More womanly than he ...
>
> (1.4.5-7)

Less open to nuanced interpretation than the play's gender dynamics is its persistently misogynist background tone. Using an image that emphasizes the hard collision of opposites,

---

[33] For a recent treatment of the topic see David Schalkwyk's *Shakespeare, Love and Service* (Cambridge: Cambridge University Press, 2008), 197-213; and his 'Is Love an Emotion? Shakespeare's *Twelfth Night* and *Antony and Cleopatra*', *symplokē* 18:1-2 (2010), 99-130.

[34] Neill, 'Introduction', 109.

so characteristic of this play, Cleopatra sees Antony switching register as soon as a 'Roman thought hath struck him' (1.2.88), which makes him suspend the love talk and brand her instead an 'enchanting queen' (1.2.122), 'cunning past man's thought' (152). After what he initially sees as her betrayal in the final battle, he attacks her verbally as a 'foul Egyptian' (4.12.10), '[t]riple-turned whore' (13), 'false soul' (25), 'gipsy' (28), 'witch' (47), 'vile lady' (4.14.22). Other characters are no less abusive. Philo calls her 'gipsy' and 'strumpet' (1.1.10; 13), Enobarbus an 'Egyptian dish' (2.6.128), Octavius a 'whore' (3.6.68), and Scarrus a 'nag' (3.10.10), a slang term for a prostitute. Scarrus also hopes Cleopatra will suffer from leprosy, believed to be a venereal disease. The flip side of the poetic hymn to love is aggressive misogyny.

Augustan propaganda had its fair share in perpetuating this negative image of Cleopatra, just as she fears might happen in her anticipation of a posthumous comedy version of her 'Alexandrian revels'.[35] Many Roman poets supported Octavius' official version: Horace saw Cleopatra as the mad queen who turned Antony's head;[36] for Lucan she was a second Helen, threatening to destroy Rome;[37] and in Virgil's *Aeneid* her example served as the negative foil for the heroic deeds of Aeneas.[38] Unlike Antony, Aeneas listened to the gods, resisted female temptation by leaving Dido (another African queen), and performed his dynastic duty by founding Rome. Most Roman historians toed the same moralistic line.

Shakespeare managed to transform this one-sided version into a tragic conflict between private passion and public responsibility. He was helped in this by North's English translation of Plutarch and by the protean transformations of Cleopatra's image, which remained in flux, despite the best efforts of Octavius' propaganda machine.[39] Like Cleopatra, Plutarch was Greek, and he was writing about a century after Antony's death, when the immediate political pressure of the events had passed. He was less interested in myth-making than in an assessment of his protagonist's character flaws. Plutarch's Antony is prone to wastefulness, he is promiscuous and a glutton, he parties excessively and is susceptible to flattery. These faults are partially redeemed by his noble character, liberal mind, magnanimity, and natural authority. The contact with Cleopatra brings his self-destructive streak to the fore: '[she] did waken and stirre vp many vices yet hidden in him ... and if any sparke of goodnesse or hope of rising were left him, Cleopatra quenched it straight, and made it worse then before.'[40] On this point Plutarch differs little from the Augustan propagandists. But importantly, he does not reduce Cleopatra to a power-crazed, oriental enchantress, who casts an erotic spell over men, and instead emphasizes her elegance and beauty, her social grace, political talent, and language skills, which ensured that she never required an interpreter for her diplomatic negotiations.

In the early modern period Cleopatra continues to figure as the femme fatale of antiquity: Dante places her in the second circle of hell;[41]Boccaccio includes a hostile biography of her in his *De mulieribus claris (Of Famous Women)*;[42] Spenser places her among the

---

[35] On Cleopatra's many after-lives in history, literature, poetry, film, criticism, and the arts see Lucy Hughes-Hallett, *Cleopatra: Histories, Dreams, Distortions*, 2nd edn (London: Pimlico, 1997); and Mary Hamer, *Signs of Cleopatra: History, Politics, Representation* (London: Routledge, 1993).

[36] Horace, *Odes*, 1.37.   [37] Lucan, *Pharsalia*, 10.70-7.   [38] Virgil, *Aeneid*, 8.671-713.

[39] For Shakespeare's sources, see Geoffrey Bullough (ed.), *Narrative and Dramatic Sources of Shakespeare*, vol. 5: *The Roman Plays* (London: Routledge and Kegan Paul, 1964), 215–449.

[40] Plutarch, 'Life of Marcus Antonius', 981.   [41] Dante Alighieri, *Inferno* (c.1308-21), 5.63.

[42] Giovanni Boccaccio, *De mulieribus claris* (1374), biography 88.

characters in the House of Pride in Book 1 of *The Faerie Queene*, and later in Book 5 reflects on the 'wondrous powre' of women that made Antony neglect the 'worlds whole rule for *Cleopatras* sight'.[43] Yet Spenser's epithet for Cleopatra, 'high minded',[44] which she earns on account of her courageous decision to take her own life, faintly echoes another tradition, the reworked image of Cleopatra as a martyr to love, for which Chaucer's *Legend of Good Women* (1385/6) and John Gower's *Confessio Amantis* (*A Lover's Confession*; 1390) are two of the earliest examples. In two contemporary English closet plays, which Shakespeare probably knew—Mary Sidney Herbert's *The Tragedie of Antonie* (1590), based on a French original by Robert Garnier (1578), and Samuel Daniel's *The Tragedie of Cleopatra* (1594)[45]— she is no lascivious temptress but a paragon of marital loyalty. While Antony styles himself in these plays as a victim of female treachery, lamenting the loss of empire, honour, and life, Cleopatra—who freely followed her lover into death—gains in heroic stature.

In one way or another, Shakespeare borrows from all these various traditions, perhaps most so in his choice to give not a single scene to the lovers themselves, showing how their private passion has become public property in the after-lives of history. His Cleopatra is subject to extreme mood swings, her love to Antony an erotic frenzy, always linked to the moment; yet at the same time she is a calculating player, who keeps Antony's interest alive through the carefully controlled performance of contrasting moods:

> If you find him sad,
> Say I am dancing; if in mirth, report
> That I am sudden sick

> (1.3.3-5)

When Cleopatra finally absolves from this ingenious scheming ('Now from head to foot | I am marble-constant', 5.2.239-40) the change is not a late moment of moral catharsis but the realization that in the face of her own death she is no longer dependent on strong male allies. The 'salad days' (1.5.76) of her youth, when she was politically naïve but sexually attractive enough to seduce Julius Caesar, the most powerful man in the world, are long gone; to hold on to Antony, she constantly has to reinvent herself as fascinating and desirable.[46]

Only in the eyes of others will her legendary beauty never fade. Enobarbus may be quoting Cleopatra when he claims '[t]hat she did make defect perfection' (2.2.238), but his ensuing excursion into paradox and hyperbole ('Age cannot wither her, nor custom stale | Her infinite variety', 242-3) continues the conventional praise of women in exactly the same style. As in the case of Antony, the gap between myth and reality is constitutive for Cleopatra's dramatic presence, accounting for the wild divergence between the image projected onto her by others and the one she herself presents to us on stage. For example, Antony's fatal decision to fight Octavius by sea rather than by land is explained clearly (though perhaps not very convincingly) through male rivalry:

---

[43] Edmund Spenser, *The Faerie Queene* (1590/96), 5.8.2.6-7; 1.5.50.7-8.

[44] *Faerie Queene*, 1.5.50.7.

[45] Both plays have been reprinted in Bullough (ed.), *Narrative and Dramatic Sources*. For a recent discussion of both plays in relation to Shakespeare's see Jane Pettegree, 'English Cleopatra in the 1590s: The Queen's Body', *Foreign and Native on the English Stage, 1588-1611* (Basingstoke: Palgrave-Macmillan, 2011), 27–48.

[46] See Fitz, 'Egyptian Queens'.

CANIDIUS Why will my lord do so?
ANTONY For that he [Octavius] *dares us to't.*

(3.7.29; my emphasis)

Yet only a few lines further on Canidius blames Cleopatra for being behind the decision: 'So our leader's led, | And we are women's men' (3.7.69-70). In the same scene Cleopatra refutes Enobarbus' suggestion that women should stay off the field of battle because their presence 'must puzzle' (3.7.10) masculine warriors, insisting instead on her political responsibility, which few of the male characters in the play seem to take very seriously:

A charge we bear i'th' war,
And, as the president of my kingdom, will
Appear there for a man....
I will not stay behind.

(3.7.16-19)

Infinite variety of the imagination is the privilege of the lovers, the self-proclaimed myth of unique, world-encompassing passion is the stuff of legend. 'We stand up peerless' (1.1.41), Antony claims, and the association of both protagonists with mythical deities thickens the epic strand of the love tragedy. Antony's god-like radiance is strengthened through the comparison with Mars, the Roman god of war, who got caught up in an erotic liaison with Venus, the goddess of love (associated with Cleopatra), an episode alternatively seen as the triumph of love over war or the wilful surrender of masculine power. In his debauchery, lustful self-submission, and penchant for the East, Antony is a self-styled new Dionysus; in virility, heroic stature, and promiscuity he is modelled on Hercules (supposedly an ancestor, according to Plutarch, though one who shamefully abandons Antony in Act 4). Hercules' humiliation by the Lydian queen Omphale, who made him wear female dress and spin wool, was another exemplary case study in masculine capitulation at the hands of a crafty female. Cleopatra's most important mythological counterpart, apart from her association with Venus, is the Egyptian deity Isis, focus of ancient fertility rites, on whose protective maternal instincts Cleopatra skilfully drew for political advantage. In the public ceremony mentioned earlier, when she and Antony handed out kingdoms to their offspring, she appeared '[i]n th'habiliments of the goddess Isis' (3.6.17; another detail Shakespeare borrowed from Plutarch). But despite (or perhaps because of) their divine properties, the scenes between the lovers are marked by petty quarrelling, and Antony's boasting about their legendary, transcendental love only draws a cynical comment from Cleopatra: 'Excellent falsehood!' (1.1.41).

The political plotline foregrounds the destructive entanglement of sexuality and power.[47] Antony succumbs to the illusion that he can keep his erotic adventures in Egypt separate from his political office in Rome ('My being in Egypt Caesar, what was't to you?', 2.2.40), expounding an outrageous fantasy of Rome melting into Tiber (1.1.34) while he is feasting in the East. The example of Aeneas should have signalled to him that passion and politics do not mix. The degree of his delusion becomes fully apparent after Actium when he has lost everything but still believes a single kiss from Cleopatra will 'repay' him

---

[47] See also Neill, 'Introduction', 91.

(3.11.71). The notion must have horrified contemporaries who believed that erotic infatu-ation was inimical to political reason. Whoever thinks of kingdoms as clay (1.1.37) while in the throes of passion cannot run an empire. No one knows better than Cleopatra, who is forced to use her sexuality for political ends, that international diplomacy is no arena for romantics. The harshness of politics is echoed in the play's culinary metaphors with their implication of voracious consumption. Cleopatra is an 'Egyptian dish' (2.6.128), gulped down by Antony; she in turn keeps him 'at dinner' (2.1.12) in Egypt with the use of 'Epicurean cooks' who '[s]harpen with cloyless sauce his appetite' (24-5). Already in her 'salad days' (1.5.76) she was a 'morsel for a monarch' (32), devoured by Julius Caesar, and upon hearing of Lepidus' fall, world politics is fittingly summarized by Enobarbus as one all-consuming orgy:

> Then, world, thou hast a pair of chops, no more,
> And throw between them all the food thou hast,
> They'll grind the one the other
>
> (3.5.12-14)

The pervasive dramatic motif of mutual destruction, as in this image of two grinding jaws that will eventually devour one another, is prominently linked to the theme of dis-solution and self-surrender. No realm of contemporary experience is more closely related to this thematic cluster than the sea. In the play the sea is both a real, physical space, where a truce is agreed and an eastern empire lost, and a metaphorical idea: as Fortune's traditional domain, it is associated with risk, hazard, uncertainty, forgetting, dissolu-tion, ecstasy, swoon—all properties central to the characters in this play. *Antony and Cleopatra* is perhaps Shakespeare's most maritime play,[48] and it is no accident that one of its key scenes is set aboard a ship. Pompey, who briefly 'commands | The empire of the sea' (1.2.183-4), hosts the feast on board his galley at which the triumvirs celebrate the momentary prevention of a political crisis (2.6), though the revels already hint darkly at the deepening rift between Octavius and Antony. The rocking boat reflects the unstable world of politics, and the respective degree of intoxication of Pompey's guests anticipates their later fate: Octavius stays sober; Lepidus loses control half way through; Antony drinks to Lethe, the river of oblivion. The persistent association between Antony, who 'o'er green Neptune's back | With ships made cities' (4.15.58-9), and the properties of the sea reveal the ocean as his true 'symbolic element'.[49] His later decision to fight Octavius at sea rather than on land is entirely in keeping with his Dionysiac temperament, and the self-reflective comment on cloud formations losing shape and becoming as 'indistinct | As water is in water' (4.15.10-11)—the element traditionally seen as female in terms of Galenic physiology—pushes his oceanic self-dissolution to the point of complete visual annihilation.

Antony's persona and power begin to dissolve into nothing soon after Actium: 'Authority melts from me' (3.13.94). The verb chosen here, 'melt' (disintegrate, dissolve, liquefy,

---

[48] I make this claim at more length in 'Staying Afloat: Literary Shipboard Encounters from Columbus to Equiano', in Bernhard Klein and Gesa Mackenthun, eds., *Sea Changes. Historicizing the Ocean* (New York: Routledge, 2004), 91–109 (97–9). A similar argument has been advanced more recently by Laurence Publicover in 'Shakespeare at Sea', *Essays in Criticism* 64:2 (2014), 138–57.

[49] Gillies, *Geography of Difference*, 116.

'discandy'), is a kind of maritime keyword in the play; it appears only six times, used exclusively by the two protagonists. Antony's shocking announcement in Act 1, 'Let Rome in Tiber melt!' (1.1.34), is furiously echoed by Cleopatra in Act 2: 'Melt Egypt into Nile' (2.5.79). Both images take the idea of dissolution to its physical extreme, with whole empires sinking into rivers, and both testify to an exaggerated sense of personal clout (insofar as they are phrased as imperatives). Both are also outward projections of the characters' desires, the first intended as a gesture of liberation—Antony ridding himself of Roman oppression— the second as a gesture of revenge born out of anger—Cleopatra's response to the news of Antony's marriage to Octavia. Dissolution, 'melting', is here actively willed upon others. The reversal of their fortunes is reflected in the final three uses of the term. After Antony sees his authority melting away in Act 3, his followers 'discandy' (dissolve) and abandon him to 'melt their sweets | On blossoming Caesar' (4.13.22-3). The vision of decay is pushed to its extreme at the moment of Antony's death, when 'melt' describes a complete loss of structure and form, leaving behind an empty and meaningless sublunary world:

> The crown o'th' earth doth melt....
> The soldier's pole is fall'n ...
> And there is nothing left remarkable
> Beneath the visiting moon.
>
> (4.16.65-70)

Even Octavius comments—indirectly—on the oceanic dimension of the two protagonists' fate in the speech that ends the play: 'No grave *upon the earth* shall clip in it | A pair so famous' (5.2.357-8; my emphasis).

The ocean is a key literary motif in the work of one of the most prominent readers of Shakespeare's play in modern times, the Caribbean poet and Nobel laureate Derek Walcott. In one of the poems from Walcott's 1979 collection *The Star-Apple Kingdom*, which contains his magnificent revisionist lyric 'The Sea Is History', Antony re-emerges as the colossus of Cleopatra's dreams, though not this time as the erect statue presiding over the globe but as a 'fallen column', forming a kind of imaginary bridge between old world and new: 'He lies like a copper palm | tree at three in the afternoon | by a hot sea | and a river, in Egypt, Tobago'.[50] The fusion of continents in the imaginary toponym is a theme continued in Walcott's stage play *A Branch of the Blue Nile* (1983), in which a group of Caribbean actors stage *Antony and Cleopatra* in the West Indies, with the clown's speeches in 5.2 rewritten in local dialect. The project fails spectacularly, throwing into doubt the very possibility of translating Shakespeare to the tropics.[51] Yet the choice of this particular play, both by Walcott and by his fictional group of players, suggests parallels across space and time that are neither accidental nor spurious. Seamus Heaney could see the analogy: 'Walcott's Caribbean and Cleopatra's Nile have the same sweltering awareness of the cynicism and brutality of political adventures.'[52] In Walcott's play, the actress Sheila Harris, cast to play

---

[50] Derek Walcott, 'Egypt, Tobago' [1979], *Collected Poems 1948-1984* (London: Faber, 1992), 368-71 (369).

[51] See Tobias Döring, 'A Branch of the Blue Nile: Derek Walcott and the Tropic of Shakespeare', in Sonia Massai, ed., *World-Wide Shakespeares: Local Appropriations in Film and Performance* (London: Routledge, 2005), 15-22.

[52] Seamus Heaney, 'The Murmur of Malvern', *The Government of the Tongue. Selected Prose, 1978-1987* (London: Faber, 1988), 23-9 (28).

Cleopatra, pulls out before the opening night, citing as her reason the oppressive force of Shakespeare's language:

> My body was invaded by that queen.
> Her gaze made everywhere a desert.
> When I got up in the morning, when I walked to work,
> I found myself walking in pentameter.[53]

Sheila's exposure of this discursive violence, performed by blank verse on a mind trained in Trinidadian creole, creates the paradox that the queen who resisted invasion becomes herself an invader. And yet she only turns into a tool of oppression because she has herself been forced into the linguistic shapes particular to a time and a place far removed from her own. Ancient Egypt and the Caribbean post-colony never crossed paths in 'real' history, but the colonization of minds and bodies is an experience common to both. And even though the two historical entities are separated from Jacobean England by hundreds of years and many seas, our image of the one and the cultural autonomy of the other struggle equally to step out of Shakespeare's long shadow. *Antony and Cleopatra* speaks to our own time very directly and on multiple levels, and its layers of meaning (and the criticism these have attracted) are as infinitely various as the legendary queen herself.

SELECT BIBLIOGRAPHY

Adelman, Janet, *The Common Liar. An Essay on* Antony and Cleopatra (New Haven and London: Yale University Press, 1973).

Adelman, Janet, 'Making Defect Perfection', *Suffocating Mothers: Fantasies of Maternal Origin in Shakespeare's Plays,* Hamlet *to* The Tempest (New York: Routledge, Chapman and Hall, 1992), 176–92.

Barton, Anne, '*Nature's piece "gainst fancy: The Divided Catastrophe in* Antony and Cleopatra', *An Inaugural Lecture* (Bedford College: University of London, 1973).

Brown, John Russell, ed., *Shakespeare:* Antony and Cleopatra. *A Casebook* (London: Macmillan, 1968).

Deats, Sara Munson, ed., *Antony and Cleopatra. New Critical Essays* (New York and London: Routledge, 2006).

Drakakis, John, ed., *New Casebooks: Antony and Cleopatra. Contemporary Critical Essays* (London: Macmillan, 1994).

Fitz, Linda T. [Linda Woodbridge], 'Egyptian Queens and Male Reviewers: Sexist Attitudes in "Antony and Cleopatra" Criticism' [1977], in Drakakis, ed., 182–211.

Gillies, John, *Shakespeare and the Geography of Difference* (Cambridge: Cambridge University Press, 1994), 112–22.

Hughes-Hallett, Lucy, *Cleopatra: Histories, Dreams, Distortions* [1990] (London: Pimlico, 1997).

Kahn, Coppélia, 'Antony's Wound', *Roman Shakespeare. Warriors, Wounds and Women* (London: Routledge, 1997), 110–43.

Loomba, Ania, 'The Imperial Romance of *Antony and Cleopatra*', *Shakespeare, Race and Colonialism* (Oxford: Oxford University Press, 2002), 112–34.

---

[53] Derek Walcott, *Three Plays: The Last Carnival; Beef, No Chicken; A Branch of the Blue Nile* (New York: Farrar, Straus and Giroux, 1986), 285.

MacDonald, Joyce Green, 'Sex, Race, and Empire in Shakespeare's *Antony and Cleopatra*', *Literature & History* 5:1 (1996), 60–77.

Muir, Kenneth, *Antony and Cleopatra*, Penguin Critical Studies (Harmondsworth: Penguin, 1987).

Neely, Carol Thomas, 'Gender and Genre in *Antony and Cleopatra*', *Broken Nuptials in Shakespeare's Plays* (New Haven: Yale University Press, 1985), 136–65.

Neill, Michael, 'Introduction', *The Tragedy of Anthony and Cleopatra* (Oxford: Oxford University Press, 1994), 1–130.

Neill, Michael, '*Finis coronat opus*: The Monumental Ending of *Anthony and Cleopatra*', *Issues of Death. Mortality and Identity in English Renaissance Tragedy* (Oxford: Clarendon Press, 1997), 305–27.

Reichert, Klaus, 'Formen des Launischen: *Antony and Cleopatra*', *Der fremde Shakespeare* (Munich: Hanser, 1998), 134–56.

Rutter, Carol Chillington, 'Shadowing Cleopatra: Making Whiteness Strange', *Enter the Body. Women and Representation on Shakespeare's Stage* (New York: Routledge, 2001), 57–103.

CHAPTER 29

··

CORIOLANUS
A Tragedy of Language

··

DAVID SCHALKWYK

FOR those committed to the idea that tragedy stems from the 'tragic flaw' of its hero—
Aristotle's term is 'hamartia'[1]—the Volscian Aufidius provides a surprising account of the
strengths and shortcomings of his mortal enemy, the Roman Caius Martius Coriolanus:

> All places yield to him ere he sits down,
> And the nobility of Rome are his;
> The senators and patricians love him too.
> The tribunes are no soldiers; and their people
> Will be as rash in the repeal, as hasty
> To expel him thence. I think he'll be to Rome
> As is the osprey to the fish, who takes it
> By sovereignty of nature. First he was
> A noble servant to them; but he could not
> Carry his honours even. Whether 'twas pride,
> Which out of daily fortune ever taints
> The happy man; whether defect of judgment,
> To fail in the disposing of those chances
> Which he was lord of; or whether nature,
> Not to be other than one thing, not moving
> From th' casque to th' cushion, but commanding peace
> Even with the same austerity and garb
> As he controlled the war; but one of these—
> As he hath spices of them all—not all,
> For I dare so far free him—made him feared,
> So hated, and so banished. But he has a merit,
> To choke it in the utt'rance.
>
> *(Coriolanus*, 4.7.28-57)[2]

Samuel Coleridge remarks that he 'had always thought this, in itself so beautiful speech,
the least explicable from the mood and intention of the speaker in all the works of

---

[1] Aristotle, *Poetics*, 1435a10–15.
[2] Quotations are from *Coriolanus*, ed. R. B. Parker (Oxford: Oxford University Press, 1994).

Shakespeare'.[3] Coleridge is bewildered by inconsistency of character: Aufidius, Coriolanus' implacable rival, both as enemy and ally, should not be speaking so sympathetically of the man he plans to slaughter without dignity or remorse.

The great Romantic poet pinpoints the crucial question of *Coriolanus* as tragedy. Does it lie in the character of its bewildering hero, or derive from issues that are more public: the political struggles that characterise the early years of Rome; or, as many have averred, in the nature of language itself, especially its failure to offer a bridge between the public and the private? Should we be confused by the apparent move 'out of character' by Aufidius as he pronounces on Coriolanus' character, or is Shakespeare deftly capitalising on an opportunity to reflect on Coriolanus as a figure of tragedy in what may be his final exercise in the genre?[4]

The context of the speech is the discomfort felt by Aufidius and his friends at Coriolanus' apparent displacement of Aufidius in the estimation of the Volscians—at the 'witchcraft' that enables Coriolanus to draw the Volscian soldiers to him, with the result that their own general is 'darkened in this action ... even by [his] own' (4.7.5-6). Aufidius' question at the opening of the scene, 'Do *they* still fly to *th' Roman*?' (1; emphasis added), uses the telling third person (*they*) of those whom he could formerly call his own, and pointedly distances Coriolanus as 'the Roman', despite (or because of) the latter's defection to the Volscians. Accustomed to be at the centre of power among the Volscians, Aufidius betrays his new marginality with a question that looks forward to his murderous resentment of Coriolanus. That is why what follows seems to Coleridge to be so out of character.

SERVICE

Beginning with Aufidius' disquisition on Coriolanus corrects the usual picture of Coriolanus as a man whose singular military prowess is matched by a complete lack of charisma and an intense aversion to public life. The person presented to us by the two Volscian soldiers not only has the capacity to displace Aufidius as the nourishing source of bewitched adulation—'Your soldiers use him as the grace fore meat, | Their talk at table, and their thanks at end' (4.7.4-5)—but is also a *naturally* sovereign being who will take Rome without effort: 'All places yields to him ere he sits down ... I think he'll be to Rome as the osprey is to the fish, who takes it | By sovereignty of nature' (28, 33-5).

The change in Aufidius' laudatory account comes, however, when he mentions Coriolanus not as a natural commander but as a *servant*: 'First he was | A noble servant to them, but he could not | Carry his honours even' (35-6). Seeing Coriolanus not as a sovereign raptor but rather as a 'noble servant', introduces a conceptual issue that runs throughout the play. Whom does Coriolanus serve? Who is included under Aufidius' pronoun, 'them'? He has just given us a catalogue of all the strata that make up the Rome's population: the 'nobility', 'senators and patricians', the 'tribunes', and 'their people'? Does

---

³ T. M. Raysor, ed., *Coleridge's Shakespearean Criticism*, 2 vols. (Cambridge: Cambridge University Press, 1930), 1: 81.

⁴ For a discussion of the date of *Coriolanus*, see *Coriolanus*, ed. Lee Bliss (Cambridge: Cambridge University Press, 2000), Introduction and Parker, Introduction.

Coriolanus serve all of them? We are reminded of the question by the tribune, Sicenius, 'What is the city but the people?' and the citizens' response, 'True | The people are the city' (3.1.200-1). If Coriolanus is the servant of the city—that is to say, the people—he cannot possibly be endowed with the natural sovereignty of the osprey vis-à-vis the fish. But Coriolanus himself accuses the people of reneging on *their* duty of service:

> I'll give my reasons,
> More worthier than their voices. They know the corn
> Was not our recompense, resting well assured
> That ne'er did service for't. Being pressed to th' war,
> Even when the navel of the state was touched,
> They would not thread the gates. This kind of service
> Did not deserve corn gratis.

> (3.1.122-7)

Not many critics attend to these conflicted notions of service in the play, but they are crucial to its insistent questions about the politics of obligation, representation, and deserving.

Aufidius' shift from praising Coriolanus' natural sovereignty to his flaws involves the concept of service. A 'noble servant' to the people of Rome, Coriolanus was nonetheless unable to 'carry his honours even', with proper temperament or control. Aufidius offers three possible reasons for this failing: 'pride', 'defect of judgment', or 'nature, | Not to be other than one thing', without settling on any one. Anyone who has watched Coriolanus' behaviour up to now would probably go for all three, but his companionate enemy refuses to go so far. He not only declines to attribute all such faults to Coriolanus, but he also proclaims that 'he hath merit | To choke it in the utt'rance'—that is to say, that his good qualities are able to stifle and silence his faults. That is, however, soon qualified by the common Shakespearean idea that merit depends on the evaluation of others: 'So our virtues | Lie in th' interpretation of the time'.

We are left with a curiously complex, even contradictory, summation of Coriolanus' qualities by his enemy-turned-friend and soon to be turned enemy again: a genuine admiration for his extraordinary authority, not merely as a killing machine but also as a magnetic human being capable of extraordinary charisma, and at the same time someone afflicted with one or more faults that render him incapable of maintaining his stature in the eyes of others.

CHARACTER AND POLITICS

Those who see the play as a tragedy of character have long puzzled over Coriolanus' psychology, especially his lack of a supposedly 'interior' self. Harold Bloom, who claims that, by giving us access to the inner thoughts and feelings of his characters, Shakespeare was the inventor of the 'human', states that '[i]nwardness, Shakespeare's great legacy to the Western self, vanishes in Coriolanus'.[5] For A. C. Bradley, Coriolanus is devoid of

---

[5] Harold Bloom, *Shakespeare: The Invention of the Human*, 1st edn (London: Fourth Estate, 2008), 583.

introspection,[6] and critics who wish to get at the inner workings of the hero lament the absence of the revealing soliloquies evident in *Hamlet* or even *Macbeth*. The most trenchant analysis of Coriolanus as a character stems from psychoanalysis, epitomized by Janet Adelman and elaborated along philosophical lines by Stanley Cavell.

A strong counter-movement, now prevalent, and represented by Emma Smith's chapter in this volume (Ch. 6), holds that to look for character in Shakespeare, and especially in this of all plays, is anachronistic. In this view, the play is concerned with impersonal political forces; such conflict is exemplified by the contest between aristocratic and democratic factions in the early days of Rome, when it was little more than a city-state. The play certainly resonated with the political turmoil of the early and mid-twentieth century, when the East German Marxist dramatist, Berthold Brecht, adapted Shakespeare's work to show how ordinary people may claim and embody their own political power.[7] The English poet and critic, T. S. Eliot, declared *Coriolanus* 'Shakespeare's most assured artistic success',[8] and used the play in his own poetry as 'part of his conservative, high-church Anglican, right-wing approach to the construction of nation and society'. The Arden 3 editor observes that *Coriolanus* has been 'appropriated by political right and left with equal success ... with equal refusal to see how deftly Shakespeare keeps the plot from ever being fixed in its political preferences'.[9]

The idea that in *Coriolanus* Shakespeare offers an even-handed, if bewildering, double perspective on the hero and on politics lies at the heart of Norman Rabkin's analysis of its 'strange mash of incompatible judgments and perceptions'.[10]

Rabkin endorses the Hegelian view of tragedy, according to which the tragic character (and thus the audience) is forced to choose between two equally compelling but incompatible values.[11] But such a choice is *ours*: democracy or oligarchy, the politics of the left or the right? A more difficult decision is whether the *hero* is confronted with equally compelling but incompatible choices, such as lie at the heart of Greek tragedy.

Hegel holds that the conflict central to Greek tragedy is absent from its Shakespearean equivalent. The German philosopher returns us, like Rabkin and others, to the force of *character*:

> Shakespeare ... gives us ... the finest examples of firm and consistent characters who come to ruin simply because of this decisive adherence to themselves and their aims. Without ethical justification, but upheld solely by the formal inevitability of their personality, they allow themselves to be lured to their deed by external circumstances, or they plunge blindly on and persevere by the strength of their will, even if now what they do they accomplish only from the necessity of maintaining themselves against others or because they have reached once and for all the point that they *have* reached. The passion, implicitly in keeping with the man's character, had not broken out hitherto, but now it arises and is fully

---

[6] A. C. Bradley, '*Coriolanus*', The Second British Academy Lecture (Oxford: Oxford University Press, 1912), 12: 'He has no more introspection in him than a tiger.'

[7] See *Coriolanus*, Arden 3, Peter Holland (London: Bloomsbury, 2013), 120–30.

[8] T. S. Eliot, *Selected Essays* (London: Faber, 1999), 143–4.   [9] Holland, *Coriolanus*, 3.

[10] Norman Rabkin, 'The Tragedy of Politics', *Shakespeare Quarterly* 17:3 (1966), 195–212 (196 and 201).

[11] Georg Hegel, *Introductory Lectures on Aesthetics*, trans. Bernard Bosanquet (Harmondsworth: Penguin, 2004).

developed—this progress and history of a great soul, its inner development, the picture of its self-destructive struggle against circumstances, events, and their consequences—all this is the main theme in many of Shakespeare's most interesting tragedies.[12]

Applied to *Coriolanus*, this scheme works and doesn't work: it captures the eponymous hero's intransigent passion and wilfulness, his 'self-destructive struggle against circumstances, events, and their consequences', but it misses the vacillating evaluation of that 'great soul' as expressed in Aufidius' ambivalent account of the play's hero.

MACHIAVELLI

Coleridge's bewilderment at the speech shows, first, that his expectation of consistency of character in Shakespeare is mistaken. Dramatically, Shakespeare needs a perspective on his hero that displays an intractable, contradictory, view of political and ethical agency, so he puts an evaluative disquisition in the mouth of the most ambivalent of people: Aufidius. He is both enemy and ally; his admiration is mixed with resentment, his promised revelation of the hero's 'tragic flaw' is withdrawn as soon as it is promised, and his outsider's assessment is polluted by intense self-interest, not least in the erotic engagement and rivalry that has often been noted.[13] Indeed, Aufidius' speech ends with a chilling Machiavellian turn that contrasts radically with the disposition of his subject:

> ... power, unto itself most commendable,
> Hath not a tomb so evident as a chair
> T'extol what it hath done.
> One fire drives out one fire, one nail one nail;
> Rights by rights falter, strengths by strengths do fail.
> Come, let's away. When Caius, Rome is thine,
> Thou art poor'st of all; then shortly thou art mine.

$$(4.7.51\text{-}7)$$

Aufidius allows himself to address Coriolanus intimately by his first name at the very point when he is planning and predicting his fall. This is consistent with the homoerotic nature of their conflict. More significant is what critics have tended to overlook: the invocation of Machiavellian politics, which invites us to consider *Coriolanus* as a study of its hero as anti-Machiavel, or at least as a study of what happens when the lion lacks the character of the fox.

It is thus surprising how little has been written about *Coriolanus* and Machiavelli. Some have turned to the political theorist's view on the necessary eloquence of successful soldiers in the debate about Coriolanus' attitude to and command of language in *The Art of War*, but few have looked at the play in relation to either the *Discourses* or *The Prince*. In

---

[12] G. W. Hegel, *Lectures on Aesthetics*, http://www.marxists.org/reference/archive/hegel/works/ae/part3-section3-chapter3.htm#c-c-3-b.

[13] Jonathan Goldberg, 'The Anus in *Coriolanus*', in Carla Mazzio and Douglas Trevor, eds., *Historicism, Psychoanalysis, and Early Modern Culture* (London: Routledge, 2000), 260–71.

their extended studies of Shakespeare's relation to the Italian writer, John Roe[14] considers *Coriolanus* only in passing while Hugh Grady ignores it altogether.[15]

The most apparent relation of Machiavelli to Shakespeare's play is through the republican writer of the *Discourses*, who praises the appointment of the tribunes as protectors and representatives of the citizens of Rome. For Machievalli, republican politics are always beset by two competing parties,

> that of the nobles and that of the people, and all the laws that are favorable to liberty result from the opposition of these parties to each other, as may easily be seen from the events of Rome ... If the troubles in Rome occasioned the creation of the Tribunes, then they cannot be praised too highly; for besides giving the people a share in the public administration, these Tribunes were established as the most assured guardians of Roman liberty.[16]

Machiavelli regards the clash between Coriolanus and the people as an exemplary instance of the success of legal means for expressing the liberty of the people through the capacity, via the institution of the Tribunes, to subject a politician to public accusation and trial. 'Let any one reflect on how much evil there would have resulted to the Roman Republic', Machiavelli urges, 'if [Coriolanus] had been killed in that popular outbreak', noting that, because of the safeguards to popular liberty built into the constitution of the early Roman republic, such freedom 'is effected solely by the public force of the state in accordance with the established laws, which have their prescribed limits that cannot be transcended to the injury of the public' (131-2). In Machiavelli's estimation, then, Coriolanus is hardly a tragic story: the Italian philosopher is interested only in the proper balance of political power through legal institutions, and the Roman general's banishment exemplifies the proper safeguards of the early Roman political order.

Although Shakespeare too is concerned with Republican power struggles, he is also intrigued by Coriolanus the man. This interest gains a Machiavellian spin if we turn from the *Discourses* to *The Prince*, especially Machiavelli's declaration that:

> [a] prince being obliged to know well how to act as a beast must imitate the fox and the lion, for the lion cannot protect himself from traps, and a fox cannot defend himself from wolves ... Those that wish to be only lions do not understand this.

> (Machiavelli, The Prince, 64)

It is not as if Coriolanus, who is as much a lion as anyone can be, does not understand Machiavelli's precept. He simply refuses to countenance it. Coriolanus as fox would have built on his achievements as lion by begging the people humbly for their 'voices', assumed the garment of humility with at least apparent meekness, and displayed his wounds publicly, all the while supressing his contempt for the people behind a façade of supplication. Having achieved what is in effect no more than the formality of their consent, he would then return to his role as lion with the full power of the consulate at his disposal. What

---

[14] John Roe, *Shakespeare and Machiavelli* (Cambridge: D. S. Brewer, 2002).

[15] Hugh Grady, *Shakespeare, Machiavelli, and Montaigne: Power and Subjectivity from Richard II to Hamlet* (Oxford: Oxford University Press, 2003).

[16] Niccolo Machiavelli, *The Prince and the Discourses*, Modern Library (New York: Randon House, 1950), 119 and 121.

sane person would *not* do this? Coriolanus does not; indeed, I shall argue, he *cannot*. The reason lies in the nature of language both as an instrument of political power and as the source of human subjectivity—of the very sense of one's self as an agent, of being 'enough the man you are' (3.2.19).

Machiavelli writes in the context of the Italian Renaissance, a time and place foreign to the Republicanism of classical Rome. Coriolanus is not a 'prince' in Machiavelli's sense; he is a fearsome general who (for reasons unspecified) seeks election to the consulate.[17] As a general, no matter how courageous, he remains the servant of the state. Coriolanus does not dispute his status as a servant; instead he questions the nature of the state, the entity to which he owes his allegiance and duty. Such distinctions do not come naturally, like lions or foxes—they are conceptual.

LANGUAGE

This conceptual conundrum is why so many critics have held that language lies at the heart of *Coriolanus*. The curious thing is that hardly anyone agrees about the meaning of language in the play, the nature of its use, and especially its relation to the play's eponymous hero. The latter is the subject of most disagreement. Carol M. Sicherman claims that Coriolanus 'reject[s] public utterances', and that in the play as a whole, 'the dissociation between words and meanings ... has become a hopeless disjunction'.[18] She echoes James Calderwood's earlier statement that, 'words have become meaningless'.[19] John Plotz concurs, attacking Stanley Fish's speech-act analysis of the play. Against Fish's argument that the trouble with Coriolanus lies in his refusal to accept the necessary public conventions that sustain social relationships through language,[20] Plotz claims that no proper community is possible in this Roman society, where language has lost all connection with truth and is used by everybody to achieve their own narrow ends.[21]

The most glaring differences come from critics' discrepant claims about to what extent Coriolanus himself speaks. Maurice Charney declares that he 'has a natural antipathy to eloquence', Brenton Hathen that he is 'deeply suspicious of speech', James Marlowe that he sees 'language ... largely as a threat ... eloquence itself can only serve to pollute action', John Porter Houseman that he is 'an inadequate speaker', and Calderwood that 'he

---

[17]   Why Coriolanus wants the consulate in the first place is pertinent question, but seldom asked. There are times when he does not seem to want it at all. Psychoanalytical critics attribute his desire for political power to a displaced and transferred form of his mother's desire. See Janet Adelman, *Suffocating Mothers: Fantasies of Maternal Origin in Shakespeare's Plays, Hamlet to the Tempest* (New York: Routledge, 1992).

[18]   Carol M. Sicherman, 'The Failure of Words', *ELH* 39:2 (1972), 189–207 (189).

[19]   James Calderwood, '*Coriolanus*: Wordless Meanings and Meaningless Words', *Studies in English Literature, 1500-1900* 6 (1966), 211, doi:10.2307/449633.

[20]   Stanley Fish, *Is There a Text in this Class?: The Authority of Interpretive Communities* (Cambridge, MA: Harvard University Press, 1990), 206: Coriolanus 'wants to be independent of society and of the language with which it constitutes itself and its values, seeking instead a language that is the servant of essences he alone can recognize because he alone embodies them'.

[21]   John Plotz, 'Coriolanus and the Failure of Performatives', *ELH* 63:4 (1996), 809–32.

remains taciturn wherever possible'.[22] Of course, one may be suspicious of speech without shying away from it, or be wary of only certain kinds of speech while engaging freely in language in which one feels at home.

An analysis of the number of lines spoken by the protagonists of the Shakespeare plays that have a protagonist of equivalent centrality shows that Coriolanus falls slightly below average in percentage of lines spoken, but he is certainly not the most uncommunicative. He speaks a smaller percentage of lines than Shakespeare's great talkers, Hamlet (38 per cent) and Timon (36 per cent), but at 26 per cent of the total lines spoken in *Coriolanus* he comes close to Macbeth (32 per cent) and Henry V (30 per cent) in their plays; he matches Prospero (27 per cent), Richard II (27 per cent), and Othello (26 per cent), and surpasses King Lear (21 per cent).[23] That's not bad for someone who is supposed to be taciturn and hate speaking. Indeed, citing the observation, among others, by A. C. Bradley that Coriolanus 'is very eloquent', Michael West and Michel Silberstein argue that Coriolanus displays the sort of anti-Ciceronian 'terse, plain-spoken rhetoric exemplified by Cato the Elder' that suited the growing suspicion of language and a particular kind of eloquence in the seventeenth century.[24] They pit the theory and history of rhetoric against the proponents of speech-act theory, claiming that 'speech-act theory will teach us very little about this play if we forget the more ancient theory of speech embodied in classical rhetoric' (330). They are right to show the degree and nature of Coriolanus' considerable eloquence against those who deny or overlook it, but they miss entirely the radically different goals and achievements of those who have analysed the force and failure of speech acts in the play.

Why is there such fundamental disagreement between critics about language in this play? If you want to find out whether Coriolanus is taciturn or not, just count his lines. If you want to see how he uses language publicly, follow West and Silberstein in looking at his rhetorical patterns and habits. But his *attitude* to language is more difficult to pinpoint. He is certainly suspicious of some kinds of uses of language as opposed to the efficacy of certain kinds of action, but he does not hesitate to resort to speech to provoke action when he thinks action is needed; he does not shirk from the vituperative force of words; he is capable of linguistic acts of generosity, thanks and comfort;[25] his charismatic seduction of the Volscians presumably involves some degree of speech; and his last words to his mother are as heart-wrenching as anything Shakespeare wrote for his other tragic heroes.

Aufidius' description of Coriolanus, with which I opened, provides a clue as to the cause of the disagreement amongst critics. He offers us a far from dispassionate description that combines admiration, speculation and resentment; some of what he says strikes us as true, some as prejudiced, and some is uncertain. Many critics who pronounce on Coriolanus' relation to language take as gospel what others say about him. Thus I suspect

---

[22] Calderwood, '*Coriolanus*', 211.

[23] Statistics calculated from Shakespearelinecount.com (accessed 15 February 2014).

[24] Michael West and Michel Silberstein, 'The Controversial Eloquence of Shakespeare's Coriolanus—an Anti-Ciceronian Orator?', *Modern Philology* 102:3 (2005), 307–31 (330). See also Margreta De Grazia, *Shakespeare Quarterly* 29:3 (1978), 374–88, doi:10.2307 | 2869147.

[25] See especially his comforting of his friends and family after his banishment.

that Meninius' exculpatory observation that the citizens should not expect the sweet eloquence of political oratory from a soldier underlies claims of his lack of eloquence:

> Consider further
> That when he speaks he speaks not like a citizen,
> You may find him like a soldier. Do not take
> His rougher accents for malicious sounds,
> But, as I say, such as become a soldier
> Rather than envy you.
>
> (3.3.50-5)

More accurate is the Tribune Sicenius' advice on how to inflame an intemperate response from Coriolanus through language:

> Put him to choler straight ... Being once chafed, he cannot
> Be reigned again to temperance, then he speaks
> What's in his heart, and that is there which looks
> With us to break his neck.
>
> (3.3.25-30)

This tactic works.

Act 3 opens with the confirmation that, despite his defeat, Aufidius has 'made new head'—raised a new army to attack Rome. Coriolanus sums up the situation decisively: 'So then the Volsces stand but at first, | Ready when time shall prompt them to make road | Upon's again' (3.1.4-6). Cominius responds with redoubled complacency: first, by calling Coriolanus 'lord consul' before he has secured that title, and at the very point at which he will not only lose it but also abandon his kinship with Rome itself; second, by dismissing the capacity of Aufidius and the Volscian army to launch a counter-attack. The irony is intensified by the fact that precisely Coriolanus' impending banishment from his homeland will invigorate the Volscian attack and threaten the destruction of Rome.

This returns us to Machiavelli, specifically to the point in the *Discourses* in which he weighs up the virtues of a tranquil but necessarily small and feeble state and a more warlike and expansive, but also less stable, one:

> If therefore you wish to make a people numerous and warlike, so as to create a great empire, you will have to constitute it in such manner as will cause you more difficulty in managing it; and if you keep it either small or unarmed, and you acquire other dominions, you will not be able to hold them, or you will become so feeble that you will fall prey to whoever attacks you.
>
> (*Discourses*, 127)

Coriolanus is the price you pay for imperial expansion. In the context of a republican Rome in its infancy, still developing a constitutional order of distributed power under conditions of constant external threat, Rome *needs* people like Coriolanus. The importance of military prowess for political success is nowhere more evident than in the practice of electing consuls who were exemplary generals. On the other hand, it also demands protection for a citizenship increasingly sensitive to its own powers, even if those powers are emergent rather than fully established.

Shakespeare is aware of the tension between these two demands. He therefore presents a historically specific constitutional issue as the tragedy of a particular person whose specific abilities are both crucial to the survival of the republican state and deeply inimical to it. The conflict is presented through language, not in the obvious sense that everything in a play may be traced to a linguistic source, but rather that the play focuses on the language through which power is both negotiated and constituted. Such language is not made up of big words, but rather small ones, such as we tend to overlook, but which Coriolanus, with his acute sensitivity to power and status, focusses upon with peculiar intensity: words like 'shall', 'must', 'may', 'let', and the personal pronouns, 'we', and 'they', 'I', and 'him'.

MODALS AND THE 'ABSOLUTE "SHALL"'

Van Dyke remarks perceptively that Coriolanus is 'uncommonly sensitive' to words.[26] This sensitivity has been interpreted as a 'hysterical' 'captivity' to single words (Sicherman, 199), but Sicherman's focus on the psychology of Coriolanus' response to language misses the broader, political concerns of the play.[27] The central case of such supposed hysteria is his response to the tribune's use of an apparently inconsequential and trivial word, 'shall', at the critical moment when he is held accountable before the citizens by the people:

> CORIOLANUS Choler! Were I as patient as the midnight sleep,
> By Jove, 'twould be my mind!
> SICINIUS It is a mind
> That *shall* remain a poison where it is,
> Not poison any further.
> CORIOLANUS *Shall* remain!
> Hear you this Triton of the minnows? Mark you
> His absolute '*shall*'?
> COMINIUS 'Twas from the canon.
> CORIOLANUS '*Shall*'?

(3.1.89–99)

This is a critical turning point in the play—but it turns on a point that most people might miss were it not for Coriolanus' hypersensitivity to language.

Alysia Kolentsis offers a perceptive reading of the use of modal verbs in *Coriolanus* as a means of negotiating power relations. As a way of measuring a speaker's relation to a community and its conventions of interpretation and validity, her approach is more nuanced than Fish's blunter analysis of speech-act theory. She argues that the crucial battlefield for Coriolanus is not that of the sword or spear, but involves the right to use words like 'shall' and 'must'—that far from being averse to speaking, Coriolanus understands better than anyone else the power that lies in grammar, and the right to use particular forms. Coriolanus loses that battle decisively in 3.1, when the man who is 'familiar and comfortable with familiar words, and who is able to shape them to serve his interests' (145) loses

---

[26] Joyce Van Dyke, 'Making a Scene: Language and Gesture in *Coriolanus*', *Shakespeare Survey* 30 (1977), 135.

[27] Cf. Alyasia Kolentsis, '"Mark you/His absolute Shall": Multitudinous Tongues and Contested Words in *Coriolanus*', *Shakespeare Survey* 58 (2009), 141–50. She observes that Coriolanus 'knows how social language works, and is sensitive to the power contained in words' (144).

that power, as the tribunes' *'shall'*, declared in the name of the people, overwhelms the absoluteness of his claims.

Lynne Magnusson alerts us to the importance of modals in Shakespeare, and to their peculiar status as points of transition and ambivalence in early modern England.[28] Modals (examples beyond *shall* and *must* are *would, should, could, may, might, can*) negotiate modes of action and being that are either brought into being, performatively, *in* speaking or as a prediction, command, wish or desire. They may be taken in two ways: to say 'he may come tomorrow' could mean either that I give him permission to come tomorrow or I judge it is possible that he will turn up. In the first I assume a position of power, allowing him to come; in the second I am guessing, more or less informatively. The same is true of *shall*. When Sicinius says, 'It is a mind | That shall remain a poison where it is, | Not poison any further', he is either declaring, from a position of power, that Coriolanus' influence will end, or merely predicting that it will not continue. In the first, he is the agent, and this speech is the instrument that neutralises the poison of Coriolanus' mind; in the second he assumes no such authority but merely guesses what will happen. The dynamic of the utterance lies in its uncertainty—the fact that the grammar does not tell us which of the interpretations is valid. The only thing that can do that is the context, and that is fraught and contested.

The most telling aspects of Coriolanus' response to the tribune's use of *shall* are the adjectives to which he couples the modal: 'peremptory' and 'absolute'. The first questions the power being assumed—it is illegitimate, beyond its proper bounds, impertinent. The second interrogates the extent of the assumed power—it is absolute as in being without limit, beyond any challenge, extensive and total. These are two different forms of critique. The first challenges the right of the person to the initial assumption of power: it turns the imperative *shall* into a flaccid, predictive *will*. The second goes to the heart of the play's constitutional battle: it was precisely because the patricians had absolute power (they commanded an absolute *shall*) in a situation of unrest over shortages of food and the threat from the Volscians, that they decided to cede some of their power to the people in the form of the elected tribunes. It would be ironical indeed if the absoluteness of patrician power were to be transformed into a limitless exercise of the people's power.[29] The political tension revealed by Coriolanus' sensitivity to the modality of language in Sicinius' use of *shall* is thus about the division of power, the avoidance of absoluteness, and a form of checks and balances that we recognise in democratic constitutions today. Whatever we may think of the subjective aspects of Coriolanus' character as he makes this speech, his focus on the grammar of power raises issues that go beyond his status as tragic character.

This aspect of the play certainly involves Coriolanus as a dramatically necessary antagonist to the drive by the citizens to force the patricians, in the short term, to give them grain (or corn) at a time of famine, and in the long term to forge an axis of real political power within the Roman state. It is now a critical commonplace that the local context of this representation of a putative citizens' rebellion involved the corn riots in the English Midlands in 1607, as a result of a series of bad harvests and rising food prices.[30] Commentators also point to a general pressure on structures of class power and the similarity between the citizen-class

---

[28] Magnusson, 'A Play of Modals: Grammar and Potential Action in Early Shakespeare', *Shakespeare Survey* 62 (2009), 69–80.

[29] This is the substance of Berthold Brecht's adaptation of *Coriolanus*.

[30] See Holland, *Coriolanus*, 56.

in the Rome of *Coriolanus* and the mobility of the 'middling sort' in Shakespeare's London to demonstrate the topicality of the play in its putative first performance in 1609-10.[31]

THE POLITICS OF GRAMMAR

The celebrated opening scene in which a group of angry citizens driven by hunger confronts the patricians, especially Caius Martius (Coriolanus)—'a very dog to the commonality' (1.1.26)—introduces the performativity of political speech that is at stake throughout the play:

> *Enter a company of mutinous Citizens with staves,*
> *clubs, and other weapons.*
> FIRST CITIZEN   Before we proceed any further, hear me
>   speak.
> ALL   Speak, speak!
> FIRST CITIZEN   You are all resolved rather to die than to famish?
> ALL   Resolved, resolved!
> FIRST CITIZEN   First, you know Caius Martius is chief enemy to the people.
> ALL   We know 't, we know 't!
> FIRST CITIZEN   Let us kill him, and we'll have corn at our own price. Is 't a
>   verdict?
> ALL   No more talking on 't; let it be done. Away, away!

> (1.1.1-6)

Note, first, the radical opposition of personal pronouns: *we* and *us* are staked against *him* and *they*. Upon this foundational difference Shakespeare builds the centrality of speech and the voice as the sites of political conflict and assent. Voices constantly clamour to speak, and the play's crucial political negotiation is conducted in terms of the securing the 'voices' of the citizens—their votes for Coriolanus as consul. But what power lies in those voices and their performance of particular kinds of language?

The scene opens with a request to be allowed to speak by one of their own, to which the people give their unanimous assent, 'Speak, speak', followed by an utterance that has the form of a statement but is possibly posed as a question about what the people are 'resolved' to do. Once they declare themselves resolved to die in their political cause the First Citizen tells them what they supposedly all 'know': that Martius (Coriolanus) is 'chief enemy to the people'. On the basis of such a declared fact, the First Citizen invokes the jussive form, *Let us kill him*. It is not quite a command, since the speaker is merely a citizen and thus has no power of the imperative. It is rather a plea for communal action. But it is presented as a statement of supposed fact—*and we will have corn at our own price*—whereas it is in fact mere conjecture. But see how *Let us* is quickly given a quasi-legal status: *Is't a verdict?* Do the people have the authority to deliver such a verdict? Of course, they may well kill Martius, given the chance, but it is neither clear that this would result in free food for all nor that it would be a legal act, both of which the people ignore in their headlong desire for—well, is it revenge on the ruling classes or merely food?

---

[31] Theodore B. Leinwand, 'Shakespeare and the Middling Sort', *Shakespeare Quarterly* 44:3 (1993), 284–303; Parker, *Coriolanus*, 33 and Bliss, *Coriolanus*, 17.

Martius and Meninius together succeed quite easily in diverting and demobilizing the mob, before the external threat of the Volscian attack deflects attention from the issue altogether. But the building blocks by which political power is negotiated, contested and constituted have been laid in the first few lines of the play. Let's turn to Acts 2 and 3 to see how Shakespeare constructs his edifice. He does so through repetition, replaying earlier scenes and reiterating key words to produce difference and reinforcement alike.

The opening of 2.2 replays the opening 'verdict' on Coriolanus as enemy to the people, but in a more nuanced, dialogical way, as the officers preparing the senate for the patricians' election of Coriolanus to consul offer both differing accounts of the protagonist and astute insight into the manipulative hypocrisies of political campaigning. He is accounted both someone who 'loves not the common people' and a 'brave fellow'; a 'worthy man' who 'hath deserved worthily of his country' (2.2.6, 5, 33, and 23) and also a man who is to be blamed for refusing to tread a middle path between ingratiating flattery and open disdain for the 'voices' upon which he depends. When the second officer states that it is the ethical duty of the citizens to acknowledge Coriolanus' service to them in battle, he opens the broader question of Coriolanus' reciprocal duty to the citizens.

That obligation is repeated in the opening of Scene 3, in the citizens' astute discussion of the ways in which it circumscribes their power:

> FIRST CITIZEN   Once, if he do require our voices, we ought not to deny him.
> SECOND CITIZEN   We may, sir, if we will.
> THIRD CITIZEN   We have power in ourselves to do it, but it is a power that
> we have no power to do. For if he show us his wounds and tell us his
> deeds, we are to put our tongues into those wounds and speak for them; so
> if he tell us his noble deeds we must also tell him our noble acceptance of
> them. Ingratitude is monstrous, and for the multitude to be ingrateful were
> to make a monster of the multitude.
>
> (2.3.1–12)

The key concepts of the opening scene are repeated here, but with significant variation. The question of the people's power, simply asserted then, is now subjected to critical scrutiny: they have the power to elect Coriolanus or not, but it is not a free power; it is heavily circumscribed—a 'power that we have no power to do'. The 'ought' of the first line introduces the notion of obligation or duty rather than the naked exercise of power, but is qualified by the modal 'may' of the second citizen, who wishes to assert the free will of the people. But that assertion is in turn qualified by the conditionals in the third citizen's response upon which the citizens' actions depend: 'if … we are to … if … we must'. This is a polity of reciprocal obligation—of service—in which each side depends on the other, and which ethics is central to political freedom. The gratitude of the people for Coriolanus' service, exemplified by his willingness to show them his wounds, constrains them to act within the bounds of humanity, and not to turn themselves into a 'monstrous multitude'.

Who is 'Rome'?

Such a subtle understanding of the ethics of reciprocity within an incipient republican system escapes Coriolanus entirely, who turns the citizens into a monster by his refusal to accept that, in a crucial, political sense, his wounds do not belong to him. As the effects of public service, they are in the public realm. Coriolanus' refusal to acknowledge the extent of that public realm leads to his banishment from it. Initially he acknowledges the obligation that he bears to take part in the public ceremony, turning his resistance against the 'musts' that constrain him to a resigned, 'Well, I must do't' (3.3.112).[32] But, incensed through the Machiavellian devices of the tribunes and what he perceives as their outrageous impertinence, he loses the self-control he promised to his mother and his peers: 'Well, mildly be it, then—mildly!' (3.2.147).

The critical point in the contest of competing powers and authorities comes earlier, in 3.2, when Coriolanus pinpoints the tension underlying the farcical political ceremony that he ultimately refuses to endorse:

> This double worship,
> Where one part does disdain with cause, the other
> Insult without all reason, where gentry, title, wisdom
> Cannot conclude but by the yea and no
> Of general ignorance, it must omit
> Real necessities, and give the way the while
> To unstable slightness. Purpose so barred, it follows
> Nothing is done to purpose ... Your dishonor
> Mangles true judgement, and bereaves the state
> Of that integrity which should become't ...
>
> (3.1.144-61)

The question is whether this judgement constitutes, as Brutus puts it, 'manifest treason' (173). The play is not entirely clear on this point. Theatrically, it is significant that when Sicinius gives the command that Coriolanus be arrested in the name of the people they are not present, but must be called:

> Go call the people,   [*Exit Aedile*]
> (*To Coriolanus*) in whose name myself
> Attach thee as a traitorous innovator,
> A foe to th' public weal. Obey, I charge thee,
> And follow to thine answer.
> [*He tries to seize Coriolanus*]
> CORIOLANUS Hence, old goat!
>
> (3.1.175-8)

Does Sicinius have the authority to issue these commands and charges? In J. L. Austin's terms, are the felicity conditions for a proper command met? In theatrical terms, the people in whose name he acts are missing, and his repeated commands show a straining for authority and legality that is rejected by Coriolanus' contemptuous response. The question that underlies this contest is who or what constitutes the city or the state of Rome? Against whom is one acting if one acts as a traitor? Once the people arrive to bolster Sicinius' claim to authority, one answer is quickly provided when the tribune rejects the First Senator's assumption about the constitution of the city itself:

> MENINIUS   This is the way to kindle, not to quench.
> FIRST SENATOR   To unbuild the city, and to lay all flat.

---

[32] See, '*Must* I go show them my unbarbed sconce? | *Must* I with my base tongue give to my noble heart | A lie that it *must* bear?' (3.2.101-3).

> SICINIUS   What is the city but the people?
> ALL [THE CITIZENS]   True,
> The people are the city.

$$(3.1.197-9)$$

If the people are the city, then who are the patricians, including such figures as Coriolanus? In 3.3 the claim that the city is identical to the people is slowly strengthened in the further contest with Coriolanus through the accumulation of political power via language. Sicinius' demands and charges move from the first-person singular ('I do demand ... (41)) to the more robust plural ('Answer to us ... We charge you...' (61, 63)). That communal authority is made explicit in the order of banishment itself:

> SICINIUS ... in the name o' th' people
> And in the power of us the tribunes, we,
> E'en from this instant banish him our city ... never more
> To enter our Roman gates. In the people's name
> I say it shall be so.
> ALL [THE CITIZENS] It shall be so, it shall be so! Let him away!
> He's banished and it shall be so!

$$(3.1.103-11)$$

Notice two things here: first, the way in which the insistent first-person plural, especially in its possessive form ('our city ... our Rome') banishes Coriolanus grammatically even before he is banished legally—Rome has long ceased to be Coriolanus' city; second, the return of the 'absolute shall', now unambiguously as a deontic modal—one that does not merely predict but performs power. When the Citizens repeat the Tribunes' words, 'It shall be so', they are in fact relegated to the merely epistemological model of prediction. Shakespeare makes this quite clear by having Sicinius insist on the exact moment of Coriolanus' banishment: 'e'en from this instant', which means that the banishment is complete by the time the citizens parrot their tribune: the tribunes have in fact appropriated, or themselves constituted, the authority in whose 'name' they supposedly speak.

Much has been made of Coriolanus' response, to banish the city: 'I banish you! | ... thus I turn my back. | There is a world elsewhere' (124, 135-6). Critics have observed that it is an infelicitous speech act, because it does not lie within the power of a single person to banish a city. Moreover, it signals Coriolanus' delusional sense of his own independence and incapacity to grasp the mutuality of a speech community as political and social entity. But if Coriolanus' utterance calls into question its own validity it also asks us to question the validity of the tribunes' legal capacity to banish Coriolanus and their arrogation of the city as a whole to themselves, in the name of a many-headed multitude that in fact has no single name.

POLITICS AND PSYCHOLOGY

R. B. Parker remarks that 'the brilliance of Coriolanus is its special insight into the mutual influence of psychology and politics' (43). I have so far treated politics rather than psychology. I have claimed that Shakespeare's tragedy traces the tensions within a developing constitutional republic that is still reliant on the military prowess of militaristic individuals for survival. Coriolanus is fully a tragedy because it traces the negotiation, contest, and constitution of power through the character of a single, gigantic individual who is finally destroyed by such a constitutional process, thought absolutely necessary by Machiavelli.

Whatever we may think of Coriolanus' politics (and in modern terms they are reprehensible) we shouldn't make the mistake of simplifying what Parker calls his psychology. I am not going to retrace the psychoanalytical analyses that explain him through his dependence on his mother. Rather, I want to suggest that part of Coriolanus' downfall lies in a trait that we are likely to find admirable in characters of a less militarist disposition: the strange human incapacity, in some people, to say something in which they don't believe, even if it would be the easiest thing to do and they would, moreover, benefit from it. The signal example in Shakespeare is Cordelia's incapacity to declare her love for her father when he demands it publicly in *King Lear*. This incapacity has fatal consequences—just as it does for Coriolanus.

Coriolanus does not grasp that in terms of the game he has agreed to play his wounds do not belong to him. It makes absolutely no sense that, once he has agreed to seek the consulship, he insists on avoiding the ceremonies that getting it requires. There are many ways of seeing this incapacity—or wilful refusal—which is encapsulated by the possibility that there are certain things that each of us, at some point, cannot bring ourselves to say. One is the gap between the words that the tongue may 'coin' and the heart believes, encapsulated by the concept of the actor who plays a false part. But another is the notion of integrity, which Coriolanus himself invokes in his refusal to accept the division of the state between citizen and patrician.

The problem with the concept of personal integrity, like that of conscience, is that it is often a fundamentally anti-social force. One's sense of one's own integrity is often sharply at odds with what is expected by one's society, and if there is a problem with the application of speech-act theory to *Coriolanus* it lies in a too-simple concept of the relation between language, society, and the individual (or the subject). There is something powerfully admirable about Coriolanus' determination to preserve his own sense of his integrity, no matter how much it may be at odds with our own values. Such admiration is redoubled by the terrible consequences of that determination.

The second aspect of Coriolanus' 'psychology' that gives the play its tragic character is his discovery, despite every effort, that human beings cannot cut themselves off from the ties that bind them to others. For Coriolanus there is indeed 'a world elsewhere' beyond Rome. It is the domain of the Volscians, but more specifically, it is his partnership with the man who obsesses him throughout the play: his mortal enemy, Aufidius, towards whom he gravitates inexorably: 'I wish I had cause to seek him there | To oppose his hatred fully' (3.1.20-1). Critics have suggested not merely the homosocial but also the homoerotic nature of this relationship. I leave the reader to explore those readings and will confine myself to the observation that Coriolanus' fatal discovery of his ties to others lies not in the arms of the Volscian general, whom he finally betrays, but in clasping the hand of his mother, in the presence of his wife and son.

INTEGRITY

The key utterance is one often picked out by critics as a signal of Coriolanus' deluded sense of his own absolute independence and self-sufficiency: 'I'll never | Be such a gosling to obey instinct, but stand | *As if a man were* author of himself | And knew no other kin' (5.3.34-7). Again, grammar is crucial. Coriolanus is not claiming self-sufficiency as an achieved condition. He is perfectly well aware of the importance of social, patriotic, and familial ties, not merely emotionally but also as constituents of identity. He is determined to act in the conditional: *as if* man were author of himself. This assumption of the actor's role—the resolve to play a part against human nature itself (despite the denigration of such ties as animal instinct)—signals the tragedy to come. And we know it will not befall Rome, but rather the man whose integrity is everything to him.

Coriolanus' speech to his mother is one of the most moving in Shakespeare, embodying as it does in their physical relation to each other, the general's realization that he has succumbed, that he could not do otherwise, and that his humanity will be his death:

> *He holds her by the hand, silent.*
> CORIOLANUS O mother, mother!
> What have you done? Behold, the heavens do ope,
> The gods look down, and this unnatural scene
> They laugh at. O, my mother, mother, O!
> You have won a happy victory to Rome,
> But, for your son—believe it, O, believe it!—
> Most dangerously you have with him prevailed,
> If not most mortal to him. But let it come.—
> Aufidius, though I cannot make true wars,
> I'll frame convenient peace. Now, good Aufidius,
> Were you in my stead, would you have heard
> A mother less? Or granted less, Aufidius?
>
> (5.3.183-94)

The core of this speech—ironically in a play so concerned with speech and voices—lies in silence, as Coriolanus holds his mother by the hand. He knows (and has known from the moment he declared in the face of his family that 'Like a dull actor now | I have forgot my part, and am out | Even to a full disgrace' (5,3.40-2)), that a man cannot live *as if* he were author of himself, and his acknowledgement, through the simple, human bond of hands, that he is doomed. But also that he could not have acted otherwise. There is a point at which he attempts to shift the blame onto his mother—'O mother, mother. | What have you done?'—although the enjambment suggests that the question comes after the mere vocative, the simple, invocation of his relationship to his mother, the woman he now touches in ways very different from the 'fisting' with Aufidius.

Coriolanus turns, finally into a Stoic, echoing Hamlet: 'But let it come.' He accepts death; he accepts defeat, even at the hands of his mortal enemy; and he finally accepts Rome as part of himself. On the other hand, he knows that his banishment remains; that he cannot return to Rome. For him the heavens have been emptied of *human* value, inhabited only by capricious gods who make human frailty their sport. But not for us. We are watching too, and we are moved to tears.

His attempt to incorporate Aufidius into what he has just done acknowledges its futility in its almost childish over-eagerness. Aufidius' hypocrisy stands in stark contrast to Coriolanus' culminating, unexpected, and heroic preservation of his integrity. Aufidius is utterly diminished in his ruthless and cynical murder of his rival—as Achilles is after the murder of Hector in *Troilus and Cressida*, or Caesar in the wake of the tragic ends of Antony and Cleopatra.

Coriolanus fully deserves its status as a Shakespearean tragedy. It is one of Shakespeare's most exacting and meticulous analyses of the constitution of political power at a particular point of history, especially through the power of grammar. It conforms to Machiavelli's judgement that for the republican forms of government that we value today to survive, Coriolanus was a necessary sacrifice. But insofar as Shakespeare embodies the effects of that historical development on a remarkable human being, it should move us to the core.

SELECT BIBLIOGRAPHY

Adelman, Janet, *Suffocating Mothers: Fantasies of Maternal Origin in Shakespeare's Plays, Hamlet to the Tempest* (New York: Routledge, 1992).

Bloom, Harold, *Shakespeare: The Invention of the Human* (London: Fourth Estate, 2008).

Bradley, A. C., 'Coriolanus', The Second British Academy Lecture (Oxford: Oxford University Press, 1912).

Calderwood, James L., '*Coriolanus*: Wordless Meanings and Meaningless Words', *Studies in English Literature, 1500–1900* 6:2 (1966), 211.

Cavell, Stanley, *Disowning Knowledge in Seven Plays of Shakespeare* (Cambridge: Cambridge University Press, 2014).

Engle, Lars, *Shakespearean Prgamatism: Market of his Time* (Chicago: University of Chicago Press, 1993).

Fish, Stanley, *Is There a Text in this Class? The Authority of Interpretive Communities* (Cambridge, MA: Harvard University Press, 1990).

Goldberg, Jonathan, 'The Anus in *Coriolanus*', in Carla Mazzio, and Douglas Trevor, eds., *Historicism, Psychoanalysis, and Early Modern Culture* (London and New York: Routledge, 2000), 260–71.

Kolentsis, Alyasia, ' "Mark you | His absolute Shall": Multitudinous Tongues and Contested Words in *Coriolanus*', *Shakespeare Survey* 58 (2009), 141–50.

Kuzner, James, 'Unbuilding the City: *Coriolanus* and the Birth of Republican Rome', *Shakespeare Quarterly* 58:2 (2007), 174–99.

Plotz, Plotz. 'Coriolanus and the Failure of Performatives', *ELH* 63:4 (1996), 809–32.

Shakespeare, William, *Coriolanus*. Arden 3, ed. Peter Holland (London: Bloomsbury, 2013).

Shakespeare, William, *Coriolanus*, ed. R. B. Parker (Oxford: Oxford University Press, 1994).

Shakespeare, William, *Coriolanus*, ed. Lee Bliss (Cambridge: Cambridge University Press, 2000).

PART IV

STAGE AND SCREEN

CHAPTER 30

....

EARLY MODERN TRAGEDY
AND PERFORMANCE

....

TIFFANY STERN

DESPITE the fact that theatres of Shakespeare's age did not make use of scenery, and so could offer little embellishment of fictional location, they could be arranged, visually, to make statements about genre. References bear witness to the way playhouses might be adorned with hangings that emphasized tragic stories: 'The Stage all hang'd with the sad death of Kings, | From whose bewailing story sorrow springs.'[1] More often, though, they made outright statements of tragic genre through colour—'A spatious *Theatre* first mee thought I saw, | All hang'd with black to act some tragedie'; 'when the stage of the world was hung in blacke, they jetted uppe & downe like proud Tragedians'; 'The stage is hung with blacke: and I perceive | The Auditors preparde for Tragedie'.[2] Marston advises audiences who dislike tragedy to 'hurrie amaine' from what he is offering in *Antonio's Revenge*: 'black visag'd showes'.[3] This decor borrows the black hangings used to adorn great houses and churches during funeral rites; it thus comes with suggestions of death and mourning as well as 'the social assumptions inherent in this kind of social display'.[4] There are mentions, too, of an enveloping stage blackness that may extend beyond hangings: writers often allude to the tragic 'sable Stage', or, as Shakespeare put it in *Rape of Lucrece*, describing night, 'Black stage for tragedies and murders fell' (766), perhaps implying that the dark-stained wood of the stage-floor, visible when rushes and matting were removed, had been purposefully revealed.[5] Sometimes, then, from the moment an audience entered a playhouse, and before the play actually began, 'tragedy', had already started. In such instances 'tragedy' did not need to be part of a title, or a direction in which a play tended—it could, rather, be a look, an atmosphere, a theatrical

---

[1] John Taylor, *The Water-Cormorant his Complaint* (1622), A4r.

[2] Richard Verstegan (alias Richard Rowlands), 'Visions of the Worlds Instabilitie', in *Odes in Imitation of the Seaven Penitential Psalmes* (1601), 109; Thomas Dekker, *Lanthorne and Candle-light* (1609), L1v; *A Warning for Faire Women* (1599), A3r.

[3] Anthony Marston, *Antonios Revenge* (1602), A2v.

[4] Michael Neill, *Issues of Death* (Oxford: Clarendon Press, 1997), 282.

[5] Francis Quarles, *Divine Fancies* (1632), 171; Matthew Parker, *A True and Terrible Narration* (1638), A4v; Samuel Daniel, *The Civile Wars* (1609), 154. Quotations from Shakespeare are taken from *The Oxford Shakespeare*, 2nd edn., ed. Stanley Wells and Gary Taylor (Oxford: Oxford University Press, 2005).

mood. 'Tragedy', was a kind of performance as well as a kind of drama, as this chapter will explore; the formality and insistent bleakness of the theatrical space was, on occasion, part of the interpretative meaning of what was put on there.

As genre was one of the few wordless comments regularly made by staging, it was obviously of keen importance to the theatrical thinking of the period. But of course, authors will not always have adopted such pointed staging. Shakespeare, like other writers, seems to have flirted with placing, and not placing, additional statements in stage decorations. *1 Henry VI's* 'Hung be the heavens with black' (1.1.1) states a tragic metaphorical intention—the sky should be darkened, as a tragedy is to ensue—and, almost certainly, a tragic stage fact—the 'heavens', the internal roof of the playhouse, were presumably adorned with black tragic hangings on this occasion, or the reference would be semi-redundant. On the other hand, some plays switch unexpectedly to tragedy in ways that are unlikely to have been predicted by staging. Examples include moments of generic confusion, as when, for instance, at the end of the comedy *Love's Labour's Lost*, Marcade enters, presumably in mourning black, to announce 'the King your father—', and the Princess realizes 'Dead, for my life' (5.2.712-13). This is a tragic turning point within what has hitherto seemed to be a straightforward comedy; but stating either comedy or tragedy through stage hangings would predict or query this moment. The suggestion, then, is that writers could choose to make visual statements in stage décor to bolster (or profitably confuse) their verbal one—and, equally, could choose not to.

When an author did not wish to proclaim genre from the moment the audience entered the playhouse, he could insert tragic signs later, during the performance itself. Tragedy could be placed in costume. Hamlet's black illustrates his mourning, but also declares 'tragedy', recalling the colour of tragic hangings. It draws attention to Hamlet's theatricality—does he know the kind of play he is in (or bring about the kind of play he is in)? It should be borne in mind, though, that Olivia, in the comedy *Twelfth Night*, also wears black as a private tragic statement. Characters, then, could carry personal 'tragedy' in a way that did not necessarily comment on the play beyond themselves.

Tragedy could additionally, or alternatively, be located in a bleak actor's adornment, usually imposed at some point deep within the play. This was the ultimate tragic prop, blood—a liquid so fundamental to the plot of many tragedies as to form a major part of their staging appeal: 'Goe tell the Authors of high Tragedies, | That bloudlesse quarrels are but merry fights'.[6] Highly appreciated tragic writers were said to be those whose 'Verses fits the bleeding Tragedie'; or whose tragic moment could be mawkishly anticipated—'This Scene will anon swimme in bloud'.[7] Blood was much relished by audiences, and Shakespeare's company seems to have developed a name for it. In *A Warning for Faire Women*, a play staged by the Lord Chamberlain's Men in 1599, the emblematic figure of Tragedy signifies her nature by entering with 'a bowle of bloud in her hand'.[8]

---

[6] Nicholas Breton, *Pasquils Mad-cap* (1600), 36.

[7] Anthony Scoloker, *Daiphantus* (1604), C1v; Justus Lipsius, *Two Bookes of Constancie* (1595), 91.

[8] *A Warning for Faire Women* (1599), C4v. For more on blood as an emblem of tragedy, see Andrea Stevens, 'Cosmetic Transformations', in Farah Karim-Cooper and Tiffany Stern, eds., *Shakespeare's Theatres and the Effects of Performance* (London: Methuen, 2013).

Shakespeare's own bloody staging, in particular, was legendary. An epitaph for Richard Burbage, Shakespeare's lead actor, famous for his performances of Lear, Hamlet, Othello, as well as Hieronimo in *The Spanish Tragedy*, dwells on the way, when Burbage acted:

> spectators and the rest
> of his sad crew, whilst hee but seemd to bleed
> amazed thought evn that hee died indeed.[9]

Throughout his writing career, Shakespeare used blood, probably bought from nearby meat markets, as a prop: he was perpetually taking the tragic theme of violent death to its most visual, most literal and most performative.[10] From the removal of hands in *Titus Andronicus*, to the handkerchief stained with young Rutland's blood, and given to mop his father York's eyes in 3 *Henry VI,* Shakespeare's early plays were lavishly drenched with the tragic substance.

Over time, however, Shakespeare sophisticated his use of the blood prop, so that a compelling theatrical device also became a literary one. *Richard II*, named a tragedy on its quarto title page, is a drama alert to the metaphorical import of physical blood. In this play obsessed with problems of inherited kingship, stage blood comes to mean both blood the substance and the royal bloodline. Richard II, anxious to avoid the shedding of literal blood—'Let's purge this choler without letting blood' (1.1.153)—is equally trying to keep his bloodline intact. When, at the end of the play, he is bloodily killed, the blood metaphorically stains land and killer: 'thy fierce hand | Hath with the King's blood stained the King's own land' (5.5.109-10) indicts Richard II as he dies; 'I'll make a voyage to the Holy Land | To wash this blood off from my guilty hand' says Henry IV (5.6.49-50). The blood, now symbolic, becomes a prominent motif—a physical representation of the curse on the house of Henry IV—explored in Shakespeare's related history plays. In *Macbeth*, too, blood is both a constant prop—the bloody man, the bloody baby, Banquo's bloody head, the blood-soaked hands of the Macbeths—and a symbol of the evil that forced it to be spilled. In some of the most important moments in *Macbeth*, therefore, blood is referred to (it is a constant refrain in the play) but is not actually there: the bloody dagger of the mind, or the damned spots on Lady Macbeth's clean hand.

Shakespeare, then, was alert to the staging possibilities raised by tragedy and subsumed them into his literary constructions. This chapter will look at the performative side of 'tragedy'—'tragic' ways of walking ('strutting', 'jetting', and 'stalking'), 'tragic' ways of speaking ('ranting' and 'canting' in a tragic 'tone' or 'key') and the revelation of tragic passions—arguing throughout that Shakespeare's consciousness of the staging of tragedy dictates his choice of metaphor and symbol; enacted tragedy, it will argue, helped form Shakespeare's tragic sensibility.

***

---

[9] 'On Mr Richard Burbidg an excellent both player, and painter', Folger Shakespeare Library MS, v.a.97, 90v.

[10] For the use of animal blood as a tragic stage prop, see Lucy Munro, '*They eat each others' arms*': Stage Blood and Body Parts', in Farah Karim-Cooper and Tiffany Stern eds., *Shakespeare's Theatres and the Effects of Performance* (London: Methuen, 2013), 73–93.

The word 'tragedian' had two meanings. It denoted a *writer* of tragedies—Phillips defined 'Tragedian, or Tragediographer' as 'a writer of ... a sort of Dramatick Poetry ... representing murthers, sad and mournfull actions', and a *player* of tragedies—Nashe writes of the way 'the Tragedian that represents [Talbot]' seems 'fresh bleeding' to spectators.[11] Tragedy straddled writing and performance, then; hardly surprisingly, Shakespeare, as a writer-player, was said to combine the two: when he is praised for his 'tragic' skills, it is not even always clear whether his writing or acting is being extolled. In 'Friendly Shakespeares Tragedies' wrote Scoloker, 'the Commedian rides, when the Tragedian stands on Tip-toe'—meaning both that, in writing terms, comic and tragic matter were combined and, in performance terms, the comic actors traversed a stage over which the tragic actors towered.[12] Even as a metaphor, if that is what this is, the language used for tragedy was rooted in performance.

Shakespeare himself, however, was particularly alert to the theatrical rather than writerly connotations of tragedy. In fact, he only ever used the word 'tragedian' as he used the word 'comedian', for an actor, not a playwright. Thus Rosencrantz tells Hamlet of the arrival of 'the tragedians of the city' (*Hamlet*, 2.2.330) in whose productions the prince had once taken great delight; while Cleopatra fears 'the quick comedians' (*Anthony and Cleopatra*, 5.2.212) will stage her story extemporally. For Shakespeare, then, tragedians and comedians, though they differed from one another, were similarly performative: tragedy and comedy, for him, denoted different forms of staging as much as different genres of writing.

It becomes important, then, to ask how tragic performance differed from comic performance, a question enlightened, though complicated, by classical precedent. In Hellenistic Greek theatre—notionally a model for early modern theatre—tragic actors had moved entirely differently from comic ones. Greek actors of tragedies had performed wearing raised boots known in English as 'buskins'; actors of comedies had played in low thin shoes known in English as 'socks'. As a result, tragedians and comedians had, of necessity, walked in genre-specific ways: there was literally a tragic and a comic pace.

In the early modern period the buskin and sock were not necessarily used, yet they conveyed enough meaning to be regularly mentioned as metaphors. Tragedy, like the buskin, was viewed as a raised and artificial form of performance; comedy as a lowered and homely form, like the sock. Thus when Abraham Wright addressed Ben Jonson's skill in comic and tragic writing, he wrote 'Yet was thy language and thy stile so high | Thy Sock to the ancle, Buskin reachd to th' thigh'; while, had playwrights known that a war would close their theatres, '*Shakespear* with *Chapman*' it was said, would have 'grown mad, and torn | The gentle *Soc*, and *lofty Buskins* worn'.[13] What 'buskin' and 'sock' also add to the description of the genres tragedy and comedy, however, is a continued sense that the two played differently—in particular, that each employed different methods of walking.

---

[11] Edward Phillips, *The New World of English Words* (1658), 2P3r; Thomas Nashe, *Pierce Penilesse* (1592), F3r.

[12] Anthony Scolocker, *Daiphantus* (1604), A2r.

[13] [Abraham Wright?] *Parnassus Biceps* (1656), 132; James Howell, 'Upon the great Drammatical Work of B and Fletcher, publish'd 1646', *Poems* (1664), 26.

Though almost certainly not wearing actual buskins, early modern players of tragedy seem to have stridden across the stage in particular ways, defined sometimes as 'stalking', sometimes as 'jetting' and sometimes as 'strutting'. The words, 'stalk', 'jet' and 'strut', are close enough in meaning as, perhaps, to be getting at the same motion, or at subtle variations of it: a stiff, pompous gait, with, analogies suggest, bird-like prinking—perhaps in its careful placing—about it. Post-Restoration accounts, which show how heightened tragic walking had become, help explain the formality and ridiculous nature of what they called the 'tragic gait':

> THEATRIC Monarchs in their tragic Gait
> Affect to mark the solemn Pace of State.
> One Foot put forward in Position strong,
> The other like its Vassal dragg'd along.
> So grave each Motion, so exact and slow,
> Like wooden Monarchs at a Puppet-show.[14]

In Shakespeare's time, 'stalking', the oldest word for tragic walking, was already out of date; often it was used to refer specifically to the gait that had been adopted for performance of plays by Christopher Marlowe. Thus Middleton/Dekker conceives of Death, personified, as 'rather like stalking *Tamberlaine*'; Hall thinks of the man who imagines himself to be 'the Turkish Tamberlaine' and 'conceives upon his fained stage | The stalking steps of his greate personage'; and Middleton describes spiders 'stalking' on the ceiling, 'as if they had bene conning of Tamburlayne'.[15] Such a walk may even be depicted in the famous 'Swan Theatre' drawing, made in 1596 by Johannes de Witt and surviving in a copy by Arend van Buchel: it shows two characters sitting on stage and one further character, his legs astride, apparently stalking up to them. In Shakespeare, 'stalking' carried with it the idea of brittle pride. He applied it to the over-proud—Ajax in *Troilus and Cressida*, 'stalks up and down like a peacock' (3.3.244)—but also to ghosts. So the ghost of Hamlet's father in *Hamlet* is said to have a 'martial stalk' (1.1.65), and when he takes umbrage as Horatio tactlessly describes him as 'usurp[ing]' the night, he 'stalks away' (1.1.44, 48). Perhaps Shakespeare used this term because Hamlet's ghost moved in a way that looked, befitting his nature, tragic; perhaps he used the term to imply that the ghost moved in a way redolent of past, Marlovian, acting styles. If the ghost of Hamlet's father, in his very gait, appeared old-fashioned, then it becomes important that Hamlet regularly fulminates against mannered and 'old' over-acting when he sees it in the players. Could it be that Hamlet dislikes in performative terms what he daren't dislike—or perhaps is incapable of recognizing—in real terms? The play continually compares performance with reality throughout, within the irony of being itself an enacted play, of course, but it seems that Shakespeare may here have employed historical acting style to give his drama further ironies.

'Jetting' was directly associated with actorly pride so intense that passages that describe the movement conflate the fictional pride of the character with the factual pride

---

[14] Robert Lloyd, *The Actor* (1760), 6. For more on the Restoration tragic strut, see Alan S. Downer, 'Nature to Advantage Dressed: Eighteenth Century Acting', *PMLA* 58 (1943), 1002–37 (1009–10).

[15] Thomas Dekker, *The Wonderfull Yeare* (1603), D1r; Joseph Hall, 'Satire III', *Virgidemiarum* (1598), 7; Thomas Middleton, *The Blacke Booke* (1604), D1r. For the idea that these references may refer to the specific acting style of Edward Alleyn, see Andrew J. Gurr, 'Who Strutted and Bellowed', *SHS* 16 (1963), 95–102.

of the actor performing him. So 'proude players jett in their silkes'; 'they on stage, in stately sort … jet;' 'they jetted uppe & downe like proud Tragedians'.[16] This word, which may also contain an internal pun on the jet-black clothes worn sometimes by tragedians, is used by Shakespeare parodically. He applies it to people who take themselves too seriously to have a sense of context. So Malvolio, reading the letter in the comedy *Twelfth Night*, is described as 'a rare turkeycock' who 'jets under his advanced plumes!' (2.5.29-30): Malvolio is the outsider, not only because he is a puritan, but also because he, like Olivia in her black, is performing wrongly for the genre for which his role is written.

Finally, there was 'strutting', which again signified self-importance and an overblown sense of superiority. It was what actors did in contrast to what real people did: 'His gate … is sage and grave, not affected and strouting like a stage-plaier'.[17] This was the word most associated with bad acting for Shakespeare. Indeed, whenever he addressed the forced walking style of the professional actor, it was the strutting that he singled out. The kind of players hated by Hamlet 'strutted and bellowed' and 'imitated humanity … abominably' (*Hamlet*, 3.2.32-5); Macbeth's 'poor player' 'struts and frets his hour upon the stage'—fretting meaning 'chewing', a description of the mouthing of words that will be considered later in this chapter (*Macbeth*, 5.5.23-4); Achilles is 'like a strutting player, whose conceit | Lies in his hamstring' (*Troilus and Cressida*, 1.3.153-4). Yet even then, some people are genuinely described as strutting by Shakespeare, again, often when taking themselves too seriously. Master Slender in *Merry Wives* is one who 'hold[s] up his head, as it were, and strut[s] in his gait' (1.4.27-8). More portentously, Anthony in *Anthony and Cleopatra*, observing how he and his paramour are striding to meet their fate, thinks that the gods are laughing at the two of them 'while we strut | To our confusion' (3.13.115-16). Here the point is that their descent to chaos is, as the entire relationship has been, tragically ridiculous. Shakespeare confirms and queries genre through tragic steps, though he may also have adopted them unambiguously for moments of ritualized, heightened drama. When characters are described as walking in telling ways, Shakespeare may even be prompting them to use a tragic gait: like the Fiends in *1 Henry VI* who *'walk and speak not'* (sd 5.2.12), or Lear who questions what he himself is doing and what it might mean, 'Doth Lear walk thus, speak thus?' (*King Lear*, 1.4.221).

It is no surprise to learn that tragedy matched its special pace with a range of unique and special tragic sounds. Tragic speech could be pronounced in a fashion so musical that Camden refers to 'speaking … (as folke say) in a tragicke Key upon the stage', while Davies writes of listeners who 'believe all Sounds (how sweet so ere) | Are but the accents of a Tragicke voice'.[18] Tragic speech, too, had its own vocabulary: 'tone' was used for its

[16] Letter from a soldier to Sir Francis Walsingham, Jan 25 1586 | 7, quoted in E. K. Chambers, *The Elizabethan Stage*, 4 vols. (Oxford: Clarendon Press, 1923), 4: 304; Stephen Gosson, *Pleasant Quippes for Upstart Newfangled Gentle-women* (1595), A3r; Thomas Dekker, *Lanthorne and Candle-light* (1609), L1v.

[17] Thomas Walkington, *The Optick Glasse of Humors* (1607), 80v.

[18] William Camden, *Britain* (1637), 78r; John Davies, *The Holy Roode* (1609), G4v. Very little has been written about tone on the early modern stage, and this section has been influenced by accounts of tonal speaking in the Restoration, in particular, John Harold Wilson, 'Rant, Cant, and Tone on the Restoration Stage', *Studies in Philology* 52 (1955), 592-8.

melodic quality of sound, and 'accent' for its melodic sense of emphasis. This distinctive vocal range was, like tragic pace, used, abused, parodied, and relied upon. Brome writes a play in which Philomel asks 'Ha' not I forgot my Actors tone?' and later Philomel '*speaks in a vile tone like a Player*'; Collop refers to players who perform with 'mimick gesture, and affected tone'.[19] Yet the popular Bull playhouse, where crowd-pleasing plays were performed most, embraced aural extravagance, bearing witness to its popularity with the masses—'She looks high, and speaks in a *Majestick tone*, like one playing the Queens part at the *Bull*.'[20]

'Accent', with its reference to rhythmic emphasis, was related to the rhetorical skill of declamation. Yet 'accent' likewise extended into the speeches' musical qualities: in glosses, 'voculation' is 'a giving a word its right tone or accent', 'prosodie' is 'the art of giving words their due accent, or tone' and 'barbarism' is 'a fault in the pronouncing, tone or accent of words'.[21] Hence musical accent is said to shape the sound of the tragic stage, from those who speak in 'the dismall accents of thy tragedie' to those who pronounce 'with an harmonious Accent'.[22]

Shakespeare, as player-playwright, was acutely accent-conscious. Unlike tragic movement, which he often parodied, he seems to have used the tragic vocal music available to him seriously, using tone and accent to beautify, heighten and embellish his poetry. So it is no surprise to find his characters also obsessed, metatheatrically, with speaking correctly. Boyet in *Love's Labour's Lost* describes how he watched Moth preparing to act a part in the Pageant of the Nine Worthies. He remarks in particular how Moth was carefully taught two qualities, 'Action and accent' (5.2.99). Polonius in *Hamlet,* likewise, praises the player who spoke his words 'with good accent and good discretion' (2.2.469-70). As Shakespeare wrote for performance, a number of his word choices will have been made with sonorous intent at least as prominent as meaning. Ben Jonson, another actor-writer, had done the same: to him 'the ... offices of a tragic writer' consisted of creating a text that had 'gravity and height of elocution, fulness and frequency of sentence'.[23] It was usual to write for the sound of performance.

Formal set passages are often in a different poetic register from the words around them, and are forthright about their musical qualities. Some moments in Shakespeare are as ornate in phrasing and rhythm as they are in lyricism:

> O, she doth teach the torches to burn bright!
> It seems she hangs upon the cheek of night
> As a rich jewel in an Ethiop's ear—
> Beauty too rich for use, for earth too dear.
>
> (Romeo and Juliet, 1.5.43-6).

The gorgeousness of the visual depiction—with Juliet's radiance teaching torches to flame, then exuding light like a sparkling jewel when all around it is dark—is here enhanced

[19] Richard Brome, *The Court Begger* (1653), S3r-S3v; John Collop, *Poesis Rediviva* (1656), 36.

[20] R. F. [Flecknoe] *Fifty Five Enigmatical Characters* (1665), 63.

[21] Edward Phillips, *The New World of English Words* (1658), 2R1v, 2I3r; Thomas Blount, *Glossographia or a Dictionary* (1656), F4v.

[22] Charles Fitz-Geffry, *Sir Francis Drake his Honorable Lifes Commendation* (1596), G2v; Charles Sorel, *The Extravagant Shepherd ... Translated out of French* (1653), 54.

[23] Ben Jonson, *Sejanus his Fall* (1605), π2r.

sonorously. From the first line with its repetition of 't', 'ch', 'b', and 'r' in words chiasti-
cally arranged so that long varies with short vowels, sound is part of this quatrain's music.
Alliteration softens as the couplets progress—'teach'/'torches', yields to 'burn'/'bright', yields
to 'Ethiop's ear'/'earth'; but the whole is also enriched aurally with assonance ('seems'/
'cheek', 'jewel'/'beauty'/'use'), and the ritualistic rhythm imposed by repetition: 'rich …
rich', 'too … too', 'for … for'. The quatrain is made up of two rhyming couplets that are
perhaps also a theatrical metaphor for the act of coupling, so that the second line seems
demanded by the first, and leads the listener first to the rhymed opposites of 'night' and
'bright', then to the inevitable ultimate fulfilment of 'dear'—with its combined meaning of
'expensive' and 'loved'.

It was, of course, tragical sonority that encouraged playwrights to write in verse as well
as prose: they relished the distinction and the possibility it offered for heightened verse. As
Sheppard, wrote, praising 'Mr. Websters most excellent tragedy, Called the White Devill',
'How pretty are thy lines, thy Verses stand | Like unto pretious Jewels set in gold, | And
grace thy fluent Prose'.[24] Some tragic speeches were designed to be gorgeous, with moments
of sonorous beauty that, like arias in operas, soar over the recitative that heralds them.
Soliloquies, in particular, not only exemplified skills in tragic writing, but also demanded
skills in tragic speaking. Indeed, soliloquies are important to tragedy not only because they
give privileged insight into the mind of the speaker, but also because they are set pieces for
tragic sound.

At the same time, writing tragic verse was thought of as slightly cheap: or, rather, iambic
pentameter was seen as crowd-pleasing and easy. Joseph Hall patronizingly describes the
type of audience who is lured by 'pure *Iambick* verse', particularly the tragic verse facilely
adopted by all writers: 'Unbid *Iambicks* flow from carelesse head'.[25] By indulging in sensual,
sonorous verse, Shakespeare was playing to the crowd, which is perhaps why his soliloquies
vary from the obviously lyrically pleasing, to the designedly spiky. Compare the sensuous-
ness of 2 *Henry 4*'s beautiful paean to sleep to the slow rhythms and spitting plosives of Lady
Macbeth:

> O gentle sleep,
> Nature's soft nurse, how have I frighted thee,
> That thou no more will weigh my eyelids down
> And steep my senses in forgetfulness?
> Why rather, sleep, liest thou in smoky cribs,
> Upon uneasy pallets stretching thee,
> And hushed with buzzing night-flies to thy slumber,
> Than in the perfum'd chambers of the great,
> Under the canopies of costly state,
> And lulled with sound of sweetest melody?
>
> (2 Henry IV, 3.1.5-14)

> The raven himself is hoarse
> That croaks the fatal entrance of Duncan
> Under my battlements. Come, you spirits

[24] Samuel Sheppard, *Epigrams* (1651), 133.   [25] John Hall, 'Satire IIII', *Virgidemiarum*, 10.

> That tend on mortal thoughts, unsex me here,
> And fill me from the crown to the toe top-full
> Of direst cruelty.
>
> (*Macbeth*, 1.5.37)

Yet writing to iambic rhythm was not the only way in which Shakespeare, like his contemporaries, courted the aural possibilities of language. Another was by coining or picking up words—the longer, the better. This was not entirely connected to the fact, often stated, that Shakespeare thought beyond language: though he did do that. It was because he was being populist, and looking to the same linguistic possibilities that brought audiences streaming to the Bull theatre. Spectators went to playhouses partly to hear and learn the newest, the sharpest, and the most magnificent words; the lengthier the word and the more elongated the line that contained it, the more it would be valued, particularly by the uneducated:

> I have heard, that the Poets of the Fortune and the red Bull, had alwayes a mouth-measure for their Actors (who were terrible teare-throats) and made their lines proportionable to their compasse, which were *sesquipedales*, a foot and a halfe.[26]

The use of long words resulted in a common term of opprobrium for author and actor alike, 'widemouths', for the fact that their mouths were said to need engorging to fit in or let out the huge terms and phrases they had been given. Hall writes of verses that an actor 'sees fitly frame to his wide-strained mouth'; Overburie mentions 'a wide-mouth'de *Poet*, that speakes nothing but bladders & bumbast'; Greene is obsessed with playwrights who turn 'to the spacious volubilitie of a drumming decasillabon'.[27] This habit was also often seen as easy, thoughtless and crude—particularly if the length of word, rather than its meaning, was most attractive. Writes Thomas Randolph,

> I cannot fulminate or tonitruate words
> To puzz'le intellects my ninth lasse affords
> No sycophronian buskins, nor can straine
> Gargantuan lines to Gigantize thy veine.[28]

So Shakespeare's urge to coin substantial words, or to insert newly minted words into his plays, was an example of his writing in a sound-conscious fashion (it is not always clear what his long words mean) as well as an example of his shaping his text to suit the tastes of the audience. He employed his long words both in comedies and tragedies, but in comedies he critiqued what, in tragedies, he exploited. He has comic clowns representing the types who crave long words, from the foolish Costard in *Love's Labour's Lost* who becomes delighted by 'remuneration' without ever understanding what it means—'Remuneration—O, that's the Latin word for three-farthings: ... | why, it is a fairer name than French crown. I will | never buy and sell out of this word' (*Love's Labour's Lost*, 3.1.133–9)—to Don Armado in *Love's Labour's Lost*, 'a man of fire-new

---

[26] Edmund Gayton, *Pleasant Notes upon Don Quixote* (1654), 24.

[27] Hall, 'Satire III', *Virgidemiarum*, 7; Sir Thomas Overburie, 'An Hypocrite' in *His Wife With New Elegies* (1616), G6r; Robert Greene, *Greenes Arcadia, or Menaphon* (1599), A2v.

[28] Thomas Randolph in James Shirley, *The Gratefull Servant* (1630), A3r.

words' (1.1.175), who writes a letter in which he glosses 'the posteriors of this day' with the explanation 'which the rude multitude call the afternoon' (5.2.84-5). When, in that same play, Holofernes uses the word 'peregrinate', and the impressed Sir Nathaniel takes out his 'table-book', a notebook, to record it for future use (5.1.13-15), Shakespeare is probably cocking a snook at the table-book-wielding audience who went to theatres primed to capture the newest words. Yet in tragedies he fell for the charm of audience-pleasing, mouth-stretching neologisms, creating, as a result, characters who seriously used them—'conspectuities' (*Coriolanus*, 2.1.63), 'empiricutic' (*Coriolanus*, 2.1.115), 'exsufflicate' (*Othello*, 3.3.186), 'fustilarian' (*2 Henry 4*, 2.1.61) are all Shakespearean coinings. No wonder, then, that Shakespeare in particular was criticized for the tragic length of some of his terms. Ben Jonson, who claimed in *Every Man in his Humour*, that he would never write the kind of play in which men 'with three rustie swords, | And helpe of some few foot-and-halfe-foote words, | Fight over *Yorke*, and *Lancasters* long jarres' seems to have been making a direct attack on Shakespeare.[29] In Shakespeare's *Richard III*, the play to which Ben Jonson is apparently referring, lengthy and often compound epithets abound: 'childish-foolish' (1.3.141), 'senseless-obstinate' (3.1.43), 'mortal-sharing' (5.3.43).

When Shakespeare placed the strangeness and musicality of rare and difficult words into the mouths of tragic speakers, he created characters who were distanced from others, but often had not chosen to be sidelined. Rather, they were types who had unwittingly isolated themselves because of their language; their very method of conveying content renders them exotic rather than explains them. Othello speaks gorgeously, often choosing single, outstanding, grandiloquent words in an otherwise explicable poetic context. The result is a detached, stately language that conveys what G. Wilson Knight years ago identified as 'the Othello music'. Othello's words, however, reflect 'not a soldier's language, but the quality of soldiership in all its glamour of romantic adventure'; they, like much else that he does, convey passion and intensity over meaning, for his language, then and now, was as beautiful as it was inaccessible: 'Anthropophagi' (1.3.143), 'chrysolite' (5.2.152), 'mandragora' (3.3.334), 'Propontic' (3.3.459), 'Hellespont' (3.3.459), 'promulgate' (1.2.21, 'pro-vulgate' in Q).[30]

There was also an alternative form of tragic speaking that Shakespeare used: it was the reverse of the sonorous one, and was exploited for moments of high, urgent, enraged passion. Again, this language has something to do with the very flavour of tragedy as opposed to comedy, sometimes crudely defined as 'comick Mirth and Tragick rage'.[31] Tragic rage, or 'furious vociferation', was described in a number of ways—including 'railing', 'ranting', and 'roaring'. Shakespeare employed dramatic *furor* regularly, and adopted all its various terms to describe the performance of heightened and enraged emotions: railing ('let me rail so high | That the false hussy Fortune break her wheel', *Anthony and Cleopatra*, 4.16.45), raging ('Abate thy rage, great duke!' *Henry V*, 3.2.25), ranting ('Nay, an thou'lt mouth, | I'll rant as well as thou', *Hamlet*, 5.1.280-1), and roaring ('we shall make our griefs and clamour roar | upon his death', *Macbeth*, 1.7.78). He

---

[29]   Ben Jonson, 'Prologue' to *Every Man in his Humour* in *Workes* (1616), 3.
[30]   George Wilson Knight, *The Wheel of Fire* (London: Methuen 1961), 106.
[31]   Thomas Jordan, *A Nursery of Novelties* (1665), 79.

employed high poetic anger ('Blow, winds, and crack your cheeks! Rage, blow, | You cataracts and hurricanoes ', *Tragedy of King Lear*, 3.2.1-2), and also the specific features of that anger, swearing.

Swearing and the making of oaths offered a variant of raging, just as word-coining offered a variant of tone. Dekker refers to 'tragicall and buskind oaths', and Hall describes a successful tragedy as being full of 'thrundring threats | That his poore hearers hayre quite upright sets'.[32] Thus when Kent in *The Tragedy of King Lear* starts a battle of oaths with Oswald, he is raging in tragic fashion. In this instance, the oaths have particular resonance. Kent has, of course, already referred to the way he will adopt a special 'accent' as his disguise—'if ... I other accents borrow | That can my speech diffuse, my good intent | May carry through itself', 1.4.1-3—this accent he accentuates with tragic oaths that are, additionally, also fresh coinings (or, at least, fresh amalgamations). Kent hence merges a number of tragic forms to make up a rant that is humorous but also tragically excessive:

> OSWALD What dost thou know me for?
> KENT A knave, a rascal, an eater of broken meats, a base, proud, shallow,
>   beggarly, three-suited, hundred-pound, filthy worsted-stocking knave; a
>   lily-livered, action-taking, whoreson, glass-gazing, super-serviceable,
>   finical rogue; one-trunk-inheriting slave; one that wouldst be a bawd in
>   way of good service, and art nothing but the composition of a knave,
>   beggar, coward, pander, and the son and heir of a mongrel bitch.
>
> *(King Lear*, 2.2.13-21)

It was, perhaps, complex approaches such as this that led others to praise Shakespeare for expanding rather than simply embracing tragic railing. In 'To our English Terence Mr. Will: Shake-speare', Davies congratulates the writer for advancing beyond railing to wit itself, much as the passage above does: 'Thou hast no rayling, but, a raigning Wit'.[33]

Naturally, actors preparing their performances had to have ways of knowing, from their text, how and when to walk or speak appropriately. For this, they had to study carefully. As is well known, for tragedy and comedy alike, actors received scripts in the form of 'parts' that they would learn at home.[34] These parts supplied all their speeches in full, but preceded each with only a short 'cue'—the last two or three words spoken by the interlocutor—for which the actor was to listen out. How, then, did an actor select genre, and how did he decide how to play his text correctly?

As performing from parts alerted actors more to *moment* than narrative arc, an actor, looking through his text, would divide it into units that would determine which actions he should use. These units were called 'passions': an actor would determine what passion his speeches were demanding and when, and would pay close attention to moments

---

[32] Dekker, *Wonderfull Yeare*, C2v; Hall, 'Satire III', *Virgidemiarum*, 7.

[33] John Davies, *The Scourge of Folly* (1611), 76-7.

[34] For more on actors' preparation generally, see Tiffany Stern, *Rehearsal from Shakespeare to Sheridan* (Oxford: Clarendon Press, 2000) and Simon Palfrey and Tiffany Stern, *Shakespeare in Parts* (Oxford: Oxford University Press, 2007).

when one passion transitioned into another. This is why Hamlet, when he wants to see how talented the player king is (to have 'a taste of [his] quality'), suggests hearing 'a passionate speech' (2.2.435). That is why, too, when the player responds with the passionate Hecuba speech, and Hamlet is scornful—he speaks of players who tear passions 'to tatters' (3.2.10)—he is being disingenuous. One of the earliest recorded references to performances of Shakespeare's *Hamlet,* written in 1604, describes the way Burbage played the lead character: it mentions how he 'Puts off his cloathes; his shirt he onely weares, | Much like mad-*Hamlet*; thus [at] Passion teares'.[35] Burbage's own performance was ratcheted up to a passionate extreme; indeed Hamlet himself comments on the way 'the bravery of [Laertes'] grief did put me | … into a tow'ring passion' (5.2.80-1; F only). So Hamlet admires, asks for, and despises the very passions that he himself displays. This is a metatheatrical moment that is also at the heart of *Hamlet*'s tragedy. Hamlet is a consummate player: that he cannot himself differentiate between playing and reality is one of his problems.

An actor's way of analysing a text, then, was totally emotional. Yet he interpreted those emotions through the rules of rhetoric for *pronuntio* and *actio*. His aim, in 'conning' or learning his part, was to decide the appropriate motion the part required—its 'action' or 'gesture', of which pace was an aspect; and the appropriate vocal range the part needed—its 'pronunciation' or 'emphasis', of which tone was a part. So 'the *Actor* … puts life into … mimicall Artillery by motion and voice'; and players who perform well 'are … deserving both for true action and faire deliverie of speech'.[36] As an actor established appropriate action and emphasis, so tragic or comic performance would emerge. This did, of course, allow for moments of tragedy in comedies and comedy in tragedies, for the actor would perform the lines he was given, rather than the feel of the whole play (as modern actors working from entire texts sometimes do). That is why certain phrases tell him to walk tragically, or sigh tragically, or both, like 'Twice for one step I'll groan' (*Richard II*, 5.1.91), and why there are tragic characters stranded in comedy.

Shakespeare's *penchant* for writing the passions gave him structures on which to hang his tragic devices. He was famous for larding his plays not just with passionate moments, but also with their speedy alterations. These are immediately clear from looking at plays in the parts that actors would receive, where a switch in passion is marked by a change in rhetorical tone. So Macduff, in *Macbeth*, will have seen a transition in the music of his speech from when he enters Duncan's room to when he leaves it.

> ——————————————[is] [the] door
> I'll make so bold to call,
> For 'tis my limited service.
> ——————————————[fellow] [to] it.
> O horror, horror, horror! Tongue nor heart
> Cannot conceive nor name thee!
>
> (2.3.49-63)

---

[35] Anthony Scolocker, *Daiphantus* (1604), E4v.
[36] John Gee, *New Shreds of the Old Snare* (1624), 17; *Ratseis Ghost* (1605), A3v.

His first speech is unemotional and deferential; his second speech illustrates its new negative passion not just with repetition of 'horror' but also musically: the twice-spoken 'nor'; the further emphasis of 'not', heightened by its alliteration with 'name'.

This interest in providing passionate transitions for actors is presumably behind Shakespeare's fascination with instant, extreme emotions. The suddenness with which tragic characters become entirely jealous (Othello, Leontes), entirely mad (Lear, Ophelia), entirely in love (Romeo, Juliet) is an aspect of writing for transitions. Shakespeare's characterization is partly encoded in simple transitions, or at least grows out of them. Edmund has a speech in *King Lear* that not only contains a number of transitions, but also predicts some of the major emotional switches that the play will explore:

> I should have been that I am, had the maidenliest star in the firmament twinkled on my bastardizing. [*Enter Edgar*] Pat he comes, like the catastrophe of the old comedy. My cue is villainous melancholy, with a sigh like Tom o' Bedlam. O, these eclipses do portend these divisions!

> (1.2.128–34)

Edmund here is confessional, 'I should have been that I am, had the maidenliest star … twinkled on my bastardizing'; he describes Edgar's arrival as the 'cue' to 'villainous' melancholy that it is indeed, going on to say that he will accompany it with a mock 'sigh like Tom o'Bedlam'. Then he transitions to phony portentousness: 'O, these eclipses'. But within this speech, the larger transitions of the play itself are encoded. Edmund's brother Edgar will indeed be 'cued' into action by the villainous mock-portentousness of Edmund; it is he who will later be seen on stage literally sighing like 'Tom o'Bedlam'—for that is the role in which he will disguise himself. Shakespeare's structure, his concept of play itself, is encoded in or even arises out of the performance possibilities for which he writes.

A look at what were said to be the primary skills of Richard Burbage, the actor, summarizes his talents with making transitions from one passion to another, love, to fear, to revenge, to rage:

> *Burbage* … when his part
> He acted, sent each passion to his heart;
> Would languish in a scene of love; then look
> Pallid for fear; but when revenge he took,
> Recall his bloud; when enemies were nigh,
> Grow big with wrath, and make his buttons fly …[37]

Like all actors, Burbage will, of course, have had to prepare his parts with keen alertness to the emotional clues they offered which he would manifest through a number of means, walking and speaking being some of the major ones. 'The praises of Burbadge', though written by Flecknoe some years after the actor's death, claims that when Burbage intended 'on the Stage t'appear with greater grace' he employed in particular the arts of speaking and walking: he

> Weigh'd every word, and measur'd every pace,
> And finally did on the Stage appear
> *Beauty to th'Eye* and *Musick* to the Ear.[38]

---

[37] Thomas Bancroft, *Time's Out of Tune* (1658), 44.
[38] Richard Flecknoe, *Epigrams* (1671), 56–7.

As this has it, Burbage's way of analysing a text allowed him to perform it appropriately: steps or 'pace' have an ideal measurement that Burbage could gauge; words had a heaviness that Burbage could correctly evaluate, resulting in the 'music' of his voice and 'beauty' of his movement.

Late as this epitaph is, it speaks of particular talents for which Burbage was also famous in his own time. A much copied manuscript epitaph written when Burbage died made precisely the same points, concentrating on the actor's amazing ability to calculate and then stage both words and gait 'correctly': when the result is said to be that he gave 'music' to the ear, it becomes obvious that the sing-song quality of tragic speech was one Burbage wholly embraced:

> how did thy speech become thee? and thy pace
> sute wth thy speech, and every action grace
> them both alike, while not a word did fall
> wthout just weight to ballast it wthall.

The epitaph even goes on to demand that playwrights, in the light of Burbage's death, cease to write tragic plays altogether, because they will not be performed appropriately. Other actors might manage comedies, but only Burbage had the correct tragic action:

> Poets whos glory whilome twas to heare
> yor leines so well expressd, from hens forbear
> and write noe more, or if you doe, let't bee
> in Comick sceanes, since tragick parts you see
> dy all in him.

Finally, it suggests that the theatre itself become fixedly and permanently 'tragic', to display the fact that Burbage is no more, suggesting adopting tragic black hangings for every play: 'hang all yor round wth black … and if you ever chance to play againe | Let nought but tragedies afflict your scene'.[39]

When Shakespeare was praised, it was partly for writing the kind of text that brought about the performances Burbage produced. As Jasper Mayne had it in 'On Worthy Master Shakespeare and his Poems', Shakespeare's tragedy was informed by Clio, muse of history, but also muse of proclaiming, and Calliope, muse of epic poetry, but also the muse of the beautiful voice—and his handling of both melodious pairs was determined by the 'foote', here both pace (it is compared with the 'nimble hand') and metre. 'Shakespeares … cunning braine' was 'Improv'd' by

> The buskind Muse, the Commicke Queene, the grannd
> And lowder tone of Clio; nimble hand,
> And nimbler foote of the melodious paire,
> The Silver voyced Lady; the most faire
> *Calliope*, whose speaking silence daunts:
> And she whose prayse the heavenly body chants.[40]

---

[39] 'On Mr Richard Burbidg an excellent both player, and painter', Folger Shakespeare Library MS, v.a.97, 90v.

[40] I. M. S., 'On Worthy Master Shakespeare and his Poems' in *Mr. William Shakespeares Comedies, Histories, and Tragedies* (1632), *3r.

As this chapter has suggested, Shakespeare's plays arose out of methods of performing tragedy, and were angled towards the performance skills of certain actors, Richard Burbage being a supreme example. This is because Shakespeare worked closely with actors and, of course, acted with them. Indeed, when John Davies singled out two players for his poem 'Players, I love yee', he picked 'W.S.R.B.', William Shakespeare and Richard Burbage, both of whom, he maintains, were consummate performers who also had additional strings to their bows, 'painting, poesie' respectively. Burbage (R.B.), was known for his artworks (he could 'both lime' [paint a picture or portrait], 'and act' explains the epitaph);[41] and Shakespeare (W.S.), was known for his poetic writing—'poesie'—as well for his roles on the stage. Both men, suggests Davies, suffused their other talents, writing and painting, with their primary talent, performing. And perhaps this is what Shakespeare thought too. The playwright in the epilogue to *Henry V*, claims his little worth as an author has been enhanced by performance: though he has a 'rough and all-unable pen', the next part of the tale, the *Henry VI* plays, 'oft our stage hath shown' (epilogue, 1, 13). Almost certainly performed by Shakespeare, the 'bending author' begs 'acceptance' for *Henry V* in the light of the success of *1, 2, 3 Henry VI* in performance (epilogue, 2). For Shakespeare, this chapter has argued, performance was all-important; his tragedies arose from his theatrical sense of what his stage and his fellow players could convey.

SELECT BIBLIOGRAPHY

Downer, Alan S., 'Nature to Advantage Dressed: Eighteenth Century Acting', *PMLA* 58 (1943), 1002–37.

Gurr, Andrew J., 'Who Strutted and Bellowed', *SHS* 16 (1963), 95–102.

Joseph, B. L., *Elizabethan Acting* (London: Oxford University Press, 1964).

Goldman, Michael, *Acting and Action in Shakespearean Tragedy* (Princeton: Princeton University Press, 1985).

Munro, Lucy. '*They eat each others' arms*: Stage Blood and Body Parts', in Farah Karim-Cooper and Tiffany Stern, eds., *Shakespeare's Theatres and the Effects of Performance* (London: Methuen, 2013), 73–93.

Neill, Michael, *Issues of Death* (Oxford: Clarendon Press, 1997).

Simon Palfrey and Tiffany Stern, *Shakespeare in Parts* (Oxford: Oxford University Press, 2007).

Rehearsal from Shakespeare to Sheridan (Oxford: Clarendon Press, 2000).

Stern, Tiffany, '(Re:)Historicizing Spontaneity: Original Practices, Stanislavski, and Characterisation', in Yu Jin Ko and Michael W. Shurgot, eds., *Shakespeare's Sense of Character: On the Page and from the Stage* (Aldershot: Ashgate, 2012), 99–110.

Stevens, Andrea, 'Cosmetic Transformations', in Farah Karim-Cooper and Tiffany Stern, eds., *Shakespeare's Theatres and the Effects of Performance* (London: Methuen, 2013), 94–117.

[41] 'On Mr Richard Burbidg an excellent both player, and painter', Folger Shakespeare Library MS, v.a.97, 90v.

Warren, Michael, 'Shakespearean Tragedy Printed and Performed', *The Cambridge Companion to Shakespearean Tragedy*, ed. Claire McEachern, 2nd edn. (Cambridge: Cambridge University Press, 2013), 71–88.

Wilson, John Harold. 'Rant, Cant, and Tone on the Restoration Stage', *Studies in Philology* 52 (1955), 592–98.

CHAPTER 31

....

PERFORMING SHAKESPEAREAN TRAGEDY, 1660-1780

....

PETER HOLLAND

COVERAGE of this vast subject in a chronological narrative is impossible. I offer instead a set of four case-studies for *Romeo and Juliet*, *Hamlet*, *Macbeth*, and *King Lear*, in the hope that the resonances of the theatre histories of these works indicate something of the complexities of the cultural contexts within which the re-making and re-presenting of Shakespeare on stage took place.

ROMEO AND JULIET AND THE SPACE OF DESIRE

....

I begin with one of Shakespeare's most daring moments of dramaturgy. The audience has watched Romeo, alone in the Capulet monument with the dead Paris and the 'dead' Juliet, take poison and die. The spectators know that Juliet must be just about to wake and find his corpse. But Shakespeare turns the focus away from the two to the arrival of Friar Laurence equipped 'with lantern, crow, and spade' (5.3.120.2), his encounter with the waiting Balthasar and his discovery of Romeo's and Paris's bodies before he says and we see 'The lady stirs' (5.3.147). The delay is exacerbated by the change of attention from the dead and dying to the rescuer who comes too late and whose 'speed' has been slowed by the number of times his 'old feet [have] stumbled at graves' (121-2). Indeed, our realization that he is already too late to save one leads us to expect that somehow he will be unable to save the other. This is the tragedy of both Romeo *and* Juliet after all and from the Prologue onwards we have been expecting a double death as well as the collateral damage.

The diversion works against the play's and the audience's desire. We want, now, to see her discovery of her dead husband. Indeed—and this is the crucial point here—we have wanted to see her awake as soon as possible, preferably, though we know impossibly, before Romeo takes the poison. Shakespeare refuses to give us what we want. The isolation of the living lovers from each other, their mutual unawareness of the fact of life is coldly painful, desperate in its separation.

But what would happen if she were to be fully awake just a few seconds earlier in the gap between his drinking and dying? What if the 'true apothecary' had given him drugs not quite so 'quick' (5.1.119–20)? Sometime after the theatres reopened in 1660, the Duke's Company performed *Romeo and Juliet* and, at some date after that, as John Downes, the theatre's prompter, recorded in *Roscius Anglicanus* (1708), 'This Tragedy of *Romeo* and *Juliet*, was made … into a Tragi-comedy, by Mr. *James Howard*, he preserving *Romeo* and *Juliet* alive; so that when the Tragedy was Reviv'd again, 'twas Play'd Alternately, Tragical one Day, and Tragicomical another; for several Days together' (22). Howard's adaptation has not survived—Downes's reference is all we know about it—but it is easy to see how an audience, confronted by the options of revived pre-war tragedy or version adapted to the fashionable genre of tragi-comedy, might have been fascinated by the choice. In the aftermath of the brutality of civil war and in the temporary euphoria of the return of the king, the drama of death was often less attractive than the drama of avoidance and recovery.

Crucial to the post-Restoration performance history of Shakespeare's tragedies was the approval by royal warrant on 12 December 1660 of Sir William Davenant's 'proposition of reformeinge some of the most ancient Playes that were played at Blackfriers and of makeinge them, fit, for the Company of Actors appointed vnder his direction and Com[m]and', allotting him nine Shakespeare plays, including *Hamlet, King Lear, Macbeth*, and *Romeo and Juliet*.[1] James Howard was, in effect, 'reformeinge' and 'makeinge … fit' *Romeo* in the context of a fierce competition for audiences between the two theatres licensed to perform in London. And plays can be re-adapted; hence, in 1679, Thomas Otway used *Romeo and Juliet* for his Roman tragedy *The History and Fall of Caius Marius*, a political tragedy written in the heightened tensions of the Popish Plot crisis, to which dramatists responded along party lines. While the title-page of the published text did not mention Shakespeare, Otway's Prologue did, explaining, without ever quite apologizing and without naming *Romeo*, that, 'from the Crop of his luxuriant Pen | E're since succeeding Poets humbly glean | … h'has rifled him of half a Play' (1680, sig.A3r). Romeo and Juliet become Marius Junior and Lavinia, with the nurse a cross-dressed role that gave James Nokes the nickname 'Nurse Nokes'. In the 'walled Garden' of Lavinia's father's house, this Juliet calls out 'O Marius, Marius! wherefore art thou Marius?' (18), appearing, for the first time, 'in the Balcony', giving the scene its nickname for ever after (the word 'balcony' never appears in Shakespeare's play).

Grafting the young lovers onto a complex political drama of consular elections, popular uprisings, banishment and old-fashioned villainy (with the wounded Sulpitius declaring 'A Curse on all Repentance! how I hate it!', 66), Otway adjusts the lovers' end to suit his political ends, with Lavinia killing herself in front of Marius Senior (i.e. Montague) with the sword with which Marius Senior 'butcher'd' her father (65). But Otway also invents a moment in the tomb that would have long echoes: Lavinia wakes before young Marius has died and they have time for a brief rapturous loving duet before the 'heav'nly Joys' that 'transport' him lead only to death (63). The temporal gap between them has been bridged and would stay that way for years to come. Theophilus Cibber's

---

[1] Allardyce Nicoll, *A History of English Drama 1660–1900*, vol. 1: *Restoration Drama 1660–1700* (Cambridge: Cambridge University Press, 1952), 352.

1744 adaptation, for instance, takes over Otway's lines for this reunion with only minor variation.

David Garrick loathed Cibber's version: 'I never heard so vile and scandalous a performance of it in my life; and, excepting the speaking of it, and the speaker, nothing could be more contemptible.'[2] Garrick adapted *Romeo and Juliet* three times: first in 1748, with Spranger Barry and Mrs Cibber as the leads at Drury Lane; then in 1750, playing Romeo himself with Mrs Bellamy as Juliet, warring for twelve performances with Barry and Cibber, who were then at the rival theatre, Covent Garden; finally in 1753. Spectacle was as important as great acting in the war of the *Romeos*. Each theatre created a grand funeral procession for Juliet (music by Arne at Covent Garden and by Boyce at Drury Lane); Garrick's had tolling bells, girls strewing flowers, torchbearers with flaming torches, choristers and clergy. But the greatest effect at Drury Lane was the tomb-scene, a claustrophobic space with moonlight beyond it, a set that intensified the emotion through its constriction and which allowed Garrick's massive elaboration of the lovers' reunion, now 75 lines long, its full exploration of the emotional despair of eighteenth-century tragic language.

Garrick's preface to his final version acknowledged that Otway was his source but 'it is a matter of wonder that so great a dramatic genius did not work up a scene from it of more nature, terror and distress'.[3] So he did exactly that.

> ROMEO I thought thee dead. Distracted at the sight,
> Fatal speed! drank poison, kissed thy cold lips,
> And found within thy arms a precious grave.
> But in that moment—O—
> JULIET And did I wake for this?
> ROMEO My powers are blasted,
> Twixt death and love I'm torn, I am distracted!...
> O, cruel, cursed fate! ...
> Fathers have flinty hearts, no tears can melt 'em.
> Nature pleads in vain. Children must be wretched.
>
> (5.4.119-30)[4]

Note the firm moral statement and the appeal to nature as the ultimate authority. This world is no longer an early modern one.

For Garrick's fans—who were legion—and for decades afterwards, in musical versions like Berlioz's 'Dramatic Symphony' *Roméo et Juliette* (1839), as well as on stage, there seemed a rightness in this scene so apparent that, for Francis Gentleman, 'we will venture to affirm, that no play ever received greater advantage from alteration than this tragedy ...; bringing Juliet to life before Romeo dies is undoubtedly a change of infinite merit.'[5] For the critic McNamara Morgan, praising Miss Nossiter as Juliet, Romeo's line after Juliet wakes, 'She speaks, she lives! And we shall still be blessed!' (5.4.74),[6]

---

[2] David Garrick, *The Letters*, ed. David M. Little and George M. Kahrl, 3 vols. (Cambridge, MA: Belknap Press of Harvard, 1963), Letter 28, 1: 43.

[3] 'Advertisement' in David Garrick, *The Plays*, ed. H. W. Pedicord and Frederick L. Bergmann, 7 vols. (Carbondale, IL: Southern Illinois University Press, 1980-2), 3: 79.

[4] Ibid., 3: 144.   [5] Francis Gentleman, *The Dramatic Censor*, 2 vols. (London, 1770), 1: 187.

[6] *Plays*, 3: 143.

'is perhaps, the finest Touch of Nature in any Tragedy, ancient or modern'.[7] What is more, for him Shakespeare lacks the ability to wring the last ounce of distress out of the scene: 'Shakespear's Conduct was not half so distressing as, *Within Sight of Heaven,* | *To be plunged in Hell.*'[8] Tragedy is great precisely when most movingly distressing, something I shall return to at the end of this chapter. Therefore turning up the emotional pitch even higher must be desirable and Shakespeare's scene simply lacks the easy accessibility of agony that Garrick creates.

Shakespeare's failure leads to Garrick's success both in the funeral dirge and in adapting the tomb scene. He had a tougher time negotiating with his audiences and with Shakespeare over Rosaline. Initially he left her in, arguing that, although 'many People have imagin'd that the sudden Change of Romeo's Love ... was a blemish in his Character', yet 'Shakespear has dwelt particularly upon it, and so great a Judge of Human Nature, knew that to be young and inconstant was extremely natural'; nonetheless, in spite of opposition, 'those, I am sure, who see the Play will readily excuse his leaving twenty Rosalines for Juliet.'[9] The argument did not work and Garrick removed her from his third version: 'an alteration in that Particular has been made more in compliance to that opinion, than from a conviction that Shakespeare, the best judge of human nature, was faulty.'[10] Shakespeare must be right but the public has decided: as Dr Johnson wrote in his prologue for Garrick's first season as manager of Drury Lane (1747), 'The drama's laws the drama's patrons give.' If 'Romeo' had not yet acquired its sense of 'a philanderer, a womanizer' (*OED*, 1.b, first example 1902), the play's significance in Garrick's version—for it was the most often performed of all tragedies between 1750 and the end of Garrick's management in 1776—gave the noun a renewed currency for 'a lover or sweetheart' (*OED*, 1.a).

Romeo and Juliet becomes in the popular imagination, at this point, emphatically the drama of innocent love, not of adolescent love, for the shade of Rosaline troubles the innocence of the passion. The erotics of love—and especially of love in the moment of death—create a charge, a thrill for the audience that, for all its banality by comparison with Shakespeare, could be seen as natural and true and permissible. *Romeo and Juliet* functions as the tragedy that permits the thrill of sexual desire not only on stage, albeit purged of some at least of the bawdy language of Mercutio, but also for the audience. Hence the comments of one female spectator on the comparison between Barry and Garrick as Romeo in 1750:

> Had I been Juliet to Garrick's Romeo,—so ardent and impassioned was he, I should have expected he would have *come up* to me in the balcony; but had I been Juliet to Barry's Romeo,—so ternder, so eloquent, and so seductive was he, I should certainly have *gone down* to him!"[11]

Romeo and Juliet enables the speaking of desire—and Garrick carefully changes Juliet's age to one that was at least legal: 'Come Lamas-tide at night shall she be eighteen' (1.5.21).[12]

[7] McNamara Morgan, *A Letter to Miss Nossiter* (London, 1753), 49.
[8] Ibid., 50.   [9] *Plays*, 3: 77.   [10] *Plays*, 3: 79.
[11] Quoted by Kalman A. Burnim, *David Garrick Director* (Carbondale, IL: Southern Illinois University press, 1961), 131–2.
[12] *Plays*, 3: 91.

HAMLET AND THE SPACE
OF THE PERFORMANCE TEXT

One of the plays allocated to Sir William Davenant at the Restoration was *Hamlet* and his theatre company soon staged it. Samuel Pepys saw it on 24 August 1661, noting the use of scenery and that Betterton 'did the Prince's part beyond imagination'.[13] According to Downes, Betterton was taught the role 'in every article of it' by Davenant, 'having seen *Mr. Taylor* of the *Black-Fryars* Company act it, who being Instructed by the Author *Mr. Shaksepeur* … which by his exact Performance of it, gain'd him Esteem and Reputation, Superlative to all other Plays'.[14] Never mind that the handing down of the tradition is extremely unlikely, since Joseph Taylor did not join the King's Men until 1619, three years after Shakespeare's death; what matters is that 'No succeeding Tragedy for several Years got more Reputation, or Money to the Company than this'.[15] The revived *Hamlet* was an immediate and ongoing success, not least because of Betterton's brilliance, irrespective of who taught his mentor's mentor.

The text used for those performances was not published until 1676 or, rather, a text of *Hamlet* 'As it is now Acted at his Highness the Duke of *York*'s Theatre' (sig. [A]1r) that might have its roots in the 1661 performances was published in 1676. How exactly it represents those earlier performances is impossible to know. Its cast-list has some of the same actors Downes listed but others are much more likely to be members of a later cast, closer to the publication date, even though it is certainly not the cast for performance in 1676 since Guildenstern is listed as performed by Mr Cademan who had been forced to retire from the stage after an injury in a duel in a play in 1673 left him partly paralyzed and with his memory affected.

The 1676 text is prefaced by a note 'To the Reader':

> This Play being too long to be conveniently Acted, such places as might be least prejudicial to the Plot or Sense, are left out upon the Stage: but that we may no way wrong the incomparable Author, are here inserted according to the Original Copy with this Mark "

The text announces that it will make apparent the layering of versions. On the one hand the complete Shakespeare text—even though no one then was likely to have known about the differences between Q2 and F and hence the notion of 'complete' is necessarily imprecise—while on the other there is the text as performed. The praise of Shakespeare is high— 'the incomparable Author'—but the necessities of performance length are vital: the convenience is that of the audience, not of the company, for audiences then would not want a four-hour performance. In 1767 John Brownsmith, prompter at the Theatre Royal in the Haymarket, published *The Dramatic Time-Piece*, offering precise timings for each act so that servants could be told when to collect their employers, staying at home in the meantime rather than 'assembling in *Public Houses*, or Houses of *ill Fame*, to the destructions of their *Morals, Properties*, and *Constitutions*'. His timings for *Hamlet* were, act by act, 40,

---

[13] Samuel Pepys, *The Diary*, ed. R. C. Latham and W. Matthews, 11 vols. (London: Bell, 1971-83), 1: 161.
[14] Downes, *Roscius Anglicanus*, 21.   [15] Ibid.

22, 40, 27, and 30 minutes so that the play would be over at '3 min. after 9'.[16] Performance texts are defined by audience demands.

The 1676 *Hamlet* text distinguishes the cuts as those that will not affect 'Plot or Sense' and, if the latter is a little vague, the need to tell the story clearly is still a major concern for productions. So, for instance, in the first scene Marcellus' lengthy enquiry about the reason for 24/7 work in the ordnance factory and Horatio's even longer answer are heavily cut. Out go the account of portents in Rome before Caesar's death and the behaviour of cocks near Christmas. The ghost's appearances are retained but the scene moves more quickly towards the arrival of Betterton as Hamlet in the next scene where, again, there are heavy cuts to long speeches such as Claudius on young Fortinbras' activities and on the importance of Polonius, Hamlet on his grief, Claudius on the need to limit mourning and Hamlet's first soliloquy. Each of these is sufficiently present not to affect the clarity of the plot; each is cut to keep the scene moving along.

But, in addition, the play's language, whether played or cut, is tidied up to meet the taste of the times. In 'To be or not to be', for instance, 'To grunt and sweat under a weary life' now begins 'To groan ... ' (since, as Michael Dobson comments, 'contemporary sensibilities, apparently, did not object to a prince referring to sweat but drew the line at grunting'[17]), while 'Is sicklied o'er with the pale cast of thought' becomes 'Shews sick and pale with thought', simplifying the language and harming the metre.[18] Minutely, from beginning to end, Shakespeare's style is made amenable to Restoration sensibilities, just as Garrick indicated that the aim of his *Romeo* 'was to clear the Original, as much as possible, from the Jingle and Quibble'.[19] Usually ascribed to Davenant, though the attribution deserves retesting,[20] the alterations are careful and effective, so long, that is, as one accepts the assumption that Shakespeare's language needs modernizing.

Garrick played Hamlet for nearly 35 years, from 1742 to 1776, the interpretation deepening but not altering. At the core was melancholy, of course, but also filial piety, while, for Hannah More, Garrick 'never once forgot he was a prince'.[21] As Lichtenberg wrote in 1775, of Hamlet's first soliloquy, 'O that this too, too solid flesh',

> Garrick is completely overcome by tears of grief, felt with only too good a cause, for a virtuous father and on account of a light-minded mother, ... The last of the words: 'So excellent a King', is utterly lost; one catches it only from the movement of the mouth, which quivers and shuts tight immediately afterwards, so as to restrain the all too distinct expression of grief on the lips, which could easily tremble with unmanly emotion.[22]

[16] John Brownsmith, *The Dramatic Time-piece* (London, 1767), sig. [A]2b, and p. 3.

[17] Michael Dobson, 'Improving on the Original: Actresses and Adaptations', in Jonathan Bate and Russell Jackson, eds., *Shakespeare: An Illustrated Stage History* (Oxford: Oxford University Press, 1996), 45–68 (50).

[18] *Hamlet* (1676), 39.   [19] Garrick, *Plays*, 3: 77.

[20] See Hazelton Spencer, '*Hamlet* Under the Restoration', *PMLA* 38:4 (1923), 770–91 and his *Shakespeare Improved* (Cambridge, MA: Harvard University Press, 1927), 178–87.

[21] Quoted by Vanessa Cunningham, *Shakespeare and Garrick* (Cambridge: Cambridge University Press, 2008), 142.

[22] Margaret L. Mare and W. H. Quarrell, eds., *Lichtenberg's Visits to England* (Oxford: Oxford University Press, 1938), 15.

Balancing this was, at the moment of Hamlet's meeting his father's ghost, the awe and horror felt by the character and the audience and carefully engineered by Garrick. It was rumoured that Garrick wore a trick-wig for the scene, made by a Mr Perkins, so that his hair could literally stand on end. Lichtenberg's description of the moment, lengthy and detailed as Garrick turns, staggers, drops his hat, stretches out his arms (the left further than the right), opens his mouth, and stands rooted to the spot, all 'with no loss of dignity', is also one of sympathetic response:

> His whole demeanour is so expressive of terror that it made my flesh creep even before he began to speak. The almost terror-struck silence of the audience, which preceded this appearance and filled one with a sense of insecurity, probably did much to enhance this effect.[23]

Murphy thought Garrick even managed to change colour, 'fixed in mute astonishment, … growing paler and paler'.[24] However, Partridge, going to *Hamlet* with Tom Jones in Fielding's novel (1749), found good grounds to sneer at Garrick's performance: 'He the best player! … Why, I could act as well as he himself. I am sure if I had seen a ghost, I should have looked in the very same manner, and done just as he did.'[25]

When Garrick first played the role in August 1742 he worked from the standard performance text, a version based on that used by Robert Wilks (c.1635-1732) when he played Hamlet, and published in 1718, itself derived from the 1676 version. The Wilks Hamlet was less introspective and reflective than active and various, shorn of his speech over the praying Claudius and 'How all occasions'. Garrick's was a performance to watch but he was well aware of what he was not playing. He altered the play here and there throughout his career but in 1772, to make his most radical change, he turned back to the Wilks playing text rather than to the edition of 1763 which contained his current performing version. Throughout the first four acts he restored over 600 lines, moments like the dispatch of the ambassadors to Norway which are still often cut but also much of Hamlet's role that he had not previously performed, including 'How all occasions'. The roles of Polonius, Ophelia and Laertes were built back up to Shakespearean proportions and Garrick found time for the whole of the Mousetrap (though not the dumb show). But Garrick was determined also to produce a more generically restricted version, a *Hamlet* that was properly tragic and far less funny. The impact of his recent trip to France and fascination with French drama, as well as his awareness of what French intellectuals found most unacceptable about Shakespeare, was a driving force but he had also long been annoyed by, for instance, the lead billing given to Osric; in 1754, for instance, Osric was billed higher than anyone except Hamlet. The answer was to cut Osric and the gravediggers completely and, where Shakespeare took 800 lines to move from Ophelia's last, mad exit to the end, Garrick managed it in barely 60, creating a patchwork of Shakespeare's own lines and adding very few of his own.

---

[23] Ibid., 10.

[24] Quoted by George Winchester Stone, Jr., and George M. Kahrl, *David Garrick: A Critical Biography* (Carbondale, IL: Southern Illinois University Press, 1979), 543.

[25] Quoted by Ian McIntyre, *Garrick* (London: Allen Lane, The Penguin Press, 1999), 65.

Dislike of the gravediggers was not restricted to France. An anonymous pamphlet on the play in 1736 found them 'very unbecoming such a Piece as this' while another in 1752 thought that 'To mix Comedy with Tragedy is breaking through the sacred Laws of Nature'.[26] Early reviews of Garrick's 1772 performances were mostly admiring: one commented that 'the tedious interruptions of this beautiful tale no longer disgrace it; its absurd digressions are no longer disgusting'.[27] There were also favourable reviews by George Steevens who later savagely mocked Garrick's editing as self-serving: 'Mr. Garrick ... has reduced the consequence of every character but himself; and thus excluding Osric, the Gravediggers, &c. contrived to monopolize the attention of the audience'.[28] Garrick wrote to a French friend that 'I have dar'd to alter *Hamlet*, I have thrown away the gravediggers ... & notwithstanding the Galleries were so fond of them, I have met with more applause than I did at five and twenty'.[29]

Perhaps the most sharply critical and witty response was by Arthur Murphy in a superb parody which circulated in manuscript, with Shakespeare's ghost complaining to Garrick that he was

> Doom'd for a certain term to leave my works
> Obscure and uncorrected; to endure
> The ignorance of players; the barbarous hand
> Of Gothic editors; the ponderous weight
> Of leaden commentator; fast confin'd
> In critic fires, till errors, not my own,
> Are done away, and sorely I the while
> Wish'd I had blotted for myself before.

Garrick is accused of tampering 'With juice of cursed nonsense in an inkhorn, | And o'er my fair applauded page did pour | A Manager's distilment' so that the play was 'brought upon the stage | With all your imperfections on my head!' The ghost warns Garrick against further adaptations but, after he leaves, Garrick tells his brother George:

> This Ghost is pleas'd with this my alteration,
> And now he bids me alter all his Plays.
> His plays are out of joint;—O *cursed spite!*
> That ever I was born to set them right![30]

The radical revision did not outlive Garrick's career and the playing text reverted to the kind of cut version Garrick had tried to overturn. The constrictions of playing time had meant moving both towards and away from Shakespeare. The search for the dramatic

---

[26] Both quoted by Cunningham, *Shakespeare and Garrick*, 152.

[27] Brian Vickers, ed., *Shakespeare: The Critical Heritage*, vol. 5, *1765-1774* (London: Routledge, 1979), 483. Vickers quotes extensively from reviews, 466–86.

[28] Quoted by Cunningham, *Shakespeare and Garrick*, 139.

[29] David Garrick, *The Letters*, Letter 730, 3: 841.

[30] Vickers, *Critical Heritage*, vol. 5, *1765-1774*, 466–70. On Murphy's piece, see Richard W. Schoch, ' "A Supplement to Public Laws": Arthur Murphy, David Garrick, and *Hamlet, with Alterations*', *Theatre Journal* 57 (2005), 21–32. For another playlet, by Richard Cumberland, responding to Murphy's and supporting Garrick, but with the gravediggers complaining to Garrick 'Since you have thrust us out your Play, Sir, be so good to say ... what we should put our hands to next', see Michael Dobson, *The Making of the National Poet* (Oxford: The Clarendon Press, 1992), 174–6.

rhythm of the earlier parts of the play had necessitated destroying the rhythms of the final sequence. The problem epitomizes Garrick's dilemma and the culture's ambivalence. The play to be read and the play to be seen could not be fully aligned.

MACBETH AND THE SPACE OF SPECTACLE

In 1674 Thomas Duffett published his burlesque version for the King's Company of Elkanah Settle's tragedy *The Empress of Morocco*, performed by the rival Duke's Company.[31] Tacked onto the end of the farce was an Epilogue 'Being a new Fancy after the old, and most surprising way of Macbeth, Perform'd with new and costly Machines' ([27]). At the start, after some music sung by invisible spirits, there is an elaborate stage-direction:

> The Scene opens. Thunder and lightning is discover'd, not behind Painted Tiffany to blind and amuse the Senses, but openly, by the most excellent way of Mustard-bowl, and Salt-Peter. Three Witches fly over the Pit Riding upon Beesomes. *Heccate* descends over the Stage in a Glorious Chariot, adorn'd with Pictures of Hell and Devils, and made of a large Wicker Basket. (30)

Duffett's epilogue, much like his other burlesques, which included one of the Duke's Company's *Tempest*, is more an attack on the rival theatre's production style than on the substance of their repertoire. Duffett is not mocking Shakespeare but the Duke's version of his work, in this case Davenant's adaptation of *Macbeth*, yet another of the plays that had been granted him in 1660, probably first performed in 1664. It was finally published in 1674, the title-page announcing it was printed 'With all the alterations, amendments, additions, and new songs', without mentioning either Shakespeare or Davenant. Pepys adored it, seeing it nine times between 1664 and 1669 (four times in 1667 alone) and he often commented on those additions: 'one of the best plays for a stage, and variety of dancing and music, that ever I saw'[32]; 'though I saw it lately, yet appears a most excellent play in all respects, but especially in divertisement, though it be a deep tragedy; which is a strange perfection in a tragedy, it being most proper here and suitable'.[33]

If the Hecate scenes were written by Middleton and inserted after the first performances of Shakespeare's play, then the addition of spectacle to the play started early. Davenant simply expands on it. Pepys is not interested in the cutting of the Porter (no room for low comedy in high tragedy now) nor in the substantial expansion of the role of Lady Macduff nor the addition of an onstage death for Macbeth with a moral one-liner as he dies, 'Farewel vain World, and what's most vain in it, Ambition' (60). He cares about the dancing, singing, music, and effects that the Duke's Company could add to the show, a way of mixing tragedy with matters less 'deep' and more diverting and a tradition that stretches at least as far as Verdi's grand chorus of witches in his opera (1847, revised 1865). It is not the spectacle of warfare but of the supernatural that could be expanded. Davenant's witches made their first exit 'flying' (1) and they flew in again for their next scene. The

---

[31] Thomas Duffet, *The Empress of Morocco: A Farce* (London, 1674).
[32] Pepys, *Diary*, 19 April 1667, 8: 171.   [33] Ibid., 7 Jan 1667, 8: 7.

Macduffs encountered the witches in a new scene in Act 2, where they dance and sing. Though Macduff describes their first song here as 'an hellish Song', their second is rather twee: 'And nimbly, nimbly dance we still | To th' Ecchoes from an hollow Hill' (25). In Act 3 Hecate makes her exit in a 'machine' that descends to collect her (40) while the witches dance and sing, and in the cauldron scene not only the cauldron but the whole cave set 'sinks' (44). As John Downes noted,

> being dresst all in it's Finery, as new Cloath's, new Scenes, Machines, as flyings for the Witches; with all the Singing and Dancing in it ....it being all Excellently perform'd, being in the nature of an Opera, it Recompenc'd double the Expense; it proves still a lasting Play. [34]

Macbeth as opera had no need to wait for Verdi and it was the witches that always enabled this financial triumph. When Addison mocked one female spectator in 1711, it was bound to be the witch-scenes that she most enjoyed:

> A little before the rising of the Curtain, she broke out into a loud Soliloquy, *When will the dear Witches enter*; and immediately upon their first Appearance, asked a Lady that sat three Boxes from her ... if those Witches were not charming Creatures.[35]

Garrick's first performance as Macbeth was on 7 January 1744. The playbills and newspaper notices advertising and hyping the new production both

> gave notice of his intention to revive *Macbeth* as originally written by Shakespeare ... Quin cried out, with an air of surprise, 'What does he mean? don't I play *Macbeth* as written by Shakespeare?'[36]

But Quin did not. He was still playing a version of Davenant's adaptation. As Stephen Orgel comments,

> Twenty years earlier a producer could have expected to attract audiences by advertising a wholly new *Macbeth*, bigger and better; Garrick's assertion, the invocation of the author to confer authority on the production, marks a significant moment in both theatrical and textual history.[37]

Where audiences had since the Restoration come to accept as validating for any new performance its strong connection with the growing tradition of approved star performances, Garrick, as Paul Prescott has argued, offered 'the claim of textual authenticity ... to justify, to a potentially hostile community of interpreters, Garrick's divergence from performance tradition and to locate the privileged origins of his originality'.[38] So, for instance,

---

[34] Downes, *Roscius Anglicanus*, 33.

[35] Quoted Cunningham, *Shakespeare and Garrick*, 50.

[36] Arthur Murphy, *The Life of David Garrick*, 2 vols. (London: 1801), 1: 70–1. The classic account of Garrick's adaptation is George Winchester Stone, Jr., 'Garrick's Handling of *Macbeth*', SP 38 (1941), 609–28.

[37] Stephen Orgel, 'The Authentic Shakespeare', *Representations* 21 (1988), 15.

[38] Paul Prescott, 'Doing All That Becomes a Man: The Reception and Afterlife of the Macbeth Actor, 1744-1889', *Shakespeare Survey 57* (Cambridge: Cambridge University Press, 2004), 84.

Murphy argued that Garrick published *An Essay on Acting* (1744), an apparent attack on his own way of playing the role, precisely because he

> knew that his manner of representing Macbeth would be essentially different from that of all the actors who had played it for twenty or thirty years before; and he was therefore determined to attack himself ironically to blunt, if not prevent, the remarks of others.[39]

Garrick reinstated much of Shakespeare's text and carefully eliminated much, though not quite all, of Davenant's alterations of Shakespeare's language to produce something more acceptably tasteful. Even the Porter is momentarily reinstated, though reduced to a single line, 'Faith, sir, we were carousing till the second cock' (2.1.155), in part to give Garrick as Macbeth enough time to change his costume and 'Get on [his] nightgown' (148).[40]

In one respect only did Garrick expand on Davenant's lead. Where Davenant had given Macbeth a single dying line, Garrick gave himself, alone on stage, an appropriately substantial final speech:

> 'Tis done! the scene of life will quickly close.
> Ambition's vain, delusive dreams are fled,
> And now I wake to darkness, guilt and horror.
> I cannot bear it! Let me shake it off.—
> 'Twa' not be; my soul is clogged with blood.
> I cannot rise! I dare not ask for mercy.
> It is too late, hell drags me down. I sink
> I sink—Oh!—my soul is lost forever!
> Oh! (*Dies*).
>
> (5.6.73–81)[41]

Jean Georges Noverre, a French ballet-master, described Garrick's death throes in detail—and Garrick, Thomas Davies reported, 'excelled in the expression of convulsive throes and dying agonies':[42]

> The approach of death showed each instant on his face; his eyes became dim, his voice could not support the efforts he made to speak his thoughts ... his legs gave way under him, his face lengthened, his pale and livid features bore the signs of suffering and repentance. At last, he fell; ... His plight made the audience shudder, he clawed the ground and seemed to be digging his own grave, but the dread moment was nigh, one saw death in reality, everything expressed that instant which makes all equal. In the end he expired. The death rattle and the convulsive movement of the features, arms and breasts gave the final touch to this terrible picture.[43]

Francis Gentleman, in his commentary to Shakespeare for the edition published by John Bell in 1773 from the Drury Lane prompt-books, was severe on Shakespeare here and equally severe on Garrick: where

> *Shakespeare*'s idea of having his head brought on by *Macduff*, is either ludicrous or horrid, therefore commendably changed to visible punishment—a dying speech, and a very good

---

[39] Murphy, *Life of David Garrick*, 1: 198.   [40] *Plays*, 3: 28.   [41] *Plays*, 3: 72.

[42] Thomas Davies, *Dramatic Miscellanies*, 3 vols., (Dublin, 1784), 2: 118.

[43] Jean Georges Noverre, *Letters on Dancing and Ballets*, trans. Cyril W. Beaumont (London, 1930), 84–5.

one, has been furnished by Mr. *Garrick*, to give the actor more eclat; but ... we are not fond of characters writhing and flouncing on carpets.[44]

Garrick's excellence in death scenes was not to everyone's taste. But the aim throughout was to ensure a proper affective response from the audience. And Garrick's witches, less all-singing and all-dancing than their predecessors, still exited in the cauldron scene after a new 'Dance of Furies'.[45]

Playing Macbeth was exhausting. In 1772, when asked to revive it by Lord North, Garrick politely refused: 'I am really not yet prepar'd for Macbeth, 'tis the most violent part I have.[46] But Garrick also mentioned to North's secretary that he had 'a design to exhibit yͤ Characters in yͤ old dresses'. *Macbeth* was played at Drury Lane (without Garrick) 'dressed in the Habits of the Times' in 1776.[47] But by then Charles Macklin (1699?-1797) had played the role at Covent Garden, in October 1773, and had been widely ridiculed for his performance. Nonetheless, it was Macklin who explored the possibility of historical accuracy in costuming *Macbeth* to an extent that Garrick never envisaged. Spectacle now would be less a matter of singing and dancing than of elaborate sets that claimed an antiquarian authority. Throughout his career, Garrick toyed with historicism in costume designs for Shakespeare, taking further what other contemporaries had experimented with, planning a production of *King John* in 1750 dressed 'half old English, half modern',[48] trying *Richard III* and *Henry IV, Part 2* in 'old English habits' in the 1760s, and finally playing Lear in what was conceived of as historical authenticity in his final performances in 1776.

But Macklin went much further. When preparing to play Shylock in 1741, a role he performed for 48 years, he read and reread Josephus' *History of the Jews* and went daily to watch Jewish businessmen in London coffee-houses, copying manners, gesture, and accent and wearing a red three-cornered hat because he had discovered that Venetian Jews usually wore one. For *Macbeth* he was determined to follow through his historical research. Cooke, Macklin's first biographer, noted,

> Macbeth used to be dressed in a suit of scarlet and gold, a tail wig, &c. in every respect like a modern military officer. Garrick always played it in this manner ... Macklin, however, ... saw the absurdity of exhibiting a Scotch character, existing many years before the Norman Conquest, in this manner, and therefore very properly abandoned it for the old Caledonian habit.[49]

As Zoffany's painting of Garrick's Macbeth shows, Garrick wore formal contemporary clothes as Macbeth, a court version of a military uniform for the murder, just as, for his second encounter with the witches, he wore the outfit of

> a modern fine gentleman so that ... you looked like a beau who had unfortunately slipped his foot and tumbled into a night-cellar, where a parcel of old women were boiling tripe for their supper.[50]

[44] Quoted in *Plays*, 3: 72.   [45] *Plays*, 3: 53.
[46] David Garrick, *The Letters*, Letter 726, 2: 838.
[47] Quoted in David Garrick, *The Letters*, Letter 726, 2: 838.   [48] Ibid., Letter 93, 1: 152.
[49] William Cooke, *Memoirs of Charles, Macklin, Comedian* (London, 1804), 283–4.
[50] Quoted by Burnim, *David Garrick, Director*, 121–2.

Where Garrick's experiments with historical accuracy, when they occurred at all, were limited to costume for the principals, Macklin went much further and 'shewed the same attention to the subordinate characters as well as to the scenes, decorations, music and other incidental parts of the performance'.[51] His own costume as Macbeth draped the plaid over his back, used the traditional belted tunic and a bonnet, and rightly avoided the kilt, a late innovation in Scottish wear. His first entrance, Macklin noted, 'should be preceded by fife, drum, bagpipe (query) and a bodyguard in highland dress'.[52] Even the set was to depict the world of the historical Macbeth as Macklin understood it: for the interior of Macbeth's castle, 'every room should be full of bad pictures of warriors, sword, helmet, target and dirk, escutcheons—and the Hall, boars stuffed, wolves, and full of pikes and broadswords.'[53]

Macklin's designs were full of anachronisms: the Scottish troops carried pistols and the castle battlements had cannon. But his vision of the play was far beyond anything Garrick ever attempted, the fullest attempt yet to create a design for a Shakespeare play that was both historical and imaginative. It was also, conspicuously unlike Garrick's success with *Macbeth*, something of a disaster with near-riots in the audience so that the management cancelled performances and Macklin was dismissed. Where Garrick had worked hard in 1744 to restore the Shakespeare text and oust Davenant's, as well as ensuring that it properly set off the brilliance of his own performance, Macklin was concerned only with historical authenticity, a unified production style, and detailed realism. Macklin may have been mocked, but his style of production prefigured the nineteenth-century fascination with historicism and the twentieth-century fascination with unified, conceptually driven modes of directorial interpretation in Shakespeare tragedy.

KING LEAR AND THE SPACE OF EMOTION

King Lear was the first of Nahum Tate's three Shakespeare adaptations, all written to comment on the current political situation, in particular the Exclusion Crisis, the attempt to enact legislation to block James, Duke of York, from succeeding to the throne after his brother, King Charles II. Shakespeare, at this time of severe political unrest, seemed as useful to make a cultural intervention as his works would be in the Soviet state centuries later.

Tate's *History of King Lear* has come to be the most mocked of all Shakespeare adaptations, simply for its happy ending which, as Dr Johnson knew, accorded with the reports of Lear's reign in the chronicles and which Shakespeare so brutally refused. The play had not yet become a staple of the repertory, though it had been, as John Downes noted, 'Acted exactly as Mr. Shakespear Wrote it'[54] and Tate's analysis of it was no surprise: 'I found the whole … a Heap of Jewels, unstrung and unpolisht; yet so dazzling in their Disorder, that I soon perceiv'd I had seiz'd on a Treasure.'[55] Tate's solution to 'rectifie what was wanting in

---

[51] Cooke, *Memoirs of Macklin*, 284.

[52] Quoted by Denis Donoghue, 'Macklin's Shylock and Macbeth', *Studies: An Irish Quarterly Review* 43 (1954), 428.

[53] Ibid.   [54] Downes, *Roscius*, 33.

[55] Nahum Tate, *The History of King Lear* (London, 1681), sig. A2v.

the Regularity and Probability of the Tale' was to 'run through the whole A *Love* betwixt *Edgar* and *Cordelia*, that never chang'd word with each other in the Original':

> This renders *Cordelia's* Indifference and her Father's Passion in the first Scene probable. It likewise gives Countenance to *Edgar's* Disguise, making that a generous Design that was before a poor Shift to save his Life. (A2v)

One crucial consequence for Tate was that the 'Distress of the Story is evidently heightned by it', not least in new scenes such as the attempted rape of Cordelia and her confidante Arante by two 'Ruffians' hired by Edmund and their rescue by Edgar.[56]

Tate's aims were multiple: to give the plot a coherence and probability it seemed to him to lack; to add to the emotional tensions, especially in terms of the emotional state of distress in which the characters are placed and which therefore calls for a sympathetic concern from the audience; and, not least, to make the play politically relevant to contemporary events.[57] If often limp in its writing—not least in the scene where Edmund and Regan are found 'amorously Seated, Listning to Musick' (40)—its broadening of the play's politics into the anxieties of a popular uprising is fascinating. The two are interrupted in 'A Grotto' by an officer who reports that 'The Peasants are all up in Mutiny' because

> Old *Gloster* …
> Proclaims your Cruelty, and their Oppression,
> With the King's Injuries; which so enrag'd 'em,
> That now that Mutiny which long had crept
> Takes Wing, and threatens your Best Pow'rs. (41)

Again and again Tate adds lines to emphasize the national and political over the familial and personal: Gloucester now calmly announces 'Well have I sold my Eyes, if the Event | Prove happy for the injur'd King' (41) and, at the end, wants to 'hail | His second Birth of Empire; my dear *Edgar* | Has, with himself, reveal'd the King's blest Restauration' (66). Lear, Kent and Gloucester will retire and Edgar and Cordelia will jointly rule, as Edgar envisages the change: 'Our drooping Country now erects her Head, | Peace spreads her balmy Wings, and Plenty Blooms' (67).

But the politics of *King Lear* and especially the national politics of Tate's *King Lear* would never be Garrick's concern. Even for a culture which saw an excess of sensibility relieved by the outpouring of weeping as the highest state of emotional sympathy, sometimes there can be too many tears. When Garrick played King Lear for the last time in 1776 a reviewer found no decline in his power:

> The curse at the close of the first act, his phrenetic appeal to heaven at the end of the second on Regan's ingratitude, were two such enthusiastic scenes of human exertion, that they caused a kind of momentary petrifaction thro' the house, which he soon dissolved universally into tears. Even the unfeeling Regan and Goneril forgetful of their characteristic cruelty, played through the whole of their parts with aching bosoms and streaming eyes.[58]

---

[56] Ibid., 33–4.

[57] On the links to the Exclusion crisis, see Nancy Klein Maguire, 'Nahum Tate's *King Lear*: "the king's blest restoration"', in Jean I. Marsden, ed., *The Appropriation of Shakespeare* (Hemel Hempstead: Harvester Wheatsheaf, 1992), 29–42.

[58] Quoted by George Winchester Stone, Jr., 'Garrick's Production of *King Lear*: A Study in the Temper of the Eighteenth-Century Mind', *SP* 45 (1948), 89–103 (103).

It was not exactly the actresses' fault, for they knew this was the last time that his performance, the most majestic and potent machine for generating the right response to the pathetic that the theatre had seen, would be experienced. Years earlier, when Boswell saw Garrick's Lear in 1762, the theatre was packed more than two hours before the performance. Boswell prepared himself for the experience:

> I kept myself at a distance from all acquaintances, and got into a proper frame. Mr. Garrick gave me the most perfect satisfaction. I was fully moved, and I shed an abundance of tears.[59]

It had been the same earlier still when Garrick, coached in the role by Macklin, 'exhibited such a scene of the pathetic … as drew tears of commiseration from the whole house'.[60]

Like yawning and laughter, one person's tears can generate tears in another. Garrick's Lear cried and cried. In the curse on Goneril, for instance, Samuel Foote complained in 1747 that Garrick wept:

> Nor can I easily pardon the Tears shed at the Conclusion. The whole Passage is a Climax of Rage, that strange mixture of Anger and Grief is to me highly unnatural; and besides this unmanly Sniveling lowers the Consequence of *Lear*.[61]

An anonymous pamphleteer, responding, turned back to Shakespeare:

> had he look'd into *Shakespeare*, he would not have been so severe upon *your Tears shed at the Conclusion*, or have said that the *strange mixture of Grief and Passion was highly unnatural*; for this speech immediately following the curse is your direction and authority.[62]

But Garrick's Lear did not mention 'these hot tears, which break from me perforce' or speak to his 'Old fond eyes, | Beweep this cause again, I'll pluck ye out' (1.4.296, 299–300), for the text he was then using was essentially still Tate's, and Tate's Act 1 ended with the curse, not with the rest of the scene, so that the focus is on Lear as he storms out with the added words 'Away, away'.[63] The writer knew and Garrick knew what Shakespeare had written but the text for Garrick's Lear was never to be Shakespeare's.

Throughout his career, Garrick rethought the version of *King Lear* he performed, even though the broad outlines of his performance hardly changed. He would never restore either the Fool or the tragic ending, though both were encouraged. Garrick's defender in 1747 called for 'the original, Fool and all',[64] and Davies reported that 'It was once in contemplation with Mr Garrick to restore the part of the Fool, which he designed for Woodward, who promised to be very chaste in his colouring, and not to counteract the agonies of Lear', but Garrick never dared to do it: 'the manager would not hazard so bold an attempt; he feared, with Mr Colman, that the feelings of Lear would derive no advantage from the buffooneries of the parti-coloured jester.' [65]

[59] Quoted in Cunningham, *Shakespeare and Garrick*, 27.
[60] Cooke, *Memoirs of Macklin*, 107.
[61] Vickers, *Critical Heritage*, vol. 3, 1733–52 (1975), 212.   [62] Ibid., 263.
[63] See *Plays*, 3: 324.   [64] *An Examen of the New Comedy* (London, 1747), 22.
[65] Davies, *Dramatic Miscellanies*, 2: 172.

There had been pressure to abandon Tate throughout the century, starting well before Garrick first played the role. Arthur Murphy, writing a series of articles on Shakespeare and particularly on *King Lear* in the *Gray's Inn Journal* in 1753-4, opposed restoring Shakespeare and assumed that 'after the heart-piercing sensations which we have endured through the whole piece, it would be too much to see this actually performed on the stage: from [Garrick] ... I am sure it would. I should be glad, notwithstanding, to see the experiment made'.[66] Dr Johnson, in his comments on the play in his 1765 Shakespeare edition, was less radical and more content with what 'the publick has decided' and recorded his own inability to cope with Shakespeare's ending: 'I was many years ago so shocked by *Cordelia*'s death that I know not whether I ever endured to read again the last scenes of the play till I undertook to revise them as an editor'.[67]

Garrick played *King Lear* in 1756, advertising the production's 'restorations from Shakespeare'. In truth there was little restored—only ten lines—but there were 200 fewer lines from Tate. As with the battle of the Romeos in 1750, Garrick once again deliberately put himself in direct competition with Spranger Barry and again he was the winner. A contemporary rhyme explained why:

> The town has found out different ways
> To praise the different Lears.
> To Barry they give loud huzzas,
> To Garrick—only tears.[68]

In 1768 George Colman produced a different version of the play for Covent Garden, aiming, as he announced in the preface to the published version, 'to purge the tragedy of Lear of the alloy of Tate, which has so long been suffered to debase it', though that did not mean incorporating the Fool and, as to the end, he wanted 'to reconcile the catastrophe of Tate to the story of Shakespeare'.[69] Less horrifying than Shakespeare and even than Tate (for Gloucester's blinding is performed off-stage, not on), Colman's *Lear* is, like Garrick's all about families. Murphy had argued against another essayist in *The Gray's Inn Journal* that Lear goes mad wholly as a result of his daughters' actions, that the loss of kingship plays no part compared to filial ingratitude, and that 'parental distress' creates the proper response for the audience to 'a monarch voluntarily abdicating and ... would, I fear, border upon the ridiculous'.[70] When Garrick described the play in a letter in 1770 he wrote of Lear as 'a *Weak* man', 'an Old Man full of affection, Generosity, Passion, & what not meeting with what he thought an ungrateful return from his best belov'd Cordelia, & afterwards real ingratitude from his other Daughters', a man whose 'unhappiness proceeded from good qualities carry'd to excess of folly', but he never describes Lear as a king. As for Murphy, Garrick's Lear suffers because of his daughters and 'an audience must feel his distresses & Madness which is yᵉ Consequence of them'.[71]

[66] Vickers, *Critical Heritage*, vol. 4, *1753-1765* (1976), 108.

[67] Vickers, *Critical Heritage*, vol. 5, *1765-1774*, 140

[68] Quoted by Arthur John Harris, 'Garrick, Colman and *King Lear*: A Reconsideration', *SQ* 22 (1971), 61.

[69] George Colman, *The History of King Lear* (London, 1768), in Colman, *The Dramatic Works*, 4 vols. (London, 1777), 3: 103.

[70] Vickers, *Critical Heritage*, vol. 4, *1753-1765*, 99.

[71] David Garrick, *The Letters*, Letter 574, 2: 682–83.

Feelings, distress, heart-piercing, endured—the kind of language used of Garrick's Lear was all of a piece. The recognizability of the suffering of an old man, a father, was far more important to the generation of the sympathetic tears than the sense of sovereignty. And the manageability of an emotion like the tears of distress was more appropriate to this culture's consumption of tragedy than the universal apocalyptic nihilism that late twentieth-century audiences were enabled to find in the play. Limited? Perhaps. But there is something powerful in that affective response, a finding of human sympathy that reveals its potency in a performance as extraordinary as Garrick's, even if one might wish he had been brave enough to return to Shakespeare's ending.[72]

In the concerns of a culture of playgoing—what audiences are willing to endure and feel or to reject and avoid—Shakespeare, unsurprisingly, served as the touchstone for defining those limits, limits of intensity and engagement, that served the exhilaration of more than a century of Shakespearean tragedy in performance. In the detail of the actors', adapters', and designers' decisions lies the refocusing of Shakespeare's text to fit the new cultures of affect and desire, the responses to the audience's continually reformulated tastes.

Select Bibliography

Bartholomeusz, Dennis, *Macbeth and the Players* (Cambridge: Cambridge University Press, 1969).

Bate, Jonathan, *Shakespearean Constitutions: Politics, Theatre, Criticism, 1730–1830* (Oxford: Clarendon Press, 1989).

Bate, Jonathan and Jackson, Russell, eds., *Shakespeare: An Illustrated Stage History* (Oxford: Oxford University Press, 1996).

Burnim, Kalman A., *David Garrick Director* (Carbondale, IL: Southern Illinois University Press, 1961).

Clark, Sandra, *Shakespeare Made Fit: restoration Adaptations of Shakespeare* (London: Dent, 1997).

Cunningham, Vanessa, *Shakespeare and Garrick* (Cambridge: Cambridge University Press, 2008).

Dobson, Michael, *The Making of the National Poet* (Oxford: The Clarendon Press, 1992).

Garrick, David, *The Plays*, ed. H. W. Pedicord and Frederick L. Bergmann, 7 vols. (Carbondale, IL: Southern Illinois University Press, 1980-2).

Marsden, Jean I., ed., *The Appropriation of Shakespeare* (Hemel Hempstead: Harvester Wheatsheaf, 1992).

Oya, Reiko, *Representing Shakespearean Tragedy: Garrick, the Kembles and Kean* (Cambridge: Cambridge University Press, 2007).

Ritchie, Fiona and Sabor, Peter, eds., *Shakespeare in the Eighteenth Century* (Cambridge: Cambridge University Press, 2012).

Rosenberg, Marvin, *The Masks of Hamlet* (Newark: University of Delaware Press, 1992).

Rosenberg, Marvin, *The Masks of King Lear* (Berkeley: University of California Press, 1972).

Rosenberg, Marvin, *The Masks of Macbeth* (Berkeley: University of California Press, 1978).

---

[72] See Jean Marsden, 'Shakespeare and Sympathy', in Peter Sabor and Paul Yachnin, eds., *Shakespeare and the Eighteenth Century* (Aldershot: Ashgate, 2008), 29–41, esp. 34-7.

Rosenberg, Marvin, *The Masks of Othello* (Berkeley: University of California Press, 1961).

Sabor, Peter and Yachnin, Paul, eds., *Shakespeare and the Eighteenth Century* (Aldershot: Ashgate, 2008).

Stone, George Winchester, Jr., 'Garrick's Production of *King Lear*: A Study in the Temper of the Eighteenth-Century Mind', *SP* 45 (1948), 89–103.

Stone, George Winchester, Jr. and Kahrl, George M., *David Garrick: A Critical Biography* (Carbondale, IL: Southern Illinois University Press, 1979).

Brian Vickers, ed., *Shakespeare: The Critical Heritage,* 6 vols. (London: Routledge and Kegan Paul, 1974–81).

CHAPTER 32

STAGING SHAKESPEAREAN TRAGEDY

The Nineteenth Century

RUSSELL JACKSON

TIME-TRAVELLERS from the twenty-first century, able to visit a performance of a Shakespearean tragedy in Britain or America the 1840s, would be surprised by differences in interpretive emphasis, not only the performances of the actors but also in the adapted script; the overall visual impact of a convincing and unified scenic picture behind the pro-scenium arch's picture frame; and the coordination of musical score and action. When it was achieved, this harmony of artistic effect existed alongside the persistent privileging of the brilliant individual performance. It is on some of these performances and the interplay between originality and tradition that this chapter focuses.

Some generalizations can be made regarding interpretations of character and situa-tion between the first years of the nineteenth century and the outbreak of the First World War, but we can also identify a degree of conflict in the critical responses to performances of *Othello, Hamlet, Macbeth, King Lear,* and *Romeo and Juliet*. Reviewers and audiences applauded innovation, but also respected continuity. The literary and dramatic critics of the Romantic period, in particular William Hazlitt, Charles Lamb, and Leigh Hunt, re-mained influential, as did memories (often first-hand) of actors of the late 1700s and early 1800s, particularly Sarah Siddons, John Philip Kemble, and Edmund Kean. Elements of the acting versions used by John Philip Kemble (and traces of those made by Garrick) survived on stage into the 1830s and 1840s. As the century progressed the versions made by William Charles Macready, copied meticulously for Charles Kean and other actor-managers, established a new set of traditions not only of acting but also of staging.

We can identify a consistency in critical approach, with commonly agreed bounda-ries of acceptable interpretation. Notions of the 'ideal' qualities appropriate to the tragic protagonist included a deep infusion of concern for civility and moral rectitude, so that accounts of the characters and their plays often had to negotiate some kind of special pleading in defence of passionate or aggressive behaviour and language. Peter Gay, in *The Bourgeois Experience: Victoria to Freud*, describes tensions that can be seen under-lying these responses: 'the cultural signals by which nineteenth-century bourgeois ori-ented themselves were often uncertain and anxiety-provoking. It was a time of progress and for confidence, but also one for doubt, for second thoughts, for bouts of pessimism, for questions about identity.'[1] Given the erotic dimensions of the tragedies, it is hardly surprising that what Gay describes as the 'steady' lowering of the 'thresholds of shame and disgust', should be reflected in performances: 'Respectable nineteenth-century culture found the imagination a dangerous companion, and instead celebrated delay, modulation, control.'[2] Performances of the tragedies reflect the tension, stimulating and at times dismaying, between the texts themselves and society's pursuit of these moral qualities.

Othello offered, as James R. Siemon suggests in his study of the treatment of the final scene, the spectacle of 'a culture trying to control a text that it desires to experience in the theatre but that it also strongly disapproves of'. After a survey of prompt copies and acting versions between 1766 and 1900, Siemon concludes that in them the murder 'becomes the sacrifice of a largely passive victim by a protagonist whose own emotional conflicts are the center of attention'.[3] This is rooted in attitudes to the balance between the play's principal characters, and in assumptions of race and gender in the treatment of Othello and Desdemona. British and American reviews of the Italian tragedian Tommaso Salvini draw attention to the unusual extremity of both gentleness and violence in a role that had always taxed actors' ability to lend Othello nobility and sensitivity. Henry James admitted that 'to many observers Salvini's rendering of the part is too simple, too much on two or three notes,—frank tenderness, quick suspicion, passionate rage'. Nevertheless, '[n]o more complete picture of passion can have been given to the stage in our day—passion beginning in noble repose and spending itself in black insanity.' In admitting the absence of the 'metaphysical side' in Shakespeare's 'sentiment', James asserts that 'Salvini's rendering of the part is the portrait of an African by an Italian'.[4] In 1875 The *London Figaro* had described the 'happy touches whereby Othello's trustful love in his wife were indicated' in the actor's performance by the 'deep affection' that 'constantly comes welling up to the surface, displaying itself in tender smiles, in tones of gentle sweetness, and in ineffably touching gesture and manner, too delicate and too minute for detailed description'.[5] Many regarded the passion and violence of the later acts as a revelation of the 'true' nature of the Moor. Another London paper, describing the 'vivid, awful' threats to Iago in 3.3, remarked that Othello was reverting to hereditary instinct: 'How subtly fine and true, also, the gradual return to his original savage nature, for a while civilised and transformed by love; but only slumbering.'[6]

In the final scene Salvini paced back and forth 'like a tiger weaving across his cage',[7] and when Desdemona left the bed to remonstrate with him, he maintained his composure until, maddened by her exclamation 'Alas, he is betrayed, and I undone' (5.2.83),

[1] Peter Gay, *The Bourgeois Experience: Victoria to Freud*, vol. 1, *Education of the Senses* (London: Harper Collins, 1984), 8.

[2] Ibid., 58.

[3] James R. Siemon, '"Nay, that's not next": *Othello*, V. ii in Performance, 1760-1900', *SQ* 37:1 (Spring 1986), 38-51 (38, 50).

[4] Henry James, 'Tommaso Salvini' (*Atlantic Monthly*, March 1883), in *The Scenic Art, Notes on Acting and the Drama, 1872-1901*, ed. Alan Wade (London: Hart-Davis, 1949), 171-2; 173-4.

[5] *London Figaro*, 7 April 1875.   [6] *The Hornet*, 21 April 1875.

[7] Albert Colby Sprague, *Shakespeare and the Actors. The Stage Business in his Plays, 1660-1905*, Fourth Printing (Cambridge MA: Harvard University Press, 1948), 211, quoting William Story.

He drags her to her feet, as she kneels, facing him; he then clutches her right arm with his right hand, knotting his fingers in her loose hair; and pulling back her head, as if to break her neck. Holding her thus, he swiftly forces her up the stage, and through the curtains which close behind them ... muffled sounds of the last fatal act are heard.[8]

Salvini's orchestration of violence culminated the particularly gruesome suicide of Othello, 'hacking and hewing with savage energy, and imitating the noise that escaping air and blood make together when the windpipe is severed'.[9]

Although details in its execution varied from time to time in his career, Salvini's approach remained consistent. It represents a variation on the interpretations and tactics of less adventurous actors, and focuses directly on the categories of critical debate as to how instinctively violent Othello should be, and how the 'mildness' and ennobling quality of his love for Desdemona should be shown. Given that the acting text had been purged of all but the least direct references to Desdemona's alleged adultery, the sexual rather than sentimental sources of Othello's passion were downplayed but inevitably remained as a more or less secret subtext for the actor and the more worldly among the spectators.

The diarist Charles Rice observed of the American actor Edwin Forrest's London debut in the role in 1836, that 'All Mr. Forrest's love-scenes were exceedingly whining and disagreeable.'

Towards the termination of the third act, the principal portion of the scenes with Desdemona in the fourth, where his rage, or madness, overcomes his outward show of indifference, and he roughly accuses her of the crime laid to her charge by Iago, and the latter part of the last scene, Mr. Forrest's acting was exceedingly fine, and original; he was rapturously applauded in those parts, and certainly deserved the approbation he received.[10]

This was some ten years before the break-up of the actor's marriage, and it has been suggested plausibly that in his later performances the sensational divorce underlay his expression of the play's passions. Forrest seems, though, to have achieved a degree of containment that threw into relief not only the final scene but also the anger directed against Iago in 3.3 when Othello demands 'ocular proof.' It was then, Marvin Rosenberg suggests, that 'the hands that would have gladly strangled' the alleged lover of the actor's wife, 'could now seize openly on the naked throat of Iago.' A contemporary witness describes the effect vividly:

Suddenly, with one electrifying bound, he leaped the whole gamut from mortal exhaustion to gigantic rage, his eyeballs rolling and his muscles strung, seized the cowering Iago by the throat, and, with a startling transition of voice from mellow and mournfully lingering notes to crackling thunderbolts ... shrieked 'If thou do slander her and torture me,/Never pray more, abandon all remorse.'[11]

[8] Sprague, *Shakespeare and the Actors*, 214.

[9] Joseph Knight, *Theatrical Notes* (London: Lawrence and Bullen, 1893), 24.

[10] Charles Rice, *The London Theatre in the Eighteen-Thirties*, ed. Arthur Colby Sprague and Bertram Shuttleworth (London: Society for Theatre Research, 1950), 8.

[11] Marvin Rosenberg, *The Masks of 'Othello.' The Search for the Identity of Othello, Iago, and Desdemona by Three Centuries of Actors and Critics* (Berkeley and Los Angeles: University of California Press, 1961), 96–7.

This was always a powerful moment, executed with varying degrees of melodramatic effect. Even the far more temperate Macready, whose Othello has been aptly described as 'primarily a loving husband whose domestic tranquility becomes brutally shattered', followed the example of Edmund Kean (with whom he had appeared as Iago). Variations included Edwin Booth's threatening to stab Iago with the ancient's own dagger and Salvini lifting his foot as though to trample him.[12]

The violence in the role was doubly challenging for actors who did not relish the role's contrasting and vehemently expressed passions. Edwin Booth, anxious to express his 'idea of Othello [as] not animal but poetic', asked the critic William Winter to find support for this when working on the acting editions published in his name. Dismayed by criticism of his Othello in London in 1881, Booth wrote: 'to my mind he is poetically pure and noble; even in his rage ... not over-refined, perhaps, I perceive no bestiality.'[13]

Macready's colleague and disciple Samuel Phelps followed his master in establishing 'self-respect, founded on a just consciousness of his own worth,' as a dominant characteristic of Othello, and (as *The Times* reported of a performance in 1864) 'it [was] not until his emotions become altogether unendurable that he [lost] the power of controlling them.'[14] As if in repudiation of crude racist assumptions about the 'natural' propensities of 'southern' European or African actors, the *Theatrical Times* observed in 1849 that even in 'the loudest and fiercest whirlwind of impassioned utterance' the 'African Roscius' Ira Aldridge's Othello was 'never harsh, never overstrained, never inarticulate, but always retaining a roundness of tone, which united with an overwhelming energy of natural expression, particularly distinguishes him'.[15] Such interpretations were made more secure by the customary surgery to 4.1, cutting not only the opening of the scene and the overhearing of Cassio with Bianca, but also Othello's fit and—in some cases, the arrival of Lodovico and Othello's striking of Desdemona.

Many actors found the role of Iago more congenial than that of Othello, although Macready, always conscientious, was anxious to avoid the temptation to employ stock melodramatic tricks in it. In 1840 a reviewer confirmed that the actor 'does not (as most actors do) make the performers engaged with him look fools, by making himself appear a complete villain, but ... makes us feel that, had we been in Cassio's place, we should most likely have done as he did'.[16] The play customarily ended without the final lines of Cassio and Lodovico, and with Iago either leaving the stage before Othello's death or remaining to look on the tragic loading of the bed as the curtain fell. Macready showed with his demoniacal smile that his heart was filled with 'a joy that hid designs that have worked upon him that he hated,' and Samuel Phelps's Iago glanced round 'with one look of ineffable scorn' before striding out.[17] Irving 'was brought on, arrested and bound, by two tall and

[12] Virginia Mason Vaughan, *Othello. A Contextual History* (Cambridge: Cambridge University Press, 1994), 137; Sprague, *Shakespeare and the Actors*, 199–200. Like similar expressions elsewhere in the text, 'whore' in line 363, 'Villain, be sure thou prove my love a whore', was customarily softened by the substitution of a milder word, such as 'drab' or 'wanton'.

[13] Daniel J. Watermeier, ed., *Between Actor and Critic. Selected Letters of Edwin Booth and William Winter* (Princeton: Princeton University Press, 1971), 107; 182.

[14] *The Times*, 17 October 1864.   [15] *Theatrical Times*, 15 April 1849.

[16] Julie Hankey, ed., *Plays in Performance: 'Othello'* (Bristol: Bristol Classical Press, 1987), 197.

[17] Sprague, *Shakespeare and the Actors*, 223.

burly guards, and after saying "From this time forth I never will speak word", the agony of the wound he had received made him gradually grow, until its seemed that those burly guards and every one else on stage shrank up to pygmies and the tortured figure with tightly compressed lips appeared to tower into the borders [above the stage]'.[18]

As for Desdemona, although Siemon's study leads to the conclusion that the play commonly ended with 'the sacrifice of a largely passive victim', the most effective Victorian Desdemonas were far from supine in the preceding acts, and many put up a sturdy defence in the final scenes. Helen Faucit, who had played opposite Macready in the 1830s and 1840s and made her last stage appearance in 1879, recalled in 1881 her first experience of the role: 'I did not know in those days that Desdemona is usually considered a merely amiable, simple, yielding creature, and that she is generally so represented on the stage.' This was a woman 'of the true, heroic mould, fearless as she was gentle'.[19] Macready told her that her emphasis on Desdemona's courage and spiritedness made the character 'a new creation for him', and that it 'restored the character of the play by giving her character its due weight in the action, so that, as he said, he had seen the play for the first time in its true *chiaroscuro*'.[20] In 1836 at Covent Garden the *Times* reviewer found her 'touchingly natural': 'Her repudiation, in the fourth act, of the coarse and vulgar accusation of the Moor was beautifully expressive of the agony of indignant virtue.'[21] She was 'very hard to kill' in the final scene, not only on account of her physical defiance but also through the force of her emotional appeal.[22] Not every critic found this acceptable: when she appeared with Macready at the Haymarket in 1839, some admired her 'delicate earnestness', while more traditionally-minded reviewers objected to her vigour in the murder scene and one thought her 'scream' was that of an 'untamed shrew'.[23]

Faucit's insistence on the feminine but nonetheless forceful emotional dimension of her characters was less effective in coping with the problematic personality of Lady Macbeth. Breaking with the tradition of tragic grandeur associated with Sarah Siddons and perpetuated by her many imitators, she sought to redeem Lady Macbeth as a loving helpmate to an erring husband.[24] Faucit argues that in the Scotland of the time violent deaths and succession achieved by means of murder were not uncommon, and that having been 'brought up amongst such scenes ... one murder more seemed little to her'. Despite this, she was ill prepared for personal experience: 'She did not know what it was to be personally implicated in murder, nor foresee the Nemesis that would pursue her waking, and fill her dreams with visions of the old man's blood slowly trickling down before her eyes.'[25] An enthusiastic witness quoted by Faucit in an appendix to her collection of essays on the heroines wrote: 'I said to myself: this woman ... is simply urging her husband forward

---

[18] George R. Foss, *What the Author Meant* (Oxford: Oxford University Press, 1932), 80.
[19] Helena Faucit, Lady Martin, *On Some of Shakespeare's Female Characters. New and Enlarged Edition* (Edinburgh and London: Blackwood, 1891), 60.
[20] Faucit, *On Some of Shakespeare's Female Characters*, 50.
[21] *The Times*, 22 October 1836.
[22] Faucit, *On Some of Shakespeare's Female Characters*, 77.
[23] Carol Jones Carlisle, *Helen Faucit. Fire and Ice on the Victorian Stage* (London: Society for Theatre Research, 2000), 74.
[24] On John Philip Kemble and Sarah Siddons in *Macbeth* see Dennis Bartholomeusz, *Macbeth and the Players* (Cambridge: Cambridge University Press, 1969), ch. 6.
[25] Faucit, *On Some of Shakespeare's Female Characters*, 232.

through her love for him.' The character is redeemed from moral condemnation, as the approach 'unquestionably adds new elements to the character, and not only rescues it from the terrible and revolting monotony in which it has heretofore appeared, but keeps it within the category of humanity, and gives a beautiful and significant moral to the closing scenes of the queen's life'.[26]

This interpretation seems to have come as a relief to some, and in his biography of Helen Faucit her husband quotes at length the *Morning Post*'s celebration of such touches as her speaking 'You lack the season of all natures, sleep' (3.4.140): 'The mingled love and pity conveyed in these words revealed the real character of Lady Macbeth, and the elocution was faultlessly pure and charmingly musical. It came from the heart of the actress, and went directly to the hearts of the audience.' Responses to the sleepwalking were correspondingly charged with gratitude for pathos that had been earned. 'Her countenance [was] expressive of a shuddering horror at the past, and a deep sense of the enormity of the crimes which are heaped above her head, crushing her down beyond redemption.' The audience's reaction was proportionate: 'A heavy breath of relief was drawn by the audience when she glided from the stage, and they gave vent to their feelings in prolonged bursts of applause.'[27] The admiration was not universal. Henry Morley, reviewing a performance in 1864, found her 'too essentially feminine, too exclusively gifted in the art of expressing all that is most graceful in womanhood, to succeed in inspiring anything like awe or terror' in the scenes before the murder of Duncan. Consequently, she seemed to have resorted to being 'too demonstrative and noisy' although in the 'second phase of the character ... the reaction of disappointment and hidden suffering after the crime' was 'delicately shown'. The sleepwalking scene, though 'very carefully delivered' had 'too much the air of a well-studied dramatic recitation'.[28]

Sarah Siddons's Lady Macbeth had been formidable and 'sublime.' Leigh Hunt (one among many admirers) had commented in 1809 that in a performance with the less than electrifying Charles Mayne Young, 'the scene between [Lady Macbeth] and her husband was grand and horrific, for how could it be otherwise when drawn by Shakespeare and sustained by Mrs. Siddons?'[29] Macready, for his part, seems to have found the more 'Siddonian' interpretation of the accomplished and versatile actress Mrs Warner more congenial than that of Helen Faucit, perhaps because she did not challenge him for attention as the centre of the tragedy. According to the critic and playwright Westland Marston, for all her lack of incisiveness and subtlety there was 'a constant *physique* of Lady Macbeth' in Warner's performance and 'such a propriety in her somewhat surface exhibition of the character that she was held for years to be its most satisfactory representative'.[30]

    [26] Ibid., 402.
    [27] Sir Theodore Martin, KCB, *Helena Faucit (Lady Martin)* (Edinburgh and London: William Blackwood and Sons, 1890), 227–8. The date of the *Morning Post* review is given as 5 August 1851; the other journal is not identified.
    [28] Henry Morley, *The Journal of a London Playgoer from 1851 to 1864*, ed. Michael Booth (Leicester: Leicester University Press, 1974), 290–2. Morley's review of the Drury Lane performance, with Phelps as Macbeth, appeared in the *Examiner* on 3 December 1864.
    [29] Leigh Hunt, 'Mr Young's Merits Considered' (*Examiner*, 15 January 1809), in Lawrence Huston Houtchens and Carolyn Washburn Houtchens, eds., *Leigh Hunt's Dramatic Criticism, 1808–1831* (London: Oxford University Press, 1950), 21–5 (23).
    [30] Bartholomeusz, *Macbeth and the Players*, 171.

Siddons's reputation haunted the role well into the century. According to one reviewer, Laura Addison, in Samuel Phelps's 1847 revival at Sadler's Wells, 'seemed struggling to be majestic and Siddonian in the early scenes'. Another hints at the same notion without naming the great actress: Addison's performance was 'passionate and energetic enough, but it want[ed] that calm discrimination, that intellectual power and personal dignity that belongs essentially to the character'.[31]

In the banquet scene (3.4) Macready's Macbeth, unmanned by the ghost's second appearance, looked at the spectre 'as if the sight had frozen every faculty', then fell into his chair, 'convulsively burying his head in his mantle, as if to shut out the sight, sense and recollection'. After the departure of the guests, he seemed to acquire 'a new and hardened manner', suggesting to one reviewer a swing 'from soft to stern'. Dennis Bartholomeusz suggests that this exemplified the way that 'once again in the third act Macready portrayed a man swayed by emotions primitive in their force and variety'.[32] Edwin Forrest's performance at this point, as recorded in an annotated copy of the play, suggests a variation on a move that Macready seems to have adapted from Edmund Kean. On his final defiance of the ghost, 'Unreal mockery, hence!' (105), 'Mr. Forrest used to throw his robe under his R. arm (which was left free for action) into his L. hand—which held up the robe as if to shield him from seeing the ghost & would then advance upon it—as if to waft it away—[It went] off at 'Hence' which would be repeated 4 or 5 times—(until it was off the stage) rising to great power of passion of fear & horror—& then fell back for support against the tormentor [i.e. the side of the stage, just behind the proscenium arch].' This contrasted with the mood at the end of the scene as Macbeth and Lady Macbeth are left alone. On 'You lack the season of all natures, sleep' (140), she 'gives a sigh and touches his hand in tender sympathy', then on 'that wants hard use' he 'takes her hand—leads her off—both drooping & subdued'.[33]

In his 1888 Lyceum production Irving tried at least two variations on the final moments. At the beginning of the run he took a torch from behind a pillar, suddenly hurled it to the ground and 'shroud[ed] his face in his robe as he rapidly lean[ed] forward and rest[ed] against a pillar' with Lady Macbeth kneeling beside him, 'clinging to his skirts, with an upturned face full of tragic solicitude'.[34] In the second variation, recorded by William Winter, as they left the hall Irving 'stopped and slowly turned to the spot where the ghost had appeared, wide-eyed with remembered fear'.[35] Both versions share the period's predilection for 'tableau' moments that encapsulate a mood or a moment of crisis.

By the end of the century, thanks largely to the influence of Macready, the play was given in a more complete version than had been customary hitherto. A review of Samuel Phelps's production at Sadler's Wells in October 1847 summarizes the reforms, which included the removal of traces of Davenant's Restoration version and the traditional music attributed

---

[31] *Theatrical Times*, 2 October 1847; *Dramatic Mirror*, 4 October 1847.

[32] The details quoted are assembled by Bartholomeusz, *Macbeth and the Players*, 166–7.

[33] New York Public Library Performing Arts Division, Lincoln Center, *NCP1860 (Shattuck 70) (Forrest).

[34] Alan Hughes, *Henry Irving, Shakespearean* (Cambridge: Cambridge University Press, 1978), 109, quoting 'An Old Hand' (Edward Russell) *'Macbeth' at the Lyceum* (Liverpool, 1889).

[35] Hughes, *Henry Irving*, 108 and n. 70, quoting William Winter, *Shakespeare on the Stage* (New York: 1911), 1: 485.

to Locke: 'For the first time for many years—we had almost written centuries—the inter-polated musical scenes [for Hecate and the witches] are omitted; and several portions of the tragedy, not latterly acted—such as the soliloquy of the Porter, the scene at Macduff's castle, and that in which the old man discourses of the prodigies—restored to the stage.'[36] (The introduction of Macbeth's severed head was not to all tastes: the *Theatrical Times* thought it 'brutal and melodramatic' and 'only suited to a Victoria audience'—that is, to the then scorned 'Old Vic' and its lurid melodramas.[37]) Although the preference for a fuller text was by now firmly established for this as for most other plays the restored scenes were not invariably included. The Porter scene was omitted when the German novelist Theodor Fontane saw Phelps's production in 1857, but he admired the completeness and overall artistic unity of the stage effects as well as the acting, comparing both favourably with what he had seen in Berlin. In the scene of the murder he noted the placing of the door to the king's bedchamber near the front of the stage, on the side opposite that of the Macbeths' room.

> After Macbeth has opened the little door and entered the king's room, the stage is empty for a good half-minute. Then at last lady Macbeth darts out of her room. After the first two lines ... she breaks off with 'Hark! Peace! And steps towards the door through which Macbeth disappeared a minute ago. She opens it a little, and through the narrow crack a pale light falls on the stage. This is the moment when she whispers the fatal words, 'He is about it.'[38]

Touches of this kind counterpointed such grander or more lurid effects as the awaken-ing of the inhabitants of the castle after the discovery of Duncan's murder, the scenes with the witches, and the final combat between Macbeth and Macduff. On receiving his death wound, Macready's Macbeth staggered back but caught himself and, 'with a mo-mentary suggestion of his regal stride, return[ed], only to fall on Macduff's sword in yield-ing weakness'.

> Thrusting his own sword into the ground, Macbeth raises himself by its help to his knees where he stares full in the face of his vanquisher with a resolute and defiant gaze of concen-trated majesty, hate and knowledge, and instantly falls dead.[39]

Irving's death scene was similarly memorable. At the beginning of his production's sixth act, after the supposed interval of seventeen years since his last appearance, Macbeth was 'visibly an old man ... his grey hair dishevilled, floating wildly in the wind'.[40] In his final combat, after 'a last, weary, impotent effort to kill his adversary by flinging his dagger at him', he fell, face down to hide his shame.[41]

---

[36] *Illustrated London News*, 20 October 1847.   [37] *Theatrical Times*, 2 October 1847.

[38] Theodor Fontane, *Shakespeare in the London Theatre, 1855-58*, trans. Russell Jackson (London: Society for Theatre Research, 1999), 84. The production is described in detail by Shirley S. Allen, *Samuel Phelps and Sadler's Wells Theatre* (Middletown CT: Wesleyan University Press, 1971), 233–6.

[39] Alan S. Downer, *The Eminent Tragedian. William Charles Macready* (Cambridge, MA: Harvard University Press, 1966), 338.

[40] *The Times*, 31 December 1888.   [41] *The Stage*, 4 January 1889.

The critical reactions quoted so far to these performances of *Othello* and *Macbeth* exemplify some of the common tensions between the actors' imaginative work and expectations informed by stage tradition and reading of the texts themselves. Both were dominated by a desire to establish heroic or ideal qualities in the principal characters: male actors should achieve both tragic suffering and nobility of feeling, female interpreters must reconcile 'feminine' delicacy with a degree of energy or, in the case of Lady Macbeth, criminality. George Henry Lewes, weighing his strengths and limitations, wrote that Macready 'did not belong to the stately declamatory school of [John Philip] Kemble, but in all parts strove to introduce as much familiarity of detail as was consistent with ideal representation.' He made his characters 'domestic rather than ideal', and 'was irritable where he should have been passionate, querulous where he should have been terrible'.[42] Opinions differed, of course, regarding Macready's success in any of these roles, but his 'domestic' emphasis, the 'familiar' (i.e. unaffected) detail in stage business, and the privileging of the 'real' over the 'ideal' were often remarked on. The difference lay between commentators who regarded these as signs of progress in dramatic art, and those who felt that a vital dimension of tragic acting was being slighted.

In the case of *Hamlet* the principal task was to reconcile the celebrated sensitivity and 'philosophical' insight of the Prince with the bloody action of the play. Hamlet had to be redeemed. Reviewers persisted in citing the opinion of the hero of Goethe's novel *Wilhelm Meister* regarding the predicament of the prince: an oak tree (the task) is planted in a precious vessel (Hamlet) suitable only for flowers, so that the roots extend and shatter it.[43] Hamlet's treatment of Ophelia and Gertrude, and his demeanour in general, had long been touchstones in evaluating performances. The agenda had in effect been set by William Hazlitt. Reviewing Edmund Kean in 1814, he felt that the actor's Hamlet resembled too closely his Richard III:

> It was too strong and pointed. There was too often a severity, approaching to virulence, in the common observations and answers. ... There should be as much of the gentleman and scholar as possible infused in the part, and as little of the actor. A pensive air of sadness should sit unwillingly upon his brow, but no appearance of fixed and sullen gloom.

Kean was 'highly impressive' in the scenes in Gertrude's closet (3.4) and the 'nunnery scene' (3.1), although perhaps too vehement in his 'remonstrances' to Ophelia. In the latter he turned back as he left the stage, 'from a pang of parting tenderness', to kiss her hand. This 'explained the character at once ... as one of disappointed hope, of bitter regret, of affection suspended, not obliterated, by the distractions of the scene around him!'[44]

Variations on the 'antic disposition' were nuanced according to the temperament as well as intellectual perception of the actor. At the most extreme end of the spectrum was Forrest's, in which the play became 'a sort of cautionary tale of vibrant health undermined and ruined by a malignant excess of thought and feeling', in a prince who was—in line with many of the actor's most popular roles—muscular and warlike. Tenderness in the

---

[42] George Henry Lewes, *On Actors and the Art of Acting* (London: Smith, Elder &Co., 1875), 34, 37.
[43] Johann Wolfgang von Goethe, *Wilhelm Meisters Lehrjahre* (1795-6), bk. 4, ch. 13.
[44] William Hazlitt, 'Mr. Kean's *Hamlet*' (*Morning Chronicle*, 14 March 1814), in William Archer and Robert Lowe, eds., *Hazlitt on Theatre* (London, 1895; repr. New York: Hill and Wang, 1957), 9–14 (12, 14).

words 'Nymph, in thy orisons | Be all my sins remembered' (3.1.91-2), became rage after he had caught sight of the eavesdroppers. He 'took her briefly in his arms' on 'I did love you once', but 'after that, the rest was all physical and vocal assault', with Ophelia 'shrinking away from him in fright'.[45] Macready suggested 'not anger, but grief assuming the appearance of anger—love awkwardly counterfeiting hate'.[46]

In the queen's closet, where some Victorian Hamlets could not resist the opportunity to lecture her in a manner that would now seem sanctimonious, Westland Marston reported that, although 'sterner ... than his contemporaries', Macready's indictment of her was delivered with 'an arresting concentration that had nothing in it of violence or tumult, and with a mien lofty and unrelenting, as if he had been the commissioned angel of retribution'.[47] Charles Fechter, in 1861, seems to have taken the preaching into a 'tableau' moment: 'In the closet scene when ... his mother, in going, advances towards him with outstretched hands ... he holds the portrait before her, and rapidly glances first at the portal from whence the spirit of his father—"in his habit as he lived"—has just issued, and then at the body of the murdered Polonius.[48] In an earlier article the same critic wrote that Fechter, although showing 'too little energy at first and too much bitterness afterwards', had some feelings to spare for Polonius: 'Thou wretched, rash intruding fool, farewell. | I took thee for thy better' (30-1) was spoken as if the words 'fell from the inmost recesses of his heart, which is bleeding with pity for the sad fate which his rashness has brought upon the old man'.[49] 'I must be cruel only to be kind' (162) usually marked the end of the scene, and Gertrude exited, leaving the stage to the prince. Booth, left alone, looked around suspiciously and fell into deep meditation, but in later performances he changed the business, as Marvin Rosenberg points out, to 'share the close'. Hamlet now put his arm round her waist and kissed her forehead, speaking 'I must be cruel only to be kind' so as to make clear 'that his harsh words ... have cut his heart and feelings no less than hers'.[50] In his 1892 production, after the interview with the queen Tree escorted her upstage to the 'oratory'. She knelt, and then, having taken a torch, with 'Thus bad begins, and worse remains behind', Hamlet knelt in prayer.[51]

Many critics were exercised by the question of princely demeanour—whether sane, mad, or feigning madness—and Hamlets who failed to evince aristocratic qualities, or who were over-familiar with their inferiors were sometimes rebuked. The delivery of soliloquies when seated was regarded as a radical move. A reviewer in the Birmingham *Evening Telegraph* admired Irving's approach in the 1874 Lyceum production: 'he rested on

---

[45] John A. Mills, *Hamlet on Stage. The Great Tradition* (Westport, CT, and London: Greenwood Press, 1985), 112; 117-18.

[46] *Dramatic Essays by Forster and Lewes*, ed. William Archer and Robert Lowe (London: Chatto and Windus, 1896), 161.

[47] Marston, quoted by Mills, *Hamlet on Stage*, 101.

[48] *The Players, a Dramatic, Musical and Literary Journal*, 1 June 1861.

[49] *The Players*, 23 March 1861.

[50] Marvin Rosenberg, *The Masks of Hamlet* (Newark, London, and Toronto: University of Delaware/Associated University Presses, 1992), 721.

[51] Promptbook, HBT12: '1893' (Shattuck 121), Tree Collection, University of Bristol Theatre Collection. (NB: References to promptbooks include the number assigned to them in the listing for their respective plays in Charles H. Shattuck's *The Shakespeare Promptbooks, a Descriptive Catalogue* (Urbana, IL, and London: University of Illinois Press, 1963).)

a table or lounged languidly and despairingly on a chair, overwhelmed with weariness and hopelessness, as he soliloquized rather than recited the magnificent "Oh that this too, too solid flesh" and the still more famous "To be or not to be", and the effect was impressive beyond all words.'[52] Impersonating the thinking man's hero, the actor had a duty towards the status of the soliloquies as revered and much-anthologized meditations as well as the task of incorporating them into the creation of a believable personality.

In *Women and Victorian Theatre*, Kerry Powell points out that 'actresses throughout the nineteenth century continued to find in the framework of madness a space for powerful effects that had no place in the usual female roles of ingénue and adventuress.'[53] George Bernard Shaw applauded Mrs Patrick Campbell's break with tradition in Johnston Forbes-Robertson's 1898 production:

> The part is one which has hitherto seemed incapable of progress. From generation to generation actresses have, in the mad scene, exhausted their musical skill, their ingenuity in devising fantasias in the language of flowers, and their intensest powers of portraying anxiously earnest sanity. Mrs. Patrick Campbell, with that complacent audacity of hers which is so exasperating when she is doing the wrong thing, this time does the right thing by making Ophelia really mad.[54]

Shaw's invocation of a conventional Ophelia calls for some qualification. Clement Scott, influential critic and faithful Irving acolyte, complained that Campbell 'substitute[d] weariness for innocence and indifference for love'. He was altogether unmoved by her madness, which was 'realistic, but it [struck] the note of pain, not pity'.[55] The prevailing view since the earliest years of the century had been that summarized by William Oxberry (in *The New English Drama*, 1821–4): 'Ophelia is tender, simple and affectionate, and her naturally sweet character shows through her beautiful and touching mad scenes.'[56] Connivance in her father's strategy to discover the sources of Hamlet's 'madness', and the bawdy lyrics of the mad scene remained a difficulty even for those who argued, like Helen Faucit, for a strong, noble, and more insightful character.[57] In 1827 Harriet Smithson, appearing with Charles Kemble in Paris, overwhelmed spectators— among them the ardent young composer Hector Berlioz—with the grace and pathos of her acting in this and other roles. For Ophelia's second appearance in the 'mad' scene she came on stage with a basket of flowers: 'Passing suddenly from the most wrenching grief to a kind of convulsive joy, like the sardonic laughter of a dying man, she offers the flowers to those around her, whom she no longer recognizes, and sings, without being aware that she is singing, words whose frivolity forms the most melancholy and theatrical contrast with her actual condition.'[58]

---

[52] *Evening Telegraph* (Birmingham), 23 November 1874.

[53] Kerry Powell, *Women and Victorian Theatre* (Cambridge: Cambridge University Press, 1997), 36.

[54] 'HAMLET' (*Saturday Review*, 2 October 1897), in *Our Theatres in the Nineties* by Bernard Shaw (3 vols., London: Constable, 1932) 3: 200–7 (205).

[55] Clement Scott, *Some Notable Hamlets* (London: 1899), 168–9.

[56] Quoted by Carol Jones Carlisle, *Shakespeare from the Greenroom. Actors' Criticisms of Four Major Tragedies* (Chapel Hill: University of North Carolina Press, 1969), 139.

[57] Ibid., 141.

[58] M. Moreau, *Souvenirs du théâtre anglais à Paris* (Paris, 1827), quoted by Peter Raby, *'Fair Ophelia': Harriet Smithson Berlioz* (Cambridge: Cambridge University Press, 1982), 66.

Mrs Patrick Campbell's most notable immediate predecessor in the part, Ellen Terry, had been 'picturesquely pathetic rather than horrifyingly real' in a mad scene purged of the 'indecent' songs. [59] (In the nunnery scene Irving's underlying love for Ophelia was especially marked.) A review in the *Academy* of Herbert Beerbohm Tree's 1892 production suggests another pitfall, that of class, that threatened the Victorian Ophelia: Mrs Tree made the character 'not original, but … receptive, at any rate', and was also 'the born gentlewoman'. In the mad scene she was 'exquisitely inconsequent, and at the proper moment, splendidly wild' but betrayed 'fortunately, in Mrs. Tree's hands, no revelation of the hysteria of the middle classes'.[60] At least in this scene, Hamlet being out of the country, she did not have her husband competing for the audience's attention. Tree described in a magazine article his own embellishment of Edmund Kean's business at the end of the 'nunnery' scene:

> After flinging Ophelia from him and rushing wildly from the room, Hamlet, in a sudden revulsion of feeling, returns. His first impulse is to console her. But he dare not show his heart. Unobserved, he steals up to her, tenderly kisses one of the tresses of her hair, silently steals from the room, finding his way without his eyes, giving, in one deep sigh, all his love to the winds.[61]

As was so often the case, the grief of the woman has been refocused to become the occasion of a display of the sensitivity of the man. (A version of the business, more restrained than Tree's, survived into Laurence Olivier's 1948 film.) This was a Hamlet who had uttered 'a cry of mingled sorrow and repugnance' on discovering Ophelia's complicity.[62]

As with Ophelia, interpreters of Cordelia were praised for gentleness and pathos. Goneril and Regan being usually taken by lower-ranking actresses, there was no major female role in the Victorians' *King Lear*. There was however, a notable example of kingly madness. The characteristically Victorian emphasis was probably the tenderness of Macready, vividly described by Dickens, himself a past master in such effects in fiction:

> The tenderness, the rage, the madness, the remorse and sorrow, all come of one another and are linked together in a chain. Only of such tenderness, could come such rage; of both combined, such madness; of such a strife of passions and affections, the pathetic cry 'Do not laugh at me; | For as I am a man, I think this lady | To be my child Cordelia;' only of such recognition and its sequel, such a broken heart.[63]

Macready's reintroduction of the Fool (played by a young actress) in 1833, and the removal of traces of Nahum Tate's 1680 version, contributed to a more complete rendering of *King Lear* than had previously been shown, though the excision of many of the less palatable elements of the script, including the on-stage blinding of Gloucester, made for a heroic and pathetic spectacle. Lear was the unchallenged center of the play, with little of the

---

[59] Hughes, *Henry Irving, Shakespearean*, 68.

[60] *Academy*, 30 January 1892 (by Frederick Wedmore).

[61] Herbert Beerbohm Tree, 'Hamlet—from an Actor's Prompt Book,' *Fortnightly Review*, o.s., 64 (December 1895), 863–78 (871).

[62] *Daily News*, 22 January 1892.

[63] *Examiner* (27 October 1849), in Michael Slater, ed., *Dickens' Journalism*, vol. 2, 'The Amusements of the People' and Other Papers…1834-51 (London: J. M. Dent, 1998), 171.

cruelty and pettiness explored in productions since the middle of the twentieth century. Forrest, at the Princess's in London in 1845, was lauded by the playwright and journalist Douglas Jerrold for his portrayal of madness 'true to nature—painfully so', and the 'utter absence of mannerism, affectation, noisy declamation, and striving for effect'.[64] The madness might be prefigured by rashness in the early scenes, but once Lear was on the heath, and especially in the scene at Dover with the blinded Gloucester, the heroic and pathetic image always prevailed and impressed. In 1952, some sixty years after this, his 'first sight' of the actor, Gordon Crosse recalled Irving in 1892. Gloucester announces that 'the king is coming'—

> And here he comes down the steps, a striking figure with masses of white hair. He is lean-
> ing on a huge scabbarded sword, which he raises with a wild cry in answer to the shouted
> greetings of his guards. His gait, his looks, his gestures, all reveal the noble, imperious
> mind already degenerating into senile irritability and ready to fall into utter ruin under the
> coming shocks of grief and rage.

Crosse admits that 'modern playgoers' would find Irving's final scene 'too long drawn out, as he sat on the ground by Cordelia's body, playing with the rope round her neck, then sinking down beside her, and raising his head again and again in the hope of finding in her some sign of life'. But these critics, he insists, 'have not seen Henry Irving'.[65]

The priorities of the Victorian theatre did not include listening to long explanations after the death of the tragic hero: like the final scenes of *Hamlet* (no Fortinbras), *Othello* (no promise to report the deaths to Venice), and *Macbeth* (a simple acclamation for Malcolm), that of *King Lear* almost invariably ended with the protagonist's death. Irving's script cut the scene very short, with Lear's 'Look there! Look there!' (5.3.287). Others allowed for a brief final comment: Macready included Kent's 'Vex not his ghost | O let him pass … He hates him | That would upon the rack of this tough world | Stretch him out longer' (289-91). Phelps included this and added the next half-line, Edgar's 'He is gone indeed', followed by the stage direction 'Ring [for curtain] as characters group round Lear—Roll of muffled drums. Soldiers and officers lower their weapons, and Curtain Slow'.[66] After 'stretch him out longer', Forrest's final direction notes the participation of Kent in the tableau: 'Kent lets Lear down gradually—supporting him when dead upon his right knee—Slow music till curtain.'[67]

Impatience with final-scene explanations was especially strong in the case of *Romeo and Juliet*. Many modern directors have shared their Victorian predecessors' inclination to abridge the concluding 139 lines, summarizing tragic circumstances vividly familiar to the audience but not known in their entirety by all those on stage except the Friar.[68]

---

[64] *Examiner*, 9 March 1845: quoted in Donald Mullin, ed., *Victorian Actors and Actresses in Review. A Dictionary of Contemporary Reviews of Representative British and American Actresses, 1837–1901* (Westport, CT, and London: Greenwood Press, 1983), 212.

[65] Gordon Crosse, *Shakespearean Playgoing, 1890–1952* (London: Mowbrays, 1953), 12–13.

[66] Folger Shakespeare Library promptbooks: Prompt Lear 10 (Shattuck 95) (Irving); Prompt Lear 5 (Shattuck 28) (Macready); Prompt Lear 20 (Shattuck 75) (Phelps).

[67] University of Pennsylvania, Forrest Collection Sh.155.23.1860 (Shattuck 65).

[68] On twentieth-century treatments of the scene, see Jill L. Levenson, *Shakespeare in Performance: 'Romeo and Juliet'* (Manchester: Manchester University Press, 1987), 46–123, and

Garrick's conclusion, with new speeches for both lovers simultaneously (if temporarily) conscious to share a final tragic dialogue, was discarded early in the new century, but Victorian productions regularly ended with a tableau and with some version of the Prince's summing up. At the Lyceum in 1882 Irving divided the scene into three pictures. The first took place outside the tomb, with the death of Paris. As Romeo opened the gates of the vault, the scene changed to the interior, with steep flights of steps down to the bier at stage level. 'One remembers Irving,' wrote Shaw, 'a dim figure dragging a horrible burden down through the gloom "into the rotten jaws of death".'[69] After the deaths of the lovers the curtains fell, to rise again a few moments later to reveal a crowd bearing torches, the steps thronged with the rival factions, and the Prince ready to join the hands of Capulet and Montague with a four-line curtain speech. As Alan Hughes points out, 'Irving was more interested in the lovers than in the restoration of order in Verona'—but this was simply a fine pictorial embodiment of a long-standing approach.[70]

Among the play's extra-textual features traditional since Garrick's time was a funeral procession for Juliet, complete with 'dirge', but the lovers' first encounter at a more or less resplendent ball, the balcony scene (2.2), and Juliet's 'potion' speech (4.3.14-57) were points in which any production was expected to score. The Nurse, although deprived of her bawdy earthiness, and Mercutio (similarly made respectable) were character roles eliciting virtuoso performances. In the former, Mrs. Stirling seemed to Henry James to outshine both Ellen Terry and Henry Irving, neither of them fitted in his opinion to the title roles, in the 1882 Lyceum production: 'Mrs. Stirling, today a very old woman, is a rich and accomplished actress; she belongs to a more sincere generation; she knows her art, and it is from her rendering of the garrulous, humorous, immoral attendant of the gentle Juliet that the spectator receives his one impression of the appropriate and the adequate.'[71]

For all its potential for spectacle and romantic pathos, *Romeo and Juliet* did not have the same status as the four 'canonical' tragedies: it lacked a strong role for a male actor—Romeo's grief after the death of Mercutio and the parting with Juliet were not sufficiently elevated in tone and spirit—and it was male actor-managers whose preferences dominated the theatrical world. Fanny Kemble, performing in London in 1847 under her married name as Mrs. Butler, 'was praised by the *Theatrical Times* for her 'exquisite tenderness, her poetic grace, her passion, and faultless elocution'. The balcony scene was 'thrilling and sublime', and 'it was here that the actress rose to absolute inspiration, inferior only perhaps to her own matchless aunt's'. (Siddons, invoked yet again.) William Creswick's Romeo 'had not the poetic glow of Miss Cushman's, but perhaps was more true to Shakspere [sic]'.[72] Juliet was the starring role, but a notable exception had occurred when the American actress Charlotte Cushman appeared as Romeo in London in 1846. Playing opposite her sister Susan's Juliet, Cushman seems to have lacked the inhibition in erotic ardour that hampered many a male in the part: 'Never was courtship more fervent, more apparently sincere, more reverential, and yet more impetuously passionate,' wrote the critic of the

Russell Jackson, *Shakespeare at Stratford: 'Romeo and Juliet* (London: Arden Shakespeare/Thomson Learning, 2003), 177–92.

[69] Shaw, *Our Theatres in the Nineties*, 202 (*Saturday Review*, 28 September 1895).

[70] Hughes, *Henry Irving, Shakespearean*, 166.

[71] James, *The Scenic Art*, 164 ('London Pictures and London Plays,' *Atlantic Monthly*, August 1882).

[72] *Theatrical Times*, 1 May 1843.

Athenaeum.[73] Maybe the less ardent Creswick was 'more true to Shakspere' because he provided less of an erotic thrill? Even Juliets might be too forward for some tastes. In 1881 the *Manchester Guardian* censured Adelaide Neilson in retrospect for having made the balcony scene 'to an extent "loathsome in its deliciousness" for want of the simplicity and exquisite naturalness it demands', whereas Elena Modjeska, the actress whose performance was being reveiwed, managed to combine 'tender seriousness' with 'the more obvious seductive features of the part'. Her line in the shared sonnet of the lovers' first encounter, 'Ay, pilgrim, lips that they must use in prayer' (1.5.101), was 'generally said archly and playfully', but 'Mme. Modjeska said it with an increased shade of gravity in her tone, and her eyes uplifted'.[74] On the other hand, it should be noted that Neilson's was regarded as one of the greatest embodiments of the role by many critics, not least the ever-effusive William Winter, who treasured the memory of 'its soft romance of tone, its splendor of passion, its sustained energy, its beauty of speech, and its poetic fragrance'.[75] It is hardly surprising that with such odds against him, a Victorian Romeo would struggle to win hearts and minds.

The time-travellers invoked at the beginning of this chapter would encounter not only unfamiliar approaches to the interpretation of the tragedies, but also a distinct emphasis on the characters rather than the society of the play, and a lack of attention to social context in line with twenty-first-century notions of class, status, and relations between the sexes. They would read reports by reviewers confident in appeals to 'what Shakespeare intended', and ready to assess performances with reference to notions of the 'real' and the 'ideal' in tragic stature. The meticulous reconstructions through scenery and costumes of the time and place of the play might seem a distraction in comparison with the production styles in favour since the early years of the twentieth century. The visitors would probably be frustrated by the long intervals required by the changing of elaborate scenery, and be challenged by acting techniques more demonstrative and declamatory than their own. But in compensation, these privileged visitors from the twentieth century would see picturesque stage pictures of Venice, Elsinore, Macbeth's Scotland, Lear's ancient Britain, and Renaissance Verona, inspired by landscape painting and illustration, lending support to Romantic interpretations of events and characters. Scenes, lines, and individual words would be missing, and the language of the plays would be seem uniformly decorous. They would also find themselves among audiences ready to applaud individual speeches and even moments of stage business, sometimes with 'three distinct rounds of applause', and also to make their displeasure felt by hissing loudly. At first sight the 'picture frame stage' might seem a barrier between auditorium and stage, but the active involvement of the audience and its expertise, comparable to those of crowds at sporting events, would do much to qualify that effect. And until the last decade of the century, the play would normally be part of a programme that began with a short play as a 'curtain-raiser', often included music and songs in the intervals between pieces, and might even (as appropriate to the season) end with a full-length Christmas pantomime. On the nineteenth-century stage

---

[73] Quoted in Charles H. Shattuck, *Shakespeare on the American Stage. From the Hallams to Edwin Booth* (Washington, DC: The Folger Shakespeare Library, 1976), 93.

[74] *The Manchester Stage 1880–1900. Criticisms Reprinted from 'The Manchester Guardian'* (London: Constable, 1900), 32–3.

[75] William Winter, *Shadows of the Stage* (New York and London: MacMillan, 1896), 61.

the tragedies took their place as part of a rich, popular, varied, and vigorously moving evening's entertainment.

SELECT BIBLIOGRAPHY

Allen, Shirley S., *Samuel Phelps and Sadler's Wells Theatre* (Middletown, CT: Wesleyan University Press, 1971).

Bartholomeusz, Dennis, *Macbeth and the Players* (Cambridge: Cambridge University Press, 1969).

Bate, Jonathan and Russell Jackson, eds., *The Oxford Illustrated History of Shakespeare on Stage* (Oxford: Oxford University Press, 2001).

Carlisle, Carol Jones, *Shakespeare from the Greenroom. Actors' Criticisms of Four Major Tragedies* (Chapel Hill: University of North Carolina Press, 1969).

Carlisle, Carol Jones, *Helen Faucit. Fire and Ice on the Victorian Stage* (London: Society for Theatre Research, 2000) .

Donohue, Joseph W., *Dramatic Character in the English Romantic Age* (Princeton: Princeton University Press, 1970).

Donohue, Joseph W., *Theatre in the Age of Kean* (Oxford: Blackwell, 1975).

Downer, Alan S., *The Eminent Tragedian. William Charles Macready* (Cambridge, MA: Harvard University Press, 1966).

Foulkes, Richard, ed., *Shakespeare and the Victorian Stage* (Cambridge: Cambridge University Press, 1986).

Foulkes, Richard, *Performing Shakespeare in the Age of Empire* (Cambridge: Cambridge University Press, 2002).

Hankey, Julie, ed., *Plays in Performance: 'Othello'* (Bristol: Bristol Classical Press, 1987).

Holroyd, Michael, *A Strange Eventful History. The Dramatic Lives of Ellen Terry, Henry Irving and their Remarkable Families* (London: Chatto and Windus, 2008).

Hughes, Alan, *Henry Irving, Shakespearean* (Cambridge: Cambridge University Press, 1978).

Marshall, Gail, ed., *Shakespeare in the Nineteenth Century* (Cambridge: Cambridge University Press, 2012).

Marshall, Gail, *Shakespeare and Victorian Women* (Cambridge: Cambridge University Press, 2009).

Mills, John A., *Hamlet on Stage. The Great Tradition* (Westport, CT and London: Greenwood Press, 1985),

Mullin, Donald, ed., *Victorian Actors and Actresses in Review. A Dictionary of Contemporary Reviews of Representative British and American Actresses, 1837–1901* (Westport, CT, and London: Greenwood Press, 1983).

Odell, G. C. D., *Shakespeare from Betterton to Irving*, 2 vols. (London: Constable, 1921; repr. New York: Dover Publications, Inc., 1966).

Rosenberg, Marvin, *The Masks of 'Othello.' The Search for the Identity of Othello, Iago, and Desdemona by Three Centuries of Actors and Critics* (Berkeley and Los Angeles: University of California Press, 1961).

Rosenberg, Marvin, *The Masks of Hamlet* (Newark, London and Toronto: University of Delaware/Associated University Presses, 1992).

Shattuck, Charles H., *Shakespeare on the American Stage. From the Hallams to Edwin Booth* (Washington, DC: The Folger Shakespeare Library, 1976).

Shattuck, Charles H., *Shakespeare on the American Stage. From Booth and Barrett to Sothern and Marlowe* (Washington, DC: Folger Books, 1987).

Sillars, Stuart, *Shakespeare and the Victorians* (Oxford: Oxford University Press, 2013).

Sprague, Albert Colby, *Shakespeare and the Actors. The Stage Business in his Plays, 1660–1905,* Fourth Printing (Cambridge, MA: Harvard University Press, 1948).

Sprague, Albert Colby, *Shakespearian Players and Performances* (Cambridge, MA: Harvard University Press, 1953).

Vaughan, Virginia Mason, *Othello: A Contextual History* (Cambridge: Cambridge University Press, 1994).

CHAPTER 33

TRAGEDY IN TWENTIETH AND TWENTY-FIRST CENTURY THEATRE PRODUCTION

Hamlet, Lear, *and the Politics of Intimacy*

BRIDGET ESCOLME

In 1962, fifteen years after Arthur Miller published his argument for the democratization of tragedy, 'Tragedy and the Common Man',[1] Paul Scofield played King Lear: not, in Kenneth Tynan's words, as 'the booming, righteously indignant Titan of old, but an edgy, capricious old man, intensely difficult to live with'. Tynan also described a 'Flat white setting, combining Brecht and Oriental theatre against which ponderous abstract objects dangle'.[2] This combination of realist characterization—a tragic hero flawed in ordinary, psychological rather than grandiose ways—and settings that are sparse, abstract and meta-theatrical, has become a standard *mise-en-scène* in the British theatre over the late twentieth and twenty-first centuries. In this chapter, I discuss the relationship between actor and scenography as it has emerged over this period, in productions of *Hamlet* and *King Lear*. I will argue that in some cases, the notion of tragic hero as common man reduces the plays in production to a set of psychological problems. However, in other theatrical moments, contrasts and tensions between acting style and scenography, or between acting style and theatre architecture, have created what I am going to call a theatrical politics of intimacy, making it possible for detailed, realist acting on a range of non-naturalistic stages to ask questions about the social and political meanings of human relations that emerge from these plays, whilst still fulfilling the actor's desire to explore character psychologically.

HAMLET'S POLITICS OF INTIMACY

The mid-1980s saw the publication of Catherine Belsey's *The Subject of Tragedy*, which traces the theatrical shift from the generic miracle play hero—the Everyman with his externally

---

[1] Arthur Miller, 'Tragedy and the Common Man', *New York Times*, 27 February 1947.
[2] Kenneth Tynan, 'The Triumph of Stratford's *Lear*', *Observer*, 11 November 1962.

constructed dilemma of choice between good and evil—and the internalization of that struggle in the tragic hero.[3] In the theatre, the twentieth century saw another radical shift in the construction of tragic subjectivity. Kenneth Tynan's excitement at the revelatory nature of Brook | Scofield's cantankerous old Lear reveals just how common a theatrical trope the tragedy of the common man has since become. Once one has witnessed Othello as the victim of racism in a Yorkshire pub, the London police force or the British army,[4] Lear as a child-abusing father or dementia sufferer,[5] Scofield's capricious old Lear no longer seems startling. During this century, Hamlet has become a young man who makes Fortinbras's assertion that 'he was likely, had he been put on, | To have proved most royal' (5.2.389-90), seem empty and inappropriate. The twenty-first century Hamlets I am going to discuss seem determinedly ordinary. Indeed, their ordinariness is part of what makes them a threat to Claudius' state, as they refuse his exhortation to 'be as ourself in Denmark' (1.2.122). With this line, Claudius is, of course, reassuring Hamlet that he still has royal status and can make himself at home, albeit in his own home. But even before the truth of his father's death is revealed to him, Hamlet is telling us that he has 'that within which passeth show' (85) and is unable to produce the social display of recovery from bereavement the court expects of him.

In the UK, audiences for *Hamlet* in the early twenty-first century became the intimates of a cynical student. His suits of solemn black became a student's hoodie at the RSC in 2001;[6] he flouted court convention at the 'Murder of Gonzago' by going barefoot with his tuxedo for the same company in 2008;[7] he slouched about the National Theatre's stage in jogging pants in 2010.[8] In these productions, Hamlet was a private individual and a transgressively profound and subversive thinker in a range of highly theatrically conscious versions of Elsinore, where Claudius attempted to appropriate the audience as his court. In these productions, tragic subjectivity was created in the relationship between actor and audience, as Hamlet confronted the audience directly with his questions of agency and fate, action and responsibility. A range of *Hamlet* productions, notably the first of the play at the Globe reconstruction in 2000,[9] collapsed the space between actor and audience, play-world and theatre-world. Eventually the Royal Shakespeare Company did the same with its main stage, reconfiguring the end-on, cinematic 1930s Royal Shakespeare Theatre into a thrust like that of its smaller Swan and temporary Courtyard theatres.

---

[3] Catherine Belsey, *The Subject of Tragedy: The Subject of Tragedy: Identity and Difference in Renaissance Drama* (London: Routledge, 1985), 55–92.

[4] I refer to Frantic Assembly and Theatre Royal Plymouth's *Othello*, dir. Scott Graham, Plymouth 2008; Andrew Davis's film adaptation of *Othello*, dir. Geoffrey Sax, 2001; and the National Theatre's *Othello*, dir. Nicholas Hytner, London 2013, respectively.

[5] For example the Almeida's *King Lear,* dir. Michael Attenborough, London 2012, in which a number of reviewers remarked on the abusive sexual relationship between Lear and his daughters; the Leicester Haymarket *King Lear* dir. Helena Kaut-Howson, Leicester 1997, which which opened in a geriatric ward; and the National Theatre's 2014 *King Lear*, dir. Sam Mendes.

[6] *Hamlet*, dir. Steven Pimlott, RSC, Royal Shakespeare Theatre Stratford-upon-Avon, 2001. This was not the first student Hamlet of course: David Warner's appearance in a black gown and long scarf immediately established him as an undergraduate in opposition to Elsinore's surveillance state in the RSC's Vietnam-era production of *Hamlet*, directed by Peter Hall in 1965.

[7] *Hamlet*, dir. Greg Doran, RSC Courtyard Theatre, Stratford-upon-Avon, 2008.

[8] *Hamlet* dir. Nicholas Hytner, National Theatre, London, 2010.

[9] *Hamlet*, dir. Giles Block, Shakespeare's Globe, London, 2000.

A *Hamlet* that seemed to emerge directly from a growing artistic discontent with the RST's proscenium arch was directed by the late Steven Pimlott and designed by Alison Chitty in 2001. Pimlott had produced *Richard II* the previous year, and actors and audience had shared bright, fluorescent light in the small, white-painted studio setting designed by Sue Wilmington; spectators were addressed directly throughout.[10] For *Hamlet*, the company built out beyond the RST's cinematic stage, creating a vast space in which a huge, bureaucratic conference seemed to be taking place at Elsinore, disrupted by Samuel West's refusal to join in; his Hamlet looked rather like a G8 protestor in his black hooded top. The stage extended still further into the auditorium via a hanamichi-like walkway[11] on which West delivered 'to be or not to be'; the lights were raised in the auditorium so he could share his musings on the relief and terror of suicide directly with the audience. Pimlott and Chitty appeared to be attempting to reproduce the intimacy of *Richard II*'s *mise-en-scène* in the RST. The production made Hamlet the rebellious individual in a vast, corrupt state bureaucracy and this has been Hamlet's purpose in a range of productions since: to represent the human capacity for love in the face of lust- and privilege-driven power; to represent the rebellious individual who disrupts the homogeny of the state's power structures; to be the one figure that speaks philosophical and political truths to the audience. Hamlet refuses to be like anyone else in Denmark and turns to the audience for an intimacy eschewed by power politics. Interestingly, the set for this production featured CCTV cameras, a commentary on the politics of surveillance that was to become a prominent feature of later *Hamlet*s.

Early twenty-first century *Hamlet*s have foregrounded the authenticity of Hamlet's emotional life amidst the mendacious display of Claudius' Denmark. The year before Pimlott's RSC production, Mark Rylance performed the role for the second time, at the Globe reconstruction, of which he was artistic director.[12] His first Hamlet was for the RSC in 1989.[13] In both productions, he turned a performance of intense psychological distress at his mother's marriage directly to the audience, beginning his first soliloquy, 'O that this too, too solid flesh would melt' (1.2.129) with his back to the greater part of the auditorium, then turning to face the all too solid audience, with a seeming horror at having to make public his mother's betrayal of his dead father. Shakespeare's Globe, of course, is a theatre in which shared daylight creates the possibility of direct address for every character. Even more emphatically than when he played to the darkened RST | Barbican Theatre auditorium, the audience were Hamlet's intimates as Rylance crouched downstage in black whilst the court occupied centre stage in rich red velvets, or as he undermined Polonius' confident asides on the nature of Hamlet's madness with up-staging comedy. Peter Brook's *Hamlet* in the same year, played by Adrian Lester, also liked to share an intimate joke with the audience in an otherwise ceremonially slow-paced and serious production (the filmed

---

[10] For a detailed account of this production and its effect of direct address see Bridget Escolme, *Talking to the Audience: Shakespeare, Performance Self* (London: Routledge 2005), 95–128.

[11] The hanamichi of kabuki theatre is a walkway used for exits and entrances through the audience.

[12] *Hamlet*, dir. Giles Block, Shakespeare's Globe, London, 2000.

[13] *Hamlet*, dir. Ron Daniels, Royal Shakespeare Company, Stratford-upon-Avon, 1989.

version of the production loses these comic intimacies).[14] What all of these productions have in common is their sense that in addressing the audience and becoming our intimates, Hamlet subverts the corrupted politics of Claudius' court.

INSIDE HAMLET

Direct address to audience has been associated, since Brecht's Epic theatre, with a politically motivated disinclination to absorb the audience in an illusory evocation of an eternal human condition. However, physical involvement of audiences in *Hamlet* has not, in the productions above, necessarily involved a Brechtian eschewal of character psychology. I have not been privy to all of the rehearsal processes of these *Hamlets* but am sure that they have included the consideration of Hamlet as a modern psychological subject, a 'real person'. What the meta-theatrical properties of these productions have allowed, though, has been a politics of intimacy with the audience, whereby 'that within' Hamlet is offered directly to the auditorium and subverts the performance of power. However, early twenty-first-century productions of *Hamlet* have occasionally attempted to involve the audience directly in the performance, whilst privileging psychological character study more markedly. Michael Grandage's production at the Young Vic in 2011 starred Michael Sheen, an actor celebrated for, amongst other roles, his intense and detailed psychological studies of journalist David Frost and of Tony Blair.[15] This Elsinore was a scruffy, late twentieth-century psychiatric hospital, through whose corridors the audience could choose to enter: the back-stage areas were converted to wards and decorated with notice boards announcing treatment regimes and the hospital's 'employee of the month'. Here, Hamlet was an asylum inmate, who, in a pre-performance sequence, stole a greatcoat from the top of old Hamlet's coffin to dress as the Ghost later in the play. It is doubtful whether his uncle, here the doctor in charge of the institution, committed the murder of Hamlet's father at all, as Claudius' scene of confessional prayer was deliberately muffled in an upstage office. Fortinbras entered at the end of the play, his face encased with one of the black fencing masks used in the fight between Hamlet and Laertes, only to reveal himself to be Sheen as Hamlet, ready to take over the asylum. The power of this production lay in the psychologically nuanced performances, particularly by Sheen himself, whose anxious paranoia conveyed itself in the detail of vocal variation and facial expression often reserved for film. If the plot of *Hamlet* is the delusion of a hospitalized schizophrenic, however, the stakes, as an actor might put it, are no longer very high and there is little room left for speculation about the relationship between the personal and the political, the individual and the state. The production's opening drew on London's contemporary fascination with 'immersive' theatre and attempted to immerse us in the mind of a 'mad' Hamlet who appeared to have invented the whole murder plot.

[14] *Hamlet*, dir. Peter Brook, Theatre des Bouffes du Nord, Paris 2000; performed at Young Vic, London, 2000; filmed by BBC Films, 2002.

[15] David Frost in *Frost/Nixon*, dir. Ron Howard 2008 (Michael Sheen played Frost in Peter Morgan's play version, 2006) and Tony Blair three times, in *The Deal* and *The Queen*, dir. Stephen Frears, and *The Special Relationship* dir. Richard Loncraine, 2010.

DreamThinkSpeak's 'deconstruction' of *Hamlet, The Rest is Silence*, in 2012,[16] shut its audience very deliberately out of the mind of Hamlet, whilst enclosing the them physically within the play's action. Behind a square of four perspex walls, with the audience in darkness at its centre, the machinations of the modern bureaucratic state of Elsinore were played out as if on screens. Edward Hogg's Hamlet spoke a severely cut version of his text, the 'To be or not to be' soliloquy featuring as an entry in his diary, pried into by his friends and family, its lines repeatedly jumbled as a sneering joke by Rosencrantz and Guildenstern. Hamlet was a still, often silent figure, whom it appeared no-one understood—and because no-one in this production could address an audience member directly from behind the perspex walls, those of his lines that remained had none of the revelatory intimacy of the meta-theatrical *Hamlets* described above. This Hamlet appeared almost autistic in his social isolation and whilst on one level Hogg's performance could not have been more different from Sheen's—Sheen all perpetual, detailed movement, Hogg eerily still—one might read both Hamlets as part of an older tradition of acting this role, versions in which Lawrence Olivier's 1949 film evocation of the inside of Hamlet's brain[17] was here, perhaps, taken to its logical conclusion.

HAMLET IN THE SURVEILLANCE STATE

The last two *Hamlet* productions considered here depicted a distinctive political landscape, with Hamlet in relief, a figure struggling for authenticity against a state determined to pry into every aspect of political and personal life. The Royal Shakespeare Company's 2008 production, directed by Greg Doran with David Tennant as Hamlet, recalled for a British audience that its own rulers are often on display in the costumes of past ceremonial. This Danish court was adorned with lush fabric and medals, sashes, and ceremonial swords, whilst David Tennant's Hamlet looked starkly modern in a plain black mourning suit and funeral tie, then blatantly subversive in bare feet and a red t-shirt with a skeleton torso design. He even remained bare-footed in his tuxedo for the play within the play. Refusing to let Rosencrantz and Guildenstern pluck out the heart of his mystery (3.3.357), he mockingly wore the Player King's crown from the 'Murder of Gonzago' to evidence his later assertion that 'the King is a thing … Of nothing' (4.1.27-9), or at least merely a theatrical construction of power. Hamlet was a recognizably modern young man amidst a state playing at archaic authoritarianism. In contrast to the close embrace of the Pimlott/West production, Hamlet's relationship with his father's Ghost seemed emotionally distant. Hamlet remained kneeling in stunned horror during most of his encounter with his father, then the Ghost heaved him violently up to exhort him to revenge. It was not only

---

[16] *Hamlet (The Rest is Silence)* dir. Tristan Sharps, Brighton Festival, London International Festival of Theatre, RSC, 2012. Described by the company as a 'deconstruction' of the play, http://dreamthinkspeak.com/productions (accessed 12 June 2014).

[17] *Hamlet* (film) dir. Lawrence Olivier, 1949. In this film, Hamlet's 'to be or not to be' soliloquy is famously spoken as a voiceover as Hamlet looks down over crashing waves and the image of a human brain pulses fleetingly into view.

Claudius' regime, perhaps, that had privileged stiff ceremonial and rigid inter-generational power structures.

The film version of this production[18] emphasizes the superficiality of the modern state's historical trappings by filming some of the action as if through court CCTV cameras. The presence of electronic surveillance makes the ceremonial richness of the court seem doubly hypocritical: power seems to be the open display of historical costume and ceremonial sword but is in fact predicated on secrecy. Hamlet breaks one of these cameras before announcing 'Now I am alone' and commencing the 'solid flesh' soliloquy. The turning point in his confrontation with Ophelia—the line 'Where's your father?' (3.1.130) where many productions show him suspecting Polonius' spying presence—features the sinister sound of a surveillance device turning towards him, after which Hamlet deliberately plays to the camera. On stage, Tennant's was a frenetically energetic Hamlet who leapt about barefoot in a court where everyone else moved at the careful pace of self-conscious ceremony. He represented a self-authoring energy which a state whose power is constructed in ceremony must attempt to overwhelm.

Rory Kinnear, too, at the National Theatre in 2010,[19] was a subversively authentic Hamlet in an Elsinore that demanded conformity to a totalitarian regime. From the first lines of the play, when Matthew Barker's Francisco announced that he is 'sick at heart' (1.1.9) and his fellow watchman glanced nervously at him, as if even this passing fragment of emotional honesty could be construed as dangerously individualistic, Elsinore was marked as a totalitarian surveillance state. The set comprised grey walls, which slid into position for each scene, and which revealed the ubiquitous presence of Claudius' Switzers, the not-so-secret state police who were ready to spring into paranoid action at any hint of subversion. They also pried into every intimate relationship: in 1.4, Polonius presented Ophelia with surveillance photographs of her and Hamlet together. The secret police also appeared to have an interest in arts censorship: in 2.2, when Hamlet asked for his own lines to be inserted into the Players' performance for the Court, the First Player looked nervously round at the presence of the Switzers, as if the 'Murder of Gonzago' were potentially subversive enough without additions.

Rory Kinnear's portrayal was, as Paul Taylor in the *Independent* puts it, of Hamlet 'as the ordinary man. There is little noble about him, little evident that is "likely to have proved most royal" despite what we are told.' [20] His soliloquy after the appearance of the ghost had him pounding the floor in grief and frustration: it read as a natural reaction to an unnatural dilemma. He wore a shirt and track-suit bottoms in which to retreat to a book-strewn student bedroom, playing a cynically put-on madness which the court were clearly, in Hamlet's opinion, absurdly gullible to fall for. He wore the kind of anorak to be found in every outdoor wear shop in the Western world for his return from England in 5.1. By this point, having discovered Rozencrantz and Guildenstern's betrayal, he had become more bitter and cynical still. As Michael Billington remarks, 'This Hamlet, the reasonable man in a violent, irrational world, seems contaminated and coarsened by Claudius's Elsinore: he shrugs off the deaths of Polonius and his old student friends with a casualness that was not initially part of his

[18] BBC2, 2010.   [19] *Hamlet*, dir. Nicholas Hytner, National Theatre, London, 2010.
[20] Paul Taylor, Review of *Hamlet*, dir. Nicholas Hytner, *Independent*, 8 October 2010.

character.'[21] Kinnear's Hamlet changed from being a student who had been forced to ask profound philosophical questions about personal, social, and political life by the violent death of his father, to being a cynical killer himself. The power of the portrayal was that one could imagine this happening to anyone of a sensitive intellectual bent. Hytner and Kinnear's interview with Peter Holland in the production's programme emphasizes the search for authenticity as a theme for their *Hamlet*, a theme that chimes with Arthur Miller's definition of modern tragedy as the struggle for self-realization. In a totalitarian state like this Elsinore, the struggle is ultimately futile as the state will finally end your struggle by killing you. Ophelia, it is strongly hinted, was finally murdered by the Switzers rather than accidentally drowned; even the usually silly Osrick was part of the state machine in this production, aiding Claudius in the poisoning of the foils in the final scene.

Both the meta-theatrical *Hamlet*s of the turn of the millennium and these two productions which, in their different scenographical ways, pitch Hamlet the individual against the corrupted power of the state, make tragedy a struggle for self-authorship against the pressures of conformity. Where productions have emphasized the meta-theatricality of *Hamlet* and Hamlet's relationship with the audience, we are offered a Prince who takes on a role of commentator on the rotten state of Denmark, a role which places him outside the play world and firmly in ours. In these last two 'surveillance states' *Hamlet*s, the RSC film and the National's production, the emphasis has been more on a scenographically produced and theatrically self-contained Danish prison for Hamlet. These were both strong, coherent, and well-received productions, although they were perhaps in danger of privileging the notion of individual authenticity over the political, of falling into an ultimately conservative version of politics in which politics itself is the problem, because it deals only in corrupt surfaces and public faces, whilst what is real is the psychological individual, Hamlet's 'that within which passeth show'. I now discuss *King Lear* in recent production and the ways in which a politics of intimacy, as opposed to a privileging of the psychological, has emerged in recent performances of that play.

KING LEAR: FILLED AND EMPTY SPACES

In Sam Mendes's production of *King Lear* at the National Theatre, London, the twentieth/twenty-first century theatrical trope of realist acting on bleak, spacious sets reached its apotheosis. Here the epic and the psychological were sometimes in productive tension, sometimes in odd contradiction as Simon Russell Beale enacted the symptoms of Lewy Body Dementia to which his character research had led him. Whilst the open, pale grey set suggested a focus on how the text produces meaning in space, Russell Beale's psychological approach rather suggested the mark of the actor-auteur who finds his own, often highly psychological, research path through the text. A debate amongst theatre practitioners around artistic authority in Shakespeare production emerges in a range of public proclamations during the late twentieth and early twenty- first centuries and is evidenced

---

[21] Michael Billington, Review of *Hamlet*, dir. Nicholas Hytner, *Guardian*, 7 October 2011.

in production. For example, in an interview about designing *Lear* for the 1991 National Theatre production directed by Nicholas Hytner, David Fielding references the Royal Shakespeare Company's previous production of the play, directed by David Hare in 1986:

> It was played against some imaginatively tacked-up white sheets, rather as though the decorators had just popped out and never returned. Such an 'empty space' design ethic is as alien to Hytner as it is to Fielding. Hytner is scornful of the 'look, no scenery' approach. 'It's a ghastly denial of the age in which we live, the visual intellectual world we're part of. You can't deny we are doing old plays under modern conditions by pretending to be primitives.'[22]

In 1986, too, this 'empty space' aesthetic produced a mixed critical response:

> The enormous stage is generally empty and three gigantic sails or blinds fill the void above, titled or gathered or pulled up to suggest the sky or simply to shrink the playing area. No matter how they are disposed, the actors are still required to cover great distances before reaching the front of the stage[23]

complains Mike Mills. Michael Billington was also critical, conflating scenographic simplicity with the lack of 'the tang and spice of a strong directorial vision'.[24] Others were more positive: Christopher Edward's review suggested that

> on the gigantic Olivier stage, of all places, Hare's decision to mount a spare, stripped-back production is also a sign of boldness. There must be a strong temptation to fill up those vast empty spaces with elaborate scenery but, instead, the overriding visual impression here is of an almost oriental simplicity and stillness.[25]

The 'oriental' impression was also created by the padded robes of a costume design panned for its eclecticism by a number of reviewers, who appeared weary of this version of supposed timelessness. Edward applauds Hare for having kept his 'rude thumb prints off the play and let it speak for itself'.[26] However Hare, in an interview with Mark Lawson, disagrees with director Peter Hall for suggesting 'that is is wrong for the director to impose a particular interpretation on the play'. Hare baldly states: 'I don't think it is wrong.' He cites as a key influence Peter Brook's 1962 production of *Lear*.[27] Brook, of course, both coined the notion of the 'empty space' as a description of theatrical practice and argues that if you 'let a play speak for itself, it may not make a sound'.[28] Hare's 'empty' scenography and 'oriental' aesthetic invite immediate comparison with Peter Brook's *Lear*, a production

---

[22] David Fielding, interviewed by Lyn Gardner, *Guardian,* 1991.

[23] Mike Mills, review of *King Lear* dir. David Hare, *What's On,* 23 December 1986.

[24] Michael Billington, review of *King Lear* dir. David Hare, *Guardian,* 13 December 1986.

[25] Christopher Edward, review of *King Lear* dir. David Hare, *The Spectator,* 18 December 1986.

[26] Edward, review of *King Lear.*

[27] 'That production made me want to work in the theatre. Curiously when I mentioned that to Christopher Hampton and Howard Brenton, they said it was the same for them. That it was spoken and staged with what appeared to be realism just wasn't how one had assumed Shakespeare to be.' David Hare, Interview with Mark Lawson, *Independent,* 8 December 1986.

[28] 'If you just let a play speak, it may not make a sound. If what you want is for the play to be heard, then you must conjure its sound from it. This demands many deliberate actions and the result may have great simplicity. However, setting out to "be simple" can be quite negative, an easy evasion

which, as we have seen, set standards for Shakespeare production in terms of psychological characterization and epic scenography.

I am going to consider two recent productions of *King Lear* in detail, one the Mendes/Russell Beale production with its open, 'epic' design, the other by Rupert Goold, a director known for the kind of director's theatre which critics of Hare seemed to be demanding, but whose *Lear* nevertheless attained the kind of theatrical self-consciousness that I argue is part of the politics of intimacy I am exploring.

Rupert Goold's *King Lear* was first performed at the Liverpool Everyman, then transferred to London's Young Vic;[29] it was an intriguing mix of overt theatricality and naturalistic scenographic concept. Goold is an active proponent of director's theatre. He has set *The Tempest* in a bleak Arctic wilderness, *Macbeth* in Soviet Russia and *The Merchant of Venice* in contemporary Las Vegas[30] and argues that as Shakespeare intervened in his source texts, so the director may feel free to do with Shakespeare as he pleases. Recalling the debate over 'empty' scenographies, blogger Alan Barker interestingly called his account of Goold's address to the Cheltenham Literary Festival 'The Filled Space'.[31] As we will see, this production proliferated subtext and backstory for the women in *King Lear*. The male figures are more playfully theatrical and though the *mise-en-scène*, as in many of Goold's productions, produces a highly specific period setting for the play, the proximity of performer to audience and the production's emphasis on of the role of performance in *King Lear* itself pushes the production beyond the merely psychological or a limited commentary on a particular period or politics.

The Liverpool Everyman version of this production was roundly condemned by reviewers as gimmicky.[32] Set in a Britain of late 1970s industrial decline, it even opened with lines from Margaret Thatcher's 'Francis of Assisi' speech.[33] This and other ideas that Pete Postlethwaite (Lear) seemed to agree were bewilderingly extraneous to the narrative, were cut from the Young Vic version,[34] though the late 1970s costumes and the set of neglected steps complete with weeds growing from cracks remained, to serve as symbols of a nation in cultural and economic crisis. The Young Vic version was a great deal better received

of the exacting steps to the simple answer.' Peter Brook, *The Empty Space* (New York: Simon and Schuster, 1968), 42–3.

[29] *King Lear*, dir. Rupert Goold, Liverpool Everyman, 2009; Young Vic, London, 2009.

[30] *The Tempest*, RSC, 2006; *Macbeth*, Chichester Festival Minerva Theatre, 2007; *The Merchant of Venice*, RSC, 2011.

[31] Alan Barker, 'The Filled Space: Rupert Goold defends director's theatre' http://justwriteonline.typepad.com/the_restless_rhetorician/2009/10/the-filled-space-rupert-goold-defends-directors-theatre.html 15 October 2009 (accessed 10 October 2013).

[32] See e.g. Michael Billington's review in the *Guardian*, 7 November 2008, Charles Spencer's in the *Daily Telegraph*, 7 November 2008, Christopher Hart's in *The Times*, 8 November 2008.

[33] When Margaret Thatcher was filmed on the steps of 10 Downing Street on taking power in 1979, she borrowed from the speech attributed to Francis of Assisi, paraphrasing it thus: 'Where there is discord, may we bring harmony. Where there is error, may we bring truth. Where there is doubt, may we bring faith. And where there is despair, may we bring hope', to emphasise her self-appointed role as bringer of harmony and hope to a Britain in decline. The production, with its set of an abandoned, broken industrial landcape, clearly wished to make an ironic comment on the further decline of Britain's manufacturing industries that followed.

[34] 'Postlethwaite: We Misjudged *Lear*', http://news.bbc.co.uk/1/hi/entertainment/7739158.stm (accessed 10 October 2013).

and was particularly successful in foregrounding, at least amongst the male characters, the startling, generically indecorous, and often transgressive range of role-playing contained in this play. Postlethwaite began the division of his kingdom by insisting that each of his daughters perform through a microphone and when Cordelia refused to take it, it seemed that an obvious point was being made about public performance versus personal authenticity. But the production finally offered a more slippery sense of the theatrical than this binary of depth and surface suggests. As Lear's control of the performance of power slipped from him, his first reaction was rage and disbelief. As if to emphasize the fluid relationship between performer and audience in this production, on one night I attended, a mobile phone went off during 1.1 and Postlethwaite turned to the audience to shout 'What's that? Silence!': not only had his own technology of power been subverted by Cordelia's refusal to use it, but some mere subject/audience member had dared to interrupt his performance with a device anachronistic to the late-1970s setting. Lear's descent into madness was characterized not so much by a stripping a way of performance to reveal unaccommodated man but by a renewed sense of the alternative possibilities of the theatrical: the king relinquished his performance of power to take on new, more playful and interrogatory roles. His first encounter with Edgar's Poor Tom involved a careful imitation of the madman's gestural vocabulary. His entrance in 4.6 saw him not 'fantastically dressed with flowers' (4.6.79SD) but in a floral print dress, as if he were relinquishing not only the performance of King but of masculinity too.

As I have suggested, the National Theatre's 2014 *Lear* directed by Sam Mendes, with Simon Russell Beale as Lear was the epitome of the realist acting/epic setting I have marked as a common theatrical trope in the late twentieth/early twenty-first century theatre. 'It combines a cosmic scale with an intimate sense of detail', writes Michael Billington; 'although the [first] scene has an epic quality, it is filled with human detail … This mixture of the epic and the intimate runs right through the production'.[35] For Paul Taylor, too, 'It's a powerfully searching account of the tragedy that fuses the familial and the cosmic, the epic and the intimate'.[36] Though this was another 'modern dress' Lear, director and designer sought to give the play only 'a loosely twentieth century setting, without making it specifically about any one particular historical period or place'.[37] Whilst Hytner's Elsinore emphasised the barely kept secrecy of the surveillance state, the court of *King Lear* in Mendes' production displayed its oppressive power structures more blatantly. Soldiers were intrinsic to the spectacle of totalitarian government, lining the curved wall of the arena in which Lear announced his arrangements for retirement. Later, in 2.1, Kent's stocks were tied to a monolithic statue of the king.

The seat of power in 1.1 seemed ludicrously large for the intimacies Lear asked his daughters to express, again through a microphone. Simon Russell Beale as Lear was dwarfed by it, his hunched stance making him look tiny in this vast arena. The soldier-knights were clearly there to shore up his masculinity and power but only succeeded in eroding both, as they lounged around Goneril's banqueting table looking young and arrogant, whilst an initially bullying Lear looked increasingly old, gnome-like, and vulnerable. Significantly,

[35] Michael Billington, review of King Lear dir. Sam Mendes, *Guardian*, 23 January 2014.

[36] Paul Taylor, review of King Lear dir. Sam Mendes, *Independent*, 24 January 2014.

[37] Published rehearsal notes for King Lear dir. Sam Mendes http://d1wf8hd6ovssje.cloudfront.net/documents/KingLear_NT_Background_Pack_Reh_Diaries_Final.pdf (accessed 1st May 2014).

they were seen abandoning Lear and tramping off to seek their fortunes even before Regan and Goneril had made them homeless. This military troupe seemed to accept the Fool's presence as an entertainer who is permitted not only to bate Lear with his jokes about daughters but to act as an antidote to their machismo; Adrian Scarborough's Fool was an endearing, effete, and somewhat child-like figure who served as a barrier between the self-disenfranchised Lear and the rowdy Knights.

Before the storm unites Lear with the unaccommodated man that is Poor Tom, the only properly empathetic parental relationship in *King Lear* is between Lear and this 'pretty knave', the Fool. Lear's mode of address to this figure is one of father, or kindly 'nuncle', to small child. Of course, the King threatens him with the whip but this was a common form of parental punishment in early modern culture. 'Pretty knave' is a frequent term of endearment for a child and as Goneril remarks, Lear quickly ceases to be endeared to his actual child, Cordelia, the moment she displeases him (1.1.287–91), whereas the 'all-licens'd' Fool receives unconditional love from his master. Although Lear's encounter with Poor Tom in Russell Beale's interpretation did not have quite the deliberately theatrical quality of Pete Postlethwaite's imitations of Forbes Masson's Edgar, the small, kindly gestures of protection and curiosity that Russell Beale offered Adrian Scarborough's Fool were foregrounded beautifully in the vast grey space of this set. As Lear discovered that he had 'ta'en too little care' of the poor and vulnerable, his own vulnerability shone a precise light on the politics of this play. Russell Beale's Lear learned his celebrated lesson in the stewardship of his people and the redistribution of wealth in moments of physical closeness and warm intimacy with these figures. It was as if the architecture of power in the first scene had been deliberately set up to turn intimacy—in this case the declaration of filial love—into the theatre of power politics, letting Lear keep his distance from his children. This Lear even made Cordelia stand on a chair to be disinherited, as if undergoing a public ritual of punishing shame, whereas the storm and hovel scenes made intimate scenes of Lear's declarations on the treatment of the poor. Small acts of kindness made political meaning, as they drew the audience's attention from the theatre of power to the intimate relations that might undermine that power.

The politics of *King Lear* were reburied in character research, however, at the point when, startlingly, Lear battered the Fool to death in an abandoned bath found in the Hovel. This interpretation emerged from Russell Beale's discovery of Lewy Body Dementia, a rare form of the disease whose symptoms include sudden outbursts of rage. 'In this one', says Russell Beale of his work on Lear, 'I thought I bet Shakespeare, being the acute observer of human nature that he is, would have studied old men. I thought: I'm going to do a bit of research.'[38] Russell Beale's performance successfully foregrounded Lear's self-conscious theatricality, his sense that a king is always performing on the stage of power—except, I felt, at the point where his Lear murders the Fool: this provided a solution to his disappearance from the action but undermined the dramaturgy of this play, which is underpinned by the ethics of hospitality, so conspicuously breached by Cornwall and company in their act of violence against the powerless figure of Gloucester.

---

[38] Simon Russell Beale, National Theatre Platforms, Talking Lear: 3, 5.February 2014; recording available at http://www.nationaltheatre.org.uk/discover/platforms/talking-lear-part-3-lear [accessed 30 March 2014].

MADNESS AND THEATRICALITY:
EDGAR'S POOR TOM

Edgar is a difficult figure for an actor to approach psychologically; it is hard to decide, as theatre critics still tend to remark, what psychological motivation there might be for him not to reveal himself to the blind Gloucester earlier than he does. For a modern audience, the Christian imperative to trust in Providence and not to despair may be lost in the suspense of wondering if father and son are going to be reunited. Tobias Menzies' Edgar in the Goold production at the Young Vic was a fascinating example of what happens when an essentially realist performance is extended meta-theatrically. Edgar tried out his Bedlam act (2.3)—a low voice, compulsive self-striking—whilst addressing himself directly to the audience, who were visible in the spill of stage lighting in this intimate performance space. In doing so, he appeared simultaneously to be communicating the psychological distress Edgar experiences at the moment of his exile and to be demonstrating how emotion is constructed in the psychological realist tradition—through broken voice and compulsive, repetitive movement designed to appear as the spontaneous emissions of the distressed psyche, both Edgar's and Poor Tom's. So theatrically conscious was this simultaneous performance of madness and grief that the stereotypes of 'mad homeless person' Menzies produced here could be read as both realist acting and consciously stylized performance. The audience could watch Menzies and empathize with Edgar's distress. Or they might have been provoked by the self-conscious construction of his performance to consider what it is we find disturbing about being looked at for so long by a 'mad' figure. The performance asked us to attend to what it is that we recognize in Poor Tom, what it is we find alien, and to consider whether particular kinds of mental disturbance are universal or historically particular. The potential for multiple readings of Edgar lay, I think, in the shifts from play-world to theatre-world, from fiction to reality, that this space demanded. It was not a simple matter of Brechtian *verfremdungseffekt*: Menzies' Edgar/Tom absolutely demanded empathy as well as distanced consideration. But the production asked that the audience consider not only how Edgar might be feeling when he plays poor Tom but how those 'feelings', and our feelings about him, are constructed theatrically and historically.

Edmund and Edgar were given something of a role reversal in Mendes's National Theatre production. Whilst at the Young Vic, JonJo O'Neil pushed Edmund's open villainy as close to the audience as possible, flirting with women in the audience and playing for the kinds of laughs that would later make him a brilliant Richard III in 2012,[39] Sam Troughton's Edmund at the National was a much more respectable-looking figure, in glasses, overcoat, and brief case, his villainy revealed to the audience almost nervously. Tom Brooke's Edgar in the National production was something of a slacker in jogging bottoms and t-shirt, the problem child whose legitimate inheritance clearly meant he had no need to find something productive to do. This Edgar had, it seemed, turned to self-contemplation without a concomitant self-awareness, and the idea that anyone could turn against him, or that he might have to fend for himself, was in danger of deranging

[39] *Richard III*, dir. Roxana Silbert, Royal Shakespeare Company, Stratford-upon-Avon, 2012.

him entirely, making Poor Tom an apt form of disguise. In a reversal of the more common directorial decision, Edgar was a seeming outsider to social conventions, Edmund outwardly keen to conform to them. This made Edmund a less attractive villain than he often is, as he appeared to be an example of court hypocrisy rather than a contemptuous outsider to it. However, the portrayal of Edgar as indulged legitimate son gave him a clear emotional and intellectual journey through the play, and made some engaging modern sense of his multiple roles. He had become somewhat meaningless as Gloucester's heir, and was trying on different personae, finally coming to the conclusion that action in a right cause was an important element of his humanity. Both Edgars—Menzies most particularly as Poor Tom, Brooke on the imaginary cliff with Gloucester—demonstrated the acute performativity of this role. Indeed, at their strongest, these interpretations offered intimacy as something about which one could make performance decisions. Menzies' Edgar at the Young Vic found his intimate relationships with his family radically disrupted and questioned what it meant to recognize humanity in the other, as he confronted the audience with his Poor Tom; Brooke's rapidly changing, detailed portrayals of the characters who confront Gloucester on the Dover cliff foregrounded the potential for intimate acts of kindness between strangers.

LEAR'S DAUGHTERS: A PSYCHOPATHOLOGY OF THE FEMININE

Significantly, both of these productions abandoned the performative politics of intimacy in some of the theatrical decisions made around Lear's daughters, choosing instead to narrow interpretations to the purely psychological. My first example is indicated by a lighting decision, similar in both versions of the first scene. Cordelia's comments on her sisters' declarations of love for their father are often marked as 'asides' in modern texts, and were foregrounded as such at the Young Vic and the National Theatre by lighting changes that spotlit Cordelia. 'What must Cordelia speak? Love and be silent' (1.1.61) says Lear's youngest daughter, and lighting marked her out as unheard by the rest of the court. It happened again in both productions at the next 'aside': 'Then poor Cordelia! | And yet not so, since I am sure my love's | More ponderous than my tongue' (1.1.75-7). In neither production was any other moment of 'aside' or soliloquy marked by such a stark lighting change. In theatre spaces that so clearly invite a fluid relationship between performer and audience, these lighting changes seemed unnecessarily expository. The decision shed, to use an appropriate metaphor, a particularly psychological light upon Cordelia that was not, except in the case of Russell Beale's Lewy Body Dementia concept, turned upon the male characters in the play. Lighting Cordelia here suggested that she was not turning to the audience to comment on the action but that these lines represented the spontaneous emissions of the psyche, a character talking to herself. This impression was strengthened at the Young Vic by the way in which Amanda Hale as Cordelia broke up her verse—particularly at the beginnings of lines—to suggest she was struggling with thoughts and feelings as they spontaneously emerged.

The second decision I want to mark is common to many modern productions of *King Lear*: it involves a psychological, often psycho-sexual explanation of Regan's behaviour during the torture of Gloucester (3.6).[40] At the Young Vic, despite her passion for Edmund, Regan invited a prolonged kiss with Cornwall during this scene; having watched Edmund's previous exit with obvious lust, she held and kissed Cornwall once he has plucked out Gloucester's first eye, and after a fleeting demonstration of horror, plucked out the second eye herself by sucking it into her mouth. It seemed that the idea of a woman being a willing witness to and participant in so violent an act of torture was deemed to be incomprehensibly horrible to modern audiences, unless explained by some kind of sexual psychosis. The fact that Regan shifted from wild enjoyment to horror at her own actions in at the end of this scene at the Young Vic—she spat out Gloucester's eyeball into a water trough down stage and frantically washed her mouth once the deed has been done—deepened the impression that she was somehow taken over by a sexual madness that shifted to self-loathing as quickly as it overwhelmed her. It is also worth noting that Goneril was played as pregnant in Goold's production and appeared to have been delivered of her baby at some point during Act 3. Her anger at the presence of her father's knights could thus be read as the result of feeling vulnerable or 'hormonal' whilst pregnant (indeed, on one night I overheard audience members discussing how this made her actions towards Lear more sympathetic: 'Of course she's not going to want a hundred knights staying if she's about to have a baby'). Again, it seemed that women's bad behaviour towards patriarchal figures must be explained away by additional psycho-sexual or psychosomatic problems, whilst male madness—Lear's and Edgar's as Poor Tom—can be more playful, subversive, productive.

At the National, two reviewers suggested that a similar decision had been made for Anna Maxwell Martin's Regan in Mendes' production as for Charlotte Randle's in Goold's: Charles Spenser described Randle's Regan as a 'sex kitten turned on by torture'[41] while Paul Taylor saw her as 'a posh nymphomaniac turned on by torture'. [42] Either this scene was reinterpreted later in the run or Spenser and Taylor were so used to seeing the scene thus played that they saw 'sex kitten' and 'nymphomaniac' where none existed. The Regan of the two performances I attended had a drink in her hand as she witnessed the torture of Gloucester, and lurched about the stage, one moment giggling, the next in a state of distress. Far from being 'turned on by torture' it seemed that she was unable to contemplate the logical end of her own treatment of Gloucester without half obliterating it in drunkenness. Whether or not I read the moment differently from Spenser and Taylor, there remained the implication that the relationship between women and violence in tragic performance must be one of psychological disturbance.

CONCLUSION

This reconsideration of *Hamlet* and *Lear* in recent production has, I hope, taken me beyond a simple objection, on the grounds of anachronism, to the acting practice of

---

[40] Penelope Wilton's Regan reacted with obvious sexual excitement to the torture of Gloucester in Jonathan Miller's production for the BBC (1982); more recently Dominic Dromgoole's production at the Globe (London, 2008) had Kellie Bright's Regan responding similarly, as did Fiona Glascott's Regan in Lucy Bailey's production at the Theatre Royal, Bath (2013).

[41] Charles Spencer, Review of *King Lear* dir. Sam Mendes, *Daily Telegraph*, 23 January 2014.

[42] Paul Taylor, Review of *King Lear* dir. Sam Mendes, *Independent*, 24 January 2014.

finding psychological motivation for early modern tragic subjects. Although I might still argue that attempts to explain away the horrors of *Lear* psychologically are our own versions of Nahum Tate's happy ending, in the productions I have described, *King Lear* ultimately reduces a King to the status of a common man who does small, compassionate things, and this has its own political resonance. In a range of abstract and meta-theatrical settings, the detailed physical and vocal performances of the modern actor can produce a politics of intimacy that opens up questions for a contemporary audience of what it means to relate to another human being outside dominant structures of power. The strengths of the *Hamlet* productions I have accounted for here lie, I have argued, in moments where Hamlet's inner life is opened up to the audience as a subversive force in the Danish state. Fashions for 'full' or 'empty' spaces, for director's theatre or for 'letting the text speak', will no doubt continue to wax and wane as the twenty-first century progresses. What I hope continues to develop is the potential of live theatre to offer acting styles and scenic tradition in productive tension. The modern Shakespearean actor, like Simon Russell Beale, with his belief in the transhistorical nature of psychological states, has offered great insight into the politics of tragedy when the detailed performance of interiority has been juxtaposed with the epic and the meta-theatrical.

SELECT BIBLIOGRAPHY

ADHS Performing Arts, *Designing Shakespeare* (digital archive), http://www.ahds.rhul.ac.uk|ahdscollections| (accessed 10 October 2014).

Belsey, Catherine, *The Subject of Tragedy: The Subject of Tragedy: Identity and Difference in Renaissance Drama* (London: Routledge, 1985).

Brook, Peter, *The Empty Space* (New York: Simon and Schuster, 1968).

Bulman, James C., *Shakespeare, Theory, and Performance* (London: Routledge, 1996).

Chillington Rutter, Carol, *Enter the Body: Women and Representation on Shakespeare's Stage* (London: Routledge, 2001).

Cox, Brian, *The 'King Lear' Diaries: The Story of the Royal National Theatre's Productions of Shakespeare's 'Richard III' and 'King Lear'* (London: Methuen, 1992).

Dawson, Anthony B., *Shakespeare in Performance: 'Hamlet'* (Manchester and New York: Manchester University Press, 1995).

Dessen, Alan C., *Rescripting Shakespeare: The Text, the Director, and Modern Productions* (Cambridge: Cambridge University Press, 2002).

Escolme, Bridget, *Talking to the Audience: Shakespeare, Performance, Self* (London: Routledge, 2005).

Holland, Peter, 'Shakespeare in the Twentieth Century Theatre', in Margareta de Grazia and Stanley Wells, eds., *The Cambridge Companion to Shakespeare* (Cambridge: Cambridge University Press: 2001), 199–216.

Ioppolo, Grace, 'The Performance of Text in the Royal National Theatre's 1997 Production of *King Lear*', in *Shakespeare Performed: Essays in Honor of R. A. Foakes*, ed. Grace Ioppolo (Newark: University of Delaware Press; London: Associated University Presses, 2000), 180–97.

Kennedy, Dennis, *Looking at Shakespeare: A Visual History of Twentieth-Century Performance* (Cambridge: Cambridge University Press, 2001).

Leggatt, Alexander, *King Lear*. Shakespeare in Performance (Manchester and New York: Manchester University Press, 1991).

Miller, Arthur, 'Tragedy and the Common Man', *New York Times*, 27 February 1947.

Mullin, Michael. 'Peter Brook's *King Lear:* Stage and Screen', *Literature/Film Quarterly* 11:3 (1983), 190–6.

Phelan, Peggy, 'Reconstructing Love: *King Lear* and Theatre Architecture', in Barbara Hodgdon and W. B. Worthen, eds., *A Companion to Shakespeare in Performance* (Oxford: Blackwell, 2005), 13–34.

Purcell, Steven, *Shakespeare and the Audience in Practice* (Basingstoke: Palgrave, 2014).

Rosenberg, Marvin, *The Masks of Hamlet* (Newark, DE: University of Delaware Press, 1992).

Tynan, Kenneth, 'The Triumph of Stratford's *Lear*', *Observer*, 11 November 1962.

Worthen, W. B. *Shakespeare and the Force of Modern Perfoprmance* (Cambridge: Cambridge University Press, 2003).

CHAPTER 34

ONTOLOGICAL SHIVERS
The Cinematic Afterlives of Shakespeare's Romeo and Juliet

COURTNEY LEHMANN

SHAKESPEARE IN SILENCE

PIECED together from prose chronicles, novellas, folklore, and poems, Shakespeare's *Romeo and Juliet* is a play that self-consciously reflects upon the adaptation process itself. In the cinema, adaptations of *Romeo and Juliet* have long been associated with important developments in film history. For example, *Romeo and Juliet* emerged on screen as early as 1900, when a recording of the Gounod opera was used to experiment with synchronized sound—technology that was not officially invented until 1927. A slightly later *Romeo and Juliet* film, titled *Le Diable Géant, ou Le Miracle de la Madone* (1902), may be the very first example of a Shakespeare 'spinoff'. Directed by George Méliès, one of cinema's founding fathers, this film was known not only for its surreal interpretation of the balcony scene—in which Romeo and Juliet are separated by a dancing devil until the Madonna herself intercedes—but also for its precocious mastery of visual effects. This adaptation of an adaptation set the stage for subsequent cinematic experiments that would forever change the burgeoning medium.

The Vitagraph *Romeo and Juliet*—one of three films of the play to appear in 1908—is a case-in-point. Kenneth Rothwell cites this adaptation, directed by William Ranous, as the earliest example of a Shakespeare film that 'went beyond the primitive "actualities" by using the camera not just as a recorder of but as a participant in the cinematic storytelling'.[1] With seventeen different camera set-ups—a process known as découpage—Ranous's adaptation unfolds not only through medium shots (as was typical of early cinema) but also through long shots, cross-cutting, shot-reverse-shot techniques, and off-camera editing, liberating the cinematic medium from the fixed frontal perspective associated with merely recording plays.

---

[1] Kenneth Rothwell, *A History of Shakespeare on Screen: A Century of Film and Television* (Cambridge: Cambridge University Press, 1999), 7.

Close-up: Découpage

'Découpage', a French term derived from the verb *découper*, meaning 'to cut into pieces', is essential to understanding the unique contribution of the Vitagraph *Romeo and Juliet* to cinematic history. Although découpage is often conflated with montage, the two terms are ontologically different: the former invokes shot selection prior to filming, whereas the latter refers to the effect of successive shots achieved by editing—a process typically associated with post-production. In addition to establishing camera set-ups (what we might think of as cinematic 'blocking'), découpage is concerned with the spatio-temporal relationship between two frames, also known as the shot transition. Shot transitions operate in two fundamental ways: one functions to achieve continuity between frames, while the other, less common approach serves to disrupt the visual narrative and disorient the viewer. Generally speaking, most mainstream films seek to produce narratives that unfold consistently in time and space. For example, a common means of creating temporal continuity is the shot-reverse-shot sequence, which generates the illusion of sustained conversation between two or more characters. A similar effect may be achieved through simple eye-line matches, which preserve spatial continuity between frames. In both contexts, the role of the shot transition is implicitly conservative, marking an effort to elide the perception of any temporal or spatial change in the interests of creating a seamless narrative experience.

This is why silent films may be considered more radical than their later sound counterparts. Despite aspirations to cinematic realism, silent shorts are almost implicitly avant garde, as space and time are intractably discontinuous in them. In the silent one-reeler genre, creating a seamless visual narrative is a virtually impossible feat—not only because of the disruptive effect of title cards or 'leaders' but also because of the dramatic compression demanded by the reduction of a two-hour play into fifteen minutes. The Vitagraph *Romeo and Juliet* condenses 1.2, 4–5; 2.1–4, 6; 3.1, 5; 4.1, 3, 5; and 5.1, 3 into merely 12 scenes, an accomplishment that requires major spatio-temporal ellipses. Through its plurality of shots and camera set-ups, Ranous's 1908 film demonstrates masterful découpage, exploring the many uses of the camera as a viable storytelling instrument both on—and in—its own terms.

The Vitagraph *Romeo and Juliet* also makes extensive use of location shooting throughout New York City. One of many outdoor locations exploited by Ranous is a shot of the Bethesda fountain, over which the Angel of the Waters presides—a motif that Baz Luhrmann revisits in the giant statue of the Virgin Mary that burnishes the skyline of his Mexico City-based 'Verona' in *William Shakespeare's Romeo + Juliet* (1996). Additionally, Ranous's adaptation is the first Shakespeare film to make conspicuous use of product placement—the Vitagraph 'V'—introducing a consumer-based rationale for cinema that would be taken to extremes in films made nearly a century later, such as David LaChappelle's *H&M Romeo & Juliet* (2005). As Robert Hamilton Ball observes, the 'V' above Juliet's bed as well as the entry to Friar Laurence's cell was 'not for Verona but an attempted protection against illegal duplicating by the display of the Vitagraph trademark'.[2]

---

[2] Robert Hamilton Ball, '*Shakespeare on Silent Film: A Strange Eventful History*' (London and New York: Routledge, 2013), 44.

Provocatively, Ranous himself became the subject of an intellectual property dispute when, having urged Vitagraph—as opposed to its chief rival, IMP (the Independent Motion Picture company)—to film *Romeo and Juliet* before anyone else could, he then defected to IMP one year later, when a commercial rivalry broke out between the studios; there he would become a major figure in directing Shakespeare's plays for years to come.

Romeo and Juliet was also the single most popular source of spinoffs, Shakespearean or otherwise, throughout cinema's adolescence in the 1910s and 20s. Comic interpretations of the tragedy were of particular interest, beginning with Méliès's film in 1902 and including titles as far-fetched as *Romeo in Pajamas* (1913). Western adaptations were also quite popular, as spinoffs like *The Galloping Romeo, A Depot Romeo, A Ridin' Romeo, Romeo Turns Bandit,* and *Roping Her Romeo* attest. Clearly, the Veronese setting of Shakespeare's play was no obstacle to imaginative transpositions of the play's action, leading to location-based spinoffs such as *A Seashore Romeo, Romeo of the Coal Wagon, A Tugboat Romeo, Romeo in the Stone Age, A Spanish Romeo, A Tropical Romeo, Seaside Romeos, A Prairie Romeo,* and so on. Foreign spinoffs were no exception to this rule; Ernst Lubitsch, for example, created a Bavarian farce, *Romeo und Julia im Schnee* (1920), by setting his film in a winter sporting park. Proving its remarkable adaptability, *Romeo and Juliet*, as Robert Hamilton Ball attests, 'continued to be a byword by which a producer could indicate a romance of some sort and which he could combine with the rest of his title to convey locale or activity'.[3] Other, more explicitly experimental treatments include a 'claymation' *Romeo and Juliet* (1917) as well as an educational 'Felix the Cat' cartoon, *Romeow* (1927). In an apparent reversal of the Marxist dictum, it seems that Shakespearean film history repeats itself first as farce and then as tragedy.

REALISM AND THE MGM *ROMEO AND JULIET* (1936)

Close-up: Classical Realism

Tracing the origins of film back to Egyptian embalming rites, Andre Bazin, the greatest champion of cinematic realism, argues that images—painterly, sculptural, photographic, or cinematographic—stem from the desire to preserve life. The first major Hollywood production of Shakespeare's play, the MGM *Romeo and Juliet* (George Cukor 1936), emerges in precisely this spirit. The film's classical realist style creates a perfect simulacrum of Renaissance Italy, while simultaneously producing a memorializing effect: the film is widely acknowledged as producer Irving Thalberg's dying gift to his wife, Norma Shearer, for whom he created this star vehicle. Highlighting the psychological pull of realism, or, the 'preservation of life by a representation of life', Bazin acknowledges that although no one assumes the ontological unity of 'model and image, ... all are agreed that the image helps us to remember the subject and to preserve him from a second spiritual death'.[4] Indeed, not only would Thalberg's love for his wife persist in historical memory through

---

[3] Ball, *Shakespeare on Silent Film*, 264.

[4] Andre Bazin, 'The Ontology of the Photographic Image', ed. Leo Braudy and Marshall Cohen, *Film Theory and Criticism*, 7th edn (New York and Oxford: Oxford University Press, 2009), 159–62 (159).

the MGM spectacle, but Shearer herself—then a 36-year-old actress—would also be frozen in a kind of perpetual adolescence as Juliet.

Classical realism revolves around 'the ideology of verisimilitude', or the culturally-dominant desire to produce 'the optical illusion of truth'.[5] As Robert Stam, Robert Burgoyne, and Sandy Flitterman-Lewis explain, '[b]y effacing the signs of their production, "dominant" cinema persuade[s] spectators to take constructed simulations as transparent renderings of the real'.[6] The desire to create a seamless transposition of life to a synthetic reality led Thalberg and MGM to spare no expense in the making of *Romeo and Juliet*, the first Shakespeare film to showcase the full resources of the Hollywood 'machine'. Designers were dispatched to Italy to bring home detailed impressions for the construction of the *mise-en-scène*—details that would generate virtual replicas of paintings by Da Vinci, Fra' Angelico, Botticelli, Bellini, Carpaccio, and Gozzoli—while professors were brought in to advise on the script and to create educational guides for distribution in the public schools. The stars, Leslie Howard (Romeo), John Barrymore (Mercutio), and Shearer, were deployed for promotional tours and appearances, while product tie-ins cemented the film within a consumer culture mesmerized by Hollywood high fashion. Elaborate choreography, courtesy of Agnes DeMille, was employed for the dance sequences, the musical score featured Tchaikovskian highlights, and the props included real Renaissance currency (ducats hand-carried from Italy), all of which combined to produce what the shooting script describes as 'a noisy, brightly-coloured pageant of fifteenth century Italian life under blue skies in July weather'.[7]

But for all its glossy production values, polished façades, and meticulously painted frescoes, the film failed, ironically, to come across as 'real'. In the words of one critic, 'the exact replica of Renaissance art and the like have rendered the film somewhat cumbersome, remov[ing] the possibilities of something fresh and exciting'.[8] Others described Thalberg's production as generally faithful but unimaginative, leading to the conclusion that the MGM *Romeo and Juliet* was a 'museum piece': 'the effect of it all is to convert a romantic tragedy into a sort of fashion parade of the Italian Renaissance'.[9] Indeed, in this context the pursuit of realism 'is no longer a question of survival after death, but of a larger concept, the creation of an ideal world in the likeness of the real, with its own temporal destiny'.[10]

Romeo and Juliet are characters in search of their own temporal destiny. In fact, Shakespeare's protagonists experience not only a disturbing feeling of temporal compression but also an ominous sense of having arrived too late at the scene of their own story. Consider, for example, Romeo's premonition just prior to entering the Capulet household when, reacting to the others' concern that they will arrive 'too late', he muses:

> I fear too early, for my mind misgives
> Some consequence yet hanging in the stars
> Shall bitterly begin his fearful date

---

[5] Robert Stam, Robert Burgoyne, and Sandy Flitterman-Lewis, *New Vocabularies in Film Semiotics: Structuralism, Post-structuralism and Beyond* (London and New York: Routledge), 188.

[6] Ibid.

[7] Quoted In Russell Jackson, *Shakespeare Films in the Making: Vision, Production and Reception* (Cambridge: Cambridge University Press, 2007) 133.

[8] Ibid., 156.   [9] Ibid.   [10] Bazin, 'The Ontology of the Photographic Image', 160.

> With this night's revels, and expire the term
> Of a despised life, closed in my breast,
> By some vile forfeit of untimely death.
>
> (1.4.106–11)

Shakespeare's play is unique as the only version of the Romeo and Juliet legend in which the lovers are afflicted with foreknowledge of their own doom. The product of cultural repetition compulsion, legends are driven by the force of tragic inevitability, ultimately leading to widely known and infinitely recyclable conclusions. In the above scene, Romeo experiences what we might think of as an ontological shiver—an acute sense of déjà vu or, more accurately, déjà vécu—a sense of having already *lived*. Juliet, too, seems all too aware of Romeo's legendary or 'notorious identity' when she has an uncanny flash forward to his death.[11] Upon Romeo's departure for Mantua, Juliet looks down at him as he descends the rope ladder and exclaims: 'O God, I have an ill-divining soul! | Methinks I see thee, now thou art so low, | As one dead in the bottom of a tomb. | Either my eyesight fails, or thou look'st pale' (3.5.54-7). Such morbid anticipation suggests the magnitude of the struggle that the lovers undertake to subvert realism—that is, to surmount, or at least forestall, the seamless transcription of the legend over their own (already dead) bodies. But even in a play, wherein improvisation is always possible, the only hope of autonomy for Romeo and Juliet lies in choosing death—a decision which, ironically, duplicates the desperate acts of their legendary predecessors.

NEOREALISM AND ITS DISCONTENTS: RENATO CASTELLANI'S *GIULIETTA E ROMEO*

It seems particularly significant, then, that Renato Castellani, in adapting *Romeo and Juliet* for the screen, sought to avoid an immediate association with Shakespeare's play by titling his film *Giulietta e Romeo* with the intent of following Da Porto's version of the legend. Similar to the designs of the MGM *Romeo and Juliet*, Castellani's approach to the film was to 'immers[e] it in an atmosphere of the Renaissance and of realism'.[12] At the time that the director was devising his adaptation, few terms could have been fraught with more controversy than 'realism'. Russell Jackson observes that 'by the early 1950s the "neo-realist" cinema was a storm-centre of fierce theoretical and political debate'.[13] Emerging, quite literally, from the ruins of the Second War World and the German plundering of Rome, Italian neorealism was an attempt to bring honesty back to cinema by creating films that exposed the horrors of war and Italy's devastated landscape. As the post-fascist 'new republic' began to take shape with a government intent on effacing Italy's complicity in the war, directors took risks to tell the truth, as breakthrough films such as Rosselini's *Rome, Open City* (1945) and

---

[11] Linda Charnes, *Notorious Identity: Materializing the Subject in Shakespeare* (Cambridge and London: Harvard University Press, 1993).

[12] Stelio Martini, ed., *'Giuletta e Romeo' di Renato Castellani* (Bologna: Capeli Editore, 1957), 37–46 (45).

[13] Jackson, *Shakespeare Films in the Making*, 163.

De Sica's *Bicycle Thief* (1948) introduced a new style of filmmaking to the world. Quite removed from the uninterrupted and highly polished transfer of reality associated with classical or Bazinian realism, the 'new' or 'neo' realism was based on an anti-capitalistic commitment to cinematic poverty, featuring largely open-air, on-location shooting and non-professional actors. As with classical realism, 'authenticity' was the aim of the movement, but what counted as 'real' meant something very different. 'This is how I understand realism', claimed De Sica, 'which cannot be, in my opinion, mere documentation. If there is any absurdity in this theory, it is the absurdity of those social contradictions that society wants to ignore.'[14] Intent on exposing Italy's postwar hypocrisies, the insistently rough-hewn films of the neorealists exploited the idea of form itself as a political intervention, leading to government scrutiny and criticism.

Close-up: *Realismo Rosa*

Castellani's *Giuletta e Romeo* was created during the official end of the neorealist era and has been referred to as an example of '*realismo rosa*', also known as 'pink' or 'soft' neorealism. Emerging in the 1950s, *realismo rosa* is best understood as a hybrid of two very distinct cinematic movements: the neorealism of the 1940s and the Calligraphism of the 1930s. In contrast to the grim reality presupposed by the neorealist movement, the Calligraphers movement took up the mantle of '*bello scrivere*'—or 'beautiful writing'—by establishing a formalist aesthetic that featured escapist themes and a fastidious attention to detail. As Mira Liehm explains, '"Calligraphism" denoted certain formalist preoccupations linked with the retreat to the past and resulting in films with a meticulously reconstructed décor and "beautiful" photography ... which led to essentially decorative results.'[15] These competing approaches to reality produced the compromise formation known as *realismo rosa*, which offered a 'rosier' portrait of Italy's human and physical landscapes. Not surprisingly, *realismo rosa* incited the wrath of leftist filmmakers and critics who viewed its beautifying lens as 'a romantic betrayal of political and aesthetic principles'.[16] The main complaint had less to do with the genre's at times stultifying formalism than it did with its ideological subterfuge, as Liehm attests: '"pink neorealism" presented important problems in such a way as to make them appear less serious and less difficult to solve, and their style, aiming at authenticity, made people believe that the problems as well as the offered solutions were real.'[17]

Nevertheless, during a time when Italy was attempting to whitewash its own ugliness in the aftermath of the Second World War, Castellani explicitly defied the black and white cinematography of the neorealists and deployed Technicolor as a politicized mode of cinematic *écriture*. Rather than emphasizing bold primary colours, the film traffics in subtle variations on these themes, producing a *mise-en-scène* awash with hues of thistle, ochre, sage, olive, lavender, sky blue, cobalt, tan, chartreuse, crimson, burgundy, peach,

---

[14] Quoted in David Overbey, ed., *Springtime in Italy: A Reader on Neo-realism* (London: Talisman Books, 1978), 88.

[15] Mira Liehm, *Passion and Defiance: Film in Italy from 1942 to the Present* (Berkeley and London: University of California Press, 1984), 30.

[16] Jackson, *Shakespeare Films in the Making*, 164.   [17] Liehm, *Passion and Defiance*, 89.

periwinkle, and rust. The lone exception to this chromatic scheme is Juliet, who is consistently shown wearing variations of red and, specifically, soft-to-medium shades of pink, as if she were the personification of 'pink neorealism' itself. The problem with Castellani's 'essentially decorative' approach to characterization is that at times, the protagonists appear secondary to the film's breathtaking arabesques of light and colour.

Castellani's desire to adapt *Romeo and Juliet* through a rose-tinted lens is especially evident in his systematic elimination of *all* of Shakespeare's foreshadowing. But what is missing from the screenplay returns with a vengeance in the film's visual rhetoric, as architectural images of entrapment cast an ominous shadow on the lovers. In a frequently repeated motif, Juliet is framed between enormous marble pillars on the balcony, while Romeo looks up at her from behind the bars of a similarly imposing bannister. Both are prohibited from meeting each other by a large iron grille at the entry to the balcony. Later, in their wedding scene, another grille literally separates Romeo and Juliet's faces as they awkwardly try to kiss through the iron latticework, giving the impression that both are in cages. This motif is repeated on the eve of Juliet's feigned death in the form of a disturbing mannequin that wears Juliet's wedding dress: where a face should be, there is a head comprised entirely of cross-hatched metal wires—arranged in precisely the same pattern as the grilles. Left alone with the uncanny figure, Juliet experiences an ontological shiver when she approaches the mannequin as though it were her ghostly *doppelgänger*. Becoming hysterical, she projects the ghost of her cousin onto the faceless dress form, lunging at it and crying 'Tybalt! Tybalt!'. A quick cut to the morning after shot shows evidence of a fierce struggle, as the ransacked mannequin lies on the floor wearing Juliet's newly-tattered red dress while Juliet lies 'dead' in the white wedding gown. The offspring of these macabre images is a *tableau mort* which implies that Juliet and the lifeless figure have changed ontological places.

Lawrence Harvey's Romeo endures a parallel struggle when he attempts to enter the monument where Juliet lies. As Russell Jackson observes, Romeo 'has something difficult and perplexing to achieve before he even reaches the heartbreaking confrontation with his fate'.[18] This time, it is not a grille that fences him off from Juliet but the implacable architecture that prevents him from accessing the Capulet vault. Though Romeo attempts to break in through the cathedral, the heavy doors respond to his force with complete indifference. So, too, when Romeo at last navigates his way to the Capulet vault, he cannot remove the massive slate of stone that prohibits his entry. In desperation, he grabs a giant candlestick from the cathedral, breaks the top off, and uses it to kill Paris—his own *doppelgänger*—and then, after considerable effort, successfully prongs the lid off the monument. Though Romeo attempts briefly to reason with death over Juliet's perfect, lifeless body, he quickly dispatches himself with a dagger rather than poison, and Juliet awakens, holding a single red rose to her bosom, to find him dead. The fact that Juliet is pictured with a rose reminds us that she is the figure who embodies the perceptual schemes of *realismo rosa*, but no form of aesthetic indulgence can trump the inertia of the legend. Although Castellani cannot prevail over Shakespeare's ending, he tempers its tragic force by craning up from the mourning families to focus on a rose window—a self-conscious inscription of the aesthetic *realismo rosa* over the fatal determinism of Shakespeare's play.

[18] Jackson, *Shakespeare Films in the Making*, 184–5.

Cinéma Vérité meets Verismo Opera: Franco Zeffirelli's Romeo and Juliet (1968)

When it comes to *Romeo and Juliet*, there seems to be no escape from realism—in any of its forms. Unlike most legends, the Romeo and Juliet story is the product of a long line of exclusively literary, rather than oral, transmission. In fact, Shakespeare's play might be said to suffer not so much from *déjà-vu* as from *déjà-lu*—the experience of itself as *already read*. Barthes's concept of *déjà-lu* reminds us that *Romeo and Juliet* emerged from centuries of literary accretion, which may account for the play's relentless sense of predetermination or, indeed, insuperable realism.[19] Like the films of his predecessors, Zeffirelli's adaptation is driven by an investment in authenticity and, perhaps counter-intuitively, realism. On the one hand, the director envisions Shakespeare's play as an opportunity to create a *cinéma vérité* style film of Renaissance Italy. Also known as 'truth cinema' or 'direct cinema', *cinéma vérité* emerged as a documentary technique inspired by the French *nouvelle vague*, which revolutionized the use of a hand-held camera as a means of 'authentically' capturing everyday reality. This approach appears throughout Zeffirelli's film in conjunction with Mercutio's appearances and the chaotic crowd scenes. On the other hand, the influence of the director's acclaimed work in opera—specifically the late nineteenth-century Italian tradition of '*opera verismo*'—resonates in the emotional through-line of his *Romeo and Juliet*. Like *cinéma vérité*, the *verismo* movement accorded importance to ordinary situations; the key difference is that the latter, in keeping with the operatic genre more generally, features violent themes and the dramatic expression of extreme emotions, also known as melodrama. Zeffirelli acknowledges both movements when he promises to create a version of *Romeo and Juliet* as 'a real story in a plausible medieval city at the opening of the Renaissance' in which 'emotional situations are singled out and underlined'.[20]

The principal source of this underlining in Zeffirelli's film is the music and, more specifically, Nino Rota's epic ballad, 'What is a Youth?' At once beautiful and haunting, this song conveys the zeitgeist of 1968, a year marked by turbulence around the world. While Mao's cultural revolution was raging in China, in France university students took to the streets to demand viable alternatives to consumer capitalism—in education, cultural production, and society at large, while workers led massive labour strikes in the same spirit. In the US, the civil rights movement posed a formidable challenge to racial segregation while anti-war sentiment was rising alongside the 'flower power' movement—a generally peaceful mode of engagement that culminated in the tragedy of the Kent State massacre, when the Ohio National Guard fired into a crowd of unarmed students in 1970. (Appropriately, Leonard Whiting's Romeo first appears walking toward the town square with a flower in his hand, dashing it to the ground when he realizes that the war between the Capulets and the Montagues has resurfaced in another bloody riot.) But in many ways

---

[19] Barthes explores the concept of *déjà lu* throughout *S/Z*.
[20] Franco Zeffirelli, *Zeffirelli: The Autobiography of Franco Zeffirelli* (London: Weidenfeld and Nicolson, 1986), 163.

it was the very year of Zeffirelli's production, 1968, which dealt a decisive blow to the idealism that flourished in the early part of the decade when the assassination of Martin Luther King, Jr. and Presidential hopeful Bobby Kennedy shocked the world. Indeed, the sense that 'a greater power' had 'thwarted [the] intents' (5.3.153–4) of the most promising voices for social change was lost on no one—least of all the international youth movement that Zeffirelli so aggressively courted for his audience. Fittingly, when the director cast Leonard Whiting as Romeo and Olivia Hussey as Juliet, they were then the youngest pair ever to play these roles on screen.

Commenting on the film, Jack Jorgens observes that Shakespeare's lovers 'are reckless, bored, cynical children of the feud, just as a generation of Americans were children of Vietnam'.[21] Peter Donaldson adds that the adaptation 'endorse[d] a number of the values of the international youth movement: pacifism, distrust of elders, and sexual liberation'[22]—a sentiment also registered, as the director himself insisted, in the long, unkempt hair of the younger characters. 'I told [the actors] I didn't want make-up, no gilded columns, no balconies with dangling wisteria' and, he stipulated, 'no wigs': 'they would have to grow their hair long—girls *and* boys'.[23] Nowhere was the zeitgeist of the youth movement more evident than in the music of the late 1960s, as the spirit of peace and freedom was championed by ballads like Bob Dylan's 'Blowing in the Wind', while the opposite sentiment of revolution through violence was relayed by songs like 'Street Fighting Man', which was released by The Rolling Stones in the same year as *Romeo and Juliet*. These tensions, I will argue, are replicated in the film's musical score.

Close-up: Diegetic vs. Non-Diegetic Music

The major source of diegetic music in Zeffirelli's adaptation is the performance of 'What is a Youth?' by the singing troubadour at the Capulet Ball. Also known as 'source music', diegetic music is generally connected to an on-screen source, contributing to the storyline aurally if not also visually. In this adaptation of *Romeo and Juliet*, the song, not by Shakespeare but by Nino Rota, is a variation on the Renaissance theme of life's transience:

> What is a youth?
> Impetuous fire.
> What is a maid?
> Ice and desire.
> The world wags on
> A rose will bloom,
> It then will fade.
> So does a youth,
> So does the fairest maid.

By contrast, non-diegetic music issues from a space that is outside of the story proper and cannot be linked to a source within the film; it is also known as 'commentary sound'.

---

[21] Jack Jorgens, *Shakespeare on Film* (Lanham, MD: University Press of America, 1991), 86–7.
[22] Peter Donaldson, *Shakespearean Films/Shakespearean Directors* (Boston and London: Unwin Hyman, 1990), 145.
[23] Zeffirelli, *Autobiography*, 163.

Examples of this type of sound in Zeffirelli's *Romeo and Juliet* include musical effects employed for dramatic emphasis, Lawrence Olivier's voice-over narration at the beginning and end of the film, and the various uses of mood music to establish the emotional disposition of a given scene. I suggest that the lovers' battle to escape the legend is writ small in the tensions within the film's musical score and, more precisely, in the conflict between the diegetic version of 'What is a youth?'—with its grave, premonitory lyrics—and the transcendent strains of the non-diegetic and exclusively instrumental repetitions of the song's melody.

Lyrical accompaniment in music has historically been regarded as a stabilizing force—a means of imposing order on sound's subversive capacity to bypass words and engage directly with 'music's nonverbal commerce with the passions'.[24] This was particularly the case in early modern England, where church Reformers (especially Puritans) were highly suspicious of instrumentation without lyrics, going so far as to ban organ music during the Interregnum. In Zeffirelli's film, Romeo and Juliet's first encounter is staged as a confrontation between the unruly potential of sound and the rationalizing force of the Logos. During an inspiring instrumental version of 'What is a Youth', the lovers kiss passionately and, as the song's refrain waxes triumphant, Romeo exclaims: 'O trespass sweetly urged | Give me my sin again' (1.5.106-7). With the utterance of the word 'sin', appropriately, the troubadour resumes singing as if on cue, admonishing the lovers for their rebellious passion with his sobering lyrics.

In the scene that follows Romeo and Juliet's (off-screen) consummation, Juliet begs Romeo to stay based on her conviction that the nightingale sings, rather than the lark—an example of the promiscuity of meaning that arises from music without lyrics. When Juliet attempts to manipulate the sound of what is in fact the lark rather than the nightingale, she indulges in the Renaissance association of 'music's affective power and the duplicitous nature of female speech ....'[25] But when Romeo too willingly falls for her wiles, exclaiming, 'Let me be ta'en. Let me be put to death | I am content .... | Come, death, and welcome; Juliet wills it so' (3.5.17-18, 24), Juliet changes her tune. With her face suddenly awash with horror, she cries:

> It is, it is. Hie hence, be gone, away.
> It is the lark that sings so out of tune,
> Straining harsh discords and unpleasing sharps.
> Some say the lark makes sweet division;
> This doth not so, for she divideth us.
>
> (3.5.26-30)

Importantly, the music of the lark in *Romeo and Juliet* is diegetic rather than non-diegetic; despite the fact that the source of the sound is off-screen, the lark's song contributes directly to the dramatic action, literally marking the moment of Romeo and Juliet's 'sweet division', for they will never see each other alive again.

During the making of *Romeo and Juliet*, Zeffirelli ventured the strange observation that in Shakespeare's play, the 'central idea is that of a puppeteer, Destiny, who handles all the characters. They are all puppets on a stage and no one is fully responsible. The

---

[24] Joseph Ortiz, *Broken Harmony: Shakespeare and the Politics of Music* (Ithaca and London: Cornell University Press, 2011), 23.

[25] Ortiz, *Broken Harmony*, 27.

whole tragedy is permeated with the idea of fate. There is nothing to do'.[26] In spite of such fatalism, however, Zeffirelli does what he can and, like Castellani before him, he eliminates nearly all of the foreshadowing present in Shakespeare's play. But as the film hurtles on to the tragic climax where both Romeo and Juliet, in an act of conscientious objection to their parents' war, take their lives, Rota's ballad is plucked out by a solitary guitar, softly registering the diminished efficacy of the lovers' resistance to their legendary fate. Although the love theme swells twice more—once, to denote Romeo's incredulity at Juliet's death-defying beauty when he asks 'why art thou yet so fair?' (5.3.102) and, subsequently, when Juliet realizes how little time has lapsed between Romeo's death and her discovery that 'thy lips are warm' (5.3.167)—its blissful crescendos are superceded by tragic gravitas as the chords resolve into a minor key. What Zeffirelli so delicately stresses here is that both Romeo and Juliet are mere children, and they sob—each over the other's body—like bawling infants in what is perhaps the most convincing representation of this scene in cinematic history. The relationship between music and political dissonance is especially visible in Juliet's suicide, which is staged as a battle between Rota's theme and the diegetic noise of the approaching Watch. Playing faintly, the transcendent strains of the love song are ultimately no match for the alarums that herald the intrusion of those who would thwart Juliet's efforts to join Romeo. Hence, as the off-screen, though distinctly diegetic sound of the Watch grows louder, Juliet, in a final attempt at dissonance, exclaims:

> Yea, noise? Then I'll be brief.
> O happy dagger.
> This is thy sheath! There rust, and let me die.
>
> (5.3.168-9)

As the knife plunges into her bosom, Rota's theme crescendos for a final time, resolving into the minor chord of its final phrase: 'So does a youth, so does the fairest maid'.

COLLISION MONTAGE: BAZ LUHRMANN'S *WILLIAM SHAKESPEARE'S ROMEO + JULIET* (1996)

Close-up: Montage

Undoubtedly the figure most associated with the term montage, Sergei Eisenstein famously observed that 'art is always conflict',[27] and no better word describes Baz Luhrmann's *William Shakespeare's Romeo + Juliet*. Although the film's title implies a simple mathematical equation of two lovers, the 'plus' sign can also suggest a dialectical approach to cinema, one that Eisentstein championed in his theory of montage. An editing practice first explored by the Russian Constructivists during the pre-Stalin1920s, the then-radical concept of montage as *collision* (rather than continuity) figures prominently not only in Eisenstein's films, but also in those of his colleague Grigori Kozintsev, both of

---

[26] Quoted in Jackson, *Shakespeare Films in the Making*, 195.

[27] Sergei Eisenstein, *Film Form* (New York and London: Harcourt Brace & Company, 1949), 46.

whom found Shakespeare indispensable to their theory of cinema. For these pioneering directors, Shakespeare's poetry was the written equivalent of Soviet montage, a process whereby the clash of two discrete frames produces a radically new concept—not a synthesis so much as a third term that cannot be reduced to its component parts. Hence, whereas continuity montage is always potentially co-optable by totalizing schemes, collision-based montage is intentionally disruptive, fracturing the viewer's sense of reality and frustrating attempts to resolve its inherent contradictions in culturally dominant terms.

Employing a shot vocabulary comprised of 'super-macro-slam zooms', 'static super-wide shots', and 'crash crane' camerawork—not to mention whip pans and lightning cuts, *William Shakespeare's Romeo + Juliet* takes collision for theme. Appropriately, the film's opening sequence is an elaborate montage that features accelerated intercutting between 'breaking news' coverage and static shots of newspaper headlines, magazine covers, and disturbing flash-forwards to the pending tragedy. Interspersed are aerial shots of the massive Jesus and Mary statues that preside over the corporate headquarters of the Montague and Capulet families. Meanwhile, in the militarized zone known as 'Verona Beach', helicopters hover impatiently over the city as surveillance spotlights reveal crimes in progress. The sound collisions are equally disorienting, combining the rhythmic chop of helicopters with an operatic track titled 'O Verona', a conspicuous variation on the theme of *Carmina Burana*'s 'O Fortuna'. As the chorus rises to an ominous crescendo, the prologue is repeated typographically in a rapid succession of lines that ends prematurely with the statement: 'two star cross'd lovers | take their life'. The 't' in 'take' is replaced by a cross, an image that brings us full circle back to the 'plus' sign in the film's title, which similarly doubles as a religious icon and as an example of chiasmus—the insignia of crossed purposes and, of course, star-crossed love.

When asked about his signature juxtapositions of wildly incongruous sounds, images, and cinematic styles, Luhrmann responds, incredulously: 'Well, have you ever seen a Hindi movie? Please. That idea of low comedy one minute, a song, then *Rebel Without a Cause*, is aligned with Shakespeare's need to keep changing style ... to keep surprising the audience, to keep ahead of them.'[28] But for all its jarring dislocations in space and time, Luhrmann's rapidly shifting *mise-en-scène* cannot 'keep ahead' of the legend, which returns with a vengeance in the film's conclusion. Set to the Liebestod, or 'Love-Death', from Wagner's *Tristan and Isolde*, the penultimate scene of Luhrmann's adaptation takes place, appropriately, in the Sagrado Corazon or Cathedral of the Sacred Heart. As Romeo (Leonardo DiCaprio) proceeds methodically toward the nave of the Church, the path he treads is spectacularly lined by neon blue crosses, leading him towards his final sight of Juliet (Claire Danes) at rest in a sea of candles and Mary figurines. Significantly, the camera remains relatively static at this juncture, as if deferring to the montage effects inherent in Shakespeare's own poetry. Indeed, Romeo experiences a disturbing ontological collision between death and beauty as both vie for prominence in Juliet's face, leading him to the impossible conclusion: 'Shall I believe | That unsubstantial death is amorous, | And that the lean abhorred monster keeps | Thee here in dark to be his paramour?' (5.3.102–5). Seeking a swift solution to an equation that doesn't

[28] Quoted in Pauline Adamek, 'Baz Luhrmann's *William Shakespeare's Romeo + Juliet*', *Cinema Papers* (February 1997), 1–14 (14).

add up, Romeo resolves to drink the apothecary's potion, failing to notice the signs of Juliet waking. Hence, in the very instant that he consumes the poison, Juliet dashes the vial from his lips when it is—just barely—too late. Forced to watch Romeo die before her eyes, Juliet, suddenly all alone in the enormous cathedral, sobs once, recognizing—as a mere teenager—that her only option is to find life in death, a literalization of the Liebestod. Mimicking Isolde's final effort to imagine Tristan's apotheosis before expiring with grief, Juliet pauses to look upwards as if to imagine Romeo's ascension, and then abruptly shoots herself in the head.

In seeking to elude Shakespeare's ending, Luhrmann is punished for his hubris, for in so doing, he recreates an earlier and, arguably, more painful version of the tragedy featured in the work of Mateo Bandello and Luigi Da Porto. In both cases, Juliet awakens to find Romeo in his death throes. Nevertheless, as the camera cranes higher and higher over the lovers' gracefully draped bodies, Luhrmann ventures a final attempt to subvert the legend by resorting—of all things—to *continuity* montage. In classical realist fashion, Luhrmann smoothly choreographs a series of flashbacks to Romeo and Juliet's courtship, seamlessly reconstituting their entire affair as if he were hoping to arrest time—a phenomenon that Bazin refers to as 'change mummified'.[29] Appropriately, then, as Wagner's aria resolves into an exquisite major chord, the camera freezes on Romeo and Juliet's iconic underwater kiss from the balcony scene—an image that allows us to glimpse an alternative ending. Although the slow fade to white that follows the montage convinces the audience that the film is over, it is not long before the white screen collides with a far more prosaic vision of the lovers' cheap cotton shrouds, as emergency workers load the corpses into ambulances. Bypassing the reconciliation scene between the two families, *William Shakespeare's Romeo + Juliet* leaves us with the dystopian conclusion that, in the end, Romeo + Juliet add up to nothing at all.

CONCLUSION: POST-REALISM IN DEEPA MEHTA'S *WATER* (2005)

> It is art's task to make manifest the contradictions
> of Being. To form equitable views by stirring up
> contradictions within the spectator's mind, and to
> forge accurate intellectual concepts from the
> dynamic clash of opposing passions.
>
> (Sergei Eisenstein)

Writing a decade and a half before Bazin, Eisenstein observed that '[a]bsolute realism is by no means the correct form of perception', for '[s]uch an approach overrules dialectical development, and dooms one to mere evolutionary "perfecting"'.[30] The goal of dialectical

---

[29] Bazin, 'The Ontology of the Photographic Image', 162.
[30] Eisenstein, *Film Form*, 35, 37.

filmmaking is not to resolve contradictions through the synthesis of opposites but rather to expose the means by which emergent and, often, imperfect structures of thinking can subvert sociopolitical continuity effects, such as race, class, and gender oppression. What, then, is *post*-realism? A theory developed in the context of international relations, post-realism is a movement that contests the naturalization of difference and its corresponding inequities, recognizing that the ongoing institutionalization of gender (and other) hierarchies excludes women and cultural minorities from intellectual and political power. Realism, in this context, is based on the Enlightenment principles of 'instrumental reason, binary logic, and positivist science', all of which conspire 'to impose, legitimize, and reproduce systematic inequalities'.[31] As V. Spike Peterson contends, '[a]lthough realism has never represented an accurate "story of the world" (no story can make that claim), the representation it reifies has concrete effects'.[32] Be it state-making or filmmaking, then, this is what we might think of as the social application of Bazinian realism, which occludes considerations of multiple, competing realities, while eclipsing viable alternatives to state-sanctioned ideological production. More than any other film explored here, Deepa Mehta's *Water* restores the Romeo and Juliet legend to its origins as a story of political crisis in ways that are decidedly post-realist.

Like Eisenstein, whose films were created to express opposition to the totalitarianism of the State and the perpetuation of class struggle, Mehta, too, has made it her life's work to voice opposition to the state-sanctioned oppression of women in Hindu society. The first film in her elemental trilogy, *Fire*—a story about a lesbian relationship between two women in a loveless joint marriage—was considered so controversial that enraged citizens burned down the cinema that first screened it. Mehta's next film, *Earth*, which focused on the race riots and ethnic cleansing that occurred during the partition of India in 1947, drew the wrath of Hindus, Muslims, and Sikhs alike. But *Water*, set in 1938 during India's battle for independence and the rise of Gandhi, is far and away the most subversive film in the trilogy. *Water* is focused on the plight of widows who, according to Hindu scriptures more than 2000 years old, have only three options when their husbands die: one is to marry their husband's younger brother, the other is to burn themselves on their husband's funeral pyre (a ritual known as *suttee*), and the third is to enter an ashram, a 'home' in which women and girls are cut off from the rest of society and shunned as pariahs. In the ashram, widows are forced to have their heads shaved and to wear a white sheet to signify atonement for their husband's deaths; subjected to both menial and sexual labour, their work is rewarded by a single meal each day.

Into this dysfunctional environment, Mehta's *Water* inserts a Romeo and Juliet story that revolves around a forbidden relationship between Narayan, a political idealist from the exclusive Brahmin caste, and Kalyani, a beautiful widow who, unlike any of the others, is allowed to keep her long hair—not for the sake of her personal dignity but so she can be sold to clients. Appropriately, an early encounter between Narayan and Kalyani is reimagined as a version of the balcony scene. As Kalyani and Chuyia (the child bride whom she takes under her wing) wring out sheets from the ashram's balcony, Narayan, who has been denied access to Kalyani by Madhu, the ashram's manager and procuress, is the recipient of the unintended

---

[31] V. Spike Peterson, 'The Gender of Rhetoric, Reason, and Realism', in Francis A. Beer and Robert Hariman, eds., *Post-Realism: The Rhetorical Turn in International Relations* (East Lansing: Michigan State University Press, 1996), 257–75 (268).

[32] Peterson, 'The Gender of Rhetoric, Reason, and Realism', 259.

shower. Literalizing Romeo's 'new baptism', Narayan's dousing underscores the fact that both he and Kalyani experience love at first sight as transformative, awakening their desire to be with each other at all costs. But water is also the force that separates the would-be lovers, for Narayan lives on the other side of the Ganges in a world characterized by a suffocating sense of privilege and elitism. When Narayan arrives back home, his friend Rabindra quotes Shakespeare in his greeting: 'Romeo! Oh Romeo! Wherefore art thou Romeo?' Perturbed by his friend's cynical sense of humour, Narayan complains to Rabindra that he doesn't know how he'll ever see Kalyani again. 'Stand beneath her balcony', Rabindra exclaims: 'but don't quote Shakespeare. People here don't know Shakespeare.'

To the contrary, the history of both theatrical and cinematic adaptations of Shakespeare runs very deep in India, and Mehta's spinoff constitutes another provocative reworking of the Romeo and Juliet legend. The critical difference between Mehta's film and Shakespeare's play is the fate of the lovers, for whereas Kalyani dies for love, Narayan lives for revolution as an Indian nationalist and disciple of Gandhi. After the unexpected passage of a law that allows widows to remarry, Kalyani and Narayan, like Romeo and Juliet, arrange to marry each other. Despite being admonished by his friends and family, who attempt to persuade him that marrying a widow will bring shame on the family, Narayan remains fixed in his devotion. Meanwhile, Kalyani has her head shaved in retribution by Madhu, who punishes her for seeking to escape the ashram. Undeterred, the lovers set out as planned to cross the Ganges, heading toward Narayan's home on the other side. But halfway through their journey, Kalyani glimpses the mansion in the distance, suddenly recognizing that Narayan's father has been one of her regular clients. She orders the boatman to turn around and, when Narayan questions her, Kalyani replies, simply, "Ask your father." These are her last words in the film. Forced by a patriarchal legend to live in a world that makes her die daily from the inside out, Kalyani returns to the ashram and undertakes a ritual cleansing—a ceremony that culminates in her decision to wade back into the Ganges. Refusing to conform to the systems that render her meaningless, Kalyani walks toward Narayan until she disappears beneath the water's surface.

As the final title card makes painfully clear, the 'legend' in *Water* materializes in the 200-year-old assertion that gender oppression is justifiable according to the joint prerogatives of the State and institutionalized religion: 'There are over 34 million widows in India according to the 2001 census. Many continue to live in conditions of social, economic and cultural deprivation as prescribed 2000 years ago by the Sacred Texts of Manu.'

Predictably, citizens were so outraged by the premise of the film alone that, on the eve of the very first shoot, two thousand protestors burned the set to the ground, throwing its remains into the Ganges while calling for the director's death—an incident that led Mehta herself to experience an ontological shiver of the first order. Although shooting began with the help of heavily armed anti-riot squads, it was abruptly halted by the intervention of the government only two takes into the opening frames. Threatening to arrest the crew for eroding Hindu values, authorities forced the production out of the country.

Driven by her conviction that 'Art is political and should be political',[33] Mehta eventually completed the film in Sri Lanka. Beyond the technical achievements that earned

---

[33] Nyay Bhushan, 'Salman Rushdie, Deepa Mehta: Movies Not to Blame for Real-World Violence (Q&A)', http://www.hollywoodreporter.com/news/salman-rushdie-deepa-mehta-movies-416776.

Water an Academy Award nomination for Best Foreign Film—exquisite shot composition, lighting, camerawork, and locations—Mehta's film is also distinctly Shakespearean in its persistent comingling of extreme tragedy with surpassing beauty. In fact, the oppositional realism that the film embraces is equally Eistensteinian in its insistence that it 'is art's task to make manifest the contradictions of Being'. More than a variation on the *Romeo and Juliet* theme, then, *Water* circles back to the work of the Russian masters, who remind us, in Grigori Kozintsev's words, that 'the study of Shakespeare is not like the gradual erection of a brick wall'; it is, rather, about the recognition that '[w]e achieve knowledge in conflict and struggle'.[34] Seeking to dismantle the walls, brick-by-brick, that bar women from achieving full 'personhood'—in both India and, for the matter, the US[35]—*Water* is a post-realist intervention that steps across the proverbial 'fourth wall' into our own cultural moment, imploring us to recognize that living with irreconcilable contradictions is a precondition of subverting legendary acts of inhumanity.

SELECT BIBLIOGRAPHY

Ball, Robert Hamilton, *Shakespeare on Silent Film: A Strange Eventful History* (London and New York: Routledge, 2013).

Bazin, Andre, *What is Cinema?*, vol.1, trans. Hugh Gray (Berkeley and London: University of California Press, 1967).

Braudy, Leo, and Marshall Cohen, eds., *Film Theory and Criticism*, 7th edn. (New York and Oxford: Oxford University Press, 2009).

Charnes, Linda, *Notorious Identity: Materializing the Subject in Shakespeare* (Cambridge and London: Harvard University Press, 1993).

Eisenstein, Sergei, *Film Form* (New York and London: Harcourt Brace & Company, 1949).

Jackson, Russell, *Shakespeare Films in the Making: Vision, Production and Reception* (Cambridge: Cambridge University Press, 2007).

Jorgens, Jack, *Shakespeare on Film* (Lanham, MD: University Press of America, 1991).

Kozintsev, Grigori, *Shakespeare: Time and Conscience* (New York: Hill and Wang, 1966).

Lehmann, Courtney, *Romeo and Juliet: The Relationship between Text and Film*. Methuen Series in Drama (London: A. & C. Black, 2010).

Liehm, Mira, *Passion and Defiance: Film in Italy from 1942 to the Present* (Berkeley and London: University of California Press, 1984).

Ortiz, Joseph, *Broken Harmony: Shakespeare and the Politics of Music*(Ithaca and London: Cornell University Press, 2011).

Peucker, Brigitte, *The Material Image: Art and the Real in Film* (Stanford, CA: Stanford University Press, 2007).

[34] Grigori Kozintsev, *Shakespeare: Time and Conscience* (New York: Hill and Wang, 1966), 132.

[35] In the ongoing battle in the US over women's reproductive rights, 'personhood' legislation—recently passed in several states under Republican control—is the most insidious threat to women's lives. According full legal status to zygotes but not to the bodies that harbour them, personhood legislation—in its extreme application—has resulted in murder charges for women who suffer miscarriages.

CHAPTER 35

....

HAMLET
Tragedy and Film Adaptation

....

DOUGLAS LANIER

SHAKESPEAREAN tragedy and film have never quite fitted comfortably together. Shakespearean tragedy is a medium of the word, its signature motif the soliloquy, its strength characterological interiority; film is a medium of image and action, its strength plot and *mise-en-scène*. In Shakespearean tragedy, characters readily unpack their hearts in language; since at least the advent of method acting, film characters tend to indicate emotion through verbal inexpressivity, the extent to which words fail to reveal—or actively cover over—interior states revealed through facework and action. The dominant aesthetic of film is photo-realistic, that is, its nature is indexical, specific in its fictional reality; the suspension of disbelief allows theater to work more suggestively, somewhere between the concrete and the abstract. Stage tragedy's high style and high-born protagonists are at odds with the colloquial idiom of mainstream film and its fascination with the anti-hero or with the plight of the ordinary man. Commercial film is typically oriented towards some final affirmation, even where that 'happy ending' is laced with loss, regret, or moral qualification, whereas tragedy demands a devastating confrontation with pain, fate and terrifying self-knowledge. Mainstream film's dominant genres are variations on epic and romance, tales of heroic action set in picturesque locales, or tales in which the protagonist makes a journey of self-discovery and self-reform, genres at some odds with the trajectories of Shakespearean tragedy.[1] Adapting Shakespearean tragedy to film, then, is not just a matter of 'opening up' the theatrical text to real locales. Rather, it involves different strategies for bringing Shakespeare and the formal, generic, and ideological protocols of film into some sort of alignment.

Such strategies are certainly at work in film versions of *Hamlet*, one of cinema's favourite Shakespeare plays to adapt. Speaking very generally, *Hamlet* films have tended to conceptualize tragedy in one of two ways. The predominant approach has been to follow the lead of A. C. Bradley and treat the Hamlet story as a tragedy of character. Hamlet is presented

---

[1] Harry Keyishian stresses that film genres not only provide bodies of formal conventions, but also dictate 'the psychology and philosophy of an artwork', ('Shakespeare and Movie Genre: The Case of *Hamlet*', in *The Cambridge Companion to Shakespeare on Film*, ed. Russell Jackson (Cambridge: Cambridge University Press 1990). 72–85 (75)).

as a potentially heroic figure hobbled by a character flaw that renders him incapable of completing revenge. Since Olivier's 1948 film, that character flaw has been often inflected through Oedipal psychology; even where it has not, many filmmakers both conventional and avant-garde have treated the tale of Hamlet as a psychological study. This approach dovetails with the shape of cinematic romance, portraying Hamlet as coming to some form of self-recognition and reform of his psychological fault and acting heroically in the final reel. The other approach has been to treat Hamlet as the tragedy of society, in which Hamlet resists a corrupt regime headed by Claudius. In this approach Hamlet's tragedy takes the form of martyrdom at the hands of a social system he opposes but cannot ultimately defeat. *Hamlet* films that adopt this strategy have qualities of the cinematic epic, though they often interpret Hamlet as a *film noir* anti-hero, one who risks compromising his nobility by pursuing vengeance. Such films also share affinities with satire, for they anatomize the oppressive qualities of their versions of Elsinore. In practice many filmmakers have combined elements of both approaches, sometimes to the detriment of their films' coherence. Nevertheless, these two strategies—the 'psychological' and the 'political'—form the predominant paradigms through which filmmakers have to date conceptualized Hamlet's tragedy. Space prohibits me from addressing the full history of *Hamlet* on film; I've also excluded televisual *Hamlet*s, for they involve rather different formal and ideological concerns. In what follows, I have singled out the most prominent screen *Hamlet*s for extended discussion, treating them as exemplary of the major approaches to adapting *Hamlet* to the screen.

'THE STAMP OF ONE DEFECT': CINEMATIC TRAGEDIES OF CHARACTER

One tried-and-true means to adapt *Hamlet* to film is make Shakespeare's play a tale of Hamlet's personal struggle for psychological autonomy or authenticity amidst an oppressive family or society. Often, though not always, this crisis is filtered through Oedipal dynamics, with the false father Claudius serving as Hamlet's principal nemesis, rival for the affections of Gertrude who has betrayed him by falling under Claudius' spell. By stressing the element of personal crisis, this species of film *Hamlet* can conform loosely to the conventions of domestic and romantic melodrama—among commercial cinema's favourite, most flexible and recognizable genres—and the story arc allows Hamlet to experience a moment of psychological triumph before he dies in the final reel, thereby satisfying the demand for some form of affirmation. To varying degrees, these films tend to treat the *mise-en-scène* as symbolic of Hamlet's inner state, and so they are particularly attracted to shadowy or cavernous spaces or compositional disequilibrium to communicate the prince's troubled, alienated psychology. In this approach we can discern two genealogical lines. In the first, the Oedipal nature of Hamlet's psychological crisis is overt. This set of films can trace its lineage from Laurence Olivier's *Hamlet* (1948), in many ways still *the* canonical film adaptation of the play. This group includes Claude Chabrol's *Ophélia* (1963, a film which directly cites Olivier's), Franco Zeffirelli's *Hamlet* (1989), Roger Allers and Rob Minkoff's animated *The Lion King* (1994), and Yim Ho's *Tianguo Niezi* (*The Day*

The Sun Went Cold, 1995), among others. Also belonging to this group is Edgar Ulmer's *Strange Illusion* (1945), a low-budget *film noir* that predates Olivier's *Hamlet* by three years. The other genealogical line of screen *Hamlets* focuses on Hamlet's struggle for personal or existential authenticity, a struggle less bound up with Oedipal dynamics. The Hamlet of these films often struggles to maintain a truth to himself in a psychologically or culturally hostile environment. Not surprisingly, many of these screen adaptations are products of a 1960s sensibility, and their concerns shade into the realm of cultural politics. This group includes John Gielgud's *Hamlet* (1964, starring Richard Burton), Tony Richardson's *Hamlet* (1969), Celestino Coronado's *Hamlet* (1976), and Kenneth Branagh's *In the Bleak Midwinter* (1995).

Laurence Olivier's 1948 adaptation has cast an extraordinarily long shadow over film adaptations of *Hamlet*. The film begins with an overtly Bradleian gesture, in which Olivier in voice-over attributes Hamlet's fall to a single character flaw ('this is the tragedy of a man who could not make up his mind'). Olivier gives this gesture Shakespearean warrant by quoting from Q2 (18.7–8, 11–15, 17, 19–20). Hamlet's character flaw instantly takes on the quality of fate, for as these words are uttered, we see the dead prince borne on a bier, the tragic end to which his 'stamp of one defect' will inevitably lead. Olivier also establishes the expressionistic qualities of the *mise-en-scène* on which later psychological *Hamlets* would ring variations—shadowy lighting, maze-like architecture, psychologically freighted objects or spaces like the throne, bed, or great room on which the camera lingers. Olivier's treatment of the castle draws upon the Gothic novel tradition where the dark past of a family haunts the lives of those in the present, as well as the iconography of horror film.

Olivier credits Ernest Jones's expansion of Freud's comments on Hamlet[2] as source for his Oedipal approach. Jones argued that Hamlet's delay for revenge springs from the fact that because he is erotically attached to his mother and unconsciously identifies with his uncle, who has done what Hamlet secretly wants to do—kill the father and replace him in his mother's affections. To kill Claudius implicates Hamlet's own Oedipal desire. What's more, Claudius has become for Hamlet a new father-figure, a new source of paternal repression against the son's desire.[3] Olivier pares down the cast—no Fortinbras, no Rosencrantz and Guildenstern—to focus on the central Oedipal triangle. Claudius is introduced with a riot of Freudian imagery—cups being emptied, phallic cannons blasting, swords held erect behind him. He parades like a Henry VIII wannabe, hands on his belt, arms akimbo, crown cocked back. After paddling palms with Claudius, Gertrude dotes on Hamlet, feeding his erotic attachment to her, her plea to the prince punctuated with an over-long kiss. Throughout, Hamlet pouts like a wounded lover, delivering his soliloquy in a languid voice-over, slouching in his chair.

Indeed, impotent lassitude is the hallmark of Olivier's Hamlet in the film's first half. He is literally laid out on the floor during his two confrontations with the ghost; the heartbeat

---

[2] Jones's reading of *Hamlet* was first published in 1910 in *The American Journal of Psychology*, and later twice expanded, in 1923 as a chapter in his *Essays in Applied Psycho-analysis*, and as the book *Hamlet and Oedipus*, published in 1949.

[3] For a detailed psychoanalytic reading, one that includes attention to Olivier's own psychobiography, see Peter Donaldson, *Shakespearean Films/ Shakespearean Directors*. Boston: Unwin Hyman, 1990), 31–67.

effect that marks the ghost's appearances suggests that at these moments we have moved into Hamlet's deepest subconscious, where the command to revenge leads to Oedipal impasse and so inaction. Lassitude pervades Olivier's handling of the play's most famous soliloquy. On the parapet where he first encountered the ghost, Hamlet contemplates suicide by tossing himself into the sea. Daringly, the camera penetrates his skull to reveal the roaring ocean that he sees, emblem of his psychological turmoil. But that turmoil never translates to action. When the camera pulls back, Hamlet delivers the speech in a languid pose and at a languorous pace; as he speaks, his dagger slips from his limp fingers into the sea. Walking near the parapet's edge and contemplating the fog below, he literally 'turn[s] awry' and descends stairs, only to end up, after a fade, once again slouching in his chair, now in the dark.

Despite this barrage of psychologically loaded images, Hamlet's indecision seems linked to Oedipal issues only in the film's first half, though Hamlet's bedchamber encounter with his mother suggests his acknowledgement of Oedipal attachment to his mother and a subsequent 'return of normalcy to their relationship'.[4] What lifts Hamlet out of his torpor is the arrival of the players. Theatrical performance gives Hamlet the means by which he can indirectly challenge paternal injunction and find the name of action.[5] He comes alive in the players' presence, spinning a pirouette as he announces 'the play's the thing | Wherein I'll catch the conscience of the King' (2.2.581–2). At *The Mousetrap*, he exudes new-found vigour. During the play his gaze, along with Horatio's, directs the eyes of the court to Claudius who exits, covering his eyes as if blinded like Oedipus, while Hamlet struts, standing on the king's throne, phallic torch in hand, no longer the castrated son. Henceforth, Hamlet seems newly capable of action, particularly if that action is associated with grand theatricality, a quality which, incidentally, photographs well. The duel scene suggests the growing conjunction of theatricality and action in Hamlet's psyche. The duel is conducted in the very space where *The Mousetrap* was performed before another court audience, and it replays an interplay of gazes that eventually focus on Claudius. Hamlet dispatches Claudius with an extravagantly theatrical gesture, diving from the parapet like a swashbuckler, the kind of leap he could not bring himself to make in the 'to be or not to be' sequence. Despite its Oedipal overlay, the arc of Olivier's Hamlet conforms to the conventional cinematic narrative in which an initially reluctant hero discovers his mettle and confronts the villain.

Zeffirelli's 1989 film returns to the Oedipal scenario explored in Olivier's film, configuring it more along classic Freudian lines, with Hamlet enraged by his mother's betrayal of old Hamlet by her marriage to Claudius. The film's visual prologue, old Hamlet's funeral, stresses one new element in the prince's psychology, the idealization of his dead father. An Oedipal triangle is formed around the body of old Hamlet, with Claudius asking Hamlet to 'think of us | As of a father' (1.2.106–7) and catching the eye of weeping Gertrude. Seeing this first hint of a relationship soon to be revealed as fully erotic, Hamlet exits the family crypt, horrified at his mother's betrayal of himself and his lionized father. When Hamlet

---

[4] Samuel Crowl, *Shakespeare's Hamlet: The Relationship between Text and Film* (London: Bloomsbury, 2014), 55.

[5] Following Ernest Jones, Patrick Cook argues that Olivier's Hamlet sees fictional killing onstage in The Mousetrap as 'an equivalent for fulfilling his task' (*Cinematic Hamlet: The Films of Olivier, Zeffirelli, Branagh, and Almereyda* (Athens, OH: Ohio University Press, 2011, 41)).

returns to the crypt for 'to be or not to be,' the central issue is again idealization of his father and the degrading 'afterlife' his father faces in the present, replaced and forgotten, surrounded by rotting corpses in the shadows. Gertrude's treatment of Hamlet in the 'I know not seems' scene suggests that Hamlet has heretofore served as her emotional focus, so the transfer of her affections to Claudius is deeply traumatic for her son, even though he submits to Gertrude's will when she embraces and kisses him. Hamlet's rage at his mother's betrayal of his beloved father is also rage at her betrayal of himself.

Zeffirelli weds this Oedipal scenario, seemingly incongruously, with the generic contours of the action film, casting action star Mel Gibson in the title role and paring down the soliloquies radically. Action films, so popular in the muscular Reagan/Thatcher 1980s, ultimately trace their lineage to the conventions of revenge tragedy (minus the tragedy), and so Zeffirelli's action treatment is at once a bid for box-office appeal at a time when screen Shakespeare was out of favour, a return of action film to its roots (and a restoration of its tragedy), and qualified resistance to the notion that Hamlet is constitutionally incapable of action. Like Martin Riggs from *Lethal Weapon* (1987), a role Gibson also played, Gibson's Hamlet must overcome a psychological trauma to become a successful hero. Zeffirelli adds a paranoid element by emphasizing the game of surveillance and counter-surveillance between Hamlet and his father-figure adversaries, Claudius and Polonius, an element consistent with both the action genre and the Oedipal scenario. Hamlet's problem is not action—he is not delayed, as is Olivier's Hamlet, by Oedipal intimidation or by excessive contemplativeness, for Zeffirelli severely crops the prince's soliloquies. The issue is opportunity, compounded by Hamlet's desire to preserve his relationship with his mother. Like Riggs, Hamlet pretends madness as a strategy for navigating danger, though that madness is coloured by his unresolved Oedipal crisis.

Two moments propel Hamlet into his role as action hero. The first is Claudius' unwitting revelation of his guilt at *The Mousetrap*. As he watches Gonzago pouring poison into the Player King's ear, Claudius unconsciously covers his own ear with his hand, as if recognizing that he now occupies the position of father-king and so has become the object of assassination. Though he tries to recover his mask of the smiling monarch, this primal scene is too much and he rushes away. The second and more crucial pivotal moment is the closet scene. Here Hamlet's simmering Oedipal fury is finally expressed directly to Gertrude and purged, their bond re-established. The golden light of her chamber, so different from Elsinore's icy light elsewhere, communicates the warmth Hamlet associates with her love. As the confrontation between prince and mother escalates into quasi-sexual assault, Gertrude gives her son a long kiss, in effect re-establishing Hamlet as her beloved and resolving his Oedipal crisis. At the scene's end, Gertrude pledges to be faithful to Hamlet, and thereafter mother and son emerge as a kind of conspiratorial team, the equivalent of bickering cops who unite for a climactic confrontation of their nemesis. This renewed relationship threatens Claudius' position within Gertrude's affections, and that threat becomes his principal motive for his scheming in the duel scene. Because, Claudius reveals to Laertes, the queen so adores Hamlet that 'as the star moves not but in his sphere' (4.7.15), the scenario he devises is designed so that 'even his mother shall uncharge the practice | And call it accident' (4.7.65–6).

In many action films, the protagonist's vengeance involves collateral damage. Zeffirelli draws attention to the victims of Hamlet's revenge and his lack of remorse for them, particularly Polonius, Rosencrantz, and Guildenstern. Most troubling is Ophelia's fate, intercut with the Rosencrantz and Guildenstern sequence. In Zeffirelli's film, women's pursuit of romantic desires ultimately leads to tragedy. Ophelia cannot cope with the misogyny Hamlet directs her way, a misogyny rooted in Hamlet's Oedipal jealousy of his mother. At first, her insanity takes the form of provocation: she comes on to an embarrassed guard, madly playing out her thwarted desire. Later at court, it becomes clear that she is torn between erotic desire (revealed in her songs) and grief for her father (killed by the man she desires). Without Hamlet's option of revenge, however, she mentally implodes, eventually escaping from confinement and finding freedom in suicide. Though Hamlet causes Ophelia's downfall, it is Gertrude who most registers her tragedy, relating the details of her drowning as if they were a premonition of her own death.

At the duel, Zeffirelli dwells upon the pyrrhic nature of Hamlet's ostensible moment of triumph. Hamlet goes into the duel knowing that it is a sinister set-up; as the sun sets, he voices readiness to face his uncle's machinations, quietly, heroically confident. During the duel itself, glances between Hamlet and Gertrude register their mother–son bond. Zeffirelli devotes equal screen time to their deaths, suggesting that we are watching a double tragedy, the demise of an Oedipal unit. Once the queen drinks the poison, Zeffirelli lingers on her realization that Claudius is the murderous villain her son has long perceived him to be. Finally fully identifying with Hamlet, she pays the price for their relationship, dying on the line 'oh, my dear Hamlet' (5.2.252). It is Claudius' murder of his mother, Hamlet's love interest, that motivates the savagery of his attack on the king. Claudius and Gertrude gone, Hamlet crumples, his revenge complete, but his heroic stature is hardly celebrated: there is no salute of soldiers, no procession. Zeffirelli portrays Elsinore as an insular medieval enclave, scrubbing Shakespeare's script of references to Fortinbras or broader political contexts. As the film ends the citizens of Elsinore look on the pile-up of royal bodies in stunned silence. Hamlet's Oedipal crisis is resolved at the kingdom's expense, for there is no one to take the throne. There is only the elegiac retreat of the camera, registering the tragic social costs of Hamlet's family romance.

Tony Richardson's 1969 film exemplifies a somewhat different psychological approach to *Hamlet*, one rooted in the counter-cultural spirit of the 1960s—the struggle of a rebellious youth for moral integrity and psychological stability against the forces of bourgeois conventionality embodied in the family. This approach first appeared on film in John Gielgud's 1964 *Hamlet*, a stage production later filmed television-style and briefly released theatrically. In it Richard Burton played Hamlet as an 'angry young man' directing his fury against his unctuously middle-class uncle and mother. Richardson's film too had its origins in a stage production, but he reconceptualized the production specifically for the camera, creating an extraordinarily intimate experience by shooting almost entirely in close-ups and medium shots and framing tightly, with action near the viewer in the foreground. This approach focuses us on personal relationships divorced from larger political concerns (even though references to Fortinbras remain). Though this was the first colour film of *Hamlet*, it might as well have been filmed in black and white, for the *mise-en-scène* is relentlessly dark and often cavernous, peppered with a few objects to establish particular settings, with Hamlet's face in close-up against the shadowy background.

This dark background suggests that Hamlet's struggle against mother and uncle is also a struggle against a pervading existential void that only he and perhaps Ophelia recognize as troubling. Claudius and Gertrude seem content to pursue mindless sensual pleasures, unencumbered by reflection, moral scruples about their incestuous marriage or any interest in politics. The two epitomize the unexamined life, a fact that Richardson underlines with his handling of 2.2, a reprise of the notorious eating scene in his *Tom Jones* (1963). As Polonius theorizes about Hamlet's madness, Claudius and Gertrude, uninterested, snack and smooch in bed. Nicol Williamson's quick-witted Hamlet, by contrast, is racked with angst coloured with cynicism, bitterness, and self-loathing. His statement 'I have that within which passeth show' (1.2.85), delivered against a grey void, declares his existential integrity. In 'to be or not to be' he engages in painful self-examination, musing about death as a release from angst and concluding that angst is the unavoidable condition of life: uncertainty *'makes* us rather bear those ills we have | Than fly to others that we now not of' (3.1.83–4, Williamson's emphasis). Hamlet ends with a cynical chuckle, amused that he would even entertain the thought of escape from his condition. Richardson's handling of the ghost reinforces the theme of struggle for existential authenticity. Never seen directly, the ghost is a bright light reflected in the astounded faces of those who see it. This choice addresses the constraints of low-budget filming, but it also suggests that the ghost represents an otherworldly manifestation of pure meaning experienced only in moments of revelation. Once having been visited by it, Hamlet's struggle against Claudius becomes a matter of exposing his uncle's regime of hedonistic complacency and re-establishing a principle of authentic being in Denmark.

Repeatedly Hamlet brings Claudius and Gertrude into states of existential anguish. When confronted at *The Mousetrap* with the Player King and Queen's professions of faithfulness, Claudius and Gertrude's faces fall as they are reminded of the moral standard which they have forsaken. In Gertrude's bedchamber Hamlet ruthlessly plays the existential crusader. Forcing Gertrude away from the boudoir mirror where she composes her face, Hamlet stresses the shattering power of the inward moral gaze, determined 'to set up a glass | Where you may see the inmost part of you' (3.4.19–20). Slipping into tearful anguish, he forces Gertrude to look at old Hamlet's picture, her face falling into shame as he presses her—'have you eyes? … have you eyes?' (3.4.64, 66)—about her self-indulgent sensualism. Hamlet is himself overcome as he recognizes his responsibility for Polonius' death and, more generally, his condition of 'thrownness' in the universe:

> For this same lord,
> I do repent. But heaven hath pleased it so
> To punish me with this, and this with me,
> That I must be their scourge and minister.

(3.4.156–9)

The film's most intense moment of bonding occurs when Hamlet, begging Gertrude to abstain from Claudius' bed, promises to exchange blessings with her when she is 'desirous to be blest' (3.4.155)—they are revealed as two figures united by deeply painful moral self-examination and the experience of angst. Ophelia, eerily placid in her insanity, pursues the same confrontational mission as Hamlet, but through mad song and flowers, and she has the same effect on Gertrude, who lowers her head in shame in Ophelia's presence. By contrast, Claudius responds with a show of royal authority and manipulation of Laertes, as if the issue were merely a matter of public exposure, not self-examination. Richardson's handling of the duel scene frames Hamlet's revenge in terms of resignation to his existential condition. To Horatio's advice that he forego the duel, Hamlet looks directly at the camera, replying 'the readiness is all' (5.2.160), as if resigning himself to the absurdity of his fate: 'Since no man has aught of what he leaves, what is't to leave betimes? Let be' (5.2.160–1). Though the deaths by poison of Laertes, Gertrude and Claudius are painful and utterly unredemptive, Hamlet's death is almost peaceful, a slipping into the sleep he desired for himself in 'to be or not to be,' brought on by willingly quaffed poison. His final line, drawn out by Williamson's delivery ('the ... rest ... is ... silence,' 5.2.300), bespeaks acceptance of the existential void toward which Hamlet has always been projected in this film. Freezing the frame on Hamlet's dead face, Richardson dwells on this moment, eliminating any attention to the political aftermath of the Danish kingdom or, indeed, any heroic memorializing of the prince. The killing of the king leads Hamlet only to release from the regime of existential inauthenticity that the union of Gertrude and Claudius represents.

Other examples of this mode of reimagining Hamlet vary in their portrayal of his confrontation of forces that threaten his authentic self. In Celestino Coronado's avant-garde *Hamlet* (1976), Hamlet, a literally-split queer subject (he is played by twins), struggles against the tyranny of heteronormativity nightmarishly embodied by Claudius and Gertrude. In the end, Hamlet achieves a symbolic victory when in the duel scene he reconciles with Laertes and becomes a single character, but the film's final image is of Hamlet on a funereal slab, with the viewer unsure whether he is dreaming or dead. Branagh's *In the Bleak Midwinter* (1995), a comic backstage version of the play, imagines a no-budget Christmas production of *Hamlet* as the antidote for protagonist and wannabe actor Joe's melancholy regarding his failing career and the spiritually impoverished state of the arts in Britain. His show is an unexpected success and provides all involved with a rush of artistic integrity and family reconciliations, but in the end Joe remains out of work; as he tells his girlfriend, Molly, 'despite my immense purity of soul and being cleansed by my art, I'm still always going to get depressed and mad'. In both cases, passage through the *Hamlet* narrative offers a pointedly qualified, ultimately bittersweet experience of integrity.

'SOMETHING IS ROTTEN IN THE STATE OF DENMARK': TRAGEDY OF SOCIETY

A second major group of screen *Hamlet*s treats Shakespeare's tragedy primarily as a political tale and portrays Hamlet as a crusader against a corrupt regime, of which Claudius and Gertrude are symptomatic. Films in this group pit Hamlet, often the lone perceiver of injustice, against the larger social system of Elsinore (or Denmark)—a conflict which serves as a vehicle for directorial critique of various political, economic and technological orders. This group of films tends to preserve characters and incidents that more psychologically oriented *Hamlet*s cut in order to focus on family dynamics; indeed, Guntner has observed that one mark of politically inflected *Hamlet* films is that a Fortinbras figure is often included (121), though there are myriad exceptions to this truism. The focus often falls more on the mechanics of vengeance than on Hamlet's tortuous psychological struggles; Oedipal dynamics tend to be muted, the troubling marriage between Claudius and Gertrude lumped in with other moral failings. Makers of these films anatomize the immorality or corrupting influence that saturates an entire sociopolitical formation, not just the royal family. These films also often stress a generational divide: the younger generation, represented by Hamlet, is a harbinger of change from the ideological regime of the older generation, though Hamlet himself rarely gets to see the revolution he gestures toward. *Hamlet* films of this ilk tend to fall into two subcategories. One subset targets tainted political orders, states marked by tyranny, cronyism, aristocratic decadence, and pervasive injustice. Such films include Svend Gade's *Hamlet* (1921), Grigori Kozintsev's *Hamlet* (1964), Enzo Castellari's *Quella sporca storia nel west* (*Johnny Hamlet*, 1968), Kenneth Branagh's *Hamlet* (1996), Feng Xiaogang's *Yè Yàn* (*The Banquet*, 2006), and Vishal Bhardwaj's *Haider* (2014). Another group, arguably a subset of the former, takes aim at the sins of capitalism by imagining Elsinore as an unscrupulous business empire. This strain of *Hamlet* films includes Helmut Käutner's *Der Rest ist Schweigen* (*The Rest is Silence*, 1959), Akira Kurosawa's *Warui yatsu hodo yoku nemuru* (*The Bad Sleep Well*, 1960), Aki Kaurismaki's *Hamlet liikemaailmassa* (*Hamlet Goes Business*, 1987), and Stacy Title's *Let the Devil Wear Black* (1999). Though it falls outside either of these two subcategories, Alexander Fodor's quirky *Hamlet* (2007) fits the parameters of a cinematic tragedy of society, for it reimagines Elsinore as a hipper-than-thou yuppie social set covertly beset, as in a horror film, by the murderous ghost of old Hamlet.

Gyorgi Kozintsev's *Hamlet* (1964) exemplifies how Shakespeare's play might be conceptualized for film as a political drama. It rests firmly in the tradition of double-voiced dissident Eastern European and Soviet Shakespeare productions.[6] On one level Kozintsev's Hamlet plays as a crusader against crypto-Czarist Claudius and his elitist court, who are out of touch with the people outside the confines of Elsinore. On another level, Claudius plays as a Renaissance Stalin, a tyrant at the centre of a miniature police state, surrounded by yea-saying apparatchiks, spies, and superficially cultured courtiers. A fortress walled off from the world, Elsinore epitomizes the Soviet political system, of which Claudius is both leader and symptom. Hamlet emerges as a vanguard revolutionary, often pictured from behind or walled off by bars, silently resisting Claudius' regime. Hamlet's story thereby becomes the tragedy of the alienated philosopher-intellectual who can speak truth to power only indirectly, a martyr who paves the way for a revolution that appears only after his death. To underline the point visually, Kozintsev recodes Olivier's iconography. In his version the raging sea and the shadowy castle signify not Hamlet's psychology but political elements, the sea standing for revolutionary restlessness, the castle for the imposing, implacable edifice of the Soviet state. Throughout Hamlet is drawn to the sea, and some of his most important moments occur in its presence—his encounter with the ghost, 'to be or not to be'. The castle, like Olivier's, is maze-like and grand in its public spaces, and there Hamlet often walks alone amidst throngs of courtiers, pointedly against the flow of the crowd.

For this Hamlet, Denmark is indeed a prison, and so at the heart of his tragedy is his struggle to speak truth to totalitarian power. Accordingly, Innokenty Smoktunovsky's performance as Hamlet is extraordinarily buttoned-up. Aware he is being watched, he speaks his soliloquies in voice-over, his smouldering rage registering covertly with the symbolic fire he watches. Only when the players arrive does he find a means for attacking

---

[6] Tiffany Moore, *Kozintsev's Shakespeare Films: Russian Political Protest in* Hamlet *and* King Lear (Jefferson, NC: McFarland, 2012), 74-5.

Claudius obliquely with a play—a metaphor for Kozintsev's own film. Notably, the performance of *The Mousetrap* takes place overlooking the sea. Though Claudius exerts remarkable self-control over the public situation—he even applauds the performance—he
involuntarily exposes his guilt when Lucianus poisons the Player King, and afterwards
Hamlet becomes newly energized.

Whereas in the film's first half, Hamlet exudes a Dostoevskian quality—socially alienated, intensely private, and philosophical—after his mocking confrontation with his
mother, he becomes increasingly bold, an instrument of moral exhortation willing now to
act. Upon his return to Denmark, Hamlet undergoes a transformation, taking on the role
of the *yurodivy* of the Eastern Orthodox tradition, the holy fool who gives up luxury, acts
provocatively, and purveys wisdom through riddles, in this case commenting ironically
on the evanescence of past imperial regimes at Ophelia's graveside. For the duel scene,
Hamlet changes back again to the heroic black-clad prince. Each of these changes is occasioned by Hamlet's sight of a flying bird, symbol of Ophelia's spirit freed by her death
and of the Russian landscape.

Kozintsev's film has two endings. In the first, Hamlet, wounded at the duel, dies overlooking the sea, with the camera tracking right to a rock wall. This ending underlines the
tragic cost of Hamlet's revenge and hints at its futility, since the stone wall of state seems
unaffected. The second 'heroic' ending is ushered in by the sounds of hooves—the arrival
of Fortinbras's army, the engineers of revolution. Seeing the dead prince (and not crowning himself), Fortinbras directs Hamlet's body to be paraded before soldiers and citizens
as if he were the fatherland's hero, carrying him to the symbolic sea. These two endings
allow Kozintsev to treat Hamlet's tragedy as the martyrdom of a socially alienated intellectual in a totalitarian state who dies defending his own moral integrity. His death registers individually as a loss but collectively as a harbinger of revolution.[7]

Kenneth Branagh's *Hamlet* (1996)[8] reconceives the play as a political tragedy from
within the generic protocols of heritage film, fastening upon a past era at the moment
of its passing. By using an uncut First Folio text supplemented by the Second Quarto,
Branagh gives full rein to the play's political context, especially the rise of Fortinbras,
while treating *Hamlet* as the fall of an extended aristocratic family. The contrast with
Olivier's production is pointed: where his *Hamlet* offers a shadowy castle and brooding
interiority, Branagh offers an opulent, bright winter palace filled with nineteenth-century
period detail and behind-scenes scheming. The court of Elsinore has become insular and
preoccupied with noble display, a miniature world of smart military uniforms and fencing
lessons in an era of guns and power politics. Its spectacular stateroom, where Claudius

---

[7] Taylor and Kliman both read the film's second ending pessimistically, seeing Fortinbras's arrival
as the establishment of a 'new but equally oppressive regime' (Neil Taylor, 'The Films of *Hamlet*', in
Shakespeare and the Moving Image, ed. Anthony Davies and Stanley Wells (Cambridge: Cambridge
University Press, 1994), 180–95 (187); see also Bernice Kliman, *Hamlet: Film, Television and Audio
Performance*. Rutherford NJ: Fairleigh Dickinson University Press, 1988)). However, we never see
Fortinbras crowned, and Shostakovich's music for Hamlet's funeral procession suggests triumph,
not fatalism.

[8] Branagh's *Hamlet* exists in two versions, a four-hour theatrical release and a two-hour edit
for video. Here I discuss the longer version, though in general conception the two versions share
substantially the same vision of Hamlet's tragedy.

announces his marriage and Hamlet and Laertes fight their duel before gathered courtiers, exudes aristocratic grandeur. But appearances are deceptive. Behind its mirrored doors lies the court's less noble private life, where we catch glimpses of the hypocrisy, manipulation, and decadence through which the court actually operates.

At the centre of this social order is the epic father, emblematized by the larger-than-life statue of old Hamlet outside the palace gate.[9] Hamlet sees devotion to his father as a mark of his commitment to aristocratic ideals, and so Claudius's murder of old Hamlet violates the very principle that undergirds social order. Claudius's primary motive is envy of the position of patriarch, a role which he is not quite up to. Taking the throne by marrying Gertrude, Claudius is committed to maintaining Elsinore's aristocratic appearances, projecting gentlemanly bonhomie to the court and paternal sincerity to Hamlet, but he, the exemplar of the final, decadent generation of his class, does not exude old Hamlet's authority. Ironically, Fortinbras, portrayed as an ambitious general concerned more with extending his empire than avenging his father, emerges as the kind of epic warrior-king that Hamlet's father embodies. But Fortinbras's power comes not from patriarchal right but from the might of the faceless armies he commands; he signals the end of a social order founded upon familial bonds and the birth of the political mass-movements of modernity—Communism and Fascism. Throughout, Fortinbras's absent presence hangs over events at Elsinore, more than in any other film adaptation to date.

Branagh's ambivalence about the passing of the age of aristocrats is evident in his treatment of Hamlet. Branagh portrays him both as a crusader against the failings of the *ancien régime* (especially Claudius) and as the last true aristocratic hero. His Hamlet is not plagued by delay. With the exception of his 'to be or not to be', nearly all Hamlet's soliloquies in the film's first half become statements of heroic resolve, but at first much of his battle against the court involves shattering its polite decorum and Claudius' *sang-froid* with mad wit or fury, behaviour particularly on display at the performance of *The Mousetrap*. When Hamlet returns to Denmark and Fortinbras's forces near, Hamlet's relationship to the court at Elsinore becomes more complex. As he reflects upon the 'fine revolution' (5.1.82–3) at Ophelia's grave, Hamlet reveals a bittersweet recognition of the cycles of history and a wistful acceptance of the coming end of an era. This brave but melancholy resignation surfaces again when he claims 'the readiness is all' (5.2.160) and, with tears in his eyes, adds 'let be,' giving himself over regretfully to historical inevitability. Branagh juxtaposes the duel between Hamlet and Laertes, a ritual of honour that deteriorates into a brawl, against the march of Fortinbras's army, which mercilessly kills everyone in its path and breaks into the stateroom with brutal force—the last gasp of a deteriorated aristocratic order set against the arrival of mass society. The film's final moments emphasize the ambivalence of Hamlet's tragic achievement. The prince is buried as a grand aristocrat, in black military costume. But the same soldiers who surround his casket tear down the statue of his father, symbol of the lost patriarchal regime, obscuring the name 'Hamlet', destined *not* to be remembered.

---

[9] Lisa Starks argues that the idealization of the father and the absence of maternal bonding makes Branagh's film paradoxically 'the most "Oedipal" of all filmed *Hamlets*' ('The displaced body of desire: Sexuality in Kenneth Branagh's *Hamlet*', in *Shakespeare and Appropriation*, ed. Christy Desmet and Robert Sawyer (New York: Routledge, 1999), 160).

Michael Almereyda's *Hamlet* (2000) provides a fine example of business-oriented screen adaptations of the play, crossed with the conventions of the youth-oriented adaptations of the 1990s. 'Corporate *Hamlet*' adaptations reconceive the court of Elsinore as a modern, corrupt business empire, its power often linked to shady political connections (with Nazis in *The Rest is Silence*, with property developers in *Let the Devil Wear Black*) and contemporary media (the telephone, for example, figures largely in *The Rest is Silence* and *The Bad Sleep Well*). Almereyda's version addresses corporate media culture, a topic appropriate for a filmmaker associated with independent cinema. His Claudius (Kyle MacLachlan) is the new CEO of Denmark Corporation, a New York conglomerate, whom we meet giving a press conference. The lord of a mediatized world he controls, Claudius surrounds himself with bodyguards and surveillance cameras, and conducts business through media events, intermediaries, phone calls, and faxes. Yet he is only the smiling face of a vast corporate-media apparatus symbiotic with modern urban life. That apparatus is Hamlet's true enemy, and given its genius for appropriation, Hamlet struggles to find a form of oppositional action not already co-opted by corporate media. His weapon—film—is compromised from the start. A melancholy Gen-X recluse, Hamlet (Ethan Hawke) is as alienated from social contact as Claudius. He records soliloquies on film, discussing with himself his sense of lost direction, even flirting with suicide. Yet he is also a compulsive consumer of visual culture. The paradox of Hamlet's campaign against Claudius is that he conducts it largely through the very media culture he finds so oppressive. His weapons are low-rez (a child's Pixelvision camera) and local in reach, pitted against corporate media technology that extends everywhere. Hamlet's dilemma becomes clearest in his 'to be or not to be' in a Blockbuster video store. There, walking down the action film aisle, he passes rows of tapes, all commercial products that convert his desire for justice into empty entertainment. The sheer number of videos he confronts suggests the immensity of the corporate culture he faces, bringing him to despair toward the end of the speech. Ironically Hamlet's action takes the form of an avant-garde film, *The Mousetrap*, which he screens for Claudius and Gertrude. A collage of images culled from 1950s television, cartoons, silent films, and pornography, Hamlet's film targets both Claudius' violation of what Hamlet presents as an idyllic childhood and the 'phantom empire' (in Geoffrey O'Brien's phrase) of images embedded in the public imagination and controlled by corporate media. *The Mousetrap* illustrates the nature of Hamlet's tragedy in this film, for he is implicated in the media culture he pits himself against. He carves out his identity primarily through appropriation, and so has become unable to engage in direct action. The heir to Romantic Hamlets whose poetic sensibility rendered them incapable of pursuing revenge, Hawke's Hamlet struggles to move beyond isolation and world-weariness to action.

Commentators have noted that the duel scene—handled as a fencing match—fits rather poorly with the film's contemporary setting. However, Almereyda's approach is appropriate to the themes of the film, for Hamlet and Laertes are wired up to a scoring machine and press photographers are in attendance. Gertrude's tragedy figures prominently. When Claudius offers the poisoned wine to Hamlet, she guesses the plot and drinks willingly from the cup to protect her son. In this version Laertes' sword is not unbated and envenomed. Rather, pulling the pistol Hamlet used to kill Polonius, he shoots the prince and after a struggle is shot himself. Only when Laertes reveals Claudius' treachery, passes the pistol to Hamlet, and Horatio props up the wounded prince does Hamlet finally come to action and shoot the false king. This approach suggests the communal nature of the vengeance upon Claudius—this is a generational, not merely personal, act of retribution. When Hamlet asks Horatio to tell his story, what we see are Hamlet's memories in pixelvision flashing before his eyes as he dies, in effect the trailer for the film we have just seen. If the central issue of this *Hamlet* has been the imbrication of independent cinema in the corporate mediascape, this rush of images suggests that his filmmaking enterprise will find ameliorative purpose in someone else's hands (perhaps Almereyda's?) after his death.[10]

OPHELIA

Cinematic *Hamlet*s feature yet one more form of tragedy, one that cuts across the categories discussed above. That tragedy is the tale of Ophelia, a figure typically treated as tragic collateral damage in Hamlet's pursuit of psychological resolution or vengeance against the system. Ophelia is variously a victim of patriarchy, of political machinations, of Hamlet's misogyny, of romantic disappointment, but she is the play's most innocent victim, presented as a focus of pathos and harbinger of the court's tragedy-to-come. It is the rare cinematic *Hamlet–Ophélia, Hamlet Goes Business, The Lion King, Haider*—that accords her an active, agential role, though in some versions—Richardson's, Zeffirelli's, and Almereyda's—she acts as a provocateur amidst her madness, exposing the court's hypocrisy or shattering its decorum before meeting her death. Interestingly, though the character Ophelia is typically presented as 'pure' victim, she offers the actresses playing her the opportunity for tour-de-force acting, particularly in her mad scenes. Though Shakespeare only reports her tragic demise through Gertrude, directors have found irresistible the prospect of showing us her in death. Lingering images of her dead body under water have become a cinematic commonplace, though directors rarely resolve visually the question which hangs over her death: was it suicide or an accident? Rather, Ophelia becomes in death an object of deep pathos for the viewer's contemplation, a contrast in her complete tragic victimhood to Hamlet's often equivocal tragic fall, which involves some measure of psychological or moral triumph and anagnorisis in death.

ADAPTATION AS THEORY

Every film adaptation of *Hamlet* in effect offers its own theory of what makes the play tragic, but, as I've suggested, most are variants on two dominant cinematic theories of tragedy in *Hamlet*—the psychological and the political. Psychological films of *Hamlet* tend to view the play as the prince's *bildungsroman* and locate Hamlet's tragedy in his need to resolve his relationship to the father-figure, both a source of the law and a block to his desire. The bedchamber scene is often a treated as a critical moment in Hamlet's

---

[10] For a fuller reading of the film along this line, see Douglas Lanier, 'Shakescorp Noir', *Shakespeare Quarterly* 53:2 (2002), 157–80.

psycho-biographical development, when Hamlet engages most directly his fraught relationship with his mother. Understandably, such films typically pare away the political contexts of *Hamlet* to focus on family dynamics. They also tend to present Hamlet's psychoanalytic progress as ultimately successful, resulting in an anagnorisis that enables him to fulfil his heroic potential. Hamlet may lose his life, but he does so having defeated the false father Claudius and having established his capability to assume his position as father-king, though fate deprives him of the throne. The women of the play, particularly Ophelia, often suffer the full force of Hamlet's need to work his way through psychological crisis. This conception of the tragedy of *Hamlet* dovetails nicely with mainstream film genres like the family melodrama, the historical romance and the action film, which focus on the protagonist's negotiation of a personal trauma or psychological lack that blocks his ability to mature and complete a heroic task, and this conception also allows for the film to have a (qualified) happy ending, at least for Hamlet. Exceptions to this understanding of Hamlet's tragic arc are typically found in avant-garde films, in which Hamlet's psycho-biographical journey is presented as less than complete or as having not brought him to full heroic status.[11]

By contrast, films that stress the corruption of the system against which Hamlet pits himself tend to offer a much darker view of the play's tragedy. Drawing upon ideological orientations of *film noir*, some of which can be traced to *Hamlet*, such films tend to emphasize the vast, labyrinthine nature of the system against which Hamlet must struggle. Often portrayed in terms of *mise-en-scène*, that corrupt social system is epitomized by Claudius but it is by no means limited to him. In such films Hamlet is often portrayed as an anti-hero. The arc Hamlet typically travels is not one of psychological maturation as it is of knowledge—he comes to perceive the full pervasiveness of corruption around him. Moreover, directors of these adaptations often explore how Hamlet's righteous integrity is complicated by his being drawn into rage, violence, madness, paranoia, and recklessness. Striking too is the cynicism of these films' endings. If Hamlet does indeed make a blow against the system by killing Claudius, his own death typically leads to little change in the status quo. In those cases where Fortinbras arrives, the regime he establishes is not clearly better and often worse than the one he replaces, and so Hamlet's victory over Claudius, while striking a symbolic blow against the social order, in the end accomplishes little systemic change. It becomes thereby a pyrrhic statement of Hamlet's individual moral integrity. Kozintsev's film is a notable exception, though it redeems the value of Hamlet's sacrifice only by adding what amounts to a second ending. There is, I would argue, among these films a palpable loss of faith in tragedy as a social ritual in which shared guilt is acknowledged; the emphasis tends to remain individual, on Hamlet as revolutionary martyr.

These two approaches leave out a third possibility—a vision of *Hamlet* as a tragedy of fate, in which the prince's actions are framed by paradoxes of destiny and the caprice

---

[11] See e.g. Celestino Coronado's *Hamlet* (1976), in which a psychologically split gay Hamlet negotiates his relationship to heteronormativity, embodied by Gertrude and Claudius, a negotiation which takes the form of a cinematic nightmare, or Alexander Fodor's *Hamlet* (2007), in which the oppressively tyrannical old Hamlet takes ghostly revenge upon the entire court, extinguishing all the characters with frighteningly impassivity, even Horatio.

of supernatural forces. Western films have entirely eschewed this conception of the play, but a handful of recent film adaptations from Southeast Asia have considered it. Sherwood Hu's *Prince of the Himalayas*, a Tibetan adaptation from 2006, frames the tale of Prince Lhamoklodan/Hamlet's vengeance with a battle for supremacy between old Hamlet's spirit and a Tibetan wise-woman. Hu's variations upon Shakespeare's plot underline the deep ironies of Lhamoklodan's actions, the extent to which he is merely a vehicle for supernatural agendas of which he is not fully aware; his story, recast from a Buddhist sensibility, stresses the possibility of forgiveness over revenge, unforeseen familial renewal rather than destruction. *Karmayogi*, a Malayalam film from 2012, follows the Shakespearean narrative more closely, but by contextualizing it within Keralan ritual and the myth of Shiva, director V. K. Prakash emphasizes the supernatural and spiritual dimensions of Hamlet's progress from indecision to vengeance. These films suggest how global Shakespeare has begun to enrich and expand how *Hamlet* has been adapted to the screen.

The dominant approaches to screen *Hamlet* discussed here, the psychological and the political, are not necessarily mutually exclusive. It is a matter of emphasis rather than absolutes. Richardson's *Hamlet* gains political resonance from the social context it hints at, the youthful rebellion of the 1960s against the hedonistic complacency of the 1950s generation. Branagh's heritage tragedy *Hamlet* draws upon the figure of the idealized father familiar from psychological *Hamlets*. Nonetheless, these approaches have tended to remain relatively distinct in filmic adaptation of the play. A key challenge for filmmakers of the future is to find ways of bringing them into fuller dialogue, by consistently thinking through, as Shakespeare does in his tragedy, the relationship between Hamlet the son and Hamlet the revolutionary.

SELECT BIBLIOGRAPHY

Cook, Patrick J., *Cinematic Hamlet: The Films of Olivier, Zeffirelli, Branagh, and Almereyda* (Athens, OH: Ohio University Press, 2011).

Crowl, Samuel, *Shakespeare's Hamlet: The Relationship between Text and Film* (London: Bloomsbury, 2014).

Donaldson, Peter S., *Shakespearean Films/Shakespearean Directors* (Boston: Unwin Hyman, 1990).

Jorgens, Jack, *Shakespeare on Film* (Bloomington: Indiana University Press, 1977).

Keyishian, Harry, 'Shakespeare and Movie Genre: The Case of *Hamlet*', in *The Cambridge Companion to Shakespeare on Film*, ed. Russell Jackson (Cambridge: Cambridge University Press, 1990), 72–85.

Kliman, Bernice, *Hamlet: Film, Television and Audio Performance* (Rutherford NJ: Fairleigh Dickinson University Press, 1988).

Lanier, Douglas M., 'Shakescorp Noir', *Shakespeare Quarterly* 53:2(2002), 157–80.

Moore, Tiffany Ann Conroy, *Kozintsev's Shakespeare Films: Russian Political Protest in* Hamlet *and* King Lear (Jefferson, NC: McFarland, 2012).

O'Brien, Geoffrey, *The Phantom Empire: Movies in the Mind of the 20th Century* (New York: Norton, 1995).

Starks, Lisa S., 'The Displaced Body of Desire: Sexuality in Kenneth Branagh's *Hamlet*', in *Shakespeare and Appropriation*, ed. Christy Desmet and Robert Sawyer (New York: Routledge, 1999), 160–78.

Taylor, Neil, 'The Films of *Hamlet*', in *Shakespeare and the Moving Image*, ed. Anthony Davies and Stanley Wells (Cambridge: Cambridge University Press, 1994), 18–95.

CHAPTER 36

INTERMEDIATED BODIES AND BODIES OF MEDIA
Screen Othellos

SUJATA IYENGAR

SCREEN media both appropriate and remediate *Othello*. Appropriation brings Shakespeare into dialogue with adaptors and audience; evaluating a performance as an appropriation weighs adapted text and origin text as independent artworks, each of which uncovers something hitherto unnoticed about the other.[1] In *Remediation*, Jay David Bolter and Richard Grusin argue that the specific material, technological, and user-centered capabilities (the 'affordances') of a so-called 'new' medium build upon but also attempt to erase the media that preceded them. Thus photographers adopted and adapted the conventions of painting, even as they argued that photography could represent the world more realistically than painting could; television 'variety shows' remediated music-hall or vaudeville; e-texts remediate both medieval scroll and printed book.[2] Following Friedrich Kittler, media scholars have suggested that so-called new media don't replace old ones but nudge them into a different niche in a particular 'media ecology';[3] similarly, appropriations or remediations of Shakespeare do not *replace* Folio or Quarto texts or modern printed copies of the text but reframe aspects of even their perceived content as medium-specific. Jens Schröter suggests that we consider using the term 'intermediality', rather than the words 'remediation' or even 'mediation', so that we can account for the persistence of prior affordances within new media not as failures of imagination on the part of the creators but as reflections of the rich significance of art objects. He asks whether such an intermedial art object needs to belong to a particular, defined medium, or whether we can only define such media *post facto*, by ignoring an immanent intermediality within the art object.

---

[1] I extend thanks to the editors of this volume for their comments and suggestions and to Katherine Rowe for the titular phrase. Christy Desmet and Robert Sawyer, *Shakespeare and Appropriation* (London: Routledge, 1999), 'Introduction' and *passim*.

[2] Jay David Boulter and Richard Grusin, *Remediation: Understanding New Media* (Boston: MIT Press, 2000).

[3] Friedrich Kittler, *Discourse Networks: 1800–1900*, trans. Michael Meteer (Stanford, CA: Stanford University Press, 1990).

Extending Saussure, Schröter suggests that we define a medium through differentiation—by contrasting it to what other media at that time are *not*. Thus photography might consist of rectangular pictures that are indexical, rather than iconic, that point to objects in the real world rather than representing them schematically or by analogy—until the advent of film, when photography is redefined as made up of rectangular pictures that are indexical, yes, but *static*. Each new medium or intermedium has to use metaphors developed from earlier media in order to describe and define itself. Schröter therefore speculates that 'Maybe all of this means that we have to recognize that it is not individual media that are primal and *then* move toward each other intermedially, but that it is intermediality that is primal and that the clearly separated "monomedia" are the result of purposeful and institutionally caused blockades, incisions, and mechanisms of exclusion.[4]

Media extend the reach of the human body and its senses; Hamlet's wax tables, like common-place books, desk diaries, dictaphones, and smartphones, extend memory just as the television (even in its macaronic name, tele-vision) allows us to 'see at a distance' and the telephone allows us to hear sound beyond its reach. The body itself, moreover, transmits information about itself and about its environment intermedially through its various monomedia of speech, facial expression, gesture, even odour. The actor's performing body, a 'communicative medium', in Robert Weiman's phrase, unites print, speech, gesture and sensation in the service of story or represented experience.[5] The 'primal' intermediality of the actor's body is broken up into the 'institutionally caused blockades, incisions, and mechanisms of exclusion' that enforce race, gender, class, and other social or institutional taxonomies on screen. Simply put, we have to ignore ('exclude', if we retain Schröter's terminology) certain qualities of the actor's body and all its hyper-, trans- or intermedial sensory richness if we want to perceive that body as gendered, raced, ranked, disabled, or otherwise socially classified. Seeing a multiply-coded human body at play on screen—at a double remove—accentuates that activity of exclusion. The screen screens the actor from the audience and the audience from the actor: it both displays and conceals the body's ability to communicate by establishing it as an intermedium even as it accentuates its monomedia qualities.

Screened performances screen out the qualities of 'liveness'—immediacy, unpredictability, ephemerality, spatial proximity, danger—to varying degrees according to their media, contexts, and audiences. As Philip Auslander has argued, 'liveness' itself is intermedial; in order to characterize a performance as 'live', we contrast it to a 'mediatized' version of itself and seek in it an imagined, lost 'authenticity'.[6] A fruitful discussion of the Canadian television series *Slings and Arrows* by Laurie Osborne suggests, 'Shakespeare thrives now through the creative use of intermedial performance differences' (in the case she discusses, through the interplay among multi-season television series, festival performance, and repertory theatre).[7] In this chapter I will

---

[4] Jens Schröter, 'Four Models of Intermediality', in *Travels in Intermedia[lity]: Reblurring the Boundaries*, ed. Bernd Herzogenrath (Hanover, NH: Dartmouth College Press, 2012), 15–36 (30).

[5] Robert Weimann, *Author's Pen and Actor's Voice: Playing and Writing in Shakespeare's Theatre* (Cambridge: Cambridge University Press, 2000), esp. 4–17.

[6] Philip Auslander, *Liveness* (London: Routledge, rev. edn. 2008), 23–38 (62).

[7] Laurie E. Osborne, 'Serial Shakespeare: Intermedial Performance and the Outrageous Fortunes of *Slings & Arrows*', *Borrowers and Lenders: The Journal of Shakespeare and Appropriation* 6:2 (2011), <http://www.borrowers.uga.edu/cocoon/borrowers/request?id=783090>, p. 22 of pdf.

investigate race and intermediality in bodies of media: *Othello*s on film, television, web, and Shakestream, the hybrid format that broadcasts 'live' stage performances of plays in cinemas worldwide. I will aim to show that, while these performances assert their status as 'new media', the way they represent other media reinforces what Schröter calls 'ontological intermediality'. Moreover, these bodies of media and mediatized human bodies threaten to screen out the lived experience of race for performers and audience.

FILM

Early silent films, as many have noted, both deploy and satirize the conventions of Victorian melodrama and are therefore intermedial performances. If we define old media through a process of differentiation or distinction, then we might also ask how early film represents live theatre, printed matter, and manuscripts on stage as media or intermedia. Douglas Lanier has investigated the effects of intermedial representation in the *Othello*-inspired feature films *A Double Life* and *Men Are Not Gods*. He deftly argues that these films use representations of the stage and the live theatre to offer viewers access to high-status cultural activities but also to satirize or critique accepted conventions of classical theatre (including, for example, the portrayal of Othello by a white actor wearing black-face make-up), histrionic delivery, and gesture.[8] Blackface in television and feature films of *Othello* ranges, for example, from the insensitive impersonation of Laurence Olivier's almost-purple blackness in Stuart Burge's filmed stage-production (1966) to the well-intentioned obfuscation of Anthony Hopkins's tawniness in Jonathan Miller's BBC Television Shakespeare (1981) to the clever understatement of Orson Welles in black-and-white (1952). Dmitri Buchowetzki's silent *Othello* (1922) formally exposes the clash between media conventions in order to present its hero as one who is unable to comprehend a modernity that Iago skilfully controls and manipulates. Judith Buchanan notes that the moment at which Werner Krauss's Iago expresses mimed disgust, as he wipes the brow of the heavily blacked-up Emil Jannings, turns Iago's 'disgust at coming into contact with his general's feverish sweat' into a critique or commentary, through parody, of blackface itself, of 'the very performance tradition of which it forms part'.[9]

Buchowetzki's film surprised even contemporary reviewers with Jannings's outdated or melodramatic presentation of the titular hero, in contrast on the one hand to the more naturalistic style of acting coming into vogue at the time and on the other to Krauss's gleefully vicious and self-conscious Iago. If Jannings was, perhaps, seeking a visual equivalent to the ornate rhetoric of Shakespeare's hero, such a subtlety escaped the critics of his day and present-day critics alike.[10] Film scholars today complain about the 'overloaded … inserts of intertexts' that, R. S. White accurately observes, fail to 'respect the visuality

---

[8] Douglas Lanier, 'Murdering *Othello*', in *A Companion to Literature, Film, and Adaptation*, ed. Deborah Cartmell (Chichester, UK: John Wiley & Sons, 2013), 198–213.

[9] Judith Buchanan, *Shakespeare on Silent Film* (Harlow, UK: Pearson-Longman, 2005), 246.

[10] Ibid., 241.

of film'.[11] The intertitles also, however, indicate how the intermedia of silent film can incorporate stage performance and print narrative. The film begins with a list of characters presented on screen, as do the dramatis personae in a printed play-text, or the playbill or programme at a stage-play. Intertitles both allude to and supersede the Shakespearean text, and they owe less to Shakespeare than to Cinthio or even (at least in the English versions we still have, tailored for US release) eighteenth-century versions of Othello as impulsive and 'ardent in his affection', as in Samuel Johnson's notes on the play.[12] Jannings's Othello is first described as 'intellectual, tender, lofty; warlike, impetuous' and moreover as descended both from an 'Egyptian prince' and a 'Spanish princess', that is to say from a magical ancestor and from unquestionably royal blood. As ethnic categories, 'Egyptian' and 'Spanish' preclude this Othello's being recognizably African, although Jannings's make-up, his exotic and luxurious robes, and the savagery he shows at the loss of the handkerchief all evoke early twentieth-century conventional beliefs about Africans and blackness.

The film itself interpolates then-new techniques of film in order to superimpose Othello's fantasy of Desdemona and Cassio embracing in the top left of the screen while Othello remains in the foreground, tortured by his jealous thoughts. Buchowetzki's film establishes a cinematic tradition of this imagined erotic interlude that is then continued in many other films such as Oliver Parker's *Othello* (1993), Tim Blake Nelson's modernized high-school setting, *O* (2001), Zaib Shaikh's television film *Othello: The Tragedy of the Moor* (2008) and even Volfango De Biasi's unlamented Italian 'Shakesteen' movie adaptation *Iago* (2008). Buchanan suggests that Buchowetzki's interpolated fantasy contaminates Desdemona's purity for the viewer even though Buchowetzki attempts to recuperate her during the murder scene through the 'cathedral'-like setting of Desdemona's bedchamber and through her presentation, 'brightly, almost spiritually, lit' beneath 'a statuette of the Virgin Mary'.[13] This shot, which displays Desdemona as her own funeral monument, cannot be a point-of-view shot in any literal sense because it does not correspond to Othello's sight-line. This Othello cannot see Desdemona as the audience sees her, any more than he can see through Iago's plot. Buchowetzki deploys what would become the grammar of film— alternating images of Desdemona's fear with Othello's fury—during the murder of Desdemona, but where later films used a shot followed by a reverse-shot to indicate an exchange of glances, the shots of Desdemona do not correspond to Othello's sight-line but instead to an unknown, omniscient observer—the viewer, or perhaps the reader who is aware of Othello's own comparison of Desdemona's white skin to 'monumental alablaster' (5.2.5).[14] We can therefore learn the thoughts of Jannings' Othello only through the archaic syntax of intertitles. Desdemona's angelic death makes her murder a 'sacrifice', in accordance with Othello's wishes in the play (5.2.67), but the film has to have him declaim via intertitle, 'she shall expiate even in her own bed!', an

---

[11] R. S. White, 'Sex, Lies, Videotape—and *Othello*', in *Almost Shakespeare: Reinventing his Works for Cinema and Television*, ed. James R. Keller and Leslie Stratyner (Jefferson, NC: McFarland, 2004), 86–98 (89).

[12] Samuel Johnson, ed., *Othello* (New York: Lewis and Geary, 1840), 880.

[13] Buchanan, *Shakespeare on Silent Film*, 247.

[14] Quotations from *Othello* come from *The Oxford Shakespeare: Othello: The Moor of Venice*, ed. Michael Neill (Oxford: Oxford University Press, 2008) and appear within the text as parenthetical citations.

adaptation of Iago's urgent desire to have Othello strangle Desdemona in 'even in the bed she hath contaminated' (4.1.200-1). The new medium of cinema makes possible sudden jumps between fury, terror, and sanctity, but only the viewer—not Othello himself—can access the spiritual vision of Desdemona.

Buchowetzki's film screens its Othello from modernity through both cinematic technique and the actors' choice of delivery. The two performance styles of Jannings's histrionic Othello and Werner Krauss's spritely and mocking Iago contrast enough to suggest an Othello befuddled by newfangled methods of communication—by new media, we might say. Iago's wit, speed, and ability to know things at a distance reflect the affordances of the new medium of film, which seems to extend human experience and perception. Iago controls this new medium and its techniques, but Othello cannot make sense of them (just as a stage-Othello cannot understand the stage-managing of Iago during the eavesdropping scene, nor the engineering of the handkerchief).

Thirty years later, Orson Welles's *Othello* could comment upon and transform the stage-convention of blackface and the film convention of using shot/reverse-shot to indicate point-of-view or reaction, in order to screen out the difficulties of having a white actor portray a black man. Welles decided to film his *Othello* in black-and-white not merely for financial but also for artistic reasons, and not only to evoke the disorienting world and corrupt underpinnings of *film noir,* but also to make (as Buchanan and others suggest) his blackface make-up both less obvious and more convincing. Kenneth Rothwell argues that Welles combined a visually distinctive approach to the film and a narrative transformation by beginning in flashback to the lovers' funeral procession. Welles starts us off in the '*locus classicus*' of the cage with the punished Iago, and then uses lattices, grids, webs, and other figures of entrapment throughout the film regardless of the chronological sequence of events.[15]

Once more, film technique connects Iago to modernity and Othello to a flamboyant medievalism. Daniel Juan Gil describes in an exemplary essay how Welles unsettles the conventional grammar of film—the use of shot/reverse-shot to indicate the exchange of glances, of montage to evoke the passage of time, of long, medium, and close shots to convey varying degrees of intimacy between viewer and actor, the pace and rhythm of sound and visual editing to convey urgency or malaise—in order to evoke an 'asocial' sexuality. Gil observes that the shot/reverse-shot dyads are slightly off-kilter, angled so that our sight-lines do not ally exactly with the point of view that, conventional film grammar would suggest, we are adopting. Moreover, writes Gil, Welles in *Othello* uses montage to reconstruct the passage of time not just on a global narrative scale but also during individual sequences, and uses long shots to normalize the grandly distant social relationships of Venice. Shot/reverse-shot—off-kilter or face-to-face—in Welles's film 'is radically transvalued to signify social deviance or dysfunction'.[16] Perhaps Welles also represents then-standard practices of film narrative, such as using a shot/reverse-shot unit, as

[15]   Kenneth S. Rothwell, *A History of Shakespeare on Screen: A Century of Film and Television* (Cambridge and New York: Cambridge University Press, 2004), 78.

[16]   Daniel Juan Gil, 'Avant-Garde Technique and the Visual Grammar of Sexuality in Orson Welles's Shakespeare Films', *Borrowers and Lenders: The Journal of Shakespeare and Appropriation* 1:2 (2005), <http://www.borrowers.uga.edu/781447/display>, p. 4 of.pdf. Last access: 20 March 2016.

archaic—perhaps even as an old medium. Extending Gil, we can argue that Welles's technique forces us to realize that in conventional film we generate a stable, viewing, subject-position retroactively—only after seeing the reverse-shot do we realize that we are following a character's gaze.

In this way Welles offers us a visual 'objective correlative' to the 'preposterous' or back-projected identity that Joel Altman has suggested underpins *Othello*. According to Altman, both Othello and Iago construct their sense of self after-the-fact.[17] Scholars have identified Iago as a 'sociopath' or a 'paranoid psychopath'; perhaps Altman's greatest achievement is to find a solid historical and rhetorical grounding for the psychoanalytic and psychological readings of this play and its central partnership in the rhetorical and religious canons of Shakespeare's time.[18] Altman convincingly argues that Iago succeeds in 3.3, the so-called temptation scene, in destroying Othello's prior sense of self—one based on honour, soldiery, and valour—so that, inchoate or formless, he turns instead to the historically worded self created and offered to him by Iago, now his lieutenant or place-holder in military, spatial, and rhetorical terms. Welles's treatment of 3.3 creates a spatial analogue to this sense of the inexorable limits of rhetoric and identity that confine Othello. Strolling on the battlements, Iago and Othello literally and figuratively go over the same ground again and again, as if trapped in physical space and time just as Othello is about to be mentally ensnared by Iago. The lattices, grids, bars, and networks that fragment our sight-lines in the film intensify its claustrophobic effect.

Critics disagree about the degree to which such technical innovations enhance or detract from Othello's racial isolation in Welles's film. James Stone argues that the film minimizes race in favour of an overarching aesthetic of *chiaroscuro* that turns away, literally and figuratively, from Othello's face. 'Race is reduced to a mirror-trick, an image that does not reflect the ego's ideal image of itself since the camera lens looks awry', writes Stone of the scene in which Othello looks into the mirror, encounters Iago's gaze on the words 'clime, complexion, and degree' and drops his eyes on the word 'complexion'.[19]

I am not sure, however, that the film 'reduce[s]' race as much as it uses cinematic techniques to display the intersections of race, gender, and sexuality, socially isolating forces that inexorably draw the three main protagonists, Othello, Iago, and Desdemona, towards tragedy. Welles's tragedy hinges upon the impossibility of loving, human communication in the context of the Venetian conventions that circumscribe whom one should love, and under what circumstances. A cluster of scenes surrounding the intimacy of Othello and Desdemona can serve as examples. In the scene at the Sagittary, the script alters Brabantio's angry epithet for Othello, 'such a thing as thou' (1.2.71) to 'such a thing as *that*', a change that on one level simply modernizes the text in order to register the same level of contempt that Shakespeare's Brabantio displays for the Moor. Literally, grammatically, the use of the demonstrative adjective instead of the personal pronoun demonstrates how the intersection of race and sexuality (Othello's marriage to Desdemona) has broken the friendship between Othello and Brabantio. The film also uses silhouettes or shadows

[17] Joel Altman, *The Improbability of* Othello (Chicago: University of Chicago Press, 2010).

[18] Edward Pechter, *Othello and Interpretive Traditions* (Iowa City: Iowa University Press, 1999), 62; Fred West, 'Iago the Psychopath', *South Atlantic Bulletin* 43:2 (1978), 27–35.

[19] James Stone, 'Black and White as Technique in Orson Welles's *Othello*', *Literature/Film Quarterly* 30 (2002), 190.

FIGS. 36.1–3 Screen captures from Orson Welles' *Othello* (1952). Iago (Micheál MacLiammóir) resentfully observes Othello (Orson Welles) and Desdemona (Suzanne Cloutier) embrace on Othello's words, 'I can deny thee nothing.'

FIGS. 36.1–3 (Continued).

to represent human figures indistinguishably at moments that ought rather to connote human individuality and intimacy. Othello and Desdemona's shadows come together as one inchoate shape to consummate their marriage.

Even when we do see Othello and Desdemona touch, on Othello's words 'I will deny thee nothing' (3.3.77) as Desdemona pleads for Cassio's reinstatement, their faces are hidden. Iago's envious, disgusted gaze frames their embrace, surrounding their love with contempt. Some of the obfuscation derived from financial and practical exigencies: Welles experimented with no fewer than three actresses, Italian, French, and American (Lea Padovani, Cécile Aubry, and Betsy Blair) before deciding upon Canadian Suzanne Cloutier. Virginia Mason Vaughan implies that Welles 'sought a substitute female body': it did not matter to him *who* played Desdemona, because the character exists mainly in order to trigger the eroticized hatred between Iago and Othello.[20] (See Figures 36.1–3.)

There is literally no place in space or time for these lovers, or for a husband who is unable to perform his expected role in the marital bed; Welles is on record as having considered Iago to be 'impotent' himself and therefore to have been consumed by destructive envy.[21] Just as Iago can only see the lovers awry, so Othello himself is forced by Iago's speech, 'In Venice they do let God see the pranks/They dare not show their

[20] Virginia Mason Vaughan, Othello: *A Contextual History* (Cambridge: Cambridge University Press, 1996), 204.

[21] Micheál MacLiammmóir, *Put Money in Thy Purse: The Diary of the Film of* Othello (London: Methuen, 1952), 26 and *passim*.

FIG. 36.4 Othello looks directly at Desdemona, but his mirrored self glimpses her framed as if in a mirror.

husbands' (3.3.205-6), to see Desdemona as if in a mirror, reflected back to him mentally through the words of a supposed native informant on the women of Venice. In an interpolated scene after Othello flings away Desdemona's handkerchief, in which Desdemona briefly re-enters before Emilia finds the napkin, Othello gazes upon Desdemona, who is reflected in the mirror behind him, while his own reflection, his *alter ego* in the mirror, as it were, glimpses her framed in the staircase as if in another mirror, in miniature (Figure 36.4). Gil writes that the climax of this film 'puts the spectator in a strange position' and encourages what Kathy Howlett has called a 'sadistic' scopophilia.[22] The screen 'screens out' normal social life and humanity for the spectator as well as for its characters.

TELEVISION

Welles's *Othello* comments intermedially upon cinema by subverting its supposed affordances or advantages over stage-play: breadth or *mise-en-scène*, enhanced verisimilitude through location shooting, and face-to-face intimacy. Auslander observes that television has traditionally been supposed to offer even deeper 'intimacy and immediacy' in contrast to film,

---

[22] Gil, 'Avant-Garde Technique', p. 15 of pdf.

even as television directors have deployed the conventions (multiple and mobile cameras to simulate a viewer's wandering gaze, location shooting, and post-production sound editing) of cinema. H. R. Coursen and others have further distinguished Shakespeare on television from Shakespeare on film through its conventions, rhythm, and scale. Television, writes Coursen, shrinks the world to the confines of a "living' room".[23] Something about Iago in particular appears to trigger intermedial commentary. Even in a film as conventional and popular as Oliver Parker's, Kenneth Branagh's Iago talks directly to camera, as does Ian McKellen's bluff Lancashire soldier in the television film (1990) based on Trevor Nunn's production of *Othello*.

Iago likewise breaks the 'fourth wall' in the two television adaptations I discuss below. Geoffrey Sax's production of Andrew Davies's television play, *Othello: A Modern Masterpiece* (Granada, 2001), uses a moving camera to unsettle our expectations of television Shakespeare and to assert the pernicious dominance of institutional racism in British life. Zaib Shaikh's Canadian Broadcasting Corporation television film *Othello: The Tragedy of the Moor* (2008) ostensibly foregrounds the play's concentration on religious, rather than racial, differences, but its humourless and psychopathic Iago and the clever use of the restrictions of commercial television turn what could have been a societal tragedy into a study in individual pathologies.

Davies transposes *Othello* to the London of the early twenty-first century, focusing on the fraught racial politics (and high-level denial) of the Metropolitan police. The Afro-Caribbean John Othello (a passionate and thoughtful Eamonn Walker), is promoted over his senior confidant and mentor Ben Jago (an inspired Christopher Eccleston) in the aftermath of race riots. Tricked by Jago into believing the results of a faked DNA test and the purported whereabouts of a silken dressing-gown, Othello murders his 'posh' white wife Dessie (Keeley Hawes). Barbara Hodgdon has written at length about the spectacularization of Dessie's body in this film, and Thomas Cartelli and Katherine Rowe have commented upon the film's brilliant parody of the then dominant genres of its medium—documentary, newscast, reality show—through its intermedial interpolation of fragments of documentary or news film, and still photography.[24] Cartelli and Rowe also note that Dessie is a journalist, a writer and photographer who jokes about the creeping archaism of her profession and about herself as a 'blank sheet of paper' to be written upon by John Othello (in one of the many close paraphrases of Shakespeare deployed by Andrew Davies's script).[25] This film's Cassio does not merely admire Desdemona from afar (as Shakespeare's, Buchowetzki's, Zeffirelli's, and Shaikh's Cassios arguably do) but overtly propositions her, in a departure from the Shakespearean source that unsettles us despite Dessie's spirited refusal.

Welles disoriented his viewers through slightly off-kilter shot/reverse-shot pairings, so that it seemed as though dialogue was impossible. Sax disorients us by giving Ben Jago a series of confidential, unselfconscious monologues delivered straight to

[23] H. R. Coursen, *Watching Shakespeare on Television* (Rutherford: Fairleigh Dickinson University Press; London and Toronto: Associated University Presses, 1993), 14.

[24] Barbara Hodgdon, 'Race-ing *Othello*, Re-engendering White-Out, II', in *Shakespeare, The Movie, II: Popularizing the Plays on Film, TV, Video, and DVD*, ed. Richard Burt and Lynda E. Boose (London and New York: Routledge, 2003), 89–104.

[25] Thomas Cartelli and Katherine Rowe, *New Wave Shakespeare on Screen* (London: Polity, 2007), 122.

camera in the style of the video diary familiar from so-called reality television or from the Shakespeare-inflected British television series *House of Cards* (1990; remade, with notable differences, for US television in 2013), in which the devious Chief Whip Francis Urquhart (Ian Richardson) frequently addresses the camera directly in order to point out others' obtuseness and his own canny plotting. Where such monologues usually use a fixed camera to capture the speaker within an intimate, private space, however, Eccleston's Jago walks frenziedly through corridors, facing a camera that tracks him through his frenetic, compelling, ferocious ('vertiginous', in Cartelli and Rowe's description) speeches. Spitting with rage, he explodes, 'I hate the Moor' even as he insists, in a phrase repeated at the beginning and the end of the film, that 'it's about love'.

The film uses intermedial components to emphasize the relationship between race and its shocking ending: Ben Jago *wins*. The final shot reproduces an old medium, a publicity photograph, of Jago in an archaic dress-uniform. In its gritty British context, Jago's triumphant smile and dress-uniform screens contemporary viewers from any kind of catharsis or redemption because they contextualize *Othello* as a tragedy of race. This tragedy foregrounds not the distance that present-day institutions stand from the historical confines of race but the ways in which such institutions continue to screen out racial minorities.

Shaikh's television film departs from Shakespeare's play most notably in emphasizing Othello's status as a 'Muslim' (a word that replaces Rodrigo's racialized slur, 'thick-lips', in 1.1). Retitled *Othello: The Tragedy of the Moor*, the film exploits the extra-diegetic performance history of its Othello (Carlo Rota, from the popular Canadian television situation comedy *Little Mosque on the Prairie*) both to domesticate and to make exotic the Moor and his extravagant setting (an unspecified but glamorous, vaguely Colonial Morocco). The ambiguous ethnicity of the Duke, Iago, and Bianca (all are dark-haired and olive-skinned) minimizes Othello's racial isolation in favour of his religious difference from those around him. This film's Bianca likewise wears ambiguously ethnic clothing: multiple necklaces with dangling brass coins, an elaborate head-dress, and harem pants. Shaikh's film cuts most of Othello's and Iago's major speeches (and many of the women's lines, including the willow scene), and frequently fades to black to accommodate commercial breaks. The performances of the actors themselves are understated, and the film prefers domestic, interior, studio shots over grand, exterior locations. The film, however, turns the frequent breaks necessitated by commercial television broadcast into advantages. It uses these enforced pauses to pace individual scenes imaginatively and also to transform the 'establishing shot,' which traditionally recreates the scene after a commercial break, into an interpretive decision.

Othello's final speech, in voice-over, frames the entire film as a flashback. The film opens with a crane shot of the dead bodies of Emilia (on the floor beside the bed), and of Othello and Desdemona upon the bed, before it repeatedly pans and tracks over vivid red bloodstains on the sheets. An interpolated marriage scene displays Desdemona removing a golden cross from around her neck and replacing it with a crescent-and-star pendant, even as she garlands her new husband in turn with a cross. In Othello's jealous fury, he will later snatch the crescent from his wife's throat. In a recollection of Welles, we cut to the perspective of Iago and Roderigo, watching from behind a lattice through which we can also spot Cassio.

Othello and Desdemona display their religious pendants prominently throughout the film, their shirts open to the neck, the silvery metal flickering even in bedroom scenes dimly lit by candles. Cinematic cuts connect these religious symbols, especially Desdemona's crescent, to the handkerchief and by extension to Othello's belief in her infidelity. In one sequence, Iago, gloating over the gift of the handkerchief, flings Emilia down on the bed as if for rough sex. The film cuts to the innocent Desdemona, the crescent shining around her neck, and then to the tortured Othello, leaning against a wall, as he imagines his wife with Cassio, a vision that the viewer, too, shares through the use of a digitally inserted clip of the supposed lovers which appears in the upper part of the frame, almost like the 'thought bubble' in a comic strip. When Othello demands the handkerchief of Desdemona and she claims to have mislaid it, cross and crescent catch the camera's eye. As Desdemona insists she is 'not a strumpet—as [she is] a Christian', and her husband accuses her of whoredom, he tears off her crescent. Immediately before Othello enters to murder her, we see Desdemona anxiously attempting to repair the torn clasp on the crescent necklace, until Emilia gently removes it from her.

The film's marriage ceremony also includes a ritual in which Othello adorns his wife with a *hijab*, the headscarf (literally, the *screen*) of an observant Muslim woman. The film could have used the scarf (as Jayaraaj's *Kaliyattam* (1997) does with Thamara's/Desdemona's *patta* or modesty-scarf) to replace or evoke the handkerchief. Notably, however, Shaikh's Desdemona does not retain the hijab throughout the film, and even during her wedding she wears it in the relaxed style of an urban professional, freely showing her hair and her neck, rather than concealing them. Nor do we ever see Othello or Desdemona kneel to pray towards Mecca, or even unroll a prayer mat; the hijab and the necklaces thus appear to connote symbolic cultural identity and domestic, romantic border-crossing rather than devout or exclusive religious belief.

Enhancing this domestic, rather than political, focus is the judicious use of cutting. Othello's rapid conversion from love to jealousy in 3.3 can seem implausibly sudden. Shaikh reconfigures this so-called temptation scene not as a single interlude but as a series of encounters, editing together discontinuous clips in a montage to give us the illusion that time is passing. The scene opens in a military office, where a map of Cyprus and Turkey dominates the background. The scene then cuts on 'What dost thou think?' to what is clearly a later encounter, as though Othello has been brooding for several days or even weeks. This second temptation scene occurs within a beautiful *mise-en-scène* of domestic food preparation with heaped fresh produce—red, yellow, and green glistening mounds of potatoes, peppers, onions, chillies, and grapes—in focus at every level of depth. Iago brings ingredients to Othello, and Othello wields the knife to cut the fruit, dramatically impaling it on 'What dost thou mean?' Rota's Othello shakes his head involuntarily even before he responds to Iago's words, as though he already mistrusts Cassio and can intuit what Iago is about to say. When the camera zooms onto Othello's face with Iago's words, 'look to your wife', we see the blood beating in his temple before he quietly confesses, 'I am bound to thee forever' and imagines his wife with Cassio in a naked clinch. This imagined encounter reappears at a later point to torment Othello; its reappearance also restores the film's intensity for a viewer at home whose attention might have dissipated after the commercial break.

On the one hand the kitchen setting domesticates or depoliticizes the play, but on the other it exploits the currency of food as a marker of religious prohibition or ethnic difference. Extra-diegetically, actor Carlo Rota's association with food might evoke for a Canadian

FIG. 36.5 Screen Capture from Zaib Shaikh's Canadian Broadcasting Corporation television film *Othello: The Tragedy of the Moor* (2008). The scene cross-fades from Emilia's words "belch us" to Othello brandishing a cleaver over a lamb's carcass.

viewer one of the many episodes of *Little Mosque on the Prairie* that present dietary conflicts comically (such as 'Baber is from Mars, Vegans are from Venus', in Season 3, 5 January 2009). Because we have associated Othello with the sustenance and life-giving warmth of the kitchen, we are shocked when an amazing piece of sound- and video-editing takes us from Emilia's diatribe against men, who are 'stomachs … [that] belch us' to the sound of Othello's knife hitting flesh on the word 'belch'. Othello is back in the kitchen, but he swings an enormous cleaver to dismember the bloodless (halal?) carcass of a lamb. Othello slaps Desdemona before that blanched and butchered body, supporting the suggestion of some feminist Shakespeareans that the play figures Desdemona herself as sacrificial lamb for consumption.[26] Othello wields a kitchen knife for the last time when we see his shadow, knife in hand, fall on the sleeping Desdemona as he mutters, 'It is the cause'.

Commercial television necessarily breaks up the narrative with breaks, each of which is traditionally followed by a re-establishing shot. But what's re-established here is not the same set or characters or situation as before the break but the shifting or contingent grounds of Othello's (and, in this production, Iago's) selfhood. We can return to Altman's explanation of the compelling power of 3.3 as a process of mutual unmaking undertaken by Othello and Iago. Without the rhetoric that constitutes Othello's ethos, chaos is come again; for Othello, not knowing 'what to think' means not knowing what or how to be. Recall that, according to Gil, Welles's *Othello* disorients us through its mismatched shot/reverse-shot sequences; these sequences interfere with a viewer's usually intuitive sense of who is looking at whom. I suggest that these mismatched sight-lines create in the viewer and for the characters a *post facto* sense of self that constitutes itself moment-to-moment, shot by shot, because we have to imagine a fictive self that is looking along that sight-line, next to but not identical to the characters shown in shot/reverse-shot. In this way, Welles

---

[26] Louise Noble, *Medicinal Cannibalism in Early Modern English Literature and Culture* (New York: Palgrave Macmillan, 2011); Stephanie Moss, 'The Paracelsan/Galenic Body in *Othello*', in *Disease, Diagnosis and Cure on the Early Modern Stage*, ed. Kaara L. Peterson and Stephanie Moss (London: Ashgate, 2004), 151–70.

exploits cinematic technique and Shaikh manipulates the establishing shot just as Iago's rhetoric influences Othello's post-rhetorical ethos.

Unlike the political rage and wider world of Davies's contemporary, London *Othello*, Shaikh's film presents the 'tragedy of the Moor' as the tragedy of Othello himself, and screens out the tragedy of what it might mean to be a Muslim in a Christian world. Post-9/11, however, a domestic, personal tragedy arguably makes its own political argument, one that asserts the rights of immigrant Muslims to serve and to sin, to judge and be judged, as individual, flawed human beings rather than as representatives of their faith. Rota's Othello is more than 'The Moor'.

WEB-SERIES

The 'web-series' produced by Ready Set Go Theatre queries not just the conventions of the early modern stage, of feature film, and of television broadcast, but also the expectations of traditional twenty-first-century film and television casting, such as having actors share the gender of their characters. The hastily composed shots, extreme close-ups, and occasional blurred focus connect the series to the self-made and uploaded YouTube Shakespeare videos of *Othello* that Ayanna Thompson and others have discussed.[27] YouTube or digital video blog (vlog) hypermediates personal subjectivity through a kind of recorded 'liveness' that brings us closer and more frequently than ever into the lives of others despite what may be vast physical distances. These social media connections reinforce a primary narcissism for the viewer. Classic film scholarship argues that subjects cathect the larger-than-life figures viewed in darkness on the big screen, but with mobile media we can carry these screen presences with us and subordinate their performances to a range of multimedia distractions. Even stationary, not mobile, digital screens such as computer monitors or NetTVs can foster such a narcissism by putting film into competition with the other screens and windows that a viewer can simultaneously access. A viewer glancing at the corner of a screen is a curator; she has added *Othello* to a collection of multimedia objects that reinforce her own importance as organizing principle.

The series breaks the play into twelve ten-minute 'webisodes', which were released sequentially, like a traditional television series, but are now available for viewing all at once. As in a television series, each instalment was given a title, and began and ended with music and credits. Many episodes used an alt-folk soundtrack (by singer Lora Faye), and the music registered in increasingly intermedial and meaningful ways as the series developed. The series was shot in Brooklyn and the West Village by graduates of the New School for Drama over a period of a month, funded by a Kickstarter campaign supported by 'family, friends and even customers at Dizzy's Diner in Park Slope, where both [John] Hurley and [Sue] White [founders and actors in the company] work'.[28]

---

[27] Ayanna Thompson, 'Unmooring the Moor: Researching and Teaching on You Tube', *Shakespeare Quarterly* 61:3 (2010), 337–56.

[28] Meena Hart Duerson, 'Brooklyn theater company turns Shakespeare's "Othello" into a web show broken into 12 episodes', *New York Daily News* (14 September 2012), online <http://www.nydailynews.com/entertainment/music-arts/brooklyn-theater-company-turns-shakespeare-othello-web-show-broken-12-episodes-article-1.1158910#ixzz2mhxlYeUk≥, last accessed 6 December 2013.

The webisodes break up the rhythm of the play but also make it into a web-series, as if much more time is passing and we are binge-watching (if we watch it all together) or as if it's happening in real-time (as if the characters were tweeting it on social media or uploading video logs to YouTube). The so-called 'double time scheme' of *Othello* has no effect here, because watching the story unfold in instalments at regular intervals makes it seem as though we are watching through windows into episodes of a long-standing relationship and as though off-camera events have influenced what we are seeing in ways we cannot know. The present-day setting and clothing recall other web-series such as *The Lizzie Bennet Diaries*, a modernized *Pride and Prejudice* shot for the internet as a vlog. Both reality television and vlog prove very apt platforms for Iago, who stages/scripts his play while making it seem as though it is reality.

Although this production showed signs of amateurism (a wobbling hand-held camera; inconsistent sound-editing; some delayed or partial focus; continuity errors; some mispronunciations; occasionally careless dramaturgy), it gained in sophistication through the webisodes. The shaky hand-held camera of the opening sequences was replaced for the most part by stable shots that still retained an allusive, active, mobile setting, as in episode four, in which a remorseful and drunken Cassio (Lauren Boyd) lolled in the subway while the camera faced Iago (Cory Lawson) as he walked along the platform during his soliloquy. Iago moved in and out of frame constantly, the camera tracking him. Although we could see Cassio languishing in the subway, the character could not hear Iago's words. These televisual, documentary-style techniques allied Iago's soliloquy to reality television, an analogy heightened by the quotidian setting of the New York subway, the natural lighting throughout, and Iago's muted voice.

The series cast female actor Lauren Boyd as 'Michel' Cassio, a decision that could have been interesting but that was hard to parse because the script changed its pronouns inconsistently, adapting some references but leaving others. (It also cross-cast Shannon Stewart as Montano, but without any change to the character's name.) Thus Desdemona refers to 'Michael Cassio, who came a-wooing with you', although the credits reference 'Michel'; Iago anticipates 'she'll be … full of quarrel' when he plies Cassio with drink in episode 3; and Desdemona refers to Cassio as 'a man that languishes in your displeasure'. It is unclear whether the variations were deliberately intended to challenge the notion of binary sex difference, whether the dramaturge and actors simply overlooked them, or whether we were meant to imagine Cassio as Shakespeare's Cassio still, a man's part played by a female actor (although in that case, why change from 'Michael' to 'Michel' in the credits?). Without a clear indication of where to place this Cassio on a gender continuum (as male, female, homosexual, heterosexual, trans- or cisgendered, or genderqueer), or of *whether* to place her on a gender continuum (whether sex or gender was intended to be 'read' as a theatrical sign at all), heteronormativity reasserts itself. Othello's jealousy emerges to viewers as a violent homophobia, a murderous rage triggered by his wife's imagined same-sex love affair. In the contemporary United States, the ugly extra-diegetic belief in African American homophobia on the one hand and Black male violence on the other can overwhelm the performance if not addressed in some way. My students certainly assumed that the sex of Desdemona's lover both triggered and exacerbated Othello's sexual jealousy, and that his race determined the violence of his response. The production thus screened at large the intersection of sexuality and race because it screened out a diegetic explanation for Cassio's gender.

Episode Six of the web-series beautifully intermediates music, the history of cinema, and classical stage convention to indicate that the handkerchief, that 'trifle, light as air', has already determined the ending. This episode concludes with an acoustic cover by Lora Faye (and unnamed female backing singers) of 'Do Not Forsake Me, O My Darlin'', also known as the 'Ballad of *High Noon*' immortalized in the classic Western of that name. *High Noon* (1952) notoriously adheres to the unities of place, action—and, through the loud ticking of the clock and its countdown to former sheriff Will Kane's climactic encounter with the criminal Frank Miller—time. This musical interpolation evokes heroism, time running out, and lovers who forsake 'clime, complexion, and degree' (Kane's Quaker bride Amy shoots Miller, saving her husband, despite her deeply held pacifism). In a play where the betrayal of Othello by Iago often attracts most attention, a woman's voice pleading musically with her husband not to 'forsake [her] … on this our wedding day' returns us to Desdemona.

SHAKESTREAM

Auslander pointed out that history and context determine 'liveness', so perhaps we should not be surprised to see the Royal National Theatre, Shakespeare's Globe, and the Royal Shakespeare Company describing what are usually playbacks of recorded performances as 'live' experiences. Such playbacks constitute a hybrid medium, a medium in its own right, or rather, an intermedium that combines the ephemeral, occasional, and social experience of playgoing with the recorded, repeated, and private consumption of projected film. The 'NTLive' broadcast and projection of Nicholas Hytner's *Othello* (2013), set in present-day London and an unspecified Middle Eastern military base for the Cyprus scenes, was obviously a play—it was performed on stage with live actors, and the screencast displayed not only the limited 'box' set but also audience members, their responses, the noise of the crowd before, during, and after the intermission, and the curtain call. After the curtain call, however, it scrolled its 'credits', feature-film style. The gimmick of NTLive is supposedly that these broadcasts include aspects of feature film by using multiple, variable-focus, moving cameras that can focus on characters' faces, even down to the sweat trickling down Othello's (Adrian Lester's) brow, and to the gasping supposed corpse of Emilia on the bed. The broadcasts also make use of television conventions such as a presenter, commercials for other NT live performances, and an interpolated documentary about the 'making of' the production and its military consultant screened during the mandatory intermission.

We expect our eye to be guided in auteur-driven film; such productions are shot out of temporal sequence, and the performance only happens when the director shouts, 'Action!' In a filmed stage production, the camera directs our attention like the intrusive narrator in a novel by Thomas Hardy or George Eliot, omniscient but insistently guiding. It tells you where to look and what to look at closely, and screens out the experiences of others even though we know—and this is a crucial distinction between filmed 'live' stage production and feature film—that the action continues off-camera in a performance space just out of sight. For example, the startling moment in the first mixed-race *Othello* in apartheid South Africa, Janet Suzman's ground-breaking 1989 production starring John Kani—when Othello's tribal-seeming necklace turns out to sheathe the dagger with which he will kill himself—arguably loses some of its effect on the massively distributed videotape of this historic performance. Although we follow the action of the dagger as it transforms from decorative to deadly object, we cannot—as we almost certainly would if we were able—glance quickly at Cassio or Gratiano to see whether they are surprised, sorrowful, or resigned.

As in Oliver Parker's, Jonathan Miller's, or Trevor Nunn's filmed *Othellos*, Hytner's production screened at large a domestic tragedy and screened out, through its use of close-up, an explicitly political one. Hytner's Othello, unlike Sax's, was not the only black character in his environment; the soldiers under his command came from various ethnicities and both genders. Rory Kinnear's Iago was overwhelmed with sexual jealousy and given this consistent motive throughout to explain his behaviour. This Iago's motive is to instil in his general the tortured sexual jealousy that he himself experiences with regard to his wife, and he lacks Iago's characteristic delight in designing duplicitous schemes and seeing them performed. The close-ups of Kinnear's face—even down to his twitching lips and tic-like spasms—pinpointed the suggestion that this was not a play about race but about psychology, including Othello's affronted dignity and sense of self. This production again supports Altman's suggestion that Othello constructs his sense of self rhetorically and after the fact. Once Othello starts to doubt assumptions he has taken for granted (in Altman's terms, once the balance between the 'probable' or provable and the 'improbable' or unprovable has been upset), he sees no alternative but savagery. As has always been true in the text but as we note afresh in this performance, Lester's Othello initiates the motion from uncertainty to murder; Kinnear's Iago seems startled or even overwhelmed by the events that he has set in motion.

All the domestic *Othellos* share a sense of claustrophobia, enhanced by the Shakestreamed hyper-mediacy of Hytner's production. The NT production featured smaller 'sub-sets' (Richard Forsyth's useful term) that literally boxed in the violent action of the fight scene.[29] The sub-sets reinforced the extreme insularity of the Cyprus setting at a military base. Aside from the regular melodic interruptions of the call to prayer, the production screened out the Middle Eastern setting of the world outside the base (to the extent that I wondered where Bianca lived and what kind of clothing she was wearing and who were her clients). In both the brawl and the murder of Desdemona, the confined space—a box or sub-set on the large stage and then another box (in the Shakestream broadcast or recorded projection) on the cinema screen—emphasized 'the pity of it' (4.1.190): the utter contingency or wilfulness of this tragedy, as if the world keeps shrinking even to the size of the bed. Donne's lyric 'The Sunne Rising' joyfully imagines the lovers' 'world contracted' to the bedroom and then the bed itself: 'This bed thy centre is, these walls thy sphere', but these lovers' bed-sheets become their winding-sheets, as Desdemona anticipated.

CONCLUSION

Each of these screened *Othellos* screens out a different aspect of the play, often in order to screen (to magnify) another. Buchowetzki's film screened out Othello's Black African

---

[29] Richard Forsyth, 'NT Live: Othello and Shows Coming Soon', Players-Shakespeare.com (blog), http://players-shakespeare.com/nt-live-othello-and-shows-coming-soon/, last accessed 28 January 2014.

origins and foregrounded the clash between Othello's chivalric medievalism and Iago's cinematic modernity. Welles's film screened out the possibility of human love in order to broaden the intersections of race, sexuality, and gender. Sax's television broadcast screened out the cathartic or purifying experience of tragedy and amplified the persistent institutional racism of contemporary London. Shaikh's television film screened out the association of skin colour with race and emphasized the 'tragedy of the Moor' or Muslim. The web-series screened out Cassio's gender but ultimately magnified contemporary associations about race and sexuality. Hytner's NTLive production screened out Othello's racial isolation but emphasized the claustrophobia of soldiers on a base far from home.

In all of these intermediated performances, what's excluded is the real and the unpredictable—the lived experience of race for the actor, the real bodies of the actors in the same physical space as the audience, the possibility (however unlikely) of unexpected personal catastrophe on the one hand and inappropriate comic resolution on the other. In this way screen *Othellos* magnify human, breathing, suffering bodies even as they conceal, protect, and withdraw from us from the lived truth of race in the world. The screen screens.

SELECT BIBLIOGRAPHY

Aebischer, Paschale, 'Black Rams Tupping White Ewes: Race vs. Gender in the Final Scene of Six *Othellos*', *Retrovisions: Reinventing the Past in Film and Fiction*, Ed. Deborah Cartmell, I.Q. Hunter, and Imelda Whelehan (London: Pluto, 2001), 59–73.

Altman, Joel, *The Improbability of* Othello (Chicago: University of Chicago Press, 2010).

Auslander, Philip, *Liveness* (London: Routledge, 1999).

Buchanan, Judith, *Shakespeare on Silent Film* (Harlow, UK, and New York: Pearson-Longman, 2005).

Bulman, James, and H. R. Coursen, eds., *Shakespeare on Television: An Anthology of Essays and Reviews* (Hanover and London: University Press of New England, 1988).

Burnett, Mark Thornton, *Shakespeare and World Cinema* (Cambridge: Cambridge University Press, 2013).

Cartmell, Deborah, *Interpreting Shakespeare on Screen* (London: St Martin's, 2000).

Cartelli, Thomas, and Katherine Rowe, *New Wave Shakespeare on Screen* (London: Polity, 2007).

Coursen, H. R., *Watching Shakespeare on Television* (Rutherford: Fairleigh Dickinson University Press; London and Toronto: Associated University Presses, 1993).

Davies, Anthony, '"An extravagant and wheeling stranger of here and everywhere": Characterising *Othello* on Film: Exploring seven film adaptations', *Shakespeare in Southern Africa* 23 (2011), 11–19.

Gil, Dan Juan. 'Avant-Garde Technique and the Visual Grammar of Sexuality in Orson Welles's Shakespeare Films', *Borrower and Lenders: The Journal of Shakespeare and Appropriation* 1.2 (2005), 28 pp. in pdf, <http://www.borrowers.uga.edu/781447/display>, accessed 20 March 2016.

Hodgdon, Barbara, 'Race-ing *Othello*, Re-engendering White-Out, II', in *Shakespeare, The Movie, II: Popularizing the Plays on Film, TV, Video, and DVD*, ed. Richard Burt and Lynda E. Boose (London and New York: Routledge, 2003), 89–104.

Lanier, Douglas, 'Murdering *Othello*', in Deborah Cartmell, ed., *A Companion to Literature, Film, and Adaptation* (Chichester, West Sussex, UK; Malden, MA: John Wiley & Sons, 2013), 198–213.

MacLiammóir, Micheál, *Put Money in Thy Purse: The Diary of the Film of* Othello (London: Methuen, 1952).

Osborne, Laurie E., 'Serial Shakespeare: Intermedial Performance and the Outrageous Fortunes of *Slings & Arrows*', *Borrowers and Lenders: The Journal of Shakespeare and Appropriation* 6:2 (2011), 24 pp. in pdf, http://www.borrowers.uga.edu/cocoon/borrowers/request?id=783090, accessed 20 March 2016.

Rothwell, Kenneth S., *A History of Shakespeare on Screen: A Century of Film and Television* (Cambridge and New York: Cambridge University Press, 2004).

Schröter, Jens, 'Four Models of Intermediality', In *Travels in Intermedia[lity]: Reblurring the Boundaries*, ed. Bernd Herzogenrath (Hanover, N.H.: Dartmouth College Press, 2012), 15–36.

Stone, James, 'Black and White as Technique in Orson Welles's *Othello*', *Literature/Film Quarterly* 30 (2002), 189–93.

Thompson, Ayanna, 'Unmooring the Moor: Researching and Teaching on You Tube', *Shakespeare Quarterly* 61:3 (2010), 337–56.

White, R. S., 'Sex, Lies, Videotape—and *Othello*', in *Almost Shakespeare: Reinventing his Works for Cinema and Television*, ed. James R. Keller and Leslie Stratyner (Jefferson, NC, and London: McFarland, 2004), 86–98.

Willis, Susan, *The BBC Shakespeare Plays: Making the Televised Canon* (Chapel Hill and London: University of North Carolina Press, 1991).

CHAPTER 37

....

SCREENING THE TRAGEDIES
King Lear

....

MACDONALD P. JACKSON

1

....

IN *King Lear*'s opening thirty-odd lines, which foreshadow both its plots, Gloucester and Kent converse in the presence of Edmond. Gloucester, referring to his 'whoreson', jokes that 'there was good sport at his making'. In Jonathan Miller's BBC TV production (1982) John Shrapnel's Kent reacts to Gloucester's flippant remarks about his adultery with complicit smiles and chuckles. Colin Blakely, playing Kent in Michael Elliott's version for Granada TV (1983), registers only embarrassment, his eyes downcast. Shrapnel's is the short-term response, serving the mood of the moment. Blakely is already fully 'in character', as a blunt moralist and decent man, likely enough to be disconcerted by the impropriety of Gloucester's bawdy-talk in front of Edmond.

This small difference of interpretation is of a kind that distinguishes any renderings of a script, on stage or screen. But these two versions of the episode also differ in their techniques of filming. The BBC's has been shot in a single long take from one stationary camera. The characters position themselves in relation to the lens, moving into significant groupings. Early on, for instance, Edmond can be seen conspicuously hovering behind and between Kent and Gloucester as they talk about him. Visual meaning is a matter of the movement and placing of characters, as in a stage production, though the camera brings us closer to them than we would be in a theatre. Granada's version, in contrast, uses a dozen different shots for the same opening dialogue, cutting between two-shots of Kent and Gloucester and close-ups of Edmond. Here camera-work is making the points about relationships and reactions. The sequence relies on four cameras set up in different places, so that angles on Kent and Gloucester change, while the close-ups encourage speculation about Edmond's inner feelings as he overhears his father's chatter.[1]

----

[1] There is a detailed discussion by Hardy M. Cook, 'Two Lears for Television: An Exploration of Televisual Strategies', in *Shakespeare on Television: An Anthology of Essays and Reviews*, ed. J. C. Bulman and H. R. Coursen (Hanover and London: University Press of New England, 1988), 122–9.

Any account of *King Lear* on screen must be concerned both with elements of presentation shared with the theatre and with peculiarly cinematic and televisual codes of communication. The language of drama, in the broadest sense, is already complex, including everything to be seen and heard. The filmmaker's art adds a further dimension, through the selection, sequence, and duration of *shots*, which are the basic filmic units.

This essay first compares the four best-known screen versions, two for television and two for cinema, and then more briefly discusses others that are readily available for viewing.[2]

2

Elliott's production, with Laurence Olivier in the title role, begins with the sun rising behind a misty Stonehenge, a gesture towards the play's timelessness, massiveness, and 'rough-hewn grandeur' that is undercut a little by the studio-replica look of this neolithic pile.[3] After the preliminary dialogue between Gloucester, Kent, and Edmond, Gloucester's 'The King is coming', together with appropriate music, gets the scene's business under way.[4]

King Lear begins with the brisk arbitrariness of folk-tale, the dramatic equivalent of 'Once upon a time there was a king with three daughters …'. It is this picture-book quality that Elliott's treatment of the scene captures, with its bright pastel colours, its fairy-tale old king, a toyshop crown on his head, its Rapunzel-haired youngest princess, its tendency towards moral absolutes, and its clear designs on our sympathies. The special tenderness between Cordelia and her father is established at the outset as he enters with his arm around her shoulder—after the rest of the court has assembled. This Lear, with his white hair and beard, has cast himself as Father Christmas in a gift-giving charade, and he likes to have an audience. He takes a childish delight in his royal authority and the adulation he receives. As he stands before his throne his subjects prostrate themselves, and he demands obeisance from Goneril and Regan. A mischievous gleam flickers in his eyes, but it takes him a while to focus them. He chortles ('Oh, ho ho ho!') as Regan essays to outbid her sister. When Cordelia refuses to play the game he has set up for her to win, he is indulgent, sure that there must be some misunderstanding. Even 'How, how, Cordelia? Mend your speech a little' is spoken, not peremptorily, but coaxingly, with a lilt on 'Cordelia' and 'a little', and the following 'Lest you may mar your fortunes' is conspiratorial, little more than a whisper. There is as much pain as anger in his eventual explosion. His is the disappointment of a Santa Claus thwarted. This is no mere despot, but a very vulnerable old man, as he dismisses Cordelia with a shaky wave of his hand. It hurts her to have to

---

[2] For two descriptive inventories see www.pbs.org/wnet/gperf/episodes/king-lear-film-and-print-editions/king-lear-films/563/ and king-lear.org/king_lear_on_dvd. Also, Kenneth Rothwell, *A History of Shakespeare on Screen* (Cambridge: Cambridge University Press, 1999), 299–34.

[3] The quoted phrase is by G. K. Hunter, ed., *King Lear* (Harmondsworth: Penguin, 1972), 7.

[4] Where possible I quote the play from the Folio-based *The Tragedy of King Lear* in *William Shakespeare: The Complete Works*, 2nd edn., gen. eds. Stanley Wells and Gary Taylor (Oxford: Clarendon Press, 2005), but when the words actually spoken in screen versions differ, I have reproduced them directly.

upset him. But it is not in her nature to enter this kind of contest, where declarations of love compete for material reward. Her sisters, a hardboiled Goneril and a smiling Regan, are nicely differentiated.[5] Albany's expression is one of puzzled wariness. Cornwall looks like a villain. These actors, Olivier in particular, exude personality. The production will be strong on emotion.

The camera-work and editing further this emphasis on individuals and feelings, cutting frequently from the speaker to the addressee, so as to catch nuances of expression in extreme close-up. There are cuts to high-angle long shots for overviews of the assembled court and the huge cowhide map, but the emphasis is on tightly framed shots of one or two people. For instance, Shakespeare gives Cordelia two asides with which to enlist the audience's empathy for her in her dilemma, and the camera draws her close to us as she turns back towards us to deliver them. When finally her father, bubbling over with his scheme, addresses 'our joy', as he calls her, the shot is from her point of view as he continues to talk while expectantly clambering back onto his throne. Then there is a cut to the distressed Cordelia herself in close-up, as she summons her strength for her answer, gulps, and gives it. The distance between the two selves, between Lear's preoccupations and hers, is poignantly revealed. An earlier close reaction-shot of Cordelia has shown her with an air of suppressed excitement dutifully nodding agreement to Lear's announcement that the time has come for her suitors to be answered. And then her father requires from her an extravagant protestation of her love for him at the very moment when she is preparing for marriage!

This production is built around a brilliantly inventive, engaging performance by an aged Olivier. It is studio-based but decorated with flora and fauna. Horses are ridden. The mouse that in his madness Lear tempts with a piece of toasted cheese is real, and he snares a rabbit, eviscerates it, and chews the entrails. There are dogs to track down the fleeing Edgar, and Kent's quarrel with Oswald excites loud barking, as in Brook's film. In the mock trial scene, 'Goneril' has strayed in from the fowl-yard. The designer aimed at what he called 'stylized realism'.[6] But the green turf of outdoor scenes in the middle of the play has the safe picturesqueness of the English countryside, despite being briefly muddied by lashings of studio rain. We are profoundly moved by Lear's personal tragedy, but something, more than glimpses of a polystyrene and plaster Stonehenge is needed to convey the play's rugged grandeur.

Miller's production does not attempt to supply it. In contrast to Elliott, with his montage technique, Miller continues to rely on medium and long shots from a relatively static camera, which records lengthy takes of characters manœuvred into apposite clusters. This strategy of importing theatrical space into the confines of the small screen is not without benefits. The ensemble shots allow for subtleties of characterization through movement, as when Regan is seen self-centredly edging forward to give her speech before Lear says 'Goneril, | Our eldest born, speak first'—one of several ways in which Miller foreshadows the sibling rivalry that will eventually destroy them. He does employ one meaningful cut

---

[5] Stanley Wells, review reprinted in Bulman and Coursen, *Shakespeare on Television*, 300.

[6] James P. Lusardi and June Schuelter, *Reading Shakespeare in Performance: 'King Lear'* (Cranbury, NJ: Associated University Presses, 1991), 187; the book is devoted to the BBC and Granada productions.

to similar effect, showing a reaction shot of Goneril when Regan says that her sister 'comes too short' in her protestations of filial devotion.

The Granada TV costumes are vaguely Anglo-Saxon or 'Pre-Raphaelite Arthurian', with ample colour and adornment, even for the men. Goneril and Regan are opulently gowned, while Cordelia is in white with an embroidered front and a virginal light-blue cape draped over her back. Miller's characters, in striking contrast, all wear Renaissance costumes in black or grey, with white ruffs, collars, or lace. Although variety is achieved through textures, distinctions of status are blurred.[7] Many of Miller's frames resemble seventeenth-century pictures of public occasions. The BBC Time-Life series often used 'visual quotations'—where the screen recalls a painting of some Dutch or Italian master— to create aesthetic distance and to alert us to Shakespeare's formal art of imitation. But here the effect is to suggest the world of Jacobean politics. Miller interests us in intrigue and the psychology of the power-seekers. But the family squabbles seldom feel like perturbations in a kingdom, let alone Armageddon. For the love-test and transfer of 'all the large effects | That troop with majesty' Lear wears no crown, sits on no regal throne, enters to no musical fanfare, and receives no ceremonial deference from his subjects. He is dressed like them and moves among them on their level. But, seated at a long table with the map before him, he could perhaps be in some Jacobean state chamber.

Miller's sets are simple in the extreme, bare and unparticularized. The boards trod by the actors might be those of a stage, and the purpose-built furniture, stained black, is strictly functional. Outdoor scenes have virtually no detail, no background, just a vague studio greyness created by swathes of canvas and desaturated of colour, but broken up by shafts of light. They are spaces in which an interiorized world of tragedy may be enacted.

This does make for a small-scale starkness and puts the onus on the actors and Shakespeare's words. There are some memorable performances, notably from Michael Hordern as a 'growling and worried' Lear and Gillian Barge as a sensual Goneril who uses a tone of sweet reasonableness like a rapier.[8] Brenda Blethyn as Cordelia is more prim and less sensitive than Granada's Anna Calder-Marshall. In her bonnet and simple collar, contrasting with her sisters' lavish court dress, she looks like some New England puritan, and her response to her father betrays exasperation with his silliness. Miller adds the Fool—distinguished by large red feathers in his hat and white face-paint—to Shakespeare's initial mass-entry, standing him next to Cordelia, who directs her asides to him. The critical truism that the play closely associates these two truth-tellers is thus underlined. The Fool lays a comforting hand on the young woman's shoulder after Lear's rejection of her.

In Elliott's version it is Kent who silently comforts a more obviously distressed Cordelia and France claims her tenderly with an enfolding arm. Reviewing Miller's production, Steven Urkowitz complained of 'a basic isolation of the actors from the emotional life implied by the words they speak': for instance, when Cordelia bids farewell to her sisters

---

[7] Miller's approach is detailed in Jonathan Miller, *Subsequent Performances* (London: Faber and Faber, 1986), 128–53; the introductory material to the published BBC script, *King Lear* (London: BBC Books, 1983); and Susan Willis, *The BBC Shakespeare Plays: Making the Televised Canon* (Chapel Hill: University of North Carolina Press), 127–31.

[8] The quoted phrase is by Henry Woudhuysen on a review reprinted in Bulman and Coursen, *Shakespeare on Television*, 288.

'with washed eyes' Brenda Blethyn's eyes are dry.[9] But tears do indeed trickle down Anna Calder-Marshall's cheek. On the screen, one notices such details.

In subsequent scenes, Olivier arouses sympathy for Lear by making him very quickly conscious of, and distressed by, the enormity of his initial misjudgements. In bringing them home to him, John Hurt's Fool suffers with him. Even Lear's curses against Goneril seem less horrific than usual, the reflex outbursts of impotent old age, rather than expressions of revengeful fury. Olivier stresses Lear's bewilderment, his self-recriminations at his own folly, his closeness to tears and to mental breakdown. In the mock-trial scene, when he protests 'The little dogs and all, | Tray, Blanch, and Sweetheart—see, they bark at me', 'Sweetheart' is said with a quavering voice as he remembers Cordelia.

Goneril is truculent and sour, resentful of the younger and more attractive Regan, who is suave and cajoling, though revealed as an eager sadist in the scene of Gloucester's blinding. After his torturer, Cornwall, has been mortally wounded by an outraged servant, and gasps the closing words 'Regan, I bleed apace. | Untimely comes this hurt. Give me your arm', her sole response is an icy stare.

Granada's Goneril does have some grounds for complaint during Lear's sojourn at her home. His knights are a rowdy crew. Lear rides his horse into the chamber, equipped with tables, where he calls for dinner. But in this production interiors are 'log dwellings lit by torches, rough wooden stockades', so that the distinction between indoors and outdoors is blurred.[10]

In and after the storm Olivier remains likable, as his moods tumble over one another in his struggles against his frailty. Near Dover, he is both practical and happily daft, washing his clothes in a brook, living off the meat that nature has afforded him, playing with the mouse, adorning himself with a crown and necklace of wild-flowers, amusing himself with the fantasies of second childhood. As he totters up a gentle slope to his encounter with Gloucester, he sings snatches from the song in which a lover calls to his sweetheart, 'Come o'er the bourn, Bessy, to me', imported from the mock trial to the banks of a real stream: his beloved youngest daughter is still infiltrating his thoughts.[11] The flowers are, of course, realizations of Cordelia's description in 4.4 of reported sightings of him. The Granada imagery answers to the play's shifts in emotional weather. The scene of reconciliation, where Lear struggles out of his delirium to find his youngest daughter bending solicitously over him, while musicians play softly in the background, is intensely moving, with Calder-Marshall extracting the last drop of emotion from 'And so I am, I am' and 'No cause, no cause.'[12] Her regal robes contrast with her father's white night-gown, reversing their original garb.

The screen allows Olivier to deliver his exchanges with the blind Gloucester as intimate, hushed chat, as he cradles his bloodied head. It is an episode of extraordinary sweetness,

---

[9] Steven Urkowitz in Bullman and Coursen, *Shakespeare on Televsion*, 288.

[10] Alexander Leggatt, *Shakespeare in Performance: King Lear* (Manchester: Manchester University Press, 1991), 121. Leggatt provides brilliantly perceptive accounts of all four screen versions discussed in my sections 1–3.

[11] Olivier includes 'little pretty Bessie' and 'she dare not speak' from a variant version of the song. See Stanley Wells, ed., *The History of King Lear* (Oxford: Oxford University Press, 2000), in the Oxford World Classics series, commentary on sc. 13.21.

[12] Elliott shows full awareness of the importance in Shakespeare of the tempest–music opposition first traced by G. Wilson Knight, *The Shakespearian Tempest* (Oxford: Oxford University Press, 1932).

with tinges of the comic pathos of Shallow and Silence trading memories of their youth in *2 Henry IV*. But the bitterness about injustice and the nausea at the idea of female sexuality are also vividly conveyed in sudden outbursts.

Hordern as the BBC Lear plays this scene in a strikingly different manner. He is unpredictable, alarmingly out of control, at one moment laughing with Gloucester, at another poking the sockets of his eyes. He is literally barking mad, 'a dog's obeyed in office' provoking a 'woof, woof!' While he gabbles, shouts, and twitches, Edgar, remains in the near-background, a concerned looker-on. All three stand throughout. Edgar's ravings as Poor Tom outside the hovel have precipitated Lear's madness: there we see him frantically nodding agreement to Tom's nonsense and mimicking his movements. They are *tête-à-tête*, filling the screen. Hordern's performance, though remarkable, conveys 'mental affliction' rather than 'spiritual anguish'.[13] His railing in the storm and cursing of his daughters come across as a kind of self-absorbed cantankerousness. The storm is shown almost solely through Lear's rain-spattered, lightning-lit face in close-up, even extreme close-up, while the Fool lurks behind him.

Frank Middlemas's gruff, vaudeville-style Fool, Lear's coeval, barks out his rhymes and wisecracks as the king's accusing conscience. Otherwise Miller's actors tend towards a 'light, quick, and natural' delivery of their lines, often *sotto voce*. Lear's knights are quiet and well behaved.[14] Goneril is imperiously low-key. Here Regan is the more overtly aggressive of the two. Gloucester's eyes are gouged out while he sits facing away from the camera, his screams fully conveying the horror. As Cornwall surgeon-like wipes his hands after this operation, Regan gives him an excited kiss.

Noting the Christian overtones in the text, despite its pagan world, Miller equipped Edgar with a crown of thorns and stigmata, seeing him as the counterpart to a courtly Edmond as Lucifer.[15] Cordelia kneels in prayer for her protestation that she is going about her father's business, with its New Testament echoes. But the restoration scene is weakened by the cramming into the frame of the Doctor and Kent, the latter too prominent in his skinhead disguise. More effective is Edgar's nursing of his father, as Miller begins to use more close-ups.

Miller omits the battle, showing only a defeated line of soldiers trudging across the back of the frame as in the foreground Edgar urges Gloucester 'Away, old man ... King Lear hath lost'. Elliott, in contrast, superimposes images of burning timbers and fierce fighting on Gloucester, as he sits (deposited by Edgar on 'this holy stone' rather than under a tree) hearing the uproar. For the BBC's showdown with Edmond, a white-masked Edgar (linking him to the Fool) pushes his way forward after the trumpet has sounded thrice. The brief combat is compellingly filmed in head and shoulders shots, with yelling and frenzied action. Granada's, after Edmond has turned to see Edgar as a mysterious silhouette against a bleached sky, is prolonged, well choreographed for medium and long shots, but on the screen one is more conscious than in the theatre of the pretence of violence.

After his blood-curdling howls as he enters with Cordelia in his arms, Lear vacillates between the certain knowledge that she is dead and the vain hope that she is not. Bradley controversially argued that he dies of joy, believing her to be alive—an interpretation available only in the Folio text, which adds the enigmatic lines 'Do you see this? Look on

---

[13] Benedict Nightingale, quoted by Leggatt, *Shakespeare in Performance*, 118.
[14] Leggatt, *Shakespeare in Performance*, 115.   [15] Miller, *Subsequent Performances*, 128–31.

her. Look, her lips. | Look there, look there.' Critics have also debated whether in Lear's last speech 'fool' in 'And my poor fool is hanged' is a term or endearment for Cordelia or a reference to the Fool. Of course the appellation inevitably links the two, but an actor must choose how to speak the six words. The thoughts of Hordern's Lear—as Edgar and Kent crouch either side of him and Albany takes up a position in behind them—are not in his conscious control. As the neurons erratically flicker, while his fingers trace the marks from the noose around Cordelia's neck, his mind makes the associative jump from one truth-teller to another and momentarily evokes the fate of his Fool.

Choosing neither the Bradleyan joyful rendering of Lear's last lines nor, the preference of most modern Lears, a despairing one, Hordern manages to be ambiguous. Distractedly stroking and cuffing his daughter's cheek, he feels a sudden tightness in his own bared throat, the onset of a heart-attack, and calls for the loosening of a non-existent button. He dies in a paroxysm that is more physical than emotional or spiritual. The oxygen-deprived cerebral cortex flashes for one last time, and the last words simply emerge in a death shout. In line with his earlier madness, this is a *medical* ending.

Olivier gives a virtuoso performance of Lear's switches between hope and despair. He utters Cordelia's name with the coaxing inflexion he had used for the love-test. She is his 'fool'. At 'come' in 'Thou'lt come no more' he feebly flexes a hand in a beckoning gesture. His last words are a diminuendo, neither anguished nor joyous, but expressions of love, as, like Othello, he dies upon a kiss. While a cello plays, the camera draws back to show father and daughter on the 'holy stone', encircled by attendants with flaming torches and, beyond them, by the megalith and the sun, 'a wheel of fire', on the horizon. The picture echoes the circles of the deranged Lear's benign capture, the arena in which Edgar and Edmond fought, the battle raging around Gloucester as he 'sees' it 'with [his] ears', the arrest of Lear and Cordelia, and, most significantly, the opening. As Edgar delivers the closing speech we are reminded of his 'through the sharp hawthorn blow the winds', as we hear them whistle.

3

The two television versions cut about as much text as does the average theatre production, with the BBC pruning the more lightly. Cinema typically needs fewer words. Russian director Grigori Kozintsev, while basing the script for his *King Lear* (*Korol Lir*, 1971) on Pasternak's translation, deemed that 'The poetic texture itself has to be transformed into a visual poetry, into the dynamic organization of film imagery.'[16] Peter Brook believed that place was more important than period for any setting of *King Lear*.[17] His film (1971) omitted half Shakespeare's dialogue and redeployed the residue, splitting scenes and even speeches into smaller units. But by shooting in and around a sprawling granite fortress in the snow-bound tundra of Northern Jutland he was able to convey something bleak, primitive, and

---

[16] Grigori Kozintsev, '"Hamlet" and "King Lear": Stage and Film', in Clifford Leech and J. M. R. Margeson, eds., *Shakespeare 1971* (Toronto: University of Toronto Press, 1972), 190–9, at 191.

[17] Brook, ITV's South Bank Show on *King Lear*, built around David Hare's National Theatre production with Anthony Hopkins as Lear, and broadcast 11 January 1987.

vast that is largely absent from the TV versions. The film, like Brook's famous theatre production before it, was influenced by Polish critic Jan Kott's post-Holocaust view of *King Lear* as the Shakespearean equivalent of Samuel Beckett's *Endgame*—nihilistic and without hope.[18] Brook eschewed music, heightened the play's brutal violence, and blurred distinctions between good and evil characters. The first half of Edmond's lying speech to Gloucester about Edgar's having often maintained that a son should manage his father's revenues is assigned to Edgar himself as he smilingly cues his brother to complete it. Lear's knights are genuinely riotous, pelting a fleeing Oswald and, after Lear's confrontation with Goneril, taking a cue from his overturning of a laden table to create general havoc. Gloucester's 'As flies to wanton boys are we to th' gods; | They kill us for their sport' is removed from its specific context and given the authority of voice-over, as a far-distant Edgar leads his father through icy wastes to Dover. Technically, Brook uses all the tricks of the 'New Wave' cinema, with its rapid shifts and disjunctions.

The credits come up as the camera pans in silence across a crowd of the motionless male faces of the embattled 'survival culture' society over which Lear rules. The preliminary dialogue having been jettisoned, we move to a cavernous stone chamber, with a heavy door that slams shut. The focus is on the back of a huge oval throne, with those assembled beyond. Abruptly, Lear's face fills the screen, and after several seconds he speaks: 'Know', with a pause that lets us hear the negative homophone. Whereas TV tends to personalize the actors, to the point even of individual quirkiness, Paul Scofield's grizzled, growling head transports us to a more ritualistic and generalized dramatic world. The filming in monochrome aids this impression. Lear's huge visage is immobile except for the lips, a barely perceptible swivel of the eyes as he mentions Albany and Cornwall, and a tiny twist of the head as he addresses Goneril. Each daughter must hold an orb as she speaks. A sour-looking Goneril delivers her protestation of love in dreamlike monotone, as though reciting a litany. Sweet-faced Regan manages a shade more expression. No significant glances are exchanged. Cordelia is almost sullen. Brook cuts her asides: we do not know what she thinks or feels, though a shot of her sitting alone makes its claim on our imagination. Brook also omits the closing lines of Lear's speech, where after asking 'Which of you shall we say doth love us most?', he continues, 'That we out largest bounty may extend | Where nature doth with merit challenge'. So the ulterior motives of Goneril and Regan are less clear.

There are sudden cuts between close-ups, mid-shots, and long-shots, and between the backs and fronts of heads. Though France and Burgundy are twice mentioned (as in the Folio), Lear addresses neither, and France claims Cordelia while Burgundy stands in silence. Kent's dispute with Lear is shown as two opposed half-faces in profile at extreme left and right of the frame. The confrontation, though tense, is private and quiet. As Lear stalks out the door and shoulders his way through his expectant subjects, he is clothed to resemble some great vulture, and animal furs and skins soon dehumanize others into the beasts of prey to which Shakespeare's imagery likens them. Outdoors a column of horsemen and crude carriages and carts trek through the snow.

Many conversations—between Regan and Goneril, Lear and the Fool, Edgar and Edmond—take place in the wooden-wheeled, horse-drawn vehicles. Filming techniques remain startling throughout. The camera swings to and fro between a seated Lear and the

---

[18] Jan Kott, *Shakespeare Our Contemporary*, trans. Boleslaw Taborski (London: Methuen, 1964); Brook wrote the preface to this book.

Fool (the wonderfully lugubrious, droll, and empathetic Beckett actor Jack MacGowran) to register the latter's initial entry. A jump-cut has Goneril, as angry hostess, first loom before Lear in extreme close-up. This method is especially effective when Edgar, nemesis personified, materializes unheralded to challenge Edmond and kill him with the single stroke of an axe. Dialogue is often delivered off-frame or while the image is of the speaker's back or some other body part. There are two title cards explaining locales and events in silent-movie mode. Action is punctuated by pure blackness, as when, at the words 'See't shalt thou never', Cornwall picks up an iron implement and advances on Gloucester tied in a chair; but we get a quick glimpse of the gouging of the second eye. Regan batters the protesting servant to death, but she is tearful before embracing the mortally wounded Cornwall. Although this film's violent attacks are nasty, brutish, and short, Brook does show an old servant cracking an egg (as the Fool did to create 'two crowns') and applying the white to Gloucester's eyes.

Many later shots of the head or face of Gloucester are out of focus. For the storm Brook mingles odd angles and distortions, dazzling white and sheer black frames, rapid switches as Lear's face appears at extreme left or right, the momentary superimposition of the Fool's face on Lear's, and a lens blurred by water-drops. The drenched Lear delivers 'Blow winds and crack your cheeks' while lying beside the Fool on the ground, eyes directed skyward. In the hovel, the camera tilts down the 'poor bare forked animal' that is Tom, while at 'Child Roland to the dark tower came' the screen again turns black. Goneril and Cordelia make hallucinatory appearances. The 'little dogs' that 'bark' are corralled sheep that bleat. Outside, the blizzard leaves animal corpses strewn about. In human dwellings fires blaze. 'In such a night as this' being accommodated matters for livestock too.

The stylistic keynote is fracture. But in the reunion scene Brook uses his panoply of tricks with great tact. Close-ups or mid-shots of Cordelia and recumbent Lear alternate. The Doctor's 'He's scarce awake' and Kent's 'In your own kingdom' are from unseen voices that Lear cannot yet locate. There are quick glimpses of Kent standing in the background. All are single-person shots, until 'And so I am, I am', beautifully articulated, unites Cordelia and Lear in a two-shot. The overcrowding of Miller's BBC version of the episode is skilfully avoided. The meeting of Lear and Gloucester at Dover is similarly affecting— on a long stretch of beach, where in occasional crane shots they appear like washed-up wreckage. Their talk, however, is even more confidential and intimate than in the Granada production. This is the film's dominant manner: the actors tend to 'flatten and understate', speaking 'in slow, gruff whispers'.[19] This is true of Scofield, who nevertheless can burst into vocal thunder-claps, as in 'No, you unnatural *hags*'. Though gnarled, he is sturdy, revealing old age only in hunched shoulders and uncertain adjustments of his gaze, as though struggling to get his bearings.

The battle is a blur to the noise of crackling flames, as experienced by the waiting Gloucester. Then burning boats and dwellings are displayed and Gloucester's corpse is dragged off by Edgar, who picks up a long-handled axe.

The sub-plot is stripped to the bone. Edmond incriminates Edgar by tricking him into reading aloud, while Gloucester eavesdrops, the forged letter about hastening their father's

---

[19] Jack J. Jorgens, *Shakespeare on Film* (Lanham, Maryland: University Press of America, 1991), 244.

demise. Edgar's disguise as a bedlam beggar deceives the horse-riding posse in search of him, but attracts a callous blow. Edmond's final repentance is cut. Regan murders Goneril by hurling her headlong to the stony ground. She then kneels, swaying like a cobra about to strike, and brains herself on a rock. There is a jump-cut to Cordelia hanged. Filmmakers are apt to show action that Shakespeare merely narrates. The effect here is to accentuate the horror.

A distant Lear howls as he carries Cordelia across deserted wasteland. After the camera has drawn near and he has laid her down and bent over her, reality and delusion are confused. 'This feather stirs' is spoken while Lear stands, holding a feather far from Cordelia. Kent and Edgar appear, vanish, and reappear. Cordelia momentarily stands nearby. On 'Never ...' and 'Look on her ...' Lear reclines utterly alone, staring upward, until the eyes close as his head drops slowly out of the frame to leave blank white nothingness.

If Brook's film was tinged with Theatre of the Absurd and Theatre of Cruelty, Kozintsev's owed much to a Christian-humanist tradition and the great Russian novelists, especially Dostoyevsky. His *King Lear: The Space of Tragedy* is the perfect guide to his preoccupations and his comprehensive response to Shakespeare's play.[20] His insights make most modern criticism seem trivial. Shot for wide-screen Sovscope, the equivalent of Cinemascope but in this case monochrome, Kozintsev's outdoor *mises-en-scène* are a collage from Balkan locations of boulder-strewn hills and desolate river flats, but numerous peasants, soldiers, and beggars wend their way through them. He is concerned to show the breakdown of rule affecting the people. Imagery is truly elemental—earth, water, fire, air. He wanted no hint of historical costume drama. Any attempt to recreate minutiae of a specific time and place would detract from the tragedy's essentials. His characters are dressed in gowns, cloaks, tunics, or sackcloth tatters that have been common wear for centuries. 'A mother breast-feeds her baby: a beggar wraps himself in rags to protect his body from the cold—what century do such details belong to?'[21] Objects and accoutrements were not to draw attention to themselves. Nor must there be any grandiloquence—nothing that set 'boundaries between *Lear* and contemporary life'.[22] Viewers must be made to experience a recognizable reality: 'political treachery, heads of state overturned, documents [faked], secret assassinations, a career forged out of the blood of those nearest—is this really only a theatrical fantasy?'[23] No, Lear's world is actual, though neither prehistoric nor Renaissance: 'It is like all times.'[24]

In *Korol Lir*, horses, dogs, sheep, cattle are not the animate scenic props of TV, but creatures in symbiotic relationship with humans. And Kozintsev's fluent cinematography constructs a visual poetry that imparts metaphorical resonance to what is shown, achieving 'unity of spiritual and material life on the screen'.[25] The rhythms, echoes, and contrasts of Shakespeare's scenes and speeches are translated into cinematic terms. Dmitri Shostakovich's magnificent music deepens this effect. Kozintsev had never heard an actor convey the impact of 'Blow, winds, and crack your cheeks! Rage, blow!' but had 'heard something similar and of equal weight in the tragic *forte* passages in Shostakovich's

---

[20] Grigori Kozintsev, *King Lear: The Space of Tragedy*, trans. Mary Mackintosh (London: Heinemann, 1977); hereafter 'Kozintsev'.
  [21] Kozintsev, 37.   [22] Kozintsev, 94.   [23] Kozintsev, 33.   [24] Kozintsev, 48.
  [25] Kozintsev, 51.

symphonies'.[26] The soundtrack is full also of evocative noises: the clatter of hooves or boots, the tap of walking-sticks, the barking of dogs and cries of birds, the creaking of wheels, the crackle of fire, the ripple and rush of water, the ringing of bells, the clash of weapons.

The film opens with peasant folk, some with crude hand-carts, trudging along a pathway through huge rocks, on one of which is a carved icon. We see their cloth-bound feet, legs, and staffs first. A horn is blown. The scene opens onto long files of people converging from all directions upon Lear's hill-top castle. Spear-holders on horseback force them back. Crowds stand out against the skyline, as Lear's travelling entourage will later. Kent and Gloucester converse as they stroll to the castle entrance. Kozintsev reluctantly made do with a studio interior. Councillors are assembled, the elder sisters, heads erect, stride stiffly in, Cordelia, light of foot, hurries down stairs to join them, but stands apart. Faces await the king. The Fool's bell tinkles off-frame, and a laughing Lear enters. He is white-haired and slight of build, without royal insignia, but lively and used to absolute command. Unexpectedly he takes a seat by the fire. The image is as packed with meaning as a line by Shakespeare. Certainty of deference, warmth, comfort, ease in his status—life for Lear is about to change. And his edicts from the hearth will culminate in general conflagration.

Kozintsev achieves realism in this film through various strategies. Characters move and do things as they talk. Most soliloquies, asides, and monologues are delivered wholly or partly as voice-over, sometimes when the speakers are at a distance. Lear's initial statement of intent is read out by a functionary. France has a translator to interpret what Lear and Cordelia say. Lear has already stormed out—the people expectant, fires lit and smoke billowing—as his rejection of Cordelia is completed as public denunciation. Beside a wooden cross near the ocean she and France are married by a hermit. Lear and Goneril set off to her home in a horse-drawn carriage with a regal entourage.

His quarrel with her builds gradually, as they sit together over dinner. 'Does any here know me?' and 'Hear, nature, hear' are said quietly to himself and in voice-over, as is the later 'O, reason not the need', and later still his speeches when mad. Kozintsev chose Yuri Yarvet for his Lear because of his profoundly expressive face. The camera looks into his eyes and sees all. The Fool—a boy with shaven head and 'tormented eyes'—is a village idiot 'who speaks the truth'.[27] It is the sight of a stumbling line of beggars that prompts Edgar into becoming Poor Tom and joining them. Wolves slink from the storm, as the wide sky darkens and winds rage. Rocks, rain, lightning. 'Blow winds' is filmed in long shots of the lone man battling against hostile elements. The hovel is crammed with 'rogues forlorn'. Gloucester, his chair overturned, is blinded by Cornwall's boot. Albany rebukes Goneril in his library. Multitudes, with their pathetic belongings, flee the war as troops muster. The reconciliation scene, shifting from a grotto to the open air, takes place while battle, complete with crude siege engines and scaling ladders, rages confusedly and on a massive scale. Dwellings are torched and cattle stampede from burning stalls.

Gloucester, fingering Edgar's face, dies joyfully recognizing his son, who fashions a rough cross to set above a makeshift grave. Edgar and Edmond fight ferociously with swords in an arena formed by over a hundred soldiers with helmets and pikes. As Edmond

---

[26] Kozintsev, 51.   [27] Kozintsev, 72.

writhes and pants on the ground and gives the countermand for Cordelia's release, Lear's echoing howls begin. While masses gaze upwards, he is sighted on the top of the cliff-like wall from which he had denounced Cordelia. Her hanged body appears on high in an arch of rock. Down at ground level, the feather that a standing Lear sees stir is non-existent. He lifts Cordelia and presses her face next to his ear for 'What is't thou sayst?' It is heart-breaking. But as Lear utters his anguished 'nevers', we glimpse through the vacant archway gulls gliding over the ocean, by which Cordelia had returned. 'She'll come no more', but something free, natural, and pure that is associated with her endures. Lear and Cordelia are carried out on a single bier, united in death. The weeping Fool lives on, kicked aside by a soldier as he plays a mournful tune on his pipe amid the realm's smouldering ruins. But stragglers douse fires and clear burned timbers. Painfully, life goes on.

For Kozintsev, Lear's is a journey towards redemption: the play tears from him the mask of power and, as he identifies with 'poor naked wretches', suffering makes him 'beautiful and human'.[28] And Kozintsev knows that those moments of loving tenderness—between Edgar and Gloucester, Cordelia and Lear—shine with an intense light that darkness and death cannot quench.

4

The four major screen versions of *King Lear* discussed in sections 37.1-3 are not without notable predecessors and successors. A brief historical survey of these follows, culminating in an account of the only more recent movie that is not a cross-cultural adaptation.

Early in the twentieth century, several silent *King Lear*s were made.[29] A Vitagraph production of 1909, filmed indoors with painted décor, was the first to feature a simulacrum of Stonehenge. Still readily viewed are an eleven-minute, hand-tinted Film D'Arte Italiana miming of the gist of Lear's story, without Gloucester's (*Re Lear*, 1910), and a more ambitious Thanhouser movie (1916), with Frederick B. Warde as Lear and directed by his son Ernest, who also plays the cap-and-bells Fool. In both films, which vary indoor and outdoor locations, Lear is a hirsute Methuselah-like patriarch and Cordelia a Cinderella with two Ugly Sisters. The American movie is much less obtrusively gesticulatory than the Italian and is in fact a masterpiece of its time, employing, from immobile cameras, a judicious assortment of long, medium, and close shots (including reaction shots) to cover well-organized crowd scenes and intimate exchanges. Once the plot has been outlined and the actors and the nature of their roles identified, intercut title cards are drawn, with adjustments, from Shakespeare's dialogue. The battle teems with cavalry and foot-soldiers. Lear dies falling slowly backwards, as in Brook's film. In the absence of heard speech, the organ continuo supplied on DVD is a crucial complement to the images in conveying ambience and aiding coherence.

---

[28] Kozintsev, 63.

[29] Full details can be found in Robert Hamilton Ball, *Shakespeare on Silent Film: A Strange Eventful History* (London: Allen and Unwin, 1968), and Judith Buchanan, *Shakespeare on Silent Film: An Excellent Dumb Discourse* (Cambridge: Cambridge University Press, 2009). The Italian *Re Lear* is included on the British Film Institute's DVD, *Silent Shakespeare*.

In 1953 Peter Brook had adapted *King Lear* for monochrome CBS TV. This 'Elizabethan dress' production, with Orson Welles as Lear, plays for 73 minutes. The sub-plot is excised. Gloucester is, however, retained, to have his eyes gouged out by Cornwall's thumb and to stumble, alone with staff in hand, to his encounter with the mad king. Edmond's role as object of Goneril and Regan's lust and as military general is reassigned to a reptilian Oswald. Since there is no avenging Edgar, Albany reads aloud the incriminating letter from Goneril, Oswald kills Regan as she attacks Goneril, then stabs himself. 'Poor Tom' is the crazed denizen of a windmill, which serves as the hovel. Its sails, cogs, and wheels symbolically creak, grind, and turn. It is in this 'Piranese torture chamber' that Gloucester is arrested and blinded after Kent, Lear, and the Fool have left.[30]

Several of the techniques of Brook's film are already present. The sets, backgrounded by pitch blackness, provide vivid images. Regan's castle is claustrophobic, equipped with a portcullis and drawbridge, manipulated by huge dangling chains. Kent is both stocked and encaged. Lear's retinue is boisterous, harassing one of Goneril's servants. Cordelia flaunts her virtue in elocutionary tremulo. Her asides at the love-test are heard as echoing voice-over, though her lips move. When, amid the tents of her invading army, she intones 'O dear father | It is thy business that I go about', the lighting picks out a cruciform ship-mast in the background. The Fool is court-jester sporting a coxcomb. He veers between plaintiveness and capering playfulness, and leads Lear's knights in chanting the 'Fools had ne'er grace in a year' rhymes in chorus. Virgil Thomson's music, ranging from martial drums and brass to plangent strings for Cordelia, underscores emotion or increases tension in Hollywood style. The soundtrack evokes an impressive storm, in which Lear looms out of Stygian darkness into an erratically lit foreground of hallucinatory images of a lightning-struck model tree, clumps of wind-tossed grass, and driving rain.

But the main interest for viewers now is in Welles's performance. Large and broad-shouldered, he is a Henry VIII-like monarch, first wearing a spiky crown but later, at Goneril's palace, a hat like Henry's in portraits, and finally nothing but his white woolly hair. A commanding presence, Welles uses the full gamut of his powerful base voice. In his rejection of Cordelia and banishment of Kent he is forceful and stern, rather than irate. His curses of Goneril are the more unsettling for being controlled. 'I would not be mad' is spoken with wild-eyed alarm, and as madness overtakes him, though his eyes bulge and roam, his true gaze turns inward to his own dark imagining. Now viewed in close-ups, Welles can convey an old man's bemusement, as his wits scatter, with the quiver of a lip. At Dover, where crashing waves can be heard, he is draped in a fisherman's net, his hair and clothes tangled with seaweed. His final howls announce his entry dragging Cordelia's corpse, like a rag doll, behind him. His last speeches are pared to the minimum, as he dumps her, climbs to the throne where he began, and dies, arms spread wide along the back of it, to his last 'never'. Albany, as in the quarto, delivers the play's last speech.

Although as a rendering of Shakespeare's tragedy, Brook's adaptation is fragmentary and elliptical, its nightmare images and potted dialogue give it a baroque coherence of its own. Nearly all the tragedy's essential ingredients are there, even—for all the stress on

---

[30] The phrase is Tony Howard's, in his fine essay, 'When Peter Met Orson: The CBS *King Lear*', in *Shakespeare, the Movie: Popularizing the Plays on Film, TV, and Video*, ed. Lynda E. Boose and Richard Burt (London and New York: Routledge, 1997), 121–34, at 129.

cruelty, degeneration, and sex-obsessed mania—the courage of Cornwall's servant, as he acts upon his moral revulsion at Gloucester's torture, and the beauty of Lear's resignation to being sent with Cordelia to prison. The one thing missing is any hint of the belated dawning of Lear's social conscience.

Curiously, 'O, I have ta'en too little care of this' is one of the more convincing lines in Patrick Magee's portrayal of Lear in a version directed by Tony Davenall for Thames TV in 1976. Magee, brilliant as the Marquis de Sade, seems miscast as Lear, his eccentric intonations grating on the ear. Sets, costumes, and acting are stagey, reminiscent of amateur theatricals. Camera-work is stilted. The production lacks momentum. The cutting to 110 minutes of playing time is often obtuse, omitting the key speeches of recognition from the recognition scene, for example, and all-but eliminating the Fool. There is no war, and in the comically inept single fight Edgar falls and rolls on fake grass while Edmond's repeated swipes of his sword miss his opponent's body or head by a cautious metre.

There could be no greater contrast than with Akiro Kurosawa's Japanese-language *Ran* (1985), a powerful adaptation of Shakespeare's tragedy, remixing many of its ingredients, including a sprinkling of translated key sentences, into the new work of art of a great filmmaker.[31] The Lear figure Hidetora is a sixteenth-century Japanese warlord, who divides his kingdom between his three sons, giving commanding authority to the eldest, Tarô. The second son, Jirô, plots to usurp this position. He is egged on by Tarô's wife Kaede, who becomes his mistress, combining the lust and ambition of Goneril and Regan. Jirô's estranged Buddhist wife Sué assumes something of Cordelia's role and Gloucester's blindness is shared by her flute-playing brother Tsurumaru. A ruined Buddhist temple substitutes for the hovel. Hidetora's ordeal is by fire rather than storm, but a typhoon strikes and he is long exposed to the elements. Battles are magnificent and conflagrations apocalyptic. The Fool—a Japanese kabuki court fool—is Hidetora's main companion in his mad wanderings in the wilderness. With his long white beard Hidetora looks like the typical nineteenth-century stage Lear. There is a reunion with the youngest son Saburô, who is immediately slain. In the opening scene Saburô is outspokenly critical of Hidetora, taking over Kent's vehemence.

Hidetora's crucial difference from Lear is that his power has been built through a lifetime of bloodthirsty conquest. He had gouged out Tsurumaru's eyes. Kaede, a Lady Macbeth figure, using her sexuality to promote male aggression, is motivated by desire for revenge on Hidetora's whole family, because he slaughtered hers. So the story is one of retribution. Beautiful natural surroundings are the arena for human brutality. Buddhist retreat from this life is the sole antidote. At the end, the blind Tsurumura 'still playing his reedy Noh flute, taps with his stick toward the edge of an abyss'. Empty blue sky fills the frame. Kurosawa's vibrantly coloured film has colossal scope and epic grandeur. He has not only transmuted Shakespeare's tragedy into screen imagery, but recycled it 'in the cultural iconology of Japan'.[32]

Some celebrated stage performances have been transferred to video, notably Edwin Sherin's Central Park, New York, production, with James Earl Jones as Lear and the audience present (1974); Richard Eyre's for the National Theatre (London), with Ian Holm

---

[31] A fairly recent account is by Judith Buchanan, *Shakespeare on Film* (Harlow, Essex: Pearson–Longman, 2005), 80–5.

[32] Rothwell, *History*, 200.

(1998); and Trevor Nunn's for the Royal Shakespeare Company, with Ian McKellen (2009). Eyre's, in modern dress, was most fully adapted to the screen, with the sub-plot and the Fool's part severely reduced and entries managed by cuts and dissolves, but all are perhaps best discussed in connection with the theatre.

But in 1996 Brian Blessed directed himself as Lear in a 190-minute film that has received less attention than it deserves. Outdoor scenes are in woods, clearings, and downs, and on a beach where the deranged Lear has been building sand-castles. Edgar swims across a stream to put chasing hounds off the scent. A shot over the sea to a cliff precedes Gloucester's attempted suicide at Dover. Castles are several times shown in silhouette. The moon presides at night. There are Druid rituals, and a megalith appears on the skyline as troops mass for a spectacular and clamorous battle. Ravens caw over the corpses. Dress is 'costume drama eclectic', with touches of the modern. Goneril and Regan wear scarlet lipstick.

The leonine Blessed here looks Japanese, with a lengthy mane like Hidetora's. His Lear is histrionic, a showman, volatile of mood. Even his rages seem partly mounted for effect. In the opening scene his 'while we ... crawl toward death' is a joke over which the assembly chuckles. He is the grand actor-manager, savouring his role like Olivier, and similarly confiding in and indulgent towards Cordelia. But his delayed outburst is thunderous. The theatrics have their counterpart in the mock trial, stage-managed by the crazed Lear, his hallucinations of the accused flashing onto the screen. Earlier, his parody of asking Goneril forgiveness ('Dear daughter, I confess that I am old...') is enacted with thesbian overkill. Yet his invocation of the storm is recited quietly, and largely as voice-over, while his tormented face and gestures fill the frame: the acting is entirely visual, an accompaniment to the script as read. The same technique is used for Edgar's adoption of the disguise of Poor Tom, but the camera zooms in from a high-angle long shot. Tom, daubed, lazar-like, in white and blue, maintains his subdued manner in the hovel, which, like Kozintsev's, is crowded with the ragged poor, whom Lear acknowledges as though in prayer. Tom's speeches are the more disturbing for being delivered as solemn *sententiae* betokening obsession, rather than as lunatic gabble.

Blessed curses Goneril quietly face to face, like a malevolent cleric. At Dover, he keeps apart from Gloucester as he lectures him, before drawing him into an embrace at 'I know thee well enough. Thy name is Gloucester'. For the blinding, Cornwall advances towards Gloucester with both thumbs held out for an exceptionally bloody assault, to which Regan reacts with orgasmic glee. She sits and watches her wounded husband's collapse.

Crowds welcome the returning Cordelia and her French army, but ordinary citizens are prominent among the British defenders. 'Domestic and particular broils' impinge on the larger conflict. In defence of his father against Oswald, Edgar, who has no weapon, contrives to disarm his assailant of his sword and wrestle with him, until he can drown him in a nearby stream. His dispatch of Edmond is, in contrast, immediate: the brothers advance towards each other, stand face to face, and Edgar runs Edmond through.

The reconciliation with Cordelia is moving, the ending devastating. From a view of Cordelia hanging from a bough, we cut to an interior, with alternating close shots of Lear grieving and Cordelia lying dead. So Lear's howls are very quiet. While the attendance of Kent, Albany, and Edgar is registered in brief close-ups, the prime focus is on Lear's face, staring blankly ahead, not at Cordelia. He knows she is 'gone for ever'. He repeats

'How how, Cordelia! Mend your speech a little, | Lest you may mar your fortunes' from the opening scene, lifts and drops her lifeless arm at 'No, no, no life', delivers his 'nevers' rapidly, and weeps. The camera reveals the wider scene. 'Look there' lacks external reference. Lear dies sitting by the supine Cordelia, as his eyelids are closed by Kent. The white of Lear's and Cordelia's gowns dissolves into the full moon. Their bodies are consumed on a funeral pyre.

The Fool is played by Blessed's wife, Hildegard Neil, an undisguised mature woman, incongruously called 'my boy'. She materializes at the end to declaim the 'Merlin' prophecy from 3.2. The effect is of a more sombre equivalent of the post-tragedy jig. The film has its eccentricities, but mostly adheres to Shakespeare's text and order of scenes, with light pruning. It borrows several ideas from other versions, but transforms them in an original way. Although tainted by aspects of the genre of historical drama that Kozintsev was at such pains to avoid, this is among the more notable renderings of *King Lear* on screen.

Kozintsev declared that 'The advantage of cinema over the theatre is not that you can even have horses, but that you can stare closer into a man's eyes.'[33] His statement points to the two strengths of filmed Shakespeare: the camera can draw actors close to us, to reveal facial expressions and involve us intimately in, for example, Cordelia's asides or her reunion with her father; and it can create a panorama of screen images corresponding to the interior landscape evoked by Shakespeare's dramatic verse. No production of *King Lear*, on stage, television, or film, can realize all the script's potential. But, in combination, the versions in media unimagined by the author greatly enrich our experience of his play.[34]

SELECT BIBLIOGRAPHY

Ball, Robert Hamilton, *Shakespeare on Silent Film: A Strange Eventful History* (London: Allen and Unwin, 1968).
Buchanan, Judith, *Shakespeare on Film* (Harlow, Essex: Pearson–Longman, 2005).
Buchanan, Judith, *Shakespeare on Silent Film: An Excellent Dumb Discourse* (Cambridge: Cambridge University Press, 2009).
Bulman, J. C. and H. R. Coursen, eds., *Shakespeare on Television: An Anthology of Essays and Reviews* (Hanover and London: University Press of New England, 1988).

[33] Kozintsev, 55.

[34] I have been unable to view a Bard Productions version (1982), with Mike Kellin as Lear and aiming to recreate an original Jacobean ambience. There have been dozens of screen offshoots of *King Lear*, among the most provocative being the 'feminist melodrama' *A Thousand Acres* (1996), based on Jane Smiley's novel, in which Larry Cook, hands over his Iowa farm to his married eldest daughters, Ginny and Rose, while the youngest, Caroline, rejects the legacy and pursues a career as lawyer. Our sympathies are with Ginny and Rose, who had been sexually abused by their father, revered in the community. Each develops an extra-marital attachment to neighbour Jess, while coping with the increasingly senile Cook's inability to relinquish control and descent into inebriated paranoia. Truth-teller Rose provokes Ginny's struggle to accept her repressed knowledge. The emotional scene of reconciliation is one of sisterly solidarity between G and R. Yvonne Griggs, *Screen Adaptations: Shakespeare's 'King Lear': The Relation Between Text and Film* (London: Methuen Drama, 2009) discusses many other offshoots, including Jean-Luc Goddard's misnamed *King Lear* (1987).

Cook, Hardy M., 'Two Lears for Television: An Exploration of Televisual Strategies', in J. C. Bulman and H. R. Coursen, eds., *Shakespeare on Television: An Anthology of Essays and Reviews* (Hanover and London: University Press of New England, 1988), 122–9.

Griggs, Yvonne, *Screen Adaptations: Shakespeare's 'King Lear': the Relation Between Text and Film* (London: Methuen Drama, 2009).

Howard, Tony, 'When Peter Met Orson: The CBS *King Lear*', in Lynda E. Boose and Richard Burt, eds., *Shakespeare, the Movie: Popularizing the Plays on Film, TV, and Video*, (London and New York: Routledge, 1997), 121–34.

Hunter, G. K., ed., *King Lear* (Harmondsworth: Penguin, 1972).

Jorgens, Jack J., *Shakespeare on Film* (Lanham, MD: University Press of America, 1991).

'King Lear Film and Print Editions', www.pbs.org/wnet/gperf/episodes/king-lear- film-and-print-editions/king-lear-films/563.

'King Lear. Org: The Complete King Lear Site', king-lear.org/king_lear_on_dvd.

King Lear, South Bank Show, ITV, 11 January 1987; introduced by Melvin Bragg.

Knight, G. Wilson, *The Shakespearian Tempest* (Oxford: Oxford University Press, 1932).

Kott, Jan, *Shakespeare Our Contemporary*, trans. Boleslaw Taborski (London: Methuen, 1964).

Kozintsev, Grigori, ' "Hamlet" and "King Lear": Stage and Film', in Clifford leech and J. M. R. Margeson, eds., *Shakespeare 1971* (Toronto: University of Toronto Press, 1972), 190–9.

Kozintsev, Grigori, *King Lear: The Space of Tragedy*, trans. Mary Mackintosh (London: Heinemann, 1977).

Leggatt, Alexander, *Shakespeare in Performance: King Lear* (Manchester: Manchester University Press, 1991).

Lusardi, James P. and June Schuelter, *Reading Shakespeare in Performance: 'King Lear'* (Cranbury, NJ: Associated University Presses, 1991).

Miller, Jonathan, *Subsequent Performances* (London: Faber and Faber, 1986).

Rothwell, Kenneth, *A History of Shakespeare on Screen* (Cambridge: Cambridge University Press, 1999).

Wells, Stanley, ed., *The History of King Lear*; Oxford World Classics (Oxford: Oxford University Press, 2000).

Wells, Stanley and Gary Taylor, gen. eds., *William Shakespeare: The Complete Works*, 2nd edn. (Oxford: Clarendon Press, 2005).

Wilders, John (literary consultant), *King Lear* (London: BBC Books, 1983).

Willis, Susan, *The BBC Shakespeare Plays: Making the Televised Canon* (Chapel Hill: University of North Carolina Press).

CHAPTER 38

··

MACBETH ON
CHANGING SCREENS

··

KATHERINE ROWE

'Une pensée qui forme/une forme qui pense'
Jean-Luc Godard, *Histoire(s) du cinema* (1988)

THE afterlife of *Macbeth* on screen has been lively and often brilliant. In short and long form, Shakespeare's efficient and bloody tragedy has occasioned more than a century of adaptations, appropriations, and revivals around the world, across an array of broadcast, recorded, and networked media. As scholarship in the field of Shakespeare and media studies has matured, so has our appreciation of the depth and complexity of this corpus. For his magisterial study of Shakespeare on silent film (1968), Robert Hamilton Ball identified some 14 adaptations of the play, beginning with the earliest extant 16mm short (a scant minute of sword-fighting with three actors, 1906). Kenneth Rothwell's international filmography and videography, *Shakespeare on Screen* (1990), features 68 selected *Macbeth* entries. *Shakespeares after Shakespeare* (2007; ed. Richard Burt), compiles more than 140 pop culture works that draw on the play in significant ways. The most comprehensive finding aid to date, the British Film and Video Council's database of Shakespeare on film, television, and radio, posts 651 *Macbeth* entries, a number that is still growing. No comprehensive resource exists to track the uneven but lively migration of *Macbeth* into new storage media (such as CDR, DVD, and BluRay), and into genres emerging for cable TV, ebooks, amateur video, web-based, and gaming platforms.

Students, scholars, and fans exploring this robust and diverse corpus face a number of obstacles to any attempt to generalize or systematically survey it. This chapter briefly sketches some key challenges to that work and points to some useful resources to support it. Because these challenges are endemic to all Shakespeare adaptations, they are necessarily crucial to any thoughtful approach to screen adaptations of Macbeth. Yet though they are illustrated here in *Macbeth*-centric ways, there is little *Macbeth*-specific about them. Accordingly, the second half of the chapter narrows its focus, surveying a handful of adaptation strategies that span global variations of *Macbeth* in multiple languages and periods. These may provide fruitful signposts for further study, as new engagements with *Macbeth* proliferate across media. Underpinning this essay is the principle articulated by Jean Luc Godard, in the epigraph to this chapter, from a famous 1988 intertitle in a TV series made for Canal+, which defined film as thinking medium: 'a thought that forms/a form that thinks'. This chapter follows Godard in approaching audio-visual adaptations on screen as works that think with and within the combined resources of source material and media platform.[1]

CHALLENGES OF SCOPE AND MEDIUM

Any study of Shakespeare adaptations and appropriations confronts significant challenges of scope: how to define the boundaries of analysis—by date, genre, medium, nation, language, or some other set of terms? Genre categories offer an appealing solution. Versions of *Macbeth* on screen come in diverse kinds and rubrics. The play serves as readily as a touchstone for avant-garde and experimental films, as it does for parodies and spinoffs, amateur video mash-ups, large scale Hollywood productions, documentaries, musicals, porn productions, or animated shorts. This array of genres has fostered lively scholarly commentary in Shakespeare studies. Yet these rubrics slice up adaptation practices in different ways. A closer look makes it clear how unsystematic they are, as ways to explain adaptation as a larger cultural process. 'Parody' and 'revival' name a stance toward the source material; 'experimental' and 'documentary' orient away from or towards aesthetic traditions. 'Animation' and 'mash-up' name creative techniques; 'Hollywood' refers to a production centre and distribution system, which was once geographically specific but now is much less so. It also implies a realist aesthetic that has long been associated with that production centre. Yet, as film historians have pointed out, even well-established categories such as 'Hollywood Cinema' are often fuzzier internally than they at first appear, because performances of any kind rarely conform to single modes.[2]

The medium or technology used by a given production might seem to offer sharper boundaries for organizing a study. Yet historically, *medium* has proven an unstable organizing principle, for two important reasons: first, because all media change (both their social ecosystems and their technologies), and second, because no medium is 'pure', singular, or as neatly medium-specific as it seems to be.[3] These facts have become increasingly evident over the last 50 years of Shakespeare studies, as the pace of change has accelerated in Western performance and communications media. The scholarly rubric that Ball used in the 1960s, 'Shakespeare on Film', gave way first to '…on Film and Television' (in the 1970s and 1980s), and then with the advent of home video players, to 'Shakespeare on Screen'. Through the late 1990s *screen* was still a comfortable critical shorthand in Shakespeare studies, denoting mass broadcast media such as film, television, and the long

[1] Intertitle in Jean-Luc Godard, *Histoire(s) du cinema*. 4 videodiscs (268 min.): sd., col., b&w; 4¾ in, 2007 (1989).

[2] Christopher Williams, 'After the Classic, the Classical and Ideology: The Differences of Realism', in Christine Gledhill and Linda Williams, eds., *Reinventing Film Studies* (London: Arnold, 2000), 206–20.

[3] David Thorburn and Henry Jenkins, *Rethinking Media Change: The Aesthetics of Transition* (Cambridge, MA: MIT Press, 2003), 11.

tail of their markets in electronic storage formats such as VCRs, DVDs, and BluRay. By the first decade of the twenty-first century, screen technologies comprised an extraordinarily diverse set of production and reception phenomena: captured with a camera lens or generated on a computer workstation; created by media companies and amateurs; projected on vinyl, broadcast to a CRT, or accessed on an LCD screen; watched solo, in small groups, or in large audiences, outdoors and indoors, sitting down, walking, or in a vehicle.

Beyond the explosion of phenomena that it now comprises, 'screen' has one other important limitation as a rubric for analysis. It tends to bias attention towards visual perception at the expense of aural, spatial, social, and verbal phenomena. Philip Auslander suggests 'mediatized performances', to describe 'performance that is circulated' via media formats 'based on technologies of reproduction'.[4] Though clunky, such a neutral phrase makes it easier to remember that along with camera work, editing, imagery, and other visual effects, *Macbeth* adaptations also require attention to dialogue, miking, music, and other sound effects; the space of performance and audition; audience behaviours; words on screen; and so on.

Among the most important tenets of recent media scholarship is the reminder to 'resist notions of media purity'.[5] The traffic between contemporary performance media has always been robust. As visual and audio recording media first emerged, for example, theater borrowed these technologies for acoustic and scenic design—and has continued to do so from the earliest years of film and radio to modern stage performances. Even before the advent of synchronized sound, movie-going incorporated words and ambient sound. Conversely, theater performances have periodically been broadcast live, or taped, from the beginning of broadcast technologies. Should we classify remote broadcasts such as the National Theatre Live production of *Macbeth* (Manchester, UK, 20 July 2013) as stage or screen events? The answer is both. In such performances, what Auslander terms the 'liveness' of the cineplex experience of NTLive, and the onsite shooting of live experiences (at the Manchester theater festival where NTLive recorded *Macbeth*) authorize each other in complex ways.[6] The commonplace Western understanding of a 'medium' as a distinct techno-social phenomenon makes it easy to forget that no medium 'does its cultural work in isolation from other media, any more than it works in isolation from other social and economic forces'.[7] How we understand immediacy and presence in theatere performances of *Macbeth* is shaped by the coexistence of theatre 'within a mediatic system that includes the mass media and information technologies' that communicate via screens—and vice versa.[8]

What this means in a practical sense for the student, scholar, or fan, is that any given performance of a Shakespeare play will necessarily involve a hybrid of multiple media conventions and technologies—some visible, others not, in a way that is determined as much by the media surround as by specific works. The rapid pace of media change in the first decades of the twenty-first century has made it much easier than it used to be

---

[4] Philip Auslander, *Liveness: Performance in a Mediatized Culture* (London: Routledge, 1999; repr. 2008), 4.

[5] Thorburn and Jenkins, *Rethinking*, 11.   [6] Auslander, *Liveness*, 2–6.

[7] Jay David Bolter and Richard Grusin, eds., *Remediation: Understanding New Media* (Cambridge, MA: MIT Press, 1999), 15.

[8] Auslander, *Liveness*, 5.

to recognize this hybridity. Limit cases can be especially useful in thinking through potential subcategories of 'screen'. In a scholarly survey of *Macbeth* onscreen, for example,
should immersive theatre installations such as the current New York hit *Sleep No More*
be included? The production's website describes it as follows. In an invented 'McKittrick
Hotel' (three warehouses in lower Manhattan), 'Shakespeare's classic Scottish tragedy
[is presented] through the lens of suspenseful film noir. Audiences move freely through
a transporting world at their own pace, choosing their own path through the story'.[9]
Screen conventions past and present dominate the reception experience of this production, though no actual screens are present in performance. Where the National Theatre
Live productions traffic in *liveness*, this production traffics in two kinds of *screen-ness*,
drawn from cinema and from electronic gaming. The ambient sound track derives from a
lesser-known film noir; the production spaces, paths of movement, and some few lines of
recorded dialogue riff on Alfred Hitchcock's 1940 film, *Rebecca*. (The film itself adapted
Daphne Du Maurier's 1938 gothic revival novel of the same title.) Yet the allure of *Sleep No
More*'s haunted spaces has equally to do with the addictive reception dynamics of online
gaming. Tracking actors through dark hallways and cluttered rooms, spectators 'choose
their own path through the story', pursuing each byway to find what they missed on the
previous loop.[10] This hybrid aesthetic of uncanny return along winding paths into the past
has been tremendously successful in drawing repeat audiences. It succeeds in part because
of the explicit way it layers gaming protocols over film noir aesthetics—the pull of a tracking camera through decaying architecture, which in its turn remediated the twisting prose
interiors of the gothic novel. This production transforms the endless perseverations invoked in *Macbeth* (creeping 'tomorrows', moving like a ghost, 'in blood stepped so far' …)
into a rationale for repeat ticket sales.

At a moment when the media hybrids, remediation, and trans-media borrowing are so
prominent a part of global Shakespeare performance culture, some long-standing concerns of Shakespeare adaptation studies seem less urgent. These concerns—questions of
fidelity to an original, the place of authorship in performance, the privileging or loss of
Shakespearean language—have been thoughtfully surveyed in the work of Thomas Leitch,
Elsie Walker, Thomas Cartelli, and others listed in the Select Bibliography at the end of
this chapter. They do not need to be recapitulated, but it is worth dwelling for a moment on
the shift itself. What has altered most significantly, in recent scholarship, is the perception
that the hybrid media history of Shakespeare's works should be understood as a problem.
As M. J. Kidnie observes, the regular return of adaptation as a 'problem' in Shakespeare's
studies for so many years was in part a structural effect of the difference of drama, a literary and performance form perpetuated over time.[11] As an iterative art form, drama generates not one but two concepts of textual stability in Western culture. It does so on the one
hand, via reference to prior texts and on the other hand, via reference to 'an insubstantial

[9] *Sleep No More*, Punchdrunk, New York, 2011–present. http://sleepnomorenyc.com/hotel.htm.
Consulted 4 January 2014.

[10] The game-like dynamics of the production are discussed in Jason Schreier, 'Interactive
Play', *Wired*, 3 August, 2011 and Dan Dickinson, 'Games of 2011: Sleep No More', Blogpost, 25
December, 2001.

[11] Margaret Jane Kidnie, *Shakespeare and the Problem of Adaptation* (New York: Routledge),
2009, 13.

standard—the work—that seems to exist prior to' and extend beyond any given instance of textualization.[12] The *idea* of a given work (what we think of as *Macbeth*, for example) serves specific social functions, as Kidnie explains,

> [it provides] the necessary standard by which actual instances, textual or theatrical, historical or modern, are produced and appraised. But there remains always the potential for a perceived misalignment that can be realized at any time between one's conception of the work and any particular instance of it, so transforming the previously supposed genuine instance into adaptation and adaptation into the thing itself. Because the work does not exist somewhere (not even in the First Folio), but always 'survives' somewhere else, it remains susceptible, among other things, to the ways scholars conduct and write textual histories. Inevitably, as conceptions of the work continue to alter over time, so will assessments of what will or should count as either an authentic or an adapted textual production, along with the criteria or terms by which it is recognized. (153)

To follow Kidnie's line of analysis, we can observe that the growing corpus of *Macbeth* adaptations described in the first paragraph of this essay reflects a progressively looser conception of the work known as 'Macbeth'. That loosening is reinforced in turn by an expanding archive of production. *Macbeth* is 'unmade ... and remade' in the process of adaptation, its meaning renegotiated 'in specific reception contexts'.[13] What counts as 'Macbeth' may thus be the least resolvable question for any study of the afterlife of this play, at this point in the history of Shakespeare studies. But in the very openness of this question scholarship has flourished, and our understanding of the global field of adaptations across language, culture, genre, and media platforms has deepened.

BY MEANS OF *MACBETH*

> Then yield thee ... | And live to be the show and gaze o' th' time.
>   (Macduff 5.8.23–4)

The question of whether a given production or citation counts in the expanding archive of *Macbeth*-centric works has come to seem less fruitful, therefore, than how specific elements of the play make meaning in specific performance and reception contexts. 'Shakespeare doesn't mean,' Terence Hawkes observes; '*we* mean *by* Shakespeare.'[14] The second half of this chapter explores specific opportunities for making meaning with this play, focusing on setting, social structures, and the supernatural. In each of these areas, specific patterns have emerged over more than a century of evolving screen media that enlist the play and the technical affordances of different media platforms for different

---

[12] Kidnie, *Problem of Adaptation*, 153.
[13] I am quoting first Joseph Grigley, *Textualterity: Art, Theory, and Textual Criticism* (Ann Arbor: University of Michigan Press, 1995), 33, and second Thomas Cartelli and Katherine Rowe, *New Wave Shakespeare on Screen* (Cambridge: Polity Press, 2007), 28, after Grigley.
[14] Terence Hawkes, *Meaning by Shakespeare* (New York: Routledge, 1992), 3.

ends. Picking a path through the large and diverse corpus of *Macbeth* adaptations and appropriations, to illustrate these patterns, the essay draws on examples from cinema (film and digital), television and video (broadcast, cable, and hard storage formats), and the socially networked media (such as amateur digital video and gaming) that glean these earlier forms for aesthetic conventions and material. Expanding Jean-Luc Godard's claim that cinema is the form that thinks, the works touched on here think *with Macbeth*, in their own media idioms, which depend on audio effects, interactive protocols, dialogue, writing on screen, and other verbal phenomena, as much as they depend on visual ones.

Place, Setting, Movement

> The earth hath bubbles, as the water has …
>
> (Banquo, 1.3.82)

Macbeth's ambiguous landscapes make it remarkably flexible and transportable to different periods, locales, and cultural contexts. In the playtext, dramatic setting is both unstable and relatively abstract by modern standards. This is partly a consequence of early modern geology, which understood the landscape as permeable and changeable, and partly due to plot—specifically, the supernatural actions of the witches.[15] Both factors collude to reinforce spatial abstraction in the play, from the geological phase changes that Banquo alludes to above (earth can turn to water, water to air), to the moving trees of Birnam Wood. It's worth noting that *Macbeth's* landscape is epistemologically as well as ontologically unstable. It's not just that we know that this bad weather is changeable, but that *what we know about it* changes, as we hear it described in profoundly contradictory ways.[16] Banquo will enter moments after a scene full of 'fog and filthy air', blithely remarking that 'the heaven's breath | Smells wooingly here' (1.6.6-7).

How can bad air suddenly smell sweet and why might this matter for translations of a stage play into other media? One answer has to do with the early conditions of playgoing. The same blank stage space in which these contradictory lines are uttered easily repurposes from scene to scene, as different fictional settings. In other words, the changeability of the fictional landscape in *Macbeth* aligns with playing conditions in which sudden changes of scene primarily happen through description and stage business, since few props or sets are available to do this work. (Intriguingly, Jonathan Gil Harris notes that 'filthy air' might well refer to the smell of gunpowder in the early theatres, used to create thunder—the early modern equivalent of olfactory scenography.[17]) What might seem to modern ears like a sudden reversal from 'filthy' to sweet air, then, could be understood as

[15] Kristen Poole, *Supernatural Environments in Shakespeare's England: Spaces of Demonism, Divinity, and Drama* (Cambridge: Cambridge University Press, 2011); Mary Floyd-Wilson, 'English Epicures and Scottish Witches', *Shakespeare Quarterly* 57:2 (Summer, 2006), 131–61.

[16] Floyd-Wilson, 'Epicures', 143–4.

[17] Jonathan Gil Harris, 'The Smell of Macbeth', *Shakespeare Quarterly* 58:4 (Winter, 2007), 465–86. On olfactory design see Sally Banes, 'Olfactory Performances', *TDR: The Drama Review* 45:1 (2001), 68–76.

a normal and unremarkable stage convention. Or, it would be normal and unremarkable, except that the text of *Macbeth* brings heightened awareness to this effect and colours it demonically, making it part of the play's larger category crisis of foul and fair. Taking these cues, productions of *Macbeth* tend to have a lot of bad weather and chiaroscuro lighting effects, to be thick with confusing and threatening sounds, and to be full of vertiginous movements in space. Lady Macbeth's onscreen suicide, dashing off one of the many cliffs that loom throughout Orson Welles' murky film adaptation (*Macbeth*, 1948), exemplifies this pattern.

Among the most compelling productions of *Macbeth* are those that experiment explicitly with spatial abstraction. The much admired 1979 studio recording of Trevor Nunn's RSC production (dir. Philip Casson) still feels extraordinarily fresh in part because of its blank staging. The actors form a circle, emerging from surrounding darkness into and out of a pool of light that defines the play space. Via a gracefully tracking camera, the audience describes that same circle with them. In slow zooms and continuous takes, the camera pulls auditors along a series of reversals that position Macbeth (Ian McKellen) just at our shoulder, stepping out of the near darkness like a ghost. This arrangement creates an intense sense of intimacy and complicity, used to terrific effect by Judi Dench (Lady Macbeth) and McKellen. At the other end of the production spectrum, an amateur animation, *Calum MacAskill Porter* (SkinheadNinja, 2009), plays wittily with the Porter's speech in similar ways. A delightful 1.5 minutes of invention, it riffs on the many entrances and exits afforded by a blank white screen. In this flat and abstract rectangle, the reverberating knocks at the door sound threatening by contrast, filling up moral space.

Macbeth's relatively unspecific settings (rooms in castles, doors, heath, a battlefield) have made the play transportable to locales as diverse as rural Pittsburgh (*Scotland, PA*, dir. Billy Morrisette, 2001), Yemen (*Someone is Sleeping in My Pain*, 2002), Melbourne (*Macbeth*, dir. Geoffrey Wright, 2006), or Planet Q (*Star Trek*, 1966). These qualities may also help to explain why Scotland itself rarely figures as a setting for modern adaptations. The finding-aids I have listed note a scant handful of productions set in Scotland, including Welles's medievalish, weirdly-Scottish-accented film.[18] For early modern playgoers, *Macbeth* was emphatically a play about nation and place, carefully distinguishing highland and lowland Scots, northern and southern England. Recent historicist scholarship highlights the rich textures of its social geography: its competing stereotypes of Englishness and Scottishness, its reference to contemporary political debates and to the vogue for witchcraft.[19] Yet despite the surge of literary nationalism in recent decades, a William 'Braveheart' Wallace version of the play that returns to the Scotland of the

---

[18] There are periodic efforts to mount 'authentically Scots' film productions. In 1996 *The Wall Street Journal* reported on the trials of Scottish screenwriter Steven Simpson, attempting to place 'Throne of Destiny', the story retold from George Buchanan's rather than Holinshed's version of the history.

[19] See Floyd-Wilson, 'Epicures'; Arthur Kinney, 'Scottish History, the Union of the Crowns and the Issue of Right Rule: The Case of Shakespeare's *Macbeth*', in *Renaissance Culture in Context: Theory and Practice*, ed. Jean R. Brink and William F. Gentrup (Brookfield, VT: Scolar, 1993), 18–53; and David Norbrook, '*Macbeth* and the Politics of Historiography', in *Politics of Discourse: The Literature and History of Seventeenth Century England*, ed. Kevin Sharpe and Steven N. Zwicker (Berkeley: University of California Press, 1987), 78–116.

historical Macbeth has yet to emerge for mass audiences. The 2015 *Macbeth* (dir. Justin Kurzel), starring Michael Fassbender and Marion Cotillard, was partially shot in Skye and Northumberland – capitalizing on the post-*Game-of-Thrones* vogue for medievalist northern landscapes – comes as close to that vision as any production to date has.

In adaptation, *Macbeth* turns out to be both highly localizable and quite specific in its spatial algorithms. Human place-making is ad-hoc, Julia Lupton observes; humans tend to 'envision spatial orders more as software than as hardscape'.[20] Shakespearean place-making on unlocalized stages was necessarily ad hoc, as the discussion above indicates. To approach the settings in *Macbeth* as social algorithms, in Lupton's terms, is to recognize them as engines rather than sites of uncertainty and transformation. On the battlefield, Scottish Thanes may be converted to English Earls, but only after the play passes them through England; that relocation enables the transformations that appear to resolve geo-political conflict. The elasticity of spatial orders in *Macbeth*, evoked by bubbles of earth on a heath, underwrites a troubling elasticity in social orders: a king made or unmade, a man emasculated, a woman unsexed.

Typically, movements through setting in this play consist of violent motion and cur-tailed progress. Both trajectories need to be read in political, spiritual, and psychological registers. These contradictory movement patterns are explicit in the story of usurpation and failed rule, and in Macbeth's issue-less kingship. And they are implicit in much of the language of the play that conjures processes of thought. Invoking spirits to prime her for violent action, Lady Macbeth must arrest her inner motions, 'stop up' passages through which emotions move (1.5.51). Aspiring to 'jump the life to come' (1.7.7) Macbeth slows to the 'petty', perseverating pace of despair (5.5.23).

In screen adaptations, this rule of violent movement without progress may drive edit-ing and camera action, as well as plot and character. A classic of world cinema, Akira Kurosawa's *Kumonosu-jô* (1957; *The Castle of the Spider's Web*, retitled *Throne of Blood* for its US release in 1961), illustrates the pattern vividly. Invoking Samurai-era Japan, the film's exterior settings range from grand to claustrophobic, establishing a feudal context of civil war that maps neatly onto the plot of *Macbeth*. But the camera work and editing may be the most compelling aspect of Kurosawa's encounter with the playtext, as they think through its characteristic leaps and stalls. In a famous sequence early in the film, Washizu (the Macbeth analogue, played by Toshiro Mifune) and Miki (Minoru Chiaki as the film's Banquo figure), ride ever deeper through mazelike trees to encounter an inimical forest spirit (substituting for Shakespeare's witches). As Washizu and Miki ride furiously, gradu-ally discovering they are lost, the camera alternates between tracking shots and fixed ro-tation. Screened by thick branches, the two figures move at frantic speed but make no progress. The editing reinforces their lack of progress: a repeated sequence in which the lead rider shoots an arrow teases us with the feeling that we are watching the same film clip twice. Just as language unfixes from character in *Macbeth* and seems to have its own agency, so too in Kurosawa's film the camera unfixes from character, pulling us forward or delaying us in place. Neil Forsyth describes the simultaneous excitement and anxiety

---

[20] Julia Reinhard Lupton, *Thinking with Shakespeare: Essays on Politics and Life* (Chicago: Chicago University Press, 2011), 11; after Christopher Alexander, Sara Ishikawa, and Murray Silverstein, *A Pattern Language: Towns, Buildings, Construction* (Oxford: Oxford University Press, 1982), 15.

this effect produces, rendering 'the peculiar mixture of power and helplessness essential to Shakespeare's play'.[21] A similar 'experience of conscious helplessness' evoked by occulted movements through space characterizes Orson Welles's *Macbeth* (1948), where foggy dissolves shift the spectator's distance from the action in uncomfortable ways.[22]

The most compelling adaptations of *Macbeth* to new media game environments deploy this 'experience of conscious helplessness' procedurally, in the movement of a player avatar through virtual space. 'Foul Whisperings', an immersive installation in the social gaming environment Second Life®, offers the most robust example to date. In this simulation (sim), 'dedicated to the exploration, adaptation and performance' of *Macbeth*, visitors move through a half-dozen linked rooms or settings.[23] These are arranged as a series of tour puzzles and structured thematically around scenes and problematics from the play.[24] On a blasted heath, fragments of playtext drift through the audioscape. Lines from the witches, Macbeth, and Lady Macbeth literally float free of character: spoken in multiple voices, variously male and female, as animated type dissipates. One particularly witty scene unfolds as a progress in disenchantment. Follow a rose arbor, and the avenue gradually reveals itself to be governed by Lady Macbeth's command to 'look like the innocent flower, yet be the serpent under it', as her words snake around one's virtual feet. In other rooms, scale and distance dilate or contract. A telescoping corridor leads into absolute darkness and silence, making returning not only tedious but nearly impossible. The sliver of an exit must be approached at a precise angle; failing that, the only alternative is to head into the dark.

Several rooms in 'Foul Whisperings' play with the gravitational pull of reprobation and despair—translating into the affordances of the game platform Macbeth's certainty that he has supped so full with horrors that nothing can move him further, spiritually or emotionally. The most pointed argument along these lines develops in a chamber of horrors. Surrounded by scenes of modern torture and holocaust, a crowd of ghosts lock the player in a phantom battle. The animation makes it impossible to control the player's avatar—dispossessing it of volition, as it were, while it furiously acts out a dagger fight. It takes some effort to free one's avatar, and the only way to do so is to drop through a vortex, into a mazelike, concrete Cobweb Forest. (Here and elsewhere in the sim one finds allusions to Kurosawa and Welles.) As is typical of gaming platforms, meaning in these scenes is constituted by the player's passage through them and her interaction with the sim's dynamics. Yet in the vocabulary of gaming, to drop into a hole or vortex is typically to lose the game. In a contrarian way, the experience the sim seems most invested in exploring is loss of agency. For 'Foul Whisperings', *Macbeth's* preoccupation with self-directed loss of agency sponsors critical reflection on the fantasies of control in game play.

---

[21] Neil Forsyth, 'Shakespeare the Illusionist: Filming the Supernatural', *The Cambridge Companion to Shakespeare on Film* (Cambridge: Cambridge University Press, 2007), 274–94; 286.

[22] Forsyth, 'Illusionist', 285.

[23] Angela Thomas, Kereen Ely-Harper, and Kate Richards. 'Foul Whisperings.' Literature Board of The Australian Council for the Arts, New Media Consortium. http://virtualworlds.nmc.org/2008/10/08/macbeth. Consulted 4 January 2014.

[24] These readings condense a more extended discussion in Katherine Rowe, 'Crowd-sourcing Shakespeare: Screen Work and Screen Play in Second Life™', *Shakespeare Studies* 38, 'Forum: After Shakespeare on Film' (Winter, 2010), 58–67.

Updating and Backdating

> Nor time nor place | Did then adhere ...
>
> (Lady Macbeth, 1.7.58–9)

As many scholars have observed, the Renaissance court culture depicted in Shakespeare's tragedies and histories offers significant obstacles to easy updating. Their plots and characters belong to more rigid social hierarchies than modern genres typically supply. And they incorporate deep structures of honour, purity, and revenge that may ring false for Western audiences raised after the counter-culture revolutions of the 1960s. *Hamlet* adaptations have often solved these problems by updating to a corporate *mise-en-scène*, where hierarchies are sharply defined and political stakes clear. Shakespeare's tragedies especially suit the tradition of corporate noir, as Douglas Lanier observes, where 'the dark forces of conspiracy and corruption that so often threaten the noir protagonist have been relocated in the corporate realm'.[25] For *Macbeth*, the conventions of *noir* match easily to its themes and plot: murky lighting, corrupted institutions that trap a morally compromised protagonist, monstrous femininity. Yet for *Macbeth* adaptations, the more common organizational context is not multinational corporations but their underworld equivalents, mob and gang culture. *Joe MacBeth* (dir. Ken Hughes, 1955) launched what has since become a regular strategy for updating the play. Set in Chicago, this vernacular adaptation 'filters *Macbeth* through a series of gangster and noir motifs in order to address the contradictory loyalties and paranoia of the upwardly mobile organization man of the '50s'.[26] The subgenre has flourished since, including: a Finnish noir-comic spoof (*Macbeth*, dir. Pauli Pentti, 1987), the *Godfather*-inspired *Men of Respect* (dir. William Reilly, 1991), *Macbeth-Sangrador* (dir. Leonardo Henríque, 1999, set in a bandit camp in the Venezuelan Andes), *Borough of Kings* (a mob spinoff set in Brooklyn, NY, dir. Elyse Lewin, 2000), *Maqbool* (dir. Vishal Bharadwaj, 2003, transposed to the internecine wars of a Mumbai crime family), and more.

The transposition of the play to gangster genres has the effect of localizing a production in time as well as place, since these genres are indigenous to a wide array of national film cultures, as Mark Burnett has observed.[27] For many *Macbeth* adaptations, relocalization is an opportunity to negotiate explicitly between local performance traditions and the imported source text. Such explicit negotiations foster reflection on the complex colonial and post-colonial history of which Shakespeare's works were necessarily a part. The play's focus on national assimilation and its exposure of the workings of political theatre in the service of ambitious politicians, have sponsored appropriations that 'write back' against the corruptions of empire and dictatorship.[28] Thus a film such as *Macbeth-Sangrador* uses *Macbeth*'s political theatre to 'contemplate Venezuelan militaristic authoritarianism'.[29] The Telangana-Urdu language *Yellamma* (dir. Mohan Koda, 2001), transposes the play

---

[25] Douglas Lanier, 'Shakescorp Noir', *Shakespeare Quarterly* 53:2 (2002), 170.

[26] Lanier, *Shakescorp*, 170.

[27] Burnett, Mark, *Shakespeare and World Cinema* (Cambridge: Cambridge University Press, 2012).

[28] Burnett, *World Cinema*, 165.   [29] Burnett, *World Cinema*, 7.

to the 1850s mutiny in Sepoy, that ended the East India Company's rule and inaugurated the British Raj. In *Someone is Sleeping in My Pain: An East–West Macbeth* (dir. Michael Roes, 2002), a performance of *Macbeth* becomes an opportunity to stage and reflect on present-day globalization, and the economic and cultural conflicts it generates. A subset of the Shakespeare-film-within-the-film genre, *Someone is Sleeping in My Pain* tracks the conflicts between an ambitious American auteur (Andreá Smith) and the Yemeni warriors who make up his amateur cast.[30] As Courtney Lehmann observes, the film-within-the-film conceit fosters disturbing reflections on the economic, linguistic, and political imbalances of power between West and Middle East.[31]

The structure of historical back-dating built into the plot of *Macbeth* offers politically oriented adaptations an opportunity and a cover story—just as it did in the Renaissance, when transporting a story to medieval Scotland opened a space to critique Jacobean ideas of imperial rule and the union of crowns. *Scotland PA* (dir. Billy Morrissette, 2001), a vernacular parody set in post-Vietnam, rural Pennsylvania, USA, backdates imaginatively in this way. Transposing the play into the genre codes of 1970s television cop shows, like *McCloud* and *Columbo*, the film looks back on the rise of mass media and the fast-food industry in a way that is at once irreverent and trenchant.[32] Cultural divisions backdated to medieval Scotland in Shakespeare's play—between barbaric northern Scots and civilizable, Anglicized southern Scots—are mapped 'onto the conflict between a stalled-out culture of small-town losers' who work at a burger joint (the Macbeths), 'and a counter-culture of hippies, rockers, and New Age vegetarians' (Malcolm, Donald, Lieutenant Macduff).[33] For all its gross-outs and dark humour, this is a film as suspicious of the workings of capital as any corporate noir. In *Scotland, PA*, the witches—stoners who prophesy the coming of fast-food ('like a bank, but for food')—seem to promise upwards mobility for the Macbeths. That promise is as false as the remodelled burger joint, purchased by detective Macduff (Christopher Walken) at the end of the film and converted to an alternative, vegetarian drive-in. (In the final scene we see it empty of customers.) Yet capital works its occult forces in both cases, for the 1970s counter-culture that so shakily stakes its claim at the end of the film (just as Malcolm's new order emerges at the end of Shakespeare's play) is now a billion-dollar corporate industry.[34] Backdating thus allows us to see the futility inscribed in any given Macbeth's future, since that future is the audience's 'past'—or more accurately, that fictional future tells a story about our 'past' that we wish to tell. (For example, a story about how the Western counter-culture of health food is free of the market forces that shaped fast food.) In Shakespeare's *Macbeth*, moments that highlight failed political order (such as the court banquet disrupted by Banquo's ghost) expose failed economic orders in *Scotland, PA* (a disastrous 'grand re-opening' of the drive-in).

[30] See the production description at Globalshakespeares, http://globalshakespeares.mit.edu/someone-is-sleeping-in-my-pain-roes-michael-2002, consulted 4 January 2014.

[31] Courtney Lehmann, 'Someone is Sleeping in My Pain', in Richard Burt, ed., *Shakespeares after Shakespeare: An Encyclopedia of the Bard in Mass Media and Popular Culture*, 2 vols. (London: Greenwood Press, 2007), 1: 105.

[32] The film's alignment of the rise of mass media with the rise of industrial food was missed entirely by the mainstream journalists who panned it.

[33] Cartelli and Rowe, *New Wave*, 106.

[34] Lauren Shohet, 'The Banquet of *Scotland, PA*', *Shakespeare Survey 57: Macbeth and its Afterlife*, ed. Peter Holland (Cambridge University Press, 2004), 186–95.

The closing movements of Shakespeare's *Macbeth* offer contradictory ways to tell a future history. Malcolm may represent the triumph of a new order, or he may be seen to repeat the errors of his father. Either way, he does this in a manner that assimilates Scotland to England, establishing Scotland's subordinacy to England as an 'historical fact' for those watching. Similarly, Macbeth's rise and fall can be framed as a cautionary lesson the audience can learn from, a call to action, or it can underscore the fundamentally illusory nature of any human action. In mediatized performances of this play, the direction in which a given production will go is often signalled by the treatment of Macbeth's exchange with the Doctor after Lady Macbeth's death. Three examples of this scene—from two films and one amateur video, created over more than half a century—articulate nearly opposite perspectives on the need for and efficacy of political action.

The first example of this pattern is a little known but telling moment part way through the avant-garde *Le film, est déjà commencé?* (1951), an early work by the Lettrist artist Maurice Lemaître. Screenings were part of an extended, disruptive performance event that scandalized critics at its first release in Paris, aiming to radicalize complacent audiences with disturbing events both on and off screen. (Actors planted in the audience screamed at the screen, threw objects through the crowd, audiences endured long delays in restless lines, and so on). The film itself plays with a host of discontinuity effects—including scratching and painting on the 16mm filmstrip, interjecting title cards, and separating sound and image track—that disrupt any comfortable immersion in the fictional spectacle. Lemaître's techniques for disrupting the routine conventions of movie-going in the service of a larger disruption of the social order have remained deeply influential in European experimental traditions. At one such disruptive moment in the film, Macbeth's urgent question to the Doctor flashes on a title card: 'What rhubarb, cyme, or what purgative drug would scour' the diseased land and make it healthy again (5.3.57)? The abrupt interjection of this quote on an intertitle, addressed to the audience rather than the Doctor, sums up Lemaître's call to action: in corrupt times, *we* must play the role of physician to the nation.

Twenty years later, Roman Polanski's 1971 widescreen production uses the same moment in the play to convey political disillusion, instead of a call to radical action. In Polanski's film, the counter-culture movements of the 1960s are aligned repeatedly with the witches, a nightmare version of Woodstock hippies. After two hours of horrific violence, in a drug-induced stupor, Macbeth (Jon Finch) asks the Doctor (Richard Pearson): 'Canst thou not minister to a mind diseased | ... And with some sweet oblivious antidote | Cleanse the stuffed bosom of that perilous stuff | Which weighs upon the heart?' (5.3.50–5). If the line in the play seems a request to help Lady Macbeth, here is is clearly self-reflexive. This Doctor throws Macbeth back on his own failing resources, as Polanski figuratively throws the country: 'Therein the patient | Must minister to himself.' (5.3.56–7). The psychological purge that *Macbeth* sponsored in Lemaître's revolutionary film has become for Polanski an empty provocation to violence. At the end of the film this cycle seems likely to continue. The film's final shot shows us Donaldbain seeking out the witches, in a scene that intimates a future civil war.[35]

---

[35] The reading is Neil Forsyth's, 'Illusionist', 282.

A generation later, Polanski's film (and this scene in particular) provides resonant material for a sharply conceived amateur video, 'Geto Boys/Macbeth Mashup'.[36] Clips from the film (with and without dialogue) run under the Geto Boys rap, 'Mind Playing Tricks on Me' (a classic of 1990s hip hop). 'Adroit matches between lyrics and action', as Luke McKernan observes, align Macbeth's gradual alienation from companions with hallucinatory gangsta scenarios filled with violent action and no progress ('So we speeded up the pace | Took a look back and he was right before our face').[37] The mashup climaxes with the Doctor's rejection of Macbeth's plea for care, affirming the despairing trajectory of the Geto Boys lyrics. For the haunted first person of this song, who ultimately recognizes himself as 'a fiend', there will be no exit from the dark street.

Sex Me Here

Come to my woman's breasts
(Lady Macbeth, 1.5.54)

Lady Macbeth is among the most durable of Shakespeare's iconic characters. Like Othello, Iago, and Hamlet, she circulates independently of the play, though rarely independently of her famous sleepwalking cry 'out, damned spot'.[38] The quotation carries a strong charge from the regressive arc of Lady Macbeth's plot. That 'progress from potent ambition to feminine passivity ... resists reconstruction' by new plots.[39] Indeed, so strong is this trajectory, from sexualized power to eventual abjection, that it has become the 'character function' of Lady Macbeth, a key part of the 'constellation of behaviors represented and restored by' this play as it circulates in Western and non-Western cultures.[40] Character functions this durable usually come in sets, and this one is no exception. If we call the figure that acts on oversized ambition only to discover the human cost a 'Macbeth', we can find 'Lady Macbeth' in the illegitimate authority that intensifies that ambition and illustrates its costs most punitively. What's remarkable about Lady Macbeth's character function is how broadly transnational her trajectory has become. Across a range of adaptations in a wide array of non-Western languages and cultures, she reliably returns from gender transgression to abjection and from aggressive dominance to subordinacy.[41] Interpretations of the sleepwalking scene are rarely interesting, therefore, because their outcome is so deeply scripted and standardized. By contrast, the early scenes that calculate Lady Macbeth's motives for aggressive dominance, and frame her transgression in gendered terms, allow for a much wider range

---

[36] Scartol, 'Geto Boys/Macbeth Mashup', YouTube. www.youtube.com/watch?v=9DJI2OEUKjM. Uploaded 11 February 2007. Consulted 4 January 2014.

[37] Luke McKernan, 'Geto Boys/Macbeth Mashup'. Bardbox, 20 July 2008. bardbox.wordpress. com/2008/07/20/geto-boysmacbeth-mashup. Consulted 4 January 2014. Lyrics from 'Mind is Playing Tricks on Me', in Geto Boys, *We Can't Be Stopped*. Rap-A-Lot Records, 1991.

[38] Katherine Rowe, 'The Politics of Sleepwalking: American Lady Macbeths', *Shakespeare Survey* 57: *Macbeth and its Afterlife* (2004), 147–56.

[39] Rowe, *Sleepwalking*, 128.   [40] Cartelli and Rowe, *New Wave*, 32.

[41] For a pithy summary of this dynamic with non-Anglophone film examples, see Burnett *World Cinema*, 32, quoting Aihwa Ong, *Flexible Citizenship: The Cultural Logics of Transnationality* (Durham, NC: Duke University Press, 1999), 11.

of interpretation. The key text for interpretation is Lady Macbeth's first scene. She enters the stage reading Macbeth's letter, a striking moment of 'two-in-one' voicing, as Alan Stewart has described it, and then launches her most famous soliloquy.[42] In the Trevor Nunn production discussed above, Judi Dench conjures a chilling but also deeply sensual Lady Macbeth, on the edge of her own control and already showing the cost of the self-transformation she calls for with 'unsex me here'. In Dench's interpretation, that cryptic phrase (this instance is the only *OED* citation for 'unsex'), means 'neutralize my ability to feel compassion' but not 'make me masculine', 'make me sexless', or even 'make me unhuman'. *Scotland, PA* offers no direct quotation of this phrase, but Maura Tierney's oversexed Pat Macbeth is haunted by not being able to call for such a transformation. The film makes it clear there will be no true exit for her from the repressive gender stereotypes of the middle-American 1970s; her brief co-ownership of the burger joint simply translates the ambient sexual harassment of her dead-end waitressing job into a slightly more upscale idiom. Among the least interesting interpretations are those that flatten 'unsex me' to 'fuck me now', as the BBC/Time Life Films video production (dir. Jack Gold, 1982) does. At this line Jane Lapotaire throws herself backwards onto a bed, legs spread to the camera, and gasps her way through the following lines while the camera slow-zooms to her crotch, arriving hip-height at 'stop up th'access and passage'.

The most compelling outliers to these interpretive traditions are the productions that grant real authority to Lady Macbeth's self-transformation. Isuzu Yamada, an actress renowned in Japan for playing oppressed but defiant women (scheming geishas, tough and self-aware working girls), offers a terrifying vision of Lady Macbeth's self-control, in Awaji, Washizu's terrifying consort in Kurosawa's film. Courtney Lehmann describes the conflicting strains of 'modesty and female sexuality' in her Noh-inspired movements and mask-like face:

> [her] hauntingly understated voice, dress, and expression—rendered all the more ghostly by her high-set, painted-on eyebrows located just below her hairline—continually conflict with her homicidal promptings and profoundly 'unladylike' ambition.[43]

The most interesting outliers are those that find in Lady Macbeth's plot opportunities for feminist 'writing-back' against sexual oppression. Leading Chinese actress Zhang Ziyi plays Empress Wan (a hybrid Lady-Macbeth/Gertrude figure) in this mode, in the *wuxia* epic *The Banquet/Ye Yan*, set in tenth-century China (2006, dir. Feng Xiaogang; the film was released on DVD in the US as *Legend of the Black Scorpion*). Assuming political authority and autonomous sexuality at the same time, Zhang 'ghosts' the dangerous ninja warriors she made famous in crossover action films such as *Crouching Tiger/Hidden Dragon* (2000, dir. Ang Lee) and *House of Flying Daggers* (2004, dir. Zhang Yimou). The final scene of the film turns against her rule in a particularly violent and meta-theatrical gesture (best left undescribed, in the interest of avoiding a spoiler)—as if the Shakespearean precedent were enforcing a return to type.[44] The feminist film-maker Nina Menkes may

---

[42]   Alan Stewart, *Shakespeare's Letters* (Oxford University Press, 2008), 33.

[43]   Lehmann, '*Kumonosu-jō*', *Shakespeares after Shakespeare*, 1: 389.

[44]   Rebecca Chapman, 'Spectator Violence and Queenly Desire in *The Banquet*', *Borrowers and Lenders* 4:2 (Spring/Summer 2009).

go the furthest towards embracing and repurposing the violent transgressions of gender enacted in *Macbeth*, in her extraordinary short film *The Bloody Child* (Nina Menkes). It 'combines actual Desert Storm marines, playing themselves, text from Shakespeare's MACBETH, and wife-murder ... creating a wild witch's brew'. [45] Lines from the witches haunt the film's sound-scape, re-voicing silent victims of patriarchal violence in the US and Africa, in a surreal mode that seems to share the revolutionary aims of Lemaître's earlier work.

Filming the Supernatural

> ... that, distilled by magic sleights, | Shall raise such artificial sprites
>
> (Hecate, 3.5.26-7)

In staging supernatural forces and events in *Macbeth*, screen adaptations inherit a medium-specific legacy from the early years of film, which has its roots, as Neil Forsyth describes it, in competing traditions:

> From its beginnings, the art of film has also pulled in two different directions, towards realism and towards magic. One tendency derives from the Lumière brothers, who came to film from photography, and who at first simply tried to reproduce time and event accurately—a train arriving at the station or the famous shot of workers leaving the Lumière factory. The other is the tradition of Georges Méliès, a stage magician turned cinéaste, many of whose films had the words *nightmare* or *dream* in their titles. The Lumières recorded reality; Méliès transformed it. [46]

Representations of the supernatural in Shakespeare films must navigate the push and pull of these double possibilities. In the case of *Macbeth*, as Forsyth explains, they have a rich tradition of horror film to draw on for the bloodiest scenes (a resource exemplified for Forsyth in Polanski's film). The fact that the text of this play seesaws sickeningly across the divide between supernatural and natural, questioning perception, illusion, and delusion, authorizes the deceptive tradition in cinema, but in an uneasy way. Working through the cinematic handling of key scenes—the witches, the dagger, Banquo's ghost, and the apparitions—Forsyth's detailed analysis of the opportunities they offer both naturalistic and fantastical cinematography is worth reading in full. His discussion emphasizes the ongoing instability of the film codes by which *Macbeth* adaptations navigate their competing legacies: it is easy to mishandle those codes. At the end of Polanski's film, for example, Forsyth finds camera-work devolving to 'an irremediably adolescent attitude to the supernatural and horror', as we come to realize 'we are being shown [Macbeth's death] from inside [his] severed head'. [47] For Forsyth, Welles offers a more elegant balance, for example, using deft editing to offer two alternatives for Banquo's ghost: 'On stage you have to choose whether you want a ghost or an empty chair, but Welles gives us both, cutting

---

[45] Nina Menkes, 'The Bloody Child', http://ninamenkes.com/2013/01/the-bloody-child/, consulted 1 February 2014.

[46] Forsyth, 'Illusionist', 274-5.   [47] Forsyth, 'Illusionist', 282.

between the horrified Macbeth's deep-focus vision of the ghost sitting at an empty table, and the increasingly bewildered guests who see, like Lady Macbeth, only an empty chair.[48]

A third idiom of shocking representations develops early, from the Mélies experiments, in the surrealist conventions that both Menkes and Polanski before her implicitly draw on. In the apparently one-dimensional idioms of horror film—those moments most devoted to shock and gross-out, as at the end of Polanski's film—the film historian Adam Lowenstein finds a counter-realist tradition. The graphic address of horror offers a way to look at what canonical national cinemas hide—reflect on national traumas such as the Holocaust for example (for European horror film), Hiroshima (for Japanese horror film) or the Vietnam War (in the United States).[49] Analysing horror conventions that travel across these national cinemas, Lowenstein tracks a surrealist vocabulary that synthesizes Grand Guignol theatre and the clinical address of the science film, insisting on the immediate, intimate connections between everyday life and the horrors of history. Understood in from this perspective, gestures like the severed-head's-eye-view that closes Polanski's films might be read as allegorical moments. Here symbolic narrative and graphic visuals combine in an aggressive demand to look at what is usually hidden by public history. Depending on the politics of a particular adaptation, such gestures may underscore the failures of revolutionary thinking—Polanski's suggestion that the excesses of the liberal 1960s might have contributed to their own bloody conclusion.[50] Or they may violently rearrange our understanding to reveal a trauma in apparent victory, as Menkes's film uses surreal audio to do in the aftermath of the Gulf War.

As these readings make clear, *Macbeth* has been and remains a remarkably rich resource for mediatized performances. As our screen technologies and the reception traditions that they foster continue to change, the patterns described above will evolve and surely swerve in unexpected directions. As they do so, the archive of adaptations will continue to loosen, and the meanings that can be made with this play continue to deepen.

SELECT BIBLIOGRAPHY

A | S | I | A. The Asian Intercultural Shakespeare Archive, a trilingual database of Asian Shakespeare in performance. http://a-s-i-a-web.org.

Huang, Alexander C. Y., ed. 'Asian Shakespeares on Screen: Two Films in Perspective'. Special issue of *Borrowers and Lenders* 4:2 (Spring/Summer 2009).

Ball, Robert Hamilton, *Shakespeare on Silent Film; a Strange Eventful History* (New York: Theater Arts Book, 1968).

Berger, Harry, Jr, 'The Early Scenes of Macbeth: Preface to a New Interpretation', in *Making Trifles of Terrors: Redistributing Complicities in Shakespeare* (Stanford CA: Stanford: University Press, [1980] 1997), 70–97.

---

[48] Forsyth, 'Illusionist', 292.

[49] Adam Lowenstein, *Shocking Representation: Historical Trauma, National Cinema, and the Modern Horror Film* (New York: Columbia University Press, 2005).

[50] Deanne Williams, 'Mick Jagger Macbeth', *Shakespeare Survey* 57: *Macbeth and its Afterlife*, ed. Peter Holland (Cambridge: Cambridge University Press, 2004), 145–58.

Bardbox, ed. Luke McKernan. 2008. YouTube Shakespeare collection: http://bardbox.word-press.com.

Bhardwaj, Vishal, dir. *Maqbool* (India, Kaleidoscope Productions, 2003). Film. 35mm., snd., col., 134 mins.

BFI *Screen Online*. www.screenonline.org.uk.

BUFVC International Database of Shakespeare on Film, Television, and Radio. www.bufvc.ac.uk/databases/shakespeare/index.html.

Burnett, Mark, *Filming Shakespeare in the Global Marketplace* (New York: Palgrave Macmillan, 2007).

Burnett, Mark and Roberta Wray, *Screening Shakespeare in the Twenty-First Century* (Edinburgh: Edinburgh University Press, 2006).

Burt, Richard, ed., *Shakespeares after Shakespeare: An Encyclopedia of the Bard in Mass Media and Popular Culture*, 2 vols. (London: Greenwood Press, 2007).

Globalshakespeares.org, An open-access video and performance archive. http://globalshake-speares.org/#.

Henderson, Diana, ed., *A Concise Companion to Shakespeare on Screen* (Oxford: Blackwell, 2006).

Jackson, Russell, ed., *The Cambridge Companion to Shakespeare on Film* (Cambridge: Cambridge University Press, 2007).

Lehmann, Courtney. 'Out Damned Scot: Dislocating *Macbeth* in Transnational Film and Media Culture', *Shakespeare, the Movie, II: Popularizing the Plays on Film, TV, Video, and DVD*, ed. Richard Burt and Lynda Boose (New York: Routledge, 2003).

Leitch, Thomas M., 'Twelve Fallacies in Contemporary Adaptation Theory,' *Criticism* 45:2, Spring (2003), 149–71.

Macbeth, dir. Orson Welles. Mercury Productions/Republic Pictures Corporation, 1948.

Macbeth, dir. Roman Polanski. Columbia Pictures/Caliban Films, 1971.

Macbeth, dir. Trevor Nunn-Philip Casson. RSC-Thames TV, 1979.

Macbeth, dir. Jack Gold. BBC TV Shakespeare. BBC. June 1982.

Macbeth-Sangrador. dir. Leonardo Henriquez. Centro Nacional Autónomo de Cinematografía/Post Meridian Cinema, 1999. Film.

Maqbool. dir. Vishal Bhardwaj. India, Kaleidoscope Productions, 2003. Film, 35mm, col., snd., 134 mins.

McKernan, Luke, and Olwen Terris, eds., *Walking Shadows: Shakespeare in the National Film and Television Archive* (BFI, 1994). Film/television.

National Theatre Live, *Macbeth*, broadcast from the Manchester International Festival, Manchester, UK, 20 July 2013. Broadcast. http://ntlive.nationaltheatre.org.uk/productions/ntlout4-macbeth.

Osborne, Laurie, 'iShakespeare: Digital Art/Games, Intermediality, and the Future of Shakespearean Film', *Shakespeare Studies* 38, ed Susan Zimmerman and Garrett Sullivan (Cranbury, NJ: Associated University Press, 2010), 48–57.

Rothwell, Kenneth, *A History of Shakespeare on Screen: A Century of Film and Television*, 2nd edn. (Cambridge: Cambridge University Press, 2004).

Rothwell, Kenneth, 'How the Twentieth Century Saw the Shakespeare Film: Is it Shakespeare?' *Literature/Film Quarterly* 29:2 (2001), 82–95.

Scotland, Pa, dir. Billy Morrisette. Lot 49 Films, 2001. Film.

Shakespeare in Europe (SHINE). May 2003. English Department., University of Basel, Switz. www.unibas.ch/shine/linkstragmacbethwf.html. Useful finding list of translations of *Macbeth* in multiple languages.

Skinhead Ninja. 'Calum MacAskill Porter'. Animated video, b/w 1:35. Uploaded 24 September 2009. Curated by Luke McKernan at Bardbox.wordpress.com, http://bardbox.wordpress.com/tag/macbeth. Consulted 4 January 2014.

Thompson, Ayanna, and Scott Newstok, *Weyward Macbeth: Intersections of Race and Performance* (New York: Palgrave Macmillan, 2010).

Walker, Elsie, 'Authorship: Getting Back to Shakespeare: Whose Film is it Anyway?', in *A Concise Companion to Shakespeare on Screen*, ed. Diane Henderson (Oxford: Blackwell, 2006), 8–30.

CHAPTER 39

THE ROMAN PLAYS ON SCREEN
Autonomy, Serialization, Conflation

SARAH HATCHUEL
AND NATHALIE VIENNE-GUERRIN

In 1972, Trevor Nunn directed a Roman cycle for the Royal Shakespeare Company. This cycle for the stage began with *Coriolanus*, and continued through *Julius Caesar, Antony and Cleopatra* and, finally, *Titus Andronicus*—thus following and reinforcing the boundaries of a dramatic category called the 'Roman plays' but substituting historical for compositional order (*Titus* being the first to be written by Shakespeare, and *Coriolanus* the last). In his 1973 theatre review, Peter Thomson noted that Nunn's agenda was to show the growth from small tribe (*Coriolanus*), to republic (*Julius Caesar*), to empire (*Antony and Cleopatra*) and to a decadence that was the prelude to Gothic conquest (*Titus*), an endeavour which, for Thomson, was an 'interpretative distortion'.[1] However, in a 2005 article, Barbara L. Parker—although she does not use Nunn's staged tetralogy as an illustration—proposes to consider the works 'in historical rather than compositional sequence' as collectively detailing 'a constitutional decline closely resembling that defined in Plato's *Republic*'.[2] The four Roman plays are believed to dramatize the movements from oligarchy to democracy (in *Coriolanus*), from democracy to tyranny (in *Julius Caesar*), from tyranny to imperial supremacy over the world (in *Antony and Cleopatra*) and, finally, from imperialism to a decadent, headless state (in *Titus*). Film versions have been rooted in a similar attempt to

---

[1] Peter Thomson, 'No Rome of Safety: The Royal Shakespeare Season 1972 Reviewed', *Shakespeare Survey* 26 (1973), 139–50 (141).

[2] Barbara L. Parker, 'From Monarchy to Tyranny: *Julius Caesar* among Shakespeare's Roman Works', in *Julius Caesar, New Critical Essays*, ed. Horst Zander (New York and London: Routledge, 2005), 111–26 (111). Hugh M. Richmond has even suggested that 'in a strictly chronological sense *Cymbeline* proves to be the unexpected climax of a historical Roman trilogy, covering the rise and decline of Octavius Caesar, which includes *Julius Caesar* and *Antony and Cleopatra*'. See Hugh M. Richmond, 'The Resurrection of an Expired Form: *Henry VIII* as Sequel to *Richard III*', *Medieval and Renaissance Texts and Studies* (*Shakespeare's English Histories: a quest for form*) 133 (1996), 205–27 (209). Also see Richmond, 'Shakespeare's Roman Trilogy: The Climax in *Cymbeline*', *Studies in the Literary Imagination* 5 (April 1972), 129–39.

link the stories together or to find coherence through a shared 'Romanness' made up of recurring elements—plebeian crowds, powerful matrons, stoic soldiers, the recreation of Rome as a location, and the staging of fantastically imagined orgies.

The Roman plays become representative of particular forms of cultural authority that contribute to the shaping of each nation's vision of ancient Rome as a vehicle for its own self-image (for instance, this has been the case for the United States, the United Kingdom, and Italy in their respective cinematic productions). Hollywood seems to have equated the imperial decadence of Rome with the old world of Britain by regularly having the patricians played by English actors and the plebeians by Americans, while retaining the marks of Rome's glorious days as a formative mirror for American culture and power. The United States, especially in the early years of its foundation, certainly used ideas of 'classical antiquity', to project a vision of stable identity and cultural legitimacy to the eyes of the world. Through the architecture of American monuments (such as the 'Senate' on 'Capitol Hill') or the construction of familial sagas (with the Kennedys dominated by a Volumnia-like Rose), the United States emerged as the model of an ideally imagined Roman republic, valuing liberty and civic virtue. In turn, performances of the Roman plays have been shaped by the way the ancient world was represented in the nineteenth century's spectacular popular theatre. For instance, *Ben Hur* with its spectacular chariot races was so popular that it was performed on stage from 1899 to 1920. At the same time, Hollywood produced the first epic silent films while Italy released its pseudo-historical sword-and-sandal movies. Although they may share aesthetic and ideological elements, screen adaptations of the Roman plays[3] have given rise to two narrative groupings that we will examine—*Coriolanus* and *Titus* on the one hand, which have been adapted from Shakespeare; and *Julius Caesar* and *Antony and Cleopatra* on the other, which have been serialized or conflated with stories that diverge from Shakespeare, raising the questions of their relation to the plays.

TITUS, CORIOLANUS: FILMIC AUTONOMY FROM HANNIBAL LECTER TO RED DRAGON

In the Shakespearean canon, *Titus Andronicus* and *Coriolanus* are autonomous plays unconnected by either historical event or date of composition. The former may be considered the first Shakespearean tragedy, while the latter is generally described as Shakespeare's last tragedy. It is not, however, clear that they belong to the same group of plays. Sam Crowl does not include *Titus* in his study of the 'Roman plays' on screen[4] and the BBC

---

[3] For an extensive bibliography on the subject, see José Ramón Díaz Fernández, 'The Roman Plays on Screen: An Annotated Filmo-Bibliography', in *Shakespeare on Screen: The Roman Plays*, ed. Sarah Hatchuel and Nathalie Vienne-Guerrin (Rouen: Publications des Universités de Rouen et du Havre, 2009), 329–78.

[4] Samuel Crowl, 'A world Elsewhere: The Roman Plays on Film and Television', in *Shakespeare and the Moving Image, the Plays on Film and Television*, ed. Anthony Davies and Stanley Wells (Cambridge: Cambridge University Press, 1994), 146–62.

mini-series, *The Spread of the Eagle* (1963) takes into account only three plays: *Julius Caesar, Antony and Cleopatra*, and *Coriolanus*. *Titus* and *Coriolanus* do not seem to have much in common apart from their setting and the Romanness of their eponymous heroes. Yet their filmic treatment weaves a web of correspondences between them through popular films featuring Hannibal Lecter, based on Thomas Harris's novels.

Titus Andronicus was the last production of the Shakespeare BBC series, broadcast in 1985, with Trevor Peacock as Titus. Directed by Jane Howell (who also directed the bloody *Henry VI* plays and *Richard III*, in an evocation of the Holocaust), it was broadcast several months after the rest of the series. Although this late broadcasting was due to a strike that delayed the production,[5] its place in the series suggested a difficult play not easy for the BBC series to absorb: a monstrous episode which, as Marjorie Garber notes, has often been regarded 'as a Shakespearean stepchild rather than a legitimate heir'.[6] It took a long time for film directors to stand up for this bastard play. Richard Burt notes that no fewer than four cinematic productions of *Titus Andronicus* were released in the late 1990s:[7] Lorn Richey's *Titus Andronicus: The Movie* (USA, 1997), Christopher Dunne's *Titus Andronicus* (USA, 1998), Julie Taymor's *Titus* (USA, 1999) and Richard Griffin's digital-video adaptation *William Shakespeare's Titus Andronicus* (2000).[8]

Of the four films, only Julie Taymor's version survives in collective memory, leaving the other three productions far behind in the realm of what Burt called 'Schlockspeare'.[9] Although it was not a box office success, Taymor's film has been widely celebrated in the Shakespearean world as the first noteworthy big-screen version of the play, starring Anthony Hopkins in the title role and Jessica Lange as Tamora. There is a wide gap between the 1985 BBC version and Taymor's applauded movie. Jane Howell's version unsurprisingly offers no special effects except for the first images that make a death head and young Lucius' face almost overlap. Made for television, it often looks like a filmed version of a stage production, while Taymor's film keeps showing that it is a film through conspicuous camera work. Taymor builds chaos through angle shots and montage, constructing a postmodern version of *Titus*.[10] The choreography of the first sequence anticipates *Gladiator* (dir. Ridley Scott, 2000)[11] and makes war and violence both disturbing and seductive. Taymor uses symbols, mystery and enigmas to disturb and inspire, blurring the

---

[5] http://www.screenonline.org.uk/tv/id/527846/index.html (accessed 31 December 2013). See also Susan Willis, *The BBC Shakespeare Plays. Making the Televised Canon* (Chapel Hill and London: The University of North Carolina Press, 1991), 292.

[6] Marjorie Garber, *Shakespeare After All* (New York: Pantheon Books, 2004), 75.

[7] Richard Burt, 'Shakespeare and the Holocaust. Julie Taymor's *Titus* Is Beautiful or Shakesploi Meets (the) Camp', in *Shakespeare After Mass Media*, ed. Richard Burt (Basingstoke: Palgrave, 2002), 295–329 (301).

[8] http://www.titusandronicus.8m.com/production/production.html (accessed 2 January 2013).

[9] Introduction to *Shakespeare after Mass Media*.

[10] For a detailed analysis of Taymor's film, see Elsie Walker's article, 'Julie Taymor's *Titus* (1999), Ten Years on', in Hatchuel and Vienne-Guerrin, *The Roman Plays*, 23–65.

[11] On the parallel between *Titus* (1999) and *Gladiator* (2000), see Sam Crowl's study in *Shakespeare at the Cineplex. The Kenneth Branagh Era* (Athens: Ohio University Press, 2003), 203–17. The trailer of a 2013 stage production (Vertigo Theatre Centre) of *Titus Andronicus* prolongs this connection between *Titus* and *Gladiator* by using the memorable image of the wheat field that frames *Gladiator*: http://www.youtube.com/watch?v=BRuAHQxhLiw (accessed 2 January 2014).

boundary between fiction and reality. We do not know when the action takes place, as the story seems to happen in the present, the past and the future at the same time.

Yet, different as they are, the two versions are mainly text-oriented and do not much deviate or extrapolate from Shakespeare's script. They also both use the figure of the young boy as a framing device, the spectators being invited, each time, to see the whole story through young Lucius' eyes, as if everything were his vision or dream. This device adds some metadramatic distance and focuses on the spectacle of violence[12] that pervades what the trailer of the 2013 Royal Shakespeare production described as 'Shakespeare's brutal revenge thriller'.[13] Different as they are, the two versions strive to tackle a single question: how can directors and spectators negotiate the extreme violence that characterizes this play and that conveys both unbearable, heart-rending cruelty and Grand-Guignol excess?

Excess lies at the heart of *Coriolanus* too. As Janet Adelman has shown,[14] the play is obsessed with feeding and starving. It is pregnant with grotesque, carnivalesque images of bodily dismemberment[15] and, as Stanley Cavell observes in his 1987 study subtitled 'Who does the wolf love?',[16] it is filled with evocations of cannibalism. The BBC production, directed by Elijah Moshinsky, was broadcast in 1984, with Alan Howard in the part of Coriolanus, and it was only in 2011 that Ralph Fiennes directed the very first big-screen adaptation (with a screenplay written by John Logan, also the screenwriter of *Gladiator*)[17] in which Fiennes plays the eponymous part. Just as *Titus* was Taymor's first feature, so *Coriolanus* was Ralph Fiennes's first film as a director. Taymor had put *Titus* on stage before putting it on screen;[18] Fiennes had played the part for the Almeida Theatre Company in 2000 (dir. Jonathan Kent).[19] The two films obviously played a special part in Taymor's and Fiennes's careers and undoubtedly constituted new landmarks in the screen life of the two plays. Both Taymor and Fiennes obviously knew the BBC productions, the only screen landmarks to date: Taymor uses the same framing and distancing device as Howell, while Fiennes refers to Alan Howard's performance when talking of his own.[20] Fiennes's wish is obviously to go beyond the BBC low-budget production[21] and to promote this so

[12] Anne-Kathrin Marquardt, *The Spectacle of Violence in Julie Taymor's* Titus. *Ethics and Aesthetics* (Berlin: Trafo, 2010).

[13] The trailer can be found at http://www.youtube.com/watch?v=RN6SQ-HL5b4 (accessed 2 January 2014).

[14] Janet Adelman, *Suffocating mothers. Fantasies of Maternal Origin in Shakespeare's Plays, Hamlet to The Tempest* (New York, London: Routledge, 1992), 147–64.

[15] Zvi Jagendorf, '*Coriolanus*: Body Politic and Private Parts', *Shakespeare Quarterly* 41:4 (Winter, 1990), 455–69 (458).

[16] Stanley Cavell, *Disowning Knowledge in Six Plays of Shakespeare* (Cambridge: Cambridge University Press, 1987), ch. 4, '*Coriolanus* and Interpretations of Politics ('Who does the Wolf love?'), 143–77.

[17] John Logan, *Coriolanus: The Shooting Script* (Newmarket Shooting Script, It Books, 2012).

[18] David McCandless, 'A Tale of two *Titus*es: Julie Taymor's Vision on Stage and Screen', *Shakespeare Quarterly* 53 (2002), 487–511.

[19] On this production, see Julian Curry, *Shakespeare on Stage. Thirteen Leading Actors on Thirteen Key Roles* (London: Nick Hern Books, 2010), 37–56.

[20] Curry, *Shakespeare on Stage*, 47.

[21] '[The BBC TV production] is made on a shoestring, to its detriment really' (Curry, *Shakespeare on Stage*, 47).

far undeservedly neglected play on screen. Peter Holland rightly notes that Fiennes's film was 'sold as a war film about two men who might be described as the friendly beasts' and 'offered as a buddy movie of an unusual kind'.[22] The French title of Fiennes's film, *Ennemis Jurés* ('sworn enemies'), illustrates this reading by significantly erasing the name 'Coriolanus'—not familiar to a French audience—and putting the stress on the rivalry between Martius and Aufidius. Coriolanus is the story of a man who wants to 'stand | As if a man were author of himself | And knew no other kin' (5.3.35-7). He strives to stand 'alone', a term that is emphasized several times in the play. But this absolute autonomy of the character—as well as of the play—is put into question as we shall now see.

Autonomous as the plays and Taymor's and Fiennes's films are, the same intertextual blood seems to be running in their veins, supplied by a well-known modern film series based on the cannibalistic Hannibal Lecter, which seems to irrigate the two stories. Richard Burt has described the impact that the casting of Anthony Hopkins-Hannibal Lecter as Titus had on the reception of Taymor's film:

> Because most audiences read backward from film to Shakespeare, Taymor's casting of Anthony Hopkins, given that Titus serves human flesh at his banquet, will inevitably call to the minds of many reviewers and other audiences the serial killer cannibal, Hannibal Lector (*sic*). The connection between Titus and Lector (*sic*) is underlined by Hopkins' quotation of his role in *The Silence of the Lambs*, when he sucks in the spit before slitting Chiron and Demetrius's throats.[23]

More than ten years after *Titus*, Fiennes's *Coriolanus* uncannily feeds on the same horror world and reveals a kinship with another episode of the Lecter story: *Red Dragon* (dir. Brett Ratner, 2002), based on Thomas Harris's 1981 novel of the same name, a filmic prequel to *The Silence of the Lambs* (dir. Jonathan Demme, 1991) and *Hannibal* (dir. Ridley Scott, 2001).[24] In *Red Dragon*, Fiennes plays the part of Francis Dolarhyde, a serial killer nicknamed 'The Tooth-Fairy' due to his tendency to bite his victims' bodies and to the uncommon size and sharpness of his teeth. Dolarhyde refers to his other self as 'The Great Red Dragon', after William Blake's watercolour 'The Great Red Dragon and the Women Clothed with the Sun' (1803-5), and he has the same dragon figure tattooed on his back. Although less obvious than the Hopkins-Lecter-Titus conflation, the Fiennes-Dolarhyde-Coriolanus cluster is striking to any viewer who watches the two films. One of the first images in the 2011 *Coriolanus* shows the tattooed back of a neck. We soon discover that it is the neck of Aufidius who is sharpening a big knife while watching Coriolanus on the TV news, as a manhunter would do. This focus on the tattoo is also part of the film's UK trailer[25] which significantly blurs the figures of Aufidius and Coriolanus by letting the viewer think that the tattoo is Coriolanus'. At the end of the film, during the encounter between Martius and Menenius, one finds the same blurring effect: the spectators have the impression that the tattoos are imprinted on Martius' body which in fact wears only scars. This focus on the tattoos efficiently suggests the conflation of the two rivals, Martius and Aufidius, which

---

[22] *Coriolanus*, ed. Peter Holland, 3rd Arden edn (London: Bloomsbury, 2013), 134.

[23] Burt ,'Shakespeare and the Holocaust', 308.

[24] The Hannibal Lecter films are based on Thomas Harris's tetralogy: *Red Dragon* (1981); *Silence of the Lambs*, (1988); *Hannibal* (1999), and *Hannibal Rising* (2006).

[25] http://www.youtube.com/watch?v=bsYrGIQnmxo (accessed on 2 January 2013).

is emphasized in Shakespeare's text, but it also introduces the world of *Red Dragon*—epitomized by Dolarhyde's nightmarish dragon tattoo—into the world of *Coriolanus*. When Menenius (Brian Cox) utters the famous lines 'This Martius is grown from man to dragon. He has wings; he's more than a creeping thing' (5.4.12-14), one cannot but associate Dolarhyde, the 'Red Dragon', with Coriolanus, and see in Caius Martius the figure of a bloody, cruel, dehumanized serial killer who remains indifferent to supplication. Only at the very end of the play, when the treaty of peace is signed, and during the final fight, can the spectators recognize that Coriolanus has grown from man to dragon and has become a Volscian, when we clearly see the fragment of a tattoo resembling a dragon's tail on the back of his neck. The war movie meets the thriller, the political issues of the play merge with the world of psychopathology. Dolarhyde's name actually seems to fit a Martius who refuses to show his wounds, wants to 'hide his dolour', and has a hide of dolour (a skin that is full of scars). Like Coriolanus, Dolarhyde is the monstrous fruit of maternal cruelty. The connection of Fiennes's film with the Hannibal Lecter series can also be found in the fact that Brian Cox, who plays Menenius in *Coriolanus*, was the first actor to play Hannibal Lecter 25 years earlier in *Manhunter* (dir. Michael Mann, 1986). The same Brian Cox also played the part of Titus in Deborah Warner's stage production at the Swan Theatre in 1987, a performance that he describes as 'the greatest performance I've ever given'.[26]

In these two films, Shakespeare's Roman world not only mirrors the nightmarish excesses of the twentieth and twenty-first centuries, but also proves it can take the shape of other fictional worlds, turning into a particularly attractive-though-abject object of appropriation in which a web of common metaphors and intertexts engenders a particular kind of serialization.

Julius Caesar, Antony and Cleopatra: serialization[27]

On screen, *Coriolanus* was serialized once with *Julius Caesar* and *Antony and Cleopatra*—in the 1963 BBC series *The Spread of the Eagle*, which used Shakespeare's text and turned *Coriolanus*, *Julius Caesar* and *Antony and Cleopatra* into 50-minute black-and-white episodes broadcast on a weekly basis. The three Roman plays were presented in the chronological order of real historical events—not in the order of their compositions—and were presented in nine instalments (through May and June 1963), giving the impression that the plays had been conceived by Shakespeare himself as a mini-series. However, the producers were aware that the three plays provided few opportunities for continuity between *Coriolanus*, the events of which take place around 490 BC, and the other two tragedies, that were based on events some four centuries later. This lack of continuity was compensated by strong visual connections: for example, Rome's Forum was filmed under construction in

---

[26] http://theshakespeareblog.com/2013/01/brian-coxs-titus-andronicus-the-greatest-stage-performance-ive-ever-given (accessed 2 January 2013).

[27] Sarah Hatchuel, *Shakespeare and the Cleopatra/Caesar Intertext: Sequel, Conflation, Remake* (Lanham: Fairleigh Dickinson University Press, 2011), esp. ch. 2.

Coriolanus and completed during *Julius Caesar*. The same actors also played the triumvirs in *Julius Caesar* and in *Antony and Cleopatra*. Broadcast at a time when the British empire was nearing its end through the colonial disengagement in Africa, the series used the national literary canon to appropriate the grandeur of the Roman empire, while conveying a sense of epic scale through the sequelization of three plays. The stress was on the monumental and the very title of the series evoked both imperialism and conquest through the eagle imagery. Director Peter Dews had stated that his aim was 'to show great men in great places',[28] insisting on a heroic and positive vision of the Roman empire. Millions of TV spectators were led to feel compassion for a dignified and honourable Antony through the sheer amount of screen time allotted to him. Since serialization turns Antony into the pivotal link between *Julius Caesar* and *Antony and Cleopatra*, the character generally becomes a heroic figure with a realistic and coherent psyche from one play to the next. The producers took full advantage of the sequel's inherent potential for conservative stabilization and consolidation of both aesthetics and ideology: the values of heroism and imperialism were reaffirmed across storylines, blurring the boundaries between the plays.

Shakespeare's *Antony and Cleopatra* may easily be read as *Julius Caesar*'s sequel in that it offers a chronological extension of its dramatic plot with recognizable characters from one play to the next within the same historical context. However, *Antony and Cleopatra* seems concomitantly to problematize the very logic of narrative extension through rewritings that clash with the earlier play—for example, in the second play, Antony gives us another take on the battle of Philippi, suggesting that he actually killed Brutus and Cassius, while we witness their suicides at the end of *Julius Caesar*. Intertextual links between *Antony and Cleopatra* and *Julius Caesar*, far from connecting the two play-scripts in straightforward ways, bring impermanence and irresolution to both texts, raising doubts on what is said and what is shown, and encouraging dissident reading. However, in an attempt to capitalize on the fame and emotional appeal of the first film to secure the success of the second, from the silent days of cinema onwards, screen adaptations of *Antony and Cleopatra* have been released a few months after adaptations of *Julius Caesar*. From the moment Antony became the most prominent character of *Julius Caesar* (at the very end of the nineteenth century), it has been possible to perform *Antony and Cleopatra* as *Julius Caesar*'s follow-up, playing out the story to its very end with Antony as the returning hero.[29] In 1908, American director J. Stuart Blackton directed a Vitagraph film of *Julius Caesar* with Maurice Costello as Antony, which was released almost simultaneously with his adaptation of *Antony and Cleopatra* (in which Costello reprised his role as Antony). In 1911, Frank Benson filmed *Julius Caesar* and starred as Antony. His film was immediately followed by Charles L. Gaskill's 1912 adaptation of *Antony and Cleopatra* with Helen Garner as Cleopatra (which followed a script by Victorien Sardou that had first been performed in France in 1890, with Sarah Bernhardt as Cleopatra).[30] *Antony and Cleopatra*

[28] www.screenonline.org.uk/tv/id/466545/index.html (accessed 12 November 2013).

[29] This could be inferred by comparing the stage histories of the two plays in John Ripley's *'Julius Caesar' on Stage in England & America 1599–1973* (Cambridge: Cambridge University Press, 1980) and Margaret Lamb's *Antony and Cleopatra on the English Stage* (Rutherford: Fairleigh Dickinson University Press, 1980).

[30] Before inspiring the screenplay of Gaskill's 1912 film, Victorien Sardou's French play *Cléopâtre* was translated into English and first performed in the United States at the Fifth Avenue Theatre, New York, with Fanny Davenport as Cleopatra.

worked as a film sequel to *Julius Caesar* in order to keep audiences coming back to cinema theatres to experience the continuation of the story, and 'generally make cinema-going a habit'.[31]

Richard Madelaine has considered that 'the grouped staging of Shakespeare's Roman plays' may be reflecting 'periods of political transition in which ideologies are questioned and patterns of international relations radically altered'.[32] 1972 was a beacon year in the sequelization of Shakespeare's Roman plays. While Nunn directed the Roman cycle in Stratford-upon-Avon for the British stage, Michael Kahn directed joint productions of *Julius Caesar* and *Antony and Cleopatra* in Stratford, Connecticut, for the US stage, and Charlton Heston's film of *Antony and Cleopatra* was released with strong echoes of Heston's performance as Antony in Stuart Burge's earlier 1970 *Julius Caesar*. These stage and film ventures arose in a period marked by the dire consequences of national imperialisms and political chicanery—the intensifying Troubles in Ireland led to the Bloody Sunday carnage in January 1972, while in the United States mounting political disenchantment in the wake of the Watergate scandal in June was matched by increasing demonstrations against the interminable war in Vietnam. The joint productions on stage and screen may be viewed as a denunciation of war politics, but also as reflecting a deep wish for some restoration of order and harmony, stressing, as they did, narrative continuities from one play to the next and values of national heroism. The productions of *Antony and Cleopatra* also reflected the growing fascination with Egyptian treasures: the astonishing Tutankhamun exhibition had opened in March 1972 at the British Museum in London, exciting curiosity about the Egyptian empire but also recalling Britain's own imperialism: Howard Carter had discovered and plundered the Tutankhamun tomb 50 years before, in the year when Egypt ceased to be under British rule.

Stuart Burge's 1970 *Julius Caesar* and Charlton Heston's 1972 *Antony and Cleopatra* both use Shakespeare's text in Technicolor and feature the same actor (Charlton Heston) as Antony. During the shooting of Burge's *Julius Caesar*, Heston started to imagine himself in the part of Antony again, in a film of *Antony and Cleopatra* which he wanted to control and direct on the heels of *Julius Caesar*.[33] To create links between Burge's *Caesar* and his own film, Heston suggested ideas of *mise-en-scène* that were to find their way into *Caesar*. The directorial decision to film the proscription scene in a Roman bath with Antony 'lounging naked and sweating, wreathed in steam, checking off names on a hit list while nubile slave girls filled their wine cups'[34] is to be connected with the performance of Antony as a lascivious, epicurean opportunist that Heston had in mind for the next film. This vision of Antony is in stark contrast with the performance Heston had already given in David Bradley's 1950 independent, low-budget, but highly cinematic version of *Julius Caesar* which inventively handles black-and-white and low/high-angle shots to create expressionistic, chiaroscuro effects. In Bradley's film, Heston

---

[31] Carolyn Jess-Cooke, *Film Sequels: Theory and Practice from Hollywood to Bollywood* (Edinburgh: Edinburgh University Press, 2009), 9.

[32] Richard Madelaine, ed., *Shakespeare in Production: Antony and Cleopatra* (Cambridge: Cambridge University Press, 1998), 90.

[33] Bruce Crowther, *Charlton Heston, the Epic Presence* (London: Columbus Books, 1986), 123. Also see Charlton Heston's autobiography, *In the Arena* (London: Harpers & Collins, 1995), 420, 428.

[34] Heston, *In the Arena*, 421–2.

plays Antony as a heart-riven innocent who genuinely attempts to revenge Caesar in a rapidly paced two-part story, divided by intertitles 'The Murder of Caesar' and 'The Revenge of Caesar'.

In his 1972 *Antony and Cleopatra*, Heston does not hark back to his performance in Bradley's film, but plays the hedonistic character of Burge's 1970 *Caesar*, inviting us to discover Antony in the arms of Cleopatra: 'We open focus very tightly on a woman's hand holding a makeup pot, dipping a small brush into it as we pull back to reveal Cleopatra about to paint the lips of the Emperor Antony sweating in postcoital and half-drunken slumber', anticipating Act 2 Scene 5 in which Cleopatra puts her own 'tires and mantles' on Antony.[35] Interestingly, this Cleopatra, played by Hildegard Neil, evokes 'otherness' in the same way as Janet Suzman had on stage in Trevor Nunn's RSC Roman-cycle *Antony and Cleopatra*. This production, filmed by John Scofield for ITV in 1974, used stylized sets— dazzling white for Rome, a colourful oriental tent filled with cushions for the Egyptian palace, black for the interior of Cleopatra's monument, yellowish background covered with sand for the desert, which was filmed in a blurry manner to suggest haze and dust. Janet Suzman's Cleopatra stressed impulsive sensuality and great strength of character. Both Janet Suzman and Hildegard Neil were born in South Africa in 1939. Heston explains how Neil was chosen for the part: 'I liked one of the tests very much: a South African actress, Hildegard Neil, whom I'd seen a month or so earlier as Lady Macbeth. She had the right kind of beauty, with a classical face and a contralto voice. The camera liked her, I'd found her directable in the scenes we did.'[36] The choice of Neil by Heston reveals the search for a normative form of female beauty, which has to be 'classical' and, therefore, white—a position which reflects Lucy Hughes-Hallet's claim that Cleopatra has been whitewashed for centuries, and depicted by western artists 'as a beauty of their own times and places'.[37] But Heston's discovery of Neil also betrays a 'darker', more dangerous edge—conveyed by the Otherness of her South African origins—the association with Lady Macbeth, and the 'masculine' deep vocal range. Cleopatra has to be 'other' but still tameable and 'directable' by Heston (both as Antony and as the film director)—all the more so since this Antony brings the glorious echoes of his political and military victories from the earlier *Julius Caesar*.

Heston's attempt to create a coherent vision of his own character from the first film onwards was probably intended to persuade the producers of Burge's *Julius Caesar* to back up his project for *Antony and Cleopatra*. Heston's autobiography reveals how investors first considered Heston's venture to film *Antony* in a favourable light because they considered that a sequel was less risky and more profitable, before withdrawing from the project as soon as Burge's *Caesar* did not attain its expected attendance figures.[38] Heston, therefore,

---

[35] Heston, *In the Arena*, 441.   [36] Heston, *In the Arena*, 441.

[37] Lucy Hughes-Hallet, *Cleopatra: Queen, Lover, Legend* (London: Pimlico, 2006), 254. See also Arthur L. Little Jr., *Shakespeare Jungle Fever: National-Imperial Re-Visions of Race, Rape, and Sacrifice* (Stanford: Stanford University Press, 2000); Carol Chillington Rutter, *Enter the Body: Women and Representation on Shakespeare's Stage* (London: Routledge, 2001); Celia Daileader, *Racism, Misogyny, and the Othello Myth: Inter-racial Couples from Shakespeare to Spike Lee* (Cambridge: Cambridge University Press, 2005); Ayanna Thompson, ed., *Colorblind Shakespeare: New Perspectives on Race and Performance* (New York: Routledge, 2006).

[38] Heston, *In the Arena*, 432–35.

had to raise money independently and managed to obtain distributors only in Spain and Japan, with a limited release in the United Kingdom.[39]

In this lush production of *Antony and Cleopatra* (which sometimes lacks the budget to match its ambitions), Heston reorders the succession of scenes, conflates characters and reassigns lines. The battle scenes that are hidden from the audience's view in Shakespeare's play become gory combats, with rushes of 1959 *Ben Hur* (in which Heston starred under William Wyler's direction) being recycled for the sea fight at Actium.[40] Heston creates an aesthetic tension between the land and the sea (or the river Nile), elaborating a powerful metaphor for the opposition between reason and passion. Statues, sculptures, drawings, and hieroglyphics surround the two lovers, presenting the audience with their godlike, mythical selves. The effect is to glorify Antony and Cleopatra as well as construct their myth in eternity.

The strong economic reasons for trying systematically to exploit the 'ghosting' effect of hiring the same actor to play a recurring role explain why the producers of Joseph L. Mankiewicz's *Cleopatra* (1963) first tried to hire Marlon Brando (instead of Richard Burton) to play Mark Antony, since he had played the part ten years before in Mankiewicz's cinematic adaptation of *Julius Caesar* (1953). This proved impossible since Brando was shooting Lewis Milestone's 1962 *Mutiny on the Bounty*,[41] but the attempt shows that the producers thought that Brando, beyond his bankability, would have brought legitimacy, continuity and, most of all, familiarity to the part.

CLEOPATRA: FROM CONFLATION TO INFINITE VARIETY[42]

The *Cleopatra* films—by J. Gordon Edwards in 1917 (with Theda Bara), Cecil B. DeMille in 1934 (with Claudette Colbert), Joseph Mankiewicz in 1963 (with Elizabeth Taylor) or Franc Roddam in 1999 (with Leonor Varela)—are not sequels but *conflations*. They combine three plots: (1) the affair with Julius Caesar and the Egyptian queen, as portrayed in plays such as John Fletcher and Philip Massinger's *The False One* (1620) or George Bernard Shaw's 1901 *Caesar and Cleopatra*; (2) the murder of Caesar (as dramatized by Shakespeare); and (3) the love story between Antony and Cleopatra (again as dramatized by Shakespeare).

Shakespeare refers to Cleopatra's affair with Caesar only in the form of rare, indirect allusions. What he only implies, many dramatic works have extended and detailed. Plays such as Samuel Daniel's *The Tragedy of Cleopatra* (1593), Samuel Brandon's *Octavia* (1598), the anonymous *Caesar's Revenge* (1607), Elizabeth Cary's *Mariam* (1613), Fletcher and Massinger's *The False One* (1620), Thomas May's *The Tragedy of Cleopatra* (1626), Charles Sedley's *Antony and Cleopatra* (1677), John Dryden's *All for Love* (1678), Colley Cibber's *Caesar in Egypt* (1724), Walter Savage Landor's *Antony and Octavius* (1856), or George Bernard Shaw's *Caesar and Cleopatra* (1901), have created many more narrative

---

[39] Heston, *In the Arena*, 445.   [40] Heston, *In the Arena*, 449.
[41] Pascal Mérigeau, *Mankiewicz* (Paris: Denoël, 1993), 243.
[42] Hatchuel, *Sequel, Conflation, Remake*, esp. chs. 4 and 5.

elements linking Cleopatra and Julius Caesar than Shakespeare's plays actually did—for instance through the prominence of their son Caesarion or through the dramatization of their early meeting in Egypt. The tendency of directors and spectators alike to view Shakespeare's *Antony and Cleopatra* as *Julius Caesar*'s logical follow-up may be seen as a consequence of this unusually extensive textual interplay, which not only conflated the two plots, but constructed an 'Ur-plot' of Julius Caesar's encounter with Cleopatra. While calling into question the 'natural' orders of history, determinist chronology and textual hierarchy, this intertextual network paradoxically encouraged the teleological and romantic sequelization and conflation of Shakespeare's *Julius Caesar* and *Antony and Cleopatra*. Twentieth-century films have created connections between Shakespeare's two plays by increasingly representing them as stemming from the same dramatic plot— the affair between Julius Caesar and Cleopatra. What resulted was the incremental generation of a saga.

By conflating the three plots, the films elevate Cleopatra to the metafilmic status of a star within a patriarchal world, asserting the combination of public authority with active female sexuality, and revealing how men (Caesar, Antony) gravitate around her before disappearing and being replaced. Nevertheless, the filmic conflations have tended, at the same time, to propagate imperialist and Orientalist ideologies in which Cleopatra is appropriated by the West and denied her real political importance. Through the stigmatization of the Oriental woman—especially when she visits Julius Caesar in Rome, and is banished back to Egypt after the assassination, an episode that is never depicted by Shakespeare—the films have destabilized the idea of female power. Neither totally challenging nor containing in their ideologies, the *Cleopatra* films all appear as sites where female power is continually renegotiated.

The intertextuality of the *Cleopatra* films is complex since they stem from, all at once, historical (or rather, mythical), literary, dramatic, and cinematic sources, which are not always acknowledged to the same degree. When a literary referent (other than the screenplay) is credited, it is often a contemporary play, a novel or a biography rather than any of Shakespeare's texts—Victorien Sardou and Emile Moreau's French play in the case of J. Gordon Edwards's 1917 film;[43] Margaret George's novel *The Memoirs of Cleopatra* in the case of Franc Roddam's 1999 series; or Stacy Schiff's 2010 biography *Cleopatra: A Life* in the case of the announced *Cleopatra* produced by Scott Rudin, which may feature Angelina Jolie in the title role. In their search to readapt a legendary story by focusing on accurate historical details (Roddam or Rudin) or to supersede the previous films[44] by updating the narrative elements through the use of more advanced technologies (DeMille after Edwards; Mankiewicz after DeMille, Rudin after Mankiewicz), the *Cleopatra* films oscillate between the *readaptation* and the *remake*. The various filmic *Cleopatras*, through their conflation of the plots of George Bernard Shaw's 1901 play *Caesar and Cleopatra*, Shakespeare's *Julius Caesar* and *Antony and Cleopatra*, blur the boundary between remake and sequel, since the films seem to integrate their own sequels within themselves, so that they sometimes become *films-fleuve*.

---

[43] www.imdb.com/title/tt0007801/fullcredits.

[44] Thomas Leitch, 'Twice-Told Tales: The Rhetoric of the Remake', *Literature/Film Quarterly* 18:3 (1990), 138–49.

Mankiewicz had initially wished to release two separate films, *Caesar and Cleopatra* (inspired by Shaw's play), followed by *Antony and Cleopatra* (inspired by Shakespeare's), which should have lasted three hours each. In the end, the studio chose to distribute a single film, edited from the two original projects, to create the four-hour version we know today.[45] Instead of releasing one film followed by its sequel a year or two later, Mankiewicz was pressured to prolong the viewing time and expand the narrative in one, protracted, movie experience. Twentieth Century Fox was convinced that the spectators would not have paid to see the first film (featuring Rex Harrison as Caesar) and would instead have waited for the release of the sequel, driven as they were by the on-screen sight of the real-life couple formed by Richard Burton and Elizabeth Taylor. Since the studio needed an immediate return on investment in order to avoid bankruptcy, Mankiewicz was ordered to cut his two films and turn them into one. In this reduction, the film *Caesar and Cleopatra* and its sequel *Antony and Cleopatra* became *Cleopatra*,[46] a film whose two two-hour parts mirror and echo each other on a number of occasions. Whereas film sequels may attract viewers with the promise of repeating a previous experience, Mankiewicz's four-hour film of *Cleopatra* offers to *extend* the cinematic experience.

In contrast to the titles of Shakespeare's and Shaw's plays, the names of the men (Caesar, Antony) have been suppressed from the titles of the 1917, 1934, and 1963 films, simply leaving the name of the Egyptian queen. Spectators are invited to consider Caesar and Antony through Cleopatra's eyes. This shift in focus, from male to female, has some crucial aesthetic consequences. The 1963 *Cleopatra*, for example, appears as a double act of rewriting. Mankiewicz rewrites history, reorganizing Shakespeare's scenes and discarding his texts in favour of more contemporary dialogue. At the same time he also offers another take on one of his previous films—his own 1953 *Julius Caesar*.

The fact that Mankiewicz's *Cleopatra* was shot in colour and widescreen format and displayed numerous spectacular and lavish shots may not encourage a comparison with the earlier *Julius Caesar*, which was filmed in black-and-white, used Shakespeare's text and relied on a minimalist approach with austere, tightly focused cinematic effects. Mankiewicz had notably insisted on using black and white film stock for *Julius Caesar* to distance his film from the vogue for Roman epics at the time, to evoke classical authority[47] and to recall the black-and-white newsreels showing the Führer at Nuremberg or Mussolini overlooking the crowd from his balcony.[48] However, as Karine Hildenbrand-Girard has convincingly demonstrated, there are many connections between the two films, notably some

---

[45] The six-hour director's cut is now in the process of being restored, but many scenes that were shot but not included in the final version have yet to be found in the various archives around the world.

[46] Jon Solomon, *The Ancient World in the Cinema; Revised and Expanded Edition* (New Haven and London: Yale University Press, 2001), 70; Clemens David Heymann, *Liz: An Intimate Biography of Elizabeth Taylor* (New York: Carol Publishing Group, 1995), 221.

[47] Jean Chothia, '*Julius Caesar* in Interesting Times', in *Remaking Shakespeare: Performance Across Media, Genres and Cultures*, ed. Pascale Aebisher, Edward J. Esche, and Nigel Wheale (Houndmills, Basingstoke: Palgrave, 2003), 120–1.

[48] Crowl, 'A World Elsewhere', 149. See also John Houseman's essay 'Julius Caesar on Film', in *Entertainers and the Entertained* (New York: Simon and Schuster, 1986), 83–97. Houseman was the producer of Mankiewicz's 1953 *Julius Caesar*.

structural, metafilmic junctions.[49] The two films are thought to form a story in three acts since *Cleopatra* is composed of two symmetrical parts, the central point of which—the assassination of Caesar—is the subject of *Julius Caesar*. Since Mankiewicz's 1953 *Julius Caesar* shows what remains partly hidden in the 1963 *Cleopatra*, it thus stands as both the ellipsis and the central fold of the subsequent film. As the assassination of Caesar becomes the crux of *Cleopatra*, it also offers a strong shift in standpoints, from a male to a female point of view. In the 1953 *Julius Caesar*, the spectators are encouraged to see the murder scene through the male gaze of Brutus, who, ashamed to watch, closes his eyes. The camera soon moves away from the assassination in order to hide violence, focusing on Brutus instead. In an anti-voyeuristic move, its gaze focuses on the character who refuses to see, thus denying the spectators the actual sight of the murder and reflexively imposing on the spectators Brutus' (conscious or unconscious) decision to close his eyes.

Ten years later, Mankiewicz reshot the assassination from Cleopatra's vantage-point. Although she is not actually present in the Senate, Cleopatra is watching the scene from her villa in the outskirts of Rome. An Egyptian sorceress starts a magical fire from which the vision of the murder arises. The flames which frame the murder scene metafilmically signal the act of rewriting and re-envisioning of the Shakespearean scene, while Cleopatra's face is superimposed on the images of Caesar's death, stressing the filmic palimpsest. The two special effects (the flames and the superimposition) thus reflect the double act of rewriting, as both Shakespeare as well as the earlier film are invoked only to be supplanted by a third narrative. Contrary to Brutus, Cleopatra does not close her eyes, nor does she move away from the event. She experiences the murder of her lover in her own flesh, screaming as if she herself were being stabbed. Mankiewicz's filmic trajectory seems to move from the male feelings of guilt, fear, and shame in his *Julius Caesar*, to *Cleopatra*'s female sense of love and empathy that infuses the murder with a renewed tragic quality.

As Cleopatra, in the flames produced by the sorceress, sees Caesar being stabbed, she suddenly screams 'My son!' This exclamation is highly ambiguous. The queen, in a trance, may actually be uttering the words of Caesar himself, in his shock at being slain by Brutus, a man he considered his son. 'My son!' may thus be Mankiewicz's rewriting of Shakespeare's 'Et tu, Brute?' (3.1), as a line shifted to Cleopatra in a form of ventriloquism. But Cleopatra's cry may also mean that, with Caesar's death, her son Caesarion loses political protection, any kind of legitimacy and all hopes of ever reaching power.[50] In this film, Caesar's assassination entails the eradication of a lineage stained by the mark of hybridity.

The 'Cleopatra' narrative has often been twisted, offering other versions of the story. This is the case of *Serpent of the Nile* (dir. William Castle, 1953), or Gerald Thomas's 1964 British film *Carry On Cleo* which explicitly parodied Mankiewicz's *Cleopatra*. These productions may be considered as *make-overs*, rather than remakes: the traditional narrative is rewritten, sometimes under the pretence of sequels or prequels. The Cleopatra films often

---

[49] Karine Hildenbrand-Girard, 'Mankiewicz adaptateur de Shakespeare', *Études Anglaises*, 55:2 (2002), 185–6.

[50] For the remarks on Cleopatra's ambiguous 'My son!', we are indebted to Karine Hildenbrand-Girard. 'L'Adaptation, vecteur et enjeu de plaisir dans le cinéma de J. L. Mankiewicz', paper given at the conference *From the blank page to the silver screen* organized at the University of Lorient (8–10 June 2006).

co-produced by Italy and France in the 1950s and 1960s at once challenged the American representations and more openly revealed their Orientalist agendas in which the Egyptian queen is vilified. They can be considered as direct responses to the American cultural hegemony by countries which were recovering from the human horrors and economic devastations of the Second World War. The sword-and-sandal films also gave Italy the opportunity to claim its glorious and imperial Roman past at a time when it attempted to recover from the war period and faced massive emigration. Sometimes, the European films challenged the 'Cleopatra' icon as US property so seriously that their American distribution was either delayed—Mario Mattoli's 1953 *Two Nights with Cleopatra* had to wait ten years before being released in the States—or totally cancelled. This was the case of Vittorio Cottafavi's 1960 *The Legions of the Nile*, and of Piero Pierotti and Viktor Tourjansky's 1962 *A Queen for Caesar*. Both films were bought by Twentieth Century Fox—but not released—to protect their own multi-million dollar *Cleopatra*.[51]

Other contemporary variations on the Cleopatra story can be cited, such as F. Gary Gray's 1996 film *Set It Off* (in which 'Cleo', played by Queen Latifah, is a black lesbian bank robber), Alain Chabat's 2002 French farce *Astérix et Obélix: Mission Cléopâtre* (inspired by Goscinny and Uderzo's 1965 comic book *Astérix et Cléopâtre*), the futuristic 2000-2001 TV series *Cleopatra 2525*, Osamu Tezuka's 1970 erotic anime *Kureopatora* (*Cleopatra: Queen of Sex*) or the 1989-91 three-part Japanese animated series *Cleopatra D.C.*. Sara Munson Deats notes that '[a]lthough most of these modern metamorphoses also retain Antony or Caesar as a character, the Cleopatra figure remains dominant'. Contrary to what happens when Shakespeare's *Antony and Cleopatra* is performed as *Julius Caesar*'s sequel, the focus of filmic conflations is and remains on the female character, and not on the male hero. Even if these figures of Cleopatra in popular culture are sometimes far removed from Shakespeare's own creation of the Egyptian queen, they all celebrate 'the glamourous, empowered female achieving agency in a male-dominated society'.[52] This celebration, however, should be always envisaged as a negotiation with the discourse that strives to punish the powerful, foreign woman. To use Sinfield's words, the Cleopatra story appears as one of those 'faultline stories … that require most assiduous and continuous reworking' because it addresses the 'awkward, unresolved issues, the ones in which the conditions of plausibility are in dispute'.[53] If the Cleopatra story still distresses the current conditions of plausibility, thus calling for constant repetition, it may reflect the conviction that equality between genders and among races should be able to thrive, not just in fiction but in the reality of our societies. As a sexually attractive foreign woman in power, Cleopatra still has much to say through the repetition and variations of her representational selves.

In screen adaptations of *Julius Caesar* and *Antony and Cleopatra*, the plays have been *serialized* or *conflated*. Through their emphasis on chronological and narrative orders, serialization and conflation tend to give the impression that the two plays cannot stand as

[51] Gary A. Smith, *Epic Films: Casts, Credits, and Commentary on over 250 historical spectacle movies* (Jefferson, NC: McFarland, 1991), 170.

[52] Sara Munson Deats, 'Shakespeare's Anamorphic Drama: A Survey of *Antony and Cleopatra* in Criticism, on Stage, and on Screen', in *Antony and Cleopatra: New Critical Essays*, ed. Sara Munson Deats (New York: Routledge, 2005), 77.

[53] Alan Sinfield, *Faultlines: Cultural Materialism and the Politics of Dissident Reading* (Oxford: Oxford University Press, 1992), 47.

autonomous works and that they need each other to exist—narratively and economically. Instead of temporality and spatiality challenging the predefined ideas of causality and determinism,[54] the linear time that is constructed serves a system inclined to align the notion of time with History, Progress, and Civilization, while linking space to the concepts of conservative stasis and reassuring nostalgia. The sequelization or conflation of *Julius Caesar* and *Antony and Cleopatra* appears to follow this teleological trend of 'progress' and 'nostalgia', and may stem from a partially reactionary desire, during times of upheaval, for a return to political and economic stability, or for a restoration (or celebration) of national identity through the appropriation of Roman imagery and cycles of epic history. Paul Budra and Betty A. Schellenberg wonder whether 'the phenomenon of ... desire for repetition-with-variation' is 'acute at certain historical junctures' and whether the creation of a sequel is 'possible only under certain (repeating) cultural conditions'.[55] The two plays may also be envisaged as major filters of history: directors of epic films or TV series which conflate and rewrite the two dramas can hardly ignore or bypass these cultural beacons and may use them to play with spectators' expectations. By contrast, as *Titus* and *Coriolanus* rewrite less conspicuous landmarks of Roman history, spectators do not have the same narrative expectations, giving directors more freedom to set the plays in different places and times and to introduce imagery that unmoors the stories from their Roman contexts. Paradoxically, what seem to be the most autonomous screen adaptations are irrigated by the same set of popular films. By inviting the Shakespearean audience to see *Titus Andronicus* and *Coriolanus* in the light of *Gladiator, Red Dragon,* or *The Silence of the Lambs,* the films convey a tension between respecting the Shakespearean script and departing from it. They also generate a specific form of seriality based less on Roman historical events than on the thrilling figure of the serial killer and the representation of a chaotic cycle of war.

SELECT BIBLIOGRAPHY

Cartelli, Thomas and Katherine Rowe, 'Colliding Time and Space in Taymor's *Titus*', (chapter 4), in *New Wave Shakespeare on Screen* (Cambridge: Polity Press, 2007), 69–96.

Burt, Richard, 'Shakespeare and the Holocaust. Julie Taymor's *Titus* is Beautiful or Shakesploi Meets (the) Camp', in *Shakespeare after Mass Media,* ed. Richard Burt (Basingstoke: Palgrave, 2002), 295–329.

Crowl, Sam, 'A World Elsewhere: The Roman Plays on Film and Television', in *Shakespeare and the Moving Image, the Plays on Film and Television,* ed. Anthony Davies and Stanley Wells (Cambridge: Cambridge University Press, 1994), 146–61.

Crowl, Sam, 'A Wilderness of Tigers. Taymor's *Titus*', ch. 13 in *Shakespeare at the Cineplex. The Kenneth Branagh Era* (Athens: Ohio University Press, 2003), 203–17.

Deats, Sara Munson, 'Shakespeare's Anamorphic Drama: A Survey of *Antony and Cleopatra* in Criticism, on Stage, and on Screen', in *Antony and Cleopatra: New Critical Essays,* ed. Sara Munson Deats (New York: Routledge, 2005), 1–93.

---

[54] Fredric Jameson, *Postmodernism or, The Cultural Logic of Late Capitalism* (Durham: Duke University Press, 1991), 367.

[55] Paul Budra and Betty A. Schellenberg, 'Introduction', *Part Two: Reflections on the Sequel* (Toronto, Buffalo, and London: University of Toronto Press, 1998), 17.

Hamer, Mary, *Signs of Cleopatra: History, Politics, Representation* (London: Routledge, 1993).

Hatchuel, Sarah, *Shakespeare and the Cleopatra/Caesar Intertext: Sequel, Conflation, Remake* (Lanham: Fairleigh Dickinson University Press, 2011).

Hatchuel, Sarah and Nathalie Vienne-Guerrin, eds., *Shakespeare on Screen: The Roman Plays* (Rouen: Publications des Universités de Rouen et du Havre, 2009).

Holland, Peter, ed., *Coriolanus*, 3rd Arden edn (London: Bloomsbury, 2013).

Joshel, Sandra R., Margaret Malamud, and Donald T. McGuire, Jr., eds., *Imperial Projections: Ancient Rome in Modern Popular Culture* (Baltimore and London: The Johns Hopkins University Press, 2001).

Madelaine, Richard, ed., *Shakespeare in Production: Antony and Cleopatra* (Cambridge: Cambridge University Press, 1998).

Marquardt, Anne-Kathrin, *The Spectacle of Violence in Julie Taymor's* Titus. *Ethics and Aesthetics* (Berlin: Trafo, 2010).

Rothwell, Kenneth S., *A History of Shakespeare on Screen: A Century of Film and Television* (Cambridge: Cambridge University Press, 1999).

Royster, Francesca T., *Becoming Cleopatra: The Shifting Image of an Icon* (Basingstoke: Palgrave Macmillan, 2003).

Wyke, Maria, *Projecting the Past: Ancient Rome, Cinema and History* (New York and London: Routledge, 1997).

Zander, Horst, ed., *Julius Caesar, New Critical Essays* (New York, London: Routledge, 2005).

CHAPTER 40

'THE BOWE OF ULYSSES'

Reworking the Tragedies of Shakespeare

PETER BYRNE

HAMLET   Dost thou hear me, old friend; can you play the Murder of Gonzago?
FIRST PLAYER   Ay, my lord.
HAMLET   We'll ha't to-morrow night. You could, for a need, study a speech of some
     dozen or sixteen lines, which I would set down and insert in't, could you not?
FIRST PLAYER   Ay, my lord.
HAMLET   Very well.[1]

THE dynamic portrayed in this brief exchange—revising a familiar tragedy to new purpose—is an instance in miniature of its author's career, illustrating Shakespeare's artistic
method of seizing upon convenient precedent in order to rework it for his present needs.
It is, therefore, entirely appropriate that this same technique has been applied to his own
tragedies; few of them have escaped substantial reworking by subsequent artists, their
own needs supplied by reference to or recreation of Shakespearean tragedy.

But what exactly is a 'reworking' of a Shakespearean tragedy? Ruby Cohn offers a definition: a work in which 'Shakespearean characters move through a partly or wholly non-
Shakespearean plot, sometimes with introduction of non-Shakespearean characters'[2]—
re-presentations of the tragedies that offer themselves as versions of the Shakespearean
narrative (by explicit reference to plot or character), but which distinguish themselves from
the original text by avoiding direct reference in the form of 'Shakespearean phrasal echoes'.[3]

Thus, while Tom Stoppard's *Rosencrantz and Guildenstern Are Dead* depends upon
Hamlet for its structure and context, it is less a reworking of the original as an expansion

---

[1] *Hamlet*, in G. Blakemore Evans et al., eds., *The Riverside Shakespeare*, 2nd edn. (Boston: Houghton
Mifflin Company, 1997), 2.2.537–45. All quotations from Shakespeare are from this edition.

[2] Ruby Cohn, *Modern Shakespeare Offshoots* (Princeton: Princeton University Press, 1976), 4.
Cohn's study in the field of Shakespearean revision remains one of the most substantial, and while
I have not adopted her catalogue of terminology for the various forms of such revisions—I am not in
complete agreement with the standards by which she makes her categorical determinations—I am
strongly indebted to her work.

[3] Cohn, *Modern Shakespeare*, 27.

upon it; within the play, *Hamlet* and its hero become obscure icons, larger meanings that the hapless antiheroes strive and fail to comprehend.[4] David Wroblewski's *The Story of Edgar Sawtelle,* on the other hand, takes the form of a novel, set in contemporary America, in which major characters in the original have been dropped or drastically altered (Wroblewski's 'Ophelia' is a faithful dog), and in which no use of Shakespeare's language appears. Yet the narrative pointedly derives its plot and tragic argument from the original play, encouraging that affiliation: it is a 'reworking' of *Hamlet.* 'Reworking,' then, refers to a work that establishes itself as a repetition of the Shakespearean original, and which also insists on its own artistic identity. It 'simultaneously enacts and disrupts expectations of "Shakespeare" as a generic category', creating an effect that 'becomes a significant and not necessarily alienating part of the viewing experience'.[5]

Critical response to reworking has traditionally been to evaluate the work in comparison with the original, usually expressing ridicule at the notion of trying, or contempt for the result. Harold Bloom demonstrates the source of this prejudice: 'Bardolatry, the worship of Shakespeare, ought to be even more a secular religion than it already is. The plays remain the outward limit of human achievement: aesthetically, cognitively, in certain ways morally, even spiritually. They abide beyond the end of the mind's reach; we cannot catch up to them.'[6] Such deification of Shakespeare means that reworking (which must, *ipso facto,* be produced by a lesser author) is either heresy or hubris. However simplistic and wrongheaded this conservatism may be, it is a powerful element in the Shakespearean tradition—indeed, if we are to admire these reworkings, our admiration must be prompted by the daring of artists who subject themselves to the automatic condemnation of Shakespeare's innumerable acolytes.

There is a more substantial criticism contained within the accusation of hackery, that of a false claim: when a work deviates from the Shakespearean text, one cannot unreservedly call the result 'Shakespearean'. When British television produced a series of Shakespearean modernizations in *ShakespeaRe-Told* (2005), the retellings were widely dismissed as failed attempts to articulate emotions and perspectives inextricably linked to—or contained within—the original: 'Despite the BBC's efforts to shape audience expectations to permit an at least provisional identification of the series with Shakespeare, the loss of Shakespeare's language proved for some viewers an unqualified and insurmountable barrier to recognition.'[7] If Shakespeare is contained in the language of his plays, then 'reworking' would seem a poor term. By sacrificing the distinctively Shakespearean language, we are abolishing, not reworking.

---

[4] Other instances of this approach, which view the original text as immutable and oppressive, would include the presence of *Othello* in Tayeb Salih's *Season of Migration to the North* and in Salman Rushdie's *The Satanic Verses.* We might also add 'prequels' to Shakespearean tragedies, like Gordon Bottomley's *King Lear's Wife* and John Updike's *Gertrude and Claudius,* and sequels such as Lee Blessing's *Fortinbras.*

[5] Margaret Jane Kidnie, *Shakespeare and the Problem of Adaptation* (London: Routledge, 2009), 114.

[6] Harold Bloom, *Shakespeare and the Invention of the Human* (New York: Riverhead Books, 1998), pp. xix–x.

[7] Kidnie, *Problem of Adaptation,* 114. Kidnie is far more appreciative of the *ShakespeaRe-Told* series than I am, but her defense of its artistic goals helped me to clarify my own defense of the revisionary artists discussed in this chapter.

These objections do not hold up to scrutiny. If tragedy is merely a narrative structure designed to achieve a particular kind and degree of emotional affect, we might dismiss reworkings as poor attempts to recreate the same emotional response without the inconvenience of creativity. But tragedy is not simply an emotional exhortation. It is a genre that, among its political, religious, social, and philosophical functions, is inevitably about a confrontation with precedent—with tradition and convention—and we must recognize that, for modern artists, Shakespeare is not an object of imitation, much less paraphrase. Instead, he is himself an artistic and social precedent whose authority diminishes the ability of the present to achieve significance, and his opus is the ground upon which his reworkers interpret, and challenge, their heritage.

This dynamic—the clash of the ontology of precedent and the needs of a present inadequately accounted for by that ontology—derives from the origins of tragedy as a genre. Classical Greek tragedy reworked myth as a way of confronting the present with a posterity that had to be acknowledged and rejected. It portrayed the values of the contemporary individual and of the contemporary collective in unequal conflict with a past that could not accommodate those values, and destroyed what it could not accommodate. Its Athenian authors took as their source material the age of myths and heroes that both inspired and were rendered inappropriate by the needs of the democratic state, illustrating by the destruction of those heroes the consequences of inflexible opposition to social and political context. At the same time, by basing their narratives on the works of the epic poets of the Homeric age, the Athenian playwrights acknowledged the inevitable influence of the artistic past while asserting the precedence of the contemporary in their own work:

> Tragedy establishes a distance between itself and the myths of the heroes that inspire it and that it transposes with great freedom. It scrutinizes them. It confronts heroic values and ancient religious representations with the new modes of thought that characterize the advent of the law within the city-state. The legends of the heroes are connected with ... values, social practices, forms of religion, and types of human behavior, [which] represent for the city-state the very things that it has had to condemn and reject and against which it has had to fight in order to establish itself. At the same time, however, they are what it developed from and it remains integrally linked to them.[8]

A comparison of the tragedies of classical Greece and the early modern period reveals that this formula of tragedy remains unchanged—unsurprising, given the bridging figure of Seneca, who referred to the former and inspired the latter. All that changes is the quality of the intrusive, overwhelming past, and the corresponding nature of its authority. And just as the Greek tragedy becomes the source of and precedent for Seneca's tragedies, and Seneca the same for the early modern, Shakespeare's tragedies become the modern equivalent of the myths on which classical tragedies are founded.

This attitude to Shakespeare, elevating him as it challenges him, begins in the Restoration, as does the critical justification for reworking. In his Introduction to *All for Love*, which he accurately proffers as an alternative to, rather than a reworking of *Antony*

---

[8] Jean-Pierre Vernant and Pierre Vidal-Naquet, *Myth and Tragedy in Ancient Greece*, trans. Janet Lloyd (New York: Zone Books, 1988), 26–7.

and Cleopatra, Dryden acknowledges the looming precedence of Shakespeare's play: 'The death of *Antony* and *Cleopatra*, is a Subject which has been treated by the greatest Wits of our Nation, after *Shakespeare*; and by all so variously, that their example has given me the confidence to try my self this Bowe of *Ulysses* amongst the Crowd of Sutors.'[9] The image of the bow, which will only yield to one master, provides a twofold analogy: that Shakespeare is merely one of the many who has attempted to achieve mastery of the subject of the royal lovers, and that Shakespeare is himself Ulysses, and, he having strung the bow, all other pretenders, like Homer's suitors, can only humiliate themselves in their attempt to match his achievement. This second reading is supported by his later confession that 'In my Stile, I have profess'd to imitate the Divine *Shakespeare*,'[10] the use of 'Divine' being both an acknowledgement of Shakespeare's authority and, I contend, a sardonic remark on Shakespeare's popular over-evaluation. If we concede the supremacy of heritage before we even begin, we render the contemporary at best inferior and at worst irrelevant. Instead, we must rework the past masters, argues Dryden, retaining their genius while revising for present context:

> Yet give me leave to say thus much, without injury to their Ashes, that not onely we shall never equal them, but they could never equal themselves, were they to rise and write again. We acknowledge them our Fathers in wit, but they have ruin'd their estates themselves before they came to their children's hands ... All comes sullied or wasted to us, and were they to entertain this age, they could not now make so plenteous treatments out of such decay'd Fortunes.[11]

Dryden asserts that history alters decorum, and that to worship the past is to enslave the present to an artificial standard, unreachable even by the legendary figures who created it. He proposes the conception of Shakespeare not only as a source of tragic narrative, but as the artistic and moral precedent confronted by contemporary artists in their own tragedies. The artistic needs have altered, Dryden argues. The cultures of politics, of honour, of love have all changed substantially, and to present Shakespeare as a perpetual icon is to condemn the contemporary to irrelevance.

The intervening centuries have done little to change this same reformist attitude. Herbert Blau echoes Dryden: 'Where democracy is taken for granted, and a mostly uncensored, self-determining culture, I still wince at the platitudes of community that, out of the myths of the ancient world, or the mythicizing of that world, continue to haunt the theatre.'[12] For the contemporary artist, reworking Shakespeare becomes an opportunity either to challenge his iconic status as 'artist absolute', or, less polemically, to call into question popular understandings of the play that no longer suit contemporary needs. When Jonathan Dollimore dismisses

---

[9] *All for Love*, in H. T. Swedenberg, Jr. et al., eds., *The Works of John Dryden*, 20 vols. (Berkeley: University of California Press, 1956–2000), 13: 10. All references to Dryden's writings will be to this edition, identified by volume and page number.

[10] Dryden, it should be added, argues that the 'Stile' of Shakespeare is the essential factor of his genius, but that it is possible to successfully imitate it, supporting the attempts of subsequent artists to do so. Again, the groundwork for a vindication of 'reworking' can be traced here.

[11] Dryden, 'An Essay of Dramatick Poesie', 17: 72–3.

[12] Herbert Blau, 'Who's There? Community of the Question', *PAJ: A Journal of Performance and Art* 28:2 (May 2006), 3.

both the Christian reading of *King Lear* and the humanist reading that replaced it, he as much as provides the grounds upon which the post-Marxist Edward Bond bases his reworking of the tragedy: 'The humanist view of [*King Lear*] is as inappropriate as the Christian alternative which it has generally displaced—inappropriate not least because it shares the essentialism of the later ... In fact, the play repudiates [this] essentialism ... In *Lear* ... man is decentered not through misanthropy but in order to make visible social process and its forms of ideological misrecognition.'[13] This kind of contemporary activism (the Marxism of Dollimore is one instance, but the Orientalism of Said and the work of the gender theorists have been equally fruitful), pitted against the conventional interpretation and estimation of Shakespeare, is at the heart of contemporary reworkings of his tragedies. The classical pattern of tragedy—the portrayal of the consequence of deifying precedent—is revisited by today's artists. Where the absolute of the ancient tragedies was portrayed as divinity, the reworked tragedies portray it as a cultural heritage that claims absolute authority over the present. Within this new framework, the reworking of Shakespeare is not merely a recreation of the classical pattern of tragedy, but an attempt to resolve its *agon* to the advantage of the contemporary.

In turning to specific instances of such reworking, I have, for purposes of clarity and concision, limited my examination to three modern reworkings of *King Lear*. Apart from its supreme status in the canon, the play represents one of the earliest subjects of reworking in the canon, evidenced by Nahum Tate's infamous decision to jettison Shakespeare's ending and to restore the happy conclusion of the narrative found in Shakesepeare's sources: Geoffrey of Monmouth, Spenser, and the anonymous *King Leir*. While Tate's revision is now considered sacrilege, it is, along with Davenant's *Macbeth*, the first instance of a contemporary artist insisting on privileging the decorum of the present—the presentation of a regaining of kingly authority as a propagandistic buttress for the restoration of Charles II—over the pristine retention of the Shakespearean text. (And it is worth noting that this revisionary motive is already present in Shakespeare's play, which expresses the anxiety of the basis for royal authority during the transition between the Elizabethan and Jacobean regimes.) The play, then, is a consistent presence in the tradition of reworking. In addition, Shakespeare's play is explicit in its portrayal of the clash between precedent and its heritage, enabling its contemporary re-workers to foreground the need for revisionary art. The character of Lear, clutching persistently to an outmoded order of meaning that increasingly exists only to justify his authority, has rendered the play deeply relevant to progressive artists. So it is in the case of these three instances, which demonstrate, from various cultures of contemporary identity, the attempt to resolve the *agon* between Shakespearean authority's oppressive influence and the political and artistic needs of the present to the benefit of the latter.

EDWARD BOND'S *LEAR*

One of the most obvious responses to the tragic dynamic is to reject it, acknowledging the tragic precedent set by Shakespeare, but refusing to engage in a contemporary response

---

[13] Jonathan Dollimore, *Radical Tragedy: Religion, Ideology and Power in the Drama of Shakespeare and his Contemporaries*, 3rd edn. (Durham: Duke University Press, 2004), 191.

that validates or recreates that precedent. Such refusal gains increasing popularity in the twentieth century, particularly as Marxist ideology becomes the ground for a generation of activist playwrights for whom tragedy must be artistically unacceptable. Tragedy portrays the horrors of the status quo, which it regards as cosmically unalterable, as a means of reconciling the individual to that status quo. While this reconciliation harmonizes with the pessimistic absurdity of Beckett or Ionesco, it clashes sharply with the progressivism of Ibsen, Shaw, or Brecht. Bond's *Lear* decisively locates him in the latter camp, and just as decisively places Shakespeare in the former.

If Beckett, in *Waiting for Godot* and *Endgame* (the latter frequently viewed as a version of *King Lear*[14]), draws his apocalyptic vision from *King Lear*'s conclusion—the image of the wasteland unredeemed by the grief of its few survivors—then it is easy to see why Bond draws his inspiration elsewhere: 'Bond takes his stand with Brecht ... in part to correct a prevailing misrepresentation of history as reflective of a changeless and essentially absurd human condition, but mainly to make a case for the space of human agency and the viability of intervention in history.'[15]

Bond therefore employs the techniques of Brecht's Epic Theatre: formal and presentational speech, sudden shifts in plot and on-stage authority, while offering a portrait of human nature as largely venal. The bad thrive until fortune consumes them, the kind are exploited for their troubles, and the success of the former depends largely on the weakness of the latter. Like Mother Courage, a dethroned Lear wanders on a picaresque journey through a nightmarish landscape of totalitarian oppression and the indiscriminate violence of revolutionary forces. Drawing, too, from Artaud and the Theatre of Cruelty, Bond depicts violence as the supreme mark and method of authority, surpassing Shakespeare's depiction of Gloucester's blinding with multiple acts of mutilation, dismemberment, and rape as well as murder. Bond's Lear, whose reign was marked by authority manifesting itself as dehumanizing cruelty, falls victim to this precedent in his treatment, and it is, of all people, his vicious daughter Fontanelle, who delivers the clearest indictment: 'For as long as I can remember there was misery and waste and suffering where you were. You live in your own mad world, you can't hear me. You've wasted my life and I can't even tell you. O god, where can I find justice?'[16]

Of the Shakespearean narrative of *King Lear*, little remains except fragments. A few names are unchanged. An onstage blinding occurs, though it is Lear, rather than a Gloucester-figure, who is its victim. There are two daughters who, escaping their father's authority, prove vicious. A version of the Fool appears as the Boy who helps Lear in his adversity and, murdered for doing so, returns as an accompanying Ghost, but this recasting is so different that the distinction, rather than the similarity, is notable. The same is true of Bond's Cordelia, whose name evokes the image of the merciful child, but whose actions merely recreate Lear's folly of misrule. The play is, despite its title, firmly

---

[14] R. A. Foakes gives a good account of this tradition in '*King Lear* and *Endgame*', in *Shakespeare Survey: An Annual Survey of Shakespearean Studies and Production: King Lear and its Afterlife*, ed. Peter Holland (Cambridge: Cambridge University Press 2002), 153–8.

[15] Thomas Cartelli, 'Shakespeare in Pain: Edward Bond's *Lear* and the Ghosts of History', in *Shakespeare Survey: An Annual Survey of Shakespearean Studies and Production: King Lear and its Afterlife*, 160.

[16] Edward Bond, *Lear* in *Plays: Two* (London: Eyre Methuen Ltd., 1978), 70.

un-Shakespearean in its tenor, plot, and characterization. Only in its political concerns does it relate to the original, but that continuity is, for Bond, what renders the original and his reworking essential.

To judge by his own account, Bond's *Lear* is the play that Shakespeare was unable to write. Shakespeare's play raises questions of good government and legitimate authority that he could not address: 'He did not answer his questions because historically they were not answerable at that time and art is prescribed by the political situation in which it is created.'[17] Bond's Lear—a figure of old, precedent-derived authority who misrules his kingdom because he cannot recognize that the passage of time has led to a change in the needs of his people—is a portrait of the corrupt and corrupting authority of Shakespearean tragedy. Bond composes his play in terms of names, images, decisions, and actions that reference *King Lear* in order to depict the inadequacy of its tragic vision.

Lear's early authority in the play is marked by devotion to a divisive wall, a project of a medieval mind that the modern age (which Bond illustrates with references to modern technology like rifles and photographs) has rendered absurdly obsolete. Yet the wall continues to be built. This work claims the lives of his citizens, in service to a vision of the world that, as everyone reminds him, is no longer relevant. Bond's Lear refuses to accept the arrival of modernity, and suffers because he does not address the dangerous modes of thought and conduct modernity brings with it, portrayed here in the self-serving realpolitik and casuistry of Fontanelle and Bodice. In this narrative arc—the collapse of a man devoted to an archaic order, and victimized by the heritage of that order—Bond clearly evokes Shakespeare's play and its hero.

But Shakespeare's Lear is redeemed by his submission to abjection, by his willingness to accept his helplessness in the face of a world that is not, and never was, within his power to command. For Bond, however, Lear's humility and his final despair at the death of Cordelia are just as contemptible as his earlier hubris; neither will lead the man to the action needed to change a world that Bond, at least, believes to be changeable.

Bond therefore, goes a step further. He takes his Lear to the abasement achieved by Shakespeare's king: 'Does this suffering and misery last forever? Do we work to build ruins, waste all these lives to build a desert no one could live in? There's no one to explain it to me, no one I can go to for justice. I'm old, I should know how to live by now, but I know nothing, I can do nothing, I am nothing.'[18] But Bond's Lear is ignoring the example made by young Ben, who volunteers for a suicide mission with a simple credo: 'I may not survive—but at least I'll use what time I've got left.'[19] Lear at first misreads Ben's offer as the passivity of the martyr ('If I saw Christ on his cross I would spit at him'[20]), but he is projecting himself onto the young man. Only at the play's conclusion, when Lear seizes the shovel and begins to dig up the wall's foundations, does he embrace activism, echoing Ben's words: 'I'm not as fit as I was. I can still make my mark.'[21] That he is shot and killed immediately afterwards is poignant, but it is not tragic.

---

[17] 'Introduction', in *Plays: Two*, p. xi.

[18] *Lear* in *Plays: Two*, 94. It is worth noting that the repetition of 'nothing' echoes Shakespeare's repetition of 'never' in the helpless despair of Lear over the death of Cordelia—a similarity Bond draws to illustrate distinction between the original Lear's resignation and his own Lear's eventual commitment to action.

[19] Ibid., 90.   [20] Ibid.   [21] Ibid., 102.

For Bond's play is not a tragedy. Lear dies morally and actively aligned with an approved course of action: digging up the wall that represents the oppressive folly of his reign. He is engaged in an act of positive good, and leaves the shovel protruding from the earth, its handle inviting the next rebel to take it up. Shakespeare's Lear dies in a transcendence of grief and suffering—like the hero of *Oedipus at Colonus*, he has suffered beyond the point of human existence—a moving, but pessimistic conclusion. Bond's play, despite its horrors, is optimistic about the possibility of transcending suffering through small steps, and Bond asserts this attitude by taking one of history's great statements of tragic pessimism and systematically subverting it.

Bond asserts that 'Drama comes to a crisis it cannot solve without destabilizing society instead of freeing it from ideological rigidities.'[22] The goal of drama as an instrument of political revolution can only begin when drama itself is subjected to this same revolutionary impulse; one cannot cure society with an instrument that is itself diseased. *King Lear* is a pessimistic response to the question of human agency in a pitiless cosmos framed by precedent; and, to the contemporary mind, the temptation to regard Shakespeare as an embodiment of that cosmos—his artistic authority so great as to quash any contemporary attempts to offer an equally valid answer—is clear. But Bond contends that because Shakespeare offers no answers he ought not to be considered an authority beyond the importance of the questions he has asked. For Bond, Shakespeare is an unanswered question that it falls to the present age to answer. *King Lear* ends in a wasteland. *Lear* ends with the smallest of first gestures towards recovery. The difference is profound.

KUROSAWA'S *RAN*

Michael Anderegg tasks cinematic adapters of Shakespeare with the perils of inadequate confidence in their media: 'Filmmakers seldom have the courage of their convictions. If they really believed their frequent claims that film is a visual medium, so that images can substitute for words, they would ... create an entirely new verbal structure.'[23] He then offers *Throne of Blood* as an instance of a triumphant response to this challenge, and, whether or not we consider *Ran* equally successful, Kurosawa clearly seeks to create for his Lear-narrative 'a new verbal structure' within the 'visual medium' of film. Such restructuring of meaning is essential for an artist engaged in Kurosawa's reworking of the original, inasmuch as his reworking must be filtered through a series of powerful translations.

For all of its departures from Shakespeare, Bond's play remains part of a relatively seamless tradition of language and composition; it is, after all, a theatrical play written in English by an English author. As an audience, or as readers, we experience it as part of the performative, geographical, and linguistic culture of which Shakespeare is an integral part. In *Ran*,

---

[22] Edward Bond and Peter Billingham, 'Drama and the Human: Reflections at the Start of a Millennium', *PAJ: A Journal of Performance and Art* 29:3 (September 2007), 4.

[23] Michael Anderegg, *Cinematic Shakespeare* (Lanham, MD: Rowman and Littlefield Publishers Inc., 2004), 8.

we encounter a series of disruptions: cinema rather than stage, director/screenwriter rather than playwright, and Japan rather than Britain. While Kurosawa adheres far more closely to Shakespeare's plot than Bond, the material circumstances under which we experience it are marked by disruption from the original, and we must consider whether or how those disruptions affect it as a tragic reworking of *King Lear*.

Most obviously, Kurosawa's version must, as a cinematic experience, come to us in a venue that is automatically troubled by the Aristotelian preference for plot over spectacle. But Kurosawa embraces his visual freedom of expression with great verve, often to the detriment of linguistic or performative complexity, and this has caused some critics to contemn the film as possessing 'an inflated but hollow magniloquence, which is especially inappropriate to a film that would pass itself off as a version of *King Lear*'.[24] Setting aside its derisive tone, this observation reveals Kurosawa's confrontation with the influence of the original text, as a narrative model and as a text in which the ability of language to convey meaning is rendered hollow by experience.

The articulation of identity by means of language and the attempt to fix the meaning of language by means of political authority are at the heart of the conflict of *King Lear*. The abdication of Lear creates a rupture between the king's two bodies, and there is a corresponding fragmentation of the words that once designated meaning when the two were unified. Repetitions of words like 'king', 'father', 'legitimate', 'fool', and 'man' are all part of the attempt of the characters to locate themselves in a social and political landscape in which authority is asserted primarily by the ability of the powerful to define words and their values, and thus the nature of a truth articulated by those words. *King Lear* is thus irresistible to those who wish to question the validity of this authority (especially since that authority has been the means by which Shakespeare has maintained his cultural supremacy), but perhaps more than any other play in the canon, its use of language is so essential to its meaning that the loss of that original language in reworking risks the loss of what is truly 'Shakespearean' about the narrative. Yet Kurosawa, a master of film, attempts to do for the cinematic what Shakespeare does with the theatrical articulation of ideas, and thus retain the 'Shakespearean' even in translation.

Kurosawa has claimed that he did not begin with *King Lear* in mind, but with the legend of Mōri Motonari, whose lesson to his sons on the necessity of their unity, demonstrated by their inability to break a trio of arrows, begins the action of *Ran*. But if Motonari was the initial impulse, Shakespeare's narrative quickly usurped that beginning. Motonari's legacy was untroubled by filial disobedience, whereas Hidetora, Kurosawa's hero, destroys his sons and himself by making the disastrous decision to abdicate in favour of his eldest, Taro.

Saburo, his youngest, chastises his decision in terms that resemble those by which Bond's Fontanelle condemns her father: 'You spilled an ocean of blood. You showed no mercy, no pity. We too are children of this age, weaned on strife and chaos. We are your sons, yet you count on our fidelity. In my eyes, that makes you a fool.'[25] Saburo rightly raises the argument that Hidetora's authority, deriving as it has from the cruel suppression

---

[24] Tetsuo Kishi and Graham Bradshaw, *Shakespeare in Japan* (London: Continuum, 2005), 143.

[25] *Ran*. Dir. Akira Kurosawa, Criterion Collection DVD, Greenwich Film Production S.A./Herald Ace Inc./Nippon Herald Films Inc., 1985.

and elimination of rivals, has established a precedent that can only be repaid in kind. As with Bond, there is the potential for a tragic engagement with the past, exemplified by a Shakespearean hero and narrative.

But where Bond attempts to avert this inevitability, Kurosawa appears to yield to it. The plot of *Ran* is *King Lear* told in broad strokes: Lear/Hidetora divides his land between two vicious children (Taro/Goneril and Jiro/Regan) while banishing a loving child (Saburo/Cordelia), and is subsequently driven into madness by the ungrateful abuse of his heirs. Recovering his wits after rescue by the loving child, who stages an invasion to recover the father's lost authority, he dies of grief at the murder of that child by the villains of the narrative. Where Bond's version used small similarities to distinguish itself from the original, Kurosawa's uses small differences to indicate an overall harmony with it. Even the performative break with the Shakespearean original, Kurosawa's decision to stage the performances in the theatrical style of Noh, creates a similarly traditional mode of performance. If Shakespeare's text demands, in its verse and historical idiom, a concession to tradition on the part of the actors, Kurosawa has simply replaced a traditionally Japanese mode for a traditionally Western one. If his goal were merely a statement of the universal relevance of *King Lear*—a goal he certainly achieves—then, despite its differences, *Ran* would be little more than a popularizing of the original. Yet Kurosawa is clearly attempting something else. The film reveals his awareness that his role as a cinematic director necessitates the creation of a substantial structure of meaning independent of the theatrical and verbal paradigm of Shakespeare. And here the context of film and the theatrical heritage of Japan permit Kurosawa to explore the meaning of a context opposed to Shakespeare's speech: silence.

The meaning of speechlessness explains his decision to base the appearance and performance of his actors in what, by the standards of Western theatre and cinema, is the minimalism of language and expression in Noh. The epitome of Noh is the expression of stillness. The drama is not silent, but the artistic *telos* to reduce performance to the minimal argues that silence that speaks is the height of artistic achievement. The use of silence to challenge Shakespeare's linguistic authority initially appears masterfully shrewd; if Shakespeare's version of the narrative—and of the meaning of the narrative—is contained in the language of *King Lear*, then a version that reveals the degree to which that language is unnecessary (by paring down the Western verbiage to the eloquent minimalism of the Noh) is a potent challenge to the authority of Shakespearean precedent.

The battle at the Third Castle, generally recognized as the great set piece of the film, illustrates the Kurosawan reworking of Shakespeare into silence. Until the assassination of Taro, the scene is marked by a total absence of sound effects. Instead, the score of Toru Takemitsu is the only sound. Its lush strains provide a mournful sweep to the action; it turns slaughter into something like visual poetry. The graphic violence becomes part of a symphonic whole, transforming agony into aesthetics. Without audible expression, the figures onscreen express themselves through face, body, and movement, and Kurosawa lets his camera linger on every form of death, his attention (and ours) focusing on the actors as they achieve absolute stillness.

Within the heights of the Third Castle, Hidetora, his sword broken in a pointless effort to drive off his attackers, is unable to commit seppuku, and, driven to absolute abasement, succumbs to madness. But where Lear's madness is marked by bombastic speeches at his daughters, at the gods, at nature, all ineffective, all emphasizing his impotence, Kurosawa renders his hero mute. His face rendered thoroughly mask-like in the Noh style, Hidetora descends the stair of the burning castle, trailing the visual symbol of his impotence, the empty sheath. The stunned response of the soldiers, who, moments before had driven forward to kill Hidetora, prompts our own. Hidetora walks slowly towards the camera, speechless, his face immobile. He is the epitome of silent expression, and the awe he creates silences the world around him as he disappears into the fog of war. The scene is unquestionably a tour-de-force, the more so because Kurosawa has rendered it in thoroughly un-Shakespearean terms. The ambiguity of silence replaces the uncertainty of language.

However, while the scene is a triumph for the filmmaker, we must question whether Kurosawa's silence constitutes a reworking that challenges, rather than merely translates, Shakespeare's tragedy. Both the scene and the film as a whole are marked by the display of undecidable imagery. Does the sight of the sun momentarily emerging from clouds in the pitch of battle symbolize the turn of that battle towards victory? Is it an ironic commentary on the extinguishing of Hidetora's former glory? Or is it merely a coincidental atmospheric phenomenon? Kurosawa offers no answers; he merely restates the questions throughout. Given the brevity and mildness with which he portrays it, Kurosawa's interest in the storm, so essential in Shakespeare, is perfunctory,[26] yet the storm is only one manifestation of weather upon which he consistently lavishes attention throughout the film: sun, clouds, wind, dust, and fog are always painted in striking composition, our attention forced upon them by cutaways and long takes. We are never allowed to forget the intrusive effects of a natural world indifferent to the characters who scramble to claim control of its landscape, nor are we allowed to guess as to the existence of any observing divinity, or that divinity's opinion of our conduct.

The conclusion of the film highlights this problematic silence. In a scene visually composed in the formal style of Noh, Hidetora lies dead across the body of Saburo, the tableaux completed by the flanking, seated figures of Kyoami and Tango. Kyoami berates the gods for their malice in causing or passively observing the agonies of mortals. Tango chastises him, arguing that the gods are not responsible for this horror, and that it is man who creates his own suffering in an endless cycle of cruelty and folly. Though Tango has the last word, the matter is left undecided as the film transitions to the silent progress of Hidetora's funeral, and the final image of the blind Tsurumaru on the edge of a man-made precipice (the human factor is always essential in Kurosawa), losing hold of the 'protective' Buddhist scroll given to him by his murdered sister. The image satisfies neither Kyoami's nor Tango's version of the state of humanity with any clarity, yet it could easily ratify either.

Unlike Bond's play, Kurosawa's film is a reworking that endorses, rather than challenges, Shakespeare's tragedy. Though the magnificent ambiguity of Kurosawa's images, juxtaposed with the silence of his Noh-derived composition, achieves a cinematic statement to equal the terrifying ambiguity that Shakespeare achieves verbally, the success of

---

[26] See Alexander Leggatt, *Twayne's New Critical Introductions to Shakespeare: King Lear* (Boston: Twayne Publishers, 1988), 13. Where Shakespeare's interest in the battle is minimal, and in the storm profound, Kurosawa's priorities are reversed, perhaps suggesting an advocacy for the humanist side of the debate of man's ability to achieve self-determination. See also Christopher Hoile, '*King Lear* and Kurosawa's *Ran*: Splitting, Doubling, Distancing', *Pacific Coast Philology* 22:1/2 (November 1987), 30.

the film is the success of Shakespeare's play: both are masterful portraits of the unanswer-able question of man's complicity in his own suffering. To borrow Bond's terminology, Kurosawa is apparently satisfied to repeat Shakespeare's questions, rather than answer them. *Ran* is certainly no failure in terms of its emotional or visual achievements, but of the three instances of the contemporary artist, Kurosawa appears to capitulate to the prec-edent of Shakespeare's artistry. Kurosawa achieves artistry in his own venues, and perhaps on his own terms, but only in reiterating the tragic argument of *King Lear*. In doing so, he subjects the present to the authority of the past.

SMILEY'S *A THOUSAND ACRES*

Jane Smiley's stated intentions for *A Thousand Acres* would seem, initially, to pair her with Kurosawa: 'I rewrote *King Lear* and tried to come up with exactly the same thing.' Yet she then describes her desire to 'look back on history and wonder about it and want to seri-ously engage with it and maybe rewrite it'. [27] This second assertion contradicts the first. As Dryden would have noted, altered times demand that the contemporary artist cannot duplicate his heritage, and I would argue that the novel supports her revisionist assertion. *A Thousand Acres* is the contextual result of an era of identity politics that render tragedy an unacceptable genre; if the subaltern individual is to achieve a significance other than the one prescribed for it by oppressive precedent, then tragedy cannot be permitted to endorse that precedent by portraying it as insurmountable.

By locating the narrative's perspective entirely in Ginny Smith (the Goneril of the nar-rative), Smiley does more than transfer the narrative's heroic status to her narrator; she declares the importance of individual perspective on the achievement of identity. This argu-ment explains the fidelity of Smiley to her source. The plot of *King Lear* is reproduced, with few accommodations for historical setting, faithfully; only by portraying the same events related by Shakespeare can Smiley demonstrate how something as subtle as narrative per-spective can alter their significance. At the same time, that shift in perspective is enabled and accentuated by the venue of the novel: 'That Smiley chooses narrative as the method and the novel as the instrument to articulate her transformed, female-centered version of the Shakespearean original makes available, indeed insists upon, modes of story-telling that manage the problems of causality ... and character in ways markedly different'[28] from Shakespeare's theatrical narrative.

Smiley conflates the legacy of Shakespeare with the Lear-figure of Larry Cook; both fig-ures instil a paternal order of meaning that suffocates the possibility of alternative forms of expression. This assertion causes her to draw upon the artistic feminism of Woolf's *A Room of One's Own* and its famous passage on Shakespeare's imaginary sister, Judith.[29]

---

[27] Jane Smiley and Kay Bonetti, 'An Interview with Jane Smiley', *The Missouri Review* 21:3 (1998), 99–100.

[28] Iska Alter, '*King Lear* and *A Thousand Acres*: Gender, Genre, and the Revisionary Impulse', in Marianne Novy, ed., *Transforming Shakespeare: Contemporary Women's Re-visions in Literature and Performance* (New York: Palgrave, 2000), 145.

[29] Virginia Woolf, *A Room of One's Own* (New York: Harcourt Brace & Co., 1929), 46–51.

Judith's narrative is portrayed in tragic terms, but Woolf's point is that her fate is not a matter of necessity, but of a world that modernity, with its capacity to acknowledge and encourage the female writer, proves to be alterable. Woolf does not reject Shakespeare's legacy; the poignancy of Judith's silence would mean nothing without comparison to the brilliance of her brother's achievement. But she does demonstrate that, much like Lear, Shakespeare is the beneficiary of—and thus the propagator of—a male hegemony of cultural values. Woolf herself is the evidence for a successfully contrary order of meaning, just as Smiley's status as a published author endorses her tacit argument at the validity of a feminist revision of Shakespeare.

Neither Woolf's nor Smiley's narratives are tragic, since tragedy is a depiction of the result of a conflict with the unalterable by the perversely heroic. Ginny's narrative arc is primarily the result of a world order that need not be. The novel, recognizably based on one of literature's most famous tragedies, invites us to read it as tragic, but only to enlighten us as to the self-injurious bias of that reading. The world of Zebulon County seems tragic, an absolute order that punishes even the modest ambitions of its inhabitants. Ginny longs for children, yet repeatedly miscarries, seemingly the victim of unanswerable fate. But Smiley subverts this reading by showing that this 'cosmic order' depends on secrets that, when revealed, prove that it is the result of the agency and priorities of her father. The drainage pipes (tile lines) that give fertility to the Cook farm carry toxins that, poisoning the drinking water, have caused Ginny to miscarry, and, in the novel's greatest departure from (or addition to) the narrative original, both Ginny and Rose are the victims of incestuous sexual abuse, a truth that Ginny has suppressed with a survivor's instinct of denial. Both secrets revealed, the order of Zebulon County is dissolved as the manipulative cruelties of a patriarchal monster.

As David Brauner and Mary Paniccia Carden have noted,[30] authority in the novel is marked by speech and the inability to speak; the rich interiority afforded by Smiley's first-person narrator allows us to experience what Shakespeare's performative narrative cannot: the voice of those who are silenced, and particularly the ability of the silenced 'to resist without seeming to resist, to absent yourself while seeming respectful and attentive'.[31] It is this quality of voice—the portrait of how silence in the face of overwhelming authority is not capitulation to that authority—that points us towards Smiley's escape from the tragic dynamic of the modern author oppressed by the deity of Shakespeare.

At the same time, Smiley's activism does not permit Ginny's escape from her father's ontological tyranny to serve as a comforting victory. The novel is pointedly set in the waning years of the Carter administration, when the second-wave of feminism was at high water, and the progressive politics of identity were marking successive achievements. This was also the era in which the reactionary hegemony of Reagan was imminent, the beginning of a period of regressive social engineering in which the ability of subaltern individuals to achieve identity would be severely curtailed. Larry Cook may lose his authority, but the culture that produced him will produce other autocrats.

---

[30] See David Brauner, '"Speak Again": The Politics of Rewriting in *A Thousand Acres*', *The Modern Language Review* 96:3 (July 2001), 654–6, and Mary Paniccia Carden, 'Remembering/Engendering in the Heartland: Sexed Language, Embodied Space, and America's Foundational Fictions in Jane Smiley's *A Thousand Acres*', *Frontiers: A Journal of Women's Studies* 18:2 (1997), 181–202.

[31] Jane Smiley, *A Thousand Acres* (New York: Anchor Books, 1991), 370.

While I do not believe that Smiley intends us entirely to associate Shakespeare's influence on her era's culture with Larry Cook's role as monstrous, silencing authority, Dryden's vision of 'ruin'd estates' does resonate with both figures. Like Cook, Shakespeare overrides the relevance of the subaltern voice—not only the female voice, but also the modern voice. (That the novel helplessly plays out, in contemporary America, the events of a narrative written centuries ago and an ocean away, suggests the inescapability of the Shakespearean hegemony.) Like Kurosawa, Smiley responds to the voice of Shakespeare with the silence of the contemporary. But unlike Kurosawa, her silence is eloquent, rather than ambiguous, and—however dimly—optimistic, rather than fatalistic. Ginny's last words sound very much like a characterization of Shakespeare's own foray into tragedy's abyss: 'I can't say that I forgive my father, but now I can imagine what he probably chose never to remember—the goad of an unthinkable urge, pricking him, pressing him, wrapping him in an impenetrable fog of self that must have seemed ... like the very darkness. This is the gleaming obsidian shard I safeguard above all the others.'[32]

If Smiley's goal, as originally stated, is to reproduce the achievement of the original, then her capitulation to its authority marks her, like Kurosawa, as a tragically perverse opponent to an authority that, by her own repetition, renders her its inferior. But if her goal is to reveal that such a struggle is fundamentally misguided, not because victory is impossible, but because the authority granted to Shakespeare is unjust to to the relevance of those who could not speak then, and who must speak now, then A Thousand Acres is decidedly successful. As a re-worker, Smiley rejects the Bow of Ulysses. She portrays the Homeric—and Shakespearean—challenge only to reveal that Penelope's voice, like Goneril's, like Judith's, must be heard.

But this priority, far from separating her from her Shakespearean source, may be seen as a fulfilment of its agenda. As I suggested earlier, many reworkings of Shakespeare are less in contention with the original text, than they are with popular misreadings of that text. It must be recalled that Smiley's emphasis on the value of the individual and her perspective is a quality prevalent in Shakespeare's canon. Shakespeare's language is the language of the individual's understanding of personal, contextual meaning, contrasted with a tyrannical precedent of definition—or, more simply, that we are what we can say, and if we cannot say what we mean because convention does not allow us, we must expose, subvert, and, if possible, alter convention. Shakespeare's tragedies demand that contemporary artists distinguish themselves from precedent. If he himself has become that inadequate precedent, then reworking the tragedies is not just permissible, it is essential.

Select Bibliography

Bond, Edward, Plays: Two (London: Eyre Methuen Ltd., 1978).
Bond, Edward, and Peter Billingham, 'Drama and the Human: Reflections at the Start of a Millennium'. PAJ: A Journal of Performance and Art 29:3 (September 2007): 1–14.
Cohn, Ruby, Modern Shakespeare Offshoots (Princeton: Princeton University Press, 1976).

[32] Ibid., 370–1.

Dollimore, Jonathan, *Radical Tragedy: Religion, Ideology and Power in the Drama of Shakespeare and his Contemporaries*, 3rd edn. (Durham: Duke University Press, 2004).

Evans, G. Blakemore, et al., ed., *The Riverside Shakespeare*, 2nd edn. (Boston: Houghton Mifflin Company, 1997).

Holland, Peter, ed., *Shakespeare Survey: An Annual Survey of Shakespearean Studies and Production: King Lear and its Afterlife* (Cambridge: Cambridge University Press, 2002).

Kidnie, Margaret Jane, *Shakespeare and the Problem of Adaptation* (London: Routledge, 2009).

Kurosawa, Akira, dir., *Ran*. Criterion Collection DVD, Greenwich Film Production S.A./Herald Ace Inc./Nippon Herald Films Inc., 1985.

Novy, Marianne, ed., *Transforming Shakespeare: Contemporary Women's Re-visions in Literature and Performance*, ed. Marianne Novy (New York: Palgrave, 2000).

Smiley, Jane, *A Thousand Acres* (New York: Anchor Books, 1991).

Swedenberg, H.T. Jr., et al., *The Works of John Dryden*, 20 vols. (Berkeley: University of California Press, 1956–2000).

Vernant, Jean-Pierre and Pierre Vidal-Naquet, *Myth and Tragedy in Ancient Greece*, trans. Janet Lloyd (New York: Zone Books, 1988).

Woolf, Virginia, *A Room of One's Own* (New York: Harcourt Brace & Co., 1929).

CHAPTER 41

....

SHAKESPEARE'S TRAGEDIES
ON THE OPERATIC STAGE

....

WILLIAM GERMANO

SINCE the seventeenth century, Shakespeare's tragedies have first been augmented with music, then more fully absorbed into musical versions, from song cycles to symphonic poems and ballets, that expanded and shifted the emphases of the texts. The most complex of these versions are the operatic treatments of Shakespeare's works. As old as the plays of Shakespeare, the theatrical form of opera emerged in the 1590s as an aesthetic project of the Italian humanists. In its pursuit of a revived classicism, opera (meaning 'works') was conceived as a complex theatrical entertainment combining music and the other arts. The first operas were based on Greek myths. The first of those works to establish itself in the modern repertory, *L'Orfeo* (1607) by Claudio Monteverdi, recounts the tale of Orpheus and Eurydice as tragedy redeemed by divine intervention.

The contemporaneous Stuart court masques deployed the arts, including music, to celebrate the world of the monarchy as serious fantasy. Like the Italian opera being performed in Mantua and elsewhere, the English masque was a multimedia theatrical construct, dependent on visual spectacle, the auditory pleasures of live music, and a poetical text.

Beginning around 1700, Shakespeare's tragedies were taken up as source material for opera as we recognize that term today. Shakespeare's plays already offered theatrical composers the opportunity to write music for songs within the works, and with the growth of Continental opera, the possibility of adapting Shakespeare's plays on a larger musical scale turned the playwright's work, including the tragedies, into a powerful source of inspiration for composers throughout Europe, North America, and beyond.

The Grove Dictionary of Music identifies more than 400 operas as derived from (adapted, based on, or simply 'after') Shakespeare, of which more than a third are based on the tragedies. Although that archive is extensive, the connections between Shakespeare and the operas associated with his characters and titles are often highly mediated. Many works have titles, or even plots, suggestive of a close relationship to Shakespeare's plays but that, on closer inspection, are seen to depend instead on Shakespeare's sources or on derivative works substantially different from Shakespeare's originals. Of the twelve plays identified in the 1623 Folio as tragedies all but *Titus Andronicus* have been set as operas (we are more likely today to consider *Cymbeline* a dark comedy). Of these, the most frequently set by operatic composers have been *Romeo and Juliet* and *Hamlet*, while the tragedies that have yielded the greatest operas are *Othello* and *Macbeth*.

To read the long and interwoven history of Shakespeare and opera requires acknowledging the very different objectives of a Shakespearean tragedy and a tragic opera. A tragedy is constructed entirely from language. An opera is dependent on a comparatively brief text, the words selected for dramatic impact, singability, and the capacity to inspire musical invention. The greatest of Shakespeare's scenes are rarely replicable on the operatic stage in the terms Shakespeare has provided. Instead, the goal of an operatic version is to identify some essential quality at the heart of a scene, a speech, or a phrase and to correlate that quality to music of equivalent power. Arrigo Boito (1842–1918), the finest of Shakespeare's operatic librettists, compared the process of adapting Shakespeare to squeezing the juice out of a fruit. To expect a comprehensive translation of any play into the template of a libretto, or to anticipate roles for all the characters, is to forget that music is a form of slow theatrical listening with its own priorities and temporality. When a Shakespeare play works for the operatic stage, it's because the play has been cut down to size. Without a surgical intervention, even the finest music cannot succeed.

Shakespeare's comedies have better suited the ambitions and needs of many operatic composers. The tragedies offer a complexity and heightened purpose that intensifies the disconnect between verbal and musical expression; far too much must be pared back, and what remains can easily appear little more than a shadow of a complex figure. Yet the tragedies have tempted operatic composers again and again, offering powerful musical insights into these dramas as they were reimagined in the composer's own time. Admittedly, there is no supremely great operatic *King Lear* or *Antony and Cleopatra*, though both have been set by respected twentieth-century composers. There is no distinguished *Coriolanus*. The most successful operatic *Hamlet* is merely that. There is musical beauty and theatrical brilliance throughout Shakespeare's operatic corpus, yet when it comes to Shakespeare, operatic greatness is a rare commodity, and even rarer in the case of the tragedies.

Until the work of Richard Wagner (1813–83) and the revolution in through-composed theatrical music, operas were fundamentally sequences of numbers, separated by sung dialogue, which could be accompanied or unaccompanied or, as in the German *singspiel* or French *opéra comique* tradition, not sung but spoken. A sequence of arias gave way to complex arrangements of solos, duets, trios, and larger ensembles, as well as an enhanced role for the chorus, all of which was paralleled by an increased complexity of instrumentation and the resulting growth in the size of the orchestra. Over time, that increased complexity in musical structures and materials allowed composers to approach Shakespeare's tragedies with more deeply observed musical invention. Verdi's late masterpieces—*Otello* (1887) and *Falstaff* (1893)—remain the summit of the form, excelling in economy, musical characterization, and a depth of perception through musical means. Much of their achievement as dramatic constructs relies on Boito's skilful libretti, which build on, rather than diminish or evade, the challenges inherent in Shakespeare's dramaturgy. A musical approach to Shakespeare begins with the songs within the plays themselves. Shakespeare's tragedies offer a librettist fewer passages either identified as songs or suggestive of singing. Iago's drinking song and Desdemona's 'willow' song in *Othello*, and the incantations of *Macbeth's* Witches suggest different types of moments in the tragedies that admit of musical treatment: a direct lyric (Iago's 'And let me the cannikin clink, clink, clink' in *Othello* 2.3), the distracted performance of a fragment (Desdemona's interruption of the Willow

Song 'Nay, that's not next' in *Othello* 4.3), and a chant that might be spoken or sung (the Witches' 'Double, double, toil and trouble' in *Macbeth* 4.1).

Macbeth's witches play a critical role in the earliest operatic treatment of Shakespearean tragedy, namely the Restoration stagings of the plays under the guidance of William Davenant 1606-68), poet and theatre manager (as well as self-proclaimed godson to Shakespeare). Sympathetic to the new genre of European opera, Davenant encouraged the development of Shakespeare productions that extended the musical potential of the plays. With John Dryden, Davenant produced a Restoration version of *The Tempest* that held the stage in one form or another for over a century. An unsigned text of *Macbeth*, dated 1674 text and attributed to Davenant, was advertised as containing 'alterations, additions, amendments, and new songs' (the new music has been conjecturally attributed to Matthew Locke). Augmenting Shakespeare's play with the Hecate scene (written by Thomas Middleton) and additional lyrics probably of his own devising, Davenant produced a text that not only enlarged Shakespeare's tragedy but refreshed it, too. Like other musically ambitious dramatists of the Restoration, Davenant and Dryden called their adapted texts *operas*, though they published no music to accompany their words. Unlike the Italian opera, which would be fully sung, the late seventeenth-century English use of the term *opera* or *semi-opera* meant a theatrical text designed specifically to incorporate musical numbers at crucial moments but which remained essentially a spoken theatrical event. Other English composers, notably Henry Purcell, produced elaborate musical entertainments inspired by Shakespeare (e.g. Purcell's *The Fairy Queen* after *A Midsummer Night's Dream*), but the tragedies awaited full operatic treatment by Continental hands.

If English audiences were reluctant to hear their national poet turned librettist, opera would nevertheless play a role in the dissemination of Shakespeare's work beyond the English Channel. Verdi's *Macbeth*, for example, was performed in Italy earlier than any professional staging of Shakespeare's play in the Italian language. In the 1770s, German opera based on the story of Romeo and Juliet may have provided an impetus for the earliest productions of that tragedy in German. French and German translations of the tragedies, though of doubtful accuracy and frequently made into prose versions, were nevertheless the basis for many late eighteenth and nineteenth-century operas and so contributed to a widening appreciation of the English playwright's plots and imagination.

In the history of theatrical forms, we might consider the Witches scenes in the expanded Restoration *Macbeth* as a double portal—for Macbeth and Banquo these moments provided a breach into the numinous world, while for the genre of spoken tragedy these scenes become a breach into a world where what is real is what is singable. From an operatic perspective, the witches constitute the real of Davenant's *Macbeth*, for only when they are present does the work move into the alternate, sung world familiar to us today as opera. Two centuries later, when Verdi set his version of *Macbeth*, the composer declared that there were only three characters in the work: Macbeth, Lady (as, like the Folio, he called her), and the chorus of witches. Everyone else was secondary to the work's propulsive tragic movement.

This distinction between what the English considered opera and what the Italian-driven Continental composers thought of as opera would persist for centuries. For English audiences, opera was an exercise in vocal fireworks, a form of drama in a foreign tongue with extravagant plots and an equally implausible assumption that every idea, no matter how small, could be sung. In this context, the very Englishness of Shakespeare would seem to exclude the playwright's work from operatic treatment.

During the eighteenth century, English audiences both enjoyed and distanced themselves from Italian opera. At the same time, Shakespeare's reputation grew with the rise of textual editing and the celebratory embrace of Shakespeare's 'Englishness', itself in no small part a consequence of David Garrick's great Shakespeare Jubilee in 1769. The English mid-eighteenth century, as Michael Dobson has drolly observed, envisioned a 'bourgeois Shakespeare, a master of polite letters from an age manly enough never to have heard of opera'.[1] England would prefer its Shakespeare spoken and its musical theatre vocally simple and witty rather than complex and tragic. The line from John Gay's *The Beggar's Opera* (1728) to the Victorian light opera of Gilbert and Sullivan and on to twentieth-century music hall and the Broadway musical might be considered a vernacular alternative to Continental opera. The finest quasi-operatic musical version of any Shakespearean tragedy is arguably Leonard Bernstein's *West Side Story* (New York, 1957), with book and lyrics by the young Stephen Sondheim and a production devised and choreographed by Jerome Robbins.

Italian opera turned to Shakespearean subject matter within a century of the playwright's death. Francesco Gasparini (1666-1727) composed an *Ambleto* (1706), one of the earliest operas on a Shakespearean subject and the first of several Italian treatments of the Hamlet plot. Gasparini's libretto, by the team of Apostolo Zeno and Pietro Pariati, claims its source, however, not in Shakespeare's tragedy but in the medieval *Gesta Danorum*, the chronicle that provided the textual origin of the Hamlet story. The Italian Hamlet operas point up the difficulty of identifying a work as a 'Shakespeare opera'. It's difficult to imagine that Zeno and Pariati, as well as the composers who set their words, were unaware of Shakespeare's play, yet these operas make no claim to be adapting the tragedy itself.

Gasparini's opera was in the *opera seria* tradition, in which a sequence of elaborately ornamented arias present the conflicted states of the characters. Here Fengone has murdered Orvendillo and married Gerilda, widow to the late king. As in more familiar versions of the Hamlet story, Ambleto feigns madness to escape the king's scrutiny while sustaining a love interest in the princess. The Hamlet plot, which centrally depends on the pretend madness of the title character, offered composers an irresistible opportunity for dramatic and vocal invention. Zeno's libretto provides Hamlet with not one but two scenes of costumed disguise before the restoration of justice at the final curtain. In this telling, the usurping king is subdued by a sleeping potion and killed. Exotic it may have been, yet Gasparini's *Ambleto* was given in Italian at London's Haymarket Theatre in 1712, with a libretto published by Jacob Tonson in a dual-language edition. A volume of 'Songs in the opera of Hamlet as they are perform'd at ye Queens theatre' appeared that same year (Figure 41.1).

Domenico Scarlatti reset Zeno's libretto for *Ambleto* in 1715, as did Giuseppe Carcani in 1742. By 1792, however, the genre of the Hamlet opera would be based not on Danish sources but on French versions of Shakespeare. In the last quarter of the eighteenth century, French translations would carry Shakespeare's tragedies (in versions first

---

[1] Michael Dobson, *The Making of the National Poet: Shakespeare, Adaptation and Authorship, 1660-1769* (Oxford: Oxford University Press, 1992), 158.

FIG. 41.1 Songs in the opera of Hamlet: as they are perform'd in ye Queen's Theatre. (1712).

HTC-LC M1505 G23 A4 1712 F, Houghton Library, Harvard University

by Jean-François Ducis and then by Pierre LeTourneur) into the French tongue and beyond—if with variable degrees of accuracy and success. Following the prose rendition of Ducis, Giuseppe Maria Foppa composed his *Amleto* libretto, which would serve as the text for an extravagantly melodramatic *Amleto*, bearing only some resemblance to Shakespeare, composed by Gaetano Andreozzi (1755-1826). The opera's opening scene, for example, depicts the late king's funeral monument bursting into flames as the prince and the queen approach with the new king. The operatic *Hamlet* could be set in visually arresting terms—urns on fire, dark graveyards where the prince's enemies confront un- earthly powers—episodes that allow for both musical and theatrical display. Shakespeare and opera together were now able to feed both the Gothic and Romantic sensibilities. The new Gothic Shakespeare that emerged on the operatic stage affected even the com- edies, bringing unexpectedly dark tones into the opera's favourite Shakespeare play, *The Tempest*.

In the nineteenth century, Felice Romani (1788-1865), one of the most successful of all Italian librettists, produced a melodramatic text of Hamlet based *'sulle tracce di Sackespeare e del suo imitatore Ducis'* (in the tracks of Shakespeare and his imitator, Ducis). For Romani, Hamlet was 'the Orestes of the North', and by inference Shakespeare the modern reinventor of the *Oresteia*, such was the symbolic power of Shakespeare for Continental writers and composers. Romani's text was set by Saverio Mercadante (1795-1870), whose *Amleto*, a two-act *melodramma tragico*, was premiered at La Scala in 1822.

Composer and poet Arrigo Boito, librettist for Verdi's *Otello*, had crafted his first text after Shakespeare for an operatic *Amleto* (1865) composed by Franco Faccio (1840-91), Verdi's younger contemporary. A brief success in its time, the Faccio-Boito *Amleto* has recently been reconstructed and, in 2014, given a modern performance. Where earlier Shakespeare operas had taken extensive liberties with the plot and language, Boito's *Amleto* is studiously attentive, labouring to find Italian equivalents for Shakespeare's complex and wordy play. Between his work for Faccio and Verdi two decades later, Boito learned much about condensing Shakespeare.

The best known opera based on *Hamlet* is the French version by Ambroise Thomas (1811-96), to a libretto by Michel Carré and Jules Barbier after a version of the Shakespeare's play by Alexandre Dumas, *père*. Premiered in 1868, this *Hamlet* is perhaps stronger on theatrical perfume than musical depth, but it reflects the new interests of the Romantic movement in repositioning the story as about not Hamlet's madness or even his famous indecision, but about Ophelia's madness and death. The score includes a well-known drinking song ('O vin dissipe la tristesse') and a pleasing melodic figure for the love theme associated with the 'Doubt that the stars are fire' speech. The opera's highlight is certainly the fourth of its five acts, devoted to Ophélie's madness and drowning, a showpiece for the soprano that extended and developed further mid-nineteenth-century Ophelia mania. In this version, the story concludes with Hamlet, driven on by the Ghost, killing the King and surviving to rule, albeit in despair as a result of Ophélie's death. Presumably in antici- pation of a London production, Thomas altered the denouement so that Hamlet dies; no such production is recorded during the composer's lifetime.

The first operatic adaptation of *Othello*—as well as the first operatic setting of Shakespearean tragedy by a major composer—is the 1816 opera of that name by Gioachino Rossini. Rossini's *Otello* set a new standard for operatic composition, redirecting oper- atic tastes from the world of Mozart and Paisiello and toward a more brilliantly vocal and dramatically theatrical form of theatre. The peculiar libretto by Francesco Maria Berio di Salsi barely follows the play (the entire action is set in Venice, many characters are eliminated). In his *Vie de Rossini*, Stendhal delivered an unambiguous judgement on the work: *Ce qui sauve l'Otello de Rossini, c'est le souvenir de celui de Shakspeare* ('What saves Rossini's *Otello* is the memory of Shakespeare's').[2] In this version, Roderigo is a major character, there is no handkerchief, and the suspicion of infidelity turns on a letter intended for Otello but which unfortunately bears no addressee. Despite spectacular vocal writing (there are six tenor roles), Rossini's *Otello* achieves something like Shakespearean dramatic power only in the final act, where Desdemona's Willow Song and death signal a remarkable advance over all previous operatic adaptations of the playwright's work. With its haunting melodic figure and harp accompaniment, Rossini's setting of the text conjures painful isolation, foreboding, and profound sorrow. Berio di Salsi's much-maligned text is not uniformly weak. In a brilliantly inventive suture of Italian cultural heritage to Shakespearean tragedy, composer and librettist artfully link Desdemona's grieving memory to the song of a passing gondolier, the briefest melancholic tune set to text from Dante's famous *Inferno* passage (the Paolo and Francesca episode) beginning *Nessun maggior dolore*. With the death of Desdemona, Rossini hit upon a perhaps unrepeatable success. *Otello* would be his first and last opera based on Shakespeare, and he never again crafted a death scene for a female character that struck its audiences with the same power.

Verdi clearly knew and studied both Shakespeare's text (in translation) and Rossini's setting of the death scene when he came to set the passage seven decades later. His *Otello* (Milan, 1887), with its libretto by Boito after Shakespeare, was the first opera from the composer's pen for more than a decade. This second *Otello* remains the greatest of all operatic settings of the tragedies, for its dramatic concision and (by operatic standards) fidelity to the playwright's text, for its penetrating characterizations not only of its three principals but also of its secondary figures, and for its unequalled skill in balancing the intimate with the grand. Eliminating the first act and the complications in Venice, the Boito-Verdi drama famously opens without overture, at the height of the storm that will destroy the Turks. Verdi's entrance line for Othello—*Esultate! L'orgoglio musulmano sepolto e in mar* ('Rejoice! The Moors' pride lies buried at sea')—has no equivalent at the corresponding moment of the play (2.1), yet it frames the drama as a tragedy between two epitaphs: Moorish death opens and ends this operatic *Otello*.

The critical history of *Othello* has remarked again and again on the 'Othello music', a term that G. Wilson Knight made memorable in 1930 as a way to identify the particular sonorousness of Othello's oratory as well as its lexical richness. Encouraged to think about the play in musical terms, critics easily refer to Othello's big set pieces—self-contained, frequently lapidary performances that never retreat into the solitude of monologue—as arias, so that *Othello* can emerge as 'the most lyrical—the most operatic even—of the mature tragedies'.[3] But 'the operatic' has a more tropic than descriptive force in these accounts. *Othello*, it seems, is in some sense already a musical tragedy. It is also a play of parts, and especially body parts, as if the particularity of the Moor's language made

[2] Stendhal, *La vie de Rossini* (Paris: Michel Lévy Frères, 1854), 166.
[3] Michael Neill, introduction to *Othello* (Oxford: Oxford University Press, 2006), 24.

common cause with the play's emphasis on limbs, facial features, and the singularity of one improbable prop.

The achievement of Verdi's *Otello* is inseparable from Boito's cagey theatrical decisions and his persistent encouragement of the wary and irascible composer. Stripping the play down to its essential conflicts and deceptions, Boito moved forward a text and a plan, and over the course of years, succeeded in coaxing Verdi out of what had seemed like retirement. For much of its gestation, the opera was referred to by composer and librettist simply as *Jago*, and many have suspected Rossini's achievement with the story seemed to Verdi to demand a distance from the title of Shakespeare's tragedy.

In preparing his text, Boito chose judiciously from what he could access of Shakespeare's original, a play he knew through a familiar but inadequate Italian prose retelling and the French version (also in prose) by François-Victor Hugo, son of the poet, who had undertaken the translation of Shakespeare's entire output (published between 1859 and 1866) during self-imposed political exile on the Isle of Jersey. Boito would have read Hugo's long introductory essay as well as the French text of *Othello* itself. As James Hepokoski discovered 25years ago in his important work on Verdi's *Otello*, Boito 'owned, underlined, and annotated at least three editions of Hugo's Shakespeare'.[4] In these annotations to Hugo's French Shakespeare we can see Boito's mind at work, alert to the possibility of a repetition here, a certain metrical rhythm there. While shrewdly cutting Shakespeare's play, Boito added one important passage—the famous monologue known as Iago's Creed—in which the baritone villain declares his annihilationist philosophy: *Credo in un dio crudel | che m'a creato simil a se | e che in ira io nomo* ('I believe in a cruel god who created me in his image. I name him in anger'). Man is born filthy scum, whether from human seed or from atoms (a touch of Darwinian pessimism). I'm a rogue *because* I'm a man. I can feel within me the slime out of which I was made. The showpiece aria descends into sulphur: *e dopo tanto irrision la morte. E poi? E poi? La morte e nulla—e vecchia fol il ciel!* ('After all life's deception comes death. And then?—Death is nothing. And heaven? It's just an old wives' tale'). Even Verdi, the greatest living composer of opera, knew that he risked offending the Church, but he felt that Boito's addition was powerfully Shakespearean.

Verdi's *Otello* is one of the great theatrical works of the nineteenth century, frequently compared not unfavourably to its Shakespearean source. The composer's last tragic opera is a kind of summa of everything Verdi knew about operatic structure and effect, brought to bear on one of the most powerful stories in the repertory.

This *Otello* is crowded with episodes—the gulling of the drunken Cassio, the love duet for Othello and Desdemona, Iago's arousal of Othello's suspicion, the increasingly tense interview with Desdemona, the duet in which Othello and Iago swear their terrible vow on lightning bolts and the marble halls of heaven, the Act 3 *concertato* (or extended scene for multiple singers) in which Othello is relieved of his duties and Desdemona is brutally humiliated before the visiting dignitaries, and finally the great fourth act. The haunting setting of the Willow Song is a supreme example of opera's capacity to sustain and extend the emotional import of a word or line by repeating and extending sounds, harmonies, and figural ornaments. Verdi's setting, with its unfulfilled open fifths, plays on the ballad-like

---

[4] James Hepokoski, *Giuseppe Verdi: Othello* (Cambridge: Cambridge University Press, 1987), 25.

repetition inherent in the text. Desdemona sings that she was born to love. Suddenly, she is interrupted when a cold wind rattles the window and blows through the orchestra. It passes, and she finishes her thought: she was born, she sings, to love—and to die. Unlike Shakespeare, the Boito-Verdi adaptation follows the Willow Song with an *Ave Maria*, an exceptional example of the Verdian cantilena, that long lyric line that combines ethereal beauty and a compelling physicality. The idea for the Willow Song, as Ross Duffin has shown, is in part attributable to contemporary broadsides Shakespeare may have used as the basis for Desdemona's singing, and even offer some precedent for her distracted interruptions.[5] Boito's *Ave Maria* begins as a Catholic devotional hymn sung in Latin, but soon breaks down into a more fervent, more intimate Italian. *Prega per noi*, Desdemona sings, pray for *us*, not for me. It's the traditional position of the prayerful in relation to the Madonna, but it's also Desdemona's generous plea for a *noi* that includes Otello.

The Ave Maria isn't exactly an inversion of Iago's Credo but it comes close. It's the normative theological position—God watches us, the Virgin intercedes on our behalf—but here expanded by Desdemona's touching personal grace. Desdemona's prayer finished, she bids Emilia good night. Chords of unusual finality sound three times in the orchestra, then Desdemona leaps forward in a final outburst, *Ah Emilia, addio, addio*. One of the distinctive features of operatic composition is the ability to extend musical ideas beyond the verbal and beyond the narrative present; music remembers and recalls, as Verdi's Otello does in giving the murdered Desdemona a final kiss while the orchestra plays the musical figure first heard in the love music that concludes the opera's first act. Operatic tragedy is weaker than spoken theatre at the level of language, but potentially more powerful at the level of the physical, the unspoken, the thought, the unspeakable.

Verdi, who composed *Otello* in his 74th year, had mastered the economy of musical gesture critical to achieve dramatic expression in his last two operas, both based on Shakespeare. (His *Falstaff*, also to a libretto by Boito, would be his next and final opera in 1893.) Having demonstrated elsewhere in the score his capacity to achieve massive sonic force, here in *Otello's* final scene the composer makes minimal use of crucial instruments, as in the infernal yawn of the double basses as Otello enters the chamber to murder his wife.

With its musical and dramatic opportunities, Verdi's Otello has attracted many of the greatest sopranos and baritones of the last century, but it is on the title role, written for a heroic tenor capable of almost Wagnerian power, that a performance stands or falls. Premiered by Francesco Tamagno, a singer of international reputation, the role has been a notable success for such singers of the post-war era as Mario del Monaco, Jon Vickers, and Placido Domingo, all of whom have left a recorded legacy of their interpretations.

In 1894, at the age of 81, Verdi made his last trip to the French capital, where he heard his *Falstaff* at the Opéra Comique and the French version of his *Otello* at the Garnier.[6] The last piece of Verdi's operatic output was a ballet score inserted into *Othello* for this production.

Shakespeare loomed large in Verdi's imagination. Among the great uncomposed 'what-ifs' of music history is the operatic version of *King Lear* that Verdi long wanted to take on. Other composers have also envisioned Shakespearean tragedies as Shakespearean operas. Christopher N. Wilson has identified plans for operas by Mendelssohn, Schumann, and

---

[5] Ross Duffin, *Shakespeare's Songbook* (New York: W. W. Norton, 2004), 469.
[6] See Julian Budden, *Verdi* (New York: Vintage, 1985), 346–61.

Glinka to have been based on *Hamlet*;[7] Tchaikovsky had contemplated an *Othello*; Berlioz, who did compose a solo *Mort de Cléopatre,* considered an opera of *Antony and Cleopatra*; Ernst Bloch abandoned plans for a *King Lear.* Rachmaninov considered an opera based on that most tragic of history plays, *Richard II* (which, curiously, is one of the few Shakespeare plays to have received almost no musical attention).

Shakespeare's witches, who had added drama to the English semi-operas, retreated from the operatic stage to return in the Romantic period. In 1827, Paris saw an operatic *Macbeth* by Hippolyte Chélard (1789-1861). Chélard's forgotten *Macbeth,* which emphasizes the murder of Duncan as the central event of the drama, has the distinction of a libretto after Shakespeare by Rouget de Lisle, better known as the composer of the Marseillaise. But it was Verdi—the most faithful of Shakespeare's operatic admirers—who, in the first of his three Shakespeare operas, produced a musical *Macbeth* worthy of attention. Here Verdi began to explore music's capacity to address dramatic poetry of extraordinary richness, to simplify it in order to make it complex through sound rather than words alone. With attention uncommon among composers, Verdi laboured with his librettist Francesco Maria Piave to craft the text the composer wanted. With additional verses supplied by Andrea Maffei, the libretto to *Macbeth* marks the first of Verdi's operas for which the composer made fundamental dramaturgical decisions.

Verdi's *Macbeth* minimizes the roles of Banquo and Macduff, and even Macbeth himself has less forward presence than Othello or Iago in Verdi's later opera. When he came to revise *Macbeth* for revival in Paris in 1865, Verdi gave more music to Lady and—perhaps curiously—cut a final aria for Macbeth, so that the opera ends abruptly with a battle and a triumphant chorus. Verdi also thought hard about theatrical practicalities, including how to make spectacle dramatic and not, as he feared, dull. In a remarkable letter to his French publisher Léon Escudier, Verdi sketched a diagram for the apparition of Banquo's ghosts as a rotating wheel (see Figure 41.2), explaining that it would avoid what was, at least for him, the tedium of a simple procession.

Verdi's Lady is one of his most arresting inventions, a role that feels more connected to the infernal powers than does the music he composed for his chorus of witches. It is the Sleepwalking Scene, however, that demonstrates Verdi's unique musical economy as a means to generate genuine operatic drama from Shakespearean tragedy. Verdi famously remarked that he wanted Lady's voice to be *cupo*, or covered, so as to produce the effect of a woman lost to the world and to herself. She is, he points out, *una morente*—a dying woman. Piave's text reimagines the scene in verse, choosing words that Verdi's music can repeat, stretch, and extend by musical means:

> *Una macchia*
> *E qui tutt'ora*
> *Via ti dico!*
> *O maladetta!*
> *Una, due*
> *E qui quest'ora–*
> *Fremi tu?*
> *Non osi entrar?*

('A spot—it's always here—away, I tell you! Damn it! One, two—now it's time—you're trembling? You don't dare to go in?')

---

[7] In Stanley Sadie, ed., *The Grove Dictionary of Opera* (London: Macmillan Reference, 1997), 4: 342-3.

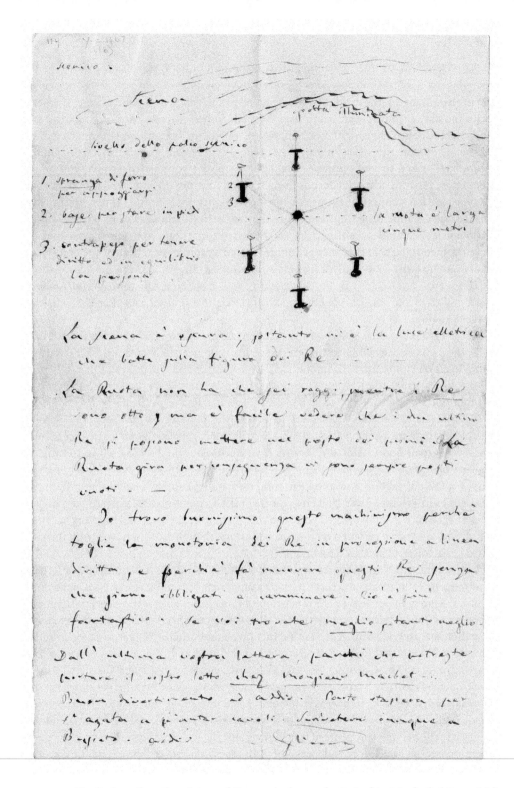

FIG. 41.2 Verdi describes the vision of Banquo's descendants in his *Macbeth* (1847; 1865). Y.c.1447 (1) folio 3 recto (1b recto) Autograph letters signed from Giuseppe Verdi, Genova and S. Agata, to various people [manuscript].

As in *Macbeth* 5.1, the Queen begins her somnambulistic traversal of the stage by focusing on a stain that only she can see. Piave condenses and readjusts the scene, permitting Lady to ask explicitly what Shakespeare's does not. While Lady Macbeth exits the play in the speech beginning 'To bed, to bed, there's knocking at the gate' and concludes by repeating the exhortation 'To bed,' the operatic setting again makes a crucial adjustment. *A letto, a letto … Andiamo Macbetto; | Non t'accusa il tuo pallor. Andiam* ('To bed to bed—let's go, Macbeth. Don't let your paleness give you away. Let's go'). Verdi's Lady grieves more succinctly, but more directly. What text cannot convey here is, of course, the music. Lady moves lightly, haltingly, as if negotiating her way across the repeating figure in the orchestra, with its cautious steps observed by a little musical creak descending from above. Verdi's writing is at its most atmospheric here. In specifying that the voice is not meant to exemplify vocal beauty, the composer is also integrating Lady's vocal line into the orchestral—that is, the musical—whole of the scene. The effect can be electrifying, as the writing for the soprano renders her both vivid and lifeless, concluding with the daunting final ascent to D flat as she leaves the stage.

Verdi was not the only composer to attempt *Macbeth*. A few years after Verdi's death in 1901, the Swiss-American Ernest Bloch (1880-1959) composed his own *Macbeth* (Geneva, 1909) to a French libretto by Edmond Fleg. Deserving of wider exposure, this rarely performed work recalls the chromatic atmosphere of Debussy while sustaining the central brutality of Shakespeare's tragedy. Some of Fleg's details are particularly apt, as in the opening scene, where the witches are gathering the ingredients for their brew among the bloody remains of the battle's victims. Bloch's underplayed Sleepwalking Scene emphasizes despair and catatonia rather than vocal display. The best known of twentieth-century operas on the Macbeth theme is Dmitri Shostakovich's 1934 *Lady Macbeth of the Mtsensk District* with a libretto by the composer. Subject to Soviet censorship but now restored to its original form, this *Lady Macbeth* is based not on Shakespeare but Nikolai Leskov's 1865 novel about a bored wife who conspires with her lover and murders her husband, Shostakovich's variation on the Macbeth story, though quite removed from Birnam Wood, is a powerful and savage work.

Like several other Shakespearean dramas, notably *The Tempest,* the tragedy of *Romeo and Juliet* took on special interest for opera composers beginning in the later eighteenth century. Among the earliest operatic versions of *Romeo and Juliet* is the German-language *Romeo und Julie* (Gotha, 1776) by the Czech-born Georg (Jiří Antonín) Benda (1722-95), Kapellmeister to Friedrich III of Saxe-Gotha. Like many 'almost Shakespeare' operas, the libretto to *Romeo und Julie* has its feet both in the Bard and in a contemporary drama, a 1767 *Trauerspiel* by Christian Felix Weisse, also entitled *Romeo und Julie.* The text is by Wilhelm Friedrich Gotter, the German writer whose work became the basis for the German-language *Tempest* operas that would come into vogue a generation later. Benda's *Romeo* singspiel may be a descendant, or at least a cousin, of Shakespeare's drama, but the opera is in the popular sub-genre of tragedy averted. The simplified plot presents the lovers, their separation, Julie's sleep and awakening, and the gathering of Romeo and the Capellet family at the tomb. There is neither poison nor fatal swordplay. When Pater Lorenzo extracts from the remorseful Capellet the vow that he would have given his daughter's hand to Romeo if only the two had lived, the curtain is pulled back, the lovers emerge from hiding, and their union is blessed. The opera ends with chorus and principals celebrating a happy, and peaceful, resolution in the tradition of the *lieto fine*, or happy ending, that had long characterized Baroque opera earlier in the eighteenth century. The work is not without skill and charm, though primarily memorable as evidence of opera's transition into a new world of sentiment and bourgeois experience.

Of the operas of Niccolò Zingarelli (1752-1837), the best known is *Romeo e Giulietta*, to a libretto by Giuseppe Foppa. With six principals, Zingarelli's original cast included one soprano, one mezzo, two tenors, as well as two castrati, one of whom is Romeo. Girolamo Crescentini, who created that role, composed his own final aria, 'Ombra adorata aspetta' (a particular favourite of Napoleon), for the tomb scene. In the nineteenth century, the prize role of Romeo was taken over by the leading female singers of the day—the *bel canto* divas Giuditta Pasta (1797-1865) and Maria Malibran (1808-36)—thereby shifting the vocal and erotic dynamics of the tragedy. The world of the castrato is even more remote to us today than the world of boy actors, but the shift from a castrato Romeo to a mezzo-soprano Romeo is one sign of the changing terms within which audiences perceived the sensuality of musical representation.

Among the *bel canto* masters, Vincenzo Bellini (1801-35) produced the most frequently performed operatic version of a tragic theme associated with Shakespeare. His *I Capuleti e i Montecchi* (Venice 1830), a two-act *tragedia lirica*, to a libretto by Romani, sounds as if it should be based on Shakespeare, yet its source is an 1818 drama by Luigi Scevola. More frequently performed than Rossini's dramatically awkward *Otello*, Bellini's version of the Romeo and Juliet story frustrates the viewer who looks for the profile of Shakespeare's plot. Romani did not, however, compose his poem with Bellini in mind. The text of *Capuleti* was first set by Nicola Vaccai (1790-1848) as *Giulietta e Romeo* (Milan, 1825). Like the majority of Shakespeare operas, Vaccai's treatment is all but unknown today.

In Bellini's version of the Romeo and Juliet story, both roles are for female singers. Immediately successful upon its premiere, the work was soon adapted further when Maria Malibran requested that Vaccai's more extensive tomb scene be performed in place of Bellini's final pages. The combined Bellini/Vaccai ending was not uncommon during the nineteenth century, demonstrating that the concept of authorial intention and textual integrity, at least in regard to operatic source material, is highly elastic.

A pleasurable, if little known, version of the Veronese tragedy is yet another *Romeo e Giulietta* by Filippo Marchetti (1831-1902), premiered in Trieste in 1865, with a libretto by Marco Marcelliano Marcello. The music has charm and emotional force, but the most striking feature of the libretto is that, unlike earlier *Romeo* operas, Marcello's text returns to the shape of Shakespeare's play, rather than the narrative in Shakespeare's Italian source material or other adaptations of it. Marchetti's opera, never performed in the composer's lifetime, received its first modern performance in 2005.

The only Romeo opera derived from Shakespeare and still widely performed is the *Roméo et Juliette* (Paris, 1867) of Charles Gounod (1818-93), a Romantic tragedy by the composer who had already been made famous for his operatic adaptation of Goethe's *Faust* in 1859. The libretto is by Carré and Barbier, who had crafted Gounod's *Faust* libretto and would provide the text for Thomas's *Hamlet* the following year. *Roméo et Juliette* capitalizes on the tragedy's ample opportunity for dancing and disguise, for surprise and intimacy, and for the irresistible pathos of young love, at once lyrical and doomed. Juliette's *Je veux vivre* and Romeo's *Ah, lève-toi, soleil!* are two often performed selections from a score that, while never achieving the summit of musical greatness, offers a surfeit of musical sweetness. If its material tends to the insistently Romantic, its denouement is recognizably Shakespearean cloth: the principals die in one another's arms. One footnotes with pleasure an antidote to operatic doom: an 1867 farce by the French composer Joseph Eugene Déjazet was entitled *Rhum et eau en juillet* (rum and water in July).

Hector Berlioz (1803-69), composer of *Symphonie fantastique* and *La damnation de Faust,* revered Shakespeare, though like his contemporaries Michael Balfe, Otto Nicolai, and Wagner, Berlioz turned his Shakespearean energies primarily to the comedies. Berlioz's signal musical contribution to Shakespearean tragedy is his *Roméo et Juliette* (1839)—not an opera at all but a *symphonie dramatique*, a large-scale musical work of groundbreaking complexity that demonstrates once again Berlioz's formal creativity.

The widespread influence of Shakespeare's plays upon the Continental imagination manifested itself in many ways, including the introduction of elements from the tragedies into operatic versions of non-tragic material. It seems probable that the theatrical force of Hamlet's ghost exerted a powerful effect on operatic works of the late eighteenth and early nineteenth centuries. In the numerous operatic treatments of *The Tempest* in the decade of the 1790s, for example, mime roles for an evil Sycorax and a corresponding 'good shade' relocate this late romance within the theatrical language of the Shakespearean spectre, linking a presumed comedy to the tragedy of Hamlet.

Twentieth- and twenty-first-century operatic versions of Shakespeare have continued the historical trend of applying more attention to the comedies than to the tragedies. (There are several post-war settings of *The Tempest.*) Some deliberately turn away from Shakespeare and toward the playwright's source material, as is the case with Riccardo Zandonai's three-act *Giulietta e Romeo* (1922), for which the libretto again looks back to Luigi da Porto's sixteenth-century novella. One of the grandest settings of a Shakespearean tragedy is the work of the American composer Samuel Barber (1910-81), commissioned to write *Antony and Cleopatra* for the opening of the new Metropolitan Opera House in New York City in 1966. The English-language libretto, arranged by Franco Zeffirelli, who also directed the premiere, is unusual in being drawn only from Shakespeare's text, though judiciously edited to playable length. The first Cleopatra was the American soprano Leontyne Price, with whom the role is closely identified. Plagued by technical difficulties on opening night, however, *Antony and Cleopatra* became notorious as an expensive failure. The composer returned to the work and produced a revised version in 1975, which has done much to restore interest in the score.

King Lear, arguably the most daunting tragedy from the perspective of musical adaptation, contains irresistible elements: storm, madness, conflict, disguise, a fool, violence, and perhaps the most piteous death in the Shakespearean canon. For most of his creative life, Verdi toyed with the idea of a *Lear* opera, even having a libretto crafted for that purpose by Salvatore Cammarano, whose premature death created only one of the many stumbling blocks for the project. In the mid-1850s, Verdi turned next to Antonio Somma for a workable text, but a Verdian *Lear* would remain one of the great 'what ifs' of operatic history. Other composers, some hardly known today, also approached the Lear theme. The last of Antonio Cagnoni's twenty operas was a *Re Lear,* with a libretto after Shakespeare by Antonio Ghislanzoni (best known for his work on Verdi's *Aida*). Cagnoni's tragedy was left unproduced at his death in 1896, published in 1990, and given its premiere only in 2009. Among contemporary works, the best known attempt to render the play in operatic terms is the German-language *Lear* (1978) of Aribert Reimann (b. 1936), set to a libretto after Shakespeare by Claus H. Henneberg. The work was written for German baritone Dietrich Fischer-Dieskau, who had suggested the theme to the composer. Even an artist of Fischer-Dieskau's accomplishment, however, remarked on the daunting challenge of the opera. No Kent and Gloucester puzzle over the King's preferences, as they do in the tragedy. Lear's own voice must open and close the opera. Eighteen sung syllables on an F#—the orchestra is completely silent—give sound to Lear's 'darker purpose' at the beginning of the play:

> *Wir haben euch hierher befohlen, um unser Reich vor euren Augen unter unserem Töchtern aufzuteilen* ('We have summoned you here to divide our kingdom, before your eyes, among our daughters').

At the end, it's Lear we hear again—no Kent takes us out of the moment; the king is left with the dead Cordelia and the cosmic darker purpose for which the play offers no consolation. The difficult score has been performed in English and French translations as well as the original German.

The Finnish composer Aulis Sallinen composed his *Kuningas Lear* in 2000, to his own libretto after Shakespeare. Sallinen's opera eliminates the role of Kent, compresses parts for the other secondary characters, and moves the blinding of Gloucester offstage. Like many of the preceding Shakespeare operas, and unlike the plays on which they are based, *Kuningas Lear* includes a chorus.

Aside from *King Lear,* contemporary operatic treatments of the tragedies have included another *Hamlet* (2009), this by the American-born, Vienna-based composer Nancy Van de Vate (1930-). The Italian composer Salva ore Sciarrino (1947-) created a *Macbeth: tre atti senza nome* (Three Nameless Acts), a work on which he laboured for 25 years and that received its premiere in Frankfurt in 2002 in a production by Achim Freyer. Sciarrino prepared his own libretto from Shakespeare's text, but in this case choosing brief, sometimes enigmatic selections from the play, so that the opera is notable for its creation of mood rather than event. Benjamin Britten composed his shattering *Rape of Lucretia* (1946) to a libretto by Ronald Duncan based on a French play by André Obey that was itself grounded not in one of Shakespeare's tragic dramas but the narrative poem 'The Rape of Lucrece'. A very different contemporary approach to Shakespeare's play drives *The Okavango Macbeth* (2009), a chamber opera with music by Tom Cunningham to a libretto by Alexander McCall Smith. The small-scale work reconceives *Macbeth* as a drama among a group of baboons observed by a team of primatologists.

A brief introduction to major and lesser operatic versions of Shakespearean tragedies can only touch on the perspectives and styles with which composers since the seventeenth century have approached these complex plays. It is important to remember that, whatever one's response to the lesser or greater alterations performed by the creative team on Shakespeare's original texts, opera is always an art in which music is first and language—however important—comes second. Which might raise the question: is there, in fact, such a thing as Shakespeare opera? The English music critic John Steane wondered whether 'any "Shakespeare" opera deserves the name', so extensive are the adaptations and alterations necessary to render an opera from a Shakespearean play. But then the same question might be asked about the tragedies themselves. Writing on the occasion of the Royal Opera's revival of Verdi's *Otello*, Stanley Wells observed that 'in a sense there is no such thing as a Shakespeare play, only an ongoing series of infinitely variable theatrical and other events stimulated by the words that Shakespeare wrote'.[8] Opera, Wells reminds us, condenses and selects in order to earn its musical autonomy. In the case of Shakespeare, there is much to carve back, and much fertile material to inspire musical invention.

The relation of Shakespearean tragedy and opera might then be best considered in terms of complementary *forms*. Shakespeare, as Stephen Orgel has reminded us, 'thought of genres not as sets of rules but as sets of expectations and possibilities. Comedy and tragedy were not rules: they were shared assumptions'.[9] The form of opera is also a set of shared assumptions—about the possibility of breaking off a moment of feeling and intensifying it through musical materials, while at the same time sustaining the musical condition in which characters are located and by means of which they are imagined. Opera can't tell us a story, not even a good Shakespearean tragic story, at least not in the way a spoken tragedy can. But opera can place its characters, instruments, voices, and time into powerful musical—that is, extra-linguistic—relationships with one another and with the audience. From such configurations are great operatic moments, and some great operas, born.

SELECT BIBLIOGRAPHY

Budden, Julian, *Verdi* (New York: Vintage, 1985).
Dean, Winton, 'Shakespeare in the Opera House', *Shakespeare Survey* (1965), 75–93.
Duffin, Ross, *Shakespeare's Songbook* (New York: W. W. Norton, 2004).
Hepokoski, James, *Giuseppe Verdi: Otello* (Cambridge: Cambridge University Press, 1987).
Kerman, Joseph, *Opera as Drama: Fiftieth Anniversary Edition* (Berkeley: University of California Press, 2005).
Neill, Michael, Introduction to *Othello* (Oxford: Oxford University Press, 2006).
Orgel, Stephen, 'Shakespeare and the Kinds of Drama', *Critical Inquiry* (Autumn 1979), 107–23.
Sadie, Stanley, ed., *The Grove Dictionary of Opera* (London: Macmillan Reference, 1997).
Schmidgall, Gary, *Shakespeare and Opera* (New York: Oxford University Press, 1990).
Schmidgall, Gary, 'Verdi's *King Lear* project', *Nineteenth-Century Music* 9: 2 (Autumn 1985), 83–101.
Stendhal, *La vie de Rossini* (Michel Lévy Frères: Paris, 1854).
Starobinski, Jean, 'Ombra adorata', *Opera Quarterly* 21:4 (Autumn 2005), 612–30.
Verdi, Giuseppe, ALS to Léon Escudier, 1865. Folger Shakespeare Library.
Wells, Stanley, 'Blogging Shakespeare,' 3 August 2012. url http://bloggingshakespeare.com/ year-of-shakespeare-verdis-otello Accessed 3 January 2014.
Wills, Garry, *Verdi's Shakespeare: Men of the Theatre* (New York: Viking, 2011).

---

[8] Stanley Wells, 'Blogging Shakespeare,' 3 August 2012. url http://bloggingshakespeare.com/year-of-shakespeare-verdis-otello Accessed 3 January 2014.

[9] Stephen Orgel, 'Shakespeare and the Kinds of Drama,' *Critical Inquiry* (Autumn 1979), 123.

PART V

THE TRAGEDIES
WORLDWIDE:
(I) EUROPEAN
RESPONSES

CHAPTER 42

···

THE TRAGEDIES IN ITALY

···

SHAUL BASSI

WE begin with a conversation between two actors, the older Gustavo Modena (1803-61) reminiscing with the younger Ernesto Rossi (1827-96) about his early Shakespearean exploit in Milan in 1842:

> He took up the manuscript of *Othello*, turned over a few pages and pointed to the first scene. 'From here to here.' 'I don't understand. Was someone taken ill? Was it necessary to abandon the performance?' 'Yes, the public was taken ill and we had to let down the curtain: here is the story. I was anxious to give the public something new, present an Author they might have only heard of by name. I took a translation of *Othello*, I shortened it, adapted it as best as I could to our habits, tastes, customs. I studied the part of the protagonist painstakingly, designed the staging, directed and instructed the actors. But to be frank with you, I had grave doubts as to the result ... Don't you know that the very word Shakespeare is hard for us to pronounce? ... Those blessed rules of Aristotle are firmly fixed in every head. Try to get outside them ... capers and somersaults ... On the night of the performance we were all seized with stage fright, no one more so than me. When the curtain went up ... at the scene between Iago and Roderigo, when the latter begins to shout from the street outside Brabantio's house, *What ho, Brabantio! Signior Brabantio, ho!* the audience began to whisper. "What is it? A tragedy or a farce?" And when at last Brabantio appeared on the balcony with his clothes all disordered and half asleep ... they began to laugh and titter. They had read 'tragedy' on the bill and thought they must be watching a scene from Goldoni or one of Gozzi's *Fiabe*. "Enough! Enough! Curtain down! Yes! No! Continue! Enough!", shouts, hisses, the curtain had to be lowered ... I took Shakespeare under my arm and put him to sleep.'[1]

Testifying that the cultural translation of Shakespearean tragedy in Italy has been far from a triumphal conquest, this anecdote recapitulates the main aspects of this tortuous process. Modena's misadventure highlights first of all the leading role played by actors (who were initially actor-directors) in what would later become a reversal of fortune. Even though by then Shakespeare had already become the focus of strenuous literary debates,

---

[1] Ernesto Rossi, *Studii Drammatici e Lettere Autobiografiche* (Florence: Le Monnier, 1885), 83–5. Partial translation in Lacy Collison-Morley, *Shakespeare in Italy* (Stratford: Shakespeare Head Press, 1916), 153.

the scene shows a nonplussed audience that welcomes *Othello* not as a classic but as an unfamiliar play, merely presumed to be a 'tragedy'. Impervious to the reverence usually associated with Shakespeare, these Italian spectators quickly appreciate how this tragic text is shot through with comic situations from its very beginning, and according to their purist (neo)classical taste—*those blessed rules of Aristotle*, the unities of time, place, and action—they reject it unconditionally. A minor detail speaks eloquently: the very name Shakespeare remains difficult to pronounce for Italians, from its first occurrence in the notes of Lorenzo Magalotti (1668) as 'Shakespier', to the earliest mention in print in Antonio Conti as 'Sasper' (1726), down to a string of 'Sachespar', 'Jhakespeare', 'Sakespir', and the unsurpassable 'Seckpaire' of Abate Gaetano Golt, emended in the errata to 'Seckspaire'—Italians can compete only with him and his contemporaries in misspelling Shakespeare.[2] But these quirky minutiae reflect a much broader phenomenon: in spite of limited pockets of admiration and periods of anglophilia, English language and literature have never been central to Italian culture.

Shakespeare came to Italy initially mediated by translations and critical interpretations made in France and, to a lesser extent, Germany. Shakespearean tragedy in Italy needs to be understood in its European context, the same context where, since Shakespeare's age, Italy started losing its cultural hegemony and became gradually peripheral. Reworking Shakespeare for Italian culture meant in cases like Modena's retranslating Italian plots and materials: out of the twelve works listed as tragedies in Shakespeare's First Folio, four are set in classical Rome, one in medieval Verona, and one in 'contemporary' Venice; another, *Cymbeline*, also includes some Italian scenes; and we can add *The Merchant of Venice*, a comedy that European history has tainted with tragedy. At the time of Modena's setback, Shakespeare was already the godhead of British civilization, but in Italy his works were still read in French, considered unsuitable, and in need of heavy editing, as our actor was well aware.

When Modena failed with his bold experiment in Milan, he was performing in Italy only in geographical terms, since politically the city belonged to the Austrian empire. Any account of Shakespeare's tragedy in Italy needs to take into consideration the political and cultural fragmentation of a country that became a unified nation only in 1861. That diversity involves different local traditions, a higher or lower proximity to French or German cultural influences, and different degrees of political and religious censorship. Last but not least, a staging of *Othello* that rapidly becomes a laughing matter may suggest that the most elusive and yet decisive factor in the reception of Shakespeare in Italy has less to do with him than with a general cultural attitude towards the *tragic*.

In an interview given in 2013, the day after a doomed bipartisan Italian coalition government was saved by an unexpected vote of confidence, a run-of-the-mill politician explained: 'Italy is not a country for Shakespearean drama, it deserves Scarpetta' (a famous Neapolitan comic author and playwright). Theatrical metaphors are recurrent in portraits and self-portraits of Italy, in *Grand Tour* travellers describing life as a *mise-en-scène* and its inhabitants as actors, as well as in a strong internal vein of national self-deprecation. Italians themselves have no doubt that their political life in particular is a comedy rather

---

[2] For this and rich historical overviews of the eighteenth and nineteenth centuries, cf. Collison-Morley, *Shakespeare in Italy* and Attilio Nulli, *Shakespeare in Italia* (Milan: Hoepli, 1918).

than a tragedy: 'Teatrino', 'Parti in commedia', 'palcoscenico', 'regista' are recurrent motifs in everyday discourse. The dominant political trope used to show how even seemingly radical changes leave the status quo fundamentally intact is 'transformism', the ability of social and political actors to transition into newer configurations without losing their standing—another theatrical metaphor. Against the historians' warning that the history of Italy is punctuated by tragic events (a regicide, political assassinations, the rise and fall of Mussolini, the Mafia, and terrorist massacres), the lingering stereotype is that of a mellow and amicable place. As we outline the different trajectories of Shakespeare in Italy, touching on both mainstream and marginal case studies, it is important to measure them against the social, political, and even anthropological matrix of a country where the fashioning of a national identity is still a work-in-progress, with all its internal contradictions and dissonances. Between Modena's *Othello interruptus* and Shakespeare's widespread presence in theatrical programmes that makes him today the most represented playwright in Italy (above any national author), there lies a rich and vexed history and an equally complex geography.

The meaning of tragedy has fluctuated in time and place since its origins in Greek culture, oscillating from a dramatic, to an aesthetic, and later to an ethical and psychological term (the *tragic*).[3] This presents special problems for Italy, a country whose collective identity is based on a shared Catholic religion and a literary canon that has a (Divine) 'comedy' as its centrepiece. As Giorgio Agamben writes, Dante Alighieri's decision to 'abandon his own "tragic" poetic project for a "comic" poem' was epochal and is still exerting its influence today: '[t]he turn registered by these words is so little a question internal to Dante scholarship that it can even be said that here, for the first time, we find one of the traits that most tenaciously characterizes Italian culture: its essential pertinence to the comic sphere and consequent refutation of tragedy.[4]

Tragedy is the genre that has most clearly registered the tension between ancient Greek and Roman values and a Christian worldview (that in post-Reformation Italy became a strictly policed cultural code), and it may be argued that Dante's monumental masterpiece in fact hybridizes tragedy with comedy. Agamben clarifies that for Dante 'tragedy' was a matter of style and content rather than of dramatic form, and it entailed a specific theological and anthropological paradigm still underlying Italian culture, even in its contemporary secularized configuration: 'It is [a] "comic" conception of the human creature, divided into innocent nature and guilty person, that Dante bequeathed to Italian culture.'[5] This is not to suggest that Italian literature has produced just an endless series of redemptive plots and happy endings, but that tragedy as a theatrical genre and as a vision of cosmic suffering of extraordinary individuals has been relegated to the margins; the Italian literary tradition 'has remained so obstinately faithful to the antitragic intention of the Divine Comedy'.[6] While Shakespeare and his contemporaries were filling up theatres in London, in Italy tragedy remained mostly a matter of intellectual debate on Aristotle's theories and a source of entertainment for an aristocratic elite. There was indeed a revival of the genre after centuries of neglect, but theory held sway. The most famous author was

---

[3] Terry Eagleton, *Sweet Violence: The Idea of the Tragic* (Oxford: Blackwell, 2003).

[4] Giorgio Agamben, *The End of the Poem. Studies in Poetics* (Stanford: Stanford University Press, 1999), 1.

[5] Ibid., 21.   [6] Ibid., 132.

Giambattista Giraldi Cinzio, destined to become one of Shakespeare's sources. The pre-dominance of theory imprisoned the plays in rigid patterns that, among other things, banned everyday speech in favour of 'magniloquent oratory'. Tragedy was too much of a challenge for the small and embattled courts of a politically fragmented country, courts that were the only patrons of theatre and favoured the inside jokes of comedy (which could also convey harsh political satire)[7] over the foreboding plots of tragedy and its representa-tion of beleaguered rulers.[8] To quote Marzia Pieri: '[o]n the plane of ideology, the concept of sin, with which the age of counter-reformation tends to identify tragic fault, does not agree with the pagan presuppositions of the genre, and the times do not allow [us] to speculate on stage about the evils of Power.'[9]

Literature is the field where society reflects and constructs an image of itself, addresses its conscious and unconscious contradictions, negotiates with authority and with differ-ent cultural and religious traditions. In this light we may better appreciate why the vicis-situdes of Shakespeare's tragedies in Italy (as opposed to his comedies, which significantly, are very little represented) are part of, and perhaps play a key role, in a larger struggle between the comic and the tragic in Italian culture. The paradox is that Shakespeare built many of his tragedies on Italian material that the Italians had articulated either in the prose tales of Giraldi Cinzio or in the philosophical speculations of Niccolò Machiavelli and Giordano Bruno, two thinkers who almost certainly influenced Shakespeare. The playwright made Italian tales and ideas into successful plays for the stage; Italians took the plays and adapted them in a variety of forms. Before they were convinced to applaud Shakespeare in his own terms, Italians had already acclaimed Rossini's opera *Otello* (1816) at the same Teatro Re where they later spurned Modena, praised Salvatore Vigano's ballet *Otello* (1820), and celebrated Francesco Hayez's painting of *Romeo's Last Kiss to Juliet* (1823). In short, the history of Shakespeare's tragedy in Italy is one of multiple displace-ments and dislocations.

Having introduced a critical framework, our account can continue with some chrono-logical coordinates. In the eighteenth century Italy produced a play called *Ambleto* (1705) that drew on Shakespeare's sources while bypassing Shakespeare, a tragedy called *Cesare* (1726) whose preface mentioned Shakespeare as the 'Corneille of the English', and the first fragment of a translation, 'Essere o no, la gran questione è questa' (Hamlet's 'To be or not to be'). The first complete Italian version of a play was made in 1756, *Julius Caesar* by Domenico Valentino, a Roman tragedy that continues to have a special standing in Italy to this day. But what characterizes the dominant approach is a set of responses to Voltaire's influential position on Shakespeare as a violator of the Aristotelian unities, which also became the Italian mainstream position. The rival view was expressed by Giuseppe Baretti's *Discours sur Shakespeare et sur Monsieur de Voltaire* (1778), appropriately consid-ered 'the first serious and extensive critical study of Shakespeare in Italy'.[10] This vigorous defence demonstrates, however, that Shakespeare in Italy was for a long time primarily a

---

[7] I thank Kent Cartwright for this observation.

[8] Marzia Pieri, *La nascita del teatro moderno in Italia tra XV e XVI secolo* (Turin: Bollati Boringhieri, 1989), 155.

[9] Ibid., 147.

[10] Agostino Lombardo, 'Shakespeare in Italy', *Proceedings of the American Philosophical Society* 141 n. 4 (December 1997), 455.

crux of literary debates, a weapon in the battle between ancients and moderns, classics and Romantics, a critical means rather than a theatrical end. And if Shakespeare is referenced by the main neoclassical authors, such as Vittorio Alfieri, Ippolito Pindemonte, Vincenzo Monti, and Ugo Foscolo, he is not contemplated by Giacomo Leopardi, the most tragic and radical poet and thinker of Italian Romanticism. This is a literary encounter that regrettably failed to occur.

The first translation of the tragedies was the work of one of the few women we can mention in a predominantly male narrative, Giustina Renier Michiel (1755-1832).[11] A Venetian noblewoman working in the years of the downfall of the millenary Republic swept away by Napoleon, Renier Michiel hosted a literary salon welcoming the likes of Foscolo, Madame de Staël, and Byron. She translated in prose *Ottello, Macbet,* and *Coriolano,* published between 1798 and 1800, at the dawn of Venice's new era. Renier Michiel's translations were read primarily by high-ranking aristocrats of her circle and never staged, at least in Venice, thwarting her ambition to produce more versions. Her prose translation was guided by a clarifying impulse that led her to paraphrase and oversimplify some of the most pregnant passages. For a single, telling example, Iago's 'I am not what I am' was rendered as 'assicuratevi che non sono qual sembro essere' (be sure I am not what I appear to be).[12] Her pioneering effort was made more innovative by her pugnacious preface, where her approach is consciously associated with her gender. Asserting a privileged relationship between Shakespeare and women (on the grounds of 'tenderness' and 'admiration'), Renier Michiel explained that she had intended to describe the 'sensations' provoked by drama and, in detail, 'the dominant feeling in each tragedy', seen as 'possibly the only subject a woman could reflect upon without fearing men's accusations'. On the other hand, she felt she had first to relate the authoritative positions of leading critics (notably Samuel Johnson), whose omission by a woman would not have been forgiven.[13]

Wavering between eighteenth-century ideals of decorum and new Romantic impulses, Renier Michiel affirmed that 'Shakespeare takes possession of us, it moves us, it interests us even in spite of us'. She portrays a democratic Shakespeare, 'a painter of humanity' who 'extended his look at the whole humankind' and saw that the 'lowest classes of Society at the same level of the most eminent were able to provide a crowd of interesting characters. Everything human was sacred to him, and every man of whatever condition was worthy of being admitted with the Kings'.[14] In that sense Shakespeare's violation of the Aristotelian unities was necessary to imitate nature and truth through the mediation of art. Her polemical conclusion was that in Italy motherhood had been reduced to little more than a 'sweet title', since women were deprived of the prerogative of educating their daughters. As the only available alternative, she offered Shakespeare to young women as reading that could entertain, educate and 'contribute to their happiness by regulating their budding passions'.[15] Unsurprisingly, this matrilinear Shakespeare had no success.

---

[11] Andrea Molesini, Anjusca Zoggia, 'Giustina Renier Michiel traduttrice di Shakespeare', in Antonia Arslan et al., *Gentildonne, Artiste, Intellettuali al tramonto della Serenissima* (Mirano Venice: Eidos, 1998), 17-27.

[12] Giustina Renier Michiel, *Opere drammatiche di Shakespeare volgarizzate da una dama veneta,* vol. 1 (Venice: eredi Costantini, 1798), 89.

[13] Ibid., 9-10.   [14] Ibid., 17.   [15] Ibid., 24.

Between 1819 and 1822 Italian readers were presented with fourteen volumes of *Le Tragedie di Shakespeare* translated by Michele Leoni and the first prose translation of the complete works, by Carlo Rusconi, followed in 1839; the same year Giulio Carcano began a verse translation, a magnum opus that was completed in 1882.[16] The gradual rise of Shakespeare's fortune in the second half of the nineteenth century is interwoven with the rising influence of French and German Romanticism and with the Risorgimento, the movement for Italian independence. Not coincidentally, some of the most prominent political and cultural protagonists of this watershed age were passionate Shakespeareans. The critic Francesco De Santis gave seminal lectures on Shakespeare in Naples; the theorist of Italian republicanism, Giuseppe Mazzini, payed tribute to his literary genius but deemed he was not an innovator and lacked a moral message; Alessandro Manzoni, the father of modern Italian prose and himself a tragedian, used a discussion of *Othello* in his *Letter to M. Chauvet* (1820) to mount a polemic that resolved the debate on the unities once and for all. Two outstanding examples of the growing interest in Shakespeare were the actor Tommaso Salvini and the composer Giuseppe Verdi, who made the Italian approach to Shakespeare's tragedies a global affair.

Tommaso Salvini, born in Milan in 1829 from a family of actors, first trod the stage in 1842. In 1849 he fought under Garibaldi against the French army, allied to the Pope; the defeat cost him imprisonment. Art, by his own admission, became a refuge from the frustrations of politics. After his release, Salvini rapidly became an international celebrity, reaping laurels throughout Europe and North and South America, and expressing a novel approach to tragic characters. In 1853, he left the stage for one year and retired to Florence to study. Salvini resisted the idea of skipping from one role to the next without reflection and psychological and philosophical understanding: 'I studied their characters, passions, costumes, leanings … I studied [each] in his environment, I tried to live with him and expound him as my imagination envisioned him.'[17] Where the English theatre privileged a representation of the social aspirations of its bourgeois audience, the Italian stage offered what its spectators were deprived of in real life. Salvini found on stage the heroic resolution that was lacking in Italian politics. While unable to read Shakespeare in the original, Salvini spared no effort to research the background he imagined for the character that made him a worlwide star, Othello:

> I read the history of the Venetian republic, the invasion of Spain by the Moors, their passions, their warfare science and their religious beliefs; nor did I neglect the novella of Cinthio Giraldi [sic] in order to better master that sublime character. It was no longer the superficial study of words or of some scenic effect, or [the use of] more or less stressed sentences to obtain a fleeting applause; it was a vaster horizon that was opening to my sight, an infinite sea where my ship navigated safely, with no fear of finding rocks.[18]

If his Italian debut of 1856 was only slightly more encouraging than that of his mentor Modena, the next year Salvini was galvanizing audiences in Paris. Many years later, when Salvini was already a fixed star of the theatrical firmament, he was invited for a *tournée*

---

[16]   Lombardo, 'Shakespeare in Italy', 458.
[17]   Tommaso Salvini, *Aneddoti, ricordi, impressioni* (Milan: Fratelli Dumolard, 1895), 104.
[18]   Ibid., 119.

in South America. The company was forced by a violent storm into an unscheduled call at Gibraltar, where Salvini had an eventful meeting:

> I was struck by a most beautiful figure of majestic gait, with a Roman physiognomy, save a slight protrusion of the lower lip. The hue of the flesh was between copper and coffee, very strong, and he wore light moustache and his chin was covered with sparse and curly hair. Up until then I had always represented Othello with my moustache only, but since I saw that proud moor I adopted also the hair on the chin and tried to imitate his gestures, motion, deportment, and, had it been possible, I would have imitated his voice too, so much did that splendid moor represent to me the true type of the Shakespearean hero.[19]

Salvini conceived Othello through a poetics of great heroes (with a possible identification of the frustrated patriot soldier with the aged warring Moor), but also through an unprecedented ethnographic approach to the character.

Salvini played in London in 1875 and in 1884, when he was reviewed by Henry James. His success was such that a legion of local actors addressed a petition to him for an extra show, and his performances are among the most documented of the pre-film era thanks to the richly detailed reports and to an American devotee who faithfully recorded the exact development of the *mise-en-scène*.[20] The English audience was especially struck by the interpretation of Othello's ethnicity, as if an Italian actor would constitute a sort of privileged intermediary to Shakespeare's moor. A sense of uncanniness must have come across from the bilingualism of the performance, in which Salvini played in Italian against an English-speaking company:

> DESDEMONA   Alas! He is betrayed and I undone!
> OTHELLO   ed ora il piangi | In faccia a me?
> DESDEMONA   O, banish me, my lord but kill me not:
> OTHELLO   Giù vil prostituta!
> DESDEMONA   Kill me tomorrow: let me live tonight.
> OTHELLO   No! se pensi | Resister ...[21]

The spectators probably knew the lines by heart, but the linguistic contrast would make Salvini's Othello that much more of an outsider.[22] One of the scenes that shocked the spectators was vividly described by G. H. Lewes:

> the whole house was swept along by the intense and finely graduated culmination of passion in the outburst, 'Villain, be sure you prove,' etc., when, seizing Iago and shaking him as lion might shake a wolf, he finishes by flinging him on the ground, raises his foot to trample on the wretch—and then a sudden revulsion of feeling checks the brutality of the act, the *gentleman* masters the *animal*, and with mingled remorse and disgust he stretches a hand to raise him up. I remember nothing so musically perfect in its tempo and intonation, so emotionally perfect in its expression, as his delivery in this passage—the fury

---

[19] Ibid., 260.

[20] Edward Tuckerman Mason, *The Othello of Tommaso Salvini* (New York: Putnam, 1890).

[21] *Othello. Tragedy in Five Acts by William Shakespeare with the English and Italian Words, as performed by Signor Salvini* (New York: Charles D. Koppel: 1889), 80.

[22] Marvin A. Carlson, *The Italian Shakespearians* (London: Associated University Presses, 1985), 63–4.

visibly growing with every word, his whole being vibrating, his face aflame, the voice becoming more and more terrible, and yet so completely under musical control that it never
approached a scream.[23]

The passage represents a standard Victorian approach to Othello, the perception of a dual
personality in precarious balance between its civilized and its animal part. Unlike his contemporary British actors, Salvini was seen to do justice to both parts, to represent well the
transition between them: the rage remains within the limits of a 'civilized' music without
degenerating into a 'wild' scream.

An even more controversial scene was that of Othello's suicide, which Salvini performed by drawing his blade 'violently across his throat, sawing backward and forward.
His head falls back, as if more than half-severed from his body ... before he can reach the
bed, he falls backward, and dies, in strong convulsions of the body and the legs'.[24] Savini
responded to the repeated objections that 'it is the custom among the Africans to cut the
abdomen of their enemies only' and that the line 'I took by the throat the circumcised
dog | And smote him, thus' made it seem 'natural that the action should suit the word'.[25]
This form of suicide was for Salvini a matter of historical and ethnographical fidelity and
wholly coherent, in its unpalatable goriness, with his poetics of grand heroic gestures. Yet
it collided inevitably with the noble, civilized Moor desired by an English public haunted
by colonial nightmares. As Great Britain was building its empire, the English Othello
depended on the containment of energy, sexuality, and violence; Salvini responded with
a perpetual *crescendo*. Finally, the way in which Salvini turned himself into Othello left a
lasting impression on Konstantin Stanislavski, the actor and director who laid the grounds
for a modern psychological approach to acting, in turn foundational for contemporary
method acting and its aspiration to total emotional identification with a role.

However vast the success of Italian *mattatori* such as Modena, Salvini, Rossi, Adelaide
Ristori, Ermete Zacconi, however, the credit must go to Giuseppe Verdi (1813-1901) if in
Italy you can still find people whose first name is Otello or Ofelia. What truly popularized
Shakespearean tragic plots was opera, the quintessential Italian genre. The first adapta-
tions came in the late eighteenth and early nineteenth century, with at least five musical
versions of *Romeo and Juliet* culminating in Vincenzo Bellini's *I Capuleti e i Montecchi*
(1830). Gioacchino Rossini's *Otello* (1816) is emblematic insofar as its libretto by Francesco
Berio di Salsa is based on J. F. Ducis's French translation, making the work a third-
degree adaptation and transmediation of Shakespeare.[26] In the second half of the century
Shakespeare became the main source for Italy's major composer, Verdi, who authored
Macbeth (1847) early in his career (preceding any notable staging of the Scottish tragedy
itself), and closed it with *Otello* (1887) and *Falstaff* (1893). He turned down a proposal for
a *Hamlet* and left plans for a *King Lear*. Verdi's Shakespeare is inextricably linked with
his main librettist Arrigo Boito, who wrote the texts for *Otello* and *Falstaff*. In *Otello* the

---

[23] George Henry Lewes, *On Actors and the Art of Acting* (1875; New York: Grove Press, 1957), 226.
[24] Tuckerman, *The Othello of Tommaso Salvini*, 107.
[25] Tommaso Salvini, 'Interpretazioni e ragionamenti su talune opere e personaggi di
G. Shakespeare. Otello', in *Fanfulla della Domenica*, 28 October 1883. English translation in 'Othello',
Putnam's Monthly, October 1907, 24.
[26] William Shakespeare, Arrigo Boito, Francesco Berio di Salsa, Jean-François Ducis, *Quattro
volti di Otello*, ed. Marco Grondona and Guido Paduano (Milan: Biblioteca Universale Rizzoli, 1996).

first act is expunged and the scene begins with the arrival of Othello and Desdemona in Cyprus. The classic point of friction between the verbal subtleties and psychological innuendos of Shakespearean drama, and a musical genre where broad brushstrokes are indispensable to convey strong passions, is Iago's famous aria 'Credo in un Dio crudel' ('I believe in a cruel God'). This parodic reversal of the Creed has been labelled by custodians of Shakespeare's integrity as one of the 'massive intrusions of alien material, or non-Shakesperean, material from other traditions' and 'a piece of high-flown nonsense'.[27] The crux of the matter is the transformation of Jago's enigmatic 'motiveless malignity', as famously defined by Coleridge, into an aria where the ensign spells out all the reasons for his evil acts. However this blasphemous invocation echoes Iago's 'I am not what I am', another mirror-like definition of God. Opera's musical idiom, on the other hand, brings its own expressive qualities and new connotations to the Shakespearean plot: in this 'symphonic' work with the orchestra 'capable of unleashing the energy of enormous phonic weights',[28] when Othello enters Desdemona's room to kill her, accompanied by a gloomy music of muted double basses, the theme associated since act I with the kiss suddenly irrupts, beautifully interweaving the murderous intentions with the memory of their passionate love.

Towards the end of the nineteenth century Shakespeare's success was undisputed, and Modena's alien playwright was now recognized as an author who had penetrated the essence of Italian civilization. Nowhere is this clearer than in the symbiosis of actor, character and place in Eleonora Duse's *Romeo and Juliet*. Duse (1858-1924) was the major Italian actress of all time (her name is still synonymous with 'great actress') and an international diva rivalling Sarah Bernhardt. From anecdotes disseminated during her lifetime (and probably cultivated by Duse herself) to more recent biographies, there is a peculiar, epiphanic moment connected to her interpretation of the young lover in Verona. Even though she affirmed her naturalistic style of acting in Ibsen and D'Annunzio, her legendary status is still linked to her debut as Juliet when she was 14 (ironically in a non-Shakespearean version). The harsh conditions and the physical and psychological exploitation that she and many child actors probably suffered was far less touching than the drama of a young Italian actress destined to international fame, impersonating the young Italian character in the city where it all began.[29] The various anecdotes were given canonical form by Duse's lover Gabriele D'Annunzio in his novel *The Flame of Life*:

> We entered Verona one evening in the month of May through the gate of the Palio, anxiety suffocated me. I held the copy-book, where I had copied out the part of Juliet with my own hand, tightly against my heart, and constantly repeated to myself the words of my first entrance: 'How now! Who calls? I am here. What is your will?' A strange coincidence had excited my imagination: I was fourteen years old on that very day,—the age of Juliet! The gossip of the Nurse buzzed in my ears; little by little my destiny seemed to be getting mixed up with the destiny of the Veronese maiden. At the corner of every street I thought I saw a

[27] Gary Schmidgall, *Shakespeare and Opera* (Oxford: Oxford University Press, 1990), 240–50.

[28] Guido Salvetti, 'Dal Verdi della maturità a Giacomo Puccini', in Alberto Basso, ed., *Musica in scena: storia dello spettacolo musicale. 2: Gli italiani all'estero; l'opera in Italia e in Francia* (Turin: UTET, 1996), 392.

[29] Roberto Cuppone, '"Io fui Giulietta". La prima volta di Eleonora', in Maria Ida Biggi and Paolo Puppa, eds., *Voci e Anime, Corpi e Scritture. Atti del convegno internazionale su Eleonora Duse* (Roma: Bulzoni, 2009), 21–38.

crowd coming towards me and accompanying a coffin covered with white roses. As soon as I saw the Arche degli Scaligeri, closed with iron nails, I cried out to my mother, 'Here is the tomb of Juliet.' And I began to weep bitterly with a desperate desire of love and death ... One Sunday in May, in the immense arena in the ancient amphitheatre under the open sky, I have been Juliet before a popular multitude that had breathed in the legend of love and death. No quiver from the most vibrating audiences, no applause, no triumph has ever meant the same to me as the fulness and the intoxication of that great hour.[30]

If Salvini was the manly master of character construction, Duse is here transfigured into the woman who literally abandons herself to the role, fusing with it. As with Salvini, the implication is that Shakespeare had captured some anthropological truth about his Italian characters, so who better than Italian actors to embody them? The fortunes of Salvini and Duse are a powerful reminder that throughout the nineteenth century and well into the twentieth, Shakespeare and his works were often interpreted through stereotypes of race and gender used to classify both characters and actors.

'4th November: Read and taken notes on Shakespeare. Italians have entered Trent and Trieste! 5th November: The armistice and the end of the war against Austria have been announced ... I have been reading Shakespeare'.[31] Those diary entries from 1918 situate the most significant critical engagement with Shakespeare by an Italian philosopher in the midst of the atrocities of the Great War. Benedetto Croce (1866-1952), an eminent public intellectual and former liberal senator who had opposed the military enterprise, had isolated himself from the conflict and concentrated on a humanistic world-view that could reconcile in the realm of literature the European countries that were killing each other in the trenches. Croce published *Shakespeare, Ariosto and Corneille* in 1920, and his publisher testified to a new attention payed to Shakespeare in schools by excerpting its chapter for a monographic volume that came out in 1925, the year Croce signed the Manifesto of Anti-Fascist Intellectuals. Croce based his reading on his long-established aesthetic theory of the autonomy of poetry defined as pure 'intuition' devoid of any moral and intellectual—let alone political—aims. 'Shakespeare did not toy with ideals of any kind and least of all with political ones; and although he represents magnificently political struggles too, he always supersedes them in their specific character and objective, always reaching, through them, the only thing that profoundly attracts him: life.'[32] His negative models were German critics and their use of *Richard II* as a doctrinaire assertion of the divine right of kings, of *The Tempest* as an apology for European colonialism and particularly of *Othello* as a warning against mixed marriages. The truth of the matter was that Shakespeare could neither agree nor disagree with 'external reality' because he is intent to 'create his own spiritual reality'.[33]

While Croce was trying to rescue Shakespeare by placing him in an abstract realm of pure art (a still lingering temptation in Italian culture), Fascist critics were trying to enact a celebration of his Italian characters and plots functional to the creation of racial and national pride (a collective effort that included a rewrite of *Julius Caesar* by Mussolini

---

[30] Gabriele D'Annunzio, *The Flame of Life*, trans. Kassandra Vivaria (Boston: Page Company, 1900), 319.

[31] Cit. in Luigi Trenti, '"*I know you what you are*": Croce e Shakespeare', *Memoria di Shakespeare* 6 (2008), 125.

[32] Benedetto Croce, *Shakespeare* (Bari: Laterza, 1925), 25.   [33] Ibid., 163.

himself, helped by Giovacchino Forzano), even though, precisely in the case of the Roman play, some characters and plots proved recalcitrant to such militant interpretations. Piero Rebora polemicized against Croce's notion of an apolitical Shakespeare and attacked the notion that Shakespeare had belittled the figure of the greatest Roman hero, expressing his republican sympathies through Brutus: 'Shakespeare is politically "Caesarean", certain of the greatness of that genius that was Caesar ... Nobody more than Shakespeare was repelled by the humanistic and republican exaltation of regicide.'[34] In 1935 *Julius Caesar* was also staged in Rome by the Opera Nazionale Dopolavoro, the institution created by the regime to organize and discipline the leisure activities of the masses. The chosen backdrop for this grandiose staging was the Basilica of Maxentius, one of the sites capable of evoking ancient Rome's imperial greatness. Reviewers were less interested in the acting than in disparaging the republican reading attributed to Victor Hugo and Mazzini: the supreme intuition of Shakespeare was to eliminate Caesar physically in the middle of the play in order to represent 'the gloriously invincible immanence of [his] spirit, ... that invests the whole tragedy with a powerful and suggestive aura'. So at the end of the play 'the effect is one and only: the soul of the spectator is in awe of the founder of the Roman empire'.[35] Two years later, an American director took this interpretation to its logical conclusion: in Orson Welles's New York production of *Julius Caesar* the Roman soldiers were dressed in brown shirts.

In 1938 Mario Praz, the greatest Italian anglicist of the century, wrote an essay called 'Come Shakespeare è letto in Italia' ('How Shakespeare is read in Italy').[36] He criticized Croce for his abstract and unproductive reading of Shakespeare and offered an impeccable philological reading of several plays to demonstrate how current Italian translations had mangled the originals. There was nothing overtly political in his intervention, but his professional correctness could be read as a response to the many contemporary ideological misreadings and appropriations of Shakespeare.

The post-war era has witnessed a steady rise of Shakespeare performances, scholarship, and translations. Michele Marrapodi usefully mapped the state of Shakespeare criticism in Italy at the end of the twentieth century, with a genealogy connecting Mario Praz with his two former students Agostino Lombardo and Giorgio Melchiori.[37] He then singled out three major schools of criticism, the structuralist-semiotic school, historical Marxism, and a last group that devotes a closer attention to formal structures and to the rhetorical and ideological uses of language. In most of these studies one can find the more or less explicit presence of the dominant Marxist matrix of post-war Italian culture. Philosophers have also addressed Shakespeare, as the disparate readings of *Hamlet* offered by feminist Adriana Cavarero and the 'unpolitical' Massimo Cacciari testify.[38] Yet we may regret that Shakespeare is hardly ever discussed by Italian thinkers (Giorgio Agamben, Antonio

[34] Piero Rebora, *Civiltà italiana e civiltà inglese. Studi e ricerche* (Florence: Le Monnier, 1936), 31.

[35] Osvaldo, Gibertini, '*Giulio Cesare* alla Basilica di Massenzio', *La Tribuna*, 3 August 1935.

[36] Mario Praz, *Caleidoscopio Shakespeariano* (Bari: Adriatica Editrice 1969), 133–55.

[37] Michele Marrapodi, 'Introduction: Shakespeare Studies in Italy Since 1964', *Italian Studies in Shakespeare and His Contemporaries* (Newark: University of Delaware Press and London: Associated University Presses, 1999), 7–18.

[38] Adriana Cavarero, *Stately Bodies: Literature, Philosophy, and the Question of Gender* (Ann Arbor: University of Michigan Press, 2002); Massimo Cacciari, *Hamletica* (Milan: Adelphi, 2009).

Negri, Roberto Esposito) whose theories—often based on analyses of early modern culture—have become influential in recent critical theory and in Shakespeare criticism. On the religious spectrum, it is interesting to find diametrically opposed readings of a textually Catholic Shakespeare set against a radical atheist who writes into his works the heretical ideas of Giordano Bruno.[39] With English gradually replacing French as the most studied second language in Italy, and with the study of English literature becoming virtually obligatory in most English language academic programmes, Shakespeare has become a basic subject in both Italian high schools and universities, with an overwhelming role given to the tragedies over the comedies and the histories, a situation that has started to alter again in the new millenium with the crisis of the humanities.

'In the post-war years, the emphasis shifted from actor to production', Paola Pugliatti reminds us, with the charismatic director replacing the lead player as the trademark of the work; 'a closer connection between the theater and Shakespeare criticism is probably the most interesting aspect of the present situation', adds Agostino Lombardo.[40] Our necessarily limited case studies must include examples of a more classical approach, where innovation is steeped in a respect for the text, as well as two radically experimental Italian Shakespeares. A colleague, friend, and political ally of Bertolt Brecht, Giorgio Strehler (1921-97) represented a new method based on a strong identification with a permanent company and a specific playhouse, the Piccolo Teatro in Milan, as well as a powerful belief in the theatre's ability to convey a political message. Strehler pursued an ideal of a 'teatro umano', with 'all the implications of human, humane and humanitarian with all their concomitant social and political overtones'.[41] If *The Tempest* was the Shakespearean play that framed his career, Strehler also directed landmark productions of *Coriolanus* (1957) and *King Lear* (1972), not to mention his versions of Verdi's *Macbeth* and *Falstaff*. *King Lear* is recognized as a point of arrival where for the first time on a mainstream stage the titular protagonist was not the centrepiece of the production.[42] Created at a tense political moment, when a new generation born after the war was calling into question the foundations of Italian society and often championing extreme and revolutionary political alternatives, Strehler described his Lear as a 'a crystal clear generational drama', where the director (himself contested by some young protesters) identified with the aging king. Within a desolate, cosmic scenario reminiscent of Beckett, Strehler still modified the close, 'we that are young | Shall never see so much, nor live so long' into 'we that are young will not allow suchlike adversities, nor claim to be eternal'.[43] The existentialist director did not renounce a progressive political message.

Against this militant but ultimately conventional theatre, the anarchist, *enfant terrible* Carmelo Bene (1937-2002) reverted to the tradition of the *mattatore*, and turned it inside

---

[39] Pietro Boitani, *The Gospel According to Shakespeare* (Notre Dame: University of Notre Dame Press, 2013); Gilberto Sacerdoti, *Nuovo cielo, nuova terra. La rivelazione copernicana di 'Antonio e Cleopatra' di Shakespeare* (Rome: Edizioni di storia e letteratura, 2008).

[40] Paola Pugliatti, 'Italy', in Michael Dobson and Stanley Wells, eds., *The Oxford Companion to Shakespeare* (Oxford: Oxford University Press, 2009), 218. Lombardo, 'Shakespeare in Italy', 462.

[41] David L. Hirst, *Giorgio Strehler* (Cambridge: Cambridge University Press, 1993), 2.

[42] Sonia Bellavia, *L'ombra di Lear: il Re Lear di Shakespeare e il teatro Italiano (1858-1995)* (Rome: Bulzoni, 2004), 261.

[43] Ibid., 269.

out. He worked with the same text and 'character' for a lifetime as Salvini had done, but in overt polemic against contemporary practitioners, he unsettled all the tenets of tradition, producing an anti-naturalistic, anti-mimetic, anti-narrative style that resembled a 'negative mould' for traditional theatre companies.[44] Bene combined the high canon of Western literature with poststructuralist theory, and tirelessly experimented with multiple media and all the new audiovisual technologies.

> From *Hamlet, Hommelette,* to *Hamlet Suite* ... the operetta of the artsy-fartsy prince is the refrain of the lives I have unlived [*svissuto*]. The assiduous, persecutory frequentation of this fine subject (five, ever changing, stage productions—'61, '67, '74, '87, '94 ... a film ('72), two widely different tv versions and radio recordings, audiotapes and compact-disc) 'defines' me as *Twentieth-Century Hamlet.*[45]

Bene's own words summarize the lifelong engagement of this idyosincratic performer, the most intellectual among Italian actors, with the Shakespearean prince. For him Hamlet represented the quintessential artist, facing his impossible existence in modern bourgeois art, a condition that led Bene to theorize a 'suspension of the tragic', where by subverting the text, the plot, and the character(s) he countered the assumption that theatre can provide the fiction of a replenished subject, radically denying any sort of catharsis to the audience. Commenting on Bene's rewrite of *Richard III*, Gilles Deleuze writes: 'The elements of power in the theatre are what ensure both the coherence of the subject in question and the coherence of the representation on stage. It is both the power of what is represented and the power of the theatre itself.'[46] Bene responds with a strategy of 'amputation and subtraction', that, as his many Hamlets demonstrate, violently manipulates the Shakespearean pre-text. Influenced by Joyce, Bene disassembled and reassembled scenes in ever more original montages, interpolated a wide variety of literary, acoustic, and visual materials, in a metatheatrical and antitheatrical postmodern gesture that has been linked to other experimentalists such as Artaud, Robert Wilson, Jerzy Grotowski. The resulting playtext aimed at a 'theatre without spectacle', a performance where, with Bene as a charismatic performer at the centre, all the conventional elements of classical Western drama were destabilized to deny audiences the comfortable bourgeois experience of attending a performance in a playhouse (or movie theatre) and receiving a unified and coherent message from it. As part of this strategy, Bene's tragic personages refuse to die, because death would offer that relief and release that the classical representation promises to jaded audiences. Instead, they agonize or repeat themselves in a sort of endless parodic cycle: 'Where there is no parody, there is no tragedy.'[47]

The lesson of Carmelo Bene has been taken to further extremes by his admirer Romeo Castellucci (1960-), whose unsettling approach is markedly different from the bland Shakespeare that is pervasive in mainstream theatres. 'Our times and our lives are completely detached from any concept of the tragic ... Disasters and slaughters of innocents

---

[44] Armando Petrini, *Amleto da Shakespeare a Laforgue per Carmelo Bene* (Pisa: ETS, 2004), 40.

[45] Carmelo Bene, *Opere. Con l'autografia di un ritratto* (Milan: Bompiani, 2008), 1351.

[46] Gilles Deleuze, 'One Less Manifesto', in Timothy Murray, ed., *Mimesis, Masochism and Mime: The Politics of Theatricality in Contemporary French Thought* (Ann Arbor: University of Michigan Press, 1997), 241.

[47] Petrini, *Amleto*, 48.

are everywhere referred to as "tragedies", but this is an idea of tragedy that does not know how to distinguish these things from the spectacle.[48] To such bleak diagnosis of the present Castellucci responds by repudiating the communicative and cognitive function of language in favour of the power of affects and new forms of subjectivity. He attacks the organic unity of the body, and his most problematic choice is to work with physically disabled actors, where 'the handicapped or sick, deformed body not only is not seen from a pathological predicament, it is treated as material of dramaturgy in itself'.[49] Writing a new, distressing chapter in the rich afterlife of *Julius Caesar* in Italy, Castellucci has Brutus and Cassius played by anorexic women and Mark Antony by a tracheotomized actor who addresses his 'Friends, Romans, countrymen' through his open blowhole.

Both acclaimed as avant-garde visionaries and lambasted as self-serving provocateurs, Bene and Castellucci hail from provincial and traditional areas of Italy. If one remembers the New Historicist argument that Elizabethan theatre absorbed and supplanted the dramatic energies of the depleted Catholic ritual, it is interesting to note how the two actors self-consciously ascribe to their strict Catholic upbringing much of the imagery of their modern, 'secular' performances. Ironically, their iconoclastic approach participates in a dialectic of transgression and reaffirmation of all establishments and rules that confirms a general pattern and somehow contradicts their intents: in a politically unstable country with very weak secular institutions and a society increasingly dominated by the logic of spectacle, the only symbolically dominant organization remains the Catholic Church (regardless of the percentages of actual observance).

No survey would be complete without a mention of cinema, an art in which Italy has received international recognition and that has paid an important tribute to Shakespearean tragedy. The best known are the spectacular, glamorous, Hollywood-style productions of Franco Zeffirelli (1923-), from *Romeo and Juliet* (1968) to *Hamlet* (1990). Besides Bene's experiments, 'minor' Shakespeares include Pier Paolo Pasolini's short and idiosyncratic adaptation of *Othello* in his *Cosa sono le nuvole?* (one of six episodes of collective film *Capriccio all'italiana*, 1967) and the more recent version of *Julius Caesar* by Paolo and Vittorio Taviani, *Cesare deve morire* (2011), chronicling a staging of the play inside a Rome prison with non-professional actors speaking in their respective dialects.

The adaptions of Shakespeare to regional languages, many of which have rich literary traditions, is another distinctive phenomenon. Luigi Meneghello (1922-2007), a novelist whose cosmopolitanism is linked to his long tenure as a professor of Italian in England, was always fuelled by his intimate memories of his provincial childhood; it also inspired a set of translations of English poetry into his native dialect, including long segments of *Hamlet* that create a fascinating dissonance between the most canonical tragedy and the intimate idiom of his small village. Playwright Giovanni Testori (1923-93) rewrote both *Hamlet* and *Macbeth* in Milanese and infused them with comedy. A rewrite of *Hamlet* had also been planned by Eduardo De Filippo (1900-84), the greatest playwright and actor in Neapolitan, who translated *The Tempest* and adapted *The Merchant of Venice*, which gave

---

[48] Audronė Žukauskaitė, 'The Post-Subjective Body, or Deleuze and Guattari Meet Romeo Castellucci', in Fintan Walsh and Matthew Causey, eds., *Performance, Identity and the Neo-Political Subject* (New York: Routledge, 2013), 111.

[49] Eleni Papalexiou, 'The Body as Dramatic Material in the Theatre of Romeo Castellucci', *Prospero. European Review. Theatre and Research* 2 (2011), 75–87.

him the opportunity to highlight the tragic potential of this comedy: 'I accuse the society in which Shakespeare lived. What was he supposed to do? What was I supposed to do during Fascism, other than make people laugh and, in the end, overturn the action and show them the tragedy?'[50]

Today Shakespeare's success in Italy appears to be unconditional. There is a Globe Theatre in Rome; a musical version of *Romeo and Juliet* attracts thousands of people, matching the thriving Shakespearean tourism in Verona at the feet of Juliet's (fake) balcony; almost every permanent company features a Shakespearean play in their season, typically a tragedy, often a bland staging; theatrical experiments continue on the fringes, while the state of Shakespeare studies reflects the shrinking role of the humanities in the educational system. We may return in conclusion to the subordinate position of tragedy in Italian culture. On the one hand, Shakespeare may have performed a compensatory function, providing iconic tragic plots to a tradition recalcitrant to the genre; on the other hand, it may be argued that the prevailingly comic disposition has often been able to subdue the unsettling energies of tragedy, as the many parodies, adaptations, and deconstructions of the plays seem to indicate. If the more traditional representations in mainstream theatres fail to be tragic because they simply reiterate the canonical status of Shakespeare for middle class audiences, the more radical, anti-representational approaches exemplified by Bene and Castellucci are programmatically anti-tragic. One hopes for new responses to this old cultural dilemma.

Select Bibliography

Carlson, Marvin A., *The Italian Shakespearians* (London: Associated University Presses, 1985).

Collison-Morley, Lacy, *Shakespeare in Italy* (Stratford: Shakespeare Head Press, 1916).

Croce, Benedetto, *Shakespeare* (Bari: Laterza, 1925).

Lombardo, Agostino, *Lettura del Macbeth* (Venice: Neri Pozza, 1969).

Lombardo, Agostino, 'Shakespeare in Italy', *Proceedings of the American Philosophical Society*, 141:4 (December 1997), 454–62.

Marrapodi, Michele et al., eds., *Italian Studies in Shakespeare and His Contemporaries* (Newark: University of Delaware Press, 1999).

Memoria di Shakespeare, Periodical (2000–).

Moretti, Franco, 'The Great Eclipse: Tragic Form as the Deconsecration of Sovereignty', *Signs Taken For Wonders,* (London: Verso, 1983).

Praz, Mario, *Caleidoscopio Shakespeariano* (Bari: Adriatica, 1969).

Schmidgall, Gary, *Shakespeare and Opera* (Oxford: Oxford University Press, 1990).

Serpieri, Alessandro, *Otello: l'Eros negato* (Naples: Liguori, 2003).

---

[50] Cit. in Agostino Lombardo, 'Eduardo e Shakespeare', *Memoria di Shakespeare* 6 (2008), 228.

CHAPTER 43

··

THE TRAGEDIES
IN GERMANY

··

ANDREAS HÖFELE

THE travelling actors in whose baggage Shakespeare arrived in Germany around 1600 were known as the English Comedians. Yet their best-remembered play is a tragedy: *Fratricide Punished*, a severely truncated version of *Hamlet*, whose original author remained unidentified. When the name of Shakespeare made its first printed appearance in German in 1682, the learned writer Daniel Morhof confessed to having read nothing of his work. Shakespeare's fame preceded first-hand knowledge well into the eighteenth century, when German Shakespeare reception took off in earnest. From around 1750, Shakespeare became a crucial force in German literary and intellectual history, and it is safe to say that his role as a catalyst rests first and foremost on the tragedies. They were the model invoked in the battle against French Classicism, the model emulated by Germany's own young *Sturm und Drang* dramatists of the 1770s. They, along with the histories, were the model that most nineteenth-century attempts at a national historical drama all too obviously strove to reproduce but failed to match, the model discussed in aesthetics and dramatic theory from Hegel onwards. Among the tragedies, *Hamlet* clearly took pride of place. It, or rather he, the prince, looms large in the German imagination, from Goethe's influential reading in *Wilhelm Meister* to Ferdinand Freiligrath's 1844 poem. The opening line of that poem, 'Germany is Hamlet', became a catchphrase that reverberated far beyond its original context into the next century.

All this is well known.[1] In the words of a recent study:

[1] For bibliographical information, see Hansjürgen Blinn, *Der deutsche Shakespeare/The German Shakespeare* (Berlin: Erich Schmidt, 1993) and Hansjürgen Blinn, Wolf Gerhard Schmidt, *Shakespeare—deutsch: Bibliographie der Übersetzungen und Bearbeitungen* (Berlin: Erich Schmidt, 2003). Collections of eighteenth and nineteenth-century source texts include Hansjürgen Blinn, ed., *Shakespeare-Rezeption: Die Diskussion um Shakespeare in Deutschland*, 2 vols. (Berlin: Erich Schmidt, 1982, 1988), and Wolfgang Stellmacher, ed., *Auseinandersetzung mit Shakespeare*, 2 vols. (Berlin: Akademie-Verlag, 1976, 1985). Excerpts from some of these texts are available in English in Roger Paulin, ed., *Voltaire, Goethe, Schlegel, Coleridge*, vol. 3, *Great Shakespeareans*, ed. Adrian Poole and Peter Holland (London and New York: Continuum, 2011). For a concise account of German Shakespeare reception, see Günter Erken's chapter on the subject in *Shakespeare-Handbuch. Die Zeit—Der Mensch—Das Werk—Die Nachwelt*, ed. Ina Schabert, 4th edn. (Stuttgart: Kröner, 2009), 635–60.

At the very outset, one fact confronts us: the sheer extent and pervasiveness of Shakespeare's influence in Germany. We encounter, in Harold Bloom's terms, a 'Shakespeare-haunted' culture. This influence involves strong proprietary claims and appropriations by the receivers ... Shakespeare can without further ado be called a German classic, akin to Goethe and Schiller. In 1849, amid crises of German national identity, the leading German Shakespeare scholar, Georg Gottfried Gervinus, could claim without exaggeration that Shakespeare 'has become a German poet almost more than any of our native writers'.[2]

This 'sheer extent and pervasiveness' is nothing short of daunting. Trying to cover it with any pretension to exhaustiveness in the space available here would be futile. Hence, the account that follows will be selective and will highlight what are the intellectually and culturally most interesting currents and individuals. My selection is obviously open to debate. I am not, for example, offering a stage history of the tragedies in Germany;[3] and even in the field I am concentrating on, the field that could be roughly designated as intellectual history, different emphases could be placed. Much more detailed accounts are not only thinkable but actually available.[4]

Shakespeare being so closely linked with the ascent of German literature from provincial obscurity to classical eminence, the history of Shakespeare in Germany has been of abiding interest and the subject of extensive reflection and academic research since the nineteenth century. A magisterial *History of Shakespearean Drama in Germany*[5] appeared as early as 1870; and when Friedrich Gundolf published *Shakespeare and the German Spirit* in 1911[6] this was the harbinger of a paradigm shift in literary studies from nineteenth-century positivism to *Geistesgeschichte*.[7] By the early twentieth century, German Shakespeare enthusiasm had created its own master narrative of 'nostrification', a veritable 'myth'. This myth, Werner Habicht writes,

> can be briefly described as follows: In eighteenth-century Germany, between the ages of rationalism and romanticism, young intellectuals began to 'discover' Shakespeare, and in doing so, they miraculously discovered themselves, a national identity, the German spirit and the potential for a national literature of the future. As a consequence, Shakespeare legitimately achieved the status of a timeless German classic.[8]

Recent critical responses to the myth have taken two main directions. One, which may be described as revisionary, replaces the generalising clichés of the myth with corrective

---

[2] Roger Paulin, *The Critical Reception of Shakespeare in Germany 1682–1914: Native Literature and Foreign Genius* (Hildesheim, Zurich, and New York: Olms, 2003), 1.

[3] Not least because such a history is so well available elsewhere: see Simon Williams, *Shakespeare on the German Stage 1586–1914* (Cambridge: Cambridge University Press, 1990), and its brilliant sequel, Wilhelm Hortmann, *Shakespeare on the German Stage: The Twentieth Century. With an Essay by Maik Hamburger* (Cambridge: Cambridge University Press, 1998).

[4] Paulin, *Critical Reception*, is exemplary here.

[5] Rudolph Genée, *Geschichte der Shakespeareschen Dramen in Deutschland* (Leipzig: Engelmann, 1870).

[6] Friedrich Gundolf, *Shakespeare und der deutsche Geist* (Berlin: Bondi, 1911).

[7] The term *Geistesgeschichte* is difficult to translate. 'History of ideas' or 'intellectual history' may serve as approximations, but fail to capture the metaphysical slant of *Geist*.

[8] Werner Habicht, *Shakespeare and the German Imagination* (Hertford: Stephen Austin and Sons for the International Shakespeare Association, 1994), 1.

facts. Roger Paulin's *Critical Reception*, which covers critical reception from 1682 (Morhof's initial name-dropping) to the First World War, is the most thorough example of this approach. The other thrust of recent research makes the myth itself the object of critical scrutiny. The numerous studies of German Hamletism fall into this bracket.[9] There is, of course, no clear-cut division between the two[10] but rather a difference of emphasis, one seeking primarily to identify the quirks and misconceptions of what might be called the authorized version, the other focussing on the cultural and political forces that went into its authorization and were, in turn, authorized by it. The latter angle predominates in studies of Shakespeare on the German stage. Traditional accounts such as E. L. Stahl's *Shakespeare and the German Theatre* (1947)[11]—much like counterpart surveys of Shakespeare's English stage history—had tended to endorse a teleological progress from distortive adaptation ('Tatification') to eventual restoration in productions that were miraculously at once 'modern' and faithful to the Bard (*werktreu*). Recent work has been at pains to avoid such teleological bias, exploring the entanglement of Shakespeare's German stage career with other strands of history instead.[12]

Theatrical and critical reception can mutually reinforce one another or can also clash, as in the case of the English Romantic critics who found the contemporary stage woefully inadequate to Shakespeare.[13] In eighteenth-century Germany, dramatic criticism almost inevitably homed in on the stage not as it was but as it should be: a virtual theatre for a nation lacking not only a nation state but also a national literature that measured up to foreign, mainly French, competition.[14] This is the context in which Shakespeare becomes the watchword of a movement, the cudgel with which to bash French classicism and its leading German advocate, Johann Christoph Gottsched, as the young Gotthold Ephraim Lessing did in his famous *17th Literary Letter* (1759). Gottsched had sought to cleanse German literature of buffoonery and the baroque bombast of the native *Trauerspiel* by prescribing a cure of regularization based on French models. His *Attempt at a Critical Poetics for the*

---

[9] See e.g. Manfred Pfister, 'Germany is Hamlet: The History of a Political Interpretation', *New Comparison* 2 (1986), 106–26; Manfred Pfister, 'German Hamletology and Beyond', in *Critical Dialogues: Current Issues in English Studies in Germany and Britain*, ed. Isobel Armstrong and Hans-Werner Ludwig (Tübingen: Narr, 1995), 41–56; Heiner O. Zimmermann, 'Is Hamlet Germany? On the Political Reception of *Hamlet*', in *New Essays on* Hamlet, ed. Mark Thornton Burnett and John Manning (New York: AMS Press, 1994), 293–318.

[10] Werner Habicht's contributions to the field, for example, tend to combine the merits of both. See e.g. his *Shakespeare and the German Imagination*; 'Romanticism, Antiromanticism, and the German Shakespeare Tradition', in *Shakespeare and Cultural Traditions*, ed. Tetsuo Kishi, Roger Pringle, and Stanley Wells (Newark, DE: University of Delaware Press, 1994), 243–52; 'Fictional Shakespeare in Nineteenth-Century Germany', in *The Globalization of Shakespeare in the Nineteenth Century*, ed. Krystyna Kujawińska Courtney, John M. Mercer, and Peter Holland (Lewiston, NY: Mellen), 235–48.

[11] E. L. Stahl, *Shakespeare und das deutsche Theater* (Stuttgart: Kohlhammer, 1947).

[12] See the two volumes on *Shakespeare on the German Stage*, by Williams (*1586–1914*) and Hortmann (*The Twentieth Century*).

[13] See e.g. Charles Lamb's famous essay 'On Garrick, and Acting; and the Plays of Shakspeare, considered with reference to their fitness for Stage Representation', *The Reflector* 2:4 (1811), 298–313.

[14] As late as 1780 Frederick II ('the Great') of Prussia's *De la Littérature Allemande* notoriously dismissed German literature as unworthy of note.

Germans (1730)[15] laid down the rules, mainly derived from Boileau; his 6-volume *German Stage* (1741-45)[16] supplied exemplary plays for a German repertory including his own *Dying Cato* (1732), an adaptation of Addison's tragedy, as well as translations from the French.

Though his merits were considerable, Gottsched is mainly remembered as the target of Lessing's attack, from which his reputation never recovered. 'Nobody', Lessing begins,

> will deny that the German stage owes a great deal of its improvement to Herr Professor Gottsched. I am this 'Nobody'; I deny it outright. One would wish that Herr Gottsched had never meddled with the theatre. His supposed improvements either bear on negligible trifles or are true changes for the worse....[17]
>
> If one had translated the masterpieces of Shakespeare for our German people, with a few modest changes, I am certain it would have been better in the end than acquainting them so well with Corneille and Racine. Firstly, our people would have found the former much more to their taste than the latter; and secondly, the former would have inspired quite a different sort of mind among us than one can say of the latter. For genius can only be sparked by genius, and most easily by genius that seems to owe everything entirely to nature and does not discourage us with the tiresome perfections of art.

Lessing's polemic is less than fair to his opponent, and much of what he says about Shakespeare is derived from Voltaire and other French sources.[18] But even though it may be claimed that Lessing's *17th Literary Letter* 'told the world nothing about Shakespeare it did not already know',[19] it does mark a new departure: the single most influential inaugural push for Shakespeare's German canonization.

And it ingeniously reconciled Shakespearean tragedy with the authority of Aristotle. 'Even judging the matter by the standards of the ancients', Lessing writes,

> Shakespeare is a far greater tragic poet than Corneille, even though the latter knew the ancients very well and the former hardly at all. Corneille approximates them in his mechanical construction, Shakespeare in what is essential. The Englishman nearly always accomplishes the purpose of tragedy, by whatever strange ways peculiar to himself that he may choose; and the Frenchman accomplishes it almost never, even though he follows the path paved by the ancients. After the *Oedipus* of Sophocles there cannot be a play in the world that has more power over our emotions than *Othello*, than *King Lear*, than *Hamlet* etc.

Defying Aristotelianism in the name of Aristotle, Lessing's argument straddles the traditional system of poetics and the modern or romantic poetics of expression.

But things were moving so fast in these years of creative unrest that Lessing's compromise seemed outdated by the end of the next decade. Aristotle's *Poetics*, the undisputed yardstick of literary excellence since the Renaissance, simply cut no ice with the young geniuses of the *Sturm und Drang*. The 22-year-old Goethe, celebrating his new-found

---

[15] Johann Christoph Gottsched, *Versuch einer critischen Dichtkunst für die Deutschen* (1730) (Darmstadt: Wissenschaftliche Buchgesellschaft, 1998).

[16] Johann Christoph Gottsched, *Die Deutsche Schaubühne*, 6 vols. (Leipzig: Breitkopf, 1741-745).

[17] Gotthold Ephraim Lessing, '17. Literaturbrief', in Lessing, *Literaturkritik, Poetik und Philologie*, ed. Jörg Schönert, vol. 5, *Werke*, ed. Herbert G. Göpfert (Darmstadt: Wissenschaftliche Buchgesellschaft, 1973), 70–3 at 70.

[18] Paulin, *Critical Reception*, 86–90.

[19] Ibid., 90; Paulin adds:'[B]ut it had effectively silenced the last authoritative anti-Shakespearean voice [in Germany].'

literary hero in an enthusiastic speech 'On Shakespeare Day' (14 October 1771), dismissed Aristotelian 'rule poetics' in the name of nature: 'And I cry: Nature! Nature! Nothing is so like Nature as Shakespeare's figures.'[20] In his own history play *Götz von Berlichingen* (1773), Goethe dispenses with the unities of place, time, and action, availing himself of well over fifty scene changes to whisk his audience all over Southern Germany. Unity of plot is programmatically discarded in favour of a unity based on powerfully individual characters; such characters, Jakob Michael Reinhold Lenz wrote, another *Sturm und Drang* dramatist, 'create their own realities (Begebenheiten)'.[21] Goethe's Götz is a character like this as are the antagonistic brothers, Karl and Franz Mohr, in Friedrich Schiller's debut play *The Robbers* (1781). Lessing had warned that 'Shakespeare should be studied, not plundered',[22] but the wave of 'irregular' tragic dramas attests to a veritable epidemic of 'Shakespearomania'.

Goethe and Schiller, in their maturity, retreated from the exuberant anti-classicism of their *Sturm und Drang* years. When Schiller adapted *Macbeth* for the Weimar Court Theatre in 1800, he tailored it to classical propriety, notoriously replacing the saucy ramblings of the porter with a pious morning song. For Weimar Classicism at its height, in the collaboration of Goethe and Schiller between 1794 and 1805, the year of Schiller's death, Shakespeare was clearly no longer suitable as a model for tragic form, let alone as a playwright to be imitated. Although Goethe never recanted his admiration for the Bard, he found fault with Shakespeare's dramaturgy: '[N]ot everything the master does is masterful. While Shakespeare's name is an essential part of the history of literature, he is only a peripheral part of the history of the theater.'[23]

By the late 1790s, the baton of Shakespeare enthusiasm had passed to a younger generation whose critical opinions differed sharply from the classicist canons of Weimar. To these founders of German Romanticism, the Schlegel brothers and Ludwig Tieck, Shakespeare was the epitome of Romantic art. Most of his plays, like most of Calderón's, 'are neither tragedies nor comedies in the sense of the ancients', August Wilhelm Schlegel wrote; 'they are romantic dramas'.[24] While the art and poetry of classical antiquity 'rigorously separate things which are dissimilar', romantic art 'delights in indissoluble mixtures', melting

> all contrarieties—nature and art, poetry and prose, seriousness and mirth, recollection and anticipation, spirituality and sensuality, terrestrial and celestial, life and death. (76)

Classical tragedy resembles 'a group in sculpture', Romantic drama more

---

[20] Johann Wolfgang von Goethe, 'Shakespeare: A Tribute' (1771), in Goethe, *Essays on Art and Literature*, ed. John Gearey, trans. Ellen von Nardoff and Ernest H. von Nardoff, vol. 3, *Goethe's Collected Works* (New York: Suhrkamp, 1986), 163–5 at 164.

[21] Jakob Michael Reinhold Lenz, 'Anmerkungen übers Theater' (1774), in *Dramaturgische Schriften des 18. Jahrhunderts*, ed. Klaus Hammer (Berlin: Henschel, 1968), 295–321 at 304.

[22] Gotthold Ephraim Lessing, *Hamburgische Dramaturgie*, ed. Klaus Bohnen, vol. 6, *Werke und Briefe*, ed. Wilfried Barner et al. (Frankfurt am Main: Deutscher Klassiker Verlag, 1985), 181–694 at 549.

[23] Goethe, 'Shakespeare Once Again' (1815), in *Essays on Art and Literature*, 166–74 at 172.

[24] August Wilhelm Schlegel, 'Lectures on Dramatic Art (1809); Lecture XXII', trans. John Black, in *Masterpieces of German Literature; Translated into English*, vol. 4, *German Classics* (New York: The German Publication Society, 1913), 71–119 at 74. Page references in the text are to this edition.

a large picture, where not merely figure and motion are exhibited in larger, richer groups, but where even all that surrounds the figures must also be portrayed; where we see not merely the nearest objects, but are indulged with the prospect of a considerable distance; and all this under a magical light which assists in giving to the impression the particular character desired. (77)

This opposition may not have much analytical force at such a level of generalization, but unlike his *Sturm und Drang* predecessors Schlegel read Shakespeare with close attention to stylistic detail—a *sine qua non* for a critic who undertook what was to be the canonical German translation of Shakespeare. Where earlier critics had seen 'wild nature', Schlegel saw form. 'The works of genius', he declares, 'cannot therefore be permitted to be without form; but of this there is no danger' (73). Nature is not opposed to form but its very principle. Only to neo-classicist sticklers for 'stiff regularity' will Shakespeare look 'formless'; but their notion of form, Schlegel argues, is 'mechanical', concerned with accidentals and external additions, and not, as 'all genuine forms are', 'organical' (73-4). 'Organical form' becomes the watchword of Schlegel's poetics; it is 'innate; it unfolds itself from within, and requires its determination contemporaneously with the perfect development of the germ' (74). Under the auspices of 'organical form', a tragedy like *Romeo and Juliet*, for all its variety and seeming incongruities, will reveal its 'inner unity' (*innere Einheit*).[25]

Gaining currency through the international success of Schlegel's lectures,[26] the notion of a form that grows rather than being mechanically assembled owes much to Johann Gottfried Herder (1744-1803).[27] It was Herder who had awakened the young Goethe's interest in Shakespeare. He also became a formative influence on the Romantics. Critics as early as Addison had defended Shakespeare against the strictures of neoclassicism, but Herder put this defence on a completely new footing. He was the first to explain Shakespeare's divergence from the norms of classical tragedy historically. Up to the present, he writes, 'Shakespeare's boldest enemies' have claimed

that though he may be a great poet, he is not a good dramatist; or if he is a good dramatist, then he is not a classical tragedian equal in rank to men such as Sophocles, Euripides, Corneille, and Voltaire, who raised this art to the highest pinnacle of perfection. And Shakespeare's boldest friends have mostly been content to *excuse*, to *defend* him from such attacks; to weigh his beauties against his transgressions of the rules and see the former as compensation for the latter; to utter the *absolvo* over the accused; and then to deify his

---

[25] August Wilhelm Schlegel, 'Ueber Shakespeares Romeo und Julia. 1797', in *Sämmtliche Werke*, 12 vols., ed. Eduard Böcking, vol. 7 (Leipzig: Weidmann, 1846), 70–97 at 76 (my trans.).

[26] Cf. Christine Roger and Roger Paulin, 'August Wilhelm Schlegel', in *Voltaire, Goethe, Schlegel, Coleridge*, ed. Paulin, 92–127 at 120. 'There is much that is Herderian in Schlegel's critical language, not least the vocabulary of organic growth and processual development that so struck Coleridge when first reading him' (104).

[27] Herder derived it from Edward Young's *Conjectures on Original Composition* (1759), which, only a year after its English publication, appeared in two German translations and became a foundational manifesto of the *Genie*-movement. 'An *Original*', Young wrote, 'may be said to be of a *vegetable* nature; it rises spontaneously from the vital root of genius; it *grows*, it is not *made*'. Edward Young, *Conjectures on Original Composition*, ed. Edith J. Morley (Manchester: Manchester University Press, 1918), 7.

greatness all the more immoderately, the more they were compelled to shrug their shoulders at his faults.[28]

This unsatisfactory state of affairs could only be overcome, Herder argued, if the conditions from which Greek tragedy arose and the very different conditions in which Shakespeare flourished were properly taken into account. The 'new Athenians of Europe', as Herder mockingly calls the French, had not realized the unbridgeable gap between antiquity and the present, making their efforts at tragedy but 'an effigy outwardly resembling Greek drama; but the effigy lacks spirit, life, nature, truth' (21-2). Greek tragedy—its unity and simplicity of form—grew naturally from the unity and simplicity of Greek life; it was the perfect expression of its time and place of origin. Hence the seeming 'artificiality of the rules of Greek drama was—not artifice at all!' (9).

The conditions under which Shakespearean drama arose were entirely different. 'Shakespeare was confronted with nothing like the simplicity of national manners, deeds, inclinations, and historical traditions that formed the Greek drama' (28-9). And thus to demand that something like 'Greek drama arise then, and in England' and that it 'develop *naturally* ... is worse than asking a sheep to give birth to lion cubs' (26).

Herder's historicizing comparison between Shakespearean and Greek tragic drama not only informed the Romantics' view of Shakespeare, it established something like a ground pattern for the theoretical discussion of tragedy in the nineteenth century. In his lectures on *Aesthetics* (given between 1817 and 1829, published posthumously 1835-8), Hegel maintains the same distinction between the 'grand simplicity' of classical tragedy[29] and 'the infinite breadth of [Shakespeare's] "world-stage"' (1227) epitomizing the greater particularity of modern or 'romantic' tragedy. The heroes of classical tragedy are single-mindedly dedicated to the one aim that defines them: 'Throughout they are what they can and must be in accordance with their essential nature', Hegel writes; 'they are simply the *one* power dominating their own specific character' (1194). For illustration of this defining singleness of purpose he borrows Schlegel's image: 'Standing on this height, where the mere accidents of the individual's purely personal life disappear, the tragic heroes of [classical Greek] dramatic art have risen to become, as it were, works of sculpture' (1195).[30] In modern tragedy, by contrast, 'the principle of subjectivity' gains sway: 'Therefore it takes for its proper subject-matter and contents the subjective inner life of the character' (1223) and it places its characters on a much broader and much more open canvas, 'in the midst of a wide field of more or less accidental circumstances and conditions within which it is possible to act either in this way or in that' (1226). Hegel's conception of modern tragedy is predominantly modelled on Shakespeare, most crucially on *Hamlet*, the play that exemplifies the specific qualities, but also the pitfalls, of romantic art. Even

---

[28] Johann Gottfried Herder, *Shakespeare* (1773), ed. and trans. Gregory Moore (Princeton, NJ, and Oxford: Princeton University Press, 2008), 2-3. Page references in the text are to this edition.

[29] In the section on 'The Principle of Dramatic Poetry' he speaks of motivation in classical tragedy as being of a 'grand simplicity' (*großartige ... Einfachheit*). T. M. Knox renders this, less than felicitously, as 'the motives are of greater simplicity'. *Hegel's Aesthetics. Lectures on Fine Art*, 2 vols., ed. and trans. T. M. Knox, vol. 2 (Oxford: Clarendon Press, 1975), 1167. Page references in the text are to this edition.

[30] '[A]nd so in this respect', the paragraph concludes, 'the statues and images of the gods, rather abstract in themselves, explain the lofty tragic characters of the Greeks better than all other commentaries and notes.'

where Hamlet is not explicitly referred to, he is implicitly evoked by the very emphasis Hegel puts on what the heroes of classical tragedy are and do, and especially on what they are not and don't do:

> [T]hey act out of this character of theirs, on *this* pathos, because this character, this pathos is precisely what they are: their act is not preceded by either hesitation or choice. It is just the strength of the great characters that they do not choose but, throughout, from start to finish, *are* what they will and accomplish. They are what they are, and never anything else, and this is their greatness. (1214)

'[W]eakness in action', on the other hand, arises from 'a cleavage between the individual and his object'. Where this is the case and 'no fixed aim is alive in the individual's soul ... he may swither irresolutely from this to that and let caprice decide. From this swithering', Hegel concludes, 'the Greek [tragic heroes] are exempt' (1214). Unlike Herder and Schlegel, who had invoked history in order to bring Shakespearean drama up to par with classical tragedy, Hegel never leaves any doubt about his preference for the latter.

As Peter Szondi points out, 'Hegel accepts modern tragedy only with reservations', and 'even within Greek tragedy, he clearly favours one of the possible tragic collisions, the one that he finds ... most perfectly in *Antigone*, which he calls "the most magnificent and satisfying artwork ... of all the masterpieces of the ancient and modern world".[31] Nowhere is the 'self-division of the ethical' (19), the clash between two equally justified ethical forces so successfully exemplified as in the collision 'between love and law as they meet and clash in the figures of Antigone and Creon' (20). If *Antigone* embodies the quintessence of classical tragedy, *Hamlet* is the epitome of the modern. '[I]n the portrayal of concretely human individuals', Hegel writes, 'Shakespeare stands at an almost unapproachable height.' (Hegel, 2: 1227) But not even the excellence of this portrayal can make up for a shift from objective to subjective and for what Hegel sees as a concomitant weakening of the tragic substance of ancient tragedy. In Sophocles' *Electra*, Orestes, whose mother has married his father's murderer, pursues 'an ethically justified revenge' while 'being forced in the process to violate the ethical order.' (1225) Shakespeare's revenge tragedy, however, turns entirely 'on Hamlet's personal character':

> His noble soul is not made for this kind of energetic activity; and, full of disgust with the world and life, what with decision, proof, arrangements for carrying out his resolve, and being bandied from pillar to post, he eventually perishes owing to his own hesitation and a complication of external circumstances. (1226)

Hegel praises Shakespeare for endowing his dramatic characters with 'spirit and imagination', thus making them 'free artists of their own selves' (1227-8). He also points out that Shakespearean tragedy is by no means limited to the 'portrayal of vacillating characters inwardly divided against themselves' but also 'gives us ... the finest examples of firm and consistent characters who come to ruin simply because of [their] decisive adherence to themselves and their aims' (1229-30). Yet there is no mistaking that Hegel regards *Hamlet*, for all its greatness, as an altogether harmful example, one to be held accountable for what he finds most objectionable in modern tragedy, 'this personal

---

[31] Peter Szondi, *An Essay on the Tragic* (1961), trans. Paul Fleming (Stanford, CA: Stanford University Press, 2002), 20. Page references in the text are to this edition.

tragedy of inner discord', about which 'there is ... something now painful and sad, now aggravating':

> But what is worst of all is to exhibit such indecision and vacillation of character, and of the whole man, as a sort of perverse and sophistical dialectic and then to make it the main theme of the entire drama. (1229)[32]

Hegel's indignation seems less directed at Shakespeare's *Tragedy of Hamlet* itself than at Hamlet as the prototype, or role model, of a specifically modern 'character'. If, as Emerson put it, the nineteenth century's 'speculative genius is a sort of living Hamlet',[33] it is no wonder that in Germany, where this speculative bent flourished most unrestrainedly, Shakespeare's pensive Dane should prove an irresistible figure of identification. The portrayal of his predicament by Wilhelm Meister, the eponymous hero of Goethe's autobiographical *Bildungsroman* (1796),[34] set the tone for much subsequent psychologizing:

> [I]t is clear to me what Shakespeare set out to portray: a heavy deed placed on a soul which is not adequate to cope with it. And it is in this sense that I find the whole play constructed. An oak tree planted in a precious pot which should only have held delicate flowers. The roots spread out, the vessel is shattered. A fine, pure, noble and highly moral person, but devoid of that emotional strength that characterizes a hero, goes to pieces beneath a burden that it can neither support nor cast off.[35]

Schlegel was enthusiastic: with the Hamlet theme in *Wilhelm Meister* Shakespeare had 'risen from the dead and walks among the living'.[36]

The identification with Hamlet took a bitter, self-accusatory turn in Ferdinand Freiligrath's poem 'Hamlet' (1844), in which the hesitant prince epitomizes the ineffectual opposition to the repressive post-Napoleonic Restoration. 'Germany is Hamlet', the poem opens, yet this equation is anything but flattering. No longer 'lovely, pure, noble and most moral', Hamlet becomes an overweight slacker ('short of breath and too fat') who has hung around too long studying and drinking at Wittenberg University:

> Think of the oath you've sworn
> Revenge your father's ghost!
> What use is brooding on and on?
> But who am I to scold an old dreamer?
> After all, I am like you,
> You old waverer and laggard![37]

---

[32] NB: *Hamlet*, though unmistakably suggested by the passage is, again, not actually mentioned in it.

[33] Ralph Waldo Emerson, 'Shakespeare; or, the Poet', *Representative Men*, in Emerson, *Essays and Lectures*, ed. Joel Porte (New York: Library of America, 1983), 710–26 at 718.

[34] For a well-informed account of Goethe's evolving views on Hamlet, see Stephen Fennell, 'Johann Wolfgang Goethe', in *Voltaire, Goethe, Schlegel, Coleridge*, ed. Paulin, 44–91 at 61–72.

[35] Johann Wolfgang von Goethe, *Wilhelm Meister's Apprenticeship* (1795/6), trans. and ed. Eric A. Blackall, vol. 9, *The Collected Works* (Princeton, NJ: Princeton University Press, 1995), 146 (Book IV, ch. 13).

[36] August Wilhelm Schlegel, 'Etwas über William Shakespeare bei Gelegenheit Wilhelm Meisters' ['Something on William Shakespeare on the Occasion of Wilhelm Meister'], *Die Horen* 4 (1796), 57–112 at 24–5.

[37] Ferdinand Freiligrath, 'Hamlet', in *Ein Glaubensbekenntniß* (Mainz: von Zabern, 1844), 253–4.

In 1877 H. H. Furness alluded to Freiligrath's opening line in the dedication of his *New Variorum Hamlet* 'To the Shakespeare-Society of Weimar, representative of a people whose recent history has proved once for all that Germany is not Hamlet'.[38] Germany's national unification and ascent to great-power status after the Franco-Prussian War (1870/1) had created an entirely different political and mental climate. This was prefigured in the founding of the German Shakespeare Society in 1864, inspired by Franz Dingelstedt's production of the history cycle for the Weimar Shakespeare tercentenary. Popularization and 'nostrification', the patriotic mission of making Shakespeare 'our own', were primary goals, and so was, at least implicitly, the fostering of a national historical drama à la Shakespeare. However, the creative genius was lacking. Instead, the period's taste for history was served by sumptuous spectacles created by actor-managers such as Dingelstedt or Heinrich Laube. Theatrical historicism culminated in the productions of the Duke of Meiningen's troupe, applauded all over Europe for pictorial splendour and carefully choreographed crowd scenes. Their *pièce de résistance* was *Julius Caesar*, the tragedy perhaps most in tune with the spirit of late nineteenth-century imperialism. Between 1874 and 1890 the troupe gave a total of 330 performances of this one play.

By this time German Shakespeare reception had passed from poet-critics to scholars. The approach of the Romantics, always aiming at the totality of Shakespeare's art, gave way to enquiries of more limited scope. Psycho-philosophical 'character studies' in the wake of Hegel's *Aesthetics* were published by Hermann Ulrici (1839) and Friedrich Theodor Vischer (1860). Georg Gottfried Gervinus' biographical *Shakespeare* (1849/50) became a standard reference work. An increasingly specialized Shakespeare philology examined texts (Nikolaus Delius, 1846), sources, and records of the author's life and times.[39]

For practising dramatists the tragedies, no longer a source of inspiration, became a burden instead. Beset with a sense of epigonic belatedness,[40] the emerging writers of the 1820s and 30s found the unattainable heights of Shakespeare just as oppressive as the august eminence of the Weimar 'Olympians'. In his spirited attack against *Shakespearomania* (1827), Christian Dietrich Grabbe gave vent to the frustration of a talented playwright who found himself bogged down by a specifically German brand of bardolatry. Grabbe complained:

> The poor dramatic poets fare worst: if one of them writes in the spirit of Shakespeare ... people say: 'The man is an imitator, and see how he comes short of his master!' But if the poet is so bold as to write in his own way, the verdict is even harsher, for then 'the man is

---

[38] Horace Howard Furness, ed., *Hamlet. A New Variorum Edition of Shakespeare*, 2 vols. (Philadelphia and London: Lipincott, 1877).

[39] Hermann Ulrici, *Ueber Shakspeare's dramatische Kunst und sein Verhältniß zu Calderon und Göthe* (Halle: Anton, 1839); Friedrich Theodor Vischer, 'Shakspeare's Hamlet', *Kritische Gänge*, N.F. 2 (Stuttgart: Klett-Cotta, 1861) 63–156; Georg Gottfried Gervinus, *Shakespeare*, 4 vols. (Leipzig: Engelmann, 1849–52); Nikolaus Delius, *Die Tieck'sche Shakespearekritik* (Bonn: König, 1846).

[40] Karl Leberecht Immermann, *Die Epigonen. Familienmemoiren in 9 Büchern, 1823–1835* (1836) (Munich: Winkler, 1981).

on the wrong track, he would do better to study truth and nature not in themselves but in their only mirror, in Shakespeare.[41]

For the creation of a national drama—still the great task to which successive writers felt obligated—Grabbe declared Shakespeare simply the wrong model: 'Shakespeare does not deserve to be called the highest known specimen of tragedy' (50). That honour belonged to the Greeks, Aeschylus and Sophocles.

> Shakespeare never equalled them in tragedy; he ends his plays without satisfaction every time (in *Lear* even with cutting dissonance through the death of Cordelia) and the greatest comfort he gives us is usually that, after the villains have brought death and misery upon the good, there are a few minor characters left who we can hope will behave better than the criminals yet to be punished or already dead. (51)

Grabbe—aged 26 at the time of writing—admits to having once, in his precocious revenge tragedy *Gothland* (1822), shown symptoms of Shakespearomania himself and fervently exhorts his countrymen to eschew it. Other contemporary writers of serious drama such as Georg Büchner and Friedrich Hebbel were less vehement in their protestations but equally wary of the Bard's gravitational pull. Franz Grillparzer, however, was only too conscious of having succumbed to it: Shakespeare, he complained on the completion of his historical tragedy *The Fortune and Fall of King Ottokar* (1825), was 'tyrannizing his mind'.[42]

Grabbe scoffed that if a critic wanted to bolster his authority, he needed only 'point his finger at the great Shakespeare and call him the standard in a few empty phrases' (Grabbe, 30). But by the 1840s at the latest, deference to such irrefutable models could hardly be expected to produce more than arid academism. This did not prevent Gustav Freytag, in his hugely successful *Technique of Drama* (1863), from referring to the grand masters of the past as a repository of 'technical rules'[43] for the improvement of contemporary dramatic writing, which he found deplorably 'casual and uncertain' (4). Indiscriminate imitation of Shakespeare's English history plays with their 'epic' plot structure is at least partly to blame for this 'artless' slackness of form (41). But in other crucial respects Shakespeare, the creator of 'Germanic' drama, is unsurpassed:

> His treatment of the tragic, his regulation of the action, his manner of developing character, and his representation of soul experiences, have established for the introduction

---

[41] Christian Dietrich Grabbe, 'Über die Shakspearo-Manie' (1827), in Grabbe, *Werke und Briefe. Historisch-kritische Gesamtausgabe*, ed. Alfred Bergmann, vol. 4 (Emsdetten: Lechte, 1966), 27–55 at 30 (my trans.). Page references in the text are to this edition.

[42] Franz Grillparzer, *Selbstbiographien, autobiographische Notizen, Erinnerungen, Tagebücher, Briefe, Zeugnisse und Gespräche in Auswahl*, vol. 4, *Sämtliche Werke, ausgewählte Briefe, Gespräche, Berichte*, 4 vols., ed. Peter Frank and Karl Pörnbacher (Munich: Hanser: 1965), 384: 'Er tyrannisiert meinen Geist; und ich will frei bleiben. Ich danke Gott, dass er da ist und dass mir das Glück ward, ihn zu lesen und aufzunehmen in mich. Nun aber geht mein Streben dahin, ihn zu vergessen. Die Alten stärken mich, die Spanier regen mich zur Produktion an … Der Riese Shakespeare aber setzt sich selbst an die Stelle der Natur, deren herrlichstes Organ er war, und wer sich *ihm* ergibt, dem wird jede Frage, an *sie* gestellt, ewig nur *er* beantworten. Nichts mehr von Shakespeare! Die deutsche Literatur wird in seinem Abgrunde untergehen, wie sie aus ihm hervorgestiegen ist.'

[43] Gustav Freytag, *The Technique of the Drama. An Exposition of Dramatic Composition and Art* (1863), trans. Elias J. MacEwan (Chicago: Grigg, 1895), 2. By 1898 the German edition was in its 8th printing. Page references in the text are to this edition.

of the drama, and for the first half to the climax, many technical laws which still guide us. (7)

Romeo and Juliet is Freytag's paradigm of dramatic composition: using a narrative source 'specially unfavourable for the drama' (31), Shakespeare manages to convert a fortuitous sequence of events into an action whose every detail contributes to the enhancement of motivation and an overall impression of 'inherent necessity' (29).

Expressly not offered as a treatise on aesthetics but more as a guideline or manual of practical advice, the book succeeded in establishing its technical terms—ascending action, falling action, aggravating factor (*erregendes Moment*)—as the standard German vocabulary for the analysis of dramatic plot. What it predictably failed to induce was a rebirth of German drama. Such stirrings of renewal as did occur—though not until the 1880s—steered clear of Shakespearean emulation: Ibsen, not Shakespeare, inspired the naturalist drama of Gerhart Hauptmann and Arno Holz.[44]

But Shakespeare did figure prominently in the gestation of nineteenth-century Germany's most important contribution to dramatic art, the music drama of Richard Wagner. Wagner's lifelong admiration for Shakespeare, 'mightiest poet of all time',[45] can be traced in echoes of Shakespearean tragedy throughout his operas—in, for example, the fated love of Tristan and Isolde (its love-potion reminiscent of *Romeo and Juliet*) or Wotan's Lear-like self-tormentings in *Die Walküre*. Wagner's most sustained reflection on Shakespearean drama occurs in his treatise on *Opera and Drama* (1851). Shakespeare's epochal achievement, he argues, is the conjoining of two hitherto separate art forms, *Roman* and *Volksschaubühne*—narrative romance[46] and popular theatre: Shakespeare 'condensed the narrative Romance into the Drama, inasmuch as he translated it, so to say, for performance on the stage'.[47] Shakespeare's discovery of the popular stage tapped into a rich 'subterranean stream of genuine Folk's-artwork' which 'till then had hidden from the Poet's eye' (127). But this provenance from the *Roman*, Wagner argues, has been a harmful legacy for the imitators of Shakespearean drama and 'the cause and starting point of an unparalleled confusion in dramatic art for over two centuries, and down to the present day' (130). Shakespeare's multi-scenic dramaturgy has proved incompatible with the development of the modern stage and its bent towards 'the most realistic actuality' (138). The dilemma is the same as pointed out by Charles Lamb: '[T]he reading of a tragedy is a fine abstraction', but in stage performance the imperfections of material illusion, 'acting, scenery, dress, the most contemptible things' distract from 'the main interest of the play'. Wagner obviously does not share Lamb's opinion 'that the plays of Shakespeare are less calculated for performance on a stage than those of almost any other dramatist whatever' (Lamb, 312). But neither does he put his hope (as Ludwig Tieck did) in a restitution of the original Elizabethan stage

---

[44] Among Hauptmann's late works, though, is *Hamlet in Wittenberg* (1935), a play using the same title as Gutzkow's 100 years earlier.

[45] Richard Wagner, 'The Art-Work of the Future' (1849), in *Richard Wagner's Prose Works*, 3 vols., trans. William Ashton Ellis, vol. 1 (London: Kegan Paul, Trench, Trübner, 1895), 69–213 at 141.

[46] German *Roman* covers both novel and romance: *War and Peace* as well as the *Aethiopica* of Heliodorus and, of course, medieval verse narrative such as the *Roman de la Rose*.

[47] Richard Wagner, *Opera and Drama* (1851), trans. William Ashton Ellis (London: Kegan Paul, Trench, Trübner, 1893), 127. Page references in the text are to this edition.

conditions. Such restorative attempts, he says, have always proved futile. In sum, then, Shakespeare is of prime historical importance and a lasting source of creative energy; but he is not, for Wagner, a model for the drama of the future. That drama 'will be born from the satisfaction of a need which Shakespearian Drama has aroused but not yet stilled' (Wagner, *Opera and Drama*, 127).

For Wagner's admirer Nietzsche, *The Birth of Tragedy from the Spirit of Music*[48] implied that its rebirth could only take place in Wagnerian music drama. It is tempting to speculate what role Shakespeare might have been allotted in this grand trajectory from ancient to modern if, as has been suggested, 'Nietzsche did indeed plan a middle section on Shakespeare, but abandoned it.[49] As it stands, *The Birth of Tragedy* is silent on Shakespearean tragedy as such but offers a telling comment on the character of Hamlet which goes to the heart of Nietzsche's argument, his exposition of the Dionysian experience. This experience with its ecstatic dissolution of boundaries 'contains ... a *lethargic* element'. A 'chasm of oblivion' separates it from 'the worlds of everyday reality'. But only for as long as it lasts. When the Dionysian experience is over and reality returns, revulsion ensues:

> In this sense the Dionysian man resembles Hamlet: both have once looked truly into the essence of things, they have *gained knowledge*, and nausea inhibits action; ... Knowledge kills action; action requires the veils of illusion: that is the doctrine of Hamlet, not that cheap wisdom of Jack the Dreamer who reflects too much and, as it were, from an excess of possibilities does not get around to action. Not reflection, no – true knowledge, an insight into the horrible truth, outweighs any motive for action, both in Hamlet and in the Dionysian man.[50]

Instead of a Werther-like flaccidity and, as Hegel had portrayed him, 'the inactivity of a beautiful inner soul which cannot make itself actual' (a 'Jack the Dreamer'), Nietzsche's Hamlet directs his unflinching gaze into the terrible abyss of existence. His inaction bespeaks not his inability to come to a 'firm decision' (Hegel, 1: 584), but his contempt for action, the 'pessimism of strength'[51] which Nietzsche pitted against both the conventional image of Hellenic serenity and the self-congratulatory optimism of the newly-united German *Reich*. While Hegel saw the *Weltgeist* reaching its telos in the Prussian state, Nietzsche sees hope for spiritual rebirth only in a turning away from that state and its self-important philistinism. In Hamlet, the disaffected outsider at the raucously festive court of Denmark, this turning away finds its iconic embodiment and Nietzsche a kind of fictional alter ego.[52] *Julius*

---

[48] Thus the original title of the book on its first publication in 1872 (*Die Geburt der Tragödie aus dem Geiste der Musik*); it was reissued in 1886 as *The Birth of Tragedy, Or: Hellenism and Pessimism* (*Die Geburt der Tragödie. Oder: Griechenthum und Pessimismus*) and augmented by a prefatory essay 'An Attempt at Self-Criticism'. Nietzsche's breach with Wagner postdates *The Birth of Tragedy* by five or six years.

[49] Paulin, *Critical Reception of Shakespeare*, 457. Paulin adduces several fragments from the *Nachlass* to corroborate his thesis but the evidence is far from conclusive.

[50] Friedrich Nietzsche, *The Birth of Tragedy*, § 7, in Nietzsche, *Basic Writings* (1967), ed. and trans. Walter Kaufmann (New York: Modern Library, 2000), 1–144 at 59–60.

[51] Nietzsche, *Birth of Tragedy*, 'Attempt at a Self-Criticism', § 1, 17.

[52] On Nietzsche's identification with Hamlet, see Peter Holbrook, 'Nietzsche's Hamlet', *Shakespeare Survey* 50 (1997), 171–86.

Caesar is another life-long reference point in Nietzsche's thinking.[53] In his final self-assessment in *Ecce Homo* (1888), the two become complementary self-portrayals of their creator (whom Nietzsche takes to be none other than Lord Bacon!), who in turn figures as a mirror image of the autobiographical subject of *Ecce Homo*:

> When I seek my ultimate formula for *Shakespeare*, I always find only this: he conceived of the type of Caesar. That sort of thing cannot be guessed: one either is it, or one is not. The great poet dips *only* from his own reality – up to the point where afterward he cannot endure his work any longer. When I have looked into my *Zarathustra*, I walk up and down in my room for half an hour, unable to master an unbearable fit of sobbing. I know no more heart-rending reading than Shakespeare: what must a man have suffered to have such a need of being a buffoon![54]

Equally disdainful of Wilhelmine culture and of liberal modernity in general as Nietzsche, the poet Stephan George and his circle cultivated an image of Shakespeare that was similarly opposed to the mainstream views and philological approaches supported by university scholarship and the German Shakespeare Society.[55] Like Dante, Goethe, and, of course, 'the Master' himself (as George was called by his disciples), Shakespeare, belonged in the exclusive pantheon of preeminent minds on whom the spiritual aristocracy of the *New Empire* would be modelled, the mystical utopia outlined in George's last volume of poems, *Das neue Reich* (1928). George himself translated, or rather 'recreated' (the word he uses is *Umdichtung*), Shakespeare's sonnets in a rigorously 'difficult', anti-romantic style.

George's disciple Friedrich Gundolf used the same deliberately elitist principles in reworking the already canonical Schlegel-Tieck translation, which he called the only lasting masterpiece of German Romanticism. Notwithstanding this exclusivist bias, Gundolf's *Shakespeare und der deutsche Geist* (1911) became that rare thing, an academic bestseller. It presents a narrative of self-discovery in which Shakespeare is the catalyst enabling 'the German spirit' to come into its own. Reaching its climax with Goethe on the one hand and the Schlegel-Tieck translation on the other, Gundolf's narrative dismisses all that followed: historicism and naturalism appear as the twin blights of the nineteenth century. For Gundolf, Shakespeare towers not only over this recent stage of cultural decline but over his own time, and indeed any time in history. He is the absolute poet, in no way dependent on or conditioned by the circumstances of his mundane existence. Transcending all moral and religious restrictions, he is 'the human embodiment of the creative force of life itself.'[56]

---

[53] See, for example, *The Gay Science* § 98; *Ecce Homo* 'Why I Am So Clever', § 4, and a school essay written in 1863, which offers 'A Character Description of Cassius from Julius Caesar'.

[54] Friedrich Nietzsche, *Ecce Homo*, 'Why I Am So Clever', § 4, in *Basic Writings*, trans./ed. Kaufmann, 655–791 at 702–3. For a detailed discussion of the passage see Christian Benne, 'Ecce Hanswurst—Ecce Hamlet: Rollenspiele in *Ecce Homo*', *Nietzscheforschung. Jahrbuch der Nietzsche-Gesellschaft* 12 (2005), 219–28; Scott Wilson, 'Reading Shakespeare with Intensity: A Commentary on Some Lines from Nietzsche's *Ecco Homo*', in *Philosophical Shakespeares*, ed. John J. Joughin (London: Routledge, 2000), 86–104; and Andreas Höfele, *Stage, Stake, and Scaffold: Human and Animals in Shakespeare's Theatre* (Oxford: Oxford University Press, 2011), 263–6.

[55] Ruth Freifrau von Ledebur, *Der Mythos vom deutschen Shakespeare: die Deutsche Shakespeare-Gesellschaft zwischen Politik und Wissenschaft, 1918-1945* (Cologne, Weimar, and Vienna: Böhlau, 2002).

[56] Gundolf, *Shakespeare und der deutsche Geist*, p. vii.

In the same year, 1928, in which Gundolf expanded this Nietzschean vision in his, again highly successful, two-volume study of Shakespeare's plays (*Shakespeare. Sein Wesen und Werk*), a publication little noticed at the time took a diametrically opposed view. This was Walter Benjamin's *Ursprung des deutschen Trauerspiels* (*Origin of the German Mourning Play*). Not time-transcending life forces, but the force of history, Benjamin argues, is the chief determinant of the baroque *Trauerspiel*, a genre radically misunderstood when measured by the standards of classicist aesthetics of tragedy. Though *Trauerspiel* and 'tragedy' have been habitually treated as synonyms (and in common usage still are), the crucial difference, he maintains, is that tragedy deals with myth, *Trauerspiel* with history. Thus it is the sovereign rather than the hero who moves centre-stage. He is 'the representative of history', Benjamin writes,[57] drawing on seventeenth-century political theology as expounded by Carl Schmitt. The sovereign appears in two contrary yet intimately related guises: the tyrant and the martyr, the latter inevitably evoking the dual, divine and human, nature of Jesus Christ. But despite these Christological overtones—and again in contrast to tragedy—'[i]n the *Trauerspiel* monarch and martyr do not shake off their immanence' (67). The fall from which the *Trauerspiel* draws its pathos, its source of *Trauer* (sorrow, mourning), is the monarch's 'fall[ing] victim to the disproportion between the unlimited hierarchical dignity with which he is divinely invested and the humble estate of his humanity' (70). Benjamin closely anticipates Ernst Kantorowicz's *The King's Two Bodies* (1957) here and especially Kantorowicz's reading of *Richard II*, the play in the Shakespeare canon that lends itself more readily than any other—except perhaps *King Lear*—to being read as a Benjaminian *Trauerspiel*. However, it should not be forgotten that Benjamin's focus is not on Shakespeare but on the German drama of the period—plays so solemn that they make *Gorboduc* look fleet-footed. Clearly Shakespeare, as well as Calderon, is included in Benjamin's ambit of the baroque and thus the *Trauerspiel*. *Hamlet*, for example, is defended against squeamish detractors of its final bloodbath: 'The death of Hamlet, which has no more in common with tragic death than the prince himself has with Ajax, is in its drastic externality characteristic of the *Trauerspiel*' (136–7). But there are just as many instances in Benjamin's treatise where Shakespeare is what the *Trauerspiel* is not: subtle, psychological, suffused with a sense of the real, dare we say: modern.

The question of whether Shakespearean tragedy can be properly subsumed under the category of 'tragedy' at all—and if so, with what qualifications—raises the more general question of the survival of tragedy in a secular modern world.[58] Where this secularism is strongest, the answer is most decisive: there is hence no place for tragedy in Brecht. Shakespeare and his contemporaries provide welcome precedents of epic and non-condescendingly popular theatre; but the tragic fall of Shakespeare's heroes can only serve to abet the two cardinal errors of what Brecht summarily calls Aristotelian dramaturgy: the arousal of empathy and a sense of inevitability. Neither can be tolerated in a theatre whose intended target audience, the 'children of the scientific age', derive particular enjoyment from being shown the changeability of the world. Shakespearean heroes

---

[57] Walter Benjamin, *The Origin of German Tragic Drama*, introd. George Steiner, trans. John Osborne (London and New York: Verso, 1998), 65. Page references in the text are to this edition.

[58] In view of the recent global resurgence of religion, we may feel less confident today to speak of the present as the 'secular modern world', but for the twentieth-century authors discussed in this chapter the label holds good.

have no place in this historical-materialist world either, except to be lampooned as remnants of a feudal past and its ideological delusions. Thus Hamlet is demoted to the status of 'introspective sponger' in Brecht's sonnet of 1938,[59] and his adaptation of *Coriolanus* for the Berlin Ensemble (begun in 1951 and never completed) drives home the idea that society neither needs heroes, nor should worship them.[60]

At the opposite end of the political spectrum, heroes and tragedies fit seamlessly into the armoury of right-wing ideologies. The theatre of the new era, as outlined by Goebbels in 1933, 'was to be 'heroic', 'steely-romantic', 'unsentimentally direct', and 'national with grand pathos', or else it would 'not be at all'.[61] By and large this new national drama failed to materialize. Yet the debate over which traditional model it should emulate generated considerable heat. The classification of Shakespeare as Germanic or Nordic, first suggested by Gerstenberg[62] and Herder[63] and now pumped up with Nazi racism,[64] would seem to have made the Bard the natural choice. But controversy ensued over whether Greek tragedy might not provide a better model than Shakespeare. Curt Langenbeck, head dramaturge at the Bavarian State Theatre and one of the Third Reich's up-and-coming dramatic talents went on record as an outspoken anti-Shakespearean. His pamphlet with the Nietzschean title *The Rebirth of Drama from the Spirit of the Times* (1940) pronounced Shakespeare obsolete: he was, Langenbeck declares, the undisputed

> king of drama in that whole epoch which we have called the epoch of tragic individualism. But because we, the Germans of today, are about to ring out this epoch, Shakespeare, much though we may still admire his art, has nothing of relevance to say to us anymore; he cannot help us advance on the new road that we know to be the right one.[65]

As that road bent more and more foreseeably towards disaster, Langenbeck's own exercise in the tragic mode surprised reviewers with a tone more Shakespearean, reminiscent of *Macbeth*, than Hellenic. *Treue* (1944) propagated an ethos of perseverance at all cost which found its dreadful realization in the self-destructive bloodshed Hitler and his paladins enforced on their own population during the final months of the war.

---

[59] Bertolt Brecht, 'On Shakespeare's Play *Hamlet*', in Brecht, *Poems*, trans. John Willet, ed. John Willet and Ralph Manheim (London: Methuen, 1981), 321. Cf. Maria Elisa Montironi, 'The Introspective Sponger: *Hamlet* in the Poetry of Bertolt Brecht', *New Readings* 12 (2012), 19–34.

[60] The Real Socialism (*real existierender Sozialismus*) under which Brecht worked was, of course, anything but averse to hero worship. 'Work Hero' (*Held der Arbeit*) was one of the highest non-military medals awarded in the GDR.

[61] Werner Habicht, 'Shakespeare and Theatre Politics in the Third Reich', in *The Play Out of Context: Transferring Plays from Culture to Culture*, ed. Hannah Scolnicov and Peter Holland (Cambridge: Cambridge University Press, 1989), 110–20 at 110.

[62] Heinrich Wilhelm von Gerstenberg, *Briefe über Merkwürdigkeiten der Litteratur*, 2 vols., vol. 2 (Schleswig and Leipzig: Hansen, 1767).

[63] Johann Gottfried Herder, 'Von Aehnlichkeit der mittlern englischen und deutschen Dichtkunst, nebst Verschiednem, das daraus folget', *Deutsches Museum* 2:11 (1777), 421–35. Herder classes not only Shakespeare but English literature as a whole as 'Germanic'.

[64] See Habicht, 'Shakespeare and Theatre Politics in the Third Reich', 112.

[65] Curt Langenbeck, *Die Wiedergeburt des Dramas aus dem Geist der Zeit. Eine Rede* (Munich: Langen Müller, 1940), 36. For a more extended discussion of Langenbeck's position see Andreas Höfele, 'The Rebirth of Tragedy, or No Time for Shakespeare (Germany 1940)', *Renaissance Drama* 38 (2010), 251–68.

After the demise of Hitler's Reich, the division of Germany produced two separate interpretative traditions focusing on the dialectics of class struggle in the East and the timeless
dilemmas of the human condition in the West. Thus the perception of Shakespeare's tragedies in the two postwar German states reflected the ideological rift of the Cold War. A curious exception to the determinedly apolitical approach to tragedy in the West was the slim
and, at the time, almost unnoticed volume on *Hamlet* published by Carl Schmitt: *Hamlet
or Hecuba, or, The Intrusion of Time into the Play*.[66] A brilliant law professor and political theorist, but compromised by his role as a prominent supporter of the Nazi regime,[67]
Schmitt turned to *Hamlet* in the firm conviction that this forever puzzling case had been
solved once for all. Sigmund Freud pointed to the Oedipal triangle, declaring, with almost
Polonius-like certainty, '*that* has made him mad'. Schmitt, dismissing Freudian and all other
extant Hamlet speculations as baseless, points to Elizabethan politics and Mary Queen of
Scots as the guilty queen whose complicity in the murder of her husband, Lord Darnley, is
neither quite admitted nor quite denied in the enigmatic figure of Gertrude. This reading of
Shakespeare's hesitant prince as the fictional doppelganger of Elizabeth's hesitant Scottish
successor James had lain well-nigh forgotten in Lilian Winstanley's quirky *Hamlet and the
Scottish Succession* (1921).[68]

Schmitt goes beyond Winstanley in making her 'findings' the basis of his own theory
of tragedy. For this he draws on Walter Benjamin's distinction between tragedy and
Trauerspiel. But whereas Benjamin had made the distinction in a bid to rehabilitate the
much-maligned genre of the baroque *Trauerspiel* and its characteristic allegorical mode,[69]
Schmitt turns the distinction into a hierarchical one, claiming for *Hamlet* the higher
status of tragedy at the same time as he relentlessly allegorizes its characters and plot. For
a play to qualify as tragedy it must become more than just 'play' (*Spiel* or, more specifically,
Trauerspiel); it must rise to the level of myth. This can only be effected through the 'genuine intrusion'[70] of a truly epochal event or figure. The fate of James I constitutes such an intrusion. The taboo of his mother's alleged complicity in the murder of his father accounts
for the major blind spot in *Hamlet*: the irresolvable question of Gertrude's guilt. And what
Schmitt calls the 'Hamletization of the avenger' is directly due to the figure of James himself, the overly thoughtful, hesitant prince entangled in 'the fate of the European religious
schism' that killed his mother and his son Charles and would eventually shatter the whole

[66] Carl Schmitt, *Hamlet oder Hekuba: Der Einbruch der Zeit in das Spiel*
(Düsseldorf: Diederichs, 1956).

[67] Deploying his legal expertise to justify the dismantling of constitutional and civil rights by
the Nazis between 1933 and 1936, Schmitt applauded both the 'night of the long knives' and the
Nuremberg race laws. The pre-eminent jurist of the Third Reich, he fell out of favour with the regime
following an intrigue hatched by Nazi rivals within the legal profession.

[68] Lilian Winstanley, *Hamlet and the Scottish Succession. Being an Examination of the Relations
of the Play of Hamlet to the Scottish Succession and the Essex Conspiracy* (Cambridge: Cambridge
University Press, 1921).

[69] The downgrading of allegory as opposed to symbol had its most influential advocate in Goethe,
who credited symbol as being directly related to 'the nature of poetry'. Johann Wolfgang von Goethe,
Maxims and Reflections, trans. Elisabeth Stopp, ed. Peter Hutchinson (Harmondsworth: Penguin,
1998), 34.

[70] Carl Schmitt, *Hamlet or Hecuba: The Intrusion of the Time into the Play*, ed. and trans. David
Pan and Jennifer R. Rust (New York: Telos Press, 2009), 25. Page references in the text are to this
edition.

royal line of 'the unhappy Stuarts' (52). Shakespeare's tragedy owes its mythical force to the fact that the intrusion of history at its inception continues to reverberate through the subsequent even greater shatterings of European history. Thus Hamlet, doomed to see, but unable to 'restrain',[71] disaster, becomes not only 'the mythical figure of the European intellectual',[72] but the 'hieroglyph of the Western world', as Schmitt notes on a postcard dated 1 August 1956 to Ernst Jünger:

> 1848: Germany is Hamlet
> 1918: Europe is Hamlet
> 1958: the whole Western world is Hamlet[73]

Schmitt, who died in 1985 at the age of 97, did not live long enough to see his pessimism reversed by the 1989 watershed in German and world history.

'The Turn' of 1989 replaced Hamlet with Fortinbras as the iconic representative of the West. Fortinbras's entrance in a business suit and a golden mask—a star warrior of capitalism—marked the end of Heiner Müller's seven-and-a-half-hour production of *Hamlet* (including, as a kind of interlude, Müller's own *Hamletmachine*), which opened at the Deutsches Theater in East Berlin in March 1990.[74] Rehearsed as the old Communist order was disintegrating and presented to the public after it had ceased to exist, Müller's *Hamlet/Machine* constituted a gigantic postmortem of the GDR as well as Shakespeare's tragedy. When Hamlet (Ulrich Mühe) speaks for the first time he utters the words that are usually his last: 'I die, Horatio. The rest is silence.'

From premises quite other than Schmitt's, Müller's engagement with Shakespeare is similarly obsessed with the 'felt ultimacies' of history. His relation to Shakespeare is that of an anatomist.[75] Following Brecht's demand that the classics be salvaged for their 'material value' (*Materialwert*), Müller's Shakespeare adaptations relentlessly strip away any moral sugarcoating, any pretensions to heroism or greatness 'that he thought euphemized or disguised barbaric historical realities'.[76] The 'fall from great height' formerly needed to give the fall of the hero its

---

[71] From the 1940s onwards, the figure of the 'restrainer' (*katéchon*) is of central importance in Schmitt's theology of history. He is the one who holds up or slows down the Antichrist's seizure of power before the Second Coming.

[72] This identification, in a lecture given in January 1957, includes Schmitt himself. Carl Schmitt, 'Hamlet als mythische Figur der Gegenwart' ('Hamlet as a Mythical Figure of the Present'), 1. The unpublished lecture is among the Schmitt papers in the Landesarchiv NRW, Abteilung Rheinland, Standort Düsseldorf, RW 265–302 II.

[73] *Ernst Jünger/Carl Schmitt: Briefe 1930–1983*, ed. Helmuth Kiesel (Stuttgart: Klett-Cotta, 1999), 310. The 'hieroglyph' also appears in a letter to Armin Mohler, 15 July 1956: *Carl Schmitt: Briefwechsel mit einem seiner Schüler*, ed. Armin Mohler (Berlin: Akademie-Verlag, 1995), 220. See my essay Andreas Höfele, 'Hamlet in Plettenberg: Carl Schmitt's Shakespeare', *Shakespeare Survey* 65 (2013), 378–97.

[74] I am drawing on my review article Andreas Höfele, 'A Theater of Exhaustion? 'Posthistoire' in Recent German Shakespeare Productions', *Shakespeare Quarterly* 43 (1992), 8–6 at 84-–5. For a more extensive review of the production see Maik Hamburger, '1989 to 1990: Hamlet at World's End. Heiner Müller's Production in East Berlin', in Hortmann, *Shakespeare on the German Stage*, 428–34.

[75] Müller's adaptation of *Titus Andronicus* is titled *Anatomie Titus Fall of Rome* and bears the motto: 'Opening up/mankind's arteries like a book/and leafing through the bloodstream'. Heiner Müller, *Shakespeare Factory* 2 (Berlin: Rotbuch Verlag, 1989), 125–226 (my trans.).

[76] Jonathan Kalb, *The Theater of Heiner Müller* (Cambridge: Cambridge University Press, 1998), 88.

tragic dimension is radically shortened; but where Brecht had cut the hero down to size in the name of enlightened rationality and historical progress, Müller discards both rationality and progress. No heroes, nor even anti-heroes, let alone anything resembling a Hegelian 'sublation' of conflict, alleviate the bleak *Grand Guignol* of his *Macbeth* (1971) and *Anatomy of Titus* (1984), 'in which bloodied and bloodthirsty puppet-like creatures try to become human beings by escaping from the string of gruesome, fragmentary dramas called "history"'.[77]

The zero point of tragedy is reached in Müller's *Hamletmachine*, the 9-page, densely packed intertextual collage that grew from his work on a *Hamlet* translation in 1976-7.[78] Stripping the most famous of tragedies 'to [its] skeleton', rid[ding] it of [its] flesh and surface',[79] *Hamletmachine* not only denies the possibility of tragic heroes, but discards the very idea of subjective identity, an idea iconically embodied in Hamlet. A score made up of floating, dislocated monologues, it is 'post-' in just about every conceivable respect. Post-dramatic, post-representational, and post-historic, it tolls not only the death of the author, whose (i.e. Müller's) photograph is solemnly torn, but the death of tragedy as well, which can only be conceived of as a remembrance of things past. *Hamletmachine* opens with: 'I was Hamlet. I stood at the shore and talked with the surf BLABLA, the ruins of Europe in back of me.' What remains of tragedy in this ventriloquizing of the undead is the sheer, irreducible pathos of suffering located in the voice of Ophelia. And here is also a perspective for the future: the victim breaking from the prison of eternal recurrence:

> I am Ophelia. The one the river didn't keep. The woman dangling from the rope. The woman with her arteries cut open. The woman with the overdose. SNOW ON HER LIPS. The woman with her head in the gas stove. Yesterday I stopped killing myself. I'm alone with my breasts my thighs my womb. I smash the tools of my captivity, the chair the table the bed. I destroy the battlefield that was my home. I fling open the doors so the wind gets in and the scream of the world. I smash the window. With my bleeding hands I tear the photos of the men I loved and who used me on the bed on the table on the chair on the ground. I set fire to my prison. I throw my clothes into the fire. I wrench the clock that was my heart out of my breast. I walk into the street clothed in my blood.[80]

SELECT BIBLIOGRAPHY

Blinn, Hansjürgen, ed., *Shakespeare-Rezeption: Die Diskussion um Shakespeare in Deutschland*, 2 vols. (Berlin: Erich Schmidt, 1982, 1988).
Habicht, Werner, 'Romanticism, Antiromanticism, and the German Shakespeare Tradition', in *Shakespeare and Cultural Traditions*, ed. Tetsuo Kishi, Roger Pringle and Stanley Wells (Newark, DE: University of Delaware Press, 1994), 243–52.

---

[77] Ibid., 92.

[78] Heiner Müller, *Hamletmachine and Other Texts for the Stage*, ed. and trans. Carl Weber (New York: PAJ, 1984); the *Hamlet*-translation (with Matthias Langhoff) is in Müller, *Shakespeare Factory* 2, 7-123.

[79] In an interview, Müller spoke of his obsession with *Hamlet*: '[S]o I tried to destroy him by writing a short text, *Hamletmachine*.... I think the main impulse is to strip things to their skeleton, to rid them of their flesh and surface. Then you are finished with them.' Heiner Müller, *Rotwelsch* (Berlin: Merve, 1982), 43.

[80] Müller, *Hamletmachine*, 53-4.

Habicht, Werner, *Shakespeare and the German Imagination* (Hertford: Stephen Austin and Sons for the International Shakespeare Association, 1994).

Habicht, Werner, 'Shakespeare and Theatre Politics in the Third Reich', in *The Play Out of Context: Transferring Plays from Culture to Culture*, ed. Hannah Scolnicov and Peter Holland (Cambridge: Cambridge University Press, 1989), 110–20.

Höfele, Andreas, *No Hamlets: German Shakespeare from Nietzsche to Carl Schmitt* (Oxford: Oxford University Press, 2016).

Hortmann, Wilhelm, *Shakespeare on the German Stage: The Twentieth Century. With an Essay by Maik Hamburger* (Cambridge: Cambridge University Press, 1998).

Ledebur, Ruth Freifrau von, *Der Mythos vom deutschen Shakespeare: die Deutsche Shakespeare-Gesellschaft zwischen Politik und Wissenschaft, 1918–1945* (Cologne, Weimar, and Vienna: Böhlau, 2002).

Ledebur, Ruth Freifrau von, *Deutsche Shakespeare-Rezeption seit 1945* (Frankfurt am Main: Akademische Verlags-Gesellschaft, 1974).

Paulin, Roger, ed., *Voltaire, Goethe, Schlegel, Coleridge*, vol. 3, *Great Shakespeareans*, ed. Adrian Poole and Peter Holland (London and New York: Continuum, 2011).

Paulin, Roger, *The Critical Reception of Shakespeare in Germany 1682–1914: Native Literature and Foreign Genius* (Hildesheim, Zurich, and New York: Olms, 2003).

Pfister, Manfred, 'Germany is Hamlet: The History of a Political Interpretation', *New Comparison* 2 (1986), 106–26.

Szondi, Peter, *An Essay on the Tragic* (1961), trans. Paul Fleming (Stanford, CA: Stanford University Press, 2002).

Williams, Simon, *Shakespeare on the German Stage 1586–1914* (Cambridge: Cambridge University Press, 1990).

CHAPTER 44

FRENCH RECEPTIONS OF SHAKESPEAREAN TRAGEDY
Between Liberty and Memory

PASCALE DROUET AND
NATHALIE RIVÈRE DE CARLES

ALAIN, in his *Essays on Aesthetics*, synthesized the twofold approach to Shakespearean tragedy in France when he mockingly announced: 'If *Hamlet* fell down to Earth, naked, without its procession of admirers, the critics would mock it, not without the semblance of a reason.'[1] Contrasting a critic's obsessive quest for the essence of a work of art as opposed to its existence, the philosopher emphasized an enduring dualism in the French reception of Shakespeare in general, and his tragic plays in particular. Between Voltaire's harsh rejection and the Romantics' blind adoration of the black sun, Shakespeare generated a dialogue in French art that made a very English playwright into a natural part of the French dramatic canon. Alain's ambiguous take on *Hamlet* reveals the key to the French fascination with Shakespeare and his tragedies: their imperfection. The elasticity and absorptive nature of the Shakespearean script makes it a malleable work of art which retains its singularity but also adapts to other forms of creativity.

Whether irreverent, excessively respectful, destructive or regenerative, the reception of Shakespearean tragedies in France involves a double dialogue: namely *a vertical one* 'between the past and the present, and also … some *lateral dialogue* in which crossing boundaries of place or language or genre is as important as crossing those of time'.[2] The vertical form of dialogue is part of the creative process of realizing a Renaissance work of art and gives it its timeless flexibility. However, the power of their reception on the French stage is best expressed in the lateral form of dialogue. This chapter will treat the vertical, historiographical dialogue as both a natural cause and consequence of the lateral dialogue, which takes four shapes: the critical reception of Shakespeare's tragedies, their linguistic reception, their stage reception, and finally their refiguration or metamorphosis

---

[1] Alain, *Propos sur l'esthétique* (Paris: Stock, 1923), 88 (our translation).
[2] Lorna Hardwick, *Reception Studies* (Oxford: Oxford University Press, 2003), 4.

into an alphabet for new works. The dialogue between the past and the present will form the thread of each lateral form of reception.

Starting with the critical reception, the chapter will show how Shakespeare's tragedy became the instrument of a reflection on Liberty. The stage dynamic of destruction and regeneration of Shakespearean tragedies called for new liberated approaches to French dramatic language. Shakespeare thus became a laboratory where translators, adaptors, stage directors and actors would put their trade to the test of a protean script and free themselves from the strictures of tradition.

CRITICAL AND LINGUISTIC DIALOGUES WITH SHAKESPEARE'S TRAGEDY

Critical familiarity with Shakespearean tragedies required French translations. Translators, whether critics or not, were the first to initiate an intellectual dialogue with Shakespeare's plays with the aim of understanding them thoroughly enough to prove worthy *transmitters of the original*. Dialogue also lies at the heart of the critical practice that aims at a fruitful, stimulating plurality of interpretations. Two writers and critics of our time have emphasized this idea. For poet and critic Yves Bonnefoy, who prefaced and translated many Shakespearean plays, the Elizabethan playwright is welcoming, in the sense that he invites reading, and favours what Bonnefoy terms a 'transitive', that is, a direct author-reader relationship.[3] For philosopher Daniel Sibony, when confronting the text, 'one is immediately connected and in dialogue with the texture of the play, with its poetic breath in the making, with the vivid, sustained plot it unfolds, with the *soul* of its atmosphere'.[4] It is as if Shakespeare invited dialogic responses from both critics and translators.

From 'upstart crow' to the Bard of Liberty

Although Voltaire's response was less dialogic than others, it contributed to introducing Shakespearean drama to eighteenth-century France. Deeming them 'without the smallest spark of taste, and void of the remotest idea of rules', Voltaire labelled Shakespearean tragedies 'monstrous farces'.[5] When Voltaire aesthetically condemned

---

[3] Yves Bonnefoy, *L'amitié et la réflexion*, ed. Daniel Lançon and Stephen Romer (Tours: Presses Universitaires François-Rabelais, 2007), 10, 37–8.

[4] Daniel Sibony, *Avec Shakespeare. Éclat et passion en douze pièces* (Paris: Éditions du Seuil, 2003), 10 (our translation). The emphasis is Sibony's.

[5] Voltaire, 'English Tragedy', in *The Works of Voltaire. A Contemporary Version*, A critique and biography by John Morley, notes by Tobias Smollett, trans. William F. Fleming, 21 vols. (New York: E. R. DuMont, 1901), vol. 19, *Philosophical Letters* [1733]. Christian Biet, 'Le Théâtre Anglois d'Antoine de La Place (1746–1749), ou la difficile émergence du théâtre de Shakespeare en France', in Patricial Dorval and Jean-Marie Maguin eds., *Shakespeare et la France* (Paris: Société Française Shakespeare, 2000), 29–49.

the gravediggers' low jokes in *Hamlet* and the shoemakers' idle jests in *Julius Caesar*, he rejected the 'untimely' irruption of burlesque elements and of a *colloquial* register unworthy of classical tragedies. He was blind to the carefully-wrought mirror-effects between low characters and high characters. He failed to perceive that what he interpreted as disparities were, in fact, intertwining and echoing effects, points and counterpoints forming a meaningful, homogeneous whole. He was deaf to Shakespeare's subtle discursive polyphony. A century later, Victor Hugo would incisively mock the misguided philosopher: 'For Voltaire, Shakespeare was an occasion to show how skilful he was at shooting. Voltaire scarcely missed him. Voltaire shot at Shakespeare like peasants shoot geese.'[6]

The Hugos, father and son, played a major part in restoring Shakespeare to favour in nineteenth-century France: the son with his pioneer translations of the complete works, the father with his dithyrambic yet insightful critical work, intended as a preface to his son's translations. To Victor Hugo, Shakespeare's dramatic work had a powerful flavour of freedom and he set him up as the tutelary genius of liberty. He had understood the all-encompassing quality of Shakespeare: the mingling of high and low characters and the coexistence of comedy and tragedy. Shakespeare possessed 'what rhetoric call[ed] antithesis, that is to say, the sovereign faculty to see the two sides of things'—'*Totus in antithesi*. Shakespeare is all in antithesis'.[7] Hugo's enthusiasm was shared by most nineteenth-century Romantic writers who saw Shakespeare as an emblem of revolutionary spirit and creative liberation—Stendhal in 1823, with his famous *Racine and Shakespeare*;[8] Alfred de Musset in 1827, with his passionate claim, 'I want to be either Shakespeare or Schiller'; Alfred de Vigny in 1829, with his verse translation of *Othello*. Historian Hippolyte Taine, in turn, contributed to bringing Shakespeare into favour in his *Histoire de la Littérature Anglaise* (1865).[9] Shakespeare became an icon of freedom, both on the page and on the stage, when Sarah Bernhardt scandalously cross-dressed to play Hamlet in Alexandre Dumas's translation in 1899. As George Steiner states, '[i]t was around Shakespearean drama that the romantic sensibility gathered its main forces. The romantic poets sought to cast their own person into the mould of Romeo, Lear, or Macbeth. Hamlet became their emblem and guardian presence. In the lives of Charles Lamb, Hazlitt, Coleridge, Keats, Victor Hugo, Musset, Stendhal, Schiller, Pushkin … the discovery of Shakespeare was the great awakener of consciousness.'[10] Casting a retrospective glance back to the first half of the twentieth century, Henry Fluchère observes that 'one of the most striking features of twentieth-century Shakespeare criticism in France is its incredible lack of boldness'.[11] And to him, Shakespeare badly needed to be de-romanticized. Things were to change in the second half of the century.

---

[6] Victor Hugo, *William Shakespeare* [1864], in *Œuvres complètes: Critique* (Paris: Robert Laffont, 1985), 321.

[7] Ibid., 345–6.

[8] 'Stendhal's Shakespeare is great, in large measure, because he affirms values contrary to Racine.' George Steiner, *The Death of Tragedy* (London: Faber and Faber, 1961), 153.

[9] Holger Klein, 'Shakespeare in French literary historiography', in Dorval and Maguin, *Shakespeare et la France*, 135–72.

[10] Steiner, *The Death of Tragedy*, 143–4.

[11] Henri Fluchère, 'Shakespeare in France: 1900-1948', *Shakespeare Survey* 2 (1949), 117.

The Shakespearean School of Tragedy:
New Episteme (1949–2010)

The Second World War and the events of May 1968 both left influential marks upon the literary critical field. The works of Roland Barthes, Gilles Deleuze, and Jacques Derrida substantially reshaped the methodological and epistemological landscape. Critics explored new analytical approaches that offered to capture the intertextual dimension and implicit meanings of literature.

Roland Barthes, the pioneer of literary structuralism, made a deep impact on the critical sphere with his 1968 landmark essay provocatively entitled 'The Death of the Author'.[12] Barthes radically departed from the traditional author-and-work approach to favour close reading and free interpretation, the main idea being that the author was no longer the unique guarantor for his text, that his text originated from language itself and produced a plurality of meanings exceeding its author's original intentions. The biographical context and the author's contingent personality were to be erased to favour the emergence of the multiplicity of voices disseminated throughout the text. As he argued, the birth of the reader necessitated the death of the author. The French university tradition has, since then, almost exclusively focused on the Shakespearean corpus as an autonomous text that speaks through the richness of its language.

For Shakespearean scholar Gisèle Venet, structuralism and close reading constituted a starting point which she enriched with the method of the School of Annals and with readings of Michel Foucault, Paul Ricoeur, and Clément Rosset.[13] Indeed, new literary and philosophical tools were needed to explore the layers and meanders of texts. In a 1972 interview, French philosopher Gilles Deleuze said that a theory should be used as a toolbox that provided useful ways of reading.[14] The concepts that he and Felix Guattari created and explored—such as deterritorialization, the distinction between the principles of cartography and decalcomania, the opposition between the war machine and the State apparatus, and between the Smooth and the Striated—proved to be useful in casting a new light upon tragedies like *King Richard II*, *King Lear*, and *Coriolanus*.[15]

But while what is now labelled as 'French Theory' was successfully appropriated abroad, it was never fashionable among French Shakespearean scholars. Neither was French philosopher Jacques Derrida, the theorist of deconstruction and post-structuralism. And yet, what Derrida aimed at favouring a subjective encounter with the text and multiplying the perspectives opened with close reading. He insisted on paying attention to the internal logic of the text, making the implicit or the unsaid resurface, analysing the presuppositions

---

[12] Roland Barthes's essay was first published in English in *Aspern Magazine*, 5/6 (1967), then it was published in French, 'La mort de l'auteur', in Revue *Manteia* 5 (1968), 12–17.

[13] Gisèle Venet, *Temps et vision tragique. Shakespeare et ses contemporains* (Paris: Service des publications de l'Université de la Sorbonne Nouvelle Paris III, 1985).

[14] Gilles Deleuze, 'Les intellectuels et le pouvoir' (entretien avec C. Deleuze; 4 mars 1972), in *Dits et écrits, 1954–1988*: vol. 2, *1970–1975* (Paris: Gallimard, 1994), 309.

[15] Gilles Deleuze and Felix Guattari's *A Thousand Plateaus. Capitalism and Schizophrenia*, translation and foreword by Brian Massumi (London and New York: Continuum, 2008). See Pascale Drouet, *Mise au ban et abus de pouvoir. Essai sur trois pièces tragiques de Shakespeare* (Paris: Presses de l'Université Paris-Sorbonne, 2012).

of the author's train of thought, exploring what the text ignores and trying to make sense out of what it passed over. This undermined the stability of meaning and either subverted the notion of genre or ignored it. Sibony might be said to be an heir to Derrida, interested as he is in the deconstruction and reconstruction of meaning in Shakespeare's tragedies and tragi-comedies. He ignores generic distinctions as he focuses on human passions and radical experiences.[16] Shakespeare himself might be said to be interested in some kind of 'deconstruction': in many plays, including major tragedies like *Hamlet* and *King Lear*, he paradoxically 'deconstructed' dramatic illusion with subtly-wrought processes of *mise en abyme*. As Gisèle Venet observes, the combination of traditional tragedy with the baroque technique of drama within drama led to a poetics of incompletion, a poetics of the open work, as Umberto Eco puts it.[17]

In 1961, the French-born American philosopher and critic, George Steiner, reassessed the gap between the Greek and the Elizabethan theatre in *The Death of Tragedy*, arguing that 'the decline of tragedy [was] inseparably related to the decline of the organic world view and of its attendant context of mythology, symbolic, and ritual reference'.[18] To him, 'tragedy is that form of art that requires the intolerable burden of God's presence. It is now dead because His shadow no longer falls upon us as it fell on Agamemnon or Macbeth or Athalie.'[19] Although he does not quote Steiner's work, as he rather leans towards German philosophy and French phenomenology, Philippe Grosos, a philosopher belonging to the younger generation, also tackles the issue of tragedy and its problematic durability. According to Grosos, it is impossible to think in terms of Greek tragedy nowadays because Biblical thought and Christian thinking have permeated Western consciousness. In Greek tragedies, men were to face some implacable Fate and take grievous faults upon themselves, although morally guiltless of them. With the acknowledgement of original sin—unknown to the ancient Greeks—tragedy in the early modern period could not be dissociated from man's (even partial) responsibility. Consequently, what was formerly considered as tragic radically evolved and opened onto what Grosos terms the tragi-comic. This, he maintains, is already to be found in Shakespeare's dramatic work, where the characters' 'tragic' fates have to do with their political and passionate aberrations, their mistakes and faults, and their sense of guilt and responsibility. With Shakespeare, Modernity departed from the Greek model and awakened to the tragi-comic (rather than tragic) dimension of its existence—a lurch into comedy threatens when characters, experiencing seemingly tragic ordeals, suffer and complain despite the fact that, because of their own flaws (Macbeth's hubris or Lear's vanity, for instance), they are partly responsible for what befalls them.[20]

---

[16] Sibony, *Avec Shakespeare*, 7.

[17] Gisèle Venet, 'Introduction', in William Shakespeare, *Tragédies I (Œuvres complètes, I)*, (Paris: Gallimard, La Pléiade, 2002), p. ccvii. Umberto Eco, *The Open Work*, Translated by Anna Cancogni (Milano: Bompiani, 1962; Radius Book, 1989). On the absence of an sense of a 'panoptic whole' or 'sense of closure' at the end of Shakespeare's tragedies, see Paul Kottman, 'What is Shakespearean Tragedy?', Ch. 1 in this volume, 3–18.

[18] Steiner, *The Death of Tragedy*, 292.   [19] Ibid., 353.

[20] Philippe Grosos, 'William Shakespeare ou l'ironie tragique des Histoires', in *L'ironie du réel à la lumière du romantisme allemande* (Lausanne: L'Age d'Homme, 2009), 137–55; 'Le tragi-comique', in *Phénoménologie de l'intotalisable* (Paris: Cerf, 2012), 100–5; *Le réversible et l'irréversible* (Paris: Hermann, 2014).

Steiner's analysis appears to have influenced Shakespearean scholar Richard Marienstras who, in his *Shakespeare au XXIe siècle. Petite introduction aux tragédies*, asserts that we now live in a post-tragic world, which he calls *un au-delà de la tragédie*, because it is impossible to create a fictitious dramatic world capable of matching the horrible events, the profusion of evil that took place throughout the twentieth century.[21] Marienstras agrees—and so do Sibony and Suhamy—with Steiner's idea that tragedy can survive only with 'the creation of characters endowed with the miracle of independent life'.[22] Marienstras acknowledges the 'extraordinary presence' of larger-than-life Shakespearean characters and observes that the foundation of the individual lies in Elizabethan drama.[23] For Sibony, this explains why Shakespeare's tragic characters are still up-to-date. Lear, Coriolanus, Othello, Hamlet, and others remain the living dramatic vehicles of 'traumatic fictions' that help us question, face, cope with, or even unknot existential knots, and meet the truth that is ours.[24] It does not come as a surprise, then, that Shakespearean scholar Henri Suhamy recently devoted a book to three Shakespearean tragic characters—Hamlet, Lear, and Macbeth—to examine how they keep being impersonated and appropriated throughout centuries, and how they seem to 'assume a sustainable existence, independent from their first inventor or main divulger, and from the work within which they were apparently bound to be confined'.[25]

Such changes in the critical episteme mirrored the evolution of methods to match the strength of Shakespearean verse to French ears. Critical appraisal of Shakespeare and translation of his works have coincided since the eighteenth century; they have led to a French Shakespeare freed from the boundaries of neoclassical dramatic poetics.

Translating Shakespearean Tragedy:
The Path to a Liberated Line

'I can with ease translate it to my will' (1.2.514), says Blanche to Louis the Dauphin in *King John*. Taken out of context, this line could easily describe how both translators and stage directors have appropriated Shakespearean texts in order to turn the dramatist into their Will. To be creatively adapted on stage and performed by French actors and actresses, Shakespearean tragedies first needed to be translated. The first attempt at translating extracts from Shakespearean tragedies may be traced back to Voltaire's 1730 translation of the 'to be or not to be' monologue. He was cautious enough to invite his readers to '[b]e indulgent to the copy, in honour to the original': 'always remember', he said, 'that when you see a translation, you perceive only a faint copy of a fine picture'.[26] This warning applied to his own attempt and that of his immediate

---

[21] Richard Marienstras, *Shakespeare au XXIe siècle. Petite introduction aux tragédies* (Paris: Éditions de Minuit, 2000), 15.

[22] Steiner, *The Death of Tragedy*, 350.   [23] Marienstras, *Shakespeare au XXIe siècle*, 38.

[24] Sibony, *Avec Shakespeare*, 393–5.

[25] Henri Suhamy, *Hamlet, Lear, Macbeth. Histoire de trois personnages shakespeariens* (Paris: Ellipses, 2010), 3 (our translation).

[26] Voltaire, 'English Tragedy', in *The Works of Voltaire. A contemporary Version*. After Voltaire, in 1745, Destouches translated a selection of scenes from *The Tempest*, but he did not attempt any scenes from Shakespeare's tragedies.

successors. Antoine de La Place initiated a departure from extracts and selected scenes to the whole play or, rather, a substantial portion of it. But his *Théâtre Anglois* (1746-9), including *Othello* and *King Lear*, was in fact a toned-down adaptation: prose and lofty alexandrines alternated regardless of the original rhythm, and some scenes were censored, summarized and critically commented upon for the sake of propriety—Jean-François Ducis's 1769 *Hamlet* for the Comédie Française was adapted according to the same principles. Pierre Le Tourneur was the first, from 1776 to 1782, to venture translations of Shakespeare's complete works. Though deemed 'mediocre' by Steiner,[27] they were at least pioneering renditions. In the second half of the nineteenth century, from 1859 to 1866, François-Victor Hugo started a new translation of Shakespeare's complete works. As his father put it in his preface, this much-improved version, faithful to the playwright's text and style and regardless of French aesthetic expectations, gave access to 'Shakespeare without a muzzle'.[28]

Since François-Victor Hugo, many famous twentieth-century writers have produced their own translations of Shakespeare's tragedies, among them André Gide (*Hamlet, Antoine et Cléopâtre*), Pierre-Jean Jouve (*Roméo et Juliette*), Pierre Leyris (*Le Roi Lear*), Maurice Maeterlinck (*Macbeth*)—all of whom were published in the 1959 Pléiade Edition. In the second half of the twentieth century, Yves Bonnefoy produced outstanding translations of most of the tragedies (*Hamlet, Le Roi Lear, Macbeth, Antoine et Cléopâtre, Othello, Roméo et Juliette*). His versions perfectly illustrate Henri Meschonnic's dictum according to which 'the strength of a successful translation is that it is a poetics for a poetics. Neither meaning for meaning, nor word for word, but what transforms an act of language into an act of literature'.[29] In 2002, Gisèle Venet and scholar and stage translator Jean-Michel Déprats edited, in two volumes, a new Pléiade version of the tragedies, but this time translators and textual editors mostly came from the scholarly sphere.

Déprats's essay on translating Shakespeare is illuminating regarding the treatment of the tragedies in France. Noticing how heavy and bombastic Shakespeare's lines could sound when voiced on stage, he banishes translations in alexandrines. To him, the target of new translations is to bridge the gap between texts and readers, between actors and spectators, and to connect the audience with what takes place on stage. He is equally critical of archaistic translations in the philological vein (they prevent non-erudite people from understanding) and of excessively modernized ones (they de-historicize the semantic substance): 'translation, like performance on stage, is the presence of the past transformed by the subjectivity of another era and by the sensitiveness of the present time that shapes it.'[30] To Déprats, the best way for the translator to remain faithful to the original dramatic text is to retain its specific nature (drama) and peculiar target (audience); this is why he advocates translation for the stage—he aims at preserving the dramatic quality of the text: 'A text by Shakespeare is first and foremost a text written for mouths, bosoms, and breaths.'[31] His translations always reveal a careful ear for the text: Déprats not only

---

[27] Steiner, *The Death of Tragedy*, 155.

[28] Hugo, *William Shakespeare*, 349 (our translation)

[29] Henri Meschonnic, *Poétique du traduire* (Lagrasse: Verdier, 1999), 57 (our translation).

[30] Jean-Michel, Déprats, 'Traduire Shakespeare: pour une poétique théâtrale de la traduction shakespearienne', in William Shakespeare, *Tragédies I (Œuvres complètes, I)* (Paris: Gallimard, La Pléiade, 2008), LXXXIX-XCVII, XCVIII.

[31] Ibid., CV.

translates from English to French, but from the page to the stage—the text is translated to be *voiced* and not only read.

Voltaire, in spite of himself, initiated a long series of French translations, which has not come to an end. As Déprats admits, 'we invent a Shakespeare for our purpose, and every era, with its specific readership, translations and performances, is in turn sensitive to different aspects of his works'.[32] If 'open-mindedness', 'dialogue', 'interbreeding', and 'de-centring' constitute the 'essence of translation'[33] according to translation theorist Antoine Berman, they may also prove a prerequisite for the dramatic transfers of Shakespeare's tragedies.

The Stage Reflector: New Directions in the Performance of Tragedy

Since the nineteenth century, the reception of Shakespearean tragedy on the French stage has been shaped by the accretive and regenerative nature of the Bard's scripts. Thus performance was guided, in turn, by the regenerative power of Shakespeare on French dramaturgy (pre-1940); by the politically committed interpretation of the Bard (since the Liberation); by the idea of Shakespearean tragedy as a dramaturgical laboratory (since the 1950s); by the obsession for recovering an authentic Shakespeare (since the 1950s); by the attempt at forgetting Shakespeare through appropriation and adaptation (since the 1970s); by the recurring use of metatheatricality (since the 1970s) and its transformation into hypertheatricality (1990s); and lastly by Babelism and the Bibliocosm (since the 1980s).[34]

These enduring trends are the historical basis of the four main avenues of reception that characterize late twentieth-century and twenty-first-century French performances of Shakespearean tragedy: the absorption of histories and the dialogue with History; the recreation of the viewer as crowd; the rise of mingled performance; and the emergence of a coupled aesthetics of speed and waste issuing from a reinterpretation of Babelism (the mix of several languages in a speech), and Bibliocosm (the moment when books escape the categories they have been confined to and communicate with one another before coalescing into a single new work).

Absorbing History

When it comes to interpreting Shakespearean tragedy from a French perspective, the genres of tragedy and history play are often confused. The absorption of history into tragedy has a double origin to be found in the French conception of historical drama and in Shakespeare's flexible notion of dramatic genres.

---

[32] Ibid., XCVIII.

[33] Antoine Berman, *L'Épreuve de l'étranger* (Paris: Gallimard, 1984), 16.

[34] Ibid., 232–5; Florence March, *Shakespeare au Festival d'Avignon. Configurations textuelles et scéniques, 2004-2010* (Montpellier: L'Entretemps, 2013), 67–71.

In his preface to the 1844 edition to *Macbeth* and *Romeo and Juliet*, Emile Deschamps writes about 'historical tragedies', illustrating less the French aversion to historical drama than its generic porosity. Within a century of its emergence in fifteenth-century France, historical drama was absorbed into tragedy, as Corneille defined History as a framework of verisimilitude reworked by the playwright's imagination.[35] Used for propagandist purposes during the Revolution, historical drama was shunned until the nineteenth-century symbolists saw in History the paradoxical medium to oppose the naturalists and to represent mankind in an aspirational form. 'There is no tragedy without transcendence'[36] and this aspiration applied both to the characters and the spectators. Including History in a tragedy meant including the familiar in the confusion of the plot so as to take the tragic character from *hamartia* to *anagnorisis*, and the spectator from collective error to individual and collective revelation. The transcendental change of the fictional character thus mirrored and participated in the deep existential metamorphosis of the spectator.

Moreover, Shakespeare's troubling play titles such as *The Tragedy of Richard II*, coupled with the vision of Man trapped in the double tension of impertinent liberation and willing servitude,[37] favoured the absorption of Shakespearean historical plays into the elastic genre of tragedy. English history became the conveniently distant sounding board for a critical view of the French historical present and for the will to transcend it. Ariane Mnouchkine's 1982 transfer of *The Tragedy of Richard II* into an oneiric medieval Asian context is an example of the absorption of historical drama in the aspirational dynamic of tragedy. Merging Shakespeare's tragic history in a dialogue with global theatre history is a means to use the transcending power of tragedy to go beyond the limitations of classical dramaturgy and to invent a new form of theatricality detached from the boundaries of time.

Consciousness of the inherent historical dialogism of Shakespearean plays was cleverly played upon by Eugène-Humbert Guitard, in his review of Charles Dullin's 1933 adaptation of *Richard III* for the Théâtre de l'Atelier, when he said 'The Atelier [Workshop] Theatre is becoming the stage of theatre history, and with *Richard III* it will stage History as such'.[38] This transcendental merger reactivated the double 'function' of drama in a Shakespearean play which is to mirror human History as well as theatre history. Thus Shakespeare became a mirror of contemporary French history as well as of an aesthetic history. Because he managed 'to liberate himself from his own national and folkloric body to act as reflector of what's within or what moves all men',[39] his plays were ready to be absorbed and used as a dramatic vehicle for the French historical and cultural psyche, especially during and after the Second World War.

The junction between history and tragedy in the French reception of Shakespeare is illustrated by Jean-Louis Barrault's decision to direct *Antony and Cleopatra* for the Comédie Française in 1945 and its definition by François Mauriac as a 1607 '*drame*' chiming with

---

[35] Pierre Corneille, 'Appian Alexandrin', *Rodogune* (1646), (Paris: Folio, théâtre, 2004).

[36] Karl Jaspers, *Tragedy is not Enough*, trans. Harald A.T. Reiche, Harry T. Moore, and Karl W. Deutsch (Boston: Archon Books, 1969), 53.

[37] Robert W. Corrigan, *Tragedy, Vision and Form* (New York: Harper and Row, 1981), 1–13.

[38] *Dyonysos*, 22:85 (1934), 319.

[39] Jacques Demeure, *Portrait souvenir W. Shakespeare*, 1964, http://www.ina.fr/video/CPF86634923 (our translation).

the anxieties of the 1945 survivor.[40] The choice of the word *drame* in French is telling as it blurs the boundary between *drame historique* ('historical drama') and *drame* as tragic action. Barrault's *Antony and Cleopatra* confirms the idea of Shakespearean tragedy as a composite of histories and tragedies and its use as a sounding board for France's political and ontological concerns.

Throughout the second half of the twentieth century and at the beginning of the twenty-first, Shakespearean tragedy has remained one of the main dramatic instruments for debating virtue and tyranny, determinism and liberty. The pivotal role of Shakespeare in this debate is illustrated by the creation of both the Théâtre Populaire and the Festival d'Avignon by Jean Vilar in 1947. The very first festival featured a Shakespearean production typical of the absorptive reception of tragedy, *The Tragedy of Richard II*, directed by Jean Vilar himself. Avignon marks the complete integration of Shakespeare into the French dramatic canon as 38 of the 64 festivals have featured his plays. Twenty-four of his plays have been produced and a good third of these productions were of tragedies or historical tragedies.[41]

This choice mirrors the French official policy of citizen education through theatre since 1945. Jean Vilar's notion of a people's theatre or popular theatre derives from a French Revolution decree defining an ideal of education through the arts and especially through dramatic art.[42] Vilar, who was a stage assistant on Charles Dullin's *Richard III*, famously decided to start a career as director on that very set, but above all perceived Shakespeare as the instrument of citizen education after the war. Vilar's vision accorded with the political will to use culture in the reconstruction of France after the war,[43] and Avignon became strongly instrumental in fashioning Shakespearean tragedy as a means to explore national identity. The festival of Avignon articulated the tenets of French cultural policies. It did this by choosing a repertory reflecting the spirit of the times, reaching a larger audience and rethinking theatre as a collective effort, a contract between players and audience. Shakespeare was the dramatic Other that enabled a reconstruction of both the individual and the collective post-war self. This cultural reconstruction relied on a redefinition of the physical experience of theatre inspired by the inclusive shape of the Shakespearean stage, and on tragic texts that questioned a collective political experience of history while relying on the imagination of the individual spectator.

After Vilar's 1947 *Richard II*, each decade was to feature productions of historical plays as tragedies, as an exploration of the national psyche. Patrice Chéreau's 1970 *Richard II* openly questioned the sociopolitical context after 1968 and tried to answer the question asked by the director himself: 'How can we live in a period of crisis?' The production did

[40] François Mauriac, *Opéra*, 9 June 1945.

[41] March, *Shakespeare au Festival d'Avignon*, 142–4.

[42] Decree of 10 March 1794 converting the black wing of the Comédie Française into the Théâtre de la Nation (the Nation's theatre), while the building was renamed Théâtre du Peuple (the People's Theatre) which would be devoted to 'performances of the people, by the people and for the people'. See Frederick W. J. Hemmings, *Theatre and State in France, 1760–1905* (New York: Cambridge University Press, 1994), 79–82.

[43] Dennis Kennedy refers to Shakespeare as 'a cultural Marshall plan' in *The Spectator and Spectacle. Audiences in Modernity and Postmodernity* (Cambridge: Cambridge University Press, 2009), 81.

not try to make the play a French theatrical object of the 1970s, but opted for an authenticity whose links with the contemporary period the director believed to be self-explanatory. Similarly, Jean-Baptiste Sastre's *Richard II* for the 2010 festival retained a medieval scenography mixed with oversized royal paraphernalia (a high pointy crown, a long sceptre, and a large gown) which upstaged the royal persona. The context of bitter national debates on the solemnity of statesmanship blended into the play's initial questioning of Richard's capacity to sustain the weight of power. The Cour d'Honneur's back wall, with its rough grey stone and crude lighting, turned the stage into a prison of power cut off from the kingdom's garden. Again, the dialogue with history was at the heart of the tragic demise of Richard and chimed with the local political crisis of representation.

Nevertheless, Shakespearean tragedy cannot be confined to the exploration of the French national psyche, since Shakespeare is primarily envisaged as a transnational cultural artefact enabling a European dialogue. Indeed, the Festival of Avignon, the Comédie Française, and other national stages all open their seasons to European directors offering their own take on Shakespearean tragedy. Avignon featured Thomas Ostermeier's *Hamlet*, Ivo Van Hove's *Roman Tragedies*, Pippo Delbono's *Enrico V*, while Dan Jemmett, a British director, has just directed *Hamlet* for the Comédie Française. All these productions are part of the long-standing tradition of welcoming European directors who will shape French reception into a less local view of Shakespearean tragedy.[44]

Shakespeare has become one of the main cultural artefacts of a European community. The end of the twentieth century and the first decade of the twenty-first century have shown a growing concern for a transnational dialogue using a transnational playwright. The citizen education desired by Vilar has now acquired European dimensions. Thomas Ostermeier's *Hamlet*, created for the Festival of Avignon in 2008, exemplifies the use of Shakespearean tragedy to explore cultural and epistemological commonalty at the European level. The production was performed in German with French surtitles, and the dramatic performance of individual characters was interspersed with live video feeds of the audience or of the stage crowd, thereby attempting to reconcile the individual self with the community while also revealing their sometimes dangerously parallel existences. Responding to the cyclical succession of traumas, French reception of Shakespearean tragedy has shown a growing concern for the notions of unity and union. The performance of Shakespearean tragedy in France has become a matter of educating the viewers to consider the dialogic nature of their identity.

Since the Romantic Age, Shakespeare has been perceived as what Vilar was later to call a dramaturgical laboratory.[45] For young post-war theatre companies, lesser-known tragedies such as *Coriolanus, Pericles*, and *Titus Andronicus* were used as means to regenerate performance and *mise-en-scène*. Shakespearean tragedy was the main instrument in an enterprise of identity-building which relied on experimenting with the textual and

---

[44] These directors who create in France or are asked to offer their vision of Shakespearean tragedy to a French audience follow the likes of Giorgio Strehler, Peter Brook, Bob Wilson, Declan Donnellan, and the Footsbarn Theatre. The hybridization of reception is also favoured by the growing use of surtitled performances of non-French productions.

[45] The phrase 'dramaturgical laboratory' was borrowed from theatre critics Paul and Victor Glachant who analysed Victor Hugo's theatre as such in their 1902 opus on the French poet and dramatist.

the dramaturgical unknown.[46] Tragedy thus became the sign of innovation as well as of the schism in French post-war theatrical productions. Classical tragic landmarks, such as *Hamlet* and *Lear*, were seen as the hallmarks of established directors and companies while lesser known tragedies acted as the ontological laboratory of the next dramatic generation.

The Shakespearean Laboratory: Restaging and Reshaping the Viewer

Questioning the political subject implies observing the political leader and the political addressee and probing the place of the subject in the *polis*. Shakespearean tragedy was made a very political instrument in France by emphasizing the importance of a character only fleetingly represented in tragedies and historical plays: the crowd. The post-war political and aesthetic enterprise of identity-building did not target the individual but the collective self. It meant redefining both the crowd as character and the audience as a crowd. Such a double endeavour was to lead to a complete change in the physical organization of the performance space and in the relationship between the viewer and the stage. As in Shakespeare's own theatre, the audience was now viewed, along with on-stage spectators, as a collective addressee of the political leader. Taking into account the presence of a crowd on the stage and of a crowd in the audience led directors and the scenographers to reconsider both the space of performance and the space of reception.

Roland Barthes recorded the first step of this redefinition in Raymond Hermantier's 1955 dramaturgy for *Julius Caesar* and *Coriolanus* in the Nîmes Arena.[47] Faced with the gigantism of a venue unfitted for theatre, Hermantier staged these two tragedies from the point of view of their common character: the *plebs*. He merged the time of the performance, the time of the play, and the time of the spectator by scattering his actors throughout the tiers of the auditorium. Warriors, messengers and torch-bearers had to walk the long distance separating them from the stage, which paradoxically conferred realism on their interventions. This expansion of the performance space to include the audience space modified the identity of the receptor, now an embedded, silent witness of the Roman wars. Symbolically, the spectator was now in the space of the performance and had to superimpose her/his existence upon that of the plays' crowds. The best position from which to fully appreciate the dramatic battlefields staged in these two plays was ironically from the cheap seats of 'the Gods'. The perspective was reversed and the stage space was envisaged from the point of view of the crowd-spectator.[48]

In a paradoxical mix of authenticity and iconoclasm, the viewer was put on the stage. The scenography reshaped the political subjectivity of the spectator as well as that of the characters. When Jacques Rosner, staged *Macbeth* in 1994, the reshaping of the audience as silent crowd occurred at the intersection of three usually distinct temporal levels: the time of the spectator, the time of the performance, and the time of the characters. This junction was enabled by the metamorphosis of the Sorano Theatre into a theatre-in-the-round. The stage was moved into the middle of what was usually the seating area and the seats were

---

[46] Fayard, *The Performance of Shakespeare in France since the Second World War*, 65–8.

[47] Roland Barthes, *Ecrits sur le théâtre* (Paris: Seuil, 2002), 173–5.   [48] Ibid., 174–5.

rearranged in tiers framing three sides of the stage. Moreover, Rosner reinforced the physical commitment of the audience to the stage, by forcing them into the heart of the tragic
action during the opening scene. The room and the stage were plunged into darkness
while the contorting figures of the three witches crawled over a dimly lit metal net hung
above the stage and the audience. The loss of the traditional distance of the fourth wall of a
proscenium-arch theatre compelled the spectators to a higher level of commitment to the
dramatic action. The spectators could not but be involved in the unfolding of the tragedy
as they were made the embedded witnesses of the slow demise of excessive ambition.

The viewer's perception depends on both the directors' playing with the constraints of
authenticity and the structuring meta-theatricality of the Shakespearean tragic script. The
reflexive mirror of the theatre looking at its own metamorphoses is another dramaturgic
experimentation occasioned by Shakespeare's text. Because it produces a constant displacement of perception levels, it creates a dramaturgy of concordant discord that pushes
spectators to redefine their own positions.[49] Moreover in the political context of the French
reception of the tragedies, it reflects the constant redefinition of the representatives of
power through the crowd's perspective. Shakespearean tragedy as laboratory transforms
the dramaturgy, the consciousness of the spectator and the performane of the actor.

From 'Mingled Drama' to Mingled Performance

Samuel Johnson's 1765 praise of Shakespeare's generic mix[50] marked the overturning of
the neoclassical doxa of dramatic unities and was embraced by the French Romantics
as the hallmark of good dramatic writing. However, by the end of the twentieth century,
Shakespeare's mingled drama still had to overcome an enduring reluctance to transcend
generic boundaries. The answer to mingled drama was to create a mingled form of tragic
performance involving the use of a histrionic non-verbal language, of comic performance,
and of a comically absurd scenography.

This reinvention of performance led to the emergence of an enduring trend during
the first decade of the twenty-first century: the comic performance of tragedy. The generic hybridity of the Shakespearean text influences both the dramaturgy and the performance. In the marginalia to his translation of Plato's *Symposium*, Racine questioned
the autonomy of dramatic genres: 'Tragedy and Comedy *is* one single genre.'[51] The greatest
French tragedian believed in the generic porosity that was the hallmark of early modern
English drama. Throughout the first decade of the twenty-first century, the performance
of Shakespearean tragedy seemed to favour a genre-less approach: French stage reception of Shakespeare turned the comic content of certain tragedies into the very form of
their performance. Jean-François Sivadier's production of *King Lear* in Avignon in 2007
inserted comic meta-commentaries in the form of interjections. Nicolas Bouchaud as Lear
punctuated the love test in Act 1 Scene 1 with impatient howls and he silently answered

---

[49] Vsevolod Meyerhold, *Meyerhold on Theatre*, trans. Edward Braun (New York: Hill and Wang,
1969), 36ff.

[50] Samuel Johnson, 'Preface to William Shakespeare', *The Works of Samuel Johnson*, vol. 7 (New
Haven: Yale University Press, 1968), 66.

[51] Quoted in Jacques Schérer, *La dramaturgie classique en France* (Paris: Nizet, 1950), 12.

the Fool's complex prophecies in Act 1 Scene 4 with a mimicry of weary desperation and impatience, thus turning these scenes into parodic moments of grotesque childishness. A similar comic performance was used when the entire troupe of actors erupted into white noise when Gloucester promised to intercede in Kent's favour. These verbal or kinesic asides created a comic complicity with the audience that revealed the dark comedy lodged at the heart of Shakespeare's tragedy. The replacement of speech by new expressive forms echoed the Renaissance introduction of the colloquial in comedy writing. However the apparent poetic shapelessness of the vernacular was pushed to an extreme by replacing words with sounds. Sivadier interspersed the established text with this new expressive form which interfered with the tragic solemnity of blank verse and testified to the comic reinterpretation of the tragic protagonist.

Comic performance is a recurrent feature of the French productions of Shakespeare's tragedies. Such a device deepens the spectator's as well as the character's entrapment in the tragic vortex. The reception of tragedy through the prism of comic dramaturgy is not only a way to complete the break with neoclassical stricture but also a means to intensify the tragic action. The point is to modify tragedy, its performance, and its reception by using semiotic and kinesic codes belonging to comic performance. Dan Jemmett's 2013 *Hamlet* at the Comédie Française revisited the performance of tragedy and opted for the fusion of a comic form and a tragic outcome within the actor's performance. Thus Hamlet's first entrance pictured him reading a book on toilets, the ghost instructed the next generation in the weary tone and clichéd garb of an aging rock star, and during the interval Claudius became the metatheatrical actor of a degrading dumbshow featuring him changing toilet rolls in the club's lavatories. This type of performance relies on a jarring clash between the tragic dimension of the character and the comic effect of trivial actions; it takes the shape of a comic performance of tragedy based on a gradual decrease in the intensity of the comic performance during a scene. The point is to give a tragicomic measure to the performance of tragedy which could be summarized as follows: initial tragic context + comic performance of the tragic speech + gradual diminution of the comic aspect of the performance in order to preserve the tragic impact of the scene. However, the danger of this strategy is that the actor's performance may not include the necessary final erasure of the scene's comic aspects. In that case, the excessive comedy of trivial things can degrade the characters to the point of thoroughly destroying their epistemological depth.

Comedy and parody are instruments to question one of the essential components of classical tragedy: heroic identity. They not only realize the intrinsically mingled character of Shakespeare's drama, but redefine the genre of tragedy as both French artists and audiences know it. Laurent Pelly, director of Théâtre National de Toulouse defines Shakespeare's theatre as 'boundless drama', free from the limits of genres. His scenography for his 2013 production of *Macbeth* showed this will to stage Shakespeare's boundlessness by blending a King-Ubu-inspired scenography with the tragedy of Macbeth. Defining this tragedy as relying on the 'grotesque nature of the couple's project', Pelly created a scenographic grotesque (as in the pictorial term defining an unnatural shape combining different forms).[52] After the murder of Duncan, Macbeth reappeared sitting on a gigantic white chair. Provoking laughter from the audience at first, the initial comic effect

[52] Interview with Laurent Pelly, Nathalie Rivère de Carles, December 2013.

slowly dissipated and was transformed into an uncomfortable oneirism as the protagonist seemed unable to move down from the chair and the actor's physical unease blended into the character's usurped new identity. Pelly blended visual codes belonging to absurdist drama and comedy to reveal the tragic essence of the show of royalty. Tragedy is no longer performed homogeneously but as a form of dramatic grotesque.

From Babelism and Bibliocosm to the Aesthetics of Speed and Waste

Inventing a new verbal idiom for the reception of Shakespearean tragedy is the ultimate step before a thorough refiguration of Shakespeare into new works. Dan Jemmett's *Hamlet*, featuring interpolated dialogues in English, is the latest avatar of the trend of multilingualism in French reception of Shakespearean drama.[53] Following in the steps of Daniel Mesguich's 1977 *Hamlet*, Jemmett entered the realm of Babelism and chose to create a polyphonic dialogue between the translated Shakespearean text and other voices. Mesguich's *Hamlet* filtered Shakespeare's tragedy through the interpolated voices of other authors, sometimes in their original language. Superimposing Borges's bibliocosm and the babelism of a multilingual script, Mesguisch received Shakespearean tragedy through the voices of translators, poets, critics, philosophers, and even politicians.[54] This erudite attempt to inscribe Shakespearean tragedy in twentieth-century intellectual life has proved an enduring trend that found a new expression in Jemmett's production. However, the bibliocosm is now degraded into absurd everyday sentences issued from mass communication. Hamlet's 'Sex? Call number…' before the 'to be or not to be' is an empty automated voice echoing the perfunctory servicing of human emotions. Shakespearean intertextuality has been taken to a trivial extreme, emphasizing the tragic emptiness of a constantly mediated life.

Van Hove's *Roman Tragedies* staged in Avignon brought together *Coriolanus, Julius Caesar,* and *Antony and Cleopatra* into a single production. The dialogue of Shakespearean tragedy with itself is superimposed on a dialogue with contemporary media technology. It questions the characters' relationship to power and the way modern audiences receive tragic performances. The bibliocosm has been replaced by the filter of communication technology. It ensures a different reception of Shakespearean tragedy predicated on speed. The immediacy of modern means of communication applied to the Shakespearean script aims to make the audience absorb a sense of the tragic rather than creating a distance between the spectator and the tragic action. Tragedy relies precisely on a sense of immediacy and omnipresence from which neither the characters nor the spectators can escape.[55]

This aesthetic of speed is often accompanied by the fragmentation of the Shakespearean script. The latter is reduced to debris and requires a reconstruction which aims at an even

[53] Nathalie Rivère de Carles, 'Academic Reviewing, Interculturalism and Committed Aesthetics', in 'Nothing if not Critical: International Perspectives on Shakespearean Theatre Reviewing', Paul Prescott, Peter J. Smith, Janice Valls-Russell, eds., *Cahiers Elisabéthains* 40th anniversary special issue (2012), 17–26.

[54] Nicole Fayard, 'Daniel Mesguich's Shakespearean Play: Performing the Shakespeare Myth', *Theatre Journal* 59:1 (March, 2007), 43.

[55] Christian M. Billing, 'The Roman Tragedies', *Shakespeare Quarterly* 61:3 (October, 2010), 415–39.

faster assimilation of the original. Vincent Macaigne's approach to *Hamlet* coupled the aesthetics of speed and waste in his production of *Au moins j'aurais laissé un beau cadavre* (*At least, I'd have left a beautiful corpse*) in Avignon in 2011. Based on *Hamlet*, the production relied on the intertextual game between James Dean's tragically prophetic quote 'Live fast, die young, and leave a beautiful corpse'[56] and the original play's tendency to leave corpses behind (Old Hamlet's corpse belonging to the unseen world of those in limbo, beneath the stage and behind the scenes, or Polonius' corpse being left behind the curtain and then dragged offstage behind Hamlet). In order to accelerate the audience's understanding of the celerity of the tragic dynamic and for the director to get to the heart of the tragedy and of its speedy ineluctability, the Shakespearean script had to be broken, destroyed, and rebuilt in the manner of Rauschenberg's *gluts* sculptures made of recycled materials. The bibliocosm is now fully intermedial. It relies on the double aesthetics of speed and waste to convey the frantic and unstoppable nature of tragic violence as well as the paradoxical fertility of chaos. This aesthetic of speed and waste is the in-between zone of the 'translation' of Shakespearean tragedy onto the French stage as it acknowledges its filiation with Shakespeare and, simultaneously, presents itself as an independent work, an experiment beyond the realm of theatre.

Transplanted Shakespeares
and Refigurative Receptions

When in the nineteenth century translators and artists such as Guizot or Berlioz evoked the existence of a 'Shakespearean System' that could be lifted off the Bard's work as the template to other artworks, they theorized their own tendency to refiguration. Berlioz admitted to having used parts of *The Merchant of Venice*, a comedy, to create his tragic opera, *The Trojans* (1863).[57] Tragedy acted once again as an absorptive genre fed by other genres. Similarly, operatic writing fed on the debris of Shakespearean drama to create new, autonomous works. The Berlioz type of open refiguration, which is fragmentational and dialogic, was progressively erased as shown by the composer's telling reluctance to admit the structural influence of Shakespeare in his other operas.[58] Refiguration moves into the realm of transplant:[59] when fragments of Shakespearean tragedies are taken into a different context; when their source cannot be identified anymore; and when they become part and parcel of a thoroughly new work.

---

[56] Dean was quoting a line from Nicholas Ray's *Knock on Any Door* (1949) adapted from the eponymous novel (1947) by Willard Motley.

[57] Letter to Ernest Legouvé, [10 June 1856], Hector Berlioz, *Correspondance générale*, ed. Pierre Citron 8 vols. (Paris: Flammarion, 1972-2003), 6: 477.

[58] Gaelle Loisel, 'La Musique au défi du drame: Berlioz et Shakespeare', Ecole Normale Supérieure de Lyon, 2012 (unpublished PhD).

[59] Lorna Hardwick redefines the concept of reception by analysing the specificity of sub-categories such as *Refiguration* ('selecting and reworking material from a previous or contrasting tradition') and *Transplant* ('to take a text or image into another context and allow it to develop'). Hardwick, *Reception Studies*, 10–11.

Poetic Refiguration

Yves Bonnefoy was luckier than Berlioz in that he had direct access to Shakespeare's works and did not have to do with imperfect translations—he translated not only tragedies but also comedies, late plays, narrative poems, and sonnets. Each translation was preceded by an essay in which Bonnefoy explained how tightly intertwined his translation choices and critical interpretations were. In the tragedies he was particularly sensitive to female characters like Ophelia, Desdemona, Cordelia, and Cleopatra, whose poetically endowed voices are dismissed and who are ultimately forced into silence.[60] These characters, as well as specific scenes from the major tragedies *Hamlet* and *Othello*, resurface in his latest poetic works, *L'heure présente* (2011) and *Le Digamma* (2012). For Bonnefoy, translation is already 'an act of poetry'.[61] Bonnefoy not only translated Shakespeare's plays, he also recaptured them poetically: his poems welcome some of Shakespeare's characters in order to pay tribute to them and bring them back to life in his own poetical sphere of creation—the rest is no longer silence. What is at stake—that is, at the core of the poetical dialogue between Bonnefoy and Shakespeare—is the refusal and rejection of subjection in favour of the human face that beckons, the hand that is held out (or not) to bring help and comfort, the deep understanding indicated by light touches and mute caresses, and the delicate question of filiation with fathers' unintentional legacies.[62]

In *L'heure présente*, Bonnefoy imagines original sets for Shakespeare's most famous tragedy, which he respectively entitles 'Première ébauche d'une mise en scène d'*Hamlet*' and '*Hamlet* en montagne'. The idea of his fictitious stage director is to leave the traditional theatre building in favour of open, immense, mountainous spaces beaten by the wind and rain: 'The playhouse is as big as the mountain. The playhouse is the mountain'.[63] Actors (many of them—several being required for the same role, because the natural stages are multiple and the scenes spatially disconnected) are scattered among huge rocks, moraines, snowy trees and precipices, and spectators (among them the first-person narrator) are required to walk from one scene to the other, to make their way through the fragmented performance, maze-like, always on the move. A derelict figure of loneliness, Bonnefoy's barefooted Ophelia in the mountains echoes 'unbonneted' Lear on the heath. She comes and goes and vanishes, to be finally evoked by the sound of running mountain torrents. But she reappears in the poetic landscape of 'L'heure présente', carried away by currents, yet offered an ultimate encounter by the poet, a tender and touching one, with her beloved Hamlet.[64] When his Ophelia lightly kisses Hamlet's temples, the reader can feel not only

---

[60] Pascale Drouet, '"Elle prend vie, elle va parler": Shakespeare et Bonnefoy à l'écoute de voix féminines', *Littérature* (Paris: Larousse/Armand Colin), 150 (June 2008), 40–55.

[61] Yves Bonnefoy, 'Yves Bonnefoy: entretien avec John Naughton à propos de Shakespeare', in *L'amitié et la réflexion* (Tours: PU François-Rabelais, 2007), 140.

[62] Pascale Drouet, '*L'heure présente* et *Hamlet*: dialoguer, dialoguer encore avec Shakespeare', in *Yves Bonnefoy. Poésie et dialogue*, ed. M. Fink and P. Werly (Strasbourg: PU de Strasbourg, 2013), 231–46; Sara Amadori, 'L'épreuve du dialogue entre Bonnefoy et Shakespeare: un rapport de paternité et de filiation', in ibid., 247–63.

[63] Yves Bonnefoy, 'Première ébauche d'une mise en scène d'*Hamlet*', in *L'heure présente* (Paris: Mercure de France, 2011), 68 (our translation).

[64] Bonnefoy, 'L'heure présente', in *L'heure présente*, 84.

her love but also her deep understanding of Hamlet's predicament. It is as if she held out her hand to him, oblivious of herself, paying attention to otherness, not afraid of transitivity. Bonnefoy endows the traditionally sacrificial figure of Ophelia with a new poetic and archetypal dimension. He also does so with Desdemona in *Le Digamma*.

In his 2012 collection of poetic prose, *Le Digamma*, Bonnefoy goes back both to *Hamlet* and *Othello*. 'Pour mettre en scène *Othello*', like 'Première ébauche d'une mise en scène d'*Hamlet*' and '*Hamlet* en montagne', presents a stage director's original attempt at directing outdoors what he considers the darkest of tragedies: *Othello*. He resorts to shadow theatre so as to eradicate human faces and concentrate on darkness, on the evil dimension of the play, with no possible redemption. 'Cast shadows', he explains, 'ignore faces, they know absolutely nothing of what faces can betray.'[65] The stage director fails however: Desdemona's movements still convey intimacy, emotions, and hope. So he forgets about actors and turns to wooden dummies activated by stagehands, as if in keeping with Iago's sinister puppeteering. Yet he fails anew: Desdemona's head, 'hanging all at one side' as if about to sing the willow song, beckons, silently calling for help. For Bonnefoy, Desdemona's tilted head, even though that of a dummy in a shadow show, is much more than a mechanically cast shadow: it retains its epiphanic quality, absolutely reminiscent of the absent human face that, according to philosopher Emmanuel Levinas, reveals the frailty of the human condition and invites responsibility, solidarity and fraternity.[66] In 'Pour mettre en scène *Othello*', Bonnefoy poetically resuscitates Desdemona, pays attention to her and takes her by the hand, the welcoming and comforting hand that matters so much to one known as 'the poet of presence'. With *Le Digamma* and *L'heure présente*, both Desdemona and Ophelia acquire a new poetic dimension that highlights their unexpected understanding and resistance, their unselfish love and trustfulness. Bonnefoy's poetic refiguration brings into light the female characters, hitherto overshadowed by the eponymous male characters, to free them from their alienation and transcend their originally tragic ending. His poetic refiguration creates the very opposite of 'that act of judging by externals which is always a risk in art, which has only appearances in mind, regardless of their roots in being—a beauty admired solely for the idea of the disembodied that imagination makes of it, an image rather than life'.[67]

Dramatic Transplants

François Tanguy's relationship with Shakespeare illustrates the strange ambivalence that makes the difference between a contrastive reworking, or refiguration, and the transplant of an aesthetic item into a new work of art. Tanguy started his work with his newly founded company in 1992 with a performance of *A Midsummer Night's Dream* as a refigurative production in dialogue with Shakespeare's text and dramaturgy. In a subsequent gesture of liberation from the strictures of architectural spaces and more ironically

---

[65] Yves Bonnefoy, *Le Digamma* (Paris: Galilée, 2012), 62 (our translation).

[66] Emmanuel Levinas, *Totalité et infini. Essai sur l'extériorité*, 4th edn. (Dordrecht: Kluwer Academic Publishers, 1988), 188.

[67] Yves Bonnefoy, *Shakespeare and the French Poet*, ed. John Naughton (Chicago and London: The University of Chicago Press, 2004), 45.

from the symbolic liberator himself, the Bard, Tanguy decided to explore ideas and sensations through intermedial creations that broke free from the limits of the theatre as building and from source playwrights. He then turned to Shakespeare's tragedies, converting them into raw material to be transplanted in intermedial creations whose author was now identified as Tanguy himself. What resulted was more than an adaptation or a cinematographic transplant; Tanguy had applied Levi-Strauss's treatment of myth to Shakespearean tragedy. The latter was now treated as a collection of what Levi-Strauss called 'mythemes' (narrative items constituting the fabric of a myth). These elements can be taken and transplanted into different aesthetic contexts and allowed to grow into an autonomous work of art.

Tanguy decided not to play Shakespearean tragedy according to its absorptive qualities, but to absorb Shakespearean tragedy into a larger polyphonic creation. Thus he dismantled *Hamlet, Lear, Othello,* and *Richard II* and kept morsels as unidentified memory items to be joined into a wider, reconstructed, creative alphabet. He detached himself from explicit quotation and pushed the audience to recognize or to ignore the source texts of his unpublished and unreferenced scripts. Now performing under an itinerant tent, free from architectural attachments, Tanguy endeavours to liberate the Bibliocosm. Joyce, Kafka, Celine, Beethoven, Schubert, Dante, Shakespeare, and recordings of historical figures become the notes of a new musical partition as shown in his 2011 creation, *Onzième Heure* (*Eleventh Hour*). The receptor either can or cannot, either wants or does not want to identify Richard II's prison monologue in dialogue with the recording of a speech by Mussolini. In this show, as well as in *Orpheon* (1998), *Cantates* (2001), *Coda* (2004), or *Ricercar* (2007), Tanguy goes beyond the *fin de siècle* Babelism and Bibliocosm and he liberates the source texts from the limiting category of quotation. He creates what he calls an 'undifferentiated theatre'[68] and frees the viewers from the pressure of identification as the origin of the compositional elements has been blurred because of their conjugation with one another. He then offers the viewer the experience of a first encounter with an autonomous work. Although Tanguy's use of Shakespearean tragedy can be inscribed in an aesthetic of speed, he actually refuses to pander to a comfortable immediacy. He uses the acceleration enabled by undifferentiated theatre as a political instrument forcing the spectator to a more active participation in the work of art. Losing the obvious reference to the Shakespearean source is not an easy solution designed to homogenize the cultural backgrounds of the audience, but a subtle tool to challenge the spectator by confronting them with both the essence and the existence of the source. The effect of the transplant in Tanguy's intermedial productions is to offer the paradoxical experience of novelty to all spectators by making them cross the boundaries between genres, authors and art forms. Shakespeare's absorptive tragedies are endowed with the freedom of spectres as they are turned into familiar yet unnamed elements of the audience's collective and individual memory. The ultimate form of reception of Shakespearean tragedy in France is thus to liberate the liberator, to free the Bard from his own myth while using his myth-like qualities, to forget him while evoking him and, with the artist's indulgence, to set him and his successors free.[69]

---

[68]   François Tanguy, press file for *Coda*, Théâtre de l'Odéon, Paris, 2004.
[69]   Peter Brook, *Evoking (and Forgetting) Shakespeare* (London: Nick Hern Books, 2002), 35–7.

Select Bibliography

Barthes, Roland, 'The Death of the Author' (1967), in *The Book History Reader*, ed. David Finkelstein and Alistair McCleery, (London: Routledge, 2002), 221–4.

Barthes, Roland, *Ecrits sur le théâtre* (Paris: Seuil, 2002).

Berman, Antoine, *L'Épreuve de l'étranger* (Paris: Gallimard, 1984).

Biet, Christian, 'Le Théâtre Anglois d'Antoine de La Place (1746–1749), ou la difficile émergence du théâtre de Shakespeare en France', in Patricial Dorval and Jean-Marie Maguin, eds., *Shakespeare et la France* (Paris: Société Française Shakespeare, 2000), 29–49.

Bonnefoy, Yves, *Shakespeare and the French Poet*, Edited by John Naughton (Chicago and London: The University of Chicago Press, 2004).

Brook, Peter, *Evoking (and Forgetting) Shakespeare* (London: Nick Hern Books, 2002).

Corrigan, Robert W., *Tragedy, Vision and Form* (New York: Harper and Row, 1981).

Deleuze, Gilles, and Guattari, Felix, *A Thousand Plateaus. Capitalism and Schizophrenia*, trans. and foreword Brian Massumi (London and New York: Continuum, 2008).

Déprats, Jean-Michel, 'Traduire Shakespeare: pour une poétique théâtrale de la traduction shakespearienne', in *William Shakespeare, Tragédies I (Œuvres complètes, I)* (Paris: Gallimard, La Pléiade, 2008), LXXIX–CXXI.

Drouet, Pascale, 'L'heure présente et *Hamlet*: dialoguer, dialoguer encore avec Shakespeare', in *Yves Bonnefoy. Poésie et dialogue*, ed. M. Fink and P. Werly (Strasbourg: PU de Strasbourg, 2013), 231–46.

Drouet, Pascale, *Mise au ban et abus de pouvoir. Essai sur trois pièces tragiques de Shakespeare* (Paris: Presses de l'Université Paris-Sorbonne, 2012).

Fayard, Nicole, 'Daniel Mesguich's Shakespearean Play: Performing the Shakespeare Myth', *Theatre Journal* 59:1(2007), 39–55.

Fluchère, Henri, 'Shakespeare in France: 1900–1948', *Shakespeare Survey* 2 ([1949]; Cambridge: Cambridge University Press, 1966), 115–25.

Hardwick, Lorna, *Reception Studies* (Oxford: Oxford University Press, 2003).

Hemmings, Frederick W. J., *Theatre and State in France, 1760–1905* (New York: Cambridge University Press, 1994).

Klein, Holger, 'Shakespeare in French literary historiography', in Dorval and Maguin, eds., *Shakespeare et la France* (Paris: Société Française Shakespeare, 2000): 135–72.

March, Florence, *Shakespeare au Festival d'Avignon. Configurations textuelles et scéniques, 2004–2010* (Montpellier: L'Entretemps, 2013).

Marienstras, Richard, *Shakespeare au XXIe siècle. Petite introduction aux tragédies* (Paris: Éditions de Minuit, 2000).

Meschonnic, Henri, *Poétique du traduire* (Lagrasse: Verdier, 1999).

Rivère de Carles, Nathalie, 'Academic Reviewing, Interculturalism and Committed Aesthetics', in 'Nothing if not Critical: International Perspectives on Shakespearean Theatre Reviewing', Paul Prescott, Peter J. Smith, Janice Valls-Russell, eds., *Cahiers Elisabéthains*, 40th anniversary special issue (2012), 17–26.

Sibony, Daniel, *Avec Shakespeare. Éclat et passion en douze pièces* (Paris: Éditions du Seuil, 2003).

Venet, Gisèle, *Temps et vision tragique. Shakespeare et ses contemporains* (Paris: Service des publications de l'Université de la Sorbonne Nouvelle Paris III, 1985).

CHAPTER 45

··

SHAKESPEAREAN TRAGEDY
IN EASTERN EUROPE

··

PAVEL DRÁBEK

Dedicated to the memory of Zdeněk Stříbrný (1922–2014), a teacher, a scholar, a kind friend, author of Shakespeare and Eastern Europe *(Oxford, 2000), and a Shakespearean hero in our times.*

EASTERN Europe is a political and cultural concept rather than a geographical description of a region. The eastern geographical frontier of Europe runs along the ridge of the Ural Mountain Range, some 2,000 kilometres deep into Russia, in latitude as far as the eastern border of Iran. The inclusive, geographical concept of Europe would place Kiev, Ukraine's capital, to the West of 'central' Europe. At the same time, what has intuitively and rather loosely been called 'Eastern Europe' very often excludes Russia. The political denotation has mostly been derived from the communist past of countries that joined or were forced to join the Soviet camp after the Second World War. The latter definition is an exclusive one, limiting the number of countries concerned to Poland, the Czech Republic, Slovakia, Hungary, Romania, Bulgaria, Albania, and the countries of former Yugoslavia: Bosnia and Herzegovina, Croatia, Kosovo, Macedonia, Montenegro, Serbia, and Slovenia. Sometimes the relevant regions of the former East Germany are also included. These, as has been observed, 'have startlingly little in common now, aside from a common historical memory of communism'.[1] A more inclusive definition adds the western former Soviet republics: Belarus, Estonia, Latvia, Lithuania, Moldova, Ukraine, and even Russia.

Eastern Europe is a fluid concept, shifting imperceptibly after each political and cultural event—from negotiations about EU accession and the European Monetary Union, to membership in the NATO, and even to proclamations of belonging or manifestations of political unrest in a region that is often no more than laterally pro-European. Frequently no more than an intuitive notion, Eastern Europe is part of the cultural-political memory: it used to be East but now tends to be oriented towards the West—a concept going back

---

[1] Anne Applebaum, *Iron Curtain: The Crushing of Eastern Europe 1944–56* (London: Penguin Books, 2013), p. xxvii.

at least to Russia's political machinations in the 'European East' in its clandestine deal-ings with Austria-Hungary, Serbia, Bulgaria, Romania, the Ottoman Empire, and other states caught in the pre-First World War deadlock of the 'Racconigi Bargain' of 1909 with Italy. The 'European East' normally referred to regions west of the Russian border; and the term, it is important to remember, is almost exclusively used in Western cultural-political discourse, from a perspective that is external to the region itself. In what follows, the use of 'Eastern Europe' is already conditioned by this Western perspective, as well as being (too often) unsettlingly muddied by the influence of political networks and spheres of influence.

Shakespeare studies—equally unsettlingly—share this perspective. 'Global Shakespeare' or 'World Shakespeare' becomes cognate with a quasi-imperial map tracing spheres of in-fluence of the Elizabethan classic in regions outside the centre, so to speak. This chapter opposes these persistent notions, and documents ways in which Shakespeare's works have long been *at home* in the region of what is intuitively tagged Eastern Europe. In a number of these countries the tradition of Shakespearean theatre reaches as far back as Shakespeare's lifetime: the paths of Elizabethan travelling actors traversed the region from the last decade of the sixteenth century, as they performed in Bohemia, in Austria (as far as today's Slovenia in the southern route), and, very importantly, in greater Poland as far as today's Kaliningrad (Königsberg) and Riga.[2] In Gdańsk (Danzig), in around 1610, a playhouse was built, known as the 'Fencing School', modelled on London's Fortune theatre.[3] Influences of these early English itinerants' activities have survived in the theatre cultures—most notably in the puppet theatres of the region. Many of the plays originated in the London theatre, such as that pillar of the genre, the marionette play of Doctor Faustus. Marlowe's play enjoyed over two centuries of outstanding popularity, fuelled by the folklore of its original domicile—the trickster-magician legends on which Marlowe's source is based (the German *Das Faustbuch*, 1587) served as the cultural stem onto which the English play was grafted.[4] There are more such cases, such as Thomas Dekker's *A Shoemakers' Holiday*; a variant of which can be found in puppet plays, folk tales, and Jesuit school dramas, and these were, in turn, eventu-ally transformed into original works of high art—for instance Antonín Dvořák's early opera *Král a uhlíř* ('The King and the Collier', 1871 and 1874). Similarly, a variant of the story of *King Lear* can be found in Czech fairy tales.[5]

Given the early presence and profound influence of seventeenth-century 'English comedy'—as the genre was called—Eastern European Shakespeare requires specific criti-cal treatment. Narrowing the cultural footprint to a history of Enlightenment/Romantic

---

[2] Pavel Drábek and M. A. Katritzky, 'Shakespearean Players in Early Modern Europe', in Bruce R. Smith, gen. ed., *The Cambridge Guide to the Worlds of Shakespeare* (Cambridge: Cambridge University Press, 2016), 1527–33.

[3] Jerzy Limon, *Gentlemen of a Company: English Players in Central and Eastern Europe, 1590–1660* (Cambridge: Cambridge University Press, 1985), 42–3.

[4] Pavel Drábek, 'English Comedy and Central European Marionette Theatre', in Robert Henke and Eric Nicholson, eds., *Transnational Mobilities in Early Modern Theater* (Farnham: Ashgate, 2014), 177–96.

[5] See Martin Procházka, 'Images of King Lear in Czechoslovak Folklore', in Werner Habicht et al., eds., *Images of Shakespeare. Proceedings of the Third World Shakespeare Congress*, West Berlin 1986 (Newark: University of Delaware Press/Toronto and London: Associated University Presses, 1988), 258–68.

classics would do insufficient justice to the reality. This is further complicated by the way in which Shakespeare's fictional worlds sometimes coincide with regions of Eastern Europe: the Illyria of *Twelfth Night* (with 'the old hermit of Prague', 4.2.13-14), the Vienna of *Measure for Measure* (which includes the 'Bohemian born' Barnardine, 4.2.132, and 'Ragozine, a most notorious pirate', named after Ragusa, today's Dubrovnik, 4.3.68), the fictional Bohemia of *The Winter's Tale*, and the Poland of *Hamlet*. These fictional sites coalesce in the respective cultures with real places—be it in imagination, in theatre productions, or in festivals and even buildings: the Croatian city of Dubrovnik has hosted a Theatre Summer Festival since 1971 (and a Dubrovnik Shakespeare Festival since 2009) with productions of *Hamlet* at their core.[6] The Romanian International Shakespeare Festival in Craiova was founded 1994 and marks Shakespeare not only as an international classic but also as an author whose work played a key role in the formation of the modern Romanian nation.[7] In Poland, the Gdańsk Shakespeare Festival, masterminded by Jerzy Limon and Władysław Zawistowski, has been held on the site of the 'English' playhouse-*cum*-fencing-school since 1993. In 2014, the efforts of the Theatrum Gedanense Foundation culminated in the opening of the Gdańsk Shakespeare Theatre, dedicated both to Shakespeare as an author and to the unique local tradition of Shakespearean theatre-culture for over four centuries.

The sense of being on Shakespearean soil is not only a sign of validation but also marks the plays' history as an intrinsic part of the local and national cultures. So, as a representative example, the opening of the provisional Czech stage in Prague in 1786 was marked by the publication of a *Makbet* (sic), Karel Hynek Thám's translation of Franz Joseph Fischer's German version for the Prague stage. In his preface, Thám promotes 'Šakespear, an Englishman ... who excelled above all in the composition of sad heroic dramas, and surpassing them, won an eternal glory in his posterity' ('Předmluva').[8] Similarly, Josef Jakub Tandler's lost 1791 *Hamlet* and Prokop Šedivý's *Král Lír a jeho nevděčné dcery* ('King Lear and his Ungrateful Daughters', manuscript of 1792), a beautiful text with a tragic ending, were created for Czech performances at the Hybern Palace in Prague. At the time of the national emancipation, Shakespeare became the harbinger of the modern age—an embodiment of a spiritual, but non-clerical and non-German, demiurge. From the 1820s onwards, Shakespeare and his humanism explicitly served to corroborate the emancipation of the modern individual and of the national culture. The first complete Eastern European translation of Shakespeare's plays was published on the initiative of the Czech National Museum

[6] I am grateful to Alexandra Portmann for providing details on Yugoslavian Shakespeare, from her conference presentation at the European Shakespeare Research Association Conference at Montpellier (July 2013), and from Hugo Klajn, 'Shakespeare in Yugoslavia', *Shakespeare Quarterly* 5:1 (1954), 41-5; Luko Paljetak, 'Dubrovnik kao Hamletište ili Shakespeare na Dubrovačkim Ljetnim Igrama', *Engleske Teme* (Rijeka, 1997); and Boris Senker, *Bard u Iliriji* (Zagreb 2006).

[7] Nicoleta Cinpoeş, *Shakespeare's Hamlet in Romania 1778-2008: A Study in Translation, Performance and Cultural Appropriation* (Lewiston: The Edwin Mellen Press, 2010). Further information on the history of Shakespeare in Romania is available in Monica Matei-Chesnoiu's *Shakespeare in the Romanian Cultural Memory* (New Jersey: Fairleigh Dickinson University Press, 2006), and her 3-volume collection *Shakespeare in Romania* (Bucharest: Humanitas, 2006, 2007, 2008).

[8] Reprinted together with early and rare Czech translations in Pavel Drábek, *České pokusy o Shakespeara* (Brno: Větrné mlýny, 2012), 340.

and the Czech Foundation (Matice česká) between 1855 and 1872. In Prague the 1864 anniversary of Shakespeare's birth turned into a manifestation of Czech national emancipation: anticipated by five productions (*Much Ado about Nothing, Coriolanus, Romeo and Juliet, The Merchant of Venice*, and Rossini's *Otello*), participants in folk costumes came from all over the country; a performance was given of Hector Berlioz's 'symphonie dramatique' *Romeo et Juliette*, and Bedřich Smetana composed a bespoke festive March (Pochod); a *tableau vivant* and a procession of Shakespearean characters were set up; a collection of coloured prints was published; and the evening concluded with performed extracts from plays, and an allegorical character of Perdita, representing '*perdita ars bohemica*' gave a festive oration. Similarly, in 1916, the Shakespeare anniversary in Prague turned into a public display of opposition against the dilapidated Austro-Hungarian Empire. The key author in the Czech national repertoire has always been Shakespeare—even more than any Czech dramatist. It was always a production of a Shakespeare play that marked a crucial moment in the country's history—a (German) performance of *Coriolanus* for the reopening of a theatre in Brno in 1785; performances of *Macbeth, Hamlet*, or *King Lear* in Prague in the following decade; Romantic productions of *Macbeth* and *King Lear* in the mid-1830s; the 'Shakespearean Decade' on the Prague stage in the 1860s; Jiří Frejka's anti-Fascist *Julius Caesar* in the National Theatre in 1936; Bohuš Stejskal's *Hamlet* in the Vinohrady theatre (1941); or, Jaroslav Gillar's *Timon of Athens* (Balustrade Theatre, 1969), reacting to the 1968 military invasion of Czechoslovakia that crushed the Prague Spring. Every generation has reinvented its Shakespeare with a new translation of the Shakespearean canon. For over two centuries artists, each in their respective media and styles—playwrights, novelists, poets, painters, sculptors, puppeteers, and composers—have found inspiration in Shakespeare. Above all, the playwright has inspired major works in the opera: Bedřich Smetana's unfinished *Viola* (1874-83), J. B. Foerster's *Jessika* (1904), Iša Krejčí's *Pozdvižení v Efesu* (The Turmoil in Ephesus, after *The Comedy of Errors*, 1943), Karel Horký's *Jed z Elsinoru* (The Poison of Elsinore, 1969), Ján Cikker's Slovak *Coriolanus* (1972), or Michal Košut's *Macbeth* (2008). To these could be added Janek Ledecký's musical *Hamlet* (1999).

In view of even this selective outline, the Czech Shakespeare cannot be taken as an 'English' author whose work has entered the Czech culture. With a history of more than four centuries, in light of increasingly volatile concepts of authorship and originality, and given the intimate familiarity of a lasting Shakespeare folklore (in both the ethnographic and modern sense of the word), Shakespeare is a 'Czech' author in his own right.[9] This example of Czech culture may stand as a representative *pars pro toto* for all

---

[9] For a historical overview, see Zdeněk Stříbrný's *Shakespeare and Eastern Europe* (Oxford: Oxford University Press, 2000). Valuable views on the Czech reception are given by Jarka Burian, 'Hamlet in postwar Czech theatre', in Dennis Kennedy, ed., *Foreign Shakespeare: Contemporary Performance* (Cambridge: Cambridge University Press, 1993), 195–210; Martin Procházka, 'Shakespeare and the Czech Resistance', in Heather Kerr et al., eds., *Shakespeare: World Views* (Newark: University of Delaware Press, 1996), 44–70; 'Shakespeare, Mácha and Czech Romantic Historicism', *Shakespeare as Cultural Catalyst: Shakespeare Survey* 64 (2011), 199–207; Marcela Kostihová, *Shakespeare in Transition: Political Appropriations in the Postcommunist Czech Republic* (New York: Palgrave Macmillan, 2010). See also Pavel Drábek, 'From the General of the Scottish Army to a Fattish Beer-Drinker: A Short History of Czech Translations of *Macbeth*', in Jana Bžochová-Wild, ed., '*In double trust*': *Shakespeare in Central Europe* (Bratislava: VŠMU, 2014), 52–72.

or most of Eastern Europe. The historical, political, ethnic, and cultural conditions are different in each of the countries in Eastern Europe; however, the profound presence that has permeated, defined, and helped to create its individual cultures for centuries is a characteristic feature of a region[10] in which Shakespeare has played a special role, both culturally and historically.

Cobbling up the Dramatic Hero in a Cynical Age

When metaphysics still existed, it meant comparatively little to be a hero. But now, with an inanimate floor of rock beneath us and an empty sky above, where we have no faith, only hunger for it, where we are so disconnected from one another, thrown back into ourselves, probably more than any preceding generation, it is at this very moment that Thomas Mann appears, wakefully and courageously placing this writer into a completely godless world.

(Bruno Frank in *Neuer Rundschau*, June 1913)[11]

An actor playing the tragic role of a foreigner or a representative of another people, for example Shakespeare's Shylock, and trying to depict the Jewish merchant of Venice as a tragic character, must often do without Jewish intonation or reduce it to a minimum, for a strongly pronounced Jewish intonation would add a comic touch to the tragic passages of the part.

(Pyotr Bogatyrev discussing Nemirovich-Danchenko in 1938)[12]

In Aristotelian terms, tragedy centres on a noble hero affected by a *hamartia*—a flaw or an error that eventually leads to the catastrophic end of an otherwise virtuous individual. Criticism has suggested that Aristotle's definition applies perfectly perhaps only to *Oedipus*; nevertheless, the core of Aristotle's theory can be extended even beyond Sophocles' tragedy or classical Greek drama. The way a tragic hero is constructed makes us sympathize with him or her, despite the persona's shortcomings and mistakes as we share the experience of a fatal journey. Our sympathy is grounded in the values we share with the hero—whether this involves care for the community or the family, the pursuit of truth or justice, or shared beliefs in human dignity and goodness. This empathic rapport is vitally dependent on social sensitivity, openness, and trust in others. It is also in this sense that theatre and culture are the litmus paper of any modern society. The turbulent decades, or even centuries, in Eastern Europe have had an overwhelming impact on social values and fiduciary relations in its societies.

Cognitive biologist and post-1989 Slovak politician Ladislav Kováč, in his incisive monograph *Natural History of Communism: An Anatomy of a Utopia*, has analysed the

---

[10] For further information on individual national Shakespeare receptions, see Select Bibliography.

[11] Cited in Florian Illies, *1913: The Year Before the Storm*, trans. Shaun Whiteside and Jamie Lee Searle (London: Clerkenwell, 2013), 143.

[12] Peter Bogatyrev, 'Znaky divadelní' [Signs in the Theatre], *Slovo a slovesnost* 4 (1938), 141.

impact of the communist project on Eastern European societies, claiming that in keeping with Marxist ideology, the communist revolutions destroyed all sociopolitical institutions—until that moment based on meritocracy in the broadest sense—and exposed people to a social vacuum that required society to be constructed anew in conditions not dissimilar to the formation of animal social units on the savannah (Kováč refers to this as the *savannization* of the society).[13] The communist social experiment has failed. However, it has reconstituted the affected societies at their very core, with consequences that are still continuing. The new system of artificially imposed and rationally designed institutions, Kováč claims, has resulted in spontaneous, wild social developments that have brought about institutions marked with as yet unprecedented irrationality.[14] In the final analysis, once the Marxist 'right to work' became a categorical, unconditional axiom, it compromised and all but annulled the inherent value of work and its purpose. Consequently this particular revolution has led to what Kováč calls *ontological cynicism*—a loss of trust in the purposefulness of work and, ultimately, of knowledge. In this interpretation, as a result of the failed and monstrous social experiment and consequent traumatic ideological turnarounds, post-communist societies are profoundly permeated by ontological cynicism—a mistrust of beliefs, shared values, and ideologies, and—very crucially—of knowledge as a tool of positive progress.

Compared to some of the sublime ideological propositions of official Marxism, a care for one's own individual development and freedom may seem mundane and unworthy of academic argument—especially as it comes down to such relatively marginal matters as being given a chance to study at a grammar school rather than being forced into technical skills training, or to enrol at a university rather than being forced to start mandatory military service (of 2 years) and then going directly to work. Any breach of this routine would result in legal persecution for work shunning and social parasitism. However, the persistency and ubiquity of minor and mundane grievances—such as a catastrophic shortage of toilet paper, sanitary napkins, and paper towels in Czechoslovakia in 1988 (tragicomically repeated in Cuba in 2009)—was a source of profound humiliation, an assault on basic human dignity that also provided opportunities for black-marketeering and everyday corruption. It was these trite embarrassments that built up the everyday social reality of official socialism. It was also part of reality that some of these humiliations and grievances were used as a way of bullying, regardless of whom or by whom. They could be prevented and traded off to some extent: by agreeing to nomination for the Communist Party membership candidate list, by writing a report on one's own working environment, agreeing to mentor a colleague anonymously as part of their acculturation to the new working environment (thereby unwittingly becoming a collaborator of the Secret Police), or applying for promotion, which in itself resulted in a sequence of moral compromises. Each of these proactive steps was double-edged in its consequences: applying for membership in the Party could be used both to one's benefit as well as to one's detriment; everyone knew this was a *quid pro quo* trade-off with an ulterior motive. The cultural mythology that grew

---

[13] Ladislav Kováč, *Prírodopis komunizmu: Anatómia jednej utópie* [Natural History of Communism: An Anatomy of a Utopia] (Bratislava: Kalligram, 2007); for an earlier version in English, see Ladislav Kováč, 'Natural History of Communism', *Central European Political Science Review* 3:8 (2002), 74–110, 111–64.

[14] Kováč, *Prírodopis komunizmu*, 21.

around this new social situation testifies to its paradoxical reality as well as helping explain the disheartening cynicism with which public life is now viewed.[15] The most shocking realization of the post-communist era is that the nature of social reality has been changing only gradually. The principles on which it was built were not ideological but hierarchical; the habits have survived until the present—in the ruthless mindset of trading off favours and advantages, in corruption, and in the cynical approach to any kind of organized activity—especially towards the state economy in favour of the grey economy.

In communism, real-time arts—theatre and music, especially songwriter concerts—because they were least controlable by surveillance and censorship—were a forum for reflecting grievances against social reality. They were not political in the immediate sense, just as everyday reality was apolitical. However, the targets of their criticism were products of the contemporary state of affairs and the political regime was easily implicated by deduction. However, that does not mean that what seemed targeted against the establishment was necessarily explosive or dissident. Satire as a genre has often been deployed as a pro-regime tool in blunting the edge of aggression and alleviating tension by laughter; the satirical *Dikobraz* journal was published by the Central Committee of the Czechoslovak Communist Party. Equally, jibes from the stage against the prevailing state of affairs were indirectly supported by the Party: the Goose on a String Theatre (Brno, CZ) was well-known for its political and satirical commentaries, very clearly manifested in their *Shakespearomania* Trilogy (1988-91), a medley of Shakespeare's plays. In these three productions (*Their Majesties' Fools*, 1988; *The Hamlet Humans*, 1990; and, *The Man of the Tempest*, 1991), director Peter Scherhaufer launched a cabaret of parodic sketches derived from Shakespeare's plays, often subverting their canonical status and creating opportunities for political (as well as other) innuendos.[16] These enjoyed long runs in the theatre, attracting enthusiastic audiences; at the same time, their real political impact was rather limited, since they operated within the persistent Marxist model of culture as a superstructure. They were a variant of the bourgeois 'good night out' model with a restricted potential for actual change. The theatre was celebrated not only by the public but also by the establishment: the company were given high state decorations and were celebrated on the title page of the official *Rudé právo* newspaper. Similarly, the popular singer Jaromír Nohavica, who has acquired a national reputation since 1989, was not only persecuted—being a Czech equivalent of the Soviet oppositional songwriters Bulat Okudzhava and Vladimir Vysotskyi—but also compromised by collaborating with the State Police, a trade-off under murky circumstances, which bought him 'a minute's mirth to wail a week' / for having sold 'eternity to get a toy' (*Rape of Lucrece*, 261-2).

[15] Here are some of the proverbial sayings, rife in communist Czechoslovakia and paralleled by others in the Eastern bloc: 'Your success will never be forgiven.' 'Who doesn't steal, robs oneself and one's own family.' The 7 miracles of socialism: (1) Everyone has a job; (2) Though everyone has a job, nobody works; (3) Though nobody works, the plan is fulfilled by 100%; (4) Though the plan is fulfilled by 100%, there is a shortage of everything; (5) Though there a shortage of everything, everyone has everything; (6) Though everyone has everything, everyone steals; (7) Though everyone steals, nothing is really missing.

[16] For more on Slovak director and playwright Peter Scherhaufer (1942-99) see Dagmar Inštitorisová, 'Playwright Peter Scherhaufer (an essay from theater archives)', in Vlasta Kunová and Martin Dolinský, eds., *Current Issues of Science and Research in the Global World* (London: Taylor and Francis, 2015), 177–86.

Whether or not Kováč's comfortless analysis is an accurate articulation of the state of post-Communist Europe, the ideological turns underlying the Cold War as well as the post-1989 power contention between the East and the West has affected the very basis of civil society in Eastern Europe. Since the early years of wild Marxist reforms, antisocial egoism and self-interest have established themselves as modes of existence and survival, placing them as the lowest common denominator of the social establishment—as opposed to the traditional perception of this behaviour as an instance of antisocial dysfunction. With a crack at the heart of the fiduciary relations and social sensibility, how is it possible to fulfil the necessary condition of tragedy—empathetic rapport with the tragic hero? Or, as Adrian Noble put it in relation to Richard III, 'Richard can only have a tragic dimension if you can find the potential for good in him'.[17] How, ultimately, can the tragic hero be constructed in this social ontology?

Responses to this conundrum lie in the generic instability of Shakespearean plays. Despite its identification as comedy, *The Merchant of Venice*, since its first Czech version in 1782, has had a double reception—as a romantic comedy which nevertheless has Shylock's tragedy at its heart. Comedy as a genre hinges on social sensibility and centres around the self-chastising life of the community where individuals are subject to laws of contingency (rather than the tragic laws of causality), while it is the community that acts as the hero of the play. Given the troubled social sensibility and heightened sense of antisocial egoism in Eastern European societies, productions of *The Merchant of Venice* have tended to rely on Shylock as the pivot of the play's action, placing his tragedy at the core of the action. Unsurprisingly—given the bouts of pogroms and ethnic cleansing, occurring in horribly irrational patterns almost irrespective of the proclaimed political trends—the Jew in the Eastern Europe of the past century has been a tragic character, in contrast to the comical portrayals of earlier folk traditions. In the interwar period, the tragic character of Shylock was taken for granted, as Prague School theorist Pyotr Bogatyrev (himself a Russian emissary based in Czechoslovakia) attests. The contentious nature of the play—and its tragic potential, one might argue— resulted in its being effectively banned in the Soviet Union and treated with suspicion in the Soviet satellites.[18] If performed at all in Eastern Europe, *The Merchant* was grouped with Shakespeare's tragic canon rather than with the comedies. The haunting presence of open anti-Semitism has made it impossible to separate Shylock's religion from his antisocial and illegal behaviour. The cult of the individual fighting against the establishment was, crucially, one of the necessary components of a tragic character, since it identified a virtue or 'potential for good' with which audiences could feel sympathy. This could happen not *despite* Shylock's antisocial behaviour but *because of* it. Stubbornly faithful to his own private beliefs, Shylock is a model tragic hero in his self-destructive sacrifice—an heroic act performed in defiance of a corrupt and malevolent establishment and its laws.

There are alternatives for the frustrated social sensibility in Eastern Europe—the 'venom of nationalism', as the Polish Shakespearean scholar and critic Andrzej Żurowski called it

---

[17] Cited in Anthony Sher, *Year of the King* (London: Nick Hern Books, 2004), 149.

[18] Mark Sokolyansky, 'The Half-Forbidden Play in Soviet Shakespeare Criticism of the 1920-50s', *Multicultural Shakespeare: Translation, Appropriation and Performance* 6–7 (2010), 71–9.

after George Steiner.[19] While Steiner coined the term in connection with the late nineteenth century, the re-emergence of the sentiment in post-war Europe is something of a pathological, retrograde anachronism—particularly in connection with Shakespeare's plays, which are primed to become the medium of a transnational cultural community rather than instruments of the nationalist agendas that had been exploited by communist establishments. Hand in hand with the new nationalism goes a rekindled interest in the Russian vision of the world, often fuelled by anti-EU and anti-American sentiments. These alternative visions of national futures respond to the difficulties of the European integration process, to people's vulnerability in the economic transformation, and to the exacting responsibilities of capitalist individualism; they proffer a centrally directed power that guarantees social, national, and cultural securities—in a faux-nostalgic attempt at bringing back a less complicated and more livable version of this world. This apparent retrograde attitude manifests itself in productions of Shakespeare too, especially in their deployment of rather primitive models—whether these involve gender simplifications, racial stereotypes, or black-and-white polarizations of characters. Such models may seem crude and even offensive to an external eye—and they are. But the offence and crudeness are intentional as realistic and verisimilar representations of the jarring social and political realities of today's Eastern Europe.

Beyond these retrograde simplifications, if Shakespeare's tragic heroes are to be recreated on the modern stage, how is one to 'find the potential for good' in an antisocially egoistic and cynical age—especially, one that prides itself in being devoid of belief and shared values? This question touches the very heart of Shakespearean dramaturgy and may be used as a prism through which to explore the particularities of the genre in Eastern Europe. The construction of the tragic hero in any given production is inseparable from the setting up of the play's fictive world and from its relation to the social reality outside the theatre walls. The examples presented here are concrete case studies, designed to be representative of broad dramaturgical tendencies rather than a catalogue of directors or ensembles; given the mind-boggling range and extent of Shakespearean activities in Eastern Europe it is probably beyond the capacity of an individual to compile such a catalogue.

Apart from various retrograde attempts at creating the illusion of a hero—righteous, brave, deserving (and mostly male)—the modern Eastern European tragic protagonist is typically imagined as a failure. Ironic and parodic approaches are common, though they tend to capture only the surface of Shakespeare's tragedies. A telling example is Vladimír Morávek's award-winning 1999 production of *Macbeth* in the Andrej Bagár Theatre in Nitra (Slovakia). Macbeth and Lady Macbeth entered the play in pyjamas and shabby nightgowns, watching TV and drinking bottled beer from their fridge. As if by miracle, they entered the dreamy 'big world' they knew from the TV screen, and performed nightmarish deeds of cruelty in a desperate attempt at maximizing the gains of their new-found ambitions. The juxtaposition of small TV-watching people with the grand world of aristocracy was emphasized not only through jarring differences in costume but also in the casting: Marián Labuda and Adela Gáborová were both short, while the actors playing Duncan and the royal train were tall, towering over Labuda by half a metre. While Morávek's casting achieved simple caricature, the irony had metaphorical potency too; it played off the cultural sentiment of disenfranchisement and the powerlessness of the 'small person' in confrontation with the power players of

---

[19] George Steiner, *The Death of Tragedy* (Oxford: Oxford University Press, 1961, 1980), 286.

the 'big world'. By birth, Labuda's Macbeth was doomed from the start. Despite—or rather because of—that, he became a noble fighter, standing up to any challenge that came his way. The comic dimension of the production, together with Labuda's status as a celebrity—he had only recently appeared as King Ubu in a film performance that clearly contributed to his characterization of Macbeth—set off this tragedy of a man dressed 'in borrowed robes' (1.3.107)—a tragicomically literal fact of this production. The tragic dimension was present also from another perspective: the newcomers in the grand world of power play were recruited, by chance, from dull beer-drinkers whose only culture was TV. As a result, *Macbeth* had turned into a tragedy of degeneration, adding a charged irony to Macbeth's false lament:

> from this instant
> There's nothing serious in mortality.
> All is but toys. Renown and grace is dead.
> The wine of life is drawn, and the mere lees
> Is left this vault to brag of.

> (2.3.91-5)

Macbeth, in a moment of blatant hypocrisy—weeping over the dead King Duncan, whom he has only just butchered in his own house—obliquely speaks of himself: to the spectator, it is he who is reduced to 'nothing serious' and 'the mere lees', even as he brags of his own power.

What Kováč dubs ontological cynicism produces other variants of flawed and cobbled-up tragic heroes. Signs of disintegration can be found on various levels, including subliminal ones. Ivan Rajmont's production of *Othello* in the Czech National Theatre (Prague, 1998) seemingly stood for a canonical rendering of the tragedy within the boundaries of 'Shakespeare our contemporary': the stage design (Jozef Ciller) created a dynamic, metaphorical space, and the costumes (Marta Roszkopfová) were vaguely modern. Martin Hilský's new translation modernized the diction but also catered for the play's canonicity. Visually, Boris Rösner's Othello was the usual Eastern European whiteface rendering, not charged with racial undertones as there is no colonial past of discrimination against blacks in Czech culture. The 'trick' of this modern tragic hero lay in Rösner's acting, and his style won him a great following, influencing many younger actors. In his delivery, Othello was disintegrated internally into three parallel (and often non-intersecting) agonic layers: the lines he spoke carried one layer of meaning, while his intonation indicated another; and both of these were complemented by Rösner's animalistic body language, which added yet another semantic layer. As a result Rösner's Othello became a polyphonic character—fickle, malleable, and multifaceted, escaping any simple understanding. To be sure, the complexities suggested by this structural analysis of Rösner's acting would have probably escaped the spectator: what came across was a certain elusive mysteriousness about Othello, as well as a menacing otherness. Evolutionary studies and music psychology have shown that intonation is the *honest signal* that reveals a character's true motivations and attitudes.[20] In the

---

[20] For music psychology see Ian Cross, 'Music and Communication in Music Psychology', *Psychology of Music* 42:6 (2014), 809-19. For evolution theory see Richard Caird, *Ape Man: The Story of Human Evolution* (London: Boxtree, 1994), or Camilla Power, 'Old Wives' Tales: The Gossip Hypothesis and the Reliability of Cheap Signals', in J. R. Hurford et al., eds., *Approaches to the Evolution of Language: Social and Cognitive Bases* (Cambridge: Cambridge University Press, 1998), 111-29.

emotional and intellectual response to Rösner's polyphonic acting, the spectator was drawn in conflicting directions. In an Aristotelian sense, this disintegrated polyphony was itself the tragic hero's *flaw*—something that eventually culminated in the catastrophe of Iago setting him 'on the rack' (3.3.340), and unleashing Othello's (that is, Othello-as-Everyman's) destructive animalistic nature as both intellect and emotions dissolved. Rösner's polyphonic acting served as an objective correlative for another cultural reality of post-communist culture—namely what the history of oppression calls mental reservation (*reservatio mentis*). The divide between what one says on the one hand, and thinks on the other, is a symptom of oppressive regimes. A refinement of the ability to navigate through coercive situations and protect one's mental (though covert) integrity, is a technique of social survival—a phenomenon powerfully analysed by the Polish Nobel Prize winning poet Czesław Miłosz in his *The Captive Mind* (1953), perhaps the best testimony to the fate of intellectuals in communist states.[21] Rösner's Othello resonated with the post-communist cultural mentality of those who had to survive 'the slings and arrows' of a perverse regime. On a profoundly intimate level—in the emotional responses to Othello's intonations as honest signals, and to the discontented anger in his bodily rhythms—Rösner keyed into a cultural sentiment that his audiences knew only too well. At the same time, Othello's vulnerability to the scheming and malicious Iago made him a hero—one of us, the oppressed and compromising survivors of social degeneracy. In this respect, Rösner catered for the mainstream standpoint of people—a profound suspicion of public heroes (dissidents, political prisoners, emigrants) and a collusive sympathy with the common folk who had to learn to survive and plod on. This affirmativeness reinforced the position of Rajmont's *Othello* as a reassuring (traditionalist and canonizing) production, rather than a provocative and taxing invention. Othello was 'other'—because each of us was someone 'other', hiding away our own mental integrity from oppressive social constraints. Uncannily similar to postmodern deconstruction—but for the name—the world of Rajmont's and Rösner's *Othello* realized the social reality of the disintegrated and socially uprooted individual.

These strategies for constituting (or cobbling up) the tragic hero may be seen as a recurrent feature of Eastern European productions of Shakespeare. On many levels, Shakespearean plays are re-presented on stage with a heightened sense of metaphoricity and vicariousness—starting with translations, through actor impersonations, to the plays as spaces of vested interests. In this way, Shakespearean drama assumes and possesses spectral bodies that operate within local cultures but are also representatives of a transnational classic.

SHAKESPEARE'S SPECTRAL PRESENCE

Shakespeare's *Hamlet* brought to the early modern stage a ground-breakingly refined version of those Senecan revenge tragedies, in which a Fury haunting stage characters exacted

---

[21] Czesław Miłosz, *The Captive Mind* (1953; London: Penguin Classics, 2001). Rather than *mental reservation*, Miłosz uses the Persian term *Ketman* for the self-protective white lie (or downright lie) pronounced in an oppressive situation (see ch. 3 'Ketman', 54ff.).

retaliation for past crimes. While Senecan protagonists were near-allegorical agents of this metaphysical duty, Hamlet is also—or perhaps first of all—an individual with a profoundly modern, fragmented notion of self. 'This quintessence of dust', the modern self, has been ghosted ever since by 'bad dreams' that disintegrate the individual, pulling him/her apart in conflicting directions. This self refuses to be contained as a unified entity, and dissolves into a colour spectrum—a visual metaphor that informs many of today's productions, not only of *Hamlet* but of other tragedies too.

A highly imaginative approach was taken by Petra Tejnorová in her staging of *Titus Andronicus*, performed by students of the Puppet and Alternative Theatre Atelier at the Academy of Performing Arts in Prague (DAMU, 2005). Tejnorová's was a daring production in many ways—not only was it a premiere of the play in Czech (followed a few weeks later by Ivan Rajmont's more traditional production in the Dlouhá Theatre), it also used puppets and inanimate objects to provide a second layer of stage business. In Tejnorová's *Titus* (subtitled '*The Flight of a Fly*'), while individual characters acted and delivered their lines in the intimate studio space, they simultaneously deployed their bodies in the form of anthropomorphic puppets and props reminiscent of dinosaur bones to create spectres of monster-like bodies. The action fluently shifted from the interplay of characters to metaphorical representations of the numerous atrocities of Shakespeare's tragedy. The visual imagery created through puppets and formations made of stylized body movement was evocative not only of the primitive social life of antediluvian reptiles but also, more intimately, as a generational message, pointing at the corrupt big players of contemporary politics—the new generation of state leaders—as well as at the imposed cultural baggage of Czech theatrical tradition, with its near-fetishistic reverence for puppet theatre (a jab at the performers' own professional training). Shakespeare's tragedy was played, spectrally, on several layers—with powerful emotional overtones materialising in the puppet stage-business.

On the modern stage—and it would be perhaps misleading to narrow it to the geopolitical frame of Eastern Europe—the unease of reconstructing Hamlet the tragic hero often spreads out into multiple projections and impersonations—with Hamlet the actor ghosted by a projection and by other *spectral bodies*—turning the stage into 'an unweeded garden' (1.2.135), and presenting a cognitive impasse overwhelming the spectator's senses. For example, the 2008 Romanian production of *Hamlet*, directed by Radu Alexandru Nica in the Radu Stanca Theatre, Sibiu (with scenography by Drahoş Buhagiar) sported 'simultaneous narratives'.[22] Ciprian Scurtea's Hamlet was only one of many impersonations of the protagonist, accompanied by projections of Lawrence Olivier's 1948 film, by intertextual references to previous productions and versions—Romanian or foreign—and by two TV screen projections of real-time or even delayed camcorder footage that Scurtea (or Hamlet?) made as he played on stage. The spectral presence of Hamlet's disintegrated self became a multifaceted metaphor that provoked the audience's cultural memory. Nica's *Hamlet* was not only a self-conscious staging of Shakespeare's play but also embodied the 'encyclopaedic cultural product the play *Hamlet* has become'—constructing a multifaceted, heteroglossic presence that juggled a variety of references.[23]

[22] Cinpoeş, *Shakespeare's Hamlet in Romania*, 271.

[23] Miruna Runcan, 'Horaţio–Hamlet: scrisoare din pântecul mausoleului—*Hamlet*' [Horatio–Hamlet: a letter from the bowels of the mausoleum], *Teatrul azi*, 5–6–7 (2008), 56; quoted in Cinpoeş, *Shakespeare's Hamlet in Romania*, 275.

In a similar vein, was the much celebrated 2004 Polish adaptation of *Hamlet* by Jan Klata, entitled simply *H.* and staged in a derelict Gdańsk shipyard—the site of the 1981 worker strikes that culminated in the *Solidarność* movement. The highly evocative venue of the production combined with the rich cultural history of *Hamlet* in the north of Poland to form the site of young Fortinbras's futile conquests. Klata's production presented an emasculated Hamlet accompanied by a metrosexual Horatio, shooting golf balls into the dilapidated warehouses. This bleak vision was overridden by an appearance of a winged hussar on horseback, clad in early modern Polish military costume, that called up the military past of Great Poland, including victories against the Turks, the Swedes, and the Moscovites—all in the name Virgin Mary, the crowned Queen of Poland.[24]

> The appearance of the winged hussar in the beginning of the play and at the very end, not only evokes memories of past traditions, but transforms the spectacle itself into a metaphoric ceremonial burial, the *pompa funebris*. In this way, the material substance and its modelling create visual commentary on two seemingly discrepant worlds, the Renaissance Elsinore and present-day Gdańsk.[25]

The factory in which the production was performed was decorated by a 1989 poster from the first Polish democratic elections. In this way, the very space of the performance became a living museum showing key moments in Polish cultural history with a Hamlet-like spleen at the current state of things.[26] The richness of meaning accrued in the production was materialized in the spectral bodies and objects within the venue. The Hamlet-haunted world of Klata's *H.* immersed its spectators in a peculiar world, confronting them with the material apparitions of Polish cultural reality—a juxtaposition of images that metaphorically expressed Klata's 'criticism of a world without genuine values,' when faced with remembrances of the magnificent past.[27]

CONCLUSION

'What's Hecuba to him, or he to Hecuba | That he should weep for her?' (2.2.561-2), ponders Hamlet over the suggestive nature of theatrical performance. His is a key question of dramaturgy, reflecting on the power of onstage 'spectres' and fictions of the 'haunted stage' that conjure up our cultural knowledge.[28] In the theatre, such public metaphors solicit shared and

---

[24] Jerzy Limon, 'Jan Klata's *H.[amlet]*—questioning the myth of Solidarity', an unpublished keynote lecture, presented at the European Shakespeare Research Association conference at Montpellier, July 2013. Limon observes that 'The official announcement took place on the 1st of April, 1656, when in Lvov Cathedral the King of Poland, Jan Casimir, declared Mary as the Queen of the Crown of Poland. This was preceded by visions of an Italian monk to whom the Blessed Virgin appeared and stated that she wanted to become the Queen of Poland' (8).

[25] Limon, 'Jan Klata's *H.[amlet]*', 12–13.

[26] The concept of scenography as the staging of a living museum is derived from Pamela Howard, *What is Scenography* (Abingdon: Routledge, 2nd edn 2009).

[27] Limon, 'Jan Klata's *H.[amlet]*', 13.

[28] Marvin Carlson, *The Haunted Stage: The Theater as Memory Machine* (Ann Arbor: University of Michigan Press, 2001).

socially aware responses, creating communities of intimacy.[29] The nature and substance of these instantaneous 'imagined communities' depend on the 'baseless fabric of this vision' and the 'insubstantial pageant[s]' (*Tem*, 4.1.151, 155) that are presented to the audience—some of which activate a national sentiment, others a political community, and others a community of global citizens, while yet others remain in the domestic and private spheres.[30] This 'Hecuba' is powerful enough to raise almost any ghost for its audiences. Similarly, Shakespeare's plays are an infinitely complex cryptogram capable of evoking images, thoughts, and epistemes that constitute our social reality. The particularity of how this occurs is commensurate with the world we inhabit, *hic et nunc*, at the moment of reading or watching.

Shakespeare as a celebrity author comes into the play as a voice from the outside—from another age as well as from another country, although his work has accompanied the Eastern European cultural past for centuries. As a phenomenon both foreign and 'our contemporary' (to cite Jan Kott), Shakespeare has been deployed to reflect on our cultural and political history. For centuries, the plays—and in particular the tragedies, thanks to their political awareness—have served as metaphors of desired freedoms—'states unborn and accents yet unknown' (*JC* 3.1.114)—and of the frustrated pasts of Eastern Europe marked by visions of a millenarian state of one's own. In a sense, the dreamworlds of Shakespeare, translated into national languages, became material embodiments of these desired states-to-come. Municipal theatres, established across Eastern Europe during the long nineteenth century, embodied the emerging civil society. Theatres became (and have, in many ways, remained) spaces of projected desires and societal models—presenting epiphanies of ideal states and behaviours. It is far from coincidental that this ideological mission went hand in hand with the establishment of Shakespeare as a canonical author and the centre of a chiliastic value system—an axiological vertical of sorts, in line with Shakespeare's spectral presence. This model, I argue, survives in the spectral visions of contemporary Eastern European theatre—an ubiquitous memento, like a ghost of Old Hamlet reminding audiences and readers that the treasured vision of the national state has not yet arrived—that, still, 'something is rotten in the state' of our troubled world.

Select Bibliography

Blumenfeld, Odette and Veronica Popescu, eds., *Shakespeare in Europe: Nation(s) and Boundaries* (Iaşi: Editura universităţi 'Alexandru Ioan Cuza' Iaşi, 2011).

Bžochová-Wild, Jana, ed., *'In double trust': Shakespeare in Central Europe* (Bratislava: VŠMU, 2014).

[29] For the power of metaphor in relation to cultural knowledge and a sense of community, see Ted Cohen, 'Metaphor and the Cultivation of Intimacy', *Critical Inquiry* 5:1 (Autumn 1978), 3–12; and Ted Cohen, *Thinking of Others: On the Talent for Metaphor* (Princeton and Oxford: Princeton University Press, 2009), esp. ch. 4 'Real Feelings, Unreal People' that contains references to Wittgenstein's ponderings on the suggestive power of art (38), and Cohen's meditation on Hamlet's Hecuba speech (39–41).

[30] For 'imagined communities' see Benedict Anderson, *Imagined Communities: Reflections on the Origin and Spread of Nationalism* (London: Verso, 1983, rev. edn. 2006). For songs as creating intimate communities and imaginary rapports, see Daniel J. Levitin, *The World in Six Songs: How the Musical Brain Created Human Nature* (London: Aurum Press, 2009). Levitin is oblivious of the dramatic/situational dimension of his analysis. Songs create situations of intimate dialogue with an imaginary partner, not only static emotions and psychological states as Levitin seems to suggest.

Cinpoeş, Nicoleta, *Shakespeare's Hamlet in Romania 1778–2008: A Study in Translation, Performance and Cultural Appropriation* (Lewiston: The Edwin Mellen Press, 2010).

Gibińska, Marta and Jerzy Limon, eds., *Hamlet East–West* (Gdańsk: Theatrum Gedanense Foundation, 1998).

Gibińska, Marta and Agnieszka Romanowska, eds., *Shakespeare in Europe: History and Memory* (Kraków: Jagiellonian University Press, 2008).

Hattaway, Michael, Boika Sokolova, and Derek Roper, eds., *Shakespeare in the New Europe* (Sheffield: Sheffield Academic Press, 1994).

Kawachi, Yoshiko and Krystyna Kujawińska Courtney, eds., *Multicultural Shakespeare: Translation, Appropriation and Performance.* Journal published by University of Łódź and Walter de Gruyter, since 1972 (http://shakespearecentre.uni.lodz.pl/multicultural-shakespeare-en/).

Klein, Holger and Péter Dávidházi, eds., *Shakespeare and Hungary, Shakespeare Yearbook* 7 (1996).

Makaryk, Irena R., *Shakespeare in the Undiscovered Bourn: Les Kurbas, Modernism, and Early Soviet Cultural Politics* (Toronto and London: University of Toronto Press, 2004).

Makaryk, Irena R. and Joseph G. Price, eds., *Shakespeare in the Worlds of Communism and Socialism* (Toronto, Buffalo, and London: University of Toronto Press, 2006).

Matei-Chesnoiu, Monica, *Shakespeare in the Romanian Cultural Memory* (New Jersey: Fairleigh Dickinson University Press, 2006).

Matei-Chesnoiu, Monica, ed. *Shakespeare în România: Texts 1836–1916* (Bucureşti: Editura Academiei Române, 2009).

Mancewicz, Aneta, *Intermedial Shakespeares on European Stages* (New York: Palgrave Macmillan, 2014).

Schandl, Veronika, *Socialist Shakespeare Productions in Kádár-regime Hungary* (Lewiston: The Edwin Mellen Press, 2009).

Shurbanov, Alexander and Boika Sokolova, *Painting Shakespeare Red: An East-European Appropriation* (Newark: University of Delaware Press, 2001).

Shurbanov, Alexander and Boika Sokolova, 'King Lear East of Berlin: Tragedy under Socialist Realism and After', in Anthony R. Guneratne, ed., *Shakespeare and Genre: From Early Modern Inheritances to Postmodern Legacies* (New York: Palgrave Macmillan, 2011), 173–88.

Stříbrný, Zdeněk, *Shakespeare and Eastern Europe* (Oxford: Oxford University Press, 2000).

CHAPTER 46

....

SHAKESPEAREAN TRAGEDY IN RUSSIA

In Equal Scale Weighing Delight and Dole

....

JOHN GIVENS

SHAKESPEARE's ascent in Russia largely coincided with the birth and eventual flour-ishing of Russia's national literature. In a fateful coincidence, the Father of English literature was an important influence on the Father of Russian literature, Alexander Pushkin. Pushkin, in turn, helped to secure Shakespeare's place in Russian culture. Since the earliest days of Russian scholarship on the bard, two models have been promoted by which to measure his importance and influence on Russian literature: *shekspirizm* (Shakespearism) and *shekspirizatsiia* (Shakespearization). The first term—*shekspirizm*—was coined by Pavel Annenkov in one of the earliest works ever de-voted to the topic of Shakespeare and Pushkin.[1] It refers to how acquaintance with Shakespeare changed the very way Pushkin looked at and understood both his times and his art. Shakespeare's 'philosophical-historical impartiality' in his plays influenced how Pushkin thought about the subjects of his own art and constituted a turning point in Pushkin's development, displacing Lord Byron as the poet's presiding English muse.[2] Thus the term speaks to a kind of artistic assimilation of Shakespeare in the outlook and literary approach of the artist. *Shekspirizatsiia*, on the other hand, describes a much more straightforward appropriation of Shakespearean themes and ideas in the works of a writer. It is a kind of textual homage to a character type or plot in Shakespeare and reflects a process by which Shakespeare's literary heritage is claimed for Russia as well. Ivan Turgenev's narrative 'A Hamlet of the Shchigrovsky District' (included in the collection *A Hunter's Sketches*, 1847–1852) and *King Lear of the Steppe* (1870) as well as Nikolai Leskov's *Lady Macbeth of the Mtsenk District* (1865) are prominent ex-amples of such stories whose titles assume their readers' familiarity with Shakespeare and whose content presents a Russian take on Shakespearean themes. Shakespeare's importance in Russian culture, established in the nineteenth century, did not wane

---

[1] Pavel Annenkov, 'Shekspirizm', in *Aleksandr Sergeevich Pushkin v Aleksandrovskuiu epokhu* (Saint Petersburg: Tipografiia M. Stasiulevicha, 1874), 293–300.

[2] Ibid., 296, 293.

in the twentieth either, where he was claimed for the socialist cause in speeches at the First Congress of Soviet Writers in 1934 and never thereafter displaced from the Russian Parnassus. Translations of six of Shakespeare's tragedies by Boris Pasternak between 1941 and 1951 have even been praised as better in some respects than their English originals,[3] and film versions by Grigorii Kozintsev using two of Pasternak's renditions—of *Hamlet* in 1962 and *King Lear* in 197—are routinely included among the best productions of those plays. Such Russian maximalism speaks to the abiding importance of Shakespeare in Russian culture. Russians may have referred to Pushkin as 'our everything', but Shakespeare has also captured the hearts and minds of Russian writers and readers for over two centuries.

Ivan the Terrible (1530-84)—himself a fitting subject for Shakespearean tragedy—first brought Russia into contact with English culture in 1555, a decade before Shakespeare's birth. English literature would yet be a long time coming to Russia, however, and Shakespeare even longer. Peter the Great (1672 -1725) brought Russia and Western Europe very close together, but it was French literature, not English, that attended the development of a Russian literary tradition 35 years after Peter's death, during the reign of Catherine II (1729-96). At this time, the French neoclassical school dominated the imaginations of Russian writers, who imitated Molière, Corneille, Racine, Boileau, and, later, Voltaire and the Encylopaedists.[4] By late-century, however, Russian Gallomania abated somewhat. At the same time, French and German admiration for English culture—steadily growing throughout the 1700s—also began to penetrate Russian intellectual circles, thanks partly to Catherine II.

Though she regarded French culture very highly and even corresponded with Voltaire, Diderot, and other of the Encylcopaedists, Catherine steered Russia towards English models of governmental, legal, and educational institutions and, eventually—through French and German translations—towards English literature as well.[5] Catherine even produced her own adaptations of Shakespeare, whom she read in German prose translations. Her Russianized version of *The Merry Wives of Windsor*—titled *This is What it Means to have a Buck-Basket and Linen* ('Vot kakovo imet' korzinu i bel'e', based on a comic exclamation at the close of Act 3 of Shakespeare's play)—was published and acted in 1786 and was followed by her Russified adaptation of *Timon of Athens*, which she retitled *The Spendthrift* ('Rastochitel''). Catherine also wrote two Russian plays on historical themes which she described as 'imitations of Shakespeare' but 'without observing the usual rules of theatre', an indication of her disdain for the rules of French neoclassical drama, with its insistence on the unities of time, place, and action and its typical themes of love and duty

---

[3] In her study of *Hamlet* in Russia, Eleanor Rowe reports how Russians would inform her 'solemnly and enthusiastically, that Hamlet is better in Pasternak's translation than in the original'. See her *Hamlet: A Window on Russia* (New York: New York University Press, 1976) 152. S. P. Tolkachov mentions the 'opinion that Pasternak's translation of *Hamlet* has more diversity of meaning and is deeper than the original text'. See his 'Pasternak and Shakespeare' on the Russian 'World of Shakespeare' website at http://world-shake.ru/en/Encyclopaedia/3907.html (last accessed 21 May 2015).

[4] Ernest J. Simmons, *English Literature and Culture in Russia: 1553-1840* (Cambridge, MA: Harvard University Press, 1935), 68.

[5] For more, see Simmons's chapter 'Anglomania During the Reign of Catherine II (1762-1796)', in *English Literature and Culture in Russia*, 73–101.

and reason versus passion.[6] As Ernest J. Simmons explains, 'At a time when the Russian theatre was still dominated by French formalism, Catherine's determination to defy the traditional rules was a step in the direction of a better understanding of Shakespeare.'[7]

Although Catherine's brief venture into adapting Shakespeare for Russian audiences produced works that are interesting today only because 'the empress had written them', her plays did stimulate greater interest in the English bard among the Russian public.[8] Her version of *Merry Wives of Windsor* also marks the first appearance of Shakespeare's name on a Russian title page, though her play was not the first translation of Shakespeare in Russian theatre. That distinction belongs to Alexander Sumarokov, the 'father of Russian drama'.

A writer and director, Sumarokov was famous for a series of original plays as well as for improving technical features and acting on Russian stages.[9] His version of *Hamlet*, published in 1748 and produced in 1750, constitutes Shakespeare's debut on Russian stages, though the play is like Shakespeare's in name only, an outcome of the eighteenth-century practice of using titles and character names of well-known plays but matching them to new content. Sumarokov retained only five characters from Shakespeare's play (Hamlet, Gertrude, Claudius, Ophelia, and Polonius). He also omitted the graveyard scene, the play-within-the-play, and the duel; made Polonius the murderer of Hamlet's father and Claudius the wooer of Ophelia; and gave the play a happy ending in which Hamlet lives happily ever after with Ophelia as the rightful ruler of Denmark.[10]

Though Sumarokov's adaptation depended in part on Voltaire's free translation of the play and a 1746 prose and verse translation by Pierre Antoine de La Place, his play was no mere imitation of foreign models, as Marcus Levitt has shown. Rather, in its own way, it poses questions that would occupy Russian writers of the next century, such as whether evil can be overcome, either within oneself or in others.[11] It also explores the role of divine agency in human affairs as well as traditional Russian Orthodox values, particularly in the religious responses of Ophelia and Gertrude to the situations in which they find themselves.[12] Thus the play, as D. M. Lang argues, may actually be 'the best independent treatment of the subject which a dramatist could hope to make acceptable to a Russian audience in the middle of the eighteenth century'.[13] Produced a full 19 years before the first French version of *Hamlet* was acted, Sumarokov's play was very popular and went through four editions by 1786.[14]

The first complete and accurate rendition of a Shakespeare play into Russian was made by Nikolai Karamzin, who published a translation of *Julius Caesar* in 1787 based primarily on the original English text. As important as Karamzin's translation was, even more noteworthy was the introduction he wrote to accompany it, which, according to Simmons,

---

[6] Simmons, *English Literature and Culture in Russia*, 206, 212; also, Zdeněk Stříbrný, *Shakespeare and Eastern Europe* (Oxford: Oxford University Press, 2000), 31–2.

[7] Simmons, *English Literature and Culture in Russia*, 212.   [8] Ibid., 213.

[9] Ibid., 205.

[10] For detailed analyses of Sumarokov's play, see Stříbrný, *Shakespeare and Eastern Europe*, 27–9, and Marcus Levitt, 'Sumarokov's Russianized "Hamlet": Texts and Contexts', *Slavic and East European Journal* 38:2 (Summer, 1994), 319–41.

[11] Levitt, 'Sumarokov's Russianized "Hamlet"', 327.   [12] Ibid., 330–4.

[13] D. M. Lang, 'Sumarokov's "Hamlet": A Misjudged Russian Tragedy of the Eighteenth Century', *The Modern Language Review* 43:1 (January, 1948), 72.

[14] Ibid., 70.

represents 'the first adequate critical presentation of Shakespeare in Russia'.[15] Karamzin argued for a reassessment of Shakespeare's importance as a playwright, taking issue with the bard's French detractors and following Catharine's lead a year before him in defending Shakespeare's violation of the classical unities. He also made a case for placing Shakespeare above Corneille and Racine as a dramatist—an astounding claim, given the dominance of French culture at the time. 'I challenge the experts of French theatre', Karamzin wrote, 'to find anything in Corneille or Racine like the Shakespearean verses pronounced by the old Lear as he wanders in the wilderness on a stormy night, exiled by his own children, to whom he had given his kingdom, his crown and his greatness.'[16]

A devotee of English and German sentimentalism and the most prominent proponent of that literary movement in Russia, Karamzin praised Shakespeare's insights into the human heart and his ability to convey 'the soft emotions of the most tender passions.'[17] In Shakespeare, Karamzin saw an artist suited to the sentimentalist outlook. Though he frequently mentions Shakespeare in his critical articles and original compositions,[18] his engagement with the bard ultimately remains in the realm of *shekspirizatsiia*, like Sumarokov and Catherine before him. A promoter of Shakespeare's place in world as well as Russian culture, Karamzin did not assimilate Shakespeare's artistic or philosophical worldview to any significant degree.

In the first decades of the next century partial translations and critical discussions appeared in greater number in the literary press and new productions appeared on Russian stages. Despite Karamzin's efforts in the previous century, these versions—of *Othello* and *Lear* in 1807, *Hamlet* in 1810 and an opera adaptation of *Romeo and Juliet* in 1817— continued to be based upon loose French translations and thus had only passing resemblance to Shakespeare's plays. With the rise of romanticism in Russia, however, a new cult of Shakespeare began to form, and with it, calls for greater fidelity to his plays. 'The young Russian romantics', Simmons reminds us, 'regarded Shakespeare as a symbol of universal genius, a writer whose mind comprehended all phases of humanity, and who dared to treat the unreal and the supernatural as well as the actions of real men and women.'[19] The most important of the Russian romantics at this time and Shakespeare's best student was undoubtedly Alexander Pushkin.

Shakespeare's influence on Pushkin is well known, originating in the poet's own statements about the English playwright, whom he referred to as 'our Father Shakespeare' while working on his tragedy, *Boris Godunov* (1825).[20] Like Karamzin and his fellow romantics, Pushkin turned to Shakespeare as an antidote to French neoclassicism in drama, particularly with regard to tragedy, which Pushkin called 'perhaps the most misunderstood genre'. Instead of the classical unities, Pushkin proposed 'verisimilitude of situations and

[15] Simmons, *English Literature and Culture in Russia*, 215.

[16] Cited in P. R. Zaborov, 'Ot klassitsizma k romantizmu', *Shekspir i russkaia kul'tura*, ed. M. P. Alekseev (Moscow and Leningrad: Nauka, 1965), 78.

[17] Nikolai Karamzin, *Iulii Tsesar, perevod s Angliskago, prozoiu* (St. Petersburg, 1787). Cited in Simmons, *English Literature and Culture in Russia*, 214.

[18] Zaborov, 'Ot klassitsizma k romantizmu', 75.

[19] Simmons, *English Literature and Culture in Russia*, 223–4.

[20] *Pushkin on Literature*, trans. and ed. Tatiana Wolff (Evanston, IL: Northwestern University Press, 1998), 221.

truth of dialogue' as 'the real rule of tragedy', traits he finds precisely in Shakespearean tragedy, which emphasizes character over dramatic action. 'I have not read Calderon or Vega', he writes, 'but what a man this Shakespeare is! I can't get over it. How paltry is Byron as tragedian in comparison with him!'[21] From Shakespeare, Pushkin learned to mix comic and serious elements in his tragedy and to cultivate a dynamic structure, covering seven years of the history of Godunov's reign through 23 different scenes in half a dozen settings. Like Shakespeare, Pushkin writes in blank verse as well as prose and creates a hero worthy of the bard, a character who, as Tatiana Wolff writes, 'combined Macbeth's visionary guilt and despair with Richard III's cunning and Henry IV's shrewdness'.[22]

But *Godunov* is no mere Russian transposition of a Shakespearean theme. For all of its affinities with Shakespearean tragedies or history plays, *Godunov* is also in many ways *sui generis*. As Caryl Emerson points out, unlike 'a chronicle play in Shakespeare's sense', it 'leads nowhere'.[23] It is also unlike Shakespeare in its 'compactness, emotional and rhetorical constraint, lack of titanic heroes, and reluctance to bring the supernatural on stage'.[24] In actuality, Shakespeare's greatest influence on Pushkin is to be found in the larger question of how he assimilated Shakespeare's artistic philosophy and worldview into his own aesthetic, what Russian critics dub his *shekspirizm*. Emerson argues that for Pushkin and others, Shakespeare's plays 'were perceived less as artistic structures than as anti-structures, as celebrations of the right to violate rules'.[25] Shakespeare's greatest service to Pushkin and his Romantic peers was to unshackle their creative genius. 'Look at Shakespeare. Read Shakespeare,' Pushkin writes in a letter describing his work on *Godunov*. 'I feel that my soul has become fully developed; I can create.'[26]

In Pushkin as in Shakespeare we see art fitted to the times and linked to national life. It was just this sort of literature that the influential critic Visarrion Belinsky, writing in the 1830s, argued Russia needed but did not yet have. After attending performances of *Hamlet* in 1837 with the mesmerizing Pavel Mochalov in the lead role, however, Belinsky seized on his own and the audience's reaction to the powerful performance as a hopeful sign that literature could engage the social as well as emotional sensibilities of the Russian public. Russia, Belinsky realized, had found a national narrative, though it came from outside its borders, and this narrative spoke directly to Russians living under Nicholas I. Hamlet, Belinsky enthused in an 1838 essay, 'is you, I, each of us', that is, anyone who has suffered from the 'incompatibility between reality and one's ideals'.[27] In Nikolai Polevoy's translation—the first accurate and idiomatic translation of the play in Russian, but still shortened by a quarter from the original—the play conveyed the sense, as Peter Holland notes, 'of the individual's powerlessness in the confrontation with a strong but inert state

---

[21] *The Letters of Alexander Pushkin*, trans. and ed. J. Thomas Shaw (Madison: University of Wisconsin Press, 1963), 237.

[22] Wolff, *Pushkin on Literature*, 105.

[23] Caryl Emerson, 'Pushkin's drama', in *Cambridge Companion to Pushkin*, ed. Andrew Kahn (Cambridge: Cambridge University Press, 2006), 64.

[24] Ibid., 62.

[25] Caryl Emerson, *Boris Godunov: Transpositions of a Russian Theme* (Bloomington: Indiana University Press, 1986), 110–11.

[26] *The Letters of Alexander Pushkin*, 238.

[27] V.G. Belinskii, 'Hamlet. Drama Shekspira. Mochalov v roli Gamleta', *Polnoe sobranie sochinenii*, 13 vols., ed. N. F. Bel'chikov et al. (Moscow: Akademiia nauk SSSR, 1953-9), 2: 254, 293.

machine'.[28] This aspect of the play was not lost on Mochalov. Mochalov's energetic performance as Hamlet revealed not a 'fragile prince, lacking in nerve, but a strong man, weakened by disillusionment with a lying world and consequent self-doubt, yet full of bitter and unconcealed abhorrence towards his enemies and his own inaction'.[29]

Simmons credits the 'powerful and wholly natural interpretations' by the two great actors Mochalov and Vasilii Karatygin (who played Hamlet in Saint Petersburg later that year to equal acclaim) along with their use of 'faithful texts and proper scenic effects' for winning Shakespeare 'a hitherto unexampled popularity in the Russian theatre'.[30] The decade that followed marked the height of Shakespeare's popularity in Russia, with more translations and performances of his plays. In 1840 the writer Nikolai Ketcher was the first to begin translating Shakespeare's complete plays, with accuracy as his main criterion. Other accurate translations also began to appear, including the popular collection *Complete Dramatic Works of Shakespeare by Russian Authors* (*Polnoe sobranie dramaticheskikh proizvedenii Shekspira v perevode russkikh pisatelei*, 1865-8) under the editorship of the poet Nikolai Nekrasov and N. V. Gerbel', which generally succeeded better at rendering the bard's style.

Of all of Shakespeare's plays published or performed in Russia, *Hamlet* continued to remain the most popular and important.[31] Frequent references to the play pepper the works of Russian writers over the next decades. Writers and critics also continued to debate the play's meaning and what came to be known as Hamletism throughout this time, starting with Belinsky, who revised his earlier opinion of the play in an 1843 essay. Whereas previously subscribing to Goethe's interpretation of Hamlet as 'a beautiful, pure, noble, highly moral nature' who is unable to control his fate,[32] Belinsky now condemned Hamlet's inaction and his predilection for talk as 'shameful' and inadequate to the task of active social engagement.[33]

The most famous articulation of Hamletism in nineteenth-century Russia belongs to Ivan Turgenev in a lecture he delivered on 10 January 1860. In it, he juxtaposed Hamlet and Don Quixote as embodying 'two contrasting basic tendencies, the two poles of the human axis'.[34] Turgenev devotes the majority of his lecture to a juxtaposition of these two tendencies. Quixote, Turgenev argues, has too long been thought of as a 'ludicrous figure' preaching 'idealistic twaddle'. In reality, he is 'an archetype of self-sacrifice' (93) who typifies faith first and foremost: 'a belief in something eternal, indestructible—in a truth that is beyond the comprehension of the individual human being'. He is a man in whom 'there is no vestige of egotism' (94), someone who 'does not probe or question' (95).

---

[28] Peter Holland, '"More Russian than a Dane: The Usefulness of Hamlet in Russia', in *Translating Life: Studies in Transpositional Aesthetics*, ed. Shirley Chew and Alistair Stead (Liverpool: Liverpool University Press, 1999), 320.

[29] Robert Hapgood, 'Introduction', *Hamlet, Prince of Denmark*, ed. Robert Hapgood, Shakespeare in Production Series (Cambridge: Cambridge University Press, 1999), 45.

[30] Simmons, *English Literature and Culture in Russia*, 232.

[31] See Eleanor Rowe, *Hamlet: A Window on Russia* (New York: New York University Press, 1976), and Peter Holland, '"More Russian than a Dane"', 315–38.

[32] J. W. von Goethe, *Wilhelm Meister's Apprenticeship*, bk. 4, ch. 3.

[33] Belinskii, *Polnoe sobranie sochinenii*, 7: 313.

[34] Ivan Turgenev, 'Hamlet and Don Quixote', trans. Moshe Spiegel, *Chicago Review* 17:4 (1965), 92–109. Further references will be given parenthetically within the text.

Hamlet (the far more common type of personality in Russia, according to Turgenev) is, on the other hand, 'above all, analysis, scrutiny and egotism—and consequently, disbelief'. He is a 'skeptic' (95) who 'pitilessly includes his own self in those doubts' (96). Thus the two types are perfect opposites. Quixote is unreflective and enthusiastic; Hamlet is self-conscious and listless. Hamlet embodies 'the creed of negation' (101); Quixote, the creed of affirmation. They are 'two forces of immobility and motion, conservatism and progress' (103).

In truth, Hamlets such as Turgenev describes had long populated Russian literature in the form of the so-called 'superfluous man' (*lishnii chelovek*), a term coined by Turgenev himself in his 1850 story 'Diary of a Superfluous Man'. The 'hero of the new literature of protest', the superfluous man was, in Isaiah Berlin's famous formulation, 'a member of the tiny minority of educated and morally sensitive men, who, unable to find a place in his native land, and driven in upon himself, is liable to escape either into fantasies or illusions, or into cynicism or despair, ending, more often than not, in self-destruction or surrender'[35]—in a word, Hamlet. The list of such characters extends as far back as Pushkin's Eugene Onegin from his eponymous novel (1833), Mikhail Lermontov's Pechorin from *Hero of Our Time* (1840) as well as many of Turgenev's own passive heroes, especially the protagonist of his first novel, *Rudin* (1856). In his essay, however, Turgenev implies that complex Hamlets are more attractive than 'the half-frantic Don Quixotes, who aid and urge forward the human race solely because they behold and know only one thing' (102)—a hint at the writer's disapprobation of the kind of single-minded radicals proliferating in Russian society at the time.

Despite the popularity of Nekrasov's and Gerbel's *Complete Dramatic Works of Shakespeare*, the 1860s saw a decline in interest in the writer, who was largely deemed irrelevant in the new debates over materialism, social justice, and the utilitarian uses of literature.[36] 'The socialists go no further than the belly', Dostoevsky complained in an unfinished article at this time. 'They admit this *with pride*: boots are better than Shakespeare'.[37] These were fighting words for Dostoevsky, on whom Shakespeare was a formative influence. *Hamlet*, in particular, frames Dostoevsky's life. He read the play at age 16 (likely in Polevoy's translation) and was much moved by it, as he mentions in an 1838 letter to his brother.[38] The play is also mentioned in *Brothers Karamazov* (1879-80) four decades later, where it is quoted at different times by Dmitry and Ivan Karamazov as well as the public prosecutor at the trial. It thus 'accompanied Dostoevsky on his entire spiritual journey', as Karen Stepanian argues in his analysis of the persistence of a Hamletian subtext in Dostoevsky's life and works.[39] While *Macbeth, Othello*, and *Henry V* are other important

[35] Isaiah Berlin, 'Fathers and Children: Turgenev and the Liberal Predicament', in his *Russian Thinkers*, ed. Henry Hardy and Aileen Kelly (New York, 1984), 261–305 (265).

[36] While Ketcher's translations from the 1840s attracted some 35 reviews, Nekrasov's and Gerbel''s 1860s edition received only fourteen. See Iu. D. Levin, 'Shestidesiatye gody,' in *Shekspir i russkaia kul'tura*, 472.

[37] F. M. Dostoevskii, *Polnoe sobranie sochinenii*, 30 vols. (Leningrad, 1972-90), 20: 192–3. Cited in Kenneth Lantz, *The Dostoevsky Encyclopedia* (Westport, CT: Greenwood Press, 2004), 393.

[38] *Selected Letters of Fyodor Dostoyevsky*, trans. Andrew MacAndrew, ed. Joseph Frank and David I. Goldstein (New Brunswick: Rutgers University Press, 1987), 7.

[39] Karen Stepanian, 'Dostoevsky and Shakespeare: Characters and Authors in 'Great Time',' trans. Liv Bliss, *Russian Studies in Literature*, 50:3 (Summer, 2014), 53–77 (54).

plays in the novelist's *oeuvre*, Dostoevsky cites *Hamlet* more frequently than any other work by Shakespeare.

Hamlet is an important subtext in *The Idiot* (1869), where the famous line 'To be or not to be'—quoted in the novel—summarizes the existential quandary at the centre of the novel. This theme only strengthens in intensity in *Demons* (1871-2), whose hero, Nikolai Stavrogin, grew directly out of the Hamlet theme, as Dostoevsky remarks in his notebooks for the novel: 'A prince—a gloomy, passionate, demonic, and disorderly character, without any sense of measure, with a lofty question, all the way to 'to be or not to be?' To live or to exterminate oneself?[40] A defence of Shakespeare himself was also to be made in the novel. According to a passage in Dostoevsky's notebooks for *Demons*, Stepan Verkhovensky was to give a speech on Shakespeare, in which he was to declare him to be 'a prophet sent by God to proclaim to us the mystery of man and the human soul'.[41]

The other giant of Russian literature, Leo Tolstoy, was of an entirely opposite opinion regarding the question of Shakespeare's value in world culture. 'What a coarse, immoral and senseless work *Hamlet* is', he complained in 1896, a harsh judgement that he extended to nearly all of Shakespeare's plays.[42] Tolstoy's distaste for Shakespeare, which dated from his youth, is most prominent in his so-called post-conversion years (roughly, 1880-1910), when he argued, in essays such as *What is Art?* (1897) and *About Shakespeare and Drama* (1906), that Shakespeare was bad theatre because it did not serve the higher function of art in society, which is to infect readers and spectators with 'simple feelings common to all men, helping to unite them (the category of universal, Christian art)'.[43] In his 1906 essay, Tolstoy uses *King Lear* as his main case study, condemning the play for the coarseness and artificiality of its language, the implausibility and arbitrariness of its plot, the lack of motivation of its characters, and its inferiority to the drama on which it was based, *The True Chronicle History of King Leir*. The 'unnatural events, and yet more unnatural speeches' and other deficiencies of Shakespeare's *Lear*, according to Tolstoy, are 'faults equally characteristic also of all the other tragedies and comedies of Shakespeare'.[44] By contrast, the earlier *Leir* is 'incomparably and in every respect superior to Shakespeare's adaptation', for it 'terminates more naturally and more in accordance with the moral demands of the spectator than does Shakespeare's', without 'the completely false "effects" of Lear running about the heath, his conversations with the fool, and all these impossible disguises, failures to recognize, and accumulated deaths'.[45] Such 'false effects' are typical of Shakespeare and constitute one of the chief reasons Tolstoy consigns his plays to the category of 'bad art'. 'The fundamental inner cause of Shakespeare's fame', Tolstoy concludes on a damning moral note, was that his dramas 'corresponded to the irreligious and immoral frame of mind of the upper classes of his time'.[46]

Tolstoy's class-conscious critique (it was published with Ernest Crosby's essay on 'Shakespeare's Attitude toward the Working Class' as an afterword) anticipates Russia's precipitous slide toward revolution in the two decades opening the twentieth century. Russian society was changing, and so was its theatre. Conventional drama was ailing, and

---

[40] Dostoevsky, *Polnoe sobranie sochinenii*, 11: 204.   [41] Ibid., 11: 237.

[42] Cited in George Gibian, *Tolsoj and Shakespeare* (The Hague, 1957), 22.   [43] Ibid., 27.

[44] Leo Tolstoy, *Tolstoy on Shakespeare: A Critical Essay on Shakespeare*, trans. V. Tchertkoff and I.F.M. (New York: Funk and Wagnalls, 1906), 23, 47.

[45] Ibid., 63.   [46] Ibid., 114.

along with it, productions of Shakespeare. Under the influence of the new drama of Henrik Ibsen, August Strindberg, and Maurice Maeterlinck in the West, Anton Chekhov introduced a new kind of drama into Russian theatre in *fin de siècle* Russia through his four major plays, *The Seagull* (1896), *Uncle Vanya* (1899), *Three Sisters* (1901), and *The Cherry Orchard* (1903), charting a course away from Shakespeare and the ruling Russian playwright of the second half of the nineteenth century, Alexander Ostrovsky. While *Hamlet* is quoted in *The Seagull* and, according to some critics, even structures its themes and action,[47] Chekhov's variety of drama is quite unlike Shakespeare's. Chekhov cultivated a theatre where dramatic events are internalized and what is implied about people's interrelations is just as important as what is shown or declared. Dramatic event is replaced by the drama of something *not* happening, and 'artfully oblique and seemingly irrelevant dialogue' became the new medium for revealing character intent and emotion.[48]

Shakespeare, of course, never left the Russian stage, and, with the advent of modernism in Russian culture, new productions ensued. The most prominent modernist take on Shakespeare is undoubtedly Edward Gordon Craig's and Konstantin Stanislavsky's collaborative 1911-12 Moscow Art Theatre production of *Hamlet*. The collaboration was somewhat stormy due to the very different creative visions of the co-directors. Stanislavsky emphasized the actor and his ability to create a realistic, psychologically compelling performance. Craig, on the other hand, wanted to turn actors into marionettes, whose movements and lines were subordinated to the aesthetic effect of the production. Shakespeare, he argued, belonged to 'the domain of symbols'—his essence was poetry, not psychology.[49] Craig conceived of the production as a kind of dream seen through Hamlet's eyes, who was to pass 'like Christ across the earth', becoming 'the victim of a cleansing sacrifice'.[50] To aid his symbolist vision, he used large screens to create abstract, constructivist sets and developed a detailed plan for the production's sound, lighting and blocking. Vasilii Kachalov played the main role, and, while his Hamlet 'thought too much, analyzed too much' in Craig's assessment,[51] Russian critics hailed him as the new Mochalov. Though it played to mixed reviews (Russian reviewers did not like Craig's innovations), it became part of the MAT repertoire and even toured Europe and America during the Civil War that followed the Revolution. In this way, as Stříbrný notes, the Moscow Art Theatre became 'instrumental in building cultural bridges between tsarist and Bolshevik Russia'.[52]

Between 1918 and 1925, Shakespeare nearly disappeared from the stage, being considered by the Bolshevik cultural establishment 'a nostalgic minstrel of the decaying feudal system

---

[47] See Tomas G. Winner, 'Chekhov's *Seagull* and Shakespeare's *Hamlet*: A Study of a Dramatic Device,' *American Slavic and East European Review* 15:1 (February, 1956), 103–11, and T. A. Stroud, '*Hamlet* and *The Seagull*,' *Shakespeare Quarterly* 9:3 (Summer, 1958), 367–72.

[48] Simon Karlinsky, *Anton Chekhov's Life and Thought: Selected Letters and Commentary*, trans. Michael Henry Heim in collaboration with Simon Karlinsky (Berkeley: University of California Press, 1973), 280–1.

[49] N. N. Chushkin, *Gamlet-Kachalov* (Moscow: Iskusstvo , 1966) 24. Cited in Rowe, *Hamlet: A Window on Russia*, 120.

[50] K. S. Stanislavsky, *My Life in Art*, trans. J. J. Robbins (Boston: Little, Brown and Co., 1924), 513. Cited in Rowe, *Hamlet: A Window on Russia*, 120.

[51] Chushkin, 24, cited in Rowe, *Hamlet: A Window on Russia*, 122.

[52] Stříbrný, *Shakespeare and Eastern Europe*, 56.

and the spokesman of a decadent aristocracy'.[53] The one notable performance in the 1920s—
the Moscow Art Theatre's production of *Hamlet* in 1924-5, with the great Mikhail Chekhov
(nephew of Anton Chekhov) in the lead role—was criticized for failing to embody the ideals
of contemporary reality.[54] The situation changed dramatically by the First Congress of Soviet
Writers in 1934, however, where Shakespeare was proclaimed the proper inheritance of the
proletariat.[55] A large portrait of the bard even decorated the congress hall in recognition of the
370th anniversary of his birth. The task was now to follow Marx's command and 'Shakespearize'
Soviet drama.[56] Of the tragedies, *Othello* and *Romeo and Juliet* were preferred to *Hamlet* and
Macbeth, largely because they fit the optimistic spirit of the time better. As Arkady Ostrovsky
points out, tragedy caused by 'an accident, a misunderstanding, or a mistake', as in *Othello* and
Romeo and Juliet, was acceptable; 'innate conflict or guilt of the protagonist', as in *Hamlet* and
Macbeth, was not.[57] 'Optimistic tragedy' became the byword of 1930s Soviet performances. As
one critic wrote in 1939, 'Dead bodies pile up at the end of Shakespeare tragedies but, in spite
of that, the dominant feeling in the end is triumph of life.'[58] Soviet director Sergei Radlov—the
most prolific Shakespeare director of the Soviet thirties—even declared *Romeo and Juliet* an
ideal play for the *Komsomol* (Communist Youth League) because it depicted 'the struggle
waged by young, strong progressive people for the right to love'.[59]

   Radlov's acclaimed 1935 production of *Othello* (in the translation of his wife, the
writer Anna Radlova) set the tone for future performances of the play, which became
a staple of Soviet theater. Othello, in Radlov's words, was to be portrayed as 'a new
progressive type of man' whose heroic qualities were to supplant his tragic ones.[60] The
lead actor, Alexander Ostuzhev, interpreted the role the way Pushkin did, as a drama
not of jealousy, but of betrayed trust. This interpretation played well in the decade of
show trials and shrill Stalinist rhetoric about counter-revolutionary saboteurs and
traitors. Rather than a tragic flaw (jealousy) leading to Othello's demise, it is 'venomous reptiles' like Iago 'who hide their poisoned fangs under a hypocritical mask' that
cause his downfall.[61] In Radlov's and Ostuzhev's interpretation, Othello at times even

   [53] Miklós Szenczi, 'Shakespeare in Recent Soviet Criticism', *Angol Filológiai Tanulmányok/
Hungarian Studies in English*, 2 (1965), 37.
   [54] See Rowe, *Hamlet: A Window on Russia*, 128, for a discussion.
   [55] *Pervyi vsesoiuznyi s'ezd sovetskikh pisatelei, 1934: Stenografischeskii otchet* (Moscow: Sovetskii
pisatel', 1990) 5. Cited in Arkady Ostrovsky, 'Shakespeare as a Founding Father of Socialist Realism:
The Soviet Affair with Shakespeare', in *Shakespeare in the Worlds of Communism and Socialism*, ed.
Irena R. Makaryk and Joseph G. Price (Toronto: University of Toronto Press, 2006), 56–83 (56).
   [56] Marx made this statement in a letter to the German socialist activist Ferdinand Lassalle: 'You
will have to Shakespearize more, while at present, I consider Schillerism ... your main fault.' Quoted
by Ostrovsky, 'Shakespeare as a Founding Father', 57.
   [57] Ostrovsky, 'Shakespeare as a Founding Father', 62.
   [58] Iu. Spasskii, 'Shekspir bez kontsa', *Teatr* 4 (1939), 14. Cited in Ostrovsky, 'Shakespeare as a
Founding Father', 62–3.
   [59] Cited in Ostrovsky, 'Shakespeare as a Founding Father', 63.
   [60] Cited in Ostrovsky, 'Shakespeare as a Founding Father', 69.
   [61] 'Alexander Ostuzhev on Othello', in *Shakespeare in the Soviet Union: A Collection of Articles*,
trans. Avril Pyman, ed. Roman Samarin and Alexander Nikolyukin (Moscow: Progress, 1966), 165.
These are part of Ostuzhev's public pronouncements about the role in 1938, the height of the Stalin
Terror, when even the most principled artists echoed state propaganda.

evoked Stalin himself—a foreigner who had achieved success as a leader in another land.[62]

That same year Radlov also staged a successful *King Lear* at the State Jewish Theatre in Moscow with the renowned Solomon Mikhoels in the title role. While Radlov, ever conscious of prevailing political winds, proposed emphasizing how Lear 'pitted himself and his impulsive will against the objective principles of the development of society and the historically progressive unification of England', Mikhoels conceived of the play instead as 'a philosophical tragedy of mistaken thought'.[63] Their disagreements during pre-production prompted Radlov to resign on several occasions, but each time Mikhoels convinced him to stay. Ultimately, Mikhoels's vision of the play prevailed. His dynamic and expressive interpretation of the role mesmerized audiences. Gordon Craig called his performance, simply, 'a song'.[64]

Radlov's other major production in the decade of Stalinist Shakespeare was his involvement as co-director of Sergei Prokofiev's ballet *Romeo and Juliet*, which premiered at the Kirov Theatre in Leningrad in 1940 with the great ballerina Galina Ulanova in the main role. Radlov was also co-author of the libretto, which followed the precepts of *drambalet* or 'dramatized ballet', a child of the official socialist realist state aesthetic of politically infused cultural production. *Drambalet* combined dramatic action with dance in order to reduce the possibility of any choreographic displays that could be construed as formalism. Prokofiev was forced to delete three exotic dances—some of the ballet's most interesting music, according to Simon Morrison—and was pressured into adding a group dance. Prokofiev's score was simplified in parts and his orchestration altered without his knowledge.[65] Even so, the ballet conquered audiences in Leningrad and in Moscow six years later.

Nikolai Akimov's *Hamlet* at the Vakhtangov Theatre in 1932 should also be mentioned among prominent performances of the Soviet thirties. Stalin's well-known dislike of the play caused *Hamlet* to fall temporarily out of the Soviet Shakespearean repertoire. Akimov, however, offered a new interpretation of the play. He staged the performance in an overtly grotesque key as a political intrigue, with a drunken and dissolute Ophelia, a plotting Horatio and a fat, buffoonish Hamlet 'with a loud voice, full of vitality', as the composer Dmitri Shostakovich, who provided incidental music, later recalled.[66] The effect was to turn the play into a comedy, one that decisively did away with any question of Hamletism in Soviet society. Critical reception was fiercely negative, though crowds of Muscovites stood in long ticket lines to see it. The play was singled out at the First All-Union Congress

---

[62] See Aydin Dzhebrailov, 'The King is Dead. Long Live the King! Post-Revolutionary and Stalinist Shakespeare', trans. Cathy Porter, *History Workshop* 32 (Autumn, 1991), 1–18 (12–16).

[63] Cited in Ostrovsky, 'Shakespeare as a Founding Father', 77. See 77–80 for a detailed description of Mikhoels's interpretation of the role of Lear.

[64] Cited in Stříbrný, *Shakespeare and Eastern Europe*, 85.

[65] These facts are from a talk Simon Morrison gave at Cornell University 15 March 2011, summarized at http://www.news.cornell.edu/stories/2011/03/dark-story-behind-romeo-and-juliet-ballet-revealed (last accessed 8 June 2015). See also Morrison's *The People's Artist: Prokofiev's Soviet Years* (Oxford: Oxford University Press, 2008).

[66] *Testimony: The Memoires of Dmitri Shostakovich*, ed. Solomon Vokov, trans. Antonina Bouis (New York: Harper & Rowe, 1979), 89.

of Directors as 'a vivid example of alien theatre art',[67] precipitating a 21-year absence of *Hamlet* from Soviet stages.

The most significant development in Soviet Shakespearean tragedy in the war years and its aftermath is undoubtedly the appearance of new translations by the writer Boris Pasternak. His versions of *Hamlet* (1940), *Romeo and Juliet, Antony and Cleopatra* (both 1944), *Othello* (1945), *King Lear* (1949), and *Macbeth* (1951) have been hailed by some as the best translations of these plays into Russian. A foe of literalism as a translator, Pasternak argued that a translation 'must produce an impression of life, not of literariness'. In his preface to the first edition of *Hamlet*, he writes, 'Instead of translating words and metaphors I turned to the translation of thoughts and scenes'.[68] The result was a very modern, vernacular Shakespeare that bore the mark of Pasternak's own poetics—an outcome not all critics welcomed. Alexander Smirnov, the founder of the Leningrad school of translation, disapproved of Pasternak's 'modernization of the text' which annulled historical and local colour.[69] Smirnov acknowledged 'the great immediacy, the lyricism, the cordiality, the warmth' of Pasternak's translations, but he could not overlook what he considered 'profound shortcomings' in the poet's versions.[70] Smirnov, however, was in the minority on this question. Pasternak's translations were enthusiastically received and appeared in separate collected editions in 1949-50, 1951, and 1953.

One admirer of the writer's translations was film and theatre director Sergei Kozintsev, who staged Pasternak's *Hamlet* in 1953, shortly after Stalin's death made it possible to bring the play back into the Soviet repertoire. In the immediate aftermath of the dictator's death, Hamlet's drama of introspection again acquired national relevance. Nikolai Okhlopkov's 1954 production of the play emphasized this point with its foregrounding on stage of a massive metal grill adorned with huge locks, shields, and spikes. The grill could be manipulated to reveal separate cells for stage action, thus establishing an 'overriding metaphor of incarceration and repression' that turned the play into a commentary on Stalinist times.[71] Pasternak, too, acknowledges the relevance of *Hamlet* for Soviet times. '[C]hance has allotted Hamlet the role of judge of his own time and servant of the future', he writes in an essay.[72] Pasternak's Hamlet is thus, as Rowe points out, 'a figure of great seriousness, virtually without the verbal irony, cutting mockery, and cynical witticisms of Shakespeare's hero'.[73]

---

[67]   http://www.vakhtangov.ru/en/persones/nakimov (last accessed 8 June 2015).

[68]   Boris Pasternak, *Polnoe sobranie sochinenii*, 11 vols. (Moscow: Slovo, 2003-5) 5:72 and 5: 43–4, respectively. Cited in Aleksei Semeninko, 'Pasternak's Shakespeare in Wartime Russia', *Shakespeare and the Second World War: Memory, Culture, Identity*, ed. Irena R. Makaryk and Mariss McHugh (Toronto: University of Toronto Press, 2012), 146.

[69]   Cited in Boris Kaganovich, 'A. A. Smirnov and Pasternak's Translations of Shakespeare', trans. Liv Bliss, *Russian Studies in Literature* 50:3 (Summer, 2014), 81.

[70]   Ibid., 84.

[71]   Laurence Senelick, '"Thus conscience doth make cowards of us all": New Documentation on the Okhlopkov *Hamlet*', in *Shakespeare in the Worlds of Communism and Socialism*, 136.

[72]   Pasternak, 'Translating Shakespeare,' trans. Manya Harrari, in Boris Pasternak, *I Remember: Sketch for an Autobiography*, ed. David Magarshack (Cambridge, MA: Harvard University Press, 1983), 130–1.

[73]   Rowe, *Hamlet: A Window on Russia*, 148.

This interpretation suited Kozintsev well, especially for his 1964 black and white film version of the play. While the film betrays the political agenda of the thaw period in post-Stalin Russia—with its 'denunciation of the state and the 'false' king, Claudius-Stalin, who has turned the country into a prison and made Ophelia a victim'[74]—its socio-political aspect is perhaps its least interesting quality. What critics hailed at home and abroad was Kozintsev's taut and nuanced adaptation of the play, with its striking cinematography and powerful performances. Kozintsev derives tension in part from the film's compression of events and lines from the play. One critic likened it to 'a series of fragments, some developed, some barely there, of the entire play', with speeches missing (Polonius' 'Neither a borrower nor a lender' speech is gone) or severely truncated (Hamlet's closing speech is rendered in one line: 'The rest is silence').[75] Kozintsev's camera maintains a spectator-like distance for much of the play, with Hamlet almost never shot in close-up—the enigmatic center of the play's dramatic action. As Barbara Hodgdon notes, 'it is a film about chiaroscuro, about contrasting masses, about closed and open spaces', something 'closer to a lyric meditation than a drama'.[76]

Kozintsev's *King Lear* (1971), on the other hand, is epic in its scale. 'In *King Lear*', Kozintsev stated, 'the whole history of human civilization is summed up.'[77] The movie encompasses the expanses of the natural world, and humanity as a whole is figured in the 'naked wretches' who open the movie then later crowd Lear's hovel and finally move through the charred landscape of burning houses at the film's conclusion. 'The range of movement', Kozintsev explains, 'is from the fire of the hearth [in the palace in Act I] to an incinerated world; from Cordelia's scarcely audible 'nothing' to Lear's scream over her body, to the howling and gnashing of space engulfed in flames.'[78] Kozintsev worked closely with Dmitri Shostakovich, who wrote the score for both of his films. Besides augmenting the film's emotional register, Shostakovich's score also enabled the director to cut whole speeches in places. 'When I hear Shostakovich's music', Kozintsev confessed, 'I think I've heard Shakespeare's verse. It is possible to cut some of the verse if you have his score to substitute.'[79] Like *Hamlet*, Kozintsev's *Lear* was universally praised as a superb cinematic adaptation of Shakespeare.

Without a doubt, Kozintsev's movies mark the high point of Soviet post-Stalin adaptations of Shakespeare. His achievement was rivalled only by the opening of Yury Lyubimov's production of *Hamlet* (also in Pasternak's translation) at the Moscow Taganka Theatre in November, 1971—the same year of the release of Kozintsev's *Lear*. The provocative and controversial production featured guitar bard Vladimir Vysotsky in its lead role, with

[74] Birgit Beumers, *A History of Russian Cinema* (Oxford: Berg, 2009), 142.

[75] Royal S. Brown, review of DVD release of Grigori Kozintsev, *Hamlet*, *Cineaste* 31:1 (Winter, 2005), 70.

[76] Barbara Hodgdon, "'The Mirror up to Nature': Notes on Kozintsev's *Hamlet*', *Comparative Drama* 9:4 (Winter, 1975-6), 315–16.

[77] 'Grigori Kozintsev: Talking about His *Lear* and *Hamlet* Films with Ronald Hayman', *The Transatlantic Review* 46/47 (Summer, 1973), 12.

[78] Girgorii Kozintsev, *Sobranie sochineni*, 5 vols., ed. V. G. Kozintseva and Ia. L. Butovskii (Leningrad: Iskusstvo, 1984) 4: 129. Cited in Joseph Troncale, 'The War and Kozintsev's Films Hamlet and King Lear', *The Red Screen: Politics, Society, Art in Soviet Cinema*, ed. Anna Lawton (London: Routledge, 1992), 204.

[79] 'Grigori Kozintsev: Talking about His *Lear*', 15.

actors in jeans and turtle-neck sweaters and a giant, coarsely woven curtain (recalling Okhlopkov's mobile grill) that moved across the stage in all directions, now 'an ambiguous symbol of the supernatural forces of death and tragic destiny', now 'a giant spider's web' catching the actors like flies, now 'a wall of earth' or 'an avid monster chasing its victims'.[80] The Taganka was known for its non-conformist spirit and its experimental approach, and its production of *Hamlet* was no exception. Vysotsky, who joined the Taganka in 1964 when Lyubimov took it over, had already gained notoriety as a singer-songwriter of so-called guitar poetry—songs in a rough street idiom on everything from crime and labour camps to the Second World War and sports. His entrance on stage in Act I with guitar in hand already signalled a blurring of identities between the Soviet singer and the Danish prince. Compounding the anachronisms, after making his entrance on the bare stage where a heavy wooden cross hung asymmetrically on a whitewashed back wall and two silhouetted gravediggers swilled vodka as they worked, Vysotsky recited Pasternak's poem 'Hamlet' from his novel *Doctor Zhivago* (banned at that time), accompanying himself on guitar: 'The stir is over. I step forth on the boards. | Leaning against an upright by the entrance | I strain to make the far-off echo yield | A cue to the events that may come in my day.'[81] The poem, which associates Hamlet with Christ, encouraged spectators to see Hamlet as a martyr for his times. Over the course of the ten years and 217 performances of its Taganka run, however, Vysotsky modulated his approach, ultimately emphasizing Hamlet's quest not for the right answer, but for the right question.[82]

Vysotsky is easily the Soviet era's Mochalov or Kachalov—the actor who defines Hamlet for his times. His sometimes frenetic performance of his lines (his 'To be or not to be' soliloquy is repeated three times in succession during the play, now in a whisper, now in a raised, gravelly voice) evoked the energy and desperation of his unofficial guitar poetry concerts, further contributing to the play's blurring of present and past times, Soviet and Shakespearean contexts. His death in 1980 marked the passing of an era and the beginning of a lull in remarkable productions of Shakespeare. Within five years of Vysotsky's death, Mikhail Gorbachev began his policies of glasnost and perestroika. As previously unpublished works held back by censorship were allowed to return to bookshelves, stages, and screens, Shakespeare became less relevant in the daily lives of Soviets reclaiming their heritage and examining their society fully and honestly for the first time in Soviet history. Russians—whether writers, directors, actors, or common citizens—could now speak for themselves; they did not need Shakespeare to speak for them.

After the final collapse of the Soviet Union on 25 December 1991, a period of economic contraction set in. Over the course of the next two decades, Russians struggled to assess their past, forge a new national identity, and rebuild their country. Theatre, formerly controlled but also financed by the government, now had freedom but it also had to answer to the market, both in terms of consumer demand and fiscal responsibility. Despite changed economic and political conditions, *Hamlet*—of all of Shakespeare's

---

[80] Alexey Bartoshevich, 'The Russian Hamlets: Cold War Years and After', *Text in Contemporary Theatre: The Baltics within the World Experience*, ed. Guna Zeltiņa and Sanita Reinsone (Newcastle upon Tyne: Cambridge Scholars Publishing, 2013), 17.

[81] Boris Pasternak, *Doctor Zhivago*, trans. Max Hayward and Manya Harrari, poems trans. Bernard Guilbert Guerney (New York: Pantheon, 1958), 527.

[82] Hapgood, *Hamlet*, 80.

plays—continued to appeal most to Russian directors wishing to speak to their times. Between 1994 and 1998, there were nine productions of the play in Moscow alone. The most sensational was staged in 1998 by the German director Peter Stein and featured a saxophone-playing Hamlet—a clear homage to Vysotsky's guitar. The play, apparently trying to appeal to post-Soviet appetites for the sensational, featured a scene in a night-club where bare-breasted women rubbed up against Hamlet's shirtless torso. Other innovations included Rosencrantz and Guildenstern strumming the Beatles' 'Can't Buy Me Love' on electric guitars and the staging of Hamlet's final duel in a boxing ring. The actor Yevgeny Mironov, who learned to play the saxophone especially for the part, was praised for his performance in the unorthodox production, but reviews of the play were generally mixed.[83]

Another important post-Soviet production is Yury Butusov's 2006 *Hamlet* at the Moscow Art Theatre—the first *Hamlet* at MAT since Stanislavsky's and Craig's in 1911-12. Like Akimov's 1932 staging, Butusov's consciously rejected historicity and instead used clowning and buffoonery to both offset and augment the play's tragedy. As Njål Mjøs notes, the play's atmosphere 'swiftly changes from grotesque and lyrical to acrobatic and clownish'. Butusov and his set designer Alexander Shishkin cultivated a kind of theatrical neo-primitivism, with bare stages populated by crude props. During his 'To be or not to be' soliloquy, for instance, Hamlet carried a large, metallic riser onstage, which he tilted towards the audience, revealing a cross made out of white stage tape. 'Through these poor, surprisingly simplistic means', Mjøs remarks, 'he creates an altar for Claudius to kneel beneath.'[84] Butusov's production was well received and remained in the repertoire for the next six years.

Finally, and perhaps fittingly, director Valery Fokin's 2010 *Hamlet* at the Alexandrinksy Theatre in St Petersburg revived the play as a vehicle for political commentary. In the era of an increasingly authoritative Russian government, Fokin's Hamlet confronted the deceit and hypocrisy of the powers-that-be in a way that evoked other Russian and Soviet performances of the past 200 years that also dared to speak truth to power. Fokin's play was realized in a mode of caustic grotesque, with Denmark symbolized by a giant soccer stadium patrolled by guard dogs and soldiers in camouflage who threw dead bodies—either shot dissidents or crushed soccer fans—into a giant pit. Hamlet was a drunken, dissolute youth; Horatio a hitchhiking student; Laertes a star soccer player; and Gertrude the coldblooded mastermind of the palace plot who kept Claudius in a state of terrified obedience. It became a play, as Alexey Bartoshevich notes, whose dominant tone is despair.[85] In Fokin's production, then, Shakespearean tragedy on Russian soil has come full circle. As drama, *Hamlet* has shaped the world-view of Russian writers, readers, and playgoers. As art, it has been claimed as part of Russia's cultural heritage. And as a vehicle for expressing political dissent, it continues to speak to the hearts and minds of Russians past and present.

[83] John Freedman, 'Stein Fails to Live Up to His Name,' *Moscow Times*, 16 October 1998. http://www.themoscowtimes.com/news/article/stein-fails-to-live-up-to-his-name/284067.html (last accessed 11 June 2015).

[84] Njål Mjøs, 'Director Yury Butusov's Shakespeare Frenzy,' http://mxatschool.theatre.ru/international/notes2007/02-01/ (last accessed 12 June 2015).

[85] Bartoshevich, 'The Russian Hamlets', 25. See 21-9 for an extended commentary on the play.

Select Bibliography

Alekseev, M. P., ed., *Shekspir i russkaia kul'tura* (Moscow-Leningrad: Nauka, 1965).

Gibian, George, *Tolstoj and Shakespeare* (The Hague: Mouton & Co., 1957).

Kozintsev, Grigori, *Shakespeare: Time and Conscience*, trans. Joyce Vining (New York: Hill and Wang, 1966).

Kozintsev, Grigori, *King Lear: The Space of Tragedy*, trans. Mary MacKintosh (London: Heinemann, 1977).

Levin, Iu. D., *Shekspir i russkaia literature XIX veka* (Leningrad: Nauka, 1988).

Morgan, Joyce Vining, *Stanislavski's Encounter with Shakespeare* (Ann Arbor, MI: UMI Research Press, 1984).

Morozov, Mikhail M., *Shakespeare on the Soviet Stage*, trans. David Magarshack (London: Soviet News, 1947).

Nels, Sof'ia Markovna, *Shekspir na sovetskoi stsene* (Moscow: Iskusstvo, 1960).

O'Neil, Catherine, *With Shakespeare's Eyes: Pushkin's Creative Appropriation of Shakespeare* (Newark: University of Delaware Press, 2003).

Palmer, Daryl W., *Writing Russia in the Age of Shakespeare* (Aldershot: Ashgate, 2004).

Rowe, Eleanor, *Hamlet: A Window on Russia* (New York: New York University Press, 1976).

Russian Essays on Shakespeare and His Contemporaries, ed. Alexandr Parfenov and Joseph G. Price (Newark: University of Delaware Press, 1998).

Samarin, Roman, and Alexander Nikolyukin, eds., *Shakespeare in the Soviet Union*, trans. Avril Pyman (Moscow: Progress, 1966).

Senelick, Laurence, *Gordon Craig's Moscow Hamlet: A Reconstruction* (Westport and London: Greenwood Press, 1982).

Shakespeare and Russian Literature, ed. John Givens, *Russian Studies in Literature* 50:3 (Summer, 2014).

Shakesepeare in the Worlds of Communism and Socialism, ed. Irena R. Makaryk and Joseph G. Price (Toronto: University of Toronto Press, 2006).

Simmons, Ernest J., *English Literature and Culture in Russia (1553–1840)*, (Cambridge, MA: Harvard University Press, 1935).

Stříbrný, Zdeněk, *Shakespeare and Eastern Europe* (Oxford: Oxford University Press, 2000).

Tolstoy, Leo, *Tolstoy on Shakespeare: A Critical Essay on Shakespeare. Followed by Shakespeare's Attitude to the Working Classes by Ernest Crosby and a Letter from G. Bernard Shaw* trans. V. Tchertkoff and I. F. M. (New York: Funk and Wagnalls, 1906).

Turgenev, Ivan, 'Hamlet and Don Quixote', trans. Moshe Spiegel, *Chicago Review* 17:4 (1965), 92–109.

PART VI

THE TRAGEDIES
WORLDWIDE:
(II) THE WIDER
WORLD

CHAPTER 47

....

SHAKESPEAREAN TRAGEDY IN THE NINETEENTH CENTURY UNITED STATES
The Case of Julius Caesar

....

GAY SMITH

SHAKESPEARE'S tragedies fell somewhat out of favour with American audiences in the second half of the nineteenth century, particularly following the Civil War (1861-5). In the aftermath of that conflict the playwright's comedies fared better, indicative of a traumatized population in need of laughter. Exceptionally, *Julius Caesar* actually gained in popularity after the war. A play about revolutionary senators attempting to restore their republic by assassinating their 'monarch' had appealed to American audiences from the time American revolutionaries won their independence from England in 1783. In England, by contrast, productions of *Julius* Caesar vanished from the English stage from the time of the American Revolution until 1812, the year in which John Kemble revived *Julius Caesar* and adapted it for the London stage. Kemble ennobled Brutus (his own part) while making the play less sympathetic to the conspirators and the 'rag-tag' commoners. With some modification American theatres imported Kemble's adaptation along with English performance traditions in productions featuring mainly British and Irish-born actors who came to America in the first half the nineteenth century. One of those actors, Junius Brutus Booth, played the major role of Cassius. His acting astounded Walt Whitman who regarded Booth as the best Shakespearean tragedian of the nineteenth century— even though English born. A decade after Booth's death, by the time of the Civil War, his American-born progeny, along with the American Charlotte Cushman, had become the most celebrated Shakespearean actors in America. The Booth brothers performed together in *Julius Caesar* six months before the end of the war. Ostensibly the occasion had nothing to do with the war, as it was a benefit performance to raise money for a statue of Shakespeare. But the play's politics became a reality when one of the Booth actors, the most promising one, abandoned his theatre career for that of assassin. Like his namesake, the radical English supporter of the American Revolution, John Wilkes, the youngest Booth was an intensely political figure, who justified his assassination of Abraham Lincoln by the belief that the President, like Caesar, aspired to be a king. Junius Brutus Booth, too, had been given a politically charged name, which remembered Lucius Junius Brutus, the heroic founder of the Roman republic. 'Junius' was probably also intended to link him to 'Junius', the anonymous writer whose published letters (1772) attacked the English king and his ministers on the threshold of the American Revolution; while 'Brutus' would also recall the idealistic republican assassin of Shakespeare's tragedy. In the years following the Civil War, however, it was the a-political surviving Booth, Edwin, who went on to produce and act in *Julius Caesar* before audiences intrigued and confounded by how Shakespeare's play reflected their own recent history.

Not to be outdone by the 1864 celebrations of Shakespeare's 300th birthday in England and Germany, American actors, theatre managers, artists, and gentlemen members of the Century Club came up with the idea and funds for a statue of Shakespeare in New York City's Central Park. Their dedication of the cornerstone for the future sculpture, 'placed at the south end of the Mall between two elms', took place on 23 April 1864. More modest in scale than the ceremony that would unveil the statue eight years later, this earlier celebration engaged Shakespearean actors and managers, from Washington, DC; Philadelphia; and New York City, who pledged to raise money for the statue by giving the proceeds from performances of Shakespeare's plays. The Niblo and Winter Garden Theatres gave benefit performances.[1] Their proceeds included $1200 raised by Hackett as Falstaff at Niblo's Theatre, and $1700 raised by Edwin Booth as Romeo and Avonia Jones as Juliet at Winter Garden.[2] Aging Shakespearean actor, James H. Hackett (1800-71), famous for his Falstaff, led the theatre contingent, and placed the stone. 'The celebration will be regarded with great interest in Europe. Mr. HACKETT having been in correspondence with Lord CARLISLE and other members of the English Committee.' The band played 'Yankee Doodle' and 'Hail Columbia'. The committee initially recommended the already well-known American-born sculptor Harriet Hosmer (1830-1908) for the commission. The design 'by our accomplished country woman, Miss Hosmer', would meet the committee's desire 'that the monument shall be *purely American*'. Close friend, in the coterie of female American artists living in Rome, with America's leading Shakespearean actor, Charlotte Cushman, Hosmer had the backing of much of the theatre world, but not all, and would be replaced by Edwin Booth's choice of Ward, who won the commission the following year. Cushman and Booth had performed Shakespeare's *Macbeth* together the previous year (1863) to raise money for the Union's Sanitary Commission. That casting pleased neither actor: the strong and forceful Cushman, playing her signature role of Lady Macbeth, complained of Booth's delicacy as Macbeth, while the smaller, effeminately built Booth was unhappy to play Macbeth opposite the domineering female actor—his request to play Hamlet to her Gertrude had been turned down by both Cushman and the Sanitary Fund Commission.[3] But Edwin Booth won his choice for the sculptor of the statue, over Cushman's. And so John Quincy Adams Ward (1830-1910) came to be known as the 'Dean of American Sculptors', not Hosmer.

---

[1] *New York Times*, 24 April 1864.   [2] *New York Times*, 23 April 1864.

[3] For a fuller account see Gay Smith, *Lady Macbeth in America* (New York: Palgrave Macmillan, 2010), 108-13. Cushman had other reasons for disliking Edwin—not a gentleman, she said—for the way he treated his first wife, a young friend of Cushman's with a promising acting career that Edwin forbade her to continue after they were married. When she died in Boston, Edwin was on a drunken spree in New York.

The playing of 'Yankee Doodle' and 'Hail Columbia' at the 1864 ceremony followed a nineteenth-century American tradition. Inspired by the American Revolution, these songs were sung regularly in American theatres on the Fourth of July to celebrate the Declaration of Independence from England, and in New York City on November 25th, 'Evacuation Day'. Overtaken by President Lincoln's Thanksgiving Day on the fourth Thursday of November, the Evacuation Day celebration died out. But for over half a century it had commemorated the withdrawal of British troops from their seven-year occupation of New York City at the end of the American Revolution. By coincidence or plan, the biggest and final benefit performance to raise money for the Shakespeare statue occurred on Evacuation Day, 25 November 1864, in New York's Winter Garden. The theatre had been recently renovated by Irish actor/manager/playwright, Dion Boucicault, who reduced its size by half and adorned the theatre with real and fake tropical plants in imitation of the Parisian theatre of the same name.[4] Here for one night only Junius Brutus Booth, Jr. (1821-83) played Cassius, his brother Edwin (1833-93) played Brutus, and the youngest of the three brothers, John Wilkes (1838-65) played Antony in a production of Shakespeare's *Julius Caesar*, the only time all three played together. *New York Times* reviewer observed how Junius played Cassius with 'careful conception and vigorous execution'; Edwin's Brutus had 'a certain classic beauty and scholarly refinement'; and John W. Booth's Antony had 'an *élan* and fire which at times fairly electrifies the audience and whirls them along with him'. To the reviewer the audience was 'itself an attraction ... distinguished by artists and literati'. As for ticket sales he reported that 'during the day ticket prices reached a fabulous height [of] $100 offered for a box, $10 to $20 for a seat. But it was next to impossible to obtain one. Proceeds: $4000'.[5]

The playbill for this *Julius Caesar* celebrates the Booths' father, Junius Brutus Booth (1794-1852), as America's leading Shakespearean actor. 'The three sons have come forward with alacrity to do honor to the immortal bard, from whose works the genius of their father caught its inspiration and of many of whose greatest creations he was the best and noblest illustrator the stage has ever seen.' These were not just 'puff' words of praise. Widely considered to have been the leading actor of Shakespearean tragedy in America for over a quarter century, Booth Sr. received like praise from Walt Whitman, an eyewitness to Booth's acting in Shakespeare's 'heavy pieces':

> As is well known to old-playgoers, Booth's most effective part was Richard III. Either that, or Iago, or Shylock ... was sure to draw a crowded house. (*Remember heavy pieces were much more in demand those days than now.*) ... I happen'd to see what has been reckon'd by experts one of the most marvelous pieces of histrionism ever known. It must have been about 1834 or '35.... I can, from my good seat in the pit, pretty well front, see again Booth's quiet entrance from the side, as, with head bent, he slowly and in silence (amid the tempest of boisterous hand-clapping) walks down the stage to the footlights with that peculiar and abstracted gesture, musingly kicking his sword, which he holds off from him by its sash. Though fifty years have pass'd since then, I can hear the clank, and feel the perfect following hush of perhaps three thousand people waiting. (I never saw an actor who could make more of the said hush or wait, and hold the audience in an indescribable, half delicious,

[4] Mary C. Henderson, *The City and the Theatre: The History of New York Playhouses* (New York: Back Stage Books, 2004), 94–5.

[5] *New York Times*, 29 November 1864.

half-irritating suspense.) And so throughout the entire play, all parts, voice, atmosphere, magnetism, from 'Now is the winter of our discontent', to the closing death fight with Richmond, were of the finest and grandest.... Especially was the dream scene very impressive. A shudder went through every nervous system in the audience; it certainly did through mine.

Ever the champion of things American over English, Whitman acknowledges that Booth, Sr. brought from his birthplace the English traditions of acting Shakespeare's tragedies—but quickly adds that he individualized them with his own electric power:

Without question Booth was royal heir and legitimate representative of the Garrick-Kemble-Siddons dramatic traditions; but he vitalized and gave an unnamable *race* to those traditions with his own electric personal idiosyncrasy. (As in all art-utterance it was the subtle and powerful something *special to the individual* that really conquer'd.)

Booth broke rules. He was spontaneous. He differentiated his characters. His characterizations took 'no stereotyped position':

... Though Booth *pére* ... was the loyal child and continuer of the traditions of orthodox English play-acting, he stood out 'himself alone' in many respects beyond any of his kind on record, and with effects and ways that broke through all rules and all traditions. .... He was singularly spontaneous and fluctuating, in the same part each rendering differ'd from any and all others. He had no stereotyped position and made no arbitrary requirements on his fellow performers.

For Walt Whitman, Booth was 'one of the grandest revelations' of his life, the exemplar of 'genius', a 'lesson of artistic expression', with his 'perfect vocalization':

To me, too, Booth stands for much else besides theatricals ... his genius was to me one of the grandest revelations of my life, a lesson of artistic expression. The words fire, energy, *abandon*, found in him unprecedented meanings. I never heard a speaker or actor who could give such a sting to hauteur or the taunt. I never heard from any other the charm of unswervingly perfect vocalization without trenching at all on mere melody, the province of music.

Booth played Cassius in *Julius Caesar*, at a time when Brutus and Cassius were regarded as the two principal roles in the play. (In America Antony would replace Cassius.) An early notice, December 1820, of young Booth playing Cassius in Drury Lane Theatre, London, describes him as 'Out Heroding, Herod'. The following year he left London for America where his Cassius would gain renown. He was small in stature for the part, but suited it with a voice, 'deep, massive, resonant, many-stringed, changeful, vast in volume, of marvelous flexibility and range'.[6] Booth's Richard III, his signature role, he played 579 times out of approximately 1500 performances of Shakespeare's tragic figures. He played Cassius 57 times.[7] Whitman concludes his encomium to Junius Brutus Booth with regret

[6] John Ripley, *Julius Caesar on Stage in England and America, 1599-1973* (Cambridge: Cambridge University Press, 1980), 108.

[7] Stephen M. Archer, *Junius Brutus Booth: Theatrical Prometheus* (Carbondale: Southern Illinois University Press, 1992), 64, 239.

that those days of 'heavy' Shakespeare tragedies and great tragic actors no longer grace the American stage. 'For though those brilliant years had many fine and even magnificent actors, undoubtedly at Booth's death (in 1852) went the last and by far the noblest Roman of them all.'[8]

At the end of Shakespeare's *Julius Caesar*, the line 'This was the noblest Roman of them all' begins Antony's speech over the dead body of Brutus. The last three lines from that speech, that end with, 'This was a man', had been chiselled into the 20-foot-high obelisk erected in 1858 in the Baltimore cemetery to honour and mark Junius Brutus Booth's grave in the family plot. Four years after the assassination of Lincoln and the reburial of his assassin in an unmarked grave in that same plot, Shakespeare's lines were covered over with a blank plaque.[9]

Before appearing together in Shakespeare's *Julius Caesar*, the Booth sons had all acted in Shakespeare's tragedies: least frequently by the oldest, Junius Jr.; more erratically by the middle son, Edwin; and most frequently in the shortest period of time by the youngest of the three, John Wilkes, who at the time of his performance of Antony in 1864, showed the most promise of filling his father's shoes as America's leading actor of Shakespeare's tragic roles. Esteemed more for his management of theatres than for his acting, Junius Jr. worked primarily as a respected and welcomed actor and manager, working mid-career in San Francisco and later in Boston. At the time of this performance of *Julius Caesar* Junius Jr'.s reputation equalled that of Edwin, who chafed to outdo both brothers. Edwin had served his apprenticeship in San Francisco under his brother's management, before returning to the East Coast in 1856. Due to personal bereavements and heavy drinking bouts, Edwin performed sporadically until the day after the November 25, 1864 performance of *Julius Caesar*, when he began acting long runs of Shakespeare's tragedies.[10]

Young John Wilkes Booth, regarded by his contemporaries as the most promising legate to his father's genius, 'the youngest star in the world' according to a reviewer in Washington, DC, began his apprenticeship (1857-60) in Richmond, Virginia, performing

[8] 'One trait of his habits, I have heard, was strict vegetarianism. He was exceptionally kind to the brute creation.... He seems to have been of beautiful private character, very honorable, affectionate, good-natured, no arrogance, glad to give other actors the best chances.... He was a marvelous linguist. He play'd Shylock once in London, giving the dialogue in Hebrew, and in New Orleans Oreste (Racine's "Andromaque") in French.' Walt Whitman, 'The Old Bowery', New York *Tribune*, 16 August 1885, repr. in *The American Stage*, ed. Laurence Senelick (New York: The Library of America, Penguin Group, 2010), 50–5.

[9] 1 May 1858 the bodies of Booth Sr. and his father Richard (both born in England) were transferred to Green Mount Cemetery, Baltimore. 'Richard Booth's original tombstone with its Hebrew inscription was discarded and replaced by a new marker decorated with a Christian cross and Latin lettering.' In February, 1869, President Andrew Johnson gave permission to have John Wilkes Booth's body removed from the arsenal burial ground in DC and reburied with the provision that no marker would be allowed to indicate the precise location of the grave. Edwin had the Antony quote '*covered over* by a marble plaque'. Did Mark Antony's lines violate 'the terms of discreet burial negotiated with the federal administration'? Or did Edwin guess how the lines would now, just four years after the assassination of Abraham Lincoln, draw attention to the assassin's grave? Nora Titone, *My Thoughts Be Bloody*, Foreword by Doris Kearns Goodwin (New York: Free Press, 2010), 166, 384–5.

[10] For a firsthand account of this formative period in Edwin Booth's career see William Winter's *Life and Art of Edwin Booth* (New York: Macmillan, 1894), 45–65.

supporting roles in Shakespeare's plays. Thereafter (1861-4) he played the lead roles in Shakespeare's tragedies for the duration of the Civil War, four seasons totalling 240 performances (not counting characters in plays other than Shakespeare's); 93 of these were as Richard III, a part to which the young actor brought his father's fiery passion. During his peak season alone (1862-3), Wilkes performed Shakespeare's tragic characters a total of 96 times: 35 as Richard III, 16 as Hamlet, 15 as Macbeth, 12 as Shylock, 9 as Othello, 7 as Romeo (in theatres from Lexington and Louisville in Kentucky to Cincinnati and Cleveland in Ohio, as well as in Chicago, St Louis, Boston, Philadelphia, and Washington, DC).[11] Reviewing Wilkes Booth's New York City performance of *Richard III* in Wallack's Theatre, March 1862, the anonymous critic praises the young actor for his 'intellectual breadth' and 'superior powers of concentration':

> John Wilkes Booth has great natural gifts for the stage, and an amount of intellectual breadth in one so young that is most remarkable.... he is not amenable to the charge of pompous diction and laboriously unnatural sounds.... [he] appears to have mastered especially the rude laconism which Shakespeare puts in the tyrant's mouth: for he never drawls, but goes on quickly and conversationally always as regards time.... a player who understand the art of making talk and action vital.... [with] superior powers of concentration.[12]

John Wilkes's extraordinarily numerous performances of leading roles in Shakespeare's tragedies ended on the night he played Antony in *Julius Caesar*. One single act, the assassination of President Abraham Lincoln in Washington DC's Ford Theatre, on Good Friday, 14 April 1865, has overshadowed and thwarted dispassionate histories of the Booths as theatre artists ever since.[13]

With the death of John Wilkes (shot in the back of the neck, while trapped in a burning barn), his father's mantle as lead American Shakespearean actor passed to Edwin, but not without personal support and public acclaim from two theatre critics Adam Badeau and William Winter. After the Evacuation Day performance of Brutus in *Julius Caesar*, Edwin Booth's career as a leading Shakespearean tragic actor began in earnest. The very next evening, 26 November 1864, he played Hamlet at the same Winter Garden Theatre in a production that ran for a record-breaking 100 performances. Edwin went on to revive *Julius Caesar* numerous times, in New York City at his own theatre, and on tour across the country. The influence of Adam Badeau (1831-95) as Edwin's mentor and friend accounts for the actor's study of paintings and literature in general and of Shakespeare's plays in

---

[11] These numbers of performances are tallied from the chronological list in Gordon Samples, *Lust for Fame: The Stage Career of John Wilkes Booth* (Jefferson, NC,and London: McFarland & Co., Inc., 1982).

[12] Smith, *Lady Macbeth*, 107, 108, 205 n. 29.

[13] Theatre historians Charles Shattuck and John Ripley have done much to countervail this imbalance. But Titone's book prefaced by historian Doris Kearns Goodwin, minimizes in-depth theatre history of the Booths, misleading Goodwin to erroneously assess Edwin Booth in superlative terms: 'that no other actor in the golden age of nineteenth-century theater was ever held in higher esteem'; and that John Wilkes Booth possessed 'neither the talent nor the discipline to become a star' (p. xii). Neither claim holds up as historical fact. See also: Michael W. Kauffman, *American Brutus: John Wilkes Booth and the Lincoln Conspiracies* (New York: Random House, 2004). Albert Furtwangler's *Assassin on Stage: Brutus, Hamlet, and the Death of Lincoln* (Urbana and Chicago: University of Illinois Press, 1991).

particular. As a theatre critic before becoming an officer in the Union Army and Secretary to Ulysses Grant, Badeau wrote reviews and articles that gave Edwin the publicity and encouragement he needed. In contrast to Walt Whitman's assessment that the great period of acting Shakespeare's tragedies died mid-century with the death of Junius Brutus Booth, Badeau announces its rebirth with the emergence of Booth's son Edwin:

> In Edwin Booth, at last, we have an actor who redeems the possibility of tragedy, who 'has made me know what tragedy is', who in the moments when the divine fire is upon him recalls those highest notions of tragedy which, as we read, were known in other ages.

In the same article Badeau relates how before Edwin's triumph, he, too, felt tragedy had declined in America.

> Consider, for instance Edwin Forrest. Although he is full of feeling, he never elevates nor refines by his performances. His conceptions are not intellectual; his effects are entirely physical; he moves us but does not inspire us; he excites horror, not sublime terror. His eye is the hyena's, not the eagle's. Miss Cushman is very like Forrest; and the reigning heroine of the realist school, Matilda Heron, although to be sure, she is full of womanly instinct and great ability to express it, yet concerns herself primarily with the coarsest details of human behavior and never suggests 'a higher sphere of art'.[14]

Refinement, intellectualism, inspiration, these are the attributes Badeau bestows on Edwin Booth's acting. With that encouragement Edwin set out to keep Shakespearean tragedy alive in American theatres, most notably with his revivals of *Julius Caesar*.

Edwin Booth's definitive production of *Julius Caesar* in 1871-2 coincided with the unveiling of the statue of Shakespeare in New York City's Central Park. In May 1872, a large crowd of 6000 watched as the statue, wrapped in the American flag, a 'muffled muse', emerged as America's Shakespeare! More emphasis on this American Shakespeare would be forthcoming from the speakers.[15] After the 'Overture to King Lear' by Berlioz, Judge Daly spoke of the English and German commemorations of Shakespeare's 300th birthday, and announced that 'America would not be outdone', and that the statue would be 'a great triumph of American art'. Schiller's 'Invocation to the Artists' by Liszt played while sculptor and pedestal architect 'grasped a silken cord and gave a simultaneous haul', so that the flag fell away from the statue 'like a cloud passing from the face of the moon' to reveal 'the immortal dramatist Shakespeare'. Henry Stebbins, of the Department of Public Parks applauded this addition to the mall of great men, erected for 'contemplation and study'. After the orchestra played Nicolai's 'Merry Wives of Windsor' the featured speaker, aging poet William Cullen Bryant, spoke of Shakespeare as comparable to the towering trees of the American far West and the 'the cataract of Niagara'. The ceremony concluded with Edwin Booth reciting R. H. Stoddard's 'Shakespeare', and the orchestra playing Schumann's 'Overture to *Julius Caesar*'. The *New York Times* reporter referred to Bryant's oration as a 'eulogy'. As a funerary speech this eulogy may be regarded as marking the transition of Shakespeare's tragedies from the stage to the page, from numerous

---

[14] Shattuck quoting Badeau. Charles H. Shattuck, *The Shakespeare Promptbooks: A Descriptive Catalogue* (Urbana and London: University of Illinois Press, 1965), 20.
[15] *New York Times*, 24 May 1872.

live productions to reading them for 'contemplation and study'. Some theatre historians regard this as a transition from popular 'low' culture to elite 'high' culture.[16]

Rather than accepting the argument that intellectuals of the *élite haute bourgeoisie* and artists prevailed in making Shakespeare's tragedies exclusively the property of high culture, no longer appealing to the world of popular culture, I would argue that the waning popularity of Shakespeare's tragedies on the American stage after the Civil War had less to do with class distinctions and more with changes in theatre practice. The European theatre movements of realism (1850s) and naturalism (1870s) changed approaches to acting, staging, and architecture, with a new emphasis on contemporary subjects performed in intimate spaces. Not until the twentieth century would the staging of Shakespeare's plays reflect these new practices. Edwin Booth adhered to the traditions of acting and staging Shakespeare's plays in huge theatres. But younger actors and designers, influenced by European experiments, would abandon these traditions.

The career of the young actor who modelled for Shakespeare's statue in Central Park exemplifies these changes in late nineteenth-century America. Steele MacKaye (1842–94) posed for the statue's body. Edwin Booth provided the costume. 'The poet is shown in doublet and hose ... his right hand holding a book, brought up to his chest, and his head bowed in a meditating pose.'[17] 'It was MacKaye who suggested the pensive pose, with Shakespeare holding a book.' Twenty-eight years old in 1870 when he posed for the statue, Steele MacKaye had just returned from France where he studied new schools of visual and theatre arts, especially the 'Harmonic Gymnastics' of Delsarte. MacKaye became Delsarte's spokesperson and teacher in America. The new method of actor training emphasized achieving relaxation and poise, foreshadowing Stanislavsky's 'thinking' actors and Meyerhold's 'gymnastic' ones.[18] After performing Hamlet in London (1874)—the first American actor to do so—he turned to writing and acting in plays with contemporary subjects in more intimate spaces. MacKaye's generation of theatre artists were moving away from the traditions that still prevailed with Edwin Booth's productions of Shakespeare's tragedies.

Actor manager Edwin Booth stoked the embers of those dying traditions, especially in his production of *Julius Caesar* that opened on Christmas Day, 1871, in his own Booth Theatre, a huge space with seating for 3000. William Winter recalls the size of the stage and its effects:

> The distance from the footlights to the back wall was fifty-five feet. The width of the proscenium opening was seventy-six feet. Beneath the stage there was a cavity thirty-two feet deep, into which an entire scene set could be sunk. (The depth of the subterraneous pit at the present Metropolitan Opera House, 1914, is twenty-seven feet, while that at the Academy of Music is only fourteen.) At Booth's Theatre scenic effects of the most

---

[16]   See esp. Part One, 'Shakespeare in America', in Lawrence W. Levine's, *Highbrow/Lowbrow: The Emergence of Cultural Hierarchy in America* (Cambridge, MA: Harvard University Press, 1988).

[17]   J. Sanford Salters and Walter E. Jiene, *Statues of New York* (New York: Putnam, 1923), quoted in Steele MacKaye archive ML5, Special Collections, Dartmouth College.

[18]   The Utica *Morning Herald*, 10 December 1885, quotes MacKaye from his lecture on 'Philosophy of Expression': 'The principle of perfect repose should be sought. When there is perfect serenity of mind, the slightest motion will make an impression' (MacKaye archive).

extraordinary kind were feasible and some effects were produced there which have never been surpassed.[19]

In both his New York *Tribune*, 26 December 1871 eyewitness review and later 1914 reflection, Winter rhapsodizes about the stage scenery for *Julius Caesar*. He looks upon the 'marvelously sumptuous attire', as in 'all points … correct, and [at] some points … gorgeous'. Especially impressive were the Senate and Forum scenes with their 'Roman architecture and ornamentation':

> The Senate … is the most impressive stage portrait that we remember. It occupied the whole of the stage, and it created a perfect illusion. The climax of the assassination … was the animating soul of this picture, and made it indescribably thrilling and painful.[20]

Here Winter reveals himself a man of his age in his admiration for grand sets that fill the stage and create 'a perfect illusion'. Mistakenly claiming that the scenery represents Roman buildings of the Augustan empire, Winter credits Edwin Booth with that choice to suggest 'a stately and beautiful setting for this superb tragedy' rather than pretending 'to give an idea of the Rome that Julius Caesar knew'. He correctly describes the assassination setting as, 'an exceedingly beautiful reproduction, slightly altered for theatrical use, of Gérôme's marvelous painting', but fails to recognize that the painting and stage scenery represent the Theatre of Pompey that was built in the final years of the Roman republic, not during the Augustan empire. Archaeological evidence and reconstruction drawings of the Theatre of Pompey, made in the nineteenth century, inspired Gérôme's draft of the Julius Caesar assassination scene (1857) as well as the final painting exhibited in Paris in 1867 that Théophile Gautier applauded as 'antiquity conceived after the manner of Shakespeare'.[21]

Crediting Booth with the sets, rather than naming the scene designer, Winter follows a customary lacuna in nineteenth-century theatre reviews. The artist responsible for these 'gorgeous' sets, Charles W. Witham (1842-1926), adapted Jean Léon Gérôme's 1867 painting, *La Mort de César* that depicts the chamber in the complex of buildings located behind the actual Theatre of Pompey.[22] Ripley mistakenly follows Winter's lead in claiming that, 'he [Booth] found the Republican period too drab, and followed his canny predecessor [Kemble] in setting the action in the resplendent Augustan era'. But Ripley justly contrasts the asymmetrical compositional value of Witham's scenery to the static symmetry of John Kemble's 1812 English staging of the assassination scene:

> Booth was particularly taken with Gérôme's placement of Caesar relative to the conspirators. The side focus and asymmetry of the arrangement offered endless opportunities for

---

[19] The ninety pages, 541–630, Winter devotes to *Julius Caesar* in his 1915 essay, lay out a history of the origins of the play, British traditions of producing the play, and finally American productions. William J. Winter, *Shakespeare on the Stage* (New York: Benjamin Blom Reprint, 1969, 1915), 2: 630, 612–16.

[20] Ibid.

[21] Fanny Field Hering, *Gérôme: The Life and Works of Jean Léon Gérôme* (New York: Casal, 1889), 120.

[22] The Theatre of Pompey, Rome's first and grandest theatre, in use for over 600 years had a large chamber behind the stage where the Senate temporarily held its meetings and where Caesar was assassinated. Luigi Canin was the first to make reconstructive drawings of the complex of buildings, a likely source for Gérôme's painting.

fluid and natural movement and picturesque groupings when contrasted with the rigid and artificial action necessitated by Kemble's location of Caesar at upstage centre with the conspirators in parallel lines from upstage to downstage on either side of the throne.[23]

This radical change in nineteenth-century staging of the assassination scene, from centere stage focus to side stage, from symmetry to asymmetry, gave the actors more dramatic diagonals upon which to move. Gérôme provided the inspiration for this new way of staging the assassination scene by first sketching only the body of Caesar on the downstage right floor, then in his final painting more dramatically adding the Senators fleeing out through the upstage portal, leaving behind the body of Caesar (and one fat senator asleep in his chair). Fortunately Witham's designs for the 1870 staging of Shakespeare's *Julius Caesar* are in the City Museum of New York. Only 22 years old when he began working for Edwin Booth, Witham designed productions for his Shakespeare tragedies from 1864 to 1874, concluding the long run of *Hamlet*, 1864-5, and the almost equally extended season of *Julius Caesar* 1871-2. Poorly paid, the young artist moved on to other theatres and to designing realistic scenery for the smaller spaces intended for more modern dramas with contemporary urban settings.[24]

The asymmetry of the assassination scene provided Edwin Booth with a dramatic ground plan. Booth's acting retained the more formal and by now traditional interpretation of the character established early in the century by John Kemble—but without matching Kemble's power. Winter found Booth's Brutus 'marked by bright intelligence and profound earnestness'. Habitually describing the physical features of actors, the critic contradicts himself in describing Edwin's appearance, at first stating that the actor's small size did not impede him from playing the part, that 'Brutus like Cassius was lean and pale'; but then admitting that Brutus 'is more impressive ... when played by a man of massive size'. Winter's description of Booth's Brutus as 'delicate', and at times 'too easy' must have gone hard on the highly competitive actor, especially as Winter goes on to give unqualified praise to Laurence Barrett's Cassius: 'a work of absolute genius.... [that] easily bore away the richest honors of last night's performance'.[25]

Edwin Booth and William Winter based their *Julius Caesar* promptbook on the English, John Kemble 1814 version. Adding passages, such as Brutus' death speech, whilst making cuts that included whole scenes, and eliminated several characters, the Booth and Winter promptbook, which Winter facilitated, edited, and published in 1877,[26] represents the last

[23] Ripley, *Julius Caesar on Stage*, 121–5.

[24] Thomas F. Marshall, 'Charles W. Witham: Scenic Artist to the Nineteenth-Century American Stage', *Anatomy of an illusion: Studies in Nineteenth-century Scene Design; Lectures of the Fourth International Congress on Theatre Research, Amsterdam 1965* (Amsterdam: Scheltema & Holkema, 1969), 26–30.

[25] *New York Tribune*, 26 December 1871.

[26] William Jefferson Winter, ed., *Dramatic Library* 1:35 (Philadelphia: Penn Publishing Co., 1896, 1878). William Winter (1836-1917) exercised an enormous influence over Edwin Booth's career, not only by writing encouraging reviews, essays, and a laudatory biography, but by working closely with him on publishing Booth's promptbooks, advising through personal correspondence, and becoming a close friend of the actor, when, apparently, close relations between reviewers and actors had not yet been regarded as unethical. The earliest recorded letter from Edwin Booth to William Winter, 1859, reads, 'Thanks for your advice'. The correspondence picks up again in 1869 when Booth offers to pay for Winter's membership fees in the Century Club. *Between Actor and Critic: Selected Letters of Edwin Booth and William Winter,* ed. Introd. and Commentary, Daniel J. Watermeier (Princeton: Princeton University Press, 1971), 18, 34.

of the Kemble adaptations of *Julius Caesar* to be performed on the American stage. I have examined four sample promptbooks in the Folger Library to see how the Booth and Winter version compares with the Kemble, as well as with Shakespeare's play as it appears in the 1623 First Folio. While Booth and Winter restore some of the Folio's lines, their promptbook falls in line with Kemble in butchering the part of Portia, Brutus's wife, cutting the speech which describes how Brutus behaved when she questioned him:

> I urged you further, then you scratched your head,
> And too impatiently stampt with your foot:
> Yet I insisted, yet you answered not
> But with an angry wafture of your hand ... [27]

Booth and Winter went on to cut even more of Portia's lines than Kemble had done, both to enhance Brutus and to diminish Portia. Portia's concern for her husband's welfare is cut: 'And is it Physicall | To walke unbraced, and sucke up the humours | Of the danke morning?' Like John Kemble, Edwin Booth removed from the script lines that would compromise their strategy of ennobling the Brutus role. Portia's observation of her husband's distracted behaviour—his stamping his feet, scratching his head, walking around with his clothes unbuttoned—did not suit either Kemble's or Booth's interpretation of Brutus. So they cut those lines from Portia's speech. Nor did Shakespeare's characterization of Portia suit Booth. He made her character even less significant to the play than his predecessors had done.

Portia had already suffered significant changes in the eighteenth-century in order to cleanse Shakespeare's play of indelicacy. In the Folio's garden scene she has stabbed herself in the thigh, revealing the wound to her husband only when she finds it opportune to convince him of her endurance and ability to be his helpmate and to keep his secrets. In English prompt books from the 1770s Portia no longer stabs herself in the thigh but in the arm. The Booth script goes further by cutting entirely Portia's appearance in 3.1. Within earshot of the Capitol, and now fully aware of her husband's secret plans, Portia anxiously awaits news, and orders Lucius to discover what is happening. She grows faint as well as restless and anxious, 'Oh, Brutus, | The heavens speed thee in thine enterprise', and 'Run, Lucius, and commend me to my lord; | Say I am merry'. This agitated state of mind and worry on behalf of her husband undergirds our understanding of her suicide and Brutus's grief later in the play. The Kemble version keeps the scene, but with some trims, most notably Portia's line: 'I have a man's mind.' Why Booth cut this scene may have to do with his fraught relations with actresses and women in general. As already noted, Edwin Booth resented playing opposite the strong and forceful actress, Charlotte Cushman, who took top billing over him. A scene in which the actress playing Portia declares that she has a man's mind would have chafed. Then again, cutting the entire scene may have had as much to do with the exigencies of scene changes as it did with Edwin Booth's gender politics. The importance of Portia (and of the boy musician, Lucius) is at issue again in 4.3, which includes the popular quarrel scene between Brutus and Cassius, when Brutus learns of Portia's suicide. Once alone, Brutus gently calls for Lucius to bring his book and to play some music, a scene-length exchange in the Folio text that shows Brutus' kindness

---

[27] First Folio edition of *Julius Caesar*, 2.1.

toward his servant. Both Kemble and Booth reduced this exchange to Brutus commanding Lucius like a general speaking to a soldier, 'Lucius! Lucius! Lucius! My book! Where
is thy instrument?'

Booth's Brutus does differ significantly from Kemble's. The English actor makes his
Brutus overtly class-conscious, armed to quell and control the lower classes. This reveals the
contrast between Kemble, a monarchist Englishman, and Booth a democratic American.
In Shakespeare's 1623 text, after the assassination Brutus appears in the Forum and goes
'into the pulpit' to speak to the 'plebeians' who have been crying out, 'We will be satisfied!
Let us be satisfied!' The Booth and Winter promptbook follows the Folio. Kemble inserts
a street scene to precede the Forum: 'Rome. Street Enter Cinna, with the *cap of Liberty*,
a Throng of Plebeians,—[the Conspirators] *with their swords drawn*, and another throng
of Plebeians, all shouting.' Here Brutus instructs Cassius to take half the crowd down another street to speak to them, while he himself will take the remainder to the Forum. But
just in case the 'tag-ragged' rabble becomes hostile, Kemble's conspirators confront them
in this street scene 'with swords drawn'. Kemble's unpredictable rabble need the control
and manipulation of their superiors: 'The Plebeians continue the uproar and bawling of
"Silence! Silence" till Brutus *lays down his dagger*.' From the 'pulpit' Brutus calms them
and then exits. Succeeding Brutus at 'the rostrum' Antony descends to be closer to the
crowd to read Caesar's will. The plebeians leave the Forum 'shouting' that they will burn
down the houses of Brutus and the other conspirators (as they do in Shakespeare's text).
Leery of blaming Antony for the chaos, Kemble cuts Antony's closing lines, 'Now let it
work. Mischief, thou art afoot, | Take thou what course thou wilt!' The Booth and Winter
promptbook does not adopt Kemble's show of weaponry and crowd control, nor the wearing of the 'Cap of Liberty'. This soft hat shaped like the ancient Phrygian cap, worn by
emancipated slaves in Rome, was made famous by French revolutionaries, but appeared
in a number of guises during the period that began with the American Revolution and
extended to the War of 1812, a second war between America and England that coincided
with Kemble's revival of *Julius Caesar* on the London stage. Kemble's placement of the cap
of liberty on the conspirator Cinna would have prompted his English audience to recognize the hat as emblematic of their enemy France and of the revolutionaries who killed the
French king. It would not have had the same meaning for an American audience of the
time, for Americans were largely supportive of the French Revolution until it turned into
a Reign of Terror.

For the American critic Winter, Shakespeare's *Julius Caesar* represented American
ideals, a defence of the fight for liberty against slavery. 'To see this great play with appreciative eyes is to learn the value of liberty, and to sympathize with some of the grandest
ideals of heroic character and pathetic experience ever offered in literature or in life.' Note
that Winter writes from the standpoint of *seeing* the play, not reading it. In his review
of Edwin Booth's 1870-1 long-running production of *Julius Caesar* for the New York
Tribune (26 December 1871), Winter sees a lesson regarding the laws of a moral government: 'Shakespeare has been as true to the great laws of the moral government of the universe as to the fact of history… A tyrant is slain—but the heart of the slayer is cleft by his
own sword, in expiation of the dread sacrifice [Brutus].'

From the time of the American Revolution to the end of the nineteenth century the play
appeared regularly, if not frequently, on the American stage, but not so in England, where
the assassination of a 'king' in defence of a republic, did not sit well with conservative

monarchists. Between 1780, at the time of the American Revolution (called a Civil War by the English), and the War of 1812, *Julius Caesar* did not appear at all on the London stage. Significantly, Elizabeth Inchbald gives two reasons for this in her 'Remarks' prefacing the publication of *Julius Caesar* in her twenty-five volume collection, *The British Theatre*. First, a practical reason—a theatre company's difficulty in finding three to four leading male actors capable of taking on the roles of Brutus, Antony, Cassius, and Caesar: 'It rarely happens, that a theatre is enriched by a number of male performers, equal to the task of representing those great historical characters.'[28] How fortunate, she claims, that there are among her contemporaries actors up to the challenge performing the play in 1773: 'The theatres of London, at the present era, can boast of actors to set all such difficulties at defiance.'[29] Her cast list indicates that she is writing this in 1773, as she gives the names [Robert] Bensley for Brutus [Covent Garden 1773], ['Gentleman' William] Smith for Antony (Covent Garden 1773, Drury Lane 1780), [Robert] Hull for Cassius, and [Matthew] Clark for Julius Caesar. Inchbald gives a second more political reason for the absence of *Julius Caesar* on the London stage. She aligns with Kemble's class-consciousness, in thinking that superior 'discriminating judges' should determine whether a piece such as *Julius Caesar* can be rightly interpreted by 'unskilled' inferiors:

> When men's thoughts are deeply engaged on public events, historical occurrences, of a similar kind, are only held proper for the contemplation of such minds as know how to distinguish, and to appreciate, the good and the evil with which they abound. Such discriminating judges do not compose the whole audience of a playhouse; therefore, when the circumstances of certain periods make certain incidents of history most interesting, those are the very seasons to interdict their exhibition.[30]

Mrs. Inchbald implies a division in London audiences somewhat similar to Hamlet's in his advice to the players, the 'censure' of the 'judicious' spectators outweighing 'a whole theatre of others'. However Inchbald stretches the point by elevating the judicious audience members to a select few capable of distinguishing good and evil in a play such as *Julius Caesar,* when current events parallel its conspiracies and savagery of war. The 'unskilled' audience members, the lower classes, the plebeians, might become over-excited by these interesting parallels between what's on stage and what's going on in the world around them, and so might mistakenly join the forces of evil in the real world's parallel incidents. Therefore censor we must: 'Till the time of the world's repose, then, the lovers of the drama will, probably, be compelled to accept of real conspiracies, assassinations, and the slaughter of war, in lieu of such spectacles, ably counterfeited.'[31] And that was indeed the case for London's audiences from the time of the American Revolution when there were wars and revolutions and no productions of *Julius Caesar* until Kemble's 1812 production that emphasized and exaggerated the class distinctions inherent in Shakespeare's text.

Walt Whitman, reminds his readers that Shakespeare was not pro-democracy, but rather a monarchist, and considers Shakespeare's plays less relevant to the young American

---

[28] Mrs. Inchbald, *The British Theatre; or A Collection of Plays, which are acted at the Theatres Royal, Drury Lane, Covent Garden, and Haymarket. Printed Under the Authority of the Managers from the Prompt Books. With Biographical and Critical Remarks by Mrs. Inchbald. In Twenty-Five volumes* (London: Longman et al., 1808), *Julius Caesar*, 4: 6.
[29] Ibid., 4: 6.   [30] Ibid., 4: 6.   [31] Ibid., 4: 3.

republic's audiences. Shakespeare was a great poet, but he had the wrong politics. The plays should be less about aristocracy and monarchy and more about American democracy:

> The inward and outward characteristics of Shakspere [*sic*] are his vast and rich variety of persons and themes, with his wondrous delineation of each and all—not only limitless funds of verbal and pictorial resource, but great excess, … aristocratic perfume …. Superb and inimitable as it all is, it is mostly an objective and physiological kind of power and beauty the soul finds in Shakspere—a style supremely grand of the sort, but in my opinion stopping short of the grandest sort, at any rate for fulfilling and satisfying modern and scientific and *democratic American* purposes.

Whitman, ever the champion of the common man and all things American, contradicts his fellow countryman and poet, Bryant, who in his speech to dedicate the statue of Shakespeare in Central Park compares Shakespeare's tragedies to the magnificence of the Redwoods and Niagara Falls. For Whitman, Shakespeare's tragedies exist in marble palaces like Witham's scenery for *Julius Caesar*: 'Think, not of growths as forests primeval, or Yellowstone geysers, or Colorado ravines, but of costly marble palaces and palace rooms … and noble owners and occupants to correspond … and you have the tally of Shakspere.'[32]

As a political play that enacts assassination and civil war, Shakespeare's *Julius Caesar* can heighten audience anxiety, especially in times of real wars and assassinations. In the 1860s, with Americans embroiled in their own Civil War, the issues of liberty and tyranny in *Julius Caesar* hit home. The roles in *Julius Caesar* that the three Booth brothers performed on stage a few months before the end of the war paralleled their divided loyalties in real life: Edwin and Junius, Jr. mildly pro-Union and their youngest brother passionately pro-Confederacy. John Wilkes wrote an essay during those last days of November, 1864, when he performed Antony, to explain how his love of peace had been shattered by the election of Abraham Lincoln, how he had loved the American flag, now 'dragged deeper and deeper into cruelty and oppression'. He refers to the plot to abduct the President and hold him hostage until the war ends, giving the South its right to secede. That plot failed, and five months later Wilkes drafted another letter, with some of the wording of this earlier one, but with a different goal. At the end of this April 1865 letter, he quotes Brutus from Shakespeare's *Julius Caesar*:

> When Caesar had conquered the enemies of Rome and the power that was his menaced the liberties of the people, Brutus arose and slew him. The stroke of his dagger was guided by his love of Rome. It was the spirit and ambition of Caesar that Brutus struck at. 'Oh that we could come by Caesar's spirit, / And not dismember Caesar! / But, alas! / Caesar must bleed for it.' I answer with Brutus: 'He who loves his country better than gold or life'. John W. Booth[33]

The young actor considered Lincoln a Caesar, a President who wanted to be King, a tyrant. Just as Brutus and the conspirators killed Caesar in a theatre, The Theatre of Pompey, in

[32] Walt Whitman, 'A Thought on Shakspere', *The American Theatre as Seen by Its Critics, 1752–1934* (New York: W. W. Norton, 1934) 67–8.

[33] *'Right or Wrong, God Judge Me'*, *The Writings of John Wilkes Booth*, ed. John Rhodehamel and Louise Taper (Urbana and Chicago: University of Illinois Press, 1997), 126, 149–50.

the capital city of Rome, John Wilkes Booth shot Lincoln in a theatre, Ford's Theatre, in the capital city of Washington, DC. Wilkes's sister Asa, appears to have shared an outrage that Lincoln in the flush of victory would attend the theatre on Good Friday (14 April 1865) instead of church. She, from a family of actors, writes:

> It desecrated his idea to have his end come in a devil's den—a theater—in fact. Conquerors cannot be too careful of themselves, as history has ever proved. That fatal visit to the theater had no pity in it; it was jubilation over fields of unburied dead, over miles of desolated homes. [John Wilkes may have] saved his country from a king, but he created for her a martyr.[34]

The popularity of Edwin Booth's productions of *Julius Caesar* and his role as Brutus in New York City, as well as in tours of the country in the years following the Civil War, must have had much to do with lingering divisive memories of Abraham Lincoln's presidency and assassination. Esteem for Lincoln grew. His assassin, John Wilkes Booth, once expected to become the equal of his great father, became characterized as a drunken and mad, two-bit actor. Even a recent history portrays Edwin and John Wilkes in melodramatic nineteenth-century terms: Edwin is presented as the good guy, and Wilkes as the villain, without taking into account how the Civil War changed these two men, their attitudes and careers. Wilkes's villainy as Lincoln's assassin is indisputable (except in the South). This villainy has eclipsed his promise as a Shakespearean actor. The post-Civil War success of Edwin's productions of *Julius Caesar* may be attributed in part to the audiences' interest in seeing the brother of Lincoln's assassin play Caesar's. The haunting memory of John Wilkes Booth's action, set beside Edwin Booth's enacted assassination of Caesar may have had a cathartic effect for audiences. Edwin did not play Brutus well, according to Winter and others. But his productions kept the play in the theatres and in the American canon of popular Shakespearean tragedies at a time when Shakespeare's 'heavy pieces' had fallen out of favour, replaced by the exciting new experiments in modern realism that had taken over the late nineteenth-century theatres.

American theatres produced *Julius Caesar* during those 32 years of revolution and war when English theatres did not (1780-1812). Already the play's republican sentiments were more to the liking of American audiences than to English ones. Then to celebrate Shakespeare's 300th birthday in 1864 by raising money for a statue of the playwright, the three American Booth brothers chose *Julius Caesar* for its three strong male roles. Nevertheless, after John Wilkes Booth assassinated Abraham Lincoln and was himself killed, and when his brother Edwin successfully produced the play for the following quarter of a century, *Julius Caesar* took on more weight as a political play, reflecting the recent events of American history. Just as the statue of Shakespeare in Central Park, wrapped in the American flag for its unveiling, became an American monument, so the English playwright's *Julius Caesar* became an American Civil War tragedy.

[34] Asa Booth Clarke, *John Wilkes Booth: A Sister's Memoir*, ed. Terry Alford (Jackson, Mississippi: University Press of Mississippi, 1996), 99.

Select Bibliography

Archer, Stephen M., *Junius Brutus Booth: Theatrical Prometheus* (Carbondale: Southern Illinois University Press, 1992).

Furtwangler, Albert, *Assassin on Stage: Brutus, Hamlet, and the Death of Lincoln* (Urbana and Chicago: University of Illinois Press, 1991).

Henderson, Mary C., *The City and the Theatre: The History of New York Playhouses* (New York: Back Stage Books, 2004).

Kauffman, Michael W., *American Brutus: John Wilkes Booth and the Lincoln Conspiracies* (New York: Random House, 2004).

Ripley, John, *Julius Caesar on stage in England and America, 1599–1973* (Cambridge: Cambridge University Press, 1980).

Senelick, Laurence, ed., *The American Stage* (New York: The Library of America, Penguin Group, 2010).

Smith, Gay, *Lady Macbeth in America* (New York: Palgrave Macmillan, 2010).

CHAPTER 48

....

UNSETTLING THE BARD
Australasia and the Pacific

....

MARK HOULAHAN

SHAKESPEARE is 'Australia's most popular playwright', and remains 'New Zealand's most performed playwright'.[1] It is a paradox of cultural formation across the vast region this chapter covers (from the Indian Ocean to the islands of Samoa in the middle of the South Pacific), that a playwright born 450 years ago, and writing 19,000 kilometres away, should still exercise such power. On the one hand Shakespeare's enduring cultural prestige means that performers and audiences feel at home in his works. On the other, distances of time and space mean that much of his work is unhomely to the Pacific, an ocean of which he knew almost nothing. At its best, Australasian and Pacific Shakespeare works fruitfully across this gap, generating new energies and cultural meanings; at its neo-imperialist worst, performers and interpreters have sought to sublimate themselves within 'Shakespeare', in the hope of replicating an impossibly ideal kind of Englishness. This ambiguously divided legacy runs like a fault-line through responses to, and reworkings of, the tragedies. Mainstream Australian and New Zealand productions are frequently attuned to international concepts, but do not always seek to make nationalist or postcolonialist gestures; and the tendency to downplay questions of nation in such contexts can seem evasive. Productions foregrounding still unresolved issues of settlement, race and land, on the other hand, have provoked memorable versions of the main tragedies. Shakespeare's tragedies may thus be thought of as exercising a contradictory cultural pressure. This chapter will seek to demonstrate these propositions through considering a range of live and filmed performances, alongside the adaptive responses of writers, audiences, and critics to the tragedies.

PERFORMANCE

....

We can date the presence of Shakespeare's works in these territories quite precisely, as a copy of the *Complete Works* was on Captain James Cook's *Endeavour* when it traversed the

---

[1] Julian Meyrick, 'Shakespeare, Classic Adaptations and the Retreat in the Theatrical', *Australian Studies* 4 (2012), 1; James McKinnon, 'Lodestone or Leadweight: How Shakespeare 'Means' at the New Zealand International Arts Festival', ADSA 2012: <http://www.adsa2012.qut.edu.au/collection/performancea/lodestoneorl.jsp>.

Pacific 1769-70, logging the Transit of Venus on Tahiti before mapping New Zealand and the east coast of Australia, claiming both the latter as British territories.[2] There is no record of a Shakespeare performance on the *Endeavour*, so the first recorded Australian Shakespeare was a staging of *Henry IV* in Robert Sidaway's Sydney theatre in 1800.[3] The playbill lists Hotspur, so the performance would have included the rousing swordfight that climaxes *I Henry IV*. If so, then the first enacted moment of tragic affect in Australia would have been the pathos of Hotspur, dying mid-line: 'No, Percy, thou are dust | and food for …' (*I Henry IV*, 5.4.84-5).

Both the *Endeavour* Shakespeare volume and the Sidaway *Henry IV* must properly be thought of as false prologues to the demonstrable performance of tragedy in this region which, archivally speaking, begins in the 1830s and 1840s, when settlements in Melbourne, Sydney, and (later) New Zealand were large enough to support newspapers (the main source for early performance histories); and when their populations were sufficient to reward visits of travelling players. Throughout the nineteenth century and the early decades of the twentieth, English troupes would have been the main vehicle for receiving tragedies in live performance. Whether these were taken as occasions for high moral seriousness, or whether the audience demanded a rambunctious good time—instead of, or as well as, 'tragic' acting—is a moot point. Detailed accounts of these performances support the comic fictional evocation of nineteenth-century acting made famous in Charles Dickens's *Nicholas Nickleby* and Mark Twain's *Huckleberry Finn*. Chapter 15 of James Tucker's 1845 convict epic *Ralph Rashleigh* gives local habitation to such scenes in its depiction of drunken actors performing at Emu Plains to the west of Sydney;[4] C. J. Dennis, in his enduringly popular book of poems, *The Sentimental Bloke*, sends his pair of Australian lovers, Bob and Doreen, to a performance of *Romeo and Juliet*. Dennis nicely calibrates the pathos of the scene against the bathos of the venue in his highly crafted version of idiomatically Australian English:

> Then Juli-et wakes up an sees 'im there,
> Turns on the water-works an' tears 'er 'air,
> 'Dear love', she sez, 'I cannot live alone!'
> An' wif a moan,
> She grabs 'is pocket knife, and ends 'er cares …
> 'Peanuts or lollies!' sez a boy upstairs.[5]

The first record of a New Zealand performance of tragedy (and the first recorded New Zealand Shakespeare) in 1848, is worth quoting at length; it too suggests an audience in search more of good times than high seriousness:

> The first actor who made his appearance was greeted with such a shout, and underwent such an impertinent cross-examination as to where he had procured his red striped pantaloons,

---

[2] The copy was in the luggage of Sydney Parkinson, an artist on the voyage. It is likely to have been Johnson's 1765 edition, but the specific copy has not survived.

[3] Sidaway was a convict on the first ships which arrived in 1788. The handbill 'does not specify *Part One*', writes Rose Gaby in an unpublished history of Australian performances of *I Henry IV*, but the cast list and the familiarity of *Part One* on the eighteenth-century stage would suggest that this was the only play mounted. See Robert Jordan's *Convict Theatres of Early Australia* (Sydney: Currency Press, 2002), for the authoritative account of Sidaway's venture.

[4] Tucker was a convict who had served out his sentence; much of the novel draws directly on his lived experiences in Australia.

[5] C. J. Dennis, *The Songs of a Sentimental Bloke* (Sydney: Angus & Robertson, 1916), 43.

how the moustache was stuck on, &c., that he could not proceed ... he was known ... as a vocalist, and was accordingly called upon for a song ... he sang ... and being in the costume of 'Macbeth', it had on the whole a pleasing effect ... The piece was then commenced, and went on smoothly for half-an-hour, when poor Macbeth happening to be left alone on the stage to get through some long soliloquy, the wayward audience, knowing him to be a dancing-master and excelling in the sailor's hornpipe, demanded it in a manner which could not bear a refusal ... poor Macbeth was obliged to start off. His long sword rather interfering with his steps, he laid it aside and went to work in capital style, which brought forth ... shouts of delight and uproarious peals of laughter.[6]

Most of this audience would have been comprised of soldiers on leave in Wellington from action in the land wars against Maori tribes, so the aggressive demand for a good time in despite of the play itself is understandable.

Twenty years later, Melbourne audiences, more patient, were prepared to be riveted by the emotionally charged high seriousness of Charles and Ellen Kean's tour of *Macbeth*, as a local reviewer suggests in describing his the pathos Ellen Kean brought to the banquet scene (3.4), commending

the silent appeals of glance and smile ... so sweet now and now so passionately remonstrating her address to Macbeth, down to her last, despairing, affrighted, imperious order to the guests to separate.[7]

Such tours, bringing Shakespeare to the farthest edge of the empire, were the norm through to the 1920s. The frisson of English gurus bringing the Bard to life was evident in the rapture with which the visits of Olivier and Vivien Leigh (1948), the Shakespeare Memorial Theatre Company on their Coronation Tour (1953), and Sir Ian McKellen with the RSC/Trevor Nunn *Lear* (2009), were received. The popular National Theatre Live screenings of the Adrian Lester *Othello* (2013), and the Tom Hiddleston/Donmar Warehouse *Coriolanus* (2014) are the contemporary, mediated shadow of these tours. For several generations, however, it has no longer been enough to rely solely on such imported cultural products. For Shakespearean tragedy to compel audiences in live performance there must be ways to play tragedies in local terms, directed and performed by local artists. But what should those terms be? Kate Flaherty surveys the best Australian responses in *Ours As We Play It: Australia Plays Shakespeare* (2010).

For New Zealand audiences, Ngaio Marsh functioned as a crucial mediator, bridging the gap between travelling Shakespeare and the development of local, professional productions. Her mother, Rose Seagar, was an actor in Christchurch, New Zealand, and played Lady Macbeth for a travelling company. Marsh was immersed in Shakespeare texts from the age of 9,when her teacher introduced her to *King Lear*. She toured New Zealand with Allan Wilkie's company in the 1920s, an experience lovingly recreated in her detective novel *Vintage Murder* (1937), where, on the stage of a small town in the middle of the North Island, the lead actress is killed with a jeroboam of champagne. Often Marsh's plots use

---

[6] Lieutenant H. F. McKillop, *Reminiscences of Twelve Months' Service in New Zealand*, 1849 (Christchurch: Capper Press, 1973), 160–70.

[7] Qtd. in Kate Flaherty and Edel Lamb, 'The 1863 Melbourne Shakespeare War: Barry Sullivan, Charles and Ellen Kean and the Play of Cultural Usurpation on the Australian Stage', *Australian Studies* 4 (2012), 8.

Shakespearean performance or Shakespearean actors, such as the vain Sir Henry Ancred, who has his portrait painted in his role as Macbeth in *Final Curtain* (1947). Marsh's last novel, *Light Thickens* (1982) describes a romanticized production of *Macbeth*, with a medieval castle as the set. The lead actor is beheaded backstage; his head is brought back on stage as an unsettlingly visceral prop for the last scene.

Marsh herself directed *Macbeth* three times. She began directing Shakespeare in 1942, when she was approached by students from the University of Canterbury, Christchurch, New Zealand. Her 1943 *Hamlet* is credited as the first modern dress Shakespeare staged in New Zealand. In her productions, which toured New Zealand and Australia, she strove to replicate the force of English performances from the late 1940s and 1950s. Her productions were highly choreographed: her promptbooks in the Alexander Turnbull Library (Wellington) show a strong disposition towards symmetrical pictorialism. These scripts also show how heavily Marsh cut the plays, encouraging speed while skimping on emotional impact.

Most importantly, these were productions in which New Zealandness was actively suppressed. For Marsh, Shakespearean tragedy was something always taking place elsewhere. Moreover, Marsh despised the New Zealand accent which she found inexpressive for generating the aural resonance she feltShakespeare required. Many professional New Zealand actors had their first experience of tragedy in her productions before embarking for England, where they received the classical training thought necessary in the mid-twentieth century, learning how to mimic an English voice as an indispensable aid to conjuring proper tragic affect. In his autobiography *All My Lives* (1980) and his solo play *Passing Through* (1991), Mervyn Thompson, one of Marsh's protégés (and an influential, controversial director and playwright), recounts the constrictions of Marsh's approach, mingling irritation with affection and admiration for his mentor.

In Australia, John Bell has been a pivotal figure in seeking local habitation for tragedy, matters he reflects on at length in his autobiography (2002) and his general book on Shakespeare (2012). Bell trained in Bristol and worked at the RSC before returning to Australia, making his home Shakespeare debut as Hamlet[8] in the 1963 Old Tote production in Sydney. Bell recalls this as Shakespeare in the received English style, simply presented and sweetly articulated in the manner derived from Gielgud and Olivier, 'a combination of effete narcissism and violent derring-do'.[9] Since then Bell has explored ways of releasing the sounds of an Australian 'accent' and showing an aggressively Australian perspective on Shakespeare.[10] The Bell Shakespeare Company tours throughout Australia, a return to the nineteenth-century mode of travelling performers, but with a local perspective. Bell has been influential too in the developing 'larrikin' Shakespeare, deploying a defensively witty, irreverent style of debate into the zone of Shakespearean classics. An early venture of this kind was the Nimrod *Hamlet on Ice* (1971), a zany *Hamlet*-themed revue. Nimrod's freewheeling approach paved the way for later productions enlivened by a similar energy and independence in the face

---

[8] My comments on *Hamlet* rework in part a section of my essay 'Australasia', in *Hamlet-Handbuch: Stoffe, Aneignungen, Deutungen*, ed. Peter Marx (Stuttgart: J. B. Metzler, 2014), 358–65.

[9] *On Shakespeare* (Sydney: Allen & Unwin, 2012), 178.

[10] Adrian Kiernander, 'John Bell and a Post-Colonial Australian Shakespeare, 1963-2000', in *O Brave New World: Two Centuries of Shakespeare on the Australian Stage*, ed. John Golder and Richard Madelaine (Sydney: Currency Press, 2001), 236–56.

of the (always potentially crippling) force of an English masterpiece. Directors and actors continue to test themselves against the force of *Hamlet*. The results, over the last twenty years, have been visible in a series of energizing and innovative productions. In 1994, for example, Neil Armfield directed Richard Roxburgh as Hamlet at the Belvoir Street Theatre, Sydney. His celebrated performance epitomized the spirit of hyper-masculinity.[11] This was not a philosophically withdrawn Hamlet, but one who was physically engaged, hurling himself with anguished glee against the walls of the Belvoir Street Theatre, and fully drawing out the witty lines in which Hamlet demonstrates his Yorick-like capacity to 'set the table on a roar'. More recent Australian Hamlets have withdrawn from 'all the uses of this world', exploring instead 'that within which passes show' (*Hamlet* 1.2.145, 85). Adam Cook's Hamlet, for the Queensland Theatre Company (2007) was seen by many as 'Emo-like' in his demeanour … and emotional directness'.[12] This tendency was pushed to an extreme by Ewen Leslie in Simon Phillips's *Hamlet* for the Melbourne Theatre Company (2011). In the first court scene (1.2), Leslie's Hamlet was a weeping mess, on the verge of complete breakdown. His grief was finely wrought yet strangely unaffecting. That production conceived Elsinore (in a set designed by Phillips himself) as an assemblage of transparent cubed rooms, placed on a large revolving platform'. Even in the most private of scenes the play's other characters could be seen busily at work. This was a vivid image of the paranoid web of surveillance the play evokes in Elsinore. Yet there was nothing inherently 'Australian' about it, as the governing concept would resonate any society dependent on modern technologies. In this sense the production was typical of much professional Shakespeare in Australia and New Zealand.

Similar forms of eclectically confident internationalism can be seen in productions designed for the state-subsidized theatres which, since the 1960s, have been the main vehicle for bringing professional local productions to New Zealand audiences. These remain underexplored. A start can be made by using the *Theatre Aotearoa Database* as well as *Theatreview*, which archives post-2006 reviews of productions across New Zealand. Lisa Warrington makes resourceful use of both in her thick descriptions of local Shakespeares.[13] For Warrington the most arresting recent New Zealand *Hamlet* was David O'Donnell's for the Fortune Theatre in Dunedin (2005).[14] His most striking device was to play the ghost as a figure from a Butoh play, and to use Butoh gestural vocabulary throughout, with exquisite slow movements in an empty space, as when Gertrude removed her shoes before Hamlet accosted her in 3.4, or when Claudius demonstrated the lugubrious leaching of blood from his veins, moments before his death. These moments contrasted with a hectic, mobile Elsinore, as actors 'slithered, climbed, fell, rolled and were pushed and rotated about'.[15] The result was a poetic yet energized *Hamlet*. O'Donnell also featured two strong female actors to begin the play as Francisco and Bernardo and cast the Maori actor and playwright Rangimoana Taylor as an amusingly digressive Polonius.[16]

---

[11] Flaherty and Lamb, 'The 1863 Melbourne Shakespeare War', 27.   [12] Ibid., 69.
[13] Lisa Warrington, '"Look here, upon this picture, and on this": Representations of *Hamlet* in Aotearoa/New Zealand, 1993-2006'. *Contemporary Theatre Review* 19: 3 (August 2009), 305-17.
[14] Founded as an alternative to the 'other' professional theatre across town, The Globe.
[15] Warrington, 'Representations of *Hamlet*', 313.
[16] Discussion with David O'Donnell, March 2014. Conservative members of the Fortune's Board were not convinced that casting two women as soldiers and a Maori as a court official would be 'proper' Shakespeare.

LITERATURE

Since the nineteenth century, Shakespeare's works have also become inextricably part of the literary cultures of Australasia, in processes paralleled closely in the former settler colonies of South Africa and North America. Talismanic copies of the 1623 First Folio can be seen in Adelaide, Sydney, and Auckland. British settlers brought many copies of the *Complete Works* with them, while Shakespeare remains a mainstay in secondary and university English programmes. As Megan Murray-Pepper has recently shown, colonial writers such as Ngaio Marsh and Katherine Mansfield sampled a standardized form of Shakespeare's canon, by way of classroom anthologies and examination questions. From this perspective Philip Mead and Marion Campbell's 1993 collection, *Shakespeare's Books: Contemporary Cultural Politics and the Persistence of Empire*,[17] remains a usefully suggestive set of essays, demonstrating specific examples of the role of Shakespeare's texts in the formation of Australian print culture. The results can readily be seen in an established early Australian classic, Joseph Furphy's 1903 comic epic *Such is Life*, 'which exhibits some of the "classic" features of what has come to be seen as stereotyped masculinist, Anglo-Celtic nationalism'.[18] The rambling fictional memoirs of Tom Collins no sooner set up these values than they deconstruct them; the linear progression of the narrative is thrown off track by constant digression, frequently in Shakespearean form. A micro-essay or mini-lecture on fate in Chapter 2 strings together quotes and observations about Othello, Hamlet, and Macbeth, and quotes from their respective plays concluding banally that 'momentous alternatives are simply the voluntary rough-hewing of our own ends'.[19] The Bradleyan insistence on these three characters as the cynosure of tragic, philosophizing experience seems as inevitable as their presence in such a self-conscious attempt to ground a national, Australian text culture.

Across the Tasman, F. E. Maning's classic memoir of his adventures in the early contact zone between the Maori and the rapidly arriving settlers, *Old New Zealand: A Tale of the Good Old Times* (1863),[20] demonstrates a strikingly similar pattern of Shakespeare citationality yoked to a quasi-nationalist agenda. The unreliable narrator struggles like Tristram Shandy to get his tale told, of his landing in New Zealand, before mingling and trading with tribes in the upper North Island. Like Furphy's Tom Collins, the self-interrupting, perpetually digressing narrator cannot help himself from quoting Shakespeare, citing *Othello, Hamlet*, and *Macbeth* to comic effect. He cannot wait to get 'New Zealand' started; his quotations show his awareness that doing so will involve reading Shakespeare's book into Pacific locations.

This became the prevailing theme of M. K. Joseph's wry campus fiction *A Pound of Saffron* (1962),[21] which uses a frame story of rehearsing Shakespeare to ironize issues of

---

[17] Melbourne University and Cultural Studies Series No. 1 (Melbourne, Department of English, University of Melbourne, 1993).

[18] Susan K. Martin, 'National Dress or National Trousers', in *The Oxford Literary History of Australia*, ed. Bruce Bennett and Jennifer Strauss (Melbourne: Oxford University Press, 1988), 103.

[19] *Such is Life* (Hawthorn, Victoria: Lloyd O'Neil, 1970), 87.

[20] F. E. Maning, *Old New Zealand and Other Writings*, ed. Alex Calder (London: Leicester University Press, 2001).

[21] Joseph decentres his Shakespeare novel by taking his title from Webster's *The White Devil*: 'O the rare tricks of a Machivillian! | He doth not come like a grosse plodding slave | And buffet you

identity and provincialism in mid-twentieth-century New Zealand. Joseph reinvents a version of Auckland University, where he taught for many years after the Second World War. An unscrupulously ambitious lecturer in Renaissance drama mounts an outdoor production of *Antony and Cleopatra*, drawing support from the University and the city to make it successful. He engineers a love match between the actors playing the two title characters. Joseph captures the pettiness of campus and town gossip, lacing the fiction with what read like fragments from his own lectures on Shakespearean drama. The production within the text is fulsomely described. A part-Maori woman plays Cleopatra. Joseph focalizes Cleopatra's lament over Antony's passing ('The crown o'the earth doth melt ...') through the mind of a Maori academic. The stately, cadenced blank verse is matched by a prose English version of *waiata tangi*, the kind of song or chant used by Maori for formal grieving: 'He is fallen, the tall tree is fallen in the midst of the bush. All the blood of her mother's race cried out in the keening for the dead warrior ...'.[22] This elaborately articulated grief anticipates by fifty years the best moments of heart-breaking lamentation in the Maori *Troilus and Cressida* which launched the Globe's World Shakespeare season, 23 April 2012 (which I discuss in the final section, 'Indigeneity').

Most recent scholarship has focused on analysing Australasian performance practices, but the literary archive also holds considerable potential for future work, especially where drawing on tragedy serves not to constrict the writers' viewpoint (as if under some neo-colonialist southern form of the anxiety of influence), but to expand their artistic practice. An excellent case study here would be Randolph Stow's *Lear*-themed early novel *To the Islands* (1958), published the same year as Joseph's *Pound of Saffron*. In the preface to the revised 1982 edition of the novel, Stow is candid about the grandness of his Shakespearean gambit: 'Nowadays I should hardly dare to tackle such a *King Lear*-like theme; but I do not regret having raised the large questions asked here.'[23] His strategy was devised to break from the strictures of mid-twentieth-century fiction, borne out of his 'irritation with the tyranny, in Australia, of social realism'.[24] He then uses the frame of *Lear* to build an overtly lyrical, symbolic structure. Stephen Heriot, a missionary in the north of Western Australia, heads towards the sea with his faithful aboriginal retainer, Justin: 'He saw himself as a great red cliff, rising from the rocks of his own ruin.'[25] He self-consciously quotes Lear, as if overhearing himself cite: 'I've got nothing to say. A very foolish, fond old man.'[26] He reaches the top of his Dover-style cliff, ready for his final unburdened journey towards death: 'he stood suddenly still, his white hair blowing against the sky, his eyes dazzled with the sea.'[27] Here the novel mirrors the ambivalence of Lear's death. Heriot is left looking out to see where 'in the heart of the blaze, might appear the islands',[28] where true insight might be found.

The fictions of Janet Frame, one of New Zealand's most powerful writers, are striated with allusions to, and quotations from, Shakespeare. Her career-long negotiations with Shakespeare are an extended version of the strategies Stow deploys in his early novel. Shakespeare helps Frame critique the banality of New Zealand; at the same time,

---

to death: No my quaint knave, | He tickles you to death; makes you die laughing |As if you had swallow'd downe a pound of saffron' (4.3.190–4).

[22] M. K. Joseph, *A Pound of Saffron* (Hamilton: Paul's Books, 1962), 197.
[23] Randolph Stow, *To the Islands*, rev. edn. (London: Picador, 1983), p. ix.   [24] Ibid., p. xi.
[25] Stow, *To the Islands*, 1958 (Harmondsworth: Penguin, 1971), 13.   [26] Ibid., 75.
[27] Ibid., 207.   [28] Ibid., 208.

invoking his writing makes a space where Frame can evade the demands of mainstream realism. A little-read, seldom-anthologized early story, 'How Now Hecate, You Look Angerly', reworks an incident Frame also tells in her 1983 autobiography, *To the Is-Land*. This uses the common motif of Shakespeare in the high school classroom. The unnamed narrator recalls a class in a girl's school where she was always the outsider, never able to compete with the ever-popular Molly Cochrane. A teacher, newly returned from England, brings the gusto of *Macbeth* into the class, beginning a lesson with the witches' chant: 'When shall we three meet again.' The narrator is captivated (as evidently Frame herself was) by these cadences. The narrator is promised the part of Lady Macbeth, and spends hours at home practising 'out damned spot' before the mirror. She is led astray by what she describes as 'the complicated embezzlements of time'.[29] The popular girl plays the part instead, leaving the narrator with the single line, 'How now Hecate, you look angerly.' The teacher who brings Shakespeare as a counterpoint to the humdrum suffers a stroke. The narrative yokes teacher and narrator together as outcasts from the norm: effectively they belong to the outland, as the witches do in the play. Through accessing Shakespeare's text they strive against the crushingly normative. Frame's 1961 novel *Faces in the Water* presents in condensed, poetic form two ways of drawing writerly strength from Shakespeare, though here, as often, Frame eschews the designs of writers like Stow, who shape the entire structure of a novel after a Shakespearean plot. Rather *Faces in the Water* powerfully evokes the idea of the Shakespeare text itself as a kind of fetish object, offering material consolation. The novel is a fictionalized memoir of Frame's incarcerations in mental institutions. The traumas are recounted by the narrator/avatar Istina Mavet. She is given (as Frame was) a pink cretonne bag with a beaded rose. Here Mavet keeps her treasures: a *Complete Works* and a copy of Rilke's poetry. 'I seldom read my book yet it became more and more dilapidated physically ... with pages unleaving as if an unknown person were devoting time to studying it ... it had decided to read itself.'[30] The process is disturbingly animistic, yet consoling at the same time. Mavet rejects obvious analogies between herself and the distracted Ophelia, satirizing glib uses of *Hamlet* and the later Yeats as 'the romantic popular idea of the insane ... the easy Opheliana recited like the pages of a seed catalog [sic] or the outpourings of Crazy Janes who provide, in fiction, an outlet for poetic abandon'.[31] Shakespeare's book, reading itself silently into her consciousness, opens the way to deeper empathy through an existentialist reading of *King Lear*. She thinks of her fellow patients in 'the desperate season of their lives', directly citing Lear's deep compassion for '*Poor naked wretches wheresoe'er you are*'. Like Stow's Hariot, her imagination leads her to the top of the cliff, like Gloucester's. The institution in which they are incarcerated is called Cliffhaven, a variation of the Seacliff Hospital where Frame herself was a patient. The recollection both of Gloucester and Lear from the wandering middle of Shakespeare's play leads not directly to the physical cliff but rather is placed as an image for the disconnectedness of the patients ('nobody at home, not in themselves or anywhere'),[32] and their detachment from the everyday beyond the hospital on its cliff.

[29] Janet Frame, *The Reservoir: Stories and Sketches* (New York: George Braziller, 1963), 60.
[30] Janet Frame, *Faces in the Water*, 1961 (London: The Women's Press, 1980), 114.
[31] Ibid., 112.   [32] Ibid., 114.

Mike Johnson's 1986 novel *Lear—The Shakespeare Company Plays Lear at Babylon* is an extreme, fantasy counterpoint to Frame's fiction, and is the most extended reworking of a tragedy by a New Zealand novelist. Johnson imagines a dystopian future in which players travel a post-apocalyptic landscape; many of them bear the scars of AIDS-like sexual diseases. In an extended application of rehearsal fiction tropes (where characters rehearse for the fictive performance of a play), Shakespeare's characters play themselves, performing *Lear* as well as engaging in complex sexual alignments in their offstage lives. Their onstage and offstage lives merge with catastrophic yet hauntingly poetical results. Just as Stow does in *To the Islands*, so Johnson works through Shakespeare, quoting *Lear* liberally, effecting an escape from the constrictions of documentary-style realism.

ADAPTATION

'Productions of Shakespeare ... in Australia are always adaptations', writes Jonathan Rayner, ' ... [t]hey stand as adaptations in an evolutionary sense, as modifications of an original to fit specific cultural conditions.'[33] The scope of adaptation then looms as almost ungraspably broad. Yet within this wide and apparently universal theatre, Australasian playwrights have frequently had recourse to the specific dramaturgy of adaptation, drawn to rewrite or reshape Shakespearean tragedies for their own cultural purposes.

Romeo and Tusi, by Oscar Kightley and Erolia Ifopo, is a telling example. First devised as a production for Pacific Underground (a collective devoted to presenting live theatre that reflected the perspective of the Pacific peoples living in New Zealand), *Romeo and Tusi* has been frequently performed to audiences made up of more Pacific Islanders than would be the norm in New Zealand for conventional Shakespeare. *Romeo and Tusi* playfully wrestles with the issue of what it means for a writer like Kightley, born in Samoa but raised in New Zealand, to grapple with Shakespeare. Kightley's adaptation is partly framed against a 1992 Samoan *Romeo and Juliet* performed at the University of Auckland and directed by Justine Simei-Barton and Alan Brunton. The production was set in a nineteenth-century civil war between two branches of the Samoan royal house, and was therefore construed as implying an incestuous relation between two of its members; and production caused deep offence in some sectors of the Auckland Samoan community: 'This is so horrible, you know someone could die for something like this', said one chief. By sampling key sections of Shakespeare's play, Kightley sets out both to claim Shakespeare as something that Samoan artists could legitimately appropriate and also, through generating an upbeat performance, make light of the intensely defensive cultural response to the 1992 production which, while heartfelt, could certainly be read as being naïve.

In *Romeo and Tusi* Anaru, a Maori, and Tusi, a Samoan, are cast as Romeo and Juliet in their high school's production. Scenes of rehearsal counterpoint scenes of negotiation with their families. Will they be allowed to take their parts? Will it be culturally permissible for them to kiss on stage? The trope of rehearsal fiction

---

[33] Jonathan Rayner, 'Meditative Tangents: Fred Schepisi's *The Eye of the Storm* (2011)', *Australian Studies* 4 (2012), 3–4.

is cross-bred with the high school musical: a live band plays throughout. The play, Kightley explains, was designed to provide a 'good times vibe' for the audience, to be accessible to those uncomfortable with the protocols of serious theatre. Shakespeare's prologue and epilogue are spoken (in modified form) by a *fa'a'fine*, a Samoan version of a transgendered male/female. S/he runs a talk show to reconcile the families. This serves a sociocultural purpose, preaching a message of inter-ethnic harmony, but it also serves to blunt or evade the core narrative of *Romeo and Juliet*; for it seems paradoxical to embrace Shakespeare's classic of young love (which operates so powerfully because love plays out as both beguiling and catastrophic) and then to seek to refute its essential premise. *West Side Story*, the most enduring template for modern versions of *Romeo and Juliet*,[34] is far braver in admitting to the tragic consequences of Shakespeare's story.[35]

Since its first performance in 1993 to commemorate the centenary of women gaining the vote in New Zealand, Jean Betts's *Ophelia Thinks Harder* has acquired the status of a national classic, and is widely studied and frequently performed by teen actors. They are energized by its earnest naivety. The play reworks *Hamlet* around basic feminist premises. The men of Elsinore are sexist fools; moreover, for any female actor, Shakespeare's tragedy presents limited scope for actualization. Betts transfers Hamlet's dilemmas and iconic speeches to Ophelia. Gertrude and a reappearing Virgin Mary take her in hand and explain how much of a man's world Shakespeare's Denmark really is. Betts borrows the device made famous in Stoppard's *Rosencrantz and Guildenstern are Dead* (1966); behind Betts's scenes we get glimpses of Shakespeare's play unfolding. Like Stoppard, Betts makes comic heroes of the visiting actors. Her Ophelia evades female roles, becoming an actor and escaping Elsinore, leaving the court to its fifth-act massacre. Stripped of philosophical poetry, Shakespeare's last scene is framed as an exuberant combination of dumb shows and noise. Betts's play allows young performers in particular to level with Shakespeare. Cultural nonchalance, however, is again achieved bought at the expense of tragic pathos.

These New Zealand adaptations of tragedy are close trans-Tasman cousins to the free-wheeling spirit of 'larrikin' Shakespeare which has energized Australian Shakespeares so vividly. Some Australian adaptations mine Shakespeare for more serious purposes, yoking tragedy directly to specific cultural debates. David Williamson brings Shakespeare (in a high starched Elizabethan collar) and Lear to life in his re-enactment of the culture wars in his *Dead White Males* (1995), pitting the two of them against English lecturers who advocate both post-structuralist and new historicist lines of thought. Williamson shows academics as fatuous and manipulative, giving Shakespeare himself a speech voicing the opposite case: ' are we not *all* born with the demons love, grief, guilt, anger, fear, scorn, loyalty, and hate!' The point is underscored by a counterpoint from Lear, '*holding*

---

[34] Largely due to the success of the filmed version and its embrace by community and amateur groups. Archives record a remarkable 'total of approximately forty thousand productions around the world in the half-century since *West Side Story* was first performed', Nigel Simeone, *Leonard Bernstein: West Side Story* (Farnham: Ashgate, 2009), 4.

[35] For contrasting perspectives, see Emma Cox, 'A Pair of Star-Crossed Lovers Take Their Feet: Polynesian Identities in *Romeo and Tusi*', *Shakespeare Studies* (The Shakespeare Society of Japan) 46 (2008), 46–61; and my '*Romeo and Tusi*: An Eclectically Musical Samoan/Maori *Romeo and Juliet* in Aotearoa/New Zealand', *Contemporary Theatre Review* 19: 3 (2009), 280–90.

an imaginary Cordelia in his arms', with the wrenching speech that issues with that entrance: 'Howl, howl, howl.'[36] In the play, Angela, a female student, must choose between essentialism and humanism and the postmodern theorizing which will reward her with a high grade. She must also negotiate her family life and dying grandfather, who is seen playing Lear's last scene upstage. Down under, Williamson insists, Lear remains an everyman whom all should readily access.

Michael Gow's *Away* is the most lyrical Australian Shakespeare adaptation, insistent on an Australian right to claim his works. The play has been hugely popular in professional performances, appealing in amateur productions, and well established on examination reading lists. Gow uses an epigraph in Viola's question in the second scene of *Twelfth Night*: 'What country friends, is this?' Gow's answer, like Williamson's, is resounding: Shakespeare's. The play recreates the summer of 1967, and the main action unfolds at a seaside summer camp, an archetypal Australasian location. Tom, the main character, is a high school actor. The play opens with his winning performances of Puck's epilogue in the end-of-year school play. Yet Gow is after a deeper resonance than this surface invoking of midsummer suggests. For Tom is dying and will not live long beyond the end of the play. Gow's play then ends with the opening of *King Lear*, the school's project for the term following the summer break. It is hard not to hear Gow's voice through the teacher, Miss Latrobe. She brings her class outside, and the stage directions indicate, the '*light becomes bright, summery, morning*'. What could be less *Lear*-like than such weather? Yet the Australian outdoors, Miss Latrobe insists, is the best place to absorb 'the power of nature, its participation in the drama' of *Lear*, which she calls Shakespeare's 'masterwork'.[37]

INDIGINEITY

In many of my examples we see descendants of British settlers assessing their ambivalent Shakespearean legacy. I will finish with the strongest recent trend in Australasian and Pacific responses to tragedy, those generated by, or reflecting the perspectives of, indigenous populations, though of course 'indigenous' is a highly contested term. Here I will take it to mean those groups who descend from peoples who inhabited Australia, New Zealand, and the other Pacific Islands before the invasive arrival of European populations from the late eighteenth century onwards. Can such indigenous artists use Shakespeare in English or their own languages to address the legacy of tragedy? Should tragic acting remain a privileged white domain? No-one who witnessed the Ngākau Toa's *Troilus and Cressida* (*A Toroihi rāua ko Kāhira*) in 2012 would have thought so, when this Maori version opened the season of plays for the Globe's World Shakespeare.[38] This striking

---

[36] David Williamson, *Dead White Males* (Sydney: Currency Press, 1996), 82.

[37] Michael Gow, *Away* (Sydney: Currency Press, 1990), 56.

[38] This was preceded by *Venus and Adonis* and, on Sunday 22 April, the recitation of sonnets in many languages, including Noongarra, an Aboriginal language. Regrettably there was no play performed in an Aboriginal or Pacific Island language, so the Maori *Troilus* was the only full South Pacific Shakespeare on offer.

production was greeted with acclaim.[39] The performance opened with a staged version of a traditional Maori entrance with visitors (in this case the Greek army) being called by way of *karanga* chanting on to the stage, approached through the yard. Both Greek and Trojan characters performed matching *haka* (war dance), made familiar through its use by the New Zealand All Blacks. In the Globe's wooden amphitheatre, the reverberation of voices and stamping feet was tremendous;—the actors clearly relished filling an English space with Maori sounds and bodies. The play was set in pre-contact New Zealand, with Greeks and Trojans as warring *iwi* (tribes). Richard Nunns, one of the actors, is also a specialist in *taonga pouro*, or traditional Maori instruments (mostly wind, with some percussion): these played throughout. Shakespeare was spoken only in Maori, though brief surtitles in English summarized each scene. . The effect was austere, and completely immersive. The final section of the play, from the death of Patroclus on, orchestrated emotion with the constant unnerving sound of music played from the rear of the stage, combined with vocalized lamentation. The actor/musicians powerfully conveyed an idea of supernatural malignity, linking Shakespeare's evocation of Homeric times with the warrior cult of traditional Maori society. This was the second full production of Shakespeare in Maori: in 1990 Don Selwyn had directed Jones's translation of *The Merchant of Venice* in Auckland, twelve years before his feature film of the Maori script. In 2003 *Toi Whakaari* (the New Zealand Drama School) performed *Troilus*, with some scenes in Maori and some in English, conceiving the play as depicting conflict between the invading English (the Greeks), and a Maori tribe defending their territory, as they did through the 30-year period known as the Land Wars. Thus the 2012 *Troilus* was a culmination of a decades-long process, aligning Shakespeare with issues of cultural survival, underpinning a determination to enhance the Maori language and its protocols (*tikanga*). The delight of the Globe audiences and the world-wide publicity surrounding the event suggests that mounting this difficult, tragical satire in Maori was a cultural triumph.

Maori motifs feature in English-language versions of tragedies as well. Kirk Torrance's *Flintlock Musket* adapts *Macbeth* to New Zealand in the 1820s, when the first tribes to gain muskets exercised supreme advantage over their enemies. Torrance's main character is a Scottish trader who falls in love with an ambitious Lady Macbeth figure. The scenario blends the world of 1820s New Zealand with Shakespeare's imaginary Scotland. By lacing Shakespeare through his scenario Torrance generates an emotionally gripping account of the nineteenth-century colonial world, a fully embodied reflection of the cultural impact of land appropriations and the intertribal use of the technologies of firearms and gunpowder.

The later period of the Land Wars (1840s–1870s) has featured in full Shakespeare productions as the most crucial (and to some extent still unresolved) period of racial conflict

---

[39] Stephen Purcell, 'Troilus and Cressida', in *A Year of Shakespeare: Re-Living the World Shakespeare Festival*, ed. Paul Edmondson, Paul Prescott, and Erin Sullivan (London: Bloomsbury, 2013), 21–13. For a nuanced cultural analysis of this performance, see Catherine Silverstone, 'Festival Showcasing and Cultural Regeneration: Aotearoa New Zealand, Shakespeare's Globe and Ngākau Toa's *A Toroihi rāua ko Kāhira* (*Troilus and Cressida*) in *Te Reo* Māori', in *Shakespeare Beyond English: A Global Experiment*, ed. Susan Bennett and Christie Carson (Cambridge: Cambridge University Press, 2013), 35–48. See also Mike Jonathan's documentary of the production's *Road to the Globe* <http://vimeo.com/ondemand/roadtotheglobe/63799760>.

in New Zealand. Though a treaty was signed between the British Crown and Maori tribes in 1840, its terms were often dishonoured, and Maori land was forcibly acquired. A resonant invocation of this was an *Othello* (2001) directed by Cathy Downes, and conceived in conjunction with Jim Moriarty, a leading Maori actor. Othello here was a 'friendly' (*kupapa*) soldier, fighting for the British against his own people. His tragic fall, performed rivetingly by Moriarty, arose then not so much from Iago's lies as from the culturally schizoid state of colonial being that Frantz Fanon famously diagnosed. Earlier in 1994 *Manawa Taua/Savage Hearts* concocted a brilliant Fanon-themed entertainment around a travelling production of *Othello*. Tupou, a Maori *rangatira* (chief) visiting England, is commanded by a comically assertive Queen Victoria to take over the title role from an English actor. Tupou proves adept at the role, bringing the character Othello to the young colony of New Zealand, but the contradiction between 'being' Maori and speaking 'Shakespeare' brings disaster, leading to the death of his sister, who plays Emilia in the inset play's scenes of *Othello*.[40]

Pacific actors have also embraced the ambiguous legacy of Shakespeare. Many were either born or raised in New Zealand (like Oscar Kightley) and work professionally in New Zealand and Australia. Nathaniel (Nat) Lees, a Tongan-New Zealander, has been in the vanguard of such performers. In 1989 he starred in Mervyn Thompson's production of *Othello*, in a small studio theatre in Auckland. This was not post-colonial in the manner of the Downes/Moriarty production, using a New Zealand setting or overtly referencing local political issues; instead, Thompson used the confined space of his theatre to unleash the terrifying force of Shakespeare's tragedy, where the actors were unconstrained by any attempts to mimic English states of being. In this context Lees delivered a bravura performance. He was later the star of a piece by Albert Wendt (the most prominent Samoan writer in English), *The Songmaker's Chair* (2003), a play which extends Wendt's career-long attempts to chronicle 'the lives of those courageous [Pacific] migrant families who have made Auckland and Aotearoa their home'.[41] An older Lees played Peseola, the patriarch of those members of the Peseola family, who have lived in Auckland as migrants for many years. The family gathers and, as the play unfolds over the Shakespearean form of five acts, Peseola prepares to die, settling in to the songmaker's chair of the title where, late in the fifth act, he can poetically recall his past, moving freely from English into Samoan. This is Wendt's second fully worked-out *Lear* variant. The first was an early, intense short novel *Pouliuli* (1977), set in a version of the Samoan village where Wendt was raised. Here Faleasa Osovae, the village elder, wakes one morning, aged 76, to discover that his life revolts him, and that his feeble children disgust him, with their immersion in the shallow materialism of a post-imperial world in thrall to work and money. He flees to the hills above the village with a club-footed fool. Abandoning their daily world, they prepare to depart for the realm of darkness (*Pouliuli*) of the title. Unlike Stow or Frame, Wendt does not quote *Lear* directly in either play or novel. Rather he assimilates a Pacific story to the *Lear* mythos. Wendt's stance towards Shakespeare is complex, though, and can be traced

---

[40] The script for *Savage Hearts* is no longer publicly accessible. For detailed discussion of the piece and its wider cultural relevance, see Michael Neill's 'Post-Colonial Shakespeare? Writing Away From the Centre', in *Post-Colonial Shakespeares*, ed. Ania Loomba and Martin Orkin (London: Routledge, 1998), 181–4.

[41] Albert Wendt, 'Introduction', *The Songmaker's Chair* (Wellington: Huia, 2004), 2.

in his classroom story 'Hamlet'; and also 'Heat', which recreates in part a Samoan performance of *Antony and Cleopatra*.[42]

The thematics of cultural death, of the consequences of physical and spiritual dispossession, echo too in Australia, where the effects of the displacement of Aboriginal peoples from their traditional lands have been profound. The statistical consequences, measuring high rates of substance abuse, infant mortality, violent crime and imprisonment, are even more horrifying for Aboriginals than for Pacific Islanders or Maori. Aboriginal artists have performed Shakespeare in many Australian theatres, most prominently Deborah Mailman, who was Cordelia in Barry Kosky's experimental *Lear* (1998) for the Bell Shakespeare Company, with John Bell as the King; and then Rosalind in Neil Armfield's *As You Like It* (1990) at Belvoir Street Theatre. Mailman explains her burden as an indigenous artist: 'It's not just me on stage but it's the rest of my people, too … it's Deb Mailman and a lot of history.'[43]

Two recent experiments attempt to trace that history through *King Lear* and *Hamlet*. Michael Kantor and Tom E. Lewis's *Lear* adaptation *The Shadow King* premiered in Melbourne late in 2013 and was performed in 2014 at festivals in Sydney, Brisbane, and Adelaide. The adaptors use modern English and the Kriol language, relocating Lear and his three daughters in the far north of Australia, bringing out with piercing clarity the land issues at the heart of the play, and the sense of dispossession from the land that is central to contemporary the Aboriginal experience. The resonant analogy between Lear's voluntary abandonment of his land and the forced surrender of it across Australia creates what one reviewer described as a series of 'looking glass moments'[44] where, as in the most effective of post-colonialized adaptations, local dilemmas take Shakespearean form.

Kantor and Lewis effect the aboriginal trans-shifting of Shakespeare by using contemporary English and Kriol, simulating on stage a dusty, drought-afflicted, mineral-rich outback terrain. In his new version of the first act of *Hamlet*, Rob Conkie adheres to Shakespeare's text, but excises reference to any specific European locales (Elsinore, Denmark, Wittenberg). His Hamlet instead is an Aboriginal philosophy student at the University of Melbourne—one of Australia's oldest and most prestigious institutions of higher learning, which, both in its architecture and its ambitions, presents as a colonial simulation of a great English or American university. Conkie's own adroit explication is the best guide to his dramaturgy. Performed by Aboriginal actors, and in site-specific locales, this too becomes a tragedy in which psychic loss is inextricable from the loss of land rather than being an incidental consequence of the plot. The play, Conkie summons us to remember, is 'a story of dispossession',[45] and a violent one at that. Fully conscious of his status as a white Australian, Conkie stages his version as an act of recovery of this Aboriginal aspect of Australia's tragic history. Conkie shows that, 250 years after their Pacific arrival, Shakespeare's tragedies retain their power to unsettle.

---

[42] *The Best of Albert Wendt's Short Stories* (Auckland: Vintage, 1999), 253–64, 302–23.

[43] Qtd. in Flaherty and Lamb, 'The 1863 Melbourne Shakespeare War', 113.

[44] Chris Boyd, 'Indigenous Lear a Deeply Affecting Adaptation', *The Australian*, 17 October 2013: http://www.theaustralian.com.au/arts/stage/indigenous-lear-a-deeply-affecting-adaptation/story-fn9d344c-1226741468176.

[45] Rob Conkie, 'Remember Me', *Australian Studies* 4 (2012), 1.

SELECT BIBLIOGRAPHY

Bell, John, *On Shakespeare* (Crows Nest, NSW: Allen & Unwin, 2012).

Bell, John, *The Time of My Life* (Crows Nest, NSW: Allen & Unwin, 2002).

Betts, Jean, and Wm. Shakespeare, *Ophelia Thinks Harder* (Wellington: Women's Play Press, 1994).

Carey, Rosalie, *A Theatre in the House: The Careys' Globe* (Otago: University of Otago Press, 1999).

Clement, Jennifer, 'Admitting to Adaptation in the Shakespeare Classroom', in *Teaching Shakespeare Beyond the Centre: Australasian Perspectives*, ed. Kate Flaherty, Penny Gay, and L. E. Semler, Palgrave Shakespeare Studies (Houndmills: Palgrave Macmillan, 2013), 51–63.

Dennis, C. J., *The Songs of a Sentimental Bloke* (Sydney: Angus & Robertson, 1916).

Flaherty, Kate, *Ours As We Play It: Australia Plays Shakespeare* (Perth: University of Western Australia Press, 2011).

Flaherty, Kate and Edel Lamb, 'The 1863 Melbourne Shakespeare War: Barry Sullivan, Charles and Ellen Kean and the Play of Cultural Usurpation on the Australian Stage', *Australian Studies* 4 (2012), 1–17.

Golder, John and Richard Madelaine, eds., *O Brave New World: Two Centuries of Shakespeare on the Australian Stage* (Sydney: Currency Press, 2001).

Houlahan, Mark, 'New Zealand', in *The Oxford Companion to Shakespeare*, ed. Michael Dobson and Stanley Wells (Oxford: Oxford University Press, 2001), 318–19.

Houlahan, Mark, 'Shakespeare in New Zealand', in *The Oxford Companion to New Zealand Literature in English*, ed. Roger Robinson and Nelson Wattie (Melbourne: Oxford University Press, 1998), 489–91.

Kelly, Philippa, *The King and I*, Shakespeare Now! (London: Continuum, 2011).

Kiernander, Adrian, 'John Bell and a Post-Colonial Australian Shakespeare, 1963–2000', in Golder and Madelaine: 236–56.

Kightley, Oscar and Erolia Ifopo, *Romeo and Tusi* (Wellington: Playmarket, 2000).

McKillop, Lieutenant H. F., *Reminiscences of Twelve Months' Service in New Zealand*, 1849 (Christchurch: Capper Press, 1973).

McKinnon, James, 'Lodestone or Leadweight: How Shakespeare 'Means' at the New Zealand International Arts Festival', ADSA 2012: http://www.adsa2012.qut.edu.au/collection/performancea/lodestoneorl.jsp. <accessed September 9 2014>.

Meyrick, Julian, 'Shakespeare, Classic Adaptations and the Retreat in the Theatrical', *Australian Studies* 4 (2012), 1–18.

Murray-Pepper, Megan, '"The Bogey of the Schoolroom": Shakespeare, "Royal Readers" and New Zealand Writers', in *Teaching Shakespeare Beyond the Centre: Australasian Perspectives*, ed. Kate Flaherty, Penny Gay, and L. E. Semler, Palgrave Shakespeare Studies (Houndmills: Palgrave Macmillan, 2013), 23–37.

Neill, Michael, 'From the Editor', Special Issue: 'Dislocating Shakespeare', *Shakespeare Quarterly* 52:4 (Winter, 2001), pp. iii–x.

Neill, Michael, ' 'Post-Colonial Shakespeare? Writing Away From the Centre', in *Post-Colonial Shakespeares*, ed. Ania Loomba and Martin Orkin, New Accents (London: Routledge, 1998), 164–86.

Rayner, Jonathan, 'Meditative Tangents: Fred Schepisi's *The Eye of the Storm* (2011)', *Australian Studies* 4 (2012), 1–15.

Silverstone, Catherine. 'Festival Showcasing and Cultural Regeneration: Aotearoa New Zealand, Shakespeare's Globe and Ngākau Toa's *A Toroihi rāua ko Kāhira* (*Troilus and*

Cressida) in *Te Reo* Maori', in *Shakespeare Beyond English: A Global Experiment*, ed. Susan Bennett and Christie Carson (Cambridge: Cambridge University Press, 2013), 35–48.

Torrance, Kirk, *Flintlock Musket* (Wellington: Playmarket, 2009).

Tucker, James, *Ralph Rashleigh*, foreword by Colin Roderick (Sydney: Angus & Robertson, 1975).

Warrington, Lisa, ' "Look here, upon this picture, and on this": Representations of *Hamlet* in Aotearoa/New Zealand, 1993–2006', *Contemporary Theatre Review* 19:3 (August, 2009), 305–17.

Wendt, Albert, *The Best of Albert Wendt's Short Stories* (Auckland: Vintage, 1999).

CHAPTER 49

SHAKESPEARE'S TRAGEDIES IN SOUTHERN AFRICA

COLETTE GORDON, DANIEL ROUX, AND DAVID SCHALKWYK

TRAGEDY, PLACE, AND LANGUAGE

Two statements by veteran South African actor-directors suggest very different under-standings of the extent to which Shakespearean tragedy finds itself 'at home' in South Africa. In 1995, John Kani declared that *Julius Caesar* is 'Shakespeare's African play',[1] while more recently, Janet Suzmann pronounced that 'Theatre is a white invention ... and white people go to it. It's in their DNA. It starts with Shakespeare ... Theatre is a totally European invention, as is tragedy. Other countries don't do tragedy. It's an invention by the Greeks'.[2] In 1987, Kani, whose anti-apartheid protest theatre had by then earned him international recognition, and Suzman, who had left the country in 1959 and made her career with the Royal Shakespeare company, collaborated on a production of *Othello* for Johannesburg's Market Theatre, Suzman directing Kani in the title role. Later televised, this apartheid-era *Othello* gained iconic status.

There is a story—which may or may not be apocryphal—that Hendrik Verwoerd, Prime Minister of South Africa, returned from a meeting of the Commonwealth in London in 1966, having seen Lawrence Olivier's film of *Othello*. He declared that the film, while showing artistic merit in itself, should not be shown in South Africa, where it would be dangerously subversive. At a time when the notorious Immorality Act, which prohibited any sexual activity between white people and those of any other race, was in full force—when 'mixed' couples were spied upon and their bedrooms invaded by the police in the dead of night—the mere representation of a marriage between a black man and a white woman, whatever the context, would have been regarded by

---

[1] David Blair, 'Shakespeare, the storyteller of Africa', *The Telegraph*, 19 April 2006.
[2] http://www.theguardian.com/stage/2014/dec/08/actor-janet-suzman-criticised-calling-theatre-white-invention, accessed 28 March 2016.

the apartheid regime and its supporters as both offensively immoral and profoundly political.[3]

We can find no evidence that Shakespeare's *Othello* was banned in apartheid South Africa, although the play was indeed prohibited from being a school textbook in a variety of educational jurisdictions.[4] *Othello* exemplifies the trap that Shakespearean tragedy represents in South Africa: specifically the ways in which race imposes itself. It thus refuses a critical distancing of the plays and their historical context from the inescapable pressures of colonialism and its quintessential embodiment in apartheid.

Concerns about tragedy's relation to time and history, and its potential for limiting or liberating social consciousness have been at the centre of debates about African tragedy, where the most sustained debate is carried on in the work of mostly Nigerian playwrights experimenting with tragic forms: Wole Soyinka, Ola Rotimi, J, P. Clarke, Femi Osofisan.[5] Critics have sought either to describe these efforts (Zulu Sofola, Timothy J. Reiss) and explain their value, or to prescribe a way out of perceived problems of fatalism and stasis, the waning power of communal ritual, and the distortions of 'bourgeois' historical tragedy. Andrew Gurr criticizes Soyinka's ritual theatre for reproducing Greek fatalism, a view put in question by Raymond Williams and Terry Eagleton's more inclusive cultural-materialist vision of tragedy and confuted by careful readers like Reiss. Biodun Jeyifo recognizes Soyinka's project as extending beyond Greek tragedy, but insists that Africa needs a contemporary tragedy more attuned to the history of class struggle, this demand echoed by Femi Osofisan.[6] The question that concerns us here is the extent to which Shakespearean tragedies have any distinctive voice in Africa, and more specifically, South Africa: to what extent Shakespearean tragedy is or is not compatible with Kani's and Suzman's statements.

The odd mixture of frustration and resignation in Suzman's comments about Shakespeare and tragedy in 'other countries' recalls the belief of the British director, Gregory Doran, and South African-born actor, Anthony Sher, upon returning to England from South Africa in 1996 after a much-criticized production of *Titus Andronicus*, that 'the demise of serious theatre in Johannesburg' had made Sher's South African homecoming impossible; that it would take English audiences back 'home' in 'a country that

---

[3] South Africa's most famous playwright, Athol Fugard, wrote a play about the effects of this prohibition in the early 1970s: *Statements After An Arrest Under the Immorality Act*, in Athol Fugard, John Kani, and Winston Ntshona, *Statements: 'SizweBansi Is Dead', 'The Island', 'Statements After an Arrest Under the Immorality Act'* (London: Oxford Paperbacks, 1985).

[4] See e.g. C. M. Tatz, 'Apartheid: Battle for the Mind', *The Australian Quarterly* 33:2 (1961), 18–29: 'Othello, for example, is considered an unsuitable matriculation text, for in the South African order of things miscegenation and mixed marriages are the evils of all evils' (20–1).

[5] See esp. Wole Soyinka, 'Drama and the Revolutionary Ideal', *In Person: Achebe, Awoonor and Soyinka*, ed. K. Morell (Seattle: Washington Institute for Comparative Studies, 1971) and *Myth, Literature and the African World* (Cambridge: Cambridge University Press, 1976); Femi Osofisan, 'Ritual and the Revolutionary Ethos', *Okike* 22 (1982), 72–81.

[6] Zulu Sofola, 'The concept of tragedy in African experience', in J. Okpaku et al., eds., *The Arts and Civilization of Black and African Peoples* (Lagos: Centre for Black and African Arts and Literature, 1986); Timothy J. Reiss, 'Using Tragedy against its Makers: Some African and Caribbean Instances', *A Companion to Tragedy*, ed. Rebecca Bushnell (Oxford: Blackwell, 2005), 505–26; Biodun Jeyifo, *The Truthful Lie: Essays in a Sociology of African Drama* (London: New Beacon Books, 1995).

truly values theatre' to appreciate the historic South African *Titus*.[7] In 2014, Suzman's comments—immediately challenged as racist—addressed the importance of appealing to more diverse audiences and blamed 'cultural DNA' for low turnout of black audiences.[8]

> they don't bloody come. They're not interested. It's not in their culture, that's why. Just as their stuff is not in white culture. Fair's fair … I've just done a South African play. My co-star is a young black man from the slums of Cape Town … I saw one black face in the room, at the Print Room. I rail against that and say why don't black people come to see a play about one of the most powerful African states?

This is an odd way to characterize *Solomon and Marion*—a domestic drama about a white South African woman's relationship with the grandson of her former servant. Suzman fails to conceive that a black audience might not receive this production 'about' them as *for* them—and not because they have not grown up with Shakespeare and Greek tragedy. In 1996, a similarly dumbfounded Sher wondered: 'how can the people of Johannesburg not be interested in our experiment with Shakespeare?'[9]

In the light of the many accessible accounts of South African Shakespeare,[10] rather than offering broad, descriptive coverage, we have chosen to pursue these themes through various instances—the imposition of apartheid and Afrikaans Shakespeare; Sol Plaatje's Setswana translations; rhetorical and allegorical treatments of Shakespearean tragedy in relation to Nelson Mandela and Thabo Mbeki—and then through discussion of three landmark South African productions in the twentieth century: Suzman's *Othello*, Doran's *Titus Andronicus*, and Welcome Msomi's *Umabatha*. We conclude with a brief discussion of Africa and the Globe-to-Globe 2012 festival.

The most significant event in recent South African theatre history (and consequently for performances of Shakespeare) was the imposition of apartheid by Afrikaner Nationalists in 1948. Racial segregation was imposed upon every level of society, including theatres, and Afrikaner nationalism transformed cultural institutions as much as they did political and commercial life. A National Theatre was built, and state-subsidized and sanctioned performing arts councils were established in the four provinces. In Wright's words, 'this expensive cultural superstructure was also designed to impose western-orientated culture almost exclusively and mask the radical theatrical and artistic energies that drew on the forces of political resistance, beyond the purview of "official" apartheid high culture'. He shows that Shakespeare moved from amateur repertory groups to the new state-driven Councils, although the Maynardville open-air theatre in Cape Town maintained its tradition, started in 1956, of staging a Shakespeare play after

---

[7] Anthony Sher, Editorial, *The Star* (26 August 1995), and Antony Sher and Greg Doran. *Woza Shakespeare: 'Titus Andronicus' in South Africa* (London: Methuen Drama, 2007), 268.

[8] Suzman apologized for her choice of words, but retained her arguments. 'Dame Janet Suzman apologises for racist remark about black theatregoers', *The Daily Maverick*, 12 December 2014, http://www.dailymaverick.co.za/article/2014-12-12-dame-janet-suzman-apologises-for-racist-remark-about-black-theatregoers/#.VMEqBWSHrNU.

[9] In Clare Bayley, 'Lines of Least Resistance', *The Independent*, 31 May 1995.

[10] For an excellent critical overview of South African Shakespeare from the nineteenth century to the twenty-first, see Laurence Wright, ' "From farce to Shakespeare": Shakespeare on the South African Stage', Internet Shakespeare Editions, http://internetshakespeare.uvic.ca/Library/Criticism/shakespearein/sa1.html (accessed 11.10.2014).

Christmas. It does so still.[11] Wright concludes that 'in terms of frequency of production [by the new Arts Councils], Shakespeare was not disproportionately represented' ('From Farce to Shakespeare'). Relative to Shakespeare's cultural standing, especially in the English-speaking world, he was '*under*-represented in South Africa'.

This is not surprising, given the close connection between the Arts Councils and a regime whose intense Afrikaner nationalism, strict Calvinism, and racist ideology sought to promote the Afrikaans language, along with cultural values that corresponded to its strict religious and political ideology. And yet the sway of Shakespeare as the world's greatest playwright could not be entirely ignored. There are some 30 published Afrikaans translations of Shakespeare (as opposed to only 18 in all the other indigenous languages—predominantly Zulu, Tswana, Xhosa).[12] The status of Shakespeare, even for Afrikaner Nationalists, was confirmed in 1971, when the Nico Malan Theatre—the government's signature cultural project for the celebration of a decade of being a republic—staged Uys Krige's translation of *King Lear* as its inaugural production. It was directed by Dieter Rieble, an immigrant German director, in what has been termed an 'experimental' production. Even this event did not quite endorse the Bard's status as a universal figure: the production originally envisaged—Barto Smit's Afrikaans play *Christine*—had been banned by the censors. Shakespeare's greatest tragedy was a mere understudy to a local play.

TRANSLATION: THE CASE OF SOL T. PLAATJE

A multi-lingual country, South Africa has a complex linguistic and cultural relation to Shakespeare. Oddly enough a Shakespeare play was first translated into a relatively minor language, Setswana, during the First World War. The first Afrikaans translation—a rather clumsy *Hamlet*—did not appear until 1945 and was performed two years later.[13] The Setswana translation was the work of the remarkable Sol T. Plaatje, born in a remote rural area, educated to grade three. He went on to be a court interpreter; a political activist who became the founding Secretary General of the African Native National Congress (forerunner of the ANC); a newspaper editor; the first African to write an English novel, *Mhudi* (heavily influenced by Shakespeare); the translator of five Shakespeare plays, including *Julius Caesar*; a collector and translator of African proverbs and folk tales; and contributor to Isaac Gollancz's 1916 *A Homage to William Shakespeare*.

---

[11] In keeping with its 'festive' purpose, Maynardville has staged a disproportionate number of comedies relative to the tragedies and especially the histories. Of the 62 productions staged between 1965 and 2005 a mere 14 are tragedies, predominantly *Macbeth* and *Othello*. See Helen Robinson, *Shakespeare at Maynardville* (Wynberg: Houghton Hose, 2005), 124–5.

[12] Alet Kruger, 'Shakespeare Translations in South Africa: A History', in Ann Beylard-Ozeroff, Jana Králová, and Barbara Moser-Mercer, *Translators' Strategies and Creativity: Selected Papers from the 9th International Conference on Translation and Interpreting, Prague, September 1995* (John Benjamins Publishing, 1998), 107–16 (108).

[13] http://internetshakespeare.uvic.ca/Library/Criticism/shakespearein/sa6.html accessed 28 March 2016.

Plaatje's uses of Shakespeare encapsulate a number of issues central to the dramatist's role beyond England, especially in colonial and post-colonial contexts. Reading 'A South African's Homage', Plaatje's contribution to this tercentennial commemorative collection, one is struck by the way in which Plaatje treats Shakespeare as material to be used and transformed rather than as an icon to be worshipped. Plaatje tells us that the consequence of his reading Shakespeare after his encounter with *Hamlet* in the theatre was that he 'always had a fresh story to tell' in 'conversations after working hours'.[14] Shakespeare thus circulated, via Plaatje, as a series of folk tales and as a source of folk wisdom in the form of proverbs or 'sayings'. Plaatje translates what we know as the plays or works of William Shakespeare as the 'sayings of William Tshikinya-Chaka' (literally, Shake-the-sword).

In his translations including *Julius Caesar, The Comedy of Errors, The Merchant of Venice, Othello* and *Much Ado About Nothing*—of which only the first two survive, Plaatje uses Shakespeare as a means rather than as an end in itself. One of Plaatje's explicit purposes in the writing and sale of *Mhudi* was 'with the reader's money, to collect and print ... Sechuana folk-tales which, with the spread of European ideas, are fast being forgotten'.[15] Shakespeare was to be mobilized in his struggle to display and preserve the richness of Setswana language and culture, rather than idolized as the pre-eminent sign of a unique European achievement.

Plaatje's translation of Shakespeare into Setswana—which involved finding an equivalence of poetic expression in both the target language and its forms of life—could achieve two things: it could show, against the prejudices of those who claimed Shakespeare as their own, that whatever could be expressed in Shakespeare's text and language could be equalled by the power and subtlety of Setswana. It could also mobilize the undoubted linguistic and cultural resources of the Shakespearean text to record and preserve in writing the power and subtlety of an oral vernacular under threat from 'English' itself. Plaatje's appropriation of Shakespeare was less an effort to introduce the bard to a backward, rural people than to harness Shakespeare as a vehicle of African language and culture: both to preserve that culture through Shakespeare and to show its value by reading Shakespeare and his society in its own terms.

Academic responses to Plaatje's engagement with Shakespeare in South Africa reflect the spectrum of post-colonial questions concerning the place of an imperialist and patriarchal cultural icon within the colony. Critics like Tim Couzens, Stephen Gray, and Brian Willan (the biographer who recovered Plaatje from relative obscurity in the 1970s and 80s) displayed what to other commentators seemed to be a liberal complacency about Shakespeare's understandable influence on Plaatje's own creative work and his openness to the work of a dead white male. The Africanist critic Mazisi Kunene considered Shakespeare a debilitating influence on Plaatje, inducing him to produce not the first novel written by an African in English, but rather 'a second-rate, badly organized hodge-podge of semihistory, semifiction, shoddy allegory—a pastiche combining fact

---

[14] Sol Plaatje, 'A South African's Homage', in Israel Gollancz, ed., *A Homage to William Shakespeare* (Oxford: Oxford University Press, 1916), 7.

[15] Sol T. Plaatje, *The Boer War Diary of Sol T. Plaatje: African at Mafeking* (London: Cardinal Books, 1976), 21.

and fiction in a most illogical manner'.[16] Targeting Plaatje's questionable politics rather than his aesthetic qualities, David Johnson finally finds him, as Natasha Distiller puts it, 'a well intentioned, but horribly mistaken, appropriated colonial subject [without] any ... real agency in the exchange with Shakespeare'.[17] Distiller's position is much more sympathetic: seeking to avoid the strict binary opposition between the openly rebellious insurgent who rejects every aspect of colonizing identity and the co-opted subject who remains subjugated by the supposedly 'non-political' aspects of humanist ideology, she argues that Plaatje, like black writers who came after him, produced a hybrid Shakespeare for his own ends.

As it turned out, the cultural and liunguistic aims of Plaatje's Shakespeare translations were frustrated. Three of his translations were not published, and were subsequently lost because of his insistence that they appear in his own orthography for Setswana (rather than the standard imposed by white Linguistics Professors); those that survive have languished, unread, in university libraries. There is only one record of a performance of a Plaatje translation: parts of his translation of *Julius Caesar* were incorporated into Yael Farber's 2001 *SeZaR*, an experimental production based partly on Plaatje's *Dintshontsho tsa bo-Juliuse Kesara* and workshopped with contributions by a Pedi, Zulu, and Tswana cast. After performances in Johannesburg and Grahamstown, it toured the United Kingdom. 'Wholly about Africa, and thoroughly controversial', Laurence Wright remarks, 'this was a confidently post-colonial Shakespeare' ('From Farce to Shakespeare').

SHAKESPEARE IN THE ACADEMY

The critical disagreement over Plaatje's relation to Shakespeare is symptomatic of a broader conflict in South Africa about the dramatist's place in a colonial and post-colonial context, and his role in the apartheid struggle. Martin Orkin's *Shakespeare Against Apartheid* burst onto the South African scene when the country seemed to be on the verge of civil war,[18] when states of emergency were declared in 1985 and 1988. Violent uprisings in the black townships were met by even more violent police oppression; detentions without trial were common, as was torture and a policy of state extra-judicial executions. Censorship of the press was extensive, while freedom of expression and assembly were savagely curtailed.

Orkin's book focused on the tragedies, with chapters on *Othello, Hamlet*, and *King Lear*. He offered his own materialist readings of these plays, seeking to release from their seventeenth-century origins messages that spoke directly to South Africa in the violent last years of apartheid: he finds in *Othello* a 'text [with] a strong antipathy to racism' (60); *Hamlet* reveals 'the true nature of state power' (23); and *King Lear* demonstrates the 'connection

---

[16] Mazisi Kunene, 'Review of Stephen Gray', *Research in African Litearatures* 11:2 (1980), 244-7 (247).

[17] Natasha Distiller, *South Africa, Shakespeare, and Post-Colonial Culture* (Lewiston, NY: Edwin Mellen Press Ltd, 2004), 119.

[18] Martin Orkin, *Shakespeare against Apartheid* (Johannesburg: Ad. Donker, 1987).

between possession of land, property and power'. In the last Orkin follows Plaatje. Plaatje had written a harrowing account of the effects of the Land Act in *Native Life in South Africa*, travelled to London to try (in vain) to persuade the British government to intervene on behalf of the dispossessed black peoples, and had himself invoked *King Lear* in his fury and despair at the Act's cruelty.

It was Orkin's introduction and polemical call to action in the epilogue of his book that provoked outrage amongst his fellow Shakespeareans. For he accused 'traditional' South African Shakespeare critics of actively abetting apartheid by habitually approaching Shakespeare, and especially the tragedies, through a conservative, Bradleyian lens by focusing on the character of the hero and 'the identification of certain moral truths about "human nature"', while ignoring the social and political context of both the text and the critic's situation (Orkin, 14).[19] Orkin's introduction accused South African Shakespeareans of inculcating in their classrooms a passive 'acceptance of the status quo' (15); his readings of each tragedy sought to show how Shakespeare could offer a revolutionary call to students that would rescue the dramatist from the charge of being irrelevant, or worse, an instrument of an imperialist, racist and capitalist hegemony. His epilogue called for the texts to be 'wrested' from 'the conservative grasp of traditionalist critics' in order to pave the way for the 'emergence, perhaps, of a people's Shakespeare' (184).

Indignant South African Shakespeareans strenuously denied their complicity with the apartheid regime. Laurence Wright, founding editor of the journal *Shakespeare in Southern Africa*, wrote a scathing review of *Shakespeare against Apartheid* in the first issue. He accused Orkin of engaging in the same kinds of humanist criticism that he castigated in others, and also of propagating a narrowly moralizing or prescriptive view of literature as the instrument of personal obsessions and narrowly prescriptive political positions.

Colin Gardner, another Shakespearean who fell foul of Orkin's charge of supporting apartheid, sought to establish his struggle credentials beyond the academy. While he agreed with Orkin that 'if in a country facing frightening socio-political injustices and conflicts … the study of Shakespeare yields no specially pressing or relevant insights, then whether we like it or not Shakespeare is on the way out' (80), he nonetheless wished to preserve for tragedy a proper sense of 'humility': 'humility towards natural or supernatural conditions that may be beyond one's control is very different from acceptance of an unjust political status quo. Indeed humility implies awareness, and a thirst for justice' (82). Literary texts must be kept open for a critique of what he calls the 'puritical' narrowness of the 'revolutionary attitude' (81).[20]

---

[19] Orkin was heavily influenced by materialist approaches to tragedy that had recently been published in the United Kingdom, especially Jonathan Dollimore's *Radical Tragedy: Religion, Ideology and Power in the Drama of Shakespeare and His Contemporaries*, 3rd edn. (Durham: Duke University Press Books, 2004) and Raymond Williams, *Modern Tragedy*, 2nd edn. (Peterborough, ON: Broadview Press, 2004).

[20] Colin Gardner, 'Teaching Shakespeare in Southern African Universities: A Response to Martin Orkin's *Shakespeare against Apartheid*', *Shakespeare in Southern Africa*, 2 (1988), 78–82 (80).

WHY SHAKESPEARE? THE ROBBEN ISLAND
SHAKESPEARE AND BEYOND

By the 1990s, after the release of Mandela and other political prisoners and the demo-cratic elections in 1994, the question moved from how Shakespearean tragedy should be used or taught in opposition to apartheid to the question of whether Shakespeare was relevant in the 'rainbow nation' of the 'new South Africa'. If *Othello* could be reinstated as a text fit for school children, the other tragedies—the very ones that Orkin had of-fered as material for liberation—did not fare so well. In 2001 a syllabus committee of an educational committee in Johannesburg found three Shakespeare tragedies unsuitable for schools:

> They rejected *Hamlet* as 'not optimistic or uplifting'. *King Lear* was 'full of violence and despair' with a plot which was 'rather unlikely and ridiculous'. *Julius Caesar* was sexist because it 'elevates men'.[21]

Anthony Sampson, the journalist and biographer who wrote the first biography of the first president of post-apartheid South Africa[22] and who reported this decision in *The Observer*, defended Shakespeare by arguing for the centrality of Shakespeare's place in Africa as a whole, from Julius Nyerere's translation of *Julius Caesar* into Swahili to the use of two lines from the same play to conclude the manifesto of the Youth League of the African Nationalist Congress of South Africa in 1944: 'The fault, dear Brutus, is not in our stars, | But in ourselves that we are underlings' (1.2.147–8).

Sampson focused especially on the 'Robben Island Shakespeare': the copy of Shakespeare's complete works that was circulated by its owner, Sonny Venkatrathnam, be-tween 1975 and 1977 among the prisoners of the single-cell section of Robben Island (which included Mandela). Venkatrathnam asked his comrades to choose their favourite passages and mark them with their signatures and the date. Thirty-two prisoners marked a poem or passage in the book. Of those, thirteen chose a passage from a tragedy, including *Julius Caesar* (4), *Hamlet* (3), *King Lear* (3), *Macbeth* (2), and *Antony and Cleopatra* (1). *Othello* is conspicuously overlooked.[23] More than a third of the prisoners in this cell section thus saw some kind of reflection of their condition in a Shakespearean tragedy.

On the occasions when the Robben Island Shakespeare has been displayed in museums and exhibitions around the world it has always displayed the same lines—'Cowards die many times before their deaths; | The valiant never taste of death but once' (*Julius Caesar*, 2.2.34–5)—the passage signed by Nelson Mandela on 16 December 1977. Whatever the irony of the speech of an imputed tyrant being marked by the South African version of the

---

[21] Anthony Sampson, 'O what men dare do', *The Observer*, Sunday 22 April 2001, (accessed 16 October 2014).

[22] Anthony Sampson, *Mandela: The Authorized Biography* (New York: Knopf : Distributed by Random House, 1999).

[23] For fuller accounts of this book see David Schalkwyk, *Hamlet's Dreams: The Robben Island Shakespeare* (London: Bloomsbury Academic, 2013) and Ashwin Desai, *Reading Revolution: Shakespeare on Robben Island* (Pretoria: Unisa Press, 2012).

conspirators, the lines do express Mandela's personal Stoicism.[24] But the book contained many more signatures than Mandela's.

Many claims have been made for the crucial importance of Shakespeare for the prisoners, Sampson's being representative: 'The prisoners included Africans, Indians and Coloureds, Muslims, Christians and atheists; but they found a common supporter and teacher in Shakespeare, whose understanding of human courage and sacrifice could reassure them that they were part of a much larger world'[25] This cannot be true, if one considers that only thirty-four members of the elite leadership group signed the copy, while most of the thousands of other prisoners in the communal cells would never have heard of Shakespeare, and many were in fact illiterate. It does indicate a prevalent fantasy of Shakespeare's indubitable value across languages, cultures and in the very heat of political struggle.

That is not to say Shakespeare did not shape the thoughts and values of many black South Africans, from Sol Plaatje to the vibrant writers of the *Drum* generation of the 1950s. Sampson quotes the black writer, Lewis Nkosi, in his declaration of the relevance of Shakespeare for this generation of writers: '*Julius Caesar* was only one of several Shakespeare plays which Africans found intensely relevant: not only because they convincingly described revolutions, tyrants and human suffering; but also because the seething life of the black townships had many resemblances with Shakespeare's London. 'It was the cacophanous, swaggering world of Elizabethan England which gave us the closest parallel to our own mode of existence,' wrote the young novelist, adding that one could sometimes escape mugging by the 'tsotsi' gangs by reciting a passage from Shakespeare. In her return to the question of Shakespeare's place in South Africa in *Shakespeare and the Coconuts* (2012), Natasha Distiller concludes that despite the presence of what she calls a 'truly South Africanized South Africa which bespeak[s] a syncretic South African identification process … Shakespeare does not have more than display value in the current South African public arena.'[26]

Shakespeare's portability across time and space is assisted by the distinctive polyvocality of his dramatic style. This confluence of a historically situated affinity for tragedy with the enduring understanding of Shakespeare as a figure of globally intelligible cultural prestige and the mission school education of many of South Africa's great resistance leaders, together with the stylistic and thematic fluidity of Shakespeare's plays, can help us to grasp the purchase that Shakespearian tragedy enjoys in South African political life. This is exemplified by Mandela's successor, Thabo Mbeki, who developed an early fascination with *Coriolanus*, ignored in the 'Robben Island Shakespeare'.

CORIOLANUS FOR PRESIDENT

In the light of Orkin's earlier optimism, Distiller's conclusion that Shakespeare does not have 'more than display value in the current South African public arena' is depressing.

---

[24] For an elaboration of Mandela's Stoicism, see David Schalkwyk, 'Mandela, the Emotions, and the Lessons of Prison', in Rita Barnard, ed., *The Cambridge Companion to Nelson Mandela* (Cambridge: Cambridge University Press, 2014), 50–69.

[25] Sampson, 'O what men dare do'.

[26] Natasha Distiller, *Shakespeare and the Coconuts: On Post-Apartheid South African Culture* (Johannesburg: Witwatersrand University Press, 2012), 165.

But that hasn't prevented speculation about the influence of *Coriolanus* on the second President of the new South Africa. Thabo Mbeki was the son of Govan Mbeki, who *was* incarcerated on the Island (and, perhaps surprisingly for a committed Marxist, chose a comedy: 'If music be the food of love …', the opening speech of *Twelfth Night* (1.1.1).

Mark Gevisser, author of a biography of Mbeki,[27] observes that the former president admired *Coriolanus*. He liked its hero's uncompromising attitude in the face of populism, for saying 'I play the man I am' (3.2.17-18). In letters written while he was in the Soviet Union (1969), Mbeki claims that Coriolanus is not the tyrant he is often portrayed as in the West, but rather a modern-day revolutionary, an antidote to the 'non-hero' of 1960s existential literature. 'We shrink at "hero-worship",' he writes, 'but to think of revolutionary struggle is to think of heroic feats by individuals … Further, this heroic person in our times fights for revolutionary socialist transformation of the world; therefore it belongs to the new forces, the masses of ordinary people, to push for these moral qualities [of truthfulness, courage, self-sacrifice, absence of self-seeking, brotherliness, heroism, optimism]' (quoted in *Dream Deferred*, 283).

Mbeki felt a particular affinity with Coriolanus himself: 'He is the scourge of the rabble, the unthinking mob, with its cowardice, its lying, its ordinary-people-ness; an inspirer of the thinking masses, who are purposeful, kindly, etc.' (284). Mbeki's developing affinity for Shakespeare while he was studying in Moscow was impelled by Soviet literary critics' fascination with the tragedies: 'Mbeki had been turned on to the Soviet critics' love of Shakespearean tragedy, and particularly their rather odd notion that Shakespeare killed off his heroes as a way of critiquing the proto-capitalist societies in which they (and he) lived' (283). We have seen in Orkin's work that this notion—the death of the tragic hero as a consequence of social disjuncture—is not that odd, and remains central to a tradition of Marxist Shakespearean scholarship that extended well beyond the Soviet Union. Its Soviet form is encapsulated by Sofia Nels's book, *Shakespeare and the Soviet Stage*:

> In socialist art, the tragic hero recognizes that the history of man involves changing the world of social evil into a world of beauty and harmony. He recognizes that in this struggle for the happiness of his people all sacrifices are justified, even his own destruction. He knows that others will continue with his cause and that he is assisting the eventual triumph of that cause through his own tragic downfall. Here lies the objective rationale of his death. In his most tense and catastrophic moments, this reconciliation and purification enables him to transcend the inevitability of death.[28]

Mbeki's response to *Coriolanus* offers a multi-layered series of the uses of Shakespeare: Gevisser, a journalist with a background in literary scholarship, uses Coriolanus as a kind of *symptom*, a key to unlocking the personality of his subject. Responding to Mbeki's reading, he engages in a recursive exegetical exercise in the service of biography. And *Coriolanus* itself, a politically charged interpretation of Plutarch's *Lives of the Noble Grecians and Romans*, deals precisely with the limits of interpretation and the relationship between external show and internal truth. (See David Schalkwyk's chapter on Coriolanus, Ch. 29 in this volume.)

---

[27] Mark Gevisser, *Thabo Mbeki: The Dream Deferred* (Johannesburg: Jonathan Ball, 2007).
[28] Sofia Nels, *Shakespeare and the Soviet Stage* (Moscow: Iskutsstvo, 1960), 105.

Such reading reiterates questions that have been central to Shakespeare in South Africa. What do people use literary works *for*? What happens to literary works as they move from one discursive domain to another? How does Shakespeare reproduce his own canonical status in practice? Gevisser claims that Mbeki has formed an attachment to a literary character in a way that makes him enact the tragic narrative of Coriolanus because he is in fact blind to Coriolanus's faults. Mbeki's life is read as a form of tragedy. Shakespeare thus presents a complex individual with a value system, an internal life, and a political philosophy that can be mapped onto Mbeki: the early modern text, itself an attempt to construct what we now recognize as a modern subjectivity, writes Gevisser's biography *for* him, imposing its own narrative structure on the biography. The biographical form enters into a formal alliance with tragedy in an attempt to make sense of a particular moment of post-apartheid South African politics.

THREE TRAGEDIES: *OTHELLO, TITUS ANDRONICUS, MACBETH/UMABATHA*

Suzman and Kani's *Othello*

Three productions exemplify these questions about the place and uses of literature, especially Shakespeare, from the crisis years of late apartheid to a post-apartheid society, after the ending of the cultural boycott made it possible for South African Shakespeare to be exported abroad as part of a 'global Shakespeare', and for exiles to return to the country to reconsider the role of Shakespeare in a post-apartheid culture.

The first is a now-famous production of *Othello* directed by the South African-born actor, Janet Suzman, with John Kani in the title role. It was first performed in the Market Theatre, Johannesburg in 1987.[29] This production provoked both local and international attention. It was the first Shakespeare play to be staged at the Market Theatre, an independent theatre established in 1976 that staged both local and international plays considered a challenge to apartheid. The Market played to mixed audiences after the relaxation of the strict separation of races at cultural venues in the early eighties: its white members came from the surrounding suburbs, while black people were bussed in from outlying townships like SOWETO.

Of Kani's acceptance of her invitation, Suzman remarks: 'For a man who had never uttered a line of iambic verse in his life, it was a brave decision. For me, who had never directed a paper bag, it was lunatic.'[30] The production was filmed for TV, and consequently received more attention abroad than it would have in its brief run in Johannesburg in

---

[29] With Winston Ntshona, Kani collaborated on a number of plays with Fugard, notably *The Island*, an imaginative representation of the production of Jean Anouilh's *Antigone* on Robben Island, and *Sizwe Bansi is Dead*.

[30] Janet Suzman, 'Who Needs Parables?', The Tanner Lectures on Human Values, Delivered at Oxford University (3 and 4 May 1995), 255. http://tannerlectures.utah.edu/_documents/a-to-z/s/Suzman96.pdf (accessed 14 October 2014).

the midst of the cultural boycott (which the ANC was persuaded to lift temporarily for this production).[31] The play, and especially Kani's performance as *Othello*, received mixed reviews in the South African press. The most notable reactions were, from the audience, those who walked out on the first kiss between Othello and the white actor, Joanna Weinberg, and from a reviewer who complained that Kani was not up to the demands of Shakespeare: he was 'swamped by the role and occasionally forgets his lines'.[32]

But it was from academic commentators that the production received the most intense attention. The South African, Elizabeth Lickendorf, felt that the explicit sexuality of the relationship between Othello and Desdemona 'robs the tragedy of ... its dignity' because it pandered to the stereotype of the hypersexual black male'.[33] British critic Richard Holmes reprised Orkin's and Johnson's materialist approach to tragedy by attacking Suzman's assumption of a universal, humanist Shakespeare—his 'inexhaustible relevance', as she put it, especially for a 'polically hungry audience [who] will sniff out double meanings like starved dogs' (Suzman, 257 and 268)—and for in fact reinforcing the values of apartheid regime: 'Suzman attempt[s] to appropriate the universalist humanism of the Shakespearean logos in the name of a revolutionary action, the aim of which is to disturb the strikingly similar humanistic universalism at work within a political system.'[34] The indefinite article is telling: writing from the UK, Holmes seems to be unaware that humanism was second only to communism as a scourge to be resisted and defeated by the 'political system' of apartheid. Natasha Distiller has shown, through a study of Shakespeare in South Africa, how humanism was a radical oppositional force against the political and racial assumptions that underpinned apartheid.[35]

More sympathetically, Barbara Hodgdon reads Suzman's mobilization of racial and patriarchal stereotypes as a series of defamiliarising strategies: noting especially the production's emphasis on Desdemona's desire—with the caveat that 'white women collude in constructing the black man's exotic sexuality'—she remarks that 'it appropriates them not as denigrating narratives of cultural othering, but by trivializing and appropriating their racist content, turns them into positive modes of self-identification'.[36]

Hodgdon's sympathetic account provoked an attack from the British theatre academic and practitioner, Robert Gordon, who charged that far from contesting racial and sexist stereotypes, Suzman's unhistoricized and theoretically naïve humanism merely confirmed such prejudices for black and white audiences alike. Amazingly confident in his assumptions of how black and white audiences would have reacted to the original staging (he bases his reading on the film), Gordon accuses Suzman of importing 'a typically British empiricism that trusts to intuition and experiment in acting and directing [derived

---

[31] See esp. John D. Battersby, 'The Drama of Staging *Othello* in Johannesburg', *New York Times*, 26 November 1987, C16.

[32] *The Star*, 18 September 1987.

[33] Elizabeth Lickendorf, 'The Verse Music of Suzman's *Othello*', *Shakespeare in Southern Africa* 1 (1987), 69–70 (70).

[34] Richard Holmes, 'A World Elsewhere: Shakespeare in South Africa', *Shakespeare Survey* 55 (2002), 271–84 (272).

[35] Distiller, *South Africa, Shakespeare*, 66–76.

[36] Barbara Hodgdon, 'Race-ing Othello: Re-engendering White-out', in Lynda E. Boose and Richard Burt, eds., *Shakespeare, The Movie: Popularizing the Plays on Film, TV and Video* (London and New York: Routledge, 1997), 23–45 (28, 29).

from the RSC performing practice of Terry Hands and John Barton] rather than to more systematic acting approaches (such as those of Stanislavski, Meyerhold or Grotowski)'.[37] He also dismisses her uncritical faith in the capacity of the Shakespeare text to speak for itself against racism. In the South African context, he opines, it could *never* do that:

> *any* representation by a black man of the narrative in the form determined by Shakespeare traps the actor into performing a ritualized enactment of the infidel's regression to barbarism as the figuration of the most fearful colonialist fantasy. Whether or not the spectator views the descent into savagery as 'inevitable', pathetic or ironic, *the form of Shakespearean tragedy can in apartheid South Africa only serve to reinforce colonial stereotypes of the black as other* ... [Suzman] naturalizes the patriarchal values of the play, manipulating white spectators – as in a Hollywood romance – to project on to the figures of Desdemona and Cassio their own personal romantic fantasies and exposing Othello's sexualized blackness as ethnic outsider. (134, 140; emphasis added)

Suzman's statements about Kani's suitability for the role of *Othello* did not help. In contrast to black-faced actors like Laurence Olivier, Kani was, in her words, 'the real thing', not just because he needed no make-up, but because, in her words:

> If, beneath my articulate, politically impassioned, urbane friend—if, as I say, there lurked the race memory of generations of warriors, and of centuries smoky African nights beneath a glittering, dipping Southern Cross, and of generous natures quick to light up, and even of warm brown skins impatient of the borrowed panoply of constricting uniforms, I'd cheer. It was going to be up to me to release that memory. (Suzman, 276)

Gordon thus claims simultaneously that 'the most fearful colonialist fantasy' is *inherent* in Shakespeare's tragic form *and* that if Suzman had not subscribed to the 'universal truth' of that tragic form she might have avoided its traps. Gordon's interest in traps is the most interesting aspect of his intervention, especially when he suggests that Kani and Weinberg, as actors untrained in the proper speaking of Shakespeare's 'verse music' (Lickindorf's phrase), are themselves ensnared into appearing 'to ventriloquize the ideology of European patriarchy ... as naive beginners unaware of how soon they are to be its sacrificial victims' (Gordon, 146). Whatever the approach of director and actor, *Othello* itself seems to be an inescapable trap for South Africans.

Doran and Sher's *Titus Andronicus*

A lure of a different sort was Shakespeare's most derided play—certainly his least popular tragedy—*Titus Andronicus*, staged at the Market Theatre in 1995, eight years after the Suzman/Kani *Othello*, and in the completely different context of a South Africa one year into its post-apartheid democracy. This Shakespeare tragedy was not a local product exported for consumption abroad but rather a peculiarly hybrid local import: it was initiated by two well-known RSC figures, Gregory Doran and Anthony Sher (as director and protagonist respectively), who filled in the rest of the cast with local actors. It, too, was filmed

---

[37] Robert Gordon, 'Iago and the Swart Gevaar: The Problems and Pleasures of a (Post)colonial Othello', *International Shakespearean Yearbook* 9 (2009), 131–51 (136).

for television (by the South African Broadcasting Corporation, which did not distribute it widely); and it reached an international audience through subsequent tours of the UK and Spain.

This production caused even more of a stir than *Othello* had in the same venue in 1987. In 1995 the Immorality Act was a receding memory, while black and white actors appearing together before mixed audiences had become commonplace. Whereas Suzman had gone out of her way *not* to make her play relevant to the local situation through staging or accent, Doran and Sher decided to offer a distinctly South African *Titus*, after an RSC production to have been directed by Doran in Nigeria was cancelled because of political uncertainty in that country. The South African context was therefore fortuitous, the result of a brainstorming session on a visit to Sher's home country after a disappointing year in England.

Doran states in the book co-authored with Sher that they had no intention of 'presenting allegory'.[38] It might have gone better for them, in South Africa at least, had they indeed worked out a coherently allegorical reading, for most of the local and subsequent academic responses claimed that the production, in the words of Catherine Silverstone, thoughtlessly 'worked to reiterate or recycle stereotypes about race without sufficient critique and to occlude and conflate the voices of others that it sought to acknowledge'.[39] From the start, according to their diarized accounts, the production was to be an occasion for Sher to rediscover his South African identity as, in his words, a member of three minority groups—as a gay, Jewish, and white South African whose voice had been shaped both by a new country and the same Royal Shakespeare Company that Gordon decried in his attack on Suzman's background and approach in the 1987 *Othello*.

Titus (the play and character) bolstered Sher's quest for his roots through his peculiar family history as an Afrikaans Jew, a homecoming that he saw expressed in the play's opening lines:

> Hail Rome, victorious in thy mourning weeds!
> Lo, as the bark that hath discharged his fraught
> Returns with precious lading to the bay
> From whence at first she weighed her anchorage,
> Cometh Andronicus, bound with laurel boughs,
> To resolute his country with his tears,
> Tears of true joy for his return to Rome.

(1.1.70–6)

Upon this quest was superimposed the partners' sense that Shakespeare's most controversial tragedy, filled with filicide, rape, mutilation, and cannibalism, was *at home* in South Africa: 'Whereas the scene can be absurd and revolting elsewhere ... in South Africa ... [t]he acts of brutality, instead of being gratuitous or extreme, seem only too familiar' (Sher and Doran, 150). There may be a degree of sense in this, given the violence perpetrated by both sides during apartheid, but when Sher's idea of authenticity through his lost identity was mapped onto *accent* as a marker of racial, cultural, and political difference in South Africa the result seemed, at least to white South Africans, grotesque and bewildering. In 1995, Doran and Sher were dealing with a predominantly white theatre establishment, and

---

[38] Sher and Doran, *Woza Shakespeare*, 179.
[39] Catherine Silverstone, *Shakespeare and Trauma* (London: Routledge, 2012), 29.

although there were some black audiences, Israel Mothlabane, writing for *The Star* suggested that 'to the theatre lover in the townships, Shakespeare is sawdust': *Titus Andronicus* would do nothing to change that.[40]

It was one thing for Sher to rediscover his father's Afrikaans accent as a vehicle of authentic acting, quite another to plot racial character through a variety of South African accents upon Shakespeare's play. 'The accent feels like a gift', Sher writes,

> It's allowing me to do things with my voice which, more typically, as an actor, I do with my body. It gives me new muscles ... My voice, my vocal range, feels liberated by this full-blooded Boer accent, and yet it is not that much closer to my original childhood accent. (Sher and Doran, 117)

The decision to cast the Andronici as staunch, bitter-end Afrikaners, the Goths as members of the mixed-race or 'coloured' group (but incongruously with Tamora as the South African equivalent of 'white trash'), and the black Aaron as a 'man brutalised by oppression' (179) was an opportunistic grasping for apparently relevant features of the South African context without thinking them through. South African critics responded with—to Sher and Doran—shocking and ignorant vitriol. Christopher Thurman offered the mildest dissent when he noted that 'despite its strong surface resonances with present concerns and past injustices ... the Market *Titus* distorted the society that it has aimed to mirror'.[41] Digby Ricci, for the *Mail & Guardian*, a newspaper with impeccable struggle credentials, judged that it was 'a botched, insultingly unsubtle production of an often misunderstood, marvellous play'; the poet and major South African literary critic, Stephen Gray, in a scathing review of the book, offered an aside on the play as 'baleful, misguided', while Mbeki's biographer Mark Gevisser, in a second opinion in the *Mail & Guardian*, wrote:

> From the moment Sher appears on stage as Titus, a dead-ringer for Eugene Terre'Blanche,[42] the production announces itself as a political allegory: the Andronici representing Afrikaners having to deal with consequences of their own belligerent past; the Goths representing the marginality and subaltern ambiguity of coloureds; Aaron the Moor representing the rage of the shackled black masses. But as racial or political allegory it does not work.

Terry Hands, ex-artistic director of the Royal Shakespeare Company, was equally bewildered, even if he expressed his confusion more subtly: 'The trouble is, I think very politically. So I couldn't work out what the parallels were ... And I was very confused by your Terre'Blanche look', he says to Sher after a performance (Sher and Doran, 279).

Distiller points out the production's myopic contradictions. She observes that the adopted accents—supposedly giving the actors access to 'rawness' and 'passion' and

---

[40] In 'The Answer to Theatre Blues' *The Star* (4 May 1995) Adele Seef argues that 'Black commentators ... reacted quite differently [from white commentators]', but provides only one example. '*Titus Andronicus*: South Africa's Shakespeare', http://www.borrowers.uga.edu/782028/display#n8.

[41] Christopher Thurman, 'Doran and Sher's *Titus Andronicus* (1995): Importing Shakespeare, Exporting South Africa', *Shakespeare in Southern Africa* 18 (2006), 29-36 (33).

[42] Eugene Terre'Blanche was the charismatic leader of the neo-Fascist *Afrikaner Weerstandsbeweging* (AWB)—the Afrikaner Resistance Movement—to whom Sher as *Titus* had a much-noted resemblance, in voice and appearance. Suzman regarded Iago as a kind of Terre'Blanche.

'muscular physicality'—were no less 'assumed' (Sher and Doran, 45) than any kind of RSC-inspired 'received pronunciation'—a 'reductive stereotyping of a series of apartheid-inflected identities at a time when South Africans were uncertainly adjusting to what it means to be post-apartheid'.[43] Her broader point concerns an assumption that is characteristic of a general attitude towards Shakespeare in Africa (which we will elaborate in due course): 'the general idea that violence suits Africa, and that blackness is a sign of barbarity' (87).

The production, viewed from contrasting British and South African perspectives, produced an anomaly. It was precisely because of its South African contextualization that the play was generally received well in the UK: its South African character showed, in the eyes of some critics, 'how stale and lifeless most English productions of Shakespeare have become [in the UK]'; it offered a more 'rich variety' than 'any such Shakespearean production over here'.[44] At the same time, in South Africa its attempt to speak from Africa as the home of violence and tragedy was regarded as fatal ballast. How else do we account for Doran's response to rehearsals, while he was in Johannesburg, of a revival of *Umabatha* or the 'Zulu Macbeth', performed entirely in Zulu, with character, plot and action adapted to an indigenous 'African' setting? 'Seeing the play done in context', Doran writes, 'in a society with a *real* relation to witchcraft—like Shakespeare's society—makes me realize why ninety-nine percent of modern British *Macbeths* fail ... It's the best production of the play I've ever seen' (237-8).

UMABATHA OR 'THE ZULU *MACBETH*'

Umabatha provides a fitting conclusion to this discussion of exemplary late twentieth-century performances of Shakespeare in South Africa because it spans some thirty years and very different cultural and political contexts. It began as a project conceived by two white members of the Drama Department of the University of Natal—its head, Professor Elizabeth Sneddon, and a Senior Lecturer, Pieter Scholtz—to do a Zulu version of *Macbeth*. It was first performed at the Open Air Theatre of the university in 1972, and immediately transferred to Peter Daubeny's 1972 World Theatre Season at the Aldwych Theatre in London.[45] In 1974 it returned to the open-air Maynardville Theatre. In *Shakespeare at Maynardville*, Helen Robinson gives the occasion a measured paragraph: 'The season was completely sold out and critics hailed "a vibrant experience" which was for "everyone who wants to see something special and truly of our country". It was an African experience at a time when cultural diversity and separation were more important than shared cultural enjoyment' (59).

Each of these terms was to be contested, as the production moved from the years of deepest apartheid to a run in Johannesburg in 1995 (where Doran saw it), and from there

---

[43] Distiller, *Shakespeare and the Coconuts On Post-Apartheid South African Culture* (Johannesburg: Wits University Press, 2012), 77.

[44] *Time Out* and the *Glasgow Herald*, quoted in Sher and Doran, *Woza Shakespeare*, 272.

[45] See Laurence Wright, '*Umabatha*: Zulu Play or Shakespeare Translation?', *Shakespearean International Yearbook* 9 (2009), 105-30.

to the opening years of the new Globe Theatre in London. In 1997 it toured the USA, and it opened the Celebrate South Africa and Globe-to-Globe festival in London in 2001. It had thus moved from a local adaptation inspired by white academics in the provincial home of South Africa's Zulus to its pre-eminent out-door Shakespeare theatre in the founding city, Cape Town, and from there then to another 'founding city' and Shakespeare venue, the new Globe in London, through New York, back to South Africa just after the end of apartheid, and then back to London. It was part of a joint venture that celebrated the new South Africa on the one hand and the growing phenomenon of Global Shakespeare at the new Globe on the other.[46] As it shifted locations and contexts *Umabatha* assumed different values, not least the contested share of Shakespeare, on the one hand, and what may be considered specifically 'Zulu', 'South African', or 'African', on the other.

Two conflicting academic judgements vie for a definitive critical account of this phenomenon—for phenomenon it was—in the form of an analysis by Natasha Distiller ('The Zulu Macbeth', 2004) and two separate essays by Laurence Wright.[47] Distiller offers a sharply critical view that makes two points: first, that *Umabatha* offered a disjunctive relation between Shakespeare and Africa to the detriment of the specificities of Africa. She observes that in *Umabatha*, 'Shakespeare brings the universal themes, and the Africans bring the music and the energetic mass of bodies' (166). Distiller also argues that, especially in its marketing, the play engaged in a reductive commodification by which its 'Zuluness' was transformed into an exotic but exciting otherness that came to stand for everything 'African': from the supposedly natural 'rhythm' in drumming and dancing and the 'primitive, warring, bloodthirsty, ambitious ... chief'[48] to the fact that bodies in motion supplanted the language and dialogue of Shakespeare's original.

In contrast, Wright adopts what he considers an 'objective' stance. In his first essay, he answers British critics like Kate McKluskie who found the play embarrassing and disturbing insofar as it seemed to be a 'form of tourist theatre that invites us to celebrate the exotic'.[49] Wright seeks to show, first, *Umabatha's* distance from Shakespeare by explicating its specific cultural forms—from the complex cultural meaning of the monotony of the drumming, the significance of its notorious bare breasts (explained misleadingly as a norm of Zulu culture), the complex significance of the beads worn as part of the costumes, to the radical difference between Shakespeare's witches and the benign *sangomas* of the adaptation. In his second essay Wright addresses more directly the play's provenance and its relation to Shakespeare. He traces the way in which the role of Welcome Msomi (initially as translator and main character) changed through the realization by the director, Scholtz, that non-professional, Zulu-speaking actors could not master the subtleties of Shakespeare's verse, and consequently that *Umabatha* should be only loosely based on *Macbeth*, and, finally, that 'the script of *Umabatha* reduces Shakespeare's text to almost comic-book simplicity' (2009, 115). In Wright's view that does not reduce the value or

[46] See Natasha Distiller, '"The Zulu Macbeth": The Value of an "African Shakespeare"', *Shakespeare Survey* 57 (2004), 159–268.

[47] See Wright, '*Umabatha*: Global *and* Local', *English Studies in Africa*, 47.2 (2004): 97–114; and '*Umabatha*: Zulu Play or Shakespeare Translation?', n. 54.

[48] *The Argus*, 9 January, 1974, 12; quoted in Distiller, '"The Zulu Macbeth"', 162.

[49] Kate McKluskie, '*Macbeth/Umabatha*: Global Shakespeare in a Post-Colonial Market', *Shakespeare Survey* 52 (1999), 154–65 (155).

significance of the production itself, which he regards as 'absolutely terrifying' (2009, 125), adding elsewhere that 'the combination of retributive violence and ubiquitously cheerful social emotion makes *Umabatha* sometimes more ethically disturbing (and oddly more modern) that most productions of the Shakespearean original' (2004, 125).

Wright's later (2009) essay is most useful in deflating the spurious claims to what he calls 'slack universalism' in the supposed parallels between Zulu culture and history and the Scottish history depicted by Shakespeare. His dismissal of the claimed parallels between Macbeth and the legendary Zulu king, Shaka, is devastating. He demonstrates that the myth of Shaka is based on completely spurious neo-colonial fictions. In 2001 the Globe-to-Globe research department stated that 'the intrigue, plots and counter plots of the play echoed the Zulu history of Shaka, a great warrior king who was also murdered by those closest to him' and that '*Umabatha* draws a parallel between the Scottish clans and Zulu tribes, and was performed in historical Zulu costume',[50] thus perpetuating a bogus notion of the universality of Shakespeare that was finally to be fully embodied in the Globe-to-Globe Festival in 2012.

Part of the problem is that, once *Umabatha's* white initiators had withdrawn to leave the stage to Msomi as its 'only begetter', Msomi himself and the publicity machine that promoted the play abroad (including, finally, the ANC) made extensive claims about it as a showcase for indigenous Zulu culture and genuine Africanness: 'to show the world our culture' and 'to take pride in the richness of our culture'.[51]

This claim was politically sensitive during the 1990s, when South Africa was riven by a near civil war between supporters of the ANC and the IFP, a political and cultural nationalist Zulu movement. But Wright demonstrates that the very notion of a genuine, recoverable, pristine Zulu culture is a myth, unreadable by audiences beyond South Africa except as a general, exotic 'otherness', and indeed beyond the memory and practice of an increasingly urbanised Zulu population.

GLOBE-TO-GLOBE 2012—AFRICAN TRAGEDY?

At the Globe to Globe festival, held in 2012 as part of the UK's Cultural Olympiad, the five companies that represented cities of the African continent at London's Globe Theatre (Nairobi, Harare, Juba, Lagos, and Cape Town) delivered a pair of comedies (*The Merry Wives of Windsor; The Two Gentlemen of Verona*), two romances (*Winter's Tale; Cymbeline*), and a musical dramatization of Shakespeare's narrative poem, *Venus and Adonis*, offered by the South African Isango Ensemble as a multilingual *UVenas No Adonisi*. There were thus no tragedies among the African-language performances, although the *Venus and Adonis* does end in death.

The absence of tragedy from Africa says nothing very coherent either about national performance cultures or about how they were reflected in the festival. There appears to

---

[50] http://www.shakespearesglobe.com/uploads/ffiles/2012/03/891356.pdf (accessed 24 October 2014).

[51] *Umabatha* programme, Natal Playhouse season, 2006, quoted in Wright, '*Umabatha*: Zulu Play or Shakespeare Translation?', 121.

have been no structured bias or oversight in the Globe's programming, which proceeded mainly by serendipity and chance encounters. If Eastern Europe took the lion's share of tragedies and Africa took no part, reasons would have to be sought on a case-by-case basis, each tangled in others. It might be more to the point to note that no *major* Shakespeare play was presented by an African company. What makes the absence of any African Shakespearean tragedy in the programming worth remarking is how strongly it was insisted on elsewhere in the festival, specifically in Gegory Doran's 'African' *Julius Caesar*.

This well attended and widely publicized Royal Shakespeare Company production offered a strong counterbalance to the African-language productions at the Globe. Doran presented John Kani's nomination of *Julius Caesar* as 'Shakespeare's African play' as a core element of the promotional material. He cast Caesar in the generic role of African dictator, offered parallels with Amin, Bokassa, and Mugabe in interviews, and suggested that the plot of *Julius Caesar* is repeated in the histories of 33 African countries.[52] But in enlisting African cultural figures to support his Africanization, the director drew almost exclusively from South Africa: John Kani, Sol Plaatje, and Nelson Mandela.[53] Each presents nuanced, highly personal insights into Shakespeare, though none so relevant to Doran's production as the playwrights, particularly in Nigeria, whose experimentation with tragic forms, and vigorous debates about tragedy *in* Africa[54] might have challenged the 'tragedy *of* Africa' narrative willingly reinforced by British journalists.[55]

Audiences and critics left the RSC show persuaded of *Julius Caesar*'s relevance and power as an African play. The quality of the production, its confident execution, attention to detail, and overall coherence fed an audience consensus that *Julius Caesar* makes as much sense (many suggested *more* sense) presented in a present-day African state than in Western 'modern dress', or 'exoticising' (Doran's words) 'original dress' togas and forums. The RSC's 'ashanti togas and wrap-around lappas' were welcomed and praised for their 'authentic' quality.[56]

---

[52] Siobhan Murphy, 'Julius Caesar director Gregory Doran: Africa lends itself well to Shakespeare', *Metro*, 13 August 2012, http://metro.co.uk/2012/08/13/julius-caesar-director-gregory-doran-on-transporting-shakespeare-to-africa-534520/.

[53] First Tanzanian president Julius Nyerere's Swahili translation received cursory mention alongside these.

[54] See Soyinka, 'Drama and the Revolutionary Ideal', and *Myth, Literature and the African World* Femi Osofisan, 'Ritual and the Revolutionary Ethos', 72–81; Sofola, 'The Concept of Tragedy in African Experience', Jeyifo, *The Truthful Lie*.

[55] Doran cites inspiration from Martin Meredith 'Power and glory: how to tackle Shakespeare's revolutions', *The Guardian*, 20 June 2012, http://www.theguardian.com/culture/2012/jun/20/gregory-doran-rupert-goold-shakespeare. Programme notes were supplied by African specialist Richard Dowden.

[56] 'Interpreting Shakespeare: An Interview with Gregory Doran', *The Oxford Culture Review*, http://theoxfordculturereview.com/2013/02/13/interpreting-shakespeare-an-interview-with-gregory-doran/; Richard Dowden, 'Shakespeare and Africa—Richard Dowden Reviews an Africanised Production of Julius Caesar', http://africanarguments.org/2012/07/04/shakespeare-and-africa-richard-dowden-reviews-an-africanised-production-of-julius-caesar/. Also republished in his blog, hosted on the Royal African Society Country Profiles, under the title: 'Shakespeare—African and universal', http://188.65.113.19/country-profiles/1008-richard-dowdens-blog.html [accessed 1 May 2013].

So strong was the claim to Shakespeare's *African* play that more than a few imagined that this *was* actually an African production, not a production of Africa by a mostly British cast. Even African specialist, Richard Dowden, who wrote the programme notes, concluded in his review that 'an all-European cast could only [come] to the play as a re-enactment of ancient history [sic]. *This African production is a news story*' [our italics]. While the journalist gestures towards Shakespeare's universality—the play's capacity to be 'global and timeless'—the real rhetorical force of his words lies in their citation of the stock imagery of the archetypal African 'news story': black dictators, khaki guerrilla uniforms, bloody coups. The 'tragedy of Africa' narrative figures this as a kind of tragic fate, which speaks to and of the whole world ('a concentration of history that allows us all a metaphor to apply to the rest of the world'). But it is also unimaginable in Shakespeare's homeland: '[c]an you imagine if someone knocked off David Cameron and we brought him into Trafalgar Square and exposed his body?'[57]

There is no question that Doran's case for arguing that 'Caesar could be Idi Amin or Jean-Bédel Bokassa, Mobutu or Robert Mugabe' was bolstered by Kani's discussion of his portrayal of Claudius in Janet Suzman's *Hamlet*, touring at the RSC.[58] Here again the actor matched the director's comments on the African tyrant (Robert Mugabe as Claudius), though in this case he defended the 'relevance' of a production that eschewed obvious political and historical parallels with South Africa's own history. There is, however, a different reason that *Julius Caesar* resonates with Kani—and why Shakespeare is, to him, as it was to Plaatje, almost a century earlier, 'like an African storyteller'.[59] We conclude with that very different story.

SHAKESPEARE'S WORDS

The answer lies not in any essentializing notion of Africa as the primary place of tragedy, but in local resonances and affinities of language. 'Shakespeare's words paint pictures in glorious colour in my language', Kani explains. 'They were written by a man whose use of words fits exactly into Xhosa.'[60] And when Shakespeare first spoke to the young John Kani, he spoke to him in Xhosa. At 16, he tells us, an encounter with Shakespeare set him on the path to becoming an actor. The play he read was *uJulius Caesar*, B. B. Mdledle's 1956 translation. Enthralled by the play's sound and imagery, he did not imagine that the sonorous, muscular lines which struck him so forcefully with their poetry could have been written in another tongue. Years later, reading the 'English version', he felt 'that Shakespeare had failed to capture the beauty of Mdledle's writing'![61] Kani returns often to this narrative and this text, although now it seems the English and the Xhosa 'versions' live alongside and within one another. For *Kani*, what makes *Julius Caesar* 'Shakespeare's African play' is, at least in part, an African play: B.B. Mdledle's literary masterpiece. *uJulius Caesar* presented itself as credibly Xhosa without any

[57] Interview, *Metro*, 13 August 2012, http://metro.co.uk/2012/08/13/julius-caesar-director-gregory-doran-on-transporting-shakespeare-to-africa-534520/ (accessed 4 August 2013).

[58] Press Release 2012 (The Lowry), http://www.thelowry.com/news/2012/09/12/julius-caesar-swaps-ancient-rome-for-africa.

[59] David Blair, 'Shakespeare, the storyteller of Africa', *The Telegraph*, 19 April 2006.

[60] Ibid.   [61] Ibid.

overt Africanization of the narrative.[62] None was required to persuade the young Kani. The question of 'relevance', raised by the interviewer, seems more relevant to Europeans anxious about Shakespeare than to Nyerere, Plaatje, and Kani. What ignited Kani's meeting with Suzman (at a party held by Athol Fugard) was a row over language—the black actor's insistence on speaking in Xhosa. 'For 400 years your people have been rude to me: how dare you say I am being rude to speak in my own language?' he demanded of her.[63] In Shakespeare, rooted in Mdledle's Xhosa accents, Kani still hears his own language.

CONCLUSION

In the end, plays and productions we have discussed exemplify the problems that beset the appropriation of Shakespeare in an alien context, and then some. These include the problem of finding both linguistic and cultural equivalents; the snare of a racial history that may have been anticipated by Shakespeare, but which tends to weigh down the more exploratory subtlety that Shakespeare is able to suggest; the transportation of stereotypes under the guise of universality; the obliteration of linguistic complexity by the vividness of movement; and the problem of meaning and value in a commodified and commodifying world. These historical and cultural encumbrances mean that in one sense Gordon is right. The invitation that Shakespeare extends to his audience to think of racial and gender stereotypes as the product of fantasy, including their own complicit projections, tends to fail in a context not only of South Africa but also of South Africa exported and globalized.[64]

Despite their differences, Distiller and Wright come together in their final despair at the economic, political, and aesthetic iniquity of 'global Shakespeare' as it is exemplified by *Umabatha* as a South African translation (in all senses of the word) of Shakespearean tragedy. 'As Msomi is claiming access to essential humanity for "Africa",' Distiller writes, 'he is claiming access to a commodity value within a world market, for whom the concepts "Shakespeare", and indeed, the "Zulu Macbeth", denote a range of performances for various kinds of profit'.[65] Here is Wright: '*Umabatha* continues to circle the globe as a rootless affirmation of cultural sharing, its impact one of carnivalesque *jouissance*, making no more sense than anything else'[66] and '[*Umabatha* demonstrates] that theatre practice (sometimes) obfuscates political and aesthetic discourse, [showing] how cultures substantively miss each other and fail to connect … and how easily specific historical, geographical and imperial associations are swamped by shallow "globalized" audience response'.[67] This may be as true of the 'African' versions of *Othello*, *Titus Andronicus*, and *Julius Caesar* as it is for the more obviously adapted 'Zulu Macbeth'.

---

[62] Peter Mtuze, 'Mdledle's Xhosa Translation of *Julius Caesar*', *Shakespeare in Southern Africa* 4 (1990), 65–72 (68).

[63] Blair, 'Shakespeare, the storyteller of Africa'.

[64] See esp. Michael Neill, 'Unproper Beds: Race, Adultery and the Hideous in *Othello*', *Shakespeare Quarterly* 40:4 (1989), 383–412.

[65] Distiller, '"The Zulu Macbeth"', 168.

[66] Wright, '*Umabatha*: Zulu Play or Shakespeare Translation?', 125.

[67] Wright, '*Umabatha*: Global *and* Local', 107.

FURTHER READING

Distiller, Natasha, *South Africa, Shakespeare, and Post-Colonial Culture* (Lewiston, NY: Edwin Mellen Press Ltd, 2004).

Distiller, Natasha, *Shakespeare and the Coconuts: On Post-Apartheid South African Culture* (Johannesburg: Wits University Press, 2012).

Gordon, Robert, 'Iago and the Swart Gevaar: The Problems and Pleasures of a (Post)colonial Othello', *International Shakespearean Yearbook* 9 (2009), 131–51.

Johnson, David, *Shakespeare in South Africa* (Oxford: Clarendon Press, 1996).

Johnson, Lemuel A., *Shakespeare in Africa: Import and the Appropriation of Culture* (Africa Research & Publications, 1998).

Orkin, Martin, *Shakespeare against Apartheid* (Johannesburg: Ad. Donker, 1987).

Plastow, Jane, ed., *African Theatre 12: Shakespeare in and out of Africa* (London: James Currey, 2013).

Robinson, Helen, *Shakespeare at Maynardville* (Wynberg: Houghton House, 2005).

Schalkwyk, David, *Hamlet's Dreams: The Robben Island Shakespeare*. 1st edn (London and Gordonsville: Bloomsbury Academic, 2013).

Shakespeare, William, *Othello*. Director Janet Suzman (2005).

Sher, Antony and Greg Doran, *Woza Shakespeare: 'Titus Andronicus' in South Africa* (London: Methuen Drama, 2007).

Suzman, Janet, 'Who Needs Parables?', The Tanner Lectures on Human Values, Delivered at Oxford University (3 and 4 May 1995), 255. http://tannerlectures.utah.edu/_documents/a-to-z/s/Suzman96.pdf.

Willan, Brian, *Sol Plaatje: South African Nationalist* (London: Heineman, 1984).

Wright, Laurence, '"From Farce to Shakespeare": Shakespeare on the South African Stage', InternetShakespeareEditions,http://internetshakespeare.uvic.ca/Library/Criticism/shakespearein/sa1.html

Wright, Laurence, '*Umabatha*: Global and Local', *English Studies in Africa*, 47:2 (2004), 97–114.

Wright, Laurence, 'Introduction', *Shakespearean International Yearbook* 9 (2009), 2–32.

Wright, Laurence, '*Umabatha*: Zulu Play or Shakespeare Translation?', *Shakespearean International Yearbook* 9 (2009), 105–30.

CHAPTER 50

···

IN BLOOD STEPPED IN
Tragedy and the Modern Israelites

···

AVRAHAM OZ

1954—SIX years after the establishment of Israel—was an intriguing year for the theatre in the new state. After nine years of conspicuous reticence following the defeat of Nazism the first Israeli play dealing directly with the holocaust was put on stage.[1] Next, on the same stage and in the same year, there appeared the first play revealing ethnically racist treatment of Jews of Oriental and North African origins, following their massive immigration into Israel in the late 1940s.[2] And *Macbeth*, long and widely studied as a matriculation exam text by Israeli high-school pupils, enjoyed its first theatrical production.[3] In a country riddled with political issues and debates, this *Macbeth* turned out to be a rather cold, aesthetically beautiful, psychologically stressed 'intimate marriage drama', as its imported Swedish director, Sandro Malmquist, described his theatrical reading of the play. What might have passed in a different time and place as yet another European-style rendering of the universal classic did not fare too well in the fermenting, boisterous atmosphere of the newborn state, still immersed in the initial stages of nation building. Shakespeare's tragedy of political ambition was met on the developing Hebrew stage by the ideological rage of critics both right and left, whose responses attempted to compensate for the alleged political lacunae in this version of the tragic text. Complaining of the evil they felt to be missing, they invoked Jewish history, Ahab and Jezebel, Ferdinand and Isabella, Hitler, McCarthy, and Dialectical Materialism, in a year when many were still trying to digest the passing of Stalin, their long-time political hero.

This local debut of one of Shakespeare's greatest tragedies became a formative moment in the cultural life of the emerging nation which, charged with the sentiments of early nationhood, looked for political readings generated by the text. Whether or not one accepts the validity of the production's hostile reception, general dissatisfaction with the rather barren aestheticism of the production seems to have resulted from a real sense of its inauthenticity. Whereas the treatment of Shakespeare's comedies on the Hebrew

---

[1] Nathan Shaham, *A New Account* (The Cameri Theatre, Tel Aviv, 1954).

[2] Igael Mosensohn, *Casablan* (The Camri Theatre, 1954).

[3] At the Habimah theatre, already occupying the status of a National Theatre of Israel, which it would officially become only a few years later.

stage—dating back to 1930, when Russian director Michael Chekhov first introduced the Hebrew-speaking audience to *Twelfth Night*—hardly exceeded the boundaries of the aesthetic realm[4] the thematic challenge posed by the tragedies to the theatrical discourse of emerging Israeli culture could not be dissociated from local issues and controversies, cultural or political. By the same token, the subsequent (fairly extensive) career of Shakespearean comedies on the Israeli stage, even apart from the frequent visits of *The Merchant of Venice* in the repertoire of professional companies, was not exempt from topical allusions or even full-fledged references; yet in the context of the comedies such topical gestures were never considered more than optional. As far as the tragedies were concerned, however, the same demand critically addressed at the first theatrical rendering of *Macbeth*—namely, to embrace and explore, whether directly or through implicit suggestions and associations, themes related to the very core of the common sensibilities of the new Hebrew-speaking nation—variously informed the responses of stage interpreters and spectators alike.

The tragic is not foreign to the historical engagement of Judaism with notions of its national identity. Indeed it is deeply ingrained in Zionist ideology, the cornerstone of modern Jewish nationhood since its inception in the last decade of the nineteenth century. There is no denying the distinct mythical, allegorical, or historical position of Zion in the Jewish historical narrative as a locus of ancient memory and an object of eschatological desire. Shakespeare himself was not unfamiliar with the philosemitic terminology, common especially in Puritan discourse, that related the British to Israelites and imagined London as 'a second Jerusalem'. However, whereas for the English Puritans the yearning towards Jerusalem was allegorical, for the Jews that desire informed both the *ennui* resulting from lack of territorial roots and the innate drive to mythologize a communal origin. There is hardly any real correlation between England's 'sea-walled garden' celebrated by Gaunt and the idea of Zion as the Jewish homeland. Rather than a tangible frame for present existence, the predicate of Jewish territorial desire is a virtual reference point devoid of well-defined borders, a symbolic womb and vault borrowed from historical narrative. Whetherone locates the era of nationalism as commencing in the late sixteenth century or the modern period following the French Revolution, the very concept of nationhood pertaining to the imagined community of Jews is denied one of its major referents, namely, its constitutive territory, not only in terms of sovereignty but also in terms of rights to material access. And in this it differs from other nationalist ideologies.

The dispersion of Jewish communities among the nations and the inherent significance of diaspora to their common self-awareness determined their notion of nationhood as tragically unattainable. One of the most incongruous tokens of that aberration is the reference of both Barabas and Shylock to their compatriots as their 'countrymen', where the material concept (country) substitutes for an abstract notion (nation). What country is being alluded to here, other than a Jerusalem that is at once historical and ahistorical? Thus the mark of otherness cannot be divorced from the sense of isolated self-integration insisted upon by the widely dispersed Jewish communities.

---

[4] With the notable and self-explanatory exception of Leopold Jessner's 1936 *The Merchant of Venice* at the Habima theatre, See Avraham Oz, *The Yoke of Love: Prophetic Riddles in 'The Merchant of Venice'* (Newark: University of Delaware Press, 1995), epilogue.

If Ernest Renan regards the nation as a solidarity growing out of the sacrifices made and those to come, Jewish nationhood was doomed to remain constantly unfulfilled. The Jewish holocaust was a climactic experience of that tragedy, being an extreme response to the oxymoronic desire of Jews to contain a peculiar or tragic sense of nationhood within their controversial subjectivity, and at the same time to integrate an idea of citizenship into their inherent tendency towards separatism and isolation vis-à-vis their host countries. Indeed the universally cathartic effect of the holocaust became a major factor in helping a Jewish national home to materialize: who could shun the moral lesson of the Auschwitz catastrophe? This fulfilled desire, however, came at a price. Once Jewish national self-determination was officially achieved and recognized by universal majority, the newly born nation-state relying on Zionist national ideology started to develop a much more complex relation to the tragic than in its diasporic phase—especially because of the Hamlet-like dilemma resulting from a failure to resolve the conflict between scourge and minister involved its creation. It is hardly fortuitous that the State of Israel has spent most years of its existence so far lacking the universally recognized borders designed to formally establish the claim to Jewish nationhood.

Lookingto Shakespearean tragedy to connect the local subjectivity of the tragic phenomenon to the tragic discourse informing a drama whose original creation corresponded to an era of budding nationalism, was thus prone to produce barren, less than satisfactory theatrical outcomes. Sometimes these resulted from a discrepancy between the sophisticated formal accomplishment of 'classical tragedy' and the crudeness of the local modernity that contextualized the productions. In other cases the disappointing discrepancy stemmed from the ideological (and convenient) desire to wrap local conflicts in an indissolubly tragic shroud; whereas the political reality often suggested that the only hindrance to resolving local conflicts lay in the clinging of the parties to stubborn ideological positions rather than in the unfathomable contradictions associated with the tragic mode. The voyage taken by Shakespearean tragedy on the Hebrew stage took various turns, yet it was generally inward bound: it moved gradually away from the monumental, remote image of its foreign origins, to a local habitation—whether in attempts to dress it up with familiar, topical themes or to lend it the intimacy of crude, experiential modes of psychological catharsis.

Romeo and Juliet, in the immediate and provocative challenge it sets any audience, may serve as a case in point. Romeo and Juliet are both victims of an unexplained feud between the two families. Shakespeare goes further than his source, Arthur Brooke's translation of Boisastuau, by omitting even a remote hint as to the origin of the feud. The tragedy lies not in the fatal errors informing a plot that leads to the death of two innocent, star-crossed lovers; rather it lies in the circumstances which make it premature, or totally impossible for the two lovers to complete their rebellion against the patriarchal order that opposes their ideal of romantic love.[5] As Dympna Callaghan convincingly argues, the advent of capitalism and centralized government are symbolized by the Prince of Verona's (rather belated, alas) support for the lovers' move towards establishing the new social structure of the modern nuclear family, which dialectically negates the feudal households represented by the Capulets and Montagues. The price the two lovers pledge to pay for their

[5] See Crystal Brotolovich, Ch. 22 in the present volume, 358–73.

radical union, namely, to give up their names, is marred and momentarily forgotten when Romeo succumbs to his abandoned name of Montague at the provocation of the murderous Tybalt, and acts, like Hamlet at his mother's bedroom, as an agent of revenge on behalf of his obsolete family ties. The lovers' determined but failed attempt to incorporate themselves into the newly established imagined community led by the monarch—rather than the patriarchal heads of the feudal household—anticipates early nationhood. In vague correspondence to its transference to the Hebrew stage, the play might perhaps bring to mind the revolt of the early Zionist settlers in the ancient-yet-new territory, pitting their nationalist aspirations against their traditional family structure in the diasporic communities which they chose to abandon. The tragic tension in this attempt may be seen in the premature or totally impossible circumstances which defy their efforts to materialize *their* own autonomous territorial nationhood, without paying the price of establishing a colonialist enterprise that withholds the right of a rival ethnic group to establish *its* own self-determination as a separate, equal, imagined community claiming the same territory.

The play's debut on the Hebrew professional stage, at the Cameri Theatre in 1957, directed by Joseph Millo, who also played Romeo, was however a romantic, if somewhat cool and cerebral, cultural bombshell targeted at the challenging high wall of world tragedy. In spite of some lively character portrayal, the production failed to provide either a fresh aesthetic interpretation or one emanating from the cultural soil of its local habitation. In a rather favourable response to the production, reviewer Nachman Ben-Ami congratulated the director for exciting the audience 'with storms of passion and lovers' tragedies even though our hearts are dispassionate nowadays, after the wars and disasters we have undergone'.[6] Most other critics censured the players portraying the lovers (both in their thirties at the time) for lack of warmth and emotional spontaneity: the 'disaffected hearts' of war-weary Israelis yearned for a youthful tragedy, but received rather cold, restrained, and reserved lovers.

Less conservative was the casting of young, rising actors of modern outlook in the main roles at the Haifa Municipal Theatre in 1975, where Romeo, Mercutio, and Benvolio, clad in contemporary modern dress, externally resembled characters from thecontemporary plays of the early 1970s, portrayed with crude realism, and lacking any touch of elevated style. The minimalist set reduced Verona to three bare scaffolds, which made one of the critics yearn for the demise of Peter Brook's influence, as represented by the bare set of his *A Midsummer's Dream* (1970).[7] The production, directed by HungarianGeza Partosh (who couldn't follow the Hebrew) failed to take advantage of the youthful casting and thereby to infuse the production with a fresh contemporary spirit. Rather than freshness, it left a feeling of unripeness. The final result hardly exceeded the standards of a common, mediocre, pseudo-'classic' production of the play, immaturely executed. Juliet, played by Gita Munte—a new immigrant from Romania who hardly knew Hebrew and who was largely unfamiliar with the rather crude manners of hasty Middle Eastern lovers—was the only one among the actors who lent her part some classical grace, in odd contrast with the hyper-realism of the others. The reviewers complained of the young cast's lack of poetic sensitivity in delivering the Shakespearean verse (rendered especially for this production in a new Hebrew version by Avraham Oz).

---

[6] *Al-Hamishmar*, 20 November 1957.   [7] Boas Evron, *Yediot Aharonot*, 4 November 1975.

The production made use of a fringe-like minimalist set of the sort that also characterized Israeli director Yoram Falk's 1978 *Romeo and Juliet* at the Be'er Sheva Municipal Theatre (which also used the same Hebrew version of the text). This time the stage was dominated by a crude pine tree arena bisected by an equally crude pine-tree bridge with ropes hanging over it. The open stage and the minimalist set, as well as the modern props (swords had become penknives), were received by the reviewers as attempting to adapt the play to a contemporary setting, which at least some critics mourned as departing from the grandeur allegedly required by Shakespeare's romantic tragedy, reducing it to 'Lilliputian measures'.[8] This attitude might simply have reflected the critical response of conservative reviewers to a ground-breaking production, had not the production itself—in spite of the aesthetic statement implied by the abstract stage and costumes and the modern props—remained in the vague space between visual novelty and a conservative grasp of the tragic.

Theatrical self-reference to the shortcomings of the Hebrew stage engagement with the play ensued shortly. Director Oded Kotler, who as artistic director of the Haifa Municipal Theatre commissioned and artistically accompanied the 1975 production, offered the same Haifa audience five years later a self-conscious adaptation of the play, where the same company of young actors belonging to the core of the theatre's 'younger troupe' made little attempt to fully grasp Shakespeare's tragic themes. Instead, the adaptation tried to dramatize the failure inherent in the attempt of young Israeli actors to mount a 'classic' version of the play. This version, dubbed *Shakesperiment* (1981), was explained in a *manifesto*-like statement in the programme by the director, who appropriated the right to explore artistically 'by trial and error … the various possibilities of presenting Shakespeare by an Israeli theatre group without falling into imitation of the way in which a British company would cope with a Shakespeare play'. On stage, Kotler multiplied the major characters of the original play: beside the traditional Romeo and Juliet, the audience was exposed to a Palestinian, Bedouin Romeo and a Jewish Juliet, as well as a third couple of ballet dancers, dancing to Prokofiev's *Romeo and Juliet*. Added passages were interpolated into the Hebrew version used by the two former productions, some of them documentary, some written by the actors themselves, who occasionally addressed the audience directly. Gang-fighting scenes reminiscent of Bernstein's *West Side Story* were converted into street fights in an Israeli local town. Exploiting Mediterranean commonalities, a connection was drawn between the heat of the Italian setting and Middle Eastern conduct, which was shown to affect characters, actions, manners, and conflicts in ways that deliberately erased the mediating marks and effects of northern decorum informing the original text. This Mediterranean heat, characterizing long love-nights and the boiling blood of youth, suggested an immanent chemistry between the loci of the original action and its transformed habitations. In his programme *manifesto*, Kotler justified his experiments with the text by suggesting that the play's deep structure is not necessarily attached to a definite place and time, and could thus be easily transformed into different period and social contexts: 'the society in which Romeo and Juliet's impossible love grows is one which always exists, in all times and all places. A society characterized by its propensity to hate, to hinder, to gather material assets, and still live in full harmony. When it tackles however a true love story, spontaneous and passionate, it gets stunned, loses direction, falls out of track,

---

[8] Boas Evron, *Yediot Aharonot*, 10 June 1978.

becomes crazy and kills.' Summing up his universalist approach to the Shakespearean text, *Shakesperiment*'s director declared: 'The love of Romeo and Juliet is our own youthful love, and in that sense we are all Romeos and all Juliets.'[9]

The critics, however, while partly commending Kotler's daring to explore the Shakespearean text in a modern context, almost unanimously complained of the discrepancy between the well-intentioned process and the pretentious result offered to the audience. The latter, the general opinion claimed, exposed the young Israeli actors' clumsiness in approaching a classical text rather than displaying a fresh treatment of Shakespeare's tragedy.[10] Rather than simplistic lab exercises in Brechtian-style alienation, addressing the audience in everyday language, the actors and the director should have been trying to dig into the Shakespearean text to uncover deep layers of meaning.[11] More radical objections to the final result addressed it as a parody[12] or mere deception: Michael Handelsaltz referred to the former production of the play at the Haifa Theatre, claiming that the shortcomings of the 1975 production, where the young Israeli actors were exposed as lacking the capacity and expertise to cope with Shakespeare's language and characters, had been turned into theatrical ideology by Kotler in 1981. 'An Arab Romeo and Jewish Juliet standing side by side on stage indeed create expectations with the audience … yet it soon becomes clear that but for the mere display, Kotler and his actors have nothing to say about this conflict.'[13] The trivial insertions of modern texts did not cover the basic difficulty of the actors in coping even with the clear and fluent translation of the Shakespearean text. The director's pretence of guiding the actors into novel pathways of coping with Shakespeare turned out to be a fake.

What was sketched in 1981, received full-fledged elaboration in the following decade. The formalistic experiment went much further in Rina Yerushalmi's abstract deconstruction of the play in a performative style reminiscent of American and European fringe productions of the 1970s and 1980s (Itim Ensemble, 1993). Establishing a common space for actors and spectators, members of the ensemble intermingled with the audience at the entrance, inviting spectators to dance with them, while whispering Shakespeare's verses in their ears and drawing them to sit around the arena placed at the centre of the white, intimate rectangular auditorium where the play took place. A central object in the arena was the sculpture of a horse, parts of which were dismantled throughout the performance and placed in various focal points. The characters were similarly fractured, in a way that echoed Kotler's 1981 production, three actresses and a male actor playing Juliet and three actors playing Romeo—enabling 'the audience to grasp them as entities, rather than psychological personalities', as the director argued in his programme note. Most critics censured the production for its lack of passion. Many complained that the meanings informing the original tragedy were sacrificed to the cold, stylized rituals that dominated the performance. Yerushalmi, who founded the Itim Ensemble in 1989 in the attempt 'to explore the essence of the theatre and uncover its function within the social and cultural changes of our time', said when interviewed on her approach to *Romeo and Juliet*, that she

---

[9] Oded Kotler, *Shakesperiment*, 1981: Director's programme note.
[10] See e.g. Elyakim Yaron, 'The Spectator as a Guinea Pig', *Ma'ariv*, 12 March 1981.
[11] Boas Evron, *Yediot Aharonot*, 10 March 1981.
[12] Hava Novak, 'Shakesperiment or Shakesparody?' *Davar*, 9 March 1981.
[13] Michael Handelsaltz, 'Shakespearebluff,' *Ha'aretz*, 25 March 1981.

tried to resist the obvious temptation of correlating the feud of the Verona families to the conflict between the rival factions in the Middle East. She considered the conflict between the force of destiny and freedom of choice to be more fundamental to the modern reading of Shakespeare. Modern anxiety, for her, results from our failure to view a whole and consistent character at a given moment. By the same token, she explained, her reading of the play involved 'parting from the character as a dramatic constituent on stage, so that character could turn into an essence'.[14] Even though her production was generally commended for paying special attention to the clarity of speech—not a habitual quality in Israeli renderings of classical texts—it was much criticized for its failure to convey meanings through the verbal core, rather than the visual effects of the performance. This may account for the much more positive reception the production enjoyed from foreign critics when it travelled to London, since the verbal nuances of the Hebrew speech were lost on an audience who could not follow the text and judged the production on the merit of its visual effectiveness alone.

If Yerushalmi's production reflected some formalistic features of 1981 *Shakesperiment*, a joint production of the Palestinian Al-Kassabah Theatre and the Jewish Khan theatre in Jerusalem, mounted a few months later, echoed its political allusions. In 1994, against the background of the recently signed Oslo Accords between Israel and the Palestinians, the tragedy underlying *Romeo and Juliet* was appropriated by an attempt to read local politics onto the 400-year-old Shakespearean tragedy. In a dual-language production, directed by a Palestinian director (Fuad Awad) and a Jewish one (Eran Baniel), the Montagues were played by Palestinian actors speaking Arabic, whereas the Jewish Capulets played in Hebrew. It soon became clear that the production was judged or celebrated more as a media event than as an artistic achievement: the artificial stress on the political analogy was claimed to come at the expense of the poetic values of the original text.[15] Moreover, in its attempt to transpose the meaning of the original tragedy into the local crisis in the Middle East, the project went awry: whereas Shakespeare makes a point of emphasizing that no-one remembers the origin of the ancient feud between the Montagues and Capulets, the cause of the conflict between Israel and the Palestinians is far from being unknown. Given the production's rationale, a play such as *Troilus and Cressida* might have better fitted the symbolic analogy. When, however, the latter was mounted at the Habima in 1980, Rumanian director David Essrig merely revived his successful production formerly created in Bucharest, and what could have served as a topical political allegory for the Middle East conflict reminded one of an East European fable, whose resonances were missed by the Israeli audience, so that it was withdrawn after a few performances.

The public reaction to the shortcomings of young Israeli actors in attempting to convey Shakespeare's early tragedy in a pseudo-classical form kept inspiring directors to approach *Romeo and Juliet* as a work calling for intimate, stylized projects, focusing on youthful energy but shunning any further attempt to read local topicality into the play. A third *Romeo and Juliet* at the Haifa Theatre (directed by Yossi Pollak, 2000) placed the dramatic action within an intimate enclosure, in which the audience seating closely bordered the acting space, with various scenes divided between different levels. The melancholy

---

[14] Tammi Lubitch, Interview with Rina Yerushalmi, *Ma'ariv* 26 November 1993.
[15] See e.g. Michael Handelzalts, *Ha'aretz*, 7 July 1994.

atmosphere of the production suggested a morbid death wish, with the two lovers brought on stage in their coffins at the outset, thus visually indicating their fatal doom. However, despite a promising cast, live music by a popular rock band ('The Tractor's Revenge' led by Avi Belleli), and the interestingly devised theatrical environment, all critics complained of its lack of 'romantic heroism',[16] its coarse poetic diction, and rather sterotypical acting.[17]

The tragedy fared better, however, in a widely praised, compact, fringe version (Tmuna Theatre, 2008), where three young directors, Dafna Rubinstein, Tal Brenner, and Ido Shaked, teamed together to offer three perspectives on the play. Their project started by dividing the tragedy into three parts, in each of which one of the three directors took command and presented their scenes according to their individual theatrical visions. Yet the united space of the production—a white circus arena surrounded by black curtains in which a couple of crosses attended the death of the lovers—with a young, energetic company, Juliet in white, a Romeo in black, and four male actors in black dividing all the other parts among them in a creative multiplicity (e.g. Chorus and Mercutio; Capulet and the Nurse; Montague and Friar Laurence; Benvolio and Lady Capulet; Tybalt and Paris), brought the three perspectives together into one dramatic unity. The production, which combined highly coordinated acting with clear poetic delivery of the verse, well-tuned movement and dance (the dying Romeo carrying the fainted Juliet in a dance from which she wakes, in a continuity of movement, to see him falling lifeless), modern sound adaptation of ancient music, creative lighting, and a well-balanced mixture of comedy and passion, impressed most critics as successfully encapsulating the exuberant richness of the original.[18] The call for emphasis on violence as the dominant motif behind the fatal feud received its expression once the play was dissociated from the confused allegory of the Middle East conflict.

In Noam Shmuel's 2011 production at the Cameri Theatre, the Capulets and Montagues were presented as two gangster families, with the Prince of Verona as a cold, politic arch-gangster and Paris as a rich manipulator buying the grace of Father Capulet. Irad Rubinsterin—who in that production played Peter as the thuggish bodyguard of the Capulet clan, tearfully mourning the death of his idol Tybalt—directed his own 2015 production at the Be'er Sheva Theatre, pushing the violence even further into a kind of post-apocalyptic world, inspired by Einstein's dictum: 'I know not with what weapons World War III will be fought, but World War IV will be fought with sticks and stones.'[19] The Montagues and Capulets of that 'sticks and stones' world were presented, in a style reminiscent of *Blade Runner*, as two rival crime families; the Court of Escalus became a nest of violent corruption, and Romeo and Juliet were two naïve lovers, innocent to the point of childishness, who met in a ragged, gas-masked ball.

The same path leading from conservative 'classical' readings to political and formalist experiments characterized the treatment of some of the mature tragedies on the Israeli stage. In fact the very earliest production of a Shakespearean tragedy on the Hebrew stage

---

[16] Naomi Dudai, *Jerusalem Post* 21 March 2000.
[17] See e.g. Elyakim Yaron, *Ma'ariv*, 15 March 2000; Michael Handelzalts, *Ha'aretz*, 14 Mar 2000; Ben-Ami Feingold, *Hatsofeh* 23 March 2000.
[18] See e.g. Zvi Goren, *Habama* 3 March 2008; Jonathan Calderon, *Epoch Times Israel*, 11 Oct 2008.
[19] Quoted from an interview with Alfred Werner, *Liberal Judaism* 16 (April-May 1949), 12.

was offered about a decade before the state of Israel was established. The Ohel Theatre, founded in 1925 with the socialist agenda of 'a workers theatre' mainly devoted to a proletarian repertory (it first introduced Brecht to the Hebrew audience with *Threepenny Opera*, 1933), broke its commitment to plays with a social agenda to recover *King Lear* from the classical repertoire. Moshe Halevi's 1941 production (in which he also played the leading role, alternating with Simcha Tzehoval), was a rather traditional one. Inspired by the conventions of Russian theatre where he, like most veterans of the Hebrew theatre, received his training, it was rather conservative in its approach, and is mainly remembered for the passionate portrayal of the leading role by Aharon Meskin (who doubled the part with Shimon Finkel).

About 50 years were needed before another major production of *Lear*, considered too heavy and dark for the audience to digest, would appear on the Israeli stage. This opportunity was granted by the Cameri Theatre of Tel Aviv to Georgian director Robert Sturua (2007). Like many East European directors to have experienced the traumatic fall of the Soviet empire, Sturua read the play as a political text suggesting the fall of tyrants and the chaotic predicament they leave behind after the rigorous repression they have exerted on their subjects for so long. The first few minutes, where nothing really happens but for a tense, wordless expectation of the coming on stage of the tyrannical head of state, was a telling representation of the powerful rule of authority. Once Lear gives up his position of power, he is trapped in the evil his very tyranny established, and the shreds of authority he would have liked to maintain in retirement prove unattainable in the chaos he has created. Sturua cut the Shakespearean text to fit his reading, and attempted to render the chaos through a rough assortment and arbitrary mixture of styles, both in the visual effects of the production and in his approach to the characters. What could work in theory, however, went amiss in the practical outcome, and the result, as both the critics' response and the audience's adverse reception made clear, was confusion rather than the attempted stylish disorder.[20] Sturua went a long way in bending the original text, through both major cuts and alterations, to conform to his exuberant reading.

A year later, the veteran Israeli director Yossi Yizraeli, offered a totally different reading of the play, as a farewell production upon retiring from Tel Aviv University, where he served a long tenure as Professor of Drama. Relying mainly on an attentive scrutiny of the text, he almost entirely shunned grand pathos and radical visual effects, and instead concentrated meticulously on particular details. Unlike Yossi Pollak, Sturua's stormy tyrant, Yitzhak Hiskia's low-keyed Lear started as a matter-of-fact chief technocrat, cold, self-assured and impervious to reasoning, moving in his madness towards a philosophical, poetic mood.

Habima put on the first Hebrew production of *Hamlet* a year after the Second World War. Resident director Zvi Friedland's production, like other debuts of Shakespearean tragedies on the Hebrew stage in that period, was pretty conservative in its reading of the play. The action took place against a monumental set, representing the columns of the regal palace of Elsinore, overburdening, as one critic described it, the pomposity of the directorial approach: the bombastic use of music (with an orchestra of 16 musicians) obscuring the words

---

[20] See e.g. Michael Handelsaltz, 'Not that nice to meet, King Lear', *Ha'aretz*, 29 May 2007; Zvi Goren, *Habama* 7 June 2007.

and contradicting 'the silence of tragedy', was reminiscent of exuberant Soviet productions, whereas the interpretation barely nodded towards British and American productions of the play. The production was received, however (in the words of the same critic) as a 'signifi- cant and monumental cultural project, educating the audience, and the youth in particular, in theatre and in thought'. Shimon Finkel's Hamlet was described by the same critic as a 'poet-philosopher and a man of action at once, fighter for justice and an awesome, heroic victim'.[21] This account betrays the production's ideological agenda: speaking about the hero as victim was a charged term in 1946, the year following the revelation of the full atrocities of Auschwitz (liberated January 1945). In spite of its historical setting, topical references and controversies could barely be avoided in the discourse surrounding a production so close to the Jewish holocaust. The reviewer of *Palestine Post*, for instance, marked the omission of Fortinbras's final speech (together with that of the entire first scene), as the director's response to the Nazi practice of presenting Shakespeare's Norwegian prince as the pure, de- termined, ultimate Arian hero.[22] Fortinbras often serves as counterpart to the doubtful, hes- itant, and melancholic Hamlet, who was compared in the nineteenth century by German poet Ferdinand Freiligrath to romantic, passive Germany (not yet the united political entity it was later to become followingt Bismarck), suggesting that 'Deutschland ist Hamlet'.[23] Suspecting that the reviewer's reading of the omission of Fortinbras may have relied on a personal knowledge of the director's interpretation of the play (an interpretation,[24] Margot Klausner comments on the *Palestine Post* review by using it indirectly to contend with the director's interpretation. Suggesting that the reviewer concurs with the directorial view that for a Jewish production of *Hamlet* in Palestine the celebration of Fortinbras as bringing new life to the story is redundant, she reminds her reader sarcastically that Shakespeare wrote his play long before the rise of the Third Reich, and thus, to judge by ideas contained in his other plays, for him Fortinbras represents the new man, universally embodying the new life reborn from the vestiges and ruins of a dead world: 'every poet knows that every death gives rise to resurrection'.[25] This, she implies, should be the valid message of the play for a Jewish community rising in the Land of Israel from the ashes of the Holocaust.

Fortinbras, immersed in his political significance and portentous as ever, received his impressive rehabilitation in Konrad Swinarski's 1966 production of *Hamlet* at the Cameri theatre. This second major challenge set for Shakespeare's tragic prince on the Hebrew stage was controversial both as a charged political piece and a theatrical achievement. Swinarski, one of the most revered Polish theatre directors in the twentieth century, had made his international reputation when he directed in 1964 the world premiere of Peter Weiss's *Marat/Sade* at the Schillertheater in Berlin. A year later he directed a famous pro- duction of Zygmunt Krasiński's romantic *Non-Divine Comedy* in Kracow Stary Teatr, in

[21] Ezra Zusman, *Davar*, 27 June 1946.   [22] F. M., *Palestine Post*, 4 June 1946.
[23] Ferdinand Freiligarth, 'Hamlet', in *Ein Glaubensbekenntnis*, 1844; and see also Michael Dobson, 'Short Cuts', *London Review of Books*, 31:15, 6 August 2009, 22; Roger Paulin, *The Critical Reception of Shakespeare in Germany, 1682-1914* (Hildesheim, Zurich, and New York: Olms, 2003). A contrary view of Hamlet is offered in Bertolt Brecht's sonnet 'Über Shakespeares Stück *Hamlet*' (1940).
[24] An interpretation which might well have intended to associate such a view of the passivity of Hamlet—congruent since the rise of Anti-Semitic stereotypes and emphasized in a populist manner by the Nazis—with some Jewish qualities.
[25] Margot Klausner, 'Bamot', *Achdut Ha'avoda*, 27 June 1946.

which the social alienation of Henrik, the protagonist, may remind one of Hamlet. In the following year Swinarski was commissioned by the Cameri Theatre of Tel Aviv to direct two plays: Kopit's *Oh Dad, Poor Dad*, and Shakespeare's *Hamlet*. Swinarski made his name both as a master of modern drama and a bold, fresh interpreter of older dramatic texts, reading a topical context onto them. Notable for his productions of *Midsummer Night's Dream* and *All's Well That Ends Well* in Poland, Swinarski never got to direct *Hamlet* in his own country, even though the project persistently loomed on his creative horizon. As he wryly remarked to Ralph Berry, '*Hamlet* is always successful with us. Hamlet is always the Pole, and Fortinbras is the Soviet Army.' Berry goes on to describe Swinarski 'mocking a cliché of Polish productions, bringing on a Fortinbras listing to port with the weight of his medals, and looking much like Marshal Rokossovski.'[26] In Swinarski's Tel Aviv production, Fortinbras, clad in a shiny white suit, symbolized the cold, threatening, brave new world approaching the rotten kingdom of Denmark. This was a reading very much in the spirit of the director's contemporary compatriot Jan Kott in his influential *Shakespeare Our Contemporary*. The static, monumental columns of the palace constituting the visual setting of the former production gave way to the busy motion of commerce at the harbour of Elsinore, where heavy sacks of merchandize went up and down incessantly to form the background of the action. Old-school reviewers mourned the ephemeral atmosphere surrounding 'the proletarian prince' of Swinarski's production, which drained the Bard's 'directives' of their felicitous pathos.[27] In their more specific references to the details of Swinarski's political reading of the play, critics may have frowned at his view of Claudius as an astute, thoughtful ruler, considering the people's welfare and appropriately replacing the tyranny of Hamlet's father, for 'reducing the play into simplicity';[28] yet at the same time they applauded the director's bold attempt to undermine monolithic classical readings of the Shakespearean text by opening it instead to modern-day interpretations: 'Swinarski may have failed … yet even in his failure he proved that classical texts are not to serve as Sanctuary for directors devoid of talent and imagination.'[29] Indeed, Swinarski, who often explained his hesitation to direct *Hamlet* in his own country since it was difficult for him to locate an ideal Hamlet and Claudius in the same company, rendered a lively, viable, and intriguing reading of the play, valid in its topical allusions—many of which were wasted on an audience that had not experienced the political tensions in Eastern Europe (as both Kott and Swinarski had done). His chief failure was chiefly in casting Shimon Bar for the title role (not his first choice, it should be pointed out: he started working on the part with Oded Kotler, who was later to direct a couple of Shakespeare plays himself—but they didn't see the part eye-to-eye and Kotler left). Bar, a romantic, sensitive, and intelligent actor, rendered Hamlet's verses poetically, yet his inexperience with major Shakespearean roles and the discrepancy between his mellow, delicate portrayal of the character and the director's bold political conception of the play were barely reconcilable.

It has become a common assumption among the theatrical community in Poland that Swinarski meant his production at the Cameri Theatre of Tel Aviv as a sort of blueprint

---

[26] Ralph Berry, '*Hamlet* Then and Now: An Overview', in Frank Occhiogrosso, ed., *Shakespearean Performance: New Studies* (Cranbury, NJ: Fairleigh Dickinson University Press, 2008), 43.

[27] Uri Keissari, 'Ephemeral Shakespeare', *Ma'ariv* 17 May 1966.

[28] Elyakim Yaron, *Mabat Hadash* 5 May 1966. [29] Moshe Natan, *Lamerhav* 5 May 1966.

for a future major project in his own country. Expected to be his most mature theatrical achievement, that project was eventually launched in 1974. Yet the rehearsals of *Hamlet* with actor Jerzy Radziwiłowicz in the main role were interrupted by Swinarski's sudden death in a plane crash over Iran in 1975. For many years since, it has become a common practice among those who either watched or were involved in his 1966 production of *Hamlet*, to respond to various queries by curious theatre persons from Poland regarding the small details of that production, by attempting to reconstruct what it would have been like had he been able to complete the projected *Hamlet* in Poland.

Reading *Hamlet* as a political tragedy in the spirit of Kott's East European approach had become a kind of theatrical legacy in Israel when, somewhat ironically, in 198, Romanian director Dinu Cernescu repeated and elaborated for the Hebrew stage his version of the play, produced in his own country a decade earlier. Allowing himself to alter the original text by adding lines or changing the order of scenes (the 'To be or not to be' soliloquy, for instance, was transplanted to the fifth act), he also converted the narrative to give a newly devised political twist to the original plot which alluded to modern practices typical of familiar oppressive regimes. Having directed Edward Bond's *Lear* in 1984 at the Beer-Sheva theatre, Cernescu was commissioned later that year to produce the Shakespearean tragedy at the Habima (which had now become the National Theatre of Israel) where its Hebrew debut had taken place four decades earlier. There was no shred of affinity between these two *Hamlet* productions, however. The set consisted this time of a dark enclosure suggesting a vault, or prison wall, with a few peeping windows, through which some shady figures were spying on the action, courtiers watched the play within the play, and the actors themselves observed the final scene till the entrance of Fortinbras. The main object on stage was the royal bed on which lay Hamlet's father, which could be converted into the throne of Denmark. The ghost was not seen by the audience, since its lines were spoken by a mysterious figure seated on the throne which was turned away from the audience. In the last minutes of the play, however, following the mass slaughter of the chief characters, the mystery was resolved. Upon Fortinbras's entrance, the revolving throne uncovered the true identity of the figure who had impersonated the Ghost of Hamlet's father throughout the play: it was Horatio, who was now revealed as the 'mole', the secret agent of the Norwegian King at the Court of Elsinore. The entire 'Ghost' story, it now became clear, was a hoax from its inception. It was an act of deception, a ruse meant to bring Denmark under foreign rule. Betrayal and deception became a pattern at Court, extending also to Gertrude and Ophelia, both treacherous pawns in the fierce attack on the hero's individuality, designed to stifle his attempts to separate truth from evil. The plain, somewhat ephemeral Hebrew translation commissioned for this production from poet David Avidan, helped to bring the modernized political narrative closer to the audience, without the mediation of a heightened poetic language.[30]

---

[30]   Contrary to what may be assumed from some of the reviews, the inception of this new Hebrew version was not deliberately designed to serve Cernescu's reading of the play. The production was initially planned to be a co-production with the Be'er-Sheva Theatre, where Cernescu had directed Bond's *Lear* just a few months earlier. Once Habima decided to produce *Hamlet* on its own, the rights for T. Carmi's recent version, commissioned by Be'er-Sheva Theatre, were not released to Habima. As a Shakespeare translator myself I was invited by the artistic director of the National Theatre to produce a Hebrew version of *Hamlet* in three months, an offer I turned down as I didn't

Rina Yerushalmi's experimental production returned the play from its political setting to a psychological one, and from Avidan's vernacular to Avraham Shlonski's old and heightened poetic version prepared almost half a century earlier for the 1946 Habima production. The minimalist spirit of the production was ascribed to the influence of Grotowski's 'poor theatre' and Peter Brook's conception of theatrical space.[31] The minimalist setting allowed Yerushalmi to focus her production on physical, choreographic and psychological imagery produced by her group of young actors, with Hamlet (Shuli Rand) walking among and behind the audience, sharing his thoughts intimately with the spectators. The concept of an 'intimate stage' differently epitomized Stephen Berkoff's 1999 production of *Hamlet* at the Haifa Municipal Theatre, where a company of actors headed by Doron Tavori have reconstructed Berkoff's 1980 English production of the play, in which Berkoff himself played the title role. The square of chairs delineating the action arena where the actors were seated (observing the action when not involved in it and the swordless fencing fight in the last scene with its percussion accompaniment) were repeated from the original production, exposing Berkoff's directorial approach to critical accusations of an externalized, narcissistic handling of the play that ignored its profound themes.

The latest Hebrew version of *Hamlet* to date, Omry Nitzan's 2005 Cameri Theatre production, attempted to combine intimacy with a more distant kind of pathos: within a specially designed 150 revolving-seat auditorium. Chief actor Itay Tiran delivered Hamlet's soliloquies heroically, yet tried to retain their psychological inwardness. However, deploying the action around focal points dispersed against the four walls of the compact auditorium, and playing the Ghost scenes or Hamlet's voyage towards England against a mystically opening horizon, created a conflicting, indeed troubling visual effect, hovering between the intimacy of the indoor scenes and the aloof figures dissociating themselves from the deliberately constricted space inhabited by the rather limited community of spectators.

Macbeth, the 1954 Habima production of which was frowned upon for ignoring the bustling energy of Middle East politics, may have become the one Shakespearean tragedy which has most given itself, over the span of half a century, to compact formal experiments. Rina Yerushalmi's 1986 production at the Haifa Municipal Theatre focused on personal poetic imagery. Michael Gurevitch's 1989 production was played at the Cameri Theatre, on an almost empty stage and in traditional costume, immersed in the psychological and sexual themes of Shakespeare's tragedy, highlighted by three Witches with explicit sexual characteristics, and focused especially on the royal couple which he led into a daring sexual entanglement in the temptation scene where Lady Macbeth challenges her husband to follow her murderous schemes.

Toby Robertson's 1994 production at the Habima stressed a physically aggressive Macbeth, portrayed by Asher Tsorfaty, whereas the *Macbeth Project* at Rina Yerushalmi's Itim Ensemble, directed by Noam Ben-Azzar (2002), Lilach Dekel-Avneri's 2008 production at Tmuna Theatre, and Amit Ulman's 2014 version for Incubator Theatre were all experimental fringe reworkings. The Tmuna version was a 90-minute multi-media

want to offend my friend Carmi, nor did I think a span of three months would allow me to do justice to this complex play. My friend and colleague David Avidan has undertaken the job.

[31] See e.g. Naomi Dudai, *Jerusalem Post* 19 January 1990.

adaptation where the plot was almost sacrificed to render a personal, impressionist image of the relations between the major characters against the background of a narrator, a cello player representing the Witches, and a dancer embodying Lady Macbeth in a combination of movement and speech.

The version of Amit Ulman and his fellow poets/performers presented both the story of the protagonist and the accursed play as a performance event in the style of 'spoken word', where the main challenge was to communicate Shakespeare's tragedy through their own poetry. The most recent mainstream *Macbeth* to date, Omry Nitzan's 2013 Cameri Theatre production, took place in the intimate space where his 2005 *Hamlet* was located. Formally, it attempted to retain the intimacy of his usual approach to Shakespearean tragedy, in contrast to the monumental productions that epitomized its initial encounter with the Hebrew stage. Yet the traces of the call for local habitation were not missing. The tension between the military and the civil in governance was marked both in costume and conduct: Macbeth, clad in rather familiar military uniform, murders and usurps the throne of a good-natured, kind, and generous Duncan; Malcolm, in the final scene, took off his military overcoat to reveal a civil suit, yet on the edge of the stage appeared the regal figure of Fleance, hinting at a future chain of military violence. The production was flawed in many ways, yet in the current political climate of the Middle East, Macbeth's 'in blood stepp'd in' as the sole persistent emblem of constancy seems to have become the major vehicle of topical meaning, lending Shakespearean tragedy a shade of local habitation.

Select Bibliography

Ben-Zvi, Linda, ed., *Theater In Israel* (Ann Arbor: University of Michigan Press, 1996).

Berry, Ralph, '*Hamlet* Then and Now: An Overview', in Frank Occhiogrosso, ed., *Shakespearean Performance: New Studies* (Cranbury, NJ: Fairleigh Dickinson University Press, 2008).

Dobson, Michael, 'Short Cuts', *London Review of Books*, 31:15, 6 Aug 2009, 22.

Kochansky, Mendel, *The Hebrew Theatre: Its First Fifty Years*, preface by Tyrone Guthrie (Jerusalem: Israel Universities Press, 1969).

Kott, Jan, *Shakespeare Our Contemporary*, trans. Boleslaw Taborski, 2nd., rev. edn. (London: Methuen, 1972).

Paulin, Roger, *The Critical Reception of Shakespeare in Germany, 1682–1914* (Hildesheim, Zurich, and New York: Olms, 2003).

Oz, Avraham, *The Yoke of Love: Prophetic Riddles in The Merchant of Venice* (Newark: University of Delaware Press, 1995).

Oz, Avraham, 'Early Mimics: Shylock, Machiavelli and the Commodification of Nationhood', in Arthur F. Marotti and Chanita Goodblatt, eds., *Religious Diversity and Early Modern English Texts: Catholic, Judaic, Feminist and Secular Dimensions* (Detroit: Wayne State University Press, 2013), 107–35.

Oz, Avraham, *Fields and Luggage: Hebrew Drama and the Zionist Narrative* (Tel Aviv: Resling, 2014). [Hebrew.]

Renan, Ernest, 'What is a Nation?' in Geoff Eley and Ronald Grigor Suny, eds., *Becoming National: A Reader* (New York and Oxford: Oxford University Press, 1996), 41–55.

Williams, Raymond, *Modern Tragedy* (London: Chatto and Windus, 1966).

···

CHAPTER 51

SHAKESPEARE'S TRAGEDIES IN NORTH AFRICA AND THE ARAB WORLD

···

KHALID AMINE

SHAKESPEARE's tragedies have a long and exciting history on the Arab stage, the roots of which go back to the nineteenth century. The various Shakespearean manifestations in Arabic have oscillated between, on the one hand, simply reproducing Shakespeare within Arabo-Islamic contexts—as in the early translations of the mid-nineteenth century—and, on the other, rewriting the texts in order to relate them to Arabic cultures. Informed by Pan-Arabism of the 1970s, Shakespeare has become part of an emerging counterculture. The urgency of the socio-political crisis has led many dissident Arab playwrights to embrace Hamlet's 'to be or not to be' as a device for political critique in Arab Theatre. Such reading is symptomatic of collective panic and loss of direction between two paths—that of the West, which refuses to open completely, and that of the East, which cannot close fully. In what follows, I will attempt to introduce an exemplary selection of Shakespeare tragedies as they have appeared in North Africa and the Arab world.

SHAKESPEARE IN THE ARAB WORLD

···

Shakespeare was introduced into the Arab world by the first half of the nineteenth century, a period characterized both by Arab retreat from the international scene and by Western dreams of colonizing the Middle East. Beginning in Egypt, foreign theatrical companies performed a number of Shakespearean plays, among other classics. In the wake of Napoleon's invasion (1798-1801), Cairo and Alexandria emerged as major cultural centres in the Arab world, in which the performance of European classics was a means of transplanting Western civilization to the so-called Orient. They served as entertainments diverting colonial troops and as cultural landmarks of superiority, insofar as they were performed in European languages and mostly destined for Europeans and 'European converts'—that is, westernized Arabs and Turks. Arab audiences were a minority made up mostly of *nouveaux riches* and privileged locals. The first Shakespearean tragedies to be performed in the Arab world were: *Antony and Cleopatra, Othello, Romeo and Juliet, Hamlet*, and *Macbeth*. The performances were presented in private clubs and elite coffee houses until 1868, when the first permanent theatre was built in Egypt and named 'Commedia'. A year later, the Khedive Ismail ordered the construction of an Opera House in commemoration of the completion of the Suez Canal. European plays were admired mainly by Arab intellectuals. In fact, this admiration stemmed primarily from the identification of audience members with a number of the characters represented in the plays.

The introduction of Shakespeare was part of the dynamics of disseminating the West into non-Western territories. The three years of the French expedition in Egypt served to acquaint the Arabs not only with the master works of Shakespeare and Molière, among other established European playwrights, but also with drama/theatre in general. This process was sustained during the reign of Mohammed Ali, who used to invite European companies to perform in Egypt, especially French theatrical troupes. Thus, reception of Shakespeare in the Arab world went through different stages. At the outset, the famous British playwright was translated from French rather than from the original English. Reliance on French was due to the widespread use of this colonial language among the newly established petit bourgeoisie of Egypt after the Napoleonic expedition. Hence, the first cultural contact with Shakespeare was established through the mediation of French translations and adaptations, which marked the subsequent use of Shakespeare by Arab translators, playwrights, directors, actors, and readers. These first translations were in fact translations of translations or supplements of other supplements, which involved a constant refashioning of the master model. The first Arab translators resorted to either the Islamization or omission of certain Christian oaths, ribald jokes, and lewd allusions that could hardly be accepted and transferred into Arabic, the sacred language of the *Quran*. The mediation through translation and cultural transformation to Arabo-Islamic standards resulted in a distortion of the original Shakespearean model. Jacob M. Landou, in *Studies in the Arab Theatre and Cinema*, comments on the Arab translations of Shakespeare as follows:

> It has already been mentioned that in the early days of the Arab theatre, approximately from its beginning until the First World War, most translated plays were 'adapted' for the benefit of the audiences ... Transpositions, however, necessitated also the changing of place names and the names of the 'dramatis personae', sometimes quite ingeniously (Othello appeared as Ata Allah).[1]

Adding scenes and changing names and locations were common practices among the early Arab translators who strove to reproduce or rather transpose Shakespeare into a different environment. Arabs thus insisted on adapting rather than translating Shakespeare. Sensitive to their audiences' religious and cultural sensibilities, early Arab translators departed radically from the Shakespeare in the process of cultural negotiations that characterized the process of exchange between the two languages and ultimately between the two cultures. The outcome of such process was a different text that was neither a translation

---

[1] Jacob M. Landou, *Studies in The Arab Theater and Cinema* (Philadelphia: University of Pennsylvania Press, 1969), 108.

nor a supplement, but rather an adaptation/negotiation that was Arabized, moulded and, in a way, hybridized to meet Arabo-Islamic standards.

The first Arabic translation of *Romeo and Juliet*[2] (by Najib al-Haddad and performed by Salama Hijazi's theatrical troupe in 1905)[3] foregrounds an important aspect of Shakespeare's reception in the Arab world. The play was subtitled *Martyrs of Love* (*Shuhada' al-Gharam*), a reference to the well-known love story in the Arab literature of the Umayyad period (661–750) called *Quays and Leila*. The Shakespearean model was thus intertextualized with an Arabic version as its counterpart. The early decades of the twentieth century saw various successful performances of *The Martyrs of Love*, which was an unprecedented commercial success. Alongside a number of other actors who excelled in their roles, the famously flamboyant singer Salama Hijazi brought this new form of theatre closer to the common people, attracting them to performances of *The Martyrs of Love* with his amazing voice and vocal talent. Hijazi 'seemed to have decided the fate of whole companies as he transferred his services from one to the other … before he formed his own house'.[4] Indeed, Hijazi's voice was a magnetic power that attracted the audience to new theatre.

Khalil Mutran[5] (1872–1949) translated four of Shakespeare's plays: *Othello, Macbeth, Hamlet*, and *The Merchant of Venice*. Mutran's translation of *Hamlet* bears no date of publication in its first edition. Moreover, he 'did not translate directly from the English text', as M. M. Badaoui informs us; instead he relied on 'George Duval's French text'.[6] As a result of its many omissions, Mutran's translation is divided into four acts instead of

---

[2] Al-Haggagi also writes: 'Translators took great liberties with Shakespeare's plays. For instance, in *Romeo and Juliet*, the first scene was omitted altogether. Other translations were filled with poetry, rhyming prose, and rhetorical figures. The critics did not denounce this, they rather encouraged it! They did not judge the translation, or the poetry by how well it kept the spirit of Shakespeare; rather, they watched how it affected the audience' (Ahmed Shams al-din Al-Haggagi, *The Origins of Arabic Theatre* (Cairo: General Egyptian Book Organization, 1981), 192–3).

[3] The same year, *Hamlet* was performed in the opening night of *Dar at-tamtil al-'Arabiy* on August 8, 1905. Salama Hijazi played the role of Hamlet, then. He was reputed as a good singer and actor. At this opening night, the play was performed without singing, yet the audience 'violently protested and insisted on hearing him [Hijazi] sing' (M. M. Badawi, 'Shakespeare and the Arabs' (Cairo: Cairo Studies in English, 1963-6), 187). Hijazi, then, went to the famous poet Ahmad Shawqi who composed some songs for that purpose. In brief, *Hamlet,* in its first reception became a 'musical'. The audience played a major role in the re-fashioning of the play in its early reception. *Othello* was performed by the same company on 31 August 1909. In 1912, George Abyad formed his Arabic troupe and acted Shakespeare's *Othello* in Arabic, wherein he played the leading role.

[4] Sameh F. Hanna, 'Hamlet Lives Happily ever after in Arabic: The Genesis of the Field of Drama Translation in Egypt', *The Translator* 11:2 (November 2005), 185.

[5] Khalil Mutran (1872–1949) is a distinguished Lebanese poet and translator. He learned French at the Roman Catholic Patriarchate College in Beirut. In 1890, he immigrated to Paris. From there he left for Egypt in 1892, where he stayed until the end of his life. In Egypt he was involved in a number of activities, including journalism, poetry writing, theatre translation, and widely contributed to the cultural scene by launching newspapers, helping in setting up literary associations, and even holding official posts in the Egyptian cultural institutions at the time.

[6] M. M. Badawi, 'Shakespeare and the Arabs', 189. Indeed, there exist at least five different Arabic translations of Shakespeare's *Hamlet* including Tanyus 'Abduh, Cairo: Al-matba'a al-'arabiya, 1902; Sami Juraydini, Cairo: al-matba'a ar-rahmaniya, 1912; Jabra Ibrahim Jabra, Cairo: Dar al-hilal, 1960; Khalil Mutran, Cairo: Dar al-ma'arif, 1971 [etc.].

the five acts of the original. Indeed, Mutran never translated a page without submitting it to some alteration and negotiation. Thus, the original first scene of the second act—which includes Polonius' bombastic instructions to Reynaldo about spying on Laertes in France, as well as Ophelia's news to her father about Hamlet's pretended/assumed madness—is temporarily dropped. This episode is transferred to the second scene. Mutran's free translation omitted almost 400 lines from the second act (2.2.169-559) resulting in the exclusion of the fascinating encounter between Hamlet and Rosencrantz and Guildenstern.

Mutran's 1912 *Othello* is believed to be the first translation to set a new standard for Arabic versions of Shakespeare. It was commissioned and staged in 1912 by the renowned actor, director, and theatrical manager Jurj Abyad (1880-1959). In fact, 'the translation was published in the same year, and was subsequently republished in several editions'.[7] In his introduction, Mutran accounts for the choice of classical Arabic as part of his strategy of Arabization (*Ta'riib*). Transposing the Shakespearean plot into an Arab milieu using classical Arabic and the strategy of Arabization in translation denotes Mutran's awareness of the political function of translation and the close relationship between language and identity. Indeed, Mutran's choice of a particular kind of language is a political attempt to construct a unifying pan-Arab identity, a supra-nationalist identity. Classical Arabic functions as a unifying language for all Arabs from Morocco to the Gulf Countries. It is the standard language that is accepted by all regardless different national dialects.

Although the majority of Shakespeare's translations into Arabic were in prose, the plays in their original form provided some Arab playwrights and poets with a model to celebrate and imitate. Ahmed Shawqi (1868-1932), in his adaptation entitled *Masra' Cleopatra* (*The Murder of Cleopatra*) (1927) resorted to borrowing some scenes from Shakespeare. Even the imagery and metaphors used by Shawqi are Shakespearean. He departs from Shakespeare, however, in the interpretation of Cleopatra's character. Shawqi conceives her as a patriotic queen of old Egypt, whereas Shakespeare presents her as a wanton, fickle woman who is erotic by nature and whose moods are unpredictable. Indeed, Shawqi's different interpretation of the character of Cleopatra is part of the dynamics of negotiating a margin within the Shakespearean text. Another obvious connection with Shakespeare is found in Tawfiq al-Hakim's play entitled *Ad-dunya Riwaya Hazliya* (*Life is a Comedy*), published in 1974. In the second part of al-Hakim's play, the balcony scene of Shakespeare's *Romeo and Juliet* is reproduced when one of the characters is incarnated in a dream as Romeo and his beloved woman as Juliet. The same characters are also reincarnated as Antony and Cleopatra, invoking Act 2, Scene 5 of the original Shakespearean play. In these two scenes, intended to parody Shakespeare, al-Hakim used practically the same diction of the original though in a humorous way. Meanwhile, Hafiz Ibrahim (1872-1932) seems to have read and enjoyed *Macbeth* to the point of being inspired by the drama, evident in his poem, *Khanjar Macbeth* (*Macbeth's Dagger*). The poem is subtitled '*An Ode translated from the English Poet Shakespeare.*' It consists of 25 verses fusing together Macbeth's soliloquy in (2. 1.33-61) and the actual dagger scene itself.

---

[7] Sameh F. Hanaa, '*Othello* in Egypt: Translation and the (Un)making of National identity', in *Translation and the Construction of Identity*, ed. Juliane House, M. Rosario, Martin Ruano, and Nicole Baumgarten (Seoul: IATIS, 2005), 112.

CONTEMPORARY ARAB SHAKESPEARE
NEGOTIATIONS AND THE DYNAMICS
OF WRITING BACK

Hamlet

If the first productions and adaptations of Shakespeare reinvent the conservative myth of artistic genius, recent representations from the late 1960s onwards have sought to represent the Shakespearean canon in a more faithful, but politically informed, fashion. The rebirth of theatrical Pan-Arabism in the late 1960s exemplifies a painful process of renewal in which political uses of Shakespeare became common practice. The period of crisis that followed 1967 Arab/Israeli war was the catalyst for the emergence of a seemingly irreconcilable struggle between political necessity and creative imagination.

Nabyl Lahlou (b. 1945) is a prominent Moroccan playwright, actor, director, and filmmaker who wrote *Ophelia is not Dead* in 1968, a significant date in the artistic and intellectual life of Paris where he was living as a student. *Ophelia is not Dead* is a play in two acts containing only two characters (Hamlet and Macbeth), and is perhaps the best example of a clear dramatic transcultural weaving. Invoking Ophelia rather than Hamlet in its title, it is an angry offshoot of Shakespeare's *Hamlet*, which resists and contradicts the original insofar as, for Lahlou, Ophelia is not dead.

Originally written in French,[8] Lahlou's play was produced between the years 1970-5 by Lahlou's own theatre company and in collaboration with Josiane Benhaïm, Michel Demaulne, Abbas Brahim, and others. In 1987 *Ophelia* was staged at the French Cultural Institut in Marrakech by Nabyl Lahlou and Rachid Fekkak. An English version of the play was staged by Hicham Regragui at the International Festival of University Theatre in Casablanca in 1993. In 1998, the play was revived by Lahlou's company under the auspices of the Moroccan Ministry of Culture. This time, Lahlou opted for female actors to play the roles of Hamlet and Macbeth. Actress Sophia Hadi played Macbeth, and Amal Ayouch played Hamlet. They first performed the play in a small theatre at the Goethe Institute in Rabat between January 4th and 13th, 1999. With Hadi and Ayouch onstage, the play became an enunciated critique of deeply rooted patriarchal power structures. The performance questioned how theatre could be utilized as a site for the marginalized and subaltern to participate both in political life and in existing regimes of theatrical representation. The history of the play's production indicates its continued appeal to different Moroccan audiences over a period of four decades. The play never ceases to challenge comfortable Moroccan notions of what constitutes acceptable theatre.

Ophelia is not Dead is a visionary text, and a strong statement about the lack of artistic freedom in the newly independent states of the Arab world, with a particular focus on Morocco. Lahlou brings together two Shakespearean tragedies, *Hamlet* and *Macbeth*, in which the two tragic characters become voluntarily paralysed actors. They role-play a series

---

[8] Nabyl Lahlou, *Ophélie n'est pas morte* (*Ophelia Is Not Dead*) (Casablanca: Edition Le fennec, 1987).

of micro-dramas mostly related to Shakespeare's 'Mousetrap', which reveal their intensely self-reflexive awareness of previous theatrical behaviour. Challenging and abusive in its language, the play subverts the audience's instinct for moral judgement and pushes them to attend to the humour and subtle humanity of the two actors till the end. The play was written during the peak of what many Moroccans call 'the years of lead', a period of repression under the rule of King Hassan II. It is informed by the prison experience of activists and political prisoners in Morocco's cruelest detention centres. For decades, Moroccan authorities have routinely practiced a regime of *garde à vue* detention (inherited from the French colonial administration), whereby a political prisoner is utterly cut off from the outside world. The acting itself is cramped by the use of crutches or wheelchairs that illustrate the actors' paralysis, frustration, and contingency. The action takes place in closed environments: a room, hospital, a prison cell, or a theatre stage. As the play progresses, the audience becomes aware of the link between the various locations. Confinement, imprisonment, and impasse become defining features of the locations in which Lahlou's drama is enacted.

Lahlou's Hamlet is an example of the post-Romantic Arab Hamlet, unable to fix the 'out-of-joint' world around him. He aspires to be 'a Che Guevara in doublet-and-hose', whose 'fierce pursuit of justice [leaves] no room for introspection or doubt'; however, he is paralysed by guilt and sadness.[9] Thus, the play is about *de facto* political structures across the Arab world, ranging from total autocracies to more liberal autocratic regimes. In Lahlou's revision, Hamlet and Macbeth become emblematic figures of Moroccan artists who devote themselves to theatre and reap only repression or frustration. Their reward is either torture or a prison cell. 'Each militant actor had his own cell', says Hamlet, commenting on his imprisonment after ten years of impasse. Yet the two actors persist in performing, despite their paralysis—even if they can no longer act onstage, generate new roles or new plays, because they are frustrated artists who have been silenced.

The Egyptian playwright and critic Mahmoud Abou Douma (b. 1953) wrote *Dance of the Scorpions* in 1988; the play was performed in Egypt in 1989 and 1991. Its five characters have Shakespearean names: Hamlet, Horatio, Claudius, Polonius, and the Ghost. Yet, various Shakespearean subtleties are either altered or omitted. The central character is Claudius, who is no other than the 'scorpion' of the title: a flagrant tyrant who conspires with the foreign enemy Fortinbras, rigging a fake war to sideline his political opponents and defraud his people.[10] Theatre Critic Nehad Selaiha underlines Abou Douma's political reading of *Hamlet* that goes beyond the hesitation of the prince of Denmark, to reveal his failure to understand 'the source of the rottenness in the State of Denmark. Like Claudius, Hamlet's father was part of a corrupt system, which Polonius and his likes manipulated behind the scenes ... Even if Hamlet kills Claudius, nothing will change; Polonius will still remain the puppet master, replacing one head of State with another to preserve the same rotten system.'[11] Indeed, Selaiha's reading predicted the present state of affairs in post-Arab-Spring Egypt after the ousting of President Morsi and the return to the military regime. For Selaiha, Abou Douma's tragedy goes far beyond

[9] Margaret Litvin, *Hamlet's Arab Journey: Shakespeare's Prince and Nasser's Ghost* (Princeton: Princeton University Press, 2011), 11.

[10] Margaret Litvin, 'Vanishing Intertexts in the Arab *Hamlet* Tradition', *Critical Survey* 19: 3 (November 2007), 74.

[11] Nehad Selaiha, 'Hamlet, again and again', http://weekly.ahram.org.eg/2010/1005/cu2.htm.

Hamlet's meditation, 'to be or not to be'; it is about the failure of the Egyptians to pursue a third path away from 'Islamic fundamentalism' and the 'military': 'the corrupt regime in Denmark is one between roasting in a fire or jumping into a frying pan.'[12] On the other hand, Margaret Litvin considers Abou Douma's *Dance of the Scorpions* as part of the ongoing international tradition of *Hamlet* rewritings. Litvin's reading of Aboudouma's undertaking considers his text within other mediating con-texts. 'He has never read Shakespeare's text in any "original" English version,' she writes, 'Aboudoma's first medi-ating text happens to be a Soviet film, Grigorii Kozintsev's *Gamlet* … His late-1980s play sends a political message of his own choosing; it does so precisely by playing off his audi-ence's expectations of a heroic Hamlet.'[13]

The Iraqi playwright and director Jawad Al-Assadi's *Inssuu Hamlet* (*Forget Hamlet*) is an-other politically loaded Shakespearean offshoot. The play is described by Al-Assadi as a sub-versive rewriting of Shakespeare's *Hamlet*. It was staged in 1994 at Cairo's Hanager Theatre. Al-Assadi (b. 1947), who has long been exiled from Iraq, departs from 'Shakespeare's plot to have Ophelia a witness of Claudius's murdering of the father king through her window. Yet even as she becomes the centre of the play, Ophelia is unable to take any effective action against Claudius's reign of terror.'[14] Saddam Hussein is the backdrop for Claudius' represen-tation in the play, referred to as 'butcher', 'barbarian', 'bull', and 'brute'. In his introduction to the play, Al-Assadi writes: 'In *Forget Hamlet* I wanted to unveil characters at the edge of madness and to open up the door of the text to their desires and their postponed hatred, to face Claudius, the State's barbarian who swallowed up his brother and sister-in law at once, only to send the former to the gravediggers and the latter to his own bed.'[15] Al-Assadi's un-dertaking keeps only the bulk of *Hamlet*'s story, while changing the focus on certain charac-ters and highlighting the tragic predicament of others, Claudius is the centre of Al-Assadi's tragedy; he is the real evil which should be eradicated.

Abdelhaq Zeraouali's play *Atqu R-ruh* (*Save Our Soul*) also deploys various facets of dra-matic conflict from Shakespeare's *Hamlet* but combines them with the story of Cain and Abel. Granting the central importance of the space occupied by Shakespeare in the play, Zerouali's main characters, Dounia, El-Mahdi, Cain and Abel become 'doubles,' 'supple-ments,' or 'shadows' of Shakespeare's Gertrude, Hamlet, Claudius, and old King Hamlet respectively. However, Zerouali's characters are not negative shadows of Shakespeare's char-acters, since they are delineated according to experimentally and ideologically subversive strategies. Dounia, El-Mahdi's mother, is described as a deceptive and deceived woman, both a victim and a victimizer at the same time. Her extra-textual reference draws atten-tion to Shakespeare's Gertrude. Like Gertrude, Dounia marries her husband's brother, Cain. Zerouali's choice of the name 'Dounia' is juxtaposed against its meaning in Arabic, which is equated to 'life'. This juxtaposition highlights her lustful desires to seize the moment with-out paying attention to morality: 'Let the grass cover this body's desert … what kind of man is that? I talk to him about love, yet he escapes away to talk about politics and war' (2.19).

Her husband is unable to satisfy her cupidity and sexuality due to his voluntary par-ticipation in various independence wars. In fact, for Dounia, he is a complete failure: 'if

¹² Ibid.   ¹³ Litvin, 'Vanishing Intertexts', 77–8.

¹⁴ Margaret Litvin, 'When the Villain Steals the Show: The Character of Claudius in Post-1975 Arab(ic) Hamlet Adaptation,' *Journal of Arabic Literature* 38:2 (2007), 210.

¹⁵ Jawad Al-Assadi, *Inssuu Hamlet* (Beirut: Dar Al-Farabi, 2000), 9.

only he admitted that the war is here and not there' (220). This confession manifests her frustration as a wife and a woman who needs the constant presence of her beloved man. In the various productions of the play, the actress playing Dounia's part (Latifa Ahrar) intensified these sexual connotations: 'The war was here' was accompanied by a physical gesture in which Dounia pointed to her body. The spoken words and the bodily gesture were fused together to produce a powerful dramatic effect that amounted to a Brechtian 'Social Gestus'.

Zerouali's Dounia makes us think of Shakespeare's Gertrude. Unlike Gertrude, however, Dounia is clearly shown as guilty of adultery before the murder of her husband in which she is, moreover, complicit:

> DOUNIA   ... he is just trying to treat us in equal terms ... and you should never forget ...
>   that El-Mahdi himself ... might be your son. (8. 61)

It is insinuated here that El-Mahdi is Cain's son, which proves her adulterous past. In the case of Shakespeare's Gertrude, by contrast, it is impossible to tell if the 'adulterate' liaison began before the old king's murder, even if the Ghost hints at her sexual relation and lustful response to Claudius' sexual invitations before the death of her first husband:

> GHOST The will of my most seeming virtuous Queen
> O Hamlet, what a falling off was there,
> From me whose love was of that dignity
> That it went hand in hand even with the vow
> I made to her in marriage, and to decline
> Upon a wretch whose natural gifts were poor
> To those of mine.
>
> (*Hamlet*, 1.5.46–52)

If Gertrude's sexual response to Claudius' invitations is revealed by the Ghost, Dounia exposes her adultery herself assuming the responsibility of her own choices.

Zerouali's rewriting of Shakespeare's *Hamlet* is informed by the desire to demythologize the Shakespeare myth rather than reproduce it.[16] In its repetition of various themes from *Hamlet*, '*Atqu R-ruh* emerges as a different text that is written for a different audience. The play's originality lies in its refashioning of old Shakespearean themes in a way that appeals to the Moroccan subject today in his post-colonial condition. Hamlet's

---

[16] The name and texts of Shakespeare, then, acquired mythical proportions in the history of English Studies, transcending the barriers of time and space. Both within academia and along the fringes of theatrical enterprises Shakespeare's stature becomes one of the richest sites of discursive and aesthetic contestation. Certainly, Shakespearean dramaturgy is a powerful literary artifact, yet the amplified mythic transcendence attributed to it is informed by a deeply rooted logocentric desire for presence, plenitude, and supremacy. His works, as constructed within the narrative of the great empire, provide the world with archetypal *dramatis personae* whose images not only imply aspects of late Elizabethan social order, but also claim a fundamental depth of human nature that had never been touched with such profundity before Shakespeare. Such eternal relevance is evident in the *mythos* that sustains the Shakespeare industry through a constant refashioning of his dramaturgical practice. Nevertheless, this practice also implies the inability of Shakespearean texts to appeal, in a positive and relevant way, to a different audience, which might be distanced temporally, spatially, and culturally—like Moroccans.

mythical hesitation is transgressed through the final action of El-Mahdi who emerges as a new character finally liberated from the Shakespearean confines. At the level of form and structure, Zerouali's play is a new kind of writing that is experimental and self-reflexive. It does not repeat the Shakespearean model, for the play is written in a post-colonial context.

The Anglo-Kuwaiti playwright and director Sulayman Al-Bassam's adaptations of Shakespeare are the most significant among many during the first decade of the third millennium. His play entitled *Hamlet in Kuwait* constitutes the first cornerstone in his experimentation in Shakespeare adaptation. *The Arab League Hamlet*, Al-Bassam's second adaptation of the Shakespearean drama, is another offshoot that may be categorized as agit-prop theatre. The play was produced first in Tunisia in 2001 and the project was much closer to the format of *The Al-Hamlet Summit*. Al-Bassam transposes Shakespeare's play into the contemporary Arab world. In so doing, he rewrites the Shakespearean script, cutting and rearranging scenes, and reducing the cast to a few principal players. The revised offshoot still maintains some lines in modern colloquial English. The 'summit' setting of *The Al-Hamlet Summit* becomes an ironic projection of the political absurdity that surrounds many of the Arab League Summits.

The Al-Hamlet Summit portrays an unstable totalitarian Arab regime holding an Arab League-style conference with nametags and microphones as civil war engulfs the country, international support withers, and Fortinbras invades. Claudius, Gertrude, Ophelia, Polonius, and Hamlet conspire, declaim, and buy weapons—mostly without leaving their desks in the conference hall.[17]

The play is divided into sections corresponding to the Islamic times of prayer: Act one: *Al-Fajr* (Dawn); Act Two: *Al-Dohr* (Noon); Act Three: *Al-Asr* (Mid-Afternoon); Act Four: *Al-Maghrib* (Sunset); Act Five: *Al-Isha'a* (Supper). Al-Bassam's Shakespeare offshoot becomes a powerful political critique of the state of affairs in the Arab world few years before political upheavals of 2011 known as 'the Arab Spring'. *The Al-Hamlet Summit* interrogates contemporary political Arab situations and provokes Arab audiences and readers to think critically about their political systems and socioeconomic conditions. *Hamlet* has thus been refashioned with a great sense of urgency to cast an ironic reflection on Arab conditions. *Hamlet* 'encapsulates a debate coeval with the largely constitutive of modern Arab identity: the problem of self-determination and authenticity'.[18] *Al-Hamlet Summit* also focuses on the middle-ground of performativity beyond Frantz Fanon's post-colonial denials of the Western legacy, so that binary relationships between colonized and colonizer, local and global, East and West dissolve and become more and more interwoven. Al-Bassam's *Hamlet* metaphor fits well in today's Arab political lexicon circulated during the Arab Spring. The urgency of the crisis leads Arabs to read 'to be or not to be' as a representation of collective loss and bewilderment.

In addition to the political dimension of the adaptation, Graham Holderness highlights another dimension of the play; he writes: 'This is best described as a mythic or imaginative dimension, in which the analogies selected to effect a convergence between Shakespeare and the present take us deeper into Arabic cultural and religious sensibilities. For instance, it opens with smart-suited delegates located in a modern political assembly, but at

---

[17] Litvin, 'When the Villain Steals the Show', 215.   [18] Litvin, *Hamlet's Arab Journey*, 2.

the centre of the stage is the burial mound of Old Hamlet the assassinated King, and the actors make formal ritual gestures towards it (laying stones on the grave).[19]

Al-Bassam's English adaptations employ an English with strong Arabic undertones. Therefore, we can say that these dramatic works (adaptations) establish new relations between English, Arabic, and other world languages. The English versions of the play, Holderness explains, have been performed in the Middle East, for Arab audiences in the West, and to mixed audiences of Arabic and English speakers.[20] Indeed, the significance of the dramatic work lies in the relational interaction of different languages, in particular, between Anglo-American English and Arabic: two languages that tend to inscribe and articulate a grammar of global conflict between the Arabo-Islamic world and the West.

The Al-Hamlet Summit remains one of the most politically challenging rewritings of Shakespeare in the Arab world. The script 'was written from a contemporary Arab perspective. It carries many concerns and issues of today's Arab world and its relationship to the West. At the same time, it addresses these concerns to an English-speaking audience. The cross-cultural construction of the piece creates a sense of implication in the affairs of the other'.[21]

Othello

Shakespeare's oeuvre encodes three explicit representations of the Moor. *Aaron* is the first to appear in the play *Titus Andronicus* (1592). Represented a hundred years after the fall of Granada, which marked the final expulsion of the Moors from Europe, Aaron is conceived as a villainous Other, a threat to order, and partly responsible for the violence inflected upon Titus and his family. He is 'a woolly-headed, thick-lipped, coal-black Moor' (3.2.78), who is buried alive up to the neck as a final punishment for his extreme villainy. The figure of the Moor appears again in the play: *The Merchant of Venice* (1596-7). This time he is represented as a prince: *The Prince of Morocco*, who is a suitor to Portia. He is described as 'a tawny Moor all in white' (2.1.44). This fact implies that Shakespeare was aware of Leo Africanus'[22] differentiation among the Moors, as Norman Sanders, among others, argues.[23]

The third appearance of the Moor in Shakespeare is the tragic character of Othello in *Othello, The Moor of Venice* (a tragedy, 1603-4). This representation is considered one of the most ambivalent and controversial portrayals as it synthesizes the two previous

---

[19] Graham Holderness, 'Silence Bleeds: *Hamlet* Across Borders, The Shakespearean Adaptation of Sulayman Al-Bassam', *European Journal of English Studies* 12:1 (April 2008), 64.

[20] Holderness, 'Silence Bleeds', 60.

[21] Shirley Dent, 'Interview: Sulayman Al-Bassam,' *Culture Wars*, 3 March 2010. <http//www/culturewars.org.uk/2003-01/albassam.htm>.

[22] Leo Africanus, born in Granada as a Muslim and travelled extensively throughout Africa. He was named 'Al-Hassan Ibn Mohammad Al-wazan Al-Fassi' and only became 'John Leo' after his work entitled *A Geographical Historarie of Africa* 'which was circulated throughout Europe, primarily in Latin but also in Italian and French, from 1550 onwards and was translated into English in 1660 by John Lorry' (Emily C. Bartels, 'Making More of the Moor: Aaron, Othello, and Renaissance Refashionings of Race', *Shakespeare Quarterly* 41:4 (1990), 433-54 (435)).

[23] Norman Sanders (ed.), *Othello* (Cambridge: Cambridge University Press, 1984), 11.

Moorish stereotypes. If Aaron stands for the Moorish Other as an evil that should be excommunicated, and the Prince of Morocco represents the outstanding qualities of an exotic but powerful oriental Other, Othello synthesizes the two representational figments as constructs of the Western imaginary. As a dramatis persona, Othello is overloaded by the other characters with prejudice that implies a profound 'anti-Moorish' sentiment.

Since 1603, Arab productions of the play have highlighted the racial conflict underwritten by Shakespeare, yet the play 'seems to incriminate western society at large for its predisposition to the periodic, ritual slaughter of marginal and aboriginal groups and all whites—especially women—who consort with them'.[24] Othello, then, epitomizes the aboriginal and marginal alien although he is introduced in the play as an ostensibly tamed barbarian—a 'noble Moor', so to speak. His taming is effected from the outset through religious conversion since he is represented as a Christian convert. He thus has strong affinities with Leo Africanus, who was himself a Moorish Christian convert from Andalusia who had considerable experience in Africa. However, Othello's supposed primordial violence and barbarity remains *untamed*. This underground self of Othello becomes functional in the fabric of the play's tragic conflict. Paul Robeson describes the play as 'a tragedy of racial conflict, a tragedy of honor rather than jealousy'.[25] However, racial violence that is supposedly smoothed and tamed at the beginning of the play is soon intensified and brought to the fore through Iago's malicious intrigues.

The Syrian playwright Mohamed Al-Maghout (1934-2006) wrote a play in 1973 entitled *al-muhar-rij* (*The Jester*) wherein he made use of Shakespeare's *Othello* in an ironic way. *Al-muhar-rij* is a play in three acts. It is so often referred to as an ironical reflection of the modern Arab world in all its 'hollowness', 'cherished values', and 'authoritarian governments'. Al-Maghout makes use of the methods of traditional itinerant players and a moving stage. The performance takes place in an open public place next to a café somewhere in an old quarter of an unnamed Arab city. The supposedly itinerant players perform the last scene of Shakespeare's play *Othello*. The role of the noble Moor is played by the most comic actor of the company who is known as the jester. Mohamad Mustapha Badawi describes the jester's acting of *Othello* in the following terms:

> He is a comic version of Othello in the exaggerated melodramatic tradition of Yusuf Wahbi, the famous Egyptian stage and film actor, while the female dancer plays Desdemona, appearing in modern costume, swinging her handbag, and chewing-gum. In a comment on the action, the Drummer attacks Shakespeare for bringing about the downfall of the Arab national hero Othello, which he sees as a British imperialist plot, in collaboration with America, with its nuclear bases.[26]

Al-Maghout's play encodes a demythologizing representation of Shakespeare's *Othello*. First, the tragic character, *Othello* the Moor of Venice, is played by the most comic actor of the theatre company. This strategy demystifies all mythical attributes allocated to the

[24] James R. Andreas, 'Othello's African American Progeny', in Ivo Kamps, ed., *Materialist Shakespeare: A History* (London and New York: Verso, 1995), 185.

[25] Paul Robeson, in Sylvan Barnet, 'Othello on Stage and Screen', *Othello*, ed. Alvin Kerman (New York: Signet, 1986), 280.

[26] M. M. Badawi, in Salma Khadra Jayyusi and Roger Allen, eds., *Modern Arabic Drama: An Anthology* (Bloomington and Indianapolis: Indiana University Press, 1995), 14.

tragic hero, for it alienates Othello's mythical proportions through a farcical doubling. And Desdemona is played by a dancer. Second, the acting is suddenly interrupted by the comments of the Drummer almost in a Brechtian manner. His words claim an Arabic origin for Othello, as the national hero who falls victim of Anglo-American plotting. Obviously, Shakespeare's *Othello* is used by Al-Maghout to reflect upon the political situation in the Middle East during the early 1970s, a situation that was characterized by the Arabs' defeat in the 1973 War against Israel.

The drama of *Othello* is soon interrupted by anti-American and anti-NATO shouts from both the fictitious public and the on-stage actor. After playing *Othello*, the itinerant players perform another micro-drama. This is about *Harun al-Rachid*, 'the paragon of Arab justice and chivalry'. The jester then appears as Harun al-Rachid comically devouring his food at a feast, dispensing mock justice in an absurdly arbitrary manner to the noisy approval of the audience'.[27] Act 1 ends with a third micro-drama of Abd al-Rahman, the Umayyad founder of Arabo-Islamic Andalusia. The man is represented in a transhistorical way, yet contrary to the historical reality of the 'Hawk of Quraysh'. 'This prompts a comment from someone in the audience … immediately the telephone rings, and Act 1 ends when the proprietor of the café announces that the Hawk is on the phone wishing to speak to the jester.'[28] In Act 2, the jester is transported to the court of Abde-al-Rahman in a coffin. The jester's journey is also transhistorical as he is transported backwards to the glorious past of the Arabs. Throughout the act, the jester describes the present conditions of the Arab world to the Hawk who is impressed by his wisdom and offers him Spain, Alexandretta or Palestine to rule; but the jester explains with sorrow that all these provinces are no longer ruled by the Arabs. In Act 3, the Hawk is transposed to the present and seen held at gunpoint by immigration officers at the borders of an Arab state. As soon as his identity is disclosed, he is put under arrest by the local Arab authorities and handed to the Spanish to be judged as a mass killer and war criminal. Thus, Mohamed Al-Maghout makes use of micro-dramas in a metatheatrical way to illuminate the predicament of the present Arab subject. The play is permeated by an apocalyptic political cynicism, as it insists on mocking the present state of affairs in the Arab world. Shakespeare's *Othello* is used as a symbol of the defeated Arab. However, the Hawk's little drama is projected against *Othello*'s fate, for Abd-al-Rahman is betrayed not only by the Other (the Anglo-American), but by the Arabs themselves. The play may be seen as one of the more politically subversive negotiations of Shakespeare in the Arab World.

Abdelkrim Berrchid's *Otayl Wal-Khayl Wal-Barud* (*Otayl, Horses and Gunpowder*)[29] brings together Shakespeare's *Othello*, on the one hand, and *Horses and Gunpowder* as icons of Moroccan tradition of fantasia, on the other. Obviously, Berrchid's title spells out a peculiar kind of combination that estranges the title character from the Shakespearean gallery only to restore him to his Atlas origins. The title implies a hybrid negotiation of Shakespeare's *Othello* insofar as the play is transposed by Berrchid both geographically and culturally into a Moroccan con/text. Berrchid's Otayl is 'a Moroccan subject who bears all the features of

[27] Salma Khadra Jayyusi and Roger Allen (eds.), *Modern Arabic Drama: An Anthology* (Bloomington and Indianapolis: Indiana University Press, 1995), 15.

[28] Ibid., 15.

[29] Abdelkrim Berrchid, *Otayl wal-Khayl Wal-Barud* (*Otheil, Horses and Gunpowder*) (Casablanca: at-taqafa Al-Jadida, 1975). The play was first performed in 1975-6 by an amateur theatrical company (at-ta'si:s al-masrahiya) of Casablanca and directed by Ibrahim Ouarda.

Moroccan people'.[30] *Otayl* can be read as the drama of the post-colonial subject's desire for freedom, liberation, and confirmation of difference. Berrchid's play starts from where Shakespeare ended; Otayl is presented already wracked with guilt after killing not only Desdemona but also his own parents and the wonderful people of his native village. Berrchid's Iago is represented as a mass killer disguised as the director of a drama that was brought to an end by Otayl. Shakespeare's drama remains a subtext throughout Berrchid's play; yet the relation between *Otayl* and its subtext is subject to an incessant tension whereby the former supervenes upon the structure of the latter. That is to say, Berrchid's drama violates Shakespeare's original plot at the very moment of repeating it (in a different way). *Otayl,* then, represents another form of coming to terms with the Shakespeare myth, yet this time from the position of subalternity and post-colonial disavowals. It is a play that rehabilitates Otayl by restoring the humanity and 'Moroccanness' that were robbed from him by Iago's evil scheming.

Otayl nevertheless retains some of Othello's features. He is still a black and brave soldier whose roots are located in North Africa. This time, however, he is self-conscious and ready to act in order to change his and other peoples' destinies: he is determined to restore his identity and humanity that was robbed from him and intentionally concealed. It is true that he had been victim of the author/director's evil plotting, but this happened perhaps in another play before even signing the contract with the anonymous director. Both characters are black Moors from North Africa, yet *Otayl* is not utterly black but colored. *Othello* is a nomad who has carried with him the shining and noble simplicity of nature and peasant life. Similarly, Berrchid's *Otayl* is represented as a man whose simplicity and spontaneity were overpowered by Iago's conspiracy and evil plotting. Shakespeare's *Othello,* at the moment of recognition of his tragic plight, is filled with guilt and is ready to accept all kinds of punishment:

> O cursed, cursed slave! Whip me ye devils,
> From the possession of this heavenly sight!
> Blow me about in winds! Roast me in sulfur!
> Wash me in steep down gulfs of liquid fire!
>
> (*Othello* 5.2.161–4)

Berrchid's Otayl, too, manifests his guilt from the beginning of the play. While lamenting the murder of his people he declaims:

> Darkness... darkness in the eye and the heart; who can guide a blind man in a city of blind people. People said why don't you cheer up, and I replied, how can I afford a smile in such a gloomy atmosphere. (2.9)

Otayl's lamentable and grievous state is made clear at the play's opening. This shows that Berrchid's drama starts from where Shakespeare's ends. The lines are supposedly spoken by Otayl the character, yet they are juxtaposed against the meta-dramatic disruptions of Otayl the actor:

> It is Otayl, my other self, my other mask. I am Otayl, son of the sun, the sea, and the Atlas; I grew up in my little peaceful village as a shepherd in the mountains, a friend of the stars, the flute, and cattle. (2.9)

---

[30] Abdelkrim Berrchid, Dialogue, [Risalat al-Um-mà] (N. 4077, 13 April 1996), 4.

This doubling produces a transformation of the aesthetic experience by decentring dramatic illusion within the representation. However, this decentring is also uncovered as a threat to the centrality of Shakespeare's (or rather Othello's) myth, for it draws attention to its fictionality rather than its assumed fixed reality. The mythical proportions of Shakespeare's Othello are jeopardized through Berrchid's strategy of doubling. This doubling of Othello's history and his mythical character displays the manoeuvres of Berrchid's representation, which draws a line between the previous fiction of Othello and the present reality of Otayl who is himself at once a character and an actor.

In sum, Abdelkrim Berrchid's *Otayl Wal-Khayl Wal-Barud* embodies post-colonial negotiations of Shakespeare's *Othello*. The play manifests a transgressive tendency that ultimately creates a different narrative. The presence of the Shakespearean master model in the play represents only a point of departure, or at best a crossroad of intertextuality. Berrchid's text exhibits a deeply rooted desire to voice the repressed narrative of the Moroccan post-colonial subject, expressed at the expense of the Shakespeare myth, which is demythologized in the process of making space for an emerging voice. Berrchid's Otayl is no longer a prisoner of guilt and lamentation, but a free and emancipated man.

Le Diner de Gala (*The Gala Dinner*)[31] exemplifies Tayeb Saddiki's theatrical lineage and Western training. The play may be seen as Saddiki's pathetic outcry at one of the tragic moments of Moroccan theatrical history, the ruthless decision to demolish one of a very limited number of theatre buildings in Morocco, Le Theatre Municipal of Casablanca, where Saddiki himself served as artistic director for about ten years. The play represents Saddiki's poignant sadness and is a tribute to this theatre's history. It is also a histrionic reflection on Le Theatre Municipal's theatrical repertoire in particular, and a critical reflection on the brief history of Moroccan theatre and its present predicament. The play is set in a micro-theatre that is situated on the stage, a fact that establishes a constant effect of double distancing. It is a theatre with its own stage and auditorium within another macro-theatre. The onstage theatre is supposedly Le Théâtre Municipal in its last breath. The whole action takes place on the last night of the onstage theatre that will be demolished.

Le Diner de Gala opens with the last scene of Shakespeare's *Othello* as the last performance in the onstage theatre before its demolition. The actor playing Othello is seen preparing himself for action on the stage, a fact that lays bare the theatricality of the role-playing-within-the-role. His speech, in fact, indicates the end of Othello's task:

> From now on, farewell peace of mind!
> Farewell happy heart!
> Farewell plumed troops and great wars that make of ambition a virtue! Farewell!
> Farewell braying charger and strident trumpet, spirited drummer and deafening fifer!
> Farewell Royal banner and all fury, arrogance, pomp and paraphernalia of glorious war!
> And you, instruments of war whose raucous noise imitates the clamor of Jupiter.
> Farewell, Othello's task is over. (2.15)

The representation of Othello's last speech on the micro-theatre marks both the end of this theatre's career and of Othello's task, indicated by his many 'farewells.' The choice of the last scene of Shakespeare's *Othello* suits Saddiki's painful outcry about the loss of a

---

[31] Tayeb Saddiki, *Le Diner de Gala* (Casablanca: Editions Eddif, 1990) (abbreviated in the text as DG).

real national pearl and the silence and conspiracy of a new Judas who betrayed this oasis of freedom. In Shakespeare's original, Othello regrets the loss of a 'pearl … richer than all his tribe'. This is the last speech of Othello as far as the demolition of theatre is concerned, and it is manipulated by Saddiki into something highly divergent from the original Shakespearean script. Rather than simply reproducing it, Saddiki changes Othello's speech, subsituting lines from Act 2, Scene 3 (ll. 349 ff.).

Ali Chatter, actor, director, and manager of a theatre company, declares that Saddiki's drama was the last performance in this theatre, yet it will remain 'engraved in our memories' (*DG* 16). For Ali Chatter, theatre is an 'oasis of freedom' (*DG* 16). In the next scene, Ali Chatter arranges the costumes in a dramatic way. Each costume reminds him of a character, a role, a dramatic situation and a theatrical history. Thus, the action is built through the fusion of a dramatic and a narrative line. The two lines operate in the form of *Al-Halqa* story-telling and histrionic dramatization. In Act 2, the tragic decision to demolish the theatre building is related by Ali Chatter along with the empty promises of the Counsellor to reconstruct an Opera house and other theatre buildings in the city of Casablanca. Chatter's words invoke the authorities' real decision in 1984 that put an end to one of the theatrical jewels of Morocco.

The presence of all these characters was made possible only through theatre. Each costume stands as a reminder of a given character in a theatrical representation. Saddiki's transhistorical gala brings together some important artists who marked their societies with their artistic genius. With the exception of Shakespeare, all the rest of the guests were ignored, misunderstood, or even condemned during their lifetimes, and canonized after death. Together, they come to witness the demolition of another theatre, another 'oasis of freedom'. Their presence is projected against the miserable conditions of the artists who will have nowhere to go after the destruction of their place. The miserable condition of the artist is the link between most of these guests, as Chatter admits: 'Poor actor, you will never see glory while alive, but maybe after death' (*DG* 2.34). Ali Chatter reminds us of other miserable artists too: Van Gogh, who lived in extreme poverty and neglect, Molière who, after falling from the king's favour, lived a miserable life yet was recognized after his death as the greatest dramatist of French theatrical history, and Mohammed Al-Kouri, the martyr of Moroccan theatre of resistance, who gave his life to the theatre. These artists are all linked by the miserable conditions under which they lived. In fact, there is an essential sameness to the artists' situation. That is to say, both the transhistorical artists and Chatter and his company are miserable and frustrated, yet generous since they were born to give.

Ali Chatter's closing statement represents his lamentable outcry about the micro-theatre that is demolished in front of the audience as the play draws to its close. Then, an actor moves towards the audience and declares: 'The Municipal Theatre of Casablanca was effectively destroyed on 31 May 1984' (*DG* 4.101). This last statement invokes a reference to the real event of the demolition of the Theatre Municipal. The play is thus informed by metatheatrical aspects. Besides the existence of a stage-within-a-stage and the representation of characters as actors in a theatrical rehearsal, the transhistorical dinner party brings to the fore different theatrical traditions in a self-reflexive way. All of the transhistorical artists are transplanted into a different time and space so as to witness the destruction of Chatter's oasis of freedom. At the end of the play Chatter is left alone and without a theatrical location. The use of Shakespeare in this play thus amounts to an appeal to an international theatre repertoire. Saddiki's undertaking highlights the fact that we are part of the world and that the refusal of Western culture does not constitute in itself a path to follow.

CONCLUSION

The reception of Shakespeare from the mid-nineteenth century to the late 1950s is characterized by Arabic translations, adaptations, and imitations. In the earliest productions the aura of Shakespeare's canon is preserved and represented as a mythical space. The second stage, from the early 1960s up to the present, has been characterized by post-colonial disavowal and revisions of power relationships through the practice of 'double critique'. The Arab World is made up of so many different cultural and historical influences and one cannot simply turn one's back on any of them. Arab cultures absorb material vestiges, remnants, echoes, remains, and tattoos of a silent history that is quite literally inaccessible until subjected to an archaeology of its silences and a process of transcription or translation.

Shakespeare's representations on the Arab stage amount to portraits of the self in a world out of joint. These negotiations are no longer parts of a resistance to Western 'masks of difference' or the Prospero–Caliban model of post-colonial writing-back—a writing characterized by the refusal of the West and the claiming of Othello back to his Atlas origins as we have seen with Berrchid. Since the end of the 1960s, these offshoots have become powerful strategies for revisions of power in the Arab world. Arab *Hamlet* offshoots, for example, became more about tyranny as dreams of Pan-Arab unity faded giving birth to totalitarian regimes. The character of Hamlet has become hesitant and inarticulate, unable to fix the 'upside-down' world around him, as Margaret Litvin eloquently puts it in *Hamlet's Arab Journey*. Arab Hamlets are rituals of empowerment fuelled by a unified ideology and a full-fledged counterculture highly sensitive to Pan-Arabism, which emerged as a painful process of renewal that grew out of attribution and contention, a post-colonial struggle affected by violent taxonomic labelling and conflicting aspirations for a better future. Hamlet is transformed into a frustrated hero full of guilt and sadness, yet angrier; his fierce pursuit of justice left no room for introspection or doubt, as we have seen with Lahlou.

The 'Arab Spring' has, at best, changed the names of some autocrats, but—thanks to the internal and external obstacles to real democracy and to real change in the ruling elites and systems of governance—not the totalitarian Arab regimes. The illusion of change on the ground is actually stuck in the stasis of utopianism. However, the Spring has created a fundamental transformation in the public sphere. It has liberated Arab artists from fear and momentarily suspended the nexus of historical causality. The so-called Spring has flourished with communal performances very much like a carnival's way of sensing the world 'with its joy at change and its joyful relativity'.[32] Gilles Deleuze reminds us that what characterized people after the students protests of 1968 was that they were in a 'state of becoming', 'a revolutionary-becoming'.[33] Deleuze's reply to the conservative critics who denounced the miserable outcomes of a revolutionary upheaval is that they remain blind to the 'dimension of becoming'. The student protests of '68 changed 'national discussion' and widened 'social

---

[32] M. Bakhtin, *Problems of Dostoevsky's Poetics*, ed. and trans. C. Emerson (Minneapolis: University of Minnesota Press, 1084), 160.

[33] The proper Deleuzian paradox is that something truly new can only emerge through responding to what is intolerable: 'Men's only hope lies in a revolutionary becoming: the only way of casting off their shame or responding to what is intolerable' (Gilles Deleuze, *Negotiations* (New York: Columbia University Press, 1990), 171).

awareness', though they led to no permanent political change. Rewriting Shakespeare in the context of 'Arab Spring' became timely and topical with the *Richard III* written by Mahfoud Ghazal and directed by Jaafar Guesmi from Tunisia in 2013. The play was performed two years after the Jasmine Revolution;[34] it weaves together selected scenes and monologues from Shakespeare's original text and local narratives of tyranny as manifested in the story of Khalid's awkward position between his mother and his wife. The course of Richard's ascension to the throne, and his reduction into tyranny, and ultimately his defeat at the battle of Bosworth Field are used as backdrops in order to critique the present situation in Tunisia. The production attempts to demonize Zin El Abidine, turning him into a tyrant as opposed to simply an ambitious ruler. Its main highlight is a poetic outcry of alarm denouncing any attempts to give birth to another Richard III among the Tunisians and the Arabs.

Select Bibliography

Al-Bassam, Sulayman, *The Al-Hamlet Summit* (Arabic and English), ed. Graham Holderness (Hatfield: University of Hertfordshire Press, 2006).

Al-Asadi, Jawad, *Insaw Hamlet* (Beirut: Dar Al-Farabi, 2000).

Al-Bahar, Nadia, 'Shakespeare in Early Arabic Adaptations', *Shakespeare Translation* 3, no. 13 (1976): 5–16.

Badawi, M. Mustapha, 'Introduction', *Modern Arabic Drama: An Anthology*, ed. Salma Khadra Jayyusi and Roger Allen (Bloomington and Indianapolis: Indiana University Press, 1995), 1–21.

Bayer, Mark, 'The Martyrs of Love and the Emergence of the Arab Cultural Consumer', *Critical Survey* 19:3 (2007): 6–26.

Hanna, Sameh. F., 'Decommercializing Shakespeare: Mutran's Translation of Othello', *Critical Survey* 19:3 (2007): 27–54.

Hanna, Sameh. F., 'Hamlet Lives Happily Ever After in Arabic: The Genesis of the Field of Drama Translation in Egypt', *The Translator* 11:2 (2005): 167–92.

Holderness, Graham, 'Introduction', in *The Al-Hamlet Summit* (Hatfield: University of Hertfordshire Press, 2006).

Holderness, Graham, 'From Summit to Tragedy: Sulayman Al-Bassam's *Richard III* and Political Theatre', *Critical Survey* 19:3 (2007): 124–43.

Lahlou, Nabyl, *Ophélie n'est pas morte* (Casablanca: Le fennec Editions, 1987).

Litvin, Margaret, *Hamlet's Arab Journey: Shakespeare's Prince and Nasser's Ghost* (Princeton: Princeton University Press, 2011).

Khadra Jayyusi, Salma, and Allen, Roger, eds., *Modern Arabic Drama: An Anthology* (Bloomington and Indianapolis: Indiana University Press, 1995).

Mutran, Khalil, 'Introduction', in *Hamlet* (Cairo: Dar Al-Ma'arif, 1976).

Saddiki, Tayeb, *Le Diner de Gala* (Casablanca: Editions Eddif, 1990).

Selaiha, Nehad, 'Hamlet Galore', Al-Ahram Weekly, 12 March 2010. <http://weekly.ahram.org.eg/2009/963/cu1.htm>.

---

[34] The Jasmine Revolution in Tunisia began on 18 December 2010 setting in motion the Arab Spring all over the Arab World. It also led to the ousting of President Zine El Abidine Ben Ali in January 2011.

CHAPTER 52

....

SHAKESPEAREAN TRAGEDY IN LATIN AMERICA AND THE CARIBBEAN

....

ALFREDO MICHEL MODENESSI AND MARGARIDA GANDARA RAUEN

THE region that we now call Latin America comprises new cultures that gradually emerged, alongside the environmental and human impact of exploration, invasion, exploitation, deprivation, extermination, miscegenation, slavery—every act of domination involved in 350 years of colonization in the Americas. Every 'post-colonial' nation of Latin America is still attempting to wrestle an identity out of the complex intermingling of the best and worst of its European—and other—legacies, and its variously conflicted relationships with the aboriginal cultures, whether destroyed or simply rendered destitute. All such 'identities' entail a strong sense of in-betweenness, as Silviano Santiago argues.[1] A postcolonial concern with place and displacement thus becomes unavoidable in a succinct account like the present one, prompting caution because a binary logic doesn't suffice to address our topic.[2]

The first challenge of Shakespearean tragedy in Latin America and the Caribbean is the sheer scale of what is involved. It isn't the only one, however. The very name 'Latin America' has been debated from numerous perspectives[3] but remains the preferred term to encompass the richly different yet patently intertwined array of cultures extending from Baja California to Tierra del Fuego and the largest islands in the Caribbean. The lexicon describing our complexity is as big as the continent. From the vernacular '*mestizo*' to the imported 'hybrid', from 'Colony' to 'Post-colonialism' to

---

[1] See Silviano Santiago, *The Space In-Between: Essays in Latin American Culture*, ed. Ana Lúcia Gazzola (Durham and London: Duke University Press, 2001).

[2] See Fernando Ortiz, *Contrapunteo cubano del tabaco y azúcar* (La Habana: Editorial de Ciencias Sociales, 1983), 90, especially his notion of '*transculturación*', abundantly elaborated upon by later writers.

[3] The literature on this is as vast as the issues and the variety of attitudes towards them. For a starting point in English, see John King, ed., *The Cambridge Companion to Latin American Culture* (Cambridge: Cambridge University Press, 2004).

'Coloniality', from '*Antropofagia*' to 'Transculturation', and anything in between,[4] the entries of that lexicon foreground an historically dynamic tension that affects every American nation expressing itself in Spanish or Portuguese—or less frequently (and more problematically) in French. Even more perplexed is the case of the natives of these lands.

Our history makes us 'others'. But if we come 'from elsewhere', like Canadians,[5] to a great extent we also come from 'here' and from a less locatable 'when', depending on var-iegated histories of mix, migration, assimilation, self-construction, and self-destruction. Silviano Santiago has accordingly used the term 'space in-between' to capture the colo-nized and unstable subject's drive to stake out zones of agency.[6] Our economies are marked by extreme polarity and tension. At the crossroads of independence and modernity, 'lib-eral ideas were applied in countries which were highly stratified, socially and racially, as well as economically underdeveloped, and in which the tradition of centralized authority ran deep. In short, in an environment which was resistant and hostile'.[7] This 'resistance' to Western economics contributed to the widening of class and educational divides, as well as to social regression and unrest, with varied results, mostly involving neo-dependence. All conditions of our region that may be prefixed 'post-', then, stem from common histo-ries, and share an outcome: 'In Latin America, a discussion of post- or neo-colonialism—or of coloniality, a term that encompasses the transhistoric expansion of colonial domin-ation and its perpetuation—is necessarily intertwined with the critique of Occidentalism and modernity. This critique requires a profound but detached understanding of imperial rationality.'[8]

Tragedy, a category that originates in, and has originated much foundational Occidental thought, has a long history of debate over its definition and provides a good example of how a Latin American mind subverts Western concepts. Consider a mere snippet from Augusto Boal's critique of 'Aristotle's Coercive System of Tragedy', at the opening of what remains one of the most influential and politically engaged exercises in theatrical theory and agency to emerge from our region: 'Aristotle constructs the first, extremely powerful poetic-political system for intimidation of the spectator, ... [which is] to this day fully utilized ... for repression.'[9] Moreover, such critique is present and strong *within* our sphere. For instance, in the most circulated essay linking Shakespeare and the region, Roberto Fernández Retamar attacks 'cultural colonialism', criticizing Jorge Luis Borges's

---

[4] For references see the massive Leslie Bethell, ed., *The Cambridge History of Latin America* (Cambridge: Cambridge University Press, 2008).

[5] Mark Fortier, 'Undead and Unsafe: Adapting Shakespeare (in Canada)', in Diana Brydon and Irena R. Makaryk, *Shakespeare in Canada. A World Elsewhere?* (Toronto: Toronto University Press, 2002), 342.

[6] Santiago draws on Montaigne's *Essays* to discuss cultural dependence from a deconstructive stance: 'Latin American Discourse: The Space In-Between', in Santiago, *The Space In-Between*, 25–39.

[7] Charles Hale, 'Political and Social Ideas in Latin America, 1870-1930', in Bethell, ed., *The Cambridge History of Latin America*, 4: 368.

[8] Mabel Moraña, Enrique Dussel, and Carlos A. Jáuregui, 'Coloniality at Large', in Mabel Moraña, Enrique Dussel, and Carlos A. Jáuregui, eds., *Coloniality at Large: Latin America and the Postcolonial Debate* (Durham: Duke University Press, 2008), 2.

[9] Augusto Boal, *Theatre of the Oppressed*, trans. Charles A. and María-Odilia Leal McBride, (London: Pluto Press, 1979), p. xiv.

and Carlos Fuentes's attachment to Western culture as mirroring Ariel's siding with Prospero.[10]

The process of transmission and reception of Shakespearean tragedy implies a similarly conflicted ebb and flow. Latin American artists not only question or interrogate European sources in their creative processes, but also re-energize *both* traditions and participate in their transformation, evident in the ways our arts have been 'devoured' across the Atlantic. More pointedly, Roberto Schwartz asks:

> Why should we suppose, even tacitly, that [Latin American] experience is of only local interest, whereas French, English, Italian, Spanish, North American, Greek or Latin experiences—or all of them taken together—are of universal significance? If the question is only asked to disguise our shortcomings as an ex-colony, it is not even worth asking. But if the intention is to question the universality of the universal and the localism of the local, then it could be a starting point for further discussion.[11]

This notion of creative interaction underlies our discussions of the sub-regions into which Latin America is usually divided. The first deals with the numerous and diverse Spanish-speaking countries, including the Caribbean nations. The second covers the likewise many-faceted Portuguese-speaking Brazil. This leaves two areas glaringly untouched: French-speaking America[12]—evidently 'Latin'—and the non-'Latin' Caribbean.[13] Space will not allow us to approach Shakespearean tragedy in these territories in anything more than a marginal fashion.

SPANISH-SPEAKING LATIN AMERICA

Twenty-five years ago, introducing Fernández Retamar's, *'Caliban' and Other Essays*, Fredric Jameson deplored how no one seemed willing to think about 'the relations between poetry and politics' anymore, and blamed such unwillingness on 'a perplexity in

---

[10]   Roberto Fernández Retamar, 'Caliban', in *'Caliban' and Other Essays*, trans. Edward Baker (Minneapolis: University of Minnesotta Press, 1989), 26–35. His treatment of the subject and positions vis-à-vis these and other writers has varied much over time: see 'Caliban Revisited', in *'Caliban' and Other Essays*, esp. 54, and the full collection: *Todo Caliban* (Buenos Aires: CLACSO, 2004).

[11]   Roberto Schwarz, 'Competing Readings in World Literature', trans. Nick Caistor, *New Left Review* 48 (November–December 2007), 98.

[12]   Needless to say, post-colonial discussion owes much to Caribbean thinkers like Aimé Césaire and Frantz Fanon, from Martinique, and the Trinidadian C. L. R. James.

[13]   On Shakespeare in the 'non-Latin' Caribbean, however, see: Helge Nowak, '"Classical and Creole": Shakespeare's Legacy in the Caribbean Theatre', in Norbert Schaffeld, ed., *Shakespeare's Legacy. The Appropriation of the Plays in Post-Colonial Drama* (Trier: WVT Wissenschaftlicher Verlag Trier, 2005), 89–104; William E. Cain, 'The Triumph of Will and the Failure of Resistance: C. L. R. James's Readings of *Moby Dick* and *Othello*', in Selwyn R. Cudjoe and William E. Cain, eds., *C. L. R. James: His Intellectual Legacies* (Amherst: University of Massachusetts Press, 1995), 260–73; and Pier Paolo Frassinelli, 'Caribbean Shakespeares: Genealogies of the Postcolonial', in Luigi Cazzato, ed., *Anglo-Southern Relations: From Deculturation to Transculturation* (Lecce: Besa, 2011), 142–67.

the West as to what politics might be: ... a perplexity no doubt meaningless to the rest of the world, ... where the political is a destiny, where human beings are condemned to politics as a result of material want and life on the edge of physical catastrophe [and] ... human violence'.[14] First, this is a reminder of how and why Shakespeare and Spanish-speaking Latin America are often associated in politically inflected discussions centred on *The Tempest*. But Jameson's 'Foreword' is relevant because it draws its binary line between 'the West' and the 'the rest' via a lexical set smacking of tragedy.

Jameson is right about 'want', 'violence', and 'catastrophe' persistently affecting the 'un-West', and about the 'West' being 'sealed' from political awareness inside 'private life' in 1989.[15] But as he tries to undermine a seemingly impregnable comfort zone, he pictures the 'rest' as tragic victims, 'destined' to 'the political'—an exoticist fiction of the *engagé*. The political isn't per se a motive for tragic rue: 'a fate in the pragmatic substance of its entanglements is never tragic'.[16] Instead, more in keeping with tragedy as *genre*, what we 'the rest' are 'condemned to' are the want, violence, and catastrophe that 'result' from a complex *combination* of whatever calamity hits us from elsewhere together *with* our own historical missteps, not mishaps.

This doesn't negate the fact that Latin America is haunted by the tragic. Well before the time that post-colonialism takes as its starting point, the Spanish and Portuguese empires had turned the region into 'the first battleground for ideas of civilization, empire, and racial difference'.[17] Thus, 'social and class relations were shaped by the violence of colonial reality', and so 'the elaboration of loss (of entire populations, cultures, territories, and natural resources) and, later, the utopian myths that accompanied modernity guide the construction of cultural identities'.[18] If tragedy is a 'means by which suffering is not disavowed but incorporated in the community'[19]—i.e. if it contributes to 'elaborating loss'—the first problem with staging tragedy in Latin America is that loss has become so pervasive and so destructive of identity.

At the beginning, however, the idea of tragedy hinged upon European definitions of genre and *self*. The first 'tragedy dealing with an American subject'[20] was staged in Buenos Aires in 1789. Manuel de Lavardén's *Siripo* dramatizes the legend of Lucía Miranda and Sebastián de Hurtado,[21] who supposedly lived in the fort of *Sancti Spiritu*, established

[14] Fredric Jameson, 'Foreword', in Fernández Retamar, *'Caliban' and Other Essays*, p. vii.

[15] Ibid., p. vii.

[16] Walter Benjamin, *The Origin of German Tragic Drama*, trans. John Osborne (London: Verso, 2003), 118.

[17] Ricardo D. Salvatore, 'The Postcolonial in Latin America and the Concept of Coloniality: A Historian's Point of View', *A Journal on Social History and Literature in Latin America* 8:1 (Fall 2010), 336.

[18] Moraña, Dussel, and Jáuregui, 'Colonialism and Its Replicants', 3.

[19] Alice Rayner, in David Román, ed., 'A Forum on Theatre and Tragedy in the Wake of September 11, 2001', *Theatre Journal* 54:1 (March 2002), 131.

[20] Laura Mogliani, '*Siripo* de Manuel de Lavardén', in Osvaldo Pellettieri, ed., *Historia del teatro argentino en Buenos Aires* (Buenos Aires: Galerna, 2005), 1: 118. (All translations from Spanish by Modenessi.)

[21] These names, among other things, have made critics argue a connection with *The Tempest*. See Luis Astrana Marín's notes to his translation of the play in William Shakespeare, *Obras Completas* (Madrid: Aguilar, 1929).

by Sebastian Cabot in 1527. Mangoré, a leader of the native *Timbús*, infatuated with Lucía, plans to abduct her during a raid. Mangoré dies, but Lucía is made prisoner by his brother Siripo, and eventually becomes his concubine. Sebastián is made a slave. The loving couple meet secretly, however, so Siripo orders her to be burned alive and him to be shot—appropriately, with arrows. This 'neoclassic' drama deployed 'the full arsenal of the Enlightenment':[22] it indicted tyranny and brute power, but strictly to legitimize European supremacy, making the 'Indian' the agent of oppression.

In 1900, another 'tragic encounter' between 'West' and 'rest' was staged: *Atzimba*, by the Mexicans Ricardo Castro and Alberto Michel. The time seemed ripe—or aptly decadent—to produce an opera in the old-world vein dealing with the new world's foundations. At the beginning of the drama, *P'urhepecha* nobles rue the surrender of the *Mexica* emperor to the Spaniards. But Princess Atzimba, torn between heart and tribe, loves Jorge de Villadiego, a herald of Cortés—and he loves her against his loyalties. Huépac, a jealous priest, lusts after Atzimba. He persuades the king, who deplores the betrayal of his own blood, to capture the aliens and—as in the best of fantasies about native Mexicans—rip out their hearts. In the end, Jorge joins Atzimba in a hopeless duet and, as he's taken to the sacrificial stone, she seizes Huépac's dagger and buries it in her own heart.

The 'story of woe' of Lucía Miranda and her Sebastián had already been dramatized in Europe: first in 1718, as *Mangora, King of the Timbusians, or The Faithful Couple*, by the Englishman Thomas Moore,[23] and secondly as *Lucía Miranda*, by the Spanish Jesuit Manuel Lassala in 1784. *Siripo*, then, together with the 'romantic' *Atzimba*, which aspired to be the 'New World's *Aida*', lined up well with certain sensibilities from the imperial world. Two centuries later, the persistence of near-feudal socio-economic structures suggests that the 'new' Latin America has remained a haven for many backward 'old' ways, and for their artistic recirculation. Presently, however, this doesn't apply much to Shakespeare, who emerged as an increasingly appreciated item in a required cultural repertoire, and who was then 'assimilated' as a token of prime repute by cultures seeking to legitimize claims on their European inheritance. But he has recently been creatively reworked in multiple ways—mostly *political*—in the assumption that whatever Shakespeare may signify in Latin America will be relevant. Farley Velázquez, head of '*Teatro Hora 25*' of Colombia, illustrates with typical, if extreme, conviction that 'in a country at war with itself, Shakespeare is a must'.[24]

Still, Latin American theatre artists mustn't be taken to validate a reductive assumption that what they produce are 'political statements' over the obvious fact that, first of all, they make *art*, whose political contents needn't be blatant or propagandistic, but which will nevertheless be critical and politically incisive about issues, in ways and within scenarios that may or may not be 'local' but have identifiable local relevance. Shakespeare is frequently prime material for such artistic endeavours. From the vast production of the nineteen countries of the region, two remarkable cases of creative appropriation may be used to contrast with the two tragedies described above, and to illustrate how, in our

---

[22] Mogliani, 'Siripo', 123.   [23] Moore's play contains an allusion to *Othello*.
[24] Farley Velázquez, 'El *spa* teatral. El estado actual del teatro colombiano', *Paso de Gato, revista mexicana de teatro* 5:24 (January–March 2006), 33.

midst, 'Western European forms have served as a focus that masks the emergence of cali-banesque, less immediately classifiable texts.'[25] Both are 'original': one is overtly 'political', and close to what is usually deemed 'adaptation'; the other, deceptively 'intimate', con-verses with Shakespeare as, and at, its point of origin.

1. The show *Mosca*,[26] derived from *Titus Andronicus*, written in 2002 and revised in 2012 by the Colombian Fabio Rubiano, probes the self-corrupting nature of the dis-courses of power, by deliberately looking at multiple forms of threat and repression, with Lavinia's body as the main battleground and prize in an unending contest over control. Shakespeare's violence is diverted into clinical explorations of the objective reasons for the abuse and torture, private and public, that wait upon an absolute patriarch—a familiar subject in Latin America, not only in general but in socio-political terms, including mul-tiple forms of dictatorship.

The play uses only nine characters and does not seek any identification with Shakespeare's 'literature'. Titus is king; he has killed Saturninus before the play begins, and Tamora is to marry him. Titus constantly exercises verbal and physical brutality, pointedly in the guise of culinary 'art', especially towards Lavinia, who must yield to his ideas of what, how, and *why* to eat. Titus' sons and sons-to-be share a sexual obsession with Lavinia, a virgin who, at 40, cannot think of a better way out of her prison and her insufferable virginity than marrying Bassianus, a butcher—a sort of inquisitor, ironically in charge of enforcing the chastity of women by brutal means, who is interested only in her remaining 'worthy'. When Titus kills Bassianus, the highly articulate Demetrius, in a disturbing feat of ironic ration-alization, persuades Lavinia that being raped by him and his subhuman brother Chiron is her best option to be free: by becoming a victim, she might break away from her nagging chastity and her father's absolute control. She goes the way of martyrdom to mutilation and death, as pre-scripted—except that an un-pre-scripted, horrifying item intervenes: a 'pear of anguish': the pear-shaped torture device that, inserted vaginally or anally, would destroy a person from within as its four segments opened with the turn of a screw. Perhaps betoken-ing Titus' ubiquitous power over and inside the world he informs and rules, this instrument also contributes to the death of the 'whore' Tamora, 'foil' to virginal Lavinia. Fittingly, once Titus has killed them all, he wishes to procreate again.

According to Rubiano, in *Titus Andronicus* 'violent acts are so frequently and so er-ratically disposed that they ultimately nullify themselves. Once a sign is rendered void, it conveys the opposite sense by extreme repetition'.[27] In *Mosca*, therefore, Rubiano strips violence of its commonplace shock value and underlines its horrors by means of hyper-objective dialogue focusing on the body. Thus, the play perhaps suggests ways to recon-struct human resistance in the face of a never-ending cycle of unsparing patriarchal rule by 'negative' means: i.e. by overloading the signs of such a cycle, and hence making them more likely to invite intellectual alertness than emotional reaction. It must be noted that all the languages used in *Mosca*—physical as well as verbal—are vernacular, readily

---

[25] Jameson, 'Foreword', p. x.

[26] This and other eight derivatives are available in: *Bordeando Shakespeare* (Mexico: Paso de Gato, 2013).

[27] León P. Sierra, 'Conversación con Fabio Rubiano. De *Mosca* a *Los puntos cardinales*', *Primer acto. Cuadernos de investigación teatral*, 306 (2004), 128.

accessible: they are active reminders that, in this play, the stage is employed as a platform for debate, rather than as a pedestal for tribute.

2. *Hamlet, por ejemplo,* by Héctor Mendoza, a show built upon the intersection of improvisation, drama, theatre, and performance, was staged in 1983 and first published in 1992.[28] As director, dramatist, and teacher of actors and directors, Mendoza was at the root of Mexican theatre from the mid-1960s to his death in 2010. What is now 'the play' *Hamlet, por ejemplo* stemmed from the preparation of a show with the four actors who eventually performed it. Two men and a woman played themselves, using their real names, as they waited to audition for the lead in a *Hamlet* to be staged by an (unidentified) director who in the end didn't show up at the appointed place: the venue where the show was actually presented. A fourth actor played the assistant director, also under his real name. The resulting script can now be performed by actors 'other than themselves'—a splendid set of stage mirrors.

The men are surprised that the woman is competing with them, at her 'advanced age' (she was in fact the oldest). A lively 'discussion including some moments by Shakespeare' (the script's subtitle) ensues; the three make their cases, using Aristotle, Coleridge, Bentley, Bradley, Kettle, Kitto, Knight, and Kott, all listed at the end under 'Desecrated Critical Essays'. For Mendoza, theatre couldn't 'be much if not profanation, collectively perpetrated'. The dialogue channels his and the actors' ideas on Shakespeare, Hamlet and *Hamlet*, love, power, gender, madness, death—and on Mexico near the end of the twentieth century. Above all, the show involves an ontological exploration of the stage out of its raw practical 'business': not just the crafts, but also the economy and power structures that regulate the life of theatres.

The actors exchange ideas, emotions, and loyalties, as they play 'moments' from *Hamlet*. Near the end, they perform the scene in the Queen's bedchamber in full. They are exhausted by the time the assistant announces the director isn't coming and already has a Hamlet. There is no commotion, but the younger man thinks he must one day play the part lest he never feel free from it. The assistant suggests *they* could stage a show from their 'notes' to *Hamlet*. The older actors make vague excuses and go. The youngest one invites the assistant to discuss it over coffee. This circular, self-referential script 'owes' as much to Shakespeare as to Sartre, Pinter, Beckett, and sundry 'authors' un-/dis-/played in the impossibly captured 'dream of passion' that was Mendoza's reason for living, and still is for those who are committed to the evanescence and precariousness of a player's life.[29] Such qualities are mirrored in the experience of Hamlet himself.

Spanish-speaking Latin Americans who interact creatively with Shakespeare regard his dramaturgy highly, but they also operate from the conviction that 'Caliban's reply to Prospero implies the vindication of his speech—his right to "babble" not as an invalid or incoherent speech but as his own valid and structured discourse'.[30] Shakespeare is, therefore, a prime choice for literary 'anthropophagy'. Bernice Kliman says that, in Latin America,

---

[28] Now in Héctor Mendoza, *Teatro Completo* (Mexico: El Milagro, La Rana, Universidad de Guanajuato, UNAM, 2010), vol. 2.

[29] Eerie but perhaps significant is the fact that the two older actors committed suicide soon after the show closed; she was chronically depressed, he terminally ill.

[30] Hugo Achugar, 'Local/Global Latin Americanisms', *Interventions: International Journal of Postcolonial Studies* 5:1 (2003), 131.

Shakespeare's works are 'cannibalized by native traditions'.[31] These 'native traditions' are only as 'native' as they're foreign, of course:[32] we are post-colonial after our own fashion, existing on a double threshold, never fully belonging: natives with an asterisk, and other-than-native with an/other asterisk. But our theatre increasingly brings Shakespeare to bear on this tragi-comic condition as a *positive* starting point for significant ends, not as the lingering legacy of an oppressive past. These processes of construction by disjunction begin with translation.

The history of Shakespeare translation in the region is long and important—and summarized elsewhere.[33] Many translations made 'for the page' in Spanish-speaking Latin America suffer from major problems, also discussed elsewhere.[34] What deserves stressing is that translations subservient to dated Spanish models and bardolatry betoken a divide between approaching Shakespeare as a canonical author and using him as a cultural resource open to interlocution. A similar problem plagues critical and academic production, which are frequently outdated, either because of a shortage of bibliographic resources, scholarly training, and systematic research, or because of the rarity of foreign scholarly engagement with Shakespeare in this region.[35] Beyond relatively numerous but mainly occasional non-specialist pieces, the scant examples of solid literature are, on the one hand, by writers who have used Shakespeare as an essayistic or literary subject—Borges, Pedro Henríquez Ureña, and Juan Villoro—or by those who have tackled pressing issues *through* his work—such as José Enrique Rodó and Fernández Retamar. There are isolated volumes and papers, of course: some are the outcome of strictly domestic events—such as the Argentine collections listed by Díaz-Fernández;[36] others belong to local academics, and are glanced at elsewhere.[37]

---

[31] 'Afterword', in Bernice W. Kliman and Rick J. Santos, eds., *Latin American Shakespeares* (Madison-Teaneck: Fairleigh Dickinson University Press, 2005), 327.

[32] The actual native traditions have had little to do with Shakespeare, as will be noted, but have never received adequate academic attention. For a minimal token in English, see Barry D. Sell and Louise M. Burkhart, *Nahuatl Theater: Death and Life in Colonial Nahua Mexico* (Norman: University of Oklahoma Press, 2004).

[33] See José Ramón Díaz-Fernández, 'Toward a Survey of Shakespeare in Latin America', in Kliman and Santos, *Latin American Shakespeares*, 293–326; and Alfredo Michel Modenessi, 'Shakespeare in Iberian and Latin American Spanishes', in Bruce Smith, ed., *The Cambridge Guide to the Worlds of Shakespeare*, vol. 2, part XV, chapter 146 (Cambridge: Cambridge University Press, 2016).

[34] See Alfredo Michel Modenessi, '"A double tongue within your mask". Translating Shakespeare in/to Spanish-speaking Latin America', in Ton Hoenselaars, ed., *Shakespeare and the Language of Translation* (London: Thomson, 2004), 240–54, and 'Traducir la alteridad a la alteridad, español mediante. Posibles Shakespeares en Latinoamérica', in Verónica Zondek and Amalia Ortiz de Zárate, eds., *Escrituras de la traducción hispánica* (Valdivia: Universidad Austral de Chile and Ediciones Kultrún, 2009), 39–70.

[35] The only volume expressly dealing with the subject in the international scene: *Latin American Shakespeares*, illustrates an evident problem in the Spanish-speaking area. Of its sixteen chapters, seven deal with Shakespeare in Brazil, four involve Mexico, two Chile, one Cuba, one explores Borges, and one is a bibliographical survey. However, five are by Brazilians working in Brazil and three teaching in the US; the others are by two scholars living in the US, one by a Canadian, one by an English scholar, three by Spaniards, and only one by a Spanish-speaker residing in the area.

[36] Díaz-Fernández, 'Toward a Survey', 314–26.

[37] See Alfredo Michel Modenessi and Margarida Gandara Rauen, 'Hamlet as a Figure of Thought in Latin America', in Peter W. Marx, ed., Hamlet-*Handbuch. Stoff—Aneignungen—Deutungen* (Stuttgart and Weimar: J. B. Metzler, 2013), 370.

The strongest bond between Spanish-speaking Latin America and Shakespearean trag-edy remains on stage. Space makes it impossible to provide other than brief hints of its rich history. As early as the mid-1810s, Shakespearean tragedies were possibly being read in Latin America, but they were certainly being performed. In 1813, Ducis's *Othello* played in Argentina and Uruguay.[38] Around 1821, in Buenos Aires, the local actor-impresario Luis Morante performed in a version of *Hamlet* called *El imperio de la verdad*. He staged another *Hamlet* in 1824, in Chile, where two years earlier Francisco Cáceres staged Ducis's *Othello*. In 1821, *Hamlet* was performed for the first time in Mexico, as it came to independence.[39]

More in keeping with the new nations' search for self-definition, however, and above this emergent taste for Shakespeare, stood plays like Vittorio Alfieri's *Bruto primo*—revealingly translated into Spanish as *Roma libre*—whose republicanism was well received by Mexicans in 1823, as the brief 'empire' of Agustín de Iturbide collapsed. Towards the mid-century, performances of *Hamlet, Othello,* and *Romeo and Juliet* were offered in Havana, Mexico, Lima, Quito, Buenos Aires, and Montevideo, mainly by Italian and Spanish companies. The years between 1860 and 1900 saw abundant proof that *Hamlet* would prove the favourite everywhere.[40] After 1900, *Romeo and Juliet, Othello,* and *Macbeth* were also often produced north and south, as well as in the Caribbean. As the century progressed, other tragedies began their journey to becoming the staples that they are today, for instance, *King Lear*, which has been staged multiple times and in many ways throughout Latin America since the 1930s. This development first coincided with times of social unrest and, subsequently, of economic growth and fleeting industrial and commercial prosperity, during which socio-political tribulations and regressions brewed, frequently ending in the brutal suppression of progress towards democracy or socialism by 'iron-fist' regimes. During better times be-tween the 1930s and 1960s theatre companies proliferated. In Mexico, new cultural endeav-ours fostered the presence of Shakespeare,[41] as they did in Uruguay and Chile. The 'National Comedy' of Argentina included Shakespeare as part of its policy to 'rescue the essence of our country and the culture of the West'.[42] By the mid-1960s Shakespeare had become famil-iar throughout Latin America—as had economic crisis, political turmoil, and repression.

The Latin American engagement with Shakespearean tragedy after the decisive 1960s was defined by a search for local or locally generated relevance. The stage has been the site of unlimited experimentation through adaptation and derivative writing, and occasional noteworthy translations.[43] Other than a word on 'direct' and 'adapted'

---

[38] Osvaldo Pellettieri, ed., *Historia del teatro argentino*, 1: 48.

[39] Enrique de Olavarría y Ferrari, *Reseña histórica del teatro en México* (Mexico: Imprenta y Litográfica La Europea, 1895), 200–1.

[40] See Modenessi and Rauen, 'Hamlet as a Figure', 368.

[41] See David Olguín, 'El "cacharro de Mesones" 42: Teatro de Ulises', 54–70; Luis Mario Moncada, 'El milagro teatral mexicano', 94–116; Olga Harmony, 'El teatro del seguro social', 117–28; and Luz Emilia Aguilar Zinser, 'La puesta en escena: los nuevos lenguajes, antes y después de *Poesía en Voz Alta*', 129–46; all in David Olguín, ed., *Un siglo de teatro en México* (Mexico: Conaculta and FCE, 2011).

[42] Camila Mansilla and Martín Rodríguez, 'El teatro oficial', in Pellettieri, ed., *Historia del teatro argentino*, 3: 389.

[43] For selected instances, see Catherine Boyle, 'Parra's Transcription of *King Lear*: The Transfiguration of the Literary Composition', 112–29; Gregary J. Racz, 'Strategies of Deletion in Pablo Neruda's *Romeo y Julieta*', 71–91; and Juan J. Zaro, 'Translating from Exile: León Felipe's Shakespeare *Paraphrases*', 92–111, all in Kliman and Santos, *Latin American Shakespeares*; and Modenessi, '"Have you made division…"'.

tragedies,[44] we will only provide a brief account of some derivative texts, as they offer intertwined advantages: an index to the variety of options that local artists find in and through Shakespearean tragedy, and a selection of entry points for research into the valuable tradition of Spanish-speaking Latin American theatre.

Since 1960, Shakespeare's tragedies have reached the stages of Latin America both in 'anthropophagous' and 'straightforward' ways. Regarding *Hamlet*, the most utilized tragedy, an overview is available,[45] but it's important to stress that *Hamlet* took a special place on Latin American stages in the dark times of military rule.[46] Likewise, even a minimal list of 'direct' productions from Argentina, Colombia, Cuba, Mexico, Uruguay, and twelve other countries, would make clear that, as 'straightforward' as they may purport to be, from 1960 to 2014 it's hard to find a remarkable production of a Shakespearean tragedy devoid of local suggestiveness.

The number of adaptations to be found in the same period would testify to the flexibility that Shakespearean tragedy affords our theatre artists to tackle their own forms of the tragic. Particularly notable is Shakespeare's reach in diasporic areas across cultural borders. An example—by no means singular—involving Spanish-speaking communities that emerged from migration or exile is the 2012 bilingual production *Hamlet: Prince of Cuba*, staged by Australian-born Michael Donald Edwards with a translation into Spanish by Pulitzer winner Nilo Cruz for the Asolo Repertory Theatre of Sarasota, Florida.

Numerous notable shows derived from Shakespeare's tragedies include *Invitación a la muerte*,[47] written in 1944 by the Mexican Xavier Villaurrutia; *Hamlet en este país de ratas retóricas*, by José Manuel Freidel (Colombia, 1985); *Romeo y Julieta en Luyanó*, by the Cuban troupe of Cheo Briñas, 1987;[48] *Ofelia o la madre muerta*, by Marco Antonio de la Parra (Chile, 1994); *Sonny* (based on *Othello*), by José Ignacio Cabrujas (Venezuela, 1995); *Yo soy Macbeth*, by Enrique Polo (Nicaragua, 2000); *La señora Macbeth*, by Griselda Gambaro (Argentina, 2003)—perhaps the best documented;[49] *Dondequiera oscuridad y*

[44] For a summary on both, see Alfredo Michel Modenessi, 'Latin America', in Michael Dobson and Stanley Wells, and Will Sharpe and Erin Sullivan, eds., *The Oxford Companion to Shakespeare*, 2nd ed. (Oxford: Oxford University Press, 2015).

[45] Modenessi and Rauen, 'Hamlet as a Figure'.

[46] The history of Argentine theatre examplifies the hardships of working under such conditions—similar to those in Uruguay, Chile, El Salvador, and all countries undergoing state terrorism. For a general introduction, see Jean Graham-Jones, *Exorcising History: Argentine Theater under Dictatorship* (London: Bucknell University Press, 2000), and 'Broken Pencils and Crouching Dictators: Issues of Censorship in Contemporary Argentine Theatre', *Theatre Journal* 53:4 (December 2001), 595–605.

[47] See Raymond Marion Watkins, *From Elsinore to Mexico City: The Pervasiveness of Shakespeare's Hamlet in Xavier Villaurrutia's Invitación a la muerte* (Saarbrücken: VDM Verlag, 2008); and Antonio Marquet, 'Invitación a la muerte y la poética del closet', *Tema y variaciones de literatura* 23 (2005), 91–122.

[48] See Donna Woodford-Gormley, 'In Fair Havana, Where We Lay Our Scene: *Romeo and Juliet* in Cuba', in Craig Dionne and Parmita Kapadia, eds., *Native Shakespeares: Indigenous Appropriations on a Global Stage* (Aldershot: Ashgate, 2008), 201–11; Woodford-Gormley also documents the ballet *Shakespeare y sus máscaras*, based on *Romeo and Juliet*, choreographed by Alicia Alonso for the National Ballet of Cuba in 2003.

[49] For a starting point, see Sharon Magnarelli, 'Staging Shadows/Seeing Ghosts: Ambiguity, Theatre, Gender, and History in Griselda Gambaro's *La señora Macbeth*', *Theatre Journal* 60:3 (October 2008), 365–82.

maquillaje, a version of *Hamlet*, by Luis Cano (Argentina, 2004);[50] *El viaje termina en Elsinor*, by Arturo Arango (Cuba, 2008); *Otelo sobre la mesa*, by Jaime Chabaud (México, 2008); *Los insensatos*, by David Olguín (Mexico, 2011), drawing on *Hamlet*; *Mendoza*, a Mexican *Macbeth* by Juan Carrillo and Antonio Zúñiga (2011); and *Hamlet de los Andes*, by the Bolivian Diego Aramburo (2012). The presence of Shakespeare in 'border' cultures also deserves exploration. Among 'Chicano' dramatists—who in addition to English and Spanish employ an increasingly independent, intermingled idiom—a good example is Edit Villarreal, whose *The Language of Flowers* (1990) is based on *Romeo and Juliet*.

Finally, although Spanish-speaking cinema has resisted filming or adapting Shakespeare, movies based on his tragedies include: *Romeo y Julieta*, a 1943 Mexican parody;[51] *Bodas trágicas*, a 1946 Mexican melodrama based on *Othello*; *Sangrador*, a version of *Macbeth* made in Venezuela in 2000;[52] *Amar te duele*, a Mexican derivative of *Romeo and Juliet*, 2002;[53] *Huapango*, based on *Othello*, Mexico, 2003;[54] and *Besos de azúcar*, another Mexican derivative of *Romeo and Juliet*, 2013.

An unprecedented case deserves greater elaboration: the first production of Shakespeare in an indigenous language.[55] *Hamlet P'urhepecha*, adapted to a pre-Columbian setting, was performed entirely by members of the native community of Zacán, in the Mexican State of Michoacán in 1990. Published in 1992, it suggests the complexities that Latin America generates, hosts, and struggles with: *Hamlet P'urhepecha* deals as much with 'Shakespearean themes' as it speaks of unresolved conflicts with whatever 'Shakespeare' may represent to the displaced natives and what they in turn make of him in a world that is in unending search of identity. Hence, it would be profitable to contrast *Hamlet P'urhepecha* with *A Soldier in Every Son—The Rise of the Aztecs*, by Luis Mario Moncada, a conflation of what was originally a trilogy charting the tumultuous conflicts between the native tribes of central Mexico that led to the establishment of the Aztec empire in pre-Columbian times.

Freely based on several Shakespearean *Histories* and sundry tragic texts, Moncada's play was performed in the UK, in English, during the 2012 World Shakespeare Festival by a combined cast from the RSC and the National Theatre Company of Mexico, receiving, at best, mixed reviews.[56] In Mexico, other than friendly publicity and some encomiastic press releases, it had a lukewarm reception, despite overtly gesturing towards contemporary

---

[50] See Modenessi and Rauen, 'Hamlet as a Figure', 369–70.

[51] See Alfredo Michel Modenessi, 'Cantinflas's *Romeo y Julieta*: The Rogue and Will', in Kliman and Santos, eds., *Latin American Shakespeares*, 219–42.

[52] See Mark Thornton Burnett, *Shakespeare and World Cinema* (Cambridge: Cambridge University Press, 2013), 89–124.

[53] See Alfredo Michel Modenessi, 'Looking for Mr. GoodWill in Rancho Grande. The "Ghostly" Presence of Shakespeare in Mexican Cinema', *Revista Alicantina de Estudios Ingleses* 25 (2012), 97–112.

[54] See Alfredo Michel Modenessi, '"Is this the noble moor?": Re-viewing Othello through "Indian" (and Indian) Eyes', *Borrowers and Lenders, the Journal of Shakespeare and Appropriation* 7:2 (Fall 2012/Winter 2013): www.borrowers.uga.edu/490/display; and Burnett, *Shakespeare and World Cinema*, 89–124.

[55] See Alfredo Michel Modenessi, 'Of Shadows and Stones: Revering and Translating "the Word" Shakespeare in Mexico', *Shakespeare Survey* 54 (2001), 152–64

[56] Michael Billington's review provides a representative illustration: www.theguardian.com/stage/2012/jul/06/a-soldier-every-son-review.

politics.[57] While on one hand, 'a British audience was only able to scratch the surface of this … culturally specific story',[58] on the other, average Mexican audiences were no less befuddled. The Shakespearean roots of the play seemed scarcely meaningful to the audience who were equally confused by its complicated plot and overelaborate staging and production. Moreover, this ambitious but problematic project sought to portray and voice the history and ways of pre-Columbian natives by means of languages and bodies significantly alien to that very people, who have been long segregated from the society wherein the show originated.

Thus, although the P'urhepecha did find in Shakespeare an appropriate vehicle for self-expression, Moncada's play raised important questions regarding the feasibility of representing the native peoples without yielding to oversimplification, condescension or sheer cynicism. Is it possible to sufficiently understand—let alone share—their past and their present? Can their voices and minds be appropriated without offence (or at all) by artists, and for audiences, that, for purposes of self-understanding, have looked more to their colonial past and colonized present than to their pre-Columbian antecedents? Can their history be legitimately fictionalized by those who somehow, or however unwittingly partake in their tragic displacement and decimation? Questions of this kind, and many more, are frequently prompted, and at times answered, by the powerful theatre traditions of the region, often through diverse forms of Shakespearean tragedy.

BRAZIL

The transmission of Shakespearean tragedy in Brazil before the late 1700s is an obscure matter, and there is no evidence regarding the introduction of Shakespeare in print during colonial times. El Far's study of reading in Brazil considers that book ownership in colonial times was limited by censorship, as well as being a privilege of individuals who could afford high import costs. Control was imposed by the Inquisition, until the 'Real Mesa Censorial' (Royal Censorship Board) was created in 1769 to scrutinize all printed matter. The first printing facility was established in 1808, as King João VI moved to Brazil following Napoleon's invasion of Portugal in 1807. British ships escorted the Royal Family to Brazil, while British troops also supported Portugal by fighting the French until the end of the Napoleonic wars in 1814.[59] As Portugal carried on its political and commercial alliance with Great Britain, the Inquisition lost power, but censorship continued. According to El Far, the 'Mesa do Desembargo do Paço' (the Palace Release Board) was created with the mission of examining all printed matter entering Brazil from overseas, as well as all of the Royal Press items—totalling 1427 official documents, political papers and literary works

[57] A telling review by the otherwise sharp Mexican critc Olga Harmony is little more than descriptive and enumerative: http://www.jornada.unam.mx/2013/11/28/opinion/a08a1cul.

[58] Christie Carson, 'Review of *A Soldier in Every Son—The Rise of the Aztecs*', in Paul Edmonson, Paul Prescott, and Erin Sullivan, eds., *A Year of Shakespeare: Re-living the World Shakespeare Festival* (London, New Delhi, New York, and Sydney: Bloomsbury, The Arden Shakespeare, 2013), 255.

[59] Eugênio Vargas Garcia, *Cronología de las Relaciones Internacionales de Brasil* (Rio de Janeiro: Contraponto, 2005).

by 1822, when Independence was proclaimed. Although bonding between Portugal and Great Britain continued, and performances of Shakespearean plays may have been staged by the 1770s, French literature and drama prevailed.[60]

Nevertheless, comparativists believe that drawing on Shakespeare's tragedies was a strategy to avoid the conventions of French melodrama. João Roberto Faria, for example, follows Décio de Almeida Prado in acknowledging *Othello* as an inspiration for Gonçalves Dias in achieving moral and psychological characterization in his play *Leonor de Mendonça* (1847).[61] Censorship was still routine, enforced since 1843 by the *Conservatório Dramático Brasileiro* (Brazilian Dramatic Conservatory).[62] The late nineteenth-century interest in Shakespeare also appears to be related to François Victor Hugo's defence of Shakespeare in his 1865 literary biography which was widely read by Brazilian authors.[63]

Eugênio Gomes has covered the appropriation of Shakespearean tragedy in fiction, poetry, and essays by several Brazilian writers,[64] having detected extensive intertextuality in Machado de Assis's novels and short stories from 1876 on,[65] when the Italian actors Rossi and Salvini began performing *Hamlet* and *Othello* in Brazil.[66] According to Gomes, *Hamlet* was de Assis's favourite play, and quotations of the 'To be, or not to be' soliloquy in English and Italian were also frequent in his chronicles. From the stance of comparative studies, Marisa Lajolo and Regina Zilberman explored the appropriation of tragic female characters to convey non-romantic role models, and again verified that Shakespeare was a source for many a Brazilian novelist.[67] Lajolo and Zilberman mention José de Alencar's novel *Senhora*, of 1875, in which the main character, Aurélia, enjoys reading Shakespearean plays, even once imagining her own death as Desdemona's.[68] Such preferences contradicted the views of romantic authors admired by Alencar's audience, such as George Sand and Lord Byron, who were then thought to provide more elegant models for a feminine audience. Lajolo and Zilberman argue that Machado de Assis and José de Alencar avoid contradicting patriarchal standards of feminine behaviour by crafting their characters as

[60] Alessandra El Far, *O Livro e a leitura no Brasil* (Rio de Janeiro: Jorge Zahar, 2006). The majority of literary works launched by the Royal Press were translations from the French.

[61] Décio de Almeida Prado, *Teatro de Anchieta a Alencar* (São Paulo: Perspectiva, 1974); João Roberto Faria, *O Teatro na Estante* (Cotia: Ateliê Editorial, 1998).

[62] Regarding theatre censorship in Brazil, see Sonia Salomão Khède, *Censores de pincenê e gravata* (Rio de Janeiro: Codecri, 1981).

[63] François Victor Hugo, *William Shakespeare*, trans. Alvaro Gonçalves (Rio de Janeiro: Editora Aurora, n.d.). Hugo recalls the times when it was dangerous to translate Shakespeare, and reacting to the conservative French who questioned the mediation of foreign works, argues that translation is always necessary in order to promote the democratic transmission of texts. Machado de Assis's works often feature quotations from Hugo.

[64] Eugênio Gomes, *Shakespeare no Brasil* (Ministério da Educação e Cultura, Serviço de Documentação, 1961), with chapters on Gonçalves Dias, Agrário de Menezes, Álvares de Azevedo, Luís Delfino, Alberto de Oliveira, Olavo Bilac, Cruz e Sousa, Coelho Neto, and Rui Barbosa.

[65] Eugênio Gomes, *Shakespeare no Brasil*, 160.

[66] For a study in-depth, see Helen Caldwell, *The Brazilian Othello of Machado de Assis* (Berkeley and Los Angeles: University of California Press; London: Cambridge University Press, 1960). Rossi and Salvini were also among the Italian artists and companies that regularly performed Shakespeare throughout the Spanish-speaking areas.

[67] Marisa Lajolo and Regina Zilberman, *A Formação da Leitura no Brasil*, 3rd edn. (São Paulo: Ática, 1999), 253–4.

[68] José de Alencar, *Senhora*, in *Obra Completa*, vol. 1 (Rio de Janeiro: José Aguilar, 1959), 1186–7.

educated and polite women who can have smart conversations with gentlemen of their own class or of a higher status.[69] Shakespeare's plays remained a privilege of those who could afford to import books or had access to theatres.

Galante de Sousa mentions the introduction of *Othello*, *Macbeth*, and *Hamlet* in Rio de Janeiro, by Adolfo Ribelli's Spanish company, in 1838.[70] Nevertheless, until João Caetano dos Santos emerged as the first Brazilian actor, and became renowned for playing the roles of Othello and Hamlet,[71] French comedy was the most frequent genre in the rare existing accounts of the theatre seasons in economically prosperous cities such as Belém, Manaus, Porto Alegre, Recife, São Luís and Rio de Janeiro during the late 1900s.

The most detailed records of the transmission, reception, and stage history of the tragedies after they were translated into the variety of Portuguese spoken in Brazil are available at the 'Escolha o seu Shakespeare' database, which reveals that such translations began to appear only after the 1940s.[72] Barbara Heliodora Carneiro de Mendonça (1923-2015) stands out for having translated all of the Shakespearean tragedies. Translation history has been well covered by Márcia A. P. Martins, indicating that *Hamlet* has been the most translated play, with 13 versions since the first version by Tristão da Cunha, in 1933, and a unique version of Q1 by José Roberto O'Shea (2010).[73] A review of the theatrical productions in the aforementioned database suggests that directors relied on various translations of the tragedies. The choice of verse or prose versions always had clear consequences for casting and acting, reflecting how the erudite assumptions of purists and the colloquial choices of revisionists, ultimately shaped productions.[74] Many Brazilian actors ventured upon tragic roles after the 1950s, but none as consistently as their master Laurence Olivier. The eclectic Paulo Autran can be singled out for his varied approaches to Othello, Macbeth, Coriolanus, Prospero, and King Lear[75] The use of Shakespeare to discuss violence and power was particularly notable in Carlos Queiroz Telles's 1974 play *O Jogo de Poder*,[76] a collage of several tragedies and histories that passed censorship during the tough period of military rule. These policies lasted through 1988, when the New Constitution allowed for greater freedom of expression in the arts.[77]

[69] Lajolo and Zilberman, *A Formação*, 255.   [70] Galante de Sousa, *O Teatro no Brasil*, 183.

[71] José Roberto O'Shea, 'Early Shakespearean Stars Performing in Brazilian Skies: João Caetano and National Theater', in Kliman and Santos, eds., *Latin American Shakespeares*, 25–36.

[72] The chronology shows that among the first tragedies to gain Brazilian translations after *Hamlet* (1933) were: *Romeo and Juliet* (with 11 versions since 1940); *Macbeth* and *King Lear* (with 13 and 10 versions, respectively, since 1948); *Othello* (with 9 versions since 1956); *Julius Caesar* (with 6 versions since 1946). The database is an ongoing project coordinated by Dr Marcia Martins at PUC-Rio, available at www.dbd.puc-rio.br/shakespeare/pdfs/traducoes_publicadas_por_peca.pdf.

[73] Marcia Amaral Peixoto Martins, 'Shakespeare em tradução no Brasil', in Marlene Soares dos Santos and Liana de Camargo Leão, eds., *Shakespeare, sua época e sua obra* (Curitiba: Beatrice, 2008), 301–19.

[74] See Margarida Gandara Rauen, 'Shakespearean Performance Reviewing in Brazil', *Cahiers Élisabéthains*, Special Issue (2012), 99–104.

[75] For a biography of actor Paulo Autran (1922-2007), see http://enciclopedia.itaucultural.org.br/pessoa13509/paulo-autran.

[76] See Marco Antônio Guerra, *Carlos Queiroz Telles* (São Paulo: Annablume, 1993), 172–4.

[77] For a sample of such constraints, see Roberto Ferreira da Rocha, 'Hero or Villain: a Brazilian *Coriolanus* during the Period of the Military Dictatorship', in Kliman and Santos, eds., *Latin American Shakespeares*, 37–53.

Audiences have welcomed updating, encompassing both what Charles Marowitz calls 'recycling', and what Desmet and Sawyer treat as 'appropriation',[78] with successes such as the 'Galpão' Group production of *Romeo and Juliet*,[79] featured in the international season of the London Globe in 2012, as well as the 'Caixa Preta' Group's cultural translation *Syncretic Hamlet*, performed at the São Pedro Psychiatric Hospital of Porto Alegre.[80] The anthropophagic drive has indeed launched our Brazilian ways of staging tragedy in Great Britain, but we still deal with the challenges of cultural dependence, aptly captured by Silviano Santiago, when he analyses the position and the role of Latin American writers, 'living between the assimilation of the original model, that is, between the love and respect for works written in the past, and the need to produce a new text that challenges and often denies the former'.[81]

FINAL REMARKS

In post-colonial theory, the concept of 'verandas' reflects the ambivalence of frontier zones. A veranda, being at once *outside* a construction and yet part of it—*in touch* with it—signifies an arena of contact where interior and exterior spaces converge.[82] Likewise, while many writers, translators, and performance artists have appropriated Shakespeare's tragedies in Latin America and the Caribbean, the scenario points to a continued division between cultural dependence and transgression, as translators, critics, and artists position themselves. Ironically, Jacques Derrida, whose concept of deconstruction provided many post-colonial critics with theoretical support, claims that he himself 'would never have the audacity to write on *Romeo and Juliet* or anything at all of Shakespeare'[83] in a book where he makes room for discussing Shakespeare's *Romeo and Juliet*. Derrida's ironic position may be said to reflect the choice of artists who, rather than turning to Shakespeare exclusively for his presumed universal and timeless appeal, have updated his tragedies for radical productions and socially oriented artistic projects throughout Latin America and the Caribbean.

In our region, Shakespeare's 'universal and timeless' themes remain appealing and allow for successful runs whenever simple stagings of the translated versions of his plays

---

[78] Charles Marowitz, *Recycling Shakespeare* (London: MacMillan, 1991); Christy Desmet and Robert Sawyer, *Shakespeare and Appropriation* (London and New York: Routledge, 1999).

[79] Images of *Romeo and Juliet* by the 'Grupo Galpão' and several other acclaimed productions of all sub-genres are now available at the MIT Global Shakespeares database at http://globalshakespeares.mit.edu/brazil/#.

[80] Anna Stegh Camati, 'A dialética da transculturação do grupo Caixa-Preta: Hamlet sincrético em espaço cênico não convencional', in *Sociopoética* 6:1 (July–December 2010), 11–19.

[81] Margarida Rauen's translation of Silviano Santiago, *Uma Literatura nos Trópicos: ensaios sobre dependência cultural* (Rio de Janeiro: Rocco, 2000), 21.

[82] David Malouf, *12 Edmonstone Street* (London: Chatto & Windus, 1985), 20. Although this notion of 'porches' as contact zones relates to Malouf's experience in Australia, we find it relevant to the Latin American and Caribbean context.

[83] Jacques Derrida, *Acts of Literature* (New York and London: Routledge, 1992), 62–3. Silviano Santiago's reading strategy strongly relies on Derrida's deconstructive approach.

are produced. Nevertheless, artists who have appropriated, or cannibalized, the plays in order to reposition their contents from postcolonial and other critical stances have not only disturbed their audiences—or at least questioned, or made them question, their assumptions—but they have also invited viewing cultures as unsettled and unsettling constructs. Such shifts in the Latin American approaches to Shakespeare, and other formerly unquestioned paradigms, have contributed to reposition the so-called subaltern subjectivity in arenas where self and other can come fruitfully, although perhaps also uncomfortably together.

SELECT BIBLIOGRAPHY

Andrade, Oswald de, 'Cannibalist Manifesto', translated by Leslie Bary, *Latin American Literary Review* 19, no. 38 (July-December 1991), 35–47.

Campos, Haroldo de, *Novas: Selected Writings*, ed. Antonio Sergio Bessa and Odile Cisneros (Evanston: Northwestern University Press, 2007).

Forbes, Curdella, 'Shakespeare, Other Shakespeares and West Indian Popular Culture: A Reading of the Erotics of Errantry and Rebellion in *Troilus and Cressida*', *Small Axe* 5, 9:1 (March 2001), 44–69.

Harrawood, Michael, 'Shakespeare in the Caribbean: The Morant Bay Massacre, Jamaica, 1865', *Modern Language Quarterly* 65:2 (June 2004), 269–92.

Larsen, Neil, *Determinations: Essays on Theory, Narrative, and Nation in the Americas* (London and New York: Verso, 2001).

Martins, Márcia A. P., ed., *Visões e identidades brasileiras de Shakespeare* (Rio de Janeiro: Lucerna, 2004).

Mignolo, Walter D., *The Darker Side of Western Modernity: Global Futures, Decolonial Options* (Durham: Duke University Press, 2011).

O'Shea, José Roberto, ed., *Accents Now Known: Shakespeare's Drama in Translation*. Vol. 36 of *Ilha do Desterro* (Florianópolis: UFSC, Jan/June 1999).

Palti, Elías José, 'The Problem of "Misplaced Ideas" Revisited: Beyond the "History of Ideas" in Latin America', *Journal of the History of Ideas* 67:1 (January 2006), 149–79.

Rama, Angel, *Writing across Cultures. Narrative Transculturation in Latin America*, trans. David Frye (Durham: Duke University Press, 2012).

Resende, Aimara da Cunha, ed., *Brazilian Readings of Shakespeare* (Newark: University of Delaware Press, 2002).

Rodríguez-Monegal, Emir, 'The *Metamorphoses of Caliban*', *Diacritics* 7 (Fall 1977), 78–83.

Santos, Marlene Soares, and Liana de Camargo Leão, eds., *Shakespeare, sua época e sua obra* (Curitiba: Beatrice, 2008).

Schwarz, Roberto, 'Brazilian Culture: Nationalism by Elimination', trans. Linda Briggs, *New Left Review* 1:167 (January–February 1988), 77–90.

Shakespeare, William, *O primeiro 'Hamlet' in Quarto de 1603*, trans. José Roberto O'Shea (São Paulo: Hedra, 2010).

Shakespeare, William, *Teatro completo*, vol. 1: *Tragédias e Comédias Sombrias*, vol. 2: *Comédias*, trans. Barbara Heliodora C. de Mendonça (Rio de Janeiro: Aguilar, 2009).

Skidmore, Thomas E., Peter H. Smith, and James N. Green, *Modern Latin America*, 8th edn (Oxford: Oxford University Press, 2013).

Taylor, Lee Scott, 'The Purpose of Playing and the Philosophy of History: C. L. R. James' Shakespeare', *Interventions: International Journal of Postcolonial Studies* 1:3 (1999), 373–83.

Wade, Peter, Carlos López-Beltrán, Eduardo Restrepo, and Ricardo Ventura-Santos, eds., *Mestizo Genomics: Race Mixture, Nation, and Science in Latin America* (Durham: Duke University Press, 2014).

CHAPTER 53

SHAKESPEAREAN TRAGEDY IN INDIA

Politics of Genre—or how Newness Entered Indian Literary Culture

POONAM TRIVEDI

THE most striking aspect of tragedy as a genre and of the tragic as a view of life in India is that they were non-existent before the introduction of Western literature—and especially of Greek and Shakespearean tragedy—with the coming of colonialism in the late eighteenth century. Since neither the dominant Indian literary and dramatic theory as embodied in the *Natya Shastra* (second century BCE–second century CE), nor the drama emerging out of it, conceived of an ending that involved the defeat and death of the protagonist, Indian literatures were innocent of tragedy till almost the nineteenth century. Not that there was no cognizance of disaster, suffering, and death in Indian literature, or no depiction of fear, anger, or pathos; but the concept of tragic fall and waste of human potential was alien to a world view which was largely governed by the laws of karma, and in which the role of art was to represent and valorize the harmonization of man with the universe, of the individual with society. The idea of tragedy was thus new to Indian writers; it caught attention, stimulated debate and was pervasively influential, leaving its mark on all the literatures of the many Indian languages. And, needless to add, it was 'discovered' largely through the most popular example, Shakespeare.

The impact of Western literature, in general, and tragedy, in particular, forms an apt illustration of the tensions attendant when 'newness' enters an old literary tradition. This chapter charts the currents and counter-currents set off by the introduction of tragedy, examining the nature of the reception of tragedy, the extent of its transformative influence and the depth of its assimilation, explicating what may be called an 'act of cultural translation'.[1] All histories of Indian literature are agreed on this issue. Sisir Kumar Das, author of the most recent and authoritative multi-volume history, reserves

---

[1] Homi Bhabha, 'How Newness Enters the World', *The Location of Culture* (London: Routledge, 1994), 226.

the last word in his epilogue to volume 8 (1800–1910) for a discussion of the significance of tragedy:

> Among all the Western literary genres to which the Indian writer responded, tragedy was the most foreign and therefore his response to it was the most significant. Whatever be the reason, the absence of tragedy in Indian literature is a fact. The Indian acceptance of this genre was itself a challenge to the age-old dramatic norms. It is not that the Indian writer showed any special competence in grafting tragedy within the Indian literary fold. In fact, most of the tragedies written in this period were imitative and contrived. But a passionate response to an unknown world of experience, a world stern and tense, was certainly very significant.... a view of life that accommodates suffering and catastrophe and death as facts of experience without imposing philosophical significance on them.[2]

Earlier, in the same volume he had pinpointed the chief source of this influence: 'Shakespeare became the most popular European author in India, and also the most influential not only in the growth of an Indian theatre but also in the emergence of a tragic vision which made nineteenth century Indian literature distinct from earlier traditions.'[3]

Sanskrit drama, which flourished from 200 BCE–1000 CE, proscribed the depiction of death and dying—as it did other things, like sex—on stage. More crucial was its determining world-view, based on Hindu philosophy in which death is not a finality, but a mere pause in the cycle of rebirths, not an end but a new beginning, held as a cause not for grief, but even for celebration. Human beings were tested by the gods and subjected to pain and failure in this drama, to prove their mettle by their endurance, and they were rewarded and released from their suffering accordingly. In such a scenario, while there may be pathos, fear, and anger, they do not overcome or defeat the good. Thus in the most well-known Sanskrit play, *Abhijnana Shakuntalam*, by Kalidasa (c.400 CE) the young heroine, pregnant with child, is rebuked and rejected in public by her husband, the king, who is a victim of a curse and is stricken with amnesia for indulging in a secret marriage. She disappears—being mysteriously whisked away to heaven—and is given up for dead. The two are finally reunited only after seven years of separation and expiation. This trajectory of human fall and recuperation is more akin to Shakespeare's romances than his tragedies and a minor tradition in Indian literary studies of comparing *Shakuntalam* with *The Winter's Tale* and *The Tempest* has developed. Earlier Sanskrit plays like *Urubhangam* and *Karnabharam* by Bhasa (c.200 BCE), based on incidents from the *Mahabharata,* may be seen as presenting a 'tragic' design of defeat and pathos, focusing as they do not on the victors, but the vanquished—but again, only as a stepping stone to remorse and redemption.

Hence, while the Greek and Shakespearean models of tragic drama extol death and suffering as proof of man's heroic resistance to fate, traditional Indian drama provides an expiatory role for the endurance of pain and adversity. It is this contrast between the Western 'extrovert humanism' of tragedy with the 'introvert humanism' of Indian literature which attracted the Indian writers to the world-view of Western tragedy. The response of the best-known Indian poet, Rabindranath Tagore (1861–1941), is illustrative: he

---

[2] Sisir Kumar Das, *A History of Indian Literature*, vol. 8: *1800–1910 Western Impact: Indian Response* (New Delhi: Sahitya Akademi, 1991), 339–40.

[3] Sisir Kumar Das, *A History*, 110.

remarks on the 'frenzied fury of passion'[4] animating Shakespearean heroes as their most arresting feature. Commenting further (1917) on 'our initiation into English Literature', he again notes the

> wildness of intoxication [in it]. The frenzy of Romeo's and Juliet's love, the fury of King Lear's impotent lamentation, the all-consuming fire of Othello's jealousy, these were the things that aroused us to enthusiastic admiration. Our restricted social life, our narrower field of activity was hedged in with such monotonous uniformity that tempestuous feelings found no entrance;—all was as calm and quiet as could be. So our hearts naturally craved the life-bringing shock of the passionate emotion in English literature.[5]

Similarly, novelist and staunch nationalist Bankimchandra Chatterjee, (1838-94) chooses the images of the sea and the garden to make an extended comparison between *Othello* and *Abhijnana Shakuntalam* in a celebrated essay which acutely reveals the perceived difference in the essence of the two plays and the world-views animating them:

> This play (*Othello*) of Shakespeare's is like the ocean, Kalidasa's play is like the garden of Eden. You cannot compare the garden with the ocean. All that is beautiful, that is good-looking, that is fragrant, that is melodious, that is pleasing, that is delightful, are to be found in this heavenly garden, abundantly, massively, multitudinously, immeasurably. And all that is deep, unfathomable, fleeting and resounding, is to be found in this ocean. This unique play of Shakespeare's is like the ocean—turbulent with the swelling tides of the heart. It is tossed by the tempest of violent anger, malice and jealousy. Its intense force, loud noise, and play of the dangling waves on the one hand, and its sweet azure, its endless sprinkling of the particles of light, its splendors, its shadows, its gems, its soft music on the other – all this is rare in the world of poetry. That is why we say that Desdemona and Sakuntala cannot be compared ... belonging to different categories.[6]

The attraction however was mixed with unease. Orientalist scholarship, which initially took a great interest in Sanskrit literature and initiated an 'Oriental Renaissance' in Europe, was, despite its enthusiasm and erudition, coloured by a superior colonial attitude. The earliest commentaries inevitably exercised a comparative analysis, examining the features of this literature alongside the known Western models. Hence, it became imperative for Horace Hayman Wilson (1786-1860), the first English Indologist to extensively translate and comment on the classical Sanskrit literary corpus, to point to the absence of tragedy in Sanskrit drama. In chapter one of his *Select Specimens of the Theatre of the Hindus* (1827) he observes:

> Another important difference from the classical drama and from that of most countries, is the total absence of the distinction between Tragedy and Comedy. The Hindu plays confine themselves neither to the 'crimes nor to the absurdities of mankind'; neither 'to the momentous changes, nor lighter vicissitudes of life'; neither 'to the terrors of distress nor the gaieties of prosperity'.... They are invariably of a mingled web, and blend 'seriousness

---

[4] Rabindranath Tagore, 'The Message of the Forest,' in *The English Writings of Rabindranath Tagore*, vol. 2: *A Miscellany*, ed. S. K. Das (New Delhi: Sahitya Akademi, 1996), 388.

[5] Rabindranath Tagore, *Reminiscences*, 1917, qtd. in *Shakespeare on the Calcutta Stage: a Checklist*, ed. Ananda Lal and Sukanta Chaudhuri (Calcutta: Papyrus, 2001), 147.

[6] Bankimchandra Chatterjee, 'Sakuntala, Miranda and Desdemona', trans. Visvanath Chaterjee in *Shakespeare: The Indian Icon*, ed. Vikram Chopra (New Delhi: The Readers Paradise, 2011), 607.

and sorrow with levity and laughter'. ... The Hindus, in fact, have no Tragedy; a defect that subverts the theory that Tragedy necessarily preceded Comedy.[7]

This foregrounding by the colonial rulers of the total lack of a genre which was perceived in the Western literary tradition as the pinnacle of literary achievement created a flutter among Indian intellectuals, provoking a counter-current in which the admiration for tragedy was tinged with ambivalence, instigating defensiveness and even a resistance to tragedy. It is well documented that the introduction of Western literature had stimulated a revival of their own classical literature among Indians as a counter to colonial hegemony. But when a lacuna was pointed out in the great ancient tradition, considerable debate arose; Indian writers and critics felt impelled into making ingenious arguments to either justify this lack or fault it by proving the pre-existence of tragedy in the classical drama. A politics of the genre resulted, which reflected a tussle between Orientalist constructivism and nationalist unease in addressing this lacuna,[8] affording a singular instance of colonial containment and native resistance. Critics argued that the proscriptions of the *Natya Shastra* had emerged to purify existing stage practice: consequently it could be assumed that death and the tragic had at one time been frequently staged—hence the necessity of the proscription.[9] Others asserted that plays like *Shakuntalam*, too, could be seen as tragic, but that the Indian notion of tragedy was different from the Greek.[10] Many, of course, cited the philosophy of Karma and the Hindu belief in rebirth as another reason for this lack of a tragic ending in Sanskrit drama.[11] Indian writers seemed to bend over backwards in their efforts to negotiate this so-called 'lack' of the tragic, as determined by Orientalist scholarship. The extent and depth of this colonial imposition/ inflexion/ indoctrination, especially in the Sanskrit scholarly sphere, is seen when, as late as 1974, Sanskrit scholar, critic and teacher G. K. Bhatt, in his book *Tragedy and Sanskrit Drama*—after a detailed discussion of the development of Western tragedy from the Greeks to Shakespeare that contrasts it with Sanskrit drama—sums up his investigation, conceding along with the Orientalists, that 'From a purely aesthetic point of view, the absence of a *formal* tragedy is itself the tragedy of Sanskrit drama; a tragedy that was inevitable.'[12] It took the post-colonial confidence of a Professor of English, V. Y. Kantak, to question this automatic application of the Aristotelian yardstick to measure all drama of every place and period, wittily quipping that to lament the lack of tragedy in Sanskrit drama is to 'commiserate [with] Sophocles for being but a feeble approach to Shakespeare and condole with Aeschylus for his total want of interest in the Elizabethan psychology of the Malcontent–hero!'[13]

    [7] Horace Hayman Wilson, *Select Specimens of the Theatre of the Hindus* (Calcutta: V. Holcroft, 1827), 11.
    [8] See V. B. Tarkeshwar, 'Translating Tragedy into Kannada: Politics of Genre and the Nationalist Elite', in *Decentering Translation Studies: India and Beyond*, ed. Judy Wakabayshi and Rita Kothari (Amsterdam: John Benjamins, 2009), 57–73.
    [9] A. R. Krishna Shastri, *Samskrita Nataka* (Sanskrit Drama) (Mysore: Prasaranga, 1937) cited in Tarkeshwar, 'Translating Tragedy', 63.
    [10] D. R. Bendre, 1974, cited in Tarakeshwar, 'Translating Tragedy', 63.
    [11] P. B. Acharya, *The Tragicomedies of Shakespeare, Kalidasa and Bhavabhuti* (New Delhi: Meherchand Lachmandas Publications, 1978), 7.
    [12] G. K. Bhat, *Tragedy and Sanskrit Drama* (Bombay: Popular Prakashan, 1974), 107.
    [13] V. Y. Kantak, 'Bharata and the Western Concept of Drama', in *Classical Literary Theory and Criticism*, ed. A.P. Dani and V. M. Madge (Delhi: Pencraft International, 2001), 31.

Despite this ambivalent reception, however, tragedy as a genre—and, especially, Shakespearean tragedies as examples—attracted extraordinary attention. Though it was the *Comedy of Errors* which was the first Shakespeare play to be translated into most Indian languages, the four great tragedies followed in quick succession: *Romeo and Juliet*(1864), *Hamlet, Macbeth*(1874), and *Othello*(1875) were translated into Bengali, *Macbeth*(1881), *Romeo and Juliet, Othello,* and *Hamlet*(1883) into Kannada; *Othello* was translated and performed in Marathi in 1867, as was *Macbeth* in 1893.Translations in Hindi came a little later: *Macbeth* in 1893, *Othello* in 1894, *Hamlet* in 1898, and *Lear* in 1906.

Most of these, prepared for the theatre in the first instance, were adaptations which specially modified the tragic ending to make the plays acceptable to public taste. As matter of fact, initially, there was a popular prejudice against the staging of tragedy since the staging of death was considered inauspicious: *Kritibilas* (1853) the first Bengali play written on the western model, and influenced by *Hamlet*, could not be staged. A few years later, in 1861, Michael Madhusudan Datta's tragic play, *Krishna Kumari*, also based on the western model could not be performed because of objections from members of his patron's family.[14] Hence, a version of *Romeo and Juliet* in Kannada, *Ramavarma Lilavati* (1889) by Anandrao, ended with a prayer to the gods (like the mangalacharan in folk theatre) to restore the young lovers to life. Whereupon god Vishnu descended, the lovers revived and the play ended in a marriage. Predictably, this was one of the most popular plays at the time and several well-known actors and companies vied to perform it.[15] Similarly, another Kannada adaptation of *Othello, Surasenacaritre* (1895) also had a happy ending.

The influence of Shakespearean tragedy, however, was pervasive. Apart from the translations, new plays on the Shakespearean tragic model were written. Bengali and Marathi theatres, given their greater proximity to the colonial centres of power and performance were the first to respond. The first Marathi 'modern' play, *Thorale Madhavrao Peshwe*, by V. J. Kirtane (1861, staged 1865), about the death of the Peshwa ruler and the death by sati of his wife, was both historical and tragic. It borrowed the structure of Shakespearean drama and in contravention of Sanskrit dramaturgy depicted Madhavrao's death on stage. It was also a nationalist undertaking to set right the negative view of Marathas as brigands propagated by the British. The sutradhar (Chorus) at the beginning of the play tells his audience:

> Dear Listeners! Lend me your ears.... I intend transporting these good people to the Maratha Durbar to give them a glimpse of its circumstances.... Why should I take them to a place where people from other isles hold command, where kings no more than parrots in their cages, do not recognize even the shadow of their past supremacy? Rather, I will take them to the elder Madhavraosaheb Peshwa, who looked after his subjects as if they were his own children ... Oh Vidushak, don't you believe that the Maratha empire was nothing but plundering.[16]

---

[14] Sisir Kumar Das, *A History*, 8: 120.

[15] Vijaya Guttal, 'Translation and Performance of Shakespeare in Kannada', in *India's Shakespeare: Translation, Interpretation and Performance* ed. Poonam Trivedi and Dennis Bartholomeusz (Delhi: Pearson, 2005), 98.

[16] Quoted by Shanta Gokhale in *Playwright at the Centre: Marathi Drama from 1843 to the Present* (Cacutta, Seagull Books, 2000), 12.

In Gujarati, Ranchodbhai Udayram, called the father of Gujarati drama, and a devotee of Shakespeare, wrote *Lalita Dukh Darsak Natak* ('Play Displaying Grief of Lalita', 1866), producing one of the earliest social reform plays as a tragedy of a Hindu girl trapped in an ill-suited marriage. This was so well received that there followed a series of such plays on social reform issues, all inspired by Shakespeare. Acceptance of this new tragic genre happened gradually: initially there was appreciation, but some hesitation to fully adopt the form, frequently resulting in a quick and rough, melodramatic approximation. This was followed by a period of critical negotiation and valuation—often via the traditional rasa aesthetics of Sanskrit literary theory which measured the merit of all art, but especially drama, through its embodiment of emotion—and only after almost a generation was there full acceptance. Crucially, it provided a new space for the expression of social and political concerns. The same process was repeated in most of the different language cultures, given a leeway of a couple of decades.

In Marathi drama, it has been noted that 'Tragedy was perceived to be a welcome addition to the [received] dramatic forms', prompting a discussion of the new genre in Marathi theatre journals. A commentary on the play *Thorale Madhavrao Peshwe* approved this new practice because it 'imitates life, which is a mixture of happiness and sorrow'—though only with the qualification that 'the hero, whose tragic end is portrayed ... must not commit a despicable act'.[17] The nature of heroism, of evil and villainy, as well as the function of drama itself, were all debated. Social-reform plays, which reflected such issues as the remarriage of widows and child marriage, had become very popular, and were enjoined not to portray a comic harmonizing end, but to choose the more appropriate tragic ending because 'virtue is not easily rewarded, and if it is shown to be so, it is less effective'.[18] Towards the end of the nineteenth century, Krishnaji Prabhakar Khadilkar's play, *Savai Madhavarava ca Mrtyu* (1895), which was based on historical figures of the Maratha royal family, was consciously modelled, not on the histories but on the tragedies. A Hamlet-like, mad, melancholic prince and an Iago-like scheming minister became the models for the hero and villian and a change of perspective on 'characterization' was observed. The older typology of the *Natya Shastra* was now giving way to a greater psychological individualization among the characters: 'the newer plays seem to move towards a notion of character with some interiority. There is reason to believe that Shakespeare's tragedies played at least a small role in this transition.'[19] By 1927, plays by Ram Ganesh Gadkari (1885-1919) took this influence further: his villains do not always reveal their motivations or show consistency—something that was ascribed to Shakespearean influence, but that was also critiqued as incomplete portrayal.[20]

In Kannada literature, the acceptance and assimilation of tragedy took a similar trajectory, with some crucial variants. The period between 1920 and 1950, especially, affords a glimpse of the 'interesting cultural maneuvers undertaken by different groups of people in responding to the genre of tragedy' as T. S. Satyanath observes in an essay on the emergence of tragedy in Kannada Literature.[21] He details how around 1926 prominent

[17] Aniket Jaaware and Urmila Bhirdikar, 'Shakespeare in Maharastra, 1892-1927: A Note on a Trend in Marathi Theatre and Theatre Criticism', in *The Shakespeare International Yearbook*. vol. 12: *Shakespeare in India*, sp. guest ed. Sukanta Chaudhuri (Farnham, Surrey: Ashgate, 2012), 44.
[18] Ibid., 46.   [19] Ibid., 48.   [20] Ibid., 50.
[21] T. S. Satyanath, 'Translation and Reception as a Cultural Process: On the Emergence of Tragedy in Kannada Literature', *Translation Today* 1:1 (March 2004), 92.

playwright B. M. Srikantia, attempting to foreground the genre of tragedy, wrote two tragic plays which adapted mythological stories from the Indian epics to the format of Greek tragedy, observing the unities and the rules of plot and characterization. This experiment, which highlighted tragic elements in the epics, as well as working within a new literary genre, was largely welcomed. However, Srikantia's necessary reinterpretation of the villain/negative characters, Duryodhana and Ashwatthama, and their elevation into tragic heroes met with serious criticism. Not only did critics feel that there was no moral ground for investing these characters with a tragic dignity, but they argued that the process had also undermined the position of the virtuous figures.[22] Others were more forthright: 'Can we consider as right the greatness (*udattate*) given to Ashwattthama and his heroic death to be moral necessities of the play? … Has the radiance of the villains like Duryodhana and Iago become the theme of poetry (*kavya-vastu*) anywhere else in the world?'[23] Nevertheless, this triggered a trend and other writers followed suit transforming many of the *pratinayakas* (negative characters) of the epics into sympathetic heroes with a tragic intensity and dignity. Srikantia defended his re-creations by pointing to the evidence of medieval Jaina epics in Kannada which took a revisionary view of the main villainous characters like Ravana, the demon king of *Ramayana*, humanizing and elevating him—a feature he had pointed out earlier in 1923 in an article titled 'A tragic Ravana'. He also referred to Shakespeare in his defence, saying that there are 'no black and white saints and devils' in his plays, and citing Milton's sympathy for Satan.[24] So keen was he to incorporate the tragic in Kannada literature that he was the first to coin a name for it, 'Rudra Naataka', saying that 'Rudra (Shiva) … the precursor of theatre and other arts, is similar to Dionysus in many respects …'. A considerable debate took place in critical discourse, not only on the merits of tragedy, searching for tragic elements in ancient and medieval literature, but also demonstrating how the newly written and produced tragic plays should be understood.[25] The novel—which was also a new literary form introduced through colonialism in India and which, according to some literary historians, had a more far-reaching influence—interestingly did not stir such debate or ruffle so many feathers. Srikantia's stirring speech towards the latter part of his life, in 1941, shows us why, as it also affirms the new acceptance of tragedy: 'What is wrong if now we stage, write or translate (tragedy)? Don't you think that a new radiation, a new experience, a new joy emerges out of tragedy? … If we don't see death on the stage and instead hear it from a messenger, isn't it then also inauspicious? … Fear of tragedy is like fear of children towards dark—only in dark do we see pole stars.'[26]

In the north, the idea of the tragic was more easily absorbed. Bhartendu Harishchandra (1850–85), considered the father of modern Hindi drama, was the first to negotiate Western drama and its conventions in his writings. He had had the benefit of a formal education in English, the effect of which is seen in his seminal essay-cum-treatise, *Natak* ('Drama', 1883), in which he puts forward his preference for a dramaturgy that modifies the classical Sanskrit rules with Western practices, strongly advocating a natural composition

---

[22] D. R. Bendre, cited by Satyanath, 'Translation and Reception', 98.
[23] K. D. Kurtukoti, cited in Satyanath, 'Translation and Reception', 100.
[24] B. M. Srikantia, cited in Tarkeshwar, 'Translating Tragedy into Kannada', 64.
[25] Satyanath, 'Translation and Reception', 104–5.
[26] Srikantia, cited in Tarkeshwar, 'Translating Tragedy into Kannada', 69.

'*swabhavikrachana*', holding a mirror up to nature, as it were, in drama. Significantly, in this essay, while enumerating the types of drama, he includes *Vijogantanatak* ('unhappy-ending play') defining it as one in which the death of the hero and heroine forms part of a calamitous catastrophe. The tragic was now being understood as involving not merely the death of the protagonists, but also unmerited disaster.[27] Bhartendu also expresses fulsome praise for Shakespeare in this essay, acknowledging him as 'a world famous poet who has won over everyone with his sweetness of expression'.[28] He goes on to describe Shakespeare's prowess as a combination of unique poetic and story-telling skills. He was also one of the first to translate Shakespeare, rendering *The Merchant of Venice* into Hindi in 1888, Indianizing the original's names and allusions, but preserving its story to contemporize the play's religious conflict. Bhartendu was attempting to create a new structural dynamic for drama, both aesthetic and political. For him theatre was an instrument for social regeneration and political sensitization and he harnessed Western conventions like the act/scene structure and the use of realistic scenery, as well as making use of tragic form to modify tradition and suit the needs of the time. Most of the eighteen plays he wrote overtly or allegorically criticize or satirize the colonial situation. None illustrates his purpose as clearly as *Bharat Durdasha* ('The Deplorable Condition of Bharat/India') written in 1876 in which the symbolic figure of Bharat, beggared and enfeebled, barely able to stand with the aid of a stick, is confronted with a series of misfortunes that satirize aspects of the political milieu, including alien rule, the treachery of collaborators, disloyalty, and the dumping of foreign goods. But at the end of the play it is not Bharat but Bharat Bhagya (Bharat's Fate) who commits suicide, stabbing himself at the end of a long and gloomy monologue encapsulating his hopeless future. Another play which was specifically termed a 'tragedy' by Bhartendu was *Nil Devi* (1880) which dramatized the story of a Rajput queen who avenges a Muslim chieftain's treacherous slaughter of her husband, by smuggling herself into the enemy camp. Disguised as a dancing girl she seduces the chieftain and then beheads him. Justice achieved, she commits sati on the funeral pyre of her husband. This play—emerging out of a turn to the past precipitated by the censorship of the Dramatic Performances Act (promulgated by the British government in 1876) which drastically restricted freedom of expression on stage—valorized the 'tragic' ending as a heroic sacrifice for the country.

However, the play which was most suggestive of Western, specifically Shakespearean, influence in its characterization, mood, and atmosphere was *Satya Harishchandra* (1875). This is the well-known story of a king famed for keeping his word and truthfulness at any cost who is so severely tested by the gods that he is forced to give up his kingdom, sell his wife and child into bondage and enslave himself at the cremation grounds before he can earn a reprieve. It is in the psychological elaboration of the king's and queen's suffering and their adverse fate that the Shakespearean sense of unease and foreboding, and echoes of Hamlet's philosophizing on life and death emerge. Surrounded by the images of death and dying at the cremation grounds, the king reflects:

> Ah, observe that head there, which was anointed once with mantras, adorned with the nine-gemmed-crown, which prided itself such that it regarded even Indra as inferior, which was

[27] Bharatendu Harishchandra, *Bharatendu Samagra* (Collected Works of Bharatendu Harishchandra), ed. Hemant Sharma (Varanasi: Hindi Pracharak Sansthan, 1988), 558.
[28] Ibid., 579.

filled with the ambition to conquer great kingdoms; today it has become the foot-ball of pishachas, and people disdain to touch it even with the tip of their toes. (*Granthavali* 1: 289)[29]

Poet and dramatist, Jaishankar Prasad (1889-1937) was the next prominent figure in Hindi to show the pervasive influence of Western literature, and especially of Shakespeare, in his dramas: copies of the complete works of Shakespeare and of Plutarch's lives were found in his library.[30] Between 1910 and 1933 he wrote 13 plays and discussed his views on theatre and dramaturgy extensively in his prefaces to the works. Like Bhartendu, he too was concerned with evolving an Indian frame for theatre, one that would blend the indigenous poetic ideal of *rasa* with the realism of the West. By now the plays of George Bernard Shaw and Ibsen had also acquired a following among Indian readers and audiences. But Prasad condemned blind imitation: in a late essay 'Rangmanch' (Theatre 1936), he writes:

> How will we evolve in the same sequential way, if we look just at the West's 'today'? ... the future is made by keeping the past and present in sight, we should not have one-dimensional aims in literature.... The West has also not found the new by taking leave of all else that it [once] possessed. [31]

In his dramaturgy he gave up many of the conventions of Sanskrit drama, like benediction, prologue, fool, sententiae, and character typology. In the treatment of character he evolved a new intense poetic style based as much on the inner truth of pain and agony as the outward reality of conflict. Prasad was also a pioneer of the Chhayavad (Romanticism) movement in Hindi poetry which was a revolt against the earlier formalism and didacticism. The new poetry was characterized by a subjective restlessness and longing, both melancholy and sensuous, protesting against the existing order. This emotional intensity found its way into Prasad's plays too. As Mahesh Anand has pointed out,

> There is no doubt that in plot development, multilevel scenic visualization, construction of theatrical flexibility, the use of dramatic conflict in establishing the individual identity of characters etc, he [Prasad] has derived inspiration from the plays of Shakespeare. The mode of depiction of the inner conflict in the life of characters in happy or unhappy circumstances seems influenced by Shakespeare. Still he does not push his characters into the anomaly of implacable fate like Shakespeare. The reason for this difference is the world view held by the Indian mind. Furthermore, questions of national unity and independence were of vital importance to Prasad. That is why his characters while struggling with political contradictions fight for the good of society at large apart from their individual purposes. This is where the inner conflict and struggle of his characters can be clearly distinguished from that of Shakespeare's characters.[32]

An early play, *Prayashchita* (Repentence 1914), about the self-destruction of a brave Rajput, Jaichand, through jealousy of his rival Prithviraj, shows several Shakespearean influences

---

[29] First pointed out by Vasudha Dalmia, *Poetics, Plays and Performances: the Politics of Modern Indian Theatre* (New Delhi: Oxford University Press, 2006), 47.

[30] Jagdish Prasad Misra, *Shakespeare's Impact on Hindi Literature* (New Delhi: Munshiram Manoharlal, 1970), 109.

[31] Mahesh Anand, *Jayashankar Prasad: Rangdrishti* (His Vision of Drama) (New Delhi: National School of Drama, 1998), 147.

[32] Mahesh Anand, *Jayashankar Prasad*, 25.

and divergences. It opens with two 'Vidyadharies' (wise women) like the Weird Sisters who however, advise the hero to repent for his sin; it has the sighting of the ghost of the dead queen as a turning point, and it shows the hero going mad due to the pricking of his conscience. In the end, Othello-like, he suddenly commits suicide, drowning himself in the river Ganga. Even though this play has been called the first real tragedy in Hindi, criticism has judged it an experimental piece lacking the severe soul-searching of Shakespearean tragic heroes. Prasad's major plays which are also historical dramas take a cue from Shakespeare to imaginatively recreate the conflicts of the past to comment on the present, and are more successful in their deployment of Shakespearean characteristics. They depict protagonists fraught with inner conflicts, who undergo huge suffering, but at the end repent and reform leading to harmonization. His plays cannot strictly be called tragedies, but as J. P. Misra, in his book *Shakespeare's Impact on Hindi Literature*, has put it, they are 'very much in the vein of Shakespearean tragedy and indeed at one moment it appears as if the play (*Skandgupta*) would end tragically'.[33] Echoes of *Lear* are to be found in the theme of filial ingratitude in *Ajatashatru* (1922), of *Hamlet* in Skandgupta's reluctance to rule (1928) and of *Titus* and *Henry V* in the political conflicts and revenges of the epical *Chandragupta* (1931).[34] The tragic ethos is mined for passionate intensity and political resonance rather than for the sacrifice of death. However, as with Bhartendu, so with Prasad, apart from some literal echoes, 'Shakespeare's influence ... is subterranean' as Vasudha Dalmia has observed. 'It is present much more as a view of history, character and morality as interpreted by the Romantic poets and nineteenth century criticism, and further propagated in British India through his decisive place in the colonial educational curriculum.'[35]

The full acceptance and incorporation of Shakespearean tragedy, however, came only after independence in 1947. The quater centenary of 1964 provided an occasion for stock-taking, as well as stimulating renewed engagement. This is best exemplified in the faithful verse translations of the four major tragedies produced by the foremost Hindi poet Harivansha Rai Bachchan between 1957 and 1972. Bachchan's prefaces to these translations show his—and by implication the literary culture's—identification with the issues of the plays. In the preface to his translation of *Hamlet*(1969) he strongly empathises with Hamlet's dilemma, calls him an 'incomplete' man and describes his tragedy as 'a conflict between the individual and the world, between the atomic and cosmic in which the individual and the atomic breaks down.... He (Hamlet) finds the world dark; he wants to lighten it up but gets consumed by his own inner fire.'[36] In the preface to his last translation, *King Lear*(1972), Bachchan adds a comment on tragedy which clearly shows the Indian assimilation of the genre. He begins by acknowledging that tragedy came to Indian literature from the West, that Hindi criticism did not even have a term for the 'unhappy-ending play',—the term 'Trasdi' being coined from tragedy. He then remarks that the genre changed from the Greeks to Shakespeare, and that 'infact it has come so close to the reality of life that unless we are totally entrenched in our own view of life, it cannot

---

[33] Misra, *Shakespeare's Impact on Hindi Literature*, 137.
[34] Misra, *Shakespeare's Impact on Hindi Literature*, 137.
[35] Vasudha Dalmia, *Poetics, Plays and Performance*, 49.
[36] Harivansh Rai Bachchan, Preface, *Hamlet* 1st edition 1969, *Bachchan Rachavali* (Bachchan Collected Works) (Delhi: Rajkamal Prakashan, 2006), 251.

be unacceptable to us'. He goes on to define Shakespearean tragedy from a non-denominational but moral perspective, arguing that it is of value in negotiating the vicissitudes of life. He says that it is a form which shows that

> life is fulfilled through the process of completion with the struggle of good with evil ... Tragedy does not happen with the destruction of the bad but with the destruction of the good. The good has to pay a price in its progress towards fulfillment. But one difference which can be seen in all tragedies is that while the bad only looks at its own helplessness during the moments of its destruction, the good, in one form or the other, is not unaware of the significance of its sacrifice. Even this is enough to lift tragedy above unrelieved sorrow, despondence, misery and suffering.[37]

The genre of tragedy in India, it is clear, has traversed a considerable distance since the early days when it was seen as failing to embody the necessary moral justice Sanskrit literary theory requires of great literature. Indeed the cultural comparativist David Damrosch, reflecting on the challenge posed by the literary history of India, with its over three-thousand-year-old traditions and twenty-two currently recognized languages, has been prompted to ask whether 'the Sanskrit cosmopolis [has] been succeeded by a Shakespearean cosmopolis'?[38]

Shakespeare today remains the most widely read and performed foreign author in India both in English and in translation. His plays and poems continue to challenge students in schools and colleges, as well as actors, both amateur and professional. Performing Shakespeare is seen as a measuring rod of a group's dramatic capability and excellence. The major tragedies are the most favoured, *Othello* being the most popular, with *Romeo and Juliet* coming a close second.

If we have to isolate one Indian instance of a typically Shakespearean 'darkness', of the remorseless reflow or return of the moral universe which seemed to have been put in abeyance, of the overtaking of the protagonists by nemesis, we have to turn, paradoxically, to subaltern folk literature and its ancient wisdom. It is best experienced in a short award-winning Hindi film *Parinati* (1989) directed by Prakash Jha, known for his politically radical films. Based on a Rajasthani folk tale recovered by writer Vijay Dan Detha, it tells of a lowly potter couple who so impress a business man with their hard work that he puts them in charge of an inn which he establishes in a remote part of Rajasthan to provide overnight stops for travelers traversing the desert. They have a young lively son who catches the eye of a rich (but childless) couple who stop for the night at their inn. The guests persuade the parents to send their son with them for a proper education in the town. The inn-keeper and his wife reluctantly agree, but after the child has left, they find themselves bereft and

---

[37] Bachchan, Preface to *King Lear*, 1st edition 1972, *Bachchan Rachavali* 383.

[38] David Damrosch, 'Literary History in a Global Age: The Legacy of Sisir Kumar Das' in *Interdisciplinary Alter-Natives in Comparative Literature* ed. E.V. Ramakrishnan, Harish Trivedi and Chandra Mohan (New Delhi: Sage, 2013), 39. Damrosch is juxtaposing two recent literary histories of India in this essay: those by Sisir Kumar Das and by Sheldon Pollock, *The Language of the Gods in the World of Men: Sanskrit, Culture and Power in Premodern India*, (Berkeley: University of California Press, 2006) where Pollock argues that at the beginning of the first millennium CE Sanskrit was transformed into a more broadly available language which spread and had far reaching implications not only in India but throughout Asia—hence Damrosch's witty equation of Sanskrit with the spread and acceptance of Shakespeare.

sorrowful. They feel that had they not been so poor they would not have had to send away their only son. They then decide that the only way to get back their child is to make money. The only way they can do so, however, is to quietly put away forever the rich guests who stop at their inn. Years pass and they await the return of their grown-up son. One day they learn that he had come, a few days earlier, but incognito, to surprise them. To their horror they realize that their last guest-victim was a handsome and wealthy young man—their own son. The film ends with a shot of a knocking on the door of the inn: the doors don't open, nor does anyone emerge, except streams of blood which slowly start oozing out under the door. The effect is reminiscent of DeQuincey's comment on the knocking on the gate in *Macbeth* after Duncan's murder as a return of the real, 'the human has made its reflux upon the fiendish'.[39] Folk art, with its freedom and flexibility from prescriptive traditions, reserves a space for the alternative and is often marked by a wry ironic take on life that makes it better able to absorb the new.

Nonetheless, it is from the stream of adaptations of Shakespeare that the more creative versions of tragedy make their mark in India. The tragic form, migrating to India under the aegis of colonialism, could not and did not produce the kind of radical mongrelisation or hybridity that Salman Rushdie valorises as a marker of the post-colonial condition. Adaptations did not reject the unhappy ending per se, but added an ameliorating postscript, as it were, conducive to a larger harmonization—as, for example, in the early versions of *Romeo and Juliet* in which the lovers revive and are married. These tragi-comic versions, an encapsulation of Indian philosophic world-views and a concession to public taste, did not challenge or subvert the meaning and value of the tragic. The depictions of suffering and death on stage in the early plays were, as seen above, nationalist appropriations of the tragic genre to present political dissent on the public stage. Thus tragedy went through a tangential process in India: from curiosity to consolidation, accommodation but not assimilation; it has remained representative of a separate and different line of thought. While the conventions and structure of the Shakespearean tragic play were freely borrowed, the plays that resulted lacked the terrible denouements and accompanying sense of waste characteristic of the originals.

Some adaptations, however, added a new dimension which may be seen as a cultural translation, or even a 'cultural contamination' since they inserted an alien element deriving from Hindu philosophy in their negotiation with the tragic. This is the interpolation of the trope of a 'saving feminine' figure, which is to be glimpsed in what Homi Bhabha has termed the space of the 'interstitial' as the location of the new, which is embedded in this particularly Indian variant in the re-working of Shakespearean tragedy. Such re-workings often incorporate a symbol/image of the avenging female, inspired from the figure of the Hindu goddess Kali, an icon of power and an avenging mother goddess, popularly imaged as dark and fearsome: with her red bulging eyes and lolling tongue, garlanded with human skulls and flourishing a bloodstained sword and other weapons in her many hands, Kali represents Shakti, the primordial creative force. Unlike Medea, this version of the heroic feminine is not made of cunning and contrivance, but contains aspects of the masculine, taking up arms for the redemption of humankind. According to

---

[39] Thomas De Quincey, 'On the knocking at the gate in *Macbeth*', *Macbeth*, Arden edition, ed. K. Muir (London: Methuen, 1966), 60.

Hinduism Kali symbolizes eternal time and hence she both gives life and destroys it. She also represents the supreme realization of truth. In the Indian variants of Shakespearean tragedy, the Kali-like saving/avenging female figure not only establishes moral order but also provides a space for a gender reversal and restitution. It is interesting to see how, recurrently, Indian writers and artists have recourse to the Kali figure to enhance the moral equilibrium at the end of their versions of the tragedies. One of the early adaptations of *Hamlet* in Kannada, *Raktakshi* ('The Blood-Eyed Girl', 1932) by prominent poet and critic Kuvempu, turns Ophelia into an avenging figure towards the end. When Ophelia hears of the death of her beloved, the Prince, she disguises herself as a madwoman in rags and sets out to seek vengeance, transforming herself into a 'blood-eyed girl', berating the heavens and calling upon the gods to aid her. With Hamlet already killed, it is Ophelia/Rudrambe, who emerges at the end as the instrument of justice.

This trope of an avenging feminine figure is more persuasively realized at the end of *Omkara*, the film of *Othello* by Vishal Bharadwaj (2006) when Omi/Othello learns the truth about Dolly/Desdemona's fidelity from Indu/Emilia but refuses to kill Langda/Iago. Instead it is Indu/Emila who suddenly transforms into an avenging fury, picks up a sickle, rushes at her husband and slashes his neck, completing in a manner the circle of moral restitution with the killing of the villain. After this there is nothing left for her, except to drown herself in the courtyard well. Other films like, Prakash Jha's *Damul* (1985, Hindi) also have recourse to the same trope: at the end of *Damul*, the submissive wife of a poor farmer, who has been harassed to death by a wily landlord, suddenly stands tall, picks up a sickle and beheads him. *Karmayogi* (2012), a Malayalam film version of *Hamlet*, has Gertrude surprising us by turning the tables on Claudius during the duel scene, when she catches hold of his anagvastram (a long ceremonial drape over the shoulders) and tries to strangle him. A much performed adaptation of *King Lear* by Tamil writer Indira Parthasarathy, *Iruthiattam* ('The Final Game', 2001)[40] underlines this trope of the saving feminine: neither Cordelia nor Lear dies at the end. She returns to save her father from the fury of the storm and both forgive each other. A student performance of *Lear* at a Delhi University women's college (2013), turned both the play and this trope inside-out in a gesture of feminist protest. It framed scenes from the play within a prologue and an epilogue deriving from the *danse macabre*: it began with three female dancers dressed in black lycra, with drum and brass music, and, as described in a review, with 'a voiced collage of every abusive curse made against women in *King Lear* [which] reverberated around the auditorium. Spinning and falling, the dancers attempted to fly against an insurmountable male-strom [sic] of rage, moving as if every word caused them physical pain. The voices got louder and louder until the overlapping of 'tigers, not daughters' and 'better thou hast not been born!' And 'Fie! Fie! Fie! Fie!' became unbearable to hear.'[41] It ended with the dancers reeling under the same chorus of abuse, leaving the Fool with the last word 'the rain it raineth everyday'.[42] Such are the 'new' deflections/ interpretations produced in the interstitial space of the contact between Indian and

---

[40] See CD authored and published by Poonam Trivedi on 'Shakespeare in India: *King Lear*' for a discussion and clips. Available at poonamtrivedi2@gmail.com.

[41] Preti Taneja, 'Lear's Indian Daughters', *Blogging Shakespeare*, 28 March 2013.

[42] Performance by students of Indraprastha College for Women, University of Delhi on the occasion of an international conference on 'Revisiting Shakespeare in Indian Literatures and Cultures', 7–9 March 2013, conceived and directed by Poonam Trivedi.

Western forms of the tragic: in them woman, in the guise of Kali, is celebrated as the source of primal energy, saving, securing, and suffering.

The tragic, as we know, has moved a long way away from its Greek and Shakespearean beginnings to a point of virtual non-existence in the modern West with its deeply sceptical view of the heroic. Tragedy's migration into Indian literary cultures has resulted in a transformation of their own norms through acts of cultural translation that have produced gendered and challenging new forms. The impact of the tragic cannot be fully estimated in isolation, because the Indo–English encounter was not just between authors, texts, or genres, but involved two widely divergent cultures; the eventual domination of one over the other influenced not only literary activities but virtually all walks of life.[43] Once again literary historian S. K. Das, at the conclusion of his discussion of the tragic in the history of Indian literature, shows its full absorption exceptionally well:

> Through his acquaintance with Western tragedy—conceptually different from the unhappy-ending texts in our own traditions, both elite and folk—did the Indian writer acquire a new vision which could not be easily reconciled to a world-order regulated by the doctrine of karma. From now onwards two streams of literary thought and exercise can be identified in Indian literature, both dealing with the theme of suffering and death. In one, suffering is regarded as part of a divine scheme to be endured silently, in another suffering is an outcome of choices made by man involving a moral dilemma.[44]

SELECT BIBLIOGRAPHY

Anand, Mahesh, *Jayashankar Prasad: Rangdrishti* (His Vision of Drama) (New Delhi: National School of Drama, 1998).

Bachchan, Harivanshrai, *Bachchan Rachavali* (Bachchan *Collected Works*) (Delhi: Rajkamal Prakashan, 2006).

Bharatendu Harishchandra, *Bharatendu Samargra* (*Collected Worksof Bharatendu Harishchandra*) ed. Hemant Sharma (Varanasi: Hindi Pracharak Sansthan, 1988).

Chaudhuri, Sukanta, sp. guest ed., *The Shakespeare International Yearbook*, vol. 12: *Shakespeare in India* (Farnham, Surrey: Ashgate, 2012).

Dalmia, Vasudha, *Poetics, Plays and Performances: The Politics of Modern Indian Theatre* (New Delhi: Oxford University Press, 2006).

Dani, A. P. and V. M. Madge, eds., *Classical Literary Theory and Criticism* (Delhi: Pencraft International, 2001).

Das, Sisir Kumar, 'Indian Ode to the West Wind', in *Indian Ode to the West Wind: Studies in Literary Encounters* (Delhi: Pencraft International, 2001).

Das, Sisir Kumar, *A History of Indian Literature*, vol. 8: *1800–1910 Western Impact: Indian Response* (New Delhi: Sahitya Akademi, 1991).

Gokhale, Shanta, *Playwright at the Centre: Marathi Drama from 1843 to the Present*, (Cacutta, Seagull Books, 2000).

---

[43] See Sisir Kumar Das, 'Indian Ode to the West Wind', in *Indian Ode to the West Wind: Studies in Literary Encounters* (Delhi: Pencraft International, 2001), 27.

[44] Sisir Kumar Das, *A History*, 340.

Lal, Ananda and Sukanta Chaudhuri, *Shakespeare on the Calcutta Stage: a Checklist.* (Calcutta: Papyrus, 2001).

Misra, Jagdish Prasad, *Shakespeare's Impact on Hindi Literature* (New Delhi: Munshiram Manoharlal, 1970).

Satyanath, T. S., 'Translation and Reception as a Cultural Process: On the Emergence of Tragedy in Kannada Literature', *Translation Today* 1:1 (March 2004).

Tagore, Rabindranath, 'The Message of the Forest', in *The English Writings of Rabindranath Tagore*, vol. 2: *A Miscellany*, ed. S. K. Das (New Delhi: Sahitya Akademi, 1996).

Taneja, Preti, 'Lear's Indian Daughters', *Blogging Shakespeare*, 28 March 2013.

Tarkeshwar, V. B., 'Translating Tragedy into Kannada: Politics of Genre and the Nationalist Elite', in *Decentering Translation Studies: India and Beyond*, ed. Judy Wakabayshi and Rita Kothari (Amsterdam: John Benjamins, 2009).

Trivedi, Poonam and Dennis Bartholomeusz, eds., *India's Shakespeare: Translation, Interpretation and Performance* (Delhi: Pearson, 2005).

Wilson, Horace Hayman, *Select Specimens of the Theatre of the Hindus* (Calcutta: V. Holcroft, 1827).

CHAPTER 54

....

'IT IS THE EAST'

Shakespearean Tragedies in East Asia

....

ALEXA HUANG

The best actors in the world, either for tragedy, comedy, history, pastoral, pastorical-comical, historical-pastoral, tragical-historical, tragical-comical-historical-pastoral, scene individable or poem unlimited.

(*Hamlet* 2.2.397–400)

FOLLOWING the sounds of Japanese temple bells, Gabriel Fauré's *Sanctus* swells softly as two elderly women pray at a gigantic set resembling a blown-up version of a *butsudan* Buddhist household altar which takes up the entire stage and dwarfs the performers and audiences. When the light comes on, witches played by Kabuki female impersonators (*onnagata*) dance to falling petals behind the semi-translucent screens in a cinematically inspired slow-motion scene. The massive shutters are opened to reveal Ninagawa Yukio's landmark 1985 stage production of *Macbeth* in Japanese (UK premiere) that seamlessly blends theatrical, cinematic, Japanese, and Western genres of presentation and music. The performance is in conversation with multiple early modern and modern Japanese stage genres, as well as with Western music, and Akira Kurosawa's (1910–98) film adaptation of *Macbeth* as *Throne of Blood* (1957). The rich audio and visual landscape of the production brings to the fore the metaphoric structure of *Macbeth*. We are witnessing one of the most innovative fusion approaches to Shakespearean tragedy in East Asia.

Fast forward to 2000. Tragedy is turned into parody. On screen. In a high-school rehearsal of *Romeo and Juliet*, a stuttering student, Fenson Wong (Pierre Png) asks his drama coach if he can play Romeo. The young lady playing Juliet, Audrey Chan (May Yee Lum) rolls her eyes and challenges her classmate: 'What makes you think that you can

Note: Part of this chapter is a revised and expanded version of the author's 'Comical Tragedies and Poly-generic Shakespeares in Contemporary China and Diasporic Chinese Culture', in *Shakespeare and Genre*, ed. Anthony Guneratne (New York: Palgrave Macmillan, 2012), 157–72 and 'Yukio Ninagawa', *Brook, Hall, Ninagawa, Lepage: Great Shakespeareans* (London: Arden Bloomsbury, 2013), 79–112.

play Romeo? You don't have the looks, and you can't even speak properly.' She is quick to point out that the other student, originally cast for the male lead, is eminently more qualified even if he cannot remember his lines: 'Nick, on the other hand, looks like Leonardo DiCaprio. That's why he's Romeo.' Her protégé promptly supports her cause and leaves the aspiring thespian speechless. The Singaporean film *Chicken Rice War* (dir. Cheah Chee Kong, aka CheeK, 2000) parodies Hollywood rhetoric and global teen culture by commenting on the popularity of Baz Luhrmann's 1996 film *William Shakespeare's Romeo + Juliet*, which starred Claire Danes and Leonardo DiCaprio and brought the classic tale of power and passion to modern-day Verona Beach.

Eventually, Fenson wins the role and gets rid of his stutter through reciting and performing Shakespeare. While recitation of Shakespearean passages seems to have 'cured' Fenson of his stuttering, other scenes expose the instability of any illusion of Shakespeare's universal utility. One family member asked during the bilingual performance: 'Hey, aren't they supposed to speak in English?' As Mark Burnett theorizes, such scenes 'demolish the illusion that Shakespeare constitutes a universal language'.[1] The text of *Romeo and Juliet* is part of the texture of the narrative in *Chicken Rice War*, not only because rehearsals and a final performance of key scenes of the play parallel the action of the film, but also because these reenactments critique the popular belief in Asia that enacting Anglo-European civilization is a staple of global progressive modernity.

So too does linguistically marked cultural difference play an important role in the film. The older generation converses in Cantonese, while the younger generation speaks mostly Singlish. Thus the feud between the two families appears both arbitrary and historically rooted: English, Singlish, and Cantonese serve as reminders of both the 'Global West' and the 'New Asia' that Singapore embodies, 'New Asia' being part of its government's slogan for tourism development. The characters are made reflexively aware of the cultural crossroads where they stand and where Singapore finds itself.

The Japanese adaptation of *Macbeth* on stage and Singaporean take on *Romeo and Juliet* on screen are but two examples of hundreds of Asian adaptations of Shakespearean tragedy. *Romeo and Juliet* has also provided raw material for cinematic parodies—aided by the device of the play-within-a-play—in Anthony Chan's *One Husband Too Many* (Hong Kong, 1988), for example, and Huo Jianqi's *A Time to Love* (China, 2005). Shakespearean tragedies have played an important part in modern and contemporary East Asian engagements with Western cultures. Japanese, Korean, Chinese, and Singaporean translations, rewritings, films, and theatre productions have three important shared characteristics, namely hybridization of genres, intra-regional and trans-historical allusions, and spirituality.

First, East Asian adaptations tend to present the plays in hybrid performative genres, sometimes turning tragedy into comedy or parody, echoing Polonius' musing on the cross-breeding of genres in his gleeful announcement to Hamlet that 'the actors are come hither'. The process of blending conventions often inspires metatheatrical takes on the Shakespearean play and on the performance itself, turning a 'big time', larger-than-life

---

[1] Mark Thornton Burnett, *Shakespeare and World Cinema* (Cambridge: Cambridge University Press, 2013), 134.

tragedy into a 'small time' comedy, and turning a tragic hero writ large into part of the fabric of the quotidian.

Secondly, intra-regional borrowing forms and reinforces a network of allusions that matter to each cultural location and to East Asia as a region. Some plays or characters have a special place in East Asian performance history because of their perceived topical relevance (female empowerment, as well as notions of Confucian duty to the family and to the state in *Hamlet*, issues of self-identity and filial piety in *King Lear*, generational gaps in *Romeo and Juliet*, and the inevitable passing of generations in *Macbeth*). East Asian adaptations of these plays tend to explore such themes in unique visual and musical presentations building an intra-regional network of trans-historical cross-references.

Last, but not least, twenty-first-century East Asian adaptations tend to interpret Shakespearean tragedies through issues of spirituality and through the artists' personal, rather than national, identities. For example, in the dramatic traditions of East Asian cultures with a Confucian inheritance, while women's agency is often undermined, women gain an upper hand when they return as ghosts or mediators in religious contexts. Along with the rise of Korean feminism in the 1990s, several South Korean adaptations of *Hamlet* recast Ophelia as a shaman who serves as a medium to console the dead and guide the living. Since a shaman is outside the Confucian social structure, she has greater agency.[2] The action of Kim Jung-ok's *Hamlet* (1993) takes place under an enormous hemp cloth that is suspended from the ceiling to resemble a house of mourning. It is customary for a mourning son to wear coarse hemp clothing, because hemp cloth is associated with funerals. Appropriately enough, the play begins with Ophelia's funeral. Possessed by the Old King's spirit, Ophelia conveys the story of his murder.[3] Kim Kwang-bo's *Ophelia: Sister, Come to My Bed* (1995) also opens with Ophelia's funeral. Caught between the incestuous love of Laertes and the romantic love of Hamlet, Ophelia is eventually abandoned by both men: there is no future with Laertes, and Hamlet must carry out his revenge mission. Ophelia is possessed by the dead king's spirit: she urges Hamlet to avenge his father's death. When the ghost of Old Hamlet appears, in the form of a large puppet operated by three monks, Ophelia moves in unison with the ghost and changes her voice to that of an old man. The use of shamanism as a thematic device reminds us, also, that *Hamlet* was perhaps used as a way to exorcise the painful loss of a son by its author.

In everyday parlance, the word tragedy often invokes inevitable suffering, moral weight, and sometimes an indifferent universe. People use the word tragic to refer to the kind of loss and suffering that they believe to have a universal valence that goes beyond its times. When something becomes a tragedy, it often carries with it a transhistorical moral tone. In other words, something of grandeur, endurance, and universality. As a dramatic genre, tragedy however, as Raymond Williams points out, is far from transhistorical or stable.[4]

---

    [2] Janice C. H. Kim, 'Processes of Feminine Power: Shamans in Central Korea', in *Korean Shamanism: Revivals, Survivals, and Change*, ed. Keith Howard (Seoul: Seoul Press, 1998), 113–32.
    [3] Alexa Huang and Peter Donaldson, eds., *Global Shakespeares* (http://globalshakespeares. org). Korean co-editor Hyon-u Lee. Accessed May 2013. Another example is Bae Yo-sup's *Hamlet Cantabile* (2005, 2007, 2008).
    [4] Raymond Williams, *Modern Tragedy*, ed. Pamela McCallum (Peterborough, Canada: Broadview, 2006), 1–35.

Studying non-Western interpretations of Shakespearean tragedies helps us gain a deeper understanding of the genre's culturally specificity.[5] What, then, constitutes a contemporary East Asian tragedy, and how are Shakespearean tragedies interpreted within that context? Why do tragedies seem more transportable from culture to culture than other genres?

As in almost all instances of transnational borrowing, a select, locally resonant group of 'privileged' plays has held continuous sway. In modern times, tragedies such as *Hamlet* are more frequently adapted around the world because of their malleability and capacity to be detached from their native cultural settings. The plays seem elastic because—as opposed to comedies that latch on to more culturally specific reference points (such as the truce between England and France in *The Comedy of Errors*, 3.2)—tragedies can be reconstructed to deal in broad strokes with more generalizable, hence transportable, issues (such as a prince's duty to his dead father and to his country). There have been more than fifty translations of *Hamlet* in India alone, while *Henry V* and *Richard II* are the only history plays to have been translated into Hindi, each translated only once.

From Tragedy to Parody

> Such welcome and unwelcome things at once.
> 'Tis hard to reconcile.
>
> *Macbeth* (4.3.136–9)

Are Asian dramatic genres, as more stylized, hybrid tragic-comic forms, reconcilable with Shakespearean tragedy as a mode of narrative? The emergence of parody can be an indication that a translated genre has matured. It is also a sign that Shakespeare's global afterlife has reached a new stage in which the *fabulae* of his plays have become so familiar to the 'cross-border' audiences that the plays can be used as a platform for artistic exploration of new genres.

One example is an adaptation of *Hamlet* in Taiwan entitled *Shamlet*. Spared the devastating Cultural Revolution and aided by its economic and political alliance with the United States (expressed formally in the 1960s and culturally since the 1980s), Taiwan has a slightly longer history of sustainable theatrical experimentation with Shakespeare than mainland China. Experimental stage works can be both mainstream and avant-garde, commercially viable and artistically interesting. In writing a critically acclaimed *huaju* (Western-style 'spoken drama') play called *Shamuleite,* or *Shamlet* (1992; continuous revivals on stage ever since), Lee Kuo-hsiu, one of the most innovative playwrights and directors to emerge in the 1980s, turned high tragedy, or what was known to Renaissance readers as 'tragical history', into comic parody. He suggests in the programme that *Shamlet* is a revenge comedy that 'has nothing to do with *Hamlet* but something to do with Shakespeare'.[6] His

[5] Helene P. Foley and Jean E. Howard. 'The Urgency of Tragedy Now', *PMLA* 129:4 (October 2014), 617–33; see esp. 618, 627.

[6] Lee, *Shamuleite*, 119.

purpose is twofold: to resist the hegemonic power of 'Shakespeare' in a global context and to offer a new way to read *Hamlet*.

Bearing a certain resemblance to Ernst Lubitsch's *To Be or Not to Be* and Kenneth Branagh's *A Midwinter's Tale*—both chronicling fictional theatre companies' comical efforts to stage *Hamlet*—Lee's seven selected scenes from *Hamlet* appear as plays within plays that document the activities of a theatre troupe named Fengping (itself a play on words pertaining to the company founded by Lee in real life, Pingfeng). The production has a playful title combining the first character of the Chinese transliteration of Shakespeare (*sha* from Shashibiya) and the last three characters for *Hamlet* (*muleite* from Hamuleite). *Shamlet* also plays with the sounds of 'sham' and 'shame'. Having no direct access to an English version of Shakespeare's *Hamlet,* Lee worked with the Franco Zeffirelli-Mel Gibson film version and two popular twentieth-century Chinese translations by Liang Shiqiu and Zhu Shenghao. As with the Singaporean *Chicken Rice War*, there are some genealogical links between *Shamlet* and the Hollywood film. Lee indicates in an interview that the film inspired him to stage *Hamlet* on his own terms. An opponent of staging straightforward literary translations of foreign plays, he claims that if one chooses to stage a 'translated foreign play' and to 'follow it slavishly line by line', one will be 'deprived of the opportunity to create and re-write'.[7]

Shamlet is an example of how East Asian playwrights and directors present Shakespearean tragedies in hybrid performative genres. Actors move from their real identities as the persons putting on the play *Shamlet* for the real audience, to their identities as actors in the story of the play, and to their phantom identities as Hamlet, Ophelia, Gertrude, and other characters in the play-within-a-play (i.e. the failed production of *Hamlet* in *Shamlet*). The framing device is a possible evocation of Tom Stoppard's award-winning play and subsequent film, *Rozencrantz and Guildenstern Are Dead*. Moving among these four different sets of identities, the characters explore their local identities as actors from a typical Taiwanese theatre troupe. They are tormented by the difficulties facing all small and experimental theatre companies. These problems echo the difficult situations that Hamlet himself faces.

Shamlet is rife with cunningly scripted errors. These range from malfunctions in the routine mechanical business of the theatre to forgotten lines and accidentally switched roles. An example of how the production embraces the contingency of theatrical performance, while highlighting the perils of translation, is the Fengping presentation of the ramparts scene from *Hamlet* (1.5), which takes place in Taichung, the second stop of their round-the-island tour of Taiwan. After informing Shamlet of his assassination and urging vengeance, the ghost prepares to ascend on a steel rope as he delivers his last lines 'Adieu, adieu, adieu. Remember me' (*Hamlet* 1.5.91). A mechanical problem traps the ghost on the stage. The actor playing Shamlet is paralysed, and Horatio enters, as directed by the script, and delivers lines of weighty irony.

> HORATIO   My lord! My lord! My lord! Anything wrong?
> SHAMLET   How strange! [*Looking at the stranded Ghost.*]
> HORATIO   Speak to it, my lord!

---

[7] Shu-hua Wang and Perng Ching-hsi. Interview with Lee Kuo-Hsiu, Taipei, 13 November 1998. Unpublished manuscript.

SHAMLET   Never ever reveal what you see tonight.

HORATIO   I will not tell. [*Improvises*] And I hope no one sees it! [*Looking at the stranded Ghost and then the audience*]

SHAMLET   Come! Swear by your conscience. Put your hand on my sword.

[*Shamlet discovers that he lacks this most vital of props*]

HORATIO   [*Filling in and improvising*] Use my sword, my lord! ...

SHAMLET   [*Soliloquizing*] Rest, rest, perturbèd spirit. I ... [*Forgetting his lines*] I've forgotten what I had to say!

HORATIO   [*Prompting*] Perturbèd spirit, please remember that whatever historical period it is, you shall keep your mouth shut [*indicating the stranded Ghost*]. The time is out of joint. O what a poor soul am I that I have to set it right!

SHAMLET   Yes, indeed!

[*The lights dim as the stranded Ghost keeps trying to see if he can ascend*]

The scene calls to mind Stoppard's transformation of the sometimes-omitted minor characters, Rosencrantz and Guildenstern, into the leads of his play. From the perspective of these two characters without memories, the performance of *The Murder of Gonzago*, the consequent turn of events, and even their own mission do not make much sense and appear farcical. If accidents and the advent of the unexpected lead to tragedy in *Hamlet,* in *Shamlet* they are turned into comedy, which is as challenging to native theatrical forms— particularly in the treatment of the bumbling director Li Xiuguo (the alter ego and the anagrammatical name of the playwright Lee Kuo-hsiu)—as they are to Renaissance antecedents. By Act 3, when the ghost still cannot ascend offstage, Laertes, seeking to impart advice to Ophelia, demands that he leave. While existentialism as a theme runs through Stoppard's play, theatrical contingency informs Lee's design. The scripted mechanical failures serve to highlight the inner workings of a stage genre, inverting the process of theatrical illusion, and inviting the audience in Stoppardian fashion to reflect on their familiarity with an editorialized, modernist *Hamlet*.

HEARING AND SEEING THE TRAGEDY

There are, of course, performances of Shakespearean tragedies that do not bend or blend genres but instead focus on innovative strategies of visual and audio presentation, such as Ninagawa's *Macbeth*. While Western audiences may expect, say, a Japanese adaptation of Shakespeare to offer something uniquely Japanese or be representative of Japanese performance traditions today, intra-regional borrowing and fusion of Asian and Western motifs are part of an increasingly common approach.

Japanese director Ninagawa Yukio's productions show that he is both a visual director and a sound engineer. It is therefore not an overstatement to say that one goes to the theatre to hear, as well as to see, his plays. Both the visual and sonic elements make important contributions to his signature metatheatrical framing devices, and his works often feature intra-Asian thematic and transhistorical allusions to styles borrowed from traditional Japan, as well as from other Asian and Western cultures. This is especially evident in the music in his productions. Over the past decades he has used atmospheric, classical music and strong visual motifs in many of his productions to blend elements of familiarity and strangeness. His theatre thus offers both visceral and intellectual experiences.

In the *Ninagawa Macbeth*, the first thing the audience heard were sounds of the gongs typically heard in temples. The gongs initially gave an impression of coherence between visual and aural motifs around the Buddhist altar. Christian music soon joined the scene. The three-minute 'Sanctus' of Gabriel Fauré's *Requiem* (1887-1900) accompanied the appearance of the two elderly women in ragged clothes praying at the Buddhist altar. An eclectic mix of music from different eras and cultures echoed Ninagawa's hybrid visual strategies. The opening scene featured temple bells and Fauré, and later on a lone flute accentuated Macbeth as he persuaded the assassins to go after Banquo. Some British theatre critics found the *Ninagawa Macbeth* 'intensely religious'[8] and appreciated the effect of the 'specifically Christian music.' Michael Ratcliffe believed the music 'made an effect of heart-breaking pathos against the dark and glittering splendor on stage.'[9]

In fact, *Sanctus* opened and closed Ninagawa's production along with the visual framing device. Following Macbeth's collapse silence ensued. The *Sanctus* swelled softly as the two old women proceeded to close the shutters. Based on the Roman Catholic Mass for the Dead, the Requiem introduced new religious elements into the otherwise Buddhist landscape, as the chorus sang:

Sanctus, sanctus, sanctus	Holy, holy, holy
Dominus Deus Sabaoth	Lord God of Hosts
Pleni sunt coeli et terra	Full are the heavens and earth
gloria tua	with the glory of you,
Hosanna in excelsis.	Hosanna in the highest.

In contrast to Verdi's *Requiem* and other compositions that are accompanied by strong vocal and instrumental expression, Fauré's *Sanctus* is simpler and more intimate in form. Its musical minimalism matched the simple visual beauty of Ninagawa's production. *Sanctus* opens with a dreamy, soft harp figure and violin, and the sopranos sing a rising and falling melody of only three notes which is repeated by male singers. The sopranos and male singers engage in a duet, responding to each other and building to the *forte* on 'excelsis' and the triumphant 'hosanna'. Towards the end of the piece, powerful major chords are joined by a horn fanfare, before the sopranos answer in diminuendo as the music softens. The dreamy harp arpeggios re-emerge to close the piece.

The gentle and shimmering *Sanctus* echoed Ninagawa's visual motif of cherry blossom. Inspired by Motojiro Kajii's (1901–32) widely circulated phrase, 'dead bodies are buried under the cherry trees', the production associated death with a cherry tree in full blossom. Cherry blossoms symbolize both beauty and death (and the repose of the soul), something which may not register in the minds of British audiences, but Ninagawa's decision to use a direct translation rather than a localized adaptation of the script of Shakespeare's *Macbeth* also introduced unfamiliar narrative patterns into the Japanese audiences' horizon of expectation. Ninagawa's rehearsal notes for 5.6 usefully sum up the significance of the

---

[8] Peter Whitebrook, Review of *The Ninagawa Macbeth*, *The Scotsman*, 23 August 1985.
[9] Michael Ratcliffe, Review of *The Ninagawa Macbeth*, *The Observer*, 25 August 1985.

Requiem and cherry blossom as the dominant visual and sonic frameworks: 'memories of cherry blossom at night [morph into] a sensuous invitation to death.'[10]

Silence is also an important element in Ninagawa's work. Komaki Kurihara's Lady Macbeth is a tour de force. A great silence envelops her sleepwalking scene as her high-pitched hysterical laughter fades into sobbing and as she rubs her hands in an imaginary stream. A profound silence frames the moment when she dies, only to be punctuated by Macbeth's remorse: 'She should have died hereafter./There would have been a time for such a word.'

Ninagawa uses the musical landscape of *Sanctus* out of context in order to contrast with the eastern spirituality represented by the *butsudan* altar. His strategy undermines both the postwar Japanese emulation of Western high culture and the stereotypical motif of 'lost' Westerners finding peace in Buddhism. It also highlights the conspicuous flaw of post-Second World War intercultural imagination in stressing either homogenizing cultural sameness or irreconcilable difference.

Another way in which Ninagawa uses music is to create varying pathways to language and sonic relations between the soundtrack and the lines delivered by his actors. In *Romeo and Juliet*, the first Shakespearean play he directed in 1974, he used music as a tool to address the shortcomings in his commercial actors who could not remember their lines and, when they did, delivered them without authenticity. Ninagawa reminisced about how he used Elton John's music to shape his strategy of appropriation, to 'drown out' the actors' awkward speech:

> When they read a line, it sounded like stereotypical samurai speech. The lines just didn't mean anything. So I thought I should submerge them under Elton John's music. Then you wouldn't hear anything when the play started, only sound. I wanted strong contrasts, such as people running, with music coming from everywhere—a sort of visual rhetoric. Otherwise, it would need a rhetoric that comes from Europe or Greece that we don't have naturally.

Ninagawa commented on the lack of agency and a 'self' in his culture, and argued that one of his most important goals is to discover a more assertive self:

> I'm still struggling with this disadvantage in our culture—we don't have a definite 'self', 'self' as an agent, an assertive, aggressive self. The core of my artistic struggle is actually to discover such a self.[11]

Ninagawa's sonic strategy is always part of his visual strategy. One of the most prominent examples is his *Macbeth*. By considering the possibility of parentless children, *Macbeth* as a historical tragedy dramatizes attacks on the order of time. Parentless children as a trope is a paradox. Macbeth pins his hope on compensating for the inevitable passing of generations through one's offspring. However, the possibility of parentless children takes this last hope away. What Macbeth fears is not fate or death, but time. Time that cannot be

---

[10] Yukio Ninagawa, *Note 1969–1988* (Tokyo, 1988), trans. Ryuta Minami; quoted in Ronnie Mulryne, 'From Text to Foreign Stage: Yukio Ninagawa's Cultural Translation of *Macbeth*', in *Shakespeare from Text to Stage*, ed. Patricia Kennan and Mariangela Tempera (Bologna: Cooperativa Libraria Universitaria Editrice Bologna, 1992), 136.

[11] 'Interview with Ninagawa Yukio', *Performing Shakespeare in Japan*, 211.

turned back, and cannot be manipulated. How might one go about staging this discourse about time? Like Peter Brook who regarded theatre as iconographic art and Kurosawa who combines Noh, American Westerns, and Japanese scroll-painting in his *Throne of Blood*, Ninagawa often works from a set of compelling images for each production as if he were a designer.[12] He does this to simultaneously spark the audience's interest and to introduce them to the play-world in the first few minutes of the performance.

This factor of surprise is certainly part of the success of many of his works. *The Ninagawa Macbeth* was the first Shakespearean play the director transposed to feudal Japan, seamlessly combining modern and traditional, Western and Japanese elements. Ninagawa found inspiration for the striking set that I discussed at the beginning of this chapter in scenes from Japanese daily life:

> When I went back home and opened up our family *butsudan* [ancestral altar] to light a candle and pray for my father, at that moment, I thought, 'this is the right image [for *Macbeth*].' I had two overlapping complex ideas: ordinary people watching *Macbeth*, and a Japanese audience looking at the stage and seeing through it to our ancestors.

He elaborated on his synaesthetic experience of a trans-temporal dialogue across different spaces:

> When I was in front of the *butsudan,* my thoughts were racing. It was like I was having a conversation with my ancestors. When I thought of *Macbeth* in this way, I thought of him appearing in the *butusdan* where we consecrate dead ancestors. Then we could change the setting when the witches appear, as in the Japanese expression, 'To be tempted by time.' We could create a setting like dusk, neither night nor day, when, according to a Japanese tradition, one often meets with demonic beings.[13]

Ninagawa was quite specific about his vision of this dialogue not only with the dead in general but with the spirits of his father and brother. Like Wu Hsing-kuo's solo Beijing opera *Lear*, which I will discuss in the next section, the *Ninagawa Macbeth* is on some level deeply personal, as the director confided:

> While I was praying [at our family altar] I recalled my dead father and elder brother and I felt as if I was conversing with them. At that time it occurred to me that if the drama of *Macbeth* were a fantasy which developed from a conversation with my dead ancestors, then this could really be my own story. Those warrior chieftains who shed so much blood could so easily be my ancestors, or they might even be what I might have been.[14]

This imaginary conversation informed a set that was evocative of a sense of spirituality. Giant sculptural warrior-god figures served as the backdrop to Malcolm and Macduff's meeting. A family Buddhist altar the size of the proscenium greeted the audience as they walked into the theatre. The screen doors were still closed. Larger shutters further divided the audience from the dimly lit stage. While the visual framing device suggested a Buddhist interpretation of *Macbeth*, the aural landscape was more complex.

---

[12] Peter Brook, *The Shifting Point, 1946–1987* (New York: Harper Collins, 1987), 78.
[13] 'Interview with Ninagawa Yukio', *Performing Shakespeare in Japan*, 208–19.
[14] Yukio Ninagawa, Programme for *The Tempest*, trans. Stefan Kaiser and Sue Henny, Edinburgh International Festival, 1988.

Throughout the performance, the two old women sat on either side of the altar that served as a stylized curtain. They watched the play with the audience. They served as stagehands and as mostly detached gatekeepers. They ate, drank, sewed, and even nodded off. They played the role of a silent chorus. They wept when Macbeth said 'my way of life | Is fallen into the sere, the yellow leaf' and at his 'Tomorrow and tomorrow and tomorrow' speech.

The two anonymous women may have been praying to comfort their ancestors, to appease evil spirits like those in the ensuing performance within the altar, or to find spiritual shelter from their traumatic past. They may have ben hallucinating or dreaming, bringing us what amounts to an old wives' tale or even a tale of their ancestors. They served as witnesses, in a similar fashion to the character of the *waki* in Noh theatre, to the heinous acts on stage, and as mediators between the audience and the play. Given that most actions were confined within the Buddhist altar, the action of *Macbeth* could be seen as made up of dreams based on their memories or their experience of divine revelation. Their utter disregard of the *Requiem* and their aloofness served as an important contrast to the earnestness and gravity of actions inside the screen doors of the altar. As Malcolm delivered the play's final lines, the old women began to close the shutters. However, they did not close the play. They merely separated the worlds of *Macbeth* and the audience and returned the performance space to the same state it had had before the show started. Their existence outside the play's narrative time parallelled *Macbeth*'s attacks on the order of time.

In conjunction with the lighting, the sliding shutters and the screen doors separated the stage into two venues for physical and allegorical actions. Action that was farther removed from the mundane took place behind the screens. The witches initially appeared behind the semi-transparent screen doors, visible through lighting and lightning. Banquo was murdered there and that was where the apparitions were seen. When Banquo's ghost appeared at Macbeth's banquet, it replaced the warrior-god statue on a pedestal upstage, and the entire banquet scene, including the courtiers, was encased behind the screens. Jolted by Banquo's ghost out of the semblance of guilt-free peace he worked so hard to maintain, Macbeth opened the screen doors to step 'outside' and therefore downstage. Fleance escaped the assassins to this area that seemed disconnected from the violent world behind the screens. Intimate scenes and casual discussions also took place in front of the screen doors; Lady Macbeth followed Macbeth there and urged him to return to the banquet to entertain his guests: 'You do not give the cheer: the feast is sold' (3.4.32).

One of the most striking visual strategies was the use of candles in Act 5 Scene 5, which opened with a single flickering candle on a dark stage, reminding the audience of Lady Macbeth's candle in her sleepwalking scene. As Macbeth mourned the passing of Lady Macbeth and the passing of time, more candles were lit on the stage floor, accentuating Macbeth's important moment of self-discovery. Macbeth lit the candles around him methodically in order to (according to Ninagawa) 'conquer his fears',[15] only to engage in futile attempts to extinguish the ever-burning candles later on. This circle of inextinguishable candles created an ironic distance between redemption and Macbeth's speech: 'Tomorrow, and tomorrow, and tomorrow.' He was encircled by the candles as he

---

[15] Ninagawa, *Note 1969-1988*.

spoke 'Out, out, brief candle! | Life's but a walking shadow' (5.5.23-4). Evident here again was Ninagawa's signature approach to creating a sense of estrangement through what would otherwise be quotidian objects. The candles might represent lost souls, including the Macbeths, soldiers who would die in the next scene, and those Macbeth had already killed. Ninagawa elaborates on Macbeth's feverish collection of the candles: 'His behavior appears just like that of a child who cannot feel at peace until he gathers all his toys around him.'[16] The visual arrangement of the candles also evoked the thousands of stone statues of Budda at Adashino Nenbutsuji Temple, an eighteenth-century Buddhist temple on a hill overlooking Kyoto. From the Heian (794-1185) to Edo (1603-1868) periods it was the site where those who could not afford proper burial rites dropped their dead. The stone Buddhas tend to the dead without graves and pray for their souls.

There was something for everyone in this production when it was staged in Japan and abroad, but it also challenged audience members to grapple with their own limitations. Self-motivated audiences may gain a passing acquaintance with a wider array of performance idioms and cultural themes when enough clues are available, but audiences may also force new meanings on the work. The framework of *Macbeth* offers spectators who are familiar with the play some semblance of control over the exotic performance event. On the other hand, the sheer grace of a backdrop of cherry blossoms can create shocking contrasts with the dark tragedy and blood. Playgoers who are unfamiliar with the connotations of cherry blossoms might see the set as an expression of beauty and a marker of Japanese identity. *Macbeth* thus becomes a twice-told and doubly removed story. This is not unusual in East Asian adaptations of Shakespearean tragedies that try to balance Asian and Western elements.

Visual framing devices surprise the audience with delight and unexpected spectacles. For example, Ninagawa's 1999 *King Lear*, an English-language intercultural work co-produced with the Royal Shakespeare Company in England, featured a rising sun in the backdrop, and made use of techniques from *noh* and *kabuki* styles; the cast included Nigel Hawthorne in the title role, and Hiroyuki Sanada as an androgynous Fool. The scene of the blinded Gloucester being led by his disguised son Edgar evoked a Japanese watercolor. Both his 1985 *Macbeth* and 2001 *Macbeth* were likewise full of visual surprises and symbolism, with many perfect painterly moments and photogenic scenes. Cherry blossoms and snowstorms are among Ninagawa's visual trademarks.

Ninagawa's *Hamlet* at the Barbican in London in May 2015 featured—as is typical of his painterly approach—a blown-up tiered *hina* dolls cabinet with actors as human-sized dolls in the play-within-a-play scene. According to the handout, he drew inspiration from the Japanese Girls' Day (Dolls' Day). The Doll's Day is a festival celebrating girls' development and offering good wishes for their future.

Like Lee Kuo-hsiu, Ninagawa often draws on metatheatricality as a theme in his productions. He prepares the audiences to take on the play-world through pre-show action (e.g. in *The Tempest* and *Titus Andronicus*) and through creative visual framing devices (*Hamlet*). Before curtain time for *Titus,* audiences rubbed shoulders with actors in Roman costumes who were warming up and walking in the aisles. In the 1995 *Hamlet* (similar to the 2015 *Hamlet*), the audience saw actors busy preparing for the performance in cubicles

---

[16]   Ninagawa, *Note 1969-1988.*

in the dressing rooms on stage before the show started. Ophelia followed the Japanese custom of arranging ornate *hina* dolls—a pastime for ladies at the court and now part of the Dolls' Festival in March celebrated by Japanese families. The dolls will eventually be set afloat to carry misfortunes away so that the family's daughters can grow up healthily and happily. Since the dolls represent hope, Ophelia's giving away dolls rather than flowers in her mad scene carried a grave suggestiveness. The metaphorical connection between drowning—dolls adrift—and despair was also evident. In the play-within-a-play scene, performers sat on a tiered platform resembling a *hina* dolls cabinet. They formed a human tableau and drew attention to the artificiality of the performance. The audience's attention was redirected away from the representational aspect of theatrical realism to the presentational aspect of Ninagawa's metatheatrical narrative.

SPIRITUALITY, EAST AND WEST

In addition to adaptions that blend genres and to visual and audio strategies of adaptation that fuse Eastern and Western aesthetics, East Asian directors have also engaged with various notions of spirituality in the twenty-first century. The self-problematizing nature of *King Lear* allowed space for Buddhist interpretations of the meanings of spiritual life. Within the realm of global Shakespeare, from Jean-Luc Godard's metacinematic film *King Lear* (1987) to Wu Hsing-kuo's Buddhist-inflected *Li'er zaici* (*Lear Is Here*, 2007), discourses of the making and unmaking of the self that echo religious formulations have played a key role in remixing Shakespeare's play as contemporary performance. Deployment of Eastern spirituality and life narratives can also be found in other directors' works, such as Michael Almereyda's film *Hamlet* in 2000 (where the Vietnamese monk Thich Nhat Hanh's scene draws upon the director's interest in Eastern spirituality); Taiwanese playwright Stan Lai's three-man production in Hong Kong in 2000, *Lear and the Thirty-seven-fold Practice of a Bodhisattva* (where Jigme Khyentse Rinpoche's recitation of a fourteenth-century Tibetan Buddhist scripture reflects Lai's interests as a practicing Buddhist); Ong Keng Sen's multimedia stage work *Desdemona* (2000) in which the Singaporean director addresses social oppression and Desdemona's endurance; the Ryutopia Noh Theatre's Japanese *Hamlet* (dir. Kurita Yoshihiro, 2007) in which the titular character's costumes and mannerism call to mind a Buddhist monk; and Akira Kurosawa's Japanese film *Ran* (1985), a re-telling of *Lear* in which Buddhist symbols such as a scroll painting of Amitabha (one of the five celestial Buddhas), Japanese calligraphy depicting the path to enlightenment, and lotus flowers play important roles. In the final scene, the blinded Gloucester figure, Tsurumaru, approaches the edge of a cliff clutching the scroll painting of Amitabha. He jolts and drops the scroll over the cliff. He steps back as the sun sets. Ophelia is recast as a shaman in several South Korean productions. As a medium between two worlds, she comforts the dead and guides the living.

How has the theatricalization of religion been used in cross-cultural readings of Shakespeare that are flirting with postmodernism?

An example of the autobiographical approach to self-knowledge and the use of Shakespearean text as a source of spiritual wisdom is Wu's solo Beijing opera *Lear Is Here* in which he plays ten characters. At centre stage stands a dispirited King Lear after the storm scene on the heath (3.2), who has just taken off his *jingju* (Beijing-opera) headdress and armour costume in full view of a packed audience. Following his powerful presentation of the scene of the mad Lear in the storm and his on-stage costume change, the actor—now dressed as if he were backstage—interrogates himself and the eyeless headdress in a somber moment while touching his own eyes, evoking Gloucester's blinding and the Lacanian gaze in a play about sight and truth. 'Who am I?' he asks. 'Doth any here know me? Why, this is not Lear. | Doth Lear walk thus? speak thus? Where are his eyes?' (1.4.217-18). Here, the performer is self-conscious of the ways in which his own eyes become Lear's eyes.

These two pairs of eyes represent the necessary split many performers experience on stage, a process of making null the performer's self identity so that he or she becomes the part being performed. This scene turns out to be somewhat controversial because it complicates the popular understanding of acting in traditional Chinese operatic theatre—which is often regarded as highly stylized and sophisticatedly coded for aesthetic appreciation by the connoisseurs, but lacking any sense of interiority and depth of character development in the Aristotelian sense. Here, perhaps for the first time in the history of Beijing opera, the process of embodiment is laid bare by Wu in a metatheatrical exposé.

Presented by the Lincoln Center Festival and produced by Taiwan's Contemporary Legend Theatre (an intercultural Beijing opera company founded by Wu in 1986, with input from his wife Lin Hsiu-wei who is a renowned modern dancer), this fine example of East Asian Shakespeare took place at the Rose Theatre in New York on the evening of 12 July 2007, with revisions of its earlier incarnations (the production was first conceived in Paris when Wu was leading a performance workshop on the invitation of Ariane Mnouchkine in 2001).

As Wu begins his transformation from 'Lear' to himself (or: 'the actor' as the programme lists this character), he removes and methodically joins the stage beard to the hairpiece, making it a faceless puppet. His work with this prop makes clear that the empty eyes raise questions about his own identity as well as that of the character whose costume he no longer inhabits. Raising it above him and pondering it intently, he asks 'Who am I,' before shifting his gaze to the audience and asking the same question, slightly revised, in the third person: 'Does any here know him?' and then answering that question himself: 'He is not Lear.' The prop thus functions as an emblem of the emptiness of stage representation and also for the actor's emptied self when not inhabited by the character. Wu's performance of Lear and the 'actor playing Lear' resonates with several metatheatrical moments in other Shakespearean plays—among them Macbeth's evocation of the 'poor player' who struts and frets and is heard no more and Hamlet's comparison of the fates of Yorick and Alexander the Great. The face sans eyes is, like 'Lear's shadow', a figure for death. When it is held aloft and gazed upon by Wu, the hollow face, like Yorick's skull, symbolizes self-knowledge through a meditation on death and embodiment, reminding the audience of his previous works that examine the meanings of death and ritual. For example, Wu has adapted *Hamlet* before and played the Prince in *The Prince's Revenge* (*Wangzi fuchouji*, 1989) and the Greek Tragedy *Medea* (*Loulan nü*, 1993).

Li'er suggests that Lear is questioning the construction of the self, a process that is similar to the meditative practices of both Christian and Buddhist traditions. As James Howe suggest in *A Buddhist's Shakespeare*, there is rich material on meditation within the Shakespearean canon which has not been explicitly defined as Christian. The meditation therefore lends itself to Buddhist interpretations. When Lear asks 'who is it that can tell me who I am', and the Fool answers 'Lear's shadow', the exchange moves close to well-known *memento mori* discourses and practices, as framed by the wisdom of the Fool's suggestion. Wu's manipulation of the faceless puppet parallels the ghost of Old Hamlet in Kim Kwang-bo's *Ophelia: Sister, Come to My Bed* (1995). Old Hamlet appears as a large puppet operated by three monks to signal a tug of war between different forms of human and spiritual agency and identities.

Wu's characters (Lear and the actor) initially reject the possibility of religious redemption. His 'decision' to return to the stage after a hiatus and the near disbandment of his company 'is tougher than entering some monastery' as he tells us on stage. Presumably it is a tougher decision to keep the show going despite seemingly insurmountable challenges because the monastery is seen as a form of escapism. Interestingly, as soon as that decision is taken, religious tropes surface again, more explicitly in the scene in which Wu as Gloucester 'looks' to Dover as a site for his redemption. In a deliberate slip of tongue during his continuous chanting of 'Duofo',—the Mandarin Chinese transliteration of 'Dover' (which rhymes with 'many Buddhas')—Gloucester conflates Duofo with Amituofo (Amitava Buddha, or Buddha of Light). Gloucester moves from contemplating suicide to seeking refuge in the Buddha and in the Buddha of Light (Amituofo). The slide from Dover to the Buddha of Light is significant because it hints at Wu's and Gloucester's wish to seek refuge in Buddhist redemption, which explains the slide later in his chant that includes a series of additional names of Buddha. The production as a whole concludes with a meditative scene in which Wu, dressed in a Buddhist monastic robe, circles the stage as himself, as Lear's ghost, as a transcendent being, or perhaps as a personification of the *jingju* tradition in crisis. The scene evokes again the performer's conflicting identities on and offstage, as a Taiwanese. His performance echoes the Buddhist circumambulation meditative practice, an act of moving around a sacred pagoda or idol. Wu as monk asks: 'Who am I? I am me.' He continues: 'And I am looking for me! I think of me; I look at me; I know me.... I kill me. I forget me! I dream about me again', thereby laying a strong claim to the centrality of the artist's self within Eastern spiritual traditions.

The Buddhist meditation highlights the contradictory nature of identities that can only be constructed in opposition to others. Eastern spirituality has also been appropriated in adaptations outside East Asia. Wu's question 'who am I?' in *Lear* parallels the performance of Hamlet's 'to be or not to be' soliloquy in Michael Almereyda's Buddhist-inflected film *Hamlet* (2000; starring Ethan Hawke). While set in modern day New York City, the film contains multiple references to Buddhism, including a clip from Ulrike Koch's documentary about a pilgrimage, *Die Salzmänner von Tibet* (*The Saltmen of Tibet*, 1998), which appears on the back-seat video monitor of Claudius' limousine. In the moment when the tribesmen pass through the boundary between the secular world and the sacred territory of the salt fields, Claudius, who has been praying, covers the screen with his hand and laments the failure of his words to reach Heaven ('what if this hand be blacker than it is with brother's blood') as he is jolted by a nasty and dangerous swerve. Hamlet is driving the limousine as Claudius' chauffeur without his knowledge.[17]

The most sustained infusion of Buddhism in the film is the appearance of Thich Nhat Hanh in a rendering of the 'to be or not to be' scene. Thich Nhat Hanh is a prolific author of Buddhist works and leader of the Engaged Buddhism movement. He appears on a video

---

[17] Alexa Huang, 'Global Shakespeare 2.0 and the Task of the Performance Archive', *Shakespeare Survey* 64 (2011), 38–51 (49).

monitor in Hamlet's apartment. His teachings on 'interbeing' ('We have the word "to be", but I propose the word "to 'interbe". Interbe. Because it is not possible to "be" alone. We must "interbe" with everything and everyone else—mother, father … uncle …'). His words echo repeated video loops of Hamlet reciting the half-line 'to be or not to be' while actively making suicidal gestures. Engrossed in his own footage of an erotic encounter with Ophelia on the hand-held monitor, Hamlet is not looking at the television or listening to Thich Nhat Hanh. Interestingly, the book Ophelia is reading, and with which she partly covers her face, is Krishnamurti's *Living and Dying* with a big photo of the sage on its cover. Even the video, however, encodes Eastern spirituality as an alternative source of wisdom.

As in Wu's *Lear*, Eastern spirituality is deployed in the film to signal the possibility of redemption and an alternative philosophy of life. The conversation that emerges between Shakespeare's *Hamlet*, Koch's *Saltmen of Tibet*, and Thich Nhat Hanh's *Peace is Every Step* video parallels Wu's Buddhist litany of contradictory states of the self at the end of his production. Both works juxtapose Buddhist teachings on the illusory and shifting nature of the self with Hamletian scepticism and with secular elements drawn from Shakespeare. Almereyda's *Hamlet* posits that the Buddhist ideal of 'interbeing' can counteract Hamlet's despair and scepticism, while Wu's Lear moves from rejecting the monastery as a site of redemption at the beginning of the production to the embodiment of the role of a monk at the end, when he literally dons the Buddhist robe. The final scene heals Wu's own identity crisis as a Taiwanese actor specializing in Beijing opera and simultaneously resolves the tension between Taiwan's need to assert its own cultural identity and the implicit demands of an art form commonly seen as an embodiment of the Chinese nation (*jingju*).

While the examples discussed in this chapter do not exhaust the rich range of interpretive possibilities of Asian adaptations of Shakespeare, they represent the three major approaches of directors: generic hybridization, intra-regional and trans-historical allusions, and the infusion of spirituality. In many ways, Wu's performance points to the future of Asian Shakespeares. He gives primacy to his personal life stories and to the interaction between his personas and his audience, rather than attempting 'authentic' representations of the Shakespearean tragedy or of 'Asia'.

SELECT BIBLIOGRAPHY

Huang, Alexa, 'Global Shakespeare 2.0 and the Task of the Performance Archive,' *Shakespeare Survey* 64 (2011), 38–51.

Huang, Alexa, and Peter Donaldson, eds., *Global Shakespeares* (http://globalshakespeares. org).

Howe, James, *A Buddhist's Shakespeare: Affirming Self-Deconstructions* (Teaneck, NJ: Fairleigh Dickinson University Press, 1994).

Kim, Janice C. H., 'Processes of Feminine Power: Shamans in Central Korea', *Korean Shamanism: Revivals, Survivals, and Change*, ed. Keith Howard (Seoul: Seoul Press, 1998), 113–32.

Lee, Kuo-hsiu, *Shamuleite* (*Shamlet*). Production in Taipei, 2000.

Minami, Ryuta, Ian Carruthers, and John Gillies, eds., *Performing Shakespeare in Japan* (Cambridge: Cambridge University Press, 2001).

Wang, Shu-hua and Perng Ching-hsi. Interview with Lee Kuo-Hsiu, Taipei, 13 November, 1998. Unpublished manuscript.

Williams, Raymond, *Modern Tragedy*, ed. Pamela McCallum (Peterborough, Canada: Broadview, 2006).

INDEX